W9-CCX-722

Handbook of
Latin American Literature
Second Edition

*Garland Reference Library
of the Humanities (Vol. 1459)*

Handbook of Latin American Literature
Second Edition

edited by
David William Foster

Garland Publishing, Inc.
New York & London
1992

Library of Congress Cataloging-in-Publication Data

Handbook of Latin American literature / edited by David William Foster.
  —2d ed.
    p. cm. — (Garland reference library of the humanities; vol. 1459)
  Includes bibliographic references and index.
  ISBN 0-8153-0343-2 (alk.)
  ISBN 0-8153-1143-5 (pbk.)
    1. Latin America—History and criticism. I. Foster, David William.
II. Series
  PQ7081.A1H36   1992
  809'.898—dc20   92-16452
                                                                 CIP

This is a second edition of *Handbook of Latin American Literature* by David
William Foster (Garland Publishing, 1987).

Printed on acid-free, 250-year-life paper
Manufactured in the United States of America

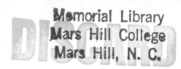
CONTENTS

PREFACE   ix

PREFACE TO SECOND EDITION   xiii

GENERAL REFERENCES   xv

ARGENTINA
Naomi Lindstrom   1

BOLIVIA
Oscar Rivera-Rodas   65

BRAZIL
Roberto Reis   95

CHILE
René Jara   123

COLOMBIA
Raymond Leslie Williams   179

COSTA RICA
Rima de Vallbona   217

CUBA
Matías Montes-Huidobro   227

DOMINICAN REPUBLIC
Doris Sommer and Esteban Torres   271

ECUADOR
Will H. Corral   287

v

GUATEMALA
  María A. Salgado   317

HAITI
  Maximilien Laroche   333

HONDURAS
  María A. Salgado   347

MEXICO
  Steven M. Bell   357

NICARAGUA
  Paul W. Borgeson, Jr.   443

PANAMA
  María A. Salgado   453

PARAGUAY
  Juan Manuel Marcos   469

PERU
  Dick Gerdes   493

PUERTO RICO
  Aníbal González   555

EL SALVADOR
  Paul W. Borgeson, Jr.   583

URUGUAY
  William H. Katra   595

VENEZUELA
  John Beverley   631

LATINO WRITING IN THE UNITED STATES
  Santa Arias and
  Erlinda Gonzales-Berry   649

PARALITERATURE
  Chuck Tatum   687

FILM
  John King   729

INDEX OF NAMES   773

PREFACE

Despite the enormous increase of interest in Latin American literature in the United States, there remain few reference works available to the scholar and general reader unable to consult literary histories and critical essays written in the languages of Latin America. Moreover, although there has been considerable opinion published on individual authors and specific topics, many of the Latin American countries lack literary histories dealing with recent writings or representing recent issues in Latin American literary scholarship. As a consequence, this compilation addresses itself to two audiences.

In the first place, it proposes to be a source of information for general readers and non-Hispanists who may require concise information concerning a particular author or work or literary tradition of Latin America. Reviews in the North American press, both in general readership magazines and in more specialized literary publications, tend to report on Latin American works as isolated phenomena, rarely placing them within the context of a national or Latin American context or relating them to the other writings of an author. The example has become legendary of the mass-circulation news magazine that began a review a few years ago with the statement: "Argentina may have no literary tradition, but it does have Borges."

In the second place, this volume of essays is also intended to meet the needs of students and researchers in the area of Latin American literature seeking reliable and comprehensive information concerning the various national literatures of Latin America and the features that set one national literature off from another. Information of this sort is often difficult to come by even in material available in English, and, as a consequence, there is the expectation that these essays will also meet the more specialized reference needs of Hispanic scholars, particularly as regards the incorporation of recent issues in Latin American culture and literary historiography.

More specifically, the contributors were charged with the preparation of essays that would constitute an ideological approach to Latin American literature. This emphasis is both a consequence of the sorts of questions being asked in current discussions of the literary and cultural traditions of Latin America, and it is also a consequence of the need to view the national literatures of Latin America as internally coherent traditions, if not as necessarily unique ones. Since the bulk of literary histories available in English discuss Latin American literature as a single tradition, with only parenthetical allusions to singular aspects from one country to the next, a series of comprehensive essays emphasizing the internal coherence of the several national traditions readily recommended itself as a goal for this volume.

The contributors were asked to focus their essays so that a consideration of general features would be complemented by reference to and discussion of major figures and texts, along with a consideration of ways in which the traditional canon could be expanded to include topics that have only recently begun to attract attention (women writers, gay-lesbian writing, a larger scope for ethnic minorities, texts that challenge traditional generic distinctions, and the like). Each scholar was free to define "ideological" as suitable for his/her interpretation of the issues and texts to be discussed; thus, there is a not unreasonable variation of approach among the essays. Each text is supplemented by an annotated bibliography of basic monographic sources for criticism and literary history, and this prefatory note is followed by a listing of general references.

The essays were either written directly in English or translated into English; all are original pieces prepared specifically for this publication. All works are cited in the original, but the first mention includes, in parentheses, the date of original publication and a nonitalicized translation of the title in the case of works that have not been translated into English or the italicized title for works that have been translated into English.

Since the essays are presented in English, every attempt has been made to use terminology easily recognizable to English-language readers and scholars. However, there are two terms that do not readily translate into English or that do not have immediate equivalents. While Brazilian scholarship uses Modernism (*modernismo*) such that it is coextensive with what American and European scholars understand by the term, Vanguardism (*vanguardismo*) is usually used in Spanish for the same phenomenon. In Spanish, *modernismo* refers to a movement between approximately 1885 and 1915 that was strongly influenced by French Parnassianism, Symbolism, and Decadentism as part of a program to "modernize" a Spanish American literature based on Hispanic traditions considered stagnant (by the same token, Brazilians speak of *parnassianis-mo* to cover something like the same set of influences and imitations).

The other term is less tricky. Costumbrism (*costumbrismo*) refers to a short prose sketch that combines elements of the essay and techniques associated with fiction and the short story in order to present details of local customs, beliefs, and lifestyles. So-called local color writing in American literature (cf. Joel Chandler Harris, Washington Irving, Mark Twain, among others) is chronologically parallel to Costumbrism, and many of the features of Dickens's novels would be considered costum-bristic from a Hispanic point of view.

I would like to express my gratitude to my research assistants, Juliette Spence and Virginia Li, for their assistance in preparing the manuscript. Katharine Kaiper Phillips provided invaluable editorial assistance in editing several of the manuscripts, especially those translated into English. And my colleagues Evar Nering and Dan Brink deserve special recognition for their enormous encouragement and advice in the computerization of my research operations. Garland's staff, especially Gary Kuris, have my unwavering gratitude for their confidence in the series of reference tools for Latin American literature of which this volume forms a part.

PREFACE TO THE SECOND EDITION

The *Handbook* was originally published in 1987. The idea of a revised edition grew out of the belief that it would be appropriate, not just to provide an update of information after its original publication, but to expand the base of coverage. Therefore, chapters have been added that deal with writing by the principal Hispanic ethnic groups in the United States and with two important topics related to conventional literary production: film and paraliterature, the latter being understood to include a series of popular/mass cultural products that involve a verbal text directly or marginally: romances, comic books, single-panel cartoons, as well as documentary and testimonial writing.

All of the original essays have been updated, with the exception of the Dominican Republic, Haiti, and Paraguay; in the case of Peru, an entirely new chapter has been included.

I would like to thank the following individuals who have contributed to the preparation of final manuscript: David Raúl Foster, Gustavo Geirola, Darrell Lockhart, and Katharine Kaiper Phillips.

GENERAL REFERENCES

Alegría, Fernando. *Nueva historia de la novela hispanoamericana.*
Hanover, N.H.: Ediciones del Norte, 1986. The historical development of the Spanish American novel since the beginning of
the nineteenth century to the present is examined; particular
emphasis is given to less studied authors.

América latina en su literatura. Ed. by César Fernández Moreno.
México, D.F.: Siglo XXI, 1972. Divided into six parts, this book
is a monumental collection of critical essays by major Latin
American scholars on a wide variety of topics central to the
definition of Latin American literature. Unfortunately, the English translation does not include the complete contents of the
original Spanish edition, which is part of a UNESCO-sponsored
series on the various cultural components of Latin American
culture: *Latin America in Its Literature.* Ed. by César Fernández
Moreno. Trans. by Mary G. Berg. New York: Holmes & Mei-
er, 1980.

Anderson Imbert, Enrique. *Spanish American Literature; a History.*
2nd ed. Trans. by John V. Falconieri. Detroit: Wayne State
University Press, 1969. 2 vols. Although this general guide is
often more a registry of names than an analytical history, it
continues to be regarded as indispensable for the vast amount
of literary production it surveys. Originally published as *Historia
de la literatura hispanoamericana.* 3a ed. México, D.F.: Fondo
de Cultura Económica, 1961.

Bravo-Elizondo, Pedro. *Teatro hispanoamericano de crítica social.* Madrid: Playor, 1975. A panoramic vision of the theater of social
protest and criticism focuses on eight representative works from
the period 1950-70.

Brotherston, Gordon. *The Emergence of the Latin American Novel.*
Cambridge: Cambridge University Press, 1977. A basic introduction to the Latin American novel with emphasis on writers
of the last three decades. After a presentation of the cultural
backgrounds, the book concentrates on principal novelists from
an essentially thematic point of view.

Brotherston, Gordon. *Latin American Poetry*. Cambridge: Cambridge University Press, 1975. The author emphasizes those poets who have strived to express a specifically Latin American moral and geographical identity since Modernism.

Brushwood, John S. *Genteel Barbarism*. Lincoln: University of Nebraska Press, 1981. Following an introductory chapter on literary movements in nineteenth-century Spanish America, Brushwood undertakes the analysis of eight key novels on the basis of a different analytical model for each text.

Brushwood, John S. *The Spanish American Novel: A Twentieth-Century Survey*. Austin: University of Texas Press, 1975. This survey deals with the unified development of the novel in Latin America in the twentieth century. Emphasis is on works rather than on authors in order to study the novel as a cultural organism. A list of the novels by years and country illustrates the basic organization which serves as a graphic representation of trends and contrasts. The material is presented in two different kinds of chapters: those that concentrate on general developments in a particular year with reference to a specific novel and those that cover periods of intervening years bridging the appearance of key works.

Conte, Rafael. *Lenguaje y violencia, introducción a la nueva novela hispanoamericana*. Madrid: Al-Borak, 1972. A brief survey of the historical evolution of the Latin American novel is followed by commentaries on the most representative novelists and their works.

Debicki, Andrew. *Poetas hispanoamericanos contemporáneos, puntos de vista, perspectiva, experiencia*. Madrid: Gredos, 1976. The author is not concerned with providing a literary history of poetic movements, but the works studied do have general implications for Spanish American poetry of this century. Rather than emphasizing the study of vocabulary and images, Debicki analyzes the perspective/point of view of the poetic voice and the role of the latter on the reader's grasp of the text.

Diccionario de la literatura latinoamericana. Washington, D.C.: Unión Panamericana, 1958-63. Although the series was never completed (alphabetically, the countries from Argentina through Ecuador, including the Central American republics and excluding Brazil, are represented in the six published volumes), this is still a useful reference source. Each author is characterized by a general description of his/her writing, followed by excellent bibliographies.

Donoso, José. *The Boom in Spanish American Literature*. Trans. by Gregory Kolovakos. New York: Columbia University Press in association with the Center for Inter-American Relations, 1977. A "personal history" written by one of the "boom" novelists. Originally published as *Historia personal del boom*. Barcelona: Anagrama, 1972.

Dramatists in Revolt. Ed. by Leon F. Lyday, and George W. Woodyard. Austin: University of Texas Press, 1976. A collection of essays on key Latin American (including Brazilian) dramatists.

Earle, Peter, and Robert G. Mead, Jr. *Historia del ensayo hispanoamericano*. México, D.F.: De Andrea, 1973. A survey of major essayists and analyses of key texts.

Foster, David William. *Alternate Voices in the Contemporary Latin American Narrative*. Columbia: University of Missouri Press, 1985. The attempt to provide a coverage for various forms of Latin American writing outside of the principal categories established by reference to privileged Western literary histories.

Foster, David William, comp. *A Dictionary of Contemporary Latin American Authors*. Tempe: Arizona State University, Center for Latin American Studies, 1975. Entries on significant Spanish and French-language writers prepared by specialists in the various national literatures. Brazil is covered in a companion publication; see Foster-Reis.

Foster, David William. *Gay and Lesbian Themes in Latin American Writing*. Austin: University of Texas Press, 1991. An examination of key texts towards establishing the identification of a tradition of Latin American writing on homoerotic issues.

Foster, David William. *Studies in the Contemporary Spanish American Short Story*. Columbia: University of Missouri Press, 1979. A series of structural and semiotic analyses of major texts in the contemporary Spanish American short story.

Foster, David William, and Roberto Reis. *A Dictionary of Contemporary Brazilian Authors*. Tempe: Arizona State University, Center for Latin American Studies, 1982. Entries on significant Brazilian writers.

Franco, Jean. *Spanish American Literature since Independence*. London: Ernest Benn; New York: Barnes and Noble, 1973. The most important literary currents in Latin America are examined.

There is a Spanish translation: *Historia de la literatura hispano-americana a partir de la independencia.* Barcelona: Ariel, 1975.

Fuentes, Carlos. *La nueva novela hispanoamericana.* México, D.F.: Joaquín Mortiz, 1969. After an examination of the traditional Latin American novel as static form within a static society, a series of major texts by new Latin American authors is examined. This book by Fuentes, as one of these authors, has been very influential as the first monographic interpretation of the so-called new novel and its challenge to fossilized Latin American traditions.

Gallagher, D. P. *Modern Latin American Literature.* London: Oxford University Press, 1973. Thirteen novelists are examined in a general introduction characterizing their contributions and place within general literary trends.

Goić, Cedomil. *Historia de la novela hispanoamericana.* Valparaíso: Universidad de Valparaíso, 1972. Pursuing an organization in terms of a generational scheme, Goić examines important modern novels as an imaginary narration presented by a personal narrator referring to a world through personal experiences. The generational organization is meant to enhance a world-view approach to the writing.

González Echevarría, Roberto. *The Voice of the Masters: Writing and Authority in Modern Latin American Literature.* Austin: University of Texas Press, 1985. An examination of major texts in terms of the relationship between language and authority and competing ideologies of culture and writing.

Harss, Luis, and Barbara Dohmann. *Into the Mainstream; Conversations with Latin American Writers.* New York: Harper and Row, 1967. Ten major writers are interviewed in depth by Harss in what, in its original Spanish version, is a landmark contribution to the definition of a new Latin American narrative: *Los nuestros.* Buenos Aires: Sudamericana, 1966.

Jackson, Richard L. *Black Writers in Latin America.* Albuquerque: University of New Mexico Press, 1977. Black writers and their place in Latin American literature are examined in terms of black self-awareness within the context of Latin American society.

Kadir, Djelal. *Questing Fictions: Latin America's Family Romance.* Minneapolis: University of Minnesota Press, 1986. An important study of the so-called family romance: the fictional modality whereby larger sociohistorical issues are cast in terms of the (typically) dysfunctionality of the familial nucleus.

Lindstrom, Naomi. *Women's Voice in Latin American Literature*. Washington, D.C.: Three Continents, 1989. A series of essays on principal women writers examined from the perspective of strategies for the expression of feminine consciousness.

Mac Adam, Alfred J. *Modern Latin American Narratives: the Dreams of Reason*. Chicago: University of Chicago Press, 1977. Major texts are examined in terms of the thesis that contemporary Latin American writing has been fundamentally satirical in nature.

McMurray, George R. *Spanish American Writing since 1941; a Critical Survey*. New York: Ungar, 1987. A solid survey of major movements, genres, and works. Although it is wanting as regards the representation of women authors, it is nevertheless a very useful coverage.

Magnarelli, Sharon. *The Lost Rib; Female Characters in the Spanish-American Novel*. Cranbury, N.J.: Bucknell University Press, 1985. Magnarelli attempts to answer the question as to why the Spanish-American novel is so nearly devoid of memorable female protagonists through a careful analysis of several female characters in works spanning one hundred years; with one exception, all of the novels studied are by men.

Martin, Gerald. *Journeys through the Labyrinth: Latin American Fiction in the Twentieth Century*. London: Verso, 1989. A useful survey of major categories of narrative forms, with a good representation of marginal phenomena.

Marting, Diane E., ed. *Spanish American Women Writers: a Bio-Biblio graphical Source Book*. Westport, Conn.: Greenwood Press, 1990. An encyclopedia of entries on over fifty major women writers with excellent characterizations of their works and bibliographical information.

Muñoz, Braulio. *Sons of the Wind; the Search for Identity in Spanish American Indian Literature*. New Brunswick, N.J.: Rutgers University Press, 1982. Through the presentation of issues concerning the cultural unity in Spanish America, this book attempts to gauge what has been gained and what has been lost in the process of imposing a hegemony of mestizo culture. Works emphasized are those dealing with the fate of the Indian caught up in the long process of Spanish America's cultural definition.

Panorama das literaturas das Américas (de 1900 a atualidade). Ed. by Joaquim de Montezume de Carvalho. Angola: Edição do Município de Nova Lisboa, 1958-63. A series of detailed essays by major specialists on each of the national literatures of Latin America.

Panorama de la actual literatura latinoamericana. La Habana: Casa de las Américas, Centro de Investigaciones Literarias, 1969. A series of position papers presented at a congress organized by the Castro government's cultural agency, the Casa de las Américas, these papers represent an important and probing array of analyses from a Marxist point of view.

Peden, Margaret Sayers, ed. *The Latin American Short Story: a Critical Survey.* Boston: G. K. Hall, 1983. A collection of four essays analyzing major figures and texts of the Spanish American (three essays) and Brazilian (one essay) short story.

Perus, François. *Literatura y sociedad en América latina: el modernismo.* La Habana: Casa de las Américas, 1976. Based on the assumption that literature is the product of a complicated historical process, this book presents a sociological interpretation of some of the most significant literary phenomena of modern Latin American literature, including Modernism and the contemporary novel.

Rivera-Rodas, Oscar. *Cinco momentos de la lírica hispanoamericana: historia literaria de un género.* La Paz: Instituto Boliviano de Cultura, 1978. A general survey of Latin American poetry in terms of five basic moments: enunciation, revelation, suggestion, dissociation, and identification.

Rojo, Grinor. *Orígenes del teatro hispanoamericano contemporáneo.* Valparaíso: Universidad Católica de Valparaíso, 1972. Developments in contemporary Latin American theater are examined, with emphasis on the assimilation of European models.

Sánchez, Luis Alberto. *Historia comparada de las literaturas americanas.* Buenos Aires: Losada, 1973-76. The purpose of this study is to consider the unity of Latin American literary expression; organization is historical.

Sánchez, Luis Alberto. *Proceso y contenido de la novela hispano-americana.* Madrid: Gredos, 1968. The generic and thematic processes underlying the evolution of the Spanish American novel are examined: generic in terms of the relationship between the

Latin American novel and the novel of Spain and other countries and thematic in the sense of general issues dealt with.

Schwartz, Ronald. *Nomads, Exiles & Emigres: the Rebirth of the Latin
American Narrative 1960-80*. Metuchen, N.J.: Scarecrow, 1980.
Ten major authors of the 1960s and 1970s are examined.

Shaw, Donald L. *Nueva narrativa hispanoamericana*. Madrid: Cátedra,
1981. A general survey of Spanish American fiction since the
1940s is provided, with emphasis on how, despite the significant
ideological and stylistic diversity of the works, the genre may
continue to be studied as a global phenomenon.

Solórzano, Carlos. *El teatro latinoamericano en el siglo XX*. México,
D.F.: Pomarca, 1964. A general panorama of developments in
the contemporary Latin American theater.

Sommer, Doris. *Foundational Fictions: the National Romances of Latin
America*. Berkeley: University of California Press, 1991. A
brilliant analysis of key nineteenth-century fictional texts expli-
cating the relationship between family romances, feminine images, and the construction of national consciousness and identity.

Stabb, Martin S. *In Quest of Identity*. Chapel Hill: University of North
Carolina Press, 1967. An excellent analysis of major essayists in
terms of their use of the essay to define Latin American identity.

Stimson, Frederick S. *The New Schools of Spanish American Poetry*.
Madrid: Castalia, 1970. A general survey provides a division of
the poets into "schools." Each such division focuses on a key
figure and the tendencies he represents.

Tittler, Jonathan. *Narrative Irony in the Contemporary Spanish-American
Novel*. Ithaca, N.Y.: Cornell University Press, 1984. Irony is examined as the motivating principle of a range of major works of
current Spanish-American fiction. Of note is the concept of
"narrative irony" as a dimension of structurally complex and
highly self-conscious texts.

Los vanguardismos en la América latina. Ed. by Oscar Collazos. Barcelona: Península, 1977. A collection of essays by various scholars
on the major features, authors, and texts of the Latin American
vanguard of the early decades of the twentieth century.

Vidal, Hernán. *Literatura hispanoamericana e ideología liberal*. Buenos
Aires: Hispamérica, 1976. In Vidal's opinion, a deleterious
liberal ideology has dominated Latin American literary discourse, creative as well as critical, and the literature is a mani-

festation of Latin America's economic and sociopolitical dependency as a consequence of that ideology. The latest manifestation of this dependency is the so-called "boom" of the new novel.
Yurkievich, Saúl. *Fundadores de la nueva poesía latinoamericana*. Barcelona: Barral, 1971. Five representative poets are examined in
detail as "founders" of contemporary Latin American poetry.

ARGENTINA
Naomi Lindstrom
University of Texas

I

Civilization—the term and the motives for invoking it—has long divided and perplexed Argentine intellectuals. Since the latter part of the nineteenth century, Argentina has stood out for its many signs of a high cultural level. Argentines have taken pride in such signs as the maintenance of an international opera house in Buenos Aires and publishers of world renown.

However, the worth of this cosmopolitan civilization—whether its benefits justify the sacrifices it requires—is a subject of endless controversy. Some of the disadvantages are easy to demonstrate, such as the overconcentration of cultural resources in the nation's capital. Other drawbacks are more difficult to assess. For instance, many observers assert that emulation of European cultural forms entails lessened appreciation for genres original to Argentina or Latin America. Such critics as David Viñas (1929) have pointed out that Argentina won its high cultural status by developing and displaying prestigious varieties of culture at the expense of more grassroots types. High art forms had their showcases in the city's impressive theaters, galleries, and bookstores. These cultural institutions are a traditional source of national self-respect. It has, in fact, been a feat to maintain such high level of activity, some of it very costly to keep operating, through years of discouraging and confusing economic conditions.

The problem, then, is not whether Argentina has achieved success in the area of culture, but whether this attainment has not involved disadvantaging other portions of the nation's total culture. Those cultural forms that are not likely to win international acclaim and that lack cosmopolitan glamour constitute, as Viñas, Adolfo Prieto (1928), and others complain, a neglected class. In this category were, for some time, Indian

1

and gaucho tradition, including folk lyric and narrative types such as ballads, refrains, and tales. By the turn of the century, though, Indian culture was nearly nonexistent, along with its practitioners, and the gaucho way of life was clearly on its way out. As these cultural strains were eliminated from living national culture, though, they acquired a certain antique value; in particular, the artifacts of now-moribund gaucho culture were regarded as worthy emblems of an essentially Argentine way of life.

In the industrial era the category of less-valued culture includes forms associated, for whatever reason, with the working class, those considered to be excessively local or provincial, and those disseminated through the mass media. In literature, the lower-prestige forms are those that seem home-grown, crude, too overtly didactic, or too directly concerned with social issues. Noé Jitrik (1929), surveying the ways in which critics and readers have categorized Argentine writing, shows the excessive ease with which much of literature becomes separated, by sometimes unthinking consensus, into high and low, refined and raw, subsets.

The years since 1955 have seen an especially vigorous production of essays by Argentines—sometimes written at home, sometimes from abroad—criticizing the understanding of civilization reflected in Argentine writing. But the abundance and variety of recent discussion should not create the impression that critics now are reacting against the stasis of a past in which shared concepts of civilization and culture were acritically accepted by most Argentines, or at least by most intellectuals. The more closely one examines earlier Argentine writings, in search of some stable, traditional notion of a desirable state of civilization, the more apparent is the absence of any concept that did not meet with opposition. Instead, many individuals and groups compete to win acceptance for their vision of what would constitute the best possible Argentine civilization. Authors return to the joined themes of civilized and primitive ways with obsessive insistence. The need to rework this subject-matter indicates that the definition of the basic terms was far from being agreed upon. Moreover, successive attempts to resolve contradictions within existing notions have had the effect of adding fresh uncertainties and contradictions to an already shifting conceptual landscape.

The question of the civilization best suited to Argentina first became explicitly formulated, though no doubt it was earlier present, with the Generation of 1837. It was in 1837-1838 that the Asociación de Mayo (Association of May) brought together young writers and social thinkers.

May was a term that summed up for them the spirit prevailing at the moment of the great drive for Argentina's independence from Spain. Though the years since Independence had obscured the vision that motivated the founding fathers, the members of the 1837 group felt they could restore it. Their common preoccupations included Romanticism, which was just then beginning to have its impact in Argentina, and the development of a postcolonial Argentine culture. To the young men of 1837, headed by Esteban Echeverría (1805-51), the great work of civilization lay entirely ahead of them. There was little feeling that Argentina could build its culture on the groundwork laid by its Indians, who, certainly, had not been among the exceptionally advanced pre-Columbian peoples, or by Spanish viceregal rule, which had been notably negligent in developing the River Plate region. Even though Argentina had lived through two decades of independence, Echeverría and his colleagues found little sign of an emerging independent culture or national self-awareness. In their analysis, the declaration of independence and the attainment of autonomous political status had been inadequate to make Argentina independent because national culture and thought had not been reworked to suit the needs of a newly postcolonial nation. Literature and social thought had no organizing program such as the Romanticism that Echeverría had seen uniting many European innovators. Educated habits of thought and expression were, at their most advanced, those of neoclassicism and the Enlightenment.

Enrique Anderson Imbert (1910) believes the group to have indeed made the 1830s the most decisive period in setting the course for Argentine intellectual life. In his analysis, Echeverría's group was not merely successful in replacing a vague, unexamined rationalism with a vigorous Romanticism. The Asociación de Mayo was also new in its eagerness to consider the nation as no longer merely extending Europe, but rather requiring a massive effort to think in American terms.

While some aspects of Echeverría's thought seem dated, other of his ideas were considerably advanced for their historical moment. Particularly notable is his analysis of the failure of traditional Enlightenment-style intellectuals to organize postcolonial Argentina. By 1830, it was evident that Argentina was not flourishing as a national entity. There were various proposals afoot for partitioning the national territory, and some areas were already sectioned, de facto, into smaller units ruled over by local bosses. Although representatives of the independence-era elite had produced a national constitution (1819) and many programmatic statements, their efforts were aggravating rather than resolving the

problem of national disunity. Echeverría pointed out that the ideals of
the Age of Reason, which Argentine intellectuals usually expressed
exactly as they had been formulated in response to European conditions,
were meaningless and offensive to many fellow countrymen. In his
analysis, the general population of Argentina was potentially democratic,
in that the citizens valued independence, but their political ideas were a
confused mix of regional interests, Hispanic traditions, and the survivalist
ethic typical of life on the frontier. As a result, the would-be governing
elites of Buenos Aires found themselves under attack from those they
sought to uplift and rule.

Of Echeverría's writings—manifestoes, speeches, poetry, and fiction—"El matadero" (The Slaughtering Grounds) is today the most read.
Written about 1839 or 1840 but not published until 1874, "El matadero"
is a short story that makes an allegorical statement about Argentina
under the 1835-52 regime of Juan Manuel Rosas. It also contains passages exhorting readers to put an end to the prevailing savagery. The
story is a work of exile literature, and accordingly it reflects the author's
great distress over the Argentina he had just fled, as had many of his
fellow intellectuals. The Rosas government, favorable to beef growers
and processors and reliant on violent repression, here appears to have
turned Argentina itself into a vast slaughtering grounds. The setting is
a stretch of riverside. In a bread-and-circuses move, Rosas has decreed
a spectacular giveaway of fresh-killed beef. While this event excites the
participants to a frenzied enthusiasm for Rosas, its effect on the reader
is intended to be quite different. Not only do the revelers let this gory
largesse determine their allegiance, but they are a cruel and bloodthirsty
mob. After trampling one another in their carnivorous excitement and
strewing blood and entrails all over the grounds, they fatally torment an
idealistic young dissident.

"El matadero" continues to attract readers and commentators. Many
examine its success in riveting readers' attention while subjecting them
to a tendentious allegory about the brutalizing effects of demagogic
dictatorship. The short narrative utilizes the shock value of realism in
describing violence and gore and the persuasive power of Romantic
rhetoric to urge the installation of a new social order.

Successful as artistic and persuasive writing, the work stands up less
well as an expression of progressive ideals—not only by today's standards
of progressive thought, but often by those Echeverría set in more critically reflective passages in his writings. Current-day readers find disturbing
the story's persistent association of brutality and non-European ancestry.

It is true that Rosas cultivated the support of gauchos and mulattos and that "El matadero" makes repulsive everything connected with the dictator. It could be argued that Echeverría shows Argentines of color the way Rosas has encouraged them to be, not as they might be under the type of liberal society the author advocates. Nonetheless, the text describes nonwhite characters in such a way as to confuse the signs of racial origin with those of savagery. (The same set of associations appears in reference to Indians in Echeverría's *La cautiva* [The Captive], a narrative poem of 1837-38.)

Echeverría exemplifies the contradictions that characterized the thought of the bright, advanced intellectuals of his generation. "El matadero" shows him neglecting principles that are evident in some, though by no means all, of the same author's essays and position papers. The fictional mob's victim is an educated young man in European dress. Though he regards the lower-class feasters with disdain, there is no hint of negative criticism of the hero. Indeed, this aristocratic, Europeanized man rises to Christlike stature. In less impassioned writings, Echeverría had warned against the taking up of European ways without considering whether they would be out of place and offensive in Argentina. He criticized the intellectual elite for its abstract Enlightenment rhetoric and unwillingness to find some common ground with a larger sector of the population. Looking through Echeverría's essays, it is possible to find such thoughtful assertions as "To be great in politics is not to be up to the civilization of the world, but to be on a level with one's own country." Echeverría warned Argentine progressives "not to wander off into abstraction, to keep a steady eye on the inner workings of our society." Yet he could express himself at a level of abstraction that leaves some of his programmatic statements almost without relation to the specific realities of Argentine life; in his creative writings, he betrayed an irreflexive horror at the Argentine people he had at other moments urged intellectuals to know and understand.

The same generation included a number of writers united by their difficulties with the Rosas regime, Romantic mode of expression, and loyalty to the ideals of the Enlightenment. José Mármol (1818-71) authored in exile the anti-Rosas novel *Amalia* (1851-55). As does Echeverría's "El matadero," *Amalia* relies on allegory and symbolism to convince readers of the need to oust Rosas and usher in a new era of high-principled democracy. But while Echeverría's slaughtering grounds provide the occasion for vivid descriptive writing, in *Amalia* the need to support an allegorical design often results in somewhat single-minded, tendentious characterization, particularly in the case of the invariably noble and freedom-loving heroine.

Juan Bautista Alberdi (1810-84) may well be the most original and nuanced thinker of the 1837 group. Readers and critics are continually being startled by the complexity and critical sharpness of his programmatic writings, newspaper articles, speeches, letters, and statesman's papers. The improved Constitution of 1853 is considered to embody his thought about national society. Alberdi was more willing than his colleagues to take economic factors into account in his analysis of Argentina's situation, a characteristic that makes him attractive to current-day thinkers with a background in Marxist thought. He recognized that concepts of rational government needed to evolve from the eighteenth-century model to which Argentine intellectuals still clung. The alternative Alberdi developed, and which he called "new rationalism," was less abstract than standard Enlightenment thought and more able to include in the reckoning specifics of the nation's historical and economic circumstances. Alberdi was also ahead of his contemporaries in seeing the limitations of romanticism and endeavoring to move beyond this mode. His creative writings today attract critical attention more for the experimental program that underlies them than for the esthetic success he obtained.

Alberdi's longstanding partner in debate and polemic was a much more literary figure: Domingo Faustino Sarmiento (1811-88). Sarmiento's foremost contribution may have been the formulation of the issue that Argentine intellectuals found so disturbing and divisive: *civilization and barbarism*. This phrase, today famous, first appeared as the main title of Sarmiento's 1848 *Civilización y barbarie: vida de Juan Facundo Quiroga* (*Civilization and Barbarism: Life of Juan Facundo Quiroga*), widely referred to as *Facundo*. Though part of anti-Rosas writing, *Facundo* has few words on the celebrated dictator, deemed a mere symptom of a vaster disorder. The work takes on the task of diagnosing Argentina's troubles up to the present in Book One, while its third segment gives Sarmiento's program for the post-Rosas future. Between these two treatises is the segment that steadily proves most attractive to literary readers and wins the work its place alongside, if not exactly within, Argentine creative literature. This is the narrative account of Facundo, a ruler over one of the rural fiefdoms into which Argentina was largely divided. Rosas cultivates and manipulates Facundo as a king would a vassal lord. When Facundo tries to move the provinces out of their feudal status, relying on his own homemade variety of the progressive program, Rosas sends his assassins.

Readers have long noted that the story of Facundo is not only vivid narrative, but also an engaging and sympathetic human portrait. Facundo first appears as an uncouth, destructive individual, whose abundant facial hair gives him a subhuman image. In subsequent scenes, though, Facundo manifests a praiseworthy desire to transform his crude self and acquire the outlook and program of action of a progressive. In his drive toward self-improvement, he is on the opposite course of Rosas, who after enjoying a privileged, urban background poses as a rustic in a cheap bid for popular support. Facundo, in his earnest struggle, dimly perceives a basic tenet of Sarmiento's thought: Argentine society needs strong progressive guidance to avoid such evils as disintegration into provincial fiefdoms, exploitation of the interior by the capital, and failure to form a national entity.

Though Facundo is not the leader needed to move society forward, the story of his well-meaning campaign to reorganize the provinces is an exemplary tale. The implication is that a stronger Facundo with a broader vision of Argentina's future could succeed in such a campaign. Sarmiento is not shy about casting himself in such a role (he did assume the presidency 1868-74) and in the next section propounds his own plan for setting Argentina to rights.

Especially since Sarmiento was one of the most important Argentine presidents, *Facundo* has become a staple of school reading lists and is often cited on public occasions. This respectful treatment, irritating to more critical readers, can give the impression that *Facundo* summarizes a set of ideas once acceptable to virtually the entire Argentine elite. While Sarmiento certainly had his supporters, *Facundo* drew polemical fire as it was first appearing as newspaper pieces, rousing fresh indignation as a book. Alberdi devoted a lengthy essay to attacking Sarmiento, his eclectic, sociological-historical-ethnographic method, and his conclusions.

Facundo, however established as an Argentine classic, continues to stir controversy not only about the accuracy of its analysis but about the statement it generates. Attentive readers have always noticed that the work is riddled with ambiguities and contradictions. The delineation of the categories *civilization* and *barbarism* shifts from passage to passage. Consider, for example, the unsteady value of urban living. On the one hand, the city offers more opportunities to gain knowledge. Facundo is not to blame for the failure of his reforms, in part because he cobbled his program together from bits of progressive thought that had reached him in his provincial isolation. Rosas is accountable for his misdeeds because he enjoyed the benefits of a cosmopolitan environment open to international currents of thought.

While the city makes available knowledge and worldly understanding, it often appears as a negative force. Sarmiento repeatedly expresses his concern over the economic exploitation of the interior by the capital city and Rosas's favoritism toward the port, the meatpacking industry, and the beef raisers of the Province of Buenos Aires, the dictator's base of power. Throughout the first and second sections of *Facundo*, Sarmiento often praises the uprightness, skill, self-reliance, and other homespun virtues of country dwellers. Sarmiento's admiration for the strengths of rural people competes with his fear that, lacking the concept of change, they will not have the drive to make Argentina progress.

The book would be considerably less controversial if it did not include among civilizing and regressive social forces those of race and ethnicity. Sarmiento was, of course, not abstractly inquiring into the relative progressive-mindedness of peoples. His purpose was to bring under control the roughly 250,000 square miles of pampa. The area was open range with unsystematically bred cattle, frontier-style social control, and a population of isolates (the part-Indian, part-Spanish gauchos) riding herd. This unregulated existence suited the gauchos, who fiercely opposed change, but to Sarmiento it was a source of national disorder. His proposal for reform included replacing the individualistic range riders with immigrant practitioners of modern agriculture. Bringing efficient farming, schooling, transportation, and communication, the settlers would rapidly build up the infrastructure. Sarmiento gave a racial reason for the hypothesized modernizing drive of the immigrant farmers. In his mind, European immigrants, and especially Northern Europeans, would be naturally eager to undertake the measures unacceptable to gauchos.

II

Rosas fell in 1852 and, despite continuing conflicts, Argentina began on the liberal, entrepreneurial path toward progress that the exiled writers had been advocating. Sarmiento proved correct in stating that the gaucho would have no place in a swiftly modernizing Argentina. The pampa, which had been almost unmarked by human civilization, was a special target of planners. Open range gave way to fenced private property. Railroads and government services altered life on the pampa. Gaucho culture was beginning to dissolve, and the formerly independent gauchos were becoming employees of farms and businesses. Just as it was clear that the real-world gaucho was vanishing, a figure of the gaucho created for literary purposes gained popularity. This stock character was a quick-witted, clear-seeing rustic, given to making sport of current developments in Argentina. A razor-tongued gaucho commentator was the mainstay of *gauchesca* poetry.

As its name indicates, *gauchesca* stood at a remove from the oral poetry that was part of gaucho culture. Its authors were educated men who spoke through fictional gauchos, partly to be amusing, and partly to benefit from the gaucho's fame as a sharp, hard-to-fool character. It little resembled the extemporaneous, abstractly philosophical verse of gaucho tradition. Taking the form of debate, gaucho verse was a competitive activity with such skilled practitioners as Gabino Ezeiza (1858-1916).

Hilario Ascasubi (1807-75) popularized the conventions of gauchesca poetry when he wrote under what were not only gaucho pseudonyms, but assumed personae: Paulino Lucero and Aniceto el Gallo. These fictional gauchos, presumably uncontaminated by ideological sophistry, could identify justice and injustice with clear eyes. The characters spoke a conventionalized adaptation of gaucho dialect; though not very true to the original, it served its purpose as a constant reminder of the speakers' special outlook. Ascasubi also developed a more literary form of gauchesca writing, full of scenes of local color and descriptions of the pampa. This decorative, florid gauchesca is the substance of his narrative poem *Santos Vega o los mellizos de la Flor* (Santos Vega or the Twin Brothers of La Flor), first published in 1850 and reworked in 1872, and of his extended elaborations of the material he had written using as his spokesmen Paulino Lucero and Aniceto el Gallo.

Estanislao del Campo (1834-80) continued the satirical use of the rough-hewn gaucho character. In his *Fausto* (1866), two gauchos discuss the visit one has paid to the Buenos Aires opera. In summarizing the opera, the two friends add a number of comical incongruities and distortions and at times seem unable to distinguish between stage acting and real-world behavior. The crucial issue in determining how to read *Fausto* is: How aware are the gauchos of the absurdities they introduce into their reconstruction of the opera? The text offers many hints that the conversation is an extended joke. Readers today generally understand the gauchos to be engaging in deadpan humor, targeted at the solemnity with which Buenos Aires took its opera. This interpretation is certainly in line with previous gauchesca writing, in which gauchos mock, among other things, pomposity and pretense. Yet Del Campo's contemporaries generally saw *Fausto* as satirizing the ignorance of gauchos. This vision of the work, which now seems hard to sustain, is probably witness to the deep conviction of the 1860s literary public that cosmopolitan civilization should always be valued above folk cultures.

El gaucho Martín Fierro (1872) by José Hernández (1834-86), continued in *La vuelta de Martín Fierro* (The Return of Martín Fierro; 1879), is thoroughly unlike other gauchesca works. Works like *Fausto* do not have the gaucho as their central concern; instead, gaucho speakers are used to give the effect of a disinterested, hard-headed perspective. In other cases, the gaucho appears in an embellished evocation of his habitat and customs, allowing for some colorful descriptive writing.

In *El gaucho Martín Fierro*, the titular character sings to protest the real-world gaucho's plight. The poem opens as Fierro begins an autobiographical song about his recent woes. All his troubles stem from his unjust treatment by the Argentine government. Fierro has lost his home, wife, children, and livelihood because of government policies and measures designed to disrupt the gaucho's way of life. He becomes an outlaw and then goes off to live among Indians. The step manifests his extreme alienation; Indians are traditional enemies of the gauchos, but stand at the furthest remove from the European-style civilization the government is promoting. Fierro takes with him an officer who, until a moment before his defection, was pursuing him. The sergeant's change of plans, a famous surprise twist in the narrative, hints at a widespread hidden dissatisfaction with the official campaign to settle the pampa. While it is unusual for a written work to have an immediate impact on an uneducated public, Hernández's work had such a reception. It became part of the literature transmitted through oral performance.

Hernández's 1872 poem reached a public that was disadvantaged by the settlement campaign and, presumably, heightened indignation. However, it does not appear to have slowed the campaign to convert the pampa to fenced private property. The project continued despite local protests and criticism from such members of the elite as Hernández, who occupied a senate seat and other positions of influence.

By 1879, Hernández felt unable to encourage further resistance. In his sequel, Martín Fierro returns from the Indian camps, the space outside civilization, and learns to live with the changing pampa. The second half of *Martín Fierro* differs from the first on significant points. While the first honors such values as autonomy and integrity, the second is colored by a survivalist ethic. The less-moral outlook is most exemplified by a scavenger who has raised Fierro's offspring to sacrifice dignity to self-interest. The pampa itself, earlier taken for granted as a natural habitat, now comes in for lyrical description. Fierro's voice, formerly the vehicle of narration, is now one of several, and his expression is less distinctively harsh and blunt. These features and others show acceptance not only of the government's plan for the pampa, but also, to some degree, of the gentility that was the ideal of the Buenos Aires governing elite.

1880 is considered an epochal year in Argentine social and cultural history. The nation began to resolve the confusion it had suffered since Independence. It was finally determined that Buenos Aires should be fully part of Argentina and serve as the national capital. General Julio A. Roca, a war hero for his Desert Campaign (to exterminate remaining Indians), was a well-liked president. The economy appeared to be endlessly booming, although by the next decade Argentines would find themselves overextended. Foreign investors considered Argentina a prime investment opportunity and Buenos Aires an ideal destination for business trips. With the nation no longer in constant crisis, writers could cultivate a literature more detached from immediate social concerns. Authors of the 1880s seem eager to display a lighthearted approach to writing. The tastes of the 1880s favored brief sketches and vignettes, often first designed as newspaper or magazine pieces and only later collected into books. Short stints of writing were virtually all that many of these authors could manage. They typically held public posts, maintained leading roles in clubs and beneficent societies, were great travelers, and in many cases exercised a profession as well. Still, their writing is copious. These gentlemen composed editorials, position papers on Argentina's best course, legislative proposals, and polemical pamphlets; when abroad, they were foreign correspondents; their correspondence was often voluminous; and some published in their professional fields.

It is easy to perceive the 1880s gentlemen-writers as almost interchangeable. Their individuality is masked by a conventional persona. In essays on national problems, the 1880s authors speak as those whose charge it is to direct Argentina. In belles-lettres, which nearly always take the form of reminiscences, they are disinterested, contemplative observers with privileged access to government and business circles and private clubs. Unselfconscious about their membership in the elite, they allude to prestigious individuals, locales, and amusements. Adding to their similarity is the off-handed attitude they seek to convey.

Yet these fellow participant-observers of the Buenos Aires and European high life give distinct emphases to their material. Lucio Vicente López (1848-94) was a politician and journalist. His work is distinguished by the insight that the Buenos Aires his contemporaries took for granted, where everyone seemed to know everyone, was already disappearing. In its place was emerging an impersonal, if elegant, modern city. López sought to preserve in writing its last years as, in his famous title, *La gran aldea* (The Big Village; 1884). This work, sometimes called a novel, is composed of scenes described out of memory, as is the equally celebrated *Juvenilia* (1884) of Miguel Cané (1851-1905), with its often critical view of upper-class schooling. A third memoir-novel is *Aguas abajo* (Downstream; 1914), never really completed by its restless and overcommitted author, Eduardo Wilde (1844-1913). Wilde, though his writings are as sketchy as those of his contemporaries, shows more evidence of a critical mind at work. While a disturbing trait of 1880s literature is the authors' hesitancy to pass judgment, even when a frivolous consumer society is under observation, Wilde's humor is not the light, bantering one typical of the 1880s, but gives glimpses of serious doubts about the worth of social arrangements and, at times, of human nature itself. Together with a tendency to throw events into an absurd perspective, Wilde's questioning of social and individual values makes him, of his generation's writers, perhaps the most easily appreciated by current-day readers.

Other associated writers of this seemingly artless prose, designed to resemble casual reminiscences, include Lucio Victorio Mansilla (1831-1913), Martín García Mérou (1862-1905), and Angel de Estrada (1872-1923). Rafael Obligado (1851-1920) was the group's poet.

However, genteel belles-lettres were not all the generation produced. Mansilla provides the most dramatically different case. At that time, military careers were still common among well-to-do Argentines, and Mansilla had become a colonel in the army. President Sarmiento had Mansilla classed among the potentially dissident young officers whom he kept far from the capital, in frontier wars with the Indians. Mansilla, on his own initiative, entered the Ranquel tribe's encampment and finalized a peace treaty before Sarmiento could reject its terms, as he seemed about to do. This venture kept Mansilla out of commission for the rest of Sarmiento's term and resulted in his best-known work, *Una excursión a los indios ranqueles* (An Excursion to the Ranquel Indians; 1870). This memoir was eagerly read by contemporaries curious to hear Mansilla's side of the famous affair. Today it retains its value as a sympathetic account of the Ranquels and their relations with the national government. Ethnographic accounts of Argentine Indian life are rare, giving Mansilla's amateur but observant description special worth.

Outside the group, the populist author Eduardo Gutiérrez (1851-1889) novelized heroic figures and episodes of Argentine history, including folkloric and mythic history. Best remembered is his *Juan Moreira* (1879-1880), the life of a wily gaucho able to outwit all comers. Although formulated from folk sources by a single author, Juan Moreira won the status of a legendary hero. Dramatized versions of the plot, often with melodramatic embellishments, became popular. Sequels were composed by many hands, and popular songs sprang up giving further episodes in the life of this hero, celebrated for his sharp eyes, lightning shrewdness, and keen sense of self-preservation.

The sanguine outlook of the early 1880s gave way to doubts over the direction Argentine society was taking. 1890 epitomizes this reversal, and indeed the year did much to erode belief in progress. 1890 brought a stock market crash and an aborted coup. The first of these was largely a result of overextended credit and unregulated trading practices that were the norm at the time. The crash made liberals begin to doubt that an unchecked market would keep the economy healthy and fuel unlimited progress, to use a favored contemporary phrase. From this time on, faith in a market free of constraints would gradually lose its place in liberal thought and become increasingly a favored tenet of conservatives. The Revolution of 1890 was really no more than a brief uprising among dissenters who were well placed in the elite and were scarcely subjected to reprisals. Though it made little actual change in the way matters of state were run, this failed coup caused the Argentine government a considerable loss of face. It drew attention to the fact that a virtual incompetent, an in-law of the popular and well-regarded Roca, was currently directing the Argentine nation. By the 1890s, too, the campaign to settle the country's underpopulated stretches with hard workers of European stock was proving to be less than well conceived. Immigrants, like most people who had become aware of the advantages of urban life, sought to settle in cities as quickly as possible, and particularly in Buenos Aires. This unintended result of immigration recruitment gave Buenos Aires the international aspect that came to be one of its great attractions. However, it drained away the talented newcomers who had been virtually promised to the provinces to stimulate and develop them. This shift aggravated the sentiment that every plan the government announced to move the country forward ended up redounding to the benefit of the capital.

The entrepreneurial spirit that had been envisioned as the force driving the nation into the future received encouragement through sparse regulation of commercial transactions. This policy helped spur the growth of transportation and the construction industry, but at the same time Buenos Aires became an international nexus for illicit forms of trade. Argentina now had many of the things that had been wished for in the mid-1880s. Its population was largely European in origin and Buenos Aires resembled a large, flourishing European city. Argentines were proud of the international renown of their more glamorous specialties, such as furs and leather goods, and of the reputation for modernity and chic that wealthy Argentines enjoyed abroad. But these attainments did not make the country any easier to govern or resolve its internal divisions.

La bolsa (The Stock Market; 1891) by Julián Martel (real name José Miró; 1867-96) reflects the overheated credit economy and complicated financial arrangements of the period, features still fairly new and strange to much of the Argentine public. The novel encourages nostalgia for a less evolved Buenos Aires in which trading was presumably a straightforward matter of exchanging tangible goods and services for other goods or for reassuringly solid metal money. A return to easily comprehensible varieties of trade is not the only regression the novel seems to advocate. The immigration policy designed to bring Argentina in line with Western European standards of living is, in this novel, a force enmiring the country in decadence. The new Argentines, epitomized by the Jewish financier Glow, are sinisterly complicated, full of hidden twists and turns. Glow's sinuous maneuvers and financier's legerdemain contrast with the straightforward frankness of Argentine characters of Spanish descent. The latter enjoy an image as upholders of time-honored virtues, loyal, dependable, and honoring their word. Yet they are shown as at a disadvantage when dealing with foreigners expert in high, and dangerous, finance.

A number of contemporary works are no more sanguine about the nation's progress. *Sin rumbo* (Aimless) by Eugenio Cambaceres (1843-88), though it appeared in 1884, is a famous example of the critical vision that would become widespread in the 1890s. The rootlessness that unbalances its protagonist will become a frequent theme in subsequent Argentine literature. Though his income arises from land holdings, this young man's excessive refinement distances him from life on his own ranch. Routine aspects of country life, such as gelding and even coarse bed linen, disturb him and reveal his estrangement from what the novel posits as the real Argentina. The young man is exploited by a diva, another figure of European guile and artifice, and in turn exploits a warm-hearted and defenseless country girl. The novel shows its protagonist as unable to return to simple home virtues even when he has resolved to do so.

The same skeptical look at society is evident in the novels of two physician-novelists, Manuel T. Podestá (1853-1920), whose much-noted *Irresponsable* was published in installments in 1889, and Francisco Sicardi (1856-1927). Both used the novel to diagnose the pathological signs of the modern, cosmopolitan scene. Carlos María Ocantos (1860-1949) was a mildly critical realist. Fray Mocho (José Sixto Alvarez; 1858-1903) was a vigorous populist known for his ability to recreate in writing the sly turns of country humor. In 1898 Fray Mocho founded (together with Eustaquio Pellicer and Manuel Majol) the celebrated belle-époque magazine *Caras y caretas* (Faces and Masks). This review managed to reach a relatively broad audience while showcasing the work of many of the era's most talented writers, and is widely regarded as an unusual achievement in combining popular appeal with fairly sophisticated writing. *Caras y caretas* was also a periodical of exceptional visual style, drawing on the talents of the foremost contemporary illustrators.

The writers conventionally linked to 1890, though their work begins before and continues past the 1890s, brought continuous narrative prose and a diagnostic scrutiny of the much-vaunted progressive civilization of Buenos Aires. Modernism, the movement that upstaged these realists and naturalists, brought a move away from direct literary presentations of social issues. On the whole, the modernists were concerned with the overall direction they saw Latin American society taking, but their alarm expressed itself in oblique and covert ways. The ideology favoring technological progress and modernization in the most visible ways—for example, improved agricultural methods—struck the modernists as fundamentally ill-conceived. These writers tended to exhibit a general attitude toward current tendencies in society rather than voicing specific complaints. They cultivated a disinterested love of beauty and the ability to establish intense esthetic bonds with objects pleasing to the senses. Accordingly, these writers were disturbed to see the mindless, showy way in which the then-flourishing bourgeoisie displayed its new ability to acquire costly things. The utilitarian emphasis that characterized much contemporary social thought repelled the modernists. Though, as their name suggests, they wanted Latin America to be modern in its culture in the manner of a city they greatly admired, Paris, they were disappointed that those in a position to plan the region's future often saw modernization as a matter of technical and material advancement rather than in spiritual and esthetic terms.

Readers who have long read modernist writing with an eye to its social implications learn to identify the vein of critical thought running through these texts at a subterranean level. Such attentive and sympathetic readers as the Mexican poet and essayist Octavio Paz have alerted the critical public to the ways in which the cultural program of the modernist writers foreshadows later critical tendencies in Latin American social thought. Nonetheless, the expression of social concerns occurs in a manner so indirect, and at times downright unclear and confused, that many perceive modernist writing either as standing in no real relation to social issues or else as inherently conservative by virtue of an elitist refusal to turn due attention to the problems of Latin American society.

Before modernism became a Buenos Aires literary movement, it had enjoyed a previous flowering, principally in Spanish American countries north of the Equator. Owing in part to the death of major figures, early modernism had lost its impetus. Rubén Darío (1867-1916), the Nicaraguan-born poet who had been foremost in the first wave of modernism, now moved to Buenos Aires, which was his base of operations during much of the 1890s. He and the Argentine writer Leopoldo Lugones (1874-1938) became leaders of a second phase of the movement. Modernism then had Buenos Aires as its capital, with Mexico City emerging somewhat later as a second major city. Buenos Aires was well suited to host an important literary movement; it enjoyed excellent connections with centers of European culture, and featured an active publishing industry and literary scene. However, Lugones was the only Argentine to become a modernist writer of the first rank. Among other Argentine participants in the movement, Enrique Larreta (1875-1961) stands out for *La gloria de don Ramiro* (The Glory of Don Ramiro; 1908), a sumptuous novel that hints Spanish American civilization arose from Spain's decadent features. Carlos Guido y Spano (1827-1918), who was an established poet already, made some move toward modernism, while Carlos Obligado (1890-1949) participated in its last years, the 1910s.

Las montañas de oro (The Golden Mountains, 1897) established Lugones as a poet with an exalted, heroic mode of expression; an anarchistic vein of cultural radicalism runs through its texts, with their seemingly disordered succession of images. Although the poems of this collection often strike current-day readers as grandiose and overwritten, the book illustrates the modernist imperative to keep generating new rhythmic and lexical experiments. Lugones won a wide readership with his application of modernist techniques to the writing of the cruel or cold short story, a subgenre then enjoying a great vogue. As exemplified by such expert practitioners as Guy de Maupassant, this type of story was distinguished by sharp and surprising turns of plot, in many cases involving supernatural phenomena, and protagonists who suffered cruel twists of fate. Readers of these stories especially valued their ability to send shivers down the spine, and it was in this respect that modernism made an apt addition to the conventions of this harrowing type of tale. Modernist writers had built up a repertory of techniques for suggesting physical sensations, with special emphasis on exceptional sensory experiences. Lugones's stories of the turn of the century, collected in *Las fuerzas extrañas* (Strange Forces; 1906) were outstanding for passages in which the narrators described in detail abnormal information they had obtained through their senses. In one story, a participant in a terrifying seance tells of being covered with glacial cold as he sat at the spirit-summoning table. In another, the friend of a mad scientist discovers the experimenter's brains evenly buttered across a wall in the wake of some ill-advised labwork. In a story not collected during the author's lifetime, "Cábala práctica" (Practical Kabbalah), the entire plot leads up to a lengthy descriptive passage giving the narrator's sensation as he grabbed hold of a friend and, with his fingers sinking into her, suddenly realized that she had no skeleton.

Once he had achieved a prominent place in national letters, Lugones often exhibited a desire to influence Argentina's esthetic values and its political culture. He gained leverage both as an arbiter of taste, promoting and attacking younger authors, and through appointments in the educational system and official or quasi-official cultural activities. During the period when he was in the public eye, from the early 1900s to his suicide in 1938, Lugones repeatedly shifted his political outlook. At the time he first gained prominence, he was espousing a lyrical anarchism. Beginning in the 1910s, he at first seemed to be settling into a stodgy, pro-Establishment stance. But by the next decade it was clear that Lugones has developed an idiosyncratic right-wing extremism. He astonished his fellow intellectuals, and revolted many, by choosing a public occasion to deliver a speech entitled "La hora de la espada" (The Hour of the Sword), tending toward fascism and colored by a peculiar fondness for authority and military severity. Lugones's vision of culture and society became increasingly characterized by fascistic and militaristic elements. At the same time, he took up a back-to-the-roots cultural nationalism and produced verse on rural Argentine themes utilizing traditional ballad meters; the implication appeared to be that the nation's true worth lay in its conservative backlands, where old-line Hispanic traditions, authoritarian and ecclesiastical, still exercised a powerful hold. Nonetheless, Lugones's mind and actions never followed a single trend. During the same period that he was rediscovering provincial Argentina, he was cultivating an expertise as an amateur Orientalist and, particularly, Egyptologist. His 1924 short story collection *Cuentos fatales* draws extensively on these studies, including lengthy disquisitions on the recent excavations of ancient Egyptian tombs. Lugones's Arabic tutor appears as a character, and a quasi-autobiographical narrator is seen avidly collecting lore and speculation about curses, amulets, and cultic initiation rites. Lugones had a special fascination with the more recondite, nonstandard aspects of the Arab world, such as the remnants of ancient cults that had somehow survived despite Islam's efforts to impose orthodoxy. These endeavors show that Lugones still harbored an admiration for cultural heterogeneity and eccentricity, even as he was advocating for his own nation a regression toward a past that his writing idealized as more uniform and regulated than the unruly present.

Toward the end of his life, Lugones went through a period of upheaval that caused him to rediscover Catholicism. He publicly declared that he had undergone a reconversion to this faith and practice. Observers who were constantly being caught off guard by Lugones's changes were surprised again when the author traveled out to an island often used by vacationers and fatally shot himself.

It would be a book-length undertaking to trace Lugones's ideological trajectory in relation to his activities as a writer and the nation's leading man of letters. It is possible, though, to give a glimpse of this intricate subject matter by considering one episode in Lugones's career as an organizer of cultural activities and one of his creative works, the poetry collection *Odas seculares* (Centennial Odes; 1910).

In 1910, Argentina celebrated the centennial of its independence from Spain. Lugones was the one to head the cultural commemorations, including the encouragement of literary works of suitably patriotic tendency. Rubén Darío, who had previously composed occasional verse to honor other nations, contributed *Canto a la Argentina* (Song to Argentina; 1910). Alberto Gerchunoff (1884-1950), representing Jewish Argentines, produced the novel *Los gauchos judíos* (*The Jewish Gauchos of the Pampas*; 1910), a rosy treatment of Argentine immigration and interior settlement. Lugones's own offering was the *Odas*. Though produced as civic verse for a specified occasion, the *Odas* are surprisingly effective in lyricizing Argentine social history. Readers who associated Lugones with an international, urbane form of experimental writing were impressed with his newfound reverence toward traditional, rural, small-town values. The *Odas* endorsed European immigration heartily, but other aspects of Argentina's program for modernization received scant attention, although industrial progress and entrepreneurial achievements were emphasized elsewhere in the festivities. Later writings confirmed that Lugones was drawn to a somewhat mystical, telluric cultural nationalism. He became preoccupied with rural Argentina and the old provincial cities. In this case, a sense of malaise with the terms of Argentina's civilization signaled, not a pluralistic mode of critical thought, but a conservative longing for a more hierarchical, set society.

During the first two decades of the century, the populist and anarchist Roberto J. Payró (1876-1928) won a readership with his picaresque narratives of country life. This author's outstanding gift was for the written representation of country talk, with its subtle ironies and deadpan humor. Unlike most contemporary realists, who tended to rely on educated narrators and to show rural people as verbally incompetent, he gave a great deal of space to the literary recreation of rural speech. This strategy not only allowed him to display the area in which he excelled as a writer, but also paid a populist homage to the ingenuity and expressivity of the population he portrayed.

Manuel Gálvez (1889-1950), who came to epitomize the Establishment, came on the scene as a figure of controversy. *Nacha Regules* (1917) is named for its pliant heroine, led into and out of prostitution by, respectively, a procurer and a social reformer (although, as many readers have noticed, he rehabilitates only one prostitute). *La maestra normal* (The Schoolmarm; 1914) features another listless young woman who falls into a stigmatized social role, this time as a partner in an illicit affair, and later regains at least a tenuous hold on social acceptance, although she remains at a permanent disadvantage. Both provoked some scandal upon publication. *La maestra normal* offended many schoolteachers and school officials, who read it as a disloyal attack on education and the behavior of school personnel authored by a real-world Inspector of Secondary Education. In addition, residents of the provincial city that the novel fictionally portrays were enraged by its image of their home town; groups were formed to defend the good name of the locality. Lugones polemicized against the author and the novel, claiming the work was a ploy to discredit public schooling and bring a return to Catholic education. Such discussion, which often seems petty in retrospect, created enough of a stir to give Gálvez the reputation of a daring author willing to take risks and disturb readers.

With the passage of time, Gálvez's novels no longer appear to be instruments of social reform. Of course, current-day readers are aware that Gálvez later evolved into an upholder of conservative Catholicism; but even without this hindsight, it is not hard to discern in his work a lack of commitment to social change. Both the above-mentioned novels contain an uneasy mixture of ideas about the causes of such problems as prostitution, sexual harassment, and the stigmatization of those who become classified as deviants.

On the one hand, there are indications that society—Buenos Aires in *Nacha Regules*, the provinces in *La maestra normal*—is not civilized enough to accommodate and assist its disadvantaged members. Nacha, for example, finds the respectable citizenry of Buenos Aires callously unhelpful when she seeks to reenter it. For much of the novel, she receives no help or sympathy in her efforts to struggle free from prostitution. On the other hand, Gálvez seems to blame Nacha for not extricating herself from her degraded life through her individual resolve and drive. The novel dwells on moments when she could not muster the will to leave her charismatic procurer. The same conflicting ideas alternate in the portrait of the schoolmarm, whose problems are attributed, now to the weak formation of a Catholic conscience, now to society's unhelpful and censorious attitudes toward her.

From the 1910s, two social essayists stand out especially. Manuel Ugarte (1878-1951) is principally important for warning against an excessive U.S. influence on Latin America. His work is also an early example of the fusion of social criticism with an existential analysis of Latin America's situation, a tendency that would grow in importance later in the century.

Ricardo Rojas (1882-1957) expounded a back-to-the-roots cultural nationalism. His insistence on an essence based in the very soil, making the region's life unique, was in line with the contemporary vogue for telluric explanations of Latin America's distinctive traits. Rojas's more lasting contribution was the publication (1917-22) of the massive *Historia de la literatura argentina* (History of Argentine Literature). An updated work of similar scope was produced 1958-1960 by a team of critics headed by Rafael Alberto Arrieta (1889-1968).

III

Buenos Aires of the 1920s was home to a good deal of avant-garde activity. When news of the European avant-garde movements first reached Argentina, information was sketchy; many of the early efforts to issue vanguardist proclamations scarcely went beyond sloganeering. By the early 1920s, though at least some Argentine experimental writers were developing well-conceived programs for aesthetic change. Two theoretically opposed, but in practice overlapping, factions won attention with their feuding, proclamations, and counterproclamations. A revolution through aesthetics was the asserted goal of the movement led by Jorge Luis Borges (1899-1986), who had spent the war years in Europe and returned to Argentina eager to start a Buenos Aires avant-garde, and Oliverio Girondo (1891-1967). This group endeavor is variously alluded to as Martinfierrism, Florida, and Ultraism. Each of these tags sums up a different aspect of the group's distinctive character. The group rallied around the tabloid *Martín Fierro* (1924-1927) and was associated with the Calle Florida for that thoroughfare's elegant modernity. Ultraism was, specifically, a poetic doctrine maintaining that unusual metaphors alone constituted the new poetry needed to revitalize Buenos Aires, and indeed world, culture. Understandably, Florida poets seldom applied this notion full force, although *Prismas* (1922) by Eduardo González Lanuza (1900) nearly sustains the principle for an entire book of poems, and Norah Lange (1906-72) also approached the goal of sheer reliance on metaphor, while Francisco Luis Bernárdez (1900-78) produced some work that was one unexpected analogy after another. Carlos Mastronardi (1901-76), Jacobo Fijman (1898-1970), Conrado Nalé Roxlo (1898-1971), and Ricardo Molinari (1898) were poetically independent affiliates of the movement. Raúl González Tuñón (1905-74), Enrique Gonález Tuñón (1901-43), Raúl Scalabrini Ortiz (1898-1959), and Nicolás Olivari (1900-66) were already showing the strong social concerns that would distinguish their work after Martinfierrism dissolved. Inevitably, some poets who were never especially innovative came to prominence during the avant-garde excitement, Horacio Jorge Molina (1899-1957) and Arturo Cancela (1892-1957) being two examples. It would be some time before the dissimilarities of the avant-gardists became clear. While Florida is here discussed in its literary aspects, it should be noted that the movement also included many experimental visual artists. Indeed, many of the Florida writers had a sideline in the visual arts, and nearly all were close followers of the art scene.

Florida's rival was Boedo, named after a more working-class street that summed up the group's emphasis. Boedo writers advocated a social or a proletarian literature, as they called it, and looked to early Soviet writing as an example. It included Elías Castelnuovo (1893-?), Leónidas Barletta (1902-75), Alvaro Yunque (1889-1982; real name Arístides Gandolfi Herrero), and Roberto Mariani (1892-1946). The last of these was a group spokesman who advocated a literary examination of the proletariat, but he turned to the "white-collar proletariat," i.e., clerical workers, for the subject matter of his most memorable short stories, the 1925 *Cuentos de la oficina* (Tales of the Office). The name of Max Dickmann (1902) sometimes appears in discussions of 1920s social writing, but he really made his impact in the 1930s with fiction whose modernity of technique threw into relief the surprising conservatism most Boedo writers manifested in the construction of their texts.

The highly innovative journalist, fiction writer, and, later, playwright Roberto Arlt (1900-42) was associated at times with both groups. Arlt's most important and influential work is the anomalous 1929 *Los siete locos* (*The Seven Madmen*). This text has been a source both of the raw urban realism typical of much subsequent Argentine fiction and of the fantastic, grotesque, and bizarre elements that have flourished in other areas of national literature. The fusion of these disparate constituents, and the novel's tantalizing promise of hidden meanings, give this erratic and enigmatic novel its enduring interest.

Florida and Boedo writers held differing notions of how to bring about massive change. The Florida program held that a new lyric vision and new expressive language could launch the desired transformation. Altered perception and communication would entail changes in all areas of life. The point of view of Boedo representatives was that social change must come first, with modifications in literary language appearing secondarily.

While the above characterizations make the groups sound clearly opposed, in practice their writing was not always so easy to distinguish. Members of each group could not resist borrowing from the other faction's repertory of innovations. Boedo writers occasionally revealed a fondness for showy literary language, even though their program favored a Spartan approach to expression. Working-class life would have seemed to be the special preserve of Boedo, but a number of Florida writers were drawn to this raw material and set to lyricizing the proletarian neighborhoods of Buenos Aires. Florida tended to favor poetry heavily, while Boedo was a movement of fiction writers. In consequence, young poets tended to publish in Florida publications even when the themes they favored would appear to align them more with Boedo. Contact between the groups was frequent. Members of each band attended the other's banquets, and all those involved kept a close eye on new developments among writers on each side. A number of beliefs and attitudes were common to Boedo and Florida writers, especially a conviction that their youth, vigor, and exceptional vision would enable them to change the character of literature and society.

Florida-Boedo avant-gardism provided a propitious environment for unusual creators who, without these movements, might have remained outsiders to literary life. The painter-poet Xul Solar (1881-1963; real name Alejandro Schulz Solari) was one such individual. The Florida writers were quick to cultivate such tribal elders as Macedonio Fernández (1874-1952) and Ricardo Güiraldes (1886-1927), although they give little evidence of a serious attempt to apprentice themselves to their proclaimed predecessors.

The attention given to these youthful movements did not entail a neglect of authors with a more standard concept of literary life. Gálvez continued to produce during this period and Lugones was highly visible, engaged in a conflict-filled relation with the new movements. The poet Alfonsina Storni (1892-1938) was an active journalist, represented feminist thought of her time, and attracted considerable notice for her daringly confessional verse. Mainstream literary journalism was well served by the magazine *Nosotros* (We; 1907-43), whose most famous editor was Roberto F. Giusti. This publication was noted for its coverage of intellectual and aesthetic tendencies in Europe and Latin America, specializing in critical social thought and reflections on the status of culture. It was sympathetic in its treatment of the avant-gardists and social writers, although the latter discounted the magazine along with the rest of the existing literary establishment.

During the period of avant-gardism, which largely coincided with the Radical government of 1916-30, reformist programs of all types were championed by literary celebrities. Storni promoted a variety of feminism that included a strong component of sexual liberationism. Lugones and Gálvez, both in the public eye, were making their way rightwards on the political spectrum. The Florida group espoused a utopian anarchism and cultural radicalism, purposely kept underdefined. The social writers had little sophisticated understanding of Marx's thought, but admired the October revolution and early Soviet culture (they knew chiefly Maxim Gorki's and Leonid Andreiev's writings).

Of the many 1920s works revealing less overt ideological concerns, Güiraldes's 1926 *Don Segundo Sombra* was exceptionally successful. This lyrical novel takes up again the figure of the gaucho. Real-world gaucho culture was, though, hardly left intact by then. Accordingly, the gaucho of the novel is not represented as a here-and-now being, but as a mythically charged presence emanating out of the gaucho tradition. His purpose in making an anachronistic apparition is to transmit the best of gaucho culture, as it once existed, to a modern-day heir who can carry this legacy into the future. The recipient of his gift is a young boy later revealed to be heir to great farm holdings.

The boy, now a responsible hacienda owner, recalls the five years he roamed the pampa with his preceptor. In his version, the most important part of his education was the acquisition of concepts and attitudes useful in the conscientious running of an estate. Don Segundo Sombra made his apprentice brave, resourceful, observant, and attentive to the needs of his animals. These virtues prevent the landowner from falling into the easy pattern of leaving the estate to a supervisor and living a refined life in Buenos Aires and Europe.

It is easy to satirize *Don Segundo Sombra* because the work is so unabashedly centered on the needs and duties of the landholding class. Though young Fabio's hacienda was no doubt carved out of the gaucho's open range, over the latter's bitter protest, his landowner role somehow becomes a way of maintaining the essence of gaucho life. Even with these obvious contradictions, the novel deserves recognition for its legendary and lyrical presentation of propositions that, in a real-world context, would seem ridiculously skewed to favor the new owners of the pampa. The novel's rapid rise to the status of a contemporary classic reflects the need for a version of recent rural history able to reconcile the disturbing conflicts left by the aggressive campaign to civilize the pampa.

In September of 1930, Argentina's half century of relatively stable democracy ended. The military takeover of that year signaled a reverse from which the country would not quickly recover. Subsequent Argentine history shows no extended period of well-accepted governance by elected officials. This record is disturbing, given the country's inherent potential for wealth, high level of education, extremely strong industrial development for the region, previous record of governance, and other favorable indexes. Argentina's vulnerability to political disruption has baffled many, but also has stimulated essayists to produce a good deal of innovative work in their attempts to diagnose the nation.

El hombre que está solo y espera (The Man Who is Alone and Waits; 1931) by Raúl Scalabrini Ortiz is the first such introspective essay to gain wide notice in post-1930 Argentina. Though it has come to sound old-fashioned, this work is certainly a fascinating document for students of contemporary culture. In a prose that owes much to the author's avant-garde background, Scalabrini espouses an urban tellurism and examines the lower-middle class, overaged adolescent who, to him, personifies Buenos Aires. Scalabrini points out that this narcissistic, misogynistic specimen is already disappearing and accurately hints that his own guidebook will soon be outdated.

A more substantial contribution to Argentina's self-analysis is *Radiografía de la pampa* (*X-Ray of the Pampa*; 1933) by Ezequiel Martínez Estrada (1895-1964). The essay continues the combination of social criticism and reflection of existential issues earlier popularized by Ugarte. *Radiografía*, despite its title, is not limited to a discussion of the famous plains, but the image of these vast empty spaces runs through its meditations on Spain and its erratic settlement of the River Plate area, the emergence and suppression of the gaucho way of life, the validity of Western civilization, the nothingness lurking under human existence, and the needs of the contemporary moment.

In contrast to the typical popular presentation of history as full of diverse and colorful actors and events, Martínez Estrada's account of Argentine history emphasizes absence, emptiness, and lack. Argentine history is, for him, exemplary of the nothingness that underlies all human endeavors, but in other circumstances is more easily ignored. He argues that the area featured no major indigenous civilization, and, indeed, no significant Indian element to contribute to future development. Moreover, once the Spanish crown noted the lack of precious metals in the area, it neglected to build up this branch of the empire. Those Spaniards who had come to settle in Argentina, imagining it to hold some promise of wealth, adventure, and meaning, confronted the vacuum central to human existence. The great progressive and liberal program of the 1880s succeeded in strewing across the pampa an occasional fence, telegraph post, or other sign of human activity, but did not alter its fundamental nature. Martínez Estrada won a place of honor among dissident critics of Argentine history because of his refusal to compose the chronicle in a heroic mode and because of his severe questioning of the doctrine of unlimited progress that justified the late ninteenth-century development programs. It is common, though, for these same revisionists to object to Martínez Estrada's relentless negativism. Only the bleakest of existences, such as that of the disillusioned conquistador facing his own nothingness in an empty land, appears to achieve authenticity.

The set of themes vaguely classifiable as existential continues to dominate Argentine intellectual life for some time. Certainly this category contains the essays and fiction of Eduardo Mallea (1903-82). *La bahía del silencio* (*The Bay of Silence*; 1940) and *Todo verdor perecerá* (*All Green Shall Perish*; 1941) show many continuities with the general mode of cultural analysis that had been being developed by the essayists discussed above. However, while such figures as Ugarte, Scalabrini, and Martínez Estrada are all associated with (if not always successful practitioners of) a skeptical revision of Argentina's developmental history, Mallea's work is generally perceived as favoring a traditional outlook. Elitism and quietism are two characteristics that hostile critics have frequently discerned in his writings, and he has never enjoyed popularity among social thinkers attempting to reassess, from a position other than the establishment one, what has been important in the making of modern Argentina.

Deserving mention in connection with the 1930s scene is the review *Sur* (South) which flourished from its founding in 1931 to the early 1940s, and continued publication until the mid 1970s. Its editor, Victoria Ocampo (1891-1979) was a well-connected woman determined to shape the Argentine reader's tastes, provide worthy translations of new European, British, and U.S. writing, and promote the careers of those Argentine writers she found of interest. *Sur*, which became considerably less innovative in the mid-1940s, drew a good deal of hostile commentary for its prominent display of non-Latin American culture and for its cliquishness. Nonetheless, during its best years, *Sur* performed a valuable cultural service in, particularly, supplying translations of high quality. Although *Sur* is often perceived as a publication unconcerned with social realities, a fair amount of social criticism appeared in its pages, with a quasi-mystical belief in primal forces being a recurring idea. Telluric views of Latin American issues appealed to Ocampo, whether enunciated by such foreigners as Count Herman von Keyserling and Waldo Frank or by such Argentine essayists as Ricardo Rojas. In some cases, writers favored by *Sur* produced work that later became useful to essayists of a much more overtly social bent. Because *Sur* and Ocampo are so strongly linked with a high-art, European-inspired notion of Argentine civilization, mention of the magazine and its editor provokes reactions based more on these associations than on any close examination of the publication itself.

1940 is the year conveniently assigned to the generation of poets who again took up the imaginative, figurative mode of the 1920s avant-garde. Oliverio Girondo, already mentioned for his promotion of the earlier Martinfierrism, now became the elder mentor to the new group of experimental poets; in addition, the generation of 1940 admired independent poets associated with 1920s innovation, such as Carlos Mastronardi. This respectful attitude toward the most recent generation of distinguished poets is one sign of the 1940s group's dissimilarity, as a literary movement, to the rebellious avant-gardists of twenty years before.

The 1940 poets were, unlike many members of the 1920s group, seriously dedicated to refining the art of poetry through assiduous study and practice more than through any special virtue inherent in being young and new. Their view of the poetic past was critical, not dismissive. A number of definitely 1940s-associated poets later became continuously innovative members of the Buenos Aires poetic scene, especially Olga Orozco (1920) and Enrique Molina (1910). Alberto Girri (1919), less representative of the 1940s movement, came to prominence at the same time. The son of the 1920s avant-gardist Baldomero Fernández Moreno (1886-1950), César Fernández Moreno (1919) was a member of the group, though his career would be at least as much that of a critic and man of letters as of a poet. Alfredo A. Roggiano (1919), the critic and editor, began his career as a 1940s poet. María Granata (1923) was with the movement but won her lasting name as a prose writer. One of the poets considered most representative of the poetic goals of 1940, Jorge Calvetti (1916), never achieved the secure place in Argentine letters accorded the above-mentioned colleagues. Of less-famed poets associated with the movement, many still deserve attention: César Rosales (1910), Miguel Angel Gómez (1911-59), Eduardo Bosco (1913-43), León Benarós (1915), Juan Rodolfo Wilcock (1919). Vicente Barbieri (1903-56) also gained prominence in the 1940s.

The 1940s group had two decades of perspective on avant-gardism and could not consider itself the "new thing under the sun" the previous generation claimed to be. The 1920s group proclaimed its great youth and included poets as young as their teens (Norah Lange and César Tiempo, both born in 1906); the overheating economy and ebullient literary scene made it possible for very young poets to publish a collection. These poets emphasized their youth and originality less, and few brought out a book before their mid- or late twenties. Not only would missionary zeal have been odd in a Buenos Aires long since socialized into avant-garde ways of expression, but it was no longer possible to mount a flamboyant youth movement in the dampened political and economic environment of the times.

The results of the 1940s movement are still unfolding. Enrique Molina has probably been the most steadfast upholder of its surrealist-influenced, dominantly metaphorical notion of poetry. In the 1950s, he and the theorist-polemicist Aldo Pellegrini (1903), ardent defender of surrealism, formed a group of Argentine poets dedicated to this aesthetic. This secondary movement, centered around the poetry magazine *A partir de cero* (Starting from Zero; 1952-1953, 1956), brought to public attention new poets as well as the underrated Juan José Ceselli (1909), whose slow emergence into belated fame is still underway. Olga Orozco's extremely original subsequent development, starting from her basis in 1940s second-generation avant-gardism, will be discussed later. César Fernández Moreno, while giving a good deal of his time to critical work, has continued to draw out the possibilities of the 1940s aesthetic program with his sophisticated incursions into intergenre forms. His combinations of poetry with elaborate visual arrangements and experiments with fragmented, poetic prose have shown his willingness to try many different directions.

Outside the 1940s group, with its commitment to experimentation in form, the decade saw a continuation of the effort to represent accurately the working class and lower middle class. Castelnuovo and other 1920s veterans extended proletarian writing into this new era of low horizons. Bernardo Verbitsky (1907-79), a newly emerging writer, specialized in the muted, meditative realism associated with 1940s realism; he also typifies the mixture of existential meditation and social criticism that has been recurrently present in twentieth-century Argentine social thought. His 1941 novel *Es difícil empezar a vivir* (It's Hard to Start Living) attracted favorable notice for its simultaneous presentation of existential concerns, the class and ethnic hierarchy of Argentina in the late 1930s, and the results of the economic stagnation and discouragement over the political process that characterized the era. The lower-middle-class hero, engaged as a reporter, is made to extract his news items from other newspapers. These resentfully gleaned items appear in the novel, offering glimpses of a world on the edge of war and hints of the genocidal campaign already underway. Many other realist works of the period could be cited, such as *El río oscuro* (The Dark River; 1943) by Alfredo Varela (1914), a notably clear case of social realism in the Argentine novel, and many instances of the fiction of Bernardo Kordon (1915). It should be noted, though, that when this last-named author was not working his melancholy vein of realism, he switched modes entirely to produce some colorful, swashbuckling adventure tales set in exotic lands. Realism and social protest were also present outside the novel. Raúl González Tuñón, previously mentioned as one of the most socially aware poets of the Martinfierrist movement, had fully emerged as a political poet with his 1935 collection *La rosa blindada* (The Armored Rose). During the 1940s he alternated between a more humanistic critique of the capitalistic world and a somewhat party-line realism that made the poet seem to be a functionary rather than an original creator. His brother Enrique, who died in 1943, shared his social awareness and produced a number of testimonial-format works that described the experience of being down and out in post-1930 Buenos Aires. Enrique Wernicke (1915-68) was influential in drama as well as fiction. José B. Pedroni (1899-1968) typifies the poet who moved from 1920s aestheticism to 1930s social protest, while José Portogallo (1904-73; real name José Ananía) is representative of poets who from the outset of their careers criticized social conditions. Raúl Scalabrini Ortiz, who had couched social commentary in imaginative figurative language, renounced this mixed mode. He subsequently concentrated on straightforward denunciatory reportage. In this later endeavor, he gained the most attention for his muckraking exposé of the British involvement in the laying and maintenance of the Argentine rail system. This early example of dependency analysis did not, however, displace Scalabrini's image with the public as the author of *El hombre que está solo y espera*, with its allusions to the spirit of the land.

Another protagonist of the 1920s, Borges, had wearied of his Ultraist obsession with metaphor, which he came to see as an immature, crudely spectacular notion of literature. In 1944 he brought out *Ficciones*, a collection of short stories or, as they may also be seen, near-essays (the title may be translated as "fictions," although the Spanish title is retained for the English-language version). Together with the stories in *El aleph* (*The Aleph*; 1949), *Ficciones* established Borges's international reputation, although worldwide recognition did not come immediately on publication of these works. Typically, Borges avoids fully developing (i.e., to the length of a novel or an exhaustively elaborated long poem) the ideas central to the text; instead, he suggests what might be done using these ideas, then appears to discard the plan or be overwhelmed by it, bringing the piece to a close. Indeed, one of the recurring suggestions in Borges's work is that the attempt to work out fully a set of ideas is doomed to result in an elaborate, ridiculous construct whose main purpose is to satisfy human beings' need for such artifacts.

A characteristic Borges piece begins by establishing in the reader's mind some system of obtaining and assembling knowledge about what exists and how the cosmos functions. As more and more elements are added to the information to be considered, and as these constituents prove more and more unwieldy, the organizing scheme seems arbitrary and absurdly inadequate. The suggestion is then put forward that generally accepted presuppositions, though useful for making sense of life on a day-to-day basis, would reveal themselves equally flimsy if subjected to the stress of difficult-to-assimilate new information or, for that matter, to a skeptical and thorough examination. Explanations and interpretations that will surely strike the reader as wild and arbitrary are made to seem no more so than the set of propositions considered self-evident by educated members of Western society.

Such an outlook, necessarily relativistic, would presumably privilege no one system or point of view over others and lead to a pluralistic acceptance of dissidence. It was surprising, then, to find the real-life Borges often making statements that showed an illiberal disregard for the well-being of political dissenters. The contradiction between Borges's liberal skepticism as a writer and his erratic dogmatism as an interviewee has generated considerable discussion. Borges at times has seemed to lack an understanding that his words could have an effect on real-world conditions. While Borges's renown as an erratic, capricious political commentator grew during the early seventies, in his last years he recovered some credibility by speaking in favor of the maintenance of human rights.

IV

At the same time that Borges was winning readers with his, in many ways, fantastic stories, other narrators specializing in nonmimetic, figurative modes were also rising to prominence. *Sur* tended to favor nonrealistic narrative, and such fiction quickly became one of the mainstays of several publishing houses. This is the period during which Adolfo Bioy Casares (1914; Borges's occasional coauthor under their shared pseudonym Honorio Bustos Domecq) and Silvina Ocampo (1906; sister of *Sur* editor Victoria Ocampo and wife of Bioy Casares) made their names. Together with Borges, these two promoted the anthologizing of Argentine fantastic short fiction, new and old.

Manuel Mujica Láinez (1910-84), who favored both fantastic narrative and an embellished fictional recreation of Buenos Aires's history, Enrique Anderson-Imbert (1910), Julio Cortázar (1914-84), and Manuel Peyrou (1902-74) all benefited from the nonrealistic vogue. Ernesto Sabato (1911; name earlier styled Sábato), a promising nuclear scientist who had renounced his first career when his faith in reason faltered, began to publish a surrealistic novel, *La fuente muda* (The Mute Fountain) in *Sur*. Alberto Vanasco (1925) in 1947 published *Sin embargo Juan vivía* (Yet Juan Was Living), a novel in the second person and future tenses. Borges, Bioy Casares, and Silvina Ocampo ransacked the Argentine literary past for examples of nonmimetic writing to anthologize. Their elegant, urbane heroes of Argentine writing included Eduardo Estanislao Holmberg (1852-1937), Atilio Chiáppori (1880-1947), and Enrique Banchs (1889-1968). The mode established by this group—to write fantastic texts and to read literature for its fantastic elements—has remained as a typical pattern available to late-emerging writers. Angel Bonomini (1929), Osvaldo Svanascini (1920; disciple of the avant-garde mystic Xul Solar), and Fernando Sorrentino (1942) follow this career type, with Sorrentino continuing the tradition of Argentine anthologies that show off narrative alternatives to realistic representation.

The acceptance of the fantastic as a vehicle for statements about political and ethical questions led many Argentine authors to have at least occasional recourse to the mode. Marco Denevi (1922), essentially a social moralist, chose the fable as his favored means of expression. Martínez Estrada, somber in his essays, became an eccentrically inventive, even lighthearted narrator. Arturo Jauretche (1900-74), best known for polemic against the spread of middle-brow culture and mindless consumerism, turned to the fable. Joaquín Gómez Bas (1907-84) wrote brief, fantastically exaggerated stories pointing to social inequities.

In 1946, Colonel Juan Domingo Perón emerged as clearly the political leader of Argentina, although he had long been edging into that position. Perón (1895-1974) had a populist program that emphasized redistribution of wealth and harassment of the traditional elites. However his regime is evaluated, it is clear that most intellectuals and creators disliked Perón and felt constrained in their expression while he was in power (until 1955). This is not to say that there were no Peronist intellectuals, including a few theorists, within the Peronist organization, but that resentment and anxiety was the typical attitude among the intelligentsia. A notable exception was Leopoldo Marechal (1900-79), former Martinfierrist. In 1948, he finally published his long-in-progress *Adán Buenosayres*. This poetic novel contains an allegory of humankind's fall and redemption, an encapsulation of Buenos Aires's cultural history, and a satire of the 1920s avant-garde, among other features. However, it provides few clues to the author's unusual political preference, which isolated him from his contemporaries and, after the fall of Perón, damaged his literary career.

The early 1950s continued to be propitious for fantastic literature, short fable-like tales, and other indirectly allusive forms. These were occasionally used to communicate negative views of Peronism, which ranged from indignation over the suppression of dissent to simple resentment of new gains by the working class. The introspective manner of social criticism firmly established by Martínez Estrada was taken up by newer practitioners. Sabato, the physicist turned surrealist, sustained a quarrel with Western rationalism and self-satisfaction. His 1952 novel *El túnel* (*The Outsider*) gained rapid popularity. This brief, brooding novel of alienation combined the themes of the essays Sabato had been producing with the Gothic fictional embellishments and phantasmagoric imagery that have drawn even idle readers to follow along. Héctor A. Murena (1923-75), an intellectual heir of Martínez Estrada, returned to the longstanding problem of Latin America's sense of identity. In *El pecado original de América Latina* (The Original Sin of Latin America; 1952) he argued that Latin America was collectively confused and tormented by the knowledge that it was not Europe, Europe being the dominant strand of civilization. Whether Latin America tries to reproduce the high civilization of Europe or whether it struggles to work out its own non-European criteria of civilization, it is living out a drama arising from the dilemma into which it was born. This situation, described as an insurmountable contradiction, seemed implausible to social critics who believed that Latin America should gain confidence in its own distinctive folkways and cultural achievements. Like previous analysts of Latin American or Argentine society who bring in notes of existential despair, Murena is open to the charge of making all proposed solutions to the problems in question sound like self-delusions. The only task urged upon Latin America is the recognition that its civilization is irreducibly paradoxical. The demand for a change in awareness, but not necessarily in the form, of Latin American civilization is a typical trait of existential social critics in this line, which extends down to the popularizer of social theories, Julio Mafud (1925).

Perón's fall in 1955 emboldened writers, whose dissent had been muted and disguised for the past decade, to criticize openly the social arrangement. The influential "parricidal" generation, associated with such figures as Noé Jitrik, David Viñas, Juan José Sebreli (1930), Ismael Viñas (1925), and Adolfo Prieto, flourished in a period in which anti-Peronism was the dominant political sentiment. But as a critical group they sought to avoid the type of unexamined anti-Peronism that many Argentine intellectuals allowed to comingle with class hostility. The members examined Argentine letters against the historical background and saw the record of various segments of society competing for wealth, power, and prestige. There was a downwards evaluation of those cultural leaders who had advocated patterning Argentine civilization along high-cultural European lines. At the same time, new attention went to the voices that had spoken out in disagreement with the ideal of progress that had prevailed. Sarmiento's contemporary critics, who came to include many besides Alberdi, and nineteenth-century observers who admired the Indians Argentina then discarded, now took on a fresh importance. The result was a greater skepticism toward the achievements of the liberal, progressive era. This period, traditionally viewed as a time of impressive modernization and swift buildup of the infrastructure, now looked like the opening a new would-be elite had found to install itself in high positions. The fact that Argentina had invited in foreign capital to move projects along was another much-criticized feature of Argentine history. The period 1880-1930 now resembled less a steady march toward civilization than a troubled move toward the type of civilization that would most favor the well-educated bourgeoisie at the expense of other sectors. Though the era was certainly less fraught with overt conflict than the period since 1930, there were now frequent expressions of doubt over and dissent from the liberal project.

The late 1950s and early 1960s brought notable narrative works by intellectuals involved in the social discussion of post-1955. David Viñas published the novels *Cayó sobre su rostro* (He Fell on His Face; 1955), *Los dueños de la tierra* (The Owners of the Land; 1958), and *Dar la cara* (Willing to Stand Up; 1962), examining the fall of a rural tyrant, the suppression of ranchhands' strikes in Patagonia, and the disillusionment of late-1950s radicals, respectively. Martínez Estrada, whose monumental essays often divert attention away from his brief, quirky fiction and poetry, deserves more scrutiny for his imaginative writing during this period. *Marta Riquelme*, a nouvelle of 1956, humorously mimics the laborious exertions of a textual exegete determined to wrest transcendental meanings from the least propitious of writings. Murena, unlike Martínez Estrada, was as dour and brooding in his imaginative writing as in his essays. The novel *Las leyes de la noche* (*The Laws of the Night*; 1958), with its numbed urban heroine, is his most recognized. Roger Pla (1927-82), principally known for his literary commentary, also contributed to the reflective, somber novel of the late 1950s and early 1960s. Sabato in 1962 brought out the massive novel *Sobre héroes y tumbas* (*On Heroes and Tombs*), full of anxiety about the course taken by Western civilization and suggesting a return to a simpler way concerned with human values rather than sophistication. Marta Lynch (1929-85), Antonio Di Benedetto (1928-86), and, to some degree, Beatriz Guido (1925-88) began to make their names as socially critical novelists. Dalmiro Sáenz (1926) was representative of liberalized Catholic thought and of writing that drew on the generic conventions of the hard-boiled detective novel.

V

The somber mood of the Argentine novel and its reliance on relatively unobtrusive narrative techniques came to an end when the "new novel" of the mid-1960s to 1970s monopolized attention on the literary scene. It is difficult to assess the significance of this narrative movement because it coincided with a suddenly heated market for Latin American literature. Publicity became overblown and commercial success was easily confounded with efficacious literary expression. To point out the prevalence of hype, though, is not to deny the existence of exceptionally original and well-conceived new novels.

Rayuela (*Hopscotch*), the 1963 novel by Julio Cortázar, is the foremost Argentine work from this innovative wave. Its most celebrated features are its "Table of Instructions," a jocular set of guidelines for reading the novel, and the appended segments that follow the chapters presenting the plot. The instructions invite the reader to proceed conventionally through that part of the work held together by a linked, if sometimes whimsically improbable, series of events. However, there is a strong suggestion that anyone content with only such a perusal is deficient in imagination and initiative. A more demanding form of reading is then mapped out for the reader. This second reading requires leafing backwards and forwards in the text and attempting to integrate with the plot-bearing chapters the seemingly miscellaneous appended segments. Diverse in length, subject-matter, and treatment, these component units nonetheless are alike in supporting the overall assertions that Cortázar and his novel put forward. The reader is urged to appreciate the random conjunction of diverse elements, either for its absurdity or because it reveals an unexpected, irrational order. The fragments also constitute an homage to many members of Cortázar's set of cultural heroes. Eccentric, whimsical, and obsessed creators, whether in the high or popular arts, merit this tribute.

Cortázar's work had a revitalizing effect on experimental writing in Argentina and led to such subsequent innovations as the novel of language. A meaningful effort in its moment, the late-1960s and early-1970s novel of language has since lost much of its appeal. Consisting of a very loosely structured outpouring of prose, usually with little punctuation and with frequent shifts in narrative voice, register of speech, and fictional setting, the form tended to run many diverse items together in a massive flow of words. Juan Carlos Martini (earlier known as Juan Carlos Martini Real to distinguish himself from a namesake fellow writer, 1944), Néstor Sánchez (1932), Héctor Libertella (1946), and Eduardo Gudiño Kieffer (1934), son of the realist novelist Luis Gudiño Kramer (1898-1973) are representative here. Since the novel of language lost momentum, relatively few prose writers have gained reputations chiefly for formal experimentation (Osvaldo Lamborghini [1934-85] is a good example). There has been a shift away from spectacular fictional structure and a drive to make more direct the relations between Argentine writing and society. A work as frolicsome as *Hopscotch* could not comment very directly on social conditions, although it could criticize, at an abstract level, some of the presuppositions behind bourgeois constraints on expression. Cortázar himself appears never to have become a very close student of society's here-and-now workings. After his youth, which extended far into his career, as a precocious, capricious literary inventor, Cortázar began to take part in left-wing political activities. His interest in radical activism surfaced in such writings as *El libro de Manuel* (*A Manual for Manuel*; 1973), which gives at least an aesthetically favorable treatment to a group of fey, whimsical urban guerrillas. Still, it would take a good deal of special pleading to argue that an approach like Cortázar's, always touched with whimsy and a cultivated element of chance, could supply a literature with focused social commentary. The frequent complaints about Cortázar from socially critical writers and commentators, which at times seem to amount to a widespread vendetta, are more understandable taking into account that this one author exercised so much influence. There was considerable anxiety that the success of flamboyantly playful writing was diminishing the chances for writers more directly concerned with the specifics of the social system.

For pointed social commentary, Argentine drama of the 1960s-1970s is generally more forthcoming than experimental fiction. As shifts in government policy at all levels left the implementation of cultural policy uncertain, newer playwrights learned to deal with obstacles to the production of their plays. Not only was censorship in its many forms a possibility, but without recourse to censorship an official body could make the logistics of production difficult by invoking various ordinances and regulations. As a consequence, and also because of precarious funding, dramas were often designed so as to be performable under improvised conditions if necessary.

Historias para ser contadas (Stories for the Telling; 1957) by Osvaldo Dragún (1929) is characteristic in its reliance on actors to carry the production. It can be performed without staging, can be abbreviated or lengthened, and offers ample opportunity for improvisational embellishment. In a Brechtian spirit, the actors present themselves as just that, and as acting and talking in order to make certain points about social ethics. Responsibility for the well-being of other members of society is reiterated as the essential principle. *Y nos dijeron que éramos inmortales* (And They Told Us We Were Immortal; 1962) also turns over to the performers the work of making the drama succeed. With little support from scenography and a text that is, in most regards, merely a guide, the actors must sing, dance, mime, recite poetry, narrate stories, and possibly improvise.

Agustín Cuzzani (1917-87) continues to be known chiefly for his 1965 *Para que se cumplan las Escrituras* (In Fulfillment of the Scriptures). The longstanding problem of free will and fate presents a fresh dilemma when a new machine proves too efficient in futurological projection. Uniting a theological issue with concern over the ethical problems brought by modernization, the play develops a complex message but is unambiguous in urging greater attention to matters of conscience in society.

Carlos Gorostiza (1920) has been active in all aspects of alternative theater. Social responsibility is a major theme in his work as well. *El pan de la locura* (The Bread of Madness; 1958) shows an outbreak of ergot poisoning and raises the issue of ethics in manufacturing. *Los prójimos* (Fellow Creatures; 1967) reminds urbanites that they, too, should be willing to help out a neighbor in trouble. *The Bread of Madness* is notable for a deliberately cartoon-like stiffness, suggesting a flattening of affect among the members of the poisoned and morally deficient community. *Los prójimos* has the unusual feature of making the audience feel like the dramatic characters cast in onlooker roles, who are willing to sit back passively and watch mayhem be visited on a neighbor.

Griselda Gambaro (1928; name previously styled Gámbaro) is best known as an Argentine practitioner of theater of the absurd. This description, though, should not be taken to indicate that Gambaro is primarily interested in the absurd for abstractly philosophical reasons, as might well be the case with European absurdists. The bond between members of society and the ridiculous and miserable results of trying to ignore this necessary solidarity take a prominent place in Gambaro's concept of the absurd. While it would be difficult to argue that Gambaro's adaptation of theater of the absurd is exclusively Latin American, it is certainly well suited to a society and a moment in which social problems are so urgent as to infiltrate themselves into existential concerns. *Los siameses* (The Siamese Twins; 1967) features two characters who, despite one's persecution of the other, are inseparably bonded. The attempt to dominate and subjugate others and the human impulses that work against this effort are recurring themes in Gambaro's work. Many other playwrights, such as Roberto M. Cossa (1934), could also be discussed for their dramatic presentation of morals in society.

Although relatively realistic fiction writers had been overshadowed by the new novel and the novel of language, a number of them claimed increasing attention over time; in general, their less spectacular careers have continued to the present time. Among these writers whose ascent was less rapid and spectacular—although all have had moments of public attention—are Elvira Orphée (1930), Marta Traba (1930-83), Daniel Moyano (1928), Leonor Picchetti (1942), the narrator and dramatist Ricardo Halac (1935), María Esther de Miguel (1930), Oscar Hermes Villordo (1928), Antonio Dal Masetto (1938), Abelardo Castillo (1935), also a dramatist, Humberto Costantini (1924-87), Pedro Orgambide (1929), and Eduardo Goligorsky (1931).

VI

Manuel Puig (1929-90) has been the only Argentine author since the boom to win a really sizable international audience through translation. At home, though, Puig never attained a secure place among the nation's leading writers. His mimicry of popular writing and allusions to gay life alarmed some critics. In addition, as Puig came to spend more time abroad, the focus of his work grew progressively less Argentine. Puig's most distinctive specialty was the imitation of pop-culture modes. His work stands in a relation to popular culture that is, to say the least, extremely complex. In some passages Puig clearly mocks mass communications, as in his deadpan recreation of product advertisements. In certain others, he can be seen paying an affectionate homage to certain popular subgenres, particularly U.S. sound films of the period 1935-1950, for which he at times almost appeared to have an aficionado's all-forgiving fondness. But in most cases, Puig's treatment of mass-audience culture is too ambivalent to be classified either under satire or nostalgic celebration. A good deal of the critical attention to Puig has gone into the attempt to specify, to whatever degree this may be possible, the statement his work generates concerning pop culture. Even when Puig's novelistic use of a given example of popular culture was not very flattering to the model, it often had the effect of resuscitating interest in the original. For example, *Heartbreak Tango* brought renewed attention to tango lyrics, excerpts from which appeared as epigraphs to chapters, while the 1976 *El beso de la mujer araña* (*Kiss of the Spider Woman*) inspired a cultish revival of certain genres of film.

Among the other constants that make Puig's writing instantly recognizable is the use of numerous and variegated types of narration within a single work. These include such oddities as a transcription of only one side of a telephone conversation and reproductions of the characters' school essays. Puig had a remarkable knack for mimicking the conventions of official reports, and narrative data in his novels often must be retrieved from such documents as the findings submitted by a coroner, detectives' case notes, and the log kept by the officer taking calls in a police station. In some passages, Puig uses an invented format resembling a bureaucratic report to provide information on an episode that was never subjected to official scrutiny.

Another hallmark of Puig's work is a disturbingly vivid evocation of the unease felt by isolated individuals, especially those who feel marked off from society because of their sexuality. During the latter part of his career, the author became increasingly bold in the presentation of gay characters and gay life. But it should be noted that he always remained concerned with many types of sexuality that fall outside the norm, so that the placing his work in the category of gay literature is insufficient to describe his sexual subject matter. The author harbored somewhat utopian notions for a future society more enlightened in its treatment of sexual matters; these reformist visions surface both in his interviews and his fiction.

Puig's first success came with *Boquitas pintadas* (*Heartbreak Tango*; 1971), which brought in turn a reprinting of the previously little-distributed *La traición de Rita Hayworth* (*Betrayed by Rita Hayworth*; 1967). After *The Buenos Aires affair* (this is the title of the original Spanish version), a 1973 work loosely patterned on the crime novel, was confiscated by authorities, Puig spent his time essentially outside Argentina and concerned with a more international range of topics. His ties were increasingly to gay cultural life and to the alternative artistic communities of his adopted cities, Rio de Janeiro and New York. He attracted specialized clienteles, including sophisticated readers of science fiction, popular culture mavens, and those interested in developing a literary culture corresponding to homosexual life. Although interest in Puig had a resurgence in the mid-1980s after Héctor Babenco directed a film version of *Kiss of the Spider Woman*, on the whole he commanded much more attention during the period 1971-76 than during the last fourteen years of his life.

It would be easy to argue that Argentina did not offer the type of civilization—accepting of differences—needed for Puig's writing to win appreciation. However, this would be too simple a statement. While there has been a tradition of primness in Argentine literature, there has also been some outstanding frankness. For example, *Fruto vedado* (Forbidden Fruit; 1884) by Paul Groussac (1848-1929) fascinated contemporary readers with its lushly elaborate presentation of adulterous pleasure. Yet Gálvez's *La maestra normal*, which manages to narrate both an illicit affair and an abortion in the most euphemistic of terms, attracted censorious denunciations. Cortázar included erotic scenes in *Hopscotch*, but resorted for this chapter to a sui generis form of pig Latin and later complained that he lacked precedents in his own language for writing such a segment. Since Puig's controversial success in the 1969-73 period, such well-established figures on the Buenos Aires literary scene as Eduardo Gudiño Kieffer and Oscar Hermes Villordo have expressed a homosexual preference, especially with the publication of the latter's matter-of-fact novelistic treatment of gay life, *La brasa en la mano* (Ahold of a Live Coal; 1983). In short, there is a good deal of variance in how much propriety readers and critics expect to see observed in literature. The likelihood of drawing adverse reactions to the literary expression of sexuality depends on many factors. As well as the author's previously established standing as a member of the literary scene, response may reflect the political and cultural weather of the moment in which the work appears. Inevitably, reaction to a given text at a given time has an unpredictable, inexplicable, and most likely random dimension.

No innovator as renowned as Puig has emerged since, though many writers born somewhat later have enjoyed fairly steady success in keeping their names and writing before the public. Jorge Asís (1946) and Enrique Medina (1937) are examples of authors who have drawn considerable publicity and their works have sold, overall, well. The critical consensus is that both these writers are skilled at drawing readers into a memorable narrative full of vivid scenes. Yet both are suspected of using their talents in an unthinking way and being careless about the type of statements their writing may generate. Asís is a journalist-novelist who practices a modern picaresque. Today he is so widely considered a popular, facile novelist that it is easy to forget the critical esteem he enjoyed during the mid-1960s to mid-1970s. His early fiction was distinguished by an affectionate, detailed evocation of life among immigrants from the Lebanon-Syria area, with special attention to their touchingly old-fashioned habits of political agitation. He also proved skillful at recreating the chaos, violence, and disorientation that afflicted Argentina during the early 1970s, as he did in his 1974 *Los reventados*, whose slangy title refers to its lower-class characters as a miserably ill-treated bunch of losers.

Starting approximately with his 1981 *Carne picada* (Chopped Meat), Asís began to produce, in swift succession, novels that were lengthier and less compact, featured more garrulous narrators, and gave a less deliberate effect than his earlier works. In addition, his work began to rely more on crudity for its effects; the narrators, in particular, manifested a somewhat jaded, even jeering, attitude. The question arose whether Asís was merely depicting glibly, irreflexively cynical speakers or whether his work actually embodied, or at least reinforced, their outlook and expression. This writing, while winning a sizable readership, attracted negative criticism for the cavalier treatment the narrators tend to accord to politically committed characters. There was also persistent concern over the derisive, sometimes rather loutish, comments these speakers made about women, especially when the women were independent and enterprising people dedicated to their careers, to intellectual and creative work, or to political activism. Even critics who find Asís too coarse and too willing to derive humor from stereotypes grant that his writing gives an accurate measure of the frayed temper of the times as the military dictatorship begun in 1976 wore on through the 1970s and into the 1980s. In part, his ability to capture the atmosphere of an era depends on the features that arouse indignation, such as the breakdown of civility manifested by his hardened narrators.

Medina earned his early fame with *Las tumbas* (The Tombs; 1972), a spare, sober account of reformatory life. His subsequent production has been very abundant and uneven. One of the most conscientiously executed of his novels is the 1981 *Las muecas del miedo* (Fear Shows on the Face).

It should be mentioned that both the above-discussed writers remained Argentine residents at a time when many of their colleagues were in exile. Those intellectuals and artists who continued to work under the repressive regime of 1976-83 are almost automatically vulnerable to the charge that they suffered no reprisals because their work posed no real challenge to the order. The inverse of this persistent notion is a suspicion often voiced concerning those colleagues who spent the period in question outside Argentina. The latter are at times seen as having benefited from their exotic and touching status as exiles from a brutal South American dictatorship. If their careers abroad prospered, some will say that they would never have done as well without the appeal to radical chic.

The controversy over these two writers and others whose talent is recognized but who are perceived as not writing at their best reflects a larger problem in the evaluation of Argentine literary production of the mid-1970s to the present. Irreverence and even insolence have their place in this literature, especially in post-1983 writing, where they may serve as restorative elements after a period in which expression was too cautious. A raw manner of writing, including an exhibition of disregard for good style, can also be counted as salutary in that it reduces the imposing weight of fixed criteria of composition. On the other hand, the writing produced with these ideas in mind may actually reflect nothing more than inattention or incompetence. It is difficult to evaluate by esthetic standards texts that are prized primarily for their fresh crudity, such as the works of Mario Szichman (1946), Germán Leopoldo García

(1944), and others. Very different is the case of the above-mentioned Osvaldo Lamborghini, author of *El fiord* (The Fjord; 1964) and *Sebregondi retrocede* (Sebregondi Retrenches; 1973). While his works certainly seek to appall, their artful composition is clearly motivated by a desire to make literature a source of esthetic pleasure. This writing, designed to create a system of symmetries and echoes within the text, has won relatively few readers, but critical readers have expressed their appreciation.

Literary life from the early 1970s well into the 1980s showed the effects of the unexpectedly sharp and upsetting political changes Argentina was undergoing. The sequence of events began when the movement to bring Perón back into power achieved its immediate goal in 1973. The second Peronist regime (1973-76) was a chaotic time. Argentine political life took on an accidental, out-of-control character. Even though Perón was back in Argentina and occupying the presidency, a longtime dream of his supporters, some former party loyalists were soon manifesting disappointment with the regime, and radical Peronists were expressing their opposition through violence. Perón was too ill to govern and died in 1974. Guerrilleros on the left became increasingly active, both in Buenos Aires and in mountain strongholds, believing that the moment was ripe to launch a revolution. Equally zealous was guerrilla activity on the right, a vigilante endeavor which attempted to police society. In 1976, the military took over, to the surpise of few. A severe law-and-order program went into effect. The antiterrorist sweeps of the late 1970s, though, created further disruption. The government's program was exclusively aimed at the left-wing side of guerrilla activity. This strategy is generally believed to have created an opportunity for right-wing extremists to take part, in various ways, in the state-sponsored attack on their longtime enemies. The targeting of suspects was so broad as to approach randomness in some instances. There was poor accounting for individuals taken into custody, so that the fate of many detainees was never clarified even after official records became available. The use of torture was frequent. The extremely wide definition of what counted as subversive activity, or as signs of possible guerrilla affiliation, had a constraining effect on public expression. During 1976-77, many writers suddenly dropped out of sight, giving rise to fearful rumors that an entire literary generation was being eliminated. Fortunately, most of the authors in question later surfaced in exile. Rodolfo Walsh, born in 1927, and Francisco Urondo, born in 1930, both died in the antiterrorist sweeps that followed the military takeover. It is generally accepted that

Haroldo Conti (1925) met a similar death, although the specifics of his fate have never been fully established. The upheaval and anxiety of this time, and the experience of detention and exile, began to be reflected in literature, although for some time nearly all works dealing openly with the subject were published outside Argentina. A great many of these texts were reissued in Argentine editions after the military was voted out in 1983, resulting in a flowering of critical debate that will be discussed below.

During the military regime, and particularly during the phase of most active repression (approximately 1976-79), adverse circumstances brought new recognition to Argentine writers whose work fell outside the bounds of literature. Rock lyricists and performers had tended to be regarded as so many purveyors of mindlessness, as indeed they frequently had been. With public expression severely hampered, certain figures in progressive rock, such as Charly García, benefited from this genre's often-noted ability to carry messages between the lines of ambiguous or unclear lyrics. The use of rock songs as a conduit for statements of opposition may be one factor in the greater respect that came to be accorded innovators in this field during the 1970s and 1980s, and that continued after constraints on public speech and writing were greatly relaxed.

A text that appeared in 1982 made evident the opening of an era of freer expression. This was *Los chicos de la guerra*, which translates as *the boys of war*, though it retained the by-now famous Spanish phrase as the principal title of the English version. The journalist Daniel Kon transcribed and edited this volume from his interviews with soldiers returned from Argentina's 1982 invasion of the islands claimed by Argentina as the Malvinas and by the United Kingdom as the Falklands. Following this frustrated territorial reclamation, rumors had circulated about the poor planning behind the venture, which was widely regarded as a ploy to distract attention from the state of the economy and, more broadly, the nation. The interviews Kon obtained confirm that the invasion force was haphazardly supplied and directed. While the brief Malvinas/Falklands affair was not an enormous drain on national resources, it exhausted goodwill toward the government. The military regime had justified itself by offering order and discipline, albeit at the expense of a number of liberties. It was now viewed as erratic and irresponsible as well as repressive, and during its remaining months in office was virtually discredited. Kon's book caught on quickly as a statement of this exasperation. In addition, it was thrilling to see a book so damaging to the still officially ruling military be openly marketed with impunity.

The restoration of civilian government, though obviously imminent for some time, was marked by the election of a Radical Party president in 1983. Many exiles returned, a general reexamination of the past regime was inaugurated, and the results of these new changes also surfaced in the writing and critical commentary of literature. The mid-1980s saw an abundant production of works—documentary, imaginative, and critical—whose principal purpose was to bring into the open subject matter that could not have been aired during the previous period.

During the time extending from, roughly, 1983 to 1987 or 1988, a great deal of discussion went toward the identification of a literature—usually, works of fiction—that would somehow epitomize the changes Argentina had undergone over the past several years. The object of this inquiry was often described as Argentine literature of the *proceso*, referring to the military government's term for its reorganization of national society. In practice, though, critics examined a wider range of works, going back to the early 1970s, when Argentines noted a sudden rise in violence and other signs of social unrest, and forward far into the 1980s, when the nation was still struggling to assimilate the bewildering events it had undergone. Certain novelists were almost inevitably cited, particularly Ricardo Piglia (1940), Andrés Rivera (1928), and Osvaldo Soriano (1943). Other authors, such as Tomás Eloy Martínez, Luis Gusmán (1944), Jorge Mansur (1949), Marcelo Cohen (1951), Juan Carlos Martelli, Miguel Bonasso, Carlos Dámaso Martínez (1944), and Héctor Tizón (1929), to give some characteristic names, came in for frequent mention. In addition, certain Argentine writers who had been well established for some time were at times cited in this context, such as Daniel Moyano, Juan Carlos Martini, Humberto Costantini, Antonio Dal Masetto, and Pedro Orgambide, all noted above. Juan José Saer (1937), who had been highly esteemed by some critics but not widely known, now had an opportunity to be read by those concerned with literature and repression. Viñas, who for a time had seemed old hat to many, became newly interesting. In exile, he had published a novel so critical of the military that it could not have appeared at home: the 1979 *Cuerpo a cuerpo* (Body to Body; also the term for hand-to-hand combat). Asís came in for frequent mention, but critics engaged in this inquiry nearly always treated this author and his works harshly; he was frequently accused of a flippant, glib treatment of the nation's most important social problems. Puig was occasionally brought into consideration. His inclusion was justified, at a literal level, by the characterization of an urban guerrillero in *Kiss of the Spider Woman*. More complexly, though, this author now seemed significant for setting a certain style of social and cultural criticism in fiction, with a special focus on the mass media. The debate over literature of the *proceso* went out of fashion as the initial euphoria over redemocratization wore off. Yet it did succeed in bringing attention to writers who had been working conscientiously for years and scoring critical successes without gaining very wide notice.

Piglia is a talented and knowledgeable critic, editor, and writer of fiction, and an acute student of popular culture. His most-noted works are *Nombre falso* (Assumed Name; 1975), a collection of short pieces that contains the intricately playful "Homenaje a Roberto Arlt" (Homage to Roberto Arlt) and the 1981 novel *Respiración artificial*. The latter sold only moderately when first published in 1980, but later caught on with readers and critics, becoming perhaps the single work most exhaustively discussed in the critical inquiry into literature of the 1976-1983 regime. One of Piglia's strengths is the literary use he makes of his knowledge of Argentine literature and popular culture from the 1920s to the present. The conventions of the hard-boiled crime novel often appear, worked into variant forms, in his imaginative writings, as is the case with many recently emerged authors.

Piglia's 1980 novel has a double plot involving two searches for information. The central figure becomes fascinated by an old photograph and begins to research the life of his uncle. In turn, this older character was investigating the life of an exiled Argentine politician from the nineteenth century. These two lines of research involve the examination and, necessarily, the interpretation of crucial periods in Argentine history. The novel is full of bits of evidence taken from letters, archives, and other sources. No matter how assiduously the researchers carry out their work, the important pieces of the puzzle have a disconcerting way of turning up in an uninvited, random fashion. All the items of evidence that are unearthed in the course of the novel appear to stand in some overall relation to one another, but the total picture never emerges very clearly. Along with the issue of how knowledge of the past is obtained and assembled, the novel brings out the question of how meanings are assigned to history. The fragmentary, inconclusive results of the investigations suggest the impossibility of ever specifying fully the facts and significance of events. Yet the novel does not promote a view of history so relativistic as to make research seem futile. The effort to become aware of the past and to interpret history, and particularly the difficult-to-comprehend history of modern Argentina, appears as a worthwhile and needed endeavor.

Rivera had been writing and publishing fiction for many years when his work was quite suddenly taken up by numbers of readers and critics in the mid-1980s. *Nada que perder* (Nothing to Lose, 1982), the short novel that introduced him to many readers, centers on the recreation of the immigrant socialism that flourished in the generation previous to that of the central figure. When his father dies, this individual must straighten out a bureaucratic tangle over the elder figure's identity, a task complicated by discrepancies in the information entered on the dead man's various identification documents. He is drawn to retrace in some detail the life of his father, a labor leader who brought with him to Argentina the radicalized intellectual culture common to many Eastern European Jews of the turn of the century. The older man's involvement in the labor movement and, more generally, in the left, becomes the main focus of his son's curiosity, and the latter's discoveries on this subject are abundantly documented in the novel. This work not only comprises a well-composed piece of fiction but also has value for the informative and sympathetic glimpses it offers of a world now in danger of vanishing from memory.

Osvaldo Soriano has, like many Argentine writers of his generation, adapted features of hard-boiled fiction to his distinctive novelistic purposes. Part of the appeal of Soriano's work is its widely-recognized ability to evoke a powerful sense of melancholy, loneliness, and bitterness; this capacity has brought the author both praise and the epithet of *sentimental*. Soriano often portrays his characters as they are living out the last days of an experience. His protagonists may have come to the end of their relationships, careers, or lives. Wrenching departures and separations loom large, to pathetic effect. Although Soriano's characters are known to have suffered extremes of isolation, during the period covered by the narration they typically enjoy consoling bonds of solidarity with other hard-bitten outsiders and losers. *Triste, solitario y final* (Sad, Lonely, and Final), Soriano's 1973 novel, tapped into already established meanings that have accumulated around Laurel and Hardy, John Wayne, and Raymond Chandler's fictional detective Philip Marlowe. The novel takes place in Southern California and includes knowing references to such U.S. phenomena as the 1940s-1950s Red Scare. Yet it features enough allusions to Argentina that readers from that country should not take it as purely a commentary on another nation's problems. Soriano's 1980 novel *No habrá más penas ni olvido*, translated into English as *A*

Funny Dirty Little War, is especially likely to come in for political readings because its plot involves a conflict between rival Peronist bands; still, this author's recurring thematic nucleus of isolated outcasts enjoying a shared warmth often upstages the political subject matter.

Tomás Eloy Martínez managed to attract both critics and a wider audience with his 1985 *La novela de Perón* (*The Peron Novel*). The title of the work gives an accurate picture of what it offers: a novelized biography of Perón. The author is a longtime investigator of Perón's life. He had published some of his findings as historical research, as his study of Perón's occasional practice of extending refuge to Nazi criminals. The material that went into the 1985 novel was also the product of his investigations, but selected to emphasize the personal, private side of the subject's life. Readers of *La novela de Perón* learn about such matters as Perón's none too successful strategies for maintaining a robust image during his last year and his relations with his closest advisor and astrologer. While it would be hard to deny the gossipy attraction the novel exercises, particularly in a nation where there is much fascination with Perón lore, it is at the same time a conscientiously executed work of fiction. The statement it makes concerning the recent Argentine past is partly the uncerebral expression of a dispirited mood, particularly disappointment over Perón's long-awaited return to Argentina. There is also a more complex interpretive analysis of national history, providing considerable occasion for critical discussion.

The work of recent writers is always hard to judge. The difficulty is compounded when their writing has been the object of an excessively intense critical vogue, as in the case of the authors just discussed. Perhaps easier to assess are the literary rediscoveries that have competed with newly emerged authors for attention. The category of reclaimed authors includes both those who have become innovative later in their careers and those whose imaginative work was not given its due until lately. The reasons for the delayed acclaim of an author's work may be political, as in the above-discussed case of Leopoldo Marechal; they may reflect the work's being ahead of its time; or the author may belong to some long undervalued class, such as women writers or authors who favor overt social commentary in a period dominated by highly figurative and fantastic modes.

Olga Orozco, first known as a member of the 1940 generation, became a bolder and more defined poet during the 1960s and has continued to gain in interest. Always concerned with the poetic invocation of unseen presences, Orozco began to refer more overtly to these beings as summoned spirits and demigods. The unorthodox supernaturalism corresponded to Orozco's poetic persona, now undisguisedly that of a shamanistic sorceress. Subsequently, her poetry successfully displayed a vast accumulation of spiritualistic lore and the thorough consideration Orozco had given to the concept of poetry as spirit-summoning.

With the new 1960s-1970s interest in women's culture, Orozco began to emphasize the womanly nature of her magical persona. *Cantos a Berenice* (Songs to Berenice; 1977) is a cycle of poems from an enchantress calling out to her feline familiar, now in the realm of the dead. Another feature of this collection, the celebration of intimate bonds between female friends, has continued to be an element in Orozco's evolution. The sorceress-persona has come to question the efficacy of her magical powers of evocation, placing greater importance on the here-and-now ties between women. The communication a magician can achieve between worlds is less triumphantly proclaimed than lamented as a poor substitute for intimacy in this world.

Juan José Ceselli for many years was chiefly known as a name associated with Argentine surrealism. Rediscovered by younger readers, he has been appearing in newly available editions. The same pattern applies to numerous other unusual cases such as that of Antonio Porchia (1886-1968), whose reputation rests on a single enigmatic volume of poetic aphorisms, *Voces* (Voices; 1943), and Juan L. Ortiz (1896-1978), an independent poet who remained far from the Buenos Aires literary scene. Macedonio Fernández, earlier much admired by the 1920s avant-gardists and long championed by Borges, finally achieved a wider audience. Macedonio, whose goal was to oblige readers to help in the assembling of the text, provided truncated narratives, suggestions for how a possible work might be elaborated, and other incomplete forms. These practices made him resemble a late twentieth-century writer more than an early one, and, indeed, his teachings appear openly reflected in the famous *Rayuela*. Güiraldes's unabashed solidarity with the landed gentry had prejudiced many later readers against him, but the ideological slant of his work was so visible that it became uninteresting to denounce it. In consequence, critics such as Eduardo Romano (1938) began to examine the literary construction of *Don Segundo Sombra* and found it surprisingly modern and innovative. Other 1920s figures, including Arlt and Juan Filloy (1894-1967), were rediscovered in large part because their unusual construction of narrative appealed to readers accustomed to the new novel. Filloy had had an eccentric career, giving away his privately printed works and attempting to prevent plans to market them. Now these idiosyncratic works, each with a title seven letters in length, obtained new editions and new readings. Written to satisfy a drive for symmetry, the novels are full of palindromes and palindromic structures. But they were not motivated purely by formal concerns. For example, *Ignitus* (1971), full of the mirror-image repetitions that mark Filloy's work, also has a denunciation of social neglect as it describes the death of a family full of children caught in a fire. The ability to combine innovative form with social statement also brought Armando Discépolo (1887-1971) back to the theatergoing public's attention. Discépolo's grotesque, but sympathetic, treatments of working-class life had enjoyed a degree of success earlier in the century (1910s-1930s especially), when they were considered important as workers' theater (whoever the actual audiences may have been). The revival of Discépolo produced a different image of the playwright's supposed audience: one sophisticated in dramatic techniques and eager for an inventive form of social theater that had developed directly out of Argentine stage tradition.

The fact that so many new discoveries are really rediscoveries should not be taken as a sign of nostalgia for simpler times. Indeed, the works now earning fresh readings are very often ones that were pushed to one side because the consideration of their innovations was too fraught with sensitive questions. In other cases, the works in question had fallen out of favor because they seemed too simplistic, but upon fresh review, they proved themselves to be charged with contradictory forces. An example of this latter situation is the recent new interest in Gerchunoff's previously mentioned Centennial novel, *Los gauchos judíos*, by such critics as Saúl Sosnowski (1943). This novel reflects simultaneously the idea that European Jews were bringing a new refinement of civilization to Argentina and the historical circumstance that they were doing some of the roughest work involved in building up the rural infrastructure. Brutal events in the immigrants' lives are rendered in a lyrical prose that smoothes over the hardships to which the newcomers were exposed. Despite evidence within the novel that the host country assigned immigrants difficult tasks indeed, the conclusion drawn is that the new Argentines should be grateful to their benefactor country. At several decades' distance from the moment that produced such a work, critics have become more able to see it as no simple celebration of an adopted land, but a complicated text that, in its strenuous efforts to reconcile ideals and facts, is highly symptomatic of a confusing experience.

While Gerchunoff draws critics' attention largely for his almost abject eagerness to please non-Jewish readers and participate in the literary establishment, other immigrant writers are newly interesting because they maintained a critical outlook. José Rabinovich (1903-79) wrote a disputative, editorializing body of work in poetry, prose, and theater. Though he arrived in Argentina in 1924, it was not until the late 1960s, with the resurgence of ethnic awareness and protest writing, that he gained a wide audience. Rabinovich began as part of Argentine-Yiddish literature, but after his early 1940s discovery by Elías Castelnuovo and other realist writers, he began to publish in Spanish. At first his work was translated; translation between Yiddish and Spanish has been a specialty of the Buenos Aires editorial world. Later, though, Rabinovich came to favor Spanish as his literary medium. His persona and literary career were themselves interesting to his belated 1960s-1970s public, for he was a veteran of Yiddish artistic activity in Buenos Aires, workers' theater, and many other less known phenomena in the capital's cultural history. The exhumation of a writer like Rabinovich entails the fresh examination of those aspects of Argentine culture most interesting to revisionist historians: populist and working-class art forms, ethnic enclaves, Old Left-style didactic literature.

The recent attention to women's writing has also brought out more clearly certain figures in Argentine literary history and their work. Alfonsina Storni, earlier mentioned as a poet and journalist, has been the subject of fresh discussion. In her case, the reception given women's writing has proved an especially complicated problem. It is clear that contemporary reactions to Storni, and many lasting attitudes about her, reveal an all too pervasive awareness that the poet was a woman. This consciousness that a woman is writing the text in question overdetermines the way her work is perceived and understood. It has been noted that the long-established practice of mentally type-casting Storni as always the confessional poetess makes it difficult to arrive at a reasonable assessment of the literary merit of her work. The problem for critics is now how to disentangle Storni's work from the accumulated beliefs surrounding it, such as the conviction that women turn to writing as an outlet for their intense emotions. Then the work could be evaluated without overwhelming concern with the author's gender.

Even when they do not present opportunities for feminist criticism, women writers have received new attention in order to remedy their previous relative neglect. There have been efforts to see a historical line of women authors stretching back to Juana Manuela Gorriti (1818-1892) and to augment the number of declared, published writers with women whose writing was in the form of personal papers. Marta Lynch, previously mentioned for her emergence during the 1960s, became the recipient of a great deal of publicity. Her special abilities, beyond a generally high level of narrative skill, were the successful fictional treatment of timely topics and the simultaneous study of the political climate and its effects on individuals. Alejandra Pizarnik (1936-72), a poet known for her focus upon extremes of experience, has attracted a posthumous cult of readers. Critics have examined, with obvious ambivalence, the generally feminist, yet increasingly petty and gossipy, best-selling novels of Silvina Bullrich (1915).

Many women writers whose careers have been generally successful may nonetheless come in for a closer reading with the new attention accorded female authors. María Elena Walsh (1930) is an unusual case because she has been so continuously visible in Argentine culture through her neofolk singing, children's books, and appearances in films and on television. Walsh can hardly be called an ignored artist, since many Argentines are familiar with her sweet singing voice and might easily identify her as a folklorist. She had been such a fixture for so long that in a sense she had been taken for granted. When a new look was taken at women authors, critics began to notice how much Walsh had innovated within such genres as urban folksong and children's literature. Walsh, who won poetic acclaim while still in her teens, has not settled into a fixed mode, but rather continues to make her material evolve to suit the needs of the time. In her work directed at a child audience, she has brought in timely concerns over the environment, gentle urging to move away from overdetermined notions of femininity and masculinity, and the promotion of an imaginative, ethical approach to social issues. Luisa Pasamanik (1930), a poet who gained prominence in the 1950s, still merits greater attention to her unspectacular but purposefully composed verse. Another longstanding talent was Sara Gallardo (1929-88), widow of the above-discussed Héctor A. Murena, whose slow-moving fictions recreate nuances of experience. These women's works could profitably receive greater attention, and not necessarily with issues of femininity and masculinity entering into the discussion. It should be noted that women have often worked conscientiously in editorial tasks, an example being Liliana Heker (1943), who wrote little but supervised the production of much new writing.

Women whose literary fame is more recent have, in many cases, become associated with women's issues. Luisa Valenzuela (1943), a novelist heavily publicized in the United States, sees herself as the practitioner of a specifically female writing. Reina Roffé (1951), a fiction writer similar to Asís in displaying a brassy, insolent outlook, has strong ties to the discussion of women's writing and to the movement to treat lesbian issues more openly.

Looking at the entire recent discussion of women and their writing, one may see a distinct tendency to present with pride aspects of women's experience that may be considered disagreeably uncivilized. This category includes folklore associated with women: spell- and curse-casting, midwifery, divining, healing and soothing arts, and conjuring. The experience of woman's body is given a new presentation in writing, with an emphasis on extremes of desire and revulsion and on alternative sexualities. The point to be made is not the wholesome-sounding precept that women are sexual beings just as are men. Instead, it is suggested that women's understanding and perception of the life of the body is distinguished by special, subtle characteristics. Recent women's writings foregrounding this general concern with women range from Roffé's rebellious *Monte de Venus* (Mons of Venus; 1973), with its youthful contempt and Lesbianism, to Griselda Gambaro's elegant *Lo impenetrable* (The Impenetrable; 1984). Gambaro, known as a grim dramatist of social morality and existential dilemmas, surprised her readers with a novel that appeared to respect the lighthearted conventions of the ribald tale. Though the work does indeed honor many traditions of the erotic narrative, it follows a well-conceived pattern and inevitably leads attention back and forth between risqué situations and the issues, requiring reflection, that these scenes manage to raise.

Part of the work of rescuing or rediscovering neglected areas of Argentine writing is the effort, dating back to the late 1960s, to bring the most original popular-culture works into the area of critical discussion. Argentina has long had students of traditional folklore whose specialty is the collection and examination of orally transmitted material. For example, Juan Draghi Lucero (1887-1952) and Jaime Dávalos (1921) made careers of disseminating the results of their folkloristic studies in written transcriptions or, more usually, adaptations. Nor is it entirely new to study those forms arising from the modern mass entertainment industry. Certain chosen areas of popular culture, particulary song and song lyrics, have frequently been topics of the Argentine essay. The tango lyric, typically offering a dismal report on the relations between the sexes, has excited the diagnostic imagination of observers. As a result, since the early 1930s Argentine writers have authored numerous works in which the tango is considered as the reflection of a special set of beliefs and attitudes characteristic of Argentina or of Buenos Aires.

Newer than these approaches is the effort to see song lyrics, radio and film scripts, and other pop forms as commercial products, rather than as some direct manifestation of the spirit of a given group. Followers of this less romantic approach examine how popular culture originated and was marketed. At the same time that the necessarily homogenizing effect of the entertainment industry is acknowledged, certain gifted individuals are seen as able to innovate within the commercial system. An example is Enrique Santos Discépolo (1901-51; often alluded to by the affectionate diminutive Discepolín), brother of the dramatist Armando. He was an author of and actor in stage plays, but his original contribution was in more mass-produced genres. His film direction and production are recognized for their stylish vigor; still, current attention goes to his lyrics for tangos, including some that have become standards. During the 1930s, he wrote several lyrics outstanding for their embittered, alienated outlook, extending beyond individual and personal concerns to express an aggrieved attitude toward society. Students of popular culture have, of course, been drawn to the correspondences between the sentiments expressed in these lyrics, which enjoyed massive success, and the frustrating political and economic conditions prevailing during the 1930s. While this case may be the clearest one of social commentary finding artistic expression in a mass medium, many other songwriters and lyricist have attracted a retrospective look. Homero Manzi (1907-57; real name Homero Manzione) is representative of those in whom current-day critics sometimes find a popular poet.

It has proven easier to find notable examples of popular culture and to present them to a new readership than to develop worthwhile critical modes for the analysis of these forms of culture. An excellent example of the showcasing of popular culture is its treatment in the magazine *Crisis* (1973-76), whose editor was the Uruguayan-born Eduardo Galeano (1940). *Crisis* was not a specialized popular-culture journal, but rather a general cultural and social issues magazine. Among its projects was the presentation of those aspects of Argentine literary history that, for one reason or another, might be neglected by readers when thinking about national culture. The category of possibly overlooked works included a range from Colonial-era poetry (the Conquistador's son Luis de Tejeda, 1604-80), through writings expressing dissent with Argentina's nineteenth-century drive toward modernization, including writers with a populist orientation and makers of popular culture itself. In this revisionist survey of Argentine culture, the presentation of popular texts made sense as part of the effort to reconsider the overall shape and significance of the nation's literary and expressive history.

Among critics who have had success in analyzing, as well as presenting, Argentine popular culture, Jorge B. Rivera (1935) and Piglia, earlier noted as a writer of fiction, stand out. Neither of these is predominantly an aficionado preoccupied with amassing items of information, although such fans are common enough in Argentina. Rather, Rivera and Piglia are historians of cultural life whose populism leads them to the study of mass-marketed forms. Rivera has a strong interest in the turn of the century, when magazine illustration, penny novels, caricature and belle-époque ornamental graphics flourished. Piglia is drawn especially to the period 1920-1950 and to written forms of popular culture. His longstanding fascination with the fiction of Roberto Arlt and the works of *noir* crime writers has extended from the study of the more literary aspects of these phenomena to the pulp-novel background from which Arlt and the talented hard-boiled writers arose. In each case, the revisionist's desire to see culture without the distortions imposed by official textbook history is the motivating idea behind the reading of the popular text. For this same reason, such critics as Noé Jitrik, Aníbal Ford (1934), and Jorge Lafforgue (1935) take popular culture into account as background for the analysis of literary works.

Of great significance during the 1980s was the role played in Argentine culture by the country's established critical intellectuals, especially senior figures who had developed and matured their thought while weathering the last several changes in the nation's political climate. The best illustration is the recent career of David Viñas. Viñas now took on a new significance, not just as a writer, but as an emblematic figure in Argentine culture. Having fled to Mexico, he represented exile, and specifically the uprooting of dissident intellectuals. He also stood for the issue of disappeared citizens, having lost people close to him. During the mid to late 1980s, the relation of Jewish Argentines and Jewish culture to overall Argentine social history was a focus of much analysis and discussion. As the son of a secular Jewish woman and a father of the more mainstream Hispanic descent, and with his brother living in Israel, Viñas stood at something of a crossroads in this entire territory of issues. This is not to say, though, that the returned Viñas simply assumed the status of elder symbolic presence. His cultural activities continued to evolve in response to the altered situation.

Viñas's most notable new job was holding a chair in Spanish American literature at the Universidad de Buenos Aires. But he also became involved in many other activities. The most surprising of these was his campaign for a post roughly equivalent to city manager, supervising the services provided by the municipal government of Buenos Aires. This campaign, though widely recognized as doomed, was not an enigmatic joke similar to Norman Mailer's running for mayor of New York City. Viñas had developed plans for encouraging artists, writers, and performers who lacked venues for their work in part because of the way the city's resources were managed. During his campaign, for instance, he drew public attention to the city's many unused theaters that could be opened to independent ventures.

Although Viñas had personal reasons to affiliate himself with the organized relatives of the disappeared, the Madres de la Plaza de Mayo, his association with them had a complex element of social criticism. He was concerned with the way in which the group continued to press the elected government for a thorough probe of recent events. The issue had grown extremely sensitive, with many urging caution lest the investigation, and subsequent trials, dangerously provoke the military right and destroy the good will needed for redemocratization. It should be noted that while Viñas has been highly significant in recent times as a literary and social critic and an organizer and participant in cultural activities, he has not been occupying such a major role as a creative writer.

While Viñas is an unusually visible example of the effort to maintain critical social and cultural thought, it should be recognized that many intellectuals were involved. Beatriz Sarlo, an acute literary analyst and Viñas's colleague and fellow chair-holder in Spanish American Literature, was active in organizing forums for the discussion of current and historical issues in culture and society. Jitrik never recovered the fame he had at one time enjoyed, perhaps because of the waning of the rather formalist manner of literary commentary with which he had become identified, but he was one of the returnees and continued as a critic.

The role played by Sabato during the 1970s and 1980s is marked by a constantly lessening involvement with the literary world. In 1974, Sabato reemerged as a productive author by finally publishing his massive novel *Abaddón el exterminador* (*Angel of Darkness*). This was an unusually heterogeneous work that contained commentary on Argentine society and discussions of the overall situation of humankind together with interweaving plot lines. Sabato appeared to be undergoing significant shifts in his identity. It was at this time that he dropped the accent mark on his already well-established name. He spoke of moving away from literature entirely (in fact, as of this writing he has not published further imaginative writing). He took up painting as his creative mode, pursuing this activity in a somewhat private, insular fashion and only occasionally letting his work be seen.

During the antiterrorist campaigns, the seemingly withdrawn Sabato began to express public concern over the writers who had disappeared and were unaccounted for. He visited the president, accompanied by Borges and other writers, and drew international attention to the problem. Because of his skill in rallying interest in the investigation of violations of human rights, Sabato was tapped by the newly elected government for the National Commission on the Disappearance of Persons. The resulting documentation was issued in a condensed form as *Nunca más* (1984-1985) and sold well to the contemporary public eager to examine the recent past. The title translates as *never again*, but the original Spanish formulation acquired such an emblematic charge that it was retained as the title of the English translation. Sabato is still the object of intense curiosity among literary people, but is not really a current participant in Argentine letters.

During the early period of democratization, roughly 1983-87, attention focused fairly easily on Argentine social history and the meaning of the recent past, even if the discussion of these matters was at times rather facile or self-congratulatory. But elected rule lost its excitement as the nation's economy continued to have seemingly intractable problems. Argentines had plenty of practice at using ingenious strategies to maintain their cash flow. Even in the worst times, such enterprises as (at least commercial) theater, night life, and luxury shops were maintained and the central parts of Buenos Aires still looked elegant, to the amazement of foreign visitors who had read dire, and true, reports on the economy. Even the publishing industry, sensitive to economic disruption, managed to flourish during the mid-1980s; many works that previously could only be published abroad, or had gone unpublished, now appeared in Argentine editions.

Under years' accumulation of financial stresses, the legendary resourcefulness of Argentine businessmen could not stave off attrition. Buenos Aires and its cultural life suffered undisguisable erosions. Publishers' lists were cut back, although not as much as might have been expected, and it became increasingly difficult to assume the risk of launching works by little-known writers. Under such pressure, the discussion of national life understandably shifted toward a concentration on economic matters. Newspapers that had earlier run analyses of human rights issues and the military mind now riveted attention on the Ministry of the Economy, reading the entrails for some indication of the next development in economic policy.

During 1988-1989, Argentines became accustomed to the idea that the reins of government were quickly passing from the Radical Party, in power since the 1983 elections, to Peronist rule. First Peronist candidates began winning local and provincial elections, then Carlos Saúl Menem won the presidency. The consensus is that the Radicals lost support because their advisors could not devise a successful means of reviving and stabilizing the economy, although many monetary and fiscal plans were tried.

The severity of the nation's economic problems appeared to be flattening out the formerly salient differences between political parties and coalitions. While the first Peronist regime had been aggressively populist, taunting the oligarchy and expropriating prized pieces of its property, by the end of the 1980s Peronists could not afford to antagonize such a powerful sector of the population. Now the Peronist president cultivated allies among the well-to-do, and posed for photographs with the nation's reputedly richest woman. In a similar situation, the Radical president had been unable to implement the progressive social measures that were supposed to be his faction's special virtue. The result is less an amicable reconciliation of differences than a depoliticization stemming from the government's inability to strike out in bold new directions, no matter who is in office.

One unusual feature of current-day Argentine literature is the absence of a leading figure active on the literary scene. Borges had filled the traditional role of the nation's leading man of letters. Cortázar had been too culturally left-wing to assume such a part, but he had been a central presence by which newer authors were measured and against whom they at times rebelled. Sabato was by consensus the third most important Argentine writer and his statements on national problems carried significant weight. Puig had attained an international reputation but had never had a place at the center of Argentine literary life. Cortázar died in 1984 and Borges in 1986; as noted above, Sabato became a more hermetic and less literary person. The result was an important literary center with no real leading lights.

While there is not an indisputably major author, there are a number of creative writers who enjoy respect from both critics and the public, such as Piglia and Rivera. Several authors produce work that is skillfully executed and stylish, even if critics do not find it so promisingly rife with complexities seeking analysis. Representative of this somewhat more accessible writing is the fiction of Mempo Giardinelli (1947), who has scored a series of successes with his generally brief and expertly-paced novels. Though less dense with potential meanings, able, fluid writing like Giardinelli's has been tapped by critics to obtain a measure of the mood of the times.

Of writers currently producing and receiving critical attention, a great many are working variants on the hard-boiled crime novel. Some feature actual detectives as lead characters, while in other cases a protagonist in some other line of work is moved to undertake the investigation of a key sequence of events. In these altered forms of the hard-boiled novel, the matter being researched may not be literally a crime, but rather some set of occurrences surrounded by mystery. Also very characteristic of these newer novels of detection is the relatively low importance assigned to obtaining the actual facts of a given case. The inquiry is often at heart a search for meanings, with the hermeneutical task facing the protagonist more prominently featured than the fact finding. Typical, too, is the practice of presenting fragments of evidence and interpretive leads to the reader with the implication that he or she should undertake some portion of the struggle toward significance. Argentine authors have been productively ringing changes on the conventions of detective and crime fiction for decades, and it is a safe prediction that they will continue to generate new forms out of this seemingly inexhaustible matrix.

The ability to work borrowings from mass culture into literature, taking advantage of the well-established connotations and associations of the popular elements, is widespread among the more newly emerged writers. It is worth remembering that when Puig's first novels appeared in the late 1960s and early 1970s, many readers were alarmed and appalled by his original utilization of mass-culture allusions and mimicry of popular cultural forms. Some Argentine literary figures expressed anxiety lest literature itself be contaminated by the often simplistic banality of the cultural repertory on which Puig was drawing. Borges, for example, told interviewers that he could never overcome the repugnance he felt at the aggressively pop titles of Puig's novels. With sucessive readings and further discussion, a sizable portion of critics became convinced that the literary use of popular culture, including commercial, mass-produced forms, could enhance rather than diminish the complexity of a literary work. Today only a minority of critics would hold a work under suspicion simply because it referred extensively to, or imitated an aspect of, mass culture. Several of the more skilled newer novelists are knowledgeable students of popular culture. Some, like Piglia, are carrying out a type of cultural history that extends backwards across the recent decades of Argentine life. Others have a predominantly contemporary focus. The most exemplary case of the latter is Marcelo Cohen, who achieved sudden prominence with his 1984 novel *El país de la dama eléctrica* (Electric Ladyland; the title is a Spanish translation of the name of Jimi Hendrix's studio), whose crucial referents are from the world of rock music. Because Argentine authors are still successfully discovering the possibilities of working with this set of allusions and models, it is more than reasonable to expect the further unfolding of this experiment in heterogeneous writing. A related development is the increased respect that has been accorded to those able to innovate in popular genres, as witness the informed reviews of progressive rock in such intellectual periodicals as *El periodista de Buenos Aires* (The Buenos Aires Journalist).

New Argentine authors still make their presence known, even though it is not as easy to do so as in some earlier periods, and Buenos Aires is still by all accounts a major publishing center. Despite the inevitable flattening and dampening effects of long-term economic adversity, the Argentine literary scene has shown unusual resilience, particularly well demonstrated in its recovery from the extremely difficult circumstances of the late 1970s.

BIBLIOGRAPHY

Arrieta, Rafael Alberto, ed. *Historia de la literatura argentina.* Buenos Aires: Peuser, 1959. 6 vols. In this ambitious, extensive reference work, the various volumes treat periods in Argentine literature, while within each volume, lengthy essays by established critics discuss the evolution of particular genres during the era. The coverage is thorough to the 1930s, thinner thereafter.

Avellaneda, Andrés. *El habla de la ideología: modos de réplica literaria en la Argentina contemporánea.* Buenos Aires: Sudamericana, 1983. The premise of this subtle study is that midcentury Argentine fiction both manifests and disguises and denies the elite's resentment toward a lower class that had become newly visible as a result of Peronist populism.

Foster, David William. *The Argentine Generation of 1880: Ideology and Cultural Texts.* Columbia: University of Missouri Press, 1990.

Both well-known and less-cited writings by authors of the Argentine generation of 1880 figure in this study. The bulk of the work consists of analyses of individual works; attention goes to their textual construction and their relation to the prevailing climate of contemporary Argentine thought, particularly the outlook of the elite that produced this writing.

Foster, David William. *Argentine Literature: A Research Guide*. 2nd. ed. New York: Garland, 1982. Revised and updated, this reference work is useful to researchers looking for orientation among the diverse sources for the study of Argentine literature. Coverage of recent Argentine literature is unusually strong for a reference work.

Foster, David William. *Currents in the Contemporary Argentine Novel*. Columbia: University of Missouri Press, 1975. The four main chapters of this study go to detailed analyses of major novels by twentieth century Argentine authors, while the introductory chapter surveys earlier manifestations of the novel in Argentina, and a closing discussion covers novels by authors who emerged during the mid to late 1960s.

Foster, David William. *Social Realism in the Argentine Narrative*. Chapel Hill: North Carolina Studies in the Romance Languages and Literatures, 1986. Consisting principally of close studies of individual narrative texts, this is a study of the realistic tendency that arose in 1920s Argentina and continued through the mid-century period.

Goldar, Ernesto. *El peronismo en la literatura argentina*. Buenos Aires: Editorial Freeland, 1971. Written from a pro-Peronist point of view, the work surveys allusions to Juan and Eva Perón and their followers in Argentine literature since the early 1940s.

Jitrik, Noé. *Ensayos y estudios de literatura argentina*. Buenos Aires: Editorial Galerna, 1970. This 1970 collection of essays shows Jitrik's widely heralded shift toward a mode of analysis more centered on issues of textual structure and language, while preserving his concern with ideological considerations.

Jitrik, Noé. *El fuego de la especie*. Buenos Aires: Siglo Veinte, 1971. This set of Jitrik's essays includes his influential "Macedonio Fernández y su 'novela del futuro',' " credited with sparking the 1970s-1980s wave of critical studies of the singular innovator.

Jitrik, Noé. *El ochenta y su mundo*. Buenos Aires: Jorge Alvarez, 1967. This volume centers on the "gentlemen-writers" of the 1880s, their privileged situationn in a rapidly developing country, and the ways in which their literary writings display the resulting cultural tensions.

Kaiser-Lenoir, Claudia. *El grotesco criollo: estilo teatral de una época.* La Habana: Casa de las Américas, 1977. Kaiser-Lenoir examines the dramatic subgenre of the *grotesco criollo*, distinctive to the River Plate region. The *grotesco criollo*'s simultaneous populist accessibility and ability to communicate a knowing critique of existing social arrangements are the subject of analysis.

Leland, Christopher Towne. *The Last Happy Men: the Generation of 1922, Fiction, and the Argentine Reality.* Syracuse: Syracuse University Press, 1986. Leland's study is valuable in presenting an English-language discussion of significant issues in the study of the literary innovators of 1920s Argentina. He follows current critical practice in seeing continuities between avant-garde experimentation and contemporary social literature.

Lichtblau, Myron I. *The Argentine Novel in the Nineteenth Century.* New York: Hispanic Institute in the United States, 1959. Lichtblau gives an informative and analytical account of the nineteenth century Argentine novel and the literary movements it exemplifies. This critic turns an expert, sympathetic eye on works that are, in many cases, difficult for a modern reader to appreciate.

Lindstrom, Naomi. *Jewish Issues in Argentine Literature: from Gerchunoff to Szichman.* Columbia: University of Missouri Press, 1989. The long introduction to this study is a historical essay on the situation of Jewish intellectuals on the Argentine cultural scene up to 1976; analyses of eight novels and collections of poetry follow, with a conclusion on Jewish Argentine writing 1976-88.

Ludmer, Josefina. *El género gauchesco: un tratado sobre la patria.* Buenos Aires: Sudamericana, 1988. This is among the most critically sophisticated examinations of *literatura gauchesca*. Ludmer is concerned with seeing the historical formation of a national identity and self-awareness during the period when *gauchesca* literature enjoyed popularity, even as real-world gaucho culture was being edged out of the national picture.

Masiello, Francine. *Lenguaje e ideología: las escuelas argentinas de vanguardia.* Buenos Aires: Hachette, 1986. This study combines the results of archival research into avant-garde periodicals and manifestos with the examination of texts representative of 1920s experimentalism. The ideological underpinnings of Argentine avant-gardism, in relation to its poetic principles, receive careful consideration.

Onega, Gladys. *La inmigración en la literatura argentina 1880-1910*. Buenos Aires: Galerna, 1969. Onega examines representations of European immigration to Argentina in literary works of 1880-1910, with an eye for the statements works generate about the ideological implications of the immigrant influx.

Orgambide, Pedro, and Roberto Yahni, eds. *Enciclopedia de la literatura argentina*. Buenos Aires: Sudamericana, 1970. This thick reference work contains principally essays on individual authors, but also entries on movements and tendencies and on works of emblematic significance. Coverage of recent authors is strong, and the book was exceptionally up to date upon its publication.

Prieto, Adolfo. *El discurso criollista en la formación de la Argentina moderna*. Buenos Aires: Sudamericana, 1988. The widespread current interest in the development of national self-awareness and cultural nationalism is reflected in Prieto's discussion. Written at a fairly high level of abstraction with relatively sparing reliance on textual analysis, Prieto's book considers types of discourse whose defining feature, for his study, is to heighten a sense of being regionally and nationally distinctive.

Rodríguez Monegal, Emir. *El juicio de los parricidas: la nueva genera ción argentina y sus maestros*. Buenos Aires: Deucalión, 1956. Published while the "parricidal" generation of Argentine critics was exciting considerable interest with its negative reassessment of well-established literary figures, this account introduces the best-known members of this tendency and their ideas.

Sarlo, Beatriz. *Una modernidad periférica, Buenos Aires 1920 y 1930*. Buenos Aires: Nueva Visión, 1988. Sarlo examines Argentine literature and intellectual culture of the 1920s and 1930s with special attention to the complicated way in which Argentine society and culture related to European concepts of the meaning of modernity. Examination of texts and consideration of the overall cultural scene are well coordinated.

Viñas, David. *El apogeo de la oligarquía: literatura argentina y realidad política*. Buenos Aires: Siglo Veinte, 1971. This work forms part of Viñas's massive project of surveying and analyzing Argentine literature against the context of national history. Viñas takes a special interest in those periods in which the nation's ruling class came to power (the latter third of the nineteenth century) and held a relatively little-questioned preeminence (through the first two decades of this century), but also takes into account more recent developments.

Viñas, David. *De Sarmiento a Cortázar: literatura argentina y realidad política*. Rev. ed. Buenos Aires: Siglo Veinte, 1971. This is the revised edition (original version 1964) of the first volume of Viñas's above-described project.

BOLIVIA
Oscar Rivera-Rodas
Louisiana State University

I

There is no way one can speak of a pre-Hispanic Bolivian literature because, as in the rest of South America, the original inhabitants lacked a written language. Yet this does not mean that the oldest cultures of Bolivian antiquity (Aymara and Quechua) did not cultivate art in the medium of language. Certainly they did, but it was through a tradition of oral expression, one that survives to the present day. The first Spanish chroniclers were familiar with and gathered, albeit only to a small degree, the examples of this art. As a consequence, this essay will begin with the Hispanic period.

II

The colonial period in Alto Perú (today, Bolivia) was not very propitious for literary production. The texts that have survived, from more or less historical chronicles to the spotty poetry and a few dramatic compositions, belong almost in their entirety to Spaniards who arrived in this land with the task of expanding the Spanish Empire and Catholicism. Mention can be made, for example, of the works of Pedro Cieza de León (1518-60), *Crónica del Perú* (Chronicle of Peru; 1552); Pedro Sarmiento de Gamboa, *Historia de los Incas* (History of the Incas; 1572); and Luis Capoche, *Historia y descripción de Potosí* (History and Description of Potosí; 1585). On the other hand, the texts remaining by native chroniclers of the Viceroyalty of Peru (which included all of what today is Bolivia and Peru, called at the time Alto Perú and Bajo Perú, respectively), belong to authors already indoctrinated with Hispanic ideas and the religious dogmas of the colonial mentality. Nevertheless, there is no doubt that they contain their own messages wherein one can recognize, as the Mexican scholar Miguel León-Portilla has observed, the "vision of the conquered" or the "other side of the Conquest." I have in mind the well-known chronicles by the Inca Garcilaso de la Vega, Guamán Poma de Ayala, and Santa Cruz Pachacuti Yampi Sal Camayagua (see the section on Peru). The extensive list of religious chroniclers (Fray Antonio de la Calancha [1584-1654], Fray Diego de Mendoza [dates unknown], Fray Diego de Córdoba y Salinas [1591-1654], Fray Juan Meléndez [dates unknown], among others) can be added to this inventory. There is no doubt that these books exemplified the concerted task of recording, in the competitive spirit of who did what and how much better, the development of the religious congregations to which their authors belonged. In addition, they also manifest aspects of the cosmovision and habits of the native communities; in general, they are characterized by a poor understanding of the events with which they dealt.

Cultural reality as grasped by the Spanish chroniclers (or those of a Hispano-Christian mentality) is limited to the most superficial features, since the dogmatic Catholic ideology of the authors was incapable of understanding native culture. The "devil" was always to be seen lurking in the background of the native cultures. As a consequence, they excluded the greater part of the cultural data from their chronicles, since the mere presence of these facts in the text, even if narrated objectively, would have resulted in condemnation.

However, despite the adverse circumstance in which the repressed native culture was preserved, drama enjoyed a certain privileged status for two basic reasons: for being an essential activity of local culture tied to ceremonial proceedings and for the use made by the evangelizers themselves of drama in transforming it into one of the most effective instruments for the imposition of Christian doctrine. Cieza de León speaks of "theater" when describing indigenous ceremonies. Theatrical spectacle, although not in the Western sense of the term, was an everyday practice in these communities. El Inca Garcilaso pointed out that "in Potosí a dialogue of faith was recited, attended by more than twelve thousand Indians." These mass audiences were only possible in the case of spectacles which the people were already used to. Within the context of this theatrical or semitheatrical activity manipulated and organized in terms of the Christian calendar, the Indians took advantage of the tolerance and disarray of the festivities to carry out more authentic activity. Thus, in the same city of Potosí in April 1555, Catholic leaders organized an extensive celebration lasting two weeks to instill in the populace veneration for the Holy Sacrament. At the end of the two weeks the inhabitants of Potosí, according to Bartolomé Arzáns Orsúa y Vela (1676-1736), "attempted to prolong the festivities with various forms of joyousness. They started out with eight plays, the first four of which were performed to the general applause of Indian nobles." Arzáns goes on to describe the indigenous content of these plays. Since Arzáns wrote at the beginning of the eighteenth century (see discussion of his work below), there is no further information available about such works. Even less can be said about the texts themselves, if such texts existed, since it is quite possible they were memorized dialogues taken in part from the oral tradition and performed by trained actors. The exceptional find of the Quechuan text *Atawallpaj p'uchukakuyninpa wankan* (The Tragedy of Atahuallpa), which seems to match one of the works described by Arzáns and of which there are three manuscript versions, leads us, however, to imagine the existence of such texts, written obviously during the colonial period by native authors.

Alongside this indigenous drama another colonial text has been preserved, *Nuestra Señora de Guadalupe y sus milagros* (Our Lady of Guadalupe and Her Miracles), written in Potosí in 1600 by the friar Diego de Ocaña. This text is recognized as one of the few works from the period to survive in its entirety, and it exemplifies the sort of religious work that can be called a "divine comedy."

Dramatic activity during the colonial period was considerable, especially in Potosí, although only a few texts have survived as examples. The same cannot be said of poetry, of which little has been discovered to date. Nevertheless, the oral tradition has been perserved in Quechua and Aymara.

The legacy of narrative has been quite different, thanks to the monumental work of Arzáns, born in Potosí and the author of the *Historia de la villa imperial de Potosí* (History of the Imperial City of Potosí). This work, to which the author devoted the greater part of his life, was written between approximately 1700 and 1736 and was interrupted by Arzáns's death. When he died, Arzáns had written only two parts with a total of 289 chapters distributed among thirteen books. Events corresponding to two centuries are dealt with, from 1545 to 1735. Arzáns's son Diego attempted to continue his father's work, but he was able to add only eight chapters more. It was only in 1964-65 that the work was published, in a three-volume critical edition by Lewis Hanke and Gunnar Mendoza.

Arzáns's exhuberant and powerful imagination strips the narrow limits of historical objectivity and converts the text, based on specific historical events, into a narrative work of complex structure. The narrative, which is ostensively historiographic, emerges as one of the richest texts produced by Latin American Baroque literature. The narrator is able to overcome with ease the boundary between the real and the unreal (or the marvelous) as well as spatial and temporal distances, and he becomes the participant in fantastic events and past actions from which he was really in some cases separated by more than a century. Or, in his guise as a historian, he is able to convert his documentary sources into texts that he intercalates in his own, inserting himself at the same time as a participant in the stories told by those same sources. One can only marvel at the author's easy control over Baroque style and the variety of narrative techniques of the day, to which he adds his own.

This rich narrative vein is the result of a mythological conception of the world confirmed by Catholic dogmas. Supernatural events, which human beings face (thereby placing themselves on a level with the imaginary beings of Christian mythology: angels, demons, holy virgins, lost souls in torment), are the vehicle for concrete messages based on an ideological code whose axiological categories split natural reality into sin and virtue, damnation and forgiveness, curse and miracle, what is permitted and what is forbidden, hell and heaven, demon and god. The semantic coordinates of the discourse finally come together, binding into a whole happenings of the most diverse sort. Certainly this sort of causality capable of ordering events is, in the final analysis, imaginary, literary, fictional. The text thereby aligns itself with the opulence of Baroque writing.

III

With a posture similar to that of Arzáns, Vicente Pazos Kanki (1779-1853) stands out as a point of transition between the colonial period and the republic. With a doctorate in theology and law, Pazos Kanki lived his age to the fullest, residing in Europe as well as the Americas. He was active in journalism in Buenos Aires and was involved in the struggle for independence. Between 1810 and 1816 he founded the newspapers *El censor* (The Censor) and *La crónica* (The Chronicle). The work that best represents his contribution to Bolivian, and Latin American, literature was *Memorias histórico-políticas* (Historical-Political Memoirs), eventually published in London in 1934. It is a refutation of the Spanish opposition, particulary that of Francisco Martínez de la

Rosa, to Latin American independence. Pazos Kanki reviews the discovery and conquest and, from a native point of view, he subjects them to a serene, dispassionate, and balanced scrutiny, transforming his readings of the chronicles into an original interpretation. Thanks to his qualities as a born narrator, the historical segments take on the vividness of fictional narrative, which does not mean that they lose in historiographic validity. Pazos Kanki enjoyed showing off his indigenous origins, which was the case with his publication in Paris of the *Compendio de la historia de los Estados Unidos de Norte América* (Compendium of the History of the United States of America; 1825), whose subtitle reads "By an Indian from the City of La Paz."

Bolivia is born in 1825 with the independence from Spain of Alto Perú. As in the rest of Latin America, this event coincides with Romanticism. But Latin American Romanticism—and Hispanic Romanticism in general—is borne of the reading of English and German Romantic texts and only later French ones. This is not to deny the personal experience of Latin American poets at this time. Rather, the point is that Romanticism in Latin America owes more to the influence of a reading that provided access to a style and, principally, to the transference of themes and emotions. As a consequence, it is possible to say that Latin American Romanticism assimilates the signs of Western language in order to transplant them into its own context.

The abundant bibliography of Latin American Romanticism represents more quantity than quality. For Bolivia, the first reference must be Vicente Ballivián (1816-91), whose *Recreos juveniles* (Youthful Pastimes; 1834) opened a long period of the sentimental novel.

Nevertheless, among the authors who stand out in this genre is Julio Lucas Jaimes (1840-1914), who began to publish his traditions in 1868 and to whom Rubén Darío (see the section on Nicaragua) dedicated the "Recreaciones arqueológicas" (Archeological Recreations) in *Prosas profanas* (Profane Proses). One of the greatest figures of Latin American Modernism, Ricardo Jaimes Freyre, is the product of his marriage to the Peruvian writer Carolina Freyre. Jaimes, who utilized the pseudonym Brocha Gorda (Paint Brush) is, along with Ricardo Palma (see the section on Peru), the creator of the genre of the tradition in this part of Latin America. His brief tales constitute a genre opposed to traditional European Romanticism. Jaimes's stories, which imply research into history and living tradition, have often been misinterpreted by readers who see no more in them than a superficial folklorism. Yet Jaimes's texts, especially *La villa imperial de Potosí* (The Imperial City of Potosí;

1905), are based on a critical stance. Jaimes felt it was necessary to return to history, which was in a certain sense inert, and to the living chronicle of culture in order better to understand the past and to explain the present.

But this rereading of history and tradition ought to be carried out with a new mentality, a rationalist one perhaps, that would lead to seeing and recognizing those areas that had hitherto remained obscure. The preliminary notes to his book lay the foundation of this idea: "It is not possible to have a clear or even approximate idea of the spirit prevalent in the imperial city of Potosí during Spanish domination toward the end of the eighteenth century until the brilliance of rational light cast by the French revolution was able to penetrate the heavy clouds that shrouded Latin American soil." Jaimes's goal is to guide the reader of his texts, appealing to the need to become reacquainted with the setting itself. This setting has been misunderstood as a consequence of the manipulation by the Hispanic tradition of which the people's consciousness has been victim. Under the light of reason and reflexion, "It becomes possible to explain with no great effort the extraordinary stories, rare legends, fantastic tales, and incredible traditions in which the imperial city abounds so richly." Without intending to turn away from Western and local heritage, Jaimes inverts and reformulates the texts taken from history and from the oral tradition with the goal of submitting them to a critical and contemporizing rereading. In this sense he is one of the most lucid writers of the nineteenth century, devoted to the task of reformulating a typically local literary discourse for the purpose of preserving the continuity and the evolution of what may be called a national literature in the process of formation.

Nataniel Aguirre (1843-88) also cultivated the genre of the tradition. Aguirre is a more comprehensive writer, and his literary production includes, besides poetry, drama and the essay. The sources of his stories were the oral tradition and history, but in the reelaboration of his stories Aguirre assumes in a very deliberate fashion the role of narrator. He is not interested only in the tale or the historical fact in its embodiment in his rereading, but he is also concerned with assigning an importance to the narrator in the structuring of his story. The text of *La bellísima Floriana* (The Beauty Floriana; published posthumously in 1911), while it may be inspired in a story by Arzáns, is a text in which the narrator stands out as the organizing element of the discourse. His novel *Juan de la Rosa* (1885) is even more revealing in this regard, and it already demonstrates what will be of concern to Latin American writers in the twentieth century: the structure and function of the narrator. Aguirre is aware of how necessary it is to abandon the privileged primacy or supremacy of the author as the active subject of the discourse, and Juan de la Rosa is introduced explicitly as the narrator of the novel. From this point of view, Aguirre's text is original and extraordinary in nineteenth-century Latin American narrative in this detail.

But Aguirre's importance is not limited to technical and structural innovations. The narrator of the story is concerned with presenting the last soldier of the independence movement. The subtitle of the novel is "Memoirs of a soldier of the independence." Thus, its theme is the most important event in the life of the country at that time, and the novel describes battles fought by the people of Cochabamba. The narrator is not the protagonist of the novel, since the people are the real protagonist, the collective author of the struggle. The interest of the author in tradition and history has misled some historians of Bolivian literature, who have seen in this novel a historiographic text. Nevertheless, the work is clear evidence of the interest in undertaking a novelistic elaboration of a segment of national history for a special sort of readers: the youth of the country, as Aguirre states in his prologue—that is, a novel for a new class of readers.

Bolivian Romantic poetry has its beginnings in the first years of independence with the works of María Josefa Mujía (1813-88), Ricardo José Bustamante (1821-86), and Néstor Galindo (1830-65). It extends to two figures in whose work it is possible to recognize the innovative features of what will be called Modernism: Rosendo Villalobos (1859-1940) and Adela Zamudio (1854-1928). The latter poet is, nevertheless, the best representative of Romantic poetry in melding Western literary models and personal experience. From her modest position as a teacher, she embodied rebellion within the narrow confines of social, political, and religious conventions which she publically challenged with vigor. One of her principal concerns was to fight in her writings and in her personal life against injustices to women, and she argued for women's rights in the home, in society, and in the political arena. Zamudio is without a doubt one of the most impressive literary protagonists of feminism in the period spanning the end of the last century and the beginning of the present one.

In the context of Latin American literature, Zamudio is part of a group of poets who adopt Romantic rebellion as part of a posture of renovation, in the manner of Salvador Díaz Mirón (see the section on Mexico), Manuel González Prada (see the section on Peru), and José

Martí (see the section on Cuba). These poets, as protagonists of the Romantic-Modernist transition, based their work on the inability to accept their society as the result of their rebellious spirit, which becomes the source of their poetry. In an apparent paradox, the origin of their poetry is the very setting they condemn. Concomitantly with this posture, as Zamudio's work clearly reveals, they recognize the superiority of the poet in relation to the other members of society. The poet seen in this light often possesses supernatural and titanic powers, although this posture may hide a certain modesty and sense of service to humanity. In any case, rebellion against the system of their own society is a point of reference that conditions them to the society they reject.

Bolivian dramatic activity in the nineteenth century provides, as is the case throughout Latin America, few works worthy of study. Of note are those of Félix Reyes Ortiz (1828-82), who in 1857 presented a play of undeniable interest, *Plan para una representación* (Plan for a Performance), which today would be considered as an example of a play within a play in the way in which it foreshadows the devices that will emerge in Western theater in the twentieth century, especially with Pirandello. Another outstanding work of his, *Los Lanza* (The Lanzas; 1875), is a historical drama about the Lanza brothers, who were independence warriors. Two of Nataniel Aguirre's plays also belong to this period, *Visionarios y mártires* (Visionaries and Martyrs; 1865) and *Represalia de héroes* (Heroes Reprisal; 1869). There is also Ricardo Jaimes Freyre's *Los conquistadores* (The Conquerors; 1928); more on Jaimes Freyre below. As can be seen, the principal characteristic of the theater of this period is historical.

IV

Modernism in Bolivia derives from two poets attuned to the transformation in Western artistic sensibility: Ricardo Jaimes Freyre (1866-1933) and Manuel María Pinto (1872-1942). Later, they were joined by a host of poets, although only two made significant contributions to Hispanic Modernism: Franz Tamayo (1879-1956) and Gregorio Reynolds (1882-1948).

Pinto's poetic work concentrated itself in a period of eight years: *Acuarelas* (Watercolors; 1892), *Palabras* (Words; 1898), and *Viridario* (1900). The latter two volumes appeared in Buenos Aires, where Pinto was active in the literary and publishing coterie headed by Rubén Darío.

His poetry reveals a variegated experimentation with language within the canons of Modernism.   Among his efforts at experimentation is the introduction of words taken from Aymara in the context of compositions written in Spanish.

Jaimes Freyre is the one Bolivian Modernist who has attained a well-deserved international reputation, not only for the intrinsic quality of his poetry but for the fact that, together with Rubén Darío, he was able to pursue his writing in professional terms: the rigorous exercise of writing, a consideration of the latter in terms of the innovations introduced into poetry in Spanish, and the distribution of his compositions in publications created specifically for the purpose of defending the new aesthetic of Modernism.   Thus, Darío and Jaimes Freyre founded the *Revista de América* (The Review of America; 1893-94) in Buenos Aires. Jaimes Freyre was twenty-seven years old at the time, but ten years previously he had already published his first significant work.   In 1883, at the age of seventeen, "Una venganza" (An Act of Vengeance), 612 verses in length, appeared in a periodical in La Paz.   The importance of this text is considerable, despite the fact that it has largely been ignored, because it may be considered one of the founding compositions of Latin American Modernism.   Only a few months before in 1882, Martí had published his *Ismaelillo*.

In "Una venganza", imagery, especially that of perception, already shows the characteristics peculiar to Modernism.   Perception, mainly visual, exercises a creative and transforming function on the imagination. Of the forms of reality, the young poet is interested in the most representative signs, signs that he employs in a fragmentary and impressionistic fashion.   In this way, his style pursues the path of suggestion, with imprecise references to the world, a world perceived among mists where things are only partially described.

Thirteen years later, in the same year Darío brought out his monumental *Prosas profanas*, Jaimes Freyre published in the Buenos Aires review *La quincena* (The Fortnightly) fragments of his poem "Castalia bárbara" (Barbarian Castalia; 1896).   Jaimes Freyre, in a brief introductory note accompanying this publication, explains that he saw how the poetry of his day had set aside the conceptual certainty of Romanticism, a certainty that applied to our ability to grasp and to know reality and things.   His two books of poetry, *Castalia bárbara* (Barbarian Castalia; 1897) and *Los sueños son vida* (Dreams are Life; 1917), solidify these ideas.   The poem "Siempre" (Always), placed as an epigraph to the first volume, is a paradigmatic text that summarizes the essential beliefs of

Modernism. Its language reveals how the semantic grounding of the sign has disappeared, giving rise to a series of signifiers (analogies, associations, correspondences) and creating a multiple text capable of generating a plurality of meanings. Language derives its tensions from the fluctuation between various referents with the goal of attaining a full and proper act of designation. The structure of discourse in this poem states what Darío will claim in the 1901 additions to his *Prosas profanas*, that he seeks a form his style cannot achieve. The poem creates in the final analysis a referencial plurality that confers upon the signifier a transforming function. Jaimes Freyre's writing was not limited to poetry, and he also wrote narratives, plays, and historical essays.

Tamayo was also an outstanding poet of this period. His first book *Odas* (Odes; 1898), although its prologue rejects the new school out of the conviction that it reduces "art to the narrow limits of the cultivation of form," is exemplary of Modernism not so much for its sensory expression as for the preoccupation with the limits of human knowledge, which will be the wellspring of post-Modernism. Tamayo takes elements from Hellenistic culture and reworks them in his writing with a fresh sense of modernity. Yet this aspect of his work has not always been appreciated by critics, who related the salient characteristic of his poetry to the Greek tradition, with the result that they have stripped it of its relationship to a regional and national context. Tamayo postulates in his *Odas* the need for a critical consciousness among Bolivians (and among Latin Americans) with respect to the past and to the collective history of which they are a part. As a poet, he underscores the melancholic and elegiac character that had characterized Romantic poetry in Latin America and proposes a new task for the poetry of the region: the reexamination of national history with the goal of deriving a vision and a clear understanding of society in order to overcome limitations and injustices. The *Odas* see Latin American communities as divided since the colonial period and after into two human groups: the guilty and the innocent, a minority that wields power and a majority deprived of any voice. Tamayo the public man—politician, journalist, writer, national representative at home and abroad, and president-elect—never abandoned his concern for Bolivian historical reality (Tamayo was prevented from assuming the presidency by a coup d'état).

La Prometheida (The Promethiad; 1917) was Tamayo's most praised work. There have been many interpretations of it, and emphasis has been on the Hellenic symbolism it utilizes. But it must be read as an extraordinary representation of the type of conflict in Modernism generated by the uncertainty of knowledge. Its dramatic structure details the unsettling consequences of this uncertainty leading up to the death of Psiquis, while Meliphron, the "invisible nightingale," sings of mankind's frustration. The work as a whole develops this conflict, which had been of concern to Modernist poets, especially during the so-called post-Modernist phase, and which Darío had summarized in a poem called "Lo fatal" (Fatality) in terms of how there is no "greater burden than conscious life" in the uncertainty of "being, yet knowing nothing."

Tamayo's poetry continues to strike the reader as original because it is the product of a rich imagination and profound thought manifest in text that derive from the poet's sure control over classical and Romance language, Sanskrit, English, and German. But Tamayo is not only a Modernist poet; as his subsequent writings indicate, he is above all else a modern poet: *Nuevos Rubayat* (New Rubayat; 1927), *Scherzos* (1932), *Scopas* (1939), and *Epigramas griegos* (Greek Epigrams; 1945). A simple reading of the titles of the works of this author suggest a certain predilection for exoticism. Nevertheless, Tamayo's poetry reveals clearly and constantly a stark place of solitude, immense and arid, montainous and cold, that is reminiscent of the silent and immeasurable Andean realm of Bolivia.

V

At the beginning of the twentieth century, Bolivia still devoted the largest portion of its economy to mining and farming in a system inherited from the colonial period. The cities were growing, especially La Paz, as the seat of public administration and some industries. Independence had not meant any bettering of the rural sector, where, by contrast, the latifundista system increased during the second half of the nineteenth century, depriving indigenous communities of their lands, communities that had hitherto been organized in terms of their own administration. In this way the subjugation and enslavement of the peasant was increased in favor of the new owners of the land, as well as the farmers' margination from productive national activity.

Prose during the first years of the twentieth century deals directly with this reality. One of its principal figures, Alcides Arguedas (1879-1946), wends his narrative activity to a historiographic and sociological approach to the problem. Immediately following the publication of his first novel, *Psagua* (1903), inspired in a historical event although with scant literary value, Arguedas initiated the tendency towards realism

with *Wata Wara* (1904). This text, published in Barcelona, is later included in the work that best represents Arguedas's talent, *Raza de bronce*
(Race of Bronze; 1919). In the latter work, Bolivian society in all its
unequal distribution appears fully: the Indian, enslaved in abject, social
solitude, lorded over by a white or semiwhite minority in control of
political and economic law and order. This social drama is enacted
particularly in the Andean setting, described with the full vigor of realism. The vast reaches and desolation of this region is as great as its
social reality. Its inhabitants are forced to struggle against a pitiless
feudal system as though against the very forces of nature. Arguedas is
a sharp observer, but above all else he is a severe critic. In 1905 he
published another novel, *Vida criolla* (Creole Life), dealing with life in
the urban centers. In this work it is already possible to discern the
Arguedas who will intensify his criticism until it becomes open accusation
in his great sociological treatise, *Pueblo enfermo* (Sick Nation; 1909),
whose readers will be divided into those who welcome his comments
enthusiastically and those who condemn them. Critical opinion on
Pueblo enfermo has been unanimous in recognizing how drastic and often
bitter Arguedas's commentaries are. Yet it is important to bear in mind
that Arguedas lived at a time when Hispanic intellectuals had assumed
the role of judges of their own countries. It had been the case with the
members of Spain's Generation of 1898, and later in 1934 Samuel Ramos
will adopt the same posture in Mexico, a posture that will be pursued in
greater depth by Agustín Yáñez, Rodolfo Usigli, Antonio Caso, and
Octavio Paz (see the section on Mexico). Arguedas's critical method is
based on the psychological doctrines of this day. His opinions are often
exaggerated and frequently result in an incomplete representation of
facts. However, there is no avoiding the fact that the reader is forced to
reflect on the nature of the Bolivian national character, which is undoubtedly what the author most surely had in mind: to besiege aggressively Bolivian consciousness and to induce critical reflection. Arguedas's
work possesses the merit of having pointed out an undeniable fact: that
Bolivia is a complex reality of diverse social and racial components.

Rigoberto Paredes Candia (1870-1951), prolific as a historian, dedicated the greater part of his work to the study of the cosmovision of
indigenous cultures. *Mitos, supersticiones y supervivencias populares de
Bolivia* (Popular Myths, Superstitions, and Surviving Ideas of Bolivia;
1920) and *El arte folklórico de Bolivia* (The Folkloric Art of Bolivia;
1949), as studies that contributed to an awareness of forms of indigenous
thought, contributed indirectly to the development of national literature

by providing information on the popular imagination based on its own myths, fears, and hopes. Magical realism in Bolivia—and perhaps it would be better to call it mythical realism—as in the rest of Latin America is born precisely of this type of popular, indigenous imagination. Paredes called attention to this spiritual reality, whereby the cosmovision of the Indian will become the direct source of literary imagination. Paredes's son, Antonio Paredes Candia (1924), has continued his father's work, and his extensive production in this field is valuable for its contribution to knowledge concerning the Bolivian character.

Jaime Mendoza (1874-1939) belonged to the same generation as Arguedas and Rigoberto Paredes, and he also was an assiduous observer of physical and social reality. He studied the natural setting and its inhabitants of various regions of Bolivia from an integrated and global perspective. His analyses concern social, political, and economic conditions. His literary imagination and the plot of his stories are inextricably tied to the physical and cultural geography of Bolivia, and his characters are always assigned the opportunity to reflect on local realities. His principal works include *En las tierras de Potosí* (In and around Potosí; 1911), which denounces exploitation in the mines, and *Páginas bárbaras* (Barbarian Pages; 1917), an exposé on the conditions of rubber workers in the Amazon region of Bolivia.

Armando Chirveches (1881-1926) provides a clear image of life in the provinces and small towns torn apart by the politics of small groups in conflict over the spoils of power, whether it be the state or the church: *La candidatura de Rojas* (Rojas's Candidacy; 1909) and *Casa solariega* (Ancestral Home; 1916).

The presence of Vanguardism—Latin America's variety of postwar European Modernism—in Bolivian literature was brief, owing in great part to sociopolitical circumstances in the country that would result in the Chaco War (1932-35). Nevertheless, Bolivia, although there was no organized Vanguard movement, did have Man Cesped (1874-1932) and Antonio Avila Jiménez (1898-1965). Octavio Campero Echazú (1898-1972), Guillermo Viscarra Fabre (1901-79), and Raúl Reich (1905-76) are representative of a more sustained experimentalism. Franz Tamayo remains an active poet during this period also. Historians are unanimous in calling the Chaco War between Bolivia and Paraguay absurd for both the cause involved and the conditions in which it was fought. The battles were not so much between opposing armies as they were between men and hostile nature and sickness. The literature of the Chaco War is primarily narrative. The authors, in their majority excombatants, offer an autobiographical testimony of frustration and despair, as well as a profound social criticism. In their narration of the specific events of the war, they consider the origins and results of the conflict: corruption and administrative failure in political, economic, and military terms, with a resulting loss of any sense of patriotism. This loss, however, concerns not just the feelings of the authors but of an entire generation. In such circumstances, a radical change becomes all the more necessary, a goal that will incubate and mature during two decades before it breaks out in the revolution of 1952.

The literature of the Chaco War, because of its anguished tone, relies on a sort of pathetic realism and a highlighted naturalism. The strength of its denunciations derives from this feature, as does the pragmatic goal of producing an impact in readers such that authorial frustration becomes translated into an image of the horror and futility of the conflict. The protagonist of these novels is the anonymous combatant, whether Indian, mestizo, or white, caught in the web of an absurdity. For the first time in Bolivian literature, reflecting a first in Bolivian social reality, Indians and whites were identified with an identical situation. The Bolivian solider, who is principally an Indian accustomed to the heights and the low temperatures of the Andes was forced to undertake in the Chaco a struggle of acclimatization in the torrid lowlands of the tropical jungle after a trek of over five-hundred miles from the recruitment centers to the battle zone (a trek that was the consequence of the lack of highways in the area). The heat and the lack of water, the impenetrable and endless jungles in which it was easy to lose one's way, the variety of dangerous and disease-bearing insects were the foremost enemy that these soldiers had to face, rather than military conflict as such. Those who most suffered in this war were the Aymara and Quechua soldiers who, paradoxically, were the ones least able to explain what happened to them during the war.

All of these facts may be found in the novels inspired by the Chaco War. Among the outstanding ones are *La tragedia del altiplano* (The Tragedy of the Highlands; 1934) by Tristán Marof (pseud. of Gustavo Navarro, 1898-1978), *Aluvión de fuego* (Flood of Fire; 1935) by Oscar Cerruto (1912-81), *Sangre de mestizos* (Mestizo Blood; 1936) by Augusto Céspedes (1903), *Los invencibles* (The Invincible; 1935) by Porfirio Díaz Machicao (1909-80), *Prisionero de guerra* (Prisoner of War; 1936) by Augusto Guzmán (1903), *Repete* (1937) by Jesús Lara (1898-1980); *La punta de los 4 degollados* (The Group of the Four Beheaded; 1946) by Roberto Leitón (1903). Raúl Otero Reich's poems also belong to this category: *Poemas de sangre y lejanía* (Poems of Blood and Distance; 1934).

The literature of the Chaco War underscored the tendency that Arguedas's writing had begun of seeing the country as a complex theme and as a set of problems that it was necessary to untangle in order the better to analyze them in terms of their constituent elements. As a consequence, Bolivian literature, especially the narrative, becomes a display of national problems. It is no accident that the 1952 revolution inspired precisely this type of writing. It has been pointed out correctly that these historical events produced no literature leading to social changes. The explanation for this fact is to be found in how Bolivian literature had begun to demand such changes two decades previously. The revolution was simply satisfying demands that had already been formulated by Bolivian writers.

In effect, the situation of the Indian, the abiding injustice of national history, reappears in a considerable number of texts, of which only a few will be mentioned here. Raúl Botelho Gosálvez (1917) sees the condition of the Indian as a threat to national unity in his novel *Altiplano* (Highlands; 1945). Alfredo Guillén Pinto (1895-1950) also published his *Utama* in 1945 in which he calls urgently for the immediate education of the Indian, since only in this way will it be possible to integrate all Bolivians into one national identity. This concern survives to the present day. Jesús Lara devoted his entire life to the problem, and this point of protest gradually became a bitter criticism of the revolution of 1952 for the latter's failure to achieve an effective liberation of the Indian; this can be seen in *Surumi* (1943) and *Yanakuna* (1952). Lara is the writer who most devoted himself to research and study of indigenous cultures, and he became the most eloquent spokesman for the majority of Bolivians, the Aymaras and the Quechuas. The lack of security and the deceit the Indians continue to suffer after the 1952 revolution is denounced by Néstor Taboada Terán (1929) in the stories of *Indios en rebelión* (Indians Rebelling; 1968).

But the denunciation of social injustice includes more than the areas of the highlands and the valleys inhabited by the majority of Bolivian citizens. It stretches to the tropics, where the extraction of sap for the production of rubber produces an exploitation of the labor force, which is once again made up mostly of Indians. Mendoza's *Páginas bárbaras* is echoed in new ways by Diómedes de Pereyra (1897) in his novel *Caucho* (Rubber; 1938) and by Botelho Gosálvez in *Borrachera verde* (Green Drunkenness; 1937).

Other social classes also have received attention. Carlos Medinaceli (1899-1949) presents a renewed vision of the mestizo in support of the reconciliation of social classes. *La Chaskañawi* (Starry-Eyed Woman; 1947) is the story of a mestizo woman whose humanness places her above white betters within the context of the model that Arguedas employed in his sociological studies. Medinaceli's analysis of deleterious social prejudice is also taken by Antonio Díaz Villamil (1897-1948) in his novel *La niña de sus ojos* (The Apple of His Eye; 1948), whose mestizo protagonist, in spite of her social origins, is able to transcend the boundaries and resentments imposed by a dominant class and maintained by those oppressed by that minority.

Another aspect dealt with by the literature of this period, in addition to the mistreatment and exploitation of one class by another, is the indiscriminate exploitation of the natural resources of the country with no resulting benefit for either the workers or national economy. Bolivia, essentially a mining country, had suffered foreign exploitation of its mineral resources since colonial times, first by the Spaniards and then by oligarchic groups allied to foreign interests. Protest against and denunciation of this situation was the goal of Augusto Céspedes in *Metal del diablo* (Devil Metal; 1946). Guided by a firm nationalistic criterion, Céspedes devoted himself to reviewing Bolivian history and to detailing the failure of political processes that could have led to the establishment of a social balance and the strengthening of a requisite spirit of national integration. Céspedes went on to deal with two types of political personalities that, in his opinion, were unable to fulfill their mission because of the instability of the Bolivian political process. These personalities are treated in his novels *El dictador suicida* (The Dictator Commits Suicide; 1956) and *El presidente colgado* (The President Who Was Hanged; 1966).

Theater in the twentieth century develops within the aforementioned context. Although during the early years of the century there is still an emphasis on historical themes, it demonstrates an interest in local customs that matches Realism. Antonio Díaz Villamil began his dramatic career with plays inspired by history: *El nieto de Tupaj Katari* (The Grandson of Tupaj Katari; 1923) and *La hoguera* (The Bonfire; 1924), the latter based on the War of the Pacific in 1879 between Bolivia and Chile. But he also dealt with themes taken from social reality, emphasizing aspects of local color: *La Rosita* (Rosita; 1925) and *Cuando vuelva mi hijo* (When My Son Returns; 1926). In these plays there is a human quality lacking in his historical works, and it is possible to see in them the concerns that Díaz Villamil will develop twenty years later in his novel *La niña de sus ojos*. Joaquín Gantier (1900) also stands out with a production of more than thirty plays, the most important of which are *Con el alma de cristal* (With a Heart of Crystal; 1933) and *El balcón de la angustia* (The Balcony of Anguish; 1976). Mario Flores (1901-65) saw the majority of his works performed in Buenos Aires. Although he wrote musical reviews and popular sentimental plays, his later plays are especially deserving of note: *Veneno para ratones* (Rat Poison; 1950), *Fuente de oro* (Fountain of Gold; 1959), and *La casa sobre la roca* (The House on the Rock; 1961).

There was a veritable revolution in Bolivian theater around 1960 in which plays went beyond topics of local color and customs in favor of an attempt to deal with more universal themes. Participants in this movement of renovation include Raúl Botelho Gosálvez, Renato Crespo Paniagua (1922), Sergio Suárez Figueroa (1923-68), Raúl Salmón (1925), Gastón Suárez (1928), Jorge Rozsa (date unknown), and Guido Calabi Abaroa (date unknown).

But there are two names that deserve special comment. Adolfo Costa du Rels (1891-1980), poet, novelist, and dramatist, spent the greater part of his life in Europe. But he remained close to Bolivian history, and his work incorporated first the Realism of the early decades of the twentieth century (*La hantise de l'or* [The Enchantment of Gold; 1930] and *Terres embrasées* [Enchanted Lands; 1932]), the thematics of the Chaco War (*Lagune H3* [Lagoon H3; 1938]), and contemporary concerns of Western literature as reflected in postwar French theater (*Les étendards du roi* [The King's Standards; 1957]). This third aspect of his work earned him international recognition. In 1972 the Paris-based Academia del Mundo Latino (The Academy of the Hispanic World) chose Costa du Rels over the famous Spanish playwright Antonio Buero Vallejo to receive the Calisto Gulbenkian Prize and the title of Doctor in Theater. While his early works were published in Bolivia—*Hacia el atardecer* (Toward Sunset; 1920) and *El traje de Arlequín* (Harlequin's Suit; 1921)—the greater part of his mature plays were written and published first in French. Only subsequently were these works translated into Spanish: *El embrujo del oro* (1948); *Tierras hechizadas* (1943), *Laguna H3* (1944), *Los estandartes del rey* (1974). In 1941 Costa du Rels published a work of considerable intellectual importance, *El drama del escritor bilingüe* (The Drama of the Bilingual Author). His last important novel was written in Spanish: *Los Andes no creen en Dios* (The Andes Do Not Believe in God; 1973).

The other writer of exceptional talent is Guillermo Francovich (1901), an essayist and dramatist who also spent the major part of his life abroad. His search for a definition of the nature of Bolivia relies on a meld of indigenous cosmology and Western philosophy, as in *Supay* (The Devil; 1939). Interested in psychological currents, he has also been interested in human types, and his interest in contemporary philosophy in particular has led him to a consideration of modern man and to a renewed humanism. His theater is principally a theater of ideas, with an emphasis on existentialism. Among his philosophic works are *Los ídolos de Bacon* (Bacon's Idols; 1942), *Toynbee, Heidegger y Whitehead* (Toynbee, Heidegger, and Whitehead; 1951), *El pensamiento boliviano en el siglo XX* (Bolivian Thought in the Twentieth Century; 1956), *El cinismo* (Cynicism; 1963), *La búsqueda* (The Quest; 1972), and *Los mitos profundos de Bolivia* (Bolivia's Profound Myths; 1980). His dramatic works include *El monje de Potosí* (The Monk from Potosí; 1952) and *Un puñal en la noche* (A Dagger in the Night; 1954). In his 1980 treatise, Francovich develops an original interpretation of the history and thought of Bolivia. Convinced that "people cannot live without myths," he identifies historical periods in terms of the myths they embody and how these myths prevail through an influence on the sensibility and consciousness of the people. This approach allows Francovich to specify the dominant myths of major stages in the development of the Bolivian national character. Francovich provides a singularly original way for studying Latin American thought through his accurate characterization of a Bolivian historical spirit within an authentically national context.

The poetry in the period following Vanguardism, while it has been influenced by a variety of European movements, particularly Surrealism, has developed its own features in a broad spectrum. It ranges from sociopolitical conflicts of national reality to an ontological concern for national character, with intermediate interests in native culture and personal experiences. The dominant figures of this period are Oscar Cerruto, Primo Castrillo (1896), Jaime Saenz (1921), Gustavo Vásquez Méndez (1927), Alcira Cardona (1926), Yolanda Bedregal (1916), Héctor Borda Leaño (1927), Julio de la Vega (1924), and Mery Flores Saavedra (1935).

VI

The Revolution of 1952 was a historical event of such importance that it introduced radical changes in the institutional organization of the country. Yet, unfortunately, it cannot be considered to have exercised any guiding influence on a new consciousness of any consequence in Bolivian literature. In the years following the revolution, the inventory of publications increased principally on the basis of new printings of the works of already established authors and only secondarily as the result of new books by authors already recognized but who have nothing new to offer to the realist and naturalist tendencies that resulted from the Chaco War.

Nevertheless, the recognition of the absence of a literary movement that might provide positive testimony of the events of 1952 is not intended to ignore the existence of writers who participated in the process devoted to the institution of a revolutionary order. As is the case in the historical examination of any other activity of that time, one must take into account also for the analysis of the literature of that period the fact that the emergence of a revolutionary consciousness in the country occurred at least twenty years prior to April 1952. As a consequence, it is necessary to confirm the basic notion, without any pretense at anachronistic paradoxes, that the 1952 revolution begins in 1932. Bolivia's experience in the Chaco War (1932-35) is the seed bed for the revolution that will specifically take place twenty years later, and intellectuals and writers participated actively in the process of radical change (Klein 238).

The Chaco War was surrounded by a sense of anguish, which was projected in a realist-naturalist cultural expression, a pragmatic relationship of marked importance that allowed the authors to give free play to their frustrations and to provoke impressive effects in the reader regarding the horrors and absurdities of war and the uselessness of national institutions. The undeniable pragmatic value of this literature is implicit in its documentary quality, which has been useful to historians in the analysis of the period. To cite just one example, Klein has converted this literature into a rich source of information essential to his research on the "origins of the national Bolivian revolution" (214-15).

What I have said up to this point may serve to define two basic propositions that will underpin my discussion of the course of Bolivian literature during the second half of the twentieth century. The first is that Bolivian literature had nothing to contribute to the 1952 revolution, since the latter in one way or another satisfied the demands that literature had been making over the past twenty years. This would seem to me to be the only explanation for the fact that the 1952 movement failed to inspire a specific literary response. The second point is that if the events of 1952 generated a new direction—which is not even an important tendency—within Bolivian literature, it does not mean that writers were indifferent to the need for the social changes implied by those events. The revolution did not nourish a literary response because literature had, since 1932, been nourishing the revolution.

One can seek proof for these two propositions in the following fashion. The changes brought about beginning in April 1952 have been supported by two radical acts that sought to change the semifeudal nature of the country: nationalization of the mines and agrarian reform. In 1974, twenty years later, one of the historians of the revolution, Frontaura Argandoña, provided an eloquent justification for both changes, based on the intertwined exploitation of the two basic elements of national wealth, silver and the indigenous population (16-17). Bolivian literature in the years leading up to 1952 had specifically and insistently focused on the Indian and on a precious metal, the two substantive elements of Bolivian reality that were addressed by the revolution in the form of agrarian reform and nationalization of the mines. Such a revision of the relationship between the 1952 revolution and Bolivian literature leads to an understanding of how the latter worked to fulfill its social function by portraying a reality requiring change and how it nourished a revolutionary consciousness that would later pursue a program of change.

The literary vacuum immediately subsequent to the revolution must be understood also as the reflex of national reality. Yet just when it was believed that the revolution was on the verge of fulfilling its goals, it fell into a pattern of lethargy from which it was never able to escape, and literature would in turn lapse into silence in the face of such a reality, perhaps sharing in the lethargy of the revolution as a way of expressing its solidarity, so to speak, with a period of social stagnation. The revolution was failing, and that failure was the only referent for a narrative that had always characterized itself for its social content. This literature, which had always "represented" Bolivian society, continued to provide an authentic representation in the form of silence and failure.

It cannot be denied that the Movimiento Nacionalista Revolucionario (MNR: Nationalist Revolutionary Movement), when it assumed the government of the country in April 1952, partially consolidated the revolutionary process with various necessary and profound changes that could no longer be deferred. Nor can it be denied that the MNR government was incapable of carrying out the revolution during the twelve years that it remained in power. It is unfortunate that that government made more of an issue over the party with which it was identified than over the revolution that it needed to carry out. One only needs look at the political texts of the period to grasp the abundant and privileged references to the "party" rather than to the "Bolivian revolution." In the context of this predominantly sectarian consciousness, the revolution came to occupy an increasingly secondary position. In the end the revolution paradoxically turned into a means for a sectarian goal: the aggrandizement of the party. Changes as important as the nationalization of mines and agrarian reform obviously emerged as failures. One of the historians of the revolution and a prominent member of the MNR, Frontaura Argandoña, concerned more with protecting the prestige of his party than the revolution, explained the failure of nationalization as the consequence of disorder and bad administration (282) and the failure of agrarian reform as the result of violence and a lack of coordination (298). These four phrases serve to define the context of Bolivian society during the period.

The historian of Bolivian literature is compelled to research the context of this failure, disorder, lack of coordination, and violence in literature immediately following 1952. There are, in my opinion, no more propitious social referents than these. It will not be my goal to attempt to determine the reasons as to why the authors of a social literature in the period prior to 1952 failed to concern themselves with these social referents. What is certain is that some of them set the practice of literature aside in order to become politicians, while others simply lapsed into silence. Literature becomes empty and isolated, and in this fashion it inevitably fulfills its function as a mimesis of reality. In terms of the semiosis of literary history, the emptiness of Bolivian literature immediately following 1952 is the imitation of the emptiness of national reality: social failure determined the crisis in literary production.

As is the case with every historical process, crises are periodic, and Bolivian literature overcame its own crisis with the appearance of a new novelistic promotion. Before examining this group of young writers who in a collective way provided a new direction for Bolivian literature, I wish to pause to comment on two books published in 1957 that highlight exceptionally well the literature of that period: *Cerco de penumbras* (Fence of Shadows) by Oscar Cerruto (1912-81) and *Los deshabitados* (The Vacant) by Marcelo Quiroga Santa Cruz (1931-80); the latter was killed by the military dictatorship. The sparse novelistic production of the moment is reflected in loneliness and emptiness, and I could even go so far as to add, availing myself metaphorically of the sense of the two works I have mentioned, that Bolivian literature enunciates a space that is a "fence of shadows" behind which the characters are "vacant" beings. Cerruto's book (although it is in reality a collection of stories and not a novel, I include it here) clearly reflects the loneliness, the social and physical isolation, and the lack of communication of Bolivians confronting the hostility of their world, and Cerruto's characters bespeak frustration.

I have examined elsewhere the solitary efforts as a precursor in the new narrative of Quiroga Santa Cruz. The efforts of critics to interpret and define the characteristics of the new generations of fiction writers in Bolivia have always underestimated *Los deshabitados*, although it is true that they have recognized its role in prefiguring recent trends. Yet they have failed to see in this novel anything other than a subjective attitude with only a slight connection to the literature of the period and even less of one with national reality. Nevertheless, if one takes into account, as I have above, the isolation in which Bolivian literature finds itself as a consequence of the historical conditions of contemporary society, it would be possible to grasp the accuracy of Cerruto and Quiroga Santa Cruz with regard to their social referent: a fence of shadows appropriate for vacant beings. Beyond narrative elements concerning space, characters, and action, there is in these two books a profound meaning that plumbs the depth of the emptiness and the absurdness of existence. In the closing pages, Quiroga Santa Cruz's characters openly express how meaningless reality is for them in an expressive register that could not be more sincere and authentic as regards the sense of failure.

In sum, *Cerco de penumbras* and *Los deshabitados* testify to the state of a consciousness isolated in its frustration and signalling an absurd existential circumstance. Beginning with these two works of fiction, Bolivian literature pursues a thematics that critics had not previously recorded: failure.

The poetry of this period emerges as the genre in which there is a reflection of national experience under the circumstances I have described. In effect, poetry in Bolivia during the past three decades reveals the experience of the sociopolitical vacuum, and it is possible to study it in particular in the work of important poets like Oscar Cerruto, Jaime Saenz (1921-86), and Gonzalo Vásquez Méndez (1927). This poetic reflection can be seen as a unique discourse that extends from the end of the 1950s to the 1990s. This poetry bears emotional testimony to national and international events that affected radically social and cultural reality in Bolivia during these decades in the context of the frustrated revolution of 1952 and its consequences.

The poetic reflex of national history in the work of Oscar Cerruto is sustained by the tension of two underlying problems. The first is the proposition that loneliness is a national legacy and that its implicit fatalistic vision of Bolivians in the twentieth century derives from local, traditional thought. The second tension is related to the first and concerns the effort, in this case by Cerruto, to transcend that vision. Although reflections on the legacy from the perspective of an adverse present orient his discourse toward the past, Cerruto's focus is above all on the future. The entire review of the past reveals the need to avoid repeating it and its errors, to emancipate oneself from it, and to perceive the power of the individual in the process of the future. "Enumeración de tu heredad" (An Account of Your Inheritance) is one of the texts from Cerruto's first volume, *Cifra de las rosas* (Cipher of the Roses; 1957), and it attests to how a constitutive element of the thought and the geography of national reality lies in loneliness. In this text, Bolivians are shown to receive at birth, along with other values, the identity of the physical reality of the land. The sense of loneliness as the inherent legacy of Bolivians is elaborated on, and it takes on new dimensions in Cerruto's second volume, *Patria de sal cautiva* (Land of Captive Salt; 1958), especially in the text titled "Soledad, única herencia" (Solitude, the Lone Heritage). Solitude is now a complex referent of not only depopulation, both physical and territorial, but also metaphysical in the face of the absence of a superior existential meaning and national history. This solitude, adverse in its threat to existence itself, nevertheless and despite its sense of permanence, is never accepted by the Bolivian as an alliance or a point of contact. Nevertheless, it remains as the only inherited wealth, as the only property that, although harmful in its dreadful, fragile, baseless, and disorienting manifestations, seeks to perpetuate itself via an equally vain effort at absurd reformulations. Gómez-Martínez asserts correctly that the feeling of an "adverse destiny" emerges "as the escapist quality in some of the members of the Chaco Generation as the consequence of the self-examination of the Bolivian." He adds, nevertheless, that "it is in the final decades and owing, undoubtedly, to the failure of the utopian dreams which idealized the 1952 revolution, that this sentiment has been generalized to the extent of becoming an article of faith" (45).

Cerruto's text postulates the deconstruction of this sort of transmission of unpropitious wealth. The text "Soledad, única herencia" describes what could be called here the dialectics of solitude as a struggle between two forces: on the one hand, the determination of solitude as the attempt at perpetuation via a legacy; and, on the other hand, the tendency to invalidate that determination and to accord a place to an alternative that would displace that appears to be consubstantial with the national character. It is important to note that this reflection is pursued only six years after the revolution. The second part of Cerruto's 1958 book is called "Por tanta altura y soledades" (At Such a Height and with Such Solitude). One of the most important texts of this section refers to "Los dioses oriundos" (Native Gods). The impact of historical reality and its adverse sociopolitical conditions, which correspond to a psychological vacuum of disorientation, result in a profound metaphysical skepticism in the description of the vanishing and absent idea of origins, foundations, and order. The poet is interested in taking up again that theme in the way in which tradition proposes it, but in order to deconstruct it and render it void. He is not interested in ratifying previously sanctified religious and metaphysical concepts when they have demonstrated their uselessness. His effort is toward demythifying the raison d'être of Bolivians, toward obliging them to seek pragmatic solutions with a view of the future, instead of always returning to the mythic past where origins and foundations, the designs of fortune or adversity, can never be recognized with certainty. Of special note in Cerruto's poetic project is the volume *Estrella segregada* (Segregated Star; 1973).

If Cerruto's poetic reflection identifies the individual segregated in the uselessness of solitude and silence, emptiness and disorientation, in the loss of knowledge and confronted by the ineffectualness of the metaphysical values of a misguided national historical process, the poetic project of Jaime Saenz emerges from the dark morass of unnamed things, a space which, although inhabited, is without knowledge or language. At issue is the experience of unintelligibility, and Saenz's poetry is devoted to the articulation of an intelligible perception of things and of the language with which they can be described, named, and known, toward assuming a creative and constructive practice of the intelligible. The quest for the intelligible is produced in the moment of fusion between the thinking subject and the things thought about. Thus, the poet recognizes that the first contact with things will be only in terms of their appearance—that is, that experience is related not so much to that which may be thought as it is to that which may be felt, and for this reason there is an appeal to the senses, especially touch, in order to know things. Such is the basis of *Muerte por el tacto* (Death by Touch; 1957). Individuals segregated in space from that which is unintelligible suffer a subjection to a process of reification in which they are converted into mere objects that survive in an adverse climate, something like a living death. Saenz's writing, as a consequence, achieves the discourse of nothingness that involves proceeding towards an annihilating operation, first, of the meanings of language and, then, of the referents correlated with the world. His poetry adopts a phenomenological attitude in its attempt to break with the meaning of ordinary language, which is unserviceable for the experience the subject is seeking. His is a language that institutes new referents divorced from all metaphysical tradition and all previous poetic experience and literary tradition. *Aniversario de una visión* (Anniversary of a Vision; 1960) is marked by the attempt to define an enunciating subject in its relationship to the "Other," the subject that is enunciated, and in his subsequent books this discourse confronts the object in general, in a very broad ontological dimension.

The writing of interiority and darkness evident in the poetry of Cerruto and carried to its limits by Saenz appears also in Gonzalo Vázquez Méndez (1927) with a new accent: hollowness. Poetic discourse, in its reflection on the reality of the individual and his affective surroundings and in circumstances in which these are radically affected by the sociopolitical crisis, achieves perception in a process of exhaustion and narrowing whose final phase is to end up hollow. The author of *Alba de ternura* (Dawn of Tenderness; 1957), Vázquez Méndez achieved recognition with the prizewinning *Del sueño y de la vigilia* (On Sleep and Wakefulness; 1966). His poetry is collected in *Del fuego en la ceniza* (On the Fire in the Ashes; 1984). By contrast to Saenz who articulates his edifying hermeneutics in his nihilistic vision of reality, Vázquez Méndez projects in his writing the referents of a reality subjected to a chronic wearing away and to destruction in a manner that is similar to Cerruto's poetry. The perception of the process of Bolivian history in the variety of its manifestations—political, economic, social, and cultural in general—is undeniably negative and the origin of the existential desolation evinced by Bolivian poetry in recent decades. It is impossible to overlook the fact that the emptiness revealed by Vázquez Méndez's discourse in the face of the unintelligible is also the emptiness of language or the absence of words able to name the incoherent and the meaningless. Hence, the poets need to engage in a process of rearticulation. It is for this reason that Vázquez Méndez also recognizes that the individual can enclose himself in language, in the absence of meaning and determine the emptiness or, especially, the hollowness that leads one to nothingness, to absolute absence, including God.

VII

The new generation of Bolivian writers, preceded by the literature that I have just surveyed, also recognizes clearly its social context of political failure, disorder, lack of coordination, and violence that give rise to an artistic expression of dissatisfaction and adversity. The frustration over social reality is reflected in this new narrative, by authors in the main around fifty years, in terms of two clearly characterized themes: the absurd and subversion. Both stem from the same feeling: the absurdness of the frustration and subversion in the face of failure. The first of these themes was explored in Quiroga Santa Cruz's novel and the second in *Los fundadores del alba* (The Founders of the Dawn; 1969) by Renato Prada Oropeza (1937), the most outstanding figure of recent Bolivian novelists. These writers begin to appear around 1969, and to espouse a markedly renovating position that opens a new period in Bolivian fiction. Prada Oropeza's production also includes two collections of short stories published in 1969, *Ya nadie espera al hombre* (No One Waits Any Longer for the Man) and *Al borde del silencio* (On the Edge of Silence).

The theme of subversion receives a decisive impulse from the guerrilla warfare of 1967 which inspires a considerable number of narrative texts. Prada Oropeza's novel, *Los fundadores del alba*, is the inaugural text of this tendency, and it won the 1969 Cuban Casa de las Américas Prize. This text demonstrates clearly the transition from the feeling of frustration to the subversion of a baneful established social order. Prada Oropeza is very conscious of the revolution's failure and the ensuing frustration of the aspirations of the people, which becomes in his novel the driving force of subversion. This writer has paid particular attention to the theme of guerrilla warfare, which he takes up again in *Larga hora; la vigilia* (The Long Hour; the Vigil; 1979). What is noteworthy in this novelist is his capacity to make lucid observations in the context of Bolivia on the drama of human consciousness under the burden of a deleterious and meaningless social reality, and the texts of this author focus on loneliness, abandonment, uncertainty, and frustration, thereby projecting the other major theme of the most recent promotion of Bolivian writers, the absurd.

The most important poet of this generation is Pedro Shimose (1940), the author of eight volumes, gathered together in 1988 under the simple title *Poemas* (Poems). In the context of the sociopolitical conditions that have been referred to, Shimose's poetry is representative of a majority production, which could be called the poetry of alteration and altercation. The version that Shimose offers of the historical reality he lives can be synthesized by the explicit affirmation of the concept of exile in his first work, *Triludio en el exilio* (Triludio in Exile; 1961). Bolivian poetic discourse has difficulty with shedding its attachment to the concepts of interiority (enclosure) and obscurity. Nevertheless, there is a very pertinent characteristic of this new discourse of the poets born in the 1940s: the complex social representation of Latin America in the second half of this century, which has seen a dramatic outbreak of violence, injustice, and misery. The denunciation of these social elements, more and more visible in the structure of Latin American societies, would become not only a new theme in the poetic discourse of the new generation, but the very function and goal of poetry.

Sardonia (1967) is Shimose's second volume of poetry. He takes up again the thinking through the labyrinth in order to reelaborate it, no longer as a referent to social reality or as an immanent structure of the authoritarian systems of Latin America, but as language. The sociopolitical labyrinth contaminates language—or, better, language, compromised by the political situation in its social setting, is unable to manifest itself as free and uncompromised by the labyrinthine nature of society. As a consequence, in his second book Shimose articulates a language whose syntagmatic and prosodic structure reflects the labyrinth. The manifestations of the labyrinth no longer occupy only the semantic and content planes, as in the first volume, where it is one of the dominant themes, but rather the very plane of expression and writing. The labyrinth is no longer simply a referent that symbolizes the immediate space of the enunciation, the referent of social reality in which this discourse is produced. Rather, it now configures a labyrinthine form and expression. Writing as labyrinth will characterize Shimose's poetic discourse even in his last books like *Reflexiones maquiavélicas* (Machiavellian Reflections; 1980), as it characterizes the Latin American poetry of his generation.

In these circumstances, this discourse enters a new phase of its development, in accord with the political situation of the reality of Bolivia and Latin America. *Poemas para un pueblo* (Poems for a People; 1968) can also serve as a model for the underlying stance of poetry in the years at the end of the 1960s and the early 1970s. Shimose's poetry provides a significant insight into the outlines of Latin American poetic discourse during the decades of the sixties and seventies, a period characterized by military dictatorship. Thus, in this period Latin American poetry adopts a position that is more political in terms of a social commitment, wherein writing convenes in and for itself his public obligation to speak out in the context of Latin American governments imposed by force during these decades.

The most recent Bolivian literature also is testimonial in nature, although it has eschewed critical social realism in favor of a writing more vigorously experimental that reflects the tendencies of contemporary Latin American literature in general. It has borrowed forms from indigenous culture, creating an atmosphere often intangible in which daily truths possess mythic transcendency. As in any form of mythic realism, even suffering assumes a paradoxical wonder marked by inverosimilar features.

The panorama of Bolivian literature in the last thirty years, seen from the perspective of literary scholarship and criticism, still reveals an imbalance between an ongoing production by authors and the scarcity of studies on that production and its individual genres. For example, between 1960 and 1980, around 300 narrative titles appeared and something like 440 books of poetry. By contrast, insufficient studies exist concerning literary developments during the same period.

Translated by David William Foster

BIBLIOGRAPHY

Alcázar, Reinaldo. *Paisaje y novela en Bolivia*. La Paz: Difusión, 1973.
    Emphasizes the influence of geography in the Bolivian novel,
    with special emphasis on the first half of the twentieth century.
Alcázar, Reinaldo. *El cuento social boliviano*. La Paz, 1981. An analy-
    sis of social themes in the short story between 1935 and 1970.
Antezana, Luis H. *Ensayos y lecturas*. La Paz: Altiplano, 1986.
Avila Echazú, Edgar. *Resumen y antología de la literatura boliviana*.
    La Paz: Gisbert, 1973.
Beltrán S., Luis Ramiro. *Panorama de la poesía boliviana*. Bogotá:
    Secretaría Ejecutiva del Convenio Andrés Bello, 1982. Although

an anthology, it is valuable for the two introductory essays on Hispanic-Indian culture and its literature and for the bibliographic registry included as an appendix.

Diez de Medina, Fernando. *Literatura boliviana*. 2a ed. Madrid: Aguilar, 1959. A general history of Bolivian authors and works, presented chronologically.

Echeverría, Evelio. *La novela social en Bolivia*. La Paz: Difusión, 1973. Themes of social protest based on political process are studied in novels published between 1900 and 1952.

Finot, Enrique. *Historia de la literatura boliviana*. 2a ed. La Paz: Gisbert, 1955. A standard reference work.

Francovich, Guillermo. *Tres poetas modernistas*. 2a ed. La Paz: Juventud, 1971. Ricardo Jaimes Freyre, Franz Tamayo, and Gregorio Reynolds are the subjects of this study.

Frontaura Argandoña, Manuel. *La revolución boliviana*. La Paz: Los Amigos del Libro, 1974.

Gisbert, Teresa. *Literatura virreinal en Bolivia*. 2a ed. La Paz: Universidad Mayor de San Andrés, 1968. An outstanding examination of literary, historiographic, and scientific writing from the colonial period.

Gómez-Martínez, José Luis, and Carmen Chaves McClendon, eds. *Bolivia: 1952-1986*. Monographic issue of *Los ensayistas; Georgia Series on Hispanic Thought* 20-21 (Summer 1986): entire issue.

Guzmán, Augusto. *Panorama de la novela en Bolivia*. La Paz: Juventud, 1973. A standard reference work on the history of Bolivian fiction.

Klein, Herbert S. *Orígenes de la revolución nacional boliviana. La crisis de la generación del Chaco*. La Paz: Juventud, 1968.

Lara, Jesús. *La literatura de los quechuas. Ensayo y antología*. 2a ed. La Paz: Juventud, 1969. The only scholarly study available on the subject by one of Bolivia's major authorities.

Moreno, Gabriel René. *Estudios de la literatura boliviana*. Potosí: Editorial Potosí, 1955-56. A two-volume collection of essays on nineteenth-century literature by one of the outstanding scholars of Bolivian literature.

Quirós, Juan. *Indice de la poesía boliviana contemporánea*. 2a ed. La Paz: Gisbert, 1983. This anthology contains an important study on twentieth-century Bolivian poetry.

Rivera-Rodas, Oscar. *La modernidad y sus hermenéuticas poéticas. Poesía boliviana del siglo XX*. La Paz: Ediciones Signo, 1991.

Rivera-Rodas, Oscar. *La nueva narrativa boliviana*. La Paz: Camarlin-ghi, 1972. A survey of recent fiction writers with an emphasis on their interest in the formal properties of the narrative.

Sanjinés, Javier C., ed. *Tendencias actuales en la literatura boliviana*. Minneapolis: Institute for the Study of Ideologies & Literature, 1985.

Siles Salinas, Jorge. *La literatura boliviana de la guerra del Chaco*. La Paz: Universidad Católica Boliviana, 1969. A study of the themes and stylistic features of writing about the Chaco War.

Soria, Mario T. *Teatro boliviano en el siglo XX*. La Paz: Casa Municipal de Cultura, 1980. With a "Prólogo" by Carlos Miguel Suárez Radillo, this anthology contains important information concerning the development of twentieth-century Bolivian drama.

BRAZIL
Roberto Reis
University of Minnesota

I

It would be inappropriate to attempt a thorough panorama of Brazilian literature within the confines of this chapter. Even less possible would be to attempt a detailed analysis of works or an exhaustive inventory of authors. Instead, my goal will be to provide an outline of the major tendencies that characterize the body of Brazilian writing. My approach, while, for didactic reasons, chronological, does not follow the rigid periodization in terms of styles so typical of historical treatments of Brazilian literature. In this sense, authors and works will be mentioned to the extent that they illustrate the tendencies developed, without any pretense to provide a complete description of an intrinsically complex phenomenon.

The other principle that I believe it important to specify from the outset is my belief that the literary text is a reading, albeit in an oblique and indirect fashion, of social reality. Guided by this conviction, I will treat the texts, to the extent possible, as intersections and dialogues with a historical process. Such a focus, scrutinizing the area in which history and literature impinge upon one another, attempts to contribute to an understanding of Brazilian culture.

II

It is important to begin by recalling Brazil's colonial status. The Portuguese arrived at the beginning of the sixteenth century, and their purpose was frankly commercial in nature. Despite the precapitalist setting, the economic model established in the tropics, based on agriculture, still contained feudal traces, traces that were already in crisis in the

95

rest of Europe, where the bourgeoisie and capitalism had begun their ascendency toward hegemony. The mentality of a rapid accumulation of wealth at any price will predominate to a large extent among Brazil's first colonizers.

Even more important for my argument will be to stress how European cultural values, Christian and white, will be transplanted to the new colony, with the result of European ethnocentrism on the one hand and, on the other, a religious justification (the dissemination of the word of God as the rationale for the conquest and as a mask for the preeminently economic motive for Portugal's overseas expansion—the same argument used during the Crusades). These two principles will serve to guide Portugal's presence in the newfound land.

Beginning with the *Carta* (Letter; 1500) by Pero Vaz de Caminha, which details the arrival of Pedro Alvares Cabral's fleet on the Brazilian coast, the texts of chroniclers and travelers are replete with passages denouncing this preconceived and distorted vision of the original inhabitants of Brazil. The European is enchanted by the wealth of the land, with its fruits and plants and animals completely unknown to the Old World. Such wonderment gets translated, on the level of texts, into the need to compare them to what one knew in Europe. This generosity of the land will be the basis of the myth of *ufanismo*, the patriotic overoptimism because of rich but as yet undeveloped resources, that has its first expression in the *Carta* by the scribe Caminha. The eye of the conquistador will also be struck by indigenous customs, especially ones like cannibalism and nudity.

A significant fragment may serve to illustrate this position. It concerns a fragment from Chapter X of the *História da província Santa Cruz* (History of the Province of Santa Cruz; 1576) by Pero de Magalhães Gandavo (?-1576). The language spoken along the coast "is lacking, it should be pointed out, three letters: it has no letter f, no letter l, no letter r, a fact that is frightening to the extent that thus they have no Faith, no Law, no King (the word for king in Portuguese begins with an r) and, as a consequence, live a completely disordered life with no basis for any other kind." Of course, Gandavo was using his own language to evaluate the language, and by extension the culture, of the Indians, and at no point does it occur to him that their language or their culture might be different. This inability to take into account cultural differences and the relativism of cultures means that, beginning with faulty linguistic observations, Gandavo is able to extrapolate a conclusion regarding the social institutions of the Indians. Using white society as a point of reference, the chronicler cannot grasp how the Indians may have another type of religion, another mechanism of social control, another notion of hierarchy.

Distortions of this sort abound in the texts of this first century of sparse colonization. The Jesuits, dedicated to catechizing, will make use of every strategem for the conversion of the populace. The theatrical pieces by Father José de Anchieta (1534-97), for example, place in the mouths of startled Indian actors the drama of the Passion, something that was obviously foreign to them.

One of the few dissenting voices, significantly, that of a Calvinist, belongs to Jean de Léry (1534-1611), who describes indigenous customs by comparing them to those of Europeans. In this way, he is able to contrast nudity with "the opposite vice, that of the superfluity of clothes"; the cruelty of anthropophagic savages is compared to a barbaric happening in Lyon. The French anthropologist Claude Lévi-Strauss believes that *Viagem à terra do Brasil* (Voyage to the Land of Brazil; 1578) by the French humanist is a "classic of ethnographic literature" because of its relativization of cultures, an approach that was unheard of among the chroniclers of Léry's day. It is important to underscore how these "literary" manifestations reveal the vision of the conquistador as he reiterates his white, European ethnocentric view of the New World and its inhabitants. It is, in a word, the discourse of the conqueror.

But we will find a break in this discursive pattern in the work of the Bahia poet Gregório de Matos (1636-96); by this time we are in the seventeenth century. In Matos's writing, perhaps the first of a nativist cast in Brazil, the colonial Baroque finds one of its fullest realizations, one worthy of standing alongside the architecture of Antônio Francisco Lisboa, known as Aleijadinho, or the paintings of Mestre Manuel da Costa Ataíde, who in reality come a bit later. We find in Matos's poetry the same conflicting dualities that figure so prominently in the poetic production of the most renowned Baroque poets of Europe: being versus seeming, reason versus emotion, silence versus declamation, sin versus repentance. Such dualities take the form, on the level of language, of antitheses. Themes like the flight of time found in the Spanish poets Luis de Góngora and Francisco de Quevedo or in the Portuguese Mannerist Luis de Camões, may be found in Matos's amorous lyrics. His sonnets often sound like those of other Baroque writers, and some of them were "rereadings" of Góngora. Yet this Baroque dimension of Matos is purely superficial. The very facets into which the poetry of Boca do Inferno (Mouth of Hell), as the poet was known, divides itself are characteristic of a typically Baroque poetic personality: amorous lyrics shading off into the most audaciously, libidinously erotic; elegies that turn into mordant satire; licentiousness that turns into sincere repentance in his religious poems. Gregório de Matos was a critic of the society of his time. And where we find the most original Baroque contradiction, the most agonizing disruption, is in the vacillation with which the poet experienced our colonial condition. On the one hand, he questioned the metropolis; on the other, he sympathized with its values, a sort of gentility of tradition clearly tied to European culture. Torn by this profound dilemma, Matos was never able to discern that, in the aspects of indigenous culture that were so vigorously condemned, there would be a possible response to his conflict, one that would make him an open anticolonial.

By this time colonial society had clearly defined itself. Sugar plantation owners made up the dominant class, with slaves at the bottom of the social scale. Brazilian economy, originally merely extractive, as was the case with the *pau-brasil* wood that gave the country its name, was now centered in the plantations that extend along the northeastern coast. In these vast land holdings in the hands of a few proprietors, a single product was cultivated with servile hand labor to meet the demands of overseas markets.

Little by little, a literary culture grew. The relationship author-work-public began to function in the eighteenth century, when there was a slight decline in the sugar culture and when the discovery of gold in Minas Gerais stimulated the beginnings of city growth, a new economic cycle, the accompanying migration of the population, and the emergence of an Arcadian literature practiced by a group of intellectuals. Many of them took part in the so-called Inconfidência Mineira in 1789, considered the most important uprising against Portuguese domination. Today, it is believed that many of the insurgents were defending the interests of the landowning class, with little concern for radical changes in the economic and social basis of the colony.

There was in the province of Minas Gerais an effervescence in arts and letters, and it has been argued that for the first time during the colonial period there was an attempt to seek an autochthonous form of artistic expression. Proof of this is to be found in Baroque architecture, less sumptuous and more modest than its European models, which made use of Brazilian soap stone, a material that Aleijadinho and other sculptors molded into artifacts that blended Medieval traditions, Oriental influences, and already marked nativist features. In the Arcadian poetry of Tomás Antônio Gonzaga (1744-1810) and Cláudio Manuel da Costa (1729-89), despite a diction still based on European models, there is an intrusion of a nativist dissonance based on the local countryside. This poetic naturism as practiced by a learned group of intellectuals belonging to an embryonic urban bourgeoisie continued to be a manifestation of dominant segments of society. But these segments were anxious to free themselves from Lisbon in order to assume power over their own internal realm. The decision of the landowners no longer to share their wealth with the metropolis (i.e., Portugal) would lead to independence in 1822. This meant merely the severing of ties with Portugal, which had been weakened anyway by the arrival in Brazil of the royal court in 1808 in the wake of the Napoleonic invasions. But the social structure of the country would remain intact, and slavery continued in place.

III

It became necessary to forge a national legendary past and to ensure political autonomy, even on the level of literary representation. Since there were no Middle Ages as a repository of heroes, the Indian became the object of mythification and the point of reference for the projection of the ideological needs of a recently created native "aristocracy." The Indian was racially pure, which freed this nobility from the flaw of the mestizo. He was glorious and brave, an honorable and loyal warrior after the fashion of a club-wielding knight who would provide the ruling elite with the genealogy of deeds and a tradition of marvelous feats it lacked.

Moreover, Indianism (the name for this ideology) fit in nicely with an imported Romanticism, with the very idealization of the savage also an imitation. Within the European context, the primitivism of the myth of the noble savage served as an indignant protest against the destructive advance of civilization. By the same token, Romanticism in the Old World was, in the final analysis, a reply to the French Revolution and the Industrial Revolution. When Chatterton, the eponymous character of Vigny's play, declares to the Lord Mayor that the place of the poet in the ship that metaphorically represents England is to "read in the stars the course signalled by the finger of the Lord," this made sense in a universe in which social relations were increasingly controlled by money. Vigny grasped the breach between artists and their audience. In a capitalist society focused on market values, the writer had lost his social and economic function. With the disappearance of patronage, the artist no longer served to distract a royalty marginated from power. Rather, the poet was called upon to defend the highest position in the social hierarchy precisely at a time when there ceased to be any function for the poet in that hierarchy. The British navy needed pilots to command the helm and personnel to fire the canons. Chatterton is sidelined. His poetry has no market value and his only capital, his emotions and his love for Kitty Bell, are meaningless in the world of competition characterized by exchange values.

The foregoing is important as an indication of the complex problems of Romantic art in Western Europe where there was a social and historic context to give it coherence. In the case of Brazil, peripheral in terms of the major capitalist centers, there was nothing analogous to the French and Industrial Revolutions (despite an incipient movement towards industrialization with the Viscount Mauá at the end of the nineteenth century). Instead, the Brazilian social pyramid remained basically divided into masters and slaves throughout the colonial period, the independence movement, and the subsequent imperial reigns. The lords of the land were complemented by merchants, bureaucrats, and coffee barons. By the middle of the nineteenth century, the economic center had shifted southeast and coffee had become the principal export product. Manufactured goods, French magazines, ice skates (!), and political ideas were all imported. The latter included political ideas like Liberalism and aesthetic ones like Romanticism. It was a nebulous body of ideas, to the extent that there was no direct point of reference in the sociohistoric reality of the country. Great subtlety is not required to grasp the outrageous incoherency of subscribing to Liberal principles in a slaveholding society.

Romanticism would also experience this process of "adaptation." In contrast to what happened in Europe, Brazilian Romanticism would have no countercultural meaning since its main function was to serve the attempt by the monarchic state to give a cosmopolitan touch to local culture. The Brazilian Romantic movement began in Paris with the review *Niterói* (1836), and it will be affirmed by the poetry of Gonçalves Dias (1823-64). This poet sought to reconcile "idea" and "passion" in a balance still marked by a Portuguese accent, despite the idealization of the savage; see his poem "I-Juca Pirama" (He Who Is Proud to Die). There is a sort of provincial Byronism in a second generation, as in Alvares de Azevedo (1831-52), who was an ultra-Romantic pursued by shadowy feminine forms and whose poetry is characterized by the repression of desire. In a third generation, Castro Alves (1847-71) will identify with the abolitionist by mythifying the figure of the black. In his poem best known for its antislavery message, "O navio negreiro" (The Slave Ship), the first verse states that "we are on the high seas." This spatial metaphor excuses the owners who were the mainstay of slavery from any crime by placing the blame on the slavetraders.

It is therefore necessary to emphasize the question of nationalism, perhaps the distinguishing characteristic of Brazilian Romanticism. It has already been mentioned how the figure of the Indian was raised to the status of prototype of the Brazilian character. Meanwhile, the indigenous tribes had already been decimated or they had taken refuge in the interior. However, the black was omnipresent in the everyday life of Brazil. Thus, to introduce the black into the pages of the novel would be to show that slaveowning society the image of its own blemishes; this reality had to be masked. Therefore, when he appears in the fiction of the period, the black is seen obliquely. The novel *A escrava Isaura* (The Slave Isaura; 1875), by Bernardo Guimarães (1825-84), shows Isaura as white, gifted, cultured, and refined. *O mulato* (The Mulatto; 1881), a novel by Aluísio Azevedo (1857-1913) published at the height of Naturalism, portrays the mulatto hero as a blue-eyed law student. All of this is far removed from the lifestyle of the sugar mills and plantations. Blacks, on the few occasions in which they are portrayed in nineteenth-century Brazilian literature, are "whitewashed" in order to make their blackness more palatable and conceal completely the violence that dominated the relations between master and slave.

But curiously, in the paradigmatic novels of José de Alencar (1829-77), the amorous relationship is metaphorized as a master-slave relation. This is certainly the case in the following speech by Aurélia, the female protagonist of *Senhora* (Lady; 1875): "What you, my sir, call slavery is nothing more than the violence practiced by the strong against the weak. . . . True slaves, I only know the tyrant that causes them, which is love." That is to say, the real problem (slavery is the violence imposed on the weak by the stronger) is diverted into the area of the "tyrant love." In *Lucíola* (1982), we read that Lúcia smiled, "constrained like a slave before the gesture of her master."

Alencar sought to portray a vast mural of Brazil, and he published an array of novels dealing with city, rural, and historic themes. The metaphorization of amorous relations in terms of "master" and "slave" is found in all of the areas he dealt with, as well as in the works of other authors. Under examination (and these comments are limited to Alencar), it may be shown that the characters who play the role of slave and master may vary, although they refer consistently to the realm of love. But the "slave" may at times be the masculine figure, at times the feminine one; at times he is the Indian, at times the man from the backlands.

Bearing in mind how being a slave is always the mark of social inferiority for an individual, let us consider some examples: in *Lucíola* the "slave" is Lúcia the prostitute and the "master" is Paulo, a student and a candidate for "good society"; in *Iracema* (1865), the "slave" is the Tabajara Indian virgin and the "master" is the white warrior Martim; in *O guaraní* (The Guarani; 1857), Peri the Goitacás Indian is the "slave," while Cecília, daughter of a castellan, is the "mistress"; in *O sertanejo* (The Bushman; 1875) the "slave" is the cowboy Arnaldo while the "mistress" is Flor, daughter of the ranch owner. Blacks do not appear in Alencar's novels. Thus, those who are shown as socially inferior—that is, seen as the "slaves" in an amorous relationship—are, respectively, woman, an Indian woman or an Indian man, and a man of the outback. It is significant that these characters are heroes in the novels in which they appear, novels that by extolling the Indian or the man of the outback are designed to contribute to a national mythology and the creation of the Brazilian character.

With the gradual decline of the Indianist vein of literature, the backwoodsman dominates in Brazilian fiction. This individual, immune from contact with the foreigners with whom coastal people had greater contact, is presumed to preserve intact his Brazilian features. Thus, it is possible to bring all of the characters of the nineteenth-century Brazilian novel into a single relationship: the relations between them are markedly hierarchical, with the dominant position occupied by the white man (the dominance of the lordly class), by man (the prevalence of the masculine order) or by the father (the preponderance of the patriarchal order). In the position of the subjugated, it is the woman (whether she be of the same social level as her partner or whether she is an Indian, a condition that in and of itself is enough to make her socially inferior), the Indian, the backwoodsman, or the black (the few times in which he appears).

These characters are exalted as heroes in the foreground of the text as prototypic representatives of the Brazilian character. Any movement of these characters toward those who occupy the position of command is immediately rejected. This is a unique sort of nationalism that chooses as the models of Brazilian character individuals who are treated as inferiors. The nationalism of the nineteenth century in Brazil, so acclaimed by one school of criticism, is contaminated by these ideological patterns. What in effect happens with Brazilian literature of the last century is that it ends up underscoring, on the level of literary representation, the hierarchical frontiers found in social reality. The dominant group is composed of landowners and their allies, and the nationalism that takes shape in the literature of the period, a literature produced and consumed, in the final analysis, by this same elite, is one that matches their interests.

Although the foregoing comments have limited themselves to Alencar's writings, they are valid for the nineteenth-century novel as a whole. This fiction either portrays the ruling class or, when it does focus on the *other*, the Indian or the backwoodsman, it does so with a distorted perspective that subjects the latter to the frame of reference of the ruling class. A text like the *Memórias de um sargento de milícias* (Memoirs of a Sergeant in the Militia; 1854-55), by Manuel Antônio de Almeida (1831-61), perhaps one of the few novels not to focus on the ruling class, cannot nevertheless escape completely the pattern that has been described.

IV

The writer who succeeded in breaking with this "narrow circle" that dominated the narrative of the period was Joaquim Maria Machado de Assis (1839-1908). The discrepancy began at the biographical level. Where the preponderance of the other writers of the nineteenth century had their origins in the landowning faction, Machado was of humble origins and, through social ascendancy and acceptance by his social betters, he came to occupy the privileged position of the "displaced": he no longer belonged among the disadvantaged nor was he completely identified with the "aristocracy" that took him in and venerated him. This contradictory condition endowed him with a mordant perspective toward the new moneyed bourgeoisie. Machado, moreover, appears to have maintained an ambiguous posture. It seemed to him a pity that the nouveaux riches were lacking in good manners and in culture, which made him a traditionalist. This traditionalism may be found, for example, in his exercise of discriminating taste as President of the Academia Brasileira de Letras (Brazilian Academy of Letters). At the same time, his challenging literature constituted a sort of writing hitherto without precedents in Brazilian letters.

Machado, rather than adhering to the models provided by the French novel of his day, sought inspiration in English fiction of the eighteenth century, notably in Laurence Sterne's *Tristram Shandy*. It should be evident that, as a result, his plots do not follow any strict causality; rather, they ebb and flow. The result is that characters acquire emphasis and special significance accrues to the narrator with respect to events narrated and the actions of the fictional beings. The story proper becomes intertwined with digressions and disquisitions of a diverse nature without respect for a strict temporal chronology, which is replaced by an incessant movement forward and backward in time. Machado specializes in the psychology of his characters to the extent of surprising in them the most hidden motivations and the most human of weaknesses and vanities, thereby demonstrating the utility of the social mask. His characters are portrayed as paradoxical and ambiguous in the extreme, far removed from the sort of maniqueism prominent in Alencar's writing.

In addition, the nature of Machado's narrator is suprisingly modern. Such a narrator is no longer a central organizing, omniscient voice who rules like a magician over the narrative. Instead, Machado's narrator brings into play a plurality of discrepant voices without establishing any hierarchy among them; these voices challenge the version of the facts narrated. As a consequence, truth is a matter of point of view and, therefore, one that is always dependent on the interests at stake. All of which brings us to two features that are of capital importance in Machado's writing. In the first place, Machado de Assis writes under the sign of relativization, which definitely identifies him with a contemporary criterion of writing. By problematizing absolute truths, the Machado text gives precedence to polyphony, the clash of versions, the relativism of values and meanings. In this sense, Machado is a breaker of hierarchies who contradicts the sense of nineteenth-century Brazilian fiction outlined in the preceding section. His narrators never assume the point of view of the dominated classes, who are essentially absent in his work. Although Machado's narrators may move among the ranks of the socially superior, they are endowed with the weapons of humor and irony and thus are able to attack from within the contradictions found among members of the ruling classes by dismantling the concept of hierarchy, to the extent that they hold power at bay and denounce the way in which meaning depends on who wields that power.

In the second place, as a consequence of the dialogic nature of his literary production as one of its defining features, Machado undertakes, in the guise of quotations from and allusions to other texts (literary, philosophic, and a wide assortment of writings from the Bible to cook-books), an intertextual dialogue that provides his writing with a semantic pluridimensionality that results in, at the very least, a double textual orientation. This relation with other texts, usually drawn from the European literary tradition, does not result in mere reverence, as was the case with Alencar. Rather, the prime feature is parody. The appropriation of other discourses, literary or otherwise, requires a parodistic adaptation that reorients their sense so that the alien text is reread with a characteristically Machadian accent. If we realize that parody—the assimilation in a new dimension of another text—will reappear in a writer like Oswald de Andrade as a highpoint of Brazilian Modernism (see section VI), it is reasonable to ask if Machado was perhaps not, avant la lettre, the sort of anthropophagic Andrade called for, that is, one who assimilates cannibalistically the foreign influences in order to produce a new cultural tradition.

In this way, all of the narrative patterns that take shape in Alencar's narrative paradigm are questioned by Machado's writing. Machado explores the level of the act of telling and brings to the inner structure of his novel the dialogic composition of his text. The narrator engages in a dialogue with his own text, with the characters, with the (implied) reader, in addition to the aforementioned dialogue with other texts and discursive models. Verisimilitude cannot help but be affected, as one outstanding example is enough to demonstrate. In *Memórias póstumas de Brás Cubas* (*Epitaph of a Small Winner*; 1881), which inaugurates the so-called second phase, we are faced with a "dead man who is an author" and not with a "dead author." The emergence of this new form of writing, which synthesizes the ruptures that have already been mentioned, must have been developed in his activities as a journalist, the authentic "fictional laboratory" of the Machadian text, and from there to the stories and novels of his "maturity": *Quincas Borba* (*Philosopher or Dog*; 1891; also translated as *The Heritage of Quincas Borba*); *Dom Casmurro* (1899); *Esaú e Jacó* (1904), and *Memorial de Aires* (Counselor Ayres' Memorial; 1908).

It is evident that language will also be affected, and beneath a style that gives the initial impression of being academically correct, Machado deconstructs common meanings, undermines clichés, dismantles high-flown and pompous rhetoric designed to impress, and satirizes superficial erudition. The critical thrust of this undertaking impinges on the inner meaning of language itself, within whose interstices the fictional Machadian narrator denounces the fossilization of commonplaces and the culture of ostentation.

Perhaps the Machado text where all this may best be seen brought together, most notably the principle of relativization, is in "O alienista" (The Psychiatrist), the first story from Machado's mature period, originally published in *Papéis avulsos* (Scattered Papers; 1882; see the translation *The Psychiatrist and Other Stories*). The text is markedly allegorical in the sense that it proposes a subtle reflexion on power (and the notion of power is pivotal if we consider that hierarchies have their origin in power). Focusing on the theme of madness, Machado problematizes more than just the pretentious scientism of the day. Shifting the French Revolution to a colonial Itaguaí and reducing it to the dimensions of *canjicas* (the Brazilian version of hominy grits and the name given the rebels in the text), that event is reread in a parodic form with new meanings. Machado works principally with the barrier that separates, in this case, sanity from madness, normality from abnormality, a decisive disjunction for indicating within the hierarchy who is crazy and what it means to be crazy. Once this frontier is established, the mad will be gathered together and the sane will be able to enjoy their freedom. But the psychiatrist, frustrated in the attempt to apply his science to the measurement of human behavior (herein lies the principle of relativization, for where does sanity end and madness begin?), ends up the only inhabitant of his asylum, a "Bastille of human reason."

Along with his formal innovations, this "dehierarchization" facet of Machado's production may be counted as the most significant break with the prevailing practice of the novel in Brazil at the time. Although he does not break free from the ruling elites (as a result, there is no reference to the downtrodden or to class struggle), Machado is able to bring the ruling segments into caustic focus. His literature, written over the period of almost a half-century, from the colonial period to the beginnings of the Republic in 1889, with its main point of reference the closing years of the Empire, constitutes in its totality one of the most trenchant documents of the transition Brazilian society was undergoing. Machado's work, aesthetically brilliant, both universal and at the same time a detailed panorama of the Brazil of the second half of the nineteenth century, is one of the highpoints of Brazilian culture.

V

The poetry written during this period is Parnassian in nature, and it is both innocuous and alienated. In spite of an occasional poet of some degree of talent, gilded sonnets speak of Greek statues and Chinese vases. Among these writers, the name of Olavo Bilac (1865-1918) should perhaps receive mention. His is a poetry of the Belle Epoque, one contemporary with Symbolism, whose best representative is João da Cruz e Sousa (1861-98), a black poet blinded by a white soul striving poetically for transcendence. Augusto dos Anjos (1884-1914) represents a similar situation with his lyrics of putrefying flesh and the cosmos falling apart, with a vocabulary replete with scientific terms through which, in spite of it all, he seeks a lost unity.

During this period of eclecticism, which has been called Premodernism, the best point of reference is the work of Euclides da Cunha (1866-1909), *Os sertões* (*The Backlands*; 1902), and the novels by Afonso Henriques de Lima Barreto (1881-1922). In the fiction of the latter, individuals drawn from suburban Rio de Janeiro make their appearance; these individuals have few ties to the dominant segments of society.

Cunha's monumental text is a mixture of sociology, journalism, history, and literature. It deals with the Canudos uprising in the interior of the state of Bahia in the 1890s. The uprising was led by the disaffected priest Antônio Conselheiro, and *Os sertões* details the military expeditions that ended up destroying the stronghold of the Conselheiro's fanatical followers. His work constitutes a significant attempt at the assessment of the other, in this case the inhabitant of the *sertão*, the outback, who is belittled by the urban citizenry and excluded, like all rural dwellers, from the political and economic structures of the country. Cunha, as a war correspondent, accompanied the Army, and he recorded the military actions from a perspective that does not deviate from the general view: the inhabitants of Canudos were religious and monarchical fanatics (Brazil had just made the transition from monarchy to republic in 1889). However, this perspective crumbles little by little, and the end of the book portrays the full extent of the carnage against Canudos. Cloaked in an outdated and turgid style, *Os sertões* represents, nevertheless, a break in Brazilian literature by providing the opportunity for a less distorted understanding of social minorities.

VI

This opportunity provided by Cunha would be explored by Modernism. Initiated by the Semana de Arte Moderna (Modern Art Week) in São Paulo in 1922, the movement renewed the Romantic goal of a literary discovery of Brazil. But this time the difference was in exposing our cultural complexes and according recognition to the colloquial and the folkloric-popular. Modernism corresponds aesthetically to a moment of transition in the social formation of Brazil. The agrarian colossus was being transformed into an urban-industrial society with a middle class that was progressively taking its place in the political arena. This transition, which resulted in a new sociohistorical reality, required a new language for its representation. The Modernists turned to the isms of the European vanguard in the attempt to modernize Brazil artistically. They would use this rejuvenated diction in order to scrutinize the multiple facets of Brazilian culture.

Modernism was a movement with its origins in the moneyed São Paulo upper-middle class, particularly coffee interests. But it would quickly fragment into a number of currents, just as politically it would bifurcate into right- and left-wing tendencies that reflected the political effervescence the country was undergoing, which would culminate in the Revolution of 1930. Modernism appeared in São Paulo, Brazil's first great metropolis, a city already relatively industrialized by the 1920s, and it is logical that it would have an essentially urban character. Thus, Modernism was the new Brazil reflected in the pages of literature, and the goal was to grasp the new times. *Paulicéia desvairada* (*Hallucinated City*; 1922), by Mário de Andrade (1893-1945), is a good example of this effort to capture the impact provoked by urban-industrial civilization.

The experimental novels of Oswald de Andrade (1890-1954) are also devoted to the urban setting. Andrade makes radical use of Cubistic and Futuristic tendencies in novels like *Memórias sentimentais de João Miramar* (Sentimental Memoirs of João Miramar; 1924) and *Serafim Ponte Grande* (1933) in order to satirize the lives of characters drawn from the coffee-industry bourgeoisie. Oswald de Andrade was also an innovator in the theater, with works like *O rei da vela* (The King of the Candle; 1937), a portrait of the genesis of the Brazilian bourgeoisie. In poetry, his joke-poems and especially his parodic rereadings of the old chronicles, and the poems on the history of Brazil, place him among the leaders of Modernism, a restless intellectual and one of the principal renovators in Brazilian literature.

But where Oswald de Andrade's contribution is most outstanding is in the "Manifesto da poesia Pau-Brasil" (Manifesto of Brazil-Wood Poetry; 1924) and the "Manifesto antropofágico" (Anthropophagic Manifesto; 1928). In the latter, he proposes the consumption of European cultural values in a mixture with native elements that will produce a new cultural artifact, one eminently mestizo as the mark of Brazilian culture. This project, already implicit in Machado de Assis (who, it is intriguing to note, was never canonized by the Modernists), continues to possess considerable validity as a proposal for any Third-World culture: to instill a difference with respect to the European tradition by rewriting it in terms of a transformational rereading that incorporates native ingredients with the goal of creating a separate cultural space that is no longer either European or indigenous, a space where the Brazilian text will thrive.

Andrade coined a number of lapidary phrases, one of which is worth quoting by way of illustration of his ideas: "Tupi or not Tupi, that's the question." Exploiting the sound similarity between the name of an indigenous tribe and the English verb "to be," the epigram echoes the famous speech from *Hamlet*, a work clearly symbolic of the entire Western literary and cultural patrimony. Thus, Andrade both appropriates and debases this tradition in his parody, and the declaration no longer belongs to Shakespeare. The question is to be Tupi or not to be Tupi—that is, to delve into native culture or to opt for the seduction of the European model. What the sentence proposes instead is the space in between. Between Tupi or not Tupi, in this crisscross of discourses, is where Brazilian cultural space is to be found.

We find the same sort of project in Mário de Andrade's novel, *Macunaíma* (1928). The novel chronicles the uprooting move of an Indian to São Paulo and his loss of cultural identity. Andrade makes use of a body of legends fathered by the German ethnographer Theodor Koch-Grünberg. These legends, combined with folkloric tales, popular proverbs, elements drawn from the Western literary tradition beginning with Rabelais, provide for the composition of a text that restores Indianism in a wholly original fashion. Mário de Andrade's task, in the manner of the ancient rhapsodists, was to forge links between the various fragments, as though working variations on a single theme in the fashion of musical rhapsody. *Macunaíma* is not really a novel, but rather a rhapsody in the form of an "impure speech": a subversive discourse that is quite far-removed from the pure, intricate Portuguese cultivated by grammarians and purists. The mestizo and anthropophagic profile of *Macunaíma*, so important for a number of reasons, makes it a landmark of Brazilian literature. While Oswald de Andrade discovered the Brazil of Plâce Clichy in Paris, Mário de Andrade traveled about the interior collecting materials for his work. His poetry, notably *Clã do jabuti* (The Clan of the Jabuti Turtle; 1927), demonstrates this effort to imagine our country in literary terms. Literary critic, poet, novelist, musicologist, short-story writer, folklorist, he is one of the most fascinating intellectual figures of Brazilian culture.

VII

Thus, the Semana de Arte Moderna would result in a host of derivations. In the 1930s, for example, literature took on a marked social connotation, with an emphasis on the novel dealing with the Northeast region. This area was undergoing an unmistakable decline. When slavetrading began to decline around 1850, the sugar plantations could no longer count on the slave laborers that were the basis of their operations; thus, the plantations began to disappear. Since they had never used paid workers and since they resisted the adoption of modern agricultural techniques, both of which practices the coffee growers in São Paulo endorsed, the plantation owners gave way to the sugar mills. This decline, a sign of the aforementioned transition occurring in Brazilian society, was chronicled by the novel of the 1930s. Perhaps the most representative example here is the cycle of five sugar cane novels written by José Lins do Rêgo (1901-57): *Menino de engenho* (Plantation Boy; 1932), *Doidinho* (1933), *Bangüê* (Sugar Mill; 1934), *O moleque Ricardo* (Kid Ricardo; 1935); *Usina* (Mill; 1936); these novels prefigure his masterpiece, *Fogo morto* (Dead Fire; 1943). These novels are marked by an autobiographical and nostalgic tone. Vacillating between criticism of the traditional order and lament for the collapse of the old structures, in the end these novels leave intact the structures of the ruling class, with its patriarchy and the dominance of masculine values.

Even in the questioning work of Graciliano Ramos (1892-1953), literarily superior in a dry, spare language stripped of all superfluity, it is possible to detect this same sort of vacillation. In *São Bernardo* (*São Bernardo*; 1934), for example, Paulo Honório, the protagonist-narrator, stands with one foot in tradition and the other in the new capitalist order, and from this dislocation arises his principal conflict. Patriarchal values no longer find an echo in modern history, and the more modern capitalists have not yet taken over completely. The figure of the patriarchal sire had been transcended historically, while that of the modern entrepreneur was historically poorly defined. The writing of both Lins do Rêgo and Graciliano Ramos is characterized by its memorialist character. Ramos, like so many writers who were more or less his contemporary, began writing *fiction* and ended up writing a *confession*, the memoirs of his childhood. And what is remembered is always the family mansion, now in ruins.

Brazilian society, in which the family plays a primordial function, is centered around the figure of the father, the master, the man. With reference to him the other social places in the family cell and outside of it are determined. This structure is hierarchic. What is curious is that Ramos's novels, almost all written in the first person and with characters involved in the writing of the book, introduce protagonists with family problems that have their origin in the father-son relationship: cf. *Caetés* (1933), *São Bernardo*, and *Angústia* (Anguish; 1936). It is interesting to note that the father-son relationship is a variant of the hierarchical structure already present in the nineteenth-century novel. Ramos's work, along with that of other regionalistic writers of the 1930s, is basically marked by a Proustian nostalgia for the family mansion and by the father-son conflict, which illustrates the degree to which the literary production of that period continued to subscribe after all to the masculine values of the master and the patriarch of the dominant class. The author of *Vidas secas* (*Barren Lives*; 1938) is one of the major names in modern Brazilian prose fiction. Nevertheless, his writing cannot avoid the painful transition of our society from the rural-agrarian to the urban-industrial. His characters are located midway, in a world in which tradition is undermined by a new order in the same way that that new order is undermined by tradition.

Even the principal poetic works of Carlos Drummond de Andrade (1902-87) will correspond to this interpretation. The poetic subject developed in Andrade's texts fulfills a circuit. Excluded from the family circle (see the poem "Infância" [Infancy; 1930], one of his earliest poems), fleeing from a narrow and provincial Itabira, he seeks the other in the modern big city. The encounter with the other does not occur, and the action of time is corrosive and implacable. Meanwhile, "there is always a little of the whole left." And it is from this residue, which survives the wearing away of time, from this "lack that loves," that memory will be born of poetic recovery on the level of language, a memory of the past, of the family, of the paternal figure, of the wealth of the blood of the patriarchal clan (see poems like "Viagem na família" [Voyage to the Family; 1942] and "A mesa" [The Table; 1951]). The autobiographical substratum, therefore, also appears in Drummond de Andrade's poetry. This return of the prodigal son is especially evident beginning with *Boitempo* (Ox-Time; 1968) and *Menino antigo* (Ancient Boy; 1973).

Echoes of this hierarchical relationship, of which the masculine and the patriarchal orders are corollaries, are discernible in a novel published in 1959 by a writer whose roots go back to the 1930s. This is *Crônica da casa assassinada* (Chronicle of the Murdered House) by Lúcio Cardoso (1913-68). The Meneses family descendents are unable to administer the land in conformance with a social norm still dominated by patriarchalism. In the over 500 pages of the novel the father of the Meneses is never mentioned. The two ancestors evoked, Maria Sinhá and Dona Malvina, the aunt and mother, respectively, of the sons Timóteo, Valdo, and Demétrio, are masculinized women. A reading of the memoirs of Maria Helena Cardoso, the novelist's sister, confirms on a biographical level this absence of a father figure, and it is important to stress how the sense of the novel reaffirms the autobiographical tenor of modern Brazilian fiction. With the center of the circle absent, the brothers conduct themselves like "turkeys in a chalk circle" and fight among themselves over control of the farm.

By contrast, novels like *Gabriela, cravo e canela* (*Gabriela, Clove and Cinnamon*; 1958), by Jorge Amado (1912), confront the old values—Coronel Ramiro Bastos and his followers—with an emergent power not tied to the land—the entrepreneur Mundinho Falcão—whose principal activity is exports. While the Coronel has his political support in the governor of the state, Mundinho is supported by forces linked to the central power. In the final analysis, vanquishers and vanquished will forge an alliance. We remain within the confines of the prevailing sectors of power.

The outstanding novel by Mário Palmério (1916), *Chapadão do Bugre* (Bugre's Plateau; 1965), also details the emergence of a centralized political power that usurps local bossism. Might this not have been the result of the movement unleashed by the revolution of 1930? Rising up against the "coffee with milk" pact of the Minas Gerais and São Paulo oligarchies, oligarchies sidelined from the sphere of political decisions reacted by coming to power in order to forge alliances and to preserve unaltered, in the last analysis, the class structure of the country. Brazil has always experienced restructurings of power and never a revolution that altered radically the country's social stratification.

VIII

The 1940s will be dominated by two major figures: Clarice Lispector (1926-77) and João Guimarães Rosa (1908-67).

Clarice Lispector, particularly in the short stories of *Laços de família* (*Family Ties*; 1960), lays bare the hypocrisy of the everyday appearances of the middle class which hides behind the fragile security of routine in order to escape the "danger of living." Bound by culture, the female characters that predominate in Lispector's writing are unable to *see* the brute and living force of nature. Thus, the prevailing accent of Lispector's writing is philosophical, the consequence of the influence of existentialism, just as her narrative style owes much to Woolf and to Joyce. Her plots are slight, and the emphasis is on the thoughts of the characters who, immersing themselves in self-contemplation in a language that is often directly essayistic, experience the perplexity of existence.

For example, the main character in the novel *A paixão segundo GH* (*Passion according to GH*; 1964) lives her passion. Standing on a "third foot," GH always shields herself from the jeopardizing chaos of the world. Savoring the cockroach, her communion with nature, she demonstrates her nonhumanness and seeks contact with "nonbeing" in order to prepare herself to know what it is to "be" human. This novel is, after all, a sort of pivotal point in Lispector's fictional production to the extent that it attempts to grasp the other that is different, a member of another social class, which in this case is the maid who inhabits a room in the back of the house. This is a preoccupation that will reappear clearly in *A hora da estrela* (The Hour of the Star; 1977). In this case, the learned narrator hovers over the figure of Macabéa, a woman from the Northeast, only to run over her in the end with a yellow Mercedes.

If we can believe that this dilemma—i.e., that of the upper or middle-class intellectual trying to identify with the lower classes—is crucial to Brazilian literature, it is possible to illustrate the problem with metaphors drawn from Lispector's writing. The narrator of *A hora da estrela* is a *writer*. He controls the written word, and writing confers power. Macabéa is a *stenographer*, that is to say, she is restricted to copying someone else's text. As long as the character from the dominated class does not cross the boundary separating stenographer from writer, there will always be the risk of being understood in a distorted manner, yielding to the temptations of a paternalistic discourse constructed in terms of the patterns dictated by the dominating segments. In Brazilian literature, where it is unusual to find a text by the dominated, their voice is to be heard repressed in the text of those who dominate. The attempt in Brazilian culture to give voice to socially repressed minorities is indeed recent.

In Rosa's *Grande sertão: veredas* (*The Devil to Pay in the Backlands*; 1956) reveals a bandit who narrates his life in an extended monologue to a learned listener. The result is that the novel is not a discourse *about* the bandit, such as we have in the majority of regionalist novels, but the discourse of the bandit himself, even if the work is considered the product of a writer, of an immensely cultured Rosa, who "masks himself" as Riobaldo Tatarana. But Rosa's fiction is much more than just this. In a true synthesis of Brazilian literature, various currents merge: regionalism/universalism, aesthetic consciousness/social preoccupation, Baroque/Modernism, to mention only a few of the main ones that come together in the vast mural the creator of *Sagarana* (1946) left as a legacy. Moreover, Rosa also evokes the entire European tradition, which he amalgamates in a magical alchemy with the Brazilian literary tradition. In *Grande sertão: veredas* we find echoes of both the medieval gesta and the language of the Western novel, of traditional myths and popular stories, and all of the principal outlines of our literary heritage come together in the saga of Riobaldo, the Urutú-Branco (The White Pit Viper). This structure of refracted forms is used by Rosa to draw together possibilities already present in the Modernist project of which his writing is such an admirable summa.

We can discover in Rosa's literary production two planes: a plane of life on a small scale, made up of common happenings, a contingent space in which life seems to be a tangle of random pieces; and a plane of life on a large scale, occupied by the large issues that hound Rosa's "person-characters," questions that have no answers although they point toward a utopian dimension of life. Most often, Rosa's characters move from the first to the second plane, and madness, love, poetry, infancy function as the transition from the privation of contingency to the plenitude of the transcendent. Rosa's emphasis is on the transition and on the attempt to reground man in the world, on the root meaning of religiousness, and on the reintegration of man with the totality. In this sense, Rosa's work comes very close to Lispector's cosmovision.

All of Rosa's rivers have three banks. His careful working of language provokes a "stylistic shock" in the novice reader. By exploring the potentialities of the linguistic system, incorporating words from other languages into Portuguese, revitalizing terms and expressions that have fallen into disuse, taking up the language of the backlands of Minas

Gerais, creating neologisms, remaking syntax, experimenting with new resonances of alliteration, Rosa forges his own unmistakable, special diction. He turns Portuguese inside out, confers on it a new expressive stature, and liberates language, in his own words, "from the mountain of ashes under which it lay."

But the care taken with language reaches beyond the aesthetic and the ludic in the sense that, for Rosa, language possesses a metaphysical dimension. Words have their own "third bank." For Rosa, language is a weapon in the defense of human dignity. By renovating language, the world is renovated. The sense of life may be recovered via a reconstruction of language whereby the latter has restored to it its naming and creating power, the original act of *poiesis* by which being is founded through the word. Concomitantly, Rosa rejects Cartesian rationality in favor of a greater role for intuition, revelation, inspiration, enchantment, and magic. As a consequence, there is a rejection of certain weaknesses of Western thought and its habit of binary thought: Good versus Evil, God versus the Devil, Reason versus Emotion and so on. Rosa shows how "everything is and nothing is," how each thing carries within it its own contrary, and how the "third bank" is a privileged space, a utopian territory in which contradictions are abolished. Neither this bank nor that bank and both at the same time, the "third bank" is the place where man wanders, where he explores the different-same waters of the river of life, free from the confines of temporality.

In *Grande sertão: veredas* Diadorim represents this privileged space, the outback, denied to the human Riobaldo who heavily treds the human outback in order to find transcendence in immanence. In accord with these metaphysical outlines, which assume universal dimensions, Rosa's work is a multifaceted panorama of the modus vivendi of the inhabitant of the outback and of the "condition of the bandit," a complex and vast mural of the outback with its customs, its language, its particular economy, its flora and fauna. Toward representing the transition in Brazilian society from the rural to the urban, the mural painted by Rosa pinpoints in all its mythic dimensions the archaic culture of the outback subdued by urban civilization. Social denunciation thus appears mediated also by language. By setting aside a fossilized language and by rejuvenating the power of revelation of the poetic word, Rosa's fiction constitutes a protest against the society that institutionalized degraded speech.

Rosa left a body of writing that not only synthesizes Brazilian literature; it also places it in the context of Western culture. It is a writing endowed with a metaphysical shape, but it is a metaphysics against metaphysics, and in this way Rosa speaks with the same voice as the most innovative philosophical contributions of our time (e.g., Foucault, Derrida, Deleuze, all contemporary readers of Nietzsche). By the same token, in line with the writing of Jorge Luis Borges and Julio Cortázar (see the section on Argentine), Rosa contributes to the rejection of a cultural heritage of the West whose gaps are only too visible to us.

IX

In the so-called Generation of 1945, which turns to traditional forms and rehabilitates the grand themes of poetry, the name of João Cabral de Melo Neto (1920) stands out, although he soon separated from that group. Situated at one extreme of Brazilian poetry, an extreme whose major characteristic is the progressive erosion of emotive lyricism, Cabral de Melo Neto's poetry is antilyrical. Determinedly lucid, a geometrician and engineer of verses, an ally of the poet-builders, Cabral de Melo Neto, beginning in particular with the trilogy of 1947 compositions "Psicologia da composição" (Psychology of Composition), "Fábula de Anfion" (Fable of Anfion), and "Antiode" (Antiode), turned more and more to the landscape of the Northeast. This and similar landscapes (e.g., that of Spain) have been reconstructed poetically in texts like "O cão sem plumas" (The Featherless Dog; 1950), or in the Pernambucan Christmas play, "Morte e vida severina" (Severinian Life and Death; 1955). With a spare diction and a constant process of rethinking the metaphors out of which his poems are made, Cabral de Melo Neto brings to Brazilian poetry a social denunciation of a high aesthetic accomplishment, and he stands alongside Drummond de Andrade as one of the greatest poets of the Portuguese language.

All of which brings us to contemporary Brazilian writing. It is more difficult to speak in definitive terms of the tendencies, constants, and derivations of the array of writers of the present moment. This is a literature that is predominantly urban, and it seems to evade the outlines that I have attempted to describe thus far. For example, it is a literature that usually accords attention to minorities. Writers are more diversified in terms of their social origins, although the book may still be a luxury item among Brazilians, an elitist commodity with a very small number of copies printed for a society of over 150 million inhabitants. On the other hand, Brazilian literature now belongs to a tradition such that it no longer identifies itself, vis-à-vis Europe, in terms of simple dependency.

Unfortunately, it is not possible to trace these outlines in any categoric sense, and a certain listing of names considered to be important is unfortunately inevitable. Alongside the established names of Murilo Mendes (1901-75), Cecília Meireles (1901-64), and Manuel Bandeira (1886-1968), contemporary poetry includes Ferreira Gullar (pseud. of José Ribamar Ferreira; 1930), author of the remarkable *Poema sujo* (Dirty Poem; 1976), and Carlos Nejar (1939). In the novel, there are established names like Erico Veríssimo (1905-75), author of the important trilogy *O tempo e o vento* (*The Time and the Wind*; 1949-61). Also of note are novelists like Autran Dourado (1926), author of *Opera dos mortos* (*The Voices of the Dead*; 1967), Adonias Filho (1915-90), Osman Lins (1924-78), Antonio Callado (1917), José J. Veiga (1915), and Márcio Souza (1946), author of the "serial" novel *Galvez, o imperador do Acre* (*The Emperor of the Amazon*; 1976). In the short story, where there has been considerable activity in recent years, the writings of Dalton Trevisan (1925), Murilo Rubião (1916-91), Lygia Fagundes Telles (1923), Rubem Fonseca (1925), João Antônio Ferreira Filho (1937), Samuel Rawet (1929), and Luiz Vilela (1943) should be mentioned.

The chronicle, a typical Brazilian genre that is a blend of pithy editorial observation and fictional elements, achieves literary status in the hands of writers like Rubem Braga (1913-90?) and Fernando Sabino (1923). In the area of the essay of literary criticism, there is a significant advance in terms of its academic format: Afrânio Coutinho (1911), Antonio Cândido (1918), Alfredo Bosi (1936), João Alexandre Barbosa (1937), Roberto Schwarz (1938), Benedito Nunes (1929), José Carlos Garbuglio (1931), Luiz Costa Lima (1937), Silviano Santiago (1936), and Flora Süssekind (1955).

A word about theater, which has remained on the margin of this discussion. Theater during the last century possesses mostly a historical value. Mention might be made of the absurd dramas of Qorpo-Santo (pseud. of José Joaquim de Campos Leão; 1829-83) and the comedies of manners of Luís Carlos Martins Pena (1815-48) and Arthur Azevedo (1855-1908), whose criticism of the society of their day anticipates more recent theatrical production.

Modern Brazilian theater, following the efforts by Oswald de Andrade, begins with the play *Vestido de noiva* (Wedding Dress; 1943) by Nélson Rodrigues (1913-80) in which different temporal levels are combined. Rodrigues's theater includes the dramatic representation of the unconscious of the characters and the deft handling of dialogue. His plays capture the sense of the suburban middle class, with its traumas, obsessions, and desires, and they constitute archetypic embodiments of a collective unconscious.

The theater of Ariano Suassuna (1927) makes use of the folk literature of the Northeast, notably in *Auto da compadecida* (*The Rogue's Trial*; 1957). Jorge Andrade (1922) deals with the decadence of the São Paulo society involved in the coffee farms, as for example in *A moratória* (1955). Alfredo Dias Gomes (1922) probes the plight of the populace of the interior, subjected to political machinations and bound to a blind mysticism, as in *O pagador de promessas* (1960). The theater of Gianfrancesco Guarnieri (1934) and Oduvaldo Vianna Filho (1936-74) also offer significant portraits of Brazilian society. In the case of Plínio Marcos (1935), texts like *Dois perdidos numa noite suja* (Two Lost Souls in a Dirty Night; 1966) and *Navalha na carne* (Razor Blade in the Flesh; 1967) focus on marginal segments of the population like prostitutes and homosexuals.

The dramatic production of recent years, as can be seen in the foregoing works, has sustained its defiant character in the denunciation of the evils of an unjust social order.

X

Other forms have not been discussed in detail, like children's literature or popular writing like the *literatura de cordel* (literally, "tied-up literature," a reference to cheaply printed pamphlets of literary composition brought in bound bundles to the market places, where they are hawked, characteristically by the authors themselves). This is not so much out of a desire to raise the question of the institutionalized corpus of Brazilian literature. Although there is no doubt that such a questioning is necessary, what has been studied is more the result of the attempt to examine that corpus within certain parameters, with particular emphasis on *how* one might read the literary patrimony of the Brazilian canon.

With access to and participation in literature basically limited to the lettered elite, making the book a veritable luxury item in Brazil, it becomes important to examine other cultural manifestations, especially those linked to the more popular forms of art. This is especially true if one's goal is to explore Brazilian culture in a more comprehensive way. By the same token, even if the goal is to retrict oneself to the literary canon, there is still a need to examine the problematics of the process of production, circulation, reproduction, and consumption of the cultural object as a part of cultural life, toward establishing more exact and complex parameters by undertaking to address these phenomena in terms of a sociology of cultural life. Recent research has approached Modernism from the perspective of these questions, with the result that the contradictions inherent in the movement and in its process within the modernization of Brazilian society have been called into question by pointing to the cooption of many of the Modernist writings by Getúlio Vargas's fascist Estado Novo (New State), which came to power originally in the 1930s. Analyses in this mold, if recast to encompass the entire corpus of Brazilian literature, should yield interesting results by demonstrating how the literary and cultural discourse of Brazil was, as a common rule, in the service of the ideology of the dominant, hegemonic discourse and that the latter was fundamentally an authoritarian discourse to the extent that it blocked the articulation of contrary voices, closed itself off to History, preventing difference and the Other from being inscribed in its own discursive texture. The limitations of this essay have allowed only for the suggestion of these possibilities as part of an expanded treatment of the corpus studied here.

From what has been developed in this essay, it is possible to identify three major strands of Brazilian literature. The first strand owes its identity to the dominant sectors of society. Certainly, if we look back from the nineteenth century, we see that authors tended to belong almost exclusively to the ruling class. Brazilian literature has never been endowed with vast numbers of readers, and this is still the case today: books continue to circulate among an intellectualized elite. Literature, it must be recognized, is a cultural manifestation of ruling groups, an observation that is all the more obvious in the case of the last century and one that is no less true in its ramifications in the twentieth century. Modernist writers, including the Generation of 1930, not surprisingly often belong to the decadent "great families of Brazil," and their literature served as a sort of mirror in which their own class could see itself reflected.

The other two strands are disruptions in the dominant one that has just been described. One strand concerns those writers and works that succeed in portraying the other, the dominated, in terms that are less prejudicial than those of the literature of dominance. Here would be included Euclides da Cunha, Lima Barreto, Mário de Andrade, and a large number of outstanding dramatic works. The other strand is that literature written under the strand of parody, of anthropophagia, whereby the European literature tradition is rewoven with native, Creole strands.

This is the case of Machado de Assis, Oswald de Andrade, Mário de Andrade here also, João Guimarães Rosa, all of whom contribute to forging a "mestizo" literature.

It should be evident that this tripartite distinction is essentially valid in illustrative terms, since in practice these strands are never that clear in any one author or in any one work. Moreover, writers that may be identified with one of these groups may suffer from radical contradictions that serve, precisely, to make their writing interesting. Gregório de Matos, Machado himself, Graciliano Ramos, while they belong to the dominant group, experienced conflicts that provide their work with its characteristic tone.

Translated by David William Foster

BIBLIOGRAPHY

Avila, Afonso, comp. *O modernismo*. São Paulo: Editora Perspectiva, 1975. Essays by a group of scholars examine Modernism on the fiftieth anniversary of the Semana de Arte Moderna. Of special note are the contributions by Francisco Iglesias and Benedito Nunes.

Bosi, Alfredo. *História concisa da literatura brasileira*. 2nd ed. São Paulo: Editora Cultrix, 1976. An indispensible guide that combines an aesthetic and a social approach with historical and critical analyses.

Brayner, Sônia. *Labirinto do espaço romanesco*. Rio de Janeiro: Editora Civilização Brasileira, 1979. An analysis of the various stages of Brazilian prose fiction in the 1880s; the Bakhtian concept of dialoguism results in a valuable consideration of Machado de Assis.

Cândido, Antonio. *Formação da literatura brasileira: momentos decisivos*. 4th ed. São Paulo: Livraria Martins Editora, 1971. In two volumes this is one of the important works of critical historiography of Brazilian letters.

Cândido, Antonio. *Literatura e sociedade*. 2nd ed. São Paulo: Editora Nacional, 1967. The relations between literature and society are examined in one of the most outstanding contributions of recent literary scholarship.

Coutinho, Afrânio, ed. *A literatura no Brasil*. Rio de Janeiro: Livraria São José, 1959. In three volumes, essays signed by a group of scholars emphasize an aesthetic and stylistic approach that is often uneven and that has been superseded by subsequent scholarship.

Foster, David William, and Walter Rela. *Brazilian literature; a research bibliography*. New York: Garland, 1990. A comprehensive registry of general references, references on special topics, and critical books and essays on specific authors.

Lima, Luiz Costa. *Lira e antilira* Rio de Janeiro: Editora Civilização Brasileira, 1968. A general overview of Brazilian poetry between the two poles of the emotional lyricism of Bandeira and the antilyricism of Cabral de Melo Neto.

Merquior, José Guilherme. *De Anchieta a Euclides*. 2nd ed. Rio de Janeiro: Livraria José Olympio Editora, 1979. Following an arrangement based on style periods developed for European literature and adapted to the Brazilian context, this brief history is inspired by the "crisis of culture" as understood by the Frankfurt School.

Miceli, Sérgio. *Intelectuais e classe dirigente no Brasil (1920-1945)*. São Paulo: DIFEL, 1979. Although this is a sociological study based on a corpus of memoirs and autobiographies written by members of the Brazilian intelligentsia, it is especially valuable for its observations on the social backgrounds of the modernist intellectuals.

Schwarz, Roberto. *Ao vencedor as batatas*. São Paulo: Livraria Duas Cidades, 1977. Although the main subject of study is paternalism in Machado de Assis's early novels, the study is important for the framework it establishes regarding the ideological contradictions of nineteeth-century Brazilian literature.

Schwarz, Roberto. *Um mestre na periferia do capitalismo*. São Paulo: Duas Cidades, 1990. A continuation of the foregoing entry, this monograph focuses on Machado de Assis's *Memórias póstumas de Bras Cubas* in order to demonstrate how in this novel he succeeded in finding a narrative form appropriate for capturing the disconcerting nature of nineteenth-century Brazilian society.

Sodré, Nélson Werneck. *História da literatura brasileira*. 4th ed. Rio de Janeiro: Editora Civilização Brasileira, 1964. Valuable for its reference to the economic basis of Brazilian literary production.

Sevcenko, Nicolau. *A literatura como missão*. São Paulo: Brasiliense, 1983. A penetrating historical study on the Brazilian *belle époque* and the thematization of its social tensions in the work of Euclides da Cunha and Lima Barreto.

Süssekind, Flora. *Tal Brasil, qual romance?* Rio de Janeiro: Achiamé, 1984. A superb overview of Brazilian fiction, demonstrating the reiteration of the naturalist aesthetic and the ideological impregnation that has been the bane of Brazilian fiction since the middle of the nineteenth century and its later ramifications in the novelistic production of the 1930s and the documentary fiction of the 1970s.

Süssekind, Flora, and Raquel Valença. *O sapateiro Silva*. Rio de Janeiro: Fundação Casa de Rui Barbosa, 1983. This is an excellent study of the production of the so-called Arcadian poets of Minas Gerais, showing the formation of a literary system by privileged poets belonging to the landowning class and holding university degrees, while marginating the shoemaker Silva, whose poetry represented a dissident voice.

CHILE

René Jara
University of Minnesota

I

The first text to be produced within the varied and elongated geography of Chile was *La Araucana* (The Araucaniad; 1569, 1578, 1589), an epic poem written by the Spanish nobleman and soldier Alonso de Ercilla y Zúñiga (1533-94). In a curious manner Ercilla's composition might be aligned with the discourse of defense and recognition of Indian values initiated by Friar Bartolomé de Las Casas and continued by the French writer René de Montaigne. Unlike Las Casas, however, Ercilla believed in the assimilation of the vanquished. Identity of values and beliefs was to be the basis for equality. Along these lines Ercilla was to discover that the Amerindian values—patriotism, liberty, and the worth assigned to courage and pride—were after all not so different from those which he esteemed. Las Casas, one must recall, insisted that equality did not require sameness, so that the natives could conceive of God according to their own traditions. Without reaching this point, Ercilla prefers an orthodoxy that hierarchizes Christianity over Indian religious beliefs. This contrast, however, allows him to express his doubts about the health of the empire, since with all their superstitions and misguidance the Araucanians had been able to preserve their love and pride for country and freedom in a state of purity long lost for the Spaniards, most of whom were moved by greed and private gain.

More than a history of conquest, *La Araucana* is a song to war that focuses not so much on the military encounter between Europeans and Amerindians as it does on the ideological conflict between the values of the empire and those of the inhabitants of the land. Despite Ercilla's attempt at balancing both ends of the conflict, one may see a subtle tilting towards the discourse of the empire. In his descriptions of the Indians, Ercilla emphasizes their faith in man, their unmodulated pride, their love of the land over the trascendental values of Christianity. For the noble Spaniard this was religious Titanism, an attitude of defiance like that of Lucifer against the Creator. The mataphor of the fallen angel to qualify the Araucanians will entail both a fatal condemnation to submission and a behavior and worldview that are characterized by resentment. The Indians lack the true religion to be equal to the Europeans. Simultaneously, however, Ercilla gives the reader a different perspective: the Spaniards have lost the purity of the same values the barbarians preserve untouched.

Ercilla's criticism of Indian religious values is, in effect, matched by his critical view of the empire. Just as his translation of Amerindian behavior at war is rendered, in order to be understood, in the language and generic conventions of his own Europe, his analysis of Spanish decadence is constructed around the symbols of Spain's imperial greatness: the battles of San Quintín and Lepanto and, to some extent, around the unification of the Peninsula under Philip II. Against the canonical views of Ercilla's epic as a disconnected text one can see the inclusion of these episodes and, in particular, of that of Dido, as being essential to the structural functioning of the work.

Thus the victory of the Spaniards in San Quintín is placed in a tactical relation to the Araucanians' siege of the by-then recently constructed fortress of Penco. Let us recall that the victory at San Quintín marked the zenith of Spanish hegemony. Philip II had humiliated France, which was then one of the major world powers. Yet, a mere twenty years after Spain's momentous victory at San Quintín the Spaniards found themselves under siege in distant Chile at the hands of a barbarous, godless horde. Ercilla's text incorporates an internal polemic that ultimately questions the very destiny of the empire. That is, between the date of the battle of San Quintín in 1557 and the publication of the second part of *La Araucana* in 1578, the glorious victory had become a nostalgic event. Spain was beginning to lose sight of its destiny.

The same strategy is adopted for the narration of Spain's victory in the Gulf of Lepanto against the Ottoman Empire. One must recall that in 1571 the Christian fleet commanded by Juan de Austria sought to end piracy in the Mediterranean, as well as the trade of Christian slaves in Africa. The Spanish victory was thus seen as the final triumph of Christianity over the infidels. This victory, together with the earlier defeat of France, created for Spain a perception of invincibility. Doubtless Ercilla did not share this perception, since he endeavors to place the battle of Lepanto next to a fiery speech by the rebellious Araucanian chieftain

Galvarino. The linking of Lepanto and Galvarino's speech allows Ercilla to question those Christian principles that supported and gave credence to the conquest. Ercilla questioned their use in a war fought largely for the private gain of the conquistadors who, despite being Christians, corrupted the values of the faith and infringed upon the law. There is no doubt that Ercilla was well acquainted with the crimes commited against the Indians by a number of Spanish governors. He also must have realized, in ironic twist, that those crimes were not any different from those perpetrated by the Turks against the Christians in the Mediterranean and in Africa. Suddenly the reader is equating abusive Turks with abusive Christians. The frame of reference for Christian values is all but lost.

The third part of *La Araucana* is published in 1589, one year after the destruction of the Spanish Armada. In this section of the poem there is more emphasis on theoretical reflection than on the representation of war. Ercilla's epic song is one of hope and concern, as the poet and his comrades meet friendly Indians in the extreme south of Chile. At the same time that the narrator is affected by a new experience with the Indians, he becomes increasingly concerned for them because he comes to the realization that civilization brings with it corruption, greed, and injustice. For him the ideal of the Christian conquest has become a nightmare, a distorted utopia.

Ercilla's attitude towards war implies both a justification and a rejection of it. War might be justified when it is declared by a just sovereign whose actions are prompted by a quest for peace and for the benefit of the subjects. Such seems to be the case with the unification of the Iberian Peninsula under Philip II, which is discussed in the last chapter of the text. On the other hand there is in *La Araucana* a rejection of war when it is waged indiscriminately for reasons of personal gain. Such had been the case in Chile, where the natives had been mistreated in the name of a predominating search for wealth. The Indians had fought back to defend their territories and their freedom.

In the subtext of Ercilla's epic poem the attitude of the Indians ressembles a love intrigue in which the natives are suitors and defenders of their loved land. It is this attitude that justifies structurally the introduction of Dido's story in the text. It is a story that relies on a heterogeneous reading of the Dido legend rather than on the canonical appropriation of Virgil. The latter version focuses on a self-consuming passion that leads to the suicide of the protagonist. The Christian version, prefered by Ercilla, stresses the sacrifice of the character in order to preserve the dignity and memory of the dead husband. Such is the case with Elisa-Dido, the Queen of Carthage, who resists the matrimonial advances by Yarbas, the tyrant of Lybia, as well as the pressures of her fellow citizens who fear for the destruction of the city. Her death must be read as a victory over selfishness and betrayal.

The recollection of this story is surprising because at the beginning of the poem the narrator had promised not to relate a love intrigue, but to focus on the Araucanian war. When one looks at the text closely, however, it becomes clear that Ercilla has kept his promise, for the love stories he represents are always entangled with the trials of war, which are recounted from the perspective of both the Spanish and the Araucanian combatants. The introduction of the Dido legend allows for a kind of symbolic intertextuality according to which the virtuous Queen replicates the values attributed by the Araucanians to their land. Just as Yarbas becomes a symbolic double for the Spanish army ready to invade the land of Arauco, so, too, the Araucanians and the Indians of the Southern part of the territory seem to press the motherland to repel aggression. Ercilla's double for Dido, however, does nor commit suicide, as the war will continue.

The Americanization of the Dido legend is brought about through the creation of the fictive Glaura, a beautiful Indian woman who wanders through forests, mountains, and encampments in search of her husband, Cariolano. She also wanders throughout the poem in search of consolation. Eventually she is found by Ercilla, the poet—and sentry—who returns her to her husband, a man whom Ercilla has captured in order to save him from the Spanish soldiers. The Spanish captain Ercilla is no less generous than Cariolano, who had come to the Spanish camp to prevent Ercilla from being killed in an Indian ambush.

La Araucana is an answer to the unilateral discourse of the empire; it encompasses, in rich dialogue, the traditions of a people in accordance with values such as love, justice, liberty, and truth. If there is a victory in *La Araucana* it is that of love over death; it is the victory of peace over war; of poetry, which affirms its existential vitality, over the destruction of the conquest. It is perhaps for these reasons that the war against the Araucanians was the most common epic theme of the Colonial period, closely followed by the deeds of Cortés. Ercilla's pattern of discourse was constructed upon the notion that the acceptance of the other was inevitable. This was to be the great topos of most of the best writings dealing with the conquest of America. This was also to be an early model for the romance of the land, which contains the structure of the nineteenth- and the first half of Latin American twentieth-century novel.

II

The nineteenth century was for Latin Americans a time to lay the foundations. Independence came unexpectedly, and there followed a long struggle for the attainment of republican stabilization. In 1866 the Spanish squadron bombarded the unprotected Chilean port of Valparaíso. Gustavo Adolfo Bécquer (1836-70), a poet from Seville with Nordic tastes, applauded the manoeuvre with Romantic enthusiasm. One of Chile's best novelists, Alberto Blest Gana (1830-1920), a notable diplomat, managed to compose a broad narrative cycle that omitted any reference to this assault on Valparaíso. Republican history, following an institutional rhythm, had already begun to show its evasive flank. Literature did not progress with the same rhythm as the administrators of the State, or it followed a beat that better matched the needs of a nation that had been organized administratively before it knew what it was. I will attempt to provide a delicate resolution for this sort of paradox.

Historians have said that the reading of Ercilla's *La Araucana* fed the fires of independence. But its consequences were broader than this. Ercilla had put his name to the base of what could be called Latin America. The change in the Spaniard, his defeat by and his sympathy for the unknown, the need to read the map of experience in order to become something else were all there in this appraisal of an irresolvable conflict, that of a writing, Spanish writing, which did not match the political and cultural reality of what it had been called upon to label. Chile, the Chile of the Antarctic region, would come into existence as the result of war. The Indians against whom the Spaniards fought in the distant days of the conquest would not yield in their heroic struggle until the close of the nineteenth century. Those natives who were friends of the Spanish, who fought fiercely against those of their own race, came to form part of the most mestizo people of Latin America, an epitome of racial homogeneity. The visual images were lacking, and the Creoles felt that lack. In truth, it was necessary to undertake a complete inventory.

This was accomplished by a Peruvian mulatto, Gil de Castro. Castro left about a hundred portraits in a Neoclassical style par excellence. The liberator Bernardo O'Higgins and a retinue of important and notable persons all exihibit in his portaits an elegant seriousness and the statuesque charm of firm and intelligent gestures. They are classic, and class, entities, exemplary men and women who were not remote and whose known and admired virtues could be easily converted into objects of emulation. Their message was not inscribed in the realm of myth or of the epic, but in the living materiality of contemporary history. Heroes had begun to visit Chilean soil in order to populate and protect it. Forearmed with the gifts of force, security, and beauty, they came to guarantee the harmony of the world. Gil's work provided a pictorial representation of the Creole hegemony over the territory, and the satisfaction of the artist who signed the portraits of the Chilean high society was homologous with the pride of a class that arose from the masses to become the protagonists of a nation's destiny.

The driving force of informed thought was public happiness, and this would be achieved once the instruments of experience were oriented toward solving the problems of culture and humanity. The myth of progress would be the touchstone of the enlightened. Juan Egaña (1768-1836), a Peruvian Creole who established himself in Chile, would attempt to put it down in writing. Both his *Ocios filosóficos y poéticos* (Philosophical and Poetical Diversions; 1829) and his memoirs, *El chileno consolado en los presidios* (The Chilean Consoled in the Prisons; 1826), transmit the philanthropic sentiment of aristocratic generosity that would be translated into the interests of the privileged groups through the economic and intellectual betterment of the people.

It is important to remember that, if enlightened discourse was enunciated in France with the characteristics of an antilanguage that the bourgeoisie directed against the patrician class, in Spain it made its peace with the nobility. Moreover, it only repudiated extreme forms of absolutism and religion. This intelligent reformism that sought the well-being of the people by eliminating their participation in power would put down deep roots in Latin America. From the distant times of the Viceroy Manuel de Amat (1761-76) down to the days of the Christian Democrats (1964-70), Chileans have lived a situation defined by the identity of objectives and strategies: the very intent to better, via opportune reforms, the condition of the people would stall the revolutionary impulse as well as its anarchic potential, thereby preserving the code of the empire. The result, as a consequence, was controlled progress: betterment, liberty, equality, social covenant for the few.

It is informative to read today the "Cuarta Noche" (Fourth Night) of Egaña's *Ocios*, in which two characters, Philotas and Polemón, converse about the theoretical principles of civil legislation; Polemón charts the outlines of a utopian world. He is cautious, for if the advisability of generalized instruction in the natural and mathematical sciences seems unquestionable to him, he cannot help but recommend special care in the diffusion of religious and political disciplines, since cultural excess would incline people toward the sentiments of pride and indocility and sow the seeds of the spirit of innovation. For similar reasons, Egaña recommended the prohibition of secret meetings, since these could serve political interests and give rise to conspiracies that would destroy the peace of the nation and upset the institutions of State. In this context, freedom of the press would become the most dangerous of political benefits. If the existence of a public opinion could be a wall of containment for the arbitrariness of government and permit the pressuring of the latter on behalf of worthwhile projects, it could simultaneously contribute to the weakening of respect toward the Chief Executive, awaken the tendency toward insubordination, and become a vehicle for social unrest. Egaña's ideal republic, as a consequence, would give freedom of the press to citizens over forty years of age; the rest would be subject to censorship.

The nature of Egaña's discourse is curious and recurrent. It is based on a concept of public opinion that involves the creation of a reader. The structure of this reader is that of an adversary. Egaña calls this reader public opinion. It does not mean the point of view shared by the majority of persons, but rather of a verbal attitude that, because it is active in the popular sector, can become a counterdiscourse. That is, it has the potential to assume a liberal aspect during authoritarian times, a revolutionary one in moments of reaction, and even a regressive one when confronted with a progressive discourse. Thus, from its earliest beginnings, Latin American writing and its readers are constituted as a political project and, as such, as the standardbearers of one sector of the population. It is important to probe more deeply the nature of this Creole Egaña.

El chileno consolado en los presidios was printed in London in 1826. Its plot centers on a series of betrayals and an absence, that of the popular sector of the citizenry. The text centers on disloyalty of the Spaniards who supported the Napoleonic invasion, the reprehensible conduct of the impostor toward the Latin Americans who supported the deposed Spanish monarch, and the betrayal of the king himself who, once restored to the throne, made common cause with the assassins of Latin America in order to pursue the savage war of reconquest. The vileness of the moral and political conduct of Spanish officials could only

lead to independence movements, and in its denouement the book provides the image of the republic organized under the direction of O'Higgins. The text assumes the form of memoirs, and it centers on Egaña's
imprisonment, along with other worthy Creoles, during the years of the
reconquest between 1814 and 1817.

If one overlooks in Egaña's text the utopian vision of consolations
dictated by a naive Gallicanism, it is possible to recognize the figures of
a romance of the land, including silent and docile peasants. The book
is dedicated to Egaña's beloved daughter, Isabel, and to his brothers.
Isabel is the embodiment of the Creole fatherland, and Egaña's legacy
is the testament of a father educated in the school of suffering, work, and
persecution. His objective is to revindicate his dignity and his Hispanic
identity. The latter is already far removed from the spirits of the indigenous emperors Huaynacápac and Moctezuma. The Latin American of
1810, on the other hand, is the Spaniard himself, although his natural
strengths might be "something less than those of the European." Paradoxically, this definition of identity involves the recognition of a lack that
constitutes itself in the form of exile and inferiority and that, with a
strange discursive twist, seems to flow from the negation of indigenous
ancestry. The Creole recognizes himself to be a man of little consequence, the product of an imaginary, European invention.

Perhaps as a result, Egaña renounces heroic virtue. Beaten, morti-
fied, turned in upon himself, he writes his memoirs and avoids addressing
the king. He is afraid because he stands alone and lacks support from
among the people. He struggles in his own name, for his own class, for
his own property, and for his own children. The otherness discovered by
Ercilla has become separation and rending. It is another turn of the
screw, but Egaña's discourse continues to look toward Europe and
continues to be inappropriate. Perhaps it is because what was appropriate, as Ercilla had already noted, was nothing more than a labyrinth of
mirrors, a substantive estrangement.

It is for this reason that, in the face of insults and blows, privations
and bodily illness, Egaña the exile seeks remedies for his soul. He soon
finds them in the ecclesiastic figure of the wise and goodly Adeodato,
whose language reinscribes in the mind of the Creole the sacred notions
of God, the felicity of the just, the goodness and the rewards of virtue.
The voice of Adeodato, "He Who Has Been Given to God," frees him
from asphyxiation and physical misery. The world Adeodato provides is
that of harmony and proportion, far from the tumult of passions and the
grossness of the body. Physical nature vanishes, the senses grow weak,

and everything becomes a mysterious mist. An observer, man, situated on an extraterrestrial platform, examines, analyzes, and determines that everything is a function of the whole, that harmony is universal and that the wisdom of the Almighty overwhelms human importance.

A nostalgia for perfection and the sentiment of exile form the basis of the Creole disdain for lesser-cultivated individuals with more brutal customs, such as those who made up the popular strata. Egaña is unable to conceal his disgust at having to deal with "the most stupid sort of soldiers, drawn from the frontier inhabited by wild Indians." Liberals and conservatives would receive with equal pleasure this legacy of absence. The people would remain apart throughout the nineteenth century, unredeemed like Taguada, the mulatto poet who suffered defeat in the face of the learned and European knowledge of Juan de la Rosa.

The story of Taguada and his rival Rosa that must be told is that of a ghost, the ghost of an institution or the institution of a ghost, the ghost of the folk culture and folk letters of Latin America. As in the rich legacy of Hispanic Romanticism, the wealth of ballads and a multitude of popular poetic forms remained virtually unknown until the rise of the middle class to political power in the 1920s. The *contrapunto* (counterpoint; a form of poetic duel) took place during the early years of independence. It was reworked by Antonio Acevedo Hernández (1886-1962) in 1925.

Taguada was one of those folk poets who used to roam the towns and villages of Chile singing compositions on divine and human topics, armed with a bass guitar, his joy, and an infinite ingenuity. The songs were rhymed jousts that were improvised on the spot. If a singer was unable to respond to his adversary, he was obliged to fall silent and to consider himself broken or defeated. His rival was authorized to remove one of the garlands from the *chupalla* or hat of the defeated poet. Considered to be the best of the Chilean poets of this genre, Taguada made an open challenge to the public in attendance at a popular festival. The only one who dared to accept his challenge was Juan de la Rosa, a wealthy man, somewhat of a Bohemian, a good guitar player, and a man knowledgeable regarding peasant ways. At the same time, Rosa was a cultivated man who knew of books and who had traveled in Europe. Rosa was, as a human being, the counterpoint to Taguada, who was the son of a Spaniard and an Indian woman whose only byways had been the roads of his own country.

The outcome had already been inscribed in the books of learned thought: the inevitable triumph of European learning. In order to pursue this essay, I would like to call on the assistance of a man like Taguada, a peasant who learned to read when he was twelve years old, who was a woodsman and roustabout, who wore boxing gloves, and who was honored with a prize from the Universidad de Concepción for his long theatrical career: Antonio Acevedo Hernández. Commenting on the Taguada-Rosa episode, Acevedo Hernández wrote the following:

> Legend has it that when Taguada was defeated, he uttered not a word. Lowering his head, he seemed buried in his thoughts and appeared not to recognize the sea of cheers that surrounded his rival nor the oblivion in which everyone suddenly abandoned him. He seemed to be on the fringes of reality.

> Thus, become truly a shadow, he awaited nightfall before setting out under the stars. Only then did he grasp the magnitude of his defeat, realizing that the soul of all Chile applauded his rival, and it struck him that even inanimate objects pitied him. He ran to hide himself far from the world, far from himself, wounded by the sorrow of having been unable to maintain his prestige, which was that of the people who now followed his rival without even attempting to understand or to justify his fall. Taguada bewailed his great ignorance and his fearsome solitude. His pain grew and grew as the shadows of night wrapped itself around him until it deprived him of life.

> Such was the end of the greatest bard the people had known, the consequence of an unequal struggle in which true knowledge had overcome his privileged intuition.

The wit and the popular tone of this expression are immediately apparent. There is a moment of luminous blindness in this text that I would like to explore. Inadvertently, Acevedo Hernández's assessment echoes the superiority that liberal thought accorded to European knowledge, and we see someone whose roots are purely popular joining ranks with Egaña to accept, although painfully and reluctantly, the backwardness of the popular sectors. The poor mulatto, writes Acevedo, was left "outside time," inept at acquiring the knowledge that now humiliated him, leaving him "on the fringes of reality," on the shores of history. With his pride wounded by the thought that "even inanimate objects pitied him," Taguada ran to hide himself from the world, fleeing from his "fearsome solitude," shrouded by the shadows of his suffering. Taguada flees "far from himself" because he was one with the world in his unaltered identity.

It is now possible to grasp how, without bothering with logic, Acevedo Hernández's judgment refers in reality to a world, to an entire culture, condemned to be forgotten and annihilated. The problem of the superiority of one form of knowledge over another is irrelevant in this case. The tragedy is that of the incompatibility of two forms of knowledge. The triumph of one implies the elimination of the other in Darwinian terms. The one that triumphs is the one that bears the signs of prestige, of progress, of philosophy, of the Enlightenment. Taguada's failure is ideological and is presented as though it were a phenomenon of nature. Significantly, the defeat of the mulatto could have been the result of his inability to respond to the theological questioning to which his adversary submitted him. His failure had been signalled by the gods and confirmed in the sublime clues provided by Adeodato. Taguada's was not an inferior world, and the mulatto was a sovereign among the bards of his land, no matter how much Juan de la Rosa informed him scornfully that in the land of the blind, the destiny of the one-eyed was to be king. Rosa utilized ingenious sentences, sprinkled with notions as abstract as the schemes of the Enlightenment that the people would never be able to understand. A liberty, an equality, a fraternity in accord with which there were always a few who were more fraternal, freer, and more equal than the majority.

This is the drama that Acevedo Hernández was only barely able to perceive. Taguada had an ascendency among his own kind because he had a function to fulfill, that of bringing respect to his culture. With his guitar in hand, he had won prestige by dint of his verses. These verses reflected the traditional wisdom of his people, a wisdom that everyone could recognize. By contrast, Rosa brought a prestige of mysterious notions and words, taken from distant lands, a wisdom adorned with the magic of the unknown.

In Taguada's world there prevailed common sense and a form of knowledge that, transmitted from one generation to the next, made it possible to maintain the direction and the order of life. These ideas and values arose from three centuries of experience on Latin American soil, from the contact between the Indian and the missionary. Proverbs, old wives' tales, miracles, ghost stories, legends in which the ghosts of the living shake hands with the dead make up the pages of an encyclopedia in which magical knowledge and scientific thought are not split asunder as provinces of a world in which magic exists in the real and the expression of the latter can only be fantastic. This world will later become the base for the writing of major poets and novelists like Pablo Neruda

(1904-73), José Donoso (1924), María Luisa Bombal (1910-80), and Isabel Allende (1942).

Yet Taguada lost the battle, and his real defeat lay in the fact that the people with whom he identified sided with his rival. I would like, once again, to do some violence to Acevedo Hernández's text. Bitterness overwhelms the world of the mulatto, blanketing him with night and overshadowing him, it would seem, forever. Taguada witnessed the retreat of his culture in the applause of his companions for his rival, the applause of his own people, whom he represented in the face of the intruder. He realized, thus, that he had become a pariah, the essence of the Other who had lost his audience and his reader and who, dispossessed of his world, was condemned to contemplate, from the fringes, the unfolding of a history of which he was no longer a part. History had become for him a parade of masks, a concert of othernesses, or a disconcert of identities. This would be the nature of the nineteenth-century Chile for popular culture, the epic of a disappropriation, a bannishing into the night. This was not, in all certainty, the passage that Acevedo Hernández had imagined.

With Taguada, Chile lost the popular strain in its poetry. The people did not sing of the armed struggle for independence, or, if they did, the texts have been lost through a lack of scholarly interest. What is most probable is that the people lacked something to sing about, since, after all, the struggle for emancipation did nothing more than unleash the ambitions of minorities. There was no rhetoric, as we know it, in Taguada's discourse because the distance between reality and language tended to be minimal. Liberal discourse during the first half of the nineteenth century, on the other hand, had identification and persuasion as its goals. The writer, because the singer had disappeared, would assume with ease the images of the publicist, the orator, the tribune, the recreator of the historical past. The task was to convince the people that they also benefited from progress and that all modernity was synonymous with republic and democracy, with justice and equality.

III

In the face of these words, grand and empty, the people, like Taguada, could only shroud themselves in the mantle of night. It was treason not to be always repeating them, and there were those who repeated them with the sincerity and religious faith of the fanatic, like Francisco

Bilbao (1823-65). There were others who pursued a tortuous and contradictory project, like José Victorino Lastarria (1817-88). Some adopted a cautious response, like Andrés Bello (1781-1865) and the writer of local-color sketches José Joaquín Vallejo (1811-58). The historian Benjamín Vicuña Mackenna (1831-86) attempted to write a history of the people, and he seemed to have the sensitivity to do it; yet he was unable to do more than concentrate on great men. Alberto Blest Gana undoubtedly represents the best attempt in the nineteenth century to aspire to a national Chilean literature. In order to continue with the chronicle of this attempt, reference must be made to the founding teacher par excellence, the Venezuelan polymath Andrés Bello and, in passing, the Spanish satirist Mariano José de Larra (1809-37). This will bring us up to the 1920s in our examination of the development of a Chilean cultural discourse.

The shifting sands of exile, the cautious and prudent empiricism that Bello acquired during the years of his exile in England, the precautions that the repressive stance of his friend, the caudillo Diego Portales, must have inspired in him joined with Bello's diplomatic skills and the breadth of his knowledge to cement, with solid intellectual principles, the bases of Chilean literature. All of this would lead, for a long period, to the denial of unchecked flights of fancy and to a juridical and historiographic solidness that would justify the dismissive judgments of Marcelino Menéndez y Pelayo, the great Spanish literary scholar and one of the first to concern himself with Latin American literature. The Chilean people, descendents of Basques, had, in the opinion of that Basque scholar, arrived late when poetic talents were handed out. But they had, in exchange, been assigned a disposition for the cultivation of history that made their books longer than those of Greece or Rome. Menéndez y Pelayo's view only served to confirm Bello's pedagogical effectiveness, for whom the principal concerns were historiography, law, and literary criticism.

One of Bello's articles written for a historiographic polemic concerning national constitutions gives us, perhaps, an indication of his line of thought. Bello affirmed that a written constitution represented only the ideas, the passions, the interests of a certain number of men who had undertaken the task of organizing public power in accord with their own inspirations. The reader, historiographer, researcher, or critic had to be able to extract the secret of history from these constitutions. In this conception, laws, grammatical norms, or stylistic conventions are not molds for shaping facts, syntactic units, or literary genres. The task of the reader was to consider the positions and the tendencies masked behind the written word, to penetrate the prescriptions that constituted the substance of institutions in order to extract their soul. This dispersive activity of disengaging cultural texts would find its complement in the immediately subsequent operation of a construct derived from the confrontation of these texts with the national, Hispanic, and universal tradition.

During his stay in London, Bello had undertaken research concerning the Spanish epic and the structure of Spanish versification that earned Menéndez y Pelayo's respect. Bello's work on the *Poema de Mio Cid* (*The Poem of the Cid*; 1140), the first modern study in Spanish on this medieval epic, and his recovery of *La Araucana* as the only epic poem commemorating the birth of a modern people served as models for future research. He established a canon based on the very tradition that the Neoclassics and the poorly named Latin American Romantics attempted to destroy. The importance was clear for him of the Spanish classics like Garcilaso de la Vega (1501?-36), Fray Luis de León (1527?-91), Miguel de Cervantes (1547-1616), Baroque theater, Gonzalo de Berceo (13th century) and the ballad tradition, as well as moderns like the Duque Alvaro de Rivas (1791-1865), Mariano José de Larra, José Cadalso (1741-82), José Zorrilla (1817-93), and José de Espronceda (1808-42). The latter were joined by the great figures of European literature, particularly the Englishmen Byron and Sir Walter Scott, Dickens, Sterne, Fielding, Staël, and the Americans Irving and Emerson. Among the French, Bello's interests ran to Madame de Staël, Lamartine, Rousseau, Beaumarchais, Chateaubriand, Dumas. Shakespeare, Goethe, and Calderón de la Barca was his favorite trinity. This was the direction that, from the family salon, the academic forum, university journals, and the official press Bello impressed upon the literary taste of enlightened youth.

The objectives that he had proposed for himself in an essay published in London in 1826 were the same that he charted for himself between 1829 and 1859 as the editor of the official newspaper of Chile, *El Araucano* (The Araucanian; 1830-76?). Bello wished to examine how to stimulate progress in the arts and sciences in the New World in order to complete its civilization, in order to bring about awareness of "the useful inventions for the adoption of new forms and the perfecting of those already in existence," of producing the germination of the "fertile seed of liberty" of the men and actions of our history by assigning them a "place in the memory of time." The education of taste, the inclination for criticism, the examination of historical and literary documents were the mainstays of the new edifice.

Bello's discourse was able to inspire the most organic and ambitious fiction writers of the nineteenth century. Alberto Blest Gana, Vicente Pérez Rosales (1807-86), and Benjamín Vicuña Mackenna reveal the realist and pragmatic traces of a bourgeoisie that knows its own possibilities and that sets for itself decisively the course of triumph. This confidence will be lost at the beginning of the twentieth century. Luis Orrego Luco (1866-1948) will show in his novel *Casa grande* (Big House; 1908), with deep regret, the decadence of the aristocracy. Federico Gana (1868-1926), in his *Días de campo* (Days in the Country; 1916), will testify to the fragmentary agony of a Bohemian nostalgia lacking in meaning. Baldomero Lillo (1867-1923) will cry out indignantly and impotently against the misery, the exploitation, and the disdain with which the triumphal classes treated miners and peasants in *Sub terra* (Underground; 1904) and *Sub sole* (Under the Sun; 1907).

Bello's political restraint is not synonymous with a simply conservative stance, but must be measured in relation to a liberalism that went hand in hand with his Romantic proclivities in literature. But even in his Romanticism he differed from his disciples. The latter were only concerned to inebriate themselves with French exoticisms, remote and distant perfumes to be found in the pages of friendly and frequently read books. Bello, on the other hand, had met in his native Venezuela the German savant Alexander von Humboldt, and he had learned from him to discern the novelty of his world in order to awaken the rhythms of Latin American nature and the needs of its inhabitants. They became close friends, and perhaps the German traveller told Bello about his brother August, the writer of political tracts and a philosopher and linguist, and about his other German colleagues, the Schlegel brothers and Schleiermacher, while commenting to him about the importance of the theories and research of Herder. Bello's Romanticism was first-hand, cultivated, enlightened, liberal in the English fashion, and touched with a pragmatic realism that harmonized with his republican and liberal beliefs.

From this blend of pragmaticism and liberalism, with its traditional vocation and its doctrinary tendency, its restoration of institutions and its construction of canons, would arise the originality of the discourse based on Bello's writings. The most immediate formulations of the latter are Blest Gana's novels, and they would acquire even greater maturity and institutional transcendency in, for example, the *mundonovista* (New

World) writing of the Venezuelan Rufino Blanco Fombona (see the section on Venezuela) and the Chilean Francisco Contreras (1877-1933) at the end of the first quarter of the twentieth century.

Neither the political value of literature nor the notion of generic hierarchy escaped the Venezuelan's scrutiny. In his 1841 criticism of the work of the Spanish grammarian José Gómez Hermosilla (1771-1837), for example, Bello established an illuminating parallel between literary and political legitimacy. He wrote: "Romantic poetry is of English origins, like representative government and trial by jury. Its manifestations have been simultaneous with those of democracy in the south of Europe. And the same writers that have struggled against progress in the areas of legislation and government have often supported the struggle against the new literary revolution, defending with vigor the antiquities sanctified by the superstitious respect of our elders, such as the poetic codes of Athens and Rome and of the France of Louis XIV. We have such an example in Gómez Hermosilla, an ultramonarchist in politics and an ultraclassicist in literature."

This path led Bello to the concept of generic hierarchy. There was never any doubt about his preference for narrative, and we have already referred to his enthusiasm for the *Poema de Mio Cid* and *La Araucana*, the romances of Scott, the Byronic epic poem, the simplicity and the narrative charm of the lyrical ballad, the stories of Gonzalo de Berceo, the sparse fabulations of the poetry of Garcilaso de la Vega and Fray Luis de León, the intrigues of the theater of Lope de Vega and Calderón de la Barca which, in his opinion, spoke the native language of human beings. Narrative seemed to him the most adequate form for portraying the nature of the period, the effects of the disturbances in the social equilibrium as concerned domestic life, the consequences of divisive and factional attitudes for moral character. These were, in his opinion, the forms of literature that, with greatest persistence and effectiveness, could serve to educate Latin Americans in a period in which resentment, political conflicts, ideological discontent, and the threat of a reconquest by Spain challenged the peace of newly-created nations.

The epic and the historical ballad were founding genres. They, along with the sketch of local customs in the style of the grace, facility, and philosophical spirit of the Spaniard Larra, could give a faithful representation of the new republican spirit of Latin America, since, as in the case of the Spaniard, these descriptions were steeped in "liberal and philanthropic principles." Bello thus returned to his conception of literature as a political project, hastening to add that "the poet does not only paint, but rather he explains, interprets, comments on and provides a mysterious meaning to whatever strikes his senses. He develops the agreeable wanderings that physical perceptions awaken in a contemplative spirit. The poetry of our contemporaries is impregnated with aspirations and thoughts, with theories and ravings, with philosophy and mysticism. It is the faithful echo of an essentially contemplative age." The result was a *costumbrismo* (study of local manners and customs) that, as a consequence, would be at the service of something, that would set the pace or serve as a diagnostics of history, that would be an illustration of ideas and not a pictorial abstraction in the conservative sense of the style of the Spaniard Ramón de Mesonero Romanos (1803-82). What Bello sought was a poetry, a writing of physical and mental action, that would participate in intrigue and contemplation.

Bello's distance, his condition as an exile, his liberal spirit in the service of an autarchic administration contribute to an explanation of his preferences for Larra. Larra's writing provides the outlines of the two Spains, that of the moderates and that of the exalted, and it is a forum for Hispanic liberalism. Everything is reduced to marks and traces, a depersonalized and abstract calligraphy, suspended between ambiguous gesture and denunciation. The speaker is a demiurge who transforms chaos into cosmos, political reality into a poetic world. The function of literature, in revolutionary periods, could only be defined, according to Larra, as compromise. Yet it is a frozen compromise, assumed at a distance. This is what Bello sought, although he effected it from the podium of *El Araucano*, a writing like the one characterized by Larra as "studious, analytical, philosophical, profound, thinking over everything and saying it in prose and in verse, putting it at the disposal of the still ignorant multitude in an apostolic fashion and as propaganda. It is the teaching of *truths* to those in whose interest it is to know them, showing individuals not *how they ought to be* but *how they are* in order to know them. Literature is, in the end, the expression of all of the science of the period, of the intellectual progress of the century." Larra, Espronceda, and Bello initiated, simultaneously, in the theory and the practice of literary discourse the triumph of the political tendency of Spanish-language literature. A periodization of an aesthetic nature like that used for Europe will not, as a consequence, be of much use for characterizing the historical development of this literature. Its principles of construction are different.

IV

   It is perhaps for these reasons that lyric poetry comes late to Chile, not really until the second decade of the twentieth century. For Bello, as for his disciples, communication and shared activity was more important than thought pondered on in a cell. Guillermo Blest Gana (1829-1905) is, undeniably, the only poet to receive any attention during the nineteenth century, and his poetry left no appreciable mark on Chilean literature. When one reads Guillermo Blest Gana in the context of the generational group to which he belonged, it is possible to imagine him balancing rhythms on the edge of chaos, disillusioned and old, skeptical and resigned.

   Guillermo Matta (1829-99), whose varied metrics attracted the attention of Rubén Darío (see the section on Nicaragua), is a different case. His poetic register marks the dominant social tone of Chilean poetry until well into the twentieth century when, during a few years, the vanguard movements interrupt it. Matta's is a poetry of excess. Like Pablo de Rokha (1894-1968), Matta knows no restraints. He is likewise melodramatic in his anathemas directed against tyranny and ideological manipulation. His speaker is an internal exile, the rebel, the libertarian. A diplomat by profession, Matta strongly felt the call of Latin Americanism. There is something satanical in his disdain for the grossness of the bourgeoisie and the lower classes, whom he believed unable to understand the greatness of sentiments or to enjoy art and liberty. Matta is a source for social and humanitarian poetry and for the Latin Americanism of Pedro Antonio González (1863-1903). José Antonio Soffia (1843-86) and Carlos Walker Martínez (1842-1905) inaugurate the line of a subjective New Worldism that will become dominant in Víctor Domingo Silva (1882-1960) and Carlos Pezoa Vélez (1879-1908), with an emphasis on the forms of a family narrative: tender, ironic, sober and simple, close to the land and to history. All of these writers are epigones of the Latin Americanist New Worldism that Bello had inspired in them in the by-now remote 1830s.

   Chilean literature in the nineteenth century followed historiography closely. Both served to support progress, and both were tools for the attainment of political and social objectives. In the words of Diego Barros Arana (1830-1907), the writer should be a judge, and in those of Benjamín Vicuña, a priest. Menéndez y Pelayo was not mistaken in his judgments at the end of the century: Bello had planned it that way from the beginning.

If there were a good academic reason to make use of European periodization, one could justify a number of exceptions in the case of Chilean literature. The first is that the splashy nineteenth-century convoy, headed by Neoclassicism and clearly continued by the chariots of Romanticism, Realism, and Symbolism, never made it across the Atlantic. Or, if it did, it never made it across the Andes. It is impossible to find any trace of the aforementioned schools, despite the best acrobatics of literary historiographers. The second is that when speaking about Latin America as a whole, there is a somewhat better chance of success, since among the writers of some twenty countries, with a little effort one can find anything, even that which does not exist, because there will be something that looks like it.

The third point ought to be that the only tendency that had any theoretical pertinence in Chile, lasting about a century, was Romanticism, thanks to the pedagogical activity of Andrés Bello. The fourth is that, if this Romanticism is defined by the predominance of the subject over the representation of the world, there was no Romanticism in Chile's early literary manifestations, but rather something more akin to what we call Realism. The fifth is that, if Romanticism were defined as a Latin American project for the affirmation and criticism of national institutions undergoing development and altering their European identity, then some difficulties might disappear, but it would be equivalent to an act of nationalization, which certainly does not contradict the sense of the period.

The sixth observation is that, in view of all the foregoing, Romanticism of European origins is still a literary school or movement and that in Latin America it was an ingredient of a writing of an enlightened and liberal nature. As a consequence, this Romanticism is valueless for purposes of definition and periodization, which brings us back to the need to nationalize Romanticism if we want to retain the term. This would be the equivalent of undertaking historical analysis in terms of a scrutiny of writing in which the founding tropisms of a political nationality take root. This would allow us to postulate the existence of discourses that follow or overlap each other along a chronological plane that requires constant reevaluation. For it is characteristic of the historical process that, with the advance of time, what has previously been identified with all of the clarity of its outlines begins suddenly to grow fuzzy and to move closer to other discursive instances until it merges with them. After all, historiography and literature can only be historic, and whatever substance they have is composed of accidents. There is no historiography, no literature, no literary history, no history of literature either that can be called essential and that can shun and escape the territorializing materiality of discourses.

This is more evident in Latin America than it is in the European countries. Latin America was not only the child of the divorce of words and things, as Michel Foucault might have said, but, moreover, it was a conglomerate of nations in a state of virtuality, a single seed in which it was possible to discern a large number of embryos. If it is true that the large part of modern states arose from a nation that could be perceived centuries before its organization as a state, in the case of each of the states of Latin America the organization of the state existed prior to the existence of nationality. That is, countries like Chile, Peru, Mexico, or Argentina crystallized politically and administratively before they had acquired the majority of the ingredients of nationalism. The cultural program of these countries must have thus been a task of foundations, of calls for the formulation of nationality. The foundations that took on a first importance, as we have seen in the case of Chile, were those of creating a historiography, an art, a literature, almost against the grain of the European model.

Chilean poets were hardly noticed when, after the bombing of Valparaíso, Rubén Darío uttered the call for Modernism under the banner of the poetic image of the color blue (hence, the title of his first work, *Azul* [Blue; 1886]). Darío was a great poet and a cosmopolitan, and a Latin American for having chosen his destiny and created his own tradition. He was the first purely Romantic poet produced by Latin America. This is the profound sense of Latin American Modernism, the fact that Latin America had become modern, attained the status of nation, and discovered itself as individuals, all at the same time. And it is for this reason that Modernism is the first contribution of Latin America to Western literature. Chile, however, lacked this Modernist Romanticism.

Alberto Blest Gana, toward the end of his life, set about retracing the origins of Chilean nationality. *Durante la reconquista* (During the Reconquest; 1897), published following the aristocratic revolution of 1891 that blocked the egalitarian ambitions of President José Manuel Balmaceda, focused on the year of 1814 when the brutality of the Spanish intervention performed the miracle of converting the civil war into a national conflict for emancipation. There was no trace in this work of a phobic and unilateral vision of Spain. Hate had vanished, and the idea of nation was understood with greater clarity. *El loco Estero* (Estero the Madman; 1909) centered its plot in the months following the 1836 triumph of the Chilean armies against the Peruvian-Bolivian Confederation, a time when Portales's dictatorship was taking final form and the institutions of nationality had begun to arise from Bello's conjuring pen. A diplomat and a witness of national emergence, Blest Gana saw that it would be inopportune to recall the nationalistic excesses of the young Sevillan bard, Bécquer. Latin American Romanticism stood in opposition to that of Europe, and 1898 would soon change the axis of confrontation. Spain's loss would align Latin America with the United States, which, by virtue of the protocol of force, would assume the apparatus of power.

V

At the outset of the twentieth century, Chilean society looks different. Paradoxically, the aristocratic revolution of 1891 became translated into a gesture of retreat and commitment for the national ruling class. The middle classes began to be incorporated into the highest spheres of the social structure, and many who had been well-to-do in the past sank into genteel poverty. Workers began to organize themselves into unions and political bodies, incorporating the intellectual petite bourgeoisie and those members of other sectors who had suffered the impact of economic crises. It is a time of social questioning. As though by chance, the characters of Blest Gana and Orrego Luco could be seen walking the streets with all their pride and clumsiness, their elegance and vices, mixing with Lillo's workers and the peasants portrayed by Federico Gana, but without their fatalism and humility. Rather, they were aware of their rights, were lovers of a justice that they had discovered in the writings of Kropotkin and Bakunin, of Tolstoi and Marx. It was, moreover, a world that would cease to be only that of men.

The courtliness of Arturo Alessandri, the Lion of Tarapacá, must have sounded ironic to less aristocratic ears than those of literary critic Hernán Díaz Arrieta (1891-1983), when the Populist leader of 1920 bowed before the beauty of Mariana Cox-Stuven to whisper in Don Juan tones, "My dear Mariana, I was born to conquer peoples, and since there are no peoples left to conquer, I dedicate myself to conquering women." The fact is that the activities of Mariana Cox (1871-1914) had, since the turn of the century, become a challenge to the norms of her class. Two texts published in 1909 were an open defiance of a time-honored norm to the effect that ladies did not write. Cox published *Un remordimiento*

(A Regret) and *La vida íntima de Marie Goetz* (The Intimate Life of Marie Goetz) half-hidden by the pseudonym Shade. In order to mitigate the consequences of the scandal, another woman, also armed with a pseudonym, Iris, came to Cox's defense. Inés Echeverría Bello de Larraín Alcalde (1869-1949) had already used the vehicle of the newspaper article to publish chronicles and fantasy stories. Later, under the name of Inés Bello, she would publish a novel in French, *Entre Deux Mondes* (Between Two Worlds; 1914).

That same year Fernando Santiván (1886-1973) had organized a poetic competition that, in addition to stimulating the economic health of the moribund Sociedad de Escritores y Artistas (Society of Writers and Artists), would serve to encourage Chilean authors. The jury awarded the first prize to an unknown writer, Gabriela Mistral, the pseudonym of Lucila Godoy Alcayaga (1889-1957), for her three "Sonetos de la muerte" (Sonnets of Death, later included in *Desolación* [Desolation; 1922]). Santiván tells of how, after a long search, Mistral was found in the Andes. But, despite all pleas, she refused to appear personally at the awards ceremony. Her poems, read by one of the members of the jury, were enthusiastically applauded, "but Gabriela, hiding among the people present, hid her feelings under the black shawl covering her head." Thirty years later, strengthened by friendship with President Pedro Aguirre Cerda, the admiration of the Spanish critic Federico de Onís, and the gratitude of José Vasconcelos (see the section on Mexico), she would, with Andean majesty, accept the Nobel Prize from the hands of the aging king of Sweden. The year was 1945.

Mistral forced official criticism to comb the annals of Chilean literature to find the forgotten names of Mercedes Marín del Solar (1804-66) and Rosario Orrego de Uribe (1834-79) and to analyze the texts of Teresa Wilms Montt (1893-1921), Winet de Rokha (1896-1951), María Monvel (1899-1936), María Tagle (1899-1946), Chela Reyes (1904), and Mila Oyarzún (1912), poets who published or had begun to publish between 1914 and 1945. Note must also be taken of prose writers like Delie Rouge, the pseudonym of Delia Rojas Garcés (1883-1950), and Amanda Labarca Huberston (1886), the author of novels and critical and historiographic essays and a theorist concerning feminist issues and Chilean education. Novelists like Bombal, Marta Brunet (1901-67), and María Carola Geel, the pseudonym of Georgina Silva Jiménez (1913), have received considerable attention. Short story writers include Luz de Viana, the pseudonym of Marta Billanueva (1894); Marcela Paz, the pseudonym of Ester Hunneus (1904); Carmen de Alonso, the pseudonym of Margarita Carrasco Barrios (1909); Teresa Hamel (1918); and Marta Jara (1919). In view of the need for adequate research on these writers, Mistral's triumph of 1914 was only partial, although it was also the year in which Amanda Labarca published her probing history of feminism in the two Americas, *Actividades femeninas en los Estados Unidos* (Feminine Activities in the United States).

Chile's first great twentieth-century poet is unquestionably Pedro Prado (1886-1952). His inaugural work, *Flores de cardo* (Thistle Flowers; 1908), was followed by *El llamado del mundo* (The Call of the World; 1913). He published a series of prose poems in 1915 under the title of *Los pájaros errantes* (Wandering Birds), which initiated a form of lyricism with roots only in Augusto d'Halmar (1880-1950) and which would be impressively developed by Vicente Huidobro, Pablo Neruda, and Rosamel del Valle (see below). His novelesque poem, *La reina de Rapa Nui* (The Queen of Rapa Nui; 1914), is another founding contribution. Prado produced two novels important for their symbolic richness and philosophical content, *Alsino* (1920) and *Un juez rural* (A Rural Judge; 1924). The publication of his drama *Androvar* (1925) was followed by a return to poetry and by the transformation of his original metrical freedom into a rigorous and magisterial respect for the sonnet form. *Camino de las horas* (The Road of the Hours; 1934), *Otoño en las dunas* (Autumn among the Dunes; 1940), and *No más que una rosa* (No More Than a Rose; 1946) are exemplary works of this latter modality.

It must be noted that Prado and his contemporaries wrote during the years of the political ascendency of the middle classes. The political effervescence produced by the triumph of the 1915-16 parliamentary elections would culminate in the presidential victory of Arturo Alessandri Palma in 1920. Although war is the issue internationally, in Chile the warlike conduct of the unions and workers groups in the struggle for basic justice had met with a repression identified with the privileged sectors of public administration.

Confusion and introversion, a silent rebellion that fed on painful solitude, an underground aggression against bourgeois conventions that disdained anyone who could be called a parvenu or an outcast, a resentful attitude toward injustice suffered, anger provoked by the irrationality of war and the futility of so many deaths, the ineffectualness of the Christian god and religious beliefs all marked to one degree or another the poetic and civic activity of the 1914 generation grouped around Prado: Gabriela Mistral, Vicente Huidobro (1893-1948), Angel Cruchaga

Santa María (1893-1964), Juan Guzmán Cruchaga (1895-1979), and Pablo de Rokha (1894-1968).

A snail contemplating the ocean, Prado's speaker is a sounding board for the harmonics of the sea and nature. Purely receptive, he reacts with the surprise of self-examination, as someone, who confronted with this strange landscape, experiences a luminous vision of an alter ego that delights in the solitude of questions, in the absence of answers, in the vigil for a miracle that will lead to the discovery of "the essence of life." The poetic voice is a breaker of codes who, aided only by a clear and simple spirit, prepares to decipher the signals and the designs of the world. The image of the shadows, the disquieting effect of the passage of time, the nostalgia for a happy universe constitute the central coordinates of Prado's sonnets. This introversion dedicated to the Arcadian configuration of a primitive nature, the references to the geographic reality of the Chilean south, the ironic tone and social concern, along with the absence of metaphysics, will become central ingredients of the homely poetry of Jorge Teillier (1935) and other poets who emerge in the 1960s.

Neither delicate nor nostalgic, far removed from any Arcadia, and alien to the elegance of a rationally assimilated despair, Mistral's poetry is volcanic and rough, exasperated and hoarse, with all of the savage vigor of a primitive passion. The young Lucila Godoy refused to accept the 1914 prize not because she lacked a proper dress, but because she was a woman who had dared to speak out in public in verses that were megaphones. This was too much and, therefore, she decided to hide herself among the audience in order to witness her own triumph from the vantage point of those of lesser fortune. She would continue, always from a distance, to write a tough and relentless poetry.

Almost a quarter of a century later, in 1938, Mistral wrote of how poetry was for her refuge and regeneration, the consolation for a tragic lack that could be defined as the "lapse into a rational and antirhythmic expression," which resulted in a flattening of an alienated language of the passion and authenticity of human drama. Mistral's poetry traces the adventure of the recovery and appropriation of language which, although it ought to belong to all, is the property of only a few, of those who can speak with the syntax of God the Father and of all those heroes who have always held sway in the world in the fullness of their masculinity.

Vicente Huidobro (1893-1948), with his intellectual brilliance, his capacity for invention, his rebellion and lack of conformity, and, above all else, his creative will, is the initiator of contemporary poetry in Chile.

Pasando y pasando (Passing and Passing; 1914) was published in the same year in which Mistral began to stretch the strings of Modernist romanticism to the breaking point. The youthful defiant tone that Huidobro was always able to preserve separates him from Pedro Prado, and his theoretical base separated him from all the rest.

In effect, Huidobro's first works, beginning with *Ecos del alma* (Echoes of the Soul; 1911), were published concomitantly with articles and declarations of principles. When he was twenty-one he read in Santiago the first of a series of manifestoes that he would subsequently publish in Paris in 1925. The Latin title, *Non serviam* (I Will Not Serve), points to a stance toward the representation of the world via language that would provide the stamp to his poetic "creationism."

Between 1911 and 1914, Huidobro began a stage of explorations that highlight the heroism of the Modernist poetic subject, the cultivation of rapid change, the respect for fashion, the close scrutiny of the tropisms of European art, and cosmopolitanism. Huidobro's quest is the opposite of Mistral's. There is a waning of the bonds of meaning, the solidness of concepts. It is a poetry in movement, attuned to the fluctuations of an alive and powerful imagination seeking to attain an alteration of the real by awakening its hidden virtualities. *Ecos del alma*, *Canciones en la noche* (Songs in the Night; 1912), *La gruta del silencio* (The Grotto of Silence; 1913), and *Las pagodas ocultas* (The Hidden Pagodas; 1914) appeared during these years. Creationism proper emerged with *Adán* (Adam; 1916) and *El espejo de agua* (The Water Mirror; 1916).

Among the most notable modifications of this period is the concept of the page as a plastic unity. The techniques of the calligram, the avoidance of punctuation, the utilization of the mass of letters, the prolongation of the line to the right or left, the presence of diagonal words convert the written text into a Cubist artifact whose space can be viewed from diverse angles. Adam proclaims the rejection of all inheritances, whether in literature or the objective world. Adam undertook the primordial act of observation, and it is he who uttered the first word. It is he who loved the first woman and in whose womb he engendered the human race. Cain and Abel, nevertheless, establish the division of unity: the pragmatic realism of the first finds its counterpart in the pantheistic mysticism of the other, and they represent the contrary poles of science and poetry, the very principles that, following Emerson, Huidobro sought to reunite in a harmonic synthesis.

Altazor (1931), composed between 1919 and 1931, completes the project of destruction initiated in *Ecuatorial* (Equatorial; 1918), where the holocaust of the universe serves as the point of beginning anew. In *Altazor* the process of destruction of the poetic word is undertaken as a pretext for the configuration of a new poetic language. The individual is split in two, becoming Altazor, who, in an act of self-questioning, witnesses the disintegration of his language and of the mechanisms of reason and grammar. Poetry lives by excess, fragmentation, scandal, beyond the limits of the language that gives it form. Reality is converted into language, into sound and primordial babble. In the preface to *Altazor*, the poet affirms that the first divine action was the creation of noise, the prime matter of speech prior to all physical reality. Then God created light, the substance of the poetic image. Later, humans were given a mouth and a tongue whose function is to create, to make poetry. Yet, this gift has been used in a way contrary to its original function. The poet of *Altazor* must, therefore, create in something other than the maternal language.

Pablo Neruda was the literary pseudonym adopted in 1946 by Neftali Reyes Basoalto. In contrast to Huidobro, Neruda is a poetic voice of earthy and vegetable essences, of a dense, monotonal rhythm, of patterns repeated to the point of assuming a physical and visceral consistency. Neruda's tone is dark and primordial and springs from the depths of his being. It is a poetry far removed from the clarity of images of Huidobro's writing, a poetry of a throbbing, embryonic world in the process of gestation. In his acceptance speech before the Swedish Academy on the occasion of accepting the Nobel Prize in 1972, Neruda affirmed that "The poet is not a 'small God.' He is not marked by a cabbalistic density superior to that of persons who engage in other occupations and professions. . . . The best poet is the person who gives us our daily bread: the neighborhood baker who does not see himself as a god."

Neruda is a poet of absences, and the process of his writing is the result of an anguish that arises from an intimate need to give form to a world that, nevertheless, slips away in its materiality. Also, because what is sought does not always exist, the poem is constituted as the imperious quest after an absence. The presence of what is absent is identified by Neruda as the call of life. Neruda's poetic voice has little time for beauty, but is rather attracted to the sublimeness of the sick and the pained that overwhelms with the depth of suffering. It is for this reason that the poems of *Residence en la tierra* (*Residence in the Land*; 1935) have such an oppressive and terrifying atmosphere. Atmosphere and rhythm are the cause and effect of the material condition of the objects of the world in the experience and perception of the subject. Neruda's world is inexhaustible as a consequence of the cross between the external and the intimate. Nature or reality are not facts that can be registered or represented, and mimesis is useless. The world takes on form through a mechanism of contiguities and displacements that arises from the polyvalence of worlds and the constitution of an alternate symbolic process that springs from a preconscious figurative plane prior to the semantics of definitions.

A double temporal dimension, epic and utopian, characterizes the structure of *Canto general* (*General Song*; 1950). The first is based on a return to the origins of Latin America and a hierarchization of the past as an absolute time. Nostalgia for plenitude, cyclical time, unity and integration of the individual with the universe, prosopopoeial fantasy, and oracular enunciations all give *Canto general* the stamp of a sacred book. The second dimension implies a goal, a will oriented toward the future in which another plenitude may be discovered once time is stopped as a consequence of social revolution.

The epic vision and the nostalgia for a Golden Age could not be a long-term enthusiasm for Neruda. Capitalism, abuse, exploitation, injustice, and social inequalities quickly led him to the ranks of a proletarian party, and Neruda very soon decided to historicize his poetry and to transform it into a militant and committed discourse. This transition is present in "Alturas de Macchu Picchu" (Heights of Macchu Picchu), the second section of *Canto general*, where one is struck by the differences of class that were also present in the Inca world. The act of solidarity with the forgotten and the marginated demands a descent into the underworld, with the realization that there is only one recourse for the reestablishment of a link to those who, in the time of history, are irrevocably dead: the recourse of writing, whose inscription will be effected with the blood of us all. And this primordial ink will assist in explaining, mythifying, the need for struggle. If there is a change here, the registry remains the same: Neruda's language retains the same ritual to be found in its epic dimension.

Beginning with *Odas elementales* (*Elementary Odes*; 1934), the poet seems to find the world at his disposal, living to be born naked and ready to be clothed in a poetry free from the complications of any pretense at originality. It is a matter of expanding the world: I have been born to be born. Prior to *Canto general*, Neruda's poetic I conceived of itself as the witness to a world in the process of construction and disintegration, and in *Canto* it assumes a voluntaristic dimension that results in mythopoesis. By contrast, *Odas elementales* inaugurates a subject that proclaims itself invisible, intensified by the urgency of "transparent" communication. Neruda sought in *Odas* to do away with poetry in which the subject annulled or substituted for the object, and the function of the poet must be that of putting the world on display, of making himself invisible, of remaining anonymous, of serving others, of being simply one more laborer. By denying poetic specificity, the specific power of communication, poetic work would deny itself as work. As a consequence, the poetic program remains unrealized in the successive collections of the *Odas* between 1948 and 1958.

Pablo de Rokha, the pseudonym of Carlos Díaz Loyola, published his first important work in 1922. *Los gemidos* (Moans) reveals a vanguard poetry with a tone of aggressiveness and instinctive exaltation that was unknown in Chilean poetry. The strongly patriarchal, antibourgeois tone, with its primitive features, complemented a concern for the mechanization of existence. Rokha's second cycle culminated in 1929 with *Escritura de Raimundo Contreras* (Raimundo Contreras's Writing), adding the discovery of the body to his legacy to Chilean poetry. Rokha, in contrast to Huidobro, the singer of the adventure of thought, Mistral, the sculptor of emotions, and Neruda, the shaper of what can be felt, is foremost a visceral poet. His world is one of instincts, and his inscriptions draw the material traces of the fruits, foods, and drink of his land, those of his own patriarchal humanity as a young bull or an aging he-man. There is a surrealistic rhythm that also emerges in this period in the rapid, disordered, jumbled, flow of obsessive, oneiric, audaciously Pantagruelic images.

Jesucristo (Jesus Christ; 1933) and *La morfología del espanto* (The Morphology of Fright; 1942) reveal a different phase in the poet's evolution. The figure of the poetic speaker assumes decidedly the shape of the prophet and redeemer who embodies the sufferings of the people, taking on the voice of those who suffer exploitation, confusion, and misfortune. The customs, the realia, the individuals, the manner of speaking, and the Chilean countryside have an authentic sound in the speech of this poetic speaker, and they are the basis of his voice. This voice is at the same time a mosaic of moving figures on behalf of a humanity that never degenerates into stereotypes. The figures of these men and women, like the language they speak, are primordial in nature, and they are bound to the values of instinct, enthusiasm, love, and generous passion.

Rokha has served as an eloquent model for Chile's most original and vital authors; for example, Carlos Droguett (1912), Antonio Skármeta

(1940), Alfonso Alcalde (1921), Mahfud Massís (1916). All of them reveal the instinctive passion that infuses their writing with a quick and breathless rhythm that translates into rapid shifts and movements such as we find in the best pages of Fernando Alegría (1918), *Angurrientso* (Anguished; 1940) by Juan Godoy (1911), and *La visita del Presidente* (The President's Visit; 1983) by Juan Villegas (1934). By the 1940s Surrealism was an important influence in the shaping of Chilean poetry.

La mandrágora (The Mandrake) published seven numbers between 1938 and 1943 and served as the official organ of Chilean Surrealists. It received the backing of Huidobro himself who, nevertheless, had asserted in his own manifestoes his decided opposition to the poetic theories of André Breton and company. A year before *La mandrágora* ceased publication, Braulio Arenas (1913) had begun a new Surrealist publication with the name of *Leitmotiv* (1942-43). Arenas published the Spanish version of Breton's later manifestoes, as well as collaborations by Benjamin Péret and Aimé Césaire. More than for the intrinsic value of its poetic creation, Surrealism is important in the development of Chilean poetry for signaling the definitive alliance of the latter with what was at the time considered to be the most universal facet of modern poetry. Huidobro and Surrealism were, at the same time, central to the formation of one of the most influential of contemporary poets, Gonzalo Rojas (1917).

A provincial and itinerant poet, a man who hates the center of things and who is free to experience ceaseless growth, Gonzalo Rojas is best defined in terms of his travels as a child and his extensive experience in and around train stations and shipping docks. He is also marked by a radical poverty that is the source of his generosity and his indignation in the face of injustice and hunger. Rojas has lived extensively and published little. His goal is to transform the world via the conduct of poetry and to be a companion of Marx and Rimbaud in the task of "changing the basic way in which Latin America breathes" through the denunciation of the hunger in the world, the prevarication of mankind, and nuclear threat. Rojas's poetry is represented by three volumes, *La miseria del hombre* (The Suffering of Mankind; 1948), *Contra la muerte* (Against Death; 1964), and *Oscuro* (Dark; 1976), and it constitutes a blending of the trends described thus far.

The principal works of Nicanor Parra (1914) were published beginning in 1950: *Poemas y antipoemas* (*Poems and Antipoems*; 1954), *Versos de salón* (Salon Verses; 1962), and *Obra gruesa* (Bulk Work; 1969). The major goal of Parra's poetic activity, from the time of the publication of

Cancionero sin nombre (Songbook without a Name; 1937), has been the democratization of poetry. García Lorca and Whitman are present here, as are the Hispanic ballad tradition, Spanish popular poetry and its nineteenth-century Chilean derivations, the Cervantine parodic vein, Francisco de Quevedo's morality, Gustavo Adolfo Bécquer's sentimentality; the absurd sense of an existence victimized by society are seen in the ingenuous gesture of someone who simply doesn't understand, in the tradition of both Kafka and Chaplin and in the representatives of popular Chilean behavior. All of these elements constitute aspects of the intertext of Parra's work, an antipoetry that melds popularism and sophistication. The profound impact of Neruda should be added to this list as the poet of material things, as well as that of Mistral, with her disdainful sincerity toward all compassion, the audaciousness of Huidobro and Rokha, Surrealism, and the belief that poetry touches the profoundest realms of our being. These are all tightly-woven strands in what Parra has challengingly called "antipoetry."

Parra assumes an unbalanced vision of the world in his rejection of the cosmic factor present in the majority of Chilean poetry. Given the fact that the world makes no sense, all transcendent language is illusory, a pretentious farce. This is the source of Parra's irreverence, his blasphemous language, the stylistic mixtures, the alienated posture, a voice that cries out in the desert of social problems, unable to understand or to be understood, the sense of the absurd in a world of simulacra rooted in an idiotized consciousness. Hence also the fact that the preferred vehicle for human anguish is humor, as in Huidobro—the moment in which knowledge fuses with a laughter that produces precisely the loss of the power of knowing and understanding. The goal is a cynicism that proclaims eccentricity, the dissolution of being in art, love, or science, all equally made into cliché, gratuitousness, convention by decree. There is at times a nostalgia for a lost unity that links Parra to the conceptual romanticism of his forebears, but his poetry is not the tension of discovery but the path of destruction. This is at least the case in the best of his writing. A tendency toward a poetry of an essayistic cast in which the lyrical is subordinated to an expository goal may be explained as a consequence of Parra's concept of antipoetry.

Enrique Lihn (1929) has carried to the limits of silence the denuding of poetry begun by Parra. Lihn is the author of *Nada se escurre* (Nothing Slips Away; 1949), *Poemas de este tiempo y otro* (Poems of This and the Other Time; 1955), *La pieza oscura* (The Dark Room; 1963), *Poesía de paso* (Poetry by Chance; 1967), *Escrito en Cuba* (Written in Cuba;

1968), *La musiquilla de las pobres esferas* (The Little Music of the Poor Spheres; 1969). These collections are touchstones for a poetry that cultivates skepticism and self-referentiality, a poetry defined by the distrust of language and the art of the word. The poetic voice tolerates itself as a creation of its own discourse, a problematic subjectivity on the fringe of time, incapable of understanding the history that both goes on around it and creates it. This history emerges equally as a product of a deceptive discourse unworthy of trust. Whatever is happening today and whatever will happen tomorrow already took place, and the laws of discourse are inescapable. Poetry, the language exalted by the Surrealists, is worthless for undertaking the leap of exploration, and the plenitude that shows through in even some of Parra's poems appears to Lihn to be a lie forged in the inferno of language. Behind words there is anger, darkness, nothingness because pain itself, linguistically expressed, is deceitful.

Lihn and Jorge Teillier have responded to the breakdown of communication provoked by the military coup of September 1973. Teillier's view of things and his poetic voice lose sight of the syntax of the sacred that binds individuals to their world. Lihn's poetic voice finds the strength to allow language to transcend distrust in order to transform itself into an ironic and detached rebelliousness that places the poetic subject safely behind a glass partition where it reflexively contemplates the maneuvers of the attack, while also providing that subject with a mirror on the other side that relfects its face drawn by the grimaces of fear. Both exemplify what has happened on the level of discourse since 1973. Language has begun to parody itself, and it is as though Parra and Neruda had changed voices with Lihn and Teillier, as if hope had become anguish; despair, irony. Language has begun to define itself in terms of the precariousness of the process of meaning, and meaning hides from expressive brilliance, taking refuge in a zone beyond the limits of representation. The very capacity for representation is denied, since it is seen as a mode of discourse whose only presence in the history of language is that of distrust and suspicion.

VI

Dramatic fiction, as a consequence of its communal, collaborative, and immediate nature, is even more recent than the other forms of fiction like the narrative or even poetry. Arising from ritual, drama emphasizes the representation of the codes of conduct whose representation by the actors is considered important for the life of a community in a specific time and place. Therefore, the emergence of a national theater followed the creation of a nationality. This explains its absence during the historical changes of the nineteenth century, which were based on the affirmation of the structures of the State, and its emergence when the middle classes began to become incorporated into political life, bringing with them a mixture of cultivated and popular traditions that were blended into a national consciousness. One of the characteristics of drama is its condition as a past made present through the mediation of the actor. Drama allows a people to recreate its history, to affirm its idiosyncracies, to relive its myths, to become spectators of its own spectacle, not via the reading of a written discourse as in the case of poetry or fiction, but through the direct mediation of other human beings, with their own limitations, questions, and hopes. Almost as in history itself.

The adaptation of French and Spanish works, the presentation of some Italian operas by some foreign companies that made stops in the country, some meritorious performances based on the ingenuity of Daniel Caldera (1852-96), Román Vial (1833-96), and Daniel Barros (1834-94), is all that remains from the nineteenth century. Eduardo Barrios (1884-1963), Antonio Acevedo Hernández, Germán Luco Cruchaga (1894-1936), and Armando Moock (1894-1942) were, in the second decade of the twentieth century, to provide Chilean theater with solid foundations.

The middle class and the retinue of the impoverished rich, parvenues, and the pretentious, the conflicts of interests and the disadvantages the latter always represent for women constituted the subject matter of Eduardo Barrios in *Lo que niega la vida* (What Life Denies; 1914) and *Vivir* (To Live; 1916). Luco Cruchaga concerned himself with bourgeois climbing and with the decadence of the aristocracy, while Moock wielded the scalpel of his local-color criticism against all social sectors, and Acevedo Hernández placed his creativity at the service of the popular sectors which, by that time, had begun to organize themselves.

Meanwhile, it is important to sketch the historical situation of Chile around 1920. The counterrevolution of 1891, which culminated in the death of President José Manuel Balmaceda, had been the product of the alliance between the aristocracy of the land and British and Chilean nitrate interests. Balmaceda's mesocratism was followed by what some historians have called the "aristocratic republic," which extended from 1891 to 1920 as a sort of government characterized by collective hypocrasy, indifference and inertia, and by a political dilettantism that was best represented by the carnival of a parade of cabinets that usually lasted a few days or even a few hours.

The vision of crisis in aristocratic values examined in detail by essayists and social historians of the period acquired a narrative projection in two complementary currents that, for convenience's sake, we can call urban Naturalism and New Worldism (*mundonovismo* in Spanish). The first had a negative cast and catastrophic vision of the urban setting in which it preferentially flourished. The second, identified with a rural and provincial setting, found the seeds of hope in the simple and authentic life of people in contact with the land. Urban Naturalism dwelt on the aristocracy and its followers: parvenues, pretentious fops, the impoverished rich, while New Worldism concerned itself with instinctive and indomitable types shaped by the land. Both followed the deterministic principles of Zola's Naturalism, adapted to Latin American circumstances. The most interesting products of Chilean fiction during the first third of the twentieth century were a result of the combination of both concerns, as can be seen in the narrative cycle of Luis Orrego Luco, *El socio* (The Partner; 1926) by Jenaro Prieto (1889-1946), *La chica del Crillón* (The Girl of the Hotel Crillón; 1935) by Joaquín Edwards Bello (1887), and *Gran señor y rajadiablos* (Great Lord and Hellraiser; 1948) by Eduardo Barrios.

In these novels, the city becomes the principal enemy of the aristocracy, and the crisis is understood as the result of the imposition of an invading culture that has ended up poisoning the people. Some of the young sought salvation in the countryside, but disintegration was inevitable. It was impossible to remain in the country, since the life blood of the modern world was to be found in the city, which imposed a love for pleasure and luxury, ostentation and conspicuous consumption. The purity of the customs of the farm, the strength of family ties, the efficacy of a system of agricultural production founded on the estate and sharecropping could not stem corruption, and very quickly the evils represented by the city and by industrialization were to invade the countryside.

This vision informs Orrego Luco's novel cycle. *Playa negra* (Black Beach; 1942-44) deals fictionally with national life between 1877 and 1880; *En familia* (Among Family; 1912) covers the period 1885 to 1888; *Al través de la tempestad* (Throughout the Tempest; 1914) evokes episodes from the 1891 revolution; *Un idilio nuevo* (A New Idyll; 1900) focuses on the closing fifteen years of the century; *Casa grande* (Big House; 1908) moves forward to about 1905; and *El tronco herido* (The

Wounded Trunk; 1929) deals with the last half of the 1920s. The decadence, irrationality of behavior, and failure of class that had lost the
orientation of its purpose appeared, in each novel, linked to the influence
of foreign models of conduct and culture and legitimated, via a dynamic
of Naturalism, by racial and environmental determinisms that turned on
the denaturalization of the practices of the colonial era.

In *Casa grande* the beginning of the end for the protagonist occurs
at the time of the stock market crisis of 1906. Weak and unable to
recover, he falls in love with the daughter of a rich American industrialist
and assassinates his wife whose fortune has been squandered by their
rhythm of life. A vague shadow pursues him as it did Cain. This shadow is precisely what Prieto gives material form to in *El socio*. In the
latter novel, a young impoverished stock market agent creates a business
ally in order to give himself a certain speculative latitude. Soon he owes
his entire fortune and good name to Mr. Walter Davis, the skillful inves-
tor of British origins. When, tired of his anonymity, he decides to reveal
his ruse, he is taken for a madman. Madness materializes as perfectly
as does Mr. Davis, and Julián Pardo commits suicide in order for the
foreigner to be found guilty of his murder.

Alienation and irrationality have taken possession of a social group,
which now can only define its rank in terms of its access to power and
money. This group has lost any real reason for being, and it lacks a goal
in life for itself and for the country. Like Orrego Luco, but with greater
precision, Edwards observed with a certain optimism the possibility of a
regeneration of the values of the aristocratic class in contact with the
country setting. *La chica del Crillón* is the story of a young woman
whose aristocratic existence has become impoverished as the consequence of her father's ill-advised business transactions that oblige them
to live on the seedy fringes of Santiago. During a trip south, she meets
a good and generous landowner who quickly becomes her husband.
Both the diary form taken by the novel and the resolution of the heroine's problem in the form of a landowner from the south who retains the
purity and the dignity of the individual in contact with the land point
toward an optimistic conclusion on behalf of the Chilean aristocracy.
Experience, suffering, a realization of the falsity of the urban upper class
and of the generous solidarity shown by humble neighbors are undoubtedly presented as a necessary route for expiation and apprenticeship.
There still exist uncontaminated places where the dearest values of the
founders of the country can prosper.

Edwards's optimism was no longer viable at the end of the half-century. The strong outlines of aristocratic features seem to fade away in the nostalgic reading provided by Barrios in *Gran señor y rajadiablos*. The novel recalls the heroic times when, by dint of fists and machetes, the founders had established the bases of the country in the conquest and domestication of the country. The intensity of patriotic fervor, the individualistic pride of the colonizing leader, the strength, astuteness, decisiveness, and indomitable will as norms of conduct make José Pedro Valverde an archetypic figure of an ancient Chilean aristocracy. His lineage stretches back to a forebear who had fought with Pizarro in the conquest of Cuzco and forward, in a disordered and abundant mestization, through the bodies of the country girls who love and fear him. Those were the days in which it was necessary to struggle bare-fisted and in open battle against the evildoers and bandits who were shielded by the weakness of justice and government authority, in which the landowner bosses had to impose respect with the noose and the knife in order to create a setting favorable to central authority. But central authority had already been formed, and the powers of the bosses like Valverde were destined to become a colonial holdover from which the democratic governments found best to separate themselves. In the end, the countryside had become an impossible place for the old Chilean aristocracy.

All of the writers mentioned thus far enjoyed ties to privileged strata of nineteenth-century Chile, but it is not the aristocracy we hear speaking in these novels. The perspective is that of the middle class, and the narrative is postulated as a relationship of characters and actions that are part of a social system that justifies and makes intelligible these descriptions. The novel is a mirror in which the bourgeoisie recognizes itself in the attempt to articulate the image of its own world and to legitimate its own self-identity. The structures of the independent society of Creole origins formed between 1820 and 1880 and constituted thanks to the activities of bosses like Valverde and the exercise of political power they organized required no written discourse to give them legitimacy. Everyone remembered very well how and why, on the basis of what struggles and battles, the outlines of Chilean society had been formed. Thus, the local-color writings of a Jotabeche, the pseudonym of José Joaquín Vallejo (1811-58), the novels of Alberto Blest Gana, the narrative essays of Lastarria, and even the *Recuerdos del pasado* (Memories of the Past; 1882) by Vicente Pérez Rosales, far from representing a pseudoscientific project for the depiction of the forms of social life as part of the documentation of social change, served as direct participation in society—as forms of ideological debate concerning what changes were desirable.

Lillo, along with Gana, founded the Chilean short story. Lillo evinced a social concern at a time when Modernist writing still prevailed. *Sub terra* (1904), for example, is a collection of eight mining stories, while his last book, *Sub sole* (1907) contains thirteen texts. Lillo's own experiences in the mines, the acuity with which he was able to grasp the economic and human implications of social problems, the depiction of the life of exploitation of the worker by the impersonal company forces in the regions of Lota and Coronel contributed to making *Sub terra* an immediate classic of Chilean literature. Lillo had learned from Bret Harte, Zola, and Turgeniev. The immediacy of the human document, the sobriety of style, his human compassion, the denunciation of exploitation via the simple story of the suffering of human beings confronting the animal hostility of their environment made Lillo a point of departure for Chile's best literature of social denunciation, as can be seen in the writings of Acevedo Hernández, Diego Muñoz (1904), Andrés Sabella (1912), and Nicomedes Guzmán (1914-65).

Luis Durand (1895-1954) was principally the teller of stories about characters. The primitive psychology of peasants, their family problems, their customs, language, traditions are accurately represented in the faithful and pleasant stories of *Tierra de Pellines* (Pellines's Land; 1929), *Campesinos* (Peasants; 1932), *Cielos del sur* (Southern Skies; 1933), *Mi amigo Pidén* (My Friend Pidén; 1933), and *Casa de la infancia* (Childhood Home; 1945). The distinctiveness of Durand's nativist style is the mimetic accuracy of the representation of the distinctive language and syntax of his peasant characters. The novel *Frontera* (Frontier; 1949), published almost at the same time as Barrios's *Gran señor y rajadiablos*, must be considered one of the key works of the grand regionalist mode of Latin American fiction. Both novels reveal in the representation of a fundamental Chilean Creole identity an importance similar to that of *Zurzulita* (1920) by Mariano Latorre (1886-1955).

Latorre has been considered Chile's leading Creolist or nativist writer. He described the different regions of the country in a cycle of "landscape" fiction. Faithful to positivistic ideals, Latorre undertook to reveal the substance of the Latin American world via the exploration of its physical and human setting, nature, and environment. Since Chile lacked a synthesizing geographic characteristic like the jungle, the Pampa, or the mountains, it was necessary to explore its corners. Each one of these zones could be assigned a homogenizing telluric feature: mountain range, ocean, frontier (in the case of the Mapuche territories), the extreme south. The lyricism of the narrator toward the landscape and the nature of his commentaries of an anthropological interest are the most outstanding features of *Cuentos del Maule* (Maule Stories; 1912), *Cuna de cóndores* (Craddle of the Condors; 1918), *Chilenos del mar* (Chileans of the Sea; 1929), and *La isla de los pájaros* (The Island of the Birds; 1925).

Augusto d'Halmar, the pseudonym of Augusto Geomine Thomson (1882-1950), began his career with a novel that followed with a certain degree of fidelity the principles of French Naturalism. *Juana Lucero, o los vicios de Chile* (Juana Lucero, or the Vices of Chile; 1902) tells the story of an illegitimate girl who, orphaned from her mother at an early age, is victim of some relatives who exploit her and abandon her in a brothel where she buries her suffering and her madness. Tired of Zola, d'Halmar soon sought a less documentary form of writing. "A rodar tierra" (Roaming Around; 1907), the most famous of his short stories, revealed an exhuberant and unrestrained fantasy. A taste for fantasy and a free and easy manner quickly led him to a prose in which one barely perceived the undercurrent of discourse, a surface woven of exotic metaphors with a metaphysical taint to them. His greatest accomplishments were in the short story and the short novel, as in *La lámpara en el molino* (The Light in the Mill; 1914) and *Gatita* (Kitten; 1917). These texts characterized perfectly his brand of musical, airy, and mysterious prose. Solitude, melancholy, sadness for a life that one accepts as it comes, that pursues the wisp of smoke vanishing in the mirror characterize his novels, *Pasión y muerte del cura Deusto* (Passion and Death of the Priest Deusto; 1924) and *La sombra del humo en el espejo* (The Shadow of Smoke in the Mirror; 1924). His influence may be reduced to this atmosphere.

Manuel Rojas (1896-1973), as a young writer, received the generous support of the anarchist poet and labor leader José Domingo Gómez Rojas (1986-1920), who died at the age of thirty-four as the result of wounds received during a police raid on the Federación de Estudiantes (Federation of Students). Gómez Rojas is Daniel, one of the characters in Rojas's novel *Mejor que el vino* (Better than Wine; 1958). Rojas first wrote stories, *Hombres del sur* (Men from the South; 1926), *El delincuente* (The Delinquent; 1929), *Travesía* (Crossing; 1934); *El bonete maulino* (Maule Cap; 1943), and a novelette, *Lanchas en la bahía* (Launches in the Bay; 1932). His writings show the elements of Creolism: docks and prisoners, boatmen and jails, slums, the fatality and misery that plague the peasant, the city worker, and the poor. Rojas also dealt with the age-old struggle between individuals and their wild and majestic environment in which they are pummeled by the forces of nature. But their fate has an epic grandeur, and human beings are not submerged by an all-consuming nature. Nature, in an act of solidarity with his characters, emerges as the ultimate witness of the dignity of their condition.

This is a world of solitary men and women, eccentrics, malcontents, bandits, thieves, and stoolpigeons—derelict human beings who live exposed to the elements. Marginality is the unifying thread in the Aniceto Hevia tetralogy: *Hijo de ladrón* (Son of a Thief; 1951), *Mejor que el vino*, *Sombras contra el muro* (Shadows on the Wall; 1963), and *La obscura vida radiante* (Radiant Obscure Life; 1971). Rojas's narrative is a paean to the solitude of the human being as someone who is the contemporary in solidarity with all individuals. It is important to remember that the pages of *Hijo de ladrón* were written at the same time as Octavio Paz's *El laberinto de la soledad* (*Labyrinth of Solitude*; 1950), where the universal solitude of the Mexican makes him one among the universe of human beings (see the section on Mexican literature).

Hijo de ladrón is undoubtedly one of the most important texts of contemporary Chilean fiction, and it marked the influence in Chilean literature of the best examples of Latin American literature. But the human density of this novel must be complemented by the fiction of other writers who constitute the full range of the novel in Chile today. *La última niebla* (The Last Mist; 1935) and *La amortajada* (The Shrouded Woman; 1938) by María Luisa Bombal, *Mundo en sombra* (World in Shadow; 1942) and *Las cenizas* (Ashes; 1942) by Mari Yan, the pseudonym of María Flora Yáñez (1901), and *Humo hacia el sur* (Smoke toward the South; 1946) by Marta Brunet all constitute a sudden revelation of women's experiences, at the mercy of an emotional climate with extensive projections in Chile's latest novelistic production.

Brunet's *Montaña adentro* (Inside the Mountain; 1926) and *Bestia dañina* (Dangerous Animal; 1926) were, as was the case with Rojas's stories from the same period, considered by critics to represent a healthy renewal of the possibilities of Creolism. But if the message in Rojas's work was different, so too was Brunet's. She introduced experiences peculiar to women, a discontent, a rebelliousness, a desire to modify the inferior status that social conventions inflicted on one half of Chile's and the world's population. Batilde, the matron of *Humo hacia el sur*, is the prototype of the strong woman, decisive to the point of crime, without precedent in Chilean literature. A stubborn woman with the stamp of colonial aristocracy, she has seen her hopes for full realization as a woman vanish in conformity with social prescriptions, and she has been denied both conjugal love and motherhood as a consequence of her husband's impotence. Matrimony has robbed her of any trace of tenderness and generosity. But in the depiction of Batilde's fight and her relationship with a little girl, Brunet's novel has all the characteristics of a paideia addressed to women.

The confessional and testimonial tone, the autobiographism of the story of human experience, the frequency of alienation and suicidal delirium, the lack of aesthetic and moral distance with respect to the interior developments of the female protagonists, the recourse to a double in order to underscore the transformation of the individual in the social world, the abandonment of rational control and chronological causality, the distrust of a world that has lost the parameters of judgment and is shaken by the ravages of war, fascist militarism, repression, and political disorientation, the postulation of eccentricity as legitimate conduct and the immediate vision of its impossible realization, the disequilibrium between thought and emotions that characterizes narrative perspective: these are the most notable features of a narrative that is as important as it is unjustly forgotten. It constitutes a challenge that a criticism subservient to a standard of masculine meaning could only reject or attribute, with a gesture of understanding gallantry, to the strangeness of the feminine soul. With Mercedes Valdivieso (pseudonym of Mercedes Valenzuela Alvarez; 1925-65), Isabel Allende (1942), and Lucía Guerra (1942), the feminist novel has acquired other aspects: the sign of evanescence, resigned or painful acceptance, the gestures of evasion or death have disappeared in favor of a hopeful and militant stance.

The narrative associated with the year 1938 discovered the archetypic dimension of the human being, and many times the adventures it described were correlatives of deeds that crowned the fortune of mythic heroes. The discovery of the unconscious would lead, with greater frequency, to the representation of multiple levels of reality. Women, especially Bombal, had shown the way with a skill that earned her the praise of the best critics of her day. A man older than the writers of the 1938 period would extend the approach to its final limits in 1951: Manuel Rojas with his *Hijo de ladrón* and subsequent fiction. The theme of the double, symptomatic of the dispersion of the poetic subject, would appear with increasing insistence. The fictional narrator would often become a point of view for a stream of consciousness in a discourse that challenged chronological order and the customary mechanism of plot order. Delving into the byways of national geography that the Creolist writers had ignored, the novelists discovered that in the suffering of each Chilean was to be found the human being of all latitudes and that the problems of Chileans were those of both Ukrainians and Spaniards.

Nicomedes Guzmán was the first Chilean writer to confront the problem of urban proletarianization. *Los hombres oscuros* (The Dark Men; 1939) and *La sangre y la esperanza* (Blood and Hope; 1943) were cause for scandal for a large sector of Chilean criticism, still accustomed to the analytical detail of Latorre's prose and the Byzantine fantasies of Augusto d'Halmar. Both novels interpreted in epic proportions the sorrowful song of the impoverished neighborhood, the story of misery, the joy of small things like a little bit of fresh air, a meaningful look, the fragrance of boldo trees. A rebelliousness, a vitalism, an authenticity of emotion, even the clumsiness of his lyricism served Guzmán's novels as though coming direct from the lips of the people. The ugly fact, the harshness of language, the promiscuity that crowds in everywhere portray a world that, out of necessity, obeys laws of decorum that have little to do with the bourgeois laws endorsed and esteemed by readers even today.

Carlos Droguett reinforces the poetic exploration, with expressionistic characteristics, already present in the world of Guzmán, as well as Reinaldo Lomboy (1910) and Juan Godoy. An agonizing sense of existence and the tenderness with which the narrator witnesses the drama of his characters link Droguett to Rojas. Droguett's originality is the presence of a poetic point of view that serves at the same time as a narrative focus, that is, the creation of a narrative voice that assumes varying temporal dimensions and takes in differing levels of reality—dreams, myth, nightmare, conscious imaginary creation, primitive speculation, delirium, madness—while also adapting itself to each one of the characters who, in turn, embody a stream of consciousness that responds easily to the surges of the unconscious. This poetics of excess, fantasy and fright, violence and terror, is at the basis of *Eloy* (1959), *Patas de perro* (Dog Feet; 1965), and *Supay el cristiano* (Supay the Christian; 1967), Droguett's most important novels. *Eloy* is the story of the final hours of a bandit cornered by the police. Eloy kidnaps a woman and then sets her free. The monologue of the hunted man parallels the actions of the hunt. Tenderness and love share narrative space with seductions and crimes, the presentment of crime with the perfume of violets.

Fernando Alegría, poet, memorialist, and dean of Chilean criticism, adds to this inventory of the contributions of the Generation of 1938 to Chilean fiction characteristics that move us toward contemporary fiction. Among his most important works are *Caballo de copas* (Jack of Hearts; 1957), *Mañana los guerreros* (Tomorrow the Warriors; 1964), *Los días contados* (The Counted Days; 1968), *El paso de los gansos* (Goose Step; 1975), *Coral de guerra* (War Chorale; 1979), and *Una especie de memoria* (A Kind of Memory; 1984).

Caballo de copas conforms, in part, to the picaresque mode that Alegría had himself recognized in Rojas's fiction. But there is something strange about the tension between the mature picaro that acts as narrator, the master of a total experience of the world, and the young man who lived the experiences narrated in the present moment of his life by objectifying himself as the protagonist of the narrative and limiting his knowledge to his physical, intellectual, and emotional possibilities. In the narrative structure, these two individuals fuse, and the temporal distance between the two subjects vanishes, with the present tense arising as an indicator of a perspective that belongs to neither of the two. This displacement underscores how, despite the separation between the young man and the adult, they are identified in the alienation that makes one speak of his easy bourgeois life and the other of his carefree youth, fearless of the future because the future has already happened in the form of the bourgeois existence of the adult.

Both Alegría's narrative and his literary scholarship appear to be founded on a concept of historicity that understands the past as imperfect tense with little aoristic precision, as a past of the present that forms part of our present history and that has the capacity to stretch into the future as a vast present future. The individual is always a chronotopos, a space and a time, a historicity from which it is possible to draw a meaning, to liberate the meaning precariously defined by memory, by texts. José Domingo Gómez Rojas, Pablo Neruda, Gabriela Mistral, Manuel Rojas, Augusto d'Halmar, Vicente Huidobro, Pablo de Rokha, Nicomedes Guzmán are objectivations, objectivities in the narration of the past, nodes of Chilean history, forms of consciousness, real once we have assumed the possibility of inscribing in the present the traces of Chilean prehistory. The result, as in Alegría's own writing, must be a history of betrayed hopes. The problem is that there is no one to blame, neither the world nor Chileans themselves, for to find those at fault solves nothing. The only solution is to assume responsibility and the determination to make the future something better than the present, to continue to trace the steps of hope.

VII

But it was not always this way. There were moments of bitterness in which failure beleaguered artistic expression. When this happened, fiction, poetry, and drama seemed to lose that sense of the future that we have identified in some of the members of the so-called Generation of 1938. The point of view seemed to change when, between 1950 and 1960, the works began to appear of a group of young writers who have often been called the Generation of 1950 or, from another point of view, the Generation of 1957. These writers include Claudio Giaconi (1927), author of *La difícil juventud* (Difficult Youth; 1954); Herbert Müller (1923), *Perceval y otros cuentos* (Percival and Other Stories (1954); Enrique Lafourcade (1927), *Pena de muerte* (Death Sentence; 1953), *La fiesta del rey Acab* (*King Ahab's Feast*; 1959), and *Novela de navidad* (Christmas Novel; 1965); Mercedes Valdivieso, *La brecha* (The Breach; 1961); Mario Espinoza (1924), *Un retrato de David* (Picture of David; 1951); Jaime Laso (1926), *El cepo* (The Trap; 1958); María Elena Gertner (1927), *Islas en la ciudad* (Islands in the City; 1958); José Manuel Vergara (1928), *Daniel y los leones dorados* (Daniel and the Golden Lions; 1956); Jaime Valdivieso (1929), *La condena de todos* (The Condemnation of Everybody; 1966) and *Nunca el mismo río* (Never the Same River; 1965); Guillermo Blanco (1926); Jorge Edwards (1931); and José Donoso (1925). The latter two are discussed in detail below. Among the dramatists of the period, mention must be made of María Asunción Requena (1915), Isidora Aguirre (1928), Sergio Vodanovic (1926), Fernando Cuadra (1925), Gabriela Roepka (1920), Fernando Debesa (1921), Egon Wolff (1926), Luis Alberto Heiremans (1928), Jorge Díaz (1930), and Alejandro Sieveking (1934).

There is a notable political and social skepticism in the work of these writers, based on an individualistic philosophy of an existential sort that, in extreme cases, defies the collectivist ethics that characterized the exponents of social realism. The individual is an outsider, a being in permanent conflict with society, and, in order to provide a defense against constant attack, one's own individualism must be maintained at all costs rather than yielding to any group, party, or ideology. The goal of the individual can be nothing other than the final goal, the absolute.

As a consequence, any group of a relative sort, like the State, with its demand for unconditional loyalty, must be attacked and questioned. The notions of party, democracy, honor, Chilean identity, and family belong, from the point of view of these writers, to a sick vocabulary, as markers of only partial truths.

This attitude represents a genuinely critical attitude that rebelled violently against the confusion over the partial truths attributed to any one group at the expense of the urgent demand for an absolute relation with the absolute. In this view, in the face of the absence of a community of facts and shared thoughts, society acquires a rare quality of darkness and obscurity. Human beings not only cut their ties with the divinity (with the exception of Catholic authors like Heiremans, Vergara, and Blanco), but they also cut themselves off from other individuals to remain prisoners of their own helplessness. Thus they found themselves inhabiting a world of useless, meaningless, absurd, and grotesque rebellion in which all that was embraced was their own deceptive, illusory shadow. It was a world of fallen beings.

This would be the dominant feeling of the young intellectuals of 1950 who sought to escape the moral tedium they found in the bourgeois or déclassé world of their parents. They saw nothing before them but a uniform destiny, a life without ideals, a philosophy of bankrupt concepts, a political system of so much mumbojumbo. Confusion was followed by outbreaks of hope, to give way once again to bitterness and pain. Writers who began their careers around 1950 have continued to create with enormous dramatic and fictional vitality. Without denying themselves the rights of Utopia, they have questioned this very concept as part of a process of analysis of their own guilt, their own weaknesses, the responsibility that each has had in the failures of their society. In writers like Donoso, Edwards, Blanco, and dramatists like Wolff and Díaz, the middle class/bourgeoisie is not only rising and falling. It is on the analyst's couch, seeking the keys for its own failure and attempting to define a destiny that seems no longer to belong to the world they have inhabited, a destiny that turns monstrous in the attempt to recover words to give sense to language and to constitute it as literary discourse. Ariel Dorfman (1942), Isabel Allende, Antonio Skármeta, Lucía Guerra, Raúl Zurita (1951), Oscar Hahn (1938), and Myriam Díaz (1951) continue this quest, younger and more vital, less experienced, sometimes a little dogmatic, both stunned and brilliant.

Isidora Aguirre's play *Los papeleros* (The Paper Gatherers) was published in 1964. It is the story of some unfortunates whose occupation is the gathering of the paper found in garbage cans; this paper is sold to an intermediary who, in turns, resells it to a paper factory. The police frustrate an attempt by the paper gatherers to unionize, and their destiny seems to be nothing more than to be like a piece of paper in the hands of the powerful, to be used, thrown away, and recycled. A child is born, the sign of hope, and one of the women sets fire to the dump as though to purge the world of misery. The spectator is introduced to poverty through the device of an outsider, in this case a country boy who arrives in the city seeking his mother, only little by little to discover the ugliness, poverty, injustice, and abuse of a dump whose geography is that of Chile. But the emphasis is on an urban Chile, whose misery seems to be an integral part of the subconscious of its inhabitants, deforming them with specters of the uselessness and servility that are their social lot, isolated from the dignity and the possibility for human freedom.

Many of Chile's writers at this time underscore, from differing points of view, the creation of a discourse of marginality, whether in terms of gender, economics, demographics, or ideology, following the lead set by the social realists of an earlier generation. The principal weapon of marginal individuals is a raising of political consciousness and organization (usually in terms of a union). The bourgeoisie and other dominant sectors appear as caricatures, with little interest in their reasons, experiences, and internal conflicts. All that is stressed is their status as oppressors and abusers, whether as their own agents or through their flunkies. The dramatic world of Díaz and Wolff will be more intricate.

Jorge Díaz, like Donoso and Edwards in the novel, posits the world of the bourgeoisie in order to force us to grasp how language itself has been an instrument in the configuration of a writing characterized by the absurd in communication and the grotesque character of his sociohistorical, technological, and metaphysical contexts. For Díaz, accusation takes a different form. Alienation is not a special feature of marginal beings, but rather of the dominant group, and it is the latter who experience a life of disintegration, the incapacity for dialogue, and the meaninglessness of actions or interpersonal relations. Thus, Díaz appears to conceive of the unconscious of his characters like a mysterious, absurd, and immediate text in whose writing the world is carnivalized, peopled with grotesque images, cruel actions, and terrifying hallucinations. The irrational openly assumes in his theater the status of an integral element of reality, as the revelation that the bourgeoisie's sense of shame is used to hiding behind a "heavy veil," an epiphany of the absurd and the grotesque whose illumination bursts forth from a sudden breach in the social surface that conceals it.   Díaz's preferred dramatic approach is in the treatment of language.

Automatism and the institutionalization of human activity presided over by the action of language are the favorite targets of Díaz's theater. In *El lugar donde mueren los mamíferos* (Where the Mammals Die; 1963), welfare is unmasked as the ceremony whereby the bourgeoisie exorcizes its egoism.   The brutal and apocalyptical parody of conventional morals, the preoccupation with marginal beings, and the denunciation of social injustice also underlie *Topografía de un desnudo* (Topography of a Nude; 1965), a text based on a massacre in Brazil in 1961 of beggars and the unemployed.   The egoism of the bourgeoisie, the characteristics of an alienation of property and power that result in an inhuman indifference, the deformations of a language and a moral conduct that mold themselves all too easily to the dictates of power and convenience, private existence shaped to the forms of commerce and advertising, the presence of a subconscious text that dictates an irrational, irresponsible, and grotesque way of life: these are all recurring motifs in Díaz's theater. However, they have little to do with the European theater of the absurd, despite frequent assertions to this effect.   The European theater of the absurd that dates from midcentury attempted to give representation to the meaninglessness of human existence and the lack of harmony between individuals and the social context and among one another.

Metaphysical anguish is not at the root of Díaz's theater, but rather it is an anguish of social roots and its motivations derive from the irresponsibility and the alienation of a class that has lost its conscience, that knows only how to live beneath the protection of masks, that has lost language and communication, isolating itself to the extent of believing that it and every individual associated with it is the totality of the world. In its egoism this class has lost the notion of the other and of society. A theater based on this perception produces anguish.   But it is not the metaphysical anguish of the meaninglessness of existence; rather—and unfortunately—it is an anguish produced by the dynamics of a type of social existence that has taken control of the rest of society by annulling it and imposing on it a behavior that can only result in numbness and destruction.   Distancing, emotiveness, laughter are all always present in Díaz, whose theater uses the absurd as an effective strategy for underscoring the task of protest and demolition.

Between *Mansión de lechuzas* (Mansion of Owls; 1958) and *Espejismos* (Mirror Images; 1978), Egon Wolff charts a parable of meaning that, in broad terms, follows the outlines of a major aspect of recent literature in Chile: the movement from openness and the hope for a renewal of traditional values through creative activities and goals that are more authentic and vital, to the end of optimism in the dark night of individual conformity deprived of social implications and any future. Wolff's most famous work, *Los invasores* (The Invaders; 1963), is a circular drama in which, following a brief introduction, the main action takes place as a dream whose images are repeated in reality. The story line concerns the invasion of a well-to-do home by the poor who live close by. It is an act of revenge, perhaps semianarchical, against the exploiters, and its message assumes the nature of a warning: revolt against the abuse of power can take place and it will take place as long as the reality of poverty is ignored.

Without a doubt Juan Radrigán (1937) is one of the most interesting figures of a theater in which the vice of despair becomes a virtue, in the sense of a world in which life itself markedly resembles death. Radrigán's setting, the world of Chile, is filled with marginal individuals, to the extent that the marginal are no longer such: all that exists is marginality. What is called normality has been set aside in a special Purgatory, on the fringes, out of sight. The rites of this theater are those of a farewell and never of a welcome. His characters never depart; they are expelled, they have been removed, cast out. They know they are alone and that this is all there is to know. Their space has no boundaries or discernible geography. There are no entrances or exits, no outside or inside. There are only displacements on the margin. Works like *Testimonio de las muertes de Sabina* (Testimony Regarding the Deaths of Sabina; 1979), *Las brutas* (The Oafish Women; 1980), *El loco y la triste* (The Crazy Man and the Sad Woman; 1980), *Hechos consumados* (Consumated Deeds; 1981), *Informe para indiferentes* (Report for the Indifferent; 1983) nevertheless reveal a great eloquence: if Radrigán's characters experience difficulties in communicating, Radrigán does it singularly well.

VIII

The discourse of marginality, with its details on internal or real exile focusing on the processes of middle-class decay, characterizes the narrative production of José Donoso and Jorge Edwards, whom literary historians have associated with the groups of writers emerging variously around 1950 and 1957.

Prior to 1970 and the publication of *El obsceno pájaro de la noche* (*The Obscene Bird of Night*), Donoso occupied himself with the painful unmasking of the absurd conventions of the middle class. Marginal individuals, manipulators of a hidden power, release the primitivism of carefully repressed instincts that had always threatened the institutions, in appearance solid and unshakeable, of Chilean society. This frame of reference did not disappear in 1970. Rather it takes on the added dimension of exile, both voluntary and forced, and the examination of the patriarchal regime of the bourgeois system. Both the probing of this theme and the events following the military coup of 1973 motivated a change in Donoso's writings (and also in Edwards's) that is much more one of intensity and penetration than it is one of content.

Donoso's characters, in effect, make up a spectrum of individuals who inhabit a world undergoing collapse because of fragmentation and the lack of an authentic social program. Bereft of any sense of solidarity, they are consumed by the defense and protection of property and what they feel is theirs by right. Their alienation usually expresses itself in the terrifying terms of madness or death, via the mediation of persons belonging to other strata of existence or other social classes. This nihilistic vision of bourgeois society underscores ironically the revindication in Donoso's writing of what is natural and pure that is to be found in a sector considered by his characters to be filthy and degrading. Yet, these persons serve to right the wrongs of the inauthenticity, the routine, and the conventional character of middle-class morals. As the impossible possibility of the authentic, the exaltation of healthy and caring values expresses itself in terms of a vandalic cosmogony that wipes everything away in an outburst of blood, annihilation, and destruction.

Both the denouement and the characteristic narrative modalities of Donoso's fiction emphasize the enigmatic character of the intrusion of the exterior in the world of the middle class. The characters who experience this intrusion do so with such intensity that one might believe that it comes from within, as something that they had repressed in the guise of the separation of classes and the use of masks, rituals, and other isolating tactics. When these invasions from without take place, the policy of bourgeois morals is to discard the person who has been touched, to pretend that nothing has taken place, and to sustain the fiction that is life—to "pull a heavy curtain over the matter," as the characters of *Casa de campo* (*A House in the Country*; 1978) are wont to say. Woman as the priestess of bourgeois rituals, as the enchantress and the maker of the world, a function that begins to emerge in *El obsceno pájaro de la noche*, also has its origins in this circumstance.

In the latter novel, the identity of young Humberto has a dual basis in rejection and desire: the rejection of his middle-class anonymity and the wish to become a writer. The fulfillment of his wish elevates him to the plane of his model, the aristocrat Jerónimo de Azcoitía. As a consequence, his identity derives from the structures of property and power to which only a few (the members of the oligarchy) have access. Thus, if he is successful in fulfilling his desire, Humberto will have a dependent identity. To become a writer would mean to have the ability to invent, to create a plot, to possess language, to elaborate a story, to narrate as an instrument for specifying an origin, to scale the labyrinthine heights of one's own making, just as Jerónimo de Azcoitía's class has done for centuries. The undertaking is unsuccessful; its structure, nevertheless, reappears in *Casa de campo*.

Casa de campo is much more than an allegory of the military coup; it is the deconstruction of the founding fantasy of the patriarchal and bourgeois system of the dominant class. Property, with its source in the control of land acquired by conquest, is based on what the Ventura family, the conquerors, must claim to be the property of the natives in order to take it away from them; that is, to rob them of it. The adventure of the theft has taught them that, in order to maintain control over what has been stolen, they must continue robbing, depriving others of the property of their acts, depriving them of liberty, enslaving them. Once this has been done, it is necessary to legitimize the structure by a process of naming, something that must be done with careful logic. Since the Indians possessed nothing—they did not recognize private property—the fact of utilizing this property or the aboriginal equivalent of the concept as a means of exchange for the value of its use is equivalent to consuming oneself, of being anthropophagous. This means existing by virtue of a practice repugnant to the bourgeoisie, that of individuals who, out of necessity, must eat something that is a part of themselves as anthropophagi or consumers of human beings. All of which is, of course, quite unnatural. If one must eat (and to eat is necessarily a transitive verb), it is best to eat what belongs to others. Thus, the Ventura adventure continues to be controlled by the notion of possession.

Edwards exemplifies the tenacity of a critical realism toward aristocratic society, but with characteristics of contemporary modes of writing. *Los convidados de piedra* (Guests of Stone; 1978), *El museo de cera* (The Wax Museum; 1981), and *La mujer imaginaria* (The Imaginary Woman;

1985) detail in a chronicle format the falling apart of the aristocracy throughout the twentieth century. Moreover, *El museo de cera* looks back toward that oligarchy's colonial roots. All three novels involve, at least partially, aspects of a collective chronicle. The narrator of that chronicle bears the features of a voyeur, and when narrative focus yields strategically to the perspective of one of the characters, the latter assumes, in turn, the original narrator's point of view. The setting for Edwards's novels is the aristocracy, but one where little happens. Yet, this lack of action, which results in the scope of knowledge, is what permits the presence of a critical content that generally functions only by allusion, although it does become more explicit in the frequent feminist analyses by Doña Inés of her class and family in *La mujer imaginaria*. By assuming in the novel the masculine or feminine perspective of the voyeur, Edwards provides an effective complication of the strategy of framing, since the reader is obliged to consider continually the conditions of the framing of what can be seen and thought, on the basis of how no perspective, not even one that points to its own visibility as privileged in terms of the reader, is gratuitous, closed or fixed, it always being possible to subject it to a new framing operation. Thus, in *La mujer imaginaria*, the dominant context in the last paragraph of the novel is that of Inés, until the final sentence, where it is replaced by that of the chronicler, who gives his affirmations an ironic twist precisely in order to end the text.

As in the case of Alegría's *Coral de guerra*, a satanic economy overcomes liberal writing in *La casa de los espíritus* (*House of Spirits*; 1982) by Isabel Allende. When Clara's luminous spirits are dislodged from the house by the forces of evil, language is obliged to testify concerning tortures that are both frightening and chimeral because of the varieties of suffering; concerning the forms of censorship wielded in order to eliminate certain lexical registers like those corresponding to liberty, basic human rights, collectives and unions, justice, protest, types of meetings, song lyrics, private conversations, the correspondence of family and lovers; and concerning the sudden changes in the world's cardinal points of reference. The signs of the world have changed, and one must struggle to recover them with love, song, poetry, and art, with Rosa la Bella's mythological animals, Blanca's beasts of the land, and Alba's paintings. It will be another language, another reality; and it will be another form of narrative discourse and, of course, another way of viewing the world. This narrative discourse does not take its place on the political platform, nor does it consist of the mere repetition of slogans. It is devoted to improving the conditions of life, to teaching the peasants (as Blanca does in the former novel), to curing the most common ailments, to teaching people to read and do math, and to preaching a sense of social justice—and a sense of reality.

IX

Two or three generations of intellectuals and writers have set for themselves the task of rethinking Chile. The activity of the eldest has not been overshadowed by that of the youngest. They listen to each other, they gather at congresses, and they read and study each other's works with care. A literary and critical community has arisen from the catastrophe of the 1973 military destruction of Chilean institutional life. It is a community that is united in the overall anguish that has erased the academic, party, and chronological rivalries of the past. The task is now to give witness, to cultivate hope, and to continue to pursue unstintingly the clues of guilt in order to be prepared for the reconstruction of a vigorous and mature Chile that will be capable of learning from its errors.

Chile, as a consequence of the social upheaval of the years following the 1973 military coup, lent itself in major ways to the creation of a postmodern horizon of experimentation in the domains of art, architecture, and literature. The way in which many writers and intellectuals were forced to leave the country, the internal exile of the majority, and the decision by a significant number of others to leave the country, the mechanisms of censorship and self-censorship, the forced closing of the spaces of public and artistic dialogue, the mediocrity of the authoritarian monologue in which only a few could recognize themselves were all conditions that could only contribute to the reformulation of the national and Latin American identity of Chileans.

The creative efforts of Enrique Lihn and Gonzalo Rojas, of José Donoso and Nicanor Parra became models of irony, experimentation, a parodic and intertextual tone of carnivalesque modulations, the irreverence of art in the face of canonical discourses, which the new writing mocked (including those of a subjective and poetic self-representation), the impartiality of the agent, and the textual pretensions of objectivity. These features synthesize the features of the most recent writing in Chile, as in the greater part of the world. Poets no longer believe in God, although they still bow down before the medieval Devil in his local manifestations. Nor do they believe in art, science, or the steel laws that govern the history of peoples. The Mona Lisa, Freud, Michelangelo, and *Das Kapital* are read and interpreted by Groucho Marx. Religion, art, science, and all of the narratives derived from Christianity have ceased to occupy a position of privilege and must compete with other, more humble constructions that multiply with alarming fecundity. Hernán Lavín Cerda (1939) saw fit to publish in Mexico a *Nueva teoría de la evolución* (A New Theory of Evolution; 1985) that brings together texts written between 1977 and 1984, and *Aquellas máscaras de gesto permanente* (Those Masks of Permanent Expression; 1989) is undoubtedly one of the most demanding and architecturally solid novels written by a Chilean in recent years.

The features that I have enumerated are perhaps those that best identify the group of writers that begin to publish around 1970. Among them is Oscar Hahn (1938), whose *Arte de morir* (Art of Dying; 1977) and *Mal de amor* (Love Sickness; 1981) assume a popular Chilean character and an eroticism that invites the reader to flirt with death. Also among this group is the previously mentioned Lavín Cerda and Jaime Quezada (1942), as well as Myriam Díaz Diocaretz (1951), whose gagged, anxiety-ridden, and anguishedly loquacious muse is evident in *Que no se pueden decir* (Because They Cannot Say; 1982). Díaz Diocaretz is not afraid to speak the language of a cheerful feminism, while at the same time providing one of the most penetrating images of recent Chilean poetry. *El arco, la flecha, el blanco* (The Bow, the Arrow, the Target; 1988) is a miracle of poetic chess, and its principal quality lies in its intensity, a characteristic that seems to recall some of the poems of Gabriela Mistral. Gonzalo Millán (1947), in the extensive poem that is *La ciudad* (The City; 1979), once again reconstructs with an indignant and strident tone the pestiferous utopia of the generals whose world denies itself in self-consumption, repeating with efficient parody, the process the henchmen of the Tyrant had used to create it. Cecilia Vicuña (1948) stands out for the respect she demonstrates for the materiality of the artistic object, which is virtually transformed into a natural entity, so to speak, by her use of a representational synesthesia in the attempt to eliminate the differences between the arts and the media of mimesis. Carla Gandi (1947), in *Los clamores y los días* (The Protests and the Days; 1990), obliges us to appreciate the beauty of a classic line bound by the mordacity of a poetic intelligence that, without removing itself from catastrophe, makes the latter its own, almost to the point of producing it via the force of a quotidian and confused outcry that seeks something, but yet is nothing more than a form of protest that is the essence of love. Needless to say, the names that have been mentioned are only a few of the many voices that are making themselves heard at this moment in Chile.

An analysis of writing in Chile from 1973 to the present, despite Pinochet's fall, can only be carried out by bearing in mind the context and the long shadows cast by the despot. Only in this context is it possible to grasp the beauty and the daring of texts by a Carla Gandi or a Myriam Díaz Diocaretz or the intense vanguardism of Diamela Eltit and Raúl Zurita. Although they are intrinsically important, this context only serves to enhance their value.

Raúl Zurita (1951) is probably the younger writer best known in and outside Chile. Ironically, Zurita has had the support of conservatives like Father Ignacio Valente Ibáñez and the newspaper *El Mercurio* (Mercury), despite his transgressions at the expense of the establishment. His first book appeared barely a half-dozen years after the coup, in 1979. The dereliction of the individual and the community constitute the semantic nucleus of *Purgatorio* (Purgatory), a text that attempted to rescue an imaginary world repressed by the institutions of the dictatorship. The psychiatric dossier exists alongside poetry, madness prevails over reason, the laws of the dirty war over the dreamlike norms of Chilean democracy. That reason is nonreason is, nevertheless, clear: there is always a body, this body is the object of torture, and sacrifice is carried out on the altar of the nation, which finds its rejoinder in the poetry of Zurita. Chile is not a country at peace, certainly not at the time Zurita wrote his poems. But there Chile stood, the site of utopias. Chile had not disappeared along with Pinochet, but rather continued to be the fertile and chosen province of the Antarctic region of which Ercilla dreamed.

There was, nevertheless, a certain bitterness of mode that Zurita later attempted to eliminate. His next publication is *Anteparaíso* (1982; the title is difficult to translate, evoking both the idea of an antechamber of Paradise and a Paradise of Yore) and involves the imaginary mimesis of Valparaíso, the port city that was once the pride of Chile and whose name means Valley of Paradise. Valparaíso, once characterized by its air of quaint nostalgia, is now the acute pain in the holds of the training ship La Esmeralda, a symbol of torture. There is an emblematic transition from Chile to the South American landscape, from helplessness to hope and the recovery of identity in the recognition of the scars of history. *Anteparaíso* is the triumph of hope and love over the forces of destruction, hate, solitude, exile, and dereliction. Zurita's writing is a rebuttal via the poetry of the generosity and faith in the future demonstrated by the fiction of Isabel Allende.

Perhaps the most stunning text in recent years is *Lumpérica* (1983) by Diamela Eltit (1949). It is stunning because of its daring, its maturity, and the deliberately primal character of its poetic undertaking. The catachresis arising from the fusing of "lumpen" and "America" and the subtraction of the graphemes that could refer to *am-or* (love)—as, for example, those of *amor*-America—function on all levels of the text. The novel speaks directly from a position of marginality without thematizing it, but rather by converting the margin into an anchor of vision. Hierarchies are subverted, and the process becomes important, while the product moves to a secondary and irrelevant plane. Deviations, as a consequence, prevail over the linear; nouns are replaced by the pronoun and the centrality of the narrator by that of the reader. The fragmentation of the feminine consciousness, the denial of identity, the identification with the lumpen, the awareness of a sacrifice demanded of the subject connote a violent rejection—precisely because it functions on the level of language—of the patriarchal forms of domination. Eltit still has much to say to us, and she takes her place in the company of the grotesque to be found in Donoso, although her writing is both more daring and more graceful.

X

The image of the combatant Araucanian Indian that Ercilla put in place became transformed into the foundational myth of Chilean nationality. In 1883, after three centuries of struggle, the henchmen of President Santa María could pride themselves that the victory over neighboring countries in the War of the Pacific had its antecedents in the courage and the strength of the Mapuche Indians. That same year, the Chief of State put the prowess of the army to the test in breaking the Araucanian people. It should not, therefore, seem strange that the motive behind the subjection of the Araucanians had first been undertaken by a Creole, a disciple of Ercilla, who had marched to Lima to put himself in the service of the very Viceroy, Don García Hurtado de Mendoza, who had expelled the author of *La Araucana*. In fact, Don Pedro de Oña, inspired by the noble wealth and splendor of the Viceroy, would undertake the epic of Don García, the epitome of Christian valor and virtue against the backdrop of the heathen and savage Araucanians. It is significant that

Oña's poem, *El Arauco domado* (The Araucanian People Broken), written in royal octaves like Ercilla's, was nothing more than the perennial and unrealizable utopian dream of the right, just as the absolute and uncontaminated liberation from the conquistadors, the colonists, and the bourgeoisie would be the fantasy of the left.

The Araucanian myth has served victors and vanquished, invaders and inhabitants of the land at the dawn of Chile, the aristocratic republic and the followers of Balmaceda in 1891, Pinochet's strongmen and those who identified with the humanitarian and Christian socialism of Salvador Allende in the early 1970s. And it has likewise served the poets.

With considerable eloquence Soledad Bianchi (1948) has discerned this relationship in her work on Chilean poetry since 1973. In a study that, to the best of my knowledge, has yet to be published, "Descubrimiento y conquistas como intertexto de la poesía chilena actual" (Discovery and Conquests as Intertext in Contemporary Chilean Poetry), Bianchi has traced the connections between a broad sector of recent Chilean poetry and colonial writing. In fact, *Zonas de peligro* (Danger Zones; 1985), *Diario de navegación* (Navigation Diary; 1986), and *El último viaje* (The Final Voyage; 1987) by Tomás Harris, as well as *Karra Maw'n* (1984) by Clemente Riedemann (1953) and *La tierra son fuegos* (The Earth on Fire; 1986) by Juan Pablo Riveros turn writing into an instrument in the persistence of the past, not only the past in the person of the chroniclers—Columbus or Pedro Valdivia—but the past to which their chronicles refer, that of the heroism and the purity sullied by the contact with what is symbolized in the Amerindias, America and the Indies. It is the imperative, both ancestral and new, that dreams and memories do not fade. The unknown is followed by the description of the known, and the latter by its defamiliarization, its estrangement in order that it may be better seen and, in this case, that it may better serve to frighten us. Writing is present in the traces of the past, and in it the world assumes the conditions of a palimpsest. The reader, like Columbus and Harris alike, is confounded by the way their readings look at them. And in this fissure, between the object and its representation, one discovers an already rotten newness, an already violated pristine quality. Columbus becomes the Viceroy of Nothingness, a Nothingness that could perhaps find its correlative in the original, untranslated language of Riedemann's text, in the language of the land—mapudungu—a land occupied from the beginning by its aboriginals, the people of the soil, the Mapuches. It is a land that knows only fear and the arrival of the invader, and from that time forward otherness, estrangement, and mistrust begin to predominate in order to emerge as abuse, exploitation, and genocide. Columbus, Ercilla, the Valdivia of the chronicles on the foundation of Chile, the Pigafetta of Magellan's adventures, Alonso de Ovalle, the first propagandist of the beauty of the fatherland and its people, and the poets of today all merge together in exultant heteroglossia and pleasant dialogue. It is a dialogue in which the subversion of Ercilla directed against the imperial monologue is transformed into the constant underlying the most recent texts of Chilean poetry.

Translated by David William Foster

BIBLIOGRAPHY

Alegría, Fernando. *Literatura chilena del siglo XX*. Santiago de Chile: Zig-Zag, 1962. Rather than a literary history, this is a collection of thoughtful essays that have as a central point of reference the author's own role as a Chilean writer, a circumstance that makes this an indispensable guide.

Alegría, Fernando. *La poesía chilena; orígenes y desarrollo del siglo XVI al XIX*. México, D.F.: Fondo de Cultura Económica, 1954. To date, this is the most reliable guide to Chilean poetry prior to Modernism, and it is especially valuable for its treatment of Chilean Romanticism.

Bianchi, Soledad. *Entre la lluvia y el arcoiris. Algunos jóvenes poetas chilenos*. Barcelona/Rotterdam: Ediciones del Instituto para el Nuevo Chile, 1983. One of the best collections of Chilean poetry since the 1973 coup. The prologue on a "disperse generation" is significant as an overview of the ten years represented by the anthology.

Bianchi, Soledad. *Poesía chilena (mirada, enfoques, apuntes)*. Santiago de Chile: CESOC Ediciones Documentas, 1990. A collection of essays on the generations, tendencies, name, and characteristics of recent Chilean poetry, with references to the influence of Gabriela Mistral and Pablo Neruda.

Castedo, Elena. *El teatro chileno de mediados del siglo XX*. Santiago de Chile: Andrés Bello, 1982. A good overview of Chilean theater between 1950 and 1970, a period of intensive dramatic activity;

Castedo's study, moreover, incorporates a contemporary European and North American critical idiom.

Foster, David William. *Chilean Literature: a Working Bibliography of Secondary Sources*. Boston: G.K. Hall, 1978. A registry of general references, references on special topics, and critical books and essays on specific authors.

Goić, Cedomil. *La novela chilena; los mitos degradados*. Santiago de Chile: Editorial Universitaria, 1968. Goić utilizes a generational approach to order Chilean novelistic production in forty-five year blocks grouped into two main divisions, modern and contemporary. This study is, however, more important for the acuity of its analyses than for the generational schemata.

Ibáñez Langlois, José Miguel. *Poesía chilena e hispanoamericana actual*. Santiago de Chile: Nascimento, 1975. North American theoretical concepts regarding poetry are used in an examination of major Chilean and Latin American figures.

Jara, René. *El revés de la arpillera. Perfil literario de Chile*. Madrid: Hiperión, 1989. An interpretive overview of Chilean writing from the Colonial period to 1985.

Medina, José Toribio. *Historia de la literatura colonial en Chile*. Santiago de Chile: Imprenta y Librería Mercurio, 1878. In three volumes, Medina's work continues to be a major source of information in its scope and the erudition with which the information is presented.

Promis, José. *Testimonios y documentos de la literatura chilena (1842-1975)*. Santiago de Chile: Nascimento, 1977. A selection of texts important for the understanding of the internal development of Chilean literature; the texts are all by major figures in Chilean letters and therefore possess a significant testimonial quality.

Silva Castro, Raúl. *Panorama literario de Chile*. Santiago de Chile: Editorial Universitaria, 1961. A general and strictly chronological survey (rather than one focusing on movements or groups) of Chilean literature, this work is a synthesis of Silva Castro's extensive publications in the field.

COLOMBIA
Raymond Leslie Williams
University of Colorado

I

The international recognition that Nobel Laureate Gabriel García Márquez brought to Colombian literature contrasts with a venerable tradition of isolation and conservativism. The major publishing houses, avant-garde journals, and literary traditions have been centered around Buenos Aires, Mexico City and, to a lesser extent, Lima, Havana, and Santiago de Chile. Bogotá, the self-styled "Athens of South America," has been a stronghold of Spanish tradition and classical literary models. Nevertheless, Colombia has produced some of the most renowned narratives in each of the major periods: Juan Rodríguez Freyle's *El carnero* (The Ram; 1638) was one of the most outstanding pieces of colonial narrative written in Latin America; one of the most accomplished Romantic novels was Jorge Isaacs's *María* (1867); José Eustasio Rivera's *La vorágine* (The Vortex; 1924) is considered a classic of its time; finally, a superb work among those that appeared with the rise of the new novel was García Márquez's masterpiece, *Cien años de soledad* (*One Hundred Years of Solitude*; 1967). From the colonial period (approximately 1500-1810) the Vice-Royalty of the Nuevo Reino de Granada was characterized by regional divisions that became even more pronounced during the period of the republic. Within a decade after the Nuevo Reino de Granada gained its independence from Spain, in fact, the old Vice-Royalty was divided among the present countries of Venezuela, Colombia, and Ecuador. Geographical barriers created five entities within Colombia's boundaries that would eventually develop five distinct historical and cultural traditions: the Caribbean coast, Greater Antioquia, the Cundinamarca-Boyac Highlands, Greater Tolima, and the Western Valley. Each of these areas has developed a specific literary tradition within the ideo-

179

logical constants determined by the region's cultural and socioeconomic history.

Spanish control of intellectual activity and the writer's isolation were predominant factors during the colonial period. The publication of literature and distribution of novels printed in Spain were prohibited. Nevertheless, it is a well-established fact that contraband copies of Cervantes's *Don Quijote* (1605) did circulate among privileged readers in the New World. The writer's isolation can be attributed to several factors. The governmental and intellectual centers, such as Bogotá and Tunja, were geographically isolated. Men and women of letters were generally priests or officials of the Catholic church's hierarchy who lived in the isolation of monasteries. Literary production of any sort, rigidly controlled by a political and ecclesiastic elite, was a privilege of a small minority. Given this direct rapport between writing and political power during the Colonial period, it is logical that the Nuevo Reino de Granada's first writers were its conquerors.

Of the major writers of the colonial period, Gonzalo Jiménez de Quesada (1499-1579) and Juan de Castellanos (1522-1607) arrived in Colombia as conquerors of the New World. The other most renowned writers of the period were Juan Rodríguez Freyle (1556-1638), Francisca Josefa de Castillo y Guevara (1671-1742), and Hernando Domínguez Camargo (?-1656). The other literary figures of the colonial period were far less important and were limited to the production of religious texts.

Gonzalo Jiménez de Quesada explored and conquered the New World motivated by a fiction—the legend of El Dorado. His failure in discovering the legendary city of gold in the Nuevo Reino de Granada, despite several ventures in the region, was the only blemish in his otherwise brilliant military, political, and literary career. Jiménez de Quesada was a true man of the Renaissance—a polyglot and author of several tomes on historical, political, and related topics. Many of his major writings, such as his *Compendio historial* (Historical Compendium) and *Gran cuaderno* (Great Notebook), were never published and have been lost; he and his contemporaries refer to these lost manuscripts in other published books. His *Antijovio* (Antijovius), written in approximately 1567 and published in the twentieth century, is the earliest literary or historical text to which the contemporary reader has access. It demonstrates the connection between writing and political power in the colonial period. Just as Jiménez de Quesada had defended Spain's world position with his sword in the conquest of New Granada, he proposes to defend Spain's image in *Antijovio*, a rewriting of history in response to the

Italian Paulo Jovii's *Historiarum sui temporis libri XLV* (1550-52). Jiménez de Quesada explains to the reader in his prologue that Jovii's principal intention was "To speak badly of our nation." He maintains in the book that no one had told the straight and simple story of Spain's feats, untarnished by the thousands of fables that people had heard about the nation. *Antijovio*, then, is a deliberate attempt at redressing the errors that had been committed in the previous historical writing about Spain.

Juan de Castellanos also came to New Granada as a conqueror, arriving in 1536 and fighting in the conquest of the Valle de Upar (present day Valledupar) in search of gold. He was named the priest of Río de la Hacha in 1559. He was appointed priest in Tunja in 1562, where he remained the rest of his life, dedicating much of it to writing. His lengthy *Elegías de varones ilustres de Indias* (Elegy of Illustrious Men of the Indies; 1589) was a voluminous (113,000 lines) chronicle in verse dealing with the conquest and colonization of the New World. It was written in the then-new Italian octave rhyme style, although Castellanos has the Spaniards speak in royal octaves and the Indians in verses of eleven syllables. *Elegías de varones ilustres de Indias* has no continuous narrative line, but rather relates individual biographies. A four-part formal structure follows a chronological and geographical development: Part I describes Columbus's four voyages, the conquest of Caribbean islands, and the feats of Pedro de Orsuna and Lope de Aguirre; Part II tells of the conquest of Venezuela, Cape Vela, and Santa Marta; Part III deals with Cartagena, Antioquia, and Popayán; Part IV is a history of New Granada. Part I was the only section of the poem that appeared in print during Castellanos's lifetime, although in 1601 he sent Part IV to Spain for official censure and publication. The four parts were published for the first time in 1914.

The major work of narrative prose written during the colonial period was *El carnero* (completed in 1638). One of the few colonial works still read in Colombia, *El carnero* is a historical chronicle of life in Santa Fe de Bogotá (present-day Bogotá) during a hundred-year period, 1539-1636. A picaresque chronicle of "tremendous amorality," *El carnero* is a synthesis of war news, changes of government, customs, psychological portraits, adventure, scandal, crime, historical fact, and legends. Scholars have tended to view Rodríguez Freyle's book as either a historical chronicle interspersed with scandalous anecdotes, usually referring to individuals belonging to New Granada's distinguished aristocracy, or a form of novel, perhaps with entertaining moments, but too primitive to compare favorably with the European seventeenth-century novel.

Like other artists writing during the Colonial period, Rodríguez Freyle confronted the problem of a necessarily ambiguous potential readership. When the book was being written, there still were no legal printing presses in New Granada. This fact accounts for *El carnero*'s ambiguous status as part of a written culture under rigid control from afar. Spanish authorities are one group of implied readers who are clearly delineated in the text: on the first page the narrator directs his words to "Phillip IV, King of Spain," and throughout the book he pays homage to the proper authorities. Nevertheless, there is another implied reader, the general populace, that will supposedly gain valuable moral instruction from the examples of the socially unacceptable behavior *El carnero* relates. It is assumed, of course, that such scandalous anecdotes are not that part of the book directed to the presumably upright authorities. This multiplicty of implied readers makes the creation of a unified text a difficult proposition. Yet, a general design can be found in precisely the interplay between the telling of the story (to prove that interesting events took place in New Granada) and the presence of the narrator (to validate the narrator's self-image as a chronicler of unimpeachable moral virtue). Despite the validity of this proposition, Rodríguez Freyle has problems with the basic principles of story telling. In addition, Rodríguez Freyle feels the necessity to employ acrobatic logic in order to confirm his right to pursue the events of the story. The right of invention will not be definitively established in Colombia for another several centuries, with the advent of García Márquez.

New Granada's two renowned poets were Hernando Domínguez Camargo and Sor Francisca Josefa del Castillo y Guevara. Domínguez Camargo, a Baroque poet who wrote in the first half of the seventeenth century, is best known for his poem *Poema heroico de San Ignacio de Loyola* (Heroic poem of St. Ignatius of Loyola; 1666), which was not published until after his death. This poem recreates the life of Saint Ignatius in five parts: Book One tells of his birth, infancy, and youth, including military exploits; Book Two relates his conversion and a miraculous visit from the Virgin; in Book Three he makes a pilgrimage to Rome, Geneva, Venice, and Jerusalem; Book Four deals with his studies in Barcelona, Salamanca, and Paris, and with his chaste life; the fifth and final book tells of his forming the Society of Jesus. Domínguez Camargo creates, in effect, a mythical character in this poem (or saint, in ecclesiastic terms). He also wrote the poems *Otras flores aunque pocas* (Other Flowers, Although Few; 1676). Sor Francisca Josefa de Castillo y Guevara was one of the most accomplished mystic writers in Latin America during the colonial period and in this sense comparable to Sor Juana Inés de la Cruz in New Spain (see the section on Mexico). In addition to Baroque poetry, Sor Francisca Josefa wrote ascetic and mystic prose. Her diary of intimate thoughts, posthumously titled *Afectos espirituales* (Spiritual Affections; date unknown) and an autobiography, which editors have named *Su vida* (Her Life; date unknown), were her most significant prose writings.

Francisco Antonio Vélez Ladrón de Guevara (1621-?) and Fernando Fernández de Valenzuela (1616-?) are among a group of noteworthy writers of this period. Vélez Ladrón de Guevara was a court poet who wrote elaborate and decorative poetry for New Granada's royalty. His themes—the daily life of the ruling elite—were petty, but he was one of Latin America's most able and fecund Rococo poets. Fernández de Valenzuela created a one-act theatrical piece, *Laurea crítica* (Critical Laurea; date unknown), Colombia's first recognized dramatic art. It is a brief and playful satire of sixteenth-century society in Santa Fe de Bogotá. A Latin scholar, Fernández de Valenzuela also published the first Latin grammar in Colombia, *Thesaurus linguae latinae* (written 1628-29).

The second half of the eighteenth century marked a notable change in Nueva Granada's intellectual life. The literature of the colonial period, as noted, was directly controlled by the Spanish governmental and ecclesiastic hierarchy. Domínguez Camargo's *Poema heroico de San Ignacio de Loyola*, for example, was preceded by nine prefatory sections, seven of which are approvals and licenses for the book's publication. Intellectual life, until the mid-eighteenth century, was an activity limited to a small economic and religious elite. Several changes in the eighteenth century brought New Granada more into the mainstream of current Western thought. The Jesuits introduced the first printing press into New Granada in 1738 and the first secular press was established in 1779. This technological advance represented a considerable change in the relative balance of power and intellectual independence for writers.

By the 1760s José Celestino Mutis (1732-1808) was teaching mathematics and astronomy for the first time in New Granda, at the Colegio del Rosario (College of the Rosary). His activity provided for the first scientific rather than religious world view. Mathematics was introduced into the curriculum at the Colegio de San Bartolomé (St. Bartholomew College) in 1782. The first public library was opened in Bogotá in 1777. The Botanical Expedition of 1783, organized by José Celestino Mutis, contributed to legitimizing a scientific approach to phenomena; again, a questioning of not only religious doctrine, but indirectly of ecclesiastic authority. During the last two decades of the eighteenth century, the first books and newspapers were printed in New Granada. Manuel del Socorro Rodríguez began publishing the first literary magazine, *Papel periódico* (Periodical Paper) in 1791, which he continued for 270 numbers. This magazine, in addition to the literary soirées (*tertulias*) that began to be held regularly in Bogotá, provided for an intellectual communication and interaction heretofore unknown in New Granada.

II

With the Declaration of Independence in 1810 and independence from Spain in 1824, political power was transferred from the Spaniards to the national aristocracy and military leaders, both groups of Creole origin, that is, citizens of Spanish descent born in New Granada. The nineteenth century was characterized by political conflict and several civil wars between Liberals and Conservatives. Liberals favored regional autonomy, diminishing the power of the Catholic church, and free international commerce. Conservatives, many of whose leaders were the landed aristocracy, favored a strong central government and church. After considerable strife during the first half of the nineteenth century, the two parties were clearly defined for the first time in 1849 with the election of the Liberal president José Hilario López. The Conservative Party wrote and published a doctrine of principles for the first time. Most of Colombia's writers were the elite political and military leaders involved in these conflicts.

Nineteenth-century literature followed a pattern similar to much of Latin America: during the independence movement and the early years of the republic, political essays and creative literature with Neo-Classic models dominated; two generations of Romantics, Realists, and the first *modernistas* (Modernists) followed. By the second half of the century, when literary culture was a more institutionalized activity than it ever had been before, its center was Bogotá. José María Vergara y Vergara (1831-72) established in Bogotá a literary group identified as *El mosaico* (The Mosaic), which published a magazine of the same name. The land-owning elite, many of whom were writers, began losing political and economic power with the mid-century liberal reforms. These social and economic processes had important literary manifestations: the paternalism of the first *costumbristas* (Costumbrists or local-color writers), the occasionally nostalgic writing of Jorge Isaacs and José Manuel Marroquín, Gregorio Gutiérrez González's exaltation of rural values, and the decadence of the large landowners witnessed in the work of Tomás Carrasquilla (see below). In 1867 Vergara y Vergara published the first history of Colombian literature, *Historia de la literatura en Nueva Granada* (History of Literature in New Granada). Despite the predominance of the capital, the first Colombian novel was written in the Caribbean coastal region, and the major Realists and Costumbrist writers came from Antioquia. At the end of the nineteenth century, in fact, the national polemic was between the traditional Antiochians and the new Modernists.

The Constitution of 1886 assured the institution of conservative principles, and the conservative political hegemony extended through the first three decades of the twentieth century, followed by a predominance of the Liberals after 1930. The 1920s and 1930s were a period of rapid modernization and industrialization: by 1930 there were two hundred factories in Bogotá, one hundred seventeen in Medellín, ninety-one in Barranquilla, and seventy-seven in Cali. Coffee had already become the major export product by the end of the nineteenth century. In the early twentieth century train and telegraph communication connected the interior highlands to the Caribbean coast.

Conservative literary trends also continued to affect Colombia into the twentieth century. Just as Colombia's Romantic poets were more "correct" in their use of traditional forms than had been many of their counterparts in other parts of Latin America, the avant-garde was only moderately influential in Colombia. Los Nuevos (The New Ones) of the 1920s, for example, did not produce such experimental literature as the Contemporáneos (Contemporaries) in Mexico (see the section on Mexico) or the avant-garde writers who were led by Jorge Luis Borges in Buenos Aires (see the section on Argentina). The poets of the Piedra y Cielo (Stone and Sky) generation, under the leadership of Jorge Rojas (1911), renovated Colombian poetry during the 1930s and 1940s. The Spanish American "New Novel" of the 1940s was initiated unobtrusively in Colombia with the publication of three relatively unheralded novels: *La hojarasca* (*Leafstorm*; 1955) by García Márquez, *Respirando el verano* (Breathing the Summer; 1962) by Héctor Rojas Herazo, and *La casa grande* (The Big House; 1962) by Alvaro Cepeda Samudio. The phenomenon of La Violencia (The Violence), an undeclared civil war that resulted in over 100,000 deaths between 1948 and 1965, was Colombia's

most important political event of the twentieth century and had a powerful impact on literary production. The decade of the 1970s saw an upsurge of the novel and theater, both of which focussed on a reconsideration of La Violencia of the 1950s. Contemporary poetry was dominated by the Nadaístas (Nothingists) of the 1960s, followed by a more recent
generation of Posnadaístas (Postnothingists).

III

The coastal region has been geographically and culturally isolated
from the interior throughout Colombia's history. The region's key role
in African slave trade resulted in a cultural and racial makeup notably
different from the remainder of Colombia. The predominantly Hispanic
Bogotá has stood in contrast with the culturally heterogeneous and
markedly African coastal region. These cultural differences, in addition
to other geographical, political, and economic factors have resulted in
vital artistic and literary traditions that have generally been at a considerable aesthetic distance from the inland traditions.

During the Colonial period Cartagena was the major city of the
coast, followed by the small town of Santa Marta and the then village of
Barranquilla. With independence, Cartagena was left a city in ruins, and
its decadence continued throughout the ninteenth century. Barranquilla,
on the other hand, grew progessively throughout the nineteenth century
and became the largest metropolitan center by the beginning of the
twentieth. The first steamboats connected the coast to the interior in the
1830s via the Magdalena River, and this fluvial transportation made
Barranquilla the major exporter when the coffee from the interior became Colombia's principal export product from the 1880s to the present.
A train line from Bogotá to Santa Marta was also completed in the first
decade of the twentieth century. By the 1920s Barranquilla was a vibrant
modern city with an expanding middle class. Cartagena and Santa Marta
also grew significantly in the twentieth century.

Unlike the comparatively isolated and old-fashioned cultural traditions of Bogotá and Medellín, the Barranquilla of the twentieth century
was progressive, less traditional, and affected by foreign influences. Two
renowned coastal poets, Candelario Obeso (1849-84) and Luis Carlos
López (1883-1950) brought to Colombian verse colloquial language and
popular themes. Ramón Vinyes, a Spaniard from Catalonia, in effect
brought modern European literature and the latest avant-garde trends to

Colombia by publishing the cultural magazine *Voces* (Voices; 1917-20) in Barranquilla. During the 1940s and 1950s, the writer José Félix Fuenmayor (1885-1966) functioned as a literary father-figure for a group of young artists and intellectuals, later to be designated the Group of Barranquilla, which consisted of Gabriel García Márquez, Alvaro Cepeda Samudio (1926-72), Alfonso Fuenmayor (1927), and Germán Vargas (1919). The Barranquilla newspaper *El heraldo* (The Herald) has played a vital role in coastal culture since the 1940s, regularly publishing the writing of García Márquez and the other members of the group. During the last two decades Germán Vargas and *El heraldo* have been key elements in the diffusion of coastal literature in Colombia and maintaining an open and cosmopolitan attitude toward the contemporary cultural scene abroad.

As in all parts of Colombia during the nineteenth century, literary production on the coast was closely allied with the ruling elite and political power. Colombia's first novelist, Juan José Nieto (1804-66), from Cartagena, was also one of Colombia's major political and military leaders of the nineteenth century. His *Ingermina, o la hija de Calamar* (Ingermina, or the Child of Calamar; 1844) is generally considered the first novel to be published in Colombia. It is a historical novel set in the sixteenth century and dealing with the conquest of the Calamar Indians. Nieto also develops a love story and intercalates descriptions of local customs. *Los moriscos* (The Moors; 1845), Nieto's second novel, deals with the expulsion of the Moors from Spain. Both novels contain clichéd character portrayals, weakly developed plots, and simplistic narrative techniques. Rafael Núñez (1825-94), also from Cartagena, was President three times between 1880 and 1892. His fame as essayist and poet during the late nineteenth century was unquestionably due more to his political career than the aesthetic quality of his poetry, which was laden with the commonplaces of pseudoneoclassic and romantic poetry. Nevertheless, his verse was praised at the time by such writers as José Asunción Silva (see below) and Rubén Darío (see the section on Nicaragua).

Two poets from the coast whose work emanated from the region were Candelario Obeso and Luis Carlos López. Obeso was the first Colombian whose project was to write an authentic Afro-American poetry. He employed the everyday language of Afro-Americans on the coast in his one published book of poems, *Cantos populares de mi tierra* (Popular Songs of My Land; 1877). It is a book of simple language enriched with the colloquial speech patterns of a culture significantly different from the literary language of the Hispanic Romantic poetry that was the dominant literary mode of the time. Obeso was from Mompós, a river port town of splendor during the colonial period that fell into decadence when the Magdalena river changed its course. Obeso knew the local culture as well as the languages and literary traditions of the English, the French, and the Italians. Luis Carlos López was a product of Cartagena, and his poetry also grew out of local traditions, customs, and language. Most of his important poetry appeared between 1908 and 1920, beginning with *De mi villorio* (Of My Town; 1908), followed by *Posturas difíciles* (Difficult Postures; 1909) and *Por el atajo* (By the Short Cut; 1920). This is the period of Modernist and Postmodernist poetry in the Hispanic world, but López's verse is an antithesis to the preciousness and exoticism of Modernist verse. The themes of López's poetry are the objects and situations of everyday life in Cartagena—he likens his feelings for Cartagena, for example, to the comfort one senses wearing an old pair of shoes. He contributed a new element to Colombian poetry—humor. His humorous attitude and implicit reverence for the common man link his poetry to the later fiction of Gabriel García Márquez.

The tradition of Afro-American poetry initiated by Obeso continued in the twentieth century by Jorge Artel (1905). His most important work, *Tambores en la noche* (Drums in the Night; 1940), integrates folklore of the Afro-Caribbean culture, particularly the tone and rhythms of this culture's music. Artel's poetry contains less linguistic imitation than Obeso's and relies less on the nostalgic evocation of the local than López's work. The sea is a constant presence, both as theme and generator of rhythm in Artel's poetry.

The other major twentieth-century poets from this region are Gregorio Castañeda Aragón (1886) and Meira Delmar (pseud. of Olga Champs, 1921). Castañeda Aragón, from Santa Marta, wrote extensively from 1916 to 1959, publishing nine books of poetry, mostly dealing with popular themes and in a nostalgic tone. Meira Delmar of Barranquilla has written a poetry closely tied to the sea and her Middle Eastern heritage. Her books include *Alba del olvido* (Dawn of Forgetting; 1942), *Sitio del amor* (Place of Love; 1944), *Verdad del sueño* (Truth of Dreams; 1946), *Secreta isla* (Secret Island; 1951), *Huésped sin sombra* (Guest without Shadow; 1971), and *Poesía* (Poetry; 1981).

During the 1920s Barranquilla's new middle class was beginning to thrive and the appearance of the modern novel accompanied this change. The initiators were José Félix Fuenmayor and Manuel García Herreros (1894-1950). Both were of the generation of writers in Barranquilla who had witnessed the publication of the magazine *Voces*. Fuenmayor's novel *Cosme* (1927) is one of the most important (and least recognized) Colombian novels of the twentieth century. It played a key role in the development of modern fiction in Colombia as a direct predecessor to the new novel that would appear in the 1950s. *Cosme* is the story of a protagonist by this name and his life in Barranquilla. The irreverent attitude toward traditional institutions (including literary institutions), ironic tone and humor make *Cosme* an exception in comparison to the main trends of Colombian and Spanish American fiction of the time. The urban environment and alienated protagonist also make it quite distinctive. Fuenmayor's second novel, *Una triste aventura de 14 sabios* (A Sad Adventure of 14 Wise Men; 1928) is science-fiction dealing with a group of fourteen scholars and scientists who depart in a flying machine for an uninhabited island to carry out secret experiments. The earth expands enormously in size, but the travelers remain the same. Consequently, they return to find that what seems to them an enormous stone is a grain of sand. There is also a character who comments on this novel during the process of its development. The imaginative quality of *Una triste aventura de 14 sabios* is its outstanding feature and an important contribution to the coastal tradition.

García Herreros's relatively unknown novels, *Lejos del mar* (Far from the Sea; 1921) and *Asaltos* (Assaults; 1929), were more traditional than Fuenmayor's inventions. *Lejos del mar* is a short novel, narrated in first person, in which the protagonist nostalgically relates the story of a youth's maturation process in a small rural town. The most interesting feature of *Asaltos* is its setting in the coastal region of Barranquilla, Calamar, a town up the Magdalena River from Barranquilla.

The modern fiction initiated on the coast by José Félix Fuenmayor is continued on the coast by Alvaro Cepeda Samudio, Héctor Rojas Herazo (1921), and Gabriel García Márquez. They each began publishing their first writings by the early 1950s. García Márquez's first story, "La tercera resignación" (The Third Resignation; 1947), had surrealistic and Kafkian overtones and was rather amateurish. Nevertheless, his initial readings of Faulkner, Kafka, and other modern writers were evident in his early fiction; this background would become important in later years. Cepeda Samudio's first stories, *Todos estábamos a la espera* (We Were All Waiting; 1954), written in New York, are modern fictions with respect to narrative technique and deal with characters who, according to the author's preface, were observed in Alma, Michigan, waiting for a train into Chattanooga, and living in Ciénaga, Colombia. They are the product of a cosmopolitan writer who was obviously well-versed in the writings of Faulkner, Saroyan, and Capote.

García Márquez's *La hojarasca*, the initiator of the new novel in Colombia, is the Faulknerian story of an invented town called Macondo, based on García Márquez's hometown of Aracataca. The focus lies primarily on four characters: three persons in a family who narrate and a doctor whose wake is the basic circumstance of the novel. The most important event to take place in this small town during the quarter century of the main action (1903-28) is the arrival and departure of the "leafstorm"—the people and unbridled progress associated with an American banana company. The parallels with the United Fruit Company's presence on the coast of Colombia are obvious, although no company is named. The once innocent and rural town becomes a center for the chaos and corruption often linked with modernity. *La hojarasca* represents García Márquez's first novelistic attempt at creating an "other reality."

The two other initial modern novels were Cepeda Samudio's *La casa grande* and Rojas Herazo's *Respirando el verano*. *La casa grande* deals with the 1928 banana worker's strike on the coast, the same event that appears in García Márquez's *Cien años de soledad*. Cepeda Samudio changes narrative techniques in each of the novel's chapters, always contributing to the reader's appreciation of the total situation. *Respirando el verano* also reminds the reader of García Márquez and Faulkner. It is a family story that relates the decadence of a coastal town during the twentieth century. The town's decay is the result of civil war and the hatred of two brothers. Past events appear in no logical sequence, in typical Faulknerian fashion.

The culminating work for García Márquez and the most outstanding product of the coastal tradition is *Cien años de soledad*. It represents a culmination for García Márquez in the sense that each of his previous novels—*La hojarasca*, *El coronel no tiene quien le escriba* (*No One Writes to the Colonel*; 1961), and *La mala hora* (*In Evil Hour*; 1962)—had dealt with the characters and situations in Macondo that would appear later in *Cien años de soledad*. It is the story of the Buendía family and the story of Macondo. José Arcadio Buendía marries his cousin, Ursula, and they are the illustrious first generation of a prodigious seven-generation family. Because of their kinship, José Arcadio Buendía and Ursula, and all of their descendents, live with the threat and terror of engendering a child with a pig's tail. The novel can also be described as the story of Macondo, which progresses from a primitive village to a modern town, after the arrival of electricity, lights, and other twentieth-century conveniences. It also suffers the vicissitudes of Colombia's history, including its civil wars.

Cien años de soledad abounds in social and political implications. It tells much of the story of social and political life in Colombia and Latin America from the Colonial period to the present. It could well be that the most appropriate description of Colombia's history is in terms of the fantastic. García Márquez himself claims that he is basically a realist and that Latin American reality abounds in the fantastic. The already-mentioned conflicts between Liberals and Conservatives in nineteenth-century Colombia did indeed have characteristics of the incredible. Once Macondo is in communication with the rest of the nation, after Ursula's discovery of a route, it lives much of what was Colombia's nineteenth-century history.

Cien años de soledad communicates a panoply of experiences to a vast range of readers. Techniques for involving the reader and creating a total fictional universe make the novel highly experiential: the reading experience itself, the process, is as important as the intellectualization that often follows reading. Seen in retrospect, after the reading, the novel contains not only a criticism of Colombia's basic institutions, but also an affirmation of mankind, present in all of García Márquez's work. It is an affirmation based on an underlying, but constant, respect for the plight of the common man. This fundamental optimism is not found necessarily in individual or collective triumphs over the immediate social circumstance, but in a faith that the human spirit will allow humans to prevail with dignity, whatever the forces in opposition may be. García Márquez has also published a novel of a dictator, *El otoño del patriarca* (*The Autumn of the Patriarch*; 1975); a brief novel entitled *Crónica de una muerte anunciada* (*Chronicle of a Death Foretold*; 1981); and a love story, *El amor en los tiempos del cólera* (*Love in the Time of Cholera*; 1985).

The other work accompanying *Cien años de soledad* in this culmination of the coastal tradition is Rojas Herazo's *En noviembre llega el arzobispo* (The Archbishop Arrives in November; 1967). Rojas Herazo employs segmented narration to penetrate the character of the coastal region. By the 1970s coastal literature, including García Márquez's fiction, participates in more of a national and international than coastal tradition.

IV

Antioquia has not been as geographically isolated from the remainder of the nation as the Caribbean coast. Nevertheless, the region of greater Antioquia (including the present-day states of Caldas and Quindío) has been willfully independent of the rest of the Colombia and quite often in direct opposition to it. There was an indigenous population of approximately 600,000 in Antioquia at the time of the Conquest, but conflicts and disease rapidly reduced their numbers. The Antiochians of the colonial period lacked the capital necessary to bring African slaves from Cartagena. Consequently, gold seekers from Antioquia went searching as independent prospectors: many Spaniards, as well as later generations of Creoles, were thus forced into productive labor on their own account. This situation gave an early impetus to Antioquia's democratic tradition of work. The tradition of independence and democracy, however, did not contribute to Antioquia's cultural development during the colonial period. On the contrary, until the end of the colonial period most observers were struck by the general backwardness, illiteracy, and poverty of the province. The situation was decisively improved in the late eighteenth century when the Spanish crown commissioned Juan Antonio Mon y Velarde to carry out needed reforms. During the three years of his administration (1784-87), he directed a cultural and economic renaissance.

Antioquia's major city, Medellín, was founded in 1616, nearly a century later than Colombia's other major cities. During the first half of the nineteenth century it was nothing more than a traditional village. A key factor in its transformation was Antioquia's vastly increased coffee production from the 1880s and the foundation of the textile industry at the turn of the century. Nascent industrialization was indicated by Antioquia's ten factories in place by 1900.

Upon gaining independence, Antioquia did have a well-established intellectual elite like that of Bogotá, Popoyán, and Cartagena. Its literary production in the early nineteenth century consisted of an unimpressive set of political speeches, patriotic poetry, and parochial essays. Antioquia's most renowned poet, Gregorio Gutiérrez González (1826-72), led the typical life of the Antioquian landowner: he grew up in the country (in a small town, La Ceja), studied law in Bogotá, and later returned to his native province. While in Bogotá he wrote romantic poetry, and in 1866 published the lengthy and at times prosaic poem *Memorial científica sobre el cultivo del maíz en los climas cálidos del Estado de Antioquia por uno de los miembros de la Escuela de Ciencias; Artes; dedicado a la misma Escuela* (Scientific Memoire on the Cultivation of Corn in the Warm Climate of the State of Antioquia by One of the Members of the School of Sciences; Arts; Dedicated to the Same School). Written in the popular language of the region, it is a detailed and realistic description of the agriculture and land of Antioquia. This poem is also a celebration of working the land. Writing in a similar vein, Epifanio Mejía (1838-1913) did not publish books of his most traditional poetry until the twentieth century, beginning with *Poesías* (Poetry; 1902). It is Romantic verse that exalts the land and the figure of the poet who inhabits it. With respect to the *artículo de costumbres* (article on local customs), the most important writer of the period was Juan de Dios Restrepo (1823-94), who usually wrote under the pseudonym Emiro Kastos.

The economic growth of Antioquia in the late nineteenth century was accompanied by an outburst of literary production that has continued through the twentieth century. The first major Antioquian novelist, Tomás Carrasquilla (1858-1940), typifies the middle class Antioquian writer who did not belong to the elite that had dominated Colombian literature up to the twentieth century. Carrasquilla, who was of a modest background, produced Realist and Costumbrist fiction in considerable volume between 1896 and 1935. His three major novels were *Frutos de mi tierra* (Fruits of My Land; 1896), *Grandeza* (Greatness; 1910), and *La marquesa de Yolombó* (The Marquise of Yolombó; 1926). In contrast with the cosmopolitan tastes of the turn-of-the-century Modernistas—mostly elitist writers from Bogotá—Carrasquilla defended a Realist-Naturalist approach to the description of man in his environment. *Frutos de mi tierra* was his first novel of Antioquian customs, daily life, and speech. *Grandeza* depends primarily on the quaint character types chosen for portrayal, although it has a more intricate structure than most of the Costumbrista work of the period. Carrasquilla creates the impression of oral storytelling by using a loose and casual tone in *La marquesa de Yolombó*, a historical novel set in the late eighteenth and early nineteenth centuries. The Antioquian Baldomero Sanín Cano (1861-1957), one of Colombia's most distinguished essayists, described Antioquian literature of the period as follows: there was a literary tradition of that region that can be defined with a characteristic love for the land, the speech of the common people, and a tradition of equality and mutual respect. Novelist Samuel Velásquez (1865-1941) participated in this tradition. His first novel, *Madre* (Mother; 1897) describes a peasant's idealized passion for her lover, set in an ambience of strong Catholicism and the Antioquian countryside. Velásquez's other novels were *Al pie del Ruiz* (At the Foot of the Ruiz; 1898) and *Hija* (Daughter; 1904). Francisco de Paula Rendón (1855-1917), author of *Inocencia* (Innocence; 1904), wrote in the regionalist manner of Carrasquilla and Velásquez.

Literary language in Antioquia, dominated through the end of the nineteenth century by popular speech, was modified at the beginning of the twentieth by Porfirio Barba Jacob (pseudonym of Miguel Angel Osorio, 1883-1942). Traces of the language of Modernism in Barba Jacob's early poetry represented a break from the Antioquian tradition of popular literary language. His *En loor de los niños* (In Praise of Children; 1915), *Rosas negras* (Black Roses; 1935), and *La canción profunda y otros poemas* (The Profound Song and Other Poems; 1937) have some resonances from the Parnassian and Symbolist poets that Barba Jacob admired, but always express the particular voice of a language constantly weighted with the words *desolación* (desolation), *fúnebre* (funereal), and *muerte* (death).

The truly radical innovation of Colombian verse arrived in Antioquia not with Barba Jacob, however, but with León de Greiff (1895-1976), a key figure of the Los Nuevos group based primarily in Bogotá. Greiff had already explored avant-garde literature since the teens with his Panida group in Medellín, but two events in 1925 marked the beginning of the avant-garde in Antioquia: one was the publication of the magazine *Los nuevos* (The New Ones; 1925-?), organ of this new generation, and the other was the publication of León de Greiff's first book, *Tergiversaciones* (Distortions; 1925). In this book and *Libro de signos* (Book of Signs; 1930), León de Greiff created a new poetic language, completely renovating Colombian verse. Although León de Greiff did create his own exotic poetic worlds, the predominant element in his poetry was technical innovation. Language became an instrument for poetry and for music. Luis Vidales (1904) also contributed to the renovation of Colombian verse, bringing surrealism to Colombia with *Suenan timbres* (Bells Ring; 1926).

Antioquia also participated in the next generation's movement for a modern literature, that associated with the magazine *Mito* (Myth; 1955-62). Rogelio Echavarría was Antioquia's representative with *Mito*, virtually the only outlet for free creative expression published during the dictatorship of Rojas Pinilla during the 1950s. Rogelio Echavarría's direction as a poet was present from his first book, *Edad sin tiempo* (Age without Time; 1948): use of modern imagery, precise language, sobriety, and moderation.

The novel in twentieth-century Antioquia has generally been more traditional than has been the poetry of the likes of León de Greiff. During the 1920s and 1930s fiction of the regionalistic and social vein was predominant. Regionalistic works portraying Antioquian life were *Lejos del nido* (Far from the Nest; 1924) by Juan José Botero (1840-1946), *Cuentos espirituales* (Spiritual Stories; 1928) by Eduardo Arias Suárez (1896), *Por los caminos de la tierra* (On the Roads of the Land; 1928) by Adel López Gómez (1901), and the novel *David, hijo de Palestina* (David, Son of Palestine; 1931) by José Restrepo Jaramillo (1895-1926). Restrepo Jaramillo's *Ventarrón* (Windstorm; published posthumously in 1984) is both a novel of a youth's maturation and a celebration of the traditional Antioquian values of independence and hard work. Novelists with explicitly social themes were César Uribe Piedrahita (1897-1951), Rafael Jaramillo Arango (1896-1953), and Bernardo Arias Trujillo (1903-38). Uribe Piedrahita's *Toá* (1933) deals with the exploitation of rubber workers in the Colombian jungle bordering Peru and *Mancha de aceite* (Oil Stain; 1935) concerns injustice perpetrated in the petroleum industry in Colombia. Jaramillo Arango's *Barrancabermeja* (1934) is a denunciation of foreign and national exploitation of the petroleum industry workers. *Risaralda* by Bernardo Arias Trujillo is a story of the plight of Afro-Americans in Colombia, whereas Jesús Botero Restrepo's (1921) *Andágueda* (1947) deals with social problems within the context of indigenous culture.

Two important figures of traditional prose fiction in Antioquia were Francisco Gómez Escobar (1873-1938), known in Colombia as "Efe" Gómez, and Arturo Echeverría Mejía (1918-64). Gómez Escobar is considered the initiator of the short story in Colombia, and had four volumes of stories published posthumously. Echeverría Mejía published five novels, and his *Marea de ratas* (Tide of Rats; 1960) is a novel of La Violencia.

Fiction in the Antioquian tradition culminates with the novels of Manuel Mejía Vallejo (1923). His most accomplished work, *El día señalado* (The Appointed Day; 1964), represents a successful synthesis of various elements outlined in his previous stories and novels. The first truly modern novel to be published in Antioquia, *El día señalado,* contains two story lines: a third-person narration of a town and the presence of unwelcome government troops, and a first-person story of personal vengeance. The general setting is La Violencia in Antioquia, but this is one of few aesthetically successful novels published in any region of Colombia dealing with this subject. As the culminating work in the Antioquian tradition, it is a synthesis of the popular language typical of Antioquian fiction, and the language and structure of the Spanish American new novel. The writers of the generations following Mejía Vallejo, such as Darío Ruiz Gómez (1936) and Darío Jaramillo Agudelo (1947), are as much Colombian and Spanish American in language, theme, and technique as Antioquian.

V

Bogotá and the region surrounding it have been privileged cultural centers since the colonial period and dominant in all aspects of literary production since independence. "Culture" in this region's context refers to the literary culture produced by the ruling elite since the colonial period: the region's indigenous population was decimated and highland culture has been strictly Hispanic. Bogotá and Tunja were centers of literary activity during the colonial period. Juan de Castellanos was named a priest in 1562 in Tunja, where he remained the rest of his life. In the seventeenth century there were renowned poetry contests (*certámenes poéticos*) in Tunja. With the influence of the Jesuits and Dominicans, literary culture flourished in the monasteries and universities of Tunja and Bogotá. Tunja would not grow into a major city after independence, and Bogotá, self-styled "Athens of South America," would multiply in population but remain culturally isolated.

Bogotá demonstrated initial signs of reception of ideas current in the West in the second half of the eighteenth century, as has been noted in the previous discussion of José Celestino Mutis, the first *tertulias* (literary soirées), and the *Papel periódico*. Bogotá's position as an intellectual center in the nineteenth century was evidenced by the publication of magazines such as *El alacrán* (The Scorpion; 1848-?) and *El mosaico* (The Mosaic; ca. 1860s), a seminal literary organ founded and directed by José María Vergara y Vergara. *El mosaico* was important not only for what it published, but also because of the fact that it brought together writers of different tendencies, providing a certain support to national literature.

The late nineteenth and early twentieth centuries were a period of conflict, growth, and the initial modernization of Bogotá. The civil war of 1884-85 resulted in the ratification of Colombia's sixth and permanent constitution of 1886, which reflected the power of the Conservatives, proclaiming the Catholic religion, for example, the official national religion. Industrialization was marked by the foundation of the brewery Cervecería Bavaria in 1891. By the turn of the century Bogotá's population was 120,000 and it had twelve factories, making it the population and industrial center of Colombia. Literary tendencies at the turn of the century reflected both the conservative hegemony and the modernization process. Conservatism was evidenced in the Neoclassic humanism in the writings of Miguel Antonio Caro (1843-1909), Rufino José Cuervo (1844-1911), and President Marco Fidel Suárez (1855-1927). Writers more in step with their Modernist contemporaries outside Colombia were José Asunción Silva (1865-96), Víctor M. Londoño (1876-1936), and later Eduardo Castillo (1889-1933).

During the twentieth century Bogotá and the highland region have been the center of major poetic movements—Los Nuevos, Piedra y Cielo, Mito, and Nadaísmo—as well as being the origin of the novelists José María Vargas Vila (1860-1933), Clímaco Soto Borda (1870-1919), Eduardo Zalamea Borda (1907-63), Tomás Vargas Osorio (1908-41), José A. Osorio Lizarazo (1900-64), and Eduardo Caballero Calderón (1910).

The Costumbrism already noted in Antioquia (Juan de Dios Restrepo, Tomás Carrasquilla) proliferated in the highland area. José María Vergara y Vergara and José María Samper (1828-88) were its main exponents. Vergara y Vergara's sketches were less important than his contribution to Colombian literature as an essayist and as publisher of *El mosaico*. Nevertheless, he penned a famous sketch titled "Las tres tazas" (The Three Cups; date unknown) ridiculing the customs associated with social reunions in Bogotá—detailing the change from chocolate in 1813 to coffee in 1848 to tea in 1865. His short novel *Olivos y aceitunas todos son unos* (Olives and Olive Trees Are All the Same; 1868) was a criticism of the local government and its politicians. José María Samper wrote local-color sketches, novels of customs, essays, and theater. Samper published no one outstanding work, but his overall production offered a vision and criticism of society in Bogotá during the second half of the century.

The nineteenth-century novelists of customs included Eugenio Díaz (1804-65), Luis Segundo de Silvestre (1838-87), Soledad Acosta de Samper (1833-1913), José Manuel Groot (1800-78), and José Manuel Marroquín (1827-1908). Eugenio Díaz's *Manuela* (1858) first appeared in Vergara y Vergara's *El mosaico* and contained numerous descriptions of the local setting and customs of the town and region. Nevertheless, it was an early example of the rural social protest novel and, unlike the provincial novels of customs, was national in vision. Díaz demonstrated a concern for not just the local scene, but also for the direction of the nation and national politics, ridiculing the protagonist's radical liberalism. Segundo de Silvestre's *Tránsito* (1886) better fits the typical mold of the rural novel of customs: its sentimental plot is regularly interrupted with description of local color, such as holiday festivities and popular folk dances. At times the plot appears to be a mere pretext for describing customs. Acosta de Samper published several novels, ranging from descriptions of customs to historical pieces, including *Los piratas en Cartagena* (The Pirates in Cartagena; 1886) and *Una holandesa en América* (A Dutch Woman in America; 1888). José María Groot (1864-1923) published sketches, literary criticism, poetry, and several novels, including *Resurección* (Resurrection; 1902) and *El triunfo de la vida* (The Triumph of Life; 1916). José Manuel Marroquín published several novels with ample descriptions of different regions of Colombia. His best novel, *El moro* (The Moor; 1897), consists of the memories of a horse, but is typical of nineteenth-century novels written by the landed aristocracy: the main point is the opposition between nature and a degrading modernity.

Nineteenth-century poetic language in the highlands was dominated by the romantic verse of Rafael Pombo (1833-1912). Pombo was a prolific poet whose language developed and changed over the second half of the nineteenth century. This early poetry, written at midcentury, is simple and sentimental. A broader cultural background, including residence in the United States, an acquaintance with English poets, and the study of the classics later resulted in a heterogeneous poetry, both in form and content. Nevertheless, this poetry, as well as Pombo's last poems, written mostly in sonnets, is basically romantic in tone. Joaquín González Camargo (1865-86) also wrote romantic poetry, published posthumously as *Poesías* (Poetry; 1889).

Miguel Antonio Caro and José Asunción Silva were representatives of opposite tendencies of poetic language at the turn of the century in Bogotá. Caro was the central figure, with Rufino José Cuervo and Marco Fidel Suárez, in the humanist movement strongly rooted in Hispanic and classic tradition. Caro's poetry is one of ideas rather than emotion; his odes and sonnets often have the academic tone to be expected of the translator of Virgil and scholarly essayist Caro was. His poetic production included five books of poetry whose sources were the classic poets. Silva, in contrast, had as his sources Baudelaire, Verlaine, Rimbaud, Poe, and other nineteenth-century Europeans. Silva's poetic language is vague and musical. To say he was a Modernist would be appropriate only with the understanding of his distance from Rubén Darío (about whom Silva wrote a satire; see the section on Nicaragua), and the very personal tone of his verse. Silva died at the age of thirty-one with relatively little of his poetry known or appreciated in Colombia. His *Poesías* (Poetry) appeared posthumously in 1908.

The most important highland representative of the group of Los Nuevos was Germán Pardo García (1902) who was educated in Bogotá and then spent most of his life in Mexico. Like Greiff and Vidales, Pardo García contributed an entirely new poetic vocabulary, a fact that is particularly evident when compared with his Modernist predecessors. An indefatigable creator, he published some thirty books, the first of poetry being *Voluntad* (Will; 1930). Cosmic metaphors, existential anguish, and the horrors of modernity are characteristics of his poetry from the 1930s through the 1950s.

During the mid-1930s the Piedra y Cielo group of poets began to establish an identity in Bogotá. Arturo Camacho Ramírez (1910), Eduardo Carranza (1913), Tomás Vargas Osorio, Jorge Rojas, and Darío Samper (1913) were members of a group that found its roots in Gerardo Diego's celebrated anthology *Poesía española* (Spanish Poetry), first published in 1932. Between 1935 and 1940 these young Colombian poets effected an extraordinary renovation of Colombian poetry, using as their models the Spaniards Juan Ramón Jiménez and Federico García Lorca and the Chilean Pablo Neruda (see the section on Chile). Of lesser importance for them were the Spaniards Jorge Guillén, Pedro Salinas, Rafael Alberti, and Vicente Aleixandre. The two key publications to establish the group's direction were Arturo Camacho Ramírez's *Espejo de naufragios* (Mirror of Castaways; 1935) and Eduardo Carranza's *Canciones para iniciar una fiesta* (Songs to Initiate Festivities; 1936). These two books contain the two general directions of the group: Camacho Ramírez is the avant-garde poet identified with Colombia; Carranza is the Spaniard and traditionalist. It was a poetry that eventually became associated with a world of metaphors—the search of metaphor for the sake of metaphor—without reference to concrete objects or emotion.

Some ten years later, in the mid-1940s, a group consisting of Fernando Charry Lara (1920), Alvaro Mutis (1923), Eduardo Mendoza Varela (1918), and others became identified with the name Cántico (Canticle), named after Jorge Guillén's 1928 book of that title. Unlike the Piedra y Cielo group, it did not have enough uniformity to allow generalization. Charry Lara, the most outstanding poet of the group, was inspired by

Vicente Aleixandre and wrote poetry with nocturnal and dream settings. Some of his poems were traditional verse and others free verse and prose poems.

The poets associated with the magazine *Mito* were the dominant force in the 1950s: Jorge Gaitán Durán (1924-62), Eduardo Cote Lemus (1928-64), Carlos Obregón (1929-65), Carlos Castro Saavedra (1924), Julio José Fajardo (1919), Dora Castellanos (1925), Jorge Eliécer Ruiz (1931), and Octavio Gamboa (1923). Gaitán Durán and Hernando Valencia Goelkel founded *Mito* in 1955 with the following statement as a kind of doctrine for the generation: "Words are in their situation. It would be vain to demand for them univocal or ideal position. . . . In order to accept them in their ambiguity, we need words *to be*." According to Gaitán Durán, it was a group more influenced by Marx, Freud, and Sartre, and interested in Jorge Luis Borges (see the section on Argentina), Alain Robbe-Grillet, Henry Miller, and Jean Genet. The poetry of this group situated itself among such foreign poets as Octavio Paz (see the section on Mexico), Vicente Aleixandre, Carlos Drummond de Andrade (see the section on Brazil), and Alfonso Reyes (see the section on Mexico). The generation of *Mito* was short-lived as a group because of the premature deaths of two of its best poets, Gaitán Durán and Cote Lemus.

The twentieth-century novel in the highland region was the fiction of official literary language, as opposed to the popular traditions of Antioquia and the oral traditions on the Caribbean coast. In ideological terms, the novels and political positions of José Manuel Marroquín and Angel Cuervo conserved the traditional. Lorenzo Marroquín (1856-1918) and José María Rivas Groot (1863-1923) coauthored *Pax* (1907), a novel criticized by conservatives (because they were satirized in it), but which nevertheless fulfilled the patriotic function of much conservative turn-of-the-century fiction.

The iconoclast during these years of Conservative political and literary hegemony was Vargas Vila. Author of over thirty novels and other writings, Vargas Vila was a vociferous opponent of the institutional Catholic church. Many of his novels were openly anticlerical. Vargas Vila's often ungrammatical language placed him squarely in opposition to the conservative grammarians Caro and Cuervo. The aesthetic quality of Vargas Vila's novels was uneven, but his most successful works were *Flor de fango* (Flower of Mud; 1895), *Ibis* (1900), *La caída del Cóndor* (The Fall of the Condor; 1913), *María Magdalena* (Mary Magdalene; 1917), *El huerto de silencio* (The Garden of Silence; 1917), *Salomé*

(1918), *Vuelo de cisnes* (Swan Flight; 1919), and *La novena sinfonía* (The Ninth Symphony; 1928). Never accepted by the conservative ruling elite during the first decades of the century, Vargas Vila was more popular abroad than in Colombia. Another writer with extravagant aesthetic tastes, Soto Borda published *Polvo y ceniza* (Dust and Ash; 1906), a volume of stories printed with blue letters and type running the long dimension of the page. In addition, he wrote *Diana cazadora* (Diana the Huntress; 1915), a satire of the Modernists.

By the 1930s Bogotá was rapidly expanding into a modern industrial center. At the same time it was suffering its worst economic crises of the twentieth century. José A. Osorio Lizarazo became the writer of the proletariat whose fiction arose out of this crisis of a changing society. It was also a period in which Colombia's workers began to develop a sense of class consciousness for the first time. In *La casa de vecindad* (The Apartment House; 1930), Osorio Lizarazo presents a narrator-protagonist's futile attempts to understand a technological society too complex for him. Each of Osorio Lizarazo's dozen novels communicates a proletarian impulse, even though the ideological implications of this fiction are not consistent. His political positions are clearly delineated, for example, in *La cosecha* (The Harvest; 1935) and *Hombres sin presente* (Men without Present; 1938). *La cosecha* is a protest against the socioeconomic structure of the coffee industry. In *Hombres sin presente* the author defends the exploited laborer and sets forth an explanation of the worker's power to strike. In other novels, such as *El criminal* (The Criminal; 1938) and *El hombre bajo la tierra* (Man below Ground; 1944), Osorio Lizarazo's stance as a proletarian writer is not as clearly articulated. *El criminal* is a documentary-type account of the protagonist's degenerating health as a consequence of syphilis. Osorio Lizarazo implicitly praises a male-dominated society by exalting the values of a masculine work ethic in *El hombre bajo la tierra*. These two novels are the least ideologically convincing of Osorio Lizarazo's total proletarian fiction.

Zalamea Borda demonstrates interest in aesthetic concerns rather than ideological stances in *Cuatro años a borde de mí mismo*. (Four Years with Myself; 1934). It relates the journey of a youth from Bogotá to the coastal Guajira area. Modernity and technology function here not to demonstrate the circumstance of the proletariat, but to contrast the folkloric rural culture of the coast and the technological urban culture of Bogotá. The focus is on an individual's transition into manhood.

Highland novelistic production participates in a venerable tradition of written culture that ranges in ideological content from the conservative writings of the turn-of-the-century grammarians to the proletarian novels of Osorio Lizarazo. The culmination of this highland tradition of literature informed by written culture is to be found in the fiction of Eduardo Caballero Calderón. He belongs to an elitist family that has been a large landowner in Boyacá since 1560. Caballero Calderón is to be located squarely within the highland's conservative Hispanic tradition: his very first published piece was in homage to Marco Fidel Suárez, recently deceased conservative president and last vestige, in the political sphere, of turn-of-the-century conservative humanism. Caballero Calderón was named a regular member of the Academia Colombiana de la Lengua in 1944, and in 1945 he compiled a volume of studies, *Cervantes en Colombia* (Cervantes in Colombia). Thereafter he was a journalist for *El tiempo* and published short stories and a total of ten novels, including *El Cristo de espaldas* (Christ Supine; 1952), *Siervo sin tierra* (Serf without Land; 1954), *Manuel Pacho* (1962), *El buen salvaje* (The Good Savage; 1966), and *Caín* (1966). The culminating novel in the highland's tradition of Hispanic written culture is *El buen salvaje*, a novel that has as its theme, appropriately enough, writing. The protagonist is a young Colombian novelist who resides in Paris, where he attempts to write a novel. It is a story of literary ambitions that satirizes Latin American intellectuals abroad. The protagonist writes of his experiences in Paris and about the plans for his excessively ambitious novel. The proposed masterpiece changes in focus according to the protagonist's immediate circumstances, including historical, Biblical, political, and Realist types of fiction. Even though *El buen salvaje* is a successful novel in itself, it also functions as a metaphor for an intellectually pretentious highland culture that has never produced the outstanding novels of Colombia it would seem to promise.

VI

Greater Tolima, which includes the region of present-day Huila, has been closely allied with Bogotá economically and the highland tradition culturally. The reasons for this economic and cultural attachment have been multifold. The road between Bogotá and Honda (in Tolima) has always served as the connecting land bridge for all river traffic from the Magdalena River destined for Bogotá. Railroad connection from Bogotá to Girardot and Puerto Salgar was also vitally important. During times of economic stagnation in the highlands, Bogotá's oligarchy has sometimes taken land in the fertile *tierra caliente* (hot lowlands) of Tolima to undertake a financial recovery. Tolima has been traditionally connected commercially with the highlands. And, culturally, Tolima has looked to the "Athens of South America" as a model and center of intellectual activity.

Literary tradition in Tolima has involved a predominant written culture and has been a part of the highland model. The Tolima region has never had a truly cosmopolitan center: it was one of Colombia's most sparsely populated areas at the independence, and at the turn of the twentieth century Tolima's population of 440,000 was less than half that of departments such as Antioquia or Cauca. Even though its two major cities, Ibagué and Neiva, were founded in the sixteenth and seventeenth centuries respectively, neither has ever been a major industrial or cultural center in the national panorama. Each founded a *colegio* (secondary professional school) for the local elite in the nineteenth century. The two major writers born in Tolima, José María Samper and José Eustasio Rivera (1889-1928), were associated with both this region and Bogotá. Samper, already mentioned as an important participant in the highland tradition, was born in Honda, where he lived his youth. A consummate man of letters, Samper published voluminously. As a literary phenomenon in himself and as part of the inner circle of Bogotá's *El mosaico*, Samper was the product and producer par excellence of the oligarchy's written culture in nineteenth-century Tolima and the highland.

In the first quarter of the twentieth century José Eustasio Rivera also went from Tolima to Bogotá to assume a role comparable to Samper's: Rivera's hyperaestheticism was matched by Samper's hyperproductivity. Even though Rivera's parents were not among the most wealthy of the elite, he belonged to a family of the landowning elite active and powerful in the politics of the region now known as Huila. His early training and career were typical of the highland's *letrados* (learned men) since the colonial period: he was educated in a private *colegio*, began a career at the age of sixteen as an *escribiente* (scribe) in the government bureaucracy, studied later in the National University in Bogotá, and during his adulthood dedicated himself to intellectual pursuits after having taught in the Colegio de San Simón in Ibagué. Analysis of the function of the narrator and the author in *La vorágine* (The Vortex; 1924) demonstrates that Rivera was concerned with his role as intellectual in Colombian society when he wrote this classic novel in Colombian literature.

The narrator-protagonist in *La vorágine*, Arturo Cova, has been described by numerous critics as a Romantic poet. Certainly much of the text supports such a characterization, but it is only a partial portrayal of the total person. Cova also has many qualities of the decadent intellectual. But in reality, Cova is neither demented nor unreliable, and the characterization as Romantic poet/decadent intellectual is quite limiting. These are characterizations that the narrator purposely projects in order to create the image of a writer. The reader observes a patently literary character creating a self-consciously "literary" text—an explicitly arranged writing.

The first matter to consider, then, is Cova's supposedly "demented" character. His relationships with women and reactions to his surroundings do indeed seem to point to unorthodox behavior. Given the social context, his decision to flee Bogotá with Alicia is not totally reasonable. What is unique about Cova's irrationality and instability, however, is its self-consciousness. Cova himself often qualifies his actions as irrational and his thoughts as malevolent. Consequently, he should be interpreted as a narrator who employs a series of strategies in order to fulfill his characterization as writer.

The predominant subject is not a fictional world projecting a simulacrum of 1924 rural Colombia—with its vacuous women and bedraggled workers—but rather the self in the process of writing. Lacking traditional subject matter, Cova's most fully developed and central subject is writing: its dynamism is found in the narrator's striving for a form of written expression. The narrator exploits his subject matter of writing by making a drama of the very act of writing itself. The fictional character named José Eustasio Rivera initiates this drama in the prologue that has as its preeminent subject matter neither Arturo Cova nor the unjust life of the rubber workers, but a manuscript. In the final sections of the novel the real drama is not Cova's struggle with nature, because neither he as person nor nature has sufficiently important fictional status. Rather, the tension involves Cova's completion of his writing. Since he has acquired his status as writer and his text's status as an act of writing, the only question remaining is the novel's dénouement as fiction: precisely how will the text be completed and under what circumstances? This drama involves Cova's mental condition under adverse conditions in the jungle. He also explains the mechanics of this text's development with some regularity. Near the end the threats to his life increase, but he defends himself: the text survives and he continues to make progress on it. At the end of Cova's writing, the drama of the text culminates in its being left for Clemente Silva. Cova concludes: "it is our story, the desolate story of the rubber workers. So many pages left blank, so many things left unsaid." The "unsaid" portion would indeed be the story of the rubber workers, which had been told only by Clemente Silva as a sidelight to Cova's obsessive focus upon himself. The news in the epilogue of Cova's death, devoured by the jungle, is of little consequence: the writer has disappeared, as had been promised in the prologue, but his writing has survived.

The roles of the author, the novel, and the reading public were still in many ways undefined in Colombia in 1924. It is appropriate to note, for example, that the first editon of *La vorágine* included a supposed photograph of the protagonist, Arturo Cova. *La vorágine* is a text about writing—its ambiguities and contradictions are all part of a text striving to attain the status of a written text. Despite the often-repeated assertion that all these early twentieth-century novels were simply variations on the same theme of "they were devoured by the jungle," *La vorágine* does not play out this pattern in a significant way. The real drama is not the death of Cova or anyone else, but rather the survival of the text. As such, *La vorágine* represents the expression of a now-mature written culture, despite its ambiguous status in society, in the Tolima and highland regions.

The major sociopolitical event to affect writing in Tolima after Rivera was the period of civil war, particularly intense during the 1950s, of La Violencia. The Tolima region was a principal focus of conflict. La Violencia produced a vast literature, to a large extent personal accounts of human suffering, vivid in imagery but generally mediocre as aesthetic experience. One outstanding exception to this generalization was *El jardín de las Hartmann* (The Garden of the Hartmanns; 1978) by Jorge Eliécer Pardo (1945), a well-wrought short novel dealing with the historical period of La Violencia in Tolima. The violent conflict appears in a relatively abstract fashion, without attaching political parties or historical names to the events. Pardo universalizes the conflict by creating a parallel between La Violencia and the anti-Nazi resistance in Germany.

The novels of Héctor Sánchez (1941) represent a culmination of Tolima's predominantly written culture: it is self-conscious fiction. Each of Sánchez's six novels is located in a small town in Sánchez's native Tolima. They are accounts of the futility and frustration of life in the *tierra caliente* of Tolima. Both *Las maniobras* (The Manoeuvers; 1969) and *Las causas supremas* (The Supreme Causes; 1969), his first two novels, demonstrate an explicit self-conscious play with language. The result is a humorous questioning of his own discourse: the narrator always maintains an ironic attitude about language itself. Sánchez's writing is a nihilistic process of constructing and destroying language. In *Sin nada entre las manos* (Empty Hands; 1976) the characters openly criticize language, questioning its inevitable emptiness and inefficacy as a mode of communication. *El tejemaneje* (The Clever One; 1979) offers the same playful and cynical attitudes present in the previous novels.

The Tolima region has had a relatively weak tradition in the production of poetry. One of the few twentieth-century poets from Tolima of national import, Jorge Ernesto Leiva (born in Ibagué in 1937), lived the experience of La Violencia in Tolima. His early poetry, *No es una canción* (It Isn't a Song; 1959), reflects this experience. Leiva's later contact with foreign cultures in France, China, and Sweden has resulted in a poetry less directly rooted in his native history and cultural traditions.

VII

The Western Valley, centered in the Valle del Cauca, but including Popayán to the south and Chocó to the north, has developed in a tradition of cultural heterogeneity. Since the colonial period Popayán has been a bastion of a conventional and elitist written culture, similar to Bogotá and well-connected with Bogotá and Spain. The Jesuits founded the University of San José in Popoyán in 1774. The Valle del Cauca, with Cali as its largest city, has had both the influence of an opulent aristocracy and the populist forces represented by the minority African population and the Antioquian pioneers who settled parts of the Valle del Cauca in the nineteenth and twentieth centuries. The Chocó region, geographically and culturally isolated, and sparsely inhabited, has been a stronghold of African traditions with relatively little production of written culture. Nevertheless, the novelist Arnoldo Palacios (1924) is from Chocó. Chocó was opened to mining in the eighteenth century, even though small settlements were established as early at the sixteenth century, the first being in 1575 in Toro. Popoyán was founded in 1535 and Cali in 1536.

The region's vast expanses of abundant land, fertile for agriculture and rich in minerals for mining, have afforded the region economic prosperity. The Valle del Cauca is one of only three regions in the world that can produce sugar year round. Wealthy families of the Valle del Cauca's large land-owning elite, with last names like Caicedo, Garcés, and Lourido, were prosperous and politically powerful during the seventeenth and eighteenth centuries. Cali had an aristocracy that considered itself "noble." Slavery was also practiced in the region by the eighteenth century, with African slaves being brought from Cartagena and sold primarily in Popayán and Chocó, although some of Cali's elite also owned slaves.

The Valle del Cauca's heterogeneity was stimulated throughout the nineteenth century because the region was virtually an obligatory stopover place for soldiers during the continuous civil wars. These wars caused a devastating instability, even for the landowners, as was evidenced in the saying from the period, "He who lost the war, lost the plantation." Nevertheless, during the second half of the nineteenth century the first large sugar plantations were developed in the Valle del Cauca. During the decade of the 1920s Cali, like most of Colombia's major cities, underwent a process of modernization. The train line connecting Cali to the port city of Buenaventura, completed in 1915, was an important predecessor to this transformation. Modern technology for sugar refining was brought to the Valle del Cauca in the 1920s. The clearest indicator of Cali's industrialization was the presence of seventy-seven factories in 1930, compared to only one at the turn of the century. The outstanding factor in the region's twentieth century was the ferocity of La Violencia, particularly in Tulu and Caicedonia.

The Western Valley region has had a stronger tradition in poetry than Tolima, although not as significant as that of the highland or Antioquia. It is a tradition initiated with the poetry of Jorge Isaacs (1837-95) and continued with the work of Guillermo Valencia (1873-1943), Rafael Maya (1897-1983), Mario Carvajal (1896-1966), Antonio Llanos (1905), Gerardo Valencia (1911), and Octavio Gamboa (1923). Isaacs's poetry represented a minor contribution to Colombian Romanticism, whereas Valencia was not only one of the Western Valley's major poets, but a Modernista poet of national and international recognition. Rafael Maya, originally from Popoyán, was an active member of Los Nuevos in Bogotá, in addition to being one of Colombia's most erudite poetry critics. Maya belonged to the humanist highland-centered tradition of Miguel Antonio Caro, Marco Fidel Suárez, Antonio Gómez Restrepo (dates unknown), and Luis López de Mesa. Mario Carvajal published a book of sonnets of mystical orientation, *La escala de Jacob* (Jacob's Ladder; 1935), and three other books of traditional poetry. Gerardo Valencia of Popayán was a minor poet of the Piedra y Cielo group. Antonio Llanos of Cali was of this group's generation, but was not associated with it and neither his mystical writing nor his poetry of the sea were in line with the

Piedra y Cielo poetry. Octavio Gamboa, whose work has gone relatively unrecognized, has written in the traditon of Carvajal and Llanos and published one book, *Canciones y elegías* (Songs and Elegies; 1963).

Poets like Carvajal, Llanos, and Gamboa represent a voice particular to a Western Valley tradition, apart from the central literary movements of the highlands. The novel in the Western Valley also has always had a strong tradition of its own, influenced by an amalgam of cultural and historical forces of oral and written culture, and quite independent from the highlands. Isaacs's *María* (1867), the major Colombian novel of the nineteenth century, is representative of the Western Valley's verbal-ideological complexity, but is predominantly a product of Isaacs's participation in an elitist written culture. His family belonged to the Valle del Cauca's upper class, and he associated with Bogota's intellectuals of *El mosaico* in the 1860s before writing *María* from 1864 to 1866, isolated in the mountains back in the Valle del Cauca. The result was a Romantic love story set in the lush Valle del Cauca of Isaacs's childhood. The basic narrative situation is as follows: an adult narrator relates in retrospective fashion the story of his adolescent love affair with María. The narrative is a chronological reconstruction of the events and feelings of the moment. A dedication to "Efraín's brothers" suggests that an unidentified editor made the text on the basis of Efraín's memoirs. There are few deviations from Isaacs's basic method. These variations appear in the form of interruptions in which the narrator reacts to these past events in the emotional framework of the present. In addition, there is a variation in the narrator's distance from the fictional world he describes: in the majority of the novel he reacts intimately to the natural world to which he belongs; during the return trip he describes a new land with more distance.

Many critics have either questioned the unity of *María* or attempted to demonstrate how Isaacs has successfully created a unified text. Seen in the context of a heterogeneous verbal-ideological world, *María* becomes less dependent on issues such as unity. Rather, this novel can be seen as a complex network of relationships between the protagonist Efraín, his parents, and María that set up a tension between the fulfillment and the sublimation of desire. The Oedipal structure is played out in both the most basic model involving the father, the son, and the mother triangle, in addition to certain variations involving substitutions. The horror of mother-son separation is announced in the first lines of the novel and repeated constantly in the first chapter. The first line deals specifically with the protagonist's separation from home. The remainder of the chapter deals with the emotional trauma involved with this separation. The characterization of María in the initial chapters also emphasizes separation—the loss of her family. More specifically, in the sixth chapter the narrator explains the family history that resulted in María's loss of her parents in the Antilles and being sent to Colombia to live with her uncle's family. Separation from the mother will remain an underlying threat and consequently functions as part of the Oedipal structure throughout the novel.

An understanding of Efraín's performance with respect to his mother depends upon the already-established association between the mother and María. This relationship is created from the first chapter, which ends with the image of María standing among the flowers adorning the mother's bedroom. In opposition to the father's rigid control over the triangle, the mother encourages Efraín's repressed and feeble initiatives. For example, after the father has fixed stern regulations to control Efraín's relationship with María, the mother communicates her disapproval to the son. The isolation from María has been too extreme, according to the mother. It is too excessive to permit the symbolic incest. At the end of the novel Efraín's relationship with his mother, despite his age and experience, is still of mother-child.

The relationship with María, of course, is considerably more elaborated in the text. The protagonist evokes images of María at the outset that associate her with the joy of childhood. She is also characterized as a mother figure, as has been discussed. The characterization of María is closely allied with nature and the evocation of sensorial images. Consequently, Efraín's emotional response to his physical surroundings is part of his sensitivity to the love relationship.

María is an impressively well-conceived and written novel not only for its period in the context of the Western Valley, but even in a Latin American context. This fact speaks well for the development of written culture in the Western Valley. A certain level of unity and dualities attests to Isaacs's mastery of the craft of fiction. An analysis of his characterization reveals a protagonist who is far from the unified personality that the unified text would require. The superficial psychic coherence of the type Efraín maintains involves a crippling of desire. He operates as the eternal child, even within the rigid and traditional nineteenth-century societal structures within which he plays out his role.

Isaacs's novel was a product of a written culture for consumption, generally speaking, by the same elite that produced it. Popular literary culture was also present in the Western Valley during the turn of the century and it had its roots in oral tradition. The creators of this popular literature were poets who were by definition "minor," such as Pedro Antonio Uribe (1854-1934). Uribe's simple verses and sonnets were written for popular consumption on the street corners of Tuluá, a town in the Valle del Cauca north of Cali. Uninterested in the classic themes of much written culture, Uribe wrote a light verse concerned with the topics of daily life in Tuluá and other nearby towns. His poems often functioned as newspapers, related orally for an illiterate populace. Consequently, they constitute an unofficial oral history of the region, published posthumously as *Los juglares de Tuluá: Don Pedro Uribe* (The Tuluá Minstrals: Don Pedro Uribe; 1934).

The oral tradition of Uribe and the popular vision communicated by its frequent use of *dizque* ("it's said") are integral elements of the fiction of the Western Valley's major twentieth-century writer, Gustavo Alvarez Gardeazábal (1945). Alvarez Gardeazábal himself has written of his indebtedness to Uribe. In addition, Alvarez Gardeazábal began writing after the publication of García Márquez's novel of the coastal oral tradition, *Cien años de soledad*, which had exercised an enormous influence on all literary production in Colombia since 1967.

Alvarez Gardeazábal's first four novels were deeply rooted in the history and oral tradition of the Valle del Cauca, primarily of Tuluá. His first two novels, *La tara del papa* (The Pope's Defect; 1971) and *Cóndores no entierran todos los días* (Condors Don't Bury Everyday; 1972), are set within the historical context of La Violencia in the Valle del Cauca. *Cóndores no entierran todos los días* relates the story of a local caudillo who terrorized the Tuluá region during La Violencia, León María Lozano. Both the author's and the narrator's source of information for this story is popular knowledge—the rumor and history that were the essence of Pedro Uribe's poetry. The popular vision of individual lives in a small town is also the primary generator of the anecdotes in *Dabeiba*, a well-elaborated story of a disaster in this town. In *El bazar de los idiotas* (The Idiots' Bazaar; 1974), Alvarez Gardeazábal relies on a parody of languages for humorous and critical effects. The parodied language involves García Márquez's *Cien años de soledad*, the speech of Tuluá's inhabitants, and the official language of the Catholic church.

Alvarez Gardeazábal initiated a new cycle of novels, distancing himself from regional tradition, with *El titiritero* (The Puppeteer; 1977), a metafiction set in Cali's Universidad del Valle (Del Valle University). The novels that follow, *Los míos* (My People; 1981) and *Pepe Botellas*

(1984), represent Alvarez Gardeazábal's rewriting of the history of the Valle del Cauca.

VIII

By the 1970s, it becomes increasingly difficult to speak of Colombian literature within the framework of regional traditions. Modernization, improved communication among the different regions, and the national presence of García Márquez since 1967 are all factors that have diminished the traditional regional boundaries, both as political entities and as determinants of cultural production.

Oral tradition and popular culture have been important in the recent upsurge of Colombian theater. With the exception of Antonio Alvarez Lleras (1892-1956), Alejandro Meza Nicholls (1896-1920) and Luis Enrique Osorio (1896), the theater has been a relatively weak genre in Colombia. It has undergone a renovation recently with the work of Enrique Buenaventura (1925) in Cali and Santiago García (1943) in Bogotá. Buenaventura's *En la diestra de Dios Padre* (On the Right-Hand Side of Our Father; 1958) and García's *Guadalupe, años sin cuenta* (Guadalupe, Uncounted Years; 1975) are both elaborate reworkings of previous texts. *En la diestra de Dios Padre* is the version by the Teatro Experimental de Cali (Cali Experimental Theater) of a story by Tomás Carrasquilla. *Guadalupe, años sin cuenta* is a collective production based on exhaustive historical research of La Violencia, primarily by means of oral history.

Novelists of the 1970s and 1980s have been participants in national and international novelistic traditions. They participate in the production of contemporary fiction as part of a now international phenomenon informed primarily by Latin American, European, and North American cultural sources. They know the contemporary European and Latin American novel as well as their own regional traditions and histories. With the increased novelistic production of the 1970s and 1980s and other international factors in play, these directions for the Colombian novel were more heterogenous than they had ever been before.

In the broadest of terms, it is possible to identify an essentially modern novelistic tradition and another fundamentally postmodern tendency over the decades of the 1970s and 1980s. The modern novel entered Colombia with the publication of three seminal works: García Márquez's *Leafstorm* (1955), Alvaro Cepeda Samudio's *La casa grande* (The Big House; translated as *La casa grande*, 1962), and Héctor Rojas

Herazo's *Respirando el verano* (Breathing the Summer, 1962). With respect to ideology, the modern texts tend to exhibit their social agenda more explicitly by portraying an identifiable Colombian empirical reality. The modern novel has been cultivated in Colombia by García Márquez, Fanny Buitrago, Rojas Herazo, Manuel Zapata Olivella, and others. A more innovative and experimental postmodern fiction, best understood within a context of theory and other literary forms, has been published by R. H. Moreno-Durán, Albucía Angel, Marco Tulio Aguilera Garramuño, Darío Jaramillo Agudelo, Andrés Caicedo, Rodrigo Parra Sandoval, and Alberto Duque López.

García Márquez's may well be the most significant enterprise of modern fiction by a single author. Since the publication of *One Hundred Years of Solitude* in 1967, a pinnacle of the modern novel in Colombia and Latin America, García Márquez has written four novels: *El otoño del patriarca* (*The Autumn of the Patriarch*; 1975), *Crónica de una muerte anunciada* (*Chronicle of a Death Foretold*; 1981), *El amor en los tiempos del cólera* (*Love in the Time of Cholera*; 1985), and *El general en su laberinto* (*The General In his Labyrinth*; 1990). After his initial experiments in his early stories with the techniques of modernism (fragmentation, collage, multiple points of view), he used these techniques in what is an identifiable modernist project—the seeking of order and the expression of the ineffable in a world lacking order and waiting to be named. García Márquez, like certain other contemporary Latin American writers (e.g., Vargas Llosa and Fuentes), is rooted in the moderns, but not consistently so. He has also read the postmoderns and in his later work participates in some of their subversive and self-conscious exercises.

Among the other writers who have assimilated the stratagems of modern fiction, Fanny Buitrago, Manuel Zapata Olivella, and Héctor Rojas Herazo have been the most active. In addition to her short fiction, Buitrago has published the novels *El hostigante verano de los dioses* (The Harassing Summer of the Gods; 1963), *Cola de zorro* (Fox's Tail; 1970), *Los pañamanes* (The Pañamanes, 1979), and *Los amores de Afrodita* (The Loves of Aphrodite, 1983). Much of her fiction emanates from coastal Caribbean culture. Several voices narrate *El hostigante verano de los dioses*, the totality of which communicates the state of boredom endured by a spiritually exhausted generation of young people. *Los pañamanes*, set on a Caribbean island, portrays the conflicts between, on the one hand, the legends and traditions in a disappearing oral culture on the island and, one the other hand, modernization and its "beautiful

people" that are taking over. In *Los amores de Afrodita* Buitrago recurs
to popular culture in a manner reminiscent of both Manuel Puig's fiction
and of the Peruvian Mario Vargas Llosa's *La tía Julia y el escribidor*
(*Aunt Julia and the Script Writer*).

Zapata Olivella has published six novels, including his two most
recent works, *Changó, el gran putas* (Changó, the Big S.O.B.; 1983) and
El fusilamiento del diablo (The Shooting of the Devil; 1986). His most
ambitious novel, the massive *Changó, el gran putas*, is broad in scope.
The novel spans three continents and six centuries of African and Afro-
American history. In *El fusilamiento del diablo*, Zapata Olivella reelabo-
rates the story of Manuel Saturion Valencia, an Afro-Colombian leader
who was executed in 1907.

Héctor Rojas Herazo uses the narrative strategies of a Faulknerian
modernity in his trilogy, *Respirando el verano* (Breathing the Summer,
1962), *En noviembre llega el arzobispo* (In November the Archbishop
Arrives, 1967), and *Celia se pudre* (Celia Rots, 1986). These novels
evoke the premodern, oral world of Celia, the central character of this
trilogy, and her family. Just as *One Hundred Years of Solitude* synthesized García Márquez's Macondo, the massive *Celia se pudre* is summa
of the world of Cedrón. Although this hermetic novel, has multiple
narrative voices, the decadence of Cedrón is filtered primarily through
Celia's memory. As in *Respirando el verano*, the central image in *Celia
se pudre* is the home—*la casa*—and the predominant tone accentuates
the hatred that permeates Cedrón as well as Celia's life.

Solipsistic experiments do not usually become bestsellers, either in
the original version or in translation. Nevertheless, R. H. Moreno-Durán
and writers such as Albalucía Angel, Marco Tulio Aguilera Garramuño,
Darío Jaramillo Agudelo, Andrés Caicedo, Rodrigo Parra Sandoval, and
Alberto Duque López did pursue an innovative, fundamentally postmodern project during the 1970s and 1980s. Cosmopolitan in interests, most
of them have preferred to write abroad; Moreno-Durán and Angel have
lived for most of their writing careers in Europe and have been as intellectually attuned to contemporary European writing and theory as to Colombia. Similarly, Duque López has been indelibly influenced by such
diverse texts as the Argentine Julio Cortázar's *Rayuela* (*Hopscotch*) and
American film. Aguilera Garramuño has postmodern texts in the sense
that they present no privileged narrator upon whom the reader can rely,
nor is there an authoritative discourse or figure to whom the reader can
turn for something like an objective, final truth regarding its fiction. The
reading difficulties with such postmodern texts are created by this ab-

sence of an organizing, potentially omniscient mediator who could filter and interpret all of the discursive performances in the text. Having immersed themselves in writing culture's recent theory and having assimilated the fiction of the moderns, the postmoderns are the most removed from oral culture of any group of Colombian writers.

Contemporary Colombian literature, in addition to responding to factors beyond regional tradition, has surpassed the limitations of a venerable tradition of a writing culture that was the exclusive domain of a ruling elite. A democratization of both the production and consumption of Colombian literature in recent years has given it a vitality heretofore unknown in the history of Colombian letters.

BIBLIOGRAPHY

Brushwood, John S. *Genteel Barbarism: New Readings of Nineteenth Century Spanish-American Novels*. Lincoln: University of Nebraska Press, 1981. Includes an analysis of Jorge Isaac's *María* using Roland Barthes's methodology.

Brushwood, John S. *The Spanish American Novel: a Twentieth-Century Survey*. Austin: University of Texas Press, 1975. Chronological discussion of Spanish America's novelistic production of the twentieth century, including analysis of major works and numerous Colombian novels.

Bushnell, David. *The Santander Regime in Gran Colombia*. Newark, Md.: University of Delaware Press, 1954. The most complete study available on the Santander regime and Colombia's early years of nationhood.

Camacho Guizado, Eduardo. "La literatura colombiana entre 1820 y 1900." In *Manual de historia de Colombia*. Bogotá: Procultura/Colcultura, 1977. II, 618-693. Discussion of nineteenth-century Colombian literature within the social context.

Curcio Altamar, Antonio. *Evolución de la novela en Colombia*. Bogotá: Instituto Colombiano de Cultura, 1975. A standard thematic history of the Colombian novel from the colonial period to the 1950s.

Davis, Robert H. *Historical Dictionary of Colombia*. Metuchen, N.J.: Scarecrow Press, 1977. Useful and complete chronological and alphabetical account of highlights of Colombian political, social, economic, and cultural history.

Fals Borda, Orlando, Germán Guzmán, and Eduardo Umaña Luna. *La Violencia en Colombia*. Bogotá: Carlos Valencia Editores, 1980. In three volumes, the most well-documented and complete study of the twentieth-century period of La Violencia available.

Gómez Restrepo, Antonio. *Historia de la literatura colombiana*. Bogotá: Biblioteca de Autores Colombianos, 1957. In four volumes, a traditional and conservative history of Colombian literature with main focus on the colonial period and nineteenth century.

Holguín, Andrés. *Antología crítica de la poesía colombiana, 1874-1974*. Bogotá: Biblioteca del Centenario del Banco de Colombia, 1974. In two volumes, an anthology of Colombian poetry with useful introductions to each poet.

Jaramillo Uribe, Jaime. *El pensamiento colombiano en el siglo XIX*. Bogotá: Editorial Temis, 1964. An examination of major movements.

Menton, Seymour. *La novela colombiana: planetas y satélites*. Bogotá: Plaza y Janés, 1977. Analysis of major Colombian novels of the nineteenth and twentieth centuries.

Pachón Padilla, Eduardo. *El cuento colombiano*. Bogotá: Plaza y Janés, 1980. In two volumes, a well-selected anthology of nineteenth- and twentieth-century short stories, including introductions to each author and brief analyses of each story.

Rivas Sacconi, José Manuel. *El latín en Colombia; bosquejo histórico del humanismo colombiano*. Bogotá: Instituto Caro y Cuervo, 1949. History of the teaching of Latin and humanism in Colombia, with main focus on the colonial period.

Vargas, Germán. *Sobre literatura colombiana*. Bogotá: Guberek, 1985. Valuable essays on Colombian writers, written by a member of García Márquez's Group of Barranquilla.

Williams, Raymond L. *Una década de la novela colombiana: la experiencia de los setenta*. Bogotá: Plaza y Janés, 1981. Analyses of Colombian novels of the 1970s.

COSTA RICA
Rima de Vallbona
University of St. Thomas

I

In Costa Rican letters five definite stages can be established wherein one can discern how writers develop an awareness of their immediate reality and establish a correlation between that environment and literary discourse: 1) the early denunciatory essay during the colonial period; 2) the formative years of the republic in which the essay predominates; 3) the Generación del 900 (Generation of 1900) and *costumbrismo* (narrative of manners) as the starting point of Costa Rican letters; 4) the Generación del 40 (Generation of 1940), characterized by social denunciation; and 5) theater and poetry in the current sociodemocratic crisis.

II

The name Costa Rica (i.e., Rich Coast) involves an irony that has been emphasized since colonial times, for it was the poorest province of the General Capitaincy of Guatemala. This poverty was due in part to Costa Rica's sparse population, the majority of which consisted of a few conquerors and colonizers who, attracted by the natural beauty and fertile land, established themselves as agriculturists. They were unable to rely on Indian labor, as the number of Indians was becoming drastically reduced through disease and death. Perhaps because of this, the province did not have the system of *encomiendas* (royal entrustments of Indians and territories) pertaining in the rest of Latin America. In reality, a peaceful and egalitarian apportionment of the lands was carried out in which each family received its share. The sociocultural isolation in which the colonists lived was so extreme that the superstructures were ignored in order to satisfy the most urgent necessities of survival. On the

217

other hand, sociologists have attributed to these special conditions some very indicative characteristics of the Costa Rican people that define the sustained democratic tradition of the country: extreme individualism, shyness, distrust, fondness of liberty, and civic-mindedness, as well as a tendency toward patriarchy and the politics of bossism.

Since very early in the colonial period, these characteristics occupied a critical space in Costa Rican literature: the first text that has been preserved is a mediocre untitled gloss written in 1574 by Domingo Jiménez (1536-1600) and based on "Byve leda sy podrás" (Live Gaily If You Can), a Spanish courtly poem of the fifteenth-century by Juan Rodríguez de la Cármen o del Padrón. This gloss makes reference to the despot Alonso Anguciana de Gamboa, governor of Costa Rica.

In his discussion of the most outstanding features of Costa Rican literature, Abelardo Bonilla points out its prematurely rational character and its essayistic tendencies. The latter feature attests to a pressing need to define the whole axiological system of Central American reality. Costa Rica had two essayists who in actions and words were influential in the historical process of America during the reign of Carlos III and who helped prepare the way for Central American independence: the friar José Antonio de Liendo y Goicoechea (1735-1814) and the priest Florencio del Castillo (1778-1834).

Liendo y Goicoechea brought about a true revolution in teaching by introducing at the University of Guatemala the ideas of Descartes, Pascal, Linneus, Newton, and other thinkers and scientists of the period. The new ideas helped eliminate the scholasticism that had for so long been an obstacle to a dialectic process of Latin American culture. Moreover, by participating actively in the Sociedad Económica de los Amigos de la Patria (Economic Society of the Friends of the Fatherland), a focal point of criticism and conspiracy against the Spanish crown, he carried his revolution into the social realm: incited by an intense fervor for social betterment, he published in *La gaceta de Guatemala* (The Guatemalan Gazette) satires in prose and verse against the vice and corruption of the privileged classes, as well as essays concerning the indigence, mendacity, and exploitation of the Indians and the working class, whom he called the "weak members of the fatherland." He, too, insisted on the need to "make education accessible throughout the realm."

Castillo was one of the most notable Latin American representatives to attend the legislative assembly of Cadiz, where he served as secretary and later president. Inspired by the ideas of Francisco de Vitoria, a Spaniard who in the sixteenth century laid down the foundations of modern international law and civil rights, he distinguished himself by his extensive and effective speeches in defense of the rights of Indians and blacks, expressing the need for both races to participate in the administration of their respective countries. Beyond the abovementioned texts and for obvious reasons, Costa Rica does not have a tradition of indigenous literature.

III

In the first decades after independence was peacefully achieved in 1821, literary creativity in the country was insignificant. Instead, eminently historical and sociopolitical essays predominated, reflecting objectives of organizing the republic and providing a structure for the new state. This effort was carried out by lawyers and men of action who subscribed to the liberal ideologies of the late nineteenth century that were available at the Universities of Guatemala and Nicaragua. These men included Mauro Fernández (1848-1905), Manuel de Jesús Jiménez (1854-1916), and Pío Víquez (1850-99).

Strengthening the nation's economy through the cultivation and exportation of coffee and the opening of new channels of communication with the outside world favored the emergence of a type of commercial plutocracy that little by little displaced the old Creole oligarchy and also facilitated development of an alternative socioeconomic system. The printing press was introduced in 1830, and numerous foreign scientists, entrepreneurs, and professors brought Krausism and positivism to Costa Rica with them. Books were imported, and professional journalism began to emerge. With the promulgation in 1866 of the Law of Public Education mandating free, obligatory lay primary education, which was Liendo y Goicoechea's dream become reality, numerous educational training centers such as the Liceo de Costa Rica (Lyceum of Costa Rica) and the Colegio Superior de Señoritas (Girls High-School) were founded in the period 1840-50. However the Casa de Enseñanza de Santo Tomás (St. Thomas Teaching Center) was closed in 1888 by Mauro Fernández, Minister of Education, because the country did not have at that time any primary and secondary educational structure to sustain the university. Mauro Fernández was ready to found a new university when he died, but Costa Rica remained without a university during half a century.

There was also an ideological confrontation between liberals and Catholics, with attendant heated polemics, which led to an awakening of religious consciousness on the part of the latter. Inspired by the papal encyclical *Rerum novarum*, the Church undertook social action on behalf of the rights of the proletariat and in 1880 began publication of the first official Catholic periodical.

IV

Only since the latter nineteenth century and the early twentieth century can one speak of an organic literary production in Costa Rica. Three generations are defined in this period: the Generation of 1900, that of 1940, and the generation that corresponds to prevailing sociodemocratic ideologies during the period following the revolution of 1948.

The Generation of 1900, made up of liberals, focused on a variety of aspects of Costa Rican reality, including colloquial language, in the form of *costumbrismo* (Costumbrism, narrative sketches of manners and social customs). This modality prevailed after a long controversy with representatives of Modernism, an essentially poetic movement inspired by European models. The controversy did not raise any fundamental aesthetic or ideological problems, but rather linguistic and other problems related to the acceptance or rejection of colloquial language in literary discourse.

Joaquín García Monge (1881-1958) was a leader of Costumbrism and was recognized internationally as the director of *Repertorio americano* (American Repertory; 1919-58), a journal that exercised considerable influence on Latin American historical and cultural discourse. Other notable followers were Carlos Gagnini (1865-1925), Jenaro Cardona (1863-1930), and, in the essay on customs, Manuel González Zeledón (1864-1936; known as Magón). The work of Luis Dobles Segreda (1891-1956) and Max Jiménez (1900-47) marked the transition toward a stylized Realism. García Monge's *El moto* (The Landmark; 1900) and *Las hijas del campo* (The Country Daughters; 1900) represent the beginnings of Costa Rican Costumbrism, with strong nuances of Naturalism. Both novels involve the recognition of painful national realities, with an emphasis on the ignorance and superstition of peasants, the patriarchal life that was a hindrance to the progress of the country, and the small-mindedness of what García Monge calls the "society of *gamonales*" (something like political bosses). This society was a direct product of independence and was bound to the oligarchic plutocracy of coffee plantations and also to the military, its instrument of power. The progressive dictatorship of Tomás Guardia ended the political rule of this plutocracy. Cardona's *El primo* (My Cousin; 1905), one of the best novels of this stage, criticizes the society of San José (the capital) in its process of evolution from agrarian patriarchalism to a frivolous, urban bourgeoisie full of vices.

It was Magón, however, who achieved popularity for his stories and articles of manners. Although he wrote the majority of his work in the United States, where he lived many years, Magón never abandoned national themes, and he was able to record to perfection both urban and rural speech of Costa Rica. But perhaps it was his long absence from Costa Rica that explains his rosy view of the world as full of abundance, a view that contrasts sharply with García Monge's exceedingly sober view of a world full of privations.

The beginnings of Costa Rican narrative would not be complete without María Isabel Carvajal (1888-1949), known by the pseudonym Carmen Lyra. Her works represent the entrance of women into the panorama of Costa Rican letters. On the other hand, *Los cuentos de mi tía Panchita* (*My Aunt Panchita's Stories*; 1920) is a harbinger of children's narrative. These are stories that derive from diverse popular sources, but Lyra adapted them with extraordinary originality to Costa Rican settings and speech patterns. They appear when primary education, already an integral part of the ideological system of the state, attains a zenith. This book beccame a favorite of Costa Rican children. The list of writers to enrich children's literature in Costa Rica is extensive. Among them Carlos Luis Sáenz (1899-1984) and Lilia Ramos (1903) stand out.

V

After the period of Costumbrism, literary texts that might be considered part of a generation were not produced for two decades. In 1940 a very well-defined generation emerged that was intimately associated with the ideology of the moment. Various historical and cultural events set the stage for its emergence: tax reforms carried out by President Alfredo González Flores; the disappearance of small private property and an increase of workers answering to an overseer or boss as a result of the new latifundismo; exploitation in the banana industry by the United Fruit Co., which led to a strike in 1934; an awakening of the anti-imperialist consciousness of the Costa Rican people; the founding of the

Communist Party as a vehicle to encourage the organization of the proletariat and its participation in the politics of the nation.

Literary activity was stimulated by the founding of the Editorial Costa Rica (Costa Rican Publishing House) and the University of Costa Rica, organs of the state's ideological apparatus. Moreover, the competition sponsored in 1940 by the American publisher Farrar & Reinhart for the best Latin American novel represented a great incentive for the writers of that period, who came to be called the Generation of 1940. This generation has two dominant facets. First, there is the rural, protest novel, represented by Carlos Luis Fallas (1909-66), Fabián Dobles (1918), Joaquín Gutiérrez (1918), and Carlos Salazar Herrera (1906). The second aspect corresponds to the so-called introspective or experimental novel, headed by Yolanda Oreamuno (1916-56). José Marín Cañas constitutes a special case because of his identification with both aspects. He has received greatest recognition for his *Infierno verde* (Green Hell; 1935), a novel that treats the disastrous Chaco War between Paraguay and Bolivia in the early 1930s.

The rural denunciatory novel is intimately bound to the realism of Creolist tendencies in Latin America and also corresponds to the Marxist ideology with which the group's members identified. It represents an effort to make readers aware of the multiple problems of the proletariat and underprivileged classes. They are linear narratives for the most part, closed and fragmentary, in which the community and not the individual is the central character. In *Mamita Yunai* (Mommy Yunai [i.e., *Uni*ted Fruit Co.]; 1941), Fallas develops the indigenous theme of the ignorance and backwardness in the jungles of Talamanca and the unscrupulous political manipulation of voters by local authorities. The inhumane exploitation by the United Fruit Co. and the anti-North American imperialism that this produced are favorite themes of denunciatory literature. Among the texts that develop this theme are *Mommy Yunai*, *Ese que llaman pueblo* (This Thing They Call the People; 1942) by Dobles, and *Puerto Limón* (1950) by Gutiérrez. Dobles's *El sitio de las abras* (Where the Clearings Are; 1950) focuses on how small landowners are cheated out of their land and the need to return the land to those who work it.

The introspective or experimental novel, represented by Oreamuno's *La ruta de su evasión* (The Route of His Escape; 1949), is not concerned with the ideological and aesthetic principles of the denunciatory novel. Nor is it interested in the sociogeographical space of the narrative. Instead, it concentrates on the psyche of its characters and on the urban environment where existential anxiety has its origins. It employs innovative devices and, as a consequence, departs radically from the traditional forms of the Costa Rican novel. Oreamuno's work is related to post-Modernism in its theme of the disintegration of the middle-class family. The binary tensions of parents vs. children that the characters portray are the result of the man/woman relationship warped by machismo. The theme of frustration in Oreamuno's novel evokes the changes that occur even in small Costa Rican towns under the pressure of corrupting lifestyles imposed by dominant foreign cultures. Thus this novel, too, follows the denunciatory pattern.

For a long time the experimental novel became stagnant while five of Oreamuno's novels remained unpublished and were lost. Seventeen years later, it made a comeback with *Los perros no ladraron* (The Dogs Did Not Bark; 1966) by Carmen Naranjo (1931), *Los juegos furtivos* (The Furtive Games; 1967) by Alfonso Chase (1945), and *Noche en vela* (Night of Vigil; 1967) by Rima de Vallbona (1931). *Ceremonia de casta* (A Ceremony of Caste; 1976) by Samuel Rovinski (1932) and other texts that incorporate trends in the new Latin American narrative complete this group. This line of writing also corresponds to the social denunciation found in authors like Quince Duncan (1940), who continues the theme of exploitation in the banana industry, introducing blacks as a theme. In *Final de calle* (End of the Street; 1978), Duncan deals with the crisis of the social democracy inaugurated in Costa Rica with the Revolution of 1948.

VI

The trajectory of Costa Rican theater up through the first decades of the twentieth century leaves much to be desired. The same is true of lyric poetry. Both genres attained a level of accomplishment beginning in the 1960s, a period that corresponds to crisis in the social democratic government and disenchantment over the results of the Central American trade agreements. Given the social democratic conditions that contribute to the nation's development, it is understandable that theater, a mass spectacle, would achieve relative popularity only at the beginning of this century with light comedies in the Teatro Trébol. In the 1960s, however, there are the beginnings of regular performances of serious theater before large audiences. The founding of the Instituto Nacional de Artes Dramáticas (National Institute of Dramatic Arts), of little theaters like El Arlequín and Las Máscaras, and the inauguration of the

Departamento de Artes Dramáticas (Department of Dramatic Arts) all contribute to this development. As a manifestation of government policies, theater is now performed throughout the country.

There are three Costa Rican dramatists who exemplify the use of modern dramatic principles like the theater of the absurd and the grotesque: Alberto Cañas (1920), Daniel Gallegos (1930), and Samuel Rovinski. Cañas sustains a commitment to national reality by focusing on the misery, vices, hypocrisy, and self-deceit of the Costa Rican middle class. His work has been criticized for its Pirandellian texture that at times borders on the fantastic. One of his plays, *La Segua* (The Segua Woman; 1974), was made into a successful film in Costa Rica. Gallegos tends to follow the outlines of European and American theater and to use less overtly national references. Rovinski is interested in both general Latin American topics (*El martirio del pastor* [The Martyrdom of the Shepherd; 1983]) and specifically Costa Rican ones (*Las fisgonas de Paso Ancho* [The Nosey Women of Paso Ancho; 1971]).

With respect to lyric poetry, Aquileo J. Echeverría (1866-1909) distinguished himself in the first generation, known as Lira Costarricense (Costa Rican Lyre). His *Concherías* (Peasant Ways; 1905) and his Costumbrism verses are the basis of the great popularity he has always enjoyed. He captures with humor and ingenuity the idiosyncrasies of the *concho*, the Costa Rican peasant, using the latter's own colloquial and colorful language.

Modernism did not establish itself as a movement in Costa Rica, although it had some followers. The first generation to take an interest in Latin American *vanguardismo* (Vanguardism; cf. European Modernism) was composed of poets who have achieved recognition beyond Costa Rica: Isaac Felipe Azofeifa (1909), Alfredo Cardona Peña (1917), and Eunice Odio (1922-74). The "lost generation" of those who published in the 1950s brought Costa Rica definitively into the vanguard movement. Poets had previously fluctuated between conformity and conflict, solidarity and solitude as a means of addressing the sociopolitical referents of the moment. The members of the Círculo de Poetas Costarricenses (Circle of Costa Rican Poets) in the 1960s are part of the attempt to address sociopolitical problems and the mediocre level of poetry then prevalent in the country. The members of the Círculo wrote a *Manifiesto trascendentalista* (Transcendentalist Manifesto; 1977) signed by Laureano Albán (1942), Julieta Dobles (1943), Ronald Bonilla (1951), and Carlos Francisco Monge (1951). The four declare their intent to put into practice a commitment to participate "in the struggle against misery, injustice, and exploitation." Jorge Debravo (1938-67), also a member of the group, initiates social poetry in Costa Rica, but without bringing about any radical break with tradition. That break occurs with the younger poets, and their compositions incorporate the most recent poetic movements like the "exteriorist" poetry pioneered by Ernesto Cardenal (see section on Nicaragua). Other poets have received wide recognition and prestigious awards in Europe and the United States. This is the case with Albán, who received Spain's 1979 Adonais Prize for *Herencia del otoño* (*Autumn's Legacy*; 1981).

It is evident that Costa Rican narrative, theater, and poetry have finally attained a level of productive relationship between reality and literature. Eunice Odio, by conceiving of the literary text as a transcendent gesture, had already provided a plurivalent mythic vision of the world and of the artist in *El tránsito del fuego* (Fire's Journey; 1957). It is possible to conclude that, after sterile attempts, the dialectic-literary process of Costa Rica has begun to reach maturity without surrendering its national or Latin American identity.

Translated by Juliette Spence.

BIBLIOGRAPHY

Baeza Flores, Alberto. *Evolución de la poesía costarricense 1574-1977.* San José: Editorial Costa Rica, 1978. Studies the development of poetry since 1574 and establishes an interesting, although debatable, generational grouping of poets.

Bonilla, Abelardo. *Historia de la literatura costarricense.* San José: Editorial Costa Rica, 1967. An important source of information that includes data concerning the sociopolitical and historical contexts of literary production.

Castro Rawson, Margarita. *El costumbrismo en Costa Rica.* San José: Editorial Costa Rica, 1966. An excellent introduction to this important movement, followed by an anthology and extensive bibliography.

Monge, Carlos Francisco. *La imagen separada. Modelos ideológicos de la poesía costarricense 1950-1980.* San José: Ministerio de Cultura, 1984. Following an ideological model based on Lucien Goldmann and Françoise Pérus, Monge underscores the evolutionary process of twentieth-century Costa Rican poetry that begins with an ontological search and culminates in a radical break by the younger poets.

Picado Gómez, Manuel. *Literatura/ideología/crítica: notas para un estudio de la literatura costarricense*. San José: Editorial Costa Rica, 1983. Following a model of social criticism, this text pursues an ideological focus with the goal of formulating a scientific model for analyzing Costa Rican literature.

Sandoval de Fonseca, Virginia. *Resumen de literatura costarricense*. San José: Editorial Costa Rica, 1978. Although coverage begins in the nineteenth century, emphasis is on the twentieth century and developments since Bonilla's history.

Valdeperas, Jorge. *Para una nueva interpretación de la literatura costarricense*. San José: Editorial Costa Rica, 1979. An analysis of texts following Georg Lukács's Marxist model, with emphasis on the relationship, in a Latin American context, between Costa Rican reality and literary production.

CUBA
Matías Montes-Huidobro
University of Hawaii

I

The process of selection that represents the search for touchstones in Cuban literature must necessarily result in the elimination of a good number of writers, even in the formative period antedating the appearance of José María Heredia, who may be called Cuba's first great literary figure in a chronological sense. This is not to say that there are no important elements before him. It is frequently remarked that, since the genes of Cuban nationality had not been established prior to the nineteenth century, literature before that time was no more than the reflection of what had arrived from the metropolis. This is only partially true, since the formation of Cuban identity was based on convergences and divergences with respect to Spain.

II

Although theater showed signs of vitality before poetry, the latter is much more evident in terms of Cuban literary history, which begins with the *Espejo de paciencia* (Mirror of Patience; 1608) by Silvestre de Balboa, who died sometime before 1644. This poem narrates the misfortunes attending the kidnapping of the Bishop of Cuba by the pirate Gilberto Girón, the former's rescue, and the death of Girón at the hands of a black slave. But in addition to historical details, the poem is noteworthy for its lexical display. Balboa's text already demonstrates a verbal consciousness, a concern for the word as word, with a strict aesthetic function that will turn out to be characteristic, with its highly elaborate, purely ornamental form, rich in classical and classical-tropical elements. The classical tradition of Cuban Baroque sought, from its inception, aculturation to the tropical landscape. In *El espejo de paciencia* the lexical contrasts establish the verbal mechanism of the classicism-anticlassicism of the Cuban Baroque. Yet one should not overlook the note of compromise, since the poem praises ecclesiastical authority and heroic rustics alike.

As national consciousness proceeded to define itself, poetry followed a path of compromise. The struggle for independence against Spanish tyranny made itself felt, and it represented a specific influence that must be taken into consideration up to the present day. It will not be enough to sing about the mano, the guayaba, and similar fruit, no matter how Cuban they may be. While the consequences of patriotic sentiment do not always mean an identification with the decorative and gustative elements of lyrical fruit trees, the cornucopia of local fruits that Silvestre de Balboa introduced in 1608 survive in Cuban poetry for more than two centuries as a key point of patriotic reference. These elements form part of a *criollista* (Creolist) and picturesque complex that will characterize a group of poets of a later generation.

Not even the work of a poet like José María Heredia (1803-39) escaped the temptation. Under the influence of Neoclassical poets, Heredia was essentially a Romantic. Rather than harmonious, he was daring, not in style but in character. His was not a poetry wherein the word is most essential, but rather the exuberance of the personal I. Arrogant, Heredia addresses the hurricane, the falls, the volcanoes, and the pyramids in familiar terms. He inaugurated monumental definitions of tyranny and liberty, and his verses opposing tyranny reflect a constant that is already two centuries old. Compromise and the definition of consciousness will vary in style and group, but their presence will persist throughout Cuba's literary history. Moreover, Heredia inaugurates one of the constants of Cuban literature, that of exile, in which a large part of Cuban literature is written today.

What is also significant about Heredia is that he typifies, in an inaugural manner, the abiding dual nature of Cuban cultural creativity deriving from the phenomenon of exile versus nonexile. Heredia wrote and published his works outside of Cuba, and a constant of Cuban culture became the looking back, no matter what sort of landscape was involved: Heredia contemplates Niagara and sees the palm trees, he lives the moment at hand and the past remains permanently in his memory. Heredia was obliged to produce his greatest works in exile and to be reborn from the ashes. His "I" does not give in; rather, it grows; and this circumstance is reflected in his stance toward the natural phenomena he describes.

If his patriotic position earned Heredia his exile, it would cost Concepción Valdés (1809-44), known by the pseudonym Plácido, his life. Plácido saw himself trapped in the circumstances of his social class, his race, and the dual nature of his poetry: the sensual and the patriotic. On the one hand, he echoed in his poetry the rebellious, aggressive, bloodied stance against tyranny. On the other, he worked with sensual components similar to those to which we have already referred. His poems were first collected in 1886. There is something Romantic in Plácido's poetry, with its concept of the union between the sexes, yet it is too sensorial and local to be limited to such classification. The amorous state described by his poetry is purely tropical, and it provides us with incandescent images. It is local in its terminology and in the prosaic components of many of its texts in that it adheres to what is elementary, basic, and earthy. But Plácido, in addition to his ties with Creolism, sought other poetic alternatives in the writing of a patriotic poetry aimed at oppression and in favor of independence. This postion, in addition to a variety of historical, economic, and ethnological factors, cost him his life when he was accused of forming part of the so-called Conspiración de la Escalera (Staircase Conspiracy); he was shot in 1844.

Poetry would continue to be enriched by the landscape, and the whole of the nineteenth century rings with a constant song to Cuban nature, which of course is the safest way of expressing patriotic fervor. Creolism would yield to *siboneyismo* (Siboneyism, after Siboney, the name of the aboriginal inhabitants of the island). José Fornaris (1827-90) was one of the most representative poets of Siboneyism. This landscape is, to a greater and lesser degree, associated with historical concerns and the concept of liberty. It is principally a fixation of memory, since it was so frequently an expressive form for poets in exile who engraved on their memory precise images in order not to lose their identity in a foreign setting. This explains why many of these poets shared the common denominator of "to Cuba" with only minor variations. And since exile was a constant, there was an extensive gallery of farewells, recollections, and returns. Precise locales and concrete evocations were abundant. All too often one has the impression that this texture of local culture was a lyrical requisite for showing one's authentic Cubanness. It was an obsession with landscapes, flowers, and fruits, and it was often given as a sign of patriotism. In the end, it was painful, because in the large majority of these writers it emerged as a true expression of the suffering of personal experience; painful also because this experience did not necessarily translate into good poetry. In any case, it is an essential feature of Cuban poetry of the nineteenth and twentieth centuries, besieged by the political pendulum, by exile, memory, and the loss of memory.

The inventory of poetry is so extensive that it is imperative to establish certain limits. In general, toward the middle of the nineteenth century historical experience of a tragic nature tends to give poetry a greater authenticity. Its common denominator is exile, and one major group owes its name to a collection of poems, *El laúd del desterrado* (The Lute of the Exiled), published in New York in 1858. This book brings together poems of a patriotic character, and some of the poets that lived the hardships described therein are Leopoldo Turla (1818-77), who lived in misery and died in New Orleans; Miguel Teurbe Tolón (1820-57), who after suffering exile in the United States returned to Cuba in 1857, to die a few months later; Pedro Angel Castellón (1820-56), who resided for years in New Orleans and preferred to die abroad rather than accept the amnesty of Spain's Isabel II; Pedro Santacilia (1826-1910), exiled in Spain, the United States, and Mexico; and José Agustín Quintero (1829-85), a student at Harvard and a friend of Emerson and Longfellow, who died in obscurity in New Orleans. These facts of Cuban literary history form a current that cannot be overlooked. At issue is a group of individualist acts that respond to a single collective consciousness.

Within this procession of authenticity and contained suffering, a more sensitive, intimate and evasive poetry evolved. This character would grow in intensity beginning with José Jacinto Milanés (1814-63), the poet of the turtledove and a precursor of the *rimas* (rhymes) of the Spaniard Gustavo Adolfo Bécquer and of Julián del Casal (1863-93). Milanés deals in lyrical abstractions, and his abiding solitude was unable to find company, even in lament. He opposes his inactive, paralyzed "I" to the collective movement oriented toward compromise. Romantic alienation in Milanés is a decisive step toward the existentialist alienation in Cuban literature that leads naturally to Casal. José María Mendive (1821-86), another exile with a profound patriotic consciousness, also follows this line in a certain sense. Even in his nostalgia for the countryside, his shading is finer and more intimate than in the other poets mentioned previously, and he confers upon the natural setting a mysterious note that is not typical in this type of lyrical evocation. Mendive plumbs the landscape and internalizes it.

There was a similar process of internalization among women writers, with a significant evolution from Gertrudis Gómez de Avellaneda (1814-73) to Luisa Pérez de Zambrana (1835-1922). Avellaneda provides Cuban literature with an important point of Romantic reference: poetry as melodrama. There is no hiding the fact that she should have felt something, not only with respect to Cuba but also with respect to her earthly and divine loves. But what is certain is that she is grandiloquent and tearful even when addressing a tree. She attempts to move us, upon her departure from Cuba, with "Al partir" (Upon Leaving; 1836), but the result is theatrical and does not rise above sensationalism. It must be said: Avellaneda was the worst poet in nineteenth-century Cuba. She wrote, as someone said, "sonorous Alexandrines," which was all the worse for her, since we cannot excuse her by saying that she didn't know how to write them. By contrast, Luisa Pérez de Zambrana achieves an intimate tone. The elegiac tone of Pérez de Zambrana extends like a lament that reaches the Republican period (post-1898) with tragic tonalities. Poetry became more and more the expression of sadness and more and more intense as colonial existence wastes away between war and frustration. Exterior exile was enlarged by the desolate concept of interior exile, already present in Milanés.

Like a brief parenthesis among the poets of sadness, the voice of Juana Borrero (1877-96) may be heard, charged with melancholy, fleeting and evasive, manifesting in her work the classic gesture of rebelliousness in the face of impotence. This was effected in terms of nihilistic paralysis, which is another long tradition that emerges in Cuban poetry as the result of the collision with immediate reality. It was, moreover, the greatest gesture of an individualism that chose to turn in upon itself. There was no apparent collective consciousness because this poetry was born of a rejection of the collectivity and as the consequence of historical, social, economic, and political components of the society in which the poet lived. Poetry proclaimed the individual "I" and germinated in its interior exile.

Before the advent of the Republic, Cuban poetry completed its cycle with two separate directions. One of these was active and involved a social conscience and a commitment by the individual and the poet to history. It implied a communion between the individual and the world. There was no contradiction between the identity of the "I" and one's social responsibilities. The poet's new, vital stance meant that s/he was part of the world. This direction is embodied in José Martí (1853-95) (see section IV).

Perhaps Juan Clemente Zenea (1832-71) is the culmination of a trajectory that began with Heredia and takes us up to Martí, with Zenea as the pre-Martí figure of greatest importance. Exiled, persecuted, besieged, finally imprisoned and shot in Cabaña, the victim of dark political machinations that put his integrity in doubt, Zenea foreshadows the climax of the nineteenth century with Martí, where the individual and the creator, life and text, culminate in a singular case in Cuban literature. Zenea fails to attain Martí's stature, but he represents nevertheless an authentic Romantic-Symbolist dramatic quality. Zenea goes beyond the pyrotechnic language of Romanticism and internalizes the external in the dark vortex of his best poems. Yet, as in the case of Martí, he is always impassioned and committed to life.

The other direction taken in Cuban poetry was passive. It involved a commitment in the sense that the individual and the poet decided to reject historical reality; as a consequence of this rejection there was an increase of individual consciousness. It implied a rupture with the ties of the real world in favor of the created, confirming that the "I" is everything and feeds on its own aesthetic substance. This nihilistic direction was embodied by Julián del Casal.

A large part of the interest of Casal's poetry lies in the personality of the poet. The author of *Hojas al viento* (Leaves in the Wind; 1890), *Nieve* (Snow; 1892), and *Bustos y rimas* (Busts and Rhymes; 1893), Casal was one of those writers who run the risk of eclipsing their texts with their own life or, more precisely, with the mystery that ends up consuming them and turning them into legends. For example, a text by Martí is interesting in itself, although it may be enriched by the associations that can be established between the individual and the text. In the case of Casal, there is an alienating process with respect to the world. Poetry serves him, as has been said innumerable times, to escape into another reality. As a consequence, he creates his reality, whose ties with the immediate world are remote. It is, in sum, a poetry that creates its own circumstance. Thus, Casal did not have to leave Cuba in order to travel, nor did he have to suffer exile. In this way, he established a point of reference that will be taken up by José Lezama Lima in the twentieth century (see below).

In order to achieve his goal, Casal created his own ornamental reality, in which he installed himself. All of his poetry speaks to us of Casal himself escaping along the strange byways that he has created. He rebels against the poetic contexts of the nineteenth century, and he rejects the scale of values that national consciousness has forged: love, fatherland, family, social rank, glory. All of these values lack meaning for him. He proposes to depart. But he does it without moving, conscious of the futility of movement and knowing that if he could travel to other worlds, he still would not be satisfied. Nor does he sense any ties with the past or obligations to the present, and he fails to conceive of any possibility for the future. Profoundly individualistic, he exists alone with his commitment to his own creative existence.

Both directions, that personified by Martí and that personified by Casal, converged at a single point: exile. Martí's work was born of the active exile of a life dedicated to a historic cause, while Casal's unfolded in the passive exile of an alienation state devoted to aesthetics.

III

With considerable theatrical sensationalism, the trajectory of colonial Cuban drama was born of a performance that never took place: the staging of *Los buenos en el cielo y los malos en el suelo* (The Good in Heaven and the Bad Cast Down), on Midsummer's Night 1598. This event has been described in a putative chronicle by a putative chronicler, Hernando de la Parra (dates unknown), whose name does not figure in the list of the citizens of Havana of the day. The implication is not only that the chronicle never existed, but also that the chronicler and the events narrated never existed. The one responsible for the labyrinth was Joaquín José García (dates unknown), who, when he published the *Protocolo de antigüedades, literatura, agricultura, industria, comercio, etcétera* (Protocols of Antiquities, Literature, Agriculture, Industry, Commerce, Etcetera; 1845), affirmed that Parra's chronicle was from 1598. García transcribed the valuable document, moth-eaten and gnawed by rats, in a style of the nineteenth century. This was necessary for the simple reason that the aforementioned original must never have existed, which means simply that the true history of Cuban theater, according to reliable facts at our disposal, began with *El príncipe jardinero y fingido Cloridano* (The Gardener Prince and False Cloridano; 1730), written by a captain from Havana named Santiago de Pita (?-1755). This work inaugurates an erotic-materialist current that is a hallmark of Cuban drama. Pita's text involves a marked erotic tonality that was surely the underlying cause of its extraordinary success. Pleasant and ingenious, fluidly rhymed, superficial despite a few long monologues, this work attracts our attention for the heavy erotic content latent in the innocent

language of the flowers. *El príncipe jardinero y fingido Cloridano* offers
an interpretive key that is very important in Cuban literature. Its florid
sensuality and sexuality are even more notable when we correlate them
with the eroticism of Avellaneda and the theatrical farce and with more
recent manifestations of a Biblical, pagan, and Yoruba stamp that we
find in the works of Abelardo Estorino, Virgilio Piñera, and Carlos
Felipe, respectively (see discussion of these dramatists below).

Milanés's theater is of a very different character. *El conde Alarcos*
(Count Alarcos; 1838) and *Un poeta en la corte* (A Poet at Court; 1840)
are two dramatic works that play an important part in the formation of
a Cuban consciousness in literature. In the first play, Milanés takes as
a protagonist a Spaniard in the service of a French monarch. The choice
is no accident. In the same way that Alarcos lacks any clearly defined
national consciousness, Cuba is still lacking one. *Un poeta en la corte* is
a much more interesting and meaningful work, and the development of
the character of the protagonist represents an ideological step forward.
Milanés himself seems to move toward defining his own political consciousness, and the dramatic conflict resides in the firmness of Pereira,
the protagonist, in the face of adverse elements that are ranged against
the preservation of his dignity and his ideological firmness. As a man,
Pereira defines himself democratically as a plebian, and as a poet he
adopts an ethical and aesthetic position where the pen achieves a commitment with the sword. This ethic, a thousand times betrayed, looks
toward the principles of José Martí. The formal composition of the work
is modern, despite its points of contact with classical Spanish theater.

Milanés's work is representative of the formation of a Cuban national consciousness. In his plays, there are ethical and aesthetic postulates
that question seriously the relations of Cuba with the metropolis, while
in his poetic works there is an alienating process that transports him to
an internal exile. This resulted in a mental imbalance that was the price
Milanés had to pay as the consequence of his historical existence. As in
the case of Heredia and Plácido, but on another level, there is a common
denominator: the conflict with colonial power. But the price that the
nineteenth-century's most famous dramatist had to pay is of another
nature. In Gertrudis Gómez de Avellaneda, as in Heredia, there are
arrogance, valor, rebelliousness, conflict, and, principally, exile, since her
work was written for the most part in Spain. Avellaneda's exile was
voluntary and, as a result, she did not agonize over the fixation of memory. Although she exaggerated, proclaimed, and declaimed in her poetry,
touting her love for Cuba and her affinity with writers like Heredia, what

is certain is that Avellaneda did not spend her life counting the hours of Cuba's misfortune, but rather writing her work and searching for suitable accomodations for her theater. Her exile represents, among other things, the desire to depart, a characteristic gesture of the Cuban writer, who, ill-adapted to reality, must rise above the asphyxia of a setting that is judged to be mediocre. Asphyxiated by the colonial system, Avellaneda identified with the lifestyle of Spain as a way to shed her chains and to become what she would otherwise be unable to. It was the exile of one who never got around to leaving. Passionate and pragmatic at the same time, Avellaneda chose to be calculating, even though this troubled her. In any case, she could not have been happy in Cuba, and like other writers in other circumstances, she wrote outside of Cuba what she would not have written there. It is only fair to say that in order to do what she did required courage. A woman and a foreigner, someone from the colonies, Avellaneda was able to gain recognition as a writer long before many Spanish women writers. She was a professional and sexually liberated woman, which was to say a lot. As though her personal life were not enough, her dramatic work is the best produced in Spanish during the nineteenth century.

What most stands out in Avellaneda's work at every turn is her audacity. As a woman she anticipates multiple aspects of the contemporary movement of feminist liberation. In a minor work, but one that is well executed, she handles skillfully the psychological analysis of matrimonial relations and articulates the problem of divorce for reasons of incompatibility. *Simpatía y antipatía* (Sympathy and Antipathy; 1855) suggests that the matrimonial union ought not be maintained when there are forces of antipathy, even though there may be sacred ties that bind. Clearly, this point of view is not carried to its logical conclusion. The dangerous thesis does not end up destroying the balance of the established order, and the cleverness of a very able theatrical mechanism is charged with harmonizing the conflicts. The audacity of a female character who dares to suggest the unmentionable is latent throughout a series of misunderstandings developed in the work, but the principle of an absurd situation that gets explained closes the work by adhering to the rules of the game.

In more ambitious works, like *Munio Alfonso* (1844), *Saúl* (1846), and *Baltasar* (1858), Avellaneda makes use of the existentialist decision as a device that serves to resolve with dramatic ingenuity situations concerning tyranny, liberty, and ideological compromise. In *La hija de las flores, o todos están locos* (The Daughter of the Flowers, or Everybody's Mad; 1852), a number of key elements in the development of Cuban literature and theater are suggested. There is once again the attention on floriculture, on the sensuality and sexuality found in *El príncipe jardinero*. As in the latter case, Avellaneda's work revolves around the same motif, the floral metaphor, which serves to create a character that is both Marian and pagan at the same time: Flora, who is born in the flowery month of May. Her character is a Marian springtime miracle conceived mythologically as the result of a transport of the gods. The act is a sort of theatrical creationism whereby theatrical aesthetics are more important than reality.

In *La hija de las flores*, Avellaneda provides another excellent psychological analysis of the relations between the sexes. In one scene, she establishes an interesting counterpoint between two characters in the work, Luis and Inés, which serves to develop a complex Versaillesque composition about flowers and sexuality. When Luis appears with a fleur-de-lis in his mouth, Inés faints. This collapse is parallel to the one that took place when Inés was raped. By leaving Inés in a state of unconsciousness in both situations, Avellaneda frees the woman of "guilt," suspends her free will, and leaves both decision and responsibility in the hands of the man. But this is done in a critical spirit: what is for the man a cause of pleasure and the climax of agreeable sensations that are the product of his free choice, is for the woman the cause of suffering and a centrifugal force that drives her away from herself. Passive, she cannot choose, but must suffer the consequences of the freedom of male choice. By the same token, she is left erotically unfulfilled and humiliated. In no other work do we find Avellaneda more stupendously feminist, as though she were defending the sexual rights of women, even though it may be done in highly ornamental terms. Intellect, aesthetics, and sensuality all come together in this work of psychological analysis.

The names of Milanés and Avellaneda must be supplemented by that of Joaquín Lorenzo Luaces (1826-67), the author of *El mendigo rojo* (The Red Beggar; 1859), of a romantic stamp; *Aristodemo* (1867), of a classic stamp; and *El becerro de oro* (The Golden Calf; 1859), a work of local customs and an interesting treatise on the trilogy of materialism—money, bread, and sex—that would serve as an important sign of Cuban letters.

These manifestations culminated in the *teatro bufo*, the comic theater, which because of its popularity dominated the nineteenth-century Cuban stage. This theater was much more active than what can be called "serious" theater, which was a theater of minorities, infrequently performed or, in the case of Luaces, not performed at all. By contrast, the comic theater was characterized by its vitality and stage presence. It was no accident that its founder was an actor and author whose importance is almost mythic: Francisco Covarrubias (1775-1850), a surgeon, became first a serious actor—the beau in household comedies—and went on to become, during the first half of the nineteenth century, Havana's favorite comic actor. Covarrubias left behind a current of popular theater, semianonymous since there were no famous names, where Cuba's urban frustrations find their liveliest and most authentic expression, always charged with a strong dose of humor and sexuality. The comic theater put in evidence Cuban maladjustment, immaturity, rebellion, and impotence in the face of a colonial state that could not be overcome. Colonial conflict was covered over by a mask of slapstick, Cuba's tragic laughter, seasoned by a wide array of popular cultural and linguistic forms. The comic stage was dominated by the trilogy of money, bread, and sex, and it would be impossible to say that it had any civic sense. It was a theater hungry for copulation and eating, one that expressed itself in an ample spectrum of economic and sexual-gustative images. These playful economic-physiological parodies possess many points of contact with the most significant works of contemporary Cuban drama.

The most interesting lexical phenomenon of the comic theater must be sought in the manifestations of the so-called professorial genre. Professorialism (*catedratismo*) emerged with the staging of *Los negros catedráticos* (The Black Professors; 1868) by Francisco Fernández (dates unknown). After that premiere, the "little black professor" was a character to appear regularly in the comic theater. Professorialism most often represented a means by which the character masked with lexical distortion his naked materialism. The result was an astounding lexical gallery and a Baroque and absurd language that constitutes one of the greatest contributions to Cuban literature of the nineteenth century because of its verbal audacity, its sense of theatricality, its parodic system, its ethnic-economic complex, its class consciousness, and, above all else, because of the primacy of language.

IV

The Cuban novel makes its appearance under the seal of an ethnic concern. But first, let us review some chronological considerations. In 1838 Félix Tanco (1797-1871) wrote *Petrona y Rosalía* (Petrona and

Rosalía), which would not be published until 1925. Juan Francisco Manzano (1797-1854), a poet born a slave who later gained his freedom, wrote his *Apuntes autobiográficos* (Biographical Notes) in 1839, although they were not published in Spanish until 1937. Because of the importance of the *Apuntes* as antislavery writing, it was first published in English translation in London in 1840, as part of a volume that included other texts. Anselo Suárez Romero (1818-78) wrote *Francisco* in 1839, but the novel was published after his death, in 1880. Cirilo Villaverde (1812-94) began to write *Cecilia Valdés*, which only in part can be considered an antislavery novel, in 1839, completing it in 1879 but not publishing it until 1882. Here too, the life and circumstances of Avellaneda assigned her a place of privilege with respect to the others. Since she was able to count on more reliable editorial outlets, she published *Sab* in 1841, long before the aforementioned novels appeared. Yet, the circumstances of the writer, although more favorable for the publication of her work, resulted in a more artificial prism. There is a greater distance between the writer and slave experience, which means that *Sab* is, inevitably, an antislavery novel that views slavery from the outside and from a distance. It is important to note that Avellaneda's defects are those characteristic of the Romantic movement, although within these limitations the novel fulfills its goal. What is certain is that while Manzano knew slavery in terms of his own body and paid with jail and persecution the price of his literary vocation, while Suárez Romero survived in the midst of an obscure colonial existence, and while Villaverde suffered prison and exile, Avellaneda took advantage of the benefits of her class and circumstance, getting the jump on the rest. And it is clear that, in terms of Manzano's direct style, Avellaneda's bookish approach pales considerably; Manzano's objective style, indeed, may be considered a harbinger of the documentary narrative.

Despite one's objections, Villaverde's *Cecilia Valdés* may be considered an archetypic novel. So, too, is the life of its author, which spanned a large period of Cuban life and the formation of Cuban nationality. Villaverde was the typical bourgeois Liberal of the last century, who defined the characteristics of his social class in terms of a solid nationalistic concept. A committed writer, Villaverde was involved in conspiracies and was jailed more than once. After his escape from jail, he fled Cuba. He is a representative figure of the constant of exile and the rebellion against the established system, and it is quite symptomatic that he was one of the intellectuals who initiated the Cuban exodus to the United States, where he worked as a Spanish teacher. *Cecilia Valdés* is, in a certain sense, an irritating novel. The protagonist provides a vivid literary experience of the subconscious complex of the mulatto. The particular preference that the Cuban bourgeoisie and the popular classes have felt toward this almost white mulatto woman constitutes an "evolutionary guarantee" for Cuban society in general. If Cecilia Valdés had not been almost white, she would have been almost black, and the fate of the novel would have been different and its popularity would not have surpassed *Sab* and *Francisco*, whose ethnic composition is different. But this very fact makes *Cecilia Valdés* a novel rich in meaningful elements. Superficially, it is a truly integrated novel, but deep down there is a subconscious racism. The protagonist is very conscious of the shades of blackness, and the novel offers multiple images of the racism of its characters. Paradoxically, this racism is the determining factor in the novel's popularity. *Cecilia Valdés* is a vivid expression of the struggles of a family clan, a frequent motif in Cuban literature. Villaverde works with the sensuality, sexuality, and materialism of Cuban society in the last century. He focuses on the bourgeoisie and on the popular classes, in a manner similar to that of the popular theater. There is no doubt about the basis of his novel. Besides being representative of *costumbrismo* (Costumbrism; sketches of local manners and characters), it bespeaks a position that is more objective and external than subjective and internal. The scant spiritual substance of the novel looks toward the frequent dehumanization found in more recent Cuban fiction. It is basically an expositive and harsh novel, treacly on the surface but flinty in the end. The novelist's attitude and the conduct of his characters are unquestionably representative of a people.

V

The discussion of colonial Cuban literature, which one must remember extends to 1898, leads inevitably to José Martí, whose historical and literary dimensions seem to be almost too vast to chart. He is a flesh and blood man who became a mythic figure in Cuban consciousness and who can be understood as the convergence of opposing poles: sensuality and spirituality, aesthetics and commitment, reality and fantasy. Man and writer reconcile the historical and literary opposites of Spain and Latin America. His writing often has a classic flavor and resonances that are genuinely Spanish. His style is based on classical traditions of Spanish letters, ones that are frequently disdained by Latin American writers.

At the same time, only a Latin American could write like Martí. Basically Cuban, he is totally Latin American but, ultimately, universal. Conscious of the aesthetic function of literary language, he does not allow himself to be carried away by the juggling of words. The man is as important as the writer. The poet stands out alongside the essayist. If his work is scantier in the narrative and the theater, the contribution is no less significant. His scraps have been the ideological bulletins of Cuban nationality. Republican politicians, revolutionaries and counter-revolutionaries have cast themselves voraciously on Martí's tomb, and each has gone away with the relic most to his advantage. To discuss Martí's literary work is, among Cubans, a ritual act that goes from the sacred to the profane.

Martí published his novel *Amistad funesta* (Baleful Friendship; 1885) in the New York periodical *El latino-americano* (The Latin American) under the pseudonym Adelaida Ral. Between 1887 and 1890, Martí conceived the plan to publish it in book form under the title *Lucía Jerez*; this did not come about, and the first appearance was in Gonzalo de Quesada's 1911 edition of Martí's complete works. If we compare Martí's novel with Villaverde's, which was published three years before in New York, where there was a major nucleus of Cuban writers and patriots, we can see how the development of the Cuban novel was taking place outside Cuba: *Sab*, *Cecilia Valdés*, *Amistad funesta*, and the English translation of Manzano's *Apuntes autobiográficos*. If in *Cecilia Valdés* Villaverde saw the novel in a Realist, traditional, and objective mode, *Amistad funesta* inaugurates a new Cuban fiction that breaks with the traditional and creates an aesthetic tendency and a narrative form very different from the formal lines of the Spanish novel of the time. This does not mean that Martí was writing a novel superior to Spanish fiction, such as we find in Benito Pérez Galdós or Leopoldo Alas. We cannot even say that he was a better novelist than Villaverde. It is simply that Martí's originality was compelling him, almost intuitively, to seek new directions for the novel.

Simplicity and complexity are the two keys to Martí's poetry, as exemplified on any page of *Ismaelillo* (1882) and *Versos sencillos* (Simple Verses; 1891), both published in New York as new confirmations of a historical current of Cuban literature which is the fact that a large part of Cuban literature, and frequently its most significant works, was published outside the island and generally as the result of political circumstances. One is once again surprised by the accomplishments of a poetry that is seen as besieged by time in its quick and fleeting rhythm, as if time were to end from one moment to the next, as it did for Martí a few years later. Martí seems to have written everything under pressure, as though conscious of the deadline that will be death's final period to the text. Martí defines himself in his poetry with simplicity and plenitude, almost in an informative fashion, without ringing language, while at the same time showing his identification with nature and revealing his omnipresence, as if the poet were to move toward everything and to be in everything. This is a humanistic omnipresence in which man, as such, seeks in continuous movement the unity of the part with the whole. Man is, for Martí, a creating creation that covers all of space in the same way that the creating and natural act does. In this way, we find in Martí the nature that has so preoccupied previous and subsequent poets, proclaimed by Martí with metaphoric simplicity and complexity at the same time. His Cuban landscape is aesthetic in nature, and it does not function as a patriotic proclamation. It is universal and local: man and the palm tree. Cuba does not need to be mentioned in order that it be everywhere, as a part of his being and as an integral part of the cosmos. His poetry is made up of unusual antitheses that are complementary.

It is unfair to say that Martí was just a precursor of Latin American Modernism (an adaptation, among other things, of French Parnassianism and Symbolism) because he did not experiment with poetic form as others did. But to classify him as a Modernist is to limit him. Martí never got carried away by bad taste, by the decadent, or by decorative Frenchification. He was too solid a poet to become superficial and dehumanized. He sought consistency rather than fashion, and his deep Hispanic roots prevented him from being attracted to French adornments. He was, simply, very Latin American.

Since Martí can be interpreted in many ways, he contributes a multitude of denotations to Cuban poetry. If it were necessary to identify one dominant trait, it would be to speak of Martí the surrealist, to the extent that so many of his images seem to result from strange dreams. Haunted by these images, the anguished poet in several poems seems carried to the edge of dementia.

Martí is also the culmination of the Cuban essay, which he expanded and enriched such that it became an act of literary creation. There is no doubt that Cuban consciousness has been molded as the result of the contribution of distinguished essayists like Francisco de Arango y Parreño (1765-1837), Félix Valera y Morales (1787-1853), José Antonio Saco (1797-1879), José de la Luz y Caballero (1800-62), and Domingo del Monte (1804-53). These and other figures constitute a broad spectrum who concern themselves with the Cuban destiny. Conscious of their responsibility, they make philosophical, political, social, and economic proposals, but they avoid purely creative writing. The word is, in these cases, a necessary evil. But this is not true for Martí. Martí's essays match the word with the idea, and metaphoric construction is used as an apt vehicle for the adequate expression of an ideological point of view. The tradition of the essay is enriched by other names that extend from the colonial period to the Republic, such as Manuel Sanguily (1848-1925) and Enrique José Varona (1849-1933), but it is Martí who melds ideology and creation into one form.

VI

When he returned to Cuba, Bonifacio Byrne (1861-1936) complained about seeing another flag that was not his flying next to the Cuban flag. After years of suffering, returning with his soul in mourning, the poet faced a new reality. His disillusionment in the face of reality inaugurated a poetic frustration that paved the way in Cuban poetry for the hermeticism of José Lezama Lima. The frustrations of colonial existence and the struggles for emancipation created a tragic sadness in Cuban poetry. The confrontation of Cuban poets with the imperfections of reality have often caused them to turn away, and confrontation with the reality of the republic between 1902 and 1959 gave rise to an alienating process. This process is certainly global, but whether we call it Modernism, Postmodernism, pure poetry, or neo-Baroque, it is a poetry that feeds on its own lyrical landscape and does not need to look beyond itself. It lives within its own aesthetic, and it is the "creationist" author of its own reality. This is its mode of rebelling against the reality of the world. Regino Boti (1878-1958), René López (1882-1909), Dulce María Borrero (1883-1945), Agustín Acosta (1886), Mariano Brull (1908-54) are only a few of the many poets who took refuge in lyrical stylization, often abstract, often decorative, a "pure" poetry in more than one sense. Even "committed" poets like Rubén Martínez Villena (1899-1934), Manuel Navarro Luna (1894), and Juan Marinello (1898-1977) "purified" the social with aesthetic incursions. The appearance of the review *Orígenes* (Origins) in 1955 represented the culmination of an alienating trajectory. Cintio Vitier (1921), Eliseo Diego (1920), Angel Gastelu (1914), Justo Rodríguez Santos (1915), Octavio Smith (1921), and Lorenzo García Vega (1926) are some of the names that are associated with *Orígenes*. Writers like

Virgilio Piñera and Gastón Baquero (1912) were associated initally with the review, although they later separated themselves from it, while others like Roberto Fernández Retamar (1930) were admitted at the last minute, almost at the moment when the "wheel of fortune" of Cuban poetry would turn ninety degrees. But in reality the key figure of all of this is José Lezama Lima, in whom poetic intransigence has its culmination.

In Lezama Lima, the barrier becomes more and more hermetic. Lezama's hermeticism proposes the celebration of a poetic ritual in which not everyone can participate. Unquestionably, it is a matter of a "verbal sect," or a "lyrical elite," and Lezama Lima serves Cuban poetry in a priestly fashion with an impact that extends to the present day. It is for this reason that he is a highly polemic figure. From a personal point of view, the position is the same one maintained by Casal: through poetry he escapes from his surroundings. This explains why Lezama never left Cuba, where he wrote and published all of his poetry: *Muerte de Narciso* (Narcissus's Death; 1937), *Enemigo Rumor* (Enemy Rumor; 1941), *Aventuras sigilosas* (Secret Adventures; 1945), *La fijeza* (Constancy; 1949); *Dador* (Giver; 1960), *Fragmentos a su imán* (Fragments of His Magnet; 1977). Eliminating ties with the collective and cutting all links of communication with the masses, Lezama lived on the edge of society's conflicts. Thus, he achieved a special form of subversive independence. As a consequence, it is important to note that before the revolutionary triumph, precisely as the result of his disillusionment with reality, Lezama expressed his nonconformity via alienation and hermeticism, with no attempt to communicate with the masses. Politically, history followed an opposite path, addressing itself to the masses. This was the historical crossroads for Cuban poetry in 1959.

At the same time as the formation of this poetry that enclosed the work in a hermetic text, there was also the emergence of a poetry in which the word flowered sonorously, although this does not suggest that its meaning was not necessarily enriched. The sensorial, gustative, olfactive, sonorous tendency, which led to the tactile, the concrete, the sexual, culminated in this period in the so-called Afro-Cuban or black poetry, a national ethnic composition that also spawned a melting pot of races to produce the Cuban mulatto. The prevalence of this and related topics has led to a serious confusion with respect to the meaning of Afro-Cuban poetry, and a simple review of what it involves leaves Cuban culture in an embarrassing position. Afro-Cuban poetry is reduced to a variation of musical and dance motifs. Even taking into consideration that the musical component might be a very significant element in black culture, this monochord emphasis in the treatment of the black results in the effect of a racist cliché. This is especially true in the sense that it involves a superficial approach to black culture, which is seen as a series of picturesque components of national culture in its most superficial form. It is almost always a picture postcard view, one that does not differ very much from the American South's racist image of blacks eating watermelons. Afro-Cuban poetry takes on its greatest authenticity when it coincides with the social poetry also to be found during this period, although dogmatism, diatribe, and political propaganda may prevail. In any case, when it exposes social injustices suffered by the blacks, it is able to transcend the beating of drums and the swaying of hips and attain true heights.

The most representative poet of this modality is Nicolás Guillén (1902), among whose most known works are *Songoro cosongo* (1931), *West Indies, Ltd.* (1934), *Cantos para soldados y sones para turistas* (Songs for Soldiers and Rhythms for Tourists; 1937); *El son entero* (The Whole Rhythm; 1947), *El soldado Miguel Paz y el sargento José Inés* (The Soldier Miguel Paz and the Sergeant José Inés; 1952), *La paloma de vuelo popular* (The Dove of Popular Flight; 1958), *Tengo* (I Have; 1964), *El Gran Zoo (Patria o Muerte!)* (*The Great Zoo*; 1967), *La rueda dentada* (The Cog; 1972), *El diario que a diario* (Day-by-Day Diary; 1972).

It has been said of Guillén that his work inaugurates a new poetic genre that is typically Cuban in nature; that he has discovered possibilities that are unique in formal character, by virtue of his way of integrating music and politics and creating new rhythmic modalities. Although the criticism that has been most enthusiastic with respect to Guillén's work recognizes that in many cases his poems seem to be local-color sketches with caricaturesque elements, it goes on to insist at the same time that Guillén paints a vivid portrait of a system of social injustices. It has also been maintained that Guillén provides an accurate image of Cuba's ethnic composition, which is dominated by the mulatto. In sum, his work has been seen as a poetic contribution that, fully inscribed in popular culture, captures Cuban ethnicity. This is accomplished via the felicitous conjoining of musical rhythm and the word, and via social denunciation. However, Guillén's writing must primarily be seen within the aforementioned context of Afro-Cuban poetry.

Lezama Lima and Guillén represent in a certain sense two opposing poles. At the time of the triumph of the Castro revolution, poetry moves between two contrary poles dominated by these two apparently antagonistic figures. The pendulum swings between the elitist and the populist.

Both poets agree on the primacy of formal elements, which in Lezama means the Baroque complexity of language and in Guillén a rhythmic sonority that is frequently nothing more than just that. Neither of the two adheres to the importance in Cuban poetry of Martí's perfect and profound matching of form and content.

VII

The first figure of importance in Cuban theater between 1902 and 1959 is José Antonio Ramos (1856-1946). Ramos was intensely interested in social problems, and works like *Almas rebeldes* (Rebel Souls; 1906) and *Una bala perdida* (A Lost Bullet; 1907) have a certain interest from this point of view, but they are theatrically poor. Ramos's ideas were extremely confusing and complex, and he fluctuated between pragmatic and democratic concepts and an idealistic point of view close to fascism. In *Calibán Rex* (1914), he proposed a dangerous set of ideas, based on the belief that the selective judgment of the masses is very dubious. Ramos established the thesis of his work when his protagonist affirmed that the masses have always condemned their founding fathers, they have been incapable of recognizing them, and they have attributed to themselves rights within a democratic framework they never understood. Ramos's position is questionable, but, unfortunately, it does correspond to the realities that Latin American history has demonstrated from time to time from the most diverse perspectives.

With *Tembladera* (Quagmire; 1916), Ramos's theater attains its maturity and establishes the outlines of a realistic orientation that will be one of the tendencies followed by contemporary Cuban theater. The work inaugurates in Cuban theater the image of voracious family struggles that acquire multiple variations in other works with diverse technical approaches. The play is an incisive analysis of the psychology, the interests, and the struggles that take place in the nucleus of a Cuban family at the beginning of the Republic, debilitating and demoralizing that family. Ramos undertakes a very complete analysis of Cuban reality, and in the play there is the dramatic convergence of ethical, social, economic, and political commitments, as well as a share of Martí's idealism. In contrast to this idealism, there is a materialistic current that constitutes a sort of deterministic degeneration, in the spirit of Naturalism. Triumph is only possible when the human being is able to impose the ascendency of idealism over materialism.

Ramos's theories did not exclude constructive pragmatism. He broke with the lyrical patriotism of the nineteenth century to face reality. He understood that the solution to Cuba's problems was not in the "Fatherland" but in work, which would offer its fruits in the historical reality of both capitalism and Marxism. In this way, the conflict of twentieth-century Cuba is contained in Ramos's work, which dates from the opening of the period of the Republic.

Ramos's *En las manos de Dios* (In God's Hands; 1933), a work that introduced Expressionism into the Cuban theater, marked a break with the realistic tradition that would be confirmed by the two most important dramatists of Cuban theater prior to 1959: Carlos Felipe (1914-75) and Virgilio Piñera (1914-79). Both writers broke definitively with the pattern of Realism and proposed a change of direction for the aesthetics of the stage. This is similar to what authors were proposing at the same time in the novel (see below). With *El chino* (The Chinaman; 1947), Felipe was able to maintain historical continuity, since within a psychological conflict that is the axis of action, he established the collision between Martí's quest for the ideal and a confrontation with the imperfections of reality. Behind the search by the female protagonist to recreate a moment of love that perhaps never took place lies the historical counterpoint of the Republic. Palma lives an anguished pendulum that keeps her traumatized, caught in a dead-end that is a microcosm of the national trap. Although this concept relates the story to *Tembladera*, Felipe works with a complex theatrical technique, which is the most important contribution of the work to Cuban theater. The constant of the theater within a theater is a characteristic that will dominate many of Cuba's most representative plays.

With *Electra Carrigó* (1948), *Jesús* (1950), and *Falsa alarma* (False Alarm; 1957), Piñera's theater left an even more profound mark on Cuban dramatists of the following generation. *Electra Carrigó* Cubanized tragedy via a parodic system that at the same time is a Cuban form of Existentialism. The traditions of the comic theater had already been assimilated into a theater of another dramatic category, with verbal and sexual components of obvious affiliation with the theater inaugurated by *El fingido Cloridano*. Charged with sexuality and sensuality, *Electra Garrigó* is an eminently political and prophetic work.

VIII

It will, however, fall to the novel to pursue in the most explicit fashion the conflicting faces of Cuban reality. Responding to their generation and to the civic concern that was to be expected in a newly created republic, it is a social novel that transcends the strictly literary. Following the lead of Realism and Naturalism, it often takes on symbolic features that are consonant with these movements. The most representative names are Emilio Bacardí Moreau (1844-1922), Miguel de Carrión (1875-1929), Jesús Castellanos (1879-1912), Carlos Loveira (1882-1928), Luis Felipe Rodríguez (1888-1947), and José Antonio Ramos. All of these novelists lived a moment of historical transition and felt themselves called upon to take stock of the position of the writer in history. This phenomenon is more emphatic in the periods of transition, as will be the case in the 1960s. With the change of political status in 1902 and the fact that such changes were accompanied by the betrayal of many ideals, novelists met the facts face to face and adopted a position that did not always lead to the best literary results. The panorama that they proposed was pessimistic, negative, frequently fatalistic. The result was a local, nationalistic novel in which what is essentially Cuban was the direct definition of problems demanding solution, even though this may not mean a solution was to be found.

Emilio Bacardí pursues Cuban reality in the historical novel with *Vía crucis* (1910, 1914) and in *Doña Guiomar* (1916-17). A few years before, Jesús Castellanos, in *La conjura* (The Conspiracy; 1909), inaugurated a more representative tendency and linked the first manifestations of the twentieth-century Cuban novel with the Realist tradition. Castellanos posits the clash between materialism and idealism, with the defeat of the latter. Miguel Carrión elaborates on the panorama and diversifies the focus of social classes, enriching it psychologically and nationalizing Naturalism with the publication of *Las honradas* (The Honorable Women; 1918) and *Las impuras* (The Impure Women; 1919). But his narrative, with its sordidness, looks in any case backwards, contemplating the world with a Zolaesque perspective, with the result that the novel leaves a sort of documentary evidence of the spirit of the age. Carlos Loveira attempted to create representative archetypes of this society in novels like *Generales y doctores* (Generals and Doctors; 1920) and *Juan Criollo* (Juan Creole; 1928). *Juan Criollo* is considered to be archetypal of Naturalism in the Cuban novel, along with Luis Felipe Rodríguez's *Ciénaga* (The Swamp; 1937).

José Antonio Ramos, tormented and upset by reality, is the author of *Humberto Fabra* (1909), *Coaybay* (1927), *Las impurezas de la realidad* (The Impurities of Reality; 1931), and *Caniquí* (1936). Ramos saw the novel as a vehicle for positing social, economic, and political problems. His novel projects an eminently civic character, abandoning the persistent erotomania that characterized so many of the novels of the period. It must be said that Ramos was in the vanguard of the struggle for women's rights in Cuban society. In a literary setting where woman is all too frequently the geometric curve of the body and a sexual object, Ramos converts her into a human being whose center lies not in her sex but in her brain. He takes her out of the narrow confines of the duties assigned to her sex, including maternity, and converts her into an active being with a conscious ideology who is not limited to primary body functions. *Coaybay* is for many reasons one of the most important novels of contemporary Cuban literature from a thematic point of view. In this novel Ramos breaks with the patriotic and flag-waving tradition inherited from the nineteenth century and betrayed in the twentieth. He goes beyond patriotism and perceives, through the generational struggle between the patriarch Don Marcelo Fernández de Mendoza and his sons, the existence of a world that survives the nationalistic traditions of the last century.

Ramos's problem was that he lived under the sign of the nineteenth century. He belonged to the first generation of the Republic, and its intellectual genesis played an important role in his mentality, which was unable to understand that freedom lay in free literary exercise, the word and the text. But in the decade of the thirties, there were a number of important events that signaled new directions. Lino Novás Calvo (1905) published *El negrero* (The Black Slaver; 1933); Alejo Carpentier (1904-80), *Ecué-yamba-ó* (1931); Enrique Labrador Ruiz (1902), *El laberinto de sí mismo* (The Labyrinth of Himself; 1933), *Cresival* (1936), and *Anteo* (1940); and Carlos Montenegro (1900), *Hombres sin mujer* (Men without a Woman; 1938). During this decade Lydia Cabrera (1899) began to publish her Afro-Cuban narratives, *Cuentos negros de Cuba* (Black Stories from Cuba; 1940). These authors are of considerable importance in Cuban literature. Their literary production extends from the pre-Castro Republican period to the period following the Castro revolution. All, with the exception of Carpentier, are exiles, confirming with this fact the tradition of the intellectual diaspora that began in the nineteenth century.

From a verbal point of view, the most radical of all is Labrador Ruiz. *El laberinto de sí mismo* is, in effect, a labyrinth of word and mind that also, as in the case of Lezama Lima's texts, seems to withdraw into a shell closed to the world. What is at issue is the domain of "I" and the text, a sortie into literature in order to save oneself from the asphyxiation of surrounding reality and historical aggression. This approach is radical, exaggerated perhaps, and possesses an originating importance as a fact of literary history as the signal for a new direction. The reading of Labrador Ruiz's texts represents a monumental effort, for he establishes an aesthetics of the subconscious whose meaning must be sought in the disentangling of the mysterious signs offered by each and every one of the words. This leads to infinite possible approximations and to a purely intellectual game. Historically, Labrador Ruiz is one of the figures of greatest significance in contemporary Cuban literature and a precursor of the present-day Latin American novel. Novás Calvo's work, however, has attracted the greater attention. There is agreement about the importance of *El negrero*. The precision of language is complemented by a blending of reality and fiction as a literary procedure. The novel is basically realistic, with little in the way of unnecessary modifiers and superfluous commentaries.

By contast, Carlos Montenegro's *Hombres sin mujer* is so violently shocking, with a language that is so unusually crude, that the ties with imagination are intentionally eliminated by the author. It is a novel of pure violence, of brutal and sordid expression. Criticism has all too often overlooked the importance of this work, which is almost a savage document of prison life in one of the most authentic narrative portrayals of a collective consciousness. The meaning in Cuban life that police repression has had within the context of a historical process that extends from one dictatorship to another makes *Hombres sin mujer* a novel of extraordinary contemporary meaning.

The beginnings of a truly documentary narrative, with an ethnic and collective consciousness, are to be found in an unparalleled fashion in the work of Lydia Cabrera in her *Cuentos negros de Cuba* and *Por qué...* (Why; 1948). Cabrera's stories are in reality transcriptions of the oral narratives of the Afro-Cuban world, whose minstrelsy passes to the printed page. If Afro-Cuban poetry has in large measure been denied its authenticity, these transcriptions of its popular expression remedy that oversight.

Although Carpentier's *Ecué-yamba-ó* has come to be considered a minor work in relation to his other novels, it is nevertheless a major point of reference within this key period of Cuban fiction. Carpentier began his long journey to magical realism and the Latin American Baroque with this novel. Its Afro-Cuban perspective is parallel to that of the Latin American indigenist novel as a mythic interpretation of what is genuinely Latin American (see the sections on Peru and Ecuador). A novel of contrasts, its language is characterized by the rich and contrapuntal composition of the text, where Carpentier's solid culture is combined with the linguistic quest for Cuban authenticity. This is carried out by conjugating language with music, which is an essential feature of Carpentier's symphonic compositions and a structural element of special importance in many Cuban novels.

Carpentier's contribution to the Cuban novel before 1959 is not limited to *Ecué-yamba-ó*. He had already published *Viaje a la semilla* (Journey to the Seed; 1944), *El reino de este mundo* (*The Kingdom of this World*; 1949), *Los pasos perdidos* (*The Lost Steps*; 1953), *El acoso* (The Chase; 1956), and *Guerra del tiempo* (*War of Time*; 1958). *El siglo de las luces* (*Explosion in a Cathedral*; 1962) was almost completed in 1959. Carpentier's creative trajectory is pregnant with the curious ambivalence of the "journey to the seed" of the autochthonous, which is never attained as a consequence of immersion in a superimposed culture. This existential dichotomy is what gives *Los pasos perdidos* its major validity and what leads Carpentier to produce a masterpiece of contemporary literature, *El reino de este mundo*. Despite the counterpoint between the cultural inauthenticity of the white man and the cultural authenticity of the black, what is certain is that *El reino de este mundo* abounds in images that are as rich in their European as in their African consistency. The result is a constant interaction between carefully wrought images on every page that constitutes the metaphoric-syncretic texture of the novel. But if, on the one hand, the black elements function subversively in the composition of white culture, it is no less true that the opposite occurs and that the "marvelously real" of the novel is subversively overshadowed by the European consciousness of the text. The richness of *El reino de este mundo* consists, precisely, in this ambivalence: an eminently "European" writer undergoing a progressive-regressive journey to the mythic womb of Latin American reality. The Baroque element of the novel emerges, marvelously, from this convergence.

Moreover, Carpentier was principally concerned with historical novels, with characters disintegrated in historic time and space, extending back to the prehistoric, although as in the case of *El siglo de las luces* he allowed himself on several occasions to be carried away by the adventure saga of history. Basically, the whole of Carpentier's fiction yields a great historical novel, with characters that project themselves onto each other. One must not forgot the pictorial-symphonic nature of his work. For example, *El reino de este mundo* and *El acoso* are conceived in terms of opposing symphonic modes. The first leads to a Baroque expression in accord with the underlying symphonic composition, while the second works with musical dissonances that are then transposed to the visual composition of the narration, which is both objective and abstract at the same time.

IX

With the triumph of the Castro revolution in 1959, a new cycle of Cuban history opens, and it is possible to say that poetry, theater, and the narrative have traveled a great distance in their development, having reached a level of true maturity. Literature has separated itself from the nineteenth-century nationalistic consciousness as a consequence of the avatars of historical reality. At the beginnning of the Republican period, writers felt that civic responsibility should be the conditioning motive for their work, but when they experienced frustrations in the face of history, they decided to divorce themselves from history and to concentrate on their own creative experience. Poetry draws increasingly into its shell and purifies itself in its hermeticism. Theater expresses the clash with reality in the form of distortions of language and action and by seeking ritual forms to portray the absurdity of the reality of the period. In narrative, there is the quest for elaborate structural and lexical forms. What emerged in Cuba during the subsequent fifty-seven years of the Republic and the ideological and formal revolution of literary language is a true revolution of the Word that asserts the realm of fiction as a determinant of literary reality. The Copernican revolution of the word proclaimed independence from any form of colonialism. But while the text is engaged in revolution, the historical context takes its cue elsewhere.

With Castro's success in 1959, the creation of a Marxist state and the subsequent diaspora, Cuba completed a historical cycle in the present century. There was a movement away from the nationalistic ideas of the last century, and Cuba became an archetypic example of forces on an international plane, passing from the orbit of capitalistic neocolonialism to that of Marxist neocolonialism. The literary repercussions are multi-

ple. With Cuba's coming to play a leading role in world events, literature is significantly divided, although in the long run it triumphs in the
face of adversity. Gradually, the divergent elements of literature's historical development take on a convergent and complementary meaning in
what at first glance might appear to be a phenomenon of dispersion.
The sum of what is written within and outside the island constitutes,
without a doubt, an exceedingy rich corpus for an evaluation of twentieth-century Cuban literature.

The existence of the aforementioned diaspora literature does not
mean that there are two Cuban literatures. The line of continuity of this
creative crisis of divergencies advances during the present century within
two periods of Cuban history: before and after 1959. Consequently,
political history determines the conditions of literary history, and this
must be understood in terms of a temporal dichotomy (before and after
1959) and a spatial one (inside and outside Cuba). Twentieth-century
Cuban literature must be grasped as the interplay of complementary
elements that will only become clear with the passage of time. Cuban
writers after 1959 found themselves trapped in a vortex of international
forces. Insularity became an accident of geography. History, with all its
paradoxes, contributed to a literary enrichment, and historical phenomena like the Mariel exodus served to increase the diaspora and to give it
new meaning.

When the curtain opens on the second act of the saga of Cuban
literature in the twentieth century, the action begins on the morning of
1959, and the conflict emerges from a position where the antagonists
have yet to find an accomodation between literature and revolution or
between textual and historical revolution, which is a fundamental dichotomy. At the outset, both facts would seem to go hand in hand, and if
there had not been growing signs of dissidence, the present characteristics of Cuban literature would be very different. But one revolution
could not agree with the other, and the Marxist definition, which was not
subscribed to by all of the writers, increased the conflict. The immediate
struggle was around *Lunes de revolución* (Monday), the weekly magazine
of the newspaper *Revolución* (Revolution), which under the direction of
Guillermo Cabrera Infante (1929) is the most representative case of
textual revolution in conflict with the impositions of history. The weekly
first engaged in a symptomatic gesture: it inverted the R in the word
revolution; this gesture was not gratuitous. It was consciously or subcon-
sciously intentional and served to explain singlehandedly the subsequent
process whereby writers were to understand revolution as they saw fit.

Lunes de revolución appeared between 1959 and the end of 1961, but its disappearance would not eliminate the conflict, which would only re-emerge in a different fashion in an array of historical-literary episodes. What happened is very simple: the revolutionary spirit of many writers sooner or later followed the individualist path of the diaspora, and texts prohibited explicitly or implicitly by the "Index" would continue to appear outside Cuba. Others would understand literary revolution within the canons of Marxism, meeting these principles with a greater or lesser degree of flexibility.

X

First in the pages of *Revolución* and then in the pages of *Lunes de revolución*, José Alvarez Baragaño (1932-62) undertook the iconoclastic destruction of Cuban poetry. The attack was concentrated on Lezama Lima's *Orígenes* group. The poets of the new generation felt the break with preceding modalities and identified the revolution with the destruction of the alienated idols of prerevolutionary poetry. Paradoxically, many perished in the combat, but Lezama Lima, in a gesture of passive resistance, survived and continued to write. In this way, he continued to preside over his own world in the company of some of the members of the "old guard" of *Orígenes*. Spiritually, he fulfilled the same function as those who left Cuba. Nicolás Guillén pursued his own work, transformed into the poetic figure who best represents the popular character of the revolution, followed closely by Samuel Feijóo (1914), another poet of a popular strain with an established reputation that antedated the revolution. For his part, Roberto Fernández Retamar became an archetypal figure of the poetic bureaucracy. Fernández Retamar belonged to what has been called the Generation of 1959, which also included the previously mentioned Baragaño and Pablo Armando Fernández (1930), as well as three poets who were more authentic: Rolando Escardó (1925-60), Fayad Jamis (1930), and Luis Marré (1929). Escardó was deeply identified with the revolution, and his poetry transcends commitment in order to situate the reader, with profound simplicity, in the realm of the dark and the mysterious. Jamis was also a tormented poet and, although he too wrote a poetry that defined him politically, he escaped being declamatory. He was essentially a poet of final questions, of rich and surprising images that have little to do with Fernández Retamar's calculating poetry (in both a lyrical and a political sense). Finally,

Luis Marré manifested a humble tonality that spoke of work in terms of simple, objective, and visual images.

Three women poets who had already achieved some reknown, Fina García Marruz (1923), Clarilda Oliver Labra (1924), and Rafaela Chacón Nardi (1926), expanded their poetic activity. Poets like Eugenio Florit (1903) and Gastón Baquero continued to write abroad.

In order to avoid being overwhelmed by the problem of "all who are somebody are not included, and not everybody included is somebody," which is one of the problems that have plagued criticism on Cuban literature of the past twenty-five years, this discussion will be limited to the positing of the difficulties involved, to offering some general perspectives, and to providing information on what is most noteworthy.

Of special notoriety is the case of Heberto Padilla (1932), who in 1968 received the prize awarded by the Unión Nacional de Escritores y Artistas (Nacional Union of Writers and Artists) for his book *Fuera de juego* (*Out of the Game*; 1968) and in 1971 was jailed as a consequence of a number of repressive actions related to the cultural politics of the Castro government. The "Padilla Case" possesses extraordinary importance since it focuses attention, once again, on the conflict arising from the relations between the writer and the revolution, although in fact what is involved is a process begun in 1961 when Castro pronounced his "Palabras a los intelectuales" (Words to the Intellectuals) and defined clearly the position of the writer within revolutionary Cuban society, which is to say the cultural position of Castroism. The swift closing of *Lunes de revolución* was a concrete fact that left no doubt about the future position of the writer in Cuba. What happens with *Fuera de juego* is the logical extension of this first episode of cultural repression and the only surprising thing is that it took so long for a crisis of this nature to arise. *Fuera de juego* is, therefore, of considerable importance within Cuban literary history, quite apart from its literary value. It is a book where the individual consciousness of the poetic act sees itself within a collective context, and it offers a very valuable synthesis, expressed with poetic precision, of the relations between the individual and the collectivity.

From the point of view of the literary politics of the revolutionary government, Castroism committed a grave error. Despite the fact that *Fuera de juego* is a good book, it would probably have passed unnoticed had it not been the center of controversy. But history, like poetry, has its weaknesses and its Achilles's heel. The most serious problem was that the impact of this repressive act left the door open for the future emphasis of a poetry that, written from behind bars, united twentieth-century Cuban poetry with the tradition of poets who, like Juan Clemente Zenea in the last century, wrote their poetry in jail. *Fuera de fuego* opened Pandora's box for the revolution. Angel Cuadra (1931), Jorge Valls (1933), Armando Valladares (1937), and Miguel Sales (1951) deserve special mention among other writers who wrote in jail and who have attained special recognition in recent yers for the quality of their writing and for the historical experience from which it arises.

XI

The dramatists of the last prerevolutionary generation and newer voices that emerged with the triumph of the revolution—which for the first time offered them the opportunity to participate actively in the life of the theater—worked with a number of dramatic experiments in one of the most productive periods of Cuban theater. Rolando Ferrer (1925-76), already known for works like *Cita en el espejo* (Appointment in the Mirror; 1949), *Lila la mariposa* (Lila the Butterfly; 1950), *La hija de Nacho* (Nacho's Daughter; 1951), produced *La taza de café* (The Cup of Coffee; 1959), which may be considered the first success of postrevolutionary Cuban theater. *La taza de café* brings together the characteristics of "serious" theater and those of popular theater as a sort of parodic melodrama of the existence of the upper bourgeoisie prior to 1959.

As a whole, the dramatists of the 1960s moved in two directions at once, although these shared some points of contact. There is first an absurdist and ritualistic theater, complemented by one closer to the old canons of Realism, with the latter more explicit in its theses. But in neither case is there a turning away from reality, which is too strongly present to be ignored. Many of these points of view can be found in the development of the theater of Matías Montes Huidobro (1931), which begins with *Sobre las mismas rocas* (On the Same Rocks; 1951), a nonrealistic work. Without being completely so, *Los acosados* (The Besieged; 1959) is a work about characters "besieged" by social and economic reality, while *Gas en los poros* (Gas in the Pores; 1961) concerns itself with family struggle in terms of the techniques of theater within theater, a political microcosm. By contrast, *La botija* (Buried Treasure; 1959) and *El tiro por la culata* (Backfire; 1961) are ideological responses to Cuban history of the moment, as was Virgilio Piñera's *La sorpresa* (The Surprise; 1961).

The absurd and ritual consciousness characterize the theater of José Triana (1932). *El mayor general hablará de Teogonía* (The Major General Will Speak of Theogony; 1960) is one of the most daring examples of a theater of the absurd in Cuba, one where the thorough distortion of language and situations results in an almost irrational state that, nevertheless, is not without some meaning within the context of Cuba's historical logic. This admirable use of language takes on a very different character in *Medea en el espejo* (Medea in the Mirror; 1960), where Triana pursues the principles of the Cubanization of Greek tragedy utilized by Virgilio Piñera in *Electra Garrigó*. What is especially significant in *Medea en el espejo*, moreover, is the verbal chaining, which constitutes a sort of fatalistic linguistic sequence that ends up leading Medea to the fulfillment of her tragic destiny. All of this is carried out within a strictly Cuban setting and with a dazzling variety of lexical plays.

Julio Matas (1931) and Antón Arrufat (1935) are two other representatives of the theater of ritual and the absurd. *La crónica y el suceso* (The Chronicle and the Event; 1964) is Matas's most accomplished work, marked by a constant confusion of the planes of fiction and reality. Arrufat for his part has cultivated the absurd beginning with *El caso se investiga* (The Case Is Under Investigation; 1957), which he extends in subsequent works: *La zona cero* (Zone Zero; 1963), *El último tren* (The Last Train; 1963), and *La repetición* (The Repetition; 1963). *Todos los domingos* (Every Sunday; 1965) stresses the ritual act and theater within theater in order to detail the psychological state of the protagonist.

On the other hand, there is a realistic tendency, characterized by a more direct confrontation with the Cuban reality of the recent past and the revolutionary moment. Fermín Borges (1931), Manuel Reguera Saumell (1928), and Abelardo Estorino have been the most representative dramatists in this regard.

Two younger authors, Raúl de Cárdenas (1935) and Nicolás Dorr (1947), produced works in 1961 that are a sort of synthesis of the two tendencies described. Although Cárdenas's *La palangana* (The Basin) has some elements of the absurd, it follows the outlines of the traditional Cuban melodrama previously mentioned. The inhabitants of a Cuban tenement decide to buy a golden basin, which represents everybody's dreams. These are not practical dreams, but absurd ones that point to the lack of logic in Cuban life. There ensue the disputes that the basin creates among the inhabitants, with the result that they all end up in a brawl that is more festive than tragic. Dorr's *Las pericas* (The Parrots) was equally successful. It is an absurd delirium and, when it opened, the young dramatist (really only a teenager) earned the backing of those who felt that ideological pressures were undermining culture. The counterpoint between aesthetics and revolution has been very clearly exemplified since 1961, and it is for this reason that Dorr represents the most important theatrical event of the period, not for the quality of his work but for the intuitive rebellion it embodies within the context of cultural polemics.

Teatro Escambray (Escambray Theater; 1978) defines perfectly the goals and the procedures of collective theater in particular and the exact function of theater within the context of revolutionary Cuba. It is a fundamental book, and clear as regards its point. The original nucleus of the Teatro Escambray was formed in 1968. A group of theater people abandoned the Havana stage for the Escambray mountains. This area had been especially neglected during the Republican period prior to Castro, and it was the belief of these people that work in Escambray could be particularly useful, since it was an area where counterrevolutionary activity was focused. In order to carry out their "stage" work, it was necessary to count on the support of political organizations, and the leadership of the Communist Party provided such support. This position, according to the beliefs of the organizers and participants in this movement, was very different from that of previous theatrical movements. The function of the theater could no longer be simply an exercise in rhetoric. Rather, it should serve to purify the people via the sacrifice of individual personality. The Teatro Escambray arose from these principles. From an official point of view in accord with the principles of the revolutionary government at the end of the 1960s, this was the sort of theater that Cuba needed.

As a vehicle for doctrinal principles and as the embodiment of the procedures and results of the dramatic elaborations of the group, *Teatro Escambray* offers contemporary Latin American drama a methodology for revolutionary theater, one that obviously differs considerably from what was being done before. And it left no room for doubt about one fact: all of prior Cuban theater was out of the game.

In recent years and with the waning of enthusiasm for a theater of collective creation for both historical and political reasons, there has been something of a resurgence of the so-called author-centered theater. Certain figures have been reassessed, like Rolando Ferrer, who has come to be considered a contemporary classic, along with Virgilio Piñera, whose *Un arropamiento sartorial en la caverna pública* (Sartorial Raiment in the Platonic Cave; 1971) was only published in January 1988 in the magazine *Tablas* (Boards). This in itself constitutes recognition for a work that, according to Rine Leal in the same number, had been silenced and, therefore, practically unknown in Cuba. On the other hand, 1986 saw the publication abroad, also after a long delay, of *Una caja de zapatos vacía* (An Empty Shoe Box; 1968), which was given its first performance in Miami in 1988 during the II Festival de Teatro Hispano (Second Hispanic Theater Festival).

With the exile of José Triana and other dramatists, Abelardo Estorino emerges as the most important dramatist within Cuba. His theater, without ever moving away from its initial realism, is enriched by an experimentation with scenic time and space that gives it great flexibility and imagination and establishes a line of continuity with the experimental procedures that characterized Cuban theater in the 1960s. Estorino's *La dolorosa historia del amor secreto de don José Jacinto Milanés* (The Sad Story of Don José Jacinto Milanés's Secret Love; 1974), *Ni un sí ni un no* (Neither Yes nor No; 1979), and especially *Morir del cuento* (To Die in the Telling; 1984) can rightly be called the best of contemporary Cuban theater.

An examination of the prerevolutionary past and its fratricidal struggles becomes more systematic within the purview of a Marxist interpretation that insists repeatedly on exposing the defects of the capitalist system. The division at the heart of the Cuban family, which since the time of José Antonio Ramos has been of interest to many Cuban dramatists, is expanded within the context of the revolutionary framework. Without abandoning the familial nucleus, the emphasis on the family goes beyond the narrow limits of the home to explore collective organisms like the Comités de Defensa de la Revolución (Revolution Defense Committees). Some of the dramatists who were already known at the beginning of the revolution and others that will become known afterwards are involved in working with these elements. Among those who had already established themselves, Raúl González de Cascorro (1922) counts several works of this nature among his production, like *Piezas de museo* (Museum Pieces; 1969), *Traición en Villa Feliz* (Betrayal in Villa Feliz; 1972), and *El hijo de Arturo Estévez* (Arturo Estévez's Son; 1974). In this latter play, family conflicts are expanded to include the "struggle against the bandits" that takes place in the Escambray area during the 1970s. Freddy Artiles (1946), *Adriana en dos tiempos* (Adriana in Two Times; 1971), is representative of a younger author with a concern for the dualities in Cuban history. Gerardo Fernández (1941) locates such conflicts in a more recent time period, at the time when a mass exodus is taking place at the beginning of the 1980s. In *La familia de Benjamín García* (Benjamín

García's Family; 1982), a betrayal from within the family, seen as an act of patriotic and revolutionary service, the struggle between parents and children along the lines of the traditional realism of Estorino's *El robo del cochino* (The Theft of the Pig) provide a new perspective in terms of an archetypal thematics of the Cuban experience.

In fact, one of the most interesting phenomena of contemporary Cuban theater is to be found in a principle of continuity and rupture, both historical and territorial, where one side is always engaged in watching the other, like Siamese twins who detest each other but cannot be separated. There is a national obsession with contemplating the other side. The irreconcilable positions confront each other without ever reaching a common accord. Beginning with David Camps (1939) and his enigmatic *En el viaje sueño* (In the Trip a Dream; 1971), through Nicolás Dorr's *Una casa colonial* (A Colonial House; 1984) and his other extensive dramatic production, down to *Week-end en Bahía* (Weekend in Bahía; date unknown), which presents in the form of a comedy of manners the reencounter in Cuba of a couple separated by exile, various authors have elaborated this disjunctive thematics with diverse procedures but with a predominance of realism. Outside of Cuba, Leopoldo Hernández (1921), *Siempre tuvimos miedo* (We Were Always Afraid; 1985), and Matías Montes-Huidobro, *Exilio* (Exile; 1986), also work with this double perspectivist play.

Historical theater has come to acquire a marked importance in Cuba. On some occasions it demonstrates a partially allegorical character, while at other times it is partially historical, as in the case of *Ceremonial de guerra* (War Ceremonial; 1973) by José Triana, which was only published in 1989 outside of Cuba. On other occasions the element of historical documentation is more precise. It is therefore possible to survey Cuban history, which is at times a matter of literary history, through the optics of a new interpretation. Gerardo Fulleda León (1942) goes back to 1604 for inspiration in Silvestre de Balboa's *Espejo de paciencia* (Mirror of Patience) in order to recreate in *Azoque* (Quicksilver; 1979) the kidnapping of the bishop of Cuba. Previously, José Brene, one of the first dramatists to work within this new historical dimension, looks back to 1682 in his *Los demonios de Remedios* (Remedios's Demons; 1965), while Ignacio Gutiérrez (1929) in *La casa del marinero* (The Sailor's House; 1964) sets his play in 1762 with the occupation of Havana by the English. Fulleda León in *Los profanadores* (The Profaners; 1975) and *Plácido* (1981) and Abilio Estévez (1954) with *La verdadera culpa de Juan Clemente Zenea* (Juan Clemente Zenea's True Guilt; 1984) present two different moments of Cuban history in the nineteenth century. These two works, both with a specific historical content, engage in the reconstruction of the history of Cuba within a perspective that conforms to the goals of the revolution. As a consequence, there is an opposition between history as it was understood before the revolution and historical understanding subsequent to it. In dramatic terms, there is a subordination to this objective, and the result is a negative one, particularly as concerns schematic characterizations. There is the attempt to provide a mural of colonial Cuban life via an informative-narrative procedure, with a broad but conventional chronology. There is an endless number of characters, but only on occasion is their any profundity to them. The various representatives of colonial power (governing officials, military men, priests, merchants), accomplices of the Creole bourgeoisie which, except on rare occasion, functions in conformance with its basest of interests, are the determining agents of the action. The values of the nineteenth-century Liberal bourgeoisie in Cuba are subjected to a devastating analysis. And, to be sure, there is no absence of a counterresponse from the perspective of exile, as for example in case of Raúl de Cárdenas's image of José Martí in *Un cubano de importancia* (A Cuban of Importance; 1989), which received the 1989 Premio Letras de Oro (Golden Letters Award) from the University of Miami.

Some of these works provide important historical postulates with respect to racism in Cuba. Afro-Cuban mythical elements, beginning with José Brene's *Santa Camila de la Habana vieja* (Santa Camila of Old Havana; 1962), take second place in the context of more concrete problems like racial discrimination. Nevertheless, Eugenio Hernández (1936) in *María Antonia* (1967) and *Obedí el cazador* (Obedí the Hunter; 1980) maintains alive these mythic elements that constitute such an important ingredient of Cuban ethnicity. *Chocolate Campeón* (Champion Chocolate; 1981), by Jesús Gregorio (birth date unknown), offers refreshing perspectives on the treatment of ethnic conflicts.

Finally, the problems of the revolution are treated in a direct way, although with an evasion of central concerns, in the sense that the purpose is fundamentally didactic. As a consequence, many works have a local interest that is oriented toward questions affecting Cuban society at a specific moment. Héctor Quintero (1942) began in the 1960s to write comedies of manners that could well have been very funny at the time, although they have tended to age very rapidly; see, for example, *Mambrú se fue a la guerra* (Johnny Went Off to War; 1970) and *Si llueve te mojas como los demás* (If It Rains You'll Get Wet Like All the Rest;

1974). Sometimes the problems can refer to the conduct of professors and students, like *Molinos de viento* (Windmills; 1982) by Rafael González (1950), were students cheat on their exams and professors are bad teachers, which means that none of them meet their obligations like good revolutionaries; the entire proposition is developed in the most superficial manner possible. In other texts, problems of the work place are dealt with, with references to negative opinions of men with respect to women, as in *Ramona* (1978) by Roberto Orihuela (1950) and *Aprendiendo a mirar las grúas* (Learning How to Watch the Cranes; 1979) by Mauricio Coll (1951), works that could be of only the slightest interest outside of Cuba or beyond their immediate point of reference.

In other works, the conflicts attain an internationalist frame of reference. Ignacio Gutiérrez, in *Los capuzones* (Splashing Around; 1972), focuses on issues related to fishing vessels captured by the U.S. Coast Guard, while Cuban participation in Angola is dealt with in *Kunene* (1980). This is also the setting of David Camps's *El traidor* (The Traitor; 1977), a play that was accompanied in its published version by a Bundó glossary. Gerardo Fernández incorporates law enforcement and international intrigue in *Ernesto* (1976) or musical comedy elements in *A nivel de cuadra* (Seen from the Level of the Neighborhood Block; 1978). All of these works are characterized by the absence of psychological conflicts and by the presence of a schematic characterization of Good versus Bad, the presentation of exemplary characters and model situations in opposition to negative attitudes. Within these norms, "patriotic" denunciation, public confession of errors, and the absolute dedication to production all constitute goals exalted by the Cuban revolutionary theater.

XII

The success of the revolution took many writers by surprise, but especially fiction writers. Faced with the need to narrate something specific, they found themselves in what we might call an uncomfortable position. After all, poets can always justify their escape from reality in the name of poetry itself, but fiction writers, at least up until now, have had the obligation to face facts. The problem was, nevertheless, that the facts were exotic. Like good bourgeois writers (although not all of them were so well off), they had all been doing their own thing, "business as usual," while the revolution was taking place and some poor unknowns were passing over to the great beyond.

The background elements of the reality of the Cuban writer upon the arrival of Castroism are fundamental to understanding his situation and to avoiding hypocritical preconceptions. There were those Cuban writers who were obliged (or felt themselves obligated) to write the novel of the revolution, which was for them such an exotic event. Fortunately, at the time it was believed that the revolution had been carried out by the bourgeoisie and not by the working or peasant class, which provided a favorable link when the time came to tell about it. The result would be novels dealing directly with the subject, among them *El sol a plomo* (Lead Sun; 1959) by Humberto Arenal (1926), *Bertillón 166* (1959) by José Soler Puig (1916), *Mañana es 26* (Tomorrow is the 26th; 1960) by Hilda Perera (1926), and *El perseguido* (The Persecuted; 1964) by César Leante (1926).

But the bourgeois writer feels the particular necessity to explain everything ethically for himself and for others, even what is inexplicable. The revolution in which these writers have not participated directly begins by burdening them with a bourgeois guilt complex, which is a good way of shackling them. As a consequence, if it is not possible to narrate revolutionary events exactly as they took place, at least they should be narrated to the private degree in which they did not take place for the writer. The novel, instead of moving outward, relating an unknown or poorly known experience, can direct itself inward. This determines a self-preoccupation that has been understood as existentialist. The analysis of one's self and of the circumstances of a prerevolutionary world is an imperative for the individual with an honest and justified position. Thus one finds novels like *La búsqueda* (The Quest; 1961) by Jaime Sarusky (1931), *Pequeñas maniobras* (Small Maneuvers; 1963) by Virgilio Piñera, *Después de la Z* (After the Letter Z; 1964) by Mariano Rodríguez Herrera (1935), *El sol ese enemigo* (That Enemy the Sun; 1962) by José Lorenzo Fuentes (1928), and *No hay problema* (No Problem; 1961) by Edmundo Desnoes (1930). A representative case of the counterpoint existentialism-revolution involving a well-defined historical coincidence is Desnoes's *Memorias del subdesarrollo* (*Inconsolable Memories*; 1965), which involves inserting the protagonist's past within the immediate reality being lived in revolutionary Cuba. Three other novels of a similar nature are *Padres e hijos* (Fathers and Sons; 1967) by César Leante, *Los animales sagrados* (The Sacred Animals; 1967) by Humberto Arenal, and *El plano inclinado* (The Inclined Plane; 1968) by Noel Navarro (1931). But perhaps *Presiones y diamantes* (Pressures and Diamonds; 1968) by Virgilio Piñera is one of the most important novels in this category, since Piñera makes use here of the existentialism and the absurd that characterize his theater, recreating a Kafkaesque situation in terms of a machinery of the state that asphyxiates the individual.

The historical-existentialist composition, sustained by a variety of more or less complex structures, may be found also in *En ciudad semejante* (In a City like This; 1970) by Leandro Otero (1932). Otero's importance as a novelist in the general panorama of Cuban fiction of the period consists in part of his official position, which counters the dissident line being taken more and more markedly by Cuban writers. Otero represents an orthodox position that is naturally reflected in his mode of narrative as well as the content of his novel. He represents an official historical consciousness, one that Pablo Armando Fernández also manifests, in a manner even more complex, in his *Los niños se despiden* (The Children's Farewell; 1968).

During the decade of the seventies, Cuban fiction demonstrates an extraordinary variety and richness, and it is not possible here to survey all of its manifestations. But beginning with the publication of Lezama Lima's *Paradiso* (1966), the divergencies will reach a crisis point. By this time Severo Sarduy (1937) had already published *Gestos* (Gestures; 1963), which, although thematically a political novel, is in essence an experimental work with a Cubist composition pictorial in nature, accompanied by a dissonant musical structure that results in an objective dehumanization that sets it apart from the novels mentioned above. But *Gestos* in reality is a formally conservative novel, if we compare it with what will come after *Paradiso*.

Although it is undeniable that in *Paradiso* there is a historical consciousness, language, in the manner of Lezama Lima, is the real protagonist. Criticism has often repeated this observation for the simple reason that the novel turns out to be a labyrinth so complex that not to understand everything being said becomes confused with the virtues of the vocabulary, since one is uncomfortable with the possibility that things can be comprehended in a straightforward manner. Whatever the case may be, the Cuban novel becomes identified with the "boom" of the Latin American narrative, which is literarily very important to the extent that it involves an anti-mass-reader novel that seems almost to be a parodic gesture in the face of the government's literacy campaign. The preoccupations of *Paradiso* continue in *Oppiano Licario* (1977)

Sarduy's *De donde son los cantantes* (*From Cuba with a Song*; 1967) is very different in character and much more complex than *Gestos*. Mythic-ethnic composition constitutes a new type of novel that is in part historical, within the framework of a rich musical spectrum. At first fragmentary and confusing in appearance, the elements become integrated via a system where, once again, the primacy of language is stressed.

The transition of Sarduy from a writer who will go on from publishing in Cuba to attracting international attention as a writer in exile is discrete and gradual. But the case of Guillermo Cabrera Infante will have a much more pronounced and polemic political-literary importance. Cabrera Infante's prestige and his controversial nature have been recognized in Cuban literary circles since 1959. His work as a movie critic for the review *Carteles* (Billboard; 1954-60) and his short stories had already appeared in different publications and awakened the admiration of writers of his generation. It was no surprise, then, that when he assumed the editorship of *Lunes de revolución* after the Castro victory, he would become the most important writer of the new movement. A rebel and an individualist as well as a spokesman for revolutionary change, Cabrera Infante had a position different from those who identified with the orthodox revolutionary line. As a consequence, *Lunes de revolución* reflected vividly his personality and ended up representing something different from the doctrinal interests of the revolution. Definitively alienated from the direction being taken by the revolution, Cabrera Infante would find his personal liberation via the exorcisms of language. His lexical existentialism culminated in *Tres tristes tigres* (*Three Trapped Tigers*; 1964). This novel has been extensively studied by critics, and the unraveling of his verbal games, many of them touched by a strange sense of humor, has given rise to a multiplicity of approaches. It has been said that this novel reflects the loquacity, spontaneity, and improvisation of the Cuban character, a superficial interpretation of the national temperament. History has assumed the task of demonstrating quite the opposite, for behind the apparent improvisation and the spontaneity, there is an iron hand in line with the national character. But the vision of Cabrera Infante invents a new and higher individual reality. The world offered by *Tres tristes tigres* is very personal, and its greatest accomplishment is to transport the reader, not to the Havana of underdevelopment, but to the one that exists in the mind of the novelist himself, one that is expressed via the overdevelopment of his language. In *Vista del amanecer en el trópico* (*Dawn in the Tropics*; 1974), he created a unique novel on the basis of nominal omissions, a process of objective dehumanization, a lexical cleansing and/or sterilization, and a visual reconstruction of Cuban history in the form of fixed precinematographic visions. Cabrera Infante has always been an original writer who has kept Cuban fiction in a state of alert and constant movement, and his role in the political-literary game has been no less audacious than his novelistic experiments.

In the face of Cuban history, Cabrera Infante has articulated a postion of an essentially lexical basis. But the role of history weighs heavily on the Cuban novel, and the solution to the conflict between history and language is a major goal. Alejo Carpentier seeks this reconciliation in a number of works. *El recurso del método* (*Reasons of State*; 1974) brings together his own concept of the historical novel and a certain sense of parody. Also historical in nature are *El arpa y la sombra* (The Harp and the Shadow; 1979) and, in another sense, *La consagración de la primavera* (The Consecration of Spring; 1978).

In any case, the conflict between language and history required a new outlet. Miguel Barnet (1941) sought the answer in the invention of the "documentary novel." There is no question that *Biografía de un cimarrón* (*Biography of a Runaway Slave*; 1968) has the virtue of transporting us, through the medium of a verbal transcription that seems to be exact, to the world of Esteban Montejo, who had been a slave in the period before independence. At the same time the experience of the individual is narrated, the reader is led to perceive the historical context of the narrative. But the limitations of the documentary novel are obvious in *Canción de Rachel* (Rachel's Song; 1969), where the "transcription" of the story of an aging courtesan produces the effect of a falsified, partialized document and, what is worse, one of scant interest.

Long before Cabrera Infante left Cuba in 1965, a Cuban novel of exile was being written, in the face of a critical reaction that was rather condescending. Historical events imply a process of revaluation, and there is no escaping the embarrassing fact that among the "novels of the revolution" are numerous works written by authors who have ceased to be "revolutionary" novelists and whose texts, seen in perspective, are not so either. It becomes necessary to view the complex of Cuban novels in a more universal way in terms of thematic and/or formal variations. For example, the novels of Juan Arcocha (1927) reveal in their style a political consciousness parallel to that of others published in Cuba. This is also the case with *A Candle in the Wind* (1967), written originally in English, and *Una bala perdida* (A Lost Bullet; 1973). Hilda Perera is another novelist who deals in direct statements concerning her social reality and the consequences of historical events for her characters, as in *El sitio de nadie* (A Place for Nobody; 1972), *Felices Pascuas* (Happy Holidays; 1977), and *Plantado* (Left in the Lurch; 1981).

Carlos Alberto Montaner (1943) continues the violently realistic and naturalistic tradition in *Perromundo* (Dogworld; 1972), and José Sánchez-Boudy (1929) has an extensive production of humorous novels like *Lilayando* (1971), exemplifying a verbal play that is very characteristic of popular Cuban culture. He has also written more structurally elaborate novels like *Los cruzados de la aurora* (The Crusaders of Dawn; 1972). The novelistic production of Luis Ricardo Alonso (1927) analyzes the behavior of different social classes within the context of a complex Cuban reality, with well-developed characters, as in *El candidato* (*The Candidate*; 1970), *Los dioses ajenos* (Alien Gods; 1972), and *El palacio y la furia* (The Palace and the Fury; 1976). Humor in the novel acquires skillful expression in *Los primos* (The Cousins; 1971) by Celedonio González (1923) and culminates in *Desnudo en Caracas* (Naked in Caracas; 1974) by Fausto Masó (1934). It would be appropriate to consider these and other novels an integral part of recent Cuban fiction and neither marginal nor inconsequential manifestations.

The history of Cuban literature would not be complete without taking into account an extensive tradition of dissident writers and a production strongly intertwined with the meaning of this dissidence and the concomitant exile involved. This tradition in the case of postrevolutionary exile is to be seen in Matías Montes Huidobro's *Desterrados al fuego* (Exiles into Fire; 1975). The subsequent dissidence of novelists like César Leante, Antonio Benítez Rojo (1931), and Reinaldo Arenas (1943-90) favors a global analysis of Cuban narrative beyond the confines of the island. In this sense, the trajectory of Arenas is especially prominent, since he went into exile with an appreciable prestige based on *Celestino antes del alba* (Celestino before Dawn; 1967) and *El mundo alucinante* (The Hallucinating World; 1969), novels that have been called "escapist," an inapt term to describe the commitment of the author. Arenas's more recent fiction includes *El palacio de las blanquísimas mofetas* (The Palace of the Pure White Skunks; 1980), *Termina el desfile* (The Parade is Over; 1981), *Cantando en el pozo* (Singing in the Well; 1982), and *Arturo, la estrella más brillante* (Arturo, the Brightest Star; 1984). Arenas's work is, in its structural experimentation and its fantastic and imaginative conception of reality, a synthesis of multiple tendencies embodied in an original narrative mode.

In sum, one can say that Cuba's historical crisis has only served to enrich its literature, whether as an affirmation or as a negation of the political process. The result has been a quarter of a century of extraordinary vigor in Cuban letters.

Translated by David William Foster

BIBLIOGRAPHY

Aguirre, Yolanda. *Apuntes sobre el teatro colonial (1790-1833)*. La Habana: Universidad de La Habana, 1968. A useful guide to Cuban colonial theater.

Arrom, José Juan. *Historia de la literatura dramática cubana*. New Haven: Yale University Press, 1944. A brief but well-documented study on the evolution of Cuban theater.

Barreda-Tomás, Pedro M. *The Black Protagonist in the Cuban Novel*. Amherst: University of Massachusetts Press, 1979. Despite the restrictive nature of the theme, this study covers a wide spectrum of Cuban narrative.

Bueno, Salvador. *Historia de la literatura cubana*. La Habana: Ministerio de Educación, 1963. Although Bueno's works are not always profound, they are useful sources for a panoramic view of Cuban literary history and its major figures.

Bueno, Salvador. *Medio siglo de literatura cubana, 1902-1952*. La Habana: Comisión Nacional Cubana de la UNESCO, 1953. A survey of the major writing of the republican period.

Carrió Ibietatorremendía, Raquel. *Dramaturgia cubana contemporánea*. La Habana: Editorial Pueblo y Educación, 1988. A collection of critical studies that, although at times ambiguous and contradictory, provide noteworthy insights.

Cohen, J. M. *En tiempos difíciles. La poesía cubana de la Revolución*. Barcelona: Tusquets, 1970. A brief but fascinating discussion of contemporary Cuban poetry.

Colón, Edwin Teurbe, and José Antonio González. *Historia del teatro en La Habana*. Santa Clara, Cuba: Letras Cubanas, Academia de Ciencias de Cuba, 1980. A definitive work on the history of the Cuban theater.

Diccionario de la literatura cubana. La Habana: Letras Cubanas, Academia de Ciencias de Cuba, 1980.

Fernández Retamar, Roberto. *La poesía contemporánea en Cuba (1927-1953)*. La Habana: Orígenes, 1954. A better critic than poet, Fernández Retamar makes valid observations on Cuban poetry and some of its most distinguished representatives.

Fernández Vázquez, Antonio. *La novelística cubana de la revolución (testimonios y evocación de las novelas cubanas escritas fuera de Cuba: 1959-1975)*. Miami: Ediciones Universal, 1980. An informative book dealing with an area of Cuban narrative frequently neglected.

Foster, David William. *Cuban Literature: a Research Guide*. New York: Garland, 1985. A registry of general references, references on special topics, and critical books and essays on specific authors.

González Freire, Natividad. *Teatro cubano contemporáneo (1927-1961)*. La Habana: Ministerio de Relaciones Exteriores, 1961. A thorough survey of Cuban theater and dramatists.

Henríquez Ureña, Max. *Panorama histórico de la literatura cubana*. San Juan, P.R.: Mirador, 1963. Probably the best survey of Cuban literature available.

Jiménez, José Olivio. *Estudios sobre poesía cubana contemporánea*. New York: Las Américas, 1967. A detailed discussion of the basic features of Cuban poetry.

Lazo, Raimundo. *Historia de la literatura cubana*. México, D.F.: Universidad Nacional Autónoma de México, 1965. Useful but not probing.

Lazo, Raimundo. *La literatura cubana; esquema histórico desde sus orígenes hasta 1964*. México: Universidad Nacional Autónoma de México, 1965. A general outline history.

Leal, Rine. *En primera persona: 1954-1966*. La Habana: Instituto del Libro, 1967. A vivid account of Cuban theater during one of its most important periods.

Méndez y Soto, Ernesto. *Panorama de la novela cubana de la revolución (1959-1970)*. Miami: Ediciones Universal, 1973. Next to Seymour Menton's book, this is the most extensive examination of contemporary Cuban narrative during the first decade of the revolution.

Menton, Seymour. *Prose Fiction of the Cuban Revolution*. Austin: University of Texas Press, 1975. A major study on contemporary Cuban fiction.

Montes-Huidobro, Matías. *Persona, vida y máscara en el teatro cubano.* Miami: Ediciones Universal, 1973. A documentary and critical examination of contemporary Cuban drama.

Mugercia, Magaly. *El teatro cubano en vísperas de la revolución.* La Habana: Editorial Letras Cubanas, 1988. An analysis, quite well documented, on theater in Cuba between 1936 and 1958.

Portuondo, José Antonio. *Bosquejo histórico de las letras cubanas.* La Habana: Ministerio de Relaciones Exteriores, 1960. Brief but useful.

Remos, Juan J. *Historia de la literatura cubana.* La Habana: Cárdenas y Cía., 1945. A thorough account of Cuban literary history, but marked by considerable imprecision in approach.

Souza, Raymond. *Major Cuban Novelists: Innovation and Tradition.* Columbia: University of Missouri Press, 1976. Detailed analyses of major figures.

Vitier, Cintio. *Lo cubano en la poesía.* Santa Clara, Cuba: Universidad de Las Villas, 1958. Controversial in its definition of what is "Cuban" in Cuban poetry; therefore, worth consulting.

DOMINICAN REPUBLIC
Doris Sommer
Harvard University
and
Esteban Torres
Hostos Community College

I

To say that Columbus's initial reports from the New World are the earliest texts of Dominican literature doesn't stretch the truth very much; whatever the author's personal national identity may have been, his response to America becomes part of its literary and general history. This at least was the assumption made by Dominican literary historians who added to Columbus the names of many distinguished representatives of Crown and Church who at least began their American careers in this first outpost. Among them we should mention Fray Román Pané (dates unknown), a Catalan Jeronimite who was the first to learn the indigenous language and to compile local lore, and of course Gonzalo Fernández de Oviedo (1478-1557), official chronicler and author of *Historia general y natural de las Indias* (General and Natural History of the Indies; 1526), and Bartolomé de las Casas (1474-1566), defender of the Indians and author of *Historia de las Indias* (History of the Indies; 1560).

Recently, however, some Dominican literary historians have chosen to exchange the presumed dignity of this venerable Hispanic tradition for a more patently national one. Most notably the poet and novelist Pedro Mir, in *La noción de período en la historia dominicana* (The Concept of Period in Dominican History; 1981), and Abelardo Vicioso, in *El freno hatero en la literatura dominicana* (The Ranchers' Restraints on Dominican Literature; 1983), have dated the beginning of "Dominicanness" in literature from the seventeenth century on. Before this moment of violent rupture with the Spanish authorities, they argue, no truly national impulse existed. But despite their understandable pride in so early a tradition of resistance to Spain, modern Dominicans also tend to pride themselves as the scions of Europe's first settlers in the Americas. And perhaps the ensuing centuries of relative isolation have made that history of independent resistence mixed with filial affection all the more precious. In any case, it has been the motive of some of the most inspired literary works in an island that still celebrates its indigenous name of Quisqueya (meaning Great Land in Taíno) along with its adopted name, by metonymic extension of the motherland, of Hispaniola.

The "great" island, however, was not to be unified nor prosperous for very long. The lucrative contraband business with heretic Hollanders, Englishmen, and Frenchmen was effectively wiped out in 1605 when Governor Antonio Osorio ordered the region evacuated and then set to fire. The flames spread farther than anyone had intended and virtually burned out or sent into exile much of the commercial and intellectual activity in the Spanish colony, so much so that resistance to the French incursions in the Western part of the island became impossible. Except for the continuing immigration of gifted clerics and for a lively life of the theater, first in then outside the Church, Dominican letters generally languished during the seventeenth and eighteenth centuries.

As a consequence of these devastations, Spain's loss of interest allowed the eventual establishment of the French colony Saint Domingue in 1672. After that colony evicted the French and initiated the independence movement in Latin America, many privileged Dominicans emigrated. Those who stayed later declared their freedom from Spain in 1822, an event that was greeted by a Haitian occupation that lasted until 1844. This is the period when a popular, Afro-Dominican folkloric poetry flourished and when the Creole Juan Vázquez (?-1805), priest of his native Santiago de los Caballeros, wrote the following famed lines: "Yesterday I was born Spanish,/ by noon I was French,/ at night I was an Ethiope,/ I'm English today, they say:/ What indeed will become of me!" To avoid the double threat of Haiti and the U.S., some Dominicans favored the Republic's reversal to the status of Spanish colony from 1861-1864. And with Spain's second retreat a long period of civil wars followed; it paused for the dictatorship of Lilís (Ulises Hereaux) and ended only with the U.S. armed intervention of 1916. The occupying forces left Rafael Leonidas Trujillo to safeguard the country's stability, which he did, implacably, until he became president and then for thirty years more. The ensuing regime of Joaquín Balaguer, the coup that toppled the popularly elected Juan Bosch in 1963, the aborted revolution of 1965, and the following White Terror under Joaquín Balaguer again, all extended the nation's experience of being the object rather than the subject of history, somehow at the margins where isolation and frustration meet.

The history of Dominican independence begins with a clandestine group of intellectuals who seconded as soldiers. The group was known as the Trinitarian, because of the three-person nucleus that multiplied itself always by three. It was founded in 1838 by Juan Pablo Duarte (1813-76) with a mere twenty-one followers. Primarily a political conspiracy for Dominican independence from Haiti, like many movements during Latin America's period of nation-building, it did not simply distinguish politics from the literary production. In fact, its broad based and public "club," called the Philanthropic Society, helped to create mass support for the Trinitarians through intellectual and artistic work. For example, Duarte's most important writing is probably the first attempt at a national Constitution, although he is known for his patriotic verse as well.

The next generation of Dominican writers, known as the patriotic poets, featured Félix María del Monte (1819-99), author of the first national hymn as well as other poems dedicated to the renewed republic. Javier Angulo y Guridi (1816-84), shared the patriotic inspiration as did del Monte's wife, Encarnación Echavarría Vilaseca (1821-90), and Nicolás Ureña de Mendoza (1822-75). But the greatest poets of this period are probably José Joaquín Pérez (1845-1900), considered the foremost poet of Dominican exiles, and Salomé Ureña Henríquez (1850-97), whom Max Henríquez Ureña (1885-1970) calls Dominican nationality itself. Her optimistic and forward-looking verses include titles like "La gloria del progreso" (The Glory of Progress) and "La fe en el porvenir" (Faith in the Future), both published in *Poesías completas* (Complete Poetry; 1950). And if she lamented past defeats, she concentrated on turning them around. Her foundational work was more than rhetorical, as is evident from the fact that with the help of Eugenio María Hostos (see the section on Puerto Rico) she founded the first Normal School for Women in the Dominican Republic.

Other important patriotic poets were Gastón Fernando Deligne (1861-1913), Emilio Prud'homme (1856-1932), writer of the poem that popular consensus made the national anthem, Juan Isidro Ortea (1849-81), and Federico Henríquez y Carvajal (1848-1951), author also of *Romances históricos* (Historical Ballads; 1937) that trace the period from the Trinitarian to the United States' frustrated efforts to annex the republic. The poems coordinate an epic scope with the oral traditions popular during the Restoration (of independence from Spain).

It is significant that standard histories of Dominican literature deal almost exclusively with poetry; it is evidently the genre that excells. But the importance of prose will be felt increasingly from the turn of the century on. Certainly the foremost novel produced during this period of patriotic national consolidation, after various options of annexation had virtually been cancelled, was *Enriquillo, leyenda histórica dominicana* (Enriquillo, Dominican Historical Legend; 1882), by Manuel de Jesús Galván (1834-1910). It was thanks to this legend that the myth of an Indian or mestizo nation was created, at the end of long external and internal race-related wars. Galván's brilliant solution for assuaging the racism that inhibited political and economic unity was simply to exclude blacks from what would become the national epic, by tracing Dominican roots to noble Spaniards and Indians. Other patriotic novels published during periods of renewed civil war include the trilogy by Federico García Godoy (1857-1924), *Rufinito* (1908), *Alma dominicana* (Dominican Soul; 1911), and *Guanuma* (published 1908-14), in which contemporary local color combines with social criticism of local caudillismo. The tone of *La sangre* (Blood; 1914), by Tulio Cestero (1877-1955), is not less loving but certainly more outraged as it recalls caudillismo at the national level under the tyranny of Hereaux.

II

With the death of Lilís in 1899, a new and freer era was ushered in, although freedom did not at all amount to political stability. In this atmosphere the most notable poets took the opportunity that Modernismo (Modernism, a movement influenced by French Parnassianism and Symbolism) afforded to put politics at some distance. Dominican Modernism, as elsewhere in Latin America, attempts to break with classical Spanish prosody and concerns. The *fin de siecle* atmosphere of exotic and mythological themes was cultivated in the Dominican Republic most notably by Ricardo Pérez Alfonseca (1892-1950).

Vedrismo (Vedrism) follows on and breaks with Modernism to inaugurate a vanguard poetry in the Dominican Republic. This movement strove to destroy established forms in favor of euphoric exaltation; it gives free reign to free verse and to various intuitive forms. Its name comes from an ingenious French pilot who fought in the First World

War, Jules Vedrines (1881-1919), famed for his daring and graceful airborne antics using free forms to overcome enemy aggression. Probably the most important representitive of Vedrism is Otilio Vigil Díaz (1880-1961), author of *Góndolas* ((Gondolas; 1912), *Miserere patricio* (Humble Patriarch; 1915), *Del Sena al Ozama* (From the Seine to the Ozama; 1922), *Música de ayer* (Yesterday's Music; 1925), and *Galeras de pafos* (The Gods' Galleys; 1921). This last work serves also as a manifesto for the movement, which it locates in the tradition of Baudelaire. For Díaz this meant primarily an ambition to write poetic prose, leaving rhyme and meter to follow the instincts of the godlike poets.

Postumismo (Posthumism), named for having left Modernism behind, is another specifically Dominican literary movement. It was founded by Domingo Moreno Jiménez (1894) and joined by Rafael Augusto Zorrilla (1892-1937) and Andrés Avelino (1900-75). While this tendency has its roots in Modernism, it rejects the exoticist elements and allegedly farfetched metaphors, substituting for them more immediate local and national themes, including Dominican flora and fauna. It may be said that Posthumism is the literary expression of an intermediate stage of Dominican consciousness, between a traditional patriarchalism and an emerging urbanism with its capital-based relationships. The poems produced by this movement are generally scattered in various publications, but its founder, Moreno Jiménez, collected many of his own verses in an anthology titled *Del gemido a la fragua* (From the Cry to Battle; 1975). As a poet, Moreno was like an apostle, going from town to town reciting his work and outraging correct society by the very act of making poetry a public affair. His personally extravagant style of life and his antielitist esthetic became emblematic of Posthumism.

The Independientes (Independents) of the 1940s are, as their name implies, a very loosely allied group of poets who distinguish themselves by not belonging to any specific tendency. Nevertheless, their shared concerns and themes create some sense of coherence among them. Technically, what unified them was a penchant for free verse, while thematically they all gravitated towards national themes, treating them in a rather high poetic register. The Independents set themselves off from the Posthumists by their general concern for the musicality of language via distinctive Creole rhythms and cadence. The majority of Independents, whose work has been compared to that of Pablo Neruda (see the section on Chile), César Vallejo (see the section on Peru), and Nicolás Guillén (see the section on Cuba), published in *Los cuadernos dominicanos de cultura* (Dominican Cultural Notebooks; 1943-52).

Among their representatives is Tomás Hernández Franco (1904-52), author of the epic-romance *Yelidá* (1944). The title character of this poetic celebration of hybridism is quintessentially Caribbean. She is the daughter of an African mother and a European father, both of whom become free from nostalgia for their origins as their lives meld into Yelidá. The poem is still considered the most important work of the period. Other outstanding Independents are Manuel de Cabral (1907) and Héctor Incháustegui Cabral (1912-79).

Pedro Mir (1913) has also been considered an Independent, but his continuing importance for Dominican letters, both poetry and prose, exceeds any one school or tendency. Mir's books are cited in the next part of this essay as important components of contemporary Dominican literature. As a writer of prose whose production has spanned the 1930s to the present, it is even more illusory to place Juan Bosch (1909) in a particular movement. His early novel *La mañosa* (The Wily One; 1936) deals ostensibly with the last "civil war," fought just before the United States intervention of 1916, but it comments clearly on Trujillo's appropriation of national resources. This was followed by two volumes of short stories published in exile and an important series of historical and political analyses that continue to inform national debates. Unlike Bosch, Ramón Marrero Aristy (1912-50), author of *Over* (1939; the English title refers to the superprofits North Americans were making in sugar plantations), did not go into exile. His novel seemed to serve Trujillo's plan to overtake North American sugar interests, but Marrero later joined the many victims of the dictatorship.

La Poesía Sorprendida (Poetry Surprised) is a movement that can be dated rather exactly from 1943 with the founding of a journal by that name. Its directors, the Chilean Alberto Baeza Flores (1914), Franklin Mieses Burgos (1907-77), Aída Cartagena Portolatín, (1918), and Freddy Gatón Arce (1920), published the following declaration: "We aim to promote a national poetry nourished by international currents as the only way to be authentic. We declare ourselves allied to the classics of yesterday, today, and tomorrow, with a limitless creativity blind to permanent frontiers and alive to man's mysterious world, always secret, solitary, intimate, and creative." In the journal's pages Dominicans could bring those links up to date by reading works by André Breton, Guillaume Apollinaire, André Gide, Paul Eluard, James Joyce, and others. As for the Dominicans' poetry, it tended to be innovative in an intentionally difficult way, as if to vouchsafe a space for art amid the increasingly oppressive regime that Trujillo had consolidated through the 1930s.

The so-called Generation of 1948 is a literary movement inspired by several aesthetic and historical preoccupations. Its participants were determined to overcome a certain existential pessimism and to historicize the human subject in a way that committed him/her to social concerns. Nevertheless, their language supposes no easy system of referentiality, perhaps because any overt criticism faced the obvious limit of naming the tyrant at the center of Dominican concerns. Trujillo represented, in many ways, the horizon or the containing strategy of Dominican literature for three decades. This generation was based in the southern part of the country and in 1948 launched its public image through the section named "Colaboración escolar" (Scholarly Collaboration; 1948) of the newspaper *El Caribe* (The Caribbean). Among the participants were Lupe Hernández Rueda (1930), Máximo Avilés Blonda (1931), Abelardo Vicioso (1930), Abel Fernández Mejía (1931), Rafael Valera Benítez (dates unknown), and Víctor Villegas (1924).

The Generation of 1960 refers to the group of writers who precede and promote the revolutionary moment of 1965 and who will suffer the frustration of the second United States intervention. Most of them will participate directly in the struggle, where one is killed. It is more the historical context that unites them rather than any unified aesthetic program; here one will find existentialists, nihilists, and socialists alongside one another. Among them are writers to whom we will refer in more detail as participants of the post-Trujillo period, when the project of combining politics and art seemed both more promising and more frustrating.

III

Practically all of today's Dominican critics agree that since the end of Trujillo's regime, which lasted from 1930 to 1961, the history of Dominican art can be divided into two major periods: before and after the tyrant. Nevertheless, they don't all attribute the difference to chronology, as if considering a history and a prehistory of Dominican letters. There is a certain continuity of both aesthetic and political concerns, especially after 1965 when the neo-Trujillist Balaguer regime begins its reign of twelve years, that limits the degree of social transformation after the tyrant's death.

With Trujillo's death, several writers return home, bringing with them a series of questions and formulations about the meaning of their work. The social upheaval was so severe that their intellectual and artistic intervention was not noticed until later, when the habits of criticism and dialogue were established. In general, the Dominican people, including the middle classes, had been more concerned with oration and public discourse in the general atmosphere of reinaugurating political life, including the participation of previously outlawed political parties. This urgency and catharsis tended to limit the production and the impact of literary work.

Upheaval and the apparent marginality of literature continued at least until April 1965, when United States marines invaded in order to turn around the successful popular revolt occasioned by the demand to reinstate Juan Bosch and his constitution after the right-wing coup that ousted him in 1963. After the revolt and the enforced peace (also known as the White Terror), concerted literary developments began to take stock of a situation no longer as volatile—nor as promising—as it had recently been. Outstanding among those developments was poetry, both lyric and prose poems. Once the North American intervention settled in as a Dominican reality, a kind of transcendental epic style is initiated by Miguel Alfonseca (1942), author of *Arribo de la luz* (Arrival of Light; 1965) and *La guerra y los cantos* (War and Song; 1967), and Juan José Ayuso (1940), author of *Cantos de guerra* (Songs of War; published in several literary supplements during 1965). Insofar as the intervention polarized Dominican society, it may be said that these poets also intervened directly in the historical events. This is how the first anthology-pamphlet of recent heroism is to be understood. Titled *Pueblo, sangre y canto* (The People, Blood and Song; 1965), the anthology collects poems by Jacques Viaud Renaud (1942-65; Reanud was a Haitian poet who died in combat against U.S. forces), Ramón Francisco (1929), Antonio Lockward (1943), and René del Risco (1937-72), among others. Along with the international protest, which included some of the most prominent names of Latin American letters, is that of the Dominican exile, Manuel del Cabral (1907), *La isla ofendida* (The Outraged Island; 1967). And Héctor Incháustegui Cabral, who had also belonged to the literary Independents of the 1940s, published *Diario de la guerra y los dioses ametrallados* (War Diary and the Machine-Gunned Gods; 1967).

Well known in the same period is René del Risco's *El viento frío* (The Cold Wind; 1967), an existential work that is a premonition, an "odor," of what will follow the aborted heroic moment. It may be said that this poem abandons "positivism" for a tragic nihilism, that it opens the way for the two to intersect. Without necessarily being self-conscious, the writers who participate in the Frente Cultural (Cultural Front) were caught between melancholy, deriving from the nightmare of what had happened, and the effort actively to confront the reality imposed by foreigners.

Dominican critics (including some of the poets mentioned above) generally see the literary explosion, or "boom," after 1965 as a Freudian parricide after thirty years of "castration" and gagging; but we should note that the gag could be somewhat loosened, as it had been with one of the most important literary movements in Dominican literary history, the Surprised Poetry movement of the 1940s. It was a synthesis of Dominican culture with Surrealism that undertakes to confront the oppressive regime, mainly by denying the utilitarian, "positivist" duties that Trujillo imposed on literature. It allowed for the arrogance of destabilizing signifiers, beginning with the dictator himself. This movement was an artistic and sociological response against the state, the center, the father, at a time when Trujillo was all these things. One can only speculate that the poets were relatively safe because the poems were so difficult that the Benefactor must have strained unsuccessfully to understand them.

Later generations would develop this "de(con)structive" and plurivalent impulse of Surprised Poetry. At the same time, a more overtly nationalist poetry was being developed, as we have mentioned, by the Independents. This complement to the Neobaroque surprises, whose social criticism was so subtle that it was safe, is a direct antecedent of the social poetry that reaches its greatest powers in the post-1965 generation.

Part of the power of that heroic generation is surely a consequence of aspects of its organization that differentiate it from earlier movements. Instead of adhering to particular aesthetic tendencies, these poets (and narrators) organized in aesthetically heterogeneous groups that resembled militant cells, as if the phenomenon of urban commandos resisting U.S. occupation extended into the battlefield of art. Among these groups were: El Puño (Fist), La Isla (Island), La Máscara (Mask), and La Antorcha (Torch).

Most of the work of the poets associated with these groups combines political commitment with qualified optimism about the world. Individuals are represented as parts of collective beings, so that death tends to lose its terror. See especially the masterful novel, *De abril en adelante* (From April On; 1975), by Marcio Veloz Maggiolo (1936). Understood not as a passage from consciousness to "otherness," death becomes a natural byproduct of a logical process, a kind of nontranscendent pantheism. In this mood, the elegy, which can make what is absent present and eternal, is affirmed as the ultimate poetic expression. On the other hand, life becomes a medium for social redemption, practically fetishizing self-sacrifice. Few opportunities had presented themselves since the first North American intervention of 1916, which ended only when the Marines were replaced with Trujillo.

We should point out that alongside these literary cells other writers worked alone. But even these loners conceived of their art as a potentially collective social activity. As cultural forums and debates developed, a new group began to take shape in search of the "disparate" quality of experience and art. This period begins around 1970, when the Dominican Republic is undergoing the process of full integration into the international circuit of capital. The push for economic development, and the foreign debt it brings, required a new aesthetic consciousness. At least one response was the formation of a "joven poesía dominicana" (young Dominican poetry). It has been argued that this does not constitute a new literary school, in the sense of a unified attitude towards language. Nevertheless, as a group, these poets intervened on the national literary and political scene in the first years of the Republic's full integration into the world market (1970-75).

The "young Dominican poets" are careful to point out that the meaning of this new consumer-oriented and presumably shattering intrahistory isn't really known. Their response is often a variation of existentialism, featuring a language stripped of any epic tones and describing a lost world. In this version, the individual does not vanquish the minotaur but succumbs to a monster of urbanism that converts human consciousness into machine-like beings. Poetry becomes plural and the ego discovers its own uselessness, not as it did in the liberating decentering of Poetry Surprised when the battle against Trujillo was still in the future, but as an excess, a ferocity frustrated by paranoia after the political battles have revealed their dead ends.

The participation of women in this period becomes a necessary condition of poetic production, whereas before women were either marginalized or tokenized. Representative among them are Jeannette Miller (1945), *Fórmulas para combatir el miedo* (Formulas for Fighting Fear; 1972); and Soledad Alvarez (1950), whose work is still scattered in Sunday literary supplements. The principal question both raise is how Eros and Capital combine to keep women in a relationship of class dependency or as a commodity. How far does sexuality differ from

consumer goods? How constant is the patriarchy even in light of changing economic relationships? And to what extent does a Western concept
of beauty assume a sexual, or class, or racial mode of production? This
last question is especially crucial in a country discovering its deep African
cultural roots after the decades of denial from the period of independence from Haiti (called "African" by a white elite in contrast to the
racially, mythically "Indian" Dominicans) through the racist Trujillo
regime.

Writing by and about women continues to flourish and to challenge
the vacuous romantic image (in the sense of sexual object) of the femi-
nine as well as the related deified and reified Marianist image of woman.
Among the authors of a feminist criticism are Marianne de Tolentino
(dates unknown), María del Carmen Prosdocimi (dates unknown), and
María Ugarte (dates unknown). And among the published poets are
Chiqui Vicioso (dates unknown), *Viaje desde el agua* (Voyage From the
Sea; 1981); and Sabrina Román (dates unknown), *De un tiempo a otro
tiempo* (From One Time to Another Time; 1978) and *Palabra rota* (The
Broken Word; 1983).

Dominican poetry attains a new level with a movement called Plura-
lismo (Pluralism), initiated in 1974 by the already well established Manuel Rueda (1921). In its new openness, Pluralism gets beyond an
inherited and limiting set of forms, and as a kind of disobedience it
combines self-consciousness with a self-effacing style. Pluralism asks
unanswerable questions about the nature of the poetic image and suggests that the discourse writes the author, rather than the reverse. That
is to say, it shares with contemporary philosophers of language the
observation that individuals are born into an already existing linguistic
system that they may adjust or even try to subvert but that they can
hardly create. The fundamental works of this movement appear in *Con
el tambor de las islas: Pluralemas* (With the Islands' Drum: Pluralemes;
1975), signed by various narrators and poets, including Marcio Veloz
Maggiolo, Alexis Gómez Rosa (1950), Luis Manuel Ledesma (1949),
Manuel Simó (1911), Diógenes Valdés (dates unknown), Margarita L. de
Espaillat (dates unknown), and Apolinar Núñez (1946). Manuel Rueda
himself has published many works, including *Por los mares de la dama*
(Through the Lady's Seas; 1976), *Las edades del viento* (The Ages of the
Wind; 1979), and the *Antología panorámica de la poesía dominicana
contemporánea* (General Anthology of Contemporary Dominican Poetry;
1972), coauthored with Lupe Hernández Rueda.

The end of the 1970s brought a fresh curiosity about foreign literary developments as well as a renewed creativity at home. The creativity and dialogue now receive nationwide support from special events and literary prizes (especially those financed by Siboney Inc. and Taller Publishers) and journals like *Isla abierta* (Open Island; 1981), *Escriptura* (Scripture; 1981), *Yelidá* (date unknown), the cultural supplement *Aquí* (Here; date unknown), and the magazine *Ahora* (Now; 1962), along with all the pages dedicated to literature in the country's newspapers. Debates about literature now incorporate international critical tendencies like structuralism, a poststructuralist critique associated with the French Tel Quel group, the ideas of Henry Meschonnic, and a reevaluation of Jorge Luis Borges (see the section on Argentina). All this, accompanied by an intense poetic activity and coupled with the new interest in international tendencies in criticism, has made Dominican letters face up to a traditional insularism in publishing. One challenge that presents itself is how to characterize the work being produced by Dominicans residing in this country, primarily in New York City.

IV

In this small and, until recently, rather insular country where poetry seems clearly to outweigh prose in production and interest, the Latin American nineteeenth-century phenomenon of artists-statemen has survived the division of labor that first freed the Modernists to think their aesthetic thoughts and to polish seemingly apolitical verses. As a related phenomenon, the so-called historical novel, so popular in the Romantic period of nationalist consolidation and apparently on the wane since, is still cultivated, perhaps because the thirty-one years under Trujillo made the work of establishing a national identity a renewed concern. If it were not, forgetfulness and intellectual repression may have bled the country of its recent history and the hemorrhage would consequently limit the lessons and the opportunities for change.

Related to the public function and the implied general readership of the Dominican novel is its unmistakably collective language and rhetorical assumptions, as opposed to the private style that comes to characterize literature with the rise of the bourgeoisie. If the division of labor has set in among Dominican intellectuals, it has been only lately with regard to prose; by contrast, it can be said to have characterized at least the writing of the Poetry Surprised group.

Since the early Georg Lukács, Ernst Bloch, and Mikhail Bakhtin, it has been a useful habit for critics of novels to attend to the always innovative forms of individual works, since their narrative discourses are not given but made in a symbolic act that often informs social discourse and that accounts for the explanatory power of narrative. Yet, Dominican critics have tended to be taxonomists and have typically organized their thoughts about the national novel in terms of content, understood as "theme" or intention, rather than by formal analyses. Accordingly, Dominican novels have been classified in no less than ten categories, including indigenist, historical, Creole, social, biblical, urban, plantation, and didactic novels, even if some works make the scheme untidy by appearing on more than one list.

One of the assumptions embedded in the language of contemporary Dominican criticism is that national history progresses gradually from one necessary stage to another in a way that repeats the process of development in economically more advanced countries. This observation follows from the critics' predictable evaluation of Dominican novelists as developing, unable as yet to reach a mature expression because Dominican society in general lags behind. A comparable assumption about preconceived stages of development was held by many Latin American economists before the Cuban Revolution and by defenders of socialist realism in art. And because the novel has been called the last and most advanced stage of development in a nation's literature, what Dominican critics consider poor novels are interpreted as a mark of literary and social underdevelopment. In response, contemporary Dominican novelists and critics have virtually mandated themselves to produce serious novels, almost as a matter of national pride in the general effort towards modernization.

Pedro Peix (1952), for example, introduces his anthology *La narrativa yugulada* (Strangled Narrative; 1981) by explaining that the problem of Dominican fiction is its underdevelopment. Typical as the position is, one must assume that it is adopted from Carpentier's widely read essay "Problemática de la actual novela hispanoamericana" (Issues in the Contemporary Spanish American Novel; 1964), although the same position emerges as early as the prologue by the Argentine Bartolomé Mitre to his *Soledad* (Solitude; 1847). Similar developmentalist criteria organize the allegedly necessary conditions for writing good novels. They include: a literary tradition, a constant production of prose, a critical-theoretical foundation, a fairly exclusive dedication to writing, all of which tend to professionalize the art in a way that would break with the older statesmen-novelist tradition. The absence or belatedness of these conditions convinces some critics that great Dominican prose is simply not yet possible.

Nevertheless, a significant number of contemporary Dominican novels have succeeded in gaining international recognition and have then been celebrated at home. *Escalera para Electra* (A Staircase for Electra; 1969) by Aída Cartagena Portolatín received honorable mention from the judges for the Spanish Seix Barral Prize for the best novel of the year. This modern version of the Electra story makes the father-daughter incest explicit and reveals the father as the dominating sexual presence whom his daughter cannot disobey, just as the Dominican people cannot disobey the Yankee invaders to whom the author alludes in historical asides that give resonance to the aggressive masculinity of her story. Two years later Marcio Veloz Maggiolo practically won the Seix Barral Prize, though a split decision kept the publishers from giving any prize in 1971, for *De abril en adelante*. This experimental protonovel intentionally fails to constitute itself as the narrative of the Revolt of April 1965. Attempts are made to fit the facts into a repeating pattern of Dominican history; but the facts always exceed those patterns, making narrating and history itself impossible goals. The work is therefore not only a challenge to traditional prose but also to a facile political imagination.

Another international success, and perhaps the most virtuoso performance in Dominican prose, is *Cuando amaban las tierras comuneras* (When Communal Lands Were Loved; 1978) by Pedro Mir; it was widely acclaimed after being published by Mexico's Siglo XXI. In the long, musical, and unpunctuated sentences that beg to be read aloud, and in the inexhaustable puns, Mir shows himself to be a poet who can also play masterfully at making prose. The novel is a nostalgic evocation of a time before the first armed North American intervention of 1916; that is, before land became a commodity concentrated in the hands of the few. Pedro Vergés's *Sólo cenizas hallarás (bolero)* (Only Ashes Will You Find [Bolero]; 1980), about the oppressiveness of the Trujillo years in terms of personal lives, was twice awarded in Spain. In the face of these accomplishments, a critic like Peix defends his theory about the necessary poverty of Dominican narrative by considering the prize-winning works to be atypical or premature. In general, the critics of prose have tended to lag behind the narrators who know that literary history is not an insular affair and that a Latin American, and international, tradition is also their own.

Other outstanding results of daring to be contemporary are *Currículum (el síndrome de la visa)* (Curriculum [the Visa Syndrome]; 1982), by Efraím Castillo (dates unknown), and *La otra Penélope* (The Other Penelope; 1982), by Andrés L. Mateo (1946).

BIBLIOGRAPHY

Baeza Flores, Alberto. *Los poetas dominicanos del 1965: una generación importante y distinta*. Santo Domingo: Biblioteca Nacional, 1985. This book is an extended study of those Dominican poets who are revolutionary in every sense of the term; the author combines a sociological method with a sensitivity to the various tendencies and styles that made up a generation much admired by the veteran of Poesía Sorprendida.

Contín Aybar, Néstor. *Historia de la literatura dominicana*. San Pedro de Macorís: Universidad Central del Este, 1982. Organized along the general lines of Dominican history, this book nevertheless begins before the Conquest and reconstructs something of Taíno culture from the earliest Spanish chronicles.

Cruz, Josefina de la. *La sociedad dominicana de fines de siglo a través de la novela*. Santo Domingo, 1978. A valuable attempt to read history through literature, even though the author maintains a rather elementary notion of how novels reflect their times. However, she succeeds in showing that our most accurate knowledge of the turn of the century comes from the novels themselves, that whatever history they "reflect" is also constituted by the novels.

Henríquez Ureña, Max. *Panorama histórico de la literatura dominicana*. Santo Domingo: Librería Dominicana, 1965. In two volumes and originally published in 1945, this has long been the standard literary history for the Dominican Republic.

Icháustegui Cabral, Héctor. *De literatura dominicana, siglo XX*. Santiago: UCMM, 1968. An extended study of several outstanding figures, combining in a readable fashion criticism and personal memoir of the author's own literary fortunes and those of his contemporaries.

Molinaza, José. *Historia crítica del teatro dominicano, 1492-1844*. Santo Domingo: Universidad Autónoma de Santo Domingo, 1984-.

An examination of an infrequently researched area of Dominican culture.

Rosario Chandelier, Bruno. *La imaginación insular: mitos, leyendas, utopías y fantasmas en la narrativa dominicana*. Santo Domingo: Publicaciones Siboney, 1984. This detailed study of four prose fiction writers—Juan Bosch, Sócrates Nolasco, Virgilio Díaz Grullón, and Manuel Mora Serrano—is organized around the principle that fantasy is an integral part of Dominican culture, as it is of Latin American culture in general.

Sommer, Doris. *One Master for Another: Populism as Patriarchal Rhetoric in Dominican Novels*. Lanham, Md.: University Press of America, 1983. An ideological analysis of major populist Dominican novels.

Veloz Maggiolo, Marcio. *Cultura, teatro y relatos en Santo Domingo*. Santiago: UCMM, 1972. A series of critical essays spanning genres and periods.

ECUADOR
Will H. Corral
Stanford University

I

The dismembering of Ecuadorian territory is perhaps the obligatory analogy for the development of Ecuadorian literary history. From the Spanish Royal decrees of 1563 and 1740, the demarcation of 1777, the Gran Colombia unification of 1824, and the Mosquera-Pedemonte treaty of 1830, one can rapidly proceed to the relations between the historical literary moments that lead into the twentieth century. The rapid succession of territorial treaties in 1904, 1916, and 1922 foreshadow the 1942 Rio de Janeiro Treaty, which more or less leaves Ecuador in its present territorial and literary self-perception: a small country of uneven literary production. However, the oil boom beginning in the seventies, which resulted in a windfall in 1990 and produced a deficit in 1991, has brought about a cultural politics of prosperity that the present version of this essay sees as a force to be reckoned with more and more, especially since 1992 marks a decade of unusual and highly accomplished literary activity in Ecuador, a country that is still a distinctive blend of economic liberalism and authoritarian state control.

With rare exceptions, censors, critics, distributors, editors, publishers, readers, and other selectors of the type of communication an audience is to receive have contributed, almost willy-nilly, to what is at best a misinformed reception of Ecuadorian literature. The perfunctory nature of some recent foreign evaluations of this literature's most productive century is not very different from efforts by national critics—in Ecuador and outside of it—to prove the impossibility of writing about a national literature without becoming nationalistic or impressionistic. When one considers that Ecuador was one of the first Spanish American countries to found an institution—Casa de la Cultura Ecuatoriana (House of Ecuadorian Culture; 1944)—responsible for explicit cultural policy, the unhappy state of the recuperation, upkeep, and diffusion of its literary patrimony reveals a consistent lack of self-questioning. If a good part of this literature is readily representative of the literary production of an underdeveloped country, what has been written about it has generally served to distance its writers and works even further from inclusion in the literary canons of Spanish America.

However, there is ample room for objective optimism about the quality of the works in the literary history of Ecuador. Beyond the assumed folkloric and indigenous trappings of a literature characterized by facile referentiality and rather inordinate and profuse social criticism, the literary traditions of Ecuador are as internally coherent and complex as those of any other national literature of the continent. In this regard, the intense literary production of the last two decades—as well as the positive external evaluation of it, official support, and a plethora of recalcitrant, promising new authors—is more the reflection of the recovery of an underestimated tradition than an opportune linkage with a new beginning. This recovery really has its roots in the consciousness-raising promoted by Juan León Mera (1832-94). A self-taught critic, cultural anthropologist, novelist, poet, and author of the national anthem, he is, with Juan Montalvo (1832-89), the most canonical author of nineteenth-century Ecuador. In his *Ojeada histórico-crítica sobre la poesía ecuatoriana, desde su época más remota hasta nuestros días* (Historico-critical View of Ecuadorian Poetry, from Its Earliest Period to Our Day; 1868), a work he published in expanded form in 1893, Mera initiates the correction and expansion necessary to identify a national literature. Although this work is strictly chronological and pedagogical, it is a stimulating guide to the literary history of Ecuador, an undertaking shared by Spanish American countries whose national literatures are conceived as having had their beginnings at the time of independence from Spain in the first third of the last century.

For Ecuador, whose literature of foundation reveals valid, comparatively canonical authors in the seventeenth century, the problem of its literary history is complicated by two cultural stances that have never worked in parallel fashion. One is the erroneous assumption that the establishment of the Republic changed the fundamental socioeconomic structures of the country, thereby creating an articulation of all the levels of social, cultural, political, and administrative fields. The other is the relegation of Ecuadorian literature and its development, in general surveys and well-known literary histories, to the framework of trends in strictly ethnic (and specifically Indian) literature. As a corollary, even the more exact and accepted explanations of the trends of Ecuadorian literature do not deviate, even in their differences, from the chronological organization that emphasizes authors, movements, and predictable evaluations based on the inevitability of relying on hierarchies.

Thus, Barrera's and Carrión's excellently informed, documented, but oddly incomplete literary dictionary (see Bibliography) is divided into the equally odd halves of "Ecuadorian Authors from the Colony to the Present" and "Living Ecuadorian Authors." A brief manual emphasizes a progression that covers the literatures of pre-Columbian times, the discovery and conquest, the colony (primitive and learned), the founding fathers, the interregnum (1830-60), the nineteenth-century canon (Montalvo and Mera), Modernism (the Generation of 1910), the golden age (also known as the Literature or Generation of 1930), the literature of crisis (1950-60), and the literature of the early sixties or new trends (Cueva; see Bibliography). Naturally later, another critic (Valdano Morejón; see Bibliography) stresses the encroachment of generations—eight generations, from 1734 to 1944—rather than their succession. However, the thirty-year generations do not make this approach any more revealing, accountable, or devoid of lists. More recently, Cueva (in the special *Casa de las Américas* issue on Ecuador; see Bibliography), proposes a five-level revision that uses socioeconomic infrastructures as a dialectical framework that, through multiple mediations, ends up delineating "the configuration of a superstructural space (or field) in which the practices we call literary evolve." Despite this corrective effort, the reader of Ecuadorian literature must resort to a combination of these divisions and categories with provisos that are of a whole with national culture and a supranational contextualization.

Out of this necessity, pre-Columbian literature emerges as a source for Ecuador's literary history. As with other Latin American countries, this literature is difficult to gather, determine, and analyze without acknowledging its orality and the oppressive conditions that did not allow it to flourish. Although the Dominican Friar Domingo de Santo Tomás (1499-1570) published his *Gramática o arte de la lengua general de los indios de los Reynos del Perú* (Grammar or Art of the Common Speech of the Indians of the Kingdoms of Peru; 1560) in Quito, the Quechua language described therein did not provide a written tradition for its native users. The poetry, songs, fables, theater, and similar cultural expressions that existed before Columbus were linked to religious manifestations or needs. The Spaniards, as they were to do in other colonized territories, annihilated these manifestations. The information that remained regarding the existence of elegies on the death of Atahualpa or accounts about his struggles with his brother Huáscar have reached our times by word of mouth, leaving at best in their later transcriptions scattered evidence of concerted literary efforts. It is easy to think that critics summarily dismiss the pre-Columbian literature of Ecuador. But, as will be observed later, for the purposes of this essay literature is intimately bound to demographic, historical, political, economic, cultural, and literary particulars involving traceable linkages. Thus, the only literary link between early native culture and the culture that will have its foundations in the language of the colony is the literature of the chroniclers of the discovery and the conquest.

But even in those texts there can be no reference to the nation-state of Ecuador, but rather to the Kingdom of Quito. In the dozens of abundantly studied natural, general, and self- defined true histories of the Indies, what is now Ecuador serves a peripheral function as a cultural entity, although specific attention may be given to Inca royalty in the Northern part of the Kingdom of Quito. It then becomes almost un-avoidable to subject a survey of a national literature to a progression of centuries and, within it, to a selectivity of authors. For them, new formal demands were necessitated in large part by the wish to capture new experience and suggest why the sources of renewal came from the inside, from a consciousness of shared, forceful social experiences that formed a distinct milieu. For all intents and purposes the period of the conquest in Ecuador lasts until the end of the sixteenth century. The period of the colony that follows will still face the hostile circumstances of the Spanish institutions' monopoly on literacy, education, economy, legislative organi-zation, and even morality. However, the seventeeth century will provide the historical moment (the Spanish are more preoccupied with fixating their ideology than with adhering strictly to the imposition of literary taste proposed by their Crown) that enables Creoles (later, native Ecua-dorians) to choose and select beliefs and values on the basis of their own interests. These, as will be seen, did not automatically rule out Spanish tradition, but rather emulated Peninsular models, with the great differ-ence that the producers of literature were now waging on their own ability to understand their own society.

II

Antonio Bastidas (1615-81), Xacinto de Evia (1620-?), and Gaspar de Villarroel (c.1587/90-1665) are the three seventeenth-century authors who have been rescued in most literary histories as worthy of preservation. Despite the fact that the government-sponsored *Biblioteca ecuatoriana mínima* (Basic Ecuadorian Library; 1959-60) devotes nine volumes to the period, the canon of Ecuadorian colonial literature is too diffused and poor to be studied as a coherent movement or school. Most critical documentation, which is still poor for this period in Ecuadorian letters, accords the sixteenth and seventeenth centuries a few names (most were Spanish or Creole priests) or works (mainly lyric poetry) of importance in a literature characterized by descriptive language and excessively referential, anecdotal content. However, Rodríguez Castelo (1984; see bibliography) has recently gathered the writings of Ecuadorian Jesuits (expelled in 1767), who through their historiographical, hagiographic, lyrical writings, and speeches provide evidence that the literary activity covering the years 1655 to 1756 needs to be reexamined beyond its lack of a clearly determined public.

Nevertheless, Bastidas and Evia are a justifiable tandem introduction to the earliest literature of Ecuador. Both authors were born in Guayaquil, served different functions in the Jesuit order, and together published Evia's *Ramillete de varias flores recogidas y cultivadas en los primeros abriles de sus años por el Maestro Xacinto de Evia, natural de Guayaquil* (Bouquet of Assorted Flowers Gathered and Grown in the Spring of His Youth by Master Xacinto de Evia, Native of Guayaquil; 1675). The bouquet is divided into Funereal, Lyrical, Sacred, Panegyric, Amorous, and Burlesque flowers (i.e., sections). Each of these has a scholarly introduction to its contents by Evia, who admits gathering this miscellany in honor and admiration of his mentor, Bastidas. However, it is the latter who composed the funereal poems that are perhaps the best part of the bunch, as it were. But indeed both men shared in the composition of this work and its imitative character.

Reading between the lines of the bombastic or sad tone of the poems, the reader may perceive support for the nobility whom they praised elaborately. Nevertheless, in spite of successful verses like those contained in Evia's "A una rosa" (To a Rose), the work's euphemistic discourse and thematic predictability are too transparent for the reader. The work's facile symbolism and language may have prompted its initial critics to pursue a pejorative evaluation, perhaps without their knowing the totality of the work. Thus, it is equally suggestive to recall that the characteristics of Spanish American poetry of the period are not much different. A fuller appraisal of the work, then, should probably start with the analysis of the reader's own stance with respect to derivatory literary texts and the specific sociohistorical period when they were read.

Seventeenth-century Ecuadorian literature did not foresee any division between society and state or between private and public realms. Individuals still moved in familiar social strata, thereby limiting writers who wanted to co-opt complex narrative to a pseudodemocratic interest in the lives of ordinary people. Gaspar de Villarroel would aptly frame these "little histories" with the proverbial combination of social, political, religious, and autobiographical concerns that served to portray his historical period. His work at the Spanish Court and as Bishop (Santiago and Arequipa) and Archbishop (Chuquisaca) established him as a theologian and orator. He would write that upon hearing him give a sermon, a Spanish grandee was amazed that an Indian could be so white and speak Castilian so well. It is the sort of colonialism against which even early twentieth-century Ecuadorian literature was struggling.

Gaspar de Villarroel combined these talents with his ability as a chronicler, and seventeen volumes of his work were published during his lifetime. Three posthumous volumes were published in later centuries, and most critics believe at least five other volumes have been lost. Of the three his two-part *Gobierno eclesiástico pacífico y unión de los dos cuchillos, pontificio y regio* (Peaceful Ecclesiastical Government and Union of the Pontifical and Regal Branches; 1656-57) makes Gaspar de Villarroel the first and foremost writer of colonial Ecuador. His prose is denunciatory but shrewdly tempered by a tolerance that tried to establish the awareness of individual rights and a balance between Church and State, as the title clearly proposes. Villarroel wisely juxtaposes the study of the legal position of the two governments with tales of intrigue and adventure and a straightforward style, making his work a lively testimony of his troubled times. They were troubled because the Creoles, who formed the majority of a small, privileged reading public, were undergoing important internal struggles in their development as a group. Specifically, Creoles were despairing, acquiring consciousness of their "otherness," notwithstanding their willingness to show that they were part of civilized Spanish society and capable of producing complex works similar to those of the colonizers. As a consequence, the biographical changes in Villarroel's fortune illustrate the initial contradictions of Creole consciousness and are a reflection of and a spotlight on the attitude toward life and literature of an ambiguous social condition.

Literature as social interaction, or as party to social interaction, would come into its own in mid eighteenth-century Ecuador. Up to this time, and for a century before, the literary response to whatever was conceived as autochthonous was distinguished by unsympathetic treatment of American reality, by an aggravated, affected style, by scholasticism and high-flown religious oratory, and by a sort of all-purpose poetry that could signify communion with the Spanish motherland, even at a distance. The Gongorism that prevailed during this period in Ecuador is attuned to the rest of the continent in its shunning of the novel and the theater as genres that were responsive to the immediacy of their preoccupations. In contrast to another Andean country like Peru, the lack of an Ecuadorian theatrical tradition will persist well into the 1990s.

But the opening of the eighteenth century also provides the first inklings of the conception of a national entity, a distancing from the self-concept of being the audiencia of Quito or part of the consecutive viceroyalties of Peru and New Granada. This may have been the driving force that produced a really outstanding group of Ecuadorian writers, identified by their desire to assemble the human and the natural into contingent and changing unities that would reveal societal power relations through a defiant aesthetics *sub specie aeternitatis*. Although readers may form their own revisionist canon, this kind of survey must forcedly present a normative, generally known group of authors, with the proviso that their ultimate legitimation will come in a review by readers of the self-understanding of comparable or competing abstract typologies and concepts of periodization. Of those authors whose works would be published during the eigthteenth century, Juan Bautista Aguirre (1725-86), Eugenio Espejo (1747-95), Pedro Vicente Maldonado (1704-48), and Juan de Velasco (1727-92) were most responsible for the groundwork of Ecuadorian literary culture.

The above is a conditional stipulation more than an assertion, for individually these four men embodied the energetic cultural factotum who reaches beyond the specificity of his occupation. They were a Jesuit scholar, pedagogue, and poet (Aguirre); a journalist, physician, and paralegal philosopher (Espejo); a geographer and scientist (Maldonado); and a Jesuit historian and narrator (Velasco). All were bent on being poetic and combining their rhetoric with the confrontational style of their insurgent pamphlets and books. It is an insurgency that is complex in aims but at the same time full of a protonational flavor. Aguirre, for example, wrote a religious, mythological, moral, amorous, and satiric poetry of rich intertextual relations. But he may be best remembered by his "Breve diseño de las ciudades de Guayaquil e Quito" (Brief Design of the Cities of Guayaquil and Quito; date unknown), in which he postulates the centuries-old regionalism that still afflicts these rival cities. Guayaquil wins, so to speak, and this is presented by Aguirre as a serio-comic epistle whose thirty-six strophes contain language that has been alternately graceful, witty, and "crude" to a long tradition of critics. Yet, his *Versos castellanos, obras juveniles, misceláneas* (Castilian Verses, Youthful Works, Miscellany), found only in 1937, reveal him to be equally capable as a purveyor of amorous or metaphysical discourse.

Without a doubt Aguirre is the richest of the Ecuadorian poets of this period, but Espejo was to be the most representative author of a literature that did not yet have a country. A mestizo who to most critics reconciled the idiosyncracies of the Indian, the black, and the white in Ecuador, Espejo channeled his varied efforts toward a critique of the society that was to send him to his death in prison at the age of forty-eight. His eclectic *Primicias de la cultura de Quito* (First News of the Culture of Quito; 1792) was that city's first newspaper. It was to last three months, as its commitment was inappropriate for the times. This newspaper was one of the few works he was to see in print, for even his polemical longhand circulars *El nuevo Luciano de Quito...* (The New Lucian of Quito; 1779) and its countertext, *Marco Porcio Catón...* (Marcus Portius Cato; 1780), were dialogues, self-reflexive at times and calling for reform in Jesuit teaching and theology and, in the later text, an attack on moral laxity in the religious orders; both were printed after his death. His *Reflexiones sobre el contagio y transmisión de las viruelas* (Thoughts on the Contagion and Transmission of Smallpox; 1785) is a respectable precursor of scientific discourse and, as a product of a then underdeveloped social system, indicative of the challenge Espejo undertook and expanded with liberal ideas for political and administrative reforms. This struggle extended to oratory, the economy, and even literary style.

Maldonado and Velasco require an open definition as to what constitutes literariness. The former was more of a cartographer who dabbled in mathematics and physics. His 1750 map of Quito and its surroundings (actually, a good part of today's Ecuador) is considered a masterpiece in the field. He drew upon his travel experiences in his native country, about which he wrote a *Relación* (Account; 1774/78) that he started in the 1740s; he also traveled in England and France. As literature, the *Relación* is encumbered by the author's interruptions when he tries to

convince his readers that there should be greater communication between Quito and the court. But as historical understanding and harbinger of national awareness its role is undeniable.

Velasco's case is different in that it confronts the reader with a man
of exceptional literary talent. His *Historia del Reino de Quito* (History
of the Kingdom of Quito; 1789) is one of the three Ecuadorian works
(the others are by Montalvo and writers of the 1930s) included in the
canon of Latin American literature of which Venezuela's Biblioteca
Ayacucho (Ayacucho Library) has initiated publication in annotated editions. Velasco, an ex-Jesuit as a consequence of the expulsion of the
order from Ecuador in 1773, supposedly wrote this work from memory
and without notes. Be that as it may, the novelistic discourse—and all
the components that today's criticism attributes to it—that its author uses
as scaffolding makes for a very imaginative, nostalgic, and expository
view of Ecuador as a historical enterprise, if not entity. Velasco's vision
of the past and passionate interest in the Indians, a trait he shares with
other chroniclers cum "novelists," also come across in the poems, by him
and other Jesuits included in the five-volume *Colección de poesías varias,
hecha por un ocioso en la ciudad de Faenza* (Assorted Poetry Collection,
by an Idler in Faenza; 1790), which supposedly contains the entire literary production of eighteenth-century Quito. This century ends with the
planting of the seeds of the struggle for liberation, an effort whose force
will be felt for most of the first third of the next century.

III

José Mejía (1775-1813) and Vicente Solano (1791-1865) are basically
journalists and orators whose speeches, fables, and articles provide the
needed transitory calls for Independence. However, the nineteenth
century is the period of Juan León Mera and Juan Montalvo. The
reader should also be made aware first of the fabulist Rafael García
Goyena (1776-1823), whose *Fábulas y poesías varias* (Fables and Assorted Poetry; 1836) were published in Guatemala, where he died after
having spent most of his life there, thereby starting what may be the first
struggle for national attribution of exiled writers. There is also José
Joaquín de Olmedo (1780-1847), whose "La victoria de Junín, canto a
Bolívar" (Victory at Junín, Song to Bolivar; 1825-26) is a masterfully
fantastic elegy to the Liberator and the best literary expression of Creole
pleasure at the triumph over the Spaniards. His posthumous *Obras*

poéticas (Poetry; 1862) and *Poesías inéditas de Olmedo* (Unpublished Poetry by Olmedo; 1862) are not as allusive, graceful, and epic in tone as the work dedicated to Bolívar. Nevertheless, they merit study from the perspective of more current theories of poetry that may reveal an author of greater range than the poet of a single text. Something similar should be done with Dolores Veintimilla de Galindo (1830-57), a poet who experienced and rebelled against the discrimination of her time, went through a positive "No God, no boss, no husband" stage, and committed suicide when her *Necrología* (Necrology; 1857), distributed as a flier arguing for justice for an Indian condemned to death, caused diatribes against her.

The lives and works of Mera and Montalvo cover two well-defined periods of the nineteenth century: the brief interval of the struggles for independence and the strife-ridden process of the creation of the Republic. What Espejo had started was a dichotomy in which Ecuador was to be composed of the Creole republican and the mestizo. The notion of a national culture was not fully developed, nor was there societal room for anything other than some men seeking dominant roles as arbiters of taste, creators of symbolic power, or organizers of nascent economic structures. Within this context, the basic literary credo was to be Spanish in style and forms, but as native as possible in content and disdainful of the recently deposed motherland. Of itself this is the start of a process of marginalization and degeneration of the indigenous race, of the process of going toward the "new" type of Ecuadorian. In the face of this contradictory movement of self-assertion and the promotion of relationships of simple subsistence by the dominated classes, literature became more vigorous. This was a ripe moment for Mera and Montalvo, as Romantics, and also for the growth of literary creation as an institution and the appearance of an abundance of writers, very few of whom had the ability or the desire to eke out a living from their marginal writerly occupations.

Mera was not forthright in criticizing the leftover Hispanic institutions that were the basic support for the conditions described above, but we have also seen before that he was not reticent in passing negative judgment on the poetry of others in his *Ojeada*. His own work, however, has enjoyed excellent reception. Before publishing his short novels, articles, and collections of Ecuadorian folklore (works published a few years before his death), he was to be the earliest biographer and anthologizer (1873) of Sor Juana (see the section on Mexico) and the author of a Chateaubriandesque novel that is required reading in Ecuadorian schools: *Cumandá o un drama entre salvajes* (Cumanda; 1879). In this novel the forest is alive, but the savages among whom Cumandá's impossible love with Carlos (they turn out to be brother and sister) takes place are not totally noble, as portrayed by most romantics. The familiar motif of the hidden identity may be a reflection of the author's avowed sympathy for the Indians and his veiled previous support of the theocratic dictator of Ecuador, Gabriel García Moreno (1821-75). But there is no question that the Ecuadorian novel begins with Mera, especially if one considers *Un matrimonio inconveniente. Apuntes para una novela sicológica* (An Inconvenient Wedding. Notes for a Psychological Novel).

The novel, one of the many short novels Mera published as *feullitons* after the early 1870s, tells the story of a father (Don Juan) who interferes with his daughter's plans to marry a nice, rich but "nonreligious" man (Rodolfo). The psychological penetration that Mera attempts through his narrator is actually more revealing of Mera's hewing to a religious script. A 1986 inventory of the 1,858 volumes of his library revealed a preponderance of religious tomes for this father of eleven children. Besides this idealized and founding Indianist novel, Mera is the author of *Poesías* (Poetry; 1858, 1892), whose contents do not deviate much from the exalted Romanticism, pastoralness, timidity, and at times self-righteousness that characterize the rest of his production.

Montalvo, on the other hand, was loudly cathartic, more politically modern than Mera, but as full of classicity as he was of rebellion. To many, Montalvo is the intellectual author of the liberal movement of the burgeoning Ecuadorian bourgeoisie, a stance that placed him at odds with the literate García Moreno (after him Cordero and Velasco have been the only other cultured Ecuadorian presidents), whose dictatorship (1860-75) suppressed all opposition with great ferocity, tried to Gallicize Ecuador, and emulated Louis XIV's "L'état c'est moi." In a letter dated September 28, 1860 to García Moreno, Montalvo asks him: "Are you irritated by my frankness?" It is this frankness that Montalvo would embellish in concerted stylistic efforts in essays and articles as one way of rescuing the country from a period (1830-1895) that has been qualified as "The Impoverishment of the Republic."

Although his *Catilinarias* (Catilinaries; 1880-82), *Siete tratados* (Seven Treatises; 1882), and the articles of *El cosmopolita* (The Cosmopolite; 1866-69) and *El regenerador* (The Rejuvenator; 1876-78) show him to be a brilliant polemicist on moral and civil rights issues, it is the clarity of thought, expression, and assimilation of received ideas for literary style that the reader identifies immediately. Montalvo's inspired albeit archaic range of metaphors, paragraph development, lexical richness, and evident ability to correct and suggest to himself were widely praised by Latin American, Spanish, and other European writers of the period. This recognition would increase with the posthumous *Capítulos que se le olvidaron a Cervantes* (Chapters That Cervantes Forgot; 1895). Montalvo was quite aware, as would be his critics, of the implausibility of the enterprise. Nevertheless his valiant *Capítulos*, favorably compared to the master narrative, employs a novelistic discourse to narrate Don Quixote's adventures in America and to attack obliquely Montalvo's old enemies, the dictators Ignacio Veintemilla (1828-1908) and García Moreno. This middle-class mestizo, who wrote his most important work while exiled in Ipiales, Colombia, would die in Besançon, France, where he was provided the support that his native land could not give him.

The literature of nineteenth-century Ecuador can be contextualized further with the consideration of the work of Federico González Suárez (1844-1917), Federico Proaño (1848-94), Julio Zaldumbide (1833-87), even García Moreno himself (especially the two sonnets he wrote against Montalvo). They are historians, journalists, and essayists, but above all poets (sensu latu) who were part of a literary networking that sought freedom for others as a means of achieving their own peace with their lot. At this point the influence of French literature becomes clearer, as would the slow transition from the codes of Romanticism to those of Modernism. Originality was pursued only within the constraints of foreignisms, thus revealing a functional-utilitarian approach whose virtues in accounting for particularly Ecuadorian literary codes were nil. Concomitantly, the twentieth century was to start for Ecuador in 1895, when Eloy Alfaro—whose literal revolution was victorious in a short civil war—became president. His administration pushed through a number of anticlerical measures, and the Church lost control of education with the adoption of the Constitution of 1906. At about this point, the upsurge in Ecuador's literary production places its authors in the mainstream of the Spanish American literature that readily altered some of its previous traditions, giving free rein to the inventive expression that would experience the paradoxes of modernity and the fate of the market. As such, the literature of Ecuador again reveals itself to be as developed as that of any other country of the continent, but oddly lacking in recent times in 1) a self-reflexive critical tradition that is on a par with its representative works, and 2) the informed selectivity that allows other countries to discern between naïve texts and those that reach an international readership beyond nationalistic desiderata, without the help of literary cronyism.

For obvious reasons, the summary nature of this reading of Ecuadorian literary history limits its reach. By dint of conciseness, for the twentieth century some authors become basic, some authorial attitudes rule a period, generations overlap, genres become fragmentary, hybrid or lost, some aspects of literariness correctly become peripheral. Two facts remain stable: the unfairness of the exclusivity implied in a corrective approach and the need to analyze the writing that has been excluded for not being transgressive. It is a sort of dialectic that, in linking the reading moment and the past with the text, defines the rhythm of the struggle for power in twentieth-century Ecuador, where social and economic crises have not failed to find analogies in previous historical periods. The differentiating elements to be found among the critical studies on contemporary Ecuadorian letters reveal a mesmerizing activity that is far from the writing hegemonized by the virtuosi of Ecuadorian Catholicism and closer to a "literature as life" activity.

This awareness can only be isolated by presenting representative authors, genres, and movements as points of convergence. Within this kaleidoscopic disarray a good starting point is the transitory system of the Ecuadorian novel. Two years before the Constitution of 1906, Luis A. Martínez (1869-1909) published *A la costa* (To the Coast; 1904). Its subtitle, "costumbres ecuatorianas" (Ecuadorian Customs), disappears (perhaps signalling the abandonment of a literature of manners) in subsequent editions. The date of its appearance is important because Martínez has his protagonist, Salvador ("Savior") Ramírez, immersed in the immediate past of the country's civil war. Ramírez is a poor law student from Quito who goes to the coast and spends three days in Guayaquil with his wealthy friend Luciano, who is leaving for Europe. Frustrated, he ends up working as a foreman on a banana plantation on the coast, where he dies yearning for the highlands of the sierra.

A sort of Bildungsroman and historical novel that fails to combine factual and autobiographical discourse convincingly, *A la costa* shows the author's knack for the descriptiveness that has led many critics to consider him the founder of the Realist movement in Ecuadorian literature. The almost accusatory tone of this "novel of the land" (a common category among early twentieth-century scholars) and its frequent moralizing on conservative ideology do not prevent it from being a model that many subsequent Ecuadorian novelists of greater fame would follow.

The year 1930 is of extreme significance to the development of Ecuadorian literature. National pride in that decade is perfectly justifiable, and it may be recognized as providing an important model for the narrative of the rest of the continent. The problem is that the reduction of the canon to three or four prose writers overlooks what went on immediately before, in other genres and with other writers. It has been argued that the logical continuation of Martínez is the work of Fernando Chávez (1902), especially the narratives *La embrujada* (Bewitched Woman; 1923) and *Plata y bronce* (Silver and Bronze; 1927), the first evidence in Ecuador of Indigenism, that is, the attempt to portray the Indian as a vital rather than a folkloric addendum to dominant writing. But more or less the same argument could be made for Icaza's *Barro de la sierra* (Highland Clay; 1933), a collection of six short stories of similar thematics, and other works published at about the same time.

The term "narratives," or *relatos*, permits the prose canon of this period to intertwine genres and subgenres in the same physical impulses of a powerful generation, simply because readers are responding to prose created in the same sociohistorical moment. In this progression Jorge Icaza (1906-78) and his *Huasipungo* (Hut; 1934), whose theatrical version was banned in the countryside by the Ecuadorian government, are the best expression of Indigenism. It should be mentioned in passing that the change from Romantic Indianism to Indigenism ought also to include the study of the stories published by Sergio Núñez in *Novelas del páramo y de la cordillera* (Novels of the Plain and the Mountain Range; 1934) and *Tierra de lobos* (Land of Wolves; 1939).

The return to Icaza is now in better perspective. His *Huasipungo*, the original version of which undergoes many changes in subsequent editions, is widely acclaimed, translated, made into a book for children, and imitated. From actor, bookseller, bureaucrat, and union organizer Icaza goes on to become a diplomat, Director of the National Library, university lecturer, and world traveler. *Huasipungo* is considered a compendium of the suffering of the Indian. The plot of the novel is rather conventional (exploitation, foreign intervention, resistance, tragic end, hope), as is the gallery of characters that personify the elements of the progression of the plot. Although Andrés Chiliquinga is the protagonist, Icaza presents the masses as the true hero. If the transcription of Indian speech is exact, the author's carelessness in proportioning content and form allows for melodrama. What, then, made *Huasipungo* and its author the most canonical literary pairing after Montalvo? Quite simply, the succinctness and the logic of its symbolism, the epic strength of presenting in moving detail the components and workings of the systematic exploitation of the Indian. In this regard, this novel and those published up to 1958 have served perfectly to establish an accurate typology of the Indigenist novel. In that year he publishes *El Chulla Romero y Flores* (The Worthless Romero y Flores), the first Ecuadorian work to be published as part of UNESCO's prestigious Collection Archives. In this Bildungsroman a Quito *mestizo* snob achieves psychological balance by accepting the indigenous part of his being. Icaza would not write another novel until *Atrapados* (Trapped; 1972), a sort of synthesis of his personal, literary, and ultimately political life. The long gap between novels was filled with the publication of the short stories of *Seis relatos* (Six Tales; 1952), which round out the indigenous themes of the stories of *Barro de la sierra* (Highland Clay; 1933). In a way, his complete production will also round out the indigenous movement in the literature of Ecuador.

Icaza, Pablo Palacio (1906-47), José de la Cuadra (1903-41), Alfredo Pareja Diezcanseco (1908), Demetrio Aguilera Malta (1909-81), Joaquim Gallegos Lara (1909-47), and Enrique Gil Gilbert (1912-73) are the authors chosen by Pedro Jorge Vera (1914) and Jorge Enrique Adoum (1923), both excellent Ecuadorian novelists in their own right, to compose the accurately annotated anthology published by the Biblioteca Ayacucho with the title *Narradores ecuatorianos del 30* (Ecuadorian Prose Writers of the Thirties; 1980). All except Icaza and Palacio constitute what has been called the Guayaquil Group. Of these, the last three published together *Los que se van* (Those Who Leave; 1930), until now the most famous short story collection written in Ecuador. Its fame is well deserved, for the book redefined the myths of reading a canon that was indecisive and unable to provide ample appreciation for the manifold factors that create a national culture.

Los que se van would open up those possibilities of redefining the future of Ecuadorian prose. Its young authors (their ages totaled 60 years at the time of publication) had not only been at the right place at the right time, but they also knew perfectly well what they had. This is clear from the subtitle of their work, "Cuentos del cholo i [*sic*] del montuvio" (Tales of Halfbreeds and Hillbillies), to their stated aesthetic purpose, employed as frontispiece, "This book is not a bundle of egos. It has three authors: it does not have three parts. It is one single thing. It strives for the work being as unified as the dream that created it. It has been born of the fraternal march of our three spirits. Nothing else. The authors." "The Mean One," "It Was the Mother," "The Half-Breed

Who Castrated Himself" are three representative translations of the titles of the stories whose contents were to shock the readership of their time. Written with flair, crudeness of language and theme, paucity of rhetorical devices, but rich in poetic expression, *Los que se van* presents its two social groups in all their lack of sexual repression, in the brute strength they had to use for survival, and in their misery.

If the literati of the thirties found its directness objectionable, the "common reader" came to appreciate it for the positive attitudes that its antitraditionalism wrought for the literature of Ecuador. In this regard it is worth noting that there has always been a camaraderie among Ecuadorian authors that crossed gender and class lines. The very politically committed Joaquín Gallegos Lara started a novel called "Los guandos" (the indigenous name for the large basket in which Ecuadorian indians still transport large loads on their backs) in 1935. He died in 1947. In 1981 Nela Martínez, his companion of many years, revealed that *Los guandos* (1982) was a novel written in tandem. He had written "from the outside," and she took care of the "internal" representation of the suffering of Ecuadorian indians and peasants. The result is a successful variant of social realism in which many binary oppositions, not the least of which is that between the two authors, finally provide a truly dialogical voice to the downtrodden.

Returning to the three authors of *Los que se van*, Aguilera Malta is the one who maintained a symbiotic relationship with literature. As novelist and playwright, as well as biographer, he would see almost twenty of his works published in his lifetime. He was able to draw on his experiences as a journalist and moviemaker to create vast novelistic panoramas in which the search for myth, symbols, and authenticity would dominate all other themes, such as physical, spiritual, and economic tyranny. This world of Aguilera Malta's drew from the epic tradition. Of his novels, *Don Goyo* (1933), *La isla virgen* (The Virgin Island; 1942), a novel that takes up again the trite theme of the rejection of the civilizer by nature and transcends it, and *Siete lunas y siete serpientes* (*Seven Moons and Seven Serpents*; 1970) have become the trilogy on which his novelistic production is judged. Aguilera Malta is also Ecuador's best playwright (see below).

De la Cuadra is Ecuador's claim to the inclusion of one of its authors in the canon of the difficult and widely practiced genre of the short story. Among the thirteen volumes that constitute his production, one will also find novels, novellas, and ethnological studies. But it is the oxymoronic practice of psychological realism in his short stories that has earned him just praise. His search for precision and justice made the Guayaquil Group consider him the elder of the five. In 1970, Cuba's Casa de las Américas (House of the Americas) published a selection of his works under the odd title *Cuentos* (Short Stories). It is odd because it includes his novel *Las Sangurimas* (The Sangurimas; 1934) and his demographic study *El montuvio ecuatoriano* (The Ecuadorian Peasant; 1937).

The most literate of the Guayaquil Group is Pareja Diezcanseco. As a novelist, essayist, historian, and journalist, his range is wide. His forty or so titles include novels that led critics to consider him the most gifted novelist of the Group. This evaluation was to change in the mid sixties, in spite of the fact that his production has not diminished to this date. He published his first novel, *La casa de los locos* (House of the Mad) in 1929. *El muelle* (The Dock; 1933) is probably his best novel, vividly detailed in its depiction of life in the occupations of the waterfront. Similar novels will culminate with the tryptic and roman fleuve *Los nuevos años* (The New Years; 1956-64), whose three volumes are frequently reissued individually. Recent titles include *Las pequeñas estaturas* (Small Statures; 1970) and *La manticora* (The Manticore; 1974), which he considers his best novel. Pareja Diezcanseco is also considered the "conscience of the nation," but more than anything he would rather be known for holding, in his own words, "memories of history and the future."

The work of Pablo Palacio, since 1976 the object of considerable critical attention, provides Ecuadorian narrative with a quantum leap into the prose of the sixties. Obviously, it is not that nothing of quality was published in the intervening decades. It simply seems that for the forties and fifties the only novel worthy of rescue is Adalberto Ortiz's *Juyungo: historia de un negro, una isla y otros negros* (*Juyungo*; 1934). Pareja Diezcanseco published at least three novels during those two decades, but they have not had the effect that the prose of Palacio has had. Palacio published *Comedia inmortal* (Immortal Comedy; 1926), *Un hombre muerto a puntapiés* (A Man Kicked to Death; 1927), *Débora* (Debora; 1927), and *Vida del ahorcado* (Life of the Hanged Man; 1932). Together, these constitute a volume of complete works that does not exceed two hundred and fifty pages and are now being normalized for forthcoming definitive editions in Venezuela's Biblioteca Ayacucho and UNESCO's Collection Archives. However, his work gives veracity to the aesthetic position that short works can be twice as good as long ones. Palacio was artistically and personally much ahead of his time, shocking even. His sabotaging of the representation of reality, narrative self-consciousness, details bordering on the grotesque, and irony hold his readers. To many, the author's personal obsessions are thinly veiled. However, his subjective imagery ("novela subjetiva"—subjective novel—is *Débora*'s subtitle) and transcription of psychic traumas make up a corpus characterized by existentialism, self-deprecation, relegation of social criticism, and sophisticated technique, a combination subsequent narrative would emulate.

In the forties and fifties, the novel gives way to poetry, as will be seen. Of this period, Gallegos Lara's *Las cruces sobre el agua* (The Crosses on the Water; 1946) is of primary importance. The novel presages well the application of a better-assimilated social realism to urban themes, which had been looming in Palacio. For Gallegos Lara, this approach meant the ability to employ popular language with ease in combining four focuses of meaning: the city, the search for identity, character movement, and sociopolitical discourse that interprets events. These, based on the massacre of November 15, 1922 in Guayaquil, give the novel a documentary tone that never falters in its sedate reading of history. The title of the book refers to anonymous crosses put to float on the river every November 15 to commemorate the hundreds of people whose mutilated bodies were dumped there. Baldeón and Cortés, the protagonists, are from the reputedly tough neighborhood of El Astillero (Shipyard) in southern Guayaquil. There the similarities end momentarily for both men, for both acquire a self-concept by delving into their defects, virtues, and pet peeves. Baldeón joins the people's street revolt, and dies with them. Cortés later learns well that the importance of people's remembering to put crosses in the water lies in their also remembering injustices and those who did not take a stand.

A stand similar to the Spanish classic *Fuenteovejuna* by Lope de Vega is narrated in Angel F. Rojas's *El éxodo de Yangana* (The Exodus of Yangana; 1949), in which a whole town, accused of a crime, leaves. This novel, very modern in technique, closes the great cycle of the Ecuadorian novel.

To continue with the novel in Ecuador entails a considerable jump, since it is not until the sixties that an upsurge in prose (especially in the short story) starts displacing poetry. Nevertheless, the forties also see the appearance of the works of Nelson Estupiñán Bass (1915), who in *Cuando los guayacanes florecían* (When Guayacan Trees Bloomed; 1954) takes up the twenties, specifically the proliberal revolt of Carlos Concha against Plaza Gutiérrez. Like the previously mentioned Ortiz, Estupiñán

Bass is from the province of Esmeraldas, the setting for his novel, which recounts how a group of black peons decimates the regular army with guerrilla tactics. In this regard Aguilera Malta's *Una cruz en la Sierra Maestra* (A Cross in the Sierra Maestra; 1960) is indicative of the thematic concerns of the period, and perhaps of the beginnings of the short and weak lull in the narrative production that was to come.

Nevertheless, the sixties is a fortunate period for the narrative of Pareja Diezcanseco, Aguilera Malta, Miguel Donoso Pareja (1931), and Pedro Jorge Vera (1915). Donoso Pareja's *Krelko* (1962) is a well-wrought example of an antiimperialist sentiment; see also his *El hombre que mataba a sus hijos* (The Man Who Killed His Children; 1968). Vera's *La semilla estéril* (The Sterile Seed; 1962) deals with racism in Guayaquil, avarice, and U.S. usurpation of property. At this point, the country is about to experience the last surges of José María Velasco Ibarra (1893—Velasco Ibarra served five times as President), new military regimes, and the oil boom. In terms of culture, the decade is very productive and actually receives official and greater private funding, allowing for a multitude of publishing projects and what was perhaps the culminating event of the decade, the First Meeting on Ecuadorian Literature, held in November, 1978. Its extensive proceedings give an exhaustive account for all genres of the literary production of the period, in some cases taking the year 1950 as a point of departure. Indeed, the decade provides pabulum to speak of The New Novel of Ecuador. The works of Aguilera Malta, Jorge Dávila Vázquez (1947), Ivan Egüez (1944), Edmundo Ribadeneira (1920), Eliécer Cárdenas (1950), Alfonso Cuesta y Cuesta (1912), and Gustavo Alfredo Jácome (1919), with his *Por qué se fueron las garzas* (Why Did the Herons Leave; 1979), provide justifiable reasons for the start of a canonical revision.

It is natural, however, that all decades provide an exceptional year or two, and the necessary revision or creation of a literary canon's flux. If literature in countries like Ecuador unavoidably tends to project the crossroads that other cultural expressions cannot repress, the important years of the seventies in Ecuador can well start with 1972. This is the year that the magazine *La bufanda del sol* (The Sun's Scarf) began publishing with the goal of transforming national culture. Many of the members of its advisory board—Raúl Pérez, Ulises Estrella, Iván Egüez, Alejandro Moreano, Agustín Cueva, Fernando Tinajero, and Abdón Ubidia—would go on to become the cultural power brokers of the eighties through their literary production or critical work.

At this time Jaime Galarza Zavala publishes his *El festín del petróleo* (The Oil Banquet; 1972), a revealing study of corruption and maintenance of the status quo within the possibilities of the Ecuadorian oil glut, whose complement is Osvaldo Hurtado's *El poder político en el Ecuador* (Political Power in Ecuador; 1977). In 1976 three important novels appear: Jorge E. Adoum (1923) published his *Entre Marx y una mujer desnuda* (Between Marx and a Naked Woman), Egüez's *La Linares* (The Linares Woman), and Pedro Jorge Vera's *El pueblo soy yo* (I Am the People). The first two already have been the subject of much debate and writing. Adoum, excellent poet and critic, is the present dean of Ecuadorian letters. His novel partakes of the latest techniques to disarm literary discourse. Violence, literary theory, emotions, and the problems of sociocultural reality are ably juxtaposed. But what reigns is the analysis by the author/character/Adoum of the intellectual conflict produced by the self-begotten novel. Although this type of novelistic elaboration was much in vogue at the time in Spanish America, Adoum's novel stands out for its subtle treatment of characterization, especially in having the character Gálvez act as a linkage for narrative point of view. *La Linares* is really a novella whose hilarity also displaces all narrative centers. It is a valiant attempt to mix biography, social criticism, the historical novel, sarcasm, and the characteristics of the so-called novel of language within a juxtaposition of times and spaces. The title character "went far on her beauty." But she was cursed to be unlucky, and in her apocalypsis drags along a President and his corrupt entourage. But she will rise again, as the novel suggests at its end, without the "Prez," the "General of Defeats," the "Great Vilifier" and others. Within this cultural framework the prose of Alicia Yánez Cossío is an antidote to what is still a generally sexist representation of women in Ecuadorian prose. In the novel *Bruna, soroche y los tíos* (Bruna, Soroche and the Uncles; 1975), the protagonist Bruna struggles to liberate herself from the social conventions imposed by a static and stifling social milieu.

Vera's novel is the synthesis of thirty years of Ecuadorian life (1942-72?). Manuel María González Tejada, its protagonist, is a dictator. The five "acts" that make up the novel jell with difficulty. Thus the voices of the novel (wives, radio reports, official documents) do not aid readers' search for elements that may show this novel's difference from others in the same subgenre. Vera holds on too much to the representation of the manipulations that wrecked the presidencies of Velasco Ibarra, making the novel tiresome with the amplification of the protagonist's "Gonzalismo." The reader is treated better in the virtuosity of

Vera's stories, from *Luto eterno y otros relatos* (Eternal Mourning and Other Stories; 1952) to *¡Ah los militares!* (Ah, the Military!; 1986).

The seventies end with Donoso Pareja's *Día tras día* (Day after Day; 1976), a rich meditation on erotic triangles and time, and Cárdenas's *Polvo y ceniza* (Dust and Ashes; 1979). Reissued in 1983 for the series Grandes novelas ecuatorianas: los últimos 30 años (Great Ecuadorian Novels: the Last Thirty Years), Cárdenas's novel is indeed a master work. He has published the stories *Hoy, al general* (Today, to the General; 1971) and four other novels. But it is *Polvo y ceniza* that deserves rereading. The novel focuses, permeates, or hovers surreptitiously on the deeds of Naún Briones, a bandit whose deeds belong to popular mythology. A brief example is the brilliant section on the many Brioneses (even rich ones) who opportunistically stand in for El Verdadero (The Real One). It is a wonderfully hyperbolic study on the effect of the real. But for Cárdenas the myth is personalized so as to ring true to all possible readers. The myth becomes stronger, conflictive, and fulfilling. Briones and the other highwaymen acquire the human dimension that the landholders, who have made the land "a huge hacienda called the country," deny them. The novel never succumbs to predictable outcomes, even when the bandits are attacking the "boots" who eventually kill them.

The eighties are not much different in that the novel and the short story are the privileged genres. There is a flurry of activity brought about by the economic conditions of the country which, if they did not better the lot of the common reader, were certainly more positive for the literary world. Special mention should again be made of the prose of Alicia Yánez Cossío: *Yo vendo unos ojos negros* (I'm Selling Black Eyes; 1979), *Más allá de las islas* (Beyond the Islands; 1980), and *La cofradía del mullo del vestido de La Virgen Pipona* (The Brotherhood of the Potbellied Virgin's Dress Bead; 1985). The analyses of these works, still uneven or fixated on applying foreign feminist models to a different reality, have had the positive impact of empowering the recovery of the high quality of women's writing in Ecuador, especially that exemplified by the four women who make up what is being called "El Nuevo Grupo de Guayaquil." Equally deserving, are Jorge Velasco Mackenzie, author of *El rincón de los justos* (The Corner of the Just; 1983), a novel about Guayaquil's lumpen proletariat and the short stories of *Como gato en tempestad* (Like A Cat in A Storm; 1977); and two collections in the same genre by Walter Bellolio, *La sonrisa y la ira* (Smile and Wrath; 1968) and the critically acclaimed *Crónica del hombre que aprendió a llorar* (Story of the Man Who Learned to Cry; 1975).

Although it may be too early to ascertain which are the novels of the eighties that will have the resonance of Adoum's 1976 text, there are many that merit the type of consideration that can surpass the innermost politics of the cultural enclaves of Quito, Guayaquil, and Cuenca. In 1984, for example, Abdón Ubidia publishes *Ciudad de invierno* (Winter City) and Alfonso Barrera Valverde *Dos muertes en una vida* (Two Deaths in a Life; originally published in Argentina and Spain in 1971 and 1980). Both short novels deal with the contemporary ennui of urban couples in Ecuador. There is an Onettian quality to Ubidia's protagonist, Susana, while Barrera Valverde's Juan Hiedra is a victim of the type with which Benedetti prefers to fill his short stories. Ubidia and Barrera Valverde, however, cannot help resorting to symbolic enclaves that are ultimately detrimental to the construction of character. But both novels work within their generic confines.

Carlos de la Torre Reyes (1928), whose first novel ...*Y los dioses se volvieron hombres* (...And the Gods Became Men; 1981) was published in Spain, publishes *El reino de los suelos* (The Rock-Bottom Kingdom) in 1987. It is purportedly a novel about the decadent world of the high social classes of the northern Ecuadorian highlands. However the author has chosen to form a novel from seven different narratives, full of irony, for which the characters Gregorio Magno (an exbullfighter Monsignor) and the physician Timoleón Becerra serve as consciences and recoverers of narrative threads in a very contemporary novel, one full of popular cultural icons from Ecuador, Spain, and the United States. After De la Torre Reyes, the novelists who have published important works have been born in the late forties and early fifties.

El devastado jardín del paraíso (The Devastated Garden of Paradise; 1990) is Alejandro Moreano's morality tale about the adventures of a clandestine guerrilla group. It takes up terrain similar to Eliecer Cárdenas's and has in Hernán Escobar Ricaurte, "El Facineroso," a memorable character who has travelled through Chile, Nicaragua, El Salvador, and Ecuador organizing foci for uprisings. The novel plays with the strategies of testimonial narratives until "El Facineroso" (The Rogue) ends up defeated in a bus leaving Colombia. There he remembers that the constant threat of death may not have been worth trying to copy the lives of previous guerrilla heroes. Javier Ponce (1948), a major young poet, is also the author of *El insomnio de Nazario Mieles* (The Insomnia of Nazario Mieles; 1990), a novel that partakes of many of the techniques that Adoum put on display in his influential novel of 1976. Almalepra, the male protagonist of Ponce's novel, has the ability to lead simultaneous lives, and is thus reborn in the Amazonian jungle. Nazario Mieles, his antagonist, ends up in the Isla de los Muertos. Both men, aided and abetted by the sensuous Zulia Pando and Adán Negrete (an alternate narrator who is also swallowed by the jungle at the end of the novel), die, not without having their ghosts populate different moments of the novel.

But it is in the short story genre that the decade of 1990 will have to negotiate its advances. Foremost among the many Ecuadorian short story writers, who actively participate in contests organized by the major Ecuadorian newspapers for the genre, are Javier Vásconez (1946) and Raúl Pérez Torres (1941). In a way both represent the well-known split of Ecuadorian literary traditions into a somber, closed style in the highlands and a livelier, more playful representational engagement on the coast. Both men have won major international prizes in the genre (Pérez Torres won Cuba's prestigious Casa de las Americas Prize). Vásconez's *Ciudad lejana* (Far Away City; 1982) is a collection in which realism, the absurd, sensuality, and the fantastic are interwoven to produce a mosaic of urban characters not completely devoid of a religious charge. In 1989 he publishes the collection *El hombre de la mirada oblicua* (The Man with the Sidelong Glance). The title story is really a short novel, but in the other six narratives the author returns to the ghastly world of his previous stories. Again the characters are searching, not neccessarily for roots but rather for ways out of their madness, loneliness, fear, and violence.

Finally, Raúl Pérez Torres is without a doubt the most solid and "universal" of all the authors of the eighties. He has published seven collections of short stories, from which *Ana la pelota humana* (Ana the Human Ball; 1978), *Musiquero joven, musiquero viejo* (Young Musicmaker, Old Musicmaker; 1977), *En la noche y en la niebla* (At Night and in the Fog; 1980) and *Un saco de alacranes* (A Sack of Scorpions; 1989) are the most representative of his mature art. Pérez Torres has the wonderful ability to connect everyday occurrences with the political framework that informs them. The colloquial dialect of Guayaquil and the forthrightness of the characters, especially in the last collection, serve to disarm the conventionality for which most of Pérez Torres' characters have no use. The locales, however, are not exclusively national and it is because of that aspect that this author may well enter the world of Ecuadorian authors published abroad.

Although not as accomplished as Pérez Torres, the promise Huilo Ruales (1947) is showing could well transcend national barriers. The author of collections of short stories like *Y todo este rollo también a mí me jode* (And This Whole Mess also Fucks Me Up; 1984) and *Nuaycielo comuel dekito* (phonetic transcription of There Is No Heaven Like Quito's; 1985) publishes *Loca para loca la loca (cuentos para despeinarse la cara)* (Madwoman to Madwoman the Madwoman [Stories to Mess Up Your Face]; 1989). This is a collection of hybrid fragments, epigrammatic in quality, held together by the notion of madness applied to "The Gospel According to Saint I." This approach bodes well for his inclusion into a tradition of metafictional writing that at this point is for Ecuador what the so-called new historical novel is for other parts of the continent.

IV

For the twentieth century, the poetry of Ecuador cannot simply be read as before or after Jorge Carrera Andrade (1903-79), arguably the country's major poet of the century. His poetry is admittedly a result of Modernism in Ecuador (approximately 1895-1930), the first poetic movement for which guidelines have been attempted. As a movement, it is the ideal expression of the frustrations of the middle class. Yet, there is journalistic evidence that Rubén Darío (see the section on Nicaragua) and his entourage were not always the ideal model. It may not be surprising, then, that at first its authors put into play national geography, history, man, and nostalgia from similar perspectives. But they became escapists, unmitigated praisers of "better times" (for the Creoles), and their similarity extended to their stance as *poetes maudits* and suicides at an early age. They, Arturo Borja (1892-1912), Humberto Fierro (1890-1929), Ernesto Noboa Caamaño (1889-1927), and Medardo Angel Silva (1898-1919), the latter perhaps the best and not from the privileged background that spawned the other three, constitute the so-called Decapitated or 1910 Generation. Nevertheless, they also are responsible for formal and thematic renovations in the genre: Borja with *La flauta de ónix* (The Onyx Flute; 1920), Noboa Caamaño with *La romanza de las horas* (Romance of the Hours; 1922), Fierro in *El laúd en el valle* (Lute in the Valley; 1919), and Silva in *El árbol del bien y del mal* (The Tree of Good and Evil; 1918).

The publication in 1944 of the *Antología de poetas ecuatorianos* (Anthology of Ecuadorian Poets), edited by Augusto Arias, introduced the next poetic generation. They are known as the Elan Group and Alfredo Gangotena (1904-44), who wrote most of his poetry in French, stands out among them. He poeticizes American ecological forces in *La tempestad secreta* (The Secret Tempest; 1926-27) and *Ausencia* (Absence; 1928-30). In this decade the years 1946 through 1948 witness the greatest production from César Dávila Andrade, Enrique Noboa Arízaga, and Efraín Jara. The fifties seem to belong to three postmodernists, Gonzalo Escudero with his *Materia de angel* (Angel Matter; 1953) and *Autorretrato* (Self-Portrait; 1957), Carrera Andrade, and Gangotena. But the pantheism and objectivism of Carrera Andrade overtakes the first two poets, above all in *Aquí yace la espuma* (Here Lies the Foam; 1950), *Lugar de origen* (Place of Origin; 1950), and *Familia de la noche* (Family to the Night; 1953). His *Hombre planetario* (Planetary Man; 1959), to many his best work, inaugurates a cycle of poetic travelogues in which he never abandons the pains, windows, logical progressions, brevity, and general *joie de vivre* that have ruled his imagery.

The Elan Group had a sort of branch in the city of Cuenca, and César Dávila Andrade (1918-67) is its best representative, from *Oda al arquitecto* (Ode to the Architect; 1946) and *Catedral salvaje* (Savage Cathedral; 1951), through *Arco de instantes* (Arc of Moments; 1959), to the posthumous *Materia real* (Real Matter; 1970). Verbal luxury, montages of lyricism, man in rough surroundings, returns, resoluteness to abandon despair, and at the end hermetic messages, all characterize his poetry. Adoum, never part of a group, and the most solid critical conscience of Ecuadorian letters, began as a poet with *Ecuador amargo* (Bitter Ecuador; 1949). This was followed by the epic in the style of Pablo Neruda (see the section on Chile), *Los cuadernos de la tierra* (Earth Notebooks; 1952). Both and others were collected in *Poemas (1945-1961)* (Poems; 1963). *Informe personal sobre la situación* (Personal Report on Things; 1973) continues his relentless pursuit for social justice, while never falling into pamphleteering. His poetry is assertive, never agressive in its search for essence. This essence is frequently another going against the grain, which in most cases finds its referent in things that are not reported on in Ecuador, the "realism of the other reality," as he frequently posits in his essays. To shortly retrace this reading's steps, another pillar of the Cuenca branch of Elan is Efraín Jara Idrovo (1926), whose *El mundo de las evidencias* (The World of Evidences; 1979) is worthy of much study.

In the sixties a plethora of poetic groups, many attached to ephemeral journals, emerged as purported proof of new trends. Their motley names never really connected with efforts at poetic transcendence; moreover, they were practitioners of various genres. Such is the case with the

Tzántzicos (Head Shrinkers), memorable for not a few "happenings" in Ecuador. Within the group, Ulises Estrella (1940) and his *El ombligo del mundo* (The World's Navel; 1969) remains as proof of the group's best intents. For the seventies, the poetry of Carlos Eduardo Jaramillo (1932), in *Perseo ante el espejo* (Perseus in Front of the Mirror; 1974), *Tralfamadore*, and *La edad del fuego* (The Age of Fire), both from 1977, has been a consistent voice for change, pursuing the "conversational poetry" that was overwhelming Spanish America. But he also sings to fickle love, the small pleasures of everyday living. In the process he raises colloquial expression above Andean heights, uncommon in recent Ecuadorian poetry.

It is premature to speak of a "Generation of 1965" and a "Generation of 1980," because despite the obvious problems of seeing literary history in such facile compartments, there are many differences yet to be settled among the poets who generally straddle both divisions. For the eighties the poetry of Javier Ponce (1948), in the long epic poem *Postales* (Postcards; 1979) and the tripartite *A espaldas de otros lenguajes* (Behind the Backs of Other Languages; 1982), is a fountain of poetic force that devotes equal attention to the notion of narration in poetry. His *Los códices de Lorenzo Trinidad* (The Codices of Lorenzo Trinidad; 1985) is also close to the narrative strategies employed by the prose poem and the poetic sequence, both of which Ponce has down pat. Iván Carvajal, author of two poetry collections so far, *Poemas de un mal tiempo para la lírica* (Poems of a Bad Time for Poetry; 1980) and *Parajes* (Places; 1984), establishes a new rhetoric for philosophical discourse (existential) in poetry by aligning his verse with evocative conflicts that are mainly generational in nature. Antonio Preciado (1941), Humberto Vinueza (1944), and Simón Zavala Guzmán (1945) and the poets of Guayaquil's Generación Huracanada (Hurricane Generation) may be on the way to fire the canon, as may the work of Fernando Tinajero (1949).

As far as theater is concerned, Aguilera Malta's *El tigre* (The Tiger; 1955), *Lázaro* (Lazarus; 1941), and *Infierno negro* (Black Hell; 1967) may well serve to trace the development of the genre. Why? Mainly because it is only in the late second half of this century that the theater of Ecuador has tried to obliterate the popular vaudeville of Ernesto Albán Gómez (1937). Sadly, there is a good amount of theater that is put on the stage, but few of the scripts are published. Ultimately, as Ribadeneira Aguirre shows in the note he wrote for the *Revista iberoamericana* issue on Ecuador (see bibliography), it is difficult to mention even one original, strictly Ecuadorian piece that may be greeted as an important contribution to the theater of Latin America. The fact that it is matter that lacks state support or resources is only one reason for the poor condition of the genre, but it seems to be the prototypical explanation for Ecuador and the rest of the continent.

The essay as genre requires a peremptory judgment, for perhaps too many are published. When the practitioners go off on a tangent and try to insert what passes for criticism in Ecuador, the problem becomes more acute. Other than the Carrións and now Cueva and a few others, many of whom write columns for the major newspapers of Guayaquil and Quito, the essay has not found a *habitus* in Ecuador. Many of the critics mentioned here have partaken of the genre, but hardly any have achieved the kind of status that would allow for recognition outside the still very provincial realm of Ecuadorian letters.

At this point the country has gone through the military rule of 1971-79 and has entered the 1980s with an economic crisis that saw the gross national product fall 3.3 percent in 1983, and is entering the 1990s with the constant collapse of the congressional alliances that President Rodrigo Borja wants to establish. The gap between the free market and the intervention rate *sucre* is still widening. Executive-legislative confrontations, street fighting, strikes, and old networks guide politics. According to some opinions, President Febres Cordero's "free market, antistatist, proforeign capital platform" may cause social unrest. The literary response, as this reading has suggested, may be in kind.

BIBLIOGRAPHY

Alemán, Hugo. *Presencia del pasado*. Quito: Editorial Casa de la Cultura, 1953. Twenty-nine biographical sketches on contemporary writers, mainly poets.

Adoum, Jorge Enrique. "Las clases sociales en las letras contemporá neas de Ecuador." In *Panorama de la actual literatura latino-americana*. La Habana: C.I.L., Casa de las Américas, 1969. Pp. 154-66. Excellent brief introduction to the literature of the century and its social referents.

Barrera, Isaac J. *Historia de la literatura ecuatoriana*. Quito: Editorial Casa de la Cultura Ecuatoriana, 1961. Obviously dated, but fullest literary history to date.

Barrera, Isaac J., and Alejandro Carrión. *Diccionario de la literatura latinoamericana: Ecuador*. Washingtcn, D.C.: Unión Panamericana, 1962. Full biobibliographies for individual writers, but quite incomplete and full of the authors' express dislike for many.

Barrera, Isaac J., et al. *Historiadores y críticos literarios*. Puebla, México: Editorial J.M. Cajica, 1959. Sponsored by the General Secretariat of the Eleventh Interamerican Conference, a very revealing collection of the excellent state of Ecuadorian criticism during the colonial and first Republic period.

Barriga López, Franklin. *Diccionario de la literatura ecuatoriana*. 2nd. edition. Guayaquil: Casa de la Cultura Ecuatoriana, Nucleo del Guayas, 1980. Helpful as a register of authors, but overly impressionistic.

Biblioteca Nacional del Ecuador. *Bibliografía de autores ecuatorianos*. Quito: Editorial Casa de la Cultura Ecuatoriana, 1977. By far the best collection on the topic, but noticeably incomplete regarding authors of the last quarter of the century.

Bravo, Eliane Hubard de. *Roman et societé en Equateur (1930-1949)*. Cuernavaca: CIDOC, 1970. Cuaderno 48. Good sociological study of the social goals and results that the generation of 1930 textualized in its prose.

Carrasco, Adrián, et al. *Estado, nación y cultura. Los proyectos históricos en el Ecuador*. Cuenca: IDIS, Universidad de Cuenca, 1988. Excellent collection of sociological perspectives on the relations of cultural studies to literature in Ecuador. See above all Suárez and Carrasco.

Casa de las Américas 127 (julio-agosto 1981). Special issue devoted to contemporary Ecuadorian letters.

Corkill, David, and David Cubitt. *Ecuador. Fragile Democracy*. London: Latin American Bureau, 1988. Useful introduction and overview of the greater context for the production of Ecuadorian literature.

Cueva, Agustín. *Entre la ira y la esperanza (ensayos sobre la cultura nacional)*. Quito: Editorial Casa de la Cultura, 1967. Pioneering essay collection. Literate, Marxist approach to the culture by one of the best essayists of Ecuador.

Cueva, Agustín. *La literatura ecuatoriana*. Buenos Aires: Centro Editor de América Latina, 1968. Now dated but still excellent brief introduction to Ecuadorian literature.

Cueva, Agustín. *Lecturas y rupturas. Diez ensayos sociológicos sobre la literatura del Ecuador.* Quito: Planeta, 1986. Compiles some of his previously published essays, including Cueva (1968). The best may be the last one on reading codes for most recent Ecuadorian literature.

Donoso Pareja, Miguel. *Los grandes de la década del 30.* Quito: Editorial El Conejo, 1985. Contextualization of the literature of the thirties by excellent cultural promoter, author, critic.

Donoso Pareja, Miguel. *Nuevo realismo ecuatoriano. La novela después del 30.* Quito: Editorial El Conejo, 1984. Compilation of brief essays on post-1930s novels. Interestingly, the linkages he establishes among the novels is accurate for the conception of a new realism in the Ecuadorian novel.

Handelsman, Michael. *Incursiones en el mundo literario del Ecuador.* Guayaquil: Universidad de Guayaquil, 1988. Ten case studies of Ecuadorian authors, movements, journals, or literary problems, some of which have been published before by this expert on Ecuadorian modernism.

Itúrburu Rivadeneira, Fernando. *La palabra invadida. Comentarios de literatura ecuatoriana.* Quito: FEDESO, 1988. Brief but informative survey of recent literary movements and workshops in Ecuador, from a roughly semiotic perspective.

Pérez, Galo René. *Pensamiento y literatura del Ecuador (crítica y antología).* Quito: Editorial Casa de la Cultura, 1972. Very disorganized; some comments are impressionistic but review of documentation for analysis is good.

Revista iberoamericana 144-145 (julio-diciembre 1988). Special issue, organized by Gerardo Luzuriaga, on Ecuadorian literature of the previous fifty years. Most articles concentrate on narrative.

Rivera, Guillermo. *A Tentative Bibliography of the Belles Lettres of Ecuador.* Cambridge: Harvard University Press, 1934. One of the first attempts to organize bibliography of Ecuadorian letters, revealing regarding colonial letters.

Rodríguez Castelo, Hernán, ed. *Letras de la Audiencia de Quito (período jesuítico).* Caracas: Biblioteca Ayacucho, 1984. Anthology of historiographical writings, hagiographies, speeches, lyric poems, and other writings by Ecuadorian Jesuits and the nuns Gertrudis de San Ildefonso and Catalina de Jesús Herrera.

Rodríguez Castelo, Hernán, et al. *La literatura ecuatoriana en los últimos 30 años (1950-1980).* Quito: Editorial El Conejo, 1983.

Result of a seminar-symposium on the topic, made up of four studies on poetry, the short story, novelistic tendencies, and relations among writers, society, and power.

Rojas, Angel F. *La novela ecuatoriana, 1948.* México, D.F.: Fondo de Cultura Económica, 1948. By far the best study of the novel in Ecuador, well informed and judicious.

Sacoto, Antonio. *La nueva novela ecuatoriana.* Cuenca: Publicaciones del Departamento de Difusión Cultural de la Universidad de Cuenca, 1981. Obstructed by rhetoric and reliance on plot analysis, but the only source on the new novel of Ecuador.

Schyttner, Eugene. *Vida y obras de autores ecuatorianos.* Havana: Editorial Alfa, 1943. Forerunner to biographical approach employed by Aleman, *supra*, concentrates on contemporary authors.

Steinsleger, José. "Tiempo de incertidumbre. Política, literatura y sociedad en el Ecuador (1960-87)." *Casa de las Américas* 169 (julio-agosto 1988): 34-43. Updates, theoretically and in terms of information, most of Cueva's arguments in informative and well documented fashion.

Valdano Morejón, Juan. *La pluma y el cetro.* Cuenca: Publicaciones del Departamento de Difusión Cultural de la Universidad de Cuenca, 1977. Essay collection on literature and culture of Ecuador, of which the best may be his study of literary generations.

GUATEMALA

María A. Salgado
University of North Carolina at Chapel Hill

I

The few critics who have studied Guatemalan literature readily agree that the literary output of this country may be divided into three periods: pre-Columbian, Colonial, and Modern. The literature of each of these three periods is imprinted with the particular vision of the cultures represented. Each, therefore, is different in outlook and purpose; and yet critics have been careful to point out that despite cultural differences, all Guatemalan literature shares traits that give it a certain degree of homogeneity. One of the most salient is the presence of Indian elements, not only at the more obvious level of monuments, art, and cultural patterns, but, most importantly, at the psychological and spiritual levels in which the character of a people is deeply imbedded. Readily identifiable also are other important traits, such as the tendency to use magic and fantastic themes and motives; the tendency toward introspection and irony; and the tendency to emphasize psychological analysis over action and external description.

II

The most important indigenous texts to come out of Central America originated in areas comprised by today's southern Mexico, Guatemala, Honduras, and El Salvador. Their genesis is deeply intertwined with the cultural traditions of the Maya-Quichés and the Cakchiquels. The texts that have survived were written, after the Conquest, in the original Indian languages, but using the newly introduced Latin alphabet. Despite the presence of such a European "tool," the texts exhibit the typical Indian mythical mentality. Most of these manuscripts are collections of myths,

317

legends, traditions, and historical accounts predating the Spanish Conquest and coming up to the seventeenth century. The anonymous writers imbue the accounts dealing with the Conquest with the same mythical vision, thus affording the modern Western reader the rare opportunity to observe the perspective of the vanquished race. In recent times, these documents have become increasingly important for literary historians, as they are a clear source of inspiration for a large number of Guatemalan and other Central American writers. In fact, it is practically impossible to have a thorough understanding of several contemporary works without a previous acquaintance with the Indian texts.

For literature, the most famous and valuable of these documents is the *Popol Vuh* (the Mayan Bible, Book of the Council, or Book of the Quichés). This text is known also as the Manuscript of Chichicastenango, the town where it was first discovered, copied, and translated into Spanish, between 1701 and 1703, by the Dominican Francisco Ximénez (1668-1729?). The widespread diffusion of this book, however, dates from 1861, following its translation into French by the Abbot Charles Etienne Brasseur de Bourbourg (1814-74). The *Popol Vuh* is a cosmological and cosmogonical account of man and the Quiché lineage, with obvious historical and literary significance. Although the original Quiché manuscript has no divisions, modern translators divide it into four parts, subdivided into chapters; this arrangement is justified by its contents. The book has a binary structure with man's creation at its center. The story, however, is narrated from the point of view of the gods, the main protagonists. The first part narrates what the gods did and revealed before man's creation; the second part, what they did after creating man. The cyclical vision of man and the universe, conceived as an ongoing process of creation and destruction, justifies the binary structure and exemplifies the fact that for the Maya-Quiché history did not follow a linear trajectory. Rather, it moved cyclically.

Another Indian narrative of great importance is the one known by the generic name of *Books of Chilam Balam*, a collection of different versions of the same Mayan text, some with important modifications, that have been found in the different localities from which each particular book takes its name. Other significant narratives are *Memorial de Tecpán-Atitlán* (Annals of Tecpán-Atitlán), *Título de los Señores de Totonicapán* (Title of the Lords of Totonicapán), and *Título de los Señores de Otzoya* (Title of the Lords of Otzoya). The *Memorial*, written in Cakchiquel, was started in the sixteenth century by Francisco Hernández Arana Xahilá and completed early in the seventeenth by Francisco Díaz Xebutá

Quej. It was discovered in 1844 by the paleographer J. Gavarrete and later translated into French by Brasseur as *Memorial de Sololá* (Annals of Sololá; 1863) and into English by Georges Raynaud as *Annals of the Xahil*; this text is also known as *Annals of the Cakchiquels*, from the English translation by Daniel Brinton (1885). It is the story of one family, the Xahilás, from its mythical beginnings to its involvement in the sixteenth century in the war against Pedro de Alvarado (1485-1541), Conquistador of Guatemala. The *Título de los Señores de Totonicapán*, composed in 1554, tells of the Quiché beginnings, their migrations, and their struggle against the Pipiles. The *Título de los Señores de Otzoya*, dating from 1524, is one of the oldest among these manuscripts; it deals with the heroic deeds of the House of Ixcuin-Nihaib, ending with the wars against the Spaniards.

The many references to Maya-Quiché poems, dances, and dramatic performances are another clear indication of these peoples' cultural sophistication. Few of the dramatic texts have survived, but there is ample evidence of their prominence: the *Popol Vuh* speaks of the dances of the *puhuy* (owl), *cux* (weasel), *iboy* (armadillo), *ixtuzul* (centipede), and *chitic* (stilt- dancer), while the popularity of certain rituals, such as the *palo volador* (literarally, flying pole; a ritual choreography) still persists. The most important work of pre-Columbian theater is undoubtedly *Rabinal-Achí* or *Xahoh tun* (The Lord of Rabinal or Dance of the Tun or Sacred Drum). According to Brasseur, he first transcribed this text from oral tradition, dictated to him by an Indian named Bartolo Sis, in 1885. Though critics still praise Brasseur for his preservation of this work, recent investigations have thrown serious doubts on the circumstances surrounding his assertions. *Rabinal-Achí* is a drama-ballet thoroughly steeped in Indian cultural values; its originality and authenticity are unquestionable. The written text, consisting of four dialogues and one monologue, is only one part of the performance, the rest is comprised of the music and the dances that vividly execute a ritual. The "play" begins with a challenge by the Quiché-Achí, followed by his capture; it continues with a verbal duel between him and his capturer (Rabinal-Achí); next, there is a series of ceremonies and symbolic acts that precede the sacrifice; the performance ends with the human sacrifice of the Quiché-Achí. The music and dancing take place in the actual present, while the dialogues explain the circumstances—the why and how—of the Quiché warrior's capture that will lead to his sacrifice in the present.

III

The texts written during the colonial period can be divided according to three sociocultural stages of development: 1) the works of *conquistadores*, missionaries, and linguists, written for the purpose of describing the new territories and to facilitate the tasks of settling the country and converting the Indians; 2) the works of historical writers and minor poets; and 3) the works influenced by the Enlightenment. By and large, the works of the first two stages were written by Spaniards and show a culture and a language in transition. They can be characterized as utilitarian, didactic literature, with little concern for aesthetics.

Although Guatemalan literature proper may be said to begin with the letters of Pedro de Alvarado to his superior, Hernán Cortés, their literary value is minimal. The one chronicle of outstanding worth written in Guatemala is *La verdadera y notable relación de la conquista de la Nueva España* (*The True History of the Conquest of New Spain*; written 1557-1580, published 1632) by Bernal Díaz del Castillo (1495?-1584). Díaz's excellent account is still a major historical source, but his gifts as a storyteller provide the work with a significance that goes beyond its historical value. Born in Spain, Díaz came to America in 1514. He served in the conquest of Mexico, Guatemala, and Honduras, and in 1541 he settled in Guatemala. Díaz's eye for detail and ability to create mood make for exciting descriptions of the events of the conquest. The *History* is narrated in a rich, colloquial style that engages the reader in a dialogue by giving it the feeling of an oral account. This apparently simple style hides a wealth of rhetorical resources. It has many links with the epic: it narrates the deeds of a hero, Hernán Cortés, fighting to realize his destiny of Christianizing America; Cortés and his men are seen as demigods by the Indians. Moctezuma, leader of the opposing, valiant forces, also emerges as a hero, providing the typical epic confrontation. Bernal's imaginative narration also includes excellent characterizations, dramatic passages, touches of fantasy, and fresh, vivid descriptions of Nature. Its literary value can be measured by the fact that several contemporary novels, such as Miguel Angel Asturias's *Maladrón* (1969), recreate some of its mood and atmosphere.

Among several other chronicle writers, two deserve recognition for accomplishments that go beyond the simple recording of history. They are Francisco Ximénez and Bartolomé de Las Casas (1474-1566). As mentioned above, Ximénez saved the *Popol Vuh*; but he saved it because as a linguist he incorporated it into his grammatical document *Tesoro de las tres lenguas; Cakchiquel, quiché y tzutuhil* (Lexicon of Three Languages; unpublished). Besides his linguistic works, Ximénez wrote chatechisms and priestly guides, and he is the author of two historical references: *Historia natural del Reyno de Guatemala* (Natural History of the Kingdom of Guatemala; 1711-13) and *Historia de la Provincia de San Vicente de Chiapas y Guatemala* (History of the Province of Saint Vincent of Chiapas and of Guatemala; 1929), a natural history, valuable for its descriptions of flora and fauna, and a sociocultural history of the area.

Father Las Casas, a Dominican Priest and Bishop of Chiapas, became the best-known defender of the Indians. Profoundly distressed by the living conditions of the natives, he wrote his inflamatory *Brevísima relación de la destrucción de las Indias* (*Brief Account of the Destruction of the Indies*; written in 1542 but published in 1552). Although this book succeeded in helping the issuing of the New Laws against the Encomienda System (1542), it subsequently became one of the main sources of the Black Legend against Spain. Las Casas convincingly advocated the conversion of all pagans by peaceful means in *Del único modo de atraer a todos los pueblos a la verdadera religión* (The Only Method of Attracting All People to the True Faith; 1537); his *Apologética historia* (Apologetic History; 1550-1559) compares European and Indian cultures to affirm the latter's potential to rise in the scale of civilization. An important historian to write in the closing years of the seventeenth century is Francisco Antonio de Fuentes y Guzmán (1643-1700), the "father of Guatemalan history." His *Recordación florida* (Choice Remembrances; 1690), despite its flaws and intricate Baroque style, is a major source of information on the city, the land, its inhabitants, and its flora and fauna.

Not only history, but poetry, theater, and oratory were to flourish in a literary atmosphere stimulated by the establishment of the printing press in 1660 and the University of San Carlos in 1676. In the theater, alongside *autos* (allegorical religious plays) and Golden Age *comedias* from Spain, there were utilitarian plays written for missionary and scholarly purposes. However, one must record the development of a popular form of performance, unique to Guatemala, called *loas del diablo* (short plays dealing with the devil), that present, amidst fireworks, the temptation and successful rejection of the Devil by intercession of the Virgin. In poetry, the most important writer of Colonial times is the Jesuit Rafael Landívar (1731-1793), known as the "American Virgil," for his *Rusticatio mexicana* (Mexican Country Sojourn; 1781). This poem of the neo-Classical school, written in Latin in fifteen cantos, was composed and published in Italy, where Landívar lived following the expulsion of the

Jesuits from the New World in 1767. Landívar is considered the first poet to succeed in portraying the features characteristic of the New World landscape, its customs, and games. He is also one of the first writers to show a deep concern for the survival of the Indian cultures. Other poets of note are Fray Diego Sáez de Ovecure (1630-87), Fray Matías de Córdoba (1768-1828), and Rafael García Goyena (1766-1823).

During the brief period leading to independence there is an emerging conscience of nationality and a spirit of reform fomented by the establishment of *sociedades patrióticas* or *económicas* (patriotic or economic societies). The excitement and turmoil of this period and of the years immediately following the Independence is exemplified best by the works of a transitional figure, Antonio José de Irisarri (1786-1868). Besides leading an active political life in Guatemala, Chile, and Colombia, he wrote satirical verses, *Poesías satíricas y burlescas* (Satirical and Burlesque Poems; 1867), and an autobiographical narrative, *El cristiano errante* (The Wandering Christian; 1847), that reflects the adventurous and picaresque qualities of his life.

IV

Guatemala did not live through the unsettling experience of a war of independence. It was the representative of the Spanish Crown who, with one stroke, declared Independence and created the Central-American Federation (from Chiapas to Costa Rica). Belonging to the Federation would delay the actual formation of a Guatemalan conscience until 1838. The most original poet of this time, and in fact of the nineteenth century, is José Batres Montúfar (1809-44). He wrote lyric and intimate poems, in the best Romantic vein, but Batres Montúfar is best-known for his three satirical narrative poems, *Tradiciones de Guatemala* (Guatemalan Traditions; 1845). The best ninteenth-century novelist, and one of the best in Spanish America, is José Milla ("Salomé Jil," 1822-82), still one of the most popular and widely read of Guatemalan novelists. His long career afforded him the opportunity to experiment with a variety of literary schools, from Romantic, historical accounts, such as *La hija del Adelantado* (The Governor's Daughter; 1866), to realistic novels like *El esclavo de Don Dinero* (The Slave of Mr. Money; 1881) and *Historia de un Pepe* (Story of a Pepe; 1882). His convincing *Cuadros de costumbres* (Sketches of Customs; 1871) and the literary creation of a typically

Guatemalan character, Juan Chapín, count greatly among his literary accomplishments.

Although in Guatemala, political and economic conditions have impeded the development of a national theater, this genre has produced some dramatists of note. Among them a woman precursor, Vicenta Laparra de La Cerda (1834-1905), whose three plays, *Angel caído* (Fallen Angel; 1880), *Hija maldita* (Accursed Daughter; 1895) and *Los lazos del crimen* (The Bonds of Crime; 1897) are melodramatic presentations of the plight of women. The Cerna family also has made an important contribution: Ismael Cerna (1856-1901) led a romantic life and wrote his last and best play, *La penitenciería de Guatemala* (Guatemala's Penitenciary; 1891), while in exile. Other playwrights in the family were Carlos Rodríguez Cerna (1894) and Carlos Girón Cerna (1904-71), whose *Quiché-Achí* (1945) is a reworking of the Indian play and whose *Ixquic* (1935) is based on the *Popol Vuh*. Although plays have continued to be written up to the present, establishing a national theater has been a difficult task. Some prominent twentieth century authors have attempted writing for the theater, such as Arévalo Martínez, Asturias, and Soto Hall, but only a few have dedicated all their efforts to the theater. Among these are Carlos Solórzano (1922), who writes for the Mexican stage, Miguel Marsicovétere y Durán (1912), Adolfo Drago Bracco (1893-1968), and Manuel Galich (1913). Marsicovétere, a poet and founder of the group "Tepeus," has written throughout his long career abstract symbolist plays influenced by the Italian grotesque: *El espectro acróbata* (The Acrobat Ghost; 1935), *Cada cual con su fantasma* (Each Person with His Own Ghost; 1939), and *Minidramas* (Minidramas; 1971). In 1951, Marsicovétere founded the Art Theatre of Guatemala. Drago Bracco, the son of an Italian actor, has become the most active actor-writer-director associated with the Guatemalan theater. Among his plays are *Colombina quiere flores* (Columbine Wants Flowers; 1923), *Se han deshojado en el jardín las rosas* (The Roses in the Garden Have Shed their Petals; 1925), and *El viejo solar* (The Old Homestead; 1938). His earlier novels, such as *Farándula sentimental* (The Sentimental Strolling Players; 1915), also evoke the milieu of the theater. Galich is the author of more than thirty works; his early plays dramatize great moments in Guatemalan history: *El Señor Gupuk-Caki* (1939) is based on the *Popol Vuh*, while *15 de septiembre* (September 15; 1940) illustrates the struggle for independence. Later on, Galich would turn to social criticism in plays that go from the early *Papá Natas* (1938) and *M'hijo el bachiller* (My Son the Graduate; 1939) to *La mugre* (Filth; 1953), *El tren amarillo* (The Yellow Train; 1954), *El pescado indigesto* (The Indigestable Fish; 1962), and *Mr. John Ténor y yo* (Mr. John Tenor and I; 1978).

Solórzano's contribution to the theater is multiple. Not only has he written excellent plays, where he addresses the question of personal freedom, but he has written also a number of critical essays and a source book, *Teatro latinoamericano del siglo XX* (Twentieth-Century Latin American Theater; 1961). Moreover, Solórzano has exerted direct influence during his ten years as Director of the University Theater in Mexico and, more recently, as professor of drama and contemporary literature at Mexico's National University. Solórzano's best-known plays are *Doña Beatriz* (1952), a historical drama about the wife of the Conquistador Alvarado, *Las manos de Dios* (*The Hands of God*; 1956), on the oppression by church and state, the allegory *Los fantoches* (Puppets; 1959), and *Los falsos demonios* (The False Demons; 1966), a drama rewritten as a novel in the form of a psychological analysis in the first person of a dying man. In 1971 Solórzano wrote a second novel, *Las celdas* (The Cells).

In Guatemala, as in the rest of Spanish America, the period associated with Modernism would signal the creation of a truly autochthonous literature. The visits at different times of the main figures associated with Modernism—José Martí, Rubén Darío, José Santos Chocano, and Porfirio Barba Jacob—sparked and maintained a great deal of literary activity. One of the best prose writers of the period is Enrique Gómez Carrillo (1837-1927), known for his artistic prose and his contribution to the establishment of the literary chronicle, a Modernist genre, considered today instrumental in lending flexibility to the stilted Castilian prose inherited from the nineteenth century.

However, the major innovator and poet associated with Modernism is Rafael Arévalo Martínez (1884-1975). His books of poetry (from *Maya* [1911] to *Por un caminito así* [Through a Little Path Such as This; 1947]) exhibit a stylistic restraint more typical of Postmodernism. His innovations of contemporary narrative take many forms: his early autobiographical novelettes, *Una vida* (A Life; 1914) and *Manuel Aldano* (1922) introduce a new penchant for introspection and psychological analysis; the utopian novels *El mundo de los maharachías* (The World of the Maharachías; 1939) and its sequel *Viaje a Ipanda* (Journey to Ipanda; 1939), present his ideas on the role of government in a contemporary society while analyzing world events. However, it is short stories of the caliber of *El hombre que parecía un caballo* (The Man Who

Looked Like a Horse; 1915), *Las fieras del trópico* (The Wild Beasts of the Tropics; 1922), and *La signatura de la esfinge* (The Sign of the Sphinx; 1933) that are widely recognized as his major contribution to Spanish American letters. Written in a brilliant, exhuberant style clearly affiliated with Modernism, they constitute character sketches of leaders and intellectuals of his day. His imaginative mixture of real and fantastic elements combines human and animal traits into psychozoological tales that can be credited with having heralded magical realism in Spanish American narrative. Other writers formed in the tenets of Modernism are Máximo Soto Hall (1871-1976), Carlos Wyld Ospina (1891-1958), Flavio Herrera (1895-1968), César Brañas (1900-76), and Carlos Samayoa Chinchilla (1898-1973). Soto Hall's *Catalina* (1900) represents an early attempt at using the Modernists' aesthetics for dealing with the Guatemalan milieu. His novel *El problema* (The Problem; 1893) is considered the first antiimperialist novel in the country. The same theme is even more successfully developed in *La sombra de la Casa Blanca* (The Shadow of the White House; 1927), a novel that condemns the 1927 U.S. invasion of Nicaragua.

Wyld Ospina is one of the first novelists to cultivate *criollismo* (creolism). His approach to portraying Guatemalan landscape and problems reflects his early training in Naturalism, although filtered through his Modernist sensibility. His best works are *La tierra de las Nahuyacas* (The Land of the Nahuyacas; 1933), a collection of tales, and his last novel, *Los lares apagados* (The Extinguished Hearths; 1939), considered by some as one of the best *indianista* (Indianist) novels written prior to the works of Asturias and Monteforte Toledo.

Flavio Herrera's *Trópico* (1933), a collection of hai-kai poems, brought him continental fame, but he is remembered best for having established the novel of creolism in Guatemala. *El tigre* (The Jaguar; 1933), his first and best-known novel, has been compared to José Eustasio Rivera's *La vorágine* (The Vortex; see section on Colombia) and Rómulo Gallegos's *Doña Bárbara* (see section on Venezuela). And yet, in this and his other novels, particularly *Caos* (Chaos; 1949), Herrera goes beyond creolism. His control of narrative techniques, his interest in delineating visions of internal landscapes, and his imaginative treatment of fantastic elements mark him as a precursor of magical realism and the new novel.

Brañas's narrative moves from recreating the decadent world, popular at the end of the century in *Alba Emérita* (1920), to recreating the interior world of his protagonists in later novels that would culminate in

Paulita (1939). However, more important is the fact that Brañas's work as a poet of pure poetry, as a critic, and as the editor and cofounder of the newspaper *El imperial* (The Imperial) made him a powerful intellectual figure, one who provided the means for many new writers to make known their works in a country with few publishing resources. Samayoa Chinchilla also wrote works under the aegis of creolism that, like *Madre milpa* (Mother Cornfield; 1934), describe in simple and vivid terms the land and the country's traditions.

Without a doubt Miguel Angel Asturias (1899-1974) is not only Guatemala's foremost writer, but one of the most important authors to come out of Latin America. However, Asturias would not describe himself simply as a writer, but rather as a committed writer. His commitment won for him the Lenin Peace Prize in 1966, and his literary acclaim won for him the Nobel Prize in 1967. Asturias studied law in Guatemala and attended courses at the Sorbonne on the ancient religions and cultures of Central America. While in Paris, he helped in translating the *Popol Vuh* and wrote his first book, *Leyendas de Guatemala* (Legends of Guatemala; 1930), published with a laudatory prologue-letter by Paul Valéry. After returning to Guatemala, he became involved in public life; he founded the Popular University of Guatemala, became a federal deputy and, in the course of time, a cultural attaché in Mexico and Argentina and ambassador in El Salvador and France.

Asturias's first novel, *El señor Presidente* (1946), widely translated, is based on the dictatorship of Manuel Estrada Cabrera (1857-1924), who ruled the country from 1898 until 1920. Although written in the 1930s, it was not published until 1946 because of the fear it may have been taken as an attack on the current dictator-of-the-day, Jorge Ubico. Asturias uses the techniques of magical realism to recreate the nightmarish atmosphere of life under a Latin American tyrant. The rest of his novels are of two kinds: Indianist and political. In *Hombres de maíz* (*Men of Maize*; 1949), he expresses in the poetic terms of Indian myth the opposing worldviews of the two cultures, European and indigenous. Corn, the sacred seed of the Mayans, is used to expose the opresion of the Indians by men intent on the commercial exploitation of maize. What in *Men of Maize* is only a contrapuntal interweaving of myth, becomes in *Mulata de Tal* (*Mulata*; 1963), a total immersion in the bewitched and bewitching Indian and mestizo worlds. Neither work makes concessions to the uninitiated reader. *Maladrón* (1969) presents the Spaniards' search for a passage between the two oceans and their subsequent confrontation with the magical world of the Indians.

Asturias's other novels carry a heavier dose of political propaganda: his "banana trilogy" consisting of *Viento fuerte* (*Strong Wind* [also translated as *The Cyclone*]; 1950), *El Papa verde* (*The Green Pope*; 1954), and *Los ojos de los enterrados* (*The Eyes of the Interred*; 1960), denounces the economic exploitation brought about by U.S. imperialism. *Weekend en Guatemala* (Weekend in Guatemala; 1956), written as a collection of eight stories, is a scathing attack on the U.S. backed overthrow of President Arbenz's government in 1954. Most of Asturias's numerous poetic works were collected in *Poesía. Sien de alondra* (Poetry. Pulse of the Skylark; 1949), but his real contribution to the forging of a poetic language has been accomplished through the lyric qualities of his Spanish prose, endowed with peculiarly Indian resonances and syntax. Another genre used by Asturias is the theater, for which he wrote plays like *Soluna* (1955) on the survival of Indian myths in contemporary life, and *La audiencia de los confines* (The Territories of Guatemala; 1957), dealing with Father Las Casas.

The second major novelist to write in the twentieth century is Mario Monteforte Toledo (1911). His active commitment to bringing about sociopolitical changes has forced him into exile in Mexico. Monteforte's thorough knowledge of his country's problems is reflected in his narrative, where he rejects the sentimental, idyllic vision of Indian life in favor of the more genuine, human perspective he developed during the years he lived among the Indians. His first novel, *Anaité* (1938), has been compared to the Colombian José Eustasio Rivera's *La vorágine* (*The Vortex*; 1924) and the Venezuelan Rómulo Gallegos's *Doña Bárbara* (1929) because of its vivid descriptions of the exhuberant but deadly qualities of the jungle and his presentation of the theme of civilization (Guatemala City) versus barbarism (Petén). *Entre la piedra y la cruz* (Between the Stone and the Cross; 1948) is considered one Guatemalan novel that addresses the concerns of the entire nation. It attempts to show the country's need to merge into one culture by portraying a young Indian whose education places him in the situation of having to choose between what appears, at present, to be the irreconcilable divisions of Indian and *ladino* (culturally non-Indian or Hispanized) ways of life. Monteforte Toledo continues this theme on a more pessimistic note in *Donde acaban los caminos* (Where the Paths End; 1953). *Una manera de morir* (A Way of Dying; 1953) is an ideological novel that concerns a common plight among Latin American intellectuals: a man who sacrifices his ideals to submit to more traditional political thought, only to be destroyed by the self-interest prevalent in everyday power plays. As a young man, the protagonist becomes disenchanted with Communism and abandons the Party in order to enter mainstream politics. But he discovers a cynical attitude that drives him to rejoin the Party, this time resigned to give up thinking, which is "a way of dying."

An additional writer who has a clear sense of his political responsibilities and has spoken often in defense of human rights is Luis Cardoza y Aragón (1904). In fact, his committed stance has forced him to live in exile the largest part of his life. He studied painting in Europe, where he came in contact with most of the avant-garde aesthetic currents. His early poetic works show the influence of Surrealism: *Luna Park* (1923), *Maelstrom* (1926), *Soledad* (Solitude; 1936), and *El sonámbulo* (The Sleepwalker; 1937). His metaphysical search to find a new path for humanity is developed in his valuable, but difficult, lyric poem *Pequeña sinfonía del Nuevo Mundo* (Little Symphony of the New World; 1948). One of his last and most challenging poetic works is *Arte poética* (Ars Poetica; 1973). As an art critic he has written excellent essays: *Apolo y Coatlicue* (Apollo and Coatlicue; 1944), *La nube y el reloj* (The Cloud and the Clock; 1940), and *Orozco* (1959). From his exile in Mexico, Cardoza wrote a brilliant and sensitive portrait of his native land: *Guatemala, las líneas de su mano* (Guatemala, the Lines in Her Palm; 1955). The book is divided in three parts: 1) a poetic evocation of his childhood and his country's geography; 2) a historical delineation of Guatemalan letters, beginning with the *Popol Vuh*; and 3) a sociopolitical essay that portrays Guatemala as the land of eternal tyranny.

More recent poets have become known through their association with generational groups like Tepeus (1930s), Acento (Accent; 1940s), Saker-Ti (late 1940s and 1950s), and Nuevo Signo (late 1950s and 1960s). The Tepeus group, although concerned with the Indian and Guatemala, approached both subjects from an external perspective that turned them into literary motives. Oscar Mirón Alvarez (1911-38), Francisco Méndez (1907-62), José Humberto Hernández Cobos (1905-65), and Francisco Figueroa (1902) are its most prominent writers. Acento represents a reversal towards a more authentic social commitment. Raúl Leiva (1916-74), Enrique Juárez Toledo (1919), and Otto-Raúl González (1921) are the most representative members. Saker-Ti, an eclectic group composed of poets, painters, and musicians, shows an increased awareness of sociopolitical concerns. Their 1950 manifesto announced a new explicitly revolutionary commitment. Representative of this group are Huberto Alvarado (1925-74), Olga Martínez Torres (1928), Miguel Angel Vázquez (1922), Líliam Jiménez (1922), and the most prominent among them,

Antonio Brañas (1922). Nuevo Signo gathers the poets who witnessed the overthrow of Arbenz's government (1954) and the return of dictatorship. Antonio Brañas joined this group, together with Julio Fausto Aguilera (1929) and Luis Alfredo Arango (1935). A poet totally dedicated to poetry and revolution, and one who was tortured and killed for his beliefs, is Otto René Castillo (1936-67). His book *Informe de una injusticia* (Report of an Injustice; 1975) is an anthology of his most representative poems. The prologue for this book was written by the Salvadoran poet Roque Dalton (1933-75) who was himself persecuted and exiled for his political convictions and later assassinated (see section on El Salvador). Nuevo Signo was founded in 1968 by six poets: Julio Fausto Aguilera (1929), Luis Alfredo Arango (1935), Francisco Morales Santos, Antonio Brañas, José Luis Villatoro, and Delia Quiñones (1956). The Group RIN-78 is a kind of literary popular front formed by poets belonging to New Sign and the women's feminist poetry movement, as well as by younger writers. Despite these authors' committed background, RIN-78 represents a tendency to move toward literary experimentation and away from committed literature.

The decades of the 1970s and 1980s witnessed a reemergence of women's writing, which had been an important cultural contribution in the 1930s. During those early years, women had been important in their dual roles as writers and as editors of several prestigious journals (*Nosotras* [We Women] by Luz Valle [1896-1971], *Trópico* [Tropics] by Soledad Romero, *Espigas sueltas* [Loose Shoots] by Blanca Granados [1909], *Pirámide* [Pyramid] by Julia Guillermina Cienfuegos, and *Azul* [Blue] by Gloria Méndez Mina). In the 1970s, women's contributions are also dual, as writers and as social activists. Among these prominent women writers, several stand out: Luz Méndez (1919), Aleida Foppa, Margarita Carrera (1929), Ana María Rodas (1937), Delia Quiñones, Lucinda Rivas, Alenka Bermúdez, Julia Esquivel, and a host of younger names. Méndez wrote several volumes of feminist criticism and, under the pseudonym of Lina Marqués, erotic and political poetry. Foppa, a political activist, became a feminist and editor of the journal *FEM* during her exile in Mexico. She was kidnapped by the government and probably killed upon her return to Guatemala in 1980. Her best-known works are *Elogio de mi cuerpo* (Praise of My Body; 1970) and *Las palabras y el tiempo* (Words and Time; 1979). Also known for her political and feminist commitment is Carrera, author of the collection *Del noveno círculo* (From the Ninth Circle; 1976), based on Dante's *Inferno*. Rodas's *Poemas de la izquierda erótica* (Poems from the Erotic Left; 1973) is a scathing attack on traditional machismo. Rivas's *Cantar para vivir* (Singing in Order to Live; 1967) can been seen as an apt preamble to the revolutionary and feminist books of the preceding poets.

The political concerns of these authors, poets as well as prose writers, simply mirrors the country's and Central America's turmoil. The late 1970s inaugurated a new period of popular resistance. Indian lands were aggressively appropriated, a process that threatened village life. Guerrilla warfare increased and spread throughout the country. By the early 1980s, the emergence of Liberation Theology and the merging of religious, community, trade union, Indian, and political groups gave rise to new popular literary modes. Prominent among them are testimonial literature and *poesía de combate* (combat poetry). Representative of this type of poetry is the work of the poets associated with the aforementioned RIN-78. Additionally, there are a number of Indian poets who contribute their concerns for the land from the perspective of the indigenous peoples. Some of these poets are the Quiché Enrique Luis Sam Cop, author of *Versos sin refugio* (Poems without Shelter; 1978) and *La copa y la raíz* (The Glass and the Root; 1979) and Luis de Lión, who also authored a collection of short stories on land seizures and military massacres in 1984. Most of these indigenous poets, however, are women writers of testimonial poetry. Representative of them is Caby Domatila Cane'K, a Maya-Cakchiquel, who speaks of the atrocities committed against her familty.

Testimonial literature is also practiced by a number of fiction writers. Perhaps the best-known works in this genre are the texts by Mario Payeras (1950), *Días de la selva* (Jungle Days; 1980), and Rigoberta Menchú, *Me llamo Rigoberta Menchú* (*My Name is Rigoberta Menchú*; 1983). Armando Bendaña's *Grito, susurro y llanto* (Shout, Murmur, and Tears; 1985) and Carlos Menkos-Deka's *¡Abre, abre, Solare-Diez, el baúl de los gigantes!* (Open, Open the Giants' Trunk, Solare-Diez!) are vignettes of violence in Guatemala City, while José Barnoya's *Panzos y otras historias* and Catarino Mateo's *Cuentos para contar corriendo* (Stories to Tell Running; 1984) are fictional reconstructions of land massacres. Within the testimonial trend, but more experimental in nature, are the short stories of Ligia Escribá (*Cuentos* [Tales; 1985]), Francisco Nájera (*Los cómplices* [Accomplices; 1988]), and Franz Galich (*La princesa de onix* [The Onyx Princess; 1989]) who present the social horrors of the 1980s in intertextual, postmodern narratives. The novel is another genre that echoes the concern with the political pressure exercised by the government. Modernization and militarization in the countryside is explored by José Luis Perdomo in *El treno no llega* (The Train Does Not Arrive; 1984) and William Lemus in *Vida en un pueblo muerto* (Life in a Dead Town; 1984). The same trends in urban life appear in Francisco Albizúrez Palma's *Ida y vuelta* (Round Trip; 1983) and Fernando González Davison's *En los sueños no todo es reposo* (Not All Is Restful in Dreams; 1988).

Traditional narrative, as all literary genres in Guatemala, has suffered severely due to the censorship and years of political repression that have prevented Guatemalan writers from keeping pace with the revolutionary literary changes taking place in other Latin American countries. In the last few years, however, there has been an upsurge of activity that has produced a number of valuable works. As mentioned above, these works deal almost exclusively with revolution and guerrilla warfare, topics that have become associated with the Guatemalan novel since the publication of *El señor Presidente* in 1946. Among the established writers who have published on these topics are Carlos Cojulún Bedoya (1914), with *¡Violencia!* (Violence!; 1978), a fairly realistic portrayal of the violence prevalent in Guatemala City in recent years, and Miguel Angel Vázquez, with *La semilla de fuego* (Seed of Fire; 1976) an attempt at creating a "national mural" written in the vein of creolism. The works of more recent authors are more concerned with updating narrative techniques: *Los compañeros* (Comrades; 1976) by Marco Antonio Flores (1937); *Los demonios salvajes* (Savage Demons; 1978) by Mario Roberto Morales (1947), winner of Guatemala's "15 of September" Prize and the Costa Rican Educa Literary Prize (1985) for *El esplendor de la pirámide* (The Splendor of the Pyramid); *El pueblo y los atentados* (The People and Terrorism; 1979) and *La nueva esmeralda: la novela de París* (The New Emerald: the Novel of Paris; 1987) by Edwin Cienfuegos (1926); and *En la ciudad y las montañas* (In the City and the Mountains; 1975), *Después de las bombas* (After the Bombs; 1979), and *Itzam Na* (1981, winner of Cuba's Casa de las Américas Prize), by Arturo Arias (1950). Arias most recently has written the libretto for a Maya-Quiché opera, *Los caminos de Paxil* (Paxil's Paths), in collaboration with the composer Richard Cameron-Wolfe. Rodrigo Rey Sosa (1958), in exile in Morocco since 1980, has published a collection of short stories in English translation, *The Path Doubles Back* (1982), and one in Spanish, *El cuchillo del mendigo* (The Beggar's Knife; 1986), both based on the Indian myths and beliefs of his people.

BIBLIOGRAPHY

Acevedo, Ramón Luis. *La novela centroamericana (desde el Popol Vuh hasta los umbrales de la novela actual)*. Río Piedras, P.R.: Editorial Universitaria, 1982. A good overview of the development of narrative fiction in Central America, with large sections dedicated to Guatemala.

Albizúrez Palma, Francisco. *Grandes momentos de la literatura guatemalteca. Indice biobibliográfico de la literatura guatemalteca*. Guatemala: Editorial "José de Pineda Ibarra", 1983. A short listing of works by creative writers with an introduction on major trends and figures.

Albizúrez Palma, Francisco. *Historia de la literatura guatemalteca*. Guatemala: Editorial Universitaria, 1981. 2 vols. A rather complete listing and analysis of major writers and works since colonial times to the 1940s.

Carrera, Mario Alberto. *Panorama de la poesia guatemalteca del siglo XX*. Guatemala: Editorial Universidad de Guatemala, 1985. Essays on thirteen women poets writings from the early years of the century to the mid-1980s.

Cifuentes H., Juan Fernando. *Los Tepeus. Generación literaria del 30*. Guatemala: Editorial RIN-78, 1982. A study of this group and those that preceded and followed it.

Díaz Vasconcelos, Luis Antonio. *Apuntes para la historia de la literatura guatemalteca. Epocas indígena y colonial*. Guatemala: Tipografía Nacional, 1942. Articles dealing with some of the relevant figures of the past. It omits notes and bibliography.

Menton, Seymour. *Historia crítica de la novela guatemalteca*. Guatemala: Editorial Universitaria, 1960. A first, basic, and thorough study of the Guatemalan novel. The second edition (1985) revises and updates information to the date of publication.

HAITI
Maximilien Laroche
Université Laval

I

An explanation of the sociocultural background accounting for the national character of Haitian literature, an outline of the main features of its development from the eighteenth century to the present day, and a registry of the outstanding authors and works of that literature must all begin by asking what exactly constitutes Haitian literature.

One may now distinguish between a literature from within and a literature published in exile. But it is necessary not to forget that Haitian literature has always been divided into two bodies, one in French and the other in the Haitian language. Thus, there are certain distinctions to be made before undertaking a discussion of what is unique to Haitian literature.

A panorama of the evolution of literature in the two languages used in Haiti, French and Haitian, leads to significant conclusions. For example, a chronology that sees Haitian literature beginning in 1804 makes sense only for those works written in French. The political event that marks the proclamation of Haitian independence has no perceptible repercussion except for this category of texts, where January 1, 1804, stands as a clear rupture. In the proclamation uttered that day, Boisrod Tonnerre exlaimed: "The French name casts gloom over our lands." By this Tonnerre meant that if Haitians and Frenchmen continued to use the same language, henceforth they would not necessarily be saying the same thing.

By contrast, discourse in the Haitian language manifests, from colonial times to the present, a fixed identity where permanence is, after all, compatible with a specific evolution. The Haitian language arises within the territory of a Haitian acculturation that results from African languages in contact with French. This language, created by the forebears of the modern Haitians who continue to speak it, is the outcome of forces and efforts, the product of capacities, inclinations, and gifts that have survived and that are, even today, those of Haitians. Put differently, if language is the very consciousness of a people, the Haitian language is without a doubt the most reliable repository of Haiti's collective consciousness. This is why there is no gap between literature in a Creole language during the colonial period and what came after independence.

Since literature is an eminently ideological institution, there is certainly a rupture in the case of French-language texts, while in the case of texts in the Haitian language it is a question principally of transformation.

II

Texts in the Haitian language constitute the oldest examples of Haitian literature, since the first text in Creole, "Lizet kité laplenn" (Lizet Left the Countryside), the work of a colonist by the name of Duvivier de la Mahautiere (dates unknown), dates from 1749. Because of its status as an oral language, as a language of the people, and as a dominated language that, by contrast with French (the official language, the language of the schools and the elite) was not taught in school, it is easy to understand how Haitian literature suffered underdevelopment between 1749 and 1950. During this period, a few writers who may have used French for the greater part of their works also turned to the Haitian Creole in their writing: Oswald Durand (1840-1906), who published poems of which "Choukounn" (1883) is the most celebrated, and Georges Sylvain (1866-1925), whose *Cric-Crac* (1907) is a collection of La Fontaine's fables transposed into the Haitian language.

1944 marks the adoption of an orthographic system for the Haitian language and the beginnings of a grassroots literacy campaign in Haitian, important landmarks for the development of a Haitian literature in Haitian. This was especially true in the case of poetry. Félix Morisseau-Leroy (1912) is the best known of the poets, with *Diacoute* (Knapsack; 1951). It was also true for dramatists, where Morisseau-Leroy is the author of *Antigone* (1953), an adaptation in Haitian of Sophocles's play. The departure abroad of numerous intellectuals beginning in 1958 cannot curb the spirit of writing in Haitian. Quite the contrary. While in Haiti itself, Franck Etienne (1936) published the first novel in Haitian, *Dézafi* (Challenge; 1975), and penned dramatic works whose success challenged official censorship, in the United States Michel-Rolph Trouillot (dates unknown) published the first essay in the Creole language of Haiti, *Ti difé boulé sou istwa Ayiti* (Lightening Over the History of Haiti; 1977), and Georges Castera (1936) assembled his poetic works under the title *Konbèlannn* (1976). From Morisseau-Leroy's Third-World poems to Castera's Marxist texts, from the first novel by Franck Etienne to use the national language in an extended narrative to Trouillot's essay, where the history of Haiti is analyzed in the light of the Hegelian-Marxist dialectic of contradiction and class struggle, from the plays of Morisseau-Leroy, which integrate Greek myths and Haitian legends, to Franck Etienne's committed plays, we are in the presence not just of a flowering but the adaptation to the needs of the modern period of the language of the Haitian people. After a period of long eclipse, literature in Haitian appears definitively to have found its own voice. The literacy campaign, originally intended only for adults, was transformed into a program for the reform of Haitian education itself. Henceforth, there was the conviction that it would be impossible to teach someone to read and write without learning the national language.

III

French, although a foreign language, occupies meanwhile a privileged place. The language of communication outside Haiti, inside the country it has served as the language of instruction and government, the vehicle of all written communication between Haitians and between them and others. This is why the largest body of works of Haitian literature are written in the French language. Poetry occupies a special position, with Oswald Durand as its foremost exponent. Durand's collection of poems, *Rires et peurs* (Laughter and Tears; 1896), earned for him the sobriquet of national bard. As in the case of "Choukounn," certain of Durand's poems in French—"Idalina," "Chant national" (National Song), "La mort de nos cocotiers" (The Death of Our Coconut Trees)—as much for their theme as for their elaboration have become classic titles in Haiti.

The La Ronde (Round Dance) poets (1896-1915) maintained a credo of "aesthetic eclecticism," which is considered today a theory of imitation faithful to European models. Going beyond them, it is possible to associate the inspiration of the poets of the Indigenist movement (1928-56) with Durand's nationalist vein. Whereas the poet of "Choukounn" could find in the celebration of the beauties of the present or the glories of the past consolation and a source of inspiration, the Indigenist writers of the period of the American occupation of Haiti had only anguish with which to console themselves. The poetry of Magloire St. Aude (1912-71), hermetic, elliptic, and mysterious, has led some to speak of a Haitian Surrealism. But it would be better to speak of a collective neurosis. The restrained delirium, the nostalgia, the melancholy of St. Aude's *Dialogue de mes lampes* (Dialogue of My Lamps; 1941), *Tabou* (Taboo; 1941), and *Déchu* (Fallen; 1956) echo the remorse and the existential anguish of *Ecrit sur du ruban rose* (Written on a Pink Ribbon; 1927) by Carl Brouchard (dates unknown), just as the fantasy and political activism of Emile Roumer (dates unknown) in *Poemes d'Haiti et de France* (Poems of Haiti and France; 1925) and late in *Le Caiman étoilé* (*Star-Spangled Alligator*; 1963) echo the epic strain and the martial lyricism of Jean F. Brierre (1909) in *Nous garderons le dieu* (We Will Await the God; 1944) and *Black Soul* (1947). The Indigenist inspiration, at the time of its evolution from an ethnocultural thematics to a sociopolitical stance, remains marked by the circumstances of its origin. Even with the following generations, although there are thematic and stylistic differences or alternate aesthetic credos, there is as a sort of backdrop of the collective consciousness, the traumatic presence of the foreign occupation, the problematics of collective domination (colonialism, imperialism, class struggle), and the spectre of racial discrimination (racism, Jim Crow).

René Depestre (1926), in *Etincelles* (Sparks; 1945), *Gerbes de sang* (Showers of Blood; 1946), *Mineral noir* (Black Mineral; 1956), *Unar-enciel pour l'occident chrétien* (A Rainbow in the Christian West; 1967); and Paul Laraque (1920), in *Les Armes quotidiennes/poésie quotidienne* (Daily Arms/Daily Poetry; 1979), serve as the standardbearers of this militant poetic consciousness. Villard Denis (1940), with his single collection, *Idem* (1962), and Anthony Phelps (1928), in various collections like *Mon pays que voici* (Behold My Country; 1968) and *Motifs por le temps saisonnier* (Motifs for Seasonal Time; 1976), echo the concerns and anguish associated with the dominant political contexts of the sixties. To a great extent Haitians continue to live the consequences of the situation created in 1915 by the presence on native soil of the United States marines. At the time, only public finances seemed to be affected by that presence. But today, the entire field of national life is, if not occupied, at least affected, in Haiti as well as abroad, especially in the United States, where there is the greatest concentration of the Haitian diaspora. Thus, it is possible to grasp the extent to which Haitian identity itself is threatened by the tutelage begun in 1915.

It is for this reason that the novel is in Haiti a double of history and also of the essay. *Stella* (1859), by Eméric Bergeaud (1818-58), was the first Haitian novel, a fiction that involved the thinly veiled transposition of the 1804 war of independence. *La Famille des Pitite-Caille* (The Pitite-Caille Family; 1905) and *Zoune chez sa nainnainne* (Zoune at Her Grandmother's House; 1906), by Justin Lhérisson (1873-1907); and *Séna* (1905), *Les Thazar* (The Thazars; 1907), and *Romulus* (1908), by Fernand Hibbert (1873-1928) are an ironic chronicle—a bitter irony in the case of Hibbert—of the military governments of the first century of Haitian national existence.

This critique of political and social life assumes a less theoretical form with the Indigenist school. Rather than decrying Haitian collective errors on the basis of a theoretical model based on urban subjects, Indigenism resurrects the rural novel. *Gouverneurs de la rosée* (Governors of the Dew; 1944) by Jacques Roumain (1907-44), the most representative work of this genre and the best-known work internationally by a Haitian writer, represents a three-fold revolution in the Haitian novel. From the outset, history is seen in terms of the present and not as something past, as was the case for previous novelists. Furthermore, the model proposed by Roumain, rather than being that of a narrating subject, is that of a subject/reader—the narratee.

It is a commonplace that Haitian writers, since they write in French as city-based narrators addressing city dwellers, are unable to respond to a Haitian public, ninety percent of which are Creole-speaking rural inhabitants who are unable to read French and who, moreover, tolerate the parasitism of the city dwellers. The relationship of classes in Haiti can basically be described as the exploitation of rural inhabitants by townspeople. This change of novelistic perspective, in the sense of an attempt to tell as fiction real history, one lived by the majority and not the one imagined by a privileged minority, influenced the form and style of the Indigenist novel. Thus, Roumain's *Gouveneurs* serves as the most powerful and successful liason to date of French and the Haitian Creole.

The writers of the subsequent generation elaborated on the rural novel. But with his theory of "marvelous realism," which he expounded in 1956, Jacques Stéphen Alexis (1922-61) brought a new dimension to the Haitian novel. *Les Arbres musiciens* (The Musician Trees; 1957) is much more than a rural novel. It joins thematically the countryside with the city, although it is in the nature of the writing where the dynamics of history are most analyzed: novelistic technique, language, and style all go beyond regional and even national boundaries to attain a universal repre-

sentation. Marie Chauvet (1917-75) rose above the spatial and social
limitations of the rural novel in her trilogy, *Amour, colère, folie* (Love,
Hate, Madness; 1968), to attain that universality or "human-Haitian"
literature of which the La Ronde generation only dreamed. Yet by
contrast with the early twentieth-century writers, her model is no longer
located on the outside but rather on the inside of Haitian consciousness
and collective experience.

The essay has always had in Haiti the goal of representing not only
Haitians but also their art. This goal is perhaps best illustrated by the
names of Hannibal Price (1841-93), author of the revealingly titled *De la
réhabilitation de la race noir par la république d'Haïti* (Concering the
Rehabilitation of the Black Race by the Republic of Haiti; 1893); Anté-
nor Firmin (1851-1911), author of two books deserving special mention,
L'Egalité des races humaines (The Equality of Human Races; 1885) and
M. Roosevelt et la république d'Haïti (Mr. Roosevelt and the Republic of
Haiti; 1905); and Jean Price-Mars (1876-1969), author of *Ainsi parla
l'oncle* (Thus Spoke Uncle; 1928), which marked the inauguration of the
Haitian Indigenist movement; and Jacques Stéphen Alexis, who develops
his views of Haitian art in *Le Réalisme merveilleux des Haïtiens* (The
Marvelous Realism of the Haitian People; 1956). In the case of the first
two writers, who date from the period preceding the American occupation of Haiti, one can perceive a dual-faceted problem: how to understand the relationship of Haitians first to others and then to themselves.

We might say that Price-Mars's book, because of the very circumstances of its publication, belongs to the second perspective as the exposition of a sickness, the cultural alienation that has been called the "collective Bovaryism" of Haitians, and of a remedy, the return to indigenous
values. In the case of Alexis, the return to sources moves away from
ideology and closer to an aesthetic position, and the problem of identity
rises above specific features in order to take on truly universal dimensions. Alexis describes the characteristics of a national Haitian art that
shares the same values as the neighboring peoples of the Caribbean,
Latin America, and the Third World. Beyond barriers of geography,
race, and language, Haitian culture and literature joins with that of
neighboring and fellow inhabitants of Latin America and Africa in a sort
of universal integration. The Haitian contribution retains its originality,
according to Alexis, because it is characterized by this marvelous realism,
the close parallel and source of the Latin American "marvelously real"
espoused by Alejo Carpentier (see the section on Cuba) in *El reino de*

este mundo (*The Kingdom of This World*), a novel on the fate of the
Haitian king Henri Christophe.

IV

Haitian literature consists of two linguistic corpora, with the French
one more important from 1804 to 1950. Since 1950 literature more and
more has dealt with national reality in the national language as the
testimony of quite a significant transition of a writing subject and a
reader from one pole to the other in the representation of self.

Haitians, who since 1915 had emigrated sporadically to neighboring
countries like Cuba and the Dominican Republic, undertook beginning
in 1958 a massive emigration involving all social classes disbanding
indiscriminately in all possible directions. The numerous intellectuals
who have gone into exile during the last twenty years have published
their works in Montreal, New York, Paris, and Dakar. The result has
been a double locus for the representation of Haiti: one within the
country and one without.

Yet, the existence of a diaspora and of an exile population is not the
only reason for a double locus for literary activity. There is a second,
more profound factor, one that is linguistic in nature. In Haiti everyone
speaks Haitian. This language, characterized as a Creole based on
French, is the result of the acculturation to French, as well as to other
European and Amerindian languages, of the African languages spoken
by the slave ancestors of the population. Because of its vocabulary,
Haitian is close to French, but in phonology, morphology, syntax, and
semantics, it is markedly different. Nonetheless, lexical correspondences
and the fact that French has continued since independence to be the
official language of the country have led the ruling elite to ignore this
difference. Thus, French is spoken or written by only ten percent of the
population, and the large mass of illiterate Haitians only use Haitian,
customarily called "Creole," for purposes of oral communication.

This diglossic situation has created, perforce, a double locus for
written representation, as testified to by Haiti's double body of literature.
The partition of Haitian writing into an inside literature and one corresponding to the diaspora has only served to reinforce the division along
linguistic lines.

On December 6, 1492, when the Amerindians of the region of Môle
St. Nicolas came upon some Spaniards who had disembarked on their

shores, they had no idea that they were receiving their exterminators; they were not long in discovering this fact. Less than fifteen years after the arrival of the Spaniards, the conquerors had massacred a million inhabitants. As a consequence, they began to import African blacks as enslaved replacements in the gold mines and on the plantations. The Spaniards were followed by the French. In 1625, the latter took over the Western part of the island, which they rebaptized Saint-Domingue, and induced a prosperity that led to the nickname "the pearl of the Antilles." But this prosperity was a price paid with the sweat, blood, and death of thousands of slaves who throughout the eighteenth and nineteenth centuries suffered in what was also nicknamed "the hell of Saint-Domingue."

On January 1, 1804, after a war of liberation that lasted thirteen years, the slaves of Saint-Domingue proclaimed the independence of their country, to which they gave the indigenous name Haiti. This war of liberation crowned more than three centuries of resistance to slavery, racism, and colonialism. The military and political victory over the former colonizers did not, however, lead to the rejection of the French language. French continued to be used as the official language and for written communication, while Haitian, the spoken but not written language, was utilized for personal communication and remained the language of oral communication.

We are quite familiar nowadays with the phenomenon of economic, political, and cultural dependence that makes a former colony the imitator of the model propounded by its former metropolis. The double locus of representation for Haitians does not, thus, stem only from the historical circumstance of the exile of a large number of intellectuals or from an even deeper cause like linguistic duality. Rather, it derives equally from that culture alientation that Price-Mars characterized as a collective Bovaryism, that is, the tendency to represent oneself as the other. Individual and collective identity oscillate between two spaces, between two languages, and between two models. In this context, we can understand how one poet could speak of "treason" with respect to the act of writing. This, then, is the double scene: one, exterior and official, where the relationship with the other is marked by dependence with respect to the codes, models, and objectives of former or present masters; the other, interior and private, where the relationship with oneself is characterized by the will to resist exterior domination, as witnessed by the fidelity to ancestral beliefs and rites.

The two Haitian literatures, one written in French and one written in Haitian, testify to the existence of this double space. Diglossic works like *La famille des Pitite-Caille* or *Gouverneurs de la rosée* represent the attempt to chart a passage between these two spaces through the inter-communication of the two languages, French and Haitian, used in their writing. These two literatures bespeak the hierarchy of the two spaces. Diglossic writing continues to raise the question of moving from Creole to French, to accord a place to national language and culture among foreign culture and language—in short, to subordinate the first to the second. It is this subordination that the Indigenist movement sought to reverse.

V

It would be possible to consider indigenism a backdrop to all of Haitian thought. We know that the movement called Indigenism was organized in 1928 as a form of intellectual resistance to the military occupation of the country by the United States. Yet, it must be remembered that the army of Haitian revolutionaries in 1804 had already called itself an "indigenous army." On the intellectual and literary front, 1928 represented a return to 1804 since, just as the indigenous army had prepared itself to repulse the invasion of Napoleon's troops, the Indigenists of 1928 stood as a front against the new invader from North America.

Nevertheless, an earlier literary movement born in 1836 had proposed aesthetic perspectives that prefigure those of the writers of 1928, although it was cut short. It is possible to find the explanation for the failure of the earlier movement in the illusion that held sway with intellectuals between 1825 and 1915. France officially recognized Haiti's independence in 1825. After a state of siege lasting practically twenty years, the country thought itself finally recognized by the international community. Unfortunately, this was not the case. In that same year, at the instigation of the United States, Haiti was excluded from participation in the Conference of Panama, and Haitian independence was not to be recognized by the United States until 1862, despite the principles of the Monroe doctrine proclaimed in 1823. It is important especially to note that the recognition of Haitian independence by France hinged on the payment of an indemnity, which obliged Haiti to assume a debt to French banks whose conditions were even more constrictive than those of today's International Monetary Fund, there being at that time no international forum to which a country could turn for rescheduling of the debt. Haiti remained indebted to French banks until 1915, the year in which the United States assumed the debt owed those banks, a fact that helps us comprehend how 1825 was not the consecration of Haiti's independence but rather the occasion to assume new forms of struggle in order to win its liberty. By persuading themselves that the victory of 1804 had been complete, Haitian intellectuals overlooked how the war for independence was to continue on other fronts. Yesterday's political adversary had become an economic master, and while the form of the struggle had changed, the objectives remained the same. Colonialism had become neocolonialism, only to yield in time to imperialism.

The illusion of being equal to others as well as citizens of a country whose independence counted for as much as that of larger countries led Haitian writers to formulate the doctrine of the "two tendencies" that mark Haitian writing during the period between the Indigenism of 1836 and that of 1928. This doctrine is best illustrated by the La Ronde writers, a movement that had its moment of glory between 1890 and 1915. One of these tendencies was animated by the desire to create an autonomous literature—this is the everpresent indigenism of Haitian culture—while the other sought to ground Haitian writing in French literature.

This orientation was based on the theory of the two tendencies made up of the "French spirit" and the "African vitality." It is doubtful whether the fusion of these two tendencies has been anything other than the subordination of African vitality to French spirit: the function of the latter is merely to nourish the former. This conception of things represents a vision quite the opposite of what the Brazilian Modernists propounded in the guise of a doctrine of cultural anthropophagy (see the section on Brazil). The Brazilians affirmed principally that the American/Brazilian spirit would be nourished by European/French vitality. But the Haitian Indigenists of 1928, following Jean Price-Mars, underscored, without going quite so far as the Brazilians, the incongruence of a hierarchization of cultural elements such as had been encouraged by the theory of the two tendencies. National elements can only be subordinated to foreign elements at the expense of falling into what Price-Mars, in *Ainsi parla l'oncle*, stigmatized as the cultural Bovaryism of the Haitians.

As a consequence, Price-Mars and the Indigenist writers that he inspired revindicated "African" and "black" elements, as well as "indigenous" ones: if Haitian culture is undeniably marked by its African origins, no less does it bear the traces of other influences, such as Amerindian ones, a fact that has been affirmed since the birth of the country. One could even say that all of the elements of Haitian culture have been transformed and adapted by the Haitian people in the course of their history to the point that today they constitute a unique identity, as demonstrated by the popular religion (voodoo) and the national language (Haitian).

Haitian Indigenism of 1928 emerged when the Harlem Renaissance of the United States was at its height, and it is important to recognize an affinity between these two movements. Moreover, the very denomination of Indigenism derives from the intellectual movement that throughout Latin America recruited proponents of autochthonous values. Yet Haitian Indigenism is above all else the consequence of the shock over being recolonized, of the loss of the illusions of an identification with European models, and of the realization of a permanent and unyielding attitude on the part of the great powers toward people who have been colonized, races that have been dominated, and cultures that have been oppressed.

Indigenism has often mistakenly been confused with negritude. Some Indigenist writers have succumbed to the temptations of what can be called an antiracist racism. The simple fact is that, as numerous critics have insisted, Haitian Indigenism is a movement marked by a national character, while at the same time declaring an interethnic vision. Yet it is only in 1956, with the theory of marvelous realism, that Jacques Stéphen Alexis will find a way out of negritude. This was accomplished by moving the debate from the realm of the psychological (the two tendencies) and ideology (Indigenism) to that of aesthetics. In his speech on "The Marvelous Realism of the Haitians" that he presented at the First Congress of Black Writers and Artists in Paris, Alexis, while not disavowing Haitian traditional concerns, distances himself categorically from negritude. In literature and also in painting and music, Alexis discovers a characteristic Haitian expression in the alliance of realism and the marvelous. This is not a fortuitous alliance, but rather one comprehensible in terms of history, geography, social and economic conditions, the daily life and dreams, the misfortunes and the hopes of the entire Haitian people. There is no longer any need for conjectures about art on the basis of psychocultural hypotheses or ideological criteria. It will be enough to explain artistic production on the basis of the history of Haitian society. It is no longer a question of going from individuals to works, but of beginning with works in order to return to individuals. By the same token, it becomes possible to focus on the future of individuals and their artistic production. This realism is not only a technical requisite, it is a methodological imperative. It also allows for the explanation of Haiti's integration in the Caribbean, Latin American, and finally universal contexts.

Between 1749 and 1986, one can speak of a progressive Latin Americanization of Haitian literature. The eclecticism of the writers of 1900 led them to turn to Europe. The Indigenism of the 1928 generation meant a return to native soil. The marvelous realism of the 1950s, where the debt to Carpentier is as obvious as his debt to Haiti, restored Haitian art to the perspective of a national expression consonant with that of other Caribbean and Latin American nations.

Translated by David William Foster

BIBLIOGRAPHY

Berrou, F. Raphael, and Pradel Pomilus. *Histoire de la littérature haïtienne illustrée par les textes.* Port-au-Prince: Editions Caraïbes; Paris: Editions de l'Ecole, 1975-78. In three volumes, this is the principal source of information concerning the history of Haitian literature.

Cornevin, Robert. *Le théâtre haïtien des origines à nos jours.* Ottawa: Leméac, 1973. The first history of Haitian theater.

Dash, J. Michael. *Literature and Ideology in Haiti, 1915-1961.* London: Macmillan Press, 1981. An examination of a key period in the history of ideas and literature in Haiti.

Fleischmann, Ulrich. *Ideologie und Wirklichkeit in der Literatur Haiti.* Berlin: Colloquium Verlag, 1969. A superb presentation of the relations between writing and society in Haiti.

Garret, Naomi. *The Renaissance of Haitian Poetry.* Paris: Présence Africaine, 1963. A crucial period in Haiti's history is examined in terms of corresponding poetic production.

Hoffmann, Léon-François. *Le Roman Haïtien, idéologie et structure.* Sherbrooke: Editions Naaman, 1982. This is the first comprehensive monograph on Haitian fiction by one of the major specialists on Haiti.

Jahn, Janheiz. *Manuel de littérature néo-africaine du 16ème siecle à nos jours de l'Afrique à l'Amérique.* Paris: Resma, 1969. This is a most ambitious study in terms of its attempt to provide a global interpretation of the literary experience of Africans and their descendents in all of Latin America.

Laroche, Maximilien. *La littérature haïtienne, identité, langue, réalité.* Ottawa: Leméac, 1981. An integrationist interpretation of Haitian letters.

HONDURAS
María A. Salgado
University of North Carolina at Chapel Hill

I

When independence came to Central America in 1823, Honduras was very much a country without an identity. Its approximately 60,000 square miles were populated by fewer than 150,000 inhabitants of mixed Spanish, Indian, and African origin. Most of this population lived in small villages, scattered in isolated valleys throughout the mountainous interior. In large measure, geography and demography had prevented the emergence of any cultural focus to give cohesion to this area. But, perhaps to be more accurate, the blame for this state of affairs should be ascribed to the centralized viceroyalty system that had established in Guatemala the only university in Central America. In fact, Guatemala's intellectual domination was so decisive that, for Honduras, intellectual independence meant breaking away from the cultural dominance of her sister country.

Honduras accomplished this task in 1847, when its first important writer, Fray José Trinidad Reyes (1797-1855), founded the University of Honduras. Despite this major gain, however, the country's political and economic upheavals would continue to impede the orderly progress of a social milieu conducive to the dynamic promotion of artistic endeavors. For writers, especially for prose writers, an added problem has been the scarcity of printing presses and publishing houses. To remedy this situation, at least in part, there has been a proliferation of periodicals, literary journals, and in more recent years, anthologies. One result of this tendency has been that most of the literary production of the country remains unavailable, scattered in an assortment of shortlived publications. A second result has been to promote those genres that lend themselves to being fitted into the restricted space of a magazine; poetry, short stories, folkloric tales, and journalistic articles. By and large, most novels have remained unpublished or have appeared abroad.

As if to foreshadow this situation, Honduras's first writer, Reyes, was a poet. Formed in the ideas of the Enlightenment, he wrote Neoclassical verse and, although at times he becomes mocking and satiric, he never ceases to be didactic. For the most part, his patriotic poetry (fashioned after the Spaniard Manuel José Quintana) lacks inspiration. He was more successful with his political satires, called *cuandos* (whens), after the first word of each refrain. Reyes's best works are his *Pastorelas* (Rustic Plays), simple dramatic pieces in the popular vein, rendered in verse and set to music. They follow the dual traditions of the old Spanish *autos de Navidad* (Nativity plays) and of Mexican folklore by introducing shepherds who narrate the birth of Christ and the adoration of the Virgin in the simple language of the local peasants. His pastoral piece *Micol* (1841) initiated dramatic poetry in Central America.

The second great intellectual figure of this time is the politician and inspired orator José Cecilio del Valle (1790-1855). He wrote patriotic exaltations of Honduras, founded the journal *El amigo de la patria* (The Country's Friend; 1820-?), contributed to the framing of Central America's independence, and, among other things, wrote a lengthy essay dealing with the eventual union of Spanish America, *Soñaba el abad San Pedro y yo también sé soñar* (The Abbot St. Peter Used to Dream and I Too Know How to Dream; date unknown). All of his writings have been collected in his *Obras completas* (Complete Works; 1929-1930).

Despite this initial period of consolidation, Honduras continued to exist in isolation and to be ravaged by continuous bloody civil strife until 1876, date of the Liberal Reform, brought about by the writer Marco Aurelio Soto (1846-1907), during his term as President of the country. The Reform allowed the much delayed entrance of Romanticism into Honduras. The new intellectual interest was promoted by President Soto himself and by Ramón Rosa (1848-93). Although the importance of Romanticism is mainly historical, some of the writers attained distinction and contributed to the establishment of a national literary tradition. Among these writers are the poets Manuel Molina Vijil (1853-83), José Antonio Domínguez (1869-1903), and Carlos Federico Gutiérrez (1861-99), credited with writing the first Honduran novel, *Angelina* (1898). But this deed belongs instead to a woman, Lucila Gamero de Medina (1873-1964), who published three narratives prior to Gutiérrez's novel—*Amalia Montiel* (1893 now lost), *Adriana y Margarita* (1897), and *Páginas del corazón* (Pages from the Heart; 1897)—dealing with the plight of women.

Her best novel, *Blanca Olmedo* (1900), a romantic political work, represents an innovative breakthrough with the pervasive Romantic style. Gamero continued her creative growth throughout her lengthy career, which ended in 1954 with the publication of her last two novels, *Amor erótico* (Erotic Love) and *La secretaria* (The Secretary).

II

As in the rest of Spanish America, Modernism brought to Honduras continental resonance. For the first time, Honduran literature was able to develop its unmistakably American characteristics, through the creation of a language capable of projecting its own cultural and nationalistic concerns. The main exponent of this movement is Juan Ramón Molina (1875-1908). He has been called the "twin" of Rubén Darío (see section on Nicaragua), and, indeed, Darío himself described Molina as the best poet in Central America. Molina's anguished concerns led him to read voraciously, and not only literature, but science and philosophy as well. Eventually, the pessimism of his tortured soul led him to suicide. Molina's carefully wrought poetry is infused with his very personal imprint. His poems boast a wide range of tones: lyric, descriptive, elegiac, anguished. They were collected by his disciple Froylán Turcios and published under the title *Tierras, mares y cielos* (Lands, Seas, and Skys; 1913). This same Froylán Turcios (1878-1943) is the second writer of note who began his literary career associated with Modernism. He wrote his first prose work at the age of eighteen, *Mariposas* (Butterflys; 1895); other works are *Renglones (prosa y verso)* (Written Lines [prose and verse]; 1899) and *Hojas de otoño* (Autumn Leaves; 1905). His excellent *Cuentos del amor y de la muerte* (Tales of Love and Death; 1930) have obvious resonances of Villier de l'Isle Adam, while Poe's influence is suggested by his novels *Annabel Lee* (1906?; probably unpublished) and *El vampiro* (The Vampire; 1910). Turcios's influence lasted beyond the literary significance of his works because he was able to communicate to his contemporaries his personal concerns, his intellectual restlessness, and his professional dedication, traits that led him to found some of the most challenging literary reviews in Latin America: *El Pensamiento* (Thought; dates unknown), *La Revista Nueva* (The New Review; dates unknown), and *Ariel* (dates unknown).

Despite Reyes's early dramatic success with his rustic plays, Honduran theater was slow to develop due to the country's political upheavals and its lack of cultural centers. Nonetheless, there were some early practitioners of the genre who merit mentioning. Such are José María Tobías Rosa (1874-1933), a school teacher who initiated a type of *teatro escolar* (school theater) of didactic plays on local customs; Alonso A. Brito (1887-1925), a writer of satirical comedies; Julián López Pineda (1882-1958), whose melodramatic works were presented in local *soirées*; and Angela Ochoa Velásquez (1886-?), author of the social drama *El clavel rojo* (The Red Carnation; late 1920s). During the 1930s the Honduran theater had begun to deal with national politics in terms of the grotesque, but the new political turmoil and World War II were effectively to put a stop to this incipient theater.

Within the larger literary picture of the first quarter of the century, World War I would end the more exotic and external elements of Modernism. However, its most lasting qualities continued to flourish in the works of Ramón Ortega (1885-1932), Alfonso Guillén Zelaya (1888-1947), and the poet and professor Rafael Heliodoro Valle (1897-1959). Valle's professionalism as poet and critic have been exemplary. As a fiction writer, he wrote the short stories of *Flor de Mesoamérica* (Flower of Mesoamerica; 1955) and the novel *Itúrbide, varón de Dios* (Itúrbide, Man of God); as a poet, he wrote the early poems of *Como la luz del día* (Like Daylight; 1913) and his fundamental books *El perfume de la tierra natal* (The Perfume of the Native Land; 1917), *Anfora sedienta* (Thirsty Amphora; 1922), and *La sandalia del fuego* (The Fire Sandal; 1952); among his critical works, mention should be made of *La nueva poesía de América* (The New Poetry of the Americas; 1923), *El espejo historial* (The Mirror of History; 1937), and *Bibliografía mexicana* (Mexican Bibliography; 1930). Another important poet writing through the larger part of the century is Clementina Suárez (1903?). Suárez also directed the journal *Mujer* (Woman) and an important art gallery in Mexico City, but she is best known for her poetic works, the first of which was published in 1930 (*Corazón sangrante* [Bleeding Heart]) and the last in 1984 (*Engranajes* [Gears]). Her literary excellence has won her a seat in the Academia de la Lengua and Honduras's National Prize for Literature in 1970.

Social concerns were to become the main topics among the fiction writers of the group loosely called the Generation of 26, a group of prose writers of *criollista* (creolist or nativist) tendencies who searched for Honduran identity and who criticized the divisions and civil strife endemic to Honduras's politics. The most representative writer of this group is Marcos Carías Reyes (1905-49), who in his two novels—*La heredad*

(The Farm; written 1931; published 1934) and *Trópico* (Tropics; written 1948; published 1971)—presented a global picture of the country: its political, social, and economic difficulties. His aim was to offer solutions by exposing the problems. He denounces the country's dependence on the banana industry, controlled and exploited by North American interests. Other writers associated with this group are Carlos Izaguirre (1894-1956), who used his novel *Bajo el chubasco* (Beneath the Cloudburst; 1945) to advance his political ideas; Jorge Fidel Durón (1902), known for his excellent work *Opulencia y miseria* (Wealth and Poverty; 1967); Marco Antonio Ponce (1908-32), a poet of social tendencies; Argentina Díaz Lozano (1909), winner of the National Prize in Literature (1968), who writes on national themes in a simple, direct style. She is best known for *Peregrinaje* (Pilgrimage; 1944), a novelized autobiography that won two literary prizes—the Latin American Farrar and Rinehart and the Panamerican Union—which provided translation to English (*Enriqueta and I* [New York, 1944]) and immediate publication. Other works by Díaz Lozano are the tales of *Perlas de mi rosario* (The Pearls of my Rosary; 1930) and *Topacios* (Topaz; 1940) and several novels, among them *Luz en la senda* (Light on the Path; 1937), *Mayapán* (1950), *Fuego en la ciudad* (Fire in the City; 1966), and *Eran las doce* (It Was Twelve O'Clock; 1974). Ramón Amaya Amador (1916-66) is a writer whose Communist affiliation forced him to live and die in exile and prevented his novel indicting the banana company, *Prisión verde* (Green Prison), written in the 1940s from being published until 1974. His novel *Constructores* (Builders; 1959) deals with the urban milieu; most of his works have been published abroad after his death: *Operación Gorila* (Operation Gorilla; 1970), published in Russian, and *Los hijos de Ilamatepeque* (The Children of Ilamatepeque; 1979). The novels of Arturo Mejía Nieto (1910), *El solterón* (The Old Bachelor; 1931), *El tunco* (The Swine; 1932), *Liberación* (Liberation; 1939), and his short stories, *El Chele Amaya y otros cuentos* (Chele Amaya and Other Stories; 1936), are vernacular narratives on Honduran daily life.

III

After World War II Honduran theater was invigorated through the writings of poets such as Daniel Laínez (1910?-59), Claudio Barrera (1912-71), and Merardo Mejía (1907-?), who started an active theatrical renewal with his introduction of social plays. Noteworthy is his historical trilogy *Los diezmos de Olancho* (Olancho's Tithes). It was not until the mid-1950s that the Honduran government granted a subvention to the national theater, but due to this financial help the 1950s and 1960s became years of great activity. In 1954 the "Tegucigalpa" theatrical group was formed. Their success allowed for the building of their own theater in 1964. The University Theater, with its drama school was founded by the writer and director Francisco Salvador (1934), who returned from studying at Mexico's drama schools in 1958. In 1959 the Children's Theater was founded by Mercedes Agurcia (1903). In the 1960s Andrés Morris (Spain 1929) founded the TESP and the National Theater of Honduras (with F. Salvador). Morris is the author of some absurdist plays—among his best are *Oficio de hombres* (Profession of Men) and *La miel del abejorro* (The Bumblebee's Honey). Other plays of notice are F. Salvador's *El sueño de Matías Carpio* (The Dream of Matías Carpio), which follows the magical realism of Miguel Angel Asturias (see section on Guatemala), and Roberto Soto Rovelo's (1930) *Buenas tardes, señor ministro* (Good Afternoon, Mr. Secretary; 1967) and *El misionero* (The Missionary)

After the middle of this century, most writers of narrative fiction follow the more universal models—themes and techniques—offered by the so-called new Latin American novel. This breakthrough was marked by the publication of the collection of short stories *El arca* (The Arc; 1956) by Oscar Acosta (1933), who came in contact with the new narrative through Borges's writings (see section on Argentina) and his model for theme and technique. In the decade of the 1960s two writers stand out, Eduardo Bahr (1940) and Julio Escoto (1944). Active sociopolitical commitment is practiced by Bahr, who in *Fotografía del peñasco* (Photograph of the Rock; 1969) attacks militarism and racial discrimination in the United States, while *El cuento de la guerra* (Tale of the War; 1971) satirizes the 1969 war between Honduras and El Salvador. Escoto is the best-known writer of fiction outside Honduras. In 1967 he won Honduras's National Prize in Literature and in 1983 Spain's Gabriel Miró Prize. His short stories *Los guerreros de Hibueras* (The Fighters of Hibueras; 1968), *La balada del pájaro herido y otros cuentos* (The Ballad of the Wounded Bird and Other Stories; 1971), and the novel *El árbol de los pañuelos* (The Handkerchief Tree; 1972) deal with guerrilla warfare. Escoto's latest novel is *Bajo el almendro, junto al volcán* (Under the Almond Tree, Next to the Volcano; 1988). His rich personal style creates a somber but magical atmosphere around his characters' harsh daily life. Among other writers who became prominent in the 1970s are Oscar

Flores (1912)—member of an earlier generation—who discusses the urban middle class in *La voz está en el viento* (The Voice Is in the Wind; 1970), and Marcos Carías (1938), who presents a series of love conflicts in *La ternura que esperaba* (Hoped-for Tenderness; 1970). More recent works by Carías are *La memoria y sus consecuencias* (Memory and its Effects, 1976) and the unpublished *Una función con móbiles y tentetiesos* (A Function with Mobiles and Tumbler Toys). The "testimonial narrative," characteristic of recent Central American literary trends, also has taken root in Honduras. Its best example is the work of a woman peasant organizer, Elvia Alvarado's *Don't Be Afraid Gringo: A Honduran Woman Speaks from the Heart* (1987), published in English.

Some of the most successful tales among the younger writers have been collected in the anthology *El nuevo cuento hondureño* (The New Honduran Short Story; 1985). Some of these writers are Roberto Castillo (1950), a professor at the University of Honduras and author of *Subida al cielo y otros cuentos* (Up to Heaven and Other Stories; 1980), *Figuras de agradable demencia* (Figures of Agreeable Madness; 1985), and the novelette *El corneta* (The Cornetist; 1981), Edilberto Borjas (1950), and Horacio Castellanos Moya (1957; also a poet), author of two books, *¿Qué signo es Ud. niña Berta?* (What Sign Are You, Child Berta?; 1981) and *Perfil de prófugo* (Profile of a Fugitive; 1987). Castellanos, exiled in Mexico, portrays in a matter-of-fact everyday language the lives and political activities of young people at home and in exile. Two other writers to win renown in recent years are Jorge Luis Oviedo (1957) and José Porfirio Barahona, who, although unpublished, has won several literary prizes for a story reminiscent of the style of Colombia's Gabriel García Márquez, "El alfarero del cielo" (The Potter from Heaven) and his collection of poems "Mi canto como testigo" (My Song As Witness; 1972). He is also the author of the novel "El final del camino" (The End of the Road). While these authors share similar social and literary concerns with the previous generation, they also appear more eager to experiment with language, point of view, and structure.

In Honduras, political concern has continued to be the main source of inspiration in poetry. In fact, most contemporary poets deal almost exclusively with themes of Revolution. This is true even among the poets of the Generation of 35 (also called Generation of the Dictatorship): Claudio Barrera (1912), pseudonym of Vicente Alemán, a political writer deeply influenced by Vallejo and Neruda and who founded the journal *Surco* (Furrow; dates unknown); Jacobo Cárcamo (1914-59), a poet of similar tendencies, known for his collections *Flores del alma* (Flowers of

the Soul; 1941) and *Pino y sangre* (Pine Tree and Blood; 1958); Daniel
Laínez (1910?-59), a self-taught poet who wrote a spontaneous, authentic
popular poetry. Laínez's posthumous book, *Manicomio* (Madhouse;
1980), presents a series of vignettes on the people of Tegucigalpa. Other
poets are Alejandro Valladares (1910), author of *Cantos de la fragua*
(Songs of the Forge; 1933) and Constantino Suáznavar (1912), the most
original poet of the Generation and the author of *Números* (Numbers;
1940) and *La Siguanaba y otros poemas* (The Siguanaba and Other
Poems; 1954). Writing in a similar vein are two younger poets who
belong to the Generation of 45: Roberto Sosa (1930) and Oscar Acosta
(1933). Sosa received Honduras's National Prize for Literature in 1972
and is known internationally for the political commitment evident in the
titles of some of his books: *Los pobres* (The Poor; 1969, Spain's Adonaís
Prize) and *Un mundo para todos dividido* (A World Divided for All;
1971, Cuba's Casa de las Américas Prize). Other works by Sosa are
Caligrama (Calligram; 1959), *Muros* (Walls; 1966), *Mar interior* (Interior
Sea; 1967), *Secreto militar* (Military Secret; 1985), and the prose essays
of *Prosa armada* (Loaded Prose; 1981). Acosta's poetic works are characterized by an intense lyrical tone: *Poesía menor* (Minor Poems; 1957),
Tiempo detenido (Detained Time; 1962), and *Poesía [1952-65]* (Poetry;
1965).

The works of the most recent contemporary Honduran poets have
been collected regularly in anthologies representative of different trends
and themes. Some of these are *Antología de la nueva poesía hondureña*
(Anthology of the New Honduran Poetry; 1967), edited by Roberto Sosa;
Poesía negra en Honduras (Black Poetry in Honduras; 1968), edited by
Claudio Barrera; *Poesía hondureña de hoy* (Honduran Poetry of Today;
1971), edited by Oscar Acosta; *Poesía contemporánea. Once poetas
hondureños* (Contemporary Poetry. Eleven Honduran Poets; 1973);
Antología de la poesía amorosa en Honduras (An Anthology of Love
Poetry in Honduras; 1975), edited by Julio Escoto; *Cinco poetas hondure-
ños* (Five Honduran Poets; 1981), edited by Hernán Antonio Bermúdez.
The poets represented in these anthologies reflect in their works with
great accuracy the growing historical and political struggle going on in
Honduras and Central America. Exemplary are the poems collected in
Cinco poemas hondureños. The works of these five poets are characterized by a harsh, satirical presentation of life; in some cases they even
revive the inflamatory pamphlet. And yet, although their poetry bears
an undisguised political message, it is the result of a powerful existential
experience and it is written with great concern for its formal structure.

These five poets and some of their books are as follows: Alexis Ramírez (1943), *Perro contado* (Counted Dog; 1974); Rigoberto Paredes (1948), *En el lugar de los hechos* (In the Place of the Deeds; 1974), *Las cosas por su nombre* (Things by Their Name; 1978), and *Materia prima* (Raw Material; 1985); José Luis Quesada (1948), *Porque no espero nunca más volver* (Because I Hope Never To Return; 1974), *Cuaderno de testimonios* (Notebook of Testimonies; 1981), *La vida como una guerra* (Life as War; 1982), and *Sombra del blanco día* (Shadow of the White Day; 1987); Ricardo Maldonado (1949), *Me extraña araña* (I'm Surprised Spider; 1980); and Horacio Castellanos Moya (1957), already discussed as a fiction writer, who is the author of two books of poetry: *Poemas* (Poems; 1978) and *La margarita emocionante* (The Thrilling Daisy; 1979).

BIBLIOGRAPHY

Herranz, Atanasio. *Español. Antología. Introducción al estudio de la literatura hondureña*. Tegucigalpa: Editorial Guaymuras, 1983. A textbook that includes an appendix titled "Overview of Honduran Literature," composed of three essays, valuable although somewhat introductory, dealing with 1) Honduran literature in general; 2) dramatic literature in Honduras; and 3) the origins of the short story in Honduras.

Martínez, José Francisco. *Literatura hondureña y su proceso generacional*. Tegucigalpa: Editorial Universitaria, 1987. The most thorough presentation of authors and the evolution of national literature.

Oviedo, Jorge Luis. *El nuevo cuento hondureño*. Tegucigalpa: Dardo Editores, 1985. Oviedo's introduction outlines the development of the short story, indicating major trends, authors, and works.

Paredes, Rigoberto, and Manuel Salinas Paguada. *Literatura hondureña. (Selección de estudios críticos sobre su proceso creativo)*. Tegucigalpa: Editores Unidos, 1978. An overview of Honduran literature done through a series of previously published seminal articles by a variety of literary critics and authors.

Umaña, Helen. *Literatura hondureña contemporánea. (Ensayos)*. Tegucigalpa: Guaymuras, 1986. A collection of short review essays on specific authors and works.

MEXICO
Steven M. Bell
University of Arkansas

I

Mexican literature is as old as the earliest civilized inhabitants of Meso-America (we assume that literature and civilization are coterminous), and as new, we might say, as one of Carlos Fuentes's recent international best-sellers (*Gringo viejo* [*The Old Gringo*; 1985]) and its adaptation for the silver screen (an English-language film made by an international production team). This statement is meant to give some idea of the incredible distances Mexican literature has traveled in its long history, but also of the continuity underlying its diverse manifestations. Mexico has one of the most mature, complex, and representative literary traditions in all of Latin America. In fact, it is so exemplary as to border on the exceptional, and it invokes many unique considerations.

Two accidents of history account for Mexico's complexity and eccentricity, one a product of its convulsive origins, the other pertaining to its conflictive modern evolution. The first is the relative strength of the twin poles of Mexico's cultural inheritance, the pre-Hispanic and the Spanish colonial. The second is the country's immediate proximity to the United States. While these circumstances have contributed to a strong sense of the national self and a pride in Mexico's autonomous identity, these factors have also conspired to make that identity infinitely problematic. This vital dilemma may be summarized by reference to the ambiguous space the country occupies in every sense: historically, culturally, and linguistically Mexico's strongest ties are of course to Latin or Spanish America; but in geographic terms (themselves cultural and political through and through) Mexico forms part of the North American continent.

On the Hispanic side of its cultural inheritance, as a powerful Spanish viceregal capital, Mexico—New Spain—may lay claim to one of the

357

richest of all the Latin American colonial literatures. On the pre-Hispanic side of the equation, Mexico boasts within its modern territorial boundaries not one but two of the three major indigenous civilizations: the Mayan and the Aztec. As such, Mexico offers fertile ground for rebutting simplistic notions of indigenous civilization as a unitary "other" that may be opposed to the Western dominant. Mexico's unprecedented revolution of 1910 reflects indirectly the strength born of this rich, dual inheritance. But if Mexico has thus avoided certain problems of autonomy and identity faced by other Latin American and Third-World nations, its proximity to the United States has created others that also have a long history, dating back at least to the middle of the nineteenth century, when a large portion of Mexico's territory was lost to its North American neighbor. The famous epithet: "Poor Mexico, so far from God and so close to the United States," is attributed to Porfirio Díaz, a positivist, enlightened dictator from the turn of the century. In the novel *Cristóbal Nonato* (*Christopher Unborn*; 1987), contemporary author Fuentes explores this fundamental issue, presenting a darkly humorous forecast of the fate of U.S.-Mexican relations, on whose prospects the country's future, for better or worse, may depend. In the near future of 1992 in which the novel's principal action unfolds, the geopolitical boundaries of North America have been redrawn and a new entity, MexAmerica, appears along the scarred and embattled, North-South frontier. In the meantime, in the space of the Southwestern United States, once Mexican, now "North American," a rich and Mexican-American—or Chicano—culture and literature have emerged, balanced uncertainly between the two nations. This Mexican-American culture today is just as distant from mainstream Mexican literature as from that of the United States, if not more so, as evidenced by the controversy that has surrounded Octavio Paz's treatment of the *pachuco*, or Chicano, in his famous *El laberinto de la soledad* (*The Labyrinth of Solitude*; 1950).

Mexico, for these reasons and others, is in the curious position of being a leader among developing nations, an apparent contradiction in terms. But being a power among the powerless is just one of the complexities and paradoxes of Mexican being. Many of its vital contradictions are ones that Mexico shares, not only with other Latin American nations but with other Third-World countries as well. As elsewhere in the Third World, Mexico is being electronified before it has achieved complete industrialization. In many, sometimes superficial ways, Mexico is fully modern, yet in other regards it stubbornly retains a fundamental premodern character. While the dominant culture in Mexico, since the

Spanish conquest, is primordially, undeniably Western, it also preserves substantial non-Western roots, both in the non-Hispanic indigenous and at the heart of its Hispanic inheritance (at the time of the New World discovery, Iberia stood at the "frontier" of Western Europe, in both literal and more figurative senses). Much is to be learned from Mexico's confrontation of these difficult circumstances, its relative shortcomings and failures as well as its many triumphs and successes. Among other things, Mexican literature is a battleground for these vital contradictions, a testimony of this confrontation. It is a unique contribution to our stock of living fictions.

Mexican history conveniently divides itself into four, or possibly five distinct periods, whose difference is at once cultural and political. The first of these are separated by three cataclysmic, watershed events: the Spanish Conquest of Mexico (1519-21), the independence movement (1810-21), and the Mexican revolution (1910-17). In addition, though we lack sufficient historical perspective for a clear-cut determination, there is a growing consensus that the year 1968 may stand as another crucial watershed in Mexico's cultural and sociopolitical history, marked by an infamous massacre of student protestors at the Tlatelolco Plaza in Mexico City and signaling a crisis in Mexico's revolutionary institutions. The periods thus demarcated are (1) pre-Hispanic civilization, (2) the Spanish colonial years, (3) the nineteenth-century republican era, (4) twentieth-century revolutionary Mexico, and possibly now, (5) post-Tlatelolco Mexico. Whether a function of historical fact or historical perspective, it is worthwhile to note the progressive temporal compression or acceleration implied in this demarcation: the pre-Hispanic era encompasses untold centuries; the colonial period covers roughly three centuries; the republican era spans some one-hundred years; and postrevolutionary Mexico, to date, remains an experiment of hardly more than three quarters of a century.

Much has changed in Mexico through the years, but much has also stayed the same. Mexico is still struggling to attain the modernization (democracy) and liberalization (social justice) it has sought at least since the War of Independence. The effective results of independence and the revolution, undeniably events of tremendous importance and material repercussion, have often been more symbolic than real. Much the same could be said, from a social and economic vantage point, of the Spanish Conquest, when one considers that the great majority of native Mexicans simply saw a dark-skinned lord replaced by a white-skinned one. Octavio Paz, evoking central preoccupations in his work such as identity and difference, permanence and change, often speaks of "two" Mexicos: one cosmopolitan, modern, and jet set that would blindly impose its foreign models on the country, hoping to make disappear the other Mexico, the underdeveloped, "folklorish," tradition-bound Mexico, ostensibly the "dark" side of the country's being. Mexico's search for identity since its independence as a nation-state in the early nineteenth century has been an invigorating, if at times nasty struggle between the two extreme perspectives of nationalism and cosmopolitanism, between the interior (Mexico-centric) and the exterior (Eurocentric) vantage points, rhetorical inventions that often appear irreconcilable.

Mexico's dual identity has historical roots that cannot be ignored. But the "two" Mexicos of today are not simply represented by the classic division between the indigenous American and the Spanish. They are, rather, the tradition-bound Mexico that looks to the past—encompassing both the pre-Hispanic and the Spanish colonial, which in Mexico have achieved a high degree of syncretism—and the rational, modernizing impulse that looks toward a perfectible future. Indeed, Spanish colonialism's counterreformist spirit in some regards has more in common with the indigenous American worldview than it does with the reformist inspiration of the Anglo-Saxon colonization of America. Historian Edmundo O'Gorman (1906) has highlighted the fundamental differences between the Latin colonization of America and the Anglo-Saxon one. Where the latter is inspired by a creative conception of man and personal liberty, the former is linked to a closed and imitative vision of a humankind whose destiny in predetermined. Paz, for his part, has discovered a common, "patrimonial" mind-set that Mexico's Hispanic heritage shares with the pre-Hispanic civilizations, dominating the Mexican worldview right up to the present. Thus, it is not surprising that in the case of Mexico's independence movement and revolution, the effects have been somewhat superficial. These upheavals were in part natural products of social evolution, but also involved the adoption of foreign (reformist) models in an attempt to remedy a perceived insufficiency of development. The antagonists and protagonists have changed, but the struggles of indigenous, mestizo, and Creole Mexico against domination and appropriation, from within and from without, have remained little changed. It is the impossible yet necessary understanding between the North and South that Fuentes has made the object of his most recent novels, as he has moved beyond his previous preoccupation with the Hispanic roots of the Mexican soul. The problematic reception Fuentes's efforts have had, on both sides of the North-South frontier, are indicative of the many tensions that remain to be resolved.

In light of Mexico's multi-layered history of continuity and change, of historical phases coexisting and superimposed, we should perhaps abandon the necessary understanding of the two Mexicos for a more subtly nuanced appreciation of the country's many contemporary faces and its diversely transcultured literary manifestations. As a country with a central role to play in the definition of a new, postcolonial world, Mexico's central characteristic may be its defiance of definition and comprehension.

II

Popular knowledge of pre-Hispanic culture is normally limited to the vivid image of Aztec priests impiously sacrificing prisoners of war to the gods. Aztec culture, according to this common simplification, *is* pre-Hispanic civilization. Mexico itself, partly out of ignorance, partly for rhetorical convenience, has done much to perpetuate this misconception. The reality, of course, is much more complex. Most of Aztec culture is an eclectic assimilation of the customs and wisdom of previous Mesoamerican civilizations, which were both the pride and the envy of the Aztecs. Much like the Spaniards, the imperialistic Aztecs had themselves arrived from "foreign lands" to the north, some four hundred years before the Spanish conquest, to terrorize inhabitants of the central plateau. Thus the violence of the Spanish Conquest was nothing new to Mesoamerica. What was highly unprecedented was the dynamic confrontation of two radically different civilizations, each of which had previously only imagined—or "invented," as O'Gorman would have it—the existence of the other. The Aztec empire was easily defeated by the Spanish, its voices and the power of its indigenous discourse effectively silenced or destroyed. But the Indian spirit lives in Mexico today. Many aspects of popular indigenous culture have survived orally among isolated pockets of predominantly Indian population. Many more have been so assimilated into the dominant culture, at a subconscious level, as to be virtually unrecognizable. And in Mexico, it is especially important to note that the pre-Hispanic remains a central element of official rhetoric. Carlos Fuentes has often remarked the conspicuous absence in Mexico of monuments to its Spanish conqueror, Hernán Cortés, that are abundantly supplanted by statues of pre-Hispanic chieftains, rather unusual in Latin America. Too much significance should not be attached to this circumstance (key historical sites pertaining to the life of Cortés have been preserved). But this is much more than a reflection of the skill in the manipulation of historic symbols and cultural icons of the postrevolutionary institution. It is also a reflection of the strength of Mexico's always problematic "autonomous" identity, the product of a fundamental syncretism or *mestizaje* (mestization).

The study of pre-Hispanic, "indigenous" literature has a curious history, as intriguing, and significant, as that of the literature itself. Pre-Hispanic literature has certainly suffered undeserved neglect; but its impact on and presence in subsequent Mexican literary production has also at times been hyperbolically overestimated. The introduction by Ermilio Abreu Gómez to his *Clásicos, románticos, modernos* (Classics, Romantics, Moderns; 1934) might be taken as a representative overestimation of the contemporary significance of this literature. Though he makes no specific reference to pre-Hispanic literature, Abreu Gómez argues for a racially oriented approach to Mexican literature; he stresses the indigenous element and suggests that Mexican literature not be judged against European models. This is all well and good, but the racial element alone does not account for the difference of Mexican literary production vis-à-vis Europe. If Mexican literature is a purely racial designation, then it was mortally wounded by the adventure of Hernán Cortés. If, on the other hand—and Abreu Gómez's book tends to bear this out in practice though not in theory—Mexican literature is a political and cultural designation, it is an entity constantly evolving and always just eluding our grasp. Certain social and psychological factors from the Indian side of the equation (a premodern view of life and form of social organization, an acceptance of predeterminism, a certain fatalism and melancholy) have endured. But it is important to emphasize that Mexican literature as we know it today, as an established social and cultural institution and above all as a *modern* literature, need be traced back no further than the arrival of the Spanish. The opening line of *Historia de la literatura mexicana* (A History of Mexican Literature; 1928), by Carlos González Peña (1885-1955), that "Mexican literature is a branch of Spanish literature," touches the extreme of unjust neglect of the pre-Hispanic and needs qualification. But it is more on the mark than many of Abreu Gómez's polemic affirmations. Esthetic and moral judgements aside, pre-Hispanic literature is a "premodern" literature, belonging according to Alfonso Reyes (and following Vico) to the heroic or mythic stage of man's intellectual evolution. As a primarily static entity, nonetheless, it has invariably been subject to strategic manipulation.

Fray Bartolomé de las Casas (1474-1566), a Dominican missionary, is the most famed defender of the native Americans in the first century of the Spanish colony (see the section on Guatemalan literature). But it is to another missionary priest, the Franciscan Fray Bernardino de Sahagún (1499-1590), that we owe much of what has been preserved of pre-Hispanic literature. The majority of his philological and historical work—lost, found, and finally printed posthumously as *Historia general de las cosas de Nueva España* (*General History of the Things of New Spain*; 1829-30)—was accomplished under the auspices of the Colegio de Santa Cruz de Tlatelolco, established in 1536 as an institute of higher learning destined for the Indian nobility. Though the original design of the College may have been to convert and "Hispanicize" the Indian nobility, in practice it became a center for two-way cultural exchange. Surviving Aztec nobles and their descendants, such as Fernando de Alva Ixtlilxóchitl (1568?-1648?), themselves made important contributions to the preservation of pre-Hispanic culture.

Though effectively disarmed as a mainstream ideological instrument, the Indian languages during the colonial period continued to be used by the Spaniards to proselytize. Missionaries composed theatrical works and poetry in the Indian languages. Alva Ixtlilxóchitl's son published, in Nahuatl translation, plays by the Spanish Golden Age dramatists Lope de Vega and Calderón de la Barca. Nahuatl turns of phrase, and mostly insubstantial references to things Indian, are found throughout colonial poetry, partly as a function of Baroque exuberance, partly as a function of the attempted assimilation of the indigenous as unwitting Christians. With Romanticism and the anti-Spanish, anticolonial sentiment that accompanied independence, there was some effort to pen an "Indianist" literature, though the results appeared forced and mostly unconvincing. The effective recovery and recreation of the pre-Hispanic literary legacy had to await the twentieth century: the antirational vision and recuperation of pre-Hispanic motifs in poets such as Octavio Paz; social realist and neorealist, *indigenista* fiction in the 1930s; and above all the serious scholarly treatment and conscientious documentation and translation in the contributions of philologist Angel María Garibay K., anthropologist Miguel León-Portilla, and literary historian José Luis Martínez.

From the early Mayan culture the major extant works are two miscellaneous collections of religious, historical, scientific, and literary texts. The *Popol vuh* (*The Book of Counsel*) and the *Libros de Chilam Balam*

(*The Book of Chilam Balam of Cumayel*) were recreated and transcribed in Maya-Quiché using Latin characters in the years subsequent to the Conquest, but these manuscripts were not "discovered" and made public until the nineteenth century (often by European scholars). Like the work of Las Casas, Sahagún, and Alva Ixtlilxóchitl, these texts belong more to history and anthropology than to literature proper. But together with the chronicles of discovery and conquest, from the other side of Mexico's dual cultural inheritance, these "indigenous" texts remain fundamental as a source, a precedent, and an inaugural undertaking. Indeed, a work such as the *Popol vuh* is an important precursor text in unexpected ways. As a work recreated by an anonymous, indigenous informant; written, as he says, under the law of God, in "Christian"; and explicitly addressed to colonial authorities and other outsiders, it raises fundamental problems of faithful linguistic/cultural translation, and of mediating strategic or personal interests—questions also raised by many of the chronicles.

Poetry in Aztec society was apparently a noble pursuit; a specialized, even professional activity, which had both cathartic and exhortative functions. It was an essential aspect of public rites and functions, both sacred and profane. Though the poets were a salaried caste of considerable social status, poetic composition was mostly collective or anonymous; transmission was primarily oral. This said, what is today most striking about this literary production is its uncanny pertinence. Certain of its lyric manifestations seem closer to our contemporary sensibility than the Baroque verse of the colonial period, or even nineteenth-century verse of Neoclassical and Romantic inspiration. This is perhaps a testimony to the timelessness of certain aspects of the human condition and its poetic expression, but also a reflection of the twentieth century's rejection both of modern, Western rationalism, and of many of the commonplaces of the Western literary tradition.

Thematically, Nahuatl poetry is rich and varied, comparable in this regard even to contemporary verse. Both epic and lyric compositions were common, and often the songs were dramatized. Technically and stylistically, on the other hand, there is considerable monotony, as is to be expected of a relatively closed, isolated society whose culture is primarily oral. There is a constant and fixed repertoire of metaphors and images, the primary bases of comparison being flowers, birds of bright plumage, and precious stones. Warriors are eagles. The poet is a large-headed parrot. Poems are flowers. Blood is divine water or the nectar of flowers. Curiously, many of these elements were "imported" into the central plateau from more tropical regions, suggesting that exoticism has a long history indeed. Garibay groups the themes into five loose classifications: religious compositions in praise of the gods, such as "Nos enloquece el dador de la vida" (The giver of life enraptures us); heroic poems in praise of war, in memory of famous warriors, or invoking the glory of death in war, such as "Mientras que con escudos" (While with shields) or "¡Esmeraldas, oro!" (Emeralds, Gold!); philosophical poems which lament misfortune, which express fear of the mystery of death, which question the meaning of existence, or which take on the form of the classic Western *ubi sunt*; and finally "personal" themes, compositions in praise of poets and poetry. Notable for their absence in this classification scheme are composition of amorous or erotic subject matter. Equally notable and intriguing is the last thematic category and the artistic self-consciousness it betrays in the poets. In colonial poetry such self-glorification in poets and their work is rare, probably because it would seem sacrilegious in a counterreformist climate. No such prudishness or humility is evident in Nahuatl poetry. On this basis Martínez contends that Nahuatl poetry at the time of the Conquest was moving towards a new, modern conception of literature, emphasizing individual creativity and personal expression. In his critical study and anthology of Netzahualcóyotl, an Aztec noble legendary for his promotion of the arts and his humanitarianism, Martínez convincingly attributes to the Texcoco statesman some thirty-six extant poems.

If pre-Hispanic literature, since its "discovery" by Western man, has never ceased to be a strange, a truly "other" culture, its place in any full and adequate history of Mexican literature is ineluctable as an alternative source and precedent. Moreover, though themselves "immigrants" of sorts, these people cannot but be considered "natives" of the land. They had a real political sovereignty which the Spanish colonizers never knew.

III

As soon as Europeans (in this case, Spaniards) were born in America, the question of cultural identity, consciously or not, took on a special complexity. The colonial period (1519-1810) is full of contradictions often manifest only in the deeper structures of social, political, and literary expression. Spain represented authority, imposed not only from above but from without. The Creole (Spaniard born in America) quickly came to play up to the home country for favor and simultaneously to resent this self-denigration. By a not unusual twist of psychological compensation and sublimation, culturally the colony of New Spain frequently appears more Spanish than Spain itself. The colonial regime, politically and socioeconomically, was authoritarian or even tyrannical. In the cultural and artistic arenas, though equally hierarchical, things were more open and ambiguous. Restrictive measures were taken, such as the famous prohibition of works of fiction, in order to maintain the snugness of the colonial yoke. But the same physical distances that made the restrictions necessary permitted a certain laxity in their implementation.

Colonial literature is a transplanted literature, as Octavio Paz insists, or a literature that was "born mature," to borrow an expression from José Emilio Pacheco, this contradiction of terms being just one way of expressing the inner tension inherent to the Mexican circumstance. The importance of the colonial heritage—personalism, centralism, dogma, and rhetoric—can hardly be overemphasized in its molding of the Mexican mind-set to this day. It is paradoxical that in colonial Mexico we do not find the first true "Mexicans," but we do have the real origins of modern Mexican literature. Out of a mixture (*mestizaje*, mestization) of the unconscious psychophysiological inheritance from the Indian and the more conscious cultural heritage of the Spanish empire, the modern Mexican character will be formed.

The years 1521 to 1600, very roughly, are those of the edification and consolidation of the transplanted Euro-Hispanic culture. Once this tradition has rooted, it blossoms in the seventeenth century: the Baroque is extensively, perhaps excessively, cultivated in Mexico, bearing original fruit in the formidable figure of a nun, Sor Juana Inés de la Cruz (1648-95). The eighteenth century in Mexico witnesses a gradual withering of Baroque ornamentation and ingenuity and a weak assimilation of Neoclassical scholarship that was to help prepare Mexico's political independence from the Spanish colonial empire.

It is an exaggeration to suggest that the colonizers of the sixteenth century did not have time for literature, a simplistic determination belied by historical fact. But it is true that in certain realms other tasks, other concerns had precedence over purely aesthetic motivations. We should question the cliché that would have actions, during this time, speak louder than words; but words, in order to be widely heard, did have to await the arrival of the printing press on American soil, the first being imported to Mexico from Spain in 1537. For the new culture to be implanted, for the new institutions to be housed, the Spanish Renaissance tradition had first literally to be "edified," and frequently this was done over the demolished ruins of pre-Hispanic civilization. Church, state, and university were the three pillars of the Spanish empire's religious and political crusade. Literature, before it could settle down into the elaboration of objects for purely aesthetic contemplation, had its role to play in this arguably plunderous and self-righteous undertaking. Corresponding to the State's political mission, there appeared the famous "chronicles" of the Conquest. Corresponding to the Church's religious mission, there was an evangelical theater, designed to indoctrinate and convert.

It has become fashionable today to treat history as fiction, as imaginative literature. We may find this perspective particularly applicable to the "fantastic" chronicles of early Spanish settlers, which in retrospect appear fanciful indeed. It is tempting, though neither accurate nor sufficient, to suggest that real life was more unbelievable than fiction for the first Western inhabitants of the New World. Rather, the early chronicles did not see fact and fiction quite as we do today. Many scholars have documented how the conquerors' perceptions were influenced by works of what we now would consider fiction. In other words, the appearance of the chronicles does not explain the late appearance of fiction-writing in the Spanish colonies. But their basis in "fiction" may, on the other hand, go some way toward accounting for the popularity of these chronicles of the Conquest, particularly in Europe. The chronicles take a variety of forms, and adopt as many distinct vantage points as they have authors. Second-hand accounts were numerous, but the most intriguing ones are written by the participants themselves, outstanding among them those by Hernán Cortés and Bernal Díaz del Castillo.

Hernán Cortés (1485-1547) sent five letters to the King of Spain between 1519 and 1526. Published as the *Cartas de relación* (*Five Letters*), they were immediately popular in Europe. Beyond dutifully relating to the King his adventures, with an eye to justifying the importance of his mission, the leader of the expedition surely had in mind the perpetuation of his own notoriety. Yet Cortés does not focus attention exclusively on his own exploits; he quite frankly discusses his setbacks as well as his successes, as if he were aware that the magnitude of events and settings would speak for themselves on his behalf. His astonishment at what he found, his mostly respectful appreciation for the "other" civilization he encountered, are noteworthy; they shine through his cruelty, and the martial stoicism of his narration.

The *Verdadera historia de la conquista de la Nueva España* (*The Discovery and Conquest of Mexico: 1517-1521*; 1632), by Bernal Díaz del

Castillo (1492-1580?) is, understandably, the most popular of the chronicles of the Conquest. This narration by one of Cortés's soldiers serves nicely as counterpoint to the account of his Captain. Díaz wrote in response to such flowery accounts as the *Historia general de las Indias* (General History of the Indies; 1578) by Francisco López de Gómara (1511-66). Scholars have convincingly argued that the feats of the conquerors were at least partially inspired by the books of chivalry so popular in Spain at the time of the Conquest. If López de Gómara's account is the *Amadís de Gaula* of chronicles of the Conquest, because of its blatant idealizations, Díaz del Castillo's *Verdadera historia* is the *Tirante el blanco* of the chronicles, bringing the adventures down to earth by balancing the bravery of triumph with frank expressions of mortal fear and misery. There are in Díaz's account no pretensions to polished style or sophistication of lexicon. Nor does he pretend to Cortés's orthodox stoicism: his own emotions are never far from the surface of his descriptions and narrations. Just as his indignation at the idealization of the conqueror shines through, so does his "Americanist" sentiment, in hyperbolic descriptions of the grandeur of the New World and its autochthonous civilizations. Cortés, with the sobriety of his accounts, reflects the Spanish spirit of the political and religious crusade. Díaz del Castillo, nearing his deathbed in the New World, might seem to evidence the sincere pride in things American, which will contribute to the erosion of ties with the Spanish mainland. For Mexican literature, and for Latin-American literature generally, these chronicles are an important inaugural undertaking.

Like the chronicles, early Mexican theater in the sixteenth century does not properly belong to the history of literature, if by literature we understand a clear predominance of the so-called aesthetic function. The theater's subsequent irregular development as a national, Mexican genre seems at first glance curious in light of its beginnings: it is the one genre that largely succeeds in synthesizing Hispanic elements and pre-Hispanic ones. Authors and actors were not professionals; they were missionaries and Indians. Though some of the plays were in Spanish, most were composed and staged in Indian languages, the intermingling of elements from pre-Hispanic song and dance being inherent in such a practice. These functions served as flattering spectacles for high officials of church and state, confirming in their eyes the success of their program of indoctrination (and subjugation). Not infrequently in these "live" performances, however, there occurred improvisations that scandalized or outraged the patrons. Understandably, given their functionalism and anonymous authorship, few of these scripts survive today.

As colonial life became solidly institutionalized, as theatrical stagings moved from the church to the convent, and from the convent to the royal court, what could be called a Creole theater emerged and began to distance itself from the popular processions and festival air of the missionary theater. Collective authorship begins to disappear; language and versification are refined; structure is tightened; and secular themes begin to appear, though orthodox religious ones continue to predominate. As soon as theater appeared among the colonial aristocracy, native productions competed poorly with the aesthetically more polished productions imported from the Peninsula. The case of Juan Ruíz de Alarcón (1580-1639?) is in this regard representative of literary relations between the Iberian Peninsula and its colonies. Mexican-born, Ruíz de Alarcón sought the measure of his abundant talent in the theater houses of Spain. His "Mexican" character has been amply demonstrated in absurd polemics. He belongs to the history of Spanish Golden-Age theater. But personally and literarily he was unique among Golden Age theatrical bards. It is possible to suggest that the eye for detail and the strong moralizing bent of works such as *La verdad sospechosa* (Suspicious Truth; 1634) are owing to a putatively objective perspective as a physical, social, and political outsider in Spanish society. His life was a bitter struggle for personal and literary acceptance, which he himself only partially saw achieved.

Poetry does not emerge in colonial Mexico with the urgency with which the chronicle and the theater appeared, but this is as should be expected: where the chronicle and the drama were primarily functional, poetry during the colonial period was ornamental, and in this regard the polar opposite of early narrative and drama. Yet poetry soon eclipsed these other forms. It was the colonizer's genre par excellence. Only poetry, among the major forms, is a literary expression produced primarily by and for the colonizers and their descendants. The chronicles, in contrast, were directed primarily at Europe, while many of the early theatrical productions were destined for the indigenous population. Colonial poetry in this respect is literally the seed from which Mexican literature will grow. This audience factor is one that has been neglected when poetry has been affirmed as the genre historically and temperamentally most akin to the Mexican spirit, and as the genre evidencing the most complex and continuous development in Mexico.

Though a rude simplification, it is fair to suggest that as military contests waned in colonial Mexico, they were gradually replaced by the ever more popular and abundant poetic jousts as outlets for a gentleman's dexterity and ingenuity. But poetry is never a simple pastime. These poetic contests were also a form of mutual self-flattery, a way for men on the frontiers of what was considered civilization to prove to themselves, and to anyone else who would listen, that they were as refined as the society they had left on the shores of the European continent. And of course the less nobility in one's blood, the more one had to produce to demonstrate and confirm one's culture. Hernán González de Eslava (1534-1601?), a dramatist and himself a poet, is the author of the oft-cited hyperbole that there were "more poets than dung." Colonial Mexico was not only an extension of Spain; it was a province which for understandable political, social, and psychological reasons (hopes of public and private reward) sought almost desperately to emulate the homeland. Pre-Hispanic poetry surprises us for the timelessness of its thematic universality, because we expect it to be so other. Colonial poetry evidences a similar thematic universality, but because we expect it to be culturally more our own, it is by contrast more prone today to bore or even disgust for its conformism and conventionality. Certainly, it does not adhere to our postromantic concepts of originality and authenticity of individual expression, and for this at least colonial poetry may be closer to pre-Hispanic poetry than to poetry's contemporary manifestations.

The Italianate and humanist poetic tradition of the Spanish Renaissance travelled to the New World, figuratively speaking, on the wings of Spanish poets. The novelist Mateo Alemán was one of the first Peninsular writers to visit New Spain, though his direct literary influence is doubtful. The poets Juan de la Cueva and Gutierre de Cetina also make the voyage to America early on. Considered to be the first Mexican-born poet of some renown, Francisco de Terrazas (1525?-1600?) was the son of a Spanish conqueror. Terrazas apparently did not publish a collection of his poetry during his lifetime, which was not uncommon. Poetry was to remain for many years within the oral and manuscript modes of transmission; it was not revolutionized overnight with the printing press, which in the early colonial years was reserved for official and doctrinaire functions. Three of Terrazas's sonnets have survived thanks to their inclusion in a manuscript anthology of 1577 entitled *Flores de varia poesía* (Flowers of Varied Verse; 1577).

Bernardo de Balbuena (1561?-1627) is the poet who in Mexico marks the transition from the Renaissance manner of Garcilaso to the Baroque of Góngora, the latter rapidly assimilated among the many poets in seventeenth-century New Spain. Balbuena, for his seemingly natural exuberance in form and content, anticipates the full-fledged arrival of Gongorism. He is best remembered for the descriptive composition *Grandeza mexicana* (Mexican Grandeur; 1604). The poem is carefully constructed, each "chapter" elaborating one of the eight verses of an introductory summary. The poem's deep structure dramatizes the complex of sentiments and motivations that characterize the Mexican colonial experience. The poem describes in accurate and illuminating detail aristocratic social customs in Mexico, but the reputed virtues of the viceregal capital are exaggerated out of all proportion. The poem praises the grandeur of Mexico City not because it is "Mexican," but rather as an achievement of the Spanish empire and its political and religious lords. To describe the capital of New Spain to a woman who will soon enter the convent is the ostensible intention. But the real impetus behind the poem is glimpsed in the verse dedication with which it opens. Balbuena feigns personal humility and devotes himself to the service of the head of the Royal Indies Council, whose virtues he praises through lofty comparisons and classical allusions. In other words, the ambitious Balbuena, later named Bishop of Puerto Rico, was surely driven in part by hopes of political favor, and used literature as an occasion to demonstrate his literary prowess and erudition. Balbuena is perhaps an extreme case, but such dedications were standard practice until the printing press became a viable, independent enterprise. Only the very brave (or foolish) mocked the patronage system. Political and cultural tensions always lie just below the surface of these dedications: the writers' pride mixes with resentment of their dependence on patrons.

In the seventeenth century poetry blossoms, quantitatively if not always qualitatively. Mexican colonial poetry is perhaps not so much characterized by mediocrity, as critics of the Baroque would have it, but rather by monotony. Arias de Villalobos, Matías de Bocanegra, Luis de Sandoval y Zapata, and Agustín de Salazar y Torres are the representative Mexican poets; but everything they have to offer and more can be found in the unprecedented appearance of Sor Juana Inés de la Cruz. She and Carlos de Sigüenza y Góngora (1645-1700)—priest, poet, historian, and scientist—are in Mexico the outstanding cultural figures of the age. The emergence of a certain friction between the divine and the profane, between faith and intellect, seem retrospectively inevitable in a world where scholars are almost without exception affiliated with the church. Sor Juana and Sigüenza are admirable for their pursuit of new ideas and what today we would call scientific knowledge. By the same token, they never came to question the essence of their religious faith. They were extremely adept at maintaining a distinction between articles of faith and questions of intellect. Neither was completely successful at this game, however, as evidenced by a certain bitterness which surfaces in both as a result of conflicts with official church-state authority.

Sigüenza's *Primavera indiana* (Indian Spring; 1668) is a poetic hymn to the Virgin of Guadalupe, the patron saint of Mexico and a key symbolic figure in the development of Mexican national consciousness. Similar nationalist implications, more fully drawn out, are found in the *Teatro de virtudes políticas* (Theater of Political Virtues; 1680): legendary Aztec leaders are juxtaposed with figures of classical and biblical times, as examples to be followed by a wise and prudent leader. Sigüenza implies here a marked continuity between the Aztec empire and imperial Mexico, exemplifying the Jesuit view of the Aztec leaders as unwitting Christians. But we should not be too hasty, the above notwithstanding, in attributing to Sigüenza an unambiguously proindigenous position. His was rather an incipient Creole nationalism, as confirmed by his disgust with the popular uprising of 1692, in which a library he risked his life to save was set afire. Sigüenza was also the author of a significant Mexican precursor to Fernández de Lizardi's "first" Latin American novel (see below). Whether the picaresque-styled *Los infortunios de Alonso Ramírez* (The Misfortunes of Alonso Ramírez; 1690) belongs more properly to history or to literature is a topic of some critical debate, as is the case with the earlier chronicles of discovery and conquest.

The first and most obvious tension dramatized in the life and work of Sor Juana Inés de la Cruz is the simple fact that she was a learned and influential woman. It is in her case glaringly apparent that the orthodox severity of the colony was relative and arbitrary: as long as Sor Juana was a diverting curiosity, she was amply tolerated; but toward the end of her life she began to ruffle feathers, and as a consequence suffered censorship. Few figures of any place or time so clearly transcend their immediate circumstance. Sor Juana accepted with resignation and ultimately obeyed the limiting conventions of her time, but her works exude the unique spirit of her precocity and rebelliousness. Above and beyond her confessed self-doubts, she was a self-assured and even vain genius who by convention had to feign humility; a passionate soul who the severity of orthodoxy seems only to have inflamed; a brilliant, logical, and rational mind that was employed in defense of matters of faith. If Sigüenza seems to anticipate the rationalism and encyclopedic tendencies of Neoclassicism, Sor Juana appears to forecast the modern spirit and its present-day crisis, in what Octavio Paz terms her "revelation of the impossibility of ultimate revelation."

Sor Juana, a nun in the San Jerónimo convent for most of her life, was a prominent public figure who rubbed elbows with viceroys and archbishops. Much of her written work, when properly glossed, sheds light on political intrigue and posturing among New Spain's seventeenth-century ruling class. Her most often cited work, the *Respuesta a Sor Filotea* (*Answer to Sor Filotea*; 1691/1700; also translated as *A Woman of Genius; the Intellectual Biography of Sor Juana Inés de la Cruz*), is an autobiographical sketch recounting the history of her intellectual drive and curiosity; a defense not only of secular literature but also of her very womanhood. The *Respuesta* exposes many of the pressures Sor Juana felt as Catholic nun and public figure, as well as the potential contradictions between her confession of fervent intellectual passion and her profession of religious humility. The defenses that she undertakes in the *Respuesta* necessarily overlap in the orthodox religious climate in which she wrote: woman literally, Biblically we might say, was considered the more profane of the sexes. Though she makes several concessions to orthodox convention, citing authorities she argues that private study is beneficial, and goes on to enumerate a long list of precedents of classical and biblical women prominent in politics and literature. In a vein similar to her famous invective poem "Hombres necios" (Injudicious Men; 1689), she enjoins that if women are to be denied the privileges of study, there are many unqualified men who also should be refused these privileges. She explains her entrance into the convent as a "decent" option, given her concern for salvation, her aversion to official service and to marriage, and her interest in pursuing studies.

Sor Juana wrote in all of the popular and official genres of her time. Her strongest suit was perhaps lyric poetry; she comments in the *Respuesta* on the facility with which she composed in verse. As was standard for clergy with literary inclinations, she wrote didactic and theological tracts in prose. One such piece, the *Carta atenagórica* (Athenian Letter; 1690), sparked the controversy that led her to write her famous *Respuesta* and then abandon literature in her final years. Sor Juana also wrote plays for both the religious and the secular theater, all following the lines marked out by the Spanish dramatist Calderón de la Barca. The best known of these works is *Los empeños de una casa* (Household Intrigue;

1692), set in the Spanish Court in Toledo and consisting of an endless series of amorous complications and confusions.

It is Sor Juana's love poetry that has inspired much speculation as to possible amorous liaisons during her pre-convent days at court. This of course says as much about her critics and biographers as it does about Sor Juana herself. But she had obviously acquainted herself with the posturing and intrigues of courtly love. The power of fantasy is the principal theme of her most celebrated love poem, the sonnet "Detente, sombra de mi bien esquivo" (Stop, shadow of my elusive joy; 1692). Her preoccupation with the interaction of rational faculties and irrational passions is apparent in the poem "En que describe racionalmente los efectos irracionales del amor" (In which are described rationally the irrational effects of love; 1692). The struggle between reason and passion, the relative merits of possession and nonposession, is a frequent theme, as in the sonnet "Al que ingrato me deja, busco amante" (I seek lovingly the one who ungratefully abandons me; 1689). This poem is among those which best reveal Sor Juana's not infrequent disgust for the pettiness of human affairs generally. It does little to disguise a self-assuredness, pretended or real, which borders on arrogance, vanity, and implied condescension. For Sor Juana unrequitedness is "the most sublime quality of love." This notion of noncorrespondence as the height of love is present in her love poems, in her poems on loving friendship, and even in writings on divine love or of a theological bent such as the *Carta atenagórica*. There is some heresy in all this, especially as it concerns divine love: the temptation of self-divinization, of which Sor Juana may not have been fully conscious, is a definite undercurrent in such works.

Among Sor Juana's moral and philosophical poems, the most memorable are the celebrated satirical invective that begins "Hombres necios," and two sonnets that refer indirectly to art. The first, "Este que ves, engaño colorido" (This colorful deception that you see; 1689), is an attack on the immortalizing pretensions of painting, though part of its beauty is that it can be read as a variant on the poetic topic of the ephemeralness of physical beauty, combined with a defense of the intellectual and spiritual life that is indirectly a defense of her own writing.

The great majority of Sor Juana's verse is comprised of occasional pieces: she wrote for the church and she wrote for the court. Indeed, her skill in serving—we might say flattering and manipulating—the authorities probably goes some way toward explaining how her freedom to write and exist as public figure lasted as long as it did. She was especially adept, for example, at the *villancico*, a popular poetic form used for religious festivities. Her most ambitious poetic composition, at once her most celebrated and most maligned, she claimed in the *Respuesta* was the only one she undertook of her own volition: the extensive *silva* (medieval verse form) *Primero sueño* (First Dream; 1692). The strange confluence in her figure of conformism and rebellion/alienation are well represented in this masterpiece, an extremely difficult composition. Stylistically, the poem reflects the fashion of the times; but in the subject matter and its treatment Sor Juana breaks with conventional wisdom. The *Primero sueño* could be considered the complement of her famous *Respuesta*: both deal with the ardent search for knowledge, to some degree independent of Catholic orthodoxy, the latter in the space of a lifetime, the former in the poetically condensed span of a single night. In both works, Sor Juana anticipates the modern spirit's Nietzschean interpretation of human tragedy, recognizing the limits of reason even before reason had become fashionable.

Sor Juana was a legendary figure of her time, not only in her native Mexico but in the Spanish mainland as well. It was in Spain that her works were collected for publication, the first volume being the *Inundación castálida* (Museful Inundation; 1689). In the eighteenth and nineteenth centuries, as was the fate of most Baroque literature, Sor Juana's literary corpus was systematically ignored. Her twentieth-century revival in Mexico, owing in large measure to the group known as the Contemporáneos (Contemporaries), is attributable to the affinities modern and contemporary writers have discovered in her example. She has of course also been an inspiration to many twentieth-century feminist authors, just as she herself found encouragement in female predecessors from classical and Biblical times.

The eighteenth century in Mexico, like the sixteenth, though for rather different reasons, was not a strong one in purely imaginative literature. The unique circumstance and genius of Sor Juana was not to be repeated, though the theological obfuscation and Baroque conceit which she enlivened was endlessly imitated by idle clerics and academics. If the new ideas of Neoclassical humanism of the French Enlightenment were slow to penetrate in the Spanish mainland, it might be expected that this was even more the case in the colonies. But penetrate they did, in some senses yet more deeply than in Spain. Popular Spanish culture did not have the roots in New Spain that it had in the Peninsula. Literary culture was still more of an aristocratic and ecclesiastic preserve in the New World. Latin, for example, as if to compensate for real or imagined cultural inferiority, was more firmly rooted than in Spain. These circumstances make less surprising the fact that the new poetry that did appear in the eighteenth century was of a classical vein and commonly composed in Latin. These poets established the precedents which later the more popular Spanish-language classicists José Manuel Martínez de Navarrete (1768-1809) and Francisco Manuel Sánchez de Tagle (1782-1849) would follow, continuing the Mexican poetic tradition and carrying the Neoclassical style into the nineteenth century.

Other than the Latinate poetry, the most notable works of the Mexican eighteenth century were in the areas of historiography and philology. Though with its counterreformist climate the century could not be described as scientific in New Spain, it did seek to be enlightened and encyclopedic. Of special interest for their nationalist inspiration are two ambitious bibliographical compendiums: the unfinished *Biblioteca Mexicana* (Mexican Library; 1755), composed in Latin by Juan José de Eguiara y Eguren's (1696-1763), and the *Biblioteca hispano-americana septentrional* (Northern Hispanic-American Library; 1816-1821) by José Mariano Beristáin y Souza (1756-1817). That Eguiara y Eguren wrote his work in Latin is not necessarily, as might first be supposed, a sign of elitism or anti-Hispanic sentiment. Quite the contrary, it may be read as part of a continuing, strategic defense of New World intellectualism.

As the eighteenth century came to a close, problems at home gradually weakened the Spanish hold on the colonies. Inquisitorial censorship, schizophrenically, became alternately lax and aberrantly harsh. While in Spain French Enlightenment ideas were mostly unacceptable, in the New World they harmonized better with anti-Spanish sentiment, which had been present in some form from the first days of colonial rule. Humanist rationalism and political liberalism would come together in the formation of the precursors and protagonists of the Mexican independence movement.

IV

The Creoles and mestizos who led the independence movement were ill-prepared to form or implement a government. In Mexico, as in Spain and the rest of Latin America, conflict between liberal and conservative factions, insurrection, and veritable civil war were at first the rule rather than the exception. During the first half of the nineteenth century, to the disgrace of most Mexicans, considerable territories were lost to the United States. General Santa Anna, several times enthroned only to be subsequently deposed, alternately and simultaneously a national hero and a villain, epitomizes these turbulent times. In 1857 a group of liberals led by Benito Juárez succeeds in promulgating a progressive, democratic constitution, only to have the conservatives plot the French Intervention in 1862. With the expulsion in 1867 of Maximilian of Austria, the liberals finally won out. Relative political stability and economic development through foreign investment characterize the iron-hand "progressive" regime of Porfirio Díaz. Díaz ruled Mexico from 1876 until the revolution his authoritarianism inspired broke out in 1910.

Mexican literature, strictly speaking, was born with the independence movement just after the turn of the century. If we are discussing a "national" literature, our criterion is primarily a political one, and there can be no genuine Mexican literature until a Mexican nation has been constituted, or at least consciously postulated. Notwithstanding the importance of the pre-Hispanic and the colonial past, it is not too much of an exaggeration to say that Mexican literature at the start of the nineteenth century had to begin with a tabula rasa. It was not to be Indian nor was it to be Spanish; it was to be a third thing, a self-conscious child of this mixed parentage. The nineteenth century is a formative period for Mexican letters: tentative, stumbling and finally, all too sure of itself, self-sustaining by century's end.

It is convenient to divide the cultural history of nineteenth-century Mexico into three periods. The first runs from 1810 to 1836 and includes the literary protagonists of the independence sentiment. Using the terms in a very broad, unpolemical sense, the second period is that of the first or adolescent Romantic generation (1836-67), which assimilates in Mexico the European Romantic school. The final period, 1867-1910, represents the second or mature Romantic generation, and witnesses the arrival of Realism, Naturalism, and finally the emergence of Spanish-American *modernismo* (Modernism, but in the sense of French Parnassianism and Symbolism).

The literary heritage during the years of the independence struggle was Neoclassical. Yet there is an air to the literary production of the years 1810-1836 of remarkable originality and autonomy, as poorly assimilated Neoclassicism adapts itself to the peculiarly Mexican circumstance. Literature, as life, takes on a suddenly urgent political character, both as a response to and a cause of extraliterary circumstances. Modern literature in Mexico is born simultaneously with the need to nationalize and popularize the cultural sphere. A Romantic spirit can be discerned in the literature of this period, before Romanticism as a general movement in Western literature had formally arrived on the continent.

José Joaquín Fernández de Lizardi (1776-1827) is a truly revolutionary figure. Significantly, however, the revolutionary character of his life and work is not found in the specific political content that his actions and his writing may have had, but in the strength of his convictions and his formal intentions: he worked to transform the place and function of literature in Mexican society, and thereby to transform and revolutionize society itself. Fernández de Lizardi is known as El Pensador Mexicano (The Mexican Thinker), a pseudonym taken from the title of the most famous of the several newspapers he created and sustained during his lifetime, this one lasting from 1812 to 1814. As a liberal reformer, moralist, and patriotic supporter of the independence movement, Fernández de Lizardi's first and strongest calling was as a journalist. Indeed, the importance of the printing press and of its prodigal son, the newspaper, cannot be overemphasized during this period of Mexican history. Carlos Monsiváis has gone so far as to suggest that journalism was the constitutive instrument of the new nation, and in this regard Fernández de Lizardi is more than representative. When the Pan-Hispanic Courts in Cádiz pronounced the freedom of the press, Fernández de Lizardi was among the first to take advantage of the newly declared civil rights. He was a prolific author; a devoted, full-time, professional writer before such a thing existed in Mexico. Besides his journalism, he essayed poetry, wrote for the theater, and produced four works of fiction.

Fernández de Lizardi's prominent place in Mexican literary history is owing primarily to the first of his novelistic undertakings, *El Periquillo Sarniento* (*The Itching Parrot*; 1816, 1830-31). That he understood the power and the possibilities of the printed word is apparent in the prologue to this his most famous work. Fernández de Lizardi laments the scarcity of books in New Spain, and the high cost of printing and importation (one arm of the repression exercised by colonial authorities). He dedicates *El Periquillo Sarniento* not to any patron from whom he seeks favor, but to his readers, a move that only the technology of the printing press could allow. Fernández de Lizardi was a party to Mexico's independence, but he understood full well that independence in itself would not go very far toward satisfying Mexico's most urgent needs. He did not seek to entertain the colonial nobility, but to enlighten the masses of Mexicans whose toil had stocked the cupboards of that nobility—at least those of the masses who could read or would lend an ear as his works were read aloud. It is commonplace to suggest that Fernández de Lizardi turned to the novel from journalism as a means of deceiving the scrutiny of the censors. But there is little direct political content in the novel. It may be that Fernández de Lizardi chose the novel as a variant vehicle of expression, more effective in a broadly political sense precisely because its lessons are shrouded in the guise of entertainment.

Periquillo is a first-person narrator-protagonist; from his death bed he narrates the story of his life so that his children may learn from the errors of his ways. The numerous didactic passages are so excessive and superfluous that they become humorous. They transform Periquillo into an almost comic figure, distracting the reader from the lessons he ostensibly wants to teach. Of course the *Periquillo* is a product of its age. The scholasticism and encyclopedic humanism predominant in the second half of the eighteenth century are apparent in the constant recourse to classical and Neoclassical sources. Many critics, furthermore, proclaim the *Periquillo* a realistic depiction of Mexico City and a compendium of the customs and habits of the life of the times, though the author's intentions were surely other. He was a moralist and, rather ahead of his time, a sociologist of sorts. The narrator-protagonist recognizes that he himself must bear the final responsibility for what he is, but more frequently he indicts those around him, his environment and surroundings. Indeed, the *Periquillo*, which adapts the Spanish picaresque format, is a sort of Bildungsroman gone astray: society at large is more the protagonist than is the not-so-humble narrator. For all this, and in spite of the digressions, the *Periquillo* maintains an actuality and an enlightened air which many subsequent nineteenth-century novels fail to sustain.

V

The years 1836-67 are ones of tumultuous political activity, or anarchy. All men of letters are also men of action, either publicly or privately (women being largely excepted from these spheres). But at the same time there is a marked divorce between politics and Belles Lettres, between creativity and political statement. Imaginative literature has almost no explicit political content; yet cultural actors are sharply, polemically divided into conservatives (classicists) and liberals (Romantics), in emulation of the two factions disputing political power at the time. On the one hand, in theory and in public polemic, there are two diametrically opposed ways of conceiving literature, as Neoclassicism and Romanticism battle for supremacy on the Mexican cultural scene; on the other hand, in practice, an unstable mixture of classic and Romantic tendencies is almost uniformly observed. Literature was rarely seen as a real means of direct action. It is this implied attitude that Ignacio Altamirano, as leader of the second Romantic generation, will seek to combat. Few if any authors during this period achieve the ideological decisiveness of Fernández de Lizardi. Intuitively rather than programmatically, writers move toward a sort of acritical nationalism. The project knowingly or not, is double: a national, decolonized, autonomous literature must be created, but the need is also felt to construct literature that is "illustrated" (i.e., that will illustrate), that will be (will make) modern. The program, not unique to Mexico at the time, though acute, is to cultivate an audience to match the capabilities opened up by their newly liberated printing presses. Illustrated magazines, following the European lead, began to flourish during these years. The writers, transparently disguised behind initials and pseudonyms, were men; the readers, ostensibly if not in actuality, were women. For whatever reasons, undoubtedly quite diverse, "serious" men tended not to sign their real names to their literary creations. Imaginative literature, to some degree, still had a dubious reputation. These literary miscellanies were highly popular in the 1840s and 1850s: *Calendario de las señoritas mexicanas* (Young Mexican Misses' Calendar; 1838-41), *Semana de las señoritas mexicanas* (Young Mexican Misses' Weekly; 1841-42), and many others were published in installments and sold by subscription or at the newsstand. Soon more serious and nation-conscious publications appeared, such as the *Revista científica y literaria* (Scientific and Literary Review; 1845-46) and *La ilustración mexicana* (The Mexican Illustration; 1851-55), no longer explicitly directed to a female audience. These publications were the major organ of diffusion for all of the writers of the time.

It is the novel, prose fiction, which on the strength of Fernández de Lizardi's example will slowly emerge during the nineteenth century to forge a critical, national identity. The novel is best able to do this partly because it has little colonial past to exorcise. Theater, by way of contrast, throughout the nineteenth century will remain a colonial venture. Poetry, building upon and adapting its rich colonial heritage, will culminate at the end of the nineteenth century in Spanish-American Modernism, reputed to be the first autonomous literary school to originate on Latin American soil. It is perhaps true, from a purely aesthetic vantage point, that no worthwhile poets surface in the years spanning the death of Sor Juana and the birth of Modernism. But poetry in the nineteenth century, as a genre with an established public, had definite social functions to fulfill.

Manuel Carpio (1791-1860) and José Joaquín Pesado (1801-61) are the representative classicists of early nineteenth-century poetry. To the degree they did not take up the civic or patriotic banner, they maintain with their poetry a colonial, Neoclassical status quo, if they do not simply represent a recapitulation. That they were relatively popular poets perhaps emphasizes that society and culture were not revolutionized overnight with political independence. Poetry continues to defend and uphold traditional values; to educate sentimentally and emotionally, religiously and morally.

Ignacio Rodríguez Galván (1816-42) wrote some drama in verse and numerous short stories and custom sketches. He is one of the first unambiguous Romantics in Mexican poetry: syntax and lexicon become less convoluted; the mythological, Biblical, and allegorical references tend to disappear; the classic sonnet and *silva* forms come more and more to be replaced by the popular, eight-syllable *romance* verse. Personal or civic glorification, amorous or patriotic lament come to predominate in theme and tone. We find sincere expression of personal sentiments and an authentic nationalism, which at times even adopts a critical attitude. In Rodríguez Galván's patriotic composition "Profecía de Guatimoc" (Cuauhtémoc's Prophecy; 1851) the Aztec historical figure incarnates the poet's own longings, apprehensions, and sufferings. The poem oscillates between pessimism and optimism, the former based on imperfect human nature and on past histories of imperialism and repression, the latter on the recognition of historical cycles of renewal and possible vengeance. The recurrence to pre-Colombian figures was common at this time even among conservative and classicist poets: Pesado, with his collection entitled *Los aztecas* (The Aztecs; 1854), is considered the initiator of the indigenous subgenre of poetry. Recourse to pre-Hispanic figures was perhaps an effective tactic for a nation seeking to establish an autonomous identity and circumvent its colonial past.

Literarily, Ignacio Ramírez (1818-79) provides the best confirmation of the danger of hastily lumping nineteenth-century Mexican poets into either the classic or Romantic camps and of the equally risky correlations conservative-classic, liberal-Romantic. Ramírez, like his contemporary Guillermo Prieto (1818-97), lived a full life, dedicated more to politics and pedagogy than to literature. In politics Ramírez was a staunch liberal who combated vigorously the colonial mind-set and the power of the clergy. But his poetic output tended more toward the classicist. Prieto, for his part, is to this day called the National Poet and with good reason. He brought to poetry the nationalism of acritical sympathy and gentle satire which carries over into the *costumbrismo* (Costumbrism, the representation of local color and customs) of much of the prose fiction of the time. In his dedicated populism, though not in his acritical approach, he represents the most direct continuation of the spirit and intentions of Fernández de Lizardi.

There is a freshness and a vitality—that of treading on uncharted terrain—in the prose fiction of the early nineteenth century which is lacking in the poetry of the same period. Of course this contrast is partly inherent in the nature of the two genres. The novel is a less structured, conventionalized, and regulated form than was poetry. Where Lizardi had adapted the Spanish picaresque tradition, his successors in Mexico would adapt primarily the *costumbrista* sketch, modeled after such Spanish Romantics as Mesonero Romanos and Mariano José de Larra. These sketches appeared in most of the literary magazines of the nineteenth century from the late thirties on. In Mexico the tone was mostly sympathetic when not frankly paternalistic, though in the hands of such practitioners as the aforementioned Prieto, Francisco Zarco (1829-69), and José de Tomás Cuellar (1830-94), they approached the biting satire and ingenious wit of the pen of Larra.

The early prose works were very loosely organized constructs. Many of the early novels were published and sold in periodical installments at the newsstand, as was the case of *El fistol del diablo* (The Devil's Tie Tack; 1845-46) by Manuel Payno (1810-94) which appeared in the *Revista científica y literaria*. It is a commonplace to affirm that interest today in these novels can only be documentary. They are, in fact, a registry of people, places, customs, and usages. But they are also a document of another sort, as evidence of the state of development of the novel (or lack thereof) as a vehicle for aesthetic and ideological expression. There is little notion of the novel as a unified aesthetic form, nor could there be given the serial nature of the work's transmission. These works' effective unity derives from the continuous presence of the story-teller, and they surreptitiously fulfill their ideological function by placing a mirror of words before the reader: the implicit message is simply that the Mexican is a subject worthy of literary portrayal.

Juan Díaz Covarrubias (1837-59) was a prolific writer, producing five works of fiction before his untimely death. A man of action, his work nonetheless reveals an esthetic awareness, a consciousness of the peculiar functions and possibilities of literature, uncommon among his contemporaries. His best-known work is the Romantic historical novel *Gil Gómez el Insurgente o la hija del médico* (Gil Gómez the Insurgent, or the Doctor's Daughter; 1859). In the prologue the author reveals his decision to abandon poetry, at least momentarily. So exaggerated and full of vice were his poems, he claimed, that they could not help but to sow bad seeds among the youth. Instead he proposes to take up the historical novel as more edifying and as a better test of his strengths. All this foreshadows a common metaphor of the rhetoric of the late nineteenth-century novel, whereby poetry is linked to frivolity, idealization, and emotive hyperbole. In spite of his announced intentions, Díaz Covarrubias's descriptions have much the air of full-blown Romantic poetry. His is a delicate sensibility, and his pretensions to literary sophistication are apparent in his name-dropping references to Mexican and European literary figures of the age. No effort is made to interpose a fictional persona as narrator between author and reader. Quite the contrary, the naming of the author's father erases any possible doubt as to the identity of biographic author and narrating entity. Though utilization of the printing press was slowly revolutionizing the concept and social function of literature, it remained a personalized, "oral" institution. Authors and audiences had not yet grown accustomed to the distancing inherent in the mass transmission of the printed word. It was more appropriate to present standardized (idealized) types that were easily identifiable, so as to educate morally and sentimentally; to forge a national identity and so foment confidence and pride. The time for subtle distinctions and critical discernment had not yet arrived. As was common, the novel *Gil Gómez* develops two largely independent story lines, one public or social/political; the other private and amorous, which converge only by means of extraordinary twists to the plot.

Luis G. Inclán (1816-75), not a statesman but a rural type, is the author of a single, rather unique work of prose fiction, *Astucia* (The Shrewd One; 1865). The work is uncommon, among other things, for its natural and unpretentious form of expression, which does not preclude its possible ideological impact but, quite the contrary, tends to heighten it. It is a *costumbrista* sketch, strongly nationalist as these writings often were, which treats Mexican rural life (the state of Michoacán) and revolves around the traffic of contraband tobacco. Though the characters lack the complexity of emotion and motivation of those of Fernández de Lizardi's *Periquillo*, Inclán fairly well avoids the heavy-handedness of the Pensador's moralizing, in part by transmitting the didactic element (ethics, morals, and especially educational psychology) through the protagon-

ist's teachers. Typically, the basic conflict is between unequivocal good
and evil, heroes and villains. There is, however, within the "good" camp
a sort of subconflict which generates no small interest through several
metaphoric variations: common sense versus scholasticism; individual
versus society; anarchy versus law. Overall, the author favors the popular
wisdom, individual honor, and anarchy (freedom) embodied by the novel's heroes, but the author's attitude is not overly one-sided nor unambiguous. In the world of *Astucia*, individuals and informal rural communities tend to be trustworthy and honorable; cities, governments, and officially underwritten business are more likely than not corrupt. Inclán is
one of the few in the generally insecure and uncertain cultural ambience
of the time to suggest that civilization and illustration corrupt; one of the
few to valorize the simplicity and natural goodness of the rural setting
(barbarism); one of the few to do so in Mexico long before disillusionment with the notions of progress, reason, and civilization would become
fashionable. In this paradoxical sense, beyond the general tedium the
work presents for contemporary tastes, Inclán's *Astucia* can come across
as curiously enlightened.

VI

In the political sphere, relative stability and tranquility characterize
the "second half" of the nineteenth century, the years 1867 to 1910. In
literature there is a movement away from the divorce of political expression and imaginative literature and a coincident reconciliation of conservative and liberal cultural actors. A more refined and critical attitude
makes itself apparent as exaltant and naive nationalisms waver. Realist
and Naturalist, Parnassian and Symbolist literary currents are incorporated in unique and peculiar ways to the "romanticism" seemingly congenial
to the Mexican character. Be it effect or cause of the political climate,
there appears a growing maturity and responsibility in the cultural
sphere. Writers seem much less torn individually between arms and
letters. Literature is less and less an activity unworthy of serious public
attention. As the cultural sphere becomes more unified (professionaliz-
ed), writers of literature tend to be journalists and educators rather than
politicians. There is, on the one hand, a qualitative and quantitative
flowering of literature and a noticeable diversity and independence of
tendencies. Yet many trends from the first half of the century endure
and stand alongside newer developments. Three outstanding magazines

represent admirably the literary culture of this period: *El renacimiento* (The Renascence; 1869), the *Revista azul* (Blue Review; 1894-1896), and the *Revista moderna* (Modern Review; 1898-1911). Eons seem to separate these literary periodicals from their predecessors of the thirties, forties, and fifties, beginning with the fact that their attention was focused almost entirely on literary culture. Their format, style, and tone are modern, indeed still contemporary, and they set a standard which many literary periodicals today still seek to emulate.

El renacimiento was the brainchild of Ignacio M. Altamirano (1834-93). He was a student of Ignacio Ramírez at the Instituto Literario de Toluca, a school set up at Ramírez's instigation to educate promising students of Indian heritage and one indication that some progress towards a native nationalism had been made. Altamirano is often mentioned in the same breath with national hero Benito Juárez, his counterpart in the political sphere. Both were leaders of the Reform movement and fervent combatants of the French Intervention. Altamirano was a sort of jack-of-all-trades: he wrote poetry, fiction, *costumbrista* sketches, and copious essays and literary criticism. Most importantly, he was one of the first in Mexico to take literature seriously enough to espouse and defend a national literary program, one of the first to really appreciate the social function and ideological implications of literature as institution, above and beyond any specific social or political content it might articulate. He sought to free literature from the factionalism of naive and superficial political involvement, and in the pages of *El renacimiento*, writers of all political persuasions were welcomed. His program was in some respects outdated, in others ahead of its time. The national or Mexican side of the Mexican national literature he sought to foment had already largely been conquered, but in emphasizing also the literature side of the equation he unwittingly forecast the Modernist movement that was shortly to unfold.

La navidad en las montañas (*Christmas in the Mountains*; 1870) and *El Zarco* (*El Zarco, the Bandit*; 1901) are Altamirano's most popular works of fiction. But it is the example of his *Clemencia* (1869), first published in *El renacimiento*, which carries the novel in Mexico forward. *La navidad en las montañas* is a tender custom sketch of the simple life and traditional values. *El Zarco* provides a perspective on banditry diametrically opposed to that of Inclán's *Astucia*, consequent with Altamirano's "illustration" ideology. *Clemencia*, in substance, is conservative to the point of being reactionary. The character Valle represents a defense of Romantic literature for its embodiment of traditional moral values and ideals (patriotism, stoicism, unselfishness, "heart and soul"), at a time when some writers were turning away from Romantic idealization and hyperbole. But in form *Clemencia* is a much more sophisticated novelistic construction than any of its predecessors in Mexico. It follows a premeditated plan and is tightly structured, with its political and sentimental threads tightly woven. As in *El Zarco*, the moral of the story is presented through a clear demarcation of good and evil, embodied in contrasting characters; but the presentation is made much more subtle by the careful, if somewhat obvious, use of irony, suspense, foreboding, and recurrence. Clemencia is the more complex character whose destiny we follow, as she is torn between glamorous appearance (Flores) and moral integrity (Valle). Also noteworthy in *Clemencia* is the artistic self-consciousness apparent in the story's framing device: the novel is presented as the written record of an oral account, thus synthetically dramatizing one important aspect of the transition from pre-modern to modern literature that, in a word, is nineteenth-century literature in Mexico.

Altamirano's example clearly indicates a growing esthetic awareness and cultural sophistication in Mexico. Poets Manuel M. Flores (1840-85) and Manuel Acuña (1849-73) literally lived the Romantic ideals of metaphysical angst and amorous passion. They represent the culmination, if not the last exhalation, of the virtues and the vices of Romantic verse in Mexico. They also point the way to future developments with their crepuscular tone. Other writers, in contrast, serve to underscore that the Mexican literary scene was by no means transformed overnight. In the case of poet Juan de Dios Peza (1852-1910) the coincidence of traditional, Romantic nationalism and the coming waves of more cosmopolitan sophistication carried by Modernism and Realism/Naturalism is marked. Revered by the general public, Dios Peza came to be sharply censored by many national critics with literary pretensions, perhaps out of resentment of his popularity. He was a prolific and seemingly natural poet whose use of everyday language avoided the rhetorical excesses of many of his contemporaries. Neither a hapless romantic nor an ardent reformer, Dios Peza was an unceremonious defender of traditional values: patriotism, religion, and the family. Few Mexican poets have been so popular and widely read, abroad as well as at home.

The popularity of Costumbrism endured. Manuel Payno published *Los bandidos de Río Frío* (The Bandits of Río Frío; 1889-91) serially in Spain. In temperament this novel repeats his *El fistol del diablo* of fifty years earlier. If we had only Payno to judge by, we might conclude that little had happened in Mexico, literarily, during those intervening years. There was still a considerable public, at home and abroad, for the quaintness and provincialism that Payno's writing involves. It is common to affirm that Payno's is the most complete and detailed portrait of Mexican society of the nineteenth century. The detail and variety of his "slices of life" do seem infinite, and the work exemplifies well the self-satisfied excesses of this practice of writing. But there is in Payno no concern for the creation of a unified aesthetic object: each group of chapters is essentially an independent unit with a similar structure of development. The real hero and unifying element is the indefatigable storyteller and painter of social customs. What nuance there is grows out of the subtle oscillation between tender sympathy for the people, places, and customs inventoried on the one hand, and the much less heart-felt charge of "illustrating," of rectifying superstition, vice, and ignorance on the other.

For Emilio Rabasa (1856-1930), a distinguished lawyer, literature seems to have had still the taint of second-class citizenship. Under the pseudonym Sancho Polo, he produced in a two-year span a tetralogy of so-called *Novelas mexicanas* (Mexican Novels): *La bola* (Banditry; 1877), *La gran ciencia* (The Grand Science; 1877), *El cuarto poder* (The Fourth Power; 1888), *Moneda falsa* (Counterfeit Currency; 1888). These four works have a common narrator-protagonist and a definite continuity of action. But with the exception of the novella *La guerra de tres años* (The Three-Years War; 1891), published serially, he did not again write imaginative literature.

It is perhaps an exaggeration to see in Rabasa the originator of the Realistic novel in Mexico, but his series of novels represents a definite transition in the evolution of Mexican prose fiction. Not since Fernández de Lizardi's *Periquillo* had the novel in Mexico adopted the constructively critical stance it assumes with Rabasa. Moreover, Rabasa's four novels have in common with the *Periquillo* the utilization of a first-person narrator-protagonist. The technique allows Rabasa as author to distance himself from the narrator, while permitting the latter to move closer to the characters that surround him as protagonist. The move is strategic, perhaps unwittingly. Paradoxically, the novels can be more truly critical because they have their basis in a certain egalitarianism, not a fixed author-character relationship of control and subordination. It is as if the anticolonial, liberal reformist attitudes which surfaced in the independence movement had finally found themselves manifest in literary expression.

Objectivity and removal of the intrusive presence of the author-narrator were tenets of Realism with which Mexican authors invariably had difficulty complying. Rabasa's creation of a first-person narrator-protagonist, atypical of the Realist school, was an effective compromise between the newly fashionable objectivism and the more subjective, oral story-telling mode favored at the time in Mexico. Because narrator Quiñones is a fictional actor who confesses his passions, vacillations, doubts, and remorse, these works are by today's standards among the most readable that were produced in the Mexican nineteenth century.

The third part of the tetralogy, *El cuarto poder*, is set in Mexico City, where the protagonists' ambitions have carried him. It is thematically of special interest for its exposé on the "power of the press" and as an artistic denunciation of "unchained passions, ambitions without measure, envy, dishonesty, farce." Rabasa's largely implicit criticism transcends contemporary partisan lines and factional disputes. Left behind as well is the acritical nationalism that predominates in earlier narrative efforts. Prose fiction is not only showing signs of sophistication, which had formerly been the province of poetry in Mexican literature. Prose fiction is in fact liberating a critical ideological struggle against the Romantic, poetic sensibility that permeates the Mexican nineteenth century. That Rabasa is conscious of the dialectic interaction of aesthetics and ideology is clear in one of the unifying threads that runs throughout the Novelas Mexicanas: provincialism, unabashed idealization, and the Romantic sensibility are linked to poetry as a form of expression opposed by the modern metropolis and the stark verism that is the corresponding province of prose fiction. Much of the complexity and subtlety of the Novelas Mexicanas derives from Quiñones's interior struggle between his heart (poetry), which holds out a certain naive faith in provincial simplicity and idealism; and his head (prose), which is overrun by the images of brutality that surround him.

The criticisms implicit in the Novelas Mexicanas are leveled primarily at the vices and corruption of individuals of the middle and upper classes. The disenfranchised masses have little part in the society Rabasa depicts, and there is no evidence of the truly sociological awareness glimpsed in Fernández de Lizardi's *Periquillo*, which exposed the dialectical relationship between the subject and the system, between the individual and his environment. Nonetheless, by means of certain strategic choices, Rabasa did manage to move beyond the mixture of condescension and sympathy that two other Mexican Realist novelists, José López Portillo y Rojas (1850-1923) and Rafael Delgado (1853-1914), carry over from the acritical nationalism of Romantic prose-fiction. In general, stylistic and tonal tastes are changing; authors and audiences have developed a certain sophistication. López Portillo and Delgado are more artistically enlightened than the great majority of their predecessors; they have a clear understanding of the aesthetic object as premeditated form and proportional structure. But the problem from an ideologically liberal or radical position is that author and audience seem to want to glory in their "sophistication," which they confirm formally by maintaining a certain superiority over the characters they (re)create: author and reader remain outside the fiction, allowing them implicitly to cast judgment on it at will. As a novelist López Portillo stands for traditional Christian morality, individualism, and certain forms of social and economic progress ("modernization"). These values, together with the general tone of naive sympathy and undisguised condescension that color his presentations of the popular classes, are all readily apparent in such short stories as "La horma de su zapato" (The Measure of the Shoe; 1903), and in the novels *La parcela* (A Piece of Land; 1898), *Los precursores* (The Predecessors; 1909), and *Fuertes y débiles* (The Strong and the Weak; 1919).

Delgado was more middle class than López Portillo, but the ideology that can be deduced from novels such as *La Calandria* (The Love-Bird; 1891) and *Los parientes ricos* (Rich Relatives; 1903) comes across just as staunchly traditional and conservative. In Delgado's narrative world the upper classes are generally ambitious, pretentious, and immoral; the middle classes, at least those that are not corrupted by the rich, are generally god-fearing and humble and expected to stay that way. The principal virtue of Delgado's prose lies in his powers of observation, his eye for color and for psychological and social detail in the provincial ambience in which he found solace.

A diluted Naturalism enters late nineteenth-century prose fiction. While aesthetic consciousness evidently continues to flower, naturalism's introduction marks a step backward to the degree in Mexico it translates as a partial revival of the excesses of the Romantic sensibility. This "faulty" assimilation of the structures of the Naturalist school, or of the Romantic school or the Realist school, need not imply inauthenticity, as is often suggested. The Mexican authors of the nineteenth century are to the last one "sincere": they are committed to their country, committed to their audience, committed to the causes of art and literary expression, or at least committed to themselves as artists. Their so-called inauthenticity is always an authentic expression of something: their struggle to be modern, their desire for literary sophistication, their commitment to enlighten their audience, or simply their effort to produce a good work of literature.

If we may judge by publishing history, no Mexican novel since Fernández de Lizardi's *Periquillo* was so widely read as *Santa* (1903) by Federico Gamboa (1864-1939). Gamboa's writing invariably deals with that explosive pair of misfits, sexuality and morality. These are subjects capable of attracting a wide readership, but refined sensibility in these matters easily crosses over for particular readers into deplorable licentiousness. At times Gamboa shows keen psychological insight into human nature and motivation; at other times, his psychologizing is unplausible and his moralizing unconvincing. What is perhaps more interesting, in Gamboa as in Fernández de Lizardi, is how the seductiveness of descriptions of lascivious behavior can often subvert the moral which the tale was supposedly designed to illustrate, which may account for some part of their commercial appeal. If *Santa* invokes a surprising combination of naturalist determinism and Christian "liberation theology," Gamboa's second novel, *Suprema ley* (The Supreme Law; 1896), represents an unstable combination of Romantic, Realist, and Naturalist elements. The ostensible moral of the story is that (familial) love is the Supreme Law, but the story as a whole subverts this moral and suggests that passion and sexual desire are more powerful forces than social morality.

Heriberto Frías (1870-1925) was a poor man with a love for literature who entered Porfirio Díaz's army. It is to his military service that we owe his first and most notable novel, *Tomóchic*, which originally appeared anonymously in the opposition newspaper *El demócrata* from March to April of 1893. The novel recounts the army's extermination of the rebellious Indian village Tomóchic in northern Mexico during the final months of 1892. *Tomóchic* is an outstanding example of the mixture of European schools so characteristic of Mexican literary practice at the time. *Tomóchic* is Realist not in any Dickensian or Galdosian sense, but rather in its directness, in its economy of expression, and in its felt need to document an absolutely immediate reality. The novel is Romantic for its tragic love story, and in the characterization of the protagonist as a weak, solitary melancholic. It is Naturalist, finally, for the barbarism and melancholy which its desolate ambience supposedly inspires (determinism), and for the moral decay exposed in a scandalous case of incest. The work suffers somewhat for these excesses, perhaps concessions to contemporary literary fashion, or more likely, the trials of an inexperienced novelist who had something to say. *Tomóchic* understandably was an embarrassment for the Díaz government. Frias's attitude is sharply critical, but his implicit and explicit indictments are not onesided. He respects heroism, bravery, and humanitarianism on both sides. He abhors ineptness and corruption among the federal troops and the misguided (religious) fanaticism of the Tomochics. For all this, his work easily transcends the status of a simple partisan pamphlet. Frías's tone, style, and critical attitude are in retrospect highly reminiscent of those that will appear in Mariano Azuela's classic novel of the revolution, *Los de abajo* (see below).

While Frías and Gamboa in their novels seem to combine Naturalism with Romanticism in an improvisedly Realist manner, Amado Nervo (1870-1919) and Angel de Campo (1868-1908) demonstrate in their prose fiction that Naturalism and poetic Modernism are not as mutually exclusive as one might suspect. Nervo takes from Naturalism its interest in baser human passions and bodily drives, though he is mostly concerned with their psychological dimension in *El bachiller* (The Schoolboy; 1895) and *Pascual Aguilera* (1896). Campo takes from Naturalism a more than superficial interest, rather new in Mexican prose fiction, in the lower strata of the social scale in his novel *La rumba* (The Neighborhood; 1890) and in many of his short stories and sketches. Both enliven their prose with an eye for detail and a concern for style which come from their Modernist vein. The years of literary apprenticeship that are the nineteenth century for Mexico, in sum, are coming to fruition: long-sought artistic maturity appears as an indefinable mixture of Romanticism, Realism, and Naturalism that, much more than the sum of its parts, is always something other.

It is commonplace to attribute the development of Spanish-American Modernism to the influence of French poets. This asseveration is especially born out if Manuel Gutiérrez Nájera (1859-95) is considered both precursor and founder of the Modernist school in Mexico. But Spanish American Modernism also is a natural product of the native poetic evolution of Romanticism, as is apparent if one takes Salvador Díaz Mirón (1853-1928), an intuitive Modernist, as representative of the new style and sensibility.

Díaz Mirón wrote passionately, even when in the later part of his career as poet he sought to objectify or purify his verse. Expression of emotion always took precedent over poetic convention, even where he imposed upon himself severe formal constraint. His early poems are highly polished Romanticism. "A Gloria" (To Gloria; 1886) is interesting for the philosophical, psychological, and even sociological complexity which underlies the amorous thematics of its surface. There is a truly

Nietzschean quality to this work in the way the poet inverts explicitly the convention of the tragic love poem. Instead of lamenting obstacles, the poet affirms them with defiance, as a fortifying element: evil is the theater in which virtue is unleashed. The poem's popularity perhaps derives from its adherence to traditional, religious/mythic views on man's and woman's place in society. "El desertor" (The Deserter; 1895) and "Ejemplo" (Example; 1901) are significant for their treatment of a sociopolitical thematics. They indicate clearly the extent to which poetry had evolved in Mexico during the nineteenth century. Next to the total explicitness with which the common civic poems of the early nineteenth century expressed their patriotic praise or indignation, "El desertor" and "Ejemplo" prove the power of poetic condensation. "El desertor" uses brief, direct dialogue between a deserter and his military executioner to indirectly invoke the whole thematics of poverty and social dissidence. "Ejemplo" treats a similar theme by even more indirect means: the cadaver of a lynched man is described with repugnant, dehumanized images. In both poems the poetic effect is achieved with supreme efficiency: the tragic human element is contrasted with beautiful, yet totally indifferent natural surroundings—thus adding a metaphysical dimension to the poems' social and political elements. With Modernist poets such as Díaz Mirón, Mexican poetry has regained an affective quotient it had not seen since Sor Juana.

Fortunately for poetry, Díaz Mirón's zest for life tended to overpower his commitment to letters. Equally fortunate for poetry was Gutiérrez Nájera's commitment to writing and art. Gutiérrez Nájera represents one of the first cases in Mexican letters of the full-time, "professional" writer; ignoring all other pursuits, he began publishing at the tender age of thirteen. His vast production—criticism, custom and travel sketches, short stories (fantasies), and poetry—was written almost exclusively for newspapers and magazines. The style and substance of his work is marked by the indelible stamp impressed on it by his full-time dedication to literary pursuits. In "Non Omnis Moriar" (I Will Not Die Completely; 1896) the speaker evokes poetry as a form of immortality for himself and his beloved, poetry being no longer a way to instruct and delight, nor even seemingly any longer a part of the public domain. In "Para entonces," (By Then; 1896) the poet romantically invents for himself a young death, a death set not in the patriot's homeland, but in those immense poetic spaces, removed from human interaction, of sea and sky. Modernism's introversion as practiced by Gutiérrez Nájera is not directly nor unequivocally an effect of the Díaz regime, as is often suggested. But political stability did help the poet dedicate his energies fully to literature, and the relative prosperity of the times did make possible the consolidation of an audience receptive to the kind of literature Gutiérrez Nájera wrote, one with pretensions to European (especially French) refinement and sophistication, for example. It has quite perceptively been speculated that Gutiérrez Nájera's relationship with this audience was actually of the love-hate variety: he loved his public because it allowed him to make a living writing; but he simultaneously detested his dependence on an inferior reader. Above all, he plays with his audience. As he himself put it, he wanted to "bite with his lips." The emotions in his poetry, the angst in "To be" (1896) or the delightful frivolity of "La duquesa Job" (Duchess Job; 1896), always keep tongue in cheek.

Modernism unambiguously anticipates the alienation of the artist and the consequent gap between art and society, which to varying degrees will characterize most of twentieth-century Mexican literature. It is the final culmination of the assimilation of European Romanticism, if Romanticism represents a new, modern conception of literature as the original creation of an autonomous aesthetic object, with all the connotations of the "death of God" and his replacement by mortal man—preferably a poet—that this implies. Thus there is the musicality of the verse, the emphasis on color, the supernaturalism of synesthesia, and in general an emphasis on the image and its poetic effect. Gutiérrez Nájera's beautiful "De blanco" (On Whiteness; 1896) is a crowning decadent achievement, but above all simply a hymn to linguistic representation; an implicit, measured, but profound recognition of the power of symbolic action/creation. The Modernist poets often thought they were discovering the autonomy of literature, but they unwittingly confirm the ultimate impossibility of literature's autonomy. Díaz Mirón was a writer of sometimes violent exaltation and indignation who made poetry of action. Gutiérrez Nájera, a writer of exquisite refinement, alternately frivolous and melancholic, sacrificed his life to poetry. Together, Gutiérrez Nájera and Díaz Mirón form an intriguing pair that goes a long way toward revealing the multifarious yet ultimately unified phenomenon that Modernism was in Latin American poetry. Both are defiant and apparently self-assured, in life as in writing. Both are flamboyant and representative of what Modernism was in the broadest sense. For all its putatively European flair, Modernism represents nonetheless a significant liberation of the Latin American spirit.

VII

The social progress of the nineteenth century might be summed up in the following comparative generalization. The struggle for independence was led by Creoles and mestizos, a strange alliance of upper and middle elements of the social hierarchy. The revolution of 1910, on the other hand, was protagonized by mestizos and Indians who sought "freedom" from "independence." In other regards, the two rebellions were disconcertingly similar. Both were more spontaneous and fragmentary than premeditated or unified, encompassing uncertain mixtures of social, economic, and political dissatisfactions. Porfirio Díaz was quickly deposed, but the chaotic armed revolt endured through 1917 and beyond. The years 1920 to 1934 were ebullient ones in which the revolution's political machine was consolidated and a single-party, pseudodemocracy implemented. It was legendary President Lázaro Cárdenas (1934-40), the last of the military presidents, who succeeded in implementing many of the nationalist social reforms which had always been part of the revolution's rhetoric. Since 1940 Mexico's civilian leaders have generally emphasized modernization, industrialization, and economic development.

If the nineteenth is for Mexican literature a century of apprenticeship and formation, the twentieth century is one of experimentation and consolidation. Thanks in part to the aesthetic sophistication of Modernism and the thematically liberating cataclysm that was the revolution, literary imitation and borrowing become "optional" in the twentieth century, and they occur on an individual rather than a collective basis. A new cultural independence evolves in the twentieth century, partly symbolic and partly real, which coincides with the gradual consolidation of the social and political revolution.

Literary production in the twentieth century does not fall into the broad and relatively neat historical periods into which earlier efforts have over the years been channeled. This is partly a reflection of cultural and historic realities (confusion and multiplicity of influences and schools of practice; accelerated change), partly the result of a lack of historical perspective and canonical consensus. The year 1940, nonetheless, is a useful general period line for twentieth-century literary production in Mexico. In literature the years 1910 to 1940 are ones of self-definition and factional polemic. By 1940, postrevolutionary Mexico has established its character and a period of relative stability and consolidation is opened which propitiates appreciable growth.

It is noteworthy that the Mexican revolution of 1910 does not mark an abrupt change or a decisive interruption of Mexican literary development. Of course cultural activity was inconvenienced by the turmoil, but literature continued to be written and published. Intellectuals were for the most part not protagonists of the sociopolitical revolution, and literary activity during the years of the armed struggle rarely bore directly on the conflict itself. The so-called literature of the revolution was slow to appear, and very much after the fact.

The famous intellectual group known as the Ateneo de la Juventud, founded in 1909 and short-lived as a collective enterprise, is a case in point. Revolutionary intellectuals they were, but just plain revolutionaries they generally were not, even though their decisive public activity as a group exactly coincided with the birth of the political revolution. As a group their primary contributions were in the areas of philosophy and pedagogy: they argued for a reemphasis of the humanities and of the classics. The Ateneístas are widely credited with the professionalization of Mexican letters, but their contribution in this regard was not without precedent: specialization had become evident in several of the Modernist writers of the late nineteenth century, and various factors had already contributed to the break-up of the man of action/man of letters marriage characteristic of most of the nineteenth century. The Ateneístas continued and extended the Modernist enterprise, but they also modified it significantly by trading stridency and frivolity for a more stoic intellectual seriousness of social purpose. The value of their contribution was not fully recognized, could not be fully recognized, in a time when more passionate matters had the majority of the population enthralled.

What success the Ateneo did have in its time is owed in part to the diversity of interests of the individuals involved. None of the works of the Ateneo's individual members could be taken as representative of the whole. They were adept at fusing fiction and nonfiction, as in the narrative works of José Vasconcelos (1882-1959) and Martín Luis Guzmán (1887-1976); or poetry and prose, as in Alfonso Reyes (1889-1959) and Julio Torri (1889-1970). Their classicism is apparent in an undercurrent of longing for the purity, the innocence, the heroism of a bygone age. The Ateneístas were on the whole aristocrats of culture, elitists of a universalist and cosmopolitan bent. As a group they sided politically with the revolution at its outset, consequent with their criticism of positivism as official policy of the Díaz regime. When the stark realities of the political struggle become clear, however, their individualism and class interests shine through: the group dissolves, in part out of disillusionment and despair, in part because of the real impracticability of their grandiose cultural project amid the revolutionary chaos. Vasconcelos alone, with an army of mostly younger intellectuals, will attempt to adapt the cultural project to the revolutionary circumstance from his post as Secretary of Education.

A very different view of the beginnings of twentieth-century Mexican literature is obtained if the spotlight is thrown on two writers from the provinces, born and raised in the state of Jalisco. In many senses, Enrique González Martínez (1871-1952) and Mariano Azuela (1873-1952) are the real transition figures between the nineteenth and twentieth centuries in Mexican literature. They are more homespun Mexican than classicist; self-made writers (both were physicians) as opposed to professional intellectuals; "late bloomers" who were older than the precocious young Ateneístas. The literary heritage that they adopt and transform is not classical or European, but the more directly Latin-American one of Modernism in poetry and Realism/Naturalism in fiction.

González Martínez stands up for austerity and measure at a time when poetry was extravagant and politics corrupt and becoming chaotic. What he deplores in both is the moral decay that for him they reflect. He skillfully manipulated the new poetic forms in defense of traditional middle-class values. González Martínez is best known for the poem "Tuércele el cuello al cisne" (Wring the Swan's Neck; 1911), a literary manifesto in verse. Though by no means his best composition, it is an accurate characterization of the substance of his poetry. His opposition to Modernism, whose formal lessons he used to good advantage, is memorably summarized in his vivid juxtaposition of violence and refinement: twisting the neck of the Modernist swan. For González Martínez, Modernist poetry was admittedly graceful but in substance frivolous and purely decorative. Indignant, he opposed the owl to the swan, soulful depths to graceful superficiality. He frequently calls on the reader to accept the mysteries of life, and suggests the transcendence of vital oppositions in a sort of Platonic and pantheistic love, as in such poems as "Como hermana y hermano" (Like Sister and Brother; 1911) or "Romance del muerto vivo" (Romance of the Living Dead; 1939).

To Mariano Azuela can be ascribed many conservative, middle-class values similar to those of González Martínez. In 1908 Azuela immediately took up the cause of the revolution, traveling during the early years of the armed struggle through the central and northern provinces with various bands of soldiers. His most renowned novel, *Los de abajo* (*The Underdogs*), was first published in El Paso in 1915, but it was largely ignored until its rediscovery in 1924. Throughout his life Azuela was to remain on the fringes of the literary and political establishment. He often felt misunderstood and resentful, but his outsider status was in part a conscious choice of his own. Single-handedly the creator of the novel of the revolution, Azuela's most immediate predecessors in theme and technique were the Realist and Naturalist novelists of the late nineteenth and early twentieth century: Rabasa, López Portillo y Rojas, Gamboa, and especially Frías. The quantum leap Azuela gave to the novel seems more incidental than premeditated—this is part of its beauty—and can be ascribed to his profound commitment to literature, to his fierce non-conformism and individuality, to the obsessive strength of his moral convictions, and to his direct involvement in the revolutionary experience.

Azuela's first novels reveal his Naturalist roots and document his apprenticeship as novelist, establishing the social emphasis and the decidedly ethical bent of future efforts. With *Andrés Pérez, maderista* (Andrés Pérez, Madero Supporter; 1911), more a sketch than a full-fledged novel, he inaugurates the theme of the revolution. Its treatment of journalism is reminiscent of Rabasa's *El cuarto poder*, with obvious differences: the background love story in Azuela is treated cynically, not romantically, and Azuela's attack on contemporary politics is much more direct and urgent than Rabasa's.

For all its apparent immediacy, *Los de abajo* is nonetheless a carefully constructed novel. The critical success the novel eventually attained is owing not so much to its substance, rich and revealing though it may be. The real strength of the novel resides in its unwitting formal mimeticism: the episodic, discontinuous structure and the rapid, fervent style seem to incarnate the essence of the revolutionary movement. *Los de abajo* follows the participation in the revolution of a small rebel group from the central plateau. Though dates are not given, historical references can be retraced and the main action follows precisely, though selectively, the larger events of 1914 and 1915. The rebels are small landowners of the lower-middle classes. Demetrio Macías is their leader and the incorruptible hero of the story. The hypocritical ideologue Luis Cervantes serves as his social and moral counterpoint. More than the coherence of the storyline, Azuela emphasizes the attitudes of the characters, whom he characterizes through their words and actions in a series of powerfully direct, loosely connected episodes. It is clear that Azuela is in favor of what reform the revolution ideally represents. But the depth of his disillusionment with the barbarism, the opportunism, and the lack of respect for life and property among the revolutionaries, easily wins the day. The revolutionaries, who have lived by the sword, die by the sword one by one for their greed and moral bankruptcy. The intellectual Cervantes abandons the cause when the possibility of material gain presents itself. In the end, Macías returns alone to his point of origin; his moral strength and heroic death merit him a symbolic resurrection. The overall movement is cyclical; little has changed, and all efforts seem to have been for naught.

In 1916 Azuela settles in Mexico City to practice his profession and pursue his literary passion. *Los caciques* (The Bosses; 1917) and *Las moscas* (*The Flies*; 1918) round out Azuela's vision of the armed struggle, the former addressing its causes, the latter dealing more with its perverse effects. With the more hermetic style of *La malhora* (The Evil Hour; 1923), *El desquite* (Revenge; 1925), and *La luciérnaga* (Firefly; 1932), Azuela, still faithful to his convictions, anticipates the experimental techniques of the vanguard of the late twenties and early thirties. In subsequent novels Azuela pursues relentlessly his attack, never on the reformist ideals of the revolution as such, but on the corruption and immorality that permeate their practical implementation in leaders and common folk alike. Many of these are interesting and skillful works of fiction, though Azuela's insistent moralizing at times becomes overbearing. Arguably he himself, in his obsession with traditional moral values, is guilty of a nearsightedness similar to that of his revolutionaries in *Los de abajo*, incapable of envisioning the larger picture.

Like González Martínez and Azuela, Ramón López Velarde (1888-1921) was a product of the central provinces. Like them too, he traveled to Mexico City during the years of the revolution, seeking to make his mark in the cultural arena. Much as Azuela is the novelist of the revolution *par excellence*, López Velarde has been consecrated by posterity as the revolution's poetic bard, on the basis of such diverse compositions as the lamenting "Retorno maléfico" (Malefic Return; 1919) and the hermetically patriotic "Suave patria" (Tender Homeland; 1932). López Velarde is frequently classified as a Postmodernist, which in the Mexican context means that he serves as a bridge between the Modernist poets and the subsequent appearance of the so-called vanguard movements on Mexican terrain. López Velarde is not yet a truly modern poet, in the sense that Alfonso Reyes of the Ateneo, Juan José Tablada (1871-1945), and the vanguardists were or will be. He does not seek to move beyond traditional, middle-class values. Rather, he laments the fact that they are crumbling before his very eyes. His poetry is conservative and reactionary in more than the political sense: he seeks, nostalgically, to preserve the innocence of sensuality, the purity of youthful passion, and traditional domestic and religious values ("Hormigas" [Ants; 1919], "Todo" [Everything; 1919], "Mi prima Agueda" [My Cousin Agueda; 1916]); he reacts against change, destruction, disillusion, and the inexorable march of time ("Retorno maléfico"). The accidental emergence of a new Mexico ("modern" after the fact) is vividly dramatized in López Velarde's verse. His intimate and seemingly intuitive poetic vocation combined the awareness of language and the skillful manipulation of poetic tropes that came from the Modernist poets with a thematics that was at once profoundly personal and uniquely Mexican.

Juan José Tablada is a curious figure in Mexican poetry, and he has been the object in recent years of a critical revaluation. Where López Velarde was his own poet, neither Modernist nor vanguard, Tablada, in the numerous stages of his work, literally traces the path that links the Modernist enterprise of the late nineteenth century and the vanguard poetry of the late 1920s and 1930s. His early poems are Modernist with a vengeance. In "Onix" (Onyx; 1899), his superficial humility is not convincing enough to hide the underlying arrogance. He exalts himself as poet, much in the Romantic spirit, while lamenting the turn-of-the-century loss of absolute values such as God and Country. Tablada was a cosmopolitan world traveler before cosmopolitanism's heyday in Mexico; he visited France, Japan, New York. In "Quinta Avenida" (Fifth Avenue; 1918), the cynicism shown toward *haut monde* decadence barely disguises decadence's power of attraction. Tablada's gusto for vanguard experimentalism is clear in other works: he brings from Japan the power of suggestion of the haiku, translating it into Spanish; later, he experiments with the graphic possibilities of poetry in poems of frivolous inebriation like "Li-Po" (1928).

The twenties and thirties are crucial years that establish the polemic poles around which Mexican literature has moved ever since. An invigoratingly absurd duel to the death was liberated between the cosmopolitan Contemporáneos group and a wide variety of literary nationalisms. Of course, the realities of the cultural scene were not so simple. Often the various nationalisms fought among themselves as much as they polemicized against the Contemporáneos group. There were the famous murals of the so-called Escuela Mexicana de Pintura (Mexican School of Painting) by Diego Rivera, Alfaro Siqueiros, José Clemente Orozco, and others that celebrated the revolution as a proletarian victory of epic proportions. Theirs were compositions based more on materialist, utopian myths than on contemporary realities. Painting a quite different version of events than that depicted in the murals, a veritable barrage of "novels of the revolution" appeared, inspired by the success of the Madrid edition of Azuela's *Los de abajo* in 1928. There arose for a time the Estridentistas (Stridentists). A truly vanguardist group, they published in sporadic and brief-lived reviews numerous literary manifestos and wrote poetry and novellas whose primary intention seemed to be to shock. They attempted to unite the two electrified poles of socialism and futurism, and in the end mostly got burned: they were too hermetic for the social realists and too naively proletarianist for the cosmopolitans. While the Estridentistas turned to the future, another group of writers turned to the colonial past for their material, publishing in the twenties a group of historical novels designed in their own way to support nationalist sentiment.

These factional struggles in the cultural arena pick up right where the late nineteenth-century debate between the Modernist poets and the nationalistic defenders of Realism, Naturalism, and Romantic Costumbrismo left off. The terms of the opposition were constantly being rewritten, the polemic forever being refined: regionalism and cosmopolitanism; nationalism and vanguardism; art for art's sake and sociopolitical commitment, ad infinitum. These cultural and ideological polemics became a sort of public spectacle during the formative years of the revolution's institutions. The diversity of contrasting cultural projects (many of the above) that were underwritten in these early, postrevolution years by the State, officially and unofficially, constitutes an astonishing testimony to the reigning ebullience of the time in the cultural sphere as in others. The past did seem to have been effectively annihilated, and the future needed only to be created. The times were propitious for idealists and opportunists alike. There existed no precedent in Mexico, no experienced hand, to put into practice the social and political system envisioned by the revolution's ex post facto intellectual authors. The past, as a consequence, was to appear again and again.

The Contemporáneos—their group name derives from the most famous of their cultural publications, the review *Contemporáneos* (Contemporaries; 1928-31)—were arguably the most innovative and controversial of all literary "generations" in the history of Mexican letters. They were active in all areas of culture. Among other things, they were responsible for reaffirming the cosmopolitan literary culture that was the heritage of the Modernists, and they did so in the much less propitious climate of postrevolutionary uncertainty. Like the members of the Ateneo, the Contemporáneos added to the Modernist heritage a deep respect for the possible (social) benefits of humanist culture. But where the Ateneístas were predominantly classicists, the Contemporáneos, as their name suggests, sought out the experimental, the vanguard, the new. They saw through the reigning exuberance of their time, the noisy nationalism of epic proportions. They opposed it with a well-acted role of their own. Rather than project the proletarian, indianist image of the workers' party intellectual, which they saw as folklorish and demeaning, they played the professional intellectual in a rather unprofessional way, practicing an unusual combination of dandyism and bohemianism. Their strategic move was to emphasize Mexico's preponderantly Western heritage, and they fought to keep Mexico abreast of contemporary European culture. They opposed subtly the macho brutalism of the revolutionary hero with a more refined sensibility, which for their detractors bordered dangerously on the effeminate. They too wanted to contribute to the new revolutionary society, in their own radical way, with an equally "revolutionary" literature. Mexican society, however, was not yet ready to be quite so transformed.

All of the Contemporáneos were poets. This was clearly the genre most akin to their spirits. "Canto a un dios mineral" (Song to a Mineral God; 1942) by Jorge Cuesta (1903-41) and "Muerte sin fin" (Death Without End; 1939) by José Gorostiza (1901-73) are the poetic masterworks of the Contemporáneos generation. The group's creative fusion of the material and the spiritual, the physical and the metaphysical, are apparent in the very titles of the compositions. The poems are also representative of other characteristics which, though by no means common to all members of the generation, were widely imputed to them by their detractors, such as hermeticism and obscurantism (and thus elitism). "Canto a un dios mineral" and "Muerte sin fin" are carefully wrought urns that do not easily yield their contents. Like many other early twentieth-century poets, and much in the Romantic spirit, they see the poet as demonic visionary or mystic: poetry as a last refuge for speculative thought and organic vision. Gorostiza explores philosophy and mysticism, while Cuesta tests the path of science and logic. Each in his own way, they discover the extreme possibilities of language: Gorostiza's "Muerte sin fin" is transparent and susceptible to multiple readings (religious, philosophical, metapoetic, musical); Cuesta's "Canto a un dios mineral" is so opaque as to be essentially unintelligible. Both poems take the reader on an exhilarating adventure to the extreme of language as absolute knowledge or as no knowledge at all.

The best poetry of the Contemporáneos group, however, is not found
in these masterworks but in the minor tone of the poems that Xavier
Villaurrutia (1904-50) collected under the title *Nostalgia de la muerte*
(Deathly Nostalgia; 1938). Villaurrutia's success as poet can be described as a felicitous amalgamation of the qualities of the Contemporáneos as a group and an avoidance of many of their excesses. He tem-
pers the obstruse physics and metaphysics of some and the intimist,
personalist vein of others, combining them with great skill through the
creative use of rhetorical tropes and poetic technique. In "Poesía" (Poetry; 1926), one of his early poems, he establishes a relatively new vision
(for Mexico) of the poet as existential being, as solitary individual who
contemplates himself through the mirror of words, in a struggle to the
death with insomnia and the night, perhaps inspired by Sor Juana's "Primero Sueño." In "Nocturno de la alcoba" (Bedroom Nocturne; 1938)
Villurrutia inverts conventional wisdom at every turn. The closed space
of the bedroom is not the province of love but of death: death that permeates everything and gives life meaning, a fear of death that motivates
our every act, especially our desperate search for communion in love
(physical) and in poetry (metaphysical). In the charming and frightening
"Nocturno en que nada se oye" (Silent Nocturne; 1938) free association
recreates the illogical, nonempirical reality of dream. If López Velarde
is the poet of warmth and the "cesto policromo" (polychrome basket),
Villaurrutia is the poet of hot and cold, black and white. Poetry, in
Villaurrutia, is the communion of our solitude.

Carlos Pellicer (1899), though friendly with many Contemporáneos,
was never an active participant in group activities. Spiritually and literarily, too, he stands somewhat apart from the center of the group. It has
been pointed out that in the older members of the Contemporáneos
generation—Bernardo Ortiz de Montellano (1899-1941), Jaime Torres
Bodet (1902-74), Gorostiza—generally some part of Vasconcelos's revolutionary optimism endures, while disillusionment and anguish more
clearly win the day among such younger Contemporáneos as Gilberto
Owen (1905-52), Salvador Novo (1904-73), Villaurrutia, and Cuesta.
Pellicer might represent the epitome of such optimism. But his outlook
comes from his faith in nature and in traditional spiritual values; it is not
a faith directly tied to the sociopolitical revolution. Much like López
Velarde, Pellicer enlivens ancient poetic topics with an ingenious manipulation of language and a knack for audacious imagery. He renovates the
traditional religious outlook with an exuberant sensuality and a vehemently pantheistic vision.

Most of the Contemporáneos essayed esthetic theory and practical criticism of the arts, especially Villaurrutia and Cuesta. Cuesta excelled in this arena. He was active in most of the pressing issues of the time, molding the greater part of his considerable and often aggressive energies into the essay form. Literature, music, plastic arts, philosophy, and science were fused—rarely confused—in his voluminous essays, collected posthumously in the now five volume *Poemas y ensayos* (Poems and Essays; 1964, 1981). Several of the Contemporáneos also essayed the novella, though few produced full-fledged novels. Their innovations in the novel's form and substance lie in three principal areas: they aestheticized fiction, they interiorized and psychologized fiction, and they also urbanized it. Later novelists would incorporate into more balanced compositions the Modernist (in the term's Anglo-European sense) innovations the Contemporáneos introduced in such works as Owen's *Novela como nube* (Novel Like a Cloud; 1928) and Torres Bodet's *Primero de enero* (First of January; 1934).

One of the most valiant undertakings of the Contemporáneos group was their attempt to revitalize Mexican theater. The theater during the nineteenth century had not been an artistic or cultural function, but at best a "social," at worst a narcissistic one: to be seen was more important than to see. Indeed, indicative of its enduring colonialism, at the beginning of the twentieth century actors were still using on stage the Peninsular accent. Popular culture had had its "subliterary" comedies of political satire. But only exceptionally had the twain met. The Contemporáneos, in their own way, often seemed as snobbish as the well-to-do theater public. But this was a tactical error, for their enterprise was less egotistical and more nationalistic than they let on. The universalist, anticommercial impulse of the brief-lived Teatro de Ulises (Ulysses theater) project was continued under government auspices as the Teatro de Orientación (Theater Orientation; 1932-38). Repertoires were amazingly eclectic: from Sophocles to Gogol, from Shakespeare to Shaw, from Cervantes to Villaurrutia. A broader audience for serious theater was shakily constructed. The most talented dramatists to emerge from the Teatro de Orientación were Villaurrutia, author of numerous plays, and the founder himself, Celestino Gorostiza (1904). Villaurrutia's conceptualist, existencialist bent is apparent in such dramatic works as the one-act *Autos profanos* (Profane Allegories; 1933-37), and his *Invitación a la muerte* (Invitation to Death; 1940), a strange and moving play in which the son of a mortician struggles with his death instinct, and overcomes it. Gorostiza's early plays were vanguardist and abstractly intellectual.

He later returned to the theater a realist, concerned with national social and psychological problems, as in *El color de nuestra piel* (The Color of our Skin; 1952).

Not until after the discovery of Mariano Azuela's *Los de abajo* in 1924 did narrative accounts of the revolution of any literary sophistication begin to appear in number. In most all of the so-called novels of the revolution personal motivations and ideological intentions predominate over concern for artistic form. This was their glory in the fortunate cases, their weakness in the less fortunate ones. The general lack of concern for technique and structure, paradoxically, opened the door to a variety of rather original approaches to the material. As a uniquely Mexican phenomenon, the novel of the revolution was part and parcel of the essence of the revolutionary movement itself: in a very real sense, the novels that were most critical of the revolutionary enterprise were the ones most in tune with the true spirit of the social upheaval. The revolutionaries, alternately or simultaneously, were heroes and villains, idealists and pragmatic opportunists. The novelists, too, were often guilty of moral idealism and commercial opportunism. Few of the novelists who dared treat the theme were so audaciously reactionary as to criticize the revolution in principle. But ideological opponents are quick to point out the traditional, liberal, middle-class values of the majority of the novelists of the revolution. Some writers focused their gaze on the heroism and benevolence of the revolution's protagonists, but most felt the need to denounce the perversity of its opportunism. Whether legendizing or demystifying, documentation of the revolution frequently took the form of self-serving autobiography, sensationalist journalism, or naive sociology.

Indicative of the way circumstances and intentions tended to dictate form and procedures is the fact that a great number of the novels of the revolution to appear in the twenties and thirties took the form of autobiographical memoirs. Most of the autobiographically-based accounts of the revolution by participants and witnesses lack a truly critical edge. Their works play a role in the romanticizing (and trivialization) of Mexico's unprecedented social and political uprising. Such was not the case of Martín Luis Guzmán's *El águila y la serpiente* (*The Eagle and the Serpent*; 1928). Next to Azuela's *Los de abajo*, *El águila y la serpiente* is the outstanding account of the armed phase of the revolution. Guzmán, a member of the Ateneo, was a much more sophisticated intellectual than Azuela, but his values and his prejudices, like his gut reaction to the revolution, are practically identical. What his novel lacks in immediacy and passion it makes up for in elegance and in coldly penetrating analysis. He, like Azuela, in the end abandons the pistol for the pen. These two famous accounts of the revolution are in many ways complementary, and encompass the essence of the revolution as they see it. *El águila y la serpiente* covers roughly the same phase of the revolution that Azuela dealt with in *Los de abajo*: the rise and fall of *villismo* (i.e., the role of Pancho Villa) between 1913 and 1915. Though Guzmán deals with a wholly different sector of the revolution's pecking order, the poles between which it moves are the same. Pancho Villa is Guzmán's Demetrio Macías, and the work is in part a futile attempt to vindicate Villa's character. Venustiano Carranza is Guzmán's Luis Cervantes, and *El águila y la serpiente* is a scathing indictment of his greed and personal ambition. Guzmán, like Azuela, would prefer a gentleman's revolution. But where Azuela gets close enough to the common man to feel the revolution as a pathetic yet heroic tragedy, Guzmán is like a fish out of water, and from his perspective the revolution is an absurd, full-blown farce encompassing the strangest of incongruities. Guzmán also produced an outstanding political novel, *La sombra del caudillo* (The Shadow of the Political Boss; 1929).

The revolution was a complex, confusing, and ambiguous phenomenon. For many, in its origins it was a political movement on behalf of democratization. For others, prominently the revolutionary leader of the south, Emiliano Zapata, the struggle for social justice took predominance over the purely political. *Tierra* (Land; 1932), by Gregorio López y Fuentes (1897-1966), recounts schematically Zapata's agrarian revolution, as experienced by the farm workers of a single ranch. The technique is somewhat similar to that employed in *Los de abajo*, and is effective in showing the repercussion, and lack of it, among more isolated populations of the major events in the revolution. But *Tierra*'s attempt to tell its story from the campesinos' perspective is rather unconvincing. The characters do not appear as individuals, with their own hopes and fears, but rather as something at once more and less than human, and always as something other. The author's expressed sympathy for their lot only makes him come across as more patronizing and condescending. Commonplace criticisms of the revolution are revived, but they lack emotion and vigor, and betray a resignation and submission in López y Fuentes similar to those he reveals in the characters. He, like they, seems to take solace from the realities of postrevolutionary Mexico in the folklore, in the legends, in the myth of a Zapata larger than life. *Tierra* is written in a historical present that is a purely local, eternal past. The revolution, it implies, is a closed book.

In the thirties there appear a number of social-realist novels of the revolution that deal with the social aftermath. Many of these works, such as López y Fuentes's famed *El indio* (The Indian, translated as *El indio*; 1935), are *indigenista* novels (that is, works that treat the plight of the Indian). *El resplandor* (*Sunburst*; 1937) by Mauricio Magdaleno (1906-1984) is one such novel, outstanding because it manages to maintain a constructively critical edge. Recent criticism has seen in Magdaleno's novel a precursor of the new prose fiction to emerge in the forties and fifties, because of its artistic and psychosocial complexity. It too tends to mythologize and distance the Indian. The Indians are a timeless, immortal force tied to the land while the white man is mortal and moves in time. But in the protagonist Saturnino Herrera, who betrays his people, the Indian is humanized, paradoxically, by "dehumanizing" him and showing him to be just as mortal and capable of evil as the Creole or mestizo.

By way of summarizing the literarily ebullient twenties and thirties, the role of Carlos Noriego Hope's literary supplement to *El universal ilustrado* is worth noting. His editorial activity somewhat parallels Altamirano's efforts in the 1860s, for he encouraged with his publication the whole range of undertakings. That Mexico is really "two Mexicos," that the country throughout its modern history has stood at the crossroad of the old and the new, is nowhere more apparent than in the literature of this period. *La señorita Etcétera* (Miss Et Cetera; 1922) by Arqueles Vela (1899-1972) is representative of the vanguard novella produced by Estridentistas and the Contemporáneos. López y Fuentes's *El vagabundo* (The Vagabond; 1925) is fairly representative of the social realist tendency. Both novellas have a strong sociological element and adopt a critical attitude toward their material. Both novels attack conformism, be it dehumanizing or exploitative. But where López y Fuentes's novella is realist, Vela's is more surrealist. Where the tone is moralizing and the conflict purely exterior in *El vagabundo*, in *La señorita Etcétera* the tone is amoral and the conflict interiorized. Where López y Fuentes criticizes rural society for its stagnancy, Vela testifies to the not always positive effects of contemporary urbanization. If in López y Fuentes we glimpse a sort of love/hate relationship toward common folk, in Vela we see the attraction/repulsion that new technologies provoked. The outstanding Mexican novels of the forties and the fifties will go a long way toward blending harmonically these divergent threads: the old and the new, the rural and the urban, the psychological and the social.

Samuel Ramos (1897-1959) and Rodolfo Usigli (1905-1979), two final "pre-1940" authors, excelled not in the standard forms of prose and poetry, but in philosophy and the theater, areas where Mexico had little precedent to offer them. To Ramos and Usigli is owed much of the credibility these "classic" disciplines have today in Mexico. They successfully adapt these most Western of intellectual passions to the Mexican circumstance, and they employ them to probe the sociocultural and historical character of Mexico's being. Their work marks a sort of culmination to the artistic and intellectual ferment that accompanied the building of postrevolutionary institutions, and point the way to the cultural maturity evident in the post-1940 years.

Ramos, a prolific author, is best remembered for his *El perfil del hombre y la cultura en México* (*Profile of Man and Culture in México*; 1934). His criticism of provincialism and of servile cultural emulation and his controversial coinage of the "inferiority complex" were almost in themselves the liberating force necessary to overcome the collective neurosis. Though his work does not form, strictly speaking, part of literature proper, Mexico's twentieth-century literary revolution cannot be adequately accounted for in its absence. In the fifties the "philosophy of the Mexican" would be a fundamental debate for intellectuals and artists alike.

Usigli is a major figure in contemporary Mexican theater who always remained on the margins of the experimental and the commercial. The Ulises group had sought to shock and scandalize the Mexican cultural world with their audacious experiments. Usigli, more humbly if no less disinterestedly, enacted before the Mexican people their psychopathology in an effort to counteract the distortions of nationalist-inspired history. In this project he was unrelenting: many of his works appeared on stage long after their original composition, and some suffered official and unofficial censorship. Usigli was a realist who exposed the hypocrisy of the middle class and the decadence of the aristocracy. But his real achievement was to interweave harmoniously a national, historical, and political thematics with psychological and philosophical concerns at once excruciatingly personal and universal. His most renowned work, the realistic melodrama *El gesticulador* (*The Imposter*; 1937), deftly combines the moral predicament of ends and means with the philosophical dilemma of truth versus fiction in an X-ray of the Mexican revolution. *Corona de sombra* (*Crown of Shadows*; 1943), technically and symbolically a more complex work, rewrites the personal drama of the ill-fated French monarchs, Maximilian and Carlota, in the Mexico of the 1860s.

VIII

The men and women who mature after 1940 are the first intellectuals that are fully products of postrevolutionary society, rather than its protagonists or victims. Before 1940, the revolution had required some sort of knee-jerk reaction, publicity or vehement polemic. For the new generations, by way of contrast, the revolution was more the normal state of affairs, and the cultural arena no longer has a circus air; theorists and practitioners are no longer forced into exaggerated and untenable positions by their ideological adversaries. Artists and writers are in effect liberated, freed to assimilate the strengths of the various factions and amalgamate them as befits their temperament or intention. Social consciousness and artistic refinement are no longer made by force of circumstance to be mutually exclusive options. Mexico can be painted in its singularity and its universality with one and the same brush stroke. It is neither an exotic paradise nor a primeval aberration that must be saved or from which one must flee.

Al filo del agua (*The Edge of the Storm*; 1947), by Agustín Yáñez (1904-80), is widely heralded as the watershed work of twentieth-century Mexican fiction, too often as if it appeared out of nowhere and transformed overnight the reigning cultural milieu. Like other major works of this period, it realizes the potential universality of a profoundly Mexican thematics. Mexican literature becomes "revolutionary" by liberating itself from its obsession with *the* revolution. Significantly, *Al filo del agua* returns for its setting to the time immediately preceding the revolution of 1910, as if this were a necessary ploy to attain the aforementioned liberation. Breaking with the episodic structure of many novels of the revolution, the novel dissolves linear chronology through fragmentation and interior monologue. Its heavy, baroque style and liturgical resonance evoke Mexico's Hispanic colonial traditions, and with them questions of cultural and historical identity. The novel's style may also be related to the rehabilitation of Baroque poetry by vanguard groups such as the Contemporáneos, or the Generation of 1927 poets in Spain. Much of its balance derives from symbolic and allegorical overtones that are never quite carried to completion, and thus never seem forced or contrived. Yáñez moves in and out of the consciousness of the inhabitants of a rural village; their psychology paints the town, just as physical description of the town depicts them. That the revolution itself is finally coming into perspective is born out by the fact that it does not arrive noisily with any heroes, but as more subtle winds of change.

Yáñez was not the only author in the 1940s who was transforming the inheritance of the novel of the revolution. The concurrent presence of novelist José Revueltas (1914-76) on the literary horizon confirms that other, alternate paths had become available. Ideologically and intellectually, Revueltas is the virtual antithesis of Yáñez. But from their opposing vantage points—Yáñez was a respected cultural bureaucrat; Revueltas, an often persecuted radical activist and social misfit—they effected strategically similar modifications on the evolution of Mexican literature. Both enrich social and political themes with psychological depth and broad historical perspective. Both recognize Mexico's depth and singularity, yet stop short of any facile simplifications or mystification.

Revueltas is a powerful and intriguing figure and became the object of renewed attention among many young authors after 1968. His strength lies in his empassioned humanity, which encompasses the extremes of unfounded hope and unfathomable despair. He is unique for his very personal amalgamation of primitive Christianity, from the Hispanic tradition, and modern proletarian utopianism, which he takes from Marxist socialism. Neither his mysticism nor his utopianism, however, is sufficient to cure his rather Nietzschean delight in the human "will to power," and his deep despair in the face of human solitude and degradation, both collective and individual. These, the strengths of Revuelta's passionate vision, also determine the frequently cited weaknesses of his work, when judged by the standard of the unified and harmonious aesthetic object: extensive moral or philosophical digressions, internal contradiction, forced and unconvincing symbolisms. Always to exceed the boundaries of accepted forms was an inevitable product of his strategic design. Revueltas denudes himself as he denudes his characters, whom he often overpowers with his relentless critical sensibility. He frequently seeks to show the way to primordial human communion or "communism," but his excavation of human instinct often undercuts his ostensible message. In seeking to give testimony to social injustice, the degradation and eschatology he wants to denounce are the very elements whose recreation he seems to delight in. His capacity to penetrate into the depths of human motivation make the communal innocence he seems to long for appear naive. He discovers, in short, the primitive underside of modern society or, conversely, the psychological complexity of primitive instinct.

Revueltas's first novel, *Los muros de agua* (Walls of Water; 1941), deals with the fate of a group of political prisoners on a desolate island prison, despised by fellow inmates and brutal guards alike. *El luto humano* (*The Stone Knife*; 1943; also newly translated as *Human Mourning*) brought Revueltas some critical acclaim early in his career. It is technically, thematically, and symbolically more complex than the earlier effort, at times awkwardly so. Though a much more uneven work, *El luto humano* is considered by many to rival Yáñez's *Al filo de agua* as the watershed work in the development of contemporary Mexican fiction. Through flashbacks and interior monologues Revueltas evokes Mexico's recent and distant past, in search of the national soul. It is a vigorous denunciation of actual social injustices and a search for redemption.

The remainder of Revueltas's literary career is marked by fascinating vacillations. For example, in response to criticism from fellow communist party members, he once removed from bookstore shelves what is arguably his most successful and representative novel, *Los días terrenales* (Life on Earth; 1949). The novel was not reprinted until 1962. Revueltas's last published work of fiction, *El apando* (Solitary; 1969), is a stylistically forceful novella. It avoids many of the excesses of his longer works, but linguistically, for its extensive use of prison slang, it makes difficult reading. Symmetrically, Revueltas here returns to the prison setting (a very different one) of his first novel to explore once again human brutality and degradation. Politically, this final novel is all the more effective because its substance is not explicitly partisan.

Like the novelist Revueltas, the poet Octavio Paz (1914) assimilates fully the latest trends in modern Western social thought and cultural practice, and in the same gesture subjects them to a radical critique. For this and other reasons, their many differences notwithstanding, Paz and Revueltas, born the same year, are crucial, pivotal figures. To the degree that they receive and transform a similar cultural and historical heritage, they are part of a single literary movement. Ideologically, however, they represent opposite poles of response, and thus effectively trace the parameters within which subsequent literary developments in Mexico will unfold. As if by the force of their example, most subsequent authors will feel compelled to align themselves with one or the other. Thus, the juxtaposition of their figures suggests that the heated polemics of earlier years between literature's autonomy and its material dependence will never be fully transcended, only endlessly reenacted.

Rather than the revolution, it was the Spanish Civil War that marked the formative years for Paz and many others of his generation. What the Spanish Civil War signifies for them is a new combination of internationalist or cosmopolitan consciousness and political radicalization. Many Spanish intellectuals exiled from the Civil War were welcomed in Mexico. They have had a lasting impact of contemporary cultural developments in Mexico, as indicated by their collaboration with Paz on a number of important literary reviews published in the late 1930s and 1940s, such as *Taller* (Workshop; 1938-41).

Paz originally established his artistic identity in opposition to the supposed apoliticism of many of the Contemporáneos, whose poetry in other regards he deeply admired. However, he would soon modify the course of his poetic evolution, and he has omitted several of his early political poems from recent editions of his complete poetic works. "Elegía a un compañero muerto en el frente" (Elegy for a Comrade Killed at the Front; 1937) is one of his early compositions that survived the purges.

Paz's principal concern has always been language. Though with his rhetorical skill he can take on the appearance of a materialist, he is really an idealist, with a visionary's mystic approach to verse composition. The human artistry of linguistic creation for Paz (as for Nietzsche) should show us the way to an eternally renewable paradise in the wake of the death of our gods, not in spite but because of language's radical imperfection and inadequacy. This is clear in the very title to his first volume of collected poetry, *Libertad bajo palabra* (Freedom in Words; 1949, 1960), which saw several versions. Paz delights in binary opposition and conceptual paradox, affirming the dynamic and necessary coexistence of opposites: through poetry man finds his Other, which is in other words a return to his origin. Paz's theory of poetry is eloquently articulated in his *El arco y la lira* (*The Bow and the Lire*; 1956). The essential elements from which Paz derives his poetic practice have been summarized as follows: the major works of the Mexican cultural tradition, the Western poetic canon, Surrealism, and oriental philosophy/religion. In the early years, the poems are masterfully succinct, absolutely elemental, and blindingly clear (one thinks, for example, of "Bajo tu clara sombra," [Under Your Clear Shadow; 1937]). Though equally masterful and mythic/mystic, he becomes more allusive and elusive in such monumental masterworks as "Piedra de sol" (*Sun Stone*; 1957) and "Himno entre ruinas" (Hymn among Ruins; 1949), which through intricate symbolism and wide-ranging reference seek to condense and synthesize into the space of a poem, not just the history of humanity but literally the universe itself. Still later Paz becomes more earthy and carnal, more aloof and hermetic, more audaciously experimental: the books of poetry *Salamandra* (Salamander; 1962), *Ladera este* (The Eastern Slope; 1969), *Blanco* (White; 1967), *Vuelta* (Return; 1976) are all duly ordered annotated in his *Poemas (1935-1975)* (Poems [1935-75]; 1979; the modified English version is *The Collected Poetry of Octavio Paz [1957-87]*).

Paz is also a lucid cultural historian, literary critic, and political analyst. His work in this area is as vast as is his poetry. He has an impressive capacity to see the broad picture and interpret the underlying resonances of social and cultural evolution. But his own poetic vision of the human condition is so powerful that it arguably forces actual circumstances to fit a mold; the synthetic and dialectical capacities of his mind so great that he may lose sight of the trees for the forest. His works of sociocultural and historical analysis: *El laberinto de la soledad* (*The Labyrinth of Solitude*; 1950), *Posdata* (*The Other Mexico: Critique of the Pyramid*; 1970); his revisionary history of modern and contemporary poetry: *Los hijos del limo* (*Children of the Mire*; 1974), *La otra voz: poesía y fin de siglo* (The Other Voice: Poetry and the Turn of the Century; 1990); and his many collections of occasional essays, such as *Corriente alterna* (*Alternating Current*; 1967), are all replete with incisive and provocative analyses and interpretations. If Paz seems today to many Mexicans aloof and distant, it may be because among living Mexican authors, only Carlos Fuentes rivals him in international stature. Both have for some time been on the short list of candidates for the Nobel Prize for Literature, which Paz was just recently awarded (1990). It seems a peculiarly Mexican phenomenon that the price they have paid for their success has been a complex reception as hero and traitor, combining pride with envy and resentment.

In the work of Efraín Huerta (1914-72) the poetry of Paz finds its stylistic and ideological counterpart. Where Paz turned aestheticist and mystic, Huerta turned materialist and demonic. Where Paz painted possible utopias, Huerta denounced the earthly infernos found in modern, urban Mexico. Huerta's poetic language is fully colloquial, belligerently aggressive, and often self-effacing. Poems like "Avenida Juarez" (1956) and "La muchacha ebria" (The Drunken Girl; 1948), far from esthetic objects, are pointed attacks. Like Revueltas, Huerta has seen a recent revival at the hands of young writers seeking strategically to oppose the high cultural establishment of Paz and his followers.

The so-called Generation of 1950, comprising a varied group of individuals born roughly between 1915 and 1925, is less a unified and programmatic generation than most, but this in itself is a sign of the times. If they seem less inspired than the authors who immediately preceded them, the times themselves were perhaps less inspiring, with the deemphasis of revolutionary rhetoric and the push toward modernization and development of the civilian governments. Previous writers had begun the task of blending ethics and aesthetics, the national and the cosmopolitan, out of the ebullience of postrevolutionary polemics. The generation of 1950 inherited this cultural maturity and intellectual sophistication, a benefit and a curse. They fill commendably a tranquil interlude between the major figures that are Revueltas and Paz, and the fanfare of the high-culture establishment (often called the Mafia) that was the Spanish-American literary "boom" of the middle sixties. If there is a common denominator among the writers of this non-generation it might be their focus on the problems and circumstance of the individual, in a universal context or as it pertains to Mexico.

A similar stylistic and strategic contrast to that found in the novelists Yáñez and Revueltas, or the poets Paz and Huerta, is apparent in two master storytellers who emerged in the fifties: Juan José Arreola (1918) and Juan Rulfo (1918-86). Both are from the state of Jalisco, as were Azuela and González Martínez before them. Arreola and Rulfo seem to write for the pleasure inherent to human creation, with no ulterior motives, and for this the moral impact of their work is only increased. Both were obsessive perfectionists and as a consequence neither has been prolific. But here the similarities begin to thin. Arreola is cosmopolitan, intellectual, and philosophical; his humor is upbeat. "El guardagujas" (The Switchman; 1952) is the most widely anthologized of Arreola's short stories and vignettes, the bulk of which have been collected under the title of *Confabulario total* (*Confabulario and Other Inventions*; 1962). It is one of Arreola's rather infrequent incursions into a properly Mexican theme, yet characteristically it never ceases to resonate universality. In it, the railroad system of an unnamed country may be read, on one level, as a symbolic representation of the Mexican historical character, or at another level as an allegory of life itself. As with much of Arreola's work, "El guardagujas" is almost too neat and ingenious—what it seems to lack is sincere emotional commitment.

Rulfo, in contrast, is by all appearances provincial, instinctive, and strangely passionate in his writing. His humor—if it may be called that—is dry, dark, and macabre, as are his settings. His short stories, collected as *El llano en llamas* (*The Burning Plain and Other Stories*; 1953); and his one short novel, *Pedro Páramo* (1955), are cut from the same cloth. The character, sometimes narrator Juan Preciado arrives in Comala in search of his father; what he finds, little by little, he realizes, are the living dead, souls in purgatory, who with their multiple voices recreate fragment by fragment the story of Pedro Páramo. The novel's historical setting can be roughly reconstructed by references to the revolution and the Catholic reactionary Cristero revolt, but the novel's meanings do not bear directly on the revolution. Indeed in the Comala dominated by the *cacique* ("town boss") Pedro Páramo, the revolution appears as a minor distraction that he manipulates at will. Causes and effects are cloudy in *Pedro Páramo*; obscure passions and powerful grudges dominate this world. If the present that Juan Preciado finds is dry and suffocating, the past is humidly sensuous and brutal. The character Pedro Páramo represents the epitome of cruelty and arbitrary injustice. But significantly, of all the characters in the novel, he is the one who appears least ridiculed. The view of man Rulfo paints in *Pedro Páramo* is highly fatalistic. But Rulfo, like Pedro Páramo, refuses to lament. Herein lies the astonishing power of his vision.

Though there are isolated examples of women authors who in the history of Mexican literature implicitly or explicitly challenge the male dominance of the cultural arena, it is Elena Garro (1920) and especially Rosario Castellanos (1925-76), authors from the Generation of 1950, who effectively stake a claim to terrain in the field of serious literature. They open a space to be later occupied by subsequent women authors, just as their own work in certain respects follows the lead of such forbears as Sor Juana Inés de la Cruz and Nellie Campobello. Just as Campobello contributed her unique, personal perspective to the body of narrative accounts of the revolution (much as Raquel de Queiroz did for the Brazilian regionalist novel of the Northeast [see section on Brazilian literature]), Garro contributes to the radical transformation of the novel of the revolution alongside such contemporary works as Rulfo's *Pedro Páramo* and Fuentes's *La muerte de Artemio Cruz* (*The Death of Artemio Cruz*; 1962). Similarly, Castellanos's work is highly reminiscent of the feminist concerns and attitudes of Sor Juana, especially in her poetry and essays: Castellanos's self-defense, her search for identity and meaning, is necessarily a generic defense of women, even when she lashes out at the temerity of her sisters. Her work vividly dramatizes the dilemma, the pain and the resentment, of the female caught between the pull of traditional roles of domesticity and motherhood, on the one hand, and her intellectual passion and affirmation of the equal rights of women to public life. If Castellanos and Garro, in very different ways, appear to be feminists somewhat *avant la lettre*, it is as much out of necessity as conscious choice. It may be argued that their perceived shortcomings are owing to the fact that they worked within traditional, male-created forms and genres, rather than striking out in new formal and stylistic directions, as more recent women's writing will do.

Garro's most acclaimed work is the novel *Los recuerdos del porvenir* (*Recollections of Things to Come*; 1963), set in a small town during the Cristero revolt of the late 1920s. In both substance and technique, it elaborates anew many of the characteristic elements of Rulfo's *Pedro Páramo*, with the notable difference that its primary focus follows the divergent fates of two female protagonists. The historical element, the town's closed, reactionary conservatism, is lent an atemporal resonance by a complex manipulation of time and point of view. The town itself is a sort of collective yet singular narrator, giving events a larger-than-life air that may anticipate the type of magic realism made famous in García Márquez's *Cien años de soledad* (*One Hundred Years of Solitude*; 1967; see section on Colombian literature).

Rosario Castellanos essayed with considerable success poetry, theater, and the novel. A certain bitterness, seemingly the reflection of her struggle for intellectual respectability in a hostile sociocultural ambience, permeates much of her work. In her poetry, collected as *Poesía no eres tú* (Poetry You Are Not; 1972), she treats very personal, domestic, amorous, and carnal themes. Her works are full of erudite allusions, and she is fond of allegorical and mythic elements, which she skillfully enlivens. The poem "Lamentación de Dido" (Dido's Lament; 1957) is a powerful defense of the tragic/heroic destiny of woman, deploying like Sor Juana did the enumeration of precedents among women prominent in myth and history. The essay "La liberación del amor" (The Liberation of Love; 1972) is a scathing ironic attack on (the superficiality of) feminism in contemporary Mexico.

Castellanos's incursions in the novel, *Balún Canán* (*Nine Guardians*; 1957) and *Oficio de tinieblas* (Dark Craft; 1962), at first glance appear disconnected from the bulk of her poetry and essays, though the sterility of a prominent female character in the latter novel may provide some clue. They may be classified as *indigenista* fiction, and deploy primarily social realist techniques and structures. Better than her predecessors among indigenista novelists, Castellanos was able to give psychological depth and individuality to her Indian characters. Perhaps she took up the defense of oppressed and exploited indigenous populations in her native Chiapas because she found there some affinities between their social status and that of women. The "objective," external exploration of indigenous ritual and superstition approaches the cast of ethnology. In the evolution of indigenista fiction Castellanos's role bears some resemblance to that of the Peruvian author, José María Arguedas (see the section on Peruvian literature).

In the theater, new dramatists surface under the guidance of Salvador Novo as director of the Theater Section of the Instituto Nacional de Bellas Artes (INBA; National Institute of Fine Arts), a major institutional force behind contemporary Mexican art and literature. Emilio Carballido (1925) is the outstanding product of the Novo-inspired revival. He is a prolific playwright, a master of symbolic expression, the Western theatrical canon, and dramatic technique, who has sustained his energies over many years. Critical disapproval of human inauthenticity and sincere appreciation for human spontaneity and creativity permeate his work. He proves in Mexico that commercial success and intellectual sophistication are not necessarily mutually exclusive goals. Even his plays that deal most directly with the Mexican circumstance achieve deeply personal and universal resonance. Carballido has essayed during his career a wide variety of techniques and subgenres, from allegory to the comedy of manners. In later works, Carballido begins to freely mix realism and fantasy, while also assimilating defamiliarizing elements from Brechtian epic theater. Actors play multiple roles in *Yo también hablo de la rosa* (I Too Speak of the Rose; 1966), a title taken from a Villaurrutia poem. It is an ambitious play mixing a wide variety of elements, from the most fantastic and allegorical to the apparently documental. The spectator is witness to an array of perspectives and interpretations of a single event. The role of art is to reveal life as an intricate web that is complex and fragile, and never satisfactorily accounted for by cold theories or sophisticated rationalizations.

The predominance of individual temperament over programmatic unity among the Generation of 1950 writers is noteworthy in poetry. Also especially apparent in poetry is that for the time being there are few causes to defend or no battles to be won. Poets such as Alí Chumacero (1918) and Rubén Bonifáz Nuño (1923) can take advantage of the technical skill and refined sensibility inherited from the Contemporáneos, without carrying them to polemic extremes. The result is a treatment of amorous and quotidian themes that is moving and not infrequently provocative. Jaime Sabines (1925), on the other hand, is a much more spontaneous writer of sometimes scandalous emotional extremes, more in the vein of Huerta. For Sabines, poetry is a space in which to unleash frustrations, disappointment, and feelings of impotence; his revenge on a cruel and unjust world, or alternately a confession of the softer side of his masculinity.

As for the novel, Luis Spota (1925-84) is a uniquely polemic figure in contemporary Mexican literature. In the 1950s and 1960s he was one of very few Mexican writers who could make a living from the sale of his books, and "serious" writers disguise poorly their envy of the popular success of his allegedly second-class best-sellers. Critical polemics as to the status of his work continually resurface, much as has been the case of Jorge Amado in Brazil, albeit for different reasons (see the section on Brazil). Earlier in Mexico, novelists of the revolution such as José Rubén Romero (1890-l952) and Rafael Muñoz (1899-1972) had capitalized on their glorification of the simple life of the popular classes to reach large audiences. Spota, in a contemporary urban context, employs a variant on this tactic, counting on the public's taste for gossip, for the sensational, for purportedly behind-the-scene looks at public figures and events. In question is whether Spota's denunciations of corruption and injustice in novels such as *Casi el paraíso* (*Almost Paradise*; 1956) move to indignation or promote defeatism and negative self-imagery. In any case, Spota was a talented and prolific storyteller who proved early on that there is a substantial market in Mexico (and Latin America) with the resources to buy novels, if one has the know-how and the desire to tap it. Indeed, as more recent trends in Mexican literature fuse and confuse serious and popular art, Spota's work has elicited renewed attention.

Personal styles and sustained productivity are trademarks of Sergio Galindo (1926) and Jorge Ibargüengoitia (1928-83). Galindo specializes in careful portrayal of the subtleties of human interaction and self-realization. His sensitivity to nuance suggests promise for mankind, but the tragic destiny of his characters in *Polvos de arroz* (*Rice Powder*; 1958) and *El bordo* (*The Precipice*; 1960) reveals an underlying pessimism about human possibilities. The distinctive note of Ibargüengoitia's novelistic production is sharp humor, not often characteristic of mainstream Latin-American literature. Ibargüengoitia's delight in the human comedy is refreshing, even when he is at his most sardonic, as in the novel *Los relámpagos de agosto* (*Lightning in August*; 1964), a satire of the revolution, as well as of the rhetorical formulas of the novel of the revolution. Like the younger Vicente Leñero (see below), Galindo and Ibargüengoitia may be considered mavericks, but in a personal rather than a programmatic sense (Mariano Azuela may be a precursor in this regard):

they carried their work forward on the margins or outside of established
literary groups and movements. More than representative authors of the
Generation of 1950, then, they mark and anticipate a notable growth,
expansion and maturity of authors and audiences in Mexico, which allowed them to follow and sustain their independent enterprises. Ibargüengoitia particularly, with his later texts, has anticipated many of the
trends characteristic of new postmodern, or postboom, fiction: these
include the use of a flat, pseudodocumentary style; the recourse to popular subgenres, such as detective fiction; and the juxtaposition of popular
codes and discourses, of direct speech of characters or interior monologue, in appearance not mediated by a controlling or judgmental,
authorial presence (see *Las muertas* [*Dead Girls*; 1977] and *Dos crímenes*
[Two Crimes; 1979]).

IX

The existence of a new generation, writers born roughly between
1926 and 1936, which might be called the "boom" generation, may be
marked by the appearance of the novel *La región más transparente*
(*Where the Air is Clear*; 1958), by Carlos Fuentes (1928). With the previous generation, the arrival of relative stability, progress, and development
for a significant sector of Mexican society on the socioeconomic and
cultural planes was unpretentiously announced and quietly confirmed,
though the corruption and vice that accompanied them were often ignored, or simply had not come into full awareness. The novella *Las
batallas en el desierto* (Desert Battles; 1981; see below), by José Emilio
Pacheco (1939), will later supplement this lack of critical awareness; it
is an analeptic critique of the radical cultural and socioeconomic changes
experienced in Mexico during the years of the first civilian governments
of the revolution in the 1940s and 1950s, when development and modernization were an official policy that brought along with other ills corruption, hypocrisy, foreign domination, and considerable cultural and linguistic contamination, primarily North American.

In the meantime, as if bored with stability, the writers of the "boom"
generation turn not quietly but noisily to modern Western high culture,
which is to say to "modernism" and even to postmodernism in the Anglo-European sense of these terms. Literature and culture once again
become something of a circus and a public spectacle. Paz served as a
mentor and fountainhead of inspiration for this generation. He is also

the bridge to the Contemporáneos, whom many of them greatly admired. But where the Contemporáneos could be pioneers, the "boom" generation had little opposition, no fervent revolutionary nationalism to combat. Official cultural policy now supports demonstrations of Mexico's modern, cosmopolitan culture (many of these writers were called in 1968 to form committees to organize cultural events in support of the Olympic effort).

Times had in fact changed. There appeared to be an expanding audience, within Mexico, for a variety of cultural products and public polemics, including the high cultural—or at least enough intellectuals had been produced so that they could support and read each other. Various periodic publications coexist as organs of expression and debate for splinter groups within the generation: the *Revista mexicana de literatura* (Mexican Review of Literature; 1955-65), the *Revista de la Universidad*, *Estaciones* (directed by the older poet, Elías Nandino [Seasons; 1956-60]), and *Cuadernos de viento* (Notebooks of the Winds; 1960-67). It must be remarked that rarely, with one notable exception, did Mexican authors figure directly in the boom phenomenon, though as a whole Mexican literature was clearly a surreptitious beneficiary of the opening for serious literature that the boom represented. This broad and almost imperceptible effect of the boom is primarily manifest in the confidence and calm self-assurance that younger, postboom authors would bring to their craft. Much the same, of course, could be said of many Latin American countries. But because of Mexico's relatively strong and long-standing autonomous traditions, its literature, to a greater degree than that of other Spanish American nations, did not need the boom, and in fact from the start seemed to resent many of its implications. The problematic reception Carlos Fuentes's work has always had in Mexico, not unlike the fate of Paz ("everything can be forgiven except success abroad"), reflects directly this state of affairs, and is the exception that confirms the rule. Note should also be taken that the erudite, intimist, and experimental fiction of the *Revista mexicana de literatura* group, which came to fruition under the tutelage of Paz in the 1960s, as well as the *literatura de la onda* ("hip" literature) penned by younger authors in the 1960s, were virtually independent of the boom and were to remain predominantly national phenomena. Similarly, the often discussed "Mafia" of writers and artists in Mexico in the 1960s, while not unrelated to the general boom ambience, had national and not primarily regional or international implications.

Mexico's principal contribution to the boom of Latin-American literature is Carlos Fuentes (1928). He and his Spanish American colleagues

are truly citizens of the global village. Perhaps their international acclaim (read: fashionableness in the Western world) is still owing in part
to a Eurocentrist view, which sees Latin America as exotic and folklorish.
But as political and cultural ambassadors, the work of the boom novelists
has been decisive. In the cultural sphere they have done much to confirm McLuhan's prophecy, and with it the inevitability of global interde-
pendence, on whose necessary cultivation our very survival depends.
Fuentes, virtually by himself, has put Mexico on the literary map, a
praiseworthy undertaking that may also have certain sinister, unintended
implications, such as that of perpetuating a limited, unidimensional understanding of Mexico and the current state of its culture. Indeed, the
boom phenomenon, with its dependence on foreign audiences, harks
back in unsuspected ways to the chronicles of conquest and discovery
often evoked by the boom novelists, raising issues of neocolonialism and
evoking the proverbial wisdom by which the more things change the
more they stay the same.

Fuentes is a writer of immense talent. Each and every one of his
novels is a virtuoso performance. His works can have the unintended
effect of trivializing or romanticizing their otherwise moving material, for
substance is almost always overshadowed by the power of the design and
the ingenuity of the construction. *La región más transparente*, said to
show the influence of Dos Passos, is a mosaic symphony of voices which,
while painting the breadth of Mexico City's present, excavates the culture's past. In the first half of the twentieth century, the famous mural-
ism of Diego Rivera and others was in the artistic vanguard and pretended to capture the essence of the nation's heritage. It has been argued
that in the second half of the century Fuentes reclaims this sphere of
action (consciousness raising) for the novel.

Fuentes's most acclaimed novel, *La muerte de Artemio Cruz* (*The
Death of Artemio Cruz*; 1962), presents a counterpoint of perspectives on
an agonizing consciousness that is at once individual and collective. The
novel tells the story of one man in the context of the revolution and its
political, socioeconomic and psychological ramifications. *Aura* (1962), in
contrast, is a masterful minor work in which Fuentes allows his fantasy
free reign; it has been the subject of very diverse interpretations, including feminist critiques of its archetypal treatment of sex and death. *Cambio de piel* (*A Change of Skin*; 1967), though the principal action is set
in Mexico, moves on a more international plane. It is full of symbolisms
and allusions that run from pre-Hispanic pyramids to contemporary rock
music happenings. The monumental *Terra Nostra* (1975) is still more

pretentious and similarly allusive and elusive. As is prone to happen with works of such ambition, the parts often are greater than the whole. Sharing a common bibliography of Spanish-language masterpieces and works of cultural analysis with Fuentes's essay *Cervantes o la crítica de la lectura* (Cervantes or a Critique of Reading; 1976), *Terra Nostra* seeks to discover the mystery at the heart of the Hispanic soul. In projecting the novel as supreme instrument of human knowledge, while revealing the ultimate insufficiency and lack of transcendence of writing, it finally undermines (or transcends) its own pretensions.

Fuentes, as much as any other contemporary novelist, seeks to articulate sociohistorical and cultural particularities, as does Paz. But his fascination with myth and magic, the breadth and depth of his vision, the synthetic power of his mind more often win out, and the historical substance of his work is mystified and allegorized to the point of appearing strangely atemporal. He reveals in his novels the universality of the Mexican circumstance almost to a fault. Significantly, in some of his most recent works, Fuentes has turned away from his preoccupation with the Hispanic inheritance explored in *Terra Nostra*. In *Gringo viejo* (*The Old Gringo*; 1985) and *Cristóbal Nonato* (*Christopher Unborn*; 1987) Fuentes focuses his attention on the problematic past and future relations between Mexico and its neighbor to the North, a new preoccupation seemingly in consonance with Fuentes's increasing visibility as a public figure in the United States.

With the departure of Fuentes from the *Revista mexicana de literatura*, the review took a subtly new direction and the nucleus of a literary group was formed in the early sixties around Juan García Ponce as codirector of this magazine, and editor of the *Revista de la Universidad de México*. Where Fuentes seemed to take Paz's *El laberinto de la soledad* and its analysis of Mexican being as a point of departure, the new *Revista mexicana de literatura* group showed a marked preference for the "universal," carnal, metaphysical, and metapoetic preoccupations present in Paz's poetry. Talented, mostly self-taught, and precocious, these young writers quickly came to be seen as snobbish by those who felt excluded from the group, and by younger writers seeking to break onto the literary scene. Together with other consecrated figures in the cultural milieu, such as the plastic artist José Luis Cuevas, they came to be known as the aforementioned Mafia, a mythic group that had as many different membership lists as it had critics. In effect, what the writers of the *Revista mexicana de literatura* group sought and largely achieved was the right to explore in Mexico a prominent undercurrent of Western Romanticism and Mod-

ernism, exemplified by such authors as Goethe and Dostoyevski; Baudelaire and Bataille, Rimbaud and Mallarmé, Mann and Musil.

Juan Vicente Melo (1932) exemplifies well the kind of cult rather
than popular following this group has enjoyed. Melo has produced to
date a single novel, *La obediencia nocturna* (Nocturnal Obedience; 1969),
the object of a surprising amount of critical attention for a work that has
barely seen a second printing. It is among other things a hallucinogenic
quest for the female archetype, and perhaps for the supreme novel.
Another member of the group, Sergio Pitol (1933), was similarly dark,
arcane, and esoteric in his first novel, *El tañido de una flauta* (The Sound
of the Flute; 1972). Pitol later lived for many years in Europe, serving
in the Mexican diplomatic corps. And in contrast to Melo, Pitol has
turned out to be a fluid and even prolific narrative talent. Better than
any other member of the group, he has preserved the original goals and
concerns of the group while managing to move towards a more accessible, more "readerly"—not exactly popular—form. His most recent novels,
El desfile del amor (The Parade of Love; 1984) and *Domar a la divina
garza* (To Tame the Divine Heron; 1987), have met with great critical
success in Spain. In a sense, his work demonstrates the new possibilities
for broad critical and commercial success that now exist in Spanish,
independent of the more common route to success that is immediate
English translation. In other words, Pitol may exemplify the implicit
resistance to the boom phenomenon always present in Mexico and well
represented in the work of this group, while not relinquishing the boom's
underlying presuppositions (that Latin American fiction is the equal of
any other contemporary narrative practice). Pitol has remained faithful
to his high art commitments and his preferences for limited states of
consciousness and delirious or demented figures. But in his recent works
he has also proven very adept at assimilating new trends (the attenuation
of extreme narrative self-consciousness and the incorporation of more
popular genres, such as detective fiction). Self-conscious narration in *El
desfile del amor* and *Domar a la divina garza*, whether indirect and implicit, as in the former, or fully explicit, in the latter, is no longer a painfully involuted end in itself, but an element that lightens the reading
experience, that adds interest and, paradoxically, verisimilitude to the
story. In *El desfile del amor*, we follow the historian/writer Miguel del
Solar as he investigates from the present of the 1970s a case of international intrigue that occurred in Mexico during World War II. As a sort
of period piece, *El desfile del amor* has points of contact with Pacheco's
Las batallas en el desierto, and it sheds light on Mexican culture, politics,

and international relations past and present. In both style and substance, Pitol's recent fiction has its most remarkable parallels in the contributions Rubem Fonseca's novels have made to recent Brazilian fiction (see section on Brazil). What is perhaps most notable about Pitol is the way he moves so effortlessly and unselfconsciously between Mexico and Europe. The very fact that he refuses to make problematic this movement (Mexico/Europe) as such is significant: he is neither boisterously cosmopolitan (*malinchista*) nor obsessively preoccupied with the "unique" characteristics of Mexican being. He has transcended as well the often arcane literary and philosophical preoccupations of the early, representative authors of the *Revista mexicana de literatura* group. For all this, his work fulfills similar functions to that of a slightly younger author not a part of this group, Fernando del Paso (see below).

The second novel by Julieta Campos (1934), *Tiene los cabellos rojizos y se llama Sabina* (She Has Red Hair and is Called Sabina; 1974), combines the intimist and metaliterary preoccupations of the *Revista mexicana de literatura* group. Alluding indirectly, playfully, and unobtrusively to questions of literary theory and practice and to other works by group members, the composition of the novel becomes its principal theme. Like Melo's *La obediencia nocturna*, Campos's work may be described as a happy synthesis of the techniques and preoccupations that characterize the widely divergent literary practices of the two most renowned writers of this splinter group, Juan García Ponce (1932) and Salvador Elizondo (1932).

García Ponce and Elizondo have sustained in its more pure forms the cultural enterprise of the so-called *Revista mexicana de literatura* group. If the Contemporáneos, even more than the Modernistas before them, sought to bring Mexico in step with contemporary trends in European and North American literature, the work of García Ponce and Elizondo, for better or worse, confirms the final success of that enterprise. Their work has almost nothing that is specifically or exclusively Mexican about it. While they do not elide history entirely, their "universal" concerns are so broad (or narrow) that they appear ahistorical. To describe the essential concerns they share, we might say that they dramatize the dilemma of man as the language animal. But though they dramatize a similar dilemma, their responses to it are highly personal and widely divergent. Elizondo turns his back on life, fleeing into art, literature, and language to live out his drama there. *Farabeuf* (1965), his first novel, is a highly acclaimed, disturbing *tour de force* in which times, spaces, and persons—physical and grammatical ones—are fused and confused in a violent, *nouveau roman*-styled ritual. With *El hipogeo secreto* (The Secret Hypogeum; 1968), Elizondo turns from anti- to self-representation. In the novel, author Elizondo and the various fragments of his self that are the characters play out a game of hide and seek, discussing profound questions of metaphysics and literary theory along the way. The ploy of turning literature back upon itself, of making literature out of the impossibility of writing literature, is of course ingenious, but the effort quickly falls in upon itself. Elizondo was ready to admit in the early seventies, after producing *El grafógrafo* (The Graphographer; 1972), that he was finding himself at a dead end. In the autobiographic and self-conscious stories and essays collected as *Camera lúcida* (Camera lucida; 1983), the struggle to recover the inspiration and motivation to write, together with a certain nostalgia for the early days of enthusiasm for his idealistic pursuit of a pure form of linguistic representation, are prominent undercurrents that lend a minimal unity to the volume.

For García Ponce, too, his literature is his whole life, not ostensibly as an end in itself, but as a means of discovering a sort of neo-Proustian "art of life." Where Elizondo subverts conventional representation formally, García Ponce operates his subversion primarily at the level of content. He has an exceptional ability to immerse the reader in the consciousness of his characters, as if through incantation (the "monotony" of his style). All of his novels focus on the interaction of a limited number of personalities, among themselves and with their immediate, physical environment. The author-narrator traces the success or failure of their self-realization: they seek the spiritual in the material; they must lose themselves (their unique, individual consciousness) to find themselves (their oneness with the infinite materiality of the world). This can all be rather deep, as it sounds, but because García Ponce for the most part practices it through his narratives rather than theorizes about it, his novels can be very seductive, sometimes disturbing (of conventional morality) experiences, which is their design. In such early works as the stories of *Imagen primera* (First Image; 1963) and *La noche* (The Night; 1963), and in the novels *Figura de paja* (Straw Figure; 1964) and *La casa en la playa* (The House on the Beach; 1966), García Ponce essays a variety of subjects and techniques, seeking and eventually finding his highly personal tone and style. Later novels, all interesting in their own right, as a whole become repetitive and dogmatic because of the persistence with which García Ponce pursues the singularity of his vision. In his most recent efforts, García Ponce has tried new approaches. In *Figuraciones* (Figurations; 1981) and the monumental *Crónica de la inter-*

vencion (A Chronicle of Intervention; 1982), he balances the gravity of the characters' visionary quest with the grace and humor of the human comedy. The power of his art and his vision is only strengthened, not weakened, when the characters must again move in a world of contingency.

García Ponce and Elizondo are much admired and renowned figures in the contemporary Mexican cultural milieu. But they are better known as eccentric personages than read. If they have had a lasting influence on subsequent literary production, it is not obvious or immediately apparent. They have taken the road less travelled and thus in a way have freed younger writers to enliven the more beaten path. Vicente Leñero (1932), in contrast, has proven much more directly influential: he has encouraged by example the reinvigoration of context, the return to situation-specific history and the formulation of a new kind of "realism" all generally characteristic of postboom writing, in Mexico as elsewhere in Latin America. Not surprisingly, Leñero emerged on his own rather than as part of any literary group. A journalist originally trained as an engineer, he has had great success in melding a variety of technical approaches with a more accessible thematics. Issues of personal morality and social justice, contemporary and historical, are Leñero's forte. He is not a writer obsessed with a single problem, nor does he exhibit a unique, personal style. Sometimes it seems he has something to say, and then searches for the most appropriate means of expression. At other times his desire to experiment with a particular technique seems to be the guiding motivation. Not infrequently, the result is a harmonious integration of form and substance. The novel *Los albañiles* (The Bricklayers; 1964), for example, uses a construction site for the principal setting and a murder for a pretext. The characters' testimony is a vehicle for untangling the complex emotional and motivational web in which the construction workers are enmeshed. The murderer, it turns out, cannot be found. But all of those involved bear some form of moral guilt. Leñero successfully avoids both sentimentalism and condescension. His social commentary is all the more effective because the reader must piece it together from the characters' own unwitting revelations of self and circumstance.

Leñero has been a pioneer in Mexico of such innovations as the nonfiction novel and documentary theater. In the plays *Pueblo rechazado* (Rejected Nation; 1968), *El juicio* (The Trial; 1972), and *Martirio de Morelos* (Morelos's Martyrdom; 1983), which have provoked controversy in official circles, Leñero's documentary treatment of historical events allows him to integrate harmoniously three general preoccupations: he questions official versions of history and current events; he treats issues of personal morality and social justice; and he explores the complex relationship between truth and fiction. He has dealt with similar concerns in the novels *Redil de ovejas* (Flock of Sheep; 1973) and *El evangelio según don Lucas Gavilán* (The Gospel According to Lucas Gavilán; 1979).

While Leñero's documentary theater rewrites history, his nonfiction novels treat mostly contemporary events. *Los periodistas* (The Journalists; 1976), a key and controversial work, employs an ironic tone and a semidocumentary form to chronicle events surrounding the government orchestrated breakup of the editorial staff of the major daily *Excelsior* and its literary magazine *Plural* (1971). Along the way, it implicitly underscores the subjectivity involved in even the most carefully documented narrative by first-hand witnesses. Leñero's other incursions in a kind of nonfiction novel include *El garabato* (The Scribble; 1967), a metafictional novel within a novel, in which "Vicente Leñero" is one of the novelists involved; and *La gota de agua* (The Drop of Water; 1984), the author's account of his personal trials and tribulations with the water-supply problem in Mexico City, while trying "unsuccessfully" to compose a novel whose drafts he incorporates into the text. The juxtaposition of these two Leñero texts demonstrates how short the distance may be between such supposedly disparate practices as self-conscious narration and the testimonial.

In spite of the fundamental contributions of such dramatists as Leñero and Carballido, theater in Mexico continues to be an uphill struggle toward popular acceptance and critical viability, so much so that critics have referred to the group of new playwrights including Abelardo Villegas (1943) as a "lost" generation. National authors continue to compete for acceptance against contemporary foreign and classical theatrical productions. Subtle forms of official censorship have also been an obstacle—some of Leñero's documentary works stand as a case in point—owing perhaps to the theater's special dependence on government sponsorship and to its potential popular impact. Nonetheless, authors like Elena Garro and Luisa Josefina Hernández (1928) have contributed to the survival of a Mexican theatrical tradition and have helped keep Mexico abreast of recent trends in a climate that has not always been propitious. Another writer who has enlivened the Mexican stage is Maruxa Vilalta (1931). Where Leñero essays the new documentary theater, Vilalta, more along the lines of Emilio Carballido, skillfully combines the existential themes of contemporary theater of the absurd and the social, political, and economic concerns of Brechtian theater. The prize-winning plays *Esta noche juntos, amándonos tanto* (Together Tonight Loving Each Other; 1970) and *Nada como el piso 16* (Nothing Like the Sixteenth Floor; 1975) link interpersonal themes of human degradation and self-determination to questions of sociopolitical and economic powerlessness and dependence on an international scale.

X

There is a growing consensus that 1968 is a crucial, watershed moment in twentieth-century Mexican history and culture, second in importance only to the 1910 revolution itself, with which, indeed, it evidences many parallels. The year 1968 signals a crisis in Mexico's institutionalized revolution and a broad-based push for real, effective, participatory democracy in all areas that is still working itself out today. The Olympic Games staged in Mexico City in 1968, from the government's perspective, were to be a showcase for the country's development and modernization. As it turned out, 1968 marked Mexico's coparticipation in contemporary world events in ways not intended by the government. In Mexico, 1968 is remembered by the series of mostly student demonstrations that occurred that year, known simply as "Tlatelolco," after the central plaza where these demonstrations culminated, on 2 October, in a repressive massacre of hundreds of protestors and witnesses by government troops.

In his interpretive essay *Posdata*, Octavio Paz presents an incisive meditation on the similarities and differences among the various "youth rebellions" that in 1968 occurred in many parts of the world, from Paris to Prague, from Mexico to the United States. Significant distinctions notwithstanding, for Paz their parallels mark Mexico's participation in a new international subculture fostered in part by the spread of telecommunications; in a new revolution spirit no longer based in traditional, Marxist class distinctions; and in a radical critique of Western modernity and its faith in the future of rational progress. At the same time, *Posdata* presents a fascinating but arguably mystifying analysis, with which many commentators have taken exception, that would situate the Tlatelolco phenomenon and the events of 1968 in the larger context of a long cultural and political history in Mexico of centralized, hierarchical authority and repression, encompassing both the pre-Hispanic and the Spanish colonial heritages.

In contrast to Paz's sweeping syntheses, the highly acclaimed narrative, *La noche de Tlatelolco* (*Massacre in Mexico*; 1971) by Elena Poniatowska (1933) takes a very different approach to the representation and interpretation of the events of 1968. The very form of the work counters Paz's style of totalizing synthesis and abstraction, and it thereby resists "comprehension" and appropriation as well. *La noche de Tlatelolco* is a documentary collage of press accounts and photographs, together with transcriptions of tape-recorded, personal testimony, much of it by nature anonymous. The book poignantly captures a plurality of perspectives on the events, both in the variety of sources and discursive forms it incorporates, and in the many segments of society its voices represent, encompassing all sides of the multi-layered confrontation. For these reasons, *La noche de Tlatelolco* presents in exemplary form a number of characteristic features of postmodern, or postboom writing in Latin America, which in Mexico coincides with the post-1968 period.

The boom generation writers were mostly matured in 1968. They were witnesses to more than protagonists of this activism, an asseveration seemingly corroborated by the role Poniatowska plays in *La noche de Tlatelolco*. The authors of the postboom generation, in contrast, were at the time students, impressionable youth, and often participants in the events that culminated on 2 October 1968. Skepticism and disillusionment, based in immediate realities, are frequent ingredients in their writing. This is a gross but nonetheless useful generalization. It may be nuanced by reference to the significant leadership role played by boom generation authors and by older authors as well. I refer particularly to Paz and to José Revueltas, whose parallel yet contrasting activities illuminate the past and orient subsequent developments. Paz and Revueltas both reacted sharply and negatively to the deplorable actions of the Government at the time. But where Paz's opposition took the form of a resignation from his diplomatic post as Mexican ambassador in India, Revueltas was a direct participant and a leader of the demonstrations, who with his subsequent imprisonment effectively became a new cultural and political icon and a martyr for the students' cause. Indeed, if Paz, a figure of international stature, cosmopolitan and universal, was the de facto mentor of the *Revista mexicana de literatura* group, it is Revueltas, always a marginal figure virtually unknown outside of Mexico, who as a countercultural hero has played the role of mentor for many authors of the postboom generations. This is especially true of participants in the isolated and ultimately failed Mexican guerrilla activity in the early 1970s, the subject of a number of rather tortuous post-1968 novels, including

Muertes de Aurora (The Deaths of Aurora; 1980), by Gerardo de la Torre (1938), *¿Por qué no dijiste todo?* (Why Didn't You Tell All; 1980), by Salvador Castañeda (1946), and *Al cielo por asalto* (Conquering Heaven; 1979), by Agustín Ramos (1952).

The tragic events of 2 October 1968 were painfully real; they serve to remind us, as Fredric Jameson has put it, that history is what hurts. (Poniatowska's *La noche de Tlatelolco* is dedicated to the memory of her younger brother, who was a victim.) But it is also inevitable that with time the events' symbolic resonance has turned out to be their enduring significance. Indeed, certain capital literary works that predate 1968 seem to prefigure actual events, as if to prove that the events themselves were symptomatic rather than decisive. These might include, among works to be discussed below, the various *novelas de la onda*; or *Morirás lejos* (You Will Die Far Away; 1967), by José Emilio Pacheco (1939); or in a different way still, Fernando del Paso's radically experimental *José Trigo* (José Trigo, or "Joe Wheat"; 1966), which deals with an important railroad workers' strike in the 1950s whose action centers on the same Plaza de las Tres Culturas (Plaza of the Three Cultures, or Tlatelolco). Paz in *Posdata* highlighted the historical and symbolic significance of this site, in which icons of pre-Hispanic, Hispanic, and modern Mexican culture converge. It continues to be an intraurban locale of great significance in Mexico City. Amid the destruction wrought by the 1985 earthquake on the large public housing project located there, Tlatelolco once again became the focus of much critical attention (for such issues as public corruption and failure to adhere to quality construction standards).

Viewed retrospectively, the events of 1968 in Mexico seem dramatically to have initiated a long series of grassroots movements of opposition to the governing Revolutionary Party (PRI), initially from outside and more recently from within the party proper. This opposition continues to swell support and there are indications, especially in recent political events and the national elections of 1988, that they may be coming to fruition. The present administration of the governing party has inherited problems of legitimacy of unprecedented dimensions, to which it has responded with a new rhetoric of democratization and a real, if still very begrudging, opening of the political system. It remains to be seen whether de facto liberalization and democratization will occur, or whether the Revolutionary Party's political machine will continue effectively to assimilate dissidence.

This complex of optimism and pessimism is reflected in Poniatowska's more recent *Nada, nadie: las voces del temblor* (Nothing, Nobody:

the Voices of the Earthquake; 1988) which does for the major earthquake of 1985 what *La noche de Tlatelolco* had done for the events of
1968. Like its forebear, *Nada, nadie* takes the form of a collage of testimonial voices and documentary accounts. It stands as a scathing indictment of corruption, injustice, and ineptitude, but at the same time as a
moving tribute to the potential for broad-based, informal and extraoffi-
cial manifestations of solidarity. The student movement of 1968 remains
an implicit model and a source of inspiration for a number of new social
movements, some of which are chronicled in *Entrada libre, crónicas de
la sociedad que se organiza* (Free Admission: Chronicles of a Society in
Movement; 1988), by Carlos Monsiváis (1938).

One of the central characteristics of post-1968 life and culture in
Mexico is that the distance that traditionally separated the popular and
the intellectual continues to break down and new alliances are formed.
As older writers steeped in the high-cultural tradition move to incorporate and adapt more popular forms, ever wider segments of the population, including previously excluded or marginalized ones, have gained increased access to the organs of expression of the cultural industry, in
some ways that will be detailed below. (The origins of these developments, in another striking parallel between 1910 and 1968 and their
respective literary representations, may be traced back to the various
narratives of the Mexican revolution.)

That the events of 1968 have had great real and symbolic importance
for the Mexican people is apparent in the number of narrative works by
both younger and older authors that refer directly or indirectly to Tlatelolco. There is now an extensive critical literature arguing that the "novel
of Tlatelolco" or "of 1968" should be given thematic subgenre status
(thus, again echoing the "novel of the revolution"). Examples run from
Luis Spota's apologetic *La plaza* (The Plaza; 1972) to the bitingly satirical *El gran solitario de Palacio* (Alone in the Palace; l968), by René
Avilés Fabila (1935); from Juan García Ponce's *La invitación* (The Invitation; 1972) to Jorge Aguilar Mora's *Si muero lejos de ti* (If I Die Far
from You; 1979) and Fernando del Paso's *Palinuro de México* (Palinuro
of Mexico; 1977) (see below). María Luisa Mendoza (1931) has also
contributed to this possible subgenre with *Con él, conmigo, con nosotros
tres* (With Him, with Me, with Us Three; l971), a kaleidoscopic testimony
employing free association and colloquial language. Like Poniatowska,
Mendoza is a journalist by trade, and adept at fusing fiction and nonfiction in an original manner.

Like the novel of the revolution, the Tlatelolco novel presents vexing problems for literary classification and historical demarcation. Such is the pervasive significance of the phenomenon that virtually any novel treating social and cultural reality after 1968 could reasonably, or necessarily be classified under this heading. Thus, as a critical-historical category it may become virtually useless, more mystifying than articulate or discriminatory. Often the most effective and successful works are those that treat the phenomenon obliquely. And in this instance, time may hold little hope for a clear resolution of the historiographic dilemma. Some of the most successful early representations of the Tlatelolco experience are not found in the novel proper, but in the aforementioned works of documentation and historical interpretation by Paz and Poniatowska; in the relatively new form of the nonfictional novel or of the new journalism; and in poems by such authors as Paz and Pacheco, Castellanos, Héctor Manjarrez, and David Huerta (see below), many of them collected in the anthology *Poemas sobre el movimiento estudiantil de 1968* (Poems on the 1968 Student Movement; 1980), edited by Marco Antonio Campos (1949). The lasting and substantial effects of Tlatelolco in literary production may not be the obvious, superficial ones of explicit content or thematics, but more subtle and significant ones that affect means of representation and form (i.e., recourse to popular subgenres, or to the new journalism and nonfiction novels).

XI

With little historical perspective and no established canon, Mexican literature by authors born since 1936 appears as a myriad of tendencies and individuals. But this is not attributable solely to our lack of historical perspective. Perhaps the outstanding characteristic of "postboom" Mexican literature is its fragmentation and multiplicity. What in Mexico is spoken of as the democratization of culture has in fact become a reality. Young poets and novelists, readings and roundtables abound; so much so that an identity crisis seems to be reflected in a recent generational obsession with justifying the artistic vocation. There has undeniably been an opening: albeit improvisedly, postrevolutionary Mexico has produced an ever-growing pool of literacy and culture, largely underwritten by the State. There are women writers; there is a gay literature that has provoked invigorating polemics; there are a number of writers from the popular classes who are producing a "proletarian" literature. So much has culture flowered that one wonders whether this democratization is an intended result of government policy, an unwitting tactical blunder on the part of government leaders, or simply another ploy (placating dissidence) of the political elite, diverting the intelligence and energy of youth to the relatively innocuous field of imaginative literature. The best of this literature, as is correctly insisted in polemics, is undeservedly (and unintentionally) demeaned by giving it thematic "sub-genre" status. On the other hand, to speak of a gay or proletarian literature is perhaps a necessary evil and an important ideological strategy. The young writers have clearly benefited from their immediate predecessors, deriving a confidence in their own cultural sophistication out of the subcontinental and international success of older writers. Their writing often gains with this inherited self-assuredness a less ostentatious, deeply authentic ring. Many rebelled against what they saw as the high cultural pretentiousness of the boom-generation writers, and revived more committed writers such as Revueltas and Huerta in their search for native inspiration.

The novels of Fernando del Paso (1935) may exemplify the complex interplay of continuity and rupture between the boom generation authors and the younger authors of the postboom generations. Del Paso is a solitary and eccentric figure of unusual work habits. In a span of some thirty years he has produced only three novels: the aforementioned *José Trigo* and *Palinuro de México*, and the more recent *Noticias del Imperio* (News of Empire; 1987). Each is a work of immense proportions, combining technical virtuosity, meticulous historical documentation, and encyclopedic compendium. Comparison with Fuentes's monumental *Terra Nostra* is both inevitable and instructive. It may reasonably be asked what del Paso possibly hoped to achieve with the scope of these works. They seem a holdout from an earlier age of faith in the totalizing potential of literature. Perhaps part of their function is precisely a certain form of resistance to contemporary superficiality and immediacy. Yet significantly, del Paso's works for the most part avoid with their irrepressible humor the ponderous pretensions of many boom works. They refuse to make problematic Latin American or Mexican being as they move freely between the Old World and the New, the past and the present. Paradoxically, they are localizing and demystifying in their very disproportionality.

Like del Paso, though in very different ways, Elena Poniatowska, Carlos Monsiváis (1938), and José Emilio Pacheco (1939) are crucial transitional figures. They are a bridge between the boom generation's

Mafia, with which they each had close ties, and the more recent promotions of writers, whom they have encouraged by their very practice to be different. They demystify high culture without ever compromising their art or their commitment; rather than bring art down to the level of the common man, they seem ingeniously to raise the common man to the level of serious art (cultural historian and promoter Fernando Benítez [1912] is somewhat of a precursor in this regard). If Paz was spiritual figurehead and guru all wrapped in one, Monsiváis (guru) and Pacheco (spiritual figure head) have shared these chores in leading more recent generations. Monsiváis, a brilliant cultural historian, art critic, and essayist, is a breezy, almost facile intelligence of incisive wit, which has caused him to be both admired and despised, but always held in awe. In revealing the theatricality of Mexican politics and culture, he himself has made a popular figure of the analyst, a melodrama of valuation and interpretation.

Pacheco, primarily a poet, has brought Mexican poetry into the technological world and the atomic age. He better than anyone has responded to the natural death that high-culture poetry has suffered in recent times: psychoanalysis has made the oneiric cliché, the mass media have made the exotic into the everyday; the possibility of instant annihilation makes notions of the eternal and the immortal seem a cruel joke. His early poetry shows the influence of Octavio Paz: *Los elementos de la noche* (The Elements of the Night; 1963) and *El reposo del fuego* (Fire at Rest; 1966) demonstrate Pacheco's command of conventional poetic diction and rhetoric. In later works like *Irás y no volverás* (To Leave and Not Return; 1973) and *Islas a la deriva* (Islands Adrift; 1976) he turns witty, prosaic, epigramatic, and aphoristic. He turns literature against itself to create new literature, while demystifying the historic tradition. The death of high culture need not be lamented, Pacheco seems to say. Quite the contrary, it opens up new possibilities. For this he has inspired a large number of young poets, children of the technological age for whom recourse to the great Western cultural tradition seems a less viable alternative. With Pacheco a strange inversion suggests itself: while much of contemporary prose fiction has become poeticized, poetry, responding to changing circumstances, has found new life in the so-called prosaic.

Pacheco has also proven himself a skilled and multitalented narrator, with such efforts as the aforementioned *Las batallas en el desierto* (Desert Battles; 1981) and *Morirás lejos* (You Will Die Far Away; 1967), the latter a powerful orchestration in which plot and characterization are purposely confused. It is a typical Pacheco exploration of the theme of human degradation, making reference to the concentration camps and to the modern history of the Jew. The recourse to narrative works is also apparent in another contemporary author of verse, Homero Aridjis (1940). Aridjis's early poetry, such as *Mirándola dormir* (Watching Her Sleep; 1964), is, like Pacheco's, very much in a Pazian mold. More recently, Aridjis has turned to the historical novel, with *1492, vida y tiempos de Juan Cabezón de Castilla* (*1492, the Life and Times of Juan Cabezón of Castille*; 1985) and *Memorias del nuevo mundo* (Memories of the New World; 1988). It is as if for these younger writers the exclusive dedication to the poetic vocation exemplified by Paz were no longer sufficient.

A return to a more readerly text and to partial reconstructions of specific aspects of concrete, social reality is a salient characteristic of the most recent novelistic production in Mexico, by younger and older novelists alike, including documentary, testimonial and new historical novels. Leñero's documentary theater is an important contribution here, as are the texts of Poniatowska. Sometimes these new works take the form of period pieces, recasting a particular intersection of time and place; other times they recreate a decisive historical figure. Reference has already been made to Pacheco's *Las batallas en el desierto*, Pitol's *El desfile del amor*, and del Paso's monumental historical novel *Noticias del Imperio*. Other examples include *Intramuros* (Inner Walls; 1983) by Luis Arturo Ramos (1947), *Los pasos de López* (The Steps of López; 1982) by Ibargüengoitia, and *Madero, el otro* (The Other Madero; 1989) by Ignacio Solares (1945). Along similar lines runs the relatively new form of the journalistic chronicle, first popularized by the author Cristina Pacheco, whose microtexts have been compiled in such volumes as *Para vivir aquí* (To Live Here; 1983); *Sopita de fideo* (Alphabet Soup; 1985); and *Cuarto de Azotea* (Maid's Quarters; 1987). Other authors, such as Ignacio Trejo Fuentes (1955), with *Crónicas romanas* ("Roman" [Neighborhood] Chronicles; 1990), have subsequently pursued this new genre (which also has a considerable following in contemporary Brazil). These "chronicles" recall the controversy in the United States over a recent, Pulitzer Prize winning piece of investigative journalism that was discovered to have had some "fictional" elaboration. From a poststructuralist perspective, the Latin American press, in which the sharp distinctions between objective reporting and editorial comment are not so sharply drawn, may in this context seem curiously enlightened (as to the counterproductivity of separating these realms categorically).

One of the most noteworthy developments in post-1968 literature is the increasing number of women authors who have attained critical recognition. Especially troubling here is an inevitable tension between the political benefits of introducing their work as women's writing, on the one hand, and the potential for continued condescension in drawing categories along gender lines on the other, with its concomitant perpetuation of invidious distinctions. The immediate precedent and popular success of Poniatowska's documentary and testimonial works was no doubt decisive for many of these new authors. Also a source of inspiration for some were the little known but critically acclaimed novels of Josefina Vicens (1911-88), a laconic, solitary, Rulfian kind of figure whose *El libro vacío* (*The Empty Book*; 1958) and *Los años falsos* (False Years; 1982) are dark existential and metafictional exercises of unrelenting determination and fatalistic resignation.

Though most all of these authors share some feminist concerns, to speak of a unitary women's writing would be misleading and simplistic. Rather, new women authors have brought their alternative perspectives to bear on the whole range of contemporary practices, much as had Sor Juana and Campobello, Garro and Castellanos before them. Diversity rather than unity characterizes new womens' writing in Mexico. Thus, at one extreme stands the work of Carmen Boullosa (1946). Her *Mejor desaparece* (Better to Disappear; 1987), in a vanguardist and experimental vein (it alternates narrative text with the author's paintings), recreates in poetic and nightmarish fragments the childhood of its female narrator, particularly her relationship with siblings and the father. At another extreme there is the immediate and broad-based popularity of *Arráncame la vida* (*Mexican Bolero*; 1985), by Angeles Mastretta (1949). Its success may owe something to Poniatowska's recreation of the voice of women from the popular classes, but also perhaps to its adaptation of a Spota-like formula, playing on the public's prurient fascination with behind-the-scenes glimpses of ill-gained riches and political corruption. The novel rewrites the novel of the political aftermath of the revolution from the perspective of a state governor's wife. As the young politician's wife (the narrator-protagonist) rises to prominence she gains little moral perspective or appreciation for the broader implications of the violence and corruption she only glimpses. But she does, on a personal level, develop an incipient feminist consciousness as she derives from her milieu a sort of picaresque cunning.

Somewhere between the poles established by Boullosa and Mastretta, the work of María Luisa Puga (1944) may be situated. Her first book,

Las posibilidades del odio (The Possibilities of Hate; 1978), makes an absolutely original contribution to Mexican literature. Set in modern Kenya, it draws sensitively portrayed microhistories (case studies) against chronologies of major events in the African nation's history, which serve as a contextual backdrop. It is a groundbreaking work because it abandons the obsession with Latin America's conflictive ties to Europe, while suggesting a strategic new direction in Third World consciousness and solidarity. Another Puga novel, *Pánico o peligro* (Panic or Danger; 1983), is equally original and incisive. In this novel, a Mexico City secretary reflects upon her own life story, her relationships with women and men, friends and lovers. She in effect becomes a writer—the novel's twelve chapters are the twelve notebooks she has filled—but she rejects canonical norms and literary pretensions. Along the way, the novel critically portrays Mexico City's recent past, employing the length and breadth of a major thoroughfare, Insurgentes, as a controlling metaphor. This book contributes to the transformation and attenuation of extreme narrative self-reflexivity in an arguably poststructuralist manner: it emphasizes writing as a process and a construction of *social* identity, as Susana the narrator assimilates or questions the rhetoric of those who surround her.

If the boom marks Latin America's self-conscious contribution to the cutting edge of Western high culture, in the vein of Anglo-European Modernism, what appeared in the mid-sixties under the generic title of *literatura de la onda* ("hip" literature) was an unambiguous, spontaneous confirmation of the simultaneous emergence of the Postmodern. Along with rock music and drugs, the infamous generation gap has arrived on Mexican soil. Telecommunications and the ever more international scope of socioeconomic and cultural structures have indeed made the Western world a sort of global village, and telecommunications among these writers become both a means and an end in themselves. The arrival of the new wave is first apparent in two precocious, talented, and cunning young writers, Gustavo Sainz (1940) and José Agustín (1944). *Literatura de la onda* has been criticized as "adolescent" literature. This it was: Agustín had published his first two novels by the time he was twenty-two; Sainz published his trend-setting *Gazapo* (1965)—rapidly translated into French, Italian, Portuguese, German, and English—when he was twenty-five. But more than a style or a school, the new wave was an attitude, a thematics, a passing phase. It involved an irreverent use of base and colloquial language in the mouths of upper-middle-class youth. It involved rebellion against authority and moral bankruptcy in the name of the happening, the drug experience, and a rather naive and watered-down sexual revolution. It mostly proposed nothing of substance to replace what it debased. It did, however, serve as testimony to a crisis of values and a Mexican cultural predicament: traditional Hispanic culture and the empty rhetoric of Mexican nationalism were anachronisms, but the unquestioned assimilation of Western hippie culture seemed equally false and forced in the Mexican context. The rebelliousness of a bored and skeptical youth, as recorded in these novels, possibly foreshadows the protests of 1968.

That the *literatura de la onda* was indeed a passing thematic phase is apparent in Sainz's next novel, *Obsesivos días circulares* (Obsessive, Circular Days; 1969). It is in the judgement of many the pretentiously hermetic sort of work that his first effort was not. Agustín, for his part, after *La tumba* (The Tomb; 1964), *De perfil* (In Profile; 1966), and *Inventando que sueño* (Imagining I'm Dreaming; 1968), produces with *Se está haciendo tarde (final en laguna)* (It's Getting Late [Blank Ending]; 1973) a sort of epitaph to drug culture and the sexual revolution, and with them to the *literatura de la onda*. The early success of Agustín and Sainz has perhaps complicated their artistic development. They are dedicated writers, however, and their work continues to mature and evolve. They have mastered the media and the expanding Mexican/Latin-American cultural marketplace.

Héctor Manjarrez (1945) and Jorge Aguilar Mora (1946) also represent, though in a different way, the transnational dimension of contemporary youth culture. Their world, their sphere of action, is not Mexico but the globe. Like their predecessors of the boom, they are well versed in the attitudes and the techniques of modern and postmodern writing. But they reject in practice, as have among others Manuel Puig in Argentina, Antonio Skármeta in Chile, and Oscar Collazos in Colombia (see corresponding sections), what they see as the mystifying, romanticizing, symbolic system-building pretentiousness of some of the more renowned novels of the boom. Manjarrez, because his rejection occurs more at the level of content or substance, has of the two seen wider acceptance. His characters, less naive than the innocents of the new wave novels, at first delight in the schizophrenic possibilities of youth counterculture. In *Lapsus* (1971) literature grows out of a put-down of the solemnity of literature, much in the vein of Sterne's *Tristam Shandy*. Later, in *No todos los hombres son románticos* (Not all Men are Romantics; 1984), the characters recognize the emptiness of countercultural frivolity and find in international political causes a deeper dimension of humanity. Aguilar Mora has attempted more daring experiments in form. Though they certainly avoid hierarchy and totalization, with their Barthesian or Deleuzian proliferation of signifiers, the novels *Cadáver lleno de mundo* (Cadaver Full of World; 1971) and *Si muero lejos de ti* (If I Die Far From You; 1979) run the risk of seeming just as pretentious and more obscure than the overdetermined symbolic systems they seek to oppose. Manjarrez and Aguilar Mora have a kindred spirit in the poet David Huerta (1949), the author, among other works, of a complex book-length poem, *Incurable* (Incurable, 1987), that explodes from within this traditional genre and defines a potential new form.

New technology, mass media, and cultural syncretism are reflected in still another way by recent Mexican literature in the novels of Luis Zapata (1951) and Armando Ramírez (1950), representative of the new gay and proletarian subgenres, respectively. For Manjarrez and Aguilar Mora, the world is their playground and the whole of Western culture their field of reference. For Zapata and Ramírez, on the other hand, the city—Mexico City—*is* the world (read: a microcosm of it), and what they have gleaned from radio, television, and film seemingly their field of reference. Drug culture in Sainz and Agustín is the province of well-to-do youth who are bored and disaffected; drug and alcohol abuse in Ramírez's poverty-ridden Tepito (a popular neighborhood in Mexico City) or in Zapata's Colonia Roma (a sort of inner-city bohemia), by way of contrast, has quite different causes and effects. It is not altogether clear whether Zapata and Ramírez are serenely parodying the violence and melodrama of television and popular film or whether they themselves are its victims, and to this ambiguity can be attributed some of the appeal their work holds. Much like Argentina's Puig, they have made serious art of subliterary popular culture, or vice versa. Zapata's *El vampiro de la colonia Roma* (*Adonis García*; 1979) and *De pétalos perenes* (Of Perennial Petals; 1981); Ramírez's *Chin-Chin el teporocho* (Chin-Chin the Bum; 1972) and *Violación en Polanco* (Rape in Polanco; 1980) are moving or shocking stories that show great sensitivity to the whole range of human emotion, from the violent to the tender. They document daily life in a way that might be considered neo-costumbrista. The language is realistic, popular, and colloquial; the narrative techniques essayed are sometimes intricate and awkward but rarely obtrusive. Their following is considerable, and their works sell not because of national or international critical acclaim nor even so much because of sophisticated promotion, but rather, simply and significantly, thanks to word of mouth. This is one promising sign of the health and vigor in contemporary Mexican literature.

The diversity of styles and concerns reflected in post-1968 writing in Mexico is both chaotic and refreshing. Those somewhat arbitrarily selected here for brief mention can only be partially representative of the current climate and trends. Clearly, post-1968 writing testifies to the distance Mexican literature has traveled from its uncertain origins in the pre-Hispanic legacy, in its Spanish colonial heritage, and in its modern independence and revolutionary movements. Equally clear, however, is how post-1968 writing remains highly representative of certain fundamental characteristics of Mexican literature through the ages. This distinctive flavor may be described as a peculiar combination of worldliness and provincialism in Mexican literature, the product of a long history of dependency together with the country's strong sense of self and stubborn autonomy.

In Mexico today the number of young writers already with a substantial body of writing to their credit, from all walks and stations of life, is mildly astonishing, so much so that there is reasonable fear among the numbers of losing sight of the trees for the forest. As if in spite of the 1910 revolution's secret intentions, numerous shortcomings, and current crisis of legitimacy, the government continues begrudgingly to make good on some of its official rhetoric. The more pluralistic and egalitarian literary culture the country has lived in the wake of the boom of Latin American literature and in the aftermath of Tlatelolco may still be but a prelude to the substance of things to come.

BIBLIOGRAPHY

Anderson, Danny. "Cultural Conversation and Constructions of Reality: Mexican Narrative and Literary Theories after 1968." *Siglo XX/20th Century* 8.1-2 (1990-91): 11-30. A broad, original interpretation of contemporary trends in Mexican narrative as they correlate to recent work in critical theory.

Blanco, José Joaquín. *Crónica de la poesía mexicana*. México, D.F.: Katún, 1977. A pointed, down-to-earth ideological treatment of nineteenth- and twentieth-century poetry.

Brushwood, John S. *Mexico in Its Novel*. Austin: University of Texas Press, 1966. The outstanding reference work on the novel.

Brushwood, John S. *La novela mexicana: (1967-1982)*. México, D.F.: Grijalbo, 1985. A survey of recent developments in the novel, tracing thematic and stylistic trends.

Burgess, Ronald D. *The New Dramatists of Mexico, 1967-85*. Lexington: University Press of Kentucky, 1991. A carefully documented historical study of the problems and issues facing the recent generation of dramatists in Mexico.

Domínguez, Christopher. *Antología de la narrativa mexicana*. 2 vols. México, D.F.: Fondo de Cultura Económica, 1990. A comprehensive anthology of narrative works of all types; the anthology's various period divisions are all prefaced with introductory essays containing strong and insightful interpretations.

Foster, David William. *Estudios sobre teatro mexicano contemporáneo: semiología de la competencia teatral*. New York: Lang (Utah Studies in Language and Literature), 1984. New analyses of outstanding twentieth-century dramatic texts.

Foster, David William. *Mexican Literature; a Bibliography of Secondary Sources*. 2nd rev. ed. Metuchen, N.J.: Scarecrow Press, 1992. A comprehensive registry of general references, references on special topics, and critical books and essays on specific authors.

Franco, Jean. *Plotting Women: Gender and Representation in Mexico*. New York: Colombia University Press, 1989. An important contribution to Third-World gender studies, and to Mexican cultural history generally, focusing on prominent female intellectuals and writers from the colonial period to the present.

Garibay K., Angel María. *Panorama literario de los pueblos nahuas*. México, D.F.: Porrúa, 1963. An overview of the various genres of Náhuatl-language literature.

González Peña, Carlos. *Historia de la literatura mexicana: desde los orígenes hasta nuestros días*. México, D.F.: Porrúa, 1984. A traditional, general literary history, still useful for its comprehensiveness; it first appeared in 1928, and was revised in 1964.

Langford, Walter M. *The Mexican Novel Comes of Age*. Notre Dame: University of Notre Dame Press, 1981. An interesting overview from a North American perspective of the twentieth-century novel in Mexico.

Leonard, Irving. *Baroque Times in Old Mexico*. Ann Arbor: University of Michigan Press, 1959. A lively, traditionalist account of literature in seventeenth-century Mexico, with a sociological bent.

Martínez, José Luis. *De la naturaleza y carácter de la literatura mexicana*. México, D.F.: Fondo de Cultura Económica, 1960. A very brief overview of Mexican literature highlighting broad, general characteristics.

Martínez, José Luis. *La expresión nacional*. México, D.F.: Oasis, 1984. A collection of very diverse essays on nineteenth-century works and authors, ranging from brief notes to the rather substantial "México en busca de su expresión."

Martínez, José Luis. *Nezahualcóyotl: Vida y obra*. México, D.F.: Fondo de Cultura Económica, 1972. A ground-breaking study of the life and work of the great pre-Hispanic cultural figure, together with an anthology of poetry.

Monsiváis, Carlos. "Notas sobre la cultura mexicana en el siglo XX." In *Historia general de México*. 2.1377-1548. México, D.F.: El Colegio de México, 1981. An outstanding sociocultural treatment of literature in the twentieth century.

Ocampo, Aurora M. *Diccionario de escritores mexicanos*. México, D.F.: Universidad Nacional Autónoma de México, 1966. A fundamental reference work; includes a biobibliographic sketch, and both primary and secondary sources, for all authors included. The first volume of a revised and updated edition has recently appeared.

Paz, Octavio. *Sor Juana Inés de la Cruz o las trampas de la fe*. Barcelona: Seix Barral, 1982. A sociocultural interpretation of Mexican colonial society, together with a detailed study of the life and works of Sor Juana Inés de la Cruz.

Schneider, Luis Mario. *Ruptura y continuidad*. México, D.F.: Fondo de Cultura Económica, 1975. A very selective view of major periods in literature, highlighting in each representative public polemics concerning art and literature.

Sefchovich, Sara. *México: país de ideas, país de novelas*. México, D.F.: Grijalbo, 1987. A helpful, often illuminating approach to the history of the novel in Mexico, emphasizing sociology and history of ideas.

Sommers, Joseph. *After the Storm; Landmarks of the Modern Mexican Novel*. Albuquerque: University of New Mexico Press, 1968. General comments on contemporary fiction since the 1910 revolution, with monographic chapters on Agustín Yáñez, Juan Rulfo, and Carlos Fuentes.

Spell, Jefferson Rea. *Bridging the Gap*. México, D.F.: Libros de México, 1971. A collection of well-documented, scholarly essays mostly on early nineteenth-century literature, especially Fernández de Lizardi.

NICARAGUA
Paul W. Borgeson, Jr.
University of Illinois

I

Even more than in other countries, the literature of Nicaragua is conditioned by her social and economic history. As a land with a geographical position coveted by others and with a tradition of internal political divisions, one-man rule, and foreign intervention, these concerns affect her literature both internally, as themes, and externally, as elements in its very development. Nicaragua's economic status, having progressed slowly in the twentieth century, has resulted in a very limited reading public, an unsubstantial publishing industry, and a literature which, with a few exceptions, has as a consequence existed on the fringes of world cultural activity.

Among other characteristics that these and other circumstances have contributed to the literature of Nicaragua, we may suggest the following: 1) dominance of the *mestizo* culture (fusion of indigenous and European racial and cultural characteristics: little purely indigenous remains, and there is less still of the Afro-Nicaraguan), and the readiness to fuse the Nicaraguan heritage with influences from other countries (Spain first, later France, and more recently the United States and others); 2) a continued presence of the Colonial heritage, as the need to assimilate and transcend both the historical experience and the issues of neocolonialism in our day; 3) the search for a literature capable of being both Nicaraguan and universal, beginning with Rubén Darío (1867-1916) and intensifying in this century, with the Vanguard poetry movement of the 1920s and 1930s; 4) very limited production in the novel and theater and better representation of the shorter genres of poetry, the essay, and the short story; 5) tension between popular culture and the historical tendency for literature to be an activity of the educational and economic elite; 6) discontinuity of cultural development, affected by political turmoil,

443

dictatorships, repression, and the need to write and publish in exile; 7) continuity of a religious attitude orientation, even in movements that in other countries were neutral or even hostile to religion (the Vanguard, most notably) and continuing even under the Sandinista government; and 8) a general tendency to favor descriptive and prescriptive forms of literature (those that describe things and recommend change) more than those that transform reality or present one radically different from that of daily experience.

Evidently, two major issues join several of these characteristics: Nicaragua has always been a country in search of self as she strives to accede to her own place in world culture; her literature has both taken extreme positions and sought the synthesis of the country's varied cultural components. Writers who have brought them together have generally produced most of Nicaragua's best literature.

II

Most Nicaraguan critics agree that the nation's literary production achieves the qualities of a mature and perceptive artistic originality only late in her history. Consequently this survey will pass rapidly through the literature of the Colonial period and most of the nineteenth century, in order to concentrate on the more praiseworthy achievements of its Modernist, Vanguard, and more recent writers, who in general far surpass in quality the production of Nicaragua's first three and a half centuries.

Nicaragua's indigenous groups, in comparison to those of Mexico, Guatemala, or Peru, were neither cohesive nor large, and they did not produce the kind of cultural artifacts that serve today as a common cultural ground. The relatively easy conquest of Central America by Spain and her highly effective repression of traditional culture left Nicaragua with a very limited heritage of indigenous literature. What remains has little of the ritualistic nature characteristic of the literary production of the Amerindian, for whom "literature" is better thought of in terms of a complex ceremonial activity bringing together prayer, public celebration, dancing, and music in the reenactment of the culture's basic beliefs, thus fusing the state and the religion. This literature is largely lost to Nicaragua.

The closest thing to pre-Columbian literature, aside from a few fragments of verse in the local languages (and actually of postconquest origin, in all likelihood) is "El Güegüense," which may be called a popular farce for staged presentation ("theater" or "drama" do not apply well here). Traditionally presented in the marketplace or other public area, "El Güegüense" uses masked figures, music (flute, whistles, drums), dance movements, and highly stylized dialogue in a loosely structured story line focused on the main character, for whom the piece is named. Güegüense represents the people (as opposed to the Spanish or mixed *élite*): he is portrayed as an old man and picaroon who, having lived by his wits, uses them once again to frustrate the exploitative designs of the authorities. Unable to rebel openly, he stalls, mocking and joking, feigning deafness to protect himself. A satirical tone is implicit in the confrontation between the people (centered on Güegüense) and the authorities, and the protagonist's momentary allusion to the better days of his youth is a thinly veiled lament on the conquest itself. "El Güegüense" owes only a part of its makeup to pre-Columbian "theater": the extensive and frequently incremental repetitions, the use of dance and music, and some speech patterns and expressions of popular and hence indigenous origin. Also evident, however, is the impact of the Spanish theatrical tradition; the play seems to date only from the mid-seventeenth century and was first transcribed only in the late nineteenth. The value of "El Güegüense," then, is less that of an ancient cultural artifact (or even of a great piece of literature) than that of a candidly humorous and ironic expression of the early *mestizaje* and the tensions and possibilities of its emergence.

Throughout the Colonial period, as elsewhere in Latin America, all officially recognized art was the province of the privileged—which is to say that it was a dominantly Spanish activity both in production and consumption. (While the people, of course, produced their own cultural expressions, these were of little interest to the dominant class and are poorly preserved.) Success for these writers was less a question of innovation than of faithful imitation of Peninsular models; and one of the principal functions for the officials and aristocrats was to create the desirable illusion of being in Spain, and not in the "backwater" of Central America (such escapist literature was an important diversion throughout the Colonies). While in some countries outstanding writers emerged during the Colonial period, in Nicaragua (rather off the preferred routes to gold and glory), little was written of lasting quality, and even less was published. No book of poetry written by a Nicaraguan was published until the early nineteenth century, for example. While there are some *loas* (short stage pieces), the best literature about Nicaragua from the

Colonial period is surely that of the chroniclers of discovery, exploration, and conquest: Gil González Dávila (1480?-1526?), Pedro Mártir de Anghiería (or Anglería; 1459-1526), Gonzalo Fernández de Oviedo (1478-1557), Bartolomé de Las Casas (1474-1566)—all Spaniards—and Juan Dávila, considered the first Nicaraguan writer (*Relación circunstanciada de la provincia de Costa Rica*, in León Fernández, *Documentos para la historia de Costa Rica*, vol. 3 [San José, C.R.: Imprenta Nacional, 1883]). In general, we may stress the 1) imitative and the 2) instrumental function of Nicaraguan literature from the Colonial period, largely informative and didactic in nature, and generally showing few characteristics unique to the area.

Nicaragua, like most of Latin America, achieved political separation from Spain in the early decades of the nineteenth century—and like many of the other former Colonies, found herself plunged into decades of chaos, discontinuity, and internal strife unconducive to the production of quality literature. The failure of the Central American Federation (1838), disputes over power, civil violence, and the need to set a course for national unity and development are reflected in a literature that throughout the later eighteenth and most of the nineteenth century carried on the functional nature of Nicaragua's Colonial cultre. The essay flourished (at least by local standards) as did all sorts of other didactic works (religious instruction, histories, moral and philosophical treatises). If we may associate the term "literature" with not merely writing of historical importance but rather with aesthetic achievement, we may then suggest that Nicaraguan literature-as-art really begins its development late in the nineteenth century, and even more specifically in the period of the 1870s and 1880s. Arellano points out the rapid development of this period: the National Library was founded in 1880; the first daily newspaper (most were weekly or monthly) was begun in 1884; 1876 marks the formation of the first cohesive literary group; and the first anthology of Nicaraguan poetry is published in 1878. It is doubly remarkable, then, that the *belles lettres* of Nicaragua should have begun such a short time before producing a poet of true world stature: Darío, the leading figure of the Modernist movement throughout Latin America and also Spain, and the renovator (many would say the originator) of Nicaraguan literature. Darío, of course, came from a context, and it was one which he never forgot. Yet, in discussing Darío, one must also acknowledge that in his formation, ideals, and impact he so far exceeded the nature of his original environment (he jested of his "mental Gallicism," for example) that he is both Nicaraguan and much more.

Darío requires special attention, as the pride of Nicaraguan letters and as a figure of lasting international stature. His poetry and prose are typified by the utmost attention to form and the most thorough command of versification, in which he was a prolific renovator and creator; a rich lyricism and sonority whose resonances give the poem a physical quality, vastly enhancing its anecdotal or descriptive content; an authoritative tone going well beyond the biographical "I" and often speaking for the Latin American and even for mankind; and a fondness for all that is sensorial: music, painting, the decorative arts, the full use of the five senses. These qualities all lift Darío's poetry above the daily and common, even when such is its direct theme. Darío's pleasure in the exotic (faraway places and times, frequent uses of mythology), especially in his early works, is counteracted by a philosophical concern constant in his poetry. Although some poems also manifest a social concern ("To Roosevelt," for example), his most profound works center on the search for the Absolute, through art, religion, and even the occult mysteries that attracted the Romantics before him. Many of Darío's works, then, have multiple levels on which to be read and understood, including many poems (his famous "Sonatina," for example) apparently superficial and escapist in nature: his poetry is probably the most intense expression ever of humankind eternally seeking its perfection through perfect artistic creation.

Darío's *Azul* (Blue; 1888) announced the emergence of a far-reaching voice, and became the symbol for the new Modernist movement he promoted and led, carried on in his own work by the poetry of *Prosas profanas* (Profane Proses; 1896) and his more melancholy and confessional *Cantos de vida y esperanza* (Songs of Life and Hope; 1905), often considered his greatest work. Darío's death was an internationally felt loss, and is generally given as the date for the end of Modernism as a movement, although poets and others would be influenced by it and its leader for decades to come.

Other Modernist poets of note include Román Mayorga Rivas (1861?-1925), author of *Viejo y nuevo* (Old and New; 1915), and the Leonese poets Azarías H. Pallais (1884-1954; *Espumas y estrellas* [Foam and Stars; 1918], *Glosas* [Glosses; date unknown]), Lino Argüello (1887-1937; *Claros de alma* [Clearings in the Soul; 1908]), and Alfonso Cortés (1893-1969; *Treinta poemas* [Thirty Poems; 1952], *La Odisea del istmo* [Odyssey of the Isthmus; 1922]), whose work is scant in quantity, like that of many others of the period, but striking in quality and originality. Also worthy of mention as Modernists are Santiago Argüello (1871-1940),

Juan de Dios Vanegas (1873-1964), and Ramón Sáenz Morales (1891-1927).

Modernism, of course, ran well into the first decades of the present century; we are considering twentieth century literature as beginning with the dissolution of Modernism, whose roots belong to the nineteenth. Such was the dominance of Darío in Nicaraguan literature (and in that of Latin America in general) that one of the first needs for a new movement inevitably was to distance itself from him. The Nicaraguan Vanguard movement, usually dated from 1927 or 1929, adopted an aggressive posture toward Darío, and nearly everything else as well, seeking first to shake complacency and any tendency toward the superficially descriptive. It founded an "Anti-Academy" of the Spanish Language (as a counter to the moldy officiality of the Royal Spanish Academy), insisted upon a "sportive" attitude toward art, stressed national values (Darío wrote relatively little about Nicaragua), and was religiously and politically committed toward a restoration of conservative values and national stability, even at the price of a "benevolent" dictatorship (the dictatorship of course, did come about, but it did not prove to be particuarly benevolent). José Coronel Urtecho (1906) was in large measure the Vanguardists' mentor, announcing the fall (or displacement) of Darío and introducing Anglo-American verse to Nicaragua. Other Vanguardists of worth are Joaquín Pasos (1914-47), Luis Alberto Cabrales (1901-74), Salomón de la Selva (1893-1959), Manolo Cuadra (1907-57), and Pablo Antonio Cuadra (1912), who continues as one of Nicaragua's leading writers today.

Critics group Post-Vanguard Nicaraguan writers in varying ways: Generation of 1940, of 1950, and so forth, although there is only partial agreement as to who belongs where. Of these two generations, that of 1940 has made a lasting contribution to Nicaraguan literature: grouped around Cuadra, poets such as Ernesto Mejía Sánchez (1923), Carlos Martínez Rivas (1924), and Ernesto Cardenal (1925) began their writing in the 1940s and to our minds constitute the second promotion of Nicaraguan writers to truly transcend their country's borders, while (more, perhaps, than Darío) refusing to disregard her as a source. They have been active promoters of their country's literary and cultural tradition, are active researchers and publishers, and have compiled numerous studies and anthologies of Nicaraguan literature (such as Mejía Sánchez's outstanding edition of Darío's poetry).

In the short story, where Sergio Ramírez has observed the influence of the Salvadorean writer Salarrué, narrators of note include Adolfo

Calero Orozco (1889; *Cuentos pinoleros* [Stories of "Pinoleros" (Nicaraguans); 1945], *Cuentos nicaragüenses* [Stories of Nicaragua; 1957]), Mariano Fiallos Gil (1907-69; *Horizonte quebrado* [Broken Horizon; 1959]), Manolo Cuadra (1908; *Contra Sandino en la montaña* [Against Sandino in the Mountains; 1945], *Almidón* [Starch; 1945], and *Itinerario de Little Corn Island* [Little Corn Island Itinerary; 1936]), and Sergio Ramírez (1942). Also, Coronel Urtecho, Pasos, Cuadra, and Cardenal have contributed short stories of merit.

The one poet who most stands out from this group is Ernesto Cardenal, although he himself has considered Martínez Rivas the finest poet of his group. Cardenal has established himself as the second poet of Nicaragua, and some would say the first. In more than twenty anthologies, translated into all the principal and many smaller Western languages and the subject of a number of book-length studies, Cardenal is both admired and detested throughout the Americas and Europe, for his poetry, like the Liberationist political and religious position it expresses, tends to generate passionate reactions both for and against. Cardenal, in contrast to Darío, reaches not only the *literati* but "real people" as well. Both deal often with the past: Darío typically in a nostalgia for an idealized time that never existed in reality, Cardenal in a revisionist analysis of the causes for the crises and challenges of the present, as in *El estrecho dudoso* (The Search for the Strait; 1971). His most enduring works include *Salmos* (*Psalms*; 1964), *Homenaje a los indios americanos* (*Homage to the American Indians*; 1969), and *Oráculo sobre Managua* (*Oracle over Managua*; 1973). Yet his most recent work may turn out to be even more impressive. The *Homenaje* is still under revision; *Los ovnis de oro* (The Golden UFOs; 1988) is an incomplete collection of his poems on the indigenous theme with several new pieces. And Cardenal's latest book is his most ambitious ever: *Cántico cósmico* (Cosmic Canticle; 1989) is a massive, sweeping, and frequently inspired exploration of humankind and God in the universe. A massive and often epic single poem of nearly 600 pages, it seeks to understand the past—from the Big Bang of creation to Somoza to the Revolution of 1977—and the future of humankind's continuing evolution as a species.

At this time, Nicaragua is facing the need to rebuild herself in a new and freer image after decades of dictatorial rule. She also is generating the cultural products that will enable her to reevaluate her past and choose her future as well. Not all her writers view these tasks in the same way, although most are at least sympathetic to Sandinista ideology. Cardenal, for example, while Minister of Culture, promoted popular workshops in poetry, theater, and other cultural expressions (channeled to the defense of Sandinista ideals, be it noted). Cuadra, on the other hand, has a much less doctrinaire position than Cardenal and is seen by the stricter Sandinistas as uncommitted to Socialist objectives (he is Editor of *La Prensa*, a newspaper frequently at odds with Sandinismo). Clearly, the struggle between conflicting ideas that has characterized Nicaragua's history continues, and will be reflected in her literature for some time to come. As always, literature and not just the political arena will express the aspirations and the frustrations of Nicaraguans on all sides.

Meanwhile, there is a fresh wind in Nicaraguan literature, again primarily in poetry. The inclusion of writers from more diverse social and economic groups and the reevaluation of the people's contribution to national culture has also been accompanied by a new opening to women writers: Michèle Najlis (1946; *El viento armado* [The Armed Wind; 1969]), Rosario Murillo (1951) and others. Among these, Gioconda Belli (1948) is exceptionally eloquent, and has produced perhaps the best poetry of the Sandinista period, in which multiple commitments—Nicaragua, women, ideology—fuse in the multiple aspects of love (her recurring theme, as in Murillo) and her delicately balanced use of language: *Sobre la grama* (On the Grass; 1974), *Línea de fuego* (Firing Line; 1978), *De la costilla de Eva* (Of Eve's Rib; 1986). The excellence of the work of these and other Nicaraguan women writers already stands as one of the major cultural contributions of this period of Nicaraguan literary history.

Other young poets seek to maintain high-quality art that also speaks to and of the Nicaraguan people: Omar d'León (1929), Horacio Peña (1936), Edwin Yllescas (1941), Luis Rocha (1942). Beltrán Morales (1944) has a strongly satirical and sometimes epigrammatic tone: *Algún sol* (Some Sun; 1969), *Agua regia* (Aqua Regia; 1972). The democratization of literature seen in these poets is one of the most significant achievements in Nicaraguan cultural and literary history. Even amid ongoing discord, Nicaragua has produced a number of writers and other artists and intellectuals of high merits. This time, however, it has been as something approaching a generational experience: rather than having artists in spite of strife, as in the past, she has them because of it, and because of her renewed and intense search for her own real identity. It may well be that her writers at least have, at long last, found theirs.

BIBLIOGRAPHY

Aldaraca, Bridget, et al., eds. *Nicaragua in Revolution: The Poets Speak.* Minneapolis: MEP Publications, 1985. Poetry on Nicaragua's revolution through 1979; Spanish with English translations; editorializing limited to selections, section titles, and introduction.

Arellano, Jorge Eduardo. *Panorama de la literatura nicaragüense.* 4th ed. Managua: Nueva Nicaragua, 1982. The fundamental source on Nicaraguan literary history by its leading authority; some tendency to merely list names, but the scholarship is strong and the judgments are balanced.

Beverley, John, and Marc Zimmerman. *Literature and Politics in the Central American Revolutions.* Austin: University of Texas Press, 1990. Chapters three and four deal directly with recent Nicaraguan literature, and the first two provide useful regional background; up-to-date, well-researched, based on useful models of conjoined ideological and artistic production.

Borgeson, Paul W., Jr. *Hacia el hombre nuevo: poesía y pensamiento de Ernesto Cardenal.* London: Tamesis, 1984. Two major sections: the first relates Cardenal's artistic development and characterizes his mature work and its aesthetics; the second discusses the poet's religious and ideological position and its relationship to his poetics.

Cerutti, Franco. *"El Güegüense" y otros ensayos de literatura nicaragüense.* Roma: Bulzoni, 1983. Scholarly research and interpretation on the "Güegüense" and its cultural significance; Nicaraguan culture in the nineteenth century; the poet Salomón de la Selva; and indigenous culture in contemporary Nicaraguan poetry.

Urdanivia Bertarelli, Eduardo. *La poesía de Ernesto Cardenal: cristianismo y revolución.* Lima: Latinoamericana Editores, 1984. Useful study of Cardenal's poetry, especially strong in source material.

White, Steven F. *Poets of Nicaragua: A Bilingual Anthology (1918-1979).* Greensboro, N.C.: Unicorn Press, 1982. A well-presented and satisfactorily translated collection; the best and the most accessible in English.

Zimmerman, Marc, ed. and trans. *Nicaragua in Reconstruction and at War: The People Speak.* Minneapolis: MEP Publications, 1985. Varied materials, principally popular poetry and the author-com piler's account of the Nicaraguan Revolution; more recent than Aldaraca (q.v.), its companion piece; in English.

PANAMA
María A. Salgado
University of North Carolina at Chapel Hill

I

The destiny of Panama has been shaped and defined by the fact that it is an isthmus uniting North and South America. Thus, throughout history, Panama has seldom been the end of the trip, but rather the obligatory place of transition: a step on the way to somewhere else. From the earliest times the isthmus facilitated the free and open movement of the forces that shaped the natural and cultural idiosyncrasy of the New World. The Spanish conquistadors emphasized the strategic location of Panama by channeling through the Isthmus the conquest of South and Central America. It was hardly surprising, then, that in the twentieth century technology should heighten even more the strategic location of the Isthmus by choosing it for the construction of the long-planned passage between the two oceans. With the site chosen, Panama seceded from Colombia with the help of the U.S., to whom it granted the rights to build and control the canal. Thus, it can be said that technology created the Republic of Panama in 1903 and redirected its destiny and the course of history by changing the axis of the Isthmus. With the Canal in place and controlled by the United States, Panama became a powerless conveyer of goods between East and West; the Isthmus lost its original identification as the channel for the free flow of people and goods in a north-south direction. For Panama the consequences of this change were mixed; it gained its independence and some economic benefits, but only at the cost of splitting in two its national territory and relinquishing the rights to political and economic control over the Canal Zone (part of the national territory). The Canal that tore the land apart created a literal and spiritual barrier by isolating Panama City from the interior of the country. Eventually, the Canal came to be seen as the symbol of Yankee imperialism and national humiliation. The

453

central role played by the Canal Zone in the formation of a Panamanian identity is reflected in the predominance of "Canal topics" in national letters.

According to most critics, Panamanian literature does not surface prior to 1903. Colonial society in the Isthmus could boast some cultural accomplishments: it even had the University of San Javier, founded by the Jesuits between 1749 and 1767, but it did not develop an autochthonous literary expression. Some writers did contribute works that are considered important steps in the establishment of a literary tradition, but these works appear only sporadically as isolated examples of intellectual dedication. By and large, they belong to what is known as literature of ideas, essays, that in the specific case of Panama, deal to a large extent with historical and sociopolitical issues. The local debates questioning independence and the building of the Canal produced most of the early essays. They would be followed later on by those of other thinkers concerned with building the new nation and endowing it with a constitution, an appropriate system of government, and modern institutions. Through the years, this participation of Panamanian intellectuals in the shaping of the nation has continued to produce a wealth of essays that has given Panamanian letters their distinctive slant towards intellectual history.

Among the precursors of this kind of literature, two essayists deserve particular attention, Mariano Arosemena (1794-1868), who laid down the basis for the study of national history with his *Apuntamientos históricos* (Historical Notes; 1801-1804, published 1949), and his son, Justo Arosemena (1817-96), a dominant figure in the intellectual circles of the Isthmus, who formulated in elegant prose his ideas in favor of developing a Panamerican consciousness in *Sobre la idea de una Liga Americana* (On the Idea of a League of the Americas; 1864). Justo Arosemena first discussed his ideas on building a canal in an essay written and published in New York, *The Panama Canal in the Light of American Interests* (1879), and he had examined a similar idea earlier in *Examen sobre franca comunicación entre los dos océanos* (An Examination of Free Communication Between the Two Oceans; 1846). Some of his other important essays are *Código de moral fundado en la naturaleza del hombre* (Moral Code Based on Man's Nature; 1860) and his best-known work, *Estudios constitucionales sobre los gobiernos de América Latina* (Constitutional Studies on Latin American Governments; 1887-88), published in Paris.

Among the many important writers who continued these efforts during the formative years of the nation, mention must be made of Pablo Arosemena (1836-1920), a political leader who documented his experiences in a series of essays published posthumously in *Escritos* (Writings; 1930); three-time president Belisario Porras (1856-1942), who recorded his military and leadership experiences in the so-called One-Thousand-Day War for independence in *Memorias de las campañas del Istmo* (Memoirs of the Isthmus Campaigns; 1900) and in an autobiographical account, *Trozos de vida* (Slices of Life; 1931); Samuel Lewis (1871-1939), politician, historian, and author of two books, *Apuntes y conversaciones* (Notes and Conversations; 1926) and *Retazos* (Remnants; 1940); and the prominent intellectual and politician Ricardo J. Alfaro (1882-1971), minister of the government, diplomat, and president. He is perhaps the most prestigious Panamanian intellectual figure in modern times. Alfaro's books in the fields of law and biography and his *Diccionario de anglicismos* (Dictionary of Anglicisms; 1950) attest to his depth of knowledge in a variety of subjects.

Another area that has produced some outstanding thinkers is education. José Dolores Moscote (1879-1956), professor and educator, became associated with projects directed toward the development of sound national programs in education. He is the author of many works including the following representative books: *Páginas idealistas* (Idealistic Pages; 1917), *Introducción al estudio de la Constitución* (Introduction to the Study of the Constitution; 1929), *Actividades prácticas del maestro rural* (Practical Activities for Rural Teachers; 1936), *Itinerario* (Itinerary; 1942), and *Derecho constitucional panameño* (Panamanian Constitutional Law; 1943). Moscote further asserted his influence in education by becoming the editor and/or co-editor of journals like *La escuela primaria* (Primary School; 1906), *Educación nacional* (National Education; 1909), *La revista nueva* (The New Review; 1916-19), *El nuevo tiempo* (New Times; 1924), *El niño* (The Child; 1923-31), and *El educador* (The Educator; 1925-26).

Octavio Méndez Pereira (1887-1954), known as El Maestro de Juventudes (The Teacher of Youth), was another outstanding educator, a man of great intelligence and solid principles. He was instrumental in founding the University of Panama (1935) and served as its first president. As a writer he authored many valuable studies in a variety of genres: travel books, such as *Emociones y evocaciones* (Emotions and Evocations; 1927); the biographical novel *Vasco Núñez de Balboa* (1934), considered the best historical narrative in Panamanian letters; the biography *Justo*

Arosemena (1919); critical works on national and educational issues such as *Panamá, país y nación de tránsito* (Panama, Country and Nation of Transit; 1946), and *La universidad y la crisis actual del espíritu* (The University and Today's Spiritual Crisis; 1954). Another influential educator and writer is Ricaurte Soler (1923). He has explored the problematic of Panamanian national identity in *Pensamiento panameño y concepción de la nacionalidad en el siglo XIX* (Panamanian Thought and the Conception of Nationality in the Nineteenth Century; 1954) and *Formas ideológicas de la nación panameña* (Ideological Forms of the Panamanian Nation; 1964), and has explored the history of ideas in *Estudios sobre historia de las ideas en América* (Studies in the History of Ideas in the Americas; 1961), *Clase y nación en Hispanoamérica* (Class and Nation in Spanish America; 1975), and *El pensamiento político en Panamá en los siglos XIX y XX* (Political Thought in Panama in the XIXth and XXth Centuries; 1988).

In the field of literature proper, Panama is best known for its solid, and at times excellent, contributions to poetry. The prevalence of poetry is so overwhelming in Panamanian letters that most essayists, playwrights, and writers of fiction are known first and foremost as poets. The predominance of poetry is not surprising coming from an area that, during the Colonial period and the years it was part of Colombia, lacked the political and intellectual power to create the cultural and educational institutions, as well as the printing facilities, that, by contrast, allowed the major viceroyalties to become high-powered cultural centers. Lima, Mexico City, and even Guatemala, were such centers. Therefore, they were able to develop and support a complex literary and artistic life, but few of the outlying regions were equipped to emulate their efforts. They had to restrict literary production to poetry and short pieces suited to be published in periodicals. Thus, Panama's earliest literary manifestations are written in verse. The first book is titled *Llanto de Panamá* (Lament of Panama; 1604). It consists of a collection of forty-two Baroque poems written in Old Panama City by the Generación de 1638 (Generation of 1638) on the occasion of the death of the Governor, Don Enrique Enríquez. The poems provide valuable descriptions of the city and of life in the Isthmus in the seventeenth century. Also a poet of sorts is the first author born in Panama, Víctor de la Guardia y Ayala (1772-1824), writer of the Neoclassic tragedy in three acts and in verse, *La política del mundo* (The Politics of the World), first performed in 1809 and published in 1902. It deals with Napoleon's ambitious takeover of Europe.

II

The importance of these authors and works is strictly historical, however. In fact, it is not until the second half of the nineteenth century that there emerges a group of writers who can be considered the true precursors of Panamanian letters. This group is the first generation of Romantic writers, formed by José María Alemán (1830-87), poet, politician, and author of three books: *Recuerdos de juventud* (Remembrances of Youth; 1872) in prose and verse, *Amor y suicidio* (Love and Suicide; 1876), the only Romantic dramatic work written in Panama, and *Crepúsculos de la tarde* (Evening Dusks; 1882), a collection of poems. Gil Colunje (1831-99), also a poet and statesman, was a precocious writer who published, as a serial, the first Panamanian novel, *La verdad triunfante* (The Victorious Truth; 1849) at the tender age of seventeen. Colunje is known also for his verses of patriotic themes, his descriptive Romantic poems, such as his ode "Al Tequendama" (To Tequendama Falls; 1856), and several compositions in which he follows the lead of the Spaniard Espronceda, such as "El canto del llanero" (Plainsman's Song; 1853) and "Canto del cosaco" (Song of the Cossack; date unknown). The most genuine representative of Romantic tendencies is Tomás Martín Feuillet (1834-62). He had great facility for writing poetry and experimented freely with the new forms and rhymes introduced by Romanticism. His best poems project the pessimism, melancholy, and ennui characteristic of the period. Among his best poems are "Flor del Espíritu Santo" (Flower of the Holy Ghost—the national flower of Panama; date unknown), "Fantasía," (Fantasia; date unknown), "Cuanto tienes" (All You Have; 1856), and the self-portrait "Mi retrato" (My Portrait; 1857).

This generation of Romantic poets can boast one of the early woman writers in Panama, Amelia Denis de Icaza (1836-1911). She published most of her poems in local journals and newspapers, where they remained until they were collected and published posthumously under the title *Hojas secas* (Dry Leaves; 1927). Her poetry expresses in direct and simple verses emotions that reveal her patriotic feelings, her social concerns, and the more intimate aspects of her home and family life.

The definitive gains towards the creation of a truly national literature were accomplished by three groups of Modernist writers associated with the most important literary journals of the period. The movement was established by a first generation of poets writing from the pages of two important publications: *El Cosmos* (The Cosmos; 1896-97) and, later on,

El Heraldo del Istmo (The Isthmus Herald; 1904-1906), both directed by Guillermo Andreve (1879-1940), a tireless promoter of literary and cultural life. He is the author of a novel, *Una punta del velo* (A Corner of the Veil; 1929), and a series of essays and tales, *A la sombra del arco* (Under the Shadow of the Bow; 1925), *Sobre el agua* (Over the Water; 1933), and *Cuatro cuentos* (Four Tales; 1933).

The most important poet among these early Modernists is Darío Herrera (1870-1914), a cosmopolitan traveler and diplomat who became a member of Rubén Darío's group Azul (Blue; see section on Nicaragua) in Buenos Aires. He acquired an enormous reputation for writing harmonious poems of great formal beauty. His poems, however, have seldom been read; they remain dispersed and uncollected in various Spanish American publications. His excellent reputation as a prose writer is based on the only book he published in his lifetime, *Horas lejanas* (Distant Hours; 1903), the first book of short stories by a Panamanian writer. Although published in the cosmopolitan milieu of Buenos Aires, this book is a collection of tales that delineate an American setting in the refined style of Modernism. Another poet associated with this first group is León A. Soto (1874-1902), tortured and killed by the national police for supporting the building of the Canal. He founded two journals, *El Bohemio* (The Bohemian; 1893) and *Don Quijote* (Don Quixote; 1898). His book of poetic essays *Eclécticas* (Eclectic; 1907) and his *Poesías* (Poetry; 1918) are characterized by an intimist note, expressed in the exquisite vocabulary and musicality of the period.

The second Modernist group claims one of the most important poets in Panamanian letters, Ricardo Miró (1883-1940). Miró, together with Demetrio J. Fábrega (1881-1932), a conceptual poet, author of *Poesías* (Poems; 1918), and Zoraida Díaz (1881-1948), author of *Nieblas del alma* (Mists of the Soul; no date given), continued to stimulate the literary scene in Panama from the pages of Miró's journal, *Nuevos ritos* (New Rites; 1907-17). Miró's poetry undergoes the subtle changes characteristic of Spanish Postmodernism: he denudes his expression of excessive verbal ornamentation and creates an intimate, subjective poetic world, ruled by nostalgia. His themes are low-key, simpler and more human than those of the previous group. He wrote *Preludios* (Preludes; 1908); *La leyenda del Pacífico* (The Legend of the Pacific; 1919), dealing with Núñez de Balboa and considered his most important work; *Caminos silenciosos* (Silent Paths; 1929); and *Poema de la reencarnación* (Poem of Reincarnation; 1929). Most of his late poems appear in *Antología poética (1907-37)* (Poetic Anthology; 1937).

The third and final group associated with Modernism gathers together poets who published in the journals *Esto y Aquello* (This and That; 1915-17), directed by Enrique Geenzier (1887-1943), and *Memphis* (1916-19) directed by another important poet, Gaspar Octavio Hernández (1893-1918) who writes a poetry of intense suffering. A black writer, Hernández belonged to a family saddened by a series of suicides; he himself suffered from tuberculosis and died young. His poems show his thorough and personal assimilation of his readings of poets as varied as Bécquer and Byron, Musset and Lamartine, Baudelaire and Heredia. His books, *Iconografías* (Iconographies; 1915), *Melodías del pasado* (Melodies of the Past; 1916), and his posthumous *La copa de amatista* (The Amethyst Goblet; 1923), bring to Panamanian poetry a new depth of lyric expression. A third writer associated with this group is María Olimpia de Obaldía (1891-1985). A mother and a teacher, she was officially named National Poetess of Panama. Her works, *Orquídeas* (Orchids; 1926), *Brevario lírico* (Lyric Breviary; 1930), *Parnaso infantil* (Children's Parnassus; 1948), and *Visiones eternas* (Eternal Visions; 1961) show a delicate sensibility and high lyric quality; her *Obras completas* (Complete Works) were published in 1976. She is known for verses of patriotic fervor and her songs to nature and to the simple pleasures of family life.

In the third decade of the twentieth century Panamanian literature finally came of age. Solid gains could be claimed in all major genres. Modernism, with its emphasis on aesthetics and universal concerns, had given Panamanian writers a sense of pride in their artistic accomplishments, providing them with the tools necessary to present native themes without the old, folkloric, regionalist bent. In poetry, social themes begin to be introduced by writers of transition like Demetrio Korsi (1899-1957), who abandons the Modernism of *El viento de la fontana* (The Wind of the Fountain; 1926) to write the first *poesía negra* (black poetry) in Panama: *Cumbia* (1936), based on the rhythms of the national dance. In addition, he wrote social poetry, taking his themes from urban life: *El grillo que cantó sobre el Canal* (The Cricket that Sang over the Canal; 1937), *Los gringos llegan y la cumbia se va...* (The Gringos Arrive and the Cumbia Leaves...; 1953), and *El tiempo se perdía y todo era lo mismo* (Time Was Being Wasted and All Was the Same; 1956).

III

The real break with Modernism, however, came in 1930 when Rogelio Sinán (1904), pen name of Bernardo Domínguez Alba, founded the vanguard journal *Antena* (Antenna) and became the new arbiter of literary taste. His first book, *Onda* (Wave; 1929), published in Rome, heralded this new rebelliousness, an attitude he continued in the poems of *Incendio* (Fire; 1944), *Semana Santa en la niebla* (Holy Week in the Fog; 1949), *Cuna común* (Common Cradle; 1963), and *Saloma sin sal o mar* (Saloma without Salt or Sea; 1969): the title is a play on words based on the *saloma*, a cadence or chantey sung by Panamanian peasants. Although in his books Sinán moves between pure poetry and Surrealism while experimenting with introspective and subconscious preoccupations, he never loses the human touch. Sinán's impact has been equally important in renovating all genres. In the narrative he has contributed the novel *Plenilunio* (Full Moon; 1947), and the tales of *La isla mágica* (The Magic Island; 1979) and several collections of tales—among them *Todo un conflicto de sangre* (A Bloody Conflict; 1946), *La boina roja* (The Red Beret; 1961?), *Los pájaros del sueño* (Dream Birds; 1954), *A la orilla de las estatuas maduras* (At the Edge of the Ripe Statues; 1946), *Cuentos* (Tales; 1971), and *El candelabro de los malos ofidios* (The Candelabrum of the Bad Ophidians; 1982). His plays *La cucarachita Mandinga* (Mandinga, the Little Cockroach; 1937), *Chiquilinga* (1961), and *Lobo, go home* (Wolf, Go Home), although written for children, are considered important contributions to the movement of popular theater in Panama.

Another important writer is Demetrio Herrera Sevillano (1902-50), a self-taught, bohemian poet who lived in the streets and plazas of the city. His early poems, appropriately named *Mis primeros trinos* (My First Trills; 1924), still evidence the imprint of Modernism, but this influence soon gives way to Ultraism, Futurism, and other vanguardist trends. His book *Kodak* (1937) introduces the new modalities by presenting cityscapes in sharp and original metaphors. *La fiesta de San Cristóbal* (Feast of St. Christopher; 1937) and *Los poemas del pueblo* (Poems of the People; 1938) succeed in reaching the masses despite his vanguardist approach. The same is true of Herrera Sevillano's late works, *Antología* (Anthology; 1945), *La canción del esclavo* (The Song of the Slave; 1947), and *Ventana* (Window; 1950), where his experimental verses portray human misery amidst a people destroyed by poverty and abuse.

The most surrealist among the poets associated with *vanguardismo* (Vanguardism) is Ricardo J. Bermúdez (1914), a professor of architecture and ex-Secretary of Education, who has won the Miró Prize in poetry and short story; among his books of poetry are the following: *Adán liberado* (Adam Freed; 1944), *Laurel de ceniza* (Ash Laurel; 1952), *Cuando la Isla era doncella* (When the Island Was a Maiden; 1961), and *Con la llave en el suelo* (With the Key on the Ground; 1970); among his tales, *Para rendir el animal que ronda* (To Conquer the Prowling Animal). Two women, Esther María Osses (1914) and Stella Sierra (1917), are members of this group. Osses writes natural, spontaneous verses: *Mensaje* (Message; 1946), *La niña y el mar* (The Little Girl and the Sea; 1954), *Poesía en limpio* (Poetry in Fair Copy; 1965), *Crece y camina* (Grow and Walk; 1971), *Poemas* (Poems; 1976). Sierra shows total control over her poetic resources from her first books, *Canciones de mar y luna 1939-40* (Songs of Sea and Moon; 1944), *Sinfonía jubilosa* (Jubilant Symphony; 1944—first Miró Prize in Poetry) to her most recent, *Agua dulce* (Fresh Water, a play on the name of her birthplace, the town of Aguadulce; 1969), lyrical childhood memories in poetic prose. Two other poets who belong to a younger generation begin to introduce metaphysical concerns: José Guillermo Ros-Zanet (1930) and José de Jesús Martínez (1929). Ros-Zanet writes with understated simplicity of his rather complex search for the self; his works range from the early *Poemas fundamentales* (Essential Poems; 1951), *Ceremonial del recuerdo* (Ceremonial of Remembrance; 1956), and *Sin el color del cielo* (Without the Color of the Sky; 1961) to his most recent, *Bolívar, un vendaval de la historia* (Bolivar, Cyclone of History; 1984), *Los libros de la tierra* (The Books of the Land; 1985), and *Un no rompido sueño* (An Unbroken Dream; 1985). Martínez's dual career as poet and playwright provides dramatic tension to his verses, structured along the lines of dialogues and interior monologues: *Poemas a ella* (Poems to Her; 1963), *Poemas a mí* (Poems to Myself; 1961), *One Way* (1967), and the anthology *Medio siglo de José de Jesús Martínez* (Half a Century of J de J M; 1979). His plays *La mentira* (The Lie; 1954), *Caifás* (Caiaphas; 1961), *El juicio* (The Judgment; 1962), and *El mendigo y el avaro* (The Beggar and the Miser; 1972) are masterful dramatic constructions that exemplify Martínez's metaphysical concerns.

The main representative of antipoetry is the irreverent poet César Young Núñez (1934) in books like *Poemas de rutina* (Routine Poems; 1967) and *Carta a Blancanieves* (Letter to Snow White; 1976). Several younger women writers stand out—all winners of the Miró Prize and several national and international prizes: Elsie Alvarado de Ricord (1928), author of *Holocausto de rosa* (Holocaust of the Rose; 1953), *Entre materia y sueño* (Between Matter and Dream; 1966), *Pasajeros en tránsito* (Pasangers in Transit; 1973), and *Es real y de este mundo* (It is Real and of this World; 1978); Diana Morán (1932), author of *Eva definida* (Eve Defined; 1959—in collaboration with the Costa Rican poet

Ligia Alcázar), *Soberana presencia de la patria* (Sovereign Presence of the Native Land; 1964), and *Reflexiones junto a tu piel* (Reflexions Next to Your Skin; 1965); Bertalicia Peralta (1940), author of *Canto de esperanza filial* (Song of Filial Hope; 1962), *Sendas fugitivas* (Fugitive Paths; 1963), *Un lugar de la esfera terrestre* (A Place in the Terrestrial Globe; 1971), *Himno a la alegría*, (Hymn to Happiness; 1973), *Libro de fábulas* (Book of Fables; 1976), and *Casa flotante* (Floating House; 1979); and Moravia Ochoa López (1941) author of *Raíces primordiales* (Primordial Roots; 1958), *Las savias corporales* (Corporal Saps), *Múltiple voz* (Multiple Voice; 1966), *Donde transan los ríos* (Where Rivers Settle; 1967), *Círculos y planetas* (Circles and Planets; 1977), and *Cantos para decir la noche* (Songs to Convey the Night). The distinguished social poet Pedro Rivera (1939), is also known for his short stories and several films. He was the 1969 winner of Miró Prizes both in poetry and short story; his films have won awards in Germany (1965) and the Soviet Union (1976). Among his poetic works are *Las voces del dolor que trajo el alba* (The Voices of Sorrow that Dawn Brought; 1958), *Despedida del hombre* (Farewell to Man; 1969), and *Los pájaros regresan de la niebla* (The Birds Return from the Fog), 1970 Miró Prize. One of the most prestigious younger poets is Alfredo Figueroa Navarro (1950), who shows great control over poetic structures in his works *Burbujas* (Bubbles; 1964), *Hacia un anhelo* (Towards a Desire; 1967), *Baladas populares* (Popular Ballads; 1965), and *Trenes y naciones* (Trains and Nations; 1976). Another respected young poet is Manuel Orestes Nieto (1951), also a film maker. He has won the Miró Poetry Prize on two occasions, in 1972 with *Reconstrucción de los hechos* (Reconstruction of the Facts) and in 1983 with *Panamá en la memoria de los mares* (Panama in the Memory of the Seas), and Cuba's Casa de las Americas Prize with *Dar la cara* (To Face the Consequences; 1975).

The same Rogelio Sinán who started the vanguardist movement by revolting against an outmoded style of writing poetry is responsible for the renovation of the narrative. His experimental tale "sueño de serafín del carmen" (the dream of serafin del carmen; 1931) introduced in Panamanian narrative the new Freudian concepts that incorporated into literature, dreams, interior monologues, and stream of consciousness. Sinán would continue to experiment with new narrative techniques in several short stories as well as in his novel *Full Moon*. His efforts, together with those of Roque Javier Laurenza (1910-84) and Manuel Ferrer Valdés (1914-77), opened new avenues of expression with emphasis on universality and aesthetic experimentation. A writer who coincides in time with the Vanguard without adopting its norms is the novelist Julio B. Sosa (1910-46), author of several tales and novels, such as *La india dormida* (The Sleeping Indian Woman; 1936), *Tú sola en mi vida* (You Alone in My Life; 1943), and *En la cumbre se pierden los caminos* (On the Summit the Paths are Lost; 1957), an important novel of social protest on the theme of civilization versus barbarism.

The renewed interest in narrative fiction at midcentury can be attributed to a series of literary prizes intended to stimulate interest in literature. There can be no doubt of the beneficial effect these prizes have had on Panamanian letters. In fact, almost all novels published since 1945 have seen the light in conjunction with the Concurso Ricardo Miró (Ricardo Miró Competition). Most of these novelists have written works that expose the grave social problems facing the nation, but they have done it while keeping their commitment to aesthetic concerns.

Many of these writers take a regionalist approach. César A. Candanedo (Gil Serrano [1906]) writes vigorous works of social protest in *Los clandestinos* (The Clandestine Ones; 1957), *La otra frontera* (The Other Frontier; 1967), and *Palo duro* (Hard Truncheon; 1986). José María Sánchez (1918) depicts in his works *Tres cuentos* (Three Tales; 1946) and *Shumio-Ara* (1948) the exploitation by the United Fruit Co. amidst landscapes of luxuriant vegetation. The vigorous poet Tristán Solarte (1924), pseudonym of Guillermo Sánchez Borbón, who gathered his poetry in *Aproximación poética a la muerte* (Poetic Approch to Death), has incorporated in his works of narrative fiction his poetic ability to portray the effects of the natural world on the psyche of his characters; he is best known for *El ahogado* (The Drowned Man; 1957) and the unpublished *El guitarrista* (The Guitar Player; Miró Prize 1950). Mario Augusto Rodríguez (1917) depicts the areas where the suburbs meet the countryside and condemns the helplessness of the rural masses, as he does in *Campo adentro* (Inland; 1947) and *Luna en Veraguas* (Moon in Veraguas; 1948). Other well-recognized writers of regionalistic literature are Carlos Francisco Changmarín (1922) and Eustorgio Chong Ruiz (1934). Using similar techniques but portraying the urban milieu rather than specific regions are Renato Ozores (1910) (*La calle oscura* [The Dark Street; 1955] and *Diez Cuentos* [Ten Stories; 1985]), Juan O. Díaz Lewis (1916), and the poet Tobías Díaz Blaitry (1919).

The Miró Prize in Theater started relatively late, in 1953. As with the other genres, it has helped to develop greater interest in the dramatic arts. That First Prize was won by the play *El ángel* (The Angel), written by an author better known for his narrative fiction, Renato Ozores

(1910). Aside from the several poets and novelists who write for the theater, there are some authors dedicated exclusively to this genre. Among them: Mario Riera (1920-69), whose play *La montaña encendida* (The Mountain in Flames) won second prize in this first convocation. Since that time he has also staged *La muerte va por dentro* (Death Stalks on the Inside) and *La conciencia* (Conscience); Jarl Ricardo Babot (1945), playwright and professor of dramatic art, has won the Miró Prize with *Las aves* (The Birds); and Raúl Leis (1947), has won several times; among his plays are *Viaje a la salvación y otros países* (Trip to Salvation and Other Countries), *Lucecita González, María Picana*, and *El nido de Macuá* (The Macuá Nest).

IV

Separate mention needs to be made of the many writers who deal with the question of the Canal Zone. Although Julio Ardila (1863-1918) and his novel *Josefina* (1903) are given credit for starting the narrative that depicts the Canal as the determinant force in Panamanian life, in reality the *novela canalera* (Canal novel) emerged in the 1930s and is still actively produced. This type of novel, however, is most prominent from the late 1940s through the 1960s. In part, this is due to the fact that in 1947 Sinán's *Full Moon* introduced new narrative techniques and reawakened interest in the novel; this is also the time during which the Concurso Ricardo Miró served to stimulate an interest in the narrative. The treatment of the Canal theme has been influenced by Sinán's portrayal of this controversial subject, especially his presentation of a sordid city, handicapped by a Canal that brought to its crossroads the world's worst social ills. Among other authors who have written significant works on this theme is Renato Ozores, who in *Puente del mundo* (World Bridge; 1951) introduces the problems that he will present best in *La calle oscura* (Dark Street; 1955), where he shows the miserable conditions of life in a street bordering the Canal Zone. The strongest protest and the most thorough presentation of the topic is contained in the valiant trilogy written by Joaquín Beleño (1922): *Luna verde* (Green Moon; 1951), *Curundú* (1961), and *Gamboa Road Gang* (1959). Another of his more recent novels, *Flor de banana* (Banana Flower; 1970), deals an equally strong blow against the fruit companies. Other novelists who have effectively discussed the problems of the Canal are Gil Blas Tejeira (1901) in *Pueblos perdidos* (Lost Peoples; 1962), César A. Candanedo in *La otra frontera* (The Other Border; 1967), and Yolanda Camarano de Sucre in *Los Capelli* (The Capellis; 1967).

V

The most recent Panamanian narrative exhibits a wide variety of techniques for approaching several local and universal concerns. Overall, however, it is a literature more concerned with universal problems than with local ones. Leaving aside those writers contributing to the Canal novel, there are still those who continue to emphasize a regionalistic approach with strong elements of social protest. This is the case of Carlos Francisco Changmarín in the short stories of *Faragual* (Faragua Thicket; 1962) and Eustorgio Chong Ruiz in *Techumbres, guijarros y pueblo* (Roofs, Stones, and People; 1967) and *Diario de una noche de camino* (Diary of Night's Journey; 1987). Other social topics are explored by Boris A. Zachrisson (1936), who in the tales of *La casa de los ladrillos rojos* (The Red Brick House; 1968) examines the decadent surroundings of the upper bourgeoisie. A similar condemnation of the Panamanian oligarchy is the goal of *Rosca, S.A.* (Rosca, Inc.; 1963) by Rodolfo (Fito) Aguilera.

The poet Moravia Ochoa López explores psychological analysis from a feminine perspective in the short stories of *Yesca* (Tinder; 1966) and *El espejo* (The Mirror; 1968); Pedro Rivera (1939), who is both writer and film maker, mixes subjective themes and new techniques in the tales of *Peccata minuta* (Little Sins; 1970), winner of the Miró Prize, *Libro de parábolas* (Book of Parables; 1983), *Recuentos* (Inventory; 1988—with Dimas Libio Pitty), and *Para hacer el amor con la ventana abierta* (To Make Love With the Window Open; 1989); Guillermo E. Beleño presents an apocalyptic vision of World War III in *Novela absurda* (Absurd Novel; 1963); Enrique Chuez (1934) combines creolism, the emphasis on local and nativist themes, with formal experimentation in the tales of *Tiburón y otros cuentos* (Shark and Other Stories; 1964), in his novel *Las averías* (The Breakdowns; 1972), *La mecedora* (The Rocking Chair; 1976), and *La casa de las sirenas pálidas* (The House of the Pale Mermaids; 1983); Gloria Guardia (1940) won the Central American Novel Prize with *El último juego* (The Last Game; 1976), a novel written as an uninterrupted interior monologue, where she mixes the political history of Panama with imaginative tales of fiction; she has also authored *Tinie-*

bla blanca (White Darkness; 1961), and *Despertar sin raíces* (Waking Up Without Roots; 1966).

Bessy Reyna (1942), now living in the United States, is known as a painter, poet, and short story writer; her best-known book is *Terrarium* (1975). Also living in the United States is the Afro-Panamenian Carlos Guillermo Wilson ("Cubena"; 1941), author of *Cuentos del negro Cubena* (1977), translated as *Short Stories by Cubena* (1987), *Pensamiento del negro Cubena* (The Thought of Cubena; 1977), and of the novel *Chombo* (Nigger; 1981). Enrique Jaramillo Levi (1944), another prolific writer of poetry, drama, and fiction has made his reputation in the field of poetry with books like *Los atardeceres de la memoria* (The Afternoons of Memory) and *Fugas y engranajes (1978-80)* (Flights and Gears; 1982), in the theater with *La cápsula de cianuro* (The Cyanide Capsule; 1967) and *Gigolo* (1967), and in the narrative with his short stories *El búho que dejó de latir* (The Owl Who Stopped Throbbing; 1972) and *Ahora que soy él* (Now That I Am He; 1985), and the novel *Duplicaciones* (Duplications; 1973). He also directs the journal *Maga* (Magician) and the Editorial Signos and has collected the works of others in *Antología crítica de la joven narrativa panameña* (A Critical Anthology of Recent Panamanian Fiction; 1971). Another prolific writer of the 1980s is Rosa María Britton (1936), who, after winning the Miró Prize in the novel in 1982 with *Ataúd de uso* (Coffin in Use), has published *El señor de la lluvia y el viento* (The Lord of the Rain and the Wind; 1985), *Esa esquina del paraíso* (That Corner of Paradise; 1986), *¿Quién inventó el mambo?* (Who Invented The Mambo; 1986), short story Miró Prize for 1985, and *La muerte tiene dos caras* (Death Has Two Faces; 1987).

BIBLIOGRAPHY

Alvarado de Ricard, Elsie. *Escritores panameños contemporáneos (notas y biobibliografías)*. Panamá, 1962. A succinct list of the most important writers; although very incomplete, it is helpful.

García S., Ismael. *Historia de la literatura panameña*. México, D.F.: Universidad Nacional Autónoma de México, 1972. A very thorough scholarly approach to the subject.

García S., Ismael. *Medio siglo de poesía panameña*. México, D.F., 1956. A thorough study followed by a short anthology.

García Saucedo, Jaime. "Cronología de la novela panameña (1849-1985)." *Lotería* 360 (Mayo-Junio 1986): 109-122. A detailed listing of novels publshed in Panama, plus listings of literary prizes and the winning novels.

Jaramillo Levi, Enrique, compilador. *Poesía panameña contemporánea (1929-1979)*. México, D.F.: Liberta-Sumaria, 1980. A representative and very complete anthology with good bibliographies on anthologies, critical works, and works by individual poets.

Miró, Rodrigo. *Aspectos de la literatura novelesca en Panamá*. Panamá, 1968. Short, but very informative regarding main trends and authors.

Miró, Rodrigo. *La literatura panameña (origen y proceso)*. San José, C.R.: Trejos Hermanos, 1972. An excellent source of information on all aspects of Panamanian literature.

Sepúlveda, Mélida Ruth. *El tema del Canal en la novelística panameña*. Caracas: Universidad Católica "Andrés Bello," 1975. A study of the origins and development of the novels dealing with the Canal Zone.

PARAGUAY
Juan Manuel Marcos
Biblioteca Nacional, Paraguay

I

   Asunción, founded in 1537, was the historical capital of the River
Plate area. Founders of other important cities of that region, such as
Buenos Aires, had as their base Asunción. Charles V's Royal Order of
September 12, 1537, authorized the *asuncenos* (inhabitants of Asunción)
to elect their own government. This marked the birth of many Paraguayan democratic movements. The first leader of that movement was Domingo Martínez de Irala, who served as governor beginning in 1539. He
was replaced by Alvar Núñez Cabeza de Vaca in 1542, but two years
later the creoles of Asunción restored Irala to power, and he ruled the
vast province until his death in 1556. During that period, the social
regime of the *encomienda* (Indian servitude) was established. Hernando
Arias de Saavedra, also known as Hernandarias, the first Spanish governor born in Paraguay, ruled the province from 1592 to 1621 with some
interruptions. Under his tenure a number of measures alleviating the
Indian situation were adopted. At least fifteen massive Indian insurrections occurred in Paraguay between 1537 and 1599; they continued until
1660, when a well organized resistance movement suffered cruel repression in Arecayá.
   Paraguay's Jesuit Province was established in 1604. During the seventeenth century, several *comuneros* (autonomist) movements, led by
Asunción's creoles who benefited from the encomienda system, came
into conflict with the Jesuits, who had developed a solid program of
Indian colonization in their reductions (i.e., settlements). The three most
important comuneros revolts were led by Bishop Bernardino de Cárdenas from 1644 to 1650, by José de Antequera in 1724, and by Fernando
de Mompox in 1730. The comuneros failed to defeat the military alliance of the Jesuit's Indian Army and the government of Buenos Aires,

which ultimately destroyed them in the bloody battle of Tavapy in 1735. On the other hand, the Jesuit army defended the province against the *bandeirantes*, Brazilian bandits who captured Indian slaves on the border; it defeated the invaders in 1641.

The Jesuits created a peculiar social and cultural system based on the notion of communal property and the indoctrination of the Indians using their own language and adapting their religious myths to the Christian religion. They founded numerous towns, introduced the first printing presses in the River Plate area, established schools, and implemented vigorous cattle and agricultural exploitation. They also cultivated the arts, architecture, and the theater as well as anthropology, philology, astronomy, and natural sciences. Other religious orders that played a role in Paraguay during the colonial period were the Jeromians, the Mercedarians, the Dominicans, and, above all, the Franciscans. But none of them left an impression as profound as the Jesuits.

Paraguay produced a number of major figures in Latin American colonial literature. Of course, we do not find authors as prominent as Garcilaso (see the section on Peru), Ercilla (see the section on Chile), Sor Juana (see the section on Mexico), or Peralta y Barnuevo (see the section on Peru). But we should not relegate three hundred years of Paraguayan literary history to oblivion or misinterpretation. The most common practice of literary historians is that of attributing many works produced in Paraguay to Argentine literature. In fact, these works were written by Paraguayan creoles or mestizos. The *Comentarios* (Commentaries; 1555) of Alvar Núñez Cabeza de Vaca (1490?-1564?) is the first chronicle of Paraguay, narrated by the second *adelantado* (governor with special privileges) of the River Plate area to his secretary, Pero Hernández. It is an admirable autobiographical document, rich in historical precision and ethnographic data, that attempts to vindicate the author's attitudes against the comuneros abuses during his brief tenure in Asunción (1542-44). The *Comentarios* were published in Valladolid, along with the second edition of *Naufragios* (Disasters; 1542), a chronicle of the years that Cabeza de Vaca spent among the North American Indians after his ship wrecked near Florida in 1527. Both books complement each other and offer a humane and critical vision of the colony. This work can easily be shown to belong to the Las Casas tradition in Latin America (see the section on Guatemala). The *Historia y descubrimiento del Río de la Plata y Paraguay* (History and Discovery of the River Plate and Paraguay; 1567) by Utz Schmidl, a Bavarian sergeant in Pedro Mendoza's expedition, is a chronicle full of chronological and geographic errors, written originally in German and then translated into Latin, Spanish, and other languages. It describes a world of fantasies, perils, and greed from the point of view of an ordinary, non- Hispanic soldier. Pero Hernández's *Descripción del Río de la Plata* (Description of the River Plate; written in 1545 and published in 1845) is a crude chronicle about the atrocities committed against Paraguay's Indians by Irala and his followers.

The epic poem *Argentina y conquista del Río de la Plata* (Argentina and the Conquest of the River Plate; 1602), by Asunción's archdeacon Martín del Barco Centenera (1544-1605), imitates Ercilla's *octavas reales* (royal octaves; stanzas composed of eight eleven-syllable lines) to extol Cabeza de Vaca's humanitarianism. Centenera, inspired by the Christian asceticism of the Renaissance, censures greed and violence. The poem also describes the criminal execution of an Inca in Cuzco and the indignation of the Indians, which seems to anticipate the vision of the eighteenth-century Túpac Amaru revolution. The most important work of Paraguayan colonial literature is *Anales del descubrimiento, población y conquista del Río de la Plata* (Annals of the Discovery, Settling, and Conquest of the River Plate), composed in 1612 by Ruy Díaz de Guzmán, a grandson of Irala and Leonor, a Guaraní Indian; Díaz de Guzmán was born in Asunción in 1560 and died there in 1629. A son of a Spanish captain related to many peninsular aristocratic lineages, Guzmán had the honor of being elected mayor of his native city by his own people the year before he died. The original manuscript of *Anales*, dedicated to the Duke of Medinasidonia in La Plata June 25, 1612, is lost. The work is divided into four books, according to Guzmán, but the fourth part has been lost, probably destroyed by Hernandarias's followers for political reasons after the author's death.

Guzmán's prose is clear, objective, and sometimes colorful; his style is precise yet elegant. Without hesitation he employs many Taino, Quechua, and Guaraní words and place names. Guzmán does not follow Renaissance models or the Thomistic political theology that the Inca Garcilaso would introduce in his *Comentarios* five years later in order to justify the Inca Empire to the Europeans (see the section on Peru). Guzmán is one of the first New World writers who felt and wrote as an American and not as a European. *Anales* is not only an objective account of River Plate geography and sixteenth-century political history: it is a chronicle that documents a search for an original expression with regard to both style and ideas, themes and discourse. Guzmán's "dragons" and "giants" are not medieval hyperboles, but rather mythical descriptions of American nature by an observer who considered himself a part of that environment. Guzmán shows a deep respect for the Indians whose insurrections and courage he admires and whose language, Guaraní, he knows. He is not really the founder of River Plate historiography—as many scholars from Paraguay, Argentina, and Uruguay say—because he did not have an academic background and did not write a systematic document according to colonial ideology. But Guzmán is the authentic father of Paraguayan and River Plate fiction, the founder of an imaginative practice conceived as a remythification of democratic values based on the quest for an American expression and thought: his hero is not a Spaniard or even a brave but brutish Indian. His hero is Mangoré, a Guaraní leader in love with a Spanish woman. Mangoré persuaded the other chief, his brother, that it was not good for them to obey the Spaniards because soon the latter would gain complete control of their land. Mangoré ends up dying in battle for his beliefs, but his pragmatic brother defeats the Europeans, only to begin a reign of cruelty and concupiscence.

The last great figure of Paraguayan colonial literature is the Spanish-born Félix de Azara (1752-1821). Azara researched ethnography and natural history in Paraguay from 1784 to 1798 and produced one of the most outstanding inventory studies of natural science ever compiled by an individual investigator. This work includes *Essais sur l'histoire naturelle des cuadrupedes de la Province du Paraguay* (Essays on Natural History of Quadrupeds of the Paraguayan Province; 1801), *Apuntalamientos para la historia natural de los pájaros del Paraguay y Río de la Plata* (Foundations of the Natural History of the Birds of Paraguay and the River Plate; 1802), and his *Voyages dans l'Amérique méridionale* (Travels in South America; 1809), which brought him international fame. Azara left many important works, a number of which were published posthumously; others are still unpublished. Asunción's *Cabildo* (city council) awarded him honorary Paraguayan citizenship in 1793 when he completed his *Descripción histórica, física y geográfica del Paraguay* (A Historical, Physical, and Geographic Description of Paraguay), a text written at the *Cabildo*'s request, which remains unpublished in the Argentine National Library.

II

According to the Jesuit Francisco Suárez (1548-1617), author of *Defensio fidei catholicae et apostolicae adversus anglicanae sectae errores* (A Defense of the Catholic and Apostolic Faith against the Errors of the Anglican Sect; 1613), political institutions do not have a divine origin but are simply a delegation of power from the people to the prince. If the prince becomes a tyrant, the people have the right to remove him from office. When the Jesuits were expelled from Paraguay, universities such as Córdoba in Argentina, where Suárez's ideology was flourishing, were transferred to the Franciscans. But the followers of Saint Francis could not restore Scholasticism. Suárez's theology survived along with Newton, Descartes, and Gassendi, who had also been introduced by the Jesuits. In addition, it is well documented that most of Córdoba's students read Voltaire and Rousseau much more avidly than Saint Thomas Aquinas. Paraguayan and Jesuit traditions and Córdoba's subversive intellectual atmosphere would produce one of the most radical figures of modern history and certainly the first successful statesman of Third World America: José Gaspar de Francia (1766-1840).

Francia played a major role in Paraguay's Revolution of 1811. Elected Supreme Dictator by a free congress of one-thousand delegates in 1814, he ruled the country until his death. Francia eliminated all oligarchic and ecclesiastical privileges, confiscated the church's properties, put all priests under government control, and closed the seminaries. He used to say that bullets were the best saints to defend the country's borders and that if the Pope would come to Paraguay he would make him his army chaplain. In spite of creating one of the strongest and most disciplined South American armies of his time, Francia was not a military man himself. He never allowed anyone to attain high rank, and he had a long, peaceful, and prosperous tenure. A bachelor, Francia was a very cultured and honest patriot who lived an austere and hard-working life. He isolated Paraguay from the anarchy of its neighbors, developed a robust although primitive economy based on the Jesuit tradition of communal property, eliminated illiteracy, controlled bureaucracy and corruption, and inspired innumerable biographies, novels, and essays written in several languages and by many authors, including Thomas Carlyle and Augusto Roa Bastos (see below). Francia's letters and orders reveal an ironic, energetic, preromantic style, and a critical edition of his selected writings—still to be done—would reveal one of the most interesting minds of the early nineteenth century.

After a short period of anarchy following Francia's death, a congress in 1844 elected Carlos Antonio López (1792-1862), a philosophy professor, as the first president of Paraguay. He was succeeded by his son, Marshall Francisco Solano López (1827-70), first as a provisionary president after his father's death; he was subsequently confirmed by a popular congress in 1862. Both maintained many of Francia's policies such as a state capitalist economy, an independent and antiimperialistic foreign policy, a popular program with regard to elementary education and income distribution, and a strong national defense. In addition, they also diversified industries, incorporated new technology, hired European experts, modernized the army, erected numerous public buildings, encouraged the arts, culture, and higher education, sent students to London and Paris, and broke with Francia's isolationism by establishing diplomatic relations with Argentina, Brazil, the United States, England, France, Spain, and most Latin American and European countries. They developed political relations with Argentine and Uruguayan dissident and revolutionary federalists who were not followers of the dictator Rosas.

Paraguay became one of the most prosperous and democratic Third World countries, with excellent prospects of exerting a revolutionary influence in South America against any neocolonial ambitions. Thus, England manipulated and financed the oligarchic governments of Brazil, Argentina, and Uruguay and had them sign a secret Triple Alliance War Treaty in London in 1865 to destroy Paraguay. Marshall López organized the national resistance, and the Paraguayan Army defeated the three allied armies in Kurupayty on September 22, 1866. However, after five years of bloodshed, including terrible atrocities committed against citizens, the Allies killed ninety percent of Paraguay's male population, including Solano López in 1870. Paraguayan resistance astonished the entire world, especially Latin America and the United States; its sacrifice impeded the fulfillment of the London treaty, but the devastated country lost a major part of its national territory to Brazil and Argentina and had severe sanctions imposed upon it. But Paraguay did not disappear.

Francisco Solano López is the most important figure of Paraguayan romantic literature as both an essay writer and a legend. As author of several volumes of letters, speeches, and harangues, all published posthumously, he reveals a lucid anticolonial ideology, an electrifying prose, and cosmopolitan culture. I would venture to state that his prose, along with that of Sarmiento (see the section on Argentina) and Martí (see the section on Cuba), was probably the best of nineteenth-century Latin American literature. A critical edition of his complete works would articulate the extraordinary vision of this authentic precursor of contemporary Third World liberation ideals.

Other writers of this period are Juan Andrés Gelly (1790-1856), President Carlos Antonio López (1792-1862), Fidel Maíz (1833-1920), and Natalicio Talavera (1839-67), a poet and journalist who died on the battlefront. His posthumous collection of war correspondence, *La guerra del Paraguay* (The Paraguayan War; 1958), confirms the profound national conscience of the people in defense of their freedom and sovereignty. *La república del Paraguay y sus relaciones exteriores* (The Republic of Paraguay and its Foreign Relations), by Carlos Calvo (1824-1906), published in Paris in 1864, is also a well-documented book written in superb romantic prose by the brilliant Paraguayan-Argentine diplomat and scholar. It is the best definition of revolutionary Paraguayan foreign policy. Periodicals such as *El Centinela* (The Sentinal; 1867-68), *Cabichuí* (1867-68), *Cacique Lambaré* (Warlord Lambaré; 1867-68), *La estrella* (The Star; 1869), and above all *La aurora* (Dawn; 1860-1862) contributed significantly to the formation and expression of these generations.

III

The postwar years were dominated by anti-López Paraguayans who had created in Buenos Aires the Legión Paraguaya (Paraguayan Legion), and had helped the Alliance against their own country. Under Legion governments, Paraguay's state-capitalism and democratic social institutions were dismantled; the economy was put under control of Anglo-Argentine companies; the country contracted a ruinous foreign debt with London (the Lópezes had never owed a penny); the railroad was sold to a British agency; and enormous extensions of state-owned land were undersold to foreign private capitalists, who created among other things the pathetic peasant exploitation of the *yerbales* (maté tea plantations).

However, not all postwar statesmen were associated with the Legion. Under the 1874-77 presidency of Juan Bautista Gill, the allied armies abandoned Paraguay. The governments of two of Solano López's former officers, Bernardino Caballero (1880-86) and Patricio Escobar (1886-90), in spite of being inspired in part by Legion ideologues, initiated national reconstruction. A brilliant diplomat, Benjamín Aceval, succeeded in defending the Paraguayan rights to the Chaco region, which was awarded to Paraguay by the American president Rutherford B. Hayes in a refereed controversy with Argentina in 1878. A general political amnesty was granted and the opposition returned to parliament; many public buildings were built; immigration increased; José Segundo Decoud renegotiated the London loans, obtaining a substantial reduction of the principal as well as of the interest rate; and the National University of Asunción was founded in 1889. The 1886-87 census revealed a population of 329,645 inhabitants, including the former Argentine president Sarmiento (who had helped exterminate most of the prewar 1,500,000 population), who lived in Asunción from 1887 until his death the following year. Solano López's widow, the brave Irish woman Eliza Alicia Lynch, had died in Paris on July 25, 1886 without any pension or recognition.

The most important intellectual representative of this period is José Segundo Decoud (1848-1909), who was born in Asunción. He studied at Uruguay's Colegio Nacional de Concepción and at Buenos Aires's Anglo-Argentine Seminar and National University, where he majored in philosophy and law. He contributed to the foundation of the anti-López Legion in Buenos Aires, helped convince López's lieutenant-colonel, Antonio Estigarribia, to capitulate with his modern and highly selective army in Uruguayana (Brazil) at the beginning of the war in 1865, and fought in the battle of Kurupayty under the orders of Mitre's general, Wenceslao Paunero. Decoud played a crucial role in the postwar period until 1904. He was the main author of the Constitution of 1870, which follows the model of the United States Constitution. Decoud was also the editor of several periodicals. He served as president of the Constitutional Convention, Deputy Chief-of-Mission in Washington, Secretary of State, Attorney General, Secretary of Education, Ambassador to London, National Treasurer, and Supreme Court president; he was a senator when he committed suicide in 1909.

Decoud's autobiography and other writings are still unpublished, but we know he lived his last years in a deep depression. Decoud ended up virtually erased from Paraguayan historical accounts and textbooks. His many speeches and essays were never reedited, and a great many of them remain unpublished. His major enemy, Francisco Solano López, is considered Paraguay's greatest hero, and Decoud was relegated to silence and oblivion. His work is left out or underestimated in all Paraguayan literary histories without exception. Yet, Decoud is the father of postwar thought in Paraguay and without a comprehensive, critical study of his postromantic and positivistic essays the whole period will remain ideologically unintelligible. Decoud was an extremely clever ideologue who employed a consistent patriotic rhetoric and advised Paraguayan poets to condemn the past "tyrannies" and extol at the same time "the epic glory" of López's soldiers. After Decoud, what writers associated with the Colorado (i.e., Red) Party did was exalt "the epic glory" of López himself, but they exalted him only as an ideologically neutral legend with no mention of his unmistakable presocialist and antiimperialistic character. This strategy followed the model of the aristocratic Juan Zorrilla de San Martín (see the section on Uruguay), who exalted the American-born race that Uruguayan creoles had previously exterminated in his poem *Tabaré* (1886-88).

"Villify López but spoil the people, or if you speak well of López, do not remember that he was a revolutionary" is the ideological context in which most Paraguayan postromantic literature is written, including the works of Juan Crisóstomo Centurión (1840-1903), Juansilvano Godoi (1850-1926), the Spanish-born Victorino Abente y Lago (1846-1935), Enrique Parodi (1857-1917), Venancio López (1862-1926), Adriano M. Aguiar (1859-1913), Diógenes Decoud (1859-1920), Héctor Francisco Decoud (1855-1930), and Ercilia López de Blomberg (1865-1963). Delfín Chamorro (1863-1931), a school-teacher, avoided historical themes and imitated the Spanish late romantic Gustavo Bécquer in some of his poems. José de la Cruz Ayala or Alón (1864-92) constitutes a precursor of the radical liberal ideology in his courageous essays published in several periodicals.

IV

The Paraguayan Modernist period is as complex and controversial as it is in the rest of Latin America. During this period the Liberal and Colorado (conservative) parties were founded (both in 1887). They would control Paraguay's contemporary politics until the present but not in a unidirectional way. Liberals and Colorados had Legion and López veterans among their early leaders, and both have been divided into two major internal historical tendencies, virtually to the present: the Liberal *cívicos* (civics) and *radicales* (radicals) and the Colorado *caballeristas* (for former president Bernardino Caballero) and *egusquicistas* (for former president Juan Bautista Egusquiza). No one can understand contemporary Paraguayan history without basic information about these four currents. This knowledge is also necessary to interpret modern Paraguayan culture. Both parties are pragmatic rather than ideological, representing about the same type of political alliance between a middle-class urban elite and a peasant clientele. The Colorados emphasize institutional stability, while the Liberals give priority to human rights. This is a pragmatical axis. In addition, a more subtle ideological axis divides both parties into respective oligarchic and populist internal tendencies: radicals and caballeristas are populist and seek a national model of society; civics and egusquicistas are rather oligarchic and attempt to adopt foreign models, following the authority of a strong, often military, caudillo. These four historical tendencies have changed names many times but are basically the same even today. During the Modernist period all of these forces entered into conflict, so it is not surprising to find that those twenty-five years are characterized by political violence and deep sectarian animosities.

Such was the turbulent context of the Paraguayan Modernist period. It is not accidental that its literary expression was impregnated with a strong social concern. This is the case with Cecilio Báez (1862-1951) and Blas Garay (1873-99), a radical and a caballerista, respectively, and the two best native Paraguayan essayists of this period. Other authors are inspired by the pessimistic and melancholic exoticism of the poetry of the period. This is the case with poets such as Ricardo Marrero Marengo (1879-1919), Fortunato Toranzos Bardel (1883-1941), Roberto A. Velázquez (1886-1961), and Guillermo Molinas Rolón (1891-1945). A more nationalistic poetry of a sensual heroic atmosphere and a typical New World ideological ambiguity is that of Francisco Luis Bareiro (1878-1930), Gomes Freire Esteves (1886-1970), and Pablo Max Insfrán (1894-1972).

The two most outstanding Paraguayan Modernist poets were Alejandro Guanes (1872-1925) and Eloy Fariña Núñez (1885-1929). They had many things in common: a cultural formation in Buenos Aires, a practice of professional journalism (the former in Asunción), an aesthetic evolution from the exotic to mundonovismo (i.e., New Worldism—the emphasis on Latin American referents), and a disdain for political militancy. In his only book of poetry, *De paso por la vida* (Passing through Life; 1936), which includes works written mostly in 1909, Guanes dedicates a poem to the Parnassian Catulle Mendés (who had died that year); translates Poe; evokes a *Residenta* (a symbol of postwar women); celebrates decadent life in "El almuerzo" (The Lunch); and creates in his masterpiece "Las leyendas" (The Legends) a complex metaphor of Paraguayan postwar years: an old patriarchal house visited by legendary ghosts, which can represent both the soldiers of López and the Legion. Fariña Núñez followed a similar ideological ambiguity in his *Canto secular* (Secular

Canto; 1911), a typical poem of New Worldism, published to commemorate the first centenary of Paraguayan Independence. He remembers the comuneros, the exuberant Paraguayan jungle, the Guaraní mythology, birds, harps, crafts, the native tongue, women's beauty, the children educated according to the ideals of José Enrique Rodó (see the section on Uruguay). He also censures war and praises freedom in abstract terms, but never risks a single word about Francia, the Lópezes, or any other specific national historical figure. In his poem "Al general Díaz" (To General Díaz), included in *Cármenes* (Poems; 1922), Fariña Núñez censors the "scoundrel who, stained with blood and disgrace, miserably fights against his brother" but never remembers who was the Commander-in-Chief of Díaz (i.e., López). We have to wait until Postmodernism to find the first coherent vindication of López. Fariña Núñez also produced three volumes of essays and a collection of short stories that do not reach the artistic level of his poetry.

The most important figure of Paraguayan Modernism is the Spanish-born essayist Rafael Barrett (1876-1910), one of the most original and profound thinkers of his (or any) time in Latin America. The son of an Englishman and a Spanish woman, Barrett was born in Torrelavega (Santander), studied humanities and mathematics at Paris and Madrid, moved to Buenos Aires in 1903 and to Asunción the following year. He worked as a technical officer for the government until 1906 and then as a teacher, land surveyor, and journalist. Barrett founded a revolutionary weekly, *El germinal* (The Sprout) in 1908 and gave a number of lectures for the workers. He was arrested and deported the same year, although he returned to Paraguay in 1909. The most representative essay collections of Barrett, who was a very prolific writer, are *Moralidades actuales* (Current Moral Issues; 1910), *Lo que son los yerbales* (What the Yerbales Are Like; 1910), and his posthumous *El dolor paraguayo* (The Suffering of Paraguay; 1911). He was also the author of *Cuentos breves* (Short Stories; 1911), inspired by Zola.

Barrett is the precursor of almost every progressive idea or technique in Paraguayan contemporary prose and thought: the revindication of the Guaraní language and Paraguayan bilingualism, as well as native folklore, mythical herbs, popular music, "magical realism," countercultural satire, the "intrahistorical" revision of the past as a universe of poetic symbols in the collective memory, women's liberation, psychiatric reform, social or "engaged" literature, ecological defense, pedagogical revolution, children's rights, the theory of capitalist alienation, the theory of capital as accumulated human work, land reform, worker's rights, the first critical revision of the War of the Triple Alliance as neocolonial genocide, the condemnation of torture as a repressive practice (as well as military coups d'état), the well-documented denunciation of peasant exploitation in the yerbales as a part of the pillage of the Third World, impressionistic description borrowed from cinema, a critical defense of unorthodox Marxism, the conception of socialism as an international movement, the search for a Paraguayan national identity, self-criticism of petit-bourgeois intellectuals, and always, the practice of writing as a courageous moral act.

V

After eliminating in 1912 the nightmare of the reign of Albino Jara, the radicals achieved a democratic, peaceful, and prosperous period. Paraguayan exports benefited as a consequence of the First World War, and the economy improved substantially. The country enjoyed an atmosphere of optimism, fueled by honest public administrators, and the general respect for civil authority, which was also instilled at the Military School by its new director, colonel Manlio Schenoni. The foremost radical patriarch, Manuel Gondra, a former professor of literature, was elected president in 1920.

The Postmodernist period was not a mere transition, but rather a coherent literary movement that severely criticized Modernist pseudo-cosmopolitan exoticism and bourgeois narcissism, as well as the ambiguity of so-called New Worldism. Postmodernist literature rediscovered Latin American mythical and provincial reality. It also discovered a most intimate, private world, the poet's own psyche. Paraguayan culture flourished, and it would enjoy an even more widespread development during the period of Regionalism from 1924 to 1940. Manuel Gondra (1871-1927) was one of the pioneers of Postmodernist ideology when he censured Rubén Darío's exoticism in 1898 and exalted instead Carlos Calvo and resistence of López's followers in 1901. Absorbed by politics—not by an abstract notion of it, but rather by an admirable and finally victorious crusade against militarism—Gondra ceased to write his lucid, post-parnassian essays. His young caballerista disciples continued his progressive message in the essay: Manuel Domínguez (1869-1935) fulminated against Decoud's theory of Paraguayan indolence in his anti-Legion *El alma de la raza* (The Paraguayan Spirit; 1918); Ignacio A. Pane (1879-1920) pleaded for social democracy in *Solidaridad social* (Social Solidarity; 1918) and also for feminism in *La mujer guaraní* (The Guaraní Woman; 1920); and Fulgencio R. Moreno (1872-1933) introduced Marxist historical analysis in *La ciudad de Asunción* (The City of Asunción; 1926).

A typical Postmodernist intimacy appeared in the poetry of the extremely popular Spanish-Guaraní bilingual poet Manuel Ortiz Guerrero (1897-1933), who published *Surgente* (Spring Water; 1922), and other books of poetry and plays. Other poets of this period are Facundo Recalde (1896-1969), Heriberto Fernández (1903-27), and Raúl Battilana de Gásperi (1904-23). The weakest national genre, the novel, produced the realistic *Aurora* (1920), by Juan Stefanich (1889-1976).

The most representative figure of Paraguayan Postmodernism is Juan E. O'Leary (1879-1969), who developed radical ideological concerns, especially the revindication of López resistence, in a rhetorical, noncritical fashion. He helped spawn the rebirth of caballerismo in essays like *El mariscal Solano López* (Marshall Solano López; 1920) and *El libro de los héroes* (The Book of Heroes; 1922). O'Leary was never harrassed by the radical government, which appointed him professor of the National College in 1918 (he was serving a four-year term as a Colorado congressman at the time) and as a diplomatic commissioner to Paraná, Argentina in 1920. He was accorded national public homage in 1922 as well as many subsequent honors. O'Leary was appointed director of the National Archives in 1930. This reveals that caballerista and radical ideologies were quite complementary. O'Leary's revindication of López followed Báez's revindication of Francia. They were both limited: Báez emphasized Spencer's positivistic reductionism, and O'Leary emphasized individualistic willpower in the anti-Darwinian manner of Michelet. Nevertheless, following Moreno's example, the caballerista Natalicio González in 1940 and the radical Domingo Laíno in 1976 would bring a certain unorthodox Marxism to the study of the colonial causes of the War of the Triple Alliance and its aftermath. In addition to writing a vibrant and sometimes virulent prose (probably the best post-Huguian diatribes ever produced in Latin America), O'Leary also wrote mediocre, conventionally epic poems. Not surprisingly, he never published a book of this poetry. He did, however, write brilliant Postmodernist poetry. This poetry appeared in a book, *A la memoria de mi hija Rosita* (To the Memory of My Daughter Rosita; 1924). In these intimate, intensely elegiac remembrances inspired by his child's death, O'Leary's style is free of Victor Hugo's, as it is similarly in other poems inspired by the death of his parents or by his solitude in Madrid and Paris. The craftsmanship and aesthetic coherence of O'Leary's elegy is of exceptional quality, still unsurpassed in Paraguayan poetry, and it is regrettable that it remains so unknown. In addition to his Spanish poetry, O'Leary published a few excellent poems in Guaraní; Ortiz Guerrero, however, surpassed him in this language.

Postmodernist Paraguay also produced the best guitar virtuoso of that or any period in Latin American classical music, Agustín Barrios (1885-1944), who was also a distinguished composer, poet, artist, and journalist. Encouraged by the cultural atmosphere of the 1920s, he gave numerous concerts in several Paraguayan cities. He chose Mangoré (Guzmán's hero) as his artistic name, and he lived in many European and Latin American countries, dying in San Salvador.

VI

Paraguayan Regionalism reflects the natural evolution of Postmodernism as it does in the rest of Latin America. There was no rupture or conflict between these two periods, but rather a more complete development of common concerns, feelings, and themes. Paraguayan literature continued to flourish under radical administrations. The country's economy grew austere but human rights and civil institutions were rigorously respected, and an independent yet stable foreign policy secured nonalignment and dignity. No Paraguayan presidents had had, or would have to the present, more international prestige than radicals Eligio Ayala (1923-28), José Patricio Guggiari (1928-32), Eusebio Ayala (1932-36), and Marshall José Félix Estigarribia (1939-40). In Marshall López's centenary, President Eligio Ayala publicly honored his memory, burying once and for all the Legion anathema. Latin American regionalism is often identified only with the *novela de la tierra* (novel of the land), a heterogeneous type of social and nationalistic fiction. Paraguayan regionalism produced a number of these novels, some inspired by the patriarchal evocation of the past. Representative examples are *Tradiciones del hogar* (Traditions of the Hearth; 1921-28) by Teresa Lamas de Rodríguez Alcalá (1887-1976) and *Tava'i* (1942) by María Concepción Leyes de Chaves (1889-1985). Also belonging to this category are descriptions of the Chaco War (1932-35): *Bajo las botas de una bestia rubia* (Under a Blond Beast's Boots; 1933) by Arnaldo Valdovinos (1908) and *Ocho hombres* (Eight Men; 1934) by José S. Villarejo (1907).

Latin American Regionalism also produced a vigorous essay devoted to the identification of national values and concerns. This period saw the formation and expression of many important Paraguayan essayists like Justo Pastor Benítez (1895-1962), Anselmo Jover Peralta (1895-1970), Juan Natalicio González (1897-1966), who was also a poet and novelist, Justo Prieto (1897), and Arturo Bray (1898-1974).

In the context of this Americanization of characters and minds, Latin American poetry brilliantly adapted avant-garde irreverence or developed Postmodernist colloquialism to express social or intimate universes in which surprise and even scandal served as the basis for a new existential reading of human reality. Paraguayan poets of this period shared this sensibility and manifested some aesthetic features that are typically colloquial in José Concepción Ortiz (1900-72), social in Julio Correa (1890-1953), and erotic in Dora Gómez Bueno de Acuña (1903). The most representative Paraguayan regionalistic magazine was *Juventud* (Youth; 1923-27), which attained a remarkable eighty-five issues.

During this period, José Asunción Flores (1904-72) created the *guarania* in 1925, a national musical genre that soon became internationally famous in both its popular and symphonic forms. Poets such as Ortiz Guerrero contributed with their lyrics—in Spanish and Guaraní—to many of Flores's guaranias. A realistic drama was also introduced by the playwrights Luis Ruffinelli (1889-1973) and Arturo Alsina (1897-1985) in Spanish and, most remarkably, by Correa in Guaraní.

The most important literary figure of this period is Gabriel Casaccia (1907-80), a fiction writer of unquestionable international stature who lived in Asunción until 1935 (having participated in the Chaco War in 1933), in Posadas, Argentina until 1952, and in Buenos Aires until his death. A lawyer by profession, Casaccia combined the provincial atmosphere of the novel of the land, the psychosociological analysis of the regionalistic essay, and the "scandalous" uninhibited discourse of that period's poetry to create a fascinating, pre-Kafkian microcosmos. His collections of short stories, *El guajhú* (The Howl; 1938) and *El pozo* (The Well; 1947), as well as all his novels, from *Hombres, mujeres y fantoches* (Men, Women, and Puppets; 1930) to his masterpiece, *La babosa* (The Gossiping Woman; 1952), and to his posthumous *Los Huertas* (The Huertas; 1981), are a complex denouncement of petit-bourgeois hypocrisy, and the simplistic idealization of New Worldism stories and epic poems.

Casaccia's psychological realism opened the door of international criticism for the Paraguayan narrative. In the context of the triple

Latin-Americanization of local geography, critical interpretation, and poetic language, what Casaccia did was to focus on the obscure and profound individual psychology of Paraguayans toward formulating an image of their collective unconsciousness. His study was limited to the Paraguayan society of the thirties, forties, and fifties, but it still can serve as the inspiration and model for any serious and honest attempt at anti-narcissistic literature in Latin America.

VII

President Estigarribia died in September 1940 in a plane crash many believe was the result of sabotage; thus, Paraguay lost a national hero, venerated for the Paraguayan victory in the Chaco War against Bolivia (1932-35). The radicals collapsed with him, and rightist militarism has held power since then. General Alfredo Stroesner, inaugurated in 1954, has held the longest presidential tenure in Paraguayan history. Stroessner smashed the last serious caballerista rebellion in 1959, ejected from his cabinet the last caballerista with some political power, Edgar Ynsfrán, in 1966, and became the omnipotent vertex of a military pyramid. Paraguay increased its economy, expanded its public services, and modernized its communications at the expense of human rights, national morale, and international prestige.

The Neobaroque period brought world-wide visibility to Latin American literature, which became probably the most popular literature on the international market. Not surprisingly, this literature based on cultural authenticity and extremely elaborated craftsmanship and representing poetically a major Third World revolution, was voraciously read abroad. However, this period cannot be reduced to a single ideology. Neobaroque displays a very complex system of metaphors, some of which are evidently oligarchic. This is the case with Jorge Luis Borges (see the section on Argentina), for example, who conceives the intellectual as an impotent minotaur, isolated in a labyrinth not only of words or books but, above all, of threatening social forces that he neither controls nor understands. Other Neobaroque writers, like Pablo Neruda (see the section on Chile), stand for the opposite symbolism; they understand Latin American society and think its problems can be solved by political action to which every honest intellectual should be intensely committed, not necessarily through sectarian activism but—as Cervantes showed us—through an ironic, critical subversion of the status quo. A number of Neobaroque writers oscillate between the "Minotauric" and "Cervantine" positions.

Some Paraguayan authors of this period did not assume the Neobaroque fashion, but rather prolonged some regionalistic forms and ideas, like the novelists Juan F. Bazán (1900), Reinaldo Martínez (1908), Jorge R. Ritter (1914-76), and Ana Iris Chaves de Ferreiro (1922); the essayists Efraím Cardozo (1906-75), Carlos Zubizarreta (1904-70), Julio César Chaves (1907), and Hipólito Sánchez Quell (1907); the playwrights José María Rivarola Matto (1917), and Mario Halley Mora (1924); and the poets Hugo Rodríguez Alcalé (1917), Oscar Ferreiro (1922), and Elsa Wiezell (1927). This anachronism does not necessarily imply a lack of literary quality: Cardozo, for example, is one of the most admirable figures of this period as a prose stylist, a scholar, a profound thinker, and a remarkable human being. The most curious case of this type of anachronistic writer is the Spanish born Josefina Pla (1909). Pla has cultivated the highly impressionistic regionalistic essay, the intensely pessimistic New Worldism drama (in the style of Florencio Sánchez; see the section on Uruguay), the existentialist approach of psychological, neoregionalistic fiction, and, above all, the confidential metaphysical lyric of Postmodernist poetry. In spite of this mélange, Pla has insisted that most other Paraguayan writers were anachronistic. Like other Latin American minotaurs of this period—i.e., Carlos Fuentes (see the section on Mexico) and Mario Vargas Llosa (see the section on Peru)—she engaged in literary criticism on her own behalf and fabricated the reputation of the so-called Generation of 1940, praising its modernity while denouncing the earlier periods as provincial and unsophisticated. This opportunistic theory exerted some influence in Paraguay through Pla's disciples, the poets and critics Rogue Vallejos (1943) and Francisco Pérez Maricevich (1937), who publicly committed themselves to Stroessner's regime. This view also contributed to a distorted interpretation of Paraguayan literary evolution in many literary histories and anthologies.

This brief survey reveals the limited literary production in Paraguay after the cultural diaspora of 1947. A number of intellectuals left the country, moving to Argentina, the United States, France, and other countries and giving up—involuntarily, in most cases—a leadership space, which was often filled by native adherents to the dictatorship and by similarly conservative intellectuals of foreign origin. The most successful among the latter was the Spanish-born Catholic priest César Alonso de las Heras (1913), a good poet of unengaged, abstract aestheticism, which he borrowed from the most individualistic poets of the Spanish Generation of 1927. He imparted this same literary doctrine to his disciples at the Academia Literaria (Literary Academy), a highly selective bourgeois literary workshop that opened its door in 1946. Some of Alonso's trainees, such as José Luis Appleyard (1927), Ricardo Mazó (1927), and Ramiro Domínguez (1929), followed (though sometimes in an unorthodox fashion) the minotauric path of their master in essays, plays, fiction, and especially poetry. Others became quite independent, such as the social-Christian essayists Juan Santiago Dávalos (1925-73) and Adriano Irala Burgos (1929?), the avant-garde artist, poet, and playwright Carlos Colombino (who signs his poems Esteban Cabañas; 1937), and the best representative of this period among the writers who wrote their work inside Paraguay, José María Gómez Sanjurjo (1930). In the lucid transparency of his masterpiece, *Poemas* (Poems; 1978), a collection made up of texts written mostly in the fifties and sixties, Gómez Sanjurjo assumes a personal voice not only to describe his private feelings of love and solitude, but also to embody poetically the desolation and frustration of his generation. He does not attempt a bourgeois elegy for the banquet that the Paraguayan neooligarchy did not share with the Academia elite; Gómez Sanjurjo denounces in a critical, unmistakably Cervantine way both interior and exterior exiles, and he is certainly the only member of his group who has claimed (and has gained the right to claim) as his "comrade" the leading Neobaroque social poet, Elvio Romero. *Poemas* recreates Cesare Pavese's nostalgic scenes as well as Neruda's collective ego in the deepest and warmest Paraguayan manner; the collection constitutes one of the most coherent, significant, and splendid achievements within contemporary Latin American poetry.

Almost all important Neobaroque Paraguayan writing was written in exile, including that of Herib Campos Cervera (1905- 53), Augusto Roa Bastos (1917), and Elvio Romero (1926) in Argentina; that of Carlos Villagra Marsal (1932) in Chile; Rodrigo Díaz Pérez (1924), Gustavo Gatti (1927), and Gonzalo Zubizarreta (1930) in the United States; and that of Rubén Bareiro Saguier (1930) in France. These poets are influenced by the social authors of Spain's Generation of 1927, such as Rafael Alberti in the case of Campos Cervera's *Ceniza redimida* (Liberated Ashes; 1950), and Miguel Hernández in the case of Romero's *El sol bajo las raíces* (The Sun beneath the Roots; 1956), as well as in the latter's many other books. In the manner of Neruda, they adapted a system of metaphors based on pantheistic mineral, botanical, and biological images to symbolize the peoples' mythical alchemy through which they recover freedom as well as their ancestral fatherland. Following the example of

Rulfo (see the section on Mexico) and João Guimarães Rosa (see the section on Brazil), Bareiro Saguier and Villagra Marsal have also combined myth and a highly metaphorical style to describe abuse and violence in a rural environment; cf. the latter's novelette *Mancuello y la perdiz* (Mancuello and the Partridge; 1965) and the former's short story collections *Ojo por diente* (An Eye for a Tooth; 1973) and *El séptimo pétalo del viento* (The Seventh Petal of the Wind; 1984). These books introduce a meticulous codification of Spanish prose based in part on Guaraní oral traditions. Bareiro Saguier founded the international literary journal *Alcor* (The Hill; 1955-61), and Villagra Marsal the poetry series Alcándara (The Falconry-Rack) in 1982.

The most representative author of this period is, of course, Augusto Roa Bastos, whose oeuvre has inspired an international bibliography which easily exceeds that of all the other Paraguayan writers combined. He was born in Asunción, spent his childhood in the provincial city of Iturbe, moved to Buenos Aires in 1947, and to Toulouse in 1975. Roa Bastos has worked for the most part as a scriptwriter and university professor. He was allowed to visit Paraguay in the seventies, but after being expelled in 1982, he was forced again to remain in exile. In his several short story volumes and especially in his two novels, *Hijo de hombre* (Son of Man; 1960) and *Yo el Supremo* (I the Supreme; 1974), Roa Bastos explores Paraguayan social unconsciousness, revealing not only its poetic myths but also remythifying its most noble and profound values in favor of a utopian, revolutionary project: the collective resurrection of Paraguay as a coherent community. Roa Bastos displays a Christian metaphoric system in *Hijo de hombre* in accordance with the Neobaroque concept of magical realism. In *Yo el Supremo*, however, he anticipates many postboom techniques like the carnivalization of historical discourse, transtextualization, and parody that would flourish in the late seventies and eighties. Only a few Latin Americans, and certainly no Paraguayans have ever brought more world-wide literary recognition to their country than Augusto Roa Bastos. The fact that this man, who never practiced any sectarian political activism, must reside far from his own land and people is the most overwhelming evidence of the moral decadence of this period in Paraguay. It is also a pathetic demonstration of the values of a regime that has lasted three decades and that has reached its lowest point of even proclaiming silence to be a subversive activity.

VIII

In 1967 a new Constitution was tailored to grant Stroessner a lifetime presidency. The general easily controlled the country as if it were a traditional army barracks. The Army became Stroessner's personal guard. Police played a crucial role in protecting the regime by terrorizing the people: it was well-known that torture was a systematic practice, even for nonpolitical prisoners. This practice was rigorously complemented by banishment to rural towns, deportation, exile, and the abolition of the free press. Judicial and legislative systems were entirely subordinated to the president's will. Opposition parties and movements were repressed, manipulated, or eliminated, including church groups. The dictator was supported by fellow military regimes in Argentina, Uruguay, Bolivia, Chile, and Brazil—to which Paraguay became a commercial enclave—as well as by the United States, with significant exceptions during the Kennedy and Carter administrations. Fueled by the construction of Itaipú, the world's largest hydroelectric power plant, Paraguay attained the highest economic growth rate in Latin America between 1978 and 1983.

Currently, the thirty-one year old regime can hardly deal with its decrepitude. Stroessner created an Army elite with the sole purpose of defending his own person. As the dictator is aging, however, the elite is losing its reason to maintain its unity. The political apparatus is also falling apart. His supporters, divided into irreconcilable factions, are already disputing the dictator's successor. Paradoxically, the only Colorados still defending a common cause are the dissidents who joined the opposition some time ago, gallantly keeping alive the old caballerista principle of civil authority. Stroessner's cívico partners, who serve as puppets in domesticated parliamentary camouflage, have been completely repudiated by the Liberal masses. The Itaipú boom collapsed in 1984, sinking the country into its worst social and economic crisis since 1870. The vast majority of the people, who are under forty years of age, look for a new, decent leadership capable of restoring democracy, honest administration, an independent foreign policy, economic development, social justice, national cohesion, and international prestige.

The source of new values in Paraguay has been the student demonstrations of June 1969, when a massive youth movement spontaneously rose in protest against the visit of President Nixon's commissioner; the antiimperialistic demonstration (which was brutally repressed) was not inspired by communism, but rather by the same spirit of the sixties that was impelling American young people to condemn the Vietnam War and political immorality. Stroessner's regime has done as much as possible to quash the June Spirit with sixteen years of terror.

The June Spirit has produced a vast and radical cultural revolution in Paraguayan history, which includes an enormous boom in book publishing, a massive festival, cassette industry, and popular music movement led by Maneco Galeano (1945-80), Carlos Noguera (1948)—Galeano and Segura are also poets—Mito Seguera, Jorge Krauch, the Pettengill brothers, José Antonio Galeano, Jorge Garbett, and other musicians; a renaissance in theatrical arts led by José Luis Ardissone, Edda de los Ríos, Antonio Pecci, Raquel Rojas, Rudi Torga, Gustavo Calderini, and other artists; a notable increase in visual arts, gallery attendance, and art research led by the Brazilian-born woodcut artist Livio Abramo, the designer and architect Luis Alberto Boh, the critic and gallery owner Ticio Escoba, and many others; a new wave of creative ethnological research led by, among others, the filmmaker Gregorio López Grenno and the anthropologist José Antonio Gómez Perasso; and the most unconventional and modern literary evolution ever experienced within the context of either interior and exterior exile. A brave new generation of critical journalists has also appeared, symbolized by the banned newspaper editor and 1985 Columbia University International Journalism Award winner Aldo Zuccolillo and by the broadcaster Humberto Rubén.

Criterio (Criterion), a cultural magazine and book series, founded under the direction of Basilio Bogado Gondra (1947) in 1966 and banned in 1977 played a leading role in this spiritual resistance. *Criterio* inspired the June demonstration and almost every new idea in the seventies and eighties in spite of the death of a number of its editors, such as the poets René Dávalos (1945-68) and Nelson Roura (1945-69) and the essayist Juan Carlos Da Costa (1944-76). This loss was accompanied by the exile in Venezuela of the magazine's founder; his brother, Juan Félix Bogado Gondra (1945), in West Germany; the essayists José Carlos Rodríguez (1948), in France; and Juan Carlos Herken Krauer (1953), in England. Other intellectuals also associated with *Criterio* have also spent a number of years out of Paraguay, such as the poets Guido Rodríguez Alcalá (1946), in the United States, and Jorge Canese (1947), in Argentina; the latter's brother, Ricardo Canese (1950), in the Netherlands; and the essayist José Nicolás Moringo (1947), in Costa Rica. Only Boh, the poets Adolfo Ferreiro (1946) and Emilio Pérez Chaves (1950) and the innovative novelist Jesús Ruiz Nestosa (1941) remained in Asunción; all of them, without exception, have experienced political imprisonment, as has the courageous journalist and playwright Alcíbiades González Delvalle (1936).

Latin American literature has definitely entered into a new period that is provisionally called the "postboom," characterized by parody, humor, colloquial speech, intertextualities, the kaleidoscope of genres, the introduction of women and minorities as critical characters, the utopian undermining of bourgeois reification, the more explicit representation of sexual behavior, the remythifiction of revolutionary values. Paraguayans have not avoided the possibilities of the postboom. However, they are still exposed to the bewilderment of a public insufficiently prepared by mediocre and traditional literary school programs. They suffer constant police repression as well as disdain or hostility from the older writers and critics. Reviewing a book by Josefina Pla in the sixties, René Dávalos had already critized her praise of the regime's cultural policy, stating that: "those who are not committed to the people's revolutionary needs should be quiet in cultural matters." The worst situation occurs when the police assume the role of literary critics: for example, Canese's book of poetry *Paloma blanca; paloma negra* (White Dove, Black Dove; 1982) was banned because one line read "países de mierda como el nuestro" (shit-countries like ours). Roa Bastos, who had been asked to present the volume at a public cheese and wine gathering, was abruptly taken by police to the Argentine border. The sad truth is that Canese's poem had been composed from an ironic point of view, typical of postboom colloquial and countercultural poetry. Thus, to any reader with a minimal understanding of contemporary poetic sensibility, the famous line actually implies an extremely romantic love declaration. The conclusion of the story reveals a great deal about the regime's cultural impotence: *Paloma blanca, paloma negra*, though banned, circulated widely and was sold clandestinely, becoming the biggest bestseller in the history of Paraguayan poetry.

In 1922 radicals had organized a solid front from their own peasant and middle-class followers, allied with union workers and students, to defend democracy. History proved this was the best preparation for the Chaco defense ten years later. Now, not only can they count on the same forces again, but also on small parties, caballeristas, the Church, the independent media, and honest businessmen who are ready to support a restoration of democracy. The radicals have already won a war. Now they must win peace. Paraguay can hope for many good things from this reconciliation. Among these things, good literature.

BIBLIOGRAPHY

Amaral, Raúl. *El modernismo poético en el Paraguay (1901-1916)*. Asunción: Alcándara, 1982. This introduction presents a too narrow concept of Modernism; there is a useful bibliography.

Amaral, Raúl. *El romanticismo paraguayo 1860-1910*. Asunción: Alcándara, 1985. A good introduction and bibliography.

Bareiro Saguier, Rubén, et al. *Literatura guaraní del Paraguay*. Caracas: Ayacucho, 1980. This anthology contains a very useful introduction by Bareiro Saguier.

Cardozo, Efraím. *Apuntes de historia cultural del Paraguay*. Asunción: Universidad Católica, 1985. An excellent account of colonial culture.

Díaz Pérez, Viriato, et al. *Literatura del Paraguay*. Palma de Mallorca: Luis Ripoll, 1980. In two volumes, a miscellany of critical essays.

Pérez-Maricevich, Francisco. *Diccionario de la literatura paraguaya*. Asunción: Biblioteca Colorados Contemporáneos, 1983. A literary dictionary; only the first part, letters A-C, has appeared.

PERU
Dick Gerdes
University of New Mexico

I

Peru has been called a land of many contrasts. From east to west, the country's diverse topography is a case in point. First appears the immense, lushly green, impenetrable, and relatively uninhabited Amazon basin that makes up over two-thirds of the country's land surface. This green monster is followed by the looming Andes mountains, whose jagged peaks soar tens-of-thousands of feet into the sky, and in the midst of which half of Peru's population lives a precarious existence, many still cultivating Incan terraces—*andenes*—on an inhospitable vertical medium that literally cuts off the tropical rain forest to the east from the rest of the world. Finally, there is the narrow strip of coastal arid desert, dotted with small enclaves of fertile, green valleys formed by the dozens of rivers that annually rush headlong in westward fashion down from the Andes, slicing through the desert and dumping its precious contents into the Pacific Ocean. This coastal ribbon of sand dunes and rocky abutments that regularly drop off into the ocean between Ecuador to the north and Chile to the south has been the nation's center of economic and political activity since the arrival of the Spaniards over four-hundred years ago. And it is here that other contrasts become readily apparent: extreme human poverty of epidemic proportions, existing alongside the embarrassingly crass opulence and luxury of a priviledged few. Decades of migration by Peru's rural peoples to the arid coastal region have bloated the population of the coast's burgeoning urban centers (the capital, Lima, and its main seaport, Callao, and the major provincial cities of Arequipa, Ica, Trujillo, Chimbote, Chiclayo, Piura, and Tumbes) where mushrooming slums, lack of public services, and rampant unemployment are no less tragic than trying to eke out an existence against supreme natural forces in the Andes mountains or the Amazon jungle.

Hence, Peru's topographical fragmentation has historical, cultural, and political parallels.

Stimulated by tales of cities with streets paved in gold, Francisco Pizarro and his band of conquistadores sailed from Panama in 1531 to that part of South America. Their encounter with an expanding indigenous civilization, the Inca Empire, led to the creation of a society based on economic and racial differences that even today seem far from being overcome in any foreseeable future. Throughout the Spanish colonial period (until Independence in the early 1800s), and even now in the twentieth century, a large chasm exists between a fragile yet economically dominant white European minority and a vast faceless majority of impoverished Indian and mestizo peoples, not to mention significant enclaves of blacks and orientals along the coast and, in the Amazonian rain forests, small, defenseless, nomadic tribes that Western civilization seems bent on exterminating in the name of progress.

This contemporary reality raises many questions in this Quincentennial year (1992) commemorating Columbus's arrival in the New World. The renowned Peruvian fiction writer, dramatist, and intellectual, Mario Vargas Llosa, asks, for example, "Why have the postcolonial republics of the Americas—republics that might have been expected to have deeper and broader notions of liberty, equality, and fraternity—failed so miserably to improve the lives of their Indian citizens?" Basically, then, a centuries-long cultural fragmentation has remained unresolved.

Historically, Peru shares with the rest of its neighboring countries a common set of realities: the presence of a pre-Columbian culture (the Incas); military, political, and economic conquest by Spain with the consequent imposition of a foreign language and religion; the deculturation of the existing indigenous populations; the arrival of African slaves; the Independence movement in the early nineteenth century and massive European and Asian immigration during its latter half; greater social awareness and cultural interaction in the twentieth century; slow industrialization and great economic destabilization brought about by foreign capitalistic exploitation, creating a more visible North-South polarization; continued economic stagnation and greater exposure to foreign domination and control. Herein lies Peru's—and Latin America's, for that matter—unity and sense of cultural identity.

To speak of a national literature—in this case, Peruvian literature—is to suggest the existence of a body of writing based on the identification of a nation's historical coherence, unity of language, national goals, social awareness, and cultural identity. In Peru, as in so many other Latin

American countries, the concept of a coherent national literature becomes problematical, especially in terms of fitting it into the history of
Western literature. While the concept of a national literature absorbs all
literary substrata into one single if amorphous canon, Peru, with its geographical, racial, cultural, and historical diversity, fits more easily into a
regional, Latin American concept of culture, in which diverse literatures,
both written and oral, establishment and popular, respectively, continue
to collide in kaleidoscopic fashion within a multicolored, paradoxically
static yet mobile environment.

To date, in the ongoing identification of a national literary canon for
Peru, historical and critical approaches have dealt primarily with learned
or refined texts in Spanish and little with popular literature. Indigenous
literature in Quechua has been looked at primarily from anthropological
and sociological viewpoints for its testimonial value. The project for the
future will be to incorporate all literary strata—dominant and popular,
written and oral, male and female—into a literary canon in which modern critical perspectives will help us to appreciate "Peruvian" literature
in all its multiplicity, diversity, and richness.

II

When the Spaniards arrived in South America, the Inca Empire was
in an expansionist stage and had already extended far beyond what we
know today as Peru. While the Incas' pictographic art, on ceramics,
jewelry, and cloth, provide highly valuable insights into their myths, legends, history, and legal system (a knowledge greatly enriched by the
important role of the state's statisticians—*quipucamayos*—who kept precise mathematical records on sets of colored strings with knots), their
literary production was not recorded in writing but orally transmitted
from one generation to the next. The state's wise men—*amautas*—were
responsible for documenting official history and philosophy in this fashion, just as anonymous community bards—*haravicus*—would compose
highly impressionistic lyric poetry and songs, often in choral style, that
were less geared to educating the commoner about official policy or
history than to interpreting the latter's world by expressing their feelings
and sentiments via themes dealing with planting and harvest, family
celebrations, and events related to their daily trials and tribulations.
These more intimate and personal compositions—*harawis*—dealt with
pastoral, sentimental, and erotic love themes. Another indigenous form

of poetic composition that was sung and danced to musical rhythms is the *huayno*, and an interesting bilingual compilation by Gloria and Gabriel Escobar, *Huaynos del Cusco* (Huaynos from Cuzco; 1981), provides an excellent sampling of the genre. In order to keep traditions in tact and, thus, safeguard a unified, centralized theocracy, the amautas also created epic poetry to celebrate the Inca empire's origins (i.e., the legend of Manco Capac and Mama Ocllo who appear near Lake Titicaca). The quipucamayos would maintain a living memory of these heroic deeds and, later, after the Conquest, the Spanish priests, through their knowledge of the vernacular languages, preserved fragments of these compositions in their chronicles.

Theatrical representation played an important role in lending pomp and ceremony to the religious ritual that sustained the power of the Inca empire. It is at the core of official celebrations in which drama, oratory, actors, music, and dance came together to provide an allegory of state theology. Dramatic performances were also important for warriors who communicated their heroic deeds in significant battles to their community upon their return. Near the end of the Inca empire, another type of theater—the dramatization of comedy, fables, and sarcastic poetry—became fairly widespread as a means of criticizing enemies and their gods.

While rich in oral literary material such as proverbs, fables, stories and other didactic texts, including songs, dance, and spectacle, Incan society underwent significant transformation with the arrival of the Iberians. In 1525 Charles V mandated Spanish as the official language and ordered Indian leaders to learn Spanish. The colonies provided religious instruction in Spanish, and specialists trained language teachers for the task. At the time of its arrival in Peru, the Spanish language had just come into its own, having eliminated coarse Medieval structures. Most critics agree that the influence of Spanish—a new, strong, explicit, clear, and democratic language—can be felt in two ways: first, as grass-roots speech based on popular expressions and songs, ballads, and poetry that are tied to historical events; and second, as an erudite, civilized, written language cultivated by intellectuals and nobles to demonstrate the linguistic splendor of the Spanish Golden Age. A third ingredient that further transforms New World language is the incorporation of Quechua, Aymará, and their dialects into this new Spanish language, processes that imply lexicographic transfers from one language to another, but also the adaptation of diverse elements. And so begins five centuries of painful transculturation. Thanks to trained ethnologists like José María Arguedas, an important twentieth-century intellectual who not only directed the Institute of Ethnological Studies at the National Museum of History but also was himself an important fiction writer, many fables, stories, legends, and songs have been carefully collected and presented in literary fashion to highlight their important anthropological quality.

During the first century after the Conquest, Quechua-derived but Hispanic-influenced dramatic productions assimilated the world of the indigenous nobility to Western literary tradition. Such is *El pobre más rico o Yauri Tito Inca* (The Richest Poor Man Around or Yauri Tito Inca, 1600-40?), by Gabriel Centeno de Osma (seventeenth century), structured on the *auto sacramental* (religious play), based on the eucharist, showing similarities with later European drama, and written in Quechua. Another colonial Quechua-Christian play is *Uska Paucar* (anonymous), centered on the Catechism and dedicated to the Virgin of Copacabana. *El hijo pródigo* (seventeenth century), the authorship of which is attributed to Juan de Espinoza Medrano (1629-88), known as El Lunarejo, is a religious allegory with antecedents in native drama. It uses Quechua and Spanish, creating a unique Cuzco dialect. El Lunarejo also wrote plays and essays. His tragicomedy *Amar su propia muerte* (Love Your Own Death) is based on a passage from the Old Testament, and he is most famous for his tirade against the Portuguese poet Manuel de Favia Souza in "Apologética de don Luis de Góngora, Príncipe de los Poetas Líricos de España," (The Apologetics of Don Luis de Góngora, Prince of the Spansih Lyric Poets). The essay is considered the best example of Colonial Peruvian baroque style.

Repeated references have been made to another colonial Quechua drama, *Atahualpa*, also called *Tragedia del fin de Atawallpa* (Tragedy of Death of Atawallpa) or *La muerte de Atahualpa* (The Death of Atahualpa), that bilingually recounts the fateful encounter between Atahualpa and Pizarro, using prose and poetry to induce an emotionally critical reaction on the part of Indians during a period of rebellion in the eighteenth century. By far the best-known colonial dramatic text is *Ollantay*, its origin still highly contested. With thematic antecedents in pre-Columbian culture, the play's style, structure, and characters makes it reminiscent of Spanish Golden Age theater. It is commonly believed that this form of theater provided the impetus for creating post-Conquest, anti-European indigenous dance and drama spectacles that can be perceived in contemporary indigenous choreography. The problems regarding cultural origin and authorship of indigenous literature, before and after the Spanish conquest, are best seen in the polemic surrounding *Ollantay*, first discovered in 1837 and most likely presented for the first

498 Handbook of Latin American Literature

time in the presence of rebel leader Tupac Amaru in Tinta, near Cuzco, the same year he led the most extensive of several Indian rebellions: 1780. The play is based on the legend of Ollantay, who rebels against King Inca Pachacutec for not being allowed to marry into the nobility. Now considered a true expression of Quechua literature before the Conquest, there is some agreement that the play was probably never formally preserved on a *quipu* (an abacus-like set of knotted, differently colored, strings used to keep track of things), never maintained in its original form through oral tradition, nor considered an omen of future ethnic rebellions. It is seen as a combination of an indigenous theme and Spanish colonial dramatic form, perhaps one of the first transitional texts combining the Old and the New World's literary forms.

Nevertheless, much indigenous literary expression in the form of religious prayer, drama, and spectacle, including myth, legend, and fable, poetic expression of human feelings, and ritual song would be lost, except in isolated rural areas, during the colonial period. With the creation of San Marcos University at Lima in 1551 and the arrival of the printing press shortly thereafter, poetry and song in Quechua were quickly suppressed by official colonial forms appearing in large part through printed books in Spanish, the first in Peru being Antonio Ricardo's *Doctrina cristiana y catecismo para instrucción de los indios* (Christian Doctrine and Catecism for Instructing Indians) in 1584, which was then translated into Quechua and Aymara. Not to be forgotten, however, is the simultaneous importation of popular literary forms from Spain, such as *coplas*, *refranes*, *cantares*, and *romances* (ballads, proverbs, folksongs, and lyric or narrative poems, respectively) that documented with irony and satire contemporary historical events and personal folly, like civil war and illicit love affairs among Spaniards in the New World. In fact, the romance (composed in octosyllabic meter with alternate lines in assonance) accompanied the conquistadores to Peru and served as the vehicle for anonymous soldiers to narrate actual events in critical fashion. Colonial literature, then, begins to thrive on these two opposing forms in Spanish, one of which is erudite, formal, institutional, and written, while the other is popular, spontaneous, and oral. Somewhere in between fall the early chronicles that recorded and recounted in semiofficial fashion the discovery/conquest and its fateful aftermath. Their authors were diverse: Spaniards, Indians, and mestizos; soldiers, geographers, legal experts, and men of the cloth; and those representing different schools of thought and varied projects, such as the consolidation of colonial power under Francisco de Toledo's Viceroyalty in Peru (1569-81) or the attempt to vindicate the intolerance suffered by the Incas. But the first chroniclers were men like Francisco Pizarro's secretaries, Francisco de Jerez (sixteenth century) and Pedro Sancho de la Hoz (sixteenth century), who participated in the military campaign and, in writing about it, included personal observations of the land and the people in *Verdadera relación de la conquista del Perú* (The True History of the Conquest of Peru; 1634) and *La relación para su Majestad* (A History for His Majesty; written in 1534, published in Italian in 1556), respectively. The first work ends when Atahualpa is executed, the second narrates the collapse and submission of the Inca empire afterwards between June 1533 and July 1534, and both were written in order to portray Pizarro and the conquistadores in a positive light and to justify their violent exploits to the King.

A work that is typical of the second stage of chronicle writing in Peru, offering a more carefully rendered, impartial, general history of the period is *Crónica del Perú* (Chronicle of Peru; sixteenth century), written by the Spaniard Pedro Cieza de León (1519-54?), who was already in the New World in his teens. The first part of a more extensive project was published in Seville in 1553, while other parts remained unpublished until recent times. Authored by Pedro Sarmiento de Gamboa (1532?-92?), in order to support Viceroy Toledo's political designs to strengthen his power at the time, *Historia índica* (Recent History; finished in 1572 but not published until this century) is written in scrupulous, erudite Spanish, details character well, but projects a negative, anti-Indian stance that seeks to justify the conquest from a European perspective.

Opposite views found in indigenous testimony recorded in other chronicles of that time are also extremely important in order to understand both sides of the conflicts of that age. One such testimony, *Relación de la conquista del Perú* (Account of the Conquest of Peru; sixteenth century) by Diego de Castro Titu Cusi Yupanqui, which was not published until 1916, narrates the war that was fought first by his father and then himself against the Spanish invaders. Another such document, *Relación de antigüedades deste reyno del Pirú* (Account of the Antiquities of Peru), by Joan de Santacruz Pachacuti (sixteenth century) was probably written in the early 1600s and was first published in English translation in 1873. In the document, the author carefully traces his heritage in order to prove clear Christian origins for native Indians.

Felipe Guamán Poma de Ayala (c.1535-c.1615) completed his major work, *La nueva corónica y buen gobierno* (First New Chronicle and Good Government), in 1615 and hand carried to Lima. Somehow, the manuscript made its way to Europe and was not discovered until 1908 in the

Royal Library of Copenhagen. Written to Spanish king Philip III as a defense of the Andean people, the document is almost 1,200 pages in length and contains some four hundred drawings that depict the New World inhabitants living under Spanish rule. Apparently, it generated much interest among Scandinavians for its criticism of Spanish colonial conduct, but some believe the author's purpose for writing the document was to defend Guamán Poma de Ayala for claiming a local title, to expose contemporary exploitation, and to correct a deep misunderstanding by Europeans of New World history, society, and culture. His view of the world is necessarily critical and certainly biased; in fact, he even takes the Incas to task, for his parents had belonged to an ancient caste that was eventually subsumed by the Incas. But the intent of his document was more than personal; it is said he knew of and paraphrased parts of Bartolomé de las Casas work about the mistreatment of Indians in the New World. As such, Guamán Poma's treatise to the King represents not only a strong invective, accompanied by pictures, against the Spanish conquerors, but also an appeal to rectify their iniquities. Finally, it is worth noting that since the discovery of Guamán Poma's text, his apparent incorrect use of Spanish has been widely discussed, criticized and, hence, misunderstood. Today, linguists are studying the relationship between Quechua and Spanish in order to show how uncommon usage in Spanish can be attributed to the underlying influence of grammatical and lexical structures in Quechua when no real Spanish models existed for the writer and historical reality had pitted two different linguistic structures—and, in fact, verbal and visual icons representing European and New World cultures—against each other.

Other chroniclers, that is, the indigenous and mestizo writers, occupy an important position in the literary history of colonial Peru. In fact, they set the stage for creative symbiotic relationships in art and culture from that time forward. The giant among this group of writers is Inca Garcilaso de la Vega (1539-1616). His literary fame is based primarily on two historical works, *La Florida del Inca* (The Florida of the Inca; 1605), which describes the Hernando de Soto expedition to Florida (although he did not actually participate), and his seminal work, *Comentarios reales de los Incas* (Royal Commentaries of the Incas; volume I, 1609; volume II, 1617). The latter was published in two parts, the first in Lisbon in 1609, which was dedicated to the Portuguese Duchess of Braganza, Princess Catalina, and the second, entitled *Historia general del Perú* (General History of Peru), in 1619 in Córdoba, where Garcilaso is buried.

Born of Inca and Spanish parents in Cuzco, where he grew up, Garcilaso de la Vega left for Spain in 1560, never returning to his native
land. Unable to obtain compensation in Spain for his father's participation in the campaign in Peru, he became a captain in the Spanish army
in Navarra and participated in quelling a Moorish uprising in the Alpuja-
rras. Leaving the service, he turned to educating himself. After reading
the great Rennaisance historians and literary giants, he translated the
Italian León Hebreo's *Dialogues of Love* into Spanish in 1590, having begun to compile information for his definitive work, *Comentarios reales*,
four years earlier. Understandably somewhat idealized, the first part is
interesting for its documentation of Inca civilization from its beginnings,
including its government, folklore, customs, and legends. The second
part details historical events following the conquest and has been considered an attempt to justify Spanish action in Peru. El Inca Garcilaso has
been criticized for an apparent anti-Indian stance in his work, but he is
also adept in presenting a positive image of the Incas while providing a
clear picture of European cruelty, believing the Incas were destroyed
before they were ever understood. What makes the *Comentarios* stand
out from other texts of the time is its literary nature on the one hand
and the almost ideological significance of the project on the other. His
study of Renaissance texts allowed him a much freer use of imagination
in his writing about history (his prose is much admired for its fluidity and
personal yet dramatic tone) but the text was also conceived as a profound search for personal and collective identity. Its self-reflective, autobiographical nature provides a vehicle for the modern reader to understand Garcilaso's struggle to give some sense and order to a tumultuous
historical moment in the world. For all this, Garcilaso's work is considered to be the starting point for a long line of great mestizo writers from
Peru.

The transition from the early chronicle, and somewhat later historical
treatise—not to mention the standard religious document to come off the
first printing press in Peru—to fictionalized narrative, poetry, and theater
came quickly during the colonial period. While popular, imaginative
narrative, such as books of romances, was prohibited in the colonies, it
was never entirely suppressed. One of the first texts of New World
literature in Peru that sought to combine realism and imagination for a
purpose is *El lazarillo de ciegos caminantes* (The Guide for Blind Way-
farers; 1776), written by the Spaniard Alonso Carrió de la Vandera
(1715-83). The mestizo protagonist and interlocutor with the author uses
the alias Concolorcorvo to recount his trip as a postal inspector from

Buenos Aires to Lima in 1771. Several contemporary styles—picaresque narrative, travelogue, literary sketches, jokes, swear words, and Inca folklore—are fused to create humor, satire, and irony critical of the Spanish colonial empire without being caught by the censors.

Basically a travelogue secretly published in Lima, the text is an interesting account of the long trip and provides detailed information about many diverse aspects of colonial life: transportation routes, animals such as horses and mules, cost of living, food supplies and production, and the dangers of isolated travel. The work is critical of inefficient government administration and, since the author was himself a government bureaucrat, he cloaks the identity of the narrator in fictitious characters who do the work of creating the document. While some believe the work is basically a piece of literature, a protonovel, perhaps the first New World novel set in the picaresque mold, it provides much concise information about the peoples Concolorcovo met along the way, their customs and habits, and flora and fauna. Hence, for others, the text has more sociological value than anything else. In contemporary times, questions of authorship and the diverse kinds of narrative materials in the text have brought to light interesting literary considerations concerning the manipulation of point of view for specific reasons. Today, the text by Concolorcovo is considered a transitional piece toward greater awareness of those growing problems of colonial government that would eventually lead to its downfall.

And poetry flourished, especially popular poetry in the form of ballads and satiric verse—that is, coplas, that were extemporaneously composed to record historical events dealing with the conquest and colonial periods, kuje expeditions, military campaigns, hardships, executions, and scandal. However, poetry written in the classical mode for the court and family of the Viceroy, as well as for other poets, by Spaniards and Peruvians between 1550 and 1630 also flourished. Diego de Hojeda (c.1572-1615), one of many poets born in Spain but who went to Peru at an early age, wrote the important poem *La Cristiada* (The Passion of Christ; Sevilla, 1611) that draws upon classical and religious traditions to retell the Passion of Christ in twelve epic-style cantos.

Literary circles were formed. One group of poets wrote about the discovery and conquest of the Marañón River and the circumstances surrounding a rebellion against Lope de Aguirre; another, the Grupo Cervantes (The Cervantes Group), was recognized by Cervantes himself as they sought to write in his style. Still other groups were La Academia Antártica (The Antarctic Academy), notably classical in its orientation, and Los Poetas de Lope de Vega (The Followers of Lope de Vega), inspired by his writing.

This was about the time when a woman writing under the pen name "Amarilis" sent her poetry to Lope de Vega, who then published it with a response in *La Filomena* (1621). Another was an anonymous female poet who wrote a poem in tercets entitled "Discurso en Loor de la Poesía" (A Discourse in Praise of Poetry), a Neoplatonic philosophical yet highly sensual poem that appeared as a prologue in Diego Mexía de Fernangil's *El Parnaso Antártico* (Antarctic Poetry; Sevilla, 1608). Women belonging to religious orders were prolific: Sor Juana de Herrera y Mendoza (eighteenth century), Josefa de Azaña y Llano (1696-1748), Josefa Bravo de Lagunas y Villela (eighteenth century); others, like them, who wrote about the cultural world of the Viceroyalty in Peru, have been mostly forgotten. One who stands out, however, is Juana Calderón y Badillo (1726-1809). In her thirst for knowledge, she was not unlike the Mexican nun, Sor Juana Inés de la Cruz.

In general, poetry written in Peru was influenced by the great writers of the Western tradition and not only appeared in Spanish but also in combination with Latin, Italian, and Portuguese, making it erudite and cosmopolitan. Writing in the style of Luis de Góngora's *culteranismo* (baroque style stressing the use of the Latin language), the poets Pedro José Bermúdez de la Torre (1661-1746) and Pedro Peralta y Barnuevo (1664-1743) wrote erudite epic and religious poetry about Peruvian themes from European literary perspectives. The latter's *Pasión y triunfo de Cristo* (Passion and Triumph of Christ; 1738) questions the ability of science to help mankind understand eternity.

One of the most important poets of that epoch is Juan del Valle y Caviedes (c. 1650-97), who wrote much in the style of Francisco de Quevedo's *conceptismo* (baroque style stressing the use of wit and conceits). Caviedes produced hundreds of poems and several theatrical pieces, which carried his trademark of irony, satire, and biting social criticism. His work is similar in many ways to the earlier satire of Mateo Rosas de Oquendo (1559-?), the Spanish poet who satirized colonial social life in Lima in "Sátira hecha por Mateo Rosas de Oquendo a las cosas que pasan en Pirú, en 1598" (Satire on Events Taken Place in Peru in 1598). Caviedes's principal poetic work, *Diente del Parnaso* (The Tooth of Parnasus), which was written in 1689 but not published until 1873, consists of dozens of poems aimed at not only poking fun at Peruvian society in general, but also exposing and condemning the medical profession for its lack of ethical and professional standards. The poet also wrote numerous *romances amorosos* (love poems), religious poetry, and broadsides dealing with current events, such as the comet of 1681, pirate attacks along the coast, the earthquake of 1687, and the construction of a dock in Callao in 1696. Satirical poetry continues in Peru through the baroque and neoclassical writings of Andalusian Esteban de Terralla Landa (eighteenth century); his *Lima por dentro y fuera* (Lima Seen from Without and from Within; 1797) is based on the old topic of the "city with the lid off," and criticizes the way in which implanted Spanish society had been corrupted by New World miscegenation. He founded the *Diario Erudito* (The Erudite Journal) in which he maintained a two-year polemic with the writers of the prestigious journal, *Mercurio Peruano* (The Peruvian Mercury). Pablo de Olavide (1725-1803) wrote poetry and prose within the European neoclassical tradition, as noted in his *El Evangelio en triunfo* (The Triumph of the Gospel; 1798). He wrote a total of seven sentimental novels, two of which are titled *Paulina o el amor desinteresado* (Pauline, or Platonic Love; eighteenth century) and *Marcelo o los peligros de la corte* (Marcel, or the Dangers of the Court; eighteenth century).

Although the 1746 earthquake completely destroyed the old theater in Plaza San Agustín in Lima (it was rebuilt three years later), drama played a major role in colonial art, especially the short pieces aimed at a *criollo*—creole—audience that saw itself reflected in their structures and thematic content. All in all, Lima and Buenos Aires were the two colonial centers of theater. Long after Juan Ruiz de Alarcón wrote in Spain and then Sor Juana Inés de la Cruz in Mexico, Juan del Valle y Caviedes wrote three plays in Lima in the seventeenth century: *Entremés del amor alcalde* (The Mayor's Love), *Baile del amor médico* (The Dance of the Doctor's Love), *Baile del amor tahur* (Dance of the Tricker's Love), all of which are parallel in structure, consisting of several interlocutors and a protagonist who answers questions. The works compare love to jail, sickness, and gambling. In 1719 Pedro de Peralta y Barnuevo wrote *Entremés para la Comedia. La Rodoguna* (A Comedy: Rodogune), a short, mythological comedy based on Corneille's *Rodogune*, in which a father discovers his daughters Mariquita, Chepita, Panchita, and Chanita in compromising situations with their respective tutors. Peralta Barnuevo wrote other short pieces as well, and he is also known for his epic play *Lima fundada* (Lima Founded; 1732). Josefa de Azaña y Llano (16961748) wrote a traditional pastorale dedicated to Christmas entitled *Coloquio a la Natividad del Señor* (Conversation on the Birth of Christ; eighteenth century), the only one of five that was ever published.

Serious economic, social, and political problems—dwindling mineral and agricultural production, hunger, misery, exploitation, stagnating commercial profits resulting from an asphyxiating state monopoly, and burdensome taxation, among others—culminated at the end of the century and led to outright rebellion and overt protest, as seen, respectively, in the 1780 Tupac Amaru rebellion, the critical writings of a new generation of liberal intellectuals, spontaneous poems that circulated anonymously among the masses, and the new ideas espoused in numerous political speeches in Lima, one of the more famous being "Elogio" (Eulogy; 1771), delivered valiantly by José Baquíjano y Carrillo (1751-1818) in the halls of San Marcos University and directed against the tyranny and crimes of the newly arrived Viceroy.

Reformist attitudes became widespread and are readily appreciated in the writings of the ex-Jesuit priest Juan Pablo Vizcardo y Guzmán (1747-98), whose *Carta a los españoles americanos* (Letter to the Spanish-Americans) written in Paris on the eve of the third Centenary of the Discovery of America and edited and published by Rufus King in Philadelphia in 1799, is now considered the first declaration of independence. It is noteworthy that in 1792 the seminal newspaper *Mercurio Peruano* (The Peruvian Mercury) began publication, expounding ideas of the Englightenment and dealing with diverse contemporary themes like the social function of the intellectual, climatic and sociological studies, the importance of a general language in Peru, the literature of Peralta y Barnuevo, and the importance of higher education. While it was not an organ of liberation, the *Mercurio Peruano* created a space for intellectual change and growth in Peru.

III

By 1814, popular poetry inciting the masses to revolution could be heard openly on the streets. Popular poetry and song praised liberty, affirmed the notion of independence, and attempted to recuperate Peru's indigenous past by highlighting local customs. Written expressions of incipient Romantic tendencies—independence, nationalism, freedom of expression, and individualism—shifting away from neoclassical traits in poetry are best seen in the works by Mariano Melgar (1790-1815), one of Peru's most venerated literary figures. He is considered to be one of the few mestizo poets to lay the groundwork for the birth of a truly authentic Peruvian poetry. His literary accomplishments include much in traditional poetic forms—see, for example, his "Carta a Silvia" (Letter to Silvia; 1829) and his elegies, but also the revival of certain native pre-Colombian themes (i.e., feelings of abandonment and solitude, and the transformation of older love songs and poetry into *yaravíes* [poetic musical compositions]). This renovation of ancient native poetic forms marks a major step towards literary emancipation in Peru. In addition, Melgar was an important translator of classical poetry into Spanish. His poetry is known for its progressive tone, and he writes about the problems of the American-born population—Indians, mestizos, and creoles—who were constantly marginalized from society by the Spanish Crown. The idea of a literary nationalism in terms of theme, style, and tone is achieved in Melgar's work and will gain impetus through others, namely, José Santos Chocano, Abraham Valdelomar, and César Vallejo many decades later.

Under the leadership of Simón Bolívar, José de San Martín, and General Sucre, Spanish colonial rule was dealt its death blow in South America when the colonial forces were finally defeated at the battle of Ayacucho, Peru, in 1824. Yet, in Lima, several centuries of colonial splendor and aristocratic frivolity bolstered conservative, antiprogressive thinking to the point that soon after independence Peruvian intellectual forces found themselves drawing other types of battle lines. One such was between European universalist schools of thought (supported by those who, belonging to aristocratic families, distrusted the new Republican government) and national/regional nativist tendencies (found mainly in middle class writers in Lima). The former were identified with the writings—mainly sketches depicting local color, called *costumbrismo*—published in *El espejo de mi tierra* (The Mirror of My Land; 1840) by Felipe Pardo y Aliaga (1806-68). He also wrote satirical, picaresque poetry, or *letrillas*, in "Los Paraísos de Sempronio" (The Paradises of Sempronio) or "El ministro y el aspirante" (The Minister and the Candidate). Other writers, such as Manuel Ascensio Segura y Cordero (1805-71), Manuel Atanasio Fuentes (1820-89), José Antonio de Lavalle (1833-93), and Ramón Rojas y Cañas (1830-81) also typify local color sketches and they go on to write about the growing dissatisfied urban bourgeoisie in Lima and their problems. Asencio Segura's works are composed of two types: spontaneous, celebrative poetry and comedies, the latter of which are numerous and tend to be neoclassical in form and local color and satirical in theme. His best known play, *Na Catita* (1856), is a comedy about a married couple that is always fighting. Their latest conflict is over their daughter's two suitors. Na Catita is the Celestina-figure who gives conflicting advice to the parents and stirs up more and more trouble between them. Today, the majority of these writers are considered to be "colonialized writers" because of their nostalgic look backwards to colonial times and for their archconservative viewpoints with regard to commitment to sociopolitical change. Nevertheless, the opposition between the universalists and regionalists induced writers at the time to give serious attention to the function of art as a form of responsibility to society. The merits of localized expressions (slang and the like) and standard usage, for example, were fervently discussed for the first time, all of which led in 1867 to the creation of the National Academy of the Republic of Peru in order to cultivate the sciences and the arts. It was shortlived, but it did facilitate serious and heated discussions about the function of art in society that continue even today.

In fact, Peruvian literature reaches a crossroads in the nineteenth century, precisely at a point nearing the end of the century, when the works of two important writers—Ricardo Palma (1833-1919) and Manuel González Prada (1844-1918)—intersect, overlap, and chafe each other. Palma is the liberal Romantic critic and writer who helped form the Sociedad de Amigos de las Letras (Society of Friends of Letters) and became famous for creating a type of narrative that he called the *tradición*, consisting of numerous volumes of romantic local color sketches that span several decades (1863 to 1915) and spawned a myriad of imitators throughout Spanish-speaking America. González Prada is mainly known for his literary essays, *Páginas libres* (Free Pages; 1894) and *Horas de lucha* (Time to Fight; 1908), but he is also a poet.

Palma's new literary genre, a hybrid form of the short story, brings together history and literary invention through popular stories, chronicles, legends, myths, letters, old papers, andecdotes, sayings, and proverbs, to capture nostalgically, but with picaresque irony and humor, the bygone days of the aristocratic, popular, but mainly creole life at the seat of the Peruvian viceroyalty, Lima, during Spanish colonial rule. Hence, Palma is responsible for creating a mythical arcadian "City of the Kings," a true stereotypical image of the Spanish dream that did little more than mask a more unfortuante, problematical reality. This myth has spawned other responses during the present century, most notably Sebastián Salazar Bondy's essay, *Lima la horrible* (Lima, the Horrible; 1964). Nonetheless, Palma's writing represented an interesting combination of historical discourse and literary fiction. Palma was truly a gifted writer within the Romantic vein (hence, his interest in history), and his *tradiciones* are exemplary forms of masterful writing and an attempt to create a distinct national literature in Peru.

In the aftermath of losing the War of the Pacific (1879-83) to Chile, Peru finds itself destroyed and without hope. Palma's stories have been seen as a superficial attempt to restore the outmoded ways of an earlier time. Questioning Palma's seemingly retrogressive desire to return to the never-existant womb of a colonial aristocratic society through his sketches, González Prada seizes the moment to look forward and rebuild national conscience through his essays and poetry.

When novelist and *tradición* writer Clorinda Matto de Turner returned from Europe and established herself in Lima in 1887, most literary activity still gravitated around the Ateneo de Lima (The Atheneum of Lima); however, a group of radical upstarts, including González Prada, had already established the Círculo Literario (The Literary Circle) in 1886 in order to promote new ideas. They clashed immediately with Palma and the literary establishment surrounding him. González Prada's famous essay "Discurso en el Politeama" (Discourse in the Politeama; 1888) signals insurrection on the part of younger intellectuals and writers. His pronouncement "¡Los viejos a la tumba, los jóvenes a la obra!" (Send the old to the grave and the young to work) ran counter to Palma and his ideas on national reconstruction and split intellectuals into two camps on issues such as the function of literature in society. González Prada became famous for questioning everything in Peruvian society and wanting to redo it immediately. Palma and González Prada vehemently attacked each other over many issues, one of which was the value of the Spanish cultural, religious, social legacy when defining a modern, republican nation. In time, González Prada radicalized his thinking about the dominance of Spanish culture and European Positivism in Peru to the point that he perceived himself as a socialist. In essence, Palma takes refuge in Spain's glorious colonial past in Peru and González Prada becomes anti-Spanish. His essays and oratory are the vehicles by which he was able to think and analyze issues such as how a national literature might and should function as a tool for conscience-raising, for creating a literary space enabling other popular, marginalized, heretofore unknown Peruvian literary expression to have a voice and a place in the conventional literary canon. González Prada is also recongized for his excellent romantic and social poetry. Above all, he is considered the writer most responsible for altering perspectives on the future of Peruvian literature, without which great writers like José Carlos Mariátegui,

César Vallejo, and José María Arguedas might not have found their voice in the twentieth century.

During this polemical period, other intellectuals came to the forefront for important contributions in terms of fomenting cultural awareness in Peru through their literary activities and writing. Of singular importance is Clorinda Matto de Turner (1852-1909), whose ideas on socially committed literature marked the beginnings of new literary perspectives in Peru. Director of *El Perú Ilustrado* (Illustrated Peru) after its founding in 1887, Clorinda Matto de Turner also participated actively in literary groups in Cuzco and Lima. In Cuzco, she founded the literary journal, *El Recreo del Cusco* (Writing in Cuzco) in 1876. Using a pen name, she wrote regularly for several national and international newspapers and magazines and published her *Tradiciones cuzqueñas* (Cuzco Traditons; 1884-86). Her fame rests mainly on her realist-naturalist novels *Aves sin nido* (*Birds Without a Nest: A Story of Indian Life and Priestly Oppression in Peru*; 1889), *Indole* (Natural Inclination; 1889), and *Herencia* (Inheritance; 1895), all of which expose the plight of downtrodden Indians, heretofore absent in Peruvian literature. The first novel is the most widely read in contemporary times and its theme concerns the exploitation of indigenous groups that are enslaved to religious and economic institutions. In the novel, characters recognize the need for change and wonder how to bring it about. In the later novels, the characters are determined by their environment and family background. Caught up in a political revolution in 1895, Matto de Turner was forced into exile and spent her last years writing in Buenos Aires.

Also writing novels at this time from the perspective of progressive realism was Mercedes Cabello de Carbonera (1845-1909), whose principal work, *Blanca Sol* (White Sun; 1889), underscores the bankruptcy of moral values in contemporary Peruvian society by recreating the superficial and trivial life of a woman determined to get what she wants by any means available to her. She fails, is shunned by society, and becomes a lesson for the reader. Like Matto de Turner, Cabello de Carbonera wrote essays on literature, education, and philosophy. Her romantically envisioned but deterministically based essay *Sacrificio y recompensa* (Sacrifice and Compensation; 1886), which deals with the lost war with Chile, won a medal in a competition sponsored by the Ateneo de Lima in 1886. She published her second novel, *Los amores de Hortensia: historia contemporánea* (Hortensia's Loves: A Modern Story), in 1887. It narrates the trials and tribulations of urban, bourgeois family life. A third novel, *El conspirador* (The Conspirer; 1892) carries the subtitle "Autobiography of a Public Person" and deals with politics at the turn of the century. Her essay, "Las consecuencias" (The Consequences) describes certain literary influences on her own work, namely Leo Tolstoy. Another writer of this period is Abelardo Gamarra (1857-1924), a journalist whose literary sketches and essays, entitled "Rasgos de Pluma" (Pen Marks), appeared regularly in *El Nacional* (The Nation) and were published in two volumes under the same title in 1889. However, two novels by two female writers best describe this interesting era of change in Peruvian literature: *Aves sin nido* and *Blanca Sol*.

While the impact of Spanish American Modernism was being felt elsewhere through the stories and poetry of Rubén Darío and Manuel Gutiérrez Nájera, among others, this literary movement based on French Parnassianism and Symbolism was not strongly cultivated in Peru. In narrative, only *Cartas de una turista* (Letters from a Tourist; 1905), a short novel by Enrique A. Carrillo (1877-1938, alias Cabotín), and *Cuentos malévolos* (Malevolent Stories; 1904), by Clemente Palma (1872-1946), fall under the modernist rubric. Ricardo Palma's son, Clemente, did not imitate his father's *tradición* genre but wrote within the conventional model of the nineteenth-century short story written by Poe or Maupassant and developed turn-of-the-century themes of catastrophe and despair. His *Historias malignas* (Evil Stories; 1925) are similar in focus and his novel *X, Y, Z* (1934) culminates the process. Ricardo Palma's daughter, Angélica Palma y Román (1883-1935), wrote in the style of her father: *Vencida: ensayo de novela de costumbres* (Conquered: Testimony of a Novel of Local Color; 1918) narrates the early twentieth-century world of working women in a conservative society, and her *Coloniaje romántico* (Romantic Colonialism; 1923) describes colonial Peru. *Tiempos de la patria vieja* (In the Time of the Old Nation; 1926) is a historical novel that won first prize for the best historical novel at the Commemoration of the Battle of Ayachucho, held in Lima in 1924. *Sombra alucinante* (Illusionary Shade; 1924) creates a Borgesian atmosphere of the double in which the protagonist believes to have become someone else. *Por senda propia* (Taking One's Own Way; 1921) narrates urban life in Lima at the beginning of the century, while *Uno de tantos* (One Among Many; 1926) tells the life of a diplomat who is constantly moving about and, actually, recreates the way the author lived as a youngster.

In the main, Peruvian turn-of-the-century writers and intellectuals, namely, José de la Riva Agüero (1885-1944), Francisco García Calderón (1883-1953), Ventura García Calderón (1886-1959), and Víctor Andrés Belaúnde (1883-1966), wrote about Peru's long past and its relationship to the future from a position of refined elegance, conservative idealism, and an analytical, positivistic perspective. While Riva Agüero writes essays stressing the importance of fomenting a greater understanding of European culture and bolstering university research and scholarship, Ventura García Calderón recreates local environments, regional dialects, and peculiar customs in his fictional stories entitled *La venganza del cóndor* (The Revenge of the Condor; 1924). These present characters who face universal themes of cruelty, hate, injustice. A true modernista, García Calderón writes in the style of Uruguayan Horacio Quiroga, juxtaposing elegant and refined language with cruelty and misfortune. Belaunde, life-long editor of the *Mercurio peruano* (The Peruvian Mercury) published several essays such as *Peruanidad* (On Being Peruvian; 1903) and *El Perú moderno y los modernos sociólogos* (Modern Peru and Modern Sociologists; 1908), using a historical-sociological perspective.

For the most part, Peruvian Modernist poets never achieved much fame or importance. Poets such as Domingo Martínez Luján (1875-1933), Leonidas Yerovi (1881-1917), and José Eufemio Lora y Lora (1885-1907) fall into this category. However, one poet, José Santos Chocano (1875-1934), acquired great fame. A swashbuckling, romantic-turned-modernista poet who became singularly famous beyond Peru's borders, Santos Chocano was a liberal activist in both literature and politics: "Antes que ser poeta... ¡hay que ser hombre!" (Before becoming a poet, one has to be a man). He published many volumes of emotionally combative poetry and was always ready to defend noble causes with his poetry. Santos Chocano's *Alma América* (The Soul of America; 1906), subtitled *Poemas indo-españoles* (Indian-Spanish Poems) is his most famous work. Through its epiclike tone, the poet nostalgically recounts Peru's history and describes with exhuberance its geography, flora and fauna, and human cultures. His verses, he believed, carried the "majestad de Inca y orgullo de español" (the majesty of the Inca and the pride of the Spanish). World traveler on the verge of scandal wherever he went, Santos Chocano projected himself as the undisputed leader of Spanish American poetry; in fact, he once said "Walt Whitman tiene el norte, pero yo tengo el sur" (Walt Whitman has the North, but I've got the South). Peru's Poet Laureate, he became known as "El Poeta de América" (The Poet of America) during his lifetime.

Living and writing poetry at the same time was José María Eguren (1874-1942), a Modernist whose work, ironically, went beyond Modernism and brought Peruvian poetry into the twentieth century. Radically different from Chocano both in personality and poetry, Eguren kept to himself and created imaginary worlds in which he found seclusion. Steeped in French symbolism, his poetry at first blush seems to imitate the Modernists because of certain typical motifs like mystery, love, and dreams; however, his language has become a storehouse of creativity that will have tremendous impact on successive poets. His three books of poetry—*Simbólicas* (Symbolisms; 1911), *La canción de las figuras* (The Dance of the Figures; 1916), and *Poesías* (Poems; 1929)—are lyrical, telluric, symbolic, and imaginative. They enrich the Spanish language with regional words, archaic terms, neologisms, and even foreign and invented words. His works also lead Peruvian poetry into the twentieth century because themes of alienation, skepticism, doubt, and lack of creativity are the driving forces behind a poetry that takes man and woman into the esoteric spheres of the imagination and the spiritual world. Inspiration, for instance, is allegorized in the form of a small girl with a blue lamp who leads the poet into these new worlds. At one point, Eguren's poetry takes on European vanguard tendencies through metaphor and dreamlike worlds.

Other writers of the period—Enrique Bustamante y Ballivián (1883-1937) and Alberto Ureta (1885-1966)—resort to mainline themes of nostalgia and melancholy for their inspiration, but in 1927 Bustamante y Ballivián published *Antipoemas* (Antipoems), which reveals avant-garde influences in Peruvian poetry. Ureta published poems written between 1911 and 1937 in *Antología poética* (Anthology) in 1946. Another vanguard poet of that period is Carlos Oquendo de Amat (1905-36), with his strange yet fascinating book of poems, *5 metros de poemas* (Five Meters of Poems; 1927). Here, dreamlike imagery and metaphor subtly combine with logical and grammatical disorder, paradox, fragmentation, and typographical disruption to create a modern, mechanized, surrealistic, urban world of incessant movement, dynamism, chaos, and anxiety as seen from its opposite, nature. The vanguard period of the 1920s in Peru also witnessed a surge in literary journals, namely, *Amauta* (Amauta), *Flecha* (Arrow), *Poliedro* (Polyhedron), *Trampolín-Hangar-Rascacielos-Timonel* (Trampolin-Hangar-Skyscrapers-Pilot), *Guerrilla* and *Jarana* (Party Time), all of which served as organs for the diffusion of avant-garde ideas from Europe. It was in *Amauta* that María Wiesse collaborated, and she became known for her dramas like *La hermana mayor* (The Older Sister; n.d.), novels like *La Huachafita, ensayo de novela limeña* (Miss Crassy, Prototype of a Novel about Lima; 1927), short stories *Nueve relatos* (Nine Stories; 1933) and *Aves nocturnas* (Nocturnal Birds; 1941), and biographies like *José María Córdova, 1799-1829.*

But the literary giant who turned not only Peruvian but all Latin American poetry upside down was César Vallejo (1892-1938). Unlike Chocano, who was born in Lima and wrote about his glorious City of Kings on the coast, Vallejo was from a small provincial town in the northern Andes mountains. Hence, urban pomp and splendor in Chocano; rural isolation, anguish, and poverty in Vallejo. Discovered in translation along with Pablo Neruda and Vicente Huidobro in North American and European underground literary journals (i.e., the Mexican *El Corno Emplumado* [The Plumed Horn]) in the 1960s, Vallejo is mainly famous for his books of poetry, first published between 1918 and 1939: *Los heraldos negros* (*The Black Heralds*; 1990), *Trilce* (1973), *Poemas humanos* (*Poemas humanos. Human Poems*; 1968), and *España, aparta de mí este cáliz* (*Spain, let this cup pass from me*; 1972). Other English translations include *Battles in Spain: five unpublished poems* (1978) and *The Complete Posthumous Poetry* (1978), translated by Clayton Eshleman.

With the publication of *Trilce*, Vallejo leaves Peru forever, travelling to Spain and Russia and living in Paris, where he married Georgette Philipard and died at the age of forty-four. A tortured soul, Vallejo's poetic voice speaks of pain, suffering, existential isolation, in his search for identity in the modern world. Basically, his poetry seeks to define an ideal world. His first book projects a feeling of doubt about the world as it looks backward nostalgically to family and home in the mountains in a search for universal feelings of love and caring. His second book, *Trilce*, rocks the literary world in Peru by treating certain themes—the destruction of a felicitous past, love, incarceration, modern absurdity, the search for meaning—with unconventional strategies, such as experimentation with ellipsis, typographical arrangements, conceptual word play through antithesis, oxymoron, and paradox, grammatical uncoupling, repetition, colloquialisms, archaic terms, and neologisms.

Coming full circle from the expression of existential doubt in the first book and accepting the lack of any identifiable substance in contemporary absurdism, Vallejo, in his third book, seeks unity and solidarity with a proletarian audience of anonymous citizens through which love becomes an answer to the world's problems and forms the basis for a new collective human social order. Tensions abound in all three books, from dialectical forces in opposition in the first book to collective integration and salvation in the third book. A poet of the vanguard era, Vallejo's poetry represents the poetic process itself within an historical framework. Creator of a new reality, Vallejo transformed language and, in the process, changed reality. In some ways, Vallejo is like his contemporary, W.H. Auden, a lonely human being who, in the process of writing, uses his disenchantment with the world to transform his anguish and feeling of margination as an outsider into a quasi-religious affirmation of proletarian goodness that stimulates hope for the future. For instance, Vallejo moved from poetic verses in his first book that state "Hay golpes en la vida, tan fuertes... ¡Yo no sé!" (There are setbacks in life, so strong. . . I don't know!) to a position of solidarity with the proletariat in his last book: "Le hago una seña,/viene,/y le doy un abrazo, emocionado./¡Qué más da! Emocionado... Emocionado..." (I wave to him,/he comes over,/and I embrace him, moved./What else could I feel! Moved. . . Moved. . .). A significant part of his last book of poetry is "España, aparta de mí este cáliz," which represents an expression of his feelings concerning the fateful events surrounding the Spanish Civil War. It is not until the 1950s that Peruvian poetry will find itself dealing with the impact of César Vallejo.

Beyond poetry, there is no doubt that Clorinda Matto de Turner set the stage for new literary perspectives that would crystalize at this time. Based on a renewed sense of nationalism and an awareness of social problems in Peru, contemporary writers seek to define Peru's identity by focusing on regional themes and problems, characters, and styles. Along with Ventura García Calderón, one initiator of this tendency is Abraham Valdelomar (1888-1919), whose perfectly constructed short stories in *El caballero Carmelo* (Carmelo, the Gentleman; 1918) and *Los hijos del sol* (The Children of the Sun; 1921) reminisce about childhood and family in a small seaport and replicate pre-Colombian myth and legend, respectively. Taking the title Conde de Lemos, Valdelomar assumed the role of a dandy in Lima and became a key member of a generation of writers that includes Manuel González Prada (1848-1918), José Santos Chocano, José María Eguren, Percy Gibson Moller (1885-1960), Pablo Abril, and Federico More, all of whom published their writings in *Colónida* (1916), a short-lived journal that sought to overhaul Peruvian literature. Valdelomar's poetry, somewhat Modernist early on, is not unlike the poetry of Ramón López Velarde of México or the early poetry of César Vallejo, in that the emotion of family life is experienced through solitude, nostalgia, and sadness. However, it is not long before Valdelomar and others move in a new poetic direction in an anthology of poetry, *Las voces múltiples* (Multiple Voices; 1916), highlighting vulgarisms, colloquialisms, new metaphors, free verse and rhythm, and scandalous themes, which became important not only for Valdelomar but also for other poets born outside of Lima, namely, Juan Parra del Riego (1894-1925), Alberto Hidalgo (1897-1967), and Alberto Guillén (1900-35). These poets became a bridge linking Peruvian Modernism to avant-garde ideas in poetry. Alberto Hidalgo stands out as one of the more influential of the group. His *Panoplia lírica* (Lyric Panoply; 1917), *Las voces de colores* (The Voices of Colors; 1918), and *Joyería* (Jewelry Store; 1919), like many of his later books of poetry, such as *Muertos, heridos y contusos* (Dead, Wounded, and Contused; 1920), *Tu libro* (Your Book; 1923), *Química del espíritu* (Spiritual Chemistry; 1923), *Simplismo* (Simplicity; 1925), and *Descripción del cielo* (Description of the Sky and Heaven; 1928), exude newness, resonance, and rebellion against the outmoded Modernist poetry. In Buenos Aires, while Jorge Luis Borges is announcing new poetic vanguard movements, Hidalgo launches his own Simplismo movement based on innovative metaphor and outlandish typographical experimentation. His book of poetry, *La dimensión del hombre* (The Dimension of Man; 1938), will have a significant impact on poets writing after midcentury.

However, the true spokesmen for the surrealist movement in Peru are Xavier Abril (1903), César Moro (1903-56), and Emilio Adolfo Westphalen (1911). Abril was influenced by Cocteau in *Taquicardia* (Tachycardia; 1926) and *Hollywood* (1931). Moro, also influenced by French surrealism and the Estridentista group in Mexico, is known for his strange imagery and ironic cynicism in *La tortuga ecuestre* (The Equestrian Turtle; 1957). Typical of later avant-garde, stylized poetry that was more abstract and even philosophical in nature is the work by Martín Adán (1908-85), one of few Peruvian poets to achieve certain importance. More daring in fiction, Adán wrote poetry that became formal in structure and dense in meaning. Two books of poetry, *La rosa de la espinela* (The Ruby Rose; 1939) and *Travesía de extramares* (Uncharted Travails; 1950), represent well-crafted, modern verse at its best. Form and content come together to create rhythm and intensity of life for the reader. The poetry of *Travesía de extramares*, not surprisingly a set of sonnets, represents a mystical, symbolic search by a visionary for an ideal reality. The search is not without anguish, and *Escrito a ciegas* (Written Blindly; 1961) leaves the poet unsure of the poet's place in the world. Adán went on to write poetry about the Inca ruins, Machu Picchu, and additional sonnets dealing with the relationship of the poet to his or her world and the attempt to understand its meaning.

Postmodernist poetry by female poets writing in Peru at midcentury like Catalina Recavarren de Zizold and Teresa María Llona resembles the emotional, sentimental qualities of the Chilean Nobel Laureate Gabriela Mistral and the concern for women's place in society found in the poetry of the Uruguayan Juana de Ibarbourou. Recavarren's *Memorias de una desmemoriada* (Memoirs of a Memoryless One; 1976) recounts the poet's personal past that includes fourteen books of poetry and narrative published between 1925 and 1974. Llona published poetry as well and one book, *Intersección* (*Intersection*; 1950), which has a prologue by Gabriela Mistral and relives Lima customs and traditions as seen from the eyes of a creole woman who finds herself a martyr in the process.

Westphalen's poetry has made a significant contribution to the renovation and modernization of Peruvian poetry. He takes a more philosophical but also seductive stance toward universal themes of love, time, and death. *Belleza de una espada clavada en la lengua* (The Beauty of a Sword-Pierced Tongue; 1986) brings together Westphalen's poetry written between 1930 and 1986. His latest work, *Ha vuelto la diosa ambarina* (The Goddess of Beauty Has Returned; 1989), is an interesting collection of minimalist and prose poetry. Writing within a totally different sphere of Peruvian poetry is Nicomedes Santa Cruz (1925). His ten-line, eight-syllable verses, are called *Décimas* (1960); *Cumanana* (1964) is composed of more décimas, and satirical, humorous, and social-critical poems, one, for instance, about the treatment of blacks in South Africa and another dedicated to John F. Kennedy after his death.

On a broader scale, the three most important trendsetters of the period are Enrique López Albújar (1872-1966), José Carlos Mariátegui (1894-1930), and César Vallejo. Writing in their respective genres—narrative, essay, and poetry—they set the Peruvian (and, in the case of Mariátegui and Vallejo, Latin American) literary and intellectual stage for the rest of the century. López Albújar's collection of grosteque short stories, *Cuentos andinos* (Andean Stories; 1920), Vallejo's books of poetry, especially *Trilce* and *Poemas humanos*, and Mariátegui's *Siete ensayos de interpretación de la realidad peruana* (*Seven Interpretive Essays of Peruvian Reality*; 1928) solidify three major literary tendencies, respectively: sociocritical regionalist fiction, vanguard poetry, and the Marxist-based analytical essay. While López Albújar compassionately but realistically documents in his stories the harsh life of marginalized Indians in the Andes mountains of Peru and problems of discrimination among mulattos on the coast, Vallejo suffers incarceration in Trujillo and writes marginalized poetry with innovative language from tortured perspectives, and Mariátegui founds and edits *Amauta* (1926-30), one of the most important journals in Latin America, launches the publishing house

Minerva, organizes the Socialist Party of Peru, assists in establishing worker unions for the proletariat, becomes friends with Waldo Frank, and in his essays probes the ideological nature of Peruvian society and literature from an early Marxist perspective. He sought to stimulate political, social, ethnic, and economic reforms in Peru by objectifying problems through discourse with scientific, historical, and sociological perspectives: "Crear un Peru nuevo, dentro de un orden nuevo" (Create a new Peru within a new order).

In fact, these three writers, along with other prose writers such as Martín Adán, Luís E. Valcárcel (1893), César Falcón (1892-1970), and José Diez-Canseco (1904-49), do indeed pick up where Clorinda Matto de Turner left off by writing about Peru's Indians, blacks on the coast, the proletariat, and the urban middle class in a surge of novels published around 1930. This rash of narrative works suggests an awareness of Peru's vast social panorama by a small, yet growing literate middle class. López Albújar's *Matalaché* (1928), Vallejo's *El tungsteno* (*Tungsten: a Novel*; 1931), and Adán's *La casa de cartón* (*The Cardboard House*; 1927), for instance, deal respectively with diverse social problems such as discrimination faced by mulattos, deplorable working conditions in Peru's mining industry, and the absence of national cultural values in a fragmented, anonymous, urban coastal society. Adán's novel has been hailed as an excellent example of vanguard fiction, pointing the way toward more cosmopolitan perspectives in Peruvian literature.

Hence, social protest was a mainstay of contemporary fiction. César Falcón wrote *El pueblo sin Dios* (A Town Without God; 1928) and Luis E. Valcárcel published *Tempestad en los Andes* (Storm in the Andes Mountains; 1927), both of which are about the exploitation of Peru's Indian population. Valcárcel also wrote historical treatises such as *Historia de la cultura antigua del Perú* (History of Ancient Culture in Peru; 1943), *Del ayllu al imperio* (From Indian Village to Empire; 1925), and *Ruta cultural del Perú* (The Cultural Route of Peru; 1984).

The harsh living conditions of the disenfranchised poor and the abusive political machinations on the coast are recreated in *Chicha, sol y sangre* (Fermented Corn, Sun and Blood; 1946), *Taita Yoveraqué* (Chief Yoveraqué; 1956), and *La gesta del caudillo, novela histórica* (The Caudillo's Gesture, an historical novel; 1961), by Francisco Vegas Seminario (1904), all considered to be good examples of sociopolitical criticism with sarcastic insights into creole customs and habits. José Diez-Canseco (1904-1949) focused on the stigma felt by mestizos in Peru in *Estampas mulatas* (Mulatto Sketches; 1929-40), on the urban lower class in his short novels, and on Lima's superficial urban aristocracy in *Duque* (1934). Whereas the first novels fit into a brand of social realism, the latter fits into the vanguard style of unusual metaphor and language play.

The question of mestizo society in Latin America led to the famed indigenist movement in art and literature. Its most expressive mode is found in the Mexican muralist painters who sought to reevaluate the contributions of native groups to the American creative process. Not willing to align themselves with the fervent European nationalism of the 1920s and 30s, the indigenist tendency gave way to a broader approach that sought to broach the totality of American ethnic reality, the product of which is mestizo culture, considered the truly authentic expression of all societies of the New World. The tenor of this thinking is well delineated by Mexican essayist José Vasconcelos in his seminal work, *La raza cósmica* (*The Cosmic Race*; 1925), and the essays by José Carlos Mariátegui. In a way, the racial profile of America became the one projected by the new readers of Garcilaso de la Vega's works, particularly *Los comentarios reales*, written by that solitary, illegitimate son of a Spanish military captain and an Inca princess, whose portrait, ironically, is nonexistent today. A painting by Peruvian José Sabogal, a founder of indigenism in Peru, painted Garcilaso as a man with a divided face, one part Spanish and the other part Indian, each reflected by light and dark colors. Strangely enough, Sabogal's solution to the unknown face imitates the overlaying of architectural styles in Cuzco and could very well be seen as a negative force to the mestizo process, for two distinct half faces do not create a complete human face. The apparent fusion, according to some, takes on a kind of mystical, messiah symbolism that exhalts the combination of indigenous sensitivity with the best accomplishments of Western society, without denying other significant contributions coming from African or Oriental sources. Others believe that mestizo America is much more than a mixing of races: it seeks to reduce Spanish haughtiness and pride and counters the indigenous drive to return to prehistoric utopia, from which would come a true synthesis, a conciliation: mestizo society.

IV

In 1941 indigenist regionalism as a literary movement in Peru reached a crossroads and took a significant turn toward a more native cosmovision of the Andean world. Ciro Alegría (1909-67) culminates his writing career with *El mundo es ancho y ajeno* (*Broad and Alien Is the World*; 1941) and José María Arguedas (1911-69) produces his first novel, *Yawar fiesta* (*Yawar fiesta*; 1941). When we speak of indigenism, we are referring to a writing process in which author, text, and reader are not from the ethnic group being described in the novel—only the referent itself is. The process begins in the nineteenth century with Indianism, a variant of fiction writing that portrays the Indian as the typical Rous-seauan "noble savage" from a European perspective. The second vari-ant—indigenism—is seen early on in works by Clorinda Matto de Turner, mainly because her writing communicates an awareness of deeprooted social problems and a clear position of social protest. Even though her novel is basically anticlerical and the indigenous characters are portrayed in romantic fashion, the exploitation of Indians is forcefully condemned. In the twentieth century, the process continues with López Albújar's *Cuentos andinos* and García Calderón's *La venganza del cóndor*, among several others, and culminates with *El mundo es ancho y ajeno*.

During this second phase, stronger communicative ties are forged between the indigenous world, mainly in the Andes, and the rest of the country, particularly the urban white or mestizo social groups on the coast. Mariátegui's Marxist ideology also contributed to providing a deeper understanding of the social, political, and economic problems facing indigenous groups in Peru. Another contributing factor to this phase is the growing incorporation of indigenous myth, legend, story, and song into fictional texts. In poetry, Alejandro Peralta (1899-1973) con-tributed to vanguard-indigenista poetry with his two books, *Ande* (Ande-an; 1926) and *El Kollao* (1934). His poetry recreates the Andean world through descriptions of the life and customs of the Indians and the incor-poration of their native Quechua. His *Poesía de entretiempo* (Poetry for Wiling Away the Time; 1968), which includes published and nonpublish-ed poems since 1919, won the Premio Nacional de Poesía in 1968. But Peralta's poetry fits into the vanguard mold because in the 1920s it incor-porated innovative techniques. He was especially influenced by new ideas that were based on the combination of indigenous themes and vanguard aesthetics that crystalized through the Grupo Orkopata (The Orkopata Group), founded by his brother Gamaliel Churata in Puno in 1924, and found an outlet in the *Boletín Titikaka* (The Titicaca Newslet-ter; 1926-29).

A third variant—*indígena* (native) fiction—becomes evident in the works of José María Arguedas (discussed in the following pages), in which the cosmovision of indigenous groups is much more than a simple referent. It becomes a significant element of the author's world, the structure of the text, and the cosmovision of the reader.

Son of a prominent landowner in northern Peru, whose property included Indian peons, Ciro Alegría, who belongs to the second phase described above, is particularly known for three important novels—*La serpiente de oro* (*The Golden Serpent*; 1935), *Los perros hambrientos* (The Hungry Dogs; 1939), and *El mundo es ancho y ajeno*, the latter of which, after being translated into English and winning the coveted Farrar and Rinehart prize, became a widely read text by high school students in the United States. It has been translated into almost two dozen languages. The novel narrates the expulsion of an indigenous community from its lands in the northern Peruvian Andes and communicates a strong sense of injustice against the Indians. The novel has a noticeable telluric, regionalist quality about it, for it also describes the symbiotic relationship between the Indians and their sacred lands. The text is quite diffuse in terms of theme and structure; the basic story line is replete with numerous digressions that describe the problem of coca addiction, the presence of the looming jungle region to the east, and the exploitive work on the coast, stories about several characters' pasts, and ideas on social relationships among Peruvians, as well as segments that present communal stories, legends, myths, songs, and superstitions. In fact, the community's demise is foreshadowed at the very beginning when a snake crosses the path of Rosendo Maqui, the community leader, who damns his bad luck as he fails to catch the the snake and mutilate it with his machete. The narrative process moves in different directions: from a feeling of unity among the group to total fragmentation and dispersion of the community's members; from a straightforward, linear narration to an intentionally scattered series of scenes, stories, and character biographies; from characterization based on interior monologue to exaggerated stereotypes and romantic figures in society; and from a sense of hope to one of complete gloom and the feeling of loss and pessimism when, at the end, the young, progressive, future leader of the community, Benito Castro, is killed as army troops move in to expel the Indians from their lands. Similar to works by John Steinbeck, Alegría's fiction acquires at once an epic tone and yet maintains a human quality about it. Ernest Hemingway considered the novel a true classic.

The symbolic title of Alegria's first novel, *La serpiente de oro*, refers to the mighty and treacherous Marañón river and its deceptiveness, compared not only to a serpent winding along the jungle floor, but also, via its metallic reference, to its economic importance for the character

Lucas Vilca, whose livelihood depends on the river, for he ferries people and goods from one side to the other in a small boat that at any moment could be swallowed up by the enormous, intimidating river. The bond between human beings and nature becomes the theme of the novel. Differing from the traditional regional novel, in which nature wins out in the end, here both survive and triumph because, while opposites in one sense, they are intricately tied together. Also, certain notions about the opposition between civilization—that is, modern urban society—and barbarism, or backward rural communities, are questioned. In the novel, the so-called primitive people, who are closely tied to their environment, become the civilized group because they have achieved harmony without violence and destruction. Alegría places these people who live in total isolation from the rest of the world in a static, idyllic, and mythical world of timelessness and harmony, despite the apparent momentary dangers that loom hidden in the forests or the unsuspecting violence of a river swollen by hard rains. But it is this sense of constantly fighting for one's life that makes the relationship between human beings and nature not only harmonious but dynamic.

Los perros hambrientos, referring to the abject poverty under which most Indians live in the Andes, is a compelling description and severe criticism of human exploitation. Here, environment is different. It is not an encapsulated Eden of harmony, but a conflictive landscape where opposing cultures—Western and indigenous—meet head-on and clash in violence. This theme is key to understanding the novels by José María Arguedas and, while Alegría may place this conflictive world within an epic, utopian world awaiting its death knell, Arguedas will write from other perspectives that make the theme become real within a present-day context. These perspectives actuate narrative worlds heretofore unseen in literature because they had never been part of author, text, and reader, but only of the referent itself. These two writers represent a cleavage that ocurred in 1941, Alegría representing the benevolent sympathizer and observer of Peru's injustice to Indians and Arguedas incorporating not only first-hand, personal experiences as a child among Quechua-speaking Indians in southern Peru, but also as a dedicated, anthropologically trained researcher, like Mariátegui, of culture and cultural conflict. Born in the Andes, Arguedas's father was white and his mother Indian. He studied anthropology in Lima, was imprisoned in 1937 for his participation in a leftist publication, taught Quechua and ethnology at San Marcos University, and served as director of Ethnology Studies at the National Museum of History in Lima for some years before committing suicide in 1969.

The narrative worlds of Arguedas include the following indígena works: *Agua* (Water; 1935), *Runa Yupay* (1939), *Yawar fiesta, Diamantes y pedernales* (Diamonds and Cuartz; 1945), *Los ríos profundos* (*Deep Rivers*; 1958), *El sexto* (The Prison; 1961), *La agonía de Rasu Ñiti* (The Agony of Rasu Ñiti; 1962), *Todas las sangres* (All Bloods; 1964), *Amor mundo y todos los cuentos* (Worldly Love and the Short Stories; 1967), and *El zorro de arriba y el zorro de abajo* (The Fox from the Mountains and the Fox from the Coast; 1971). Whereas Alegría constructed his worlds around general themes like man against nature, man against man, and Western civilization against indigenous culture, Arguedas examines infinitely more complex worlds of opposition and conflict from decidedly cultural perspectives in an ever-widening narrative process that begins by examining not just conflict between whites and Indians but also between Indians and mestizo landowners and exploiters in *Agua* and *Yawar fiesta*; he then proceeds to examine regional cultural conflicts between populations living in the Andes and those living on the coast in *Yawar fiesta* and *Los ríos profundos*; he touches, finally, on the transnational space of conflict between first and third-world nations and the problems of commercial imperialism in *Todas las sangres* and *El zorro de arriba y el zorro de abajo*. This is a cumulative process in which Arguedas's novels carry over kernel issues into later works, thereby maintaining an awareness of exploitation at every level. By uncovering serious problems in each stage and communicating a strong defense of the Indians, Andean culture, and the Peruvian nation, respectively, this progression also demonstrates the need to be aware of the exploitation of the Indians by mestizos, the domination of coastal society and culture over the inhabitants of the Andes, and the imperialist power of transnationalism over Peru and the rest of Latin America.

Los ríos profundos is undoubtedly Arguedas's most popular novel. It narrates the rites of passage of fourteen-year-old Ernesto, whose early years were spent living in an Indian community and who now finds himself experiencing culture shock in a provincial town where he encounters exploitation of social class (rural, landless peons) and ethnic cultures (Indians) by the dominant religious, political, and economic forces in a highly stratified and fragmented society. The protagonist narrates a series of incidents while at a boarding school run by priests. From his dual cultural heritage Ernesto inherits sensitivity and emotion, empowering him to live within a world of magic and myth, while at the same time perceiving serious social problems through his ability to describe his world in minute detail, yet symbolically. The important episode involving the uprising of the women who work in the town market is a fine example of social protest in the novel. Repeatedly, common objects take on magical qualities and provide a way of understanding the delicate relationship between human beings and their world. The ancient Inca walls of Cuzco become dynamic, living forces that recall the city's glorious past; the rivers possess certain magical powers that help Ernesto to understand his environment; and the small spinning top that he plays with is a vehicle making musical sounds that carry Ernesto back in time and connect him with his cultural past. The novel's success lies in a subtle combination of varied reader experiences: universal themes like the coming of age of the young protagonist, the effect of realist, detailed description of his environment and memorable characters, the criticized effects of ethnic discrimination, and the symbolism of common objects that take on magical qualities and provide understanding of the protagonist's past and present. This combination of elements catapults Arguedas's works beyond conventional indigenist writing to a level that incorporates the indigenous world of Peru into a larger realm of cultural universalism.

El sexto is a work that fits into the subgenre known as jail novels, and *Todas las sangres* is a sweeping overview of the problem of landownership in the Peruvian Andes that documents the intricate symbiotic relationships among different types of landowners, from large, powerful, feudal landowners who are mainly non-Indian and spend most of their time on the coast, to the smaller, parasitic mestizo landowners who are easily manipulated but driven to survive. In the novel, however, this highly stratified ranking of landowners faces a new, common enemy: foreign capitalism. Alliances, betrayal, sell-outs, nationalism, racism, slavery, rebellion, and violence characterize Peru's critical social condition in the 1960s and 1970s, now acutely more serious in the 1980s and 1990s with the appearance of the Maoist forces of the Shining Path. Arguedas's unfinished, some say uneven, posthumous novel *El zorro de arriba y el zorro de abajo* is an important part of the evolution of his writing. The title's dialectical reference to two foxes symbolizes the Andean and coastal regions of Peru. The novel intercalates two story lines, one consisting of excerpts most likely from the author's personal diary and the other forming a series of narrative descriptions of the overwhelmingly massive migration of the *serranos* (people from the hills) into the northern coastal town of Chimbote. The city had mushroomed and became prosperous in the 1960s because of the burgeoning fish meal industry and is, today, all but a ghost town, filled with tens of thousands of unemployed and starving poor people. The anguish, pain, and helplessness that is communicated in the diary runs parallel to the growing general sense of failure and vulnerability, as we learn that the economic boom and bust in Chimbote is tied directly to foreign capital investments and the fluctuation of world markets and demand. Suicide for the writer, suicide for the country.

Meanwhile, efforts to stem the tide of pessimism and apocalypse in Peru could be found in the continuing proclivity for indigenist writing, particularly in the narrative works of Manuel Scorza (1928-84), who is also a poet. Scorza's political leanings led him to write about the problems of Peru's Indian communities from the perspective of a politically conscious, committed unionizer bringing modernity and justice to the rural areas. Highly readable for his storytelling abilities, criticism of injustice in the highlands, and strong doses of "magical realism," Scorza's five-volume series of novels (called *baladas* [ballads] or *cantares* [songs]) narrate not only the persistent drive of an Indian community to regain its lands and legal rights, but also the utopian hope that once again outside assistance, this time based on union consciousness and the magical collaboration of sympathetic animals and nature, will solve the Indians' problems. The novels are a curious mixture of myth-and-legend-brought-to-life and testimony of historical fact based in part on a rebellion of the Yanacocha community, in which Scorza participated, in the Department of Cerro de Pasco (1959-62) and the subsequent massacre of many of those involved. After he denounced the participation of the Peruvian military in the carnage, he was forced to flee to France, where for the next ten years he wrote the following works: *Redoble por Rancas. Balada I* (The Toll of the Bells for Rancas; 1977); *Garabombo, El invisible. Balada II*, (Garabombo, the Invisible; 1977); *El jinete insomne. Balada III*, (The Sleepless Rider; 1977); *Cantar de Agapito Robles. Balada IV*, (The Song of Agapito Reyes; 1977); *La tumba del relámpago. Balada V*, (The Tomb of the Lighting Bolt; 1979); *La danza inmóvil*, (The Stationary Dance; 1983).

As in other Latin American countries, novelists, short story writers, and literary essayists in Peru had always been the nation's true sociologists (after 1950, the creation of sociology departments in the national universities led to more scientific, but not necessarily more truthful knowledge of the country's ills). Narrating in fiction the lives of the heretofore silenced voices of disenfranchised classes of Indians, mestizos, and blacks, as well as the urban lower-class and superficial bourgeoisie, these writers, born in the 1920s and 1930s, began to document the enormous socioeconomic changes that were taking place not only in the rural provinces but also in the growing cities beginning in the 1950s. These writers debunked myths, particularly the illusion of the provincial and rural poor that going to Lima will better their lives. Their works documented the effects of dictatorship in politics, especially the nefarious effects that the Manuel Odría dictatorship in the 1950s had on an entire generation of young people. They recreated the dire results of the growing stratification and fragmentation of a society based on economic imbalances, political violence, ethnic discrimination, and cultural annihilation, and they pointed to the military as the culprits. These writers dealt with identity crises, the search for meaning, existentialism, and the age-old theme of civilization versus barbarity. They made an effort, however, to destroy the conventional meanings tied to civilization and barbarity which, in the past, associated the latter with rural, uneducated "primitive" folk and the former with cosmopolitan, progressive, urban society.

All that was turned upside down when this group of writers, namely, Sebastián Salazar Bondy (1924-65), Julio Ramón Ribeyro (1929), Oswaldo Reynoso (1932), and Enrique Congrains (1932) focused their attention on the problems facing a burgeoning urban proletariat living in shanty towns or *barriadas* and other marginalized bourgeois living on the economic and social fringes of society. Meanwhile, other writers—Eleodoro Vargas Vicuña (1924), Carlos E. Zavaleta (1928), and Julián Huanay (1907-69)—continued to develop themes that dealt with conflicts of power, culture, and society in the provinces and rural areas of Peru, involving not so much the Indians of Arguedas's novels, but more the coastal and inland mestizos and cholos (Indians). Vargas Vicuña's *Nahuín* (1953) and *Taita Cristo* (Father Christ; 1963), Zavaleta's *El Cristo Villenas* (Christ Villenas; 1955) and *Los Ingar* (The Ingars; 1955) are superb texts that deal with provincial city and rural village conflicts of cultural values tied to religion, superstition, political organization, and impinging economic forces.

When Salazar Bondy published his sociological essay *Lima la horrible* in 1964, he best characterized the demise of a national project to create a new urban Peru, centered mainly in Lima. The essay chastises the *limeño* (individual from Lima) for continuing to pretend to live in the make-believe world of the colonial period that apparently signifies power and wealth, but is now out of step with the decaying, anachronistic, sordid world of an overgrown urban environment. For those recent arrivals who populate the growing slums, Lima is considered a Mecca. Huanay's novel, *El retoño* (Reborn; 1951), is about the rites of passage of a young orphaned boy who makes his way to Lima from the provinces. Along the way, he learns about the difficulties facing poor people in different walks of life. The novel is important because it unmasks the myth of Lima as the way to happiness. Congrains's short stories in *Lima, hora cero* (Lima, Zero Hour; 1954) and *Kikuyo* (1955) deal with Lima's slum and the wretchedness newcomers find upon their arrival from the hinterlands. His novel *No una sino muchas muertes* (Not One But Several Deaths; 1958) tells the story of a young girl trapped in the sordid underworld of an informal economy in a slum where she washes used medicine bottles for resale. Violence and misery are portrayed in eery fashion, creating a disturbing view of life on the far side. Oswaldo Reynoso also writes about Lima's lower classes and their entrapment in repressive worlds of politics, religion, and sex. In his short stories *Los inocentes* (The Innocent; 1961) teenage characters rebel against the conservative values of the older generations and contemporary slang is the vehicle for expressing their discontent with society. As the title of Reynoso's novel *En octubre no hay milagros* (There Are No Miracles in October; 1965) indicates, the annual procession of Our Lord of the Miracles is the perfect backdrop and catalyst for bringing together characters from all walks of life—the rich and the poor, the exploiters and the exploited—to expose corruption, impropriety, and abuse, as well as feelings of trepidation and despair. It is a compelling novel that achieves its goal of stimulating disgust and condemnation on the part of the reader.

Peruvian theater in general began to flourish after World War II. Its renaissance is tied to three award-winning plays, *Esa luna que empieza* (That Rising Moon; 1946) by Percy Gibson Parra, *Don Quijote* (1946), by Juan Ríos (1914), and *Amor, gran laberinto* (Love, The Great Labyrinth; 1947), by Sebastián Salazar Bondy. Soon thereafter theatrical groups were formed and literary competitions were established and, after the founding of the Dirección Nacional de Teatro (National Office of Theater) in 1946, the process of renewal reached a climax in the late fifties. From then on, plays tended characteristically to become universal, psychological, and poetic. Hence, during the fifties, Peruvian theater was generally characterized by poetic expressions of human values, the use of suggestion and symbol, and a certain preference for monologue and short pieces. Since then, group theater and university-sponsored theater have dominated drama production in Peru. In fact, beginning in 1958 the undisputed leader of university theater at San Marcos University was Guillermo Ugarte Chamorro. He was responsible for taking the theater to the people, such as workers' groups, the outlying rural areas, and overseas. He organized national theater competitions, organized library archives, taught courses, and wrote extensively about theater.

Yet the impact left by Salazar Bondy, who moved away from folklore and foreign archetypes through the fifties and until his death in 1965, can only be partially matched by Ríos's production and popularity, or by an occasional single play of a spectacular nature by other dramatists, as is the case of *Collacocha* (1958), by Enrique Solari Swayne (1915), a well-constructed three-act play centering on the theme of civilization versus a hostile environment. A highway engineer fights tenaciously to build tunnels through the Andes mountains and, thus, to unify the diverse regions of Peru, whose separation has always weighed heavily on the national conscience. Juan Ríos's dramatic production is marked less by themes surrounding Peruvian reality than by his interest in delineating the human condition in general, as in *Don Quijote*. His plays have won five national awards. In one way or another his plays are tied to Peruvian or Spanish history: *Ayar Manko* (1952) develops around a story from Incan times in which four princes vie for the crown of their dead father; *El fuego* (The Fire; 1961) captures a moment during the Wars of Independence from Spain when an army officer is persecuted for his beliefs in freedom; *Los bufones* (The Fools; 1961) probes the friendship between King Philip IV and a court jester; and *La selva* (The Jungle; 1961) recreates the drama of an Indian woman who becomes a traitor to her people in her determination to help a Spaniard escape from his enemy.

Salazar Bondy is also one of Peru's most talented playwrights, and few since his death have matched the quality of his works. In fact, Salazar Bondy was not only a dramatist but also an advisor, director, and producer. In many ways, Peruvian theater since 1946 develops parallel to Salazar Bondy's career. He founded the Club de Teatro (The Theater Club) in 1953, which went on to present many plays from home and abroad. Salazar Bondy had studied existentialism in France, and his early plays reflect the anguish that the characters experience when confronted with the uselessness of reason. His later works—*No hay isla feliz* (No Happy Island; 1959), *El fabricante de deudas* (The Debt Machine; 1962), and *El Rabdomante* (The Sorcerer; 1965)—contributed to a sense of climax in Peruvian theater in the sixties because these plays not only deal with social marginalization, lack of communication, loss of freedom, and human suffering, but also portray human frailties with humor and sarcasm through Brechtian modes of dramatization as well as elements that suggest the comedy of manners. Other dramatists—Arturo Jiménez Borja (1908), Julio Ramón Ribeyro, Juan Rivera Saavedra, and Elena Portocarrero—also emerge in search of renovation. Juan Ríos seemed to oppose psychological drama, and his literary production, which includes *Los desesperados* (The Desperate; 1961) and *Medea* (1952), is more poetic in style and epic in persepective. Ribeyro's three most important plays are *Vida y pasión de Santiago el pajarero* (The Life and Passion of Santiago, the Birdman; 1958), *El último cliente* (The Last Cliente; 1966), and *Atusparia* (1981). The first play is based on one of Ricardo Palma's *tradiciones*, the second is a one-act farce portraying life in contemporary Lima, and the third is an historical drama, one of Peru's best to date, that documents an act of rebellion against injustice in the Peruvian Andes in 1885.

By the midsixties playwrights such as Víctor Zavala Cataño (1932), Alonso Alegría (1940), Julio Ortega (1942), and Sara Joffré (1935) had become known as innovators and nonconformists, sharing the common goal revitalizing Peruvian theater. For these dramatists, brevity, universality, and poetic sensitivity are seen as important guiding elements. Two plays in particular—*El cruce sobre el Niágara* (Niaagra Crossing; 1969) by Alegría, which won the "Casa de las Américas" prize in 1969, and *Historia de los tocadores de tambor* (History of the Drummers; 1966) by Sara Joffré—represent universal projects in theme and structure. Joffré's plays vary from absurdist themes and feminist stances to children's plays. Since then, these promising playwrights have drifted away from playwriting: Joffré turned to directing; Zavala's Teatro Campesino (Peasant Theater; 1969) had considerable initial impact in the rural areas, apparently lacked cosmopolitan appeal; and Alegría's work as a professional artist and administrator led him away from playwriting. Nevertheless, Zavala's efforts to restyle Andean perspectives of reality held by marginalized, peasants through Brechtian techniques of distancing, spawned several groups that use music, the oral tradition, legend, and myth to highlight social conflict and raise consciousness.

Julio Ortega is also known for writing plays from a political perspective, but mainly on an abstract level of ideas, whether social or philosophical. His first plays, like *Como cruzar la calle* (How to Cross the Street; 1965) and *El intruso* (The Intruder; 1965), capture the existential dilemma involving the consequences of a person's course of action in life and the theme of the double, respectively. *Mesa pelada* (Barren Plateau; 1972), based on an historical event, creates different versions concerning the torture and death of a forgotten historical figure who helped organize popular revolts in southern Peru. Still writing as a university professor in the United States in the eighties, Ortega penned *Balada de la dirección correcta* (Ballad of the Right Address) in 1982 that deals with the theme of rural migration to the cities, the inherent problems of exploitation, and suggests solutions through solidarity.

Perhaps the most prolific dramatist after midcentury has been Juan Rivera Saavedra (1930). With almost one hundred plays to his credit, he achieved fame in 1965 with *Los Ruperto* (The Rupertos), an expressionistic play tending toward the grotesque as it reveals everyday urban reality with all its apparent problems. Known for his subtle use of black humor, Rivera experiments with other plays, *¿Por qué la vaca tiene los ojos tristes?* (Why Does the Cow Have Sad Eyes?; 1966) and *El crédito* (The Credit; 1974), in which absurdist notions and an attack on consumerism are highlighted, respectively. Another playwright, Sarina Helgott (1928), has produced works that fall within poetic realism and tend to look at life from existential perspectives, as in *La señorita Canario* (Miss Canario; 1970?), which recreates generational conflicts wherein freedom (and death) become more meaningful than submissiveness and passivity in life. Meanwhile, other dramatists had been reading Grotowski and they became interested in theory. As a result, Eugenio Barba's theater group, El Odin Teatret (The Odin Theater), is credited with transforming Peruvian theater when its production at the 1978 Ayacucho theater competition coalesced certain theories involving the Teatro del Grupo (Group Theater) that, in turn, initiated a movement known as El teatro del cuerpo (The Theater of the Body). In fact, group theater proliferated in the seventies with Yego Teatro Ensamble (Theater Ensemble), Ayllu (Communal Theater), Cocolido, and Mesa de Teatro (Collective Theater). However, most groups were derived from two principal groups that were formed in 1971: Cuatrotablas (Four Planks) and Yuyachkani. Both sought to denounce social ills and to transform contemporary Peruvian theater. In general, urban theater with slight variations developed in similar fashion: the café-concert, street theater, and puppet theater. Alondra (Wings), founded in 1981 by Juan Rivera Saavedra and Jorge Chiarella Kruger, is based on collective dramatizations of authored works that seek to reveal problems surrounding the concept of power, terrorism, and history. José Carlos Urteaga created Magia (Magic) in 1983 as a collective theater that probes social situations in an urban context. In 1985 the Movimiento Manuela Ramos (The Manuela Ramos Movement) initiated the first competition of plays written about women, and José Enrique Mavila (1955) won with *Camino de rosas* (Path of Roses). Over the years, several theatrical organizations have been formed in Peru: Federación Nacional de Teatro Peruano (National Federation of Peruvian Theater; 1971); Asociación Nacional de Escritores y Artistas (National Association of Writers and Artists; 1983); Centro Peruano de Autores Teatrales (Center for Peruvian Dramatists; 1983); and Movimiento de Teatro Independiente (The Movement for Independent Theater; 1985), which began to sponsor the literary journal *Colectivo* (Confluence) in 1987. In general, however, an overriding commitment in Peruvian theater since Colonial times has been its efforts to capture the essence of Andean traditions and culture.

The flurry of theater production within Peru during the last two decades was complemented on an international level when fiction writer Mario Vargas Llosa (1936) published three significant plays—*La señorita de Tacna* (The Lady from Tacna; 1981), *Kathie y el hipopótamo* (Katy and the Hippopotomus; 1983), and *La Chunga* (1986)—all of which have been staged in major Latin American, U.S., and European cities. The first play premiered in Buenos Aires in 1981 and was presented in English in New York City by the INTAR Hispanic American Theater Company in 1983. The second play opened in Caracas at the Sixth International Theater Festival in 1983. In these three plays, Vargas Llosa recombines the elements of melodrama and converts them to fresh use. Actually, he stands out for his espousal of the melodramatic mode in literature. *La tía Julia y el escribidor* (*Aunt Julia and the Scriptwriter*; 1977) is his first self-consciously melodramatic work, and it creates a thematic interplay between "real" life situations and melodrama that establish a tainted relationship between an autobiographical narrative focus (the life of the young writer Vargas Llosa) and Pedro Camacho's cheap and banal soap operas, an intertextual reference that is found in the first play as the characters listen to his soap operas on the radio in the background. In the second play, ghost writer Santiago Zavala turns out to be none other than a character from the 1969 novel, *Conversación en La Catedral* (*Conversation in The Cathedral*; 1969) and, in the third play, a bordello provides an escape from reality for lower class characters living in the provincial town of Piura in northern Peru. Intertextually, the play's setting and characters first appear in Vargas Llosa's 1966 novel *La casa verde* (*The Green House*), the bordello of the same name that functions as a leitmotif for the thematic structure of the play. But for Vargas Llosa, melodrama is the single element that intensifies human sentiment, subverts the dominant aestheic models of a particular historic moment, and collapses the social mechanization of emotion. In the first play, the principal character struggles to write a story from recollected fragments as told to him by a great aunt in his childhood; the second play employs the thwarted escape plot in an absurdist play about crisis in modern society; and the third play alludes to the dark side of life and makes dynamic use of a secret, a common convention of melodrama. Together, respectively, the plays sustain a progression from veiled allegory of national ruin, set in the reconstructed family history of *La señorita de Tacna*, to a more direct treatment of bourgeois conduct in *Kathie y el hipopótamo*, and, finally, to the universal myth of capitalism in *La Chunga*. However, Mario Vargas Llosa handily avoids the conventional oppositions and solutions to the conflicts created in traditional melodrama, which forces the audience to participate emotionally in the triumph of justice. The three plays leave it to the audience to debate the social contradictions of the present historical moment.

Among the writers of this period who have been mentioned so far, the one who stands out, beginning in the 1950s, for his engaging stories and novels is Julio Ramón Ribeyro. In fact, along with Mario Vargas Llosa (1936) and Alfredo Bryce Echenique (1939), Ribeyro is among the few most important Peruvian fiction writers to continue to write in the late eighties and early nineties. Like César Vallejo, these three writers have spent much of their adult lives living abroad. Ribeyro has lived in Paris since the early 1950s, working in the Peruvian Embassy and as a translator. During that time, he has produced three novels—*Crónica de San Gabriel* (Chronicle of San Gabriel Ranch; 1960), *Los geniecillos dominicales* (The Sunday Rascals; 1965), and *Cambio de guardia* (Change of Guard; 1976), several short stories collections, mostly reprinted in the three-volume *La palabra del mudo* (The Word of a Deaf-Mute; 1972), and *Sólo para fumadores* (For Smokers Only; 1987). In addition, Ribeyro has published a short novel, *La juventud en la otra ribera* (Youth on the Other Shore; 1973), plays that were published in *Teatro* (Theater; 1975), literary essays in *La caza sutil* (The Subtle Hunt; 1976), a literary diary, *Prosas apátridas* (Narrative Without a Nation; 1975), and *Dichos de Lúder* (Luder's Sayings; 1989).

Among his early stories, two volumes are notable: *Los gallinazos sin plumas* (Vultures Without Feathers; 1955), his first, and *Tres historias sublevantes* (Three Subversive Stories; 1964). The former treat the problems of the lumpen proletariat in Lima, such as the story that serves as the title to the collection. It focuses on the exploitation of young children who are forced to sift through garbage to earn a living for their abusive grandfather. Told from the point of view of the children, the old man's greed leads to his ironic demise when a monstrous pig attacks and kills him. Other stories delve into the petty, superficial nature of the urban bourgeois. The latter collection presents socioeconomic problems of Peruvians living in three distinct regions—that is, the coast, the Andes mountains, and the Amazon jungle region ("Al pie del acantilado," "El chaco," and "Fénix," respectively). These stories are excellent examples of regional transcendentalism in that they effectively take the reader away from local environments to levels of universal condemnation of injustice and exploitation. The success of Ribeyro's stories is found in their varied themes and narrative strategies and in the use of imagination in order to create typical situations of everyday life. Ribeyro's stories are built around coincidence, fate, insanity, confusion of identity, moral values, mediocrity, and, of course, the dismal socioeconomic conditions that affect marginalized sectors of society.

Completing the panorama of well-known, widely published, and translated Peruvian fiction writers who, along with Ribeyro, today represent the solid, on-going narrative tradition of Ciro Alegría and José María Arguedas, are Mario Vargas Llosa and Alfredo Bryce Echenique. They have numerous literary works to their credit and continue to write, travel, lecture, and receive international awards. Their vast repertoire of writings not only includes novels and short stories but also short novels, literary criticism, and journalism. Vargas Llosa's novelistic trajectory spans more than thirty years. His first novel, *La ciudad y los perros* (*The Time of the Hero*; 1963), won major prizes in Spain, was the first Latin American novel to be published by Seix Barral Publishers in Barcelona, and set the stage for the almost simultaneous appearance of the so-called Boom writers of the 1960s: Gabriel García Márquez, Julio Cortázar, Carlos Fuentes, and José Donoso. Preceded by a collection of short stories entitled *Los jefes* (*The Bosses*; 1958), Vargas Llosa's first novel, along with *La casa verde* (*The Green House*; 1963) and *Conversación en La Catedral*, represent his initial neo-realist phase of writing. This trilogy of sorts attempts to create tightly structured yet panoramic "totalizations" of Peru, its people and its problems, either through the creation of a microcosm of Peruvian society, by using a real military school in Lima as a backdrop for drama and social commentary in *La ciudad y los perros*, or by juxtaposing and intertwining plots that develop simultaneously in the Peruvian jungle and in a northern, desert provincial city in *La casa verde*.

La ciudad y los perros was acclaimed as one of the best novels written in Spanish during the previous thirty years. The successful combination of theme, style, and technique in the novel creates surprise and admiration. It handily breaks with mimetic, regional fiction and relies on montage effects of film. The novel actively incorporates slang and taboo vocabulary, captures the culture of previously unmentioned marginalized sectors in literature, and portrays the subjective, emotional, and fantasized worlds of its characters. The action takes place in Lima, and the reference to dogs in the Spanish title is a derogatory name given to first-year cadets at the Leoncio Prado military school that provides the setting for a major part of the novel's action. The complexities of the juxtaposition of multiple character points of view and the chronological disjunction of time function to hide the identity of one cadet who is blamed for killing another while on military maneuvers. An investigation ensues, and the incident is ruled an accident, so that the credibility and honor of the military in Peru is not tarnished. Hence, the novel probes the effects of authoritarianism and blind discipline on morals and ethics in a dog-eat-dog world of exploiters and exploited: here, officers and cadets. The moral issues that are posed and the way in which certain characters deal with them invite the reader's participation in the overall experience of the novel. In Peru, the reaction to the novel by the military was not surprising: one thousand copies were publicly burned at the military school.

Vargas Llosa's second novel, *La casa verde*, demands even greater reader participation in the creation of its plot, themes, and artistic and aesthetic interpretations. In a structural sense, most of his novels are conceptualized in terms of discontinuity and simultaneity, and demonstrate a crafty manipulation of multiple perspectives that become the nuclear element for achieving one important goal in fiction writing: the "total" novel. It won prizes at home and abroad, including the prestigious Rómulo Gallegos Award, at which time Vargas Llosa delivered his celebrated Caracas speech, "Literature is Fire," which outlines his views on writing and society. For him, literature is a process of continuous, never-ending insurrection against ignorance and exploitation in society, and he highlights the writer's sense of rebellion because the source of the writer's vocation is his or her own discontent with society.

The action of *La casa verde* is based on at least five different plot lines that take place almost simultaneously in two opposing settings, namely, the northern desert provincial city of Piura and the jungle region to the east, where nuns operate a mission. Key to the first setting is the probable existence of a brothel, painted green, on the outskirts of the city. In 1972, Vargas Llosa published *Historia secreta de una novela*

(Secret History of a Novel), an analytical study of how the novel came into being. The juxtaposition of so many story lines is bewildering in the beginning. The reader is forced to jump back and forth among the stories, picking up on some that are left behind and leaving others temporarily in the middle of their development. Characters cross over from one story to another and acquire new names in the process. Events are presented in such a way that they seem to be part of the past when actually they are later understood to have foreshadowed future events. The first segment of each chapter deals with the nuns' mission in the jungle and how they recruit Indians to be Christianized and sent to the coast as maids for rich people; the second segment follows a conversation and accompanying flashbacks by two men as they travel downriver in the jungle; the third segment presents life in Piura and focuses on one character's mysterious arrival there and the establishment of the green house; the fourth segment is the story of a tribal Indian chief in the jungle; and the fifth takes place in Piura again and deals with life in the Mangachería neighborhood. The fragmentation of lineal structure and the juxtaposition of simultaneous action on distinct temporal planes highlight the writer's concept of the human condition, that is, his insight into circumstances that most affect people at any one moment in their lives. In this way, the novel makes a significant comment on the nature of reality as perceived by contemporary humanity—it is chaotic, fragmented, and complex.

The totalization process culminates in the third novel in which once again, but in amazingly complicated fashion, multiple voices, places, and time frames collide as in a collage but then begin to interweave throughout the novel to form a kaleidoscope of contrasting perspectives on social and political problems under dictatorship and false democracy in modern Peru. Vargas Llosa also published a short novel, *Los cachorros* (*The Cubs and Other Stories*; 1967), during this period. The novel's infantile language—diminutives and euphemisms—exposes the superficial, crass nature of Lima's petty bourgeosie by probing machismo, double standards, seeming affluence, and false social and moral values in the middle class.

Through midcentury and continuing into the 1960s, a notable spirit of progressive thinking, frank dedication to sociopolitical change, and the creation of the cultural bases of modernity among young people who grew up in that era were squelched by repressive governments that quickly led to a feeling of bitter failure and deep anxiety in a whole generation of artists and writers. In fact, moving beyond the polarizing effects of certain conventional oppositions—i.e., urban and rural environments, ethnic differences between Whites and Indians, geographical differences between the Andes mountains and the coastal region, or the long-standing theme of civilization versus barbarism—significant novels by several Peruvian fiction writers probe the effects of the *ochenio*, that is, the eight-year dictatorship (1948-56) of Manuel A. Odría, which has been characterized as having stunted the intellectual growth of a whole generation of potential future leaders by blocking, through censorship and political and moral corruption, the social mechanisms for creating contemporary culture in Peru. Novels such as *Una piel de serpiente* (A Serpent's Skin; 1964), by Luis Loayza, *Los geniecillos dominicales*, by Julio Ramón Ribeyro, *Los juegos verdaderos* (A Deadly Game; 1968), by Edmundo de los Ríos, *El escarabajo y el hombre* (The Beetle and the Man; 1970), by Oswaldo Reynoso, *Conversación en La Catedral*, by Mario Vargas Llosa, and *Un mundo para Julius* (*A World for Julius*; 1970), by Alfredo Bryce Echenique, are loosely structured around the process of the initiation of young people who suffer from anomie—the destruction of conventional social structures—and who question the possibility of ever integrating themselves into contemporary Peruvian reality, in which dictatorship has sapped the moral strength of society through corruption, theft, blackmail, assassination, and sexual taboo. Mario Vargas Llosa states that the Odría dictatorship "era muy diferente de otras que fueron o son más violentas. Esta prefirió gobernar mediante la corrupción, la intriga, el compromiso y la duplicidad. Fue una dictadura que robó a nuestra generación. No hubo héroes ni produjo mártires, pero sí muchos fracasos" (It was very different from others that were or are more violent in nature. This [dictatorship] preferred to govern by means of corruption, intrigue, promises, and duplicity. It was a dictatorship that robbed our generation. There were no heroes nor martyrs, only a lot of failures).

The characters in these powerful novels suffer from anxiety, pessimism, loss of spiritual values, apathy, and solitude. Vargas Llosa, who dedicated his novel to Luis Loayza, comments that *Una piel de serpiente* "recordará a algunos un momento particularmente triste de la historia peruana, ilustrará a todos sobre la lánguida y medrosa juventud que depara nuestra tierra a los hijos de la burguesía" (it will make some remember a particularly sad period in Peruvian history; it will present above all a languishing, fearful youth that the nation has prepared for future children of the middle class). Vargas Llosa's novel creates a panoramic mosaic of frustration and failure in multiple levels of Peruvian society through some seventy characters that move across urban and rural landscapes of poverty and wealth, exploitation and abuse, power and alienation. However, one character—Santiago Zavala—is developed more fully and the novel follows approximately twelve years of his life between the ages of eighteen and thirty, which corresponds historically to the period 1951-63 in Peru. Santiago, a journalist, communicates a feeling of malaise and pessimism throughout the novel.

Variations in focalization allow for the juxtaposition of diverse perspectives, from third-person description of the setting, including dialogue, to the interior subjectivity of the character, all of which combine to create a bitter, cynical vision of reality. In *El escarabajo y el hombre* the younger generation rejects its past and the novel focuses on language, that is, nonconventional colloquial slang, to capture the sense of alienation, rebellion, and the rejection of a morally bankrupt society. Nevertheless, a response to the feeling of entrapment by the characters in the novels of Vargas Llosa, Ribeyro, Loayza, and Reynoso is seen in *Los juegos verdaderos*, in which the protagonist Manuel responds to a conservative reformist government of Fernando Belaúnde Terry in the 1960s by joining a guerrilla movement that, like many others, was influenced by the success of the Cuban Revolution in 1959. In the novel the encarcerated guerrilla relives his remote past, immediate past, and the present moment, only to be kicked in the back and die as he mentally projects to the utopian future of a normal life. However, the protagonist communicates in the end a sense of failure, in which for him "todo había sido un gran juego" (it was all a big game). At bottom, these novels deal not only with the feeling of loss, but also with a strong sense of rejection: Santiago takes revenge against corruption in his newspaper writing and Manuel seeks answers by becoming a guerrilla. Other novels took another tactic: Alfredo Bryce Echenique's *Un mundo para Julius* is his first novel, which, like his other works, is heavily based on personal experience. Much of the novel is autobiographical, for references to Julius's childhood and schooling are similar to the author's experiences at his grandfather's mansion or at the grade school run by North American nuns and priests in Lima. A charming, well-written piece of literature, it is about a youngster's first years of life, until he reaches eleven. However, adult and child perspectives intermingle to create poignant irony, great humor, and penetrating social commentary about the relatively uncomplicated, rich, upper-class strata of Peruvian society in Lima in the 1950s.

Alfredo Marcelo Bryce Echenique was born into a distinguished aristocratic family in Lima in 1939. He seemed destined to become a writer: his mother, who admired French culture, had baptized him with the second name, Marcelo, in honor of Marcel Proust. In 1964 Bryce Echenique graduated from law school, but he also received a degree in literature, having written a thesis on the function of dialogue in the works of Ernest Hemingway. That same year he boarded a steamer for Europe in order to study and write.

Bryce Echenique is an accomplished fiction writer and journalist. To date, he has written two volumes of short stories and five other novels: *Tantas veces Pedro* (So Many Times Pedro; 1977); *La vida exagerada de Martín Romaña* (The Exaggerated Life of Martin Romaña; 1981); *La última mudanza de Felipe Carrillo* (Felipe Carrillo's Last Move; 1988); *El hombre que hablaba de Octavia de Cádiz* (The Man Who Talked about Octavia de Cadiz; 1989); *Dos señoras conversan* (Two Ladies Chat; 1990). He is also an exciting feature story writer for popular journals and newspapers throughout the Hispanic world. He has written extensively about his travels in Europe and Latin America.

The writing of *Un mundo para Julius* in 1969 and its subsequent publication in 1970 coincided with the 1969 coup d'état that took credit for expropriating vast land holdings belonging to Peru's oligarchy; not surprisingly, here literature and history fuse to symbolize the destruction of Peru's long-established ruling classes. Despite this first, political reading of the novel, making it very much a novel of its time, it won the 1972 Peruvian National Prize for Literature and continues to generate lasting interest for contemporary readers. The novel is not only an engagingly corrosive portrayal of the pretentious, morally blind Peruvian oligarchy and its transition to the dominant nouveau riche class subsidized by an influx of North American capitalism in the 1950s, but also an early postmodern urban novel in which the Bildungsroman structure and its curious, questioning, sentimental protagonist Julius bring together elements of the drama of lost innocence, black comedy of manners, playful parody, and social satire.

As we begin to review the importance of the so-called Boom period of the sixties—the fictional works of Carlos Fuentes, Mario Vargas Llosa, Julio Cortázar, and Gabriel García Márquez, among others—Bryce Echenique's *Un mundo para Julius* ranks among the first works to emphasize the art of storytelling in which the notably oral tone of the novel handily juxtaposes invention and representation, hyperbole and reality, multiple points of view and the free indirect style, in addition to interior monologue. The incorporation of these elements into the novel does not place it among those in which the allusion to societal fragmentation is the goal, as in the narrative worlds of Vargas Llosa's and Fuentes's early novels. It creates instead an obvious hierarchy of the class and ethnic differences in Peru.

It is not surprising to see the development of political themes in contemporary Peruvian fiction become more intense in the 1970s. Until then, Peru's prior twenty-five-year history is one of successive military coup d'états and, what seems not to be coincidentally, several fiction writers produced novels dealing with the military and dictatorship. While Vargas Llosa's *Conversación en La Catedral* represents the novel of dissaffected youth during the 1950s under military dictatorship, it also opens the door to a series of novels published between 1970 and 1976 that scrutinize and, ultimately, collectively condemn the dominance of the military in Peruvian society. The works mentioned include *Las rayas del tigre* (The Stripes of the Tiger; 1973), by Guillermo Thorndike, *La ronda de los generales* (The Turn of the Next General; 1973), by José B. Adolph, *Pantaleón y las visitadoras* (*Captain Pantoja and the Special Service*; 1973), by Mario Vargas Llosa, and *Cambio de guardia*, written in the mid-1960s by Julio Ramón Ribeyro.

Vargas Llosa continued his long-standing feud with machismo and military *caudillismo* (bossism) that went all the way back to his first novel, *La ciudad y los perros*. In *Pantaleón y las visitadoras*, Vargas Llosa used humor and comedy to turn the concept of professional militarism into a mockery of itself by creating a seemingly absurd story in which the military sends Captain Pantoja to the jungle region of Peru to organize a flotilla of prostitutes to service sex-starved soldiers assigned to isolated military posts, who had begun to rape women in nearby villages. The absurd plot, that is, the Captain's manic drive for organization, the irony coming out of the humorous situations, and the grotesque nature of certain events in the novel go far in condemning not only the military but also different variants of fanaticism in society, not to mention a seeming presence of a growing homophobic stance on the part of the author.

The plot of Adolph's novel develops around a coup d'état being planned by the Army in Arequipa. While historical references in the novel situate the action around the events that led to the 1968 coup that brought General Juan Velasco Alvarado and his Gobierno Revolucionario Militar (Revolutionary Military Government) to power, the novel goes beyond historical specificity and narrates a hypothetical situation that points to certain patterns in the execution of military takeovers. Hence, the novel is a strong denunciation of the established tradition of military empowerment by means of coups. However, the dynamic element of the novel is the parallel that is established in the title of the novel between this military act and children's games. While Guillermo Thorndike may have also structured his novel around specific historical incidents that took place in the late 1930s, the novel develops two parallel, alternating stories, one following an escaped thief who then goes around stealing money and explosives for a leftist political party, and the other narrating a person's rise to power as chief of internal security and finding himself plotting against the president of the nation and failing to overthrow him when he realizes he does not have the support of the armed forces. Ambition and the desire to instill fear among the populace create hypocrisy and corruption. Ironically, hatred for the dictator drives people to acquire his power.

Finally, in *Cambio de guardia*, Ribeyro shares with the reader an innovative view of Peruvian politics by presenting a collective vision of multiple characters of Peruvian society in the throes of a coup. The novel focuses on the far-reaching yet little discussed effects of the behind-the-scenes, under-the-table, covert politicking that normally accompany this type of political change. Moral indignation, disgust, and finally condemnation of military coups are typical reader responses to Ribeyro's novel. In one sense, these political novels look at society from the perspective of numerous characters that form a faceless mass of marginalized people, an aspect that communicates the unfortunate effects of military dictatorships on society at large. However, these novels also possess a particular perspective and language that serve to create a personalized, more subjective vision, based on a particular character, that allows the reader to see and feel the effects of corrupt politics on the lives of all the characters. In this sense, political themes become extremely dynamic and create interest for the reader.

Since 1950, creative fiction in Peru has maintained a strong interest in the country's reality and its successes and failures as a nation, in modern times, which under the thumb of seemingly feudal dictatorships have not only not been weakened by democratic movements throughout the world, but have been strengthened through the politics and imposition of first-world transnational capitalism that wields tremendous economic power over third-world supplier nations. In a way, literature seems to reflect these trends in an apparent dispersion of artistic endeavors that, while it generates a fiction that probes the problems of individuals in a social context, fails to produce fiction focusing on collective problems of different social groups. Before 1950, novels would analyze the problems of groups of people with common interests (i.e., *El mundo es ancho y ajeno* or *Yawar fiesta*). The new focus on individuals requires new narrative strategies, and by looking at reality from the subjective perspective of an individual, post-50s novels do seem to capture the tense interaction between character and social reality. This relationship allows the reader to perceive human attitudes that are buried deep in Peruvian culture. Readers are in a position to affirm, negate, or conform to human behavior according to social, political, and historic circumstances in Peru. As an example, several fictional works in the fifties are structured around the rites of initiation theme in order to highlight and, potentially, to subvert certain myths, like the oppositions between city and country and civilization and barbarism. Nevertheless, the move at midcentury away from traditional, particularized regional perspectives in fiction to more transcendental, universal, Latin American themes within Peruvian reality is clearly documented in works by Julio Ramón Ribeyro, Mario Vargas Llosa, and Alfredo Bryce Echenique, all of whom continued to write during the seventies and eighties.

After Vargas Llosa's 1977 novel *La tía Julia y el escribidor*, which deviates from his original social neorealist stance of the 1960s toward comedy, in a serious spoof on the act of writing both from an autobiographical perspective and from that of a fanatical soap opera writer, he has gone on to produce additional astounding works of fiction. However, this novel is important also, for its melodramatic, maudlin, humorous tone captivated a large audience, especially when the translated version was hailed in the United States as one of the top five novels of 1982. More than an entertainment piece, the novel intensifies the author's theoretical and practical concerns about the art of fiction writing. In fact, it opens the door to his world of "metafiction," that is, experimental writing in which fiction imitates other fiction. Social critics chided Vargas Llosa for turning his back on the problems of Peruvian reality. The humor in his recent novels was said to be the product of a writer who had succumbed to the lucrative enticement of literary supply and demand. It is no coincidence that Vargas Llosa's seventh novel, *La guerra del fin del mundo* (*The War of the End of the World*; 1981), a voluminous tome that is similar to his earlier neorealist works for its depiction of violence, brutality, and human chaos, is a challenging response to these charges. This novel brilliantly recreates, reinterprets, and submits to the realm of the imagination an historical incident that serves, in effect, to underscore the author's long-standing thematic obsession with ideological fanaticism. The novel deals with events that occurred at the turn of the century in the inhospitable and impoverished backlands of northeastern Brazil near Canudos, where a ghastly massacre of thousands of religious fanatics by the Brazilian army took place. Basically, the novel's retelling of the incident seems to communicate to the reader the idea that certain religious phenomena might be more important than historical influences in determining human conduct. The truth of Canudos is found less in its historical documentation than in the myths, speculation, and superstitions that still live today.

The intensification of political violence in Peru since the early sixties is documented in a fictional way in Vargas Llosa's next novel, *Historia de Mayta* (*The Real Life of Alejandro Mayta*; 1984), which narrates the attempts of a Peruvian novelist to reconstruct in dogged reporter fashion a failed leftist uprising in the Andes mountains led by an old schoolmate, Alejandro Mayta. The story revolves around interviews that the novelist conducts with family and acquaintances in order to create Mayta's confused and chaotic cosmovision. Together, Vargas Llosa's last three novels—*¿Quién mató a Palomino Molero?* (*Who Killed Palomino Molero*; 1986), *El hablador* (*The Storyteller*; 1987), *Elogio de la madrastra* (*In Praise of the Stepmother*; 1988)—represent the rich narrative diversity that has become his trademark. The first novel captures in melodramatic fashion the secret passions of men and women that make for good storytelling. Relying on those tried-and-true narrative techniques of detective fiction that create ambiguity yet stress the conviction that reality and truth are indeed illusions, Vargas Llosa plays with the reader's curiosity from the outset by posing a question in the title that is never satisfactorily answered. The second novel narrates the story of a young Jew and university student, Raúl Zuratas, who dropped out of society and joined an Amazon jungle tribe to become a storyteller. The novel deals with the theme of the collision between civilization and so-called primitive tribes and asks the question whether it is possible to integrate different cultures into modern society, or whether isolated Indian tribes should be preserved. Vargas Llosa himself has said that if forced to choose he would lean toward assimilation and modernization because the priority is to eliminate hunger, disease, misery, and painful death. The other choice is to run the risk of seeing numerous Indian tribes disappear from the face of the earth. Hence, the novel engagingly creates this dilemma for the reader as an intellectual and moral question for modern civilization. And, finally, his most recent novel, *Elogio de la madrastra* ventures prudently into the realm of erotic literature in which perversity and pleasure are experienced through the perspective and detailed descriptions of a character who revels in hedonism and the clever intertextual juxtaposition of narrations by figures that appear in paintings by the great masters of Western tradition. In essence, Vargas Llosa continues to write about themes and obsessions that began to haunt him as far back as his first novel in the 1960s. Vargas Llosa's rebellion against convention and dogma in literature has generated a progressive continuity in his growing number of works, texts that achieve a balance between objective, entertaining, and moral perspectives. His readers view humanity from many angles: the confining and alienating circumstances of corrupt social values such as machismo; the maladaptation of dominant values of society; violence in some works, the view of humankind functioning within wider parameters of historical and cultural myth; and deeply personal experiences and demonic obsessions.

Meanwhile, Vargas Llosa's international stature has not eclipsed contemporary Peruvian narrative. Bryce Echenique, for instance, as well as many others, have created their own narrative worlds alongside Vargas Llosa's looming corpus. Other significant contemporary narrative texts pick up on the earlier theme of disaffected youth in a modern, morally corrupt Peruvian society, as well as topics of societal violence, class and racial exploitation, and ethnic loss of identity: *A la hora del tiempo* (When Time Beckons; 1977), by José Antonio Bravo (1937); *El viejo saurio se retira* (The Ancient Lizard Retires; 1969), by Miguel Gutiérrez (1940); *Los hijos del orden* (Living Under Suppression; 1973), by Luis Urteaga Cabrera (1940); *El truco en los ojos* (A Trick in the Eye; 1978), by Laura Riesco (1940); *La vida a plazos de don Jacobo Lerner* (*The Fragmented Life of Don Jacobo Lerner*, 1979), and *Tiempo al tiempo* (*Play by Play*, 1984), by Isaac Goldemberg (1945). The diversity of narrative themes in contemporary Peruvian literature reflects the variety of cultural representations in Peru that makes the affirmation of a "standard" national Peruvian literature difficult. While Goldemberg narrates the historical past of a Jewish immigrant to Peru and his efforts to preserve and even affirm his identity, another important fiction writer, Gregorio Martínez (1942), creates a new panorama of heretofore unknown voices in literature, Peru's black and mulatto population on the coast, in *Tierra de Caléndula* (The Land of Calendula; 1975), *Canto de sirena* (The Siren's Song; 1977), *Crónica de músicos y diablos* (Chronicle of Musicians and Devils; 1990).

Basically, Peruvian narrative in the 1980s and 1990s develops around four general tendencies: 1) a subjective "intimist" perspective that focuses more on the development of individual characters and captures the feeling of scepticism and implicit negativity of individuals, rather than facing social and historical concerns that have led to alienation and disconformity; e.g., the works by Bryce Echenique, Alonso Cueto's (1954) *La batalla del pasado* (The Battle of the Past; 1983), *Otras tardes* (Other Afternoons; 1985) by Luis Loayza (1934), *Caballos de medianoche* (Horses on the Midnight Range; 1985) by Guillermo de Niño Guzmán (1955), and *Casi Gómez* (1982) by Marcela Romero (n.d.), in all of which social realism gives way to an exploration of individual obsessions; 2) the reconstruction of history through the incorporation of official documents and oral narratives that not only bring to life past events, but also reinterpret them in modern terms, as in *La guerra del fin del mundo* by Vargas Llosa, *Crónica de blasfemos* (Chronicles by the Blasphemous; 1986) by Félix Alvarez Sáenz (1945), and *Cuando la gloria agoniza* (When Glory Goes Into Agony; 1989) by José Antonio Bravo (1937); 3) the presentation of Peruvian reality in a crude and direct fashion that attempts to capture in an epic mode the daily travails of popular, almost carnivalesque, urban and rural poverty, first seen in works by Julio Ramón Ribeyro, now in *Montacerdos* (Pigriders; 1981) or *Patíbulo para un caballo* (Firing Squad for a Horse; 1989), or in the short stories *Las huellas del puma* (Puma Tracks; 1986) by Cromwell Jara (1951), *Jarabe de lengua* (Tongue Syrup; 1987) by Alejandro Sánchez Aizcorbe (1952); and 4) neoindigenous perspectives in *Azurita* (1978) and *Angel de Ocongate* (The Angel from Ocongate; 1986), stories by Edgardo Rivera Martínez (1943), and *Cordi-llera negra* (Black Mountain Range; 1985) by Oscar Colchado Lucio (1947), the lead one of which deals with the Atusparia rebellion that Ribeyro recreated in his historical drama, *Atusparia*. Not falling within any specific literary pattern is César Calvo's (1940) *Las tres mitades de Ino Moxo y otros brujos de la Amazonía* (The Three Halves of Ino Moxo and Other Medicine Men of the Amazon Jungle; 1981), an anthropological narrative testimony based on drug use and religious experience of the Amahuaca Indians living in the Amazon region. All in all, recent Peruvian narrative does not purport to impose current political ideologies nor reinterpret history, but rather to pose more questions than provide answers to the urgent social problems that have beset the country in recent decades.

Peru's greatest poet of the twentieth century is César Vallejo, but varying thematic elements, such as indigenism and daring aesthetic per-

spectives, namely, the avant-garde, became fused in Peru in the poetry
of Alejandro Peralta and others. Peruvian poetry after World War II
became polarized after a polemic in the fifties between the social-realists
and the so-called purists. Writing at the time was a group of poets born
in the twenties: Xavier Sologuren (1922), Francisco Carrillo (1925), Alejandro Romualdo (1926), Washington Delgado (1927), Carlos Germán
Belli (1927), Juan Gonzalo Rose (1928), and Blanca Varela (1926).
Sologuren began publishing purist poetry, that is, lyrical, balanced, architecturally structured poetry in the style of the Spaniard Jorge Guillén, in
the forties, in collections such as *El morador* (The Boarder; 1946) and
Detenimientos (Detainments; 1948), and he continued to publish regularly
through the sixties, seventies, and eighties. Sologuren published *Vida
continua: obra poética* (Continuing Life: Poetic Works) in 1989. In a
realist vein, Romualdo's *Edición extraordinaria* (Extraordinary Edition;
1958) communicates a concern for social issues and problems affecting
Peruvians from a conceptual perspective of ideas that seek to portray the
human condition as determined by politics. More in the style of Pedro
Salinas, Delgado discovered early on an endearing personal poetic formula that looks at love, nostalgia, and social commitment in unique ways.
He has published over a half-dozen books since the 1950s, winning the
Premio Nacional de Poesía in 1953. *Un mundo dividido. Poesía, 1951-
1970* (A Divided World. Poetry, 1951-1970; 1970) is a collection of po-
ems that covers twenty years of writing. A recent book of poetry by
Delgado is *Reunión elegida* (Elected Reunion; 1988).

Blanca Varela (1926), one among a few Peruvian woman poets,
began publishing poetry in 1959 with a collection entitled *Ese puerto
existe* (That Port Exists; 1959). Other significant books by Varela include
Luz de día (Daylight; 1963), *Valses y otras falsas confesiones* (Waltzes
and Other False Confessions; 1972), and *Canto villano* (Village Song;
1978). Oftentimes introspective, her poetry seeks to probe everyday
events in order to find significant, albeit disagreeable realities that provide new perspectives on life. A modern parallel to Vallejo's creative
syntax, neologisms, and daring imagery is Belli's poetry. Belli astutely
combines different types of language—scientific, archaic, slang—as well
as distortion and black humor to produce sarcastic perspectives that
capture the failure and frustration of urban dwellers in contemporary
society who are alienated from each other, their history, and their culture. His principal books of poetry include: *¡O hada cibernética!* (Oh
Cibernetic Muse; 1961), *El pie sobre el cuello* (The Foot on the Throat;
1964), *En alabanza del bolo alimenticio* (In Commemoration of Unchew-

ed Food; 1979), *Más que señora humana* (More Than a Humane Señora; 1986), and *En el restante tiempo terrenal* (The Rest of Worldly Time; 1988).

The Generation of 1960, a loosely defined group of younger poets born in the 1940s is characterized by similar concerns for contemporary humanity. It includes such notables as Rodolfo Hinostroza (1941), Antonio Cisneros (1942), Javier Heraud (1942-62), Marcos Martos (1942), Julio Ortega (1942), Mirko Lauer (1947), and Abelardo Sánchez León (1947). The group has become a significant generation linking the great poets of the past—Vallejo, Eguren, and Adán—to the urgent need for change experienced by the more recent poets of the sixties. The common denominator among these younger poets seems to be change. The concept became the driving force for the construction of new theories and ideas. Cuba, rampant urbanization and industrialization, radical political developments, and the premature death of Javier Heraud, poet-turned-guerrilla who was killed by government forces in the jungle town of Puerto Maldonado, triggered the need to formulate new attitudes and the desire not only to alter but also to reaffirm certain important values in society. Heraud's poetry, *El río* (The River, 1960) and *El viaje* (The Trip, 1961), revolves around themes involving social commitment, revolution, loneliness, love, and death. For Heraud, poetry becomes an instrument to eliminate exploitation and oppression. All in all, these poets are intensely interested in Peruvian reality and several of them tend to express their relationship with reality through personal testimony. In the process, style also changes. Antonio Cisneros has said that a sense of collective and personal anguish provided a common ground from which this group of poets could examine the contemporary world. Julio Ortega has said that they created the need to incorporate a type of experience into their poetry that is particularized by local reality. And change is seen in another way. Cisneros believes that to write poetry was not the only goal of his generation, but also to find a way to place Peruvian poetry within the international sphere that they inherited from César Vallejo. Exploring an ever-widening panorama of new realities, this group of poets develops themes concerning Peruvian history, social criticism such as alienation in contemporary society, and traditional values like family and intimate relationships.

Rodolfo Hinostroza, whose early poems were published in *Consejero del lobo* (Advisor to the Wolf) in 1965, does not choose sides between the social-realists or the purists, but rather takes a position of negativity. In many ways, the majority of these poets approach historical and social themes with the same attitude, as in Washington Delgado's critical poem, "History of Peru." Themes depicting aspects of Peruvian reality that inherently suggest badly worn yet essential cultural values are the basis for many poems: the historical past on the one hand, contemporary urban society on the other. Abelardo Sánchez León in *Las ventanas cerradas* (The Closed Windows; 1970) berates the faceless yet smug middle class that is caught up unwittingly in contradiction. And, finally, other poets see Peru—its land, people, history, and customs—subject to forces beyond man's control or even faith in divine power. More recent books of poetry by Sánchez León include *Buen lugar para morir* (A Good Place to Die; 1984) and *Antiguos papeles* (Old Papers; 1987).

Without a doubt, Antonio Cisneros is the most well-known contemporary poet, especially in international circles. His poetry includes such important works as *Destierro* (Banished; 1961), *David* (1962), *Comentarios reales* (Royal Comentaries), which won the Premio Nacional de Poesía in 1965, *Canto ceremonial contra un oso hormiguero* (see selections in *The Spider Hangs Too Far from the Ground*; 1970) that received the Cuban Casa de las Américas prize in 1968, *Agua que no has de beber* (Prohibited Waters; 1972), *Como higuera en un campo de golf* (Like a Fig Tree on a Golf Course; 1972), *El libro de Dios y de los húngaros* (The Book of God and the Hungarians; 1978), *Crónica del Niño Jesús de Chilca* (Chronicle of the Baby Jesus of Chilca; 1981), *Monólogo de la casta Susana y otros poemas* (Monologues and Other Poems; 1986). Selected poems from several books of Cisneros's poetry have been translated in *At Night the Cats* (1985). Cisneros has published numerous translations of British, North American, Hungarian, and Brazilian poetry into Spanish, in addition to traveling and teaching outside of Peru. *Comentarios reales* is an ambitious poem that deconstructs official Peruvian history using a subtle combination of contemporary language and residues of the early chronicles of Peru. Basically, Cisneros's poetry represents a confluence of personal and collective history in which poems that deal with legend, myth, and revolution stress the problems of belonging to the dominant culture.

These historical and personal concerns of the poets of the sixties produced other bifurcations, especially in language, as everyday colloquial, street language acquired renewed poetic importance and value. The intensity of movement, sounds, and noise in the cities becomes the springboard for new poetic forms. From there, things mushroomed. The poetic group Hora Cero (Zero Hour) boisterously proclaimed the rebirth of Peruvian poetry and its break with the past. At San Marcos, the group Estación Reunida (Reunited Season) was less inflammatory, as were others who were associated with the literary journal *Creación y crítica* (Creation and Criticism; 1960s and 1970s). However, the tone that captures this era is found in the hermetic, closed, asfixiating worlds of *Rastro de caracol* (Snail Track; 1977) by Abelardo Sánchez León.

Again, Peruvian poetry in the eighties is strongly marked by the feeling of deception and bitterness. A decade of seemingly leftist military dictatorship destroyed youthful enterprise and vigor, much in the same way Odría thwarted progress in the fifties. Also, the election of a conservative, rightist party in 1980 and the sudden domination of the Shining Path guerrilla movement has led Peru toward destruction in the 1990s. As a result, the relationship between poetry and society has become complicated and complex, mainly because of a process of dispersion that has hindered the creation of literary groupings or solidarity movements, which is different from earlier periods. Such is the case of the poetry of certain poets born in the fifties who publish in the 1970s and 1980s: *Una casa en la sombra* (House in the Shade; 1983) by Carlos López Degregori (1952); *Perro negro* (Black Dog; 1986) by Mario Montalbetti Solari (1953); *Violencia de sol* (Violent Rays; 1980) and *Altagracia* (Highest Pardon; 1989) by Enrique Sánchez Hernani (1953); *Itaca* (1983) by Jorge Eslava (1953); *Contaminando por la sombra del sol: conciencia* (Contaminating with the Shade of the Sun: Consciousness; 1980) and *Desde Melibea* (With Melibea; 1980) by Edgar O'Hara; *Antes de la muerte* (Before Death; 1985) and *El chico que se declaraba con la mirada* (The Boy Who Declared His Love with His Eyes; 1986) by Róger Santiváñez (1956). While these poets have not rallied around a literary journal in particular, some have found solidarity in literary circles at San Marcos University or the Catholic University. Literary magazines like *Trompa de Eustaquio* (Eustaquio's Nose), *Sic, Calandria, Macho Cabrío* (Goat Herd), *Omnibus* (Bus), the latter two from Arequipa, published initial poems by these poets that would later become integrated into books of poetry. Finally, notable books of poetry by writers mainly born in the sixties that have created positive reactions among readers include: *Prima Julianne* (Cousin Julie Anne) by Raúl Mendizábal (1956); *Poemas no recogidos en libro* (Poems Not Published in Books), *Fierro curvo* (Arced Iron), and *O un cuchillo esperándome* (Or a Knife is Waiting for Me; 1988) by Patricia Alba (1961); *Caja negra* (Black Box; 1986) and *Sacrificio* (Sacrifice; 1989) by Alonso Ruiz Rosas (1962); *Reino de la necesidad* (The Kingdom of Necessity) by Jorge Frisancho; and *Archivo de huellas digitales* (Archive of Finger Prints; 1985) by Eduardo Chirinos Arrieta (1960).

V

Peru produced a number of important literary critics during the twentieth century, most of whom have been noticeably influential for their rigorous and illuminating analyses of Peruvian literature, literary tendencies, historical movements, and cultural phenomena related to literature. Members of earlier generations of critics, writing from a historicist perspective, and current practitioners of literary criticism focus from the perspective of society and culture on canon writers, like Inca Garcilaso de la Vega, Felipe Guamán Poma de Ayala, Ricardo Palma, Manuel González Prada, José Carlos Mariátegui, José María Eguren, César Vallejo, José María Arguedas, and Ciro Alegría. Literary topics include studies of the chroniclers, emancipation literature, colonial poetry, travel literature, culture and modernization, literature and society, contemporary poetry and narrative, and indigenism.

Beginning with the past century, the most notable literary intellectual and historian is José de la Riva Agüero (1885-1944). A classicist who embraced turn-of-the-century elitist Positivism and wrote literary histories in the style of the Spaniard Marcelino Menéndez y Pelayo, Riva Agüero wrote about Peruvian history, literature, and major literary figures. He studied Peruvian poetry of the colonial period in *Discursos académicos* (Academic Lectures, 1935), and he studies Peruvian literature in general in *Paisajes peruanos* (Peruvian Landscapes; 1955). But probably the most prolific literary historian, a novelist in his own right, and now a virtual literary institution in Peru, is Luis Alberto Sánchez (1900). A fervent leader of Alianza Popular Revolucionaria Americana (American Popular Revolutionary Alliance) for most of his life, Sánchez has written widely on Peruvian history and culture. In the area of literature, he is best known for his numerous introductions to literature, literary histories, and bibliographies. Sánchez's research is diverse: *La literatura peruana, derrotero para una historia espiritual del Perú* (Peruvian Literature: The Road to a Spiritual History of Peru; 1950); *Contribución a la bibliografía de la literatura peruana* (Bibliographical Contribution to Peruvian Literature; 1969); *Panorama de la literatura del Perú: desde sus orígenes hasta nuestros días* (Panorama of Peruvian Literature From Its Origins to the Present; 1974); *La polémica del indigenismo* (The Polemic Concerning Indigenism; 1976); *El Perú: nuevo retrato de un país adoles-*

cente (Peru: New Portrait of a Young Country; 1981). For many years, *Proceso y contenido de la novela hispano-americana* (Process and Contents of the Hispanic American Novel; 1953) was widely consulted for its panoramic overview of literary tendencies in Hispanic American narrative. While he has written novelized biographies of El Inca Garcilaso, La Perricholi, and Flora Tristán, one of his more important contributions to literary research is his seminal study of José Santos Chocano.

Raúl Porras Barrenechea (1897-1960) also studied Peruvian literature, including El Inca Garcilaso, Ricardo Palma, letters written during the colonial period, myth, tradition, and history in Peru, and Peruvian chroniclers. Estuardo Núñez (1908) produced important research on Peruvian poetry, particularly on Eguren, comparative literature, and travel literature: *Viajeros de tierra adentro. Viajeros norteamericanos en el Perú* (Inland Travelers: North American Travelers in Peru; 1960), *Viajeros hispanoamericanos: temas continentales* (Hispanic American Travelers: Continental Themes; 1985), *Viajes y viajeros extranjeros por el Perú: apuntes documentales* (Travels and Foreign Travelers in Peru: Documents; 1989), and *Obras narrativas desconocidas* (Unknown Narrative Works; 1971), an anthology of novels by Pablo de Olave. Núñez, Emilia Romero de Valle (1902-68) produced meticulously researched studies on the traditional ballad in Peruvian literature, folklore studies, and biographies, especially on important women in Latin America. Augusto Tamayo Vargas (1914) is a poet, novelist, literary critic, university professor, and journalist. He taught literature courses at San Marcos from 1939 to 1969 and served in several administrative capacities. He has taught in Brazil, Chile, Puerto Rico, and the U.S.A. He has written over forty books, one of which, his two-volume *Literatura peruana* (Peruvian Literature, 4th ed.; 1976), provides an excellent panoramic overview of Peruvian literature. His books of poetry and literary criticism have won several awards, his first being *Perú en trance de novela: Mercedes Cabello de Carbonera* (Peru on the Road to Producing Novels: The Case of Mercedes Cabello de Carbonera; 1940). His novel, *Impronta del agua enferma* (The Stamp of Putrid Water; 1973), won second prize in the 1973 competition of Novela Universo (Universal Novel Editors).

Alberto Escobar (1929) broke new ground by incorporating important sociolinguistic notions into the analysis of language and literature. His work includes widely consulted texts: *El reto del multilingüismo en el Perú* (Multilingualism in Peru; 1972), *Lenguaje* (Language; 2nd ed. 1976), *Variaciones sociolingüísticas en el Perú* (Sociolinguistic Variations in Peru; 1978). Escobar has produced excellent pieces of literary scholarship as well. His best, probably, is *Como leer a Vallejo* (How to Read Vallejo; 1973), but other books of criticism—*La narración en el Perú* (Narrative Tendencies in Peru; 1956), *Patio de letras* (Patio of Letters; 1965), *La partida inconclusa* (The Unfinished Sailing; 1976), and *El imaginario nacional. Moro, Westphalen, Arguedas: una formación literaria* (National Imaginations. Moro, Westphalen, Arguedas: The Formation of a Generation; 1989)—are required reading for students of Peruvian literature.

A more recent generation of productive scholars and intellectuals who write not only about Peruvian literature but also about important literary figures from other Latin American countries include Antonio Cornejo Polar (1936), José Miguel Oviedo (1934), Mario Vargas Llosa (1936), Enrique Ballón Aguirre (1940), and Julio Ortega (1942). Vargas Llosa has produced literary criticism that has stimulated writers and critics alike to reconsider notions concerning the relationship between the writer and his or her reality. To understand the personal and cultural underpinnings of writers such as José María Arguedas, Gabriel García Márquez, Gustave Flaubert, and, equally important, Vargas Llosa's own obsessions and fantasies about writing, his critical writings are absolutely essential. For instance, his recent *La verdad de las mentiras: ensayos sobre literatura* (The Truth of Lying: Essays on Literature; 1990) is one of the most provocative incursions into the realm of the meaning of the act of writing by a writer today. Vargas Llosa's lectures on literature given at Syracuse University in 1988 were published as *A Writer's Reality* (1991).

Cornejo Polar, who, like Ortega, teaches in the United States today, founded in Lima the important literary journal *Revista de crítica literaria latinoamericana* (Journal of Latin American Literary Criticism) in 1975. Taking a notably sociological stance in his focus on literature, he is especially well-known for his exhaustive research and probing analysis of indigenist literature, the narrative of Arguedas and Alegría, and the Peruvian novel in general. For an in-depth look at Peruvian narrative, Cornejo Polar's *La novela peruana: siete estudios* (The Peruvian Novel: Seven Studies; 1977) and *La formación de la tradición literaria en el Perú* (The Formation of Literary Tradition in Peru; 1989) are key works.

Oviedo's approach to literary analysis is slightly different in that he uses structuralist theories to analyze the narrative worlds of Mario Vargas Llosa. His seminal book, *Mario Vargas Llosa: la invención de una realidad* (Mario Vargas Llosa: The Invention of Reality; 1982) deals analytically with this writer's narrative production until that date. Oviedo has also written about Ricardo Palma, Gabriel García Márquez, José Martí, Cuban poetry, and Nicaraguan literature. From a different perspective, Julio Ortega has progressively turned toward an anticipatory postmodern critical approach to analyzing Peruvian and Latin American literature. A recent study, *Crítica de identidad: la pregunta por el Perú en su literatura* (The Criticism of Identity: The Question for Peru and Its Literature; 1988) takes another look at the canonical writers since colonial times to the present from a slightly revisionist stance, relegating Mario Vargas Llosa, for instance, to a position of relative unimportance because of his apparent commercial exploitation of literature. Ortega has also produced anthologies and edited critical studies of literature in general, analyzed the works of specific writers, and written literature himself. For instance, Ortega looked at Peruvian society from interdisciplinary perspectives in *Cultura y modernización en la Lima del 900* (Culture and Modernity in Lima at The Turn of the Century; 1986) and wrote a fictionalized documentary based on the Maoist Shining Path political group in *Adiós, Ayacucho* (Goodbye, Ayacucho; 1987). In Peru, a significant group of intellectuals continue to write about Peruvian culture and literature: Ricardo González Vigil is a respected newspaper journalist who has written engaging studies on works by César Vallejo, El Inca Garcilaso, and Peruvian poetry and short story; Mirko Lauer is an interdisciplinarian in that he writes about Peruvian art (painting and Fernando de Szyszlo), politics (the Peruvian oligarchy and bourgeoisie), manifestations of regional culture (artesan activities in the Andes mountains), and literature/society: *El sitio de la literatura: escritos y política en el Perú del Siglo XX* (The Place of Literature: Writing and Politics in Peru in the Twentieth Century; 1989).

BIBLIOGRAPHY

Ballón Aguirre, Enrique. *Vallejo como paradigma*. Lima: Instituto Nacional de Cultura, 1974. A seminal study on a writer considered a crucial figure in contemporary Peruvian writing.

Cornejo Polar, Antonio. *La formación de la tradición literaria en el Perú*. Lima: Centro de Estudios y Publicaciones, 1989. A convincing sociohistorical study of the development of Peruvian literature.

Cornejo Polar, Antonio. *La novela peruana: Siete Estudios*. Lima: Editorial Horizonte, 1977. In-depth studies of seven key novels, from *Aves sin nido* to *Los geniecillos dominicales*.

Delgado, Washington. *Historia de la literatura republicana*. Lima: Rickhay Perú, 1980. Looks at the era from the perspective of the opposition between elitist and popular literatures.

Foster, David William. *Peruvian Literature. A Bibliography of Secondary Sources*. Westport, Conn.: Greenwood, 1981. An extensive, well-documented bibliography of secondary sources dealing with different literary genres.

Higgins, James. *A History of Peruvian Literature*. Liverpool, England: Francis Cairns, 1987. A panoramic yet detailed overview of Peruvian literature from pre-Columbian times to the present.

Higgins, James. *The Poet in Peru*. Liverpool: Francis Cairns, 1982. A thorough look at poetry and its development in Peru.

Losada, Alejandro. *Creación y praxis: la creación literaria como praxis social en Hispanoamérica y el Perú*. Lima: Universidad de San Marcos, 1976. Losada was Peruvian, and his general discussions on Spanish American literature are given specific application to Peru's literary production.

Mariátegui, José Carlos. *Seven Interpretive Essays on Peruvian Reality*. Austin: University of Texas Press, 1985. Considered the first Marxist analysis of Peruvian culture, this study includes an influential essay on literature.

Morris, Robert J. *The contemporary Peruvian theatre*. Lubbock: Texas Tech Press, 1977. A general survey of major figures.

Núñez, Estuardo. *La literatura peruana en el siglo XX*. México, D.F.: Pormaca,1965. A well-balanced overview of twentieth-century Peruvian literature.

Ortega, Julio. *Crítica de la identidad. La pregunta por el Perú en su literatura*. México, D.F.: Fondo de Cultura Económica, 1988. Examines Peruvian literature from a perspective of history and fiction, looking at texts by Guamán Poma de Ayala, Juan de Arona, Santos Chocano, Vallejo, Moro, Arguedas, Loayza, Vargas Llosa, and Ribeyro.

Sánchez, Luis Alberto. *La literatura peruana: derrotero para una historia cultural del Perú*. 5th ed. 5 vols. Lima: Mejía Baca, 1981. A basic, sweeping, interpretative overview of Peruvian literature from the beginnings to modern times.

Tamayo Vargas, Augusto. *Literatura peruana*. 4th ed. 2 vols. Lima: Librería Studium, 1976. Perhaps the most complete overview of Peruvian literature from its beginnings. A thorough research of sources and literary tendencies, as well as perceptive analyses of an immense number of writers and their works.

PUERTO RICO
Aníbal González
Michigan State University

I

Like many colonial and postcolonial nations, Puerto Rico has gone through massive and relatively sudden periods of cultural upheaval and revalorization in its history. Leaving aside those sociocultural transformations that occurred during the early Spanish colonial period, when the aboriginal *taino* population and its culture were virtually wiped out and when large numbers of enslaved Africans (with their own cultural manifestations and their techniques of resistance to captivity) were added to the population pool, one may discern at least four main episodes of sociocultural change in Puerto Rican history.

First, the rise of a Creole identity in the context of the policy of reinforcing Spanish political and cultural sovereignty taken towards the island in the late eighteenth century by the government of Charles III; this policy lasted until the middle of the nineteenth century. Second, the creation of an elite, Hispanicized, "new" Creole culture in the context of a conflict between the "old" Creoles and the wealthy immigrants from South America and Europe (the former were royalist refugees from the Spanish American Wars of Independence, while the latter were persons who took advantage of measures taken by the Spanish authorities to promote economic development during the early 1800s). This situation lasted until the end of the nineteenth century. Third, the cultural revalorization begun by the so-called Generation of 1930, which came as a belated aftermath to the takeover of Puerto Rico by the United States in 1898 and lasted through the change from an agrarian to an industrial economy and society in the 1950s. A fourth period is still underway, in which the idea of Puerto Rican culture generated by the 1930 intellectuals is being questioned in the context of the current postindustrial economic crisis.

The scheme proposed here is loosely based on that presented by the contemporary Puerto Rican narrator and essayist José Luis González (1926) in his influential essay, *El país de cuatro pisos* (The Four-Story Country; 1980). González's essay in turn reflects the debate that has been taking place during the past decade among Puerto Rican historians and social scientists about the historical development of Puerto Rican society. While González's "four-story" scheme is mainly concerned with the development of Puerto Rico's society and culture, it is also useful as a means of literary periodization, since it more faithfully represents the dynamics of Puerto Rico's cultural history and allows us to dispense with the usual division of Puerto Rican literary history into a sequence of foreign literary tendencies generated outside the island—Neoclassicism, Romanticism, Realism, Modernism (in its Latin American Parnassian meaning), Avant-Gardism, and so on. Needless to say, these isms also took place in Puerto Rican literary history, but they did so following the particular rhythm of Puerto Rican history and society and were often viewed with skepticism by Puerto Rican authors, who, true to their insular nature, have always been rather conservative in their adoption of foreign ideas.

II

Puerto Rican literature begins during the middle of the first period, in the early years of the nineteenth century after the arrival of the first printing press (in 1806 or 1807). Before the printing press, what literature (broadly speaking) there was in Puerto Rico consisted of a few *relaciones* (reports), chronicles, letters, municipal documents, all handwritten, of course, and a rich oral tradition that included traditional forms of Spanish poetry and folktales. To this, one might add a number of eighteenth-century travel narratives dealing with Puerto Rico that, although written by foreign visitors to the island and printed elsewhere, were incorporated by nineteenth-century writers and historians into the Puerto Rican literary tradition. The most important works of this kind are the *Memoria sobre la Isla de Puerto Rico* (Report on the Island of Puerto Rico; 1765) by Alejandro O'Reilly, *Historia geográfica, civil y política de la Isla de San Juan Bautista de Puerto Rico* (Geographic, Civil, and Political History of the Island of San Juan Bautista de Puerto Rico; 1788) by Fray Iñigo Abbad y Lasierra (1745-1813), and the *Voyage aux îles de Ténériffe, la Trinité, Saint-Thomas, Sainte-Croix, et Porto Rico* (Trip to the

Islands of Ténériffe, Trinidad, Saint Thomas, Saint Croix, and Puerto Rico; 1810) by André Pierre Ledru (1761-1825).

The arrival of the printing press coincided with the first expressions of national consciousness by the Creole elite that, in Puerto Rico as in most of Spanish America, had been slowly developing in the shadow of Spanish sovreignty. Although this elite was mainly white and slaveowning, it had common interests with a growing middle classs of free black artisans and entrepreneurs. A typical member of the white elite was the politician Ramón Power y Giralt (1775-1813), who as Puerto Rico's representative to the Spanish Parliament (*Cortes*) convened in Cádiz during the Napoleonic occupation of the peninsula, defended Creole interests vigorously as a parlamentarian.

On the other hand, a spectacular (and unusual) instance of upward mobility by a black man in eighteenth-century Puerto Rican society is the case of the mulatto privateer Miguel Henríquez (dates unknown), the shoemaker's son who by his shrewdness on land and his bravery at sea became one of the wealthiest Puerto Ricans of his time (he was resented for this, of course, and was hounded by his enemies in the government). As José Luis González reminds us, a salient characteristic of Puerto Rican demography in the late eighteenth century was the prevalence of blacks and mulattoes, a situation that the Spanish colonial authorities viewed with alarm, particularly after the events that led to Haiti's independence in 1791.

To a certain extent, the Real Cédula de Gracias (Royal Decree of Concessions) of 1815 was designed to reaffirm Spanish control over the island by fomenting the immigration of white European settlers. This was the first instance of what would become a common tactic of metropolitan governments throughout modern Puerto Rican history: the (often systematic) introduction of fresh immigrants into the island—particularly immigrants of conservative inclinations—to impede or delay the forging of a Puerto Rican national consciousness.

With the printing press came journalism, and the first tentative literary expressions of the Puerto Rican Creoles. Among the first relevant literary figures of this period is a woman, María Bibiana Benítez (1783-1873), whose poem "La ninfa de Puerto Rico" (The Nymph of Puerto Rico; 1832), was published in the government-owned *La gaceta oficial* (The Official Gazette). This text shows a mixture of Neoclassic form with Romantic ideology similar to that of the poetry being written in the already independent Spanish America of the period, like the Venezuelan Andrés Bello's *Silva a la agricultura de la zona tórrida* (Poem on Agriculture in the Torrid Zone; 1826).

In its most visible, exterior manifestations, Romanticism, in fact, did not have an enthusiastic reception in Puerto Rico during the first half of the nineteenth century. This was mainly due to the conservative aesthetic and political influence exerted by the migrants who came to the island fleeing from the newly independent territories of Santo Domingo and the Spanish American mainland. These conservative newcomers strengthened the reactionary tendencies of the Spanish colonial administration and effectively displaced most members of the Puerto Rican Creole elite from the positions of influence they had achieved during the latter half of the eighteenth century. Along with the European migrants brought by the Cédula, they also contributed to the "whitening" of Puerto Rican society. Nevertheless, the newcomers, being often wealthier and more Europeanized than the "old" Creoles they displaced, could not help acting as the source of new ideas in Puerto Rican culture. These included, willy-nilly, certain elements of Romantic ideology that had become disseminated in European culture (there was, after all, a Romantic conservatism too), like the very notion of "nationhood" or *patria* as the product of an organic fusion of a people with their natural environment.

Partly because of censorship and political repression, Puerto Rican Romanticism (like the Spanish Romanticism of José Espronceda, Ramón de Campoamor, and Gustavo Adolfo Bécquer that served as its model) tended to be formally and ideologically low-key. An outstanding exception, but one that proves this point, is the figure of the Puerto Rican revolutionary leader Ramón Emeterio Betances (1827-98). A French-educated mulatto, the few literary works he wrote were in this language: the short novels *La vierge de Borinquen* (The Virgin of Borinquen; 1859) and *Les voyages de Scaldado* (The Travels of Scaldado; 1890). *La vierge de Borinquen* in particular shows the influence of Edgar Allan Poe (whom Betances read in French translation) and Victor Hugo. However, if Betances's literary texts were not particularly distinguished as Romantic works, his rebellious life—totally committed to the abolition of slavery and the struggle for Puerto Rican independence and the Antillean Confederation—was itself Romantic to such a high degree that he could well be considered the only authentic Puerto Rican Romantic. In any case, however muted, it was under the sign of Romanticism that literary production was established in Puerto Rico and that the first great generation of Puerto Rican writers was produced. The most important of these are the *costumbrista* (local color) essayist Manuel Alonso (1822-89), the poet

José Gautier Benítez (1848-80), and the novelist, essayist, and poet Alejandro Tapia y Rivera (1826-82). Significantly, all three were of middle-class origins, either of old Creole stock or of mixed old Creole and Peninsular lineage. Alonso was by profession a physician and specialist in the treatment of mental diseases, and in his collection of essays on manners titled *El gíbaro* (The Peasant; 1849) he tried not only to draw the broad outlines of a Puerto Rican cultural identity, but also to chastise the social and cultural backwardness of his countrymen.

Gautier, grand-nephew of María Bibiana Benítez and son of Alejandrina Benítez (1819-79), who was also an important *femme de lettres* of the period, was a soldier by profession who, after being transferred to Spain in 1870, decided, because of his political liberalism and his nostalgia, to abandon the army and return to Puerto Rico in order to pursue a literary career. His poetry, although reminiscent of the late Romanticism of Bécquer in tone, was able to achieve on occasion a note of grandeur and showed a concern with formal perfection similar to that of the French Parnassians, like Théophile Gautier, to whom the Puerto Rican was not related. Several of his poems, like "A Puerto Rico (Ausencia)" (To Puerto Rico [Absence]; 1870), "A Puerto Rico (Regreso)" (To Puerto Rico [Return]; 1870), and his "Canto a Puerto Rico" (Song to Puerto Rico; 1879) have become beloved classics of Puerto Rican literature.

Finally, Tapia y Rivera is rightfully considered by most critics to be the founding father of Puerto Rican letters. An extremely prolific writer, Tapia authored eight plays, six novels, one long epic poem, *La sataniada* (The Sataniad; 1878), two biographies of Puerto Rican figures, one book of memoirs, and an anthology of verse and prose titled *El bardo de Guamaní* (The Bard of Guamaní; 1862). He also compiled the first serious collection of materials on the history of Puerto Rico in his *Biblioteca histórica* (Historical Library; 1854). Among his plays, his antislavery drama *La cuarterona* (The Quadroon; 1867) is one of his best and still bears reading today. His novel *Póstumo el transmigrado* (Posthumous the Transmigrated; 1879), about a man who discovers he is someone else's reincarnation, masks social criticism under the guise of a fantasy similar to Poe's short story "William Wilson" (1839) and Théophile Gautier's *L'Avatar* (The Avatar; 1857). A cultural animator who was also active in journalism and who helped found such important cultural institutions as the Ateneo Puertorriqueño (Puerto Rican Atheneum), Tapia was a complete intellectual, and it is difficult to single out any of his works as the key to his contribution to the dominant culture; rather, it

is the totality of his works that justifies his foundational role in Puerto
Rican culture.

The lasting impact of Alonso, Gautier, and Tapia in Puerto Rican
letters is probably due to their creation of a poetic image of Puerto Rico
and the Puerto Ricans that suited perfectly the ideological requirements
of the liberal sector of the new Creole class, composed mainly of wealthy
landowners and a small middle class of urban professionals. Gautier, for
example, contrasted in his poems the small, gentle, and serene Puerto
Rican landscape with the titanic and violent landscape of the American
continent, declaring that Puerto Rico's "moral world owes its charm/ to
the sweet influence of its exterior world." Alonso, in his sonnet titled "El
puertorriqueño" (The Puerto Rican; 1849), describes the typical Puerto
Rican as male and white, "black-bearded, pale of face,/ thin of visage,
with a well-proportioned nose," with "his soul full of illusions,/ quick-witted, free and arrogant," "Humane, affable, just, generous," and "in love
over his country, without peer." These writers' idea of Puerto Rico and
its culture was permeated by a reformist, liberal spirit (liberal in the
strict nineteenth-century political sense of the word), that sought a middle ground between the Romantic rebelliousness of a Betances and the
opressive and obscurantist dogmas of the pro-Spanish *incondicionales*
(unconditionals).

Alonso, Gautier, and Tapia were all abolitionists and believers either
in some form of autonomy for the island or at least in substantial social
and economic reforms, which would mainly benefit, of course, the new
social group to which they owed allegiance. Nevertheless, for them,
there was no question that Puerto Rico was a basically white, Hispanic
nation. For all their abolitionism, few of these writers would have accepted a Puerto Rican black as a fellow countryman, and they viewed
even the nonblack peasants who toiled in the sugar and coffee plantations as a rabble, hardly capable of understanding the meaning of nationhood.

Later in the century, still working within this common ideology,
Puerto Rican writers developed a more critical attitude, further stressing
the desire for social and political reform shown by their Romantic precursors. Authors like the great sociologist, pedagogue, and thinker Eugenio María de Hostos (1839-1903), the Realist novelist and historian Salvador Brau (1842-1912), the Naturalist novelist Manuel Zeno Gandía
(1855-1930), and the poets Lola Rodríguez de Tió (1843-1924) and Francisco Gonzalo ("Pachín") Marín (1863-96), produced trenchant analyses
of Puerto Rican history and society in works that were often overtly

anticolonial. Most of them became outright supporters of independence, and some, like Hostos, Rodríguez de Tió, and Marín, chose to live in exile and became involved in the Cuban War of Independence.

Perhaps the most typical of the end-of-the-century Puerto Rican prose writers was Manuel Zeno Gandía. A practicing physician who was also involved in journalism and politics, Zeno became the island's foremost novelist during the 1890s, and his novels *Garduña* (Marten; 1896), *La charca* (Stagnant Waters; 1894), *El negocio* (The Business Deal; 1922), and *Redentores* (Redeemers; 1925), are today regarded as Puerto Rican literary classics. Zeno is usually considered a Naturalist novelist in the vein of France's Emile Zola. Yet it is clear that Zeno viewed the Naturalist aesthetic with some skepticism, not because he deemed it too radical (as had occurred with Romanticism in the previous generation), but because he felt it was not radical enough and that it was incapable of representing Puerto Rico's colonial situation in all its chaotic complexity. His best-known work, *La charca*, portrays the exploitation of the rural proletariat in Puerto Rico's coffee plantations through the use of metaphors and devices that stress the turbulent, chaotic nature of Puerto Rico's socioeconomic system. Unlike Zola, who used mechanical and biological metaphors (that were at bottom mechanistic also) to represent and explain social processes, Zeno makes use of a system of metaphors derived from hydraulics, the branch of physics that studies liquids and their flow. Phenomena are analyzed in hydraulics through the use of probability and differential calculus, and it is therefore a less deterministic area of physics because, in dealing with the movements of molecules in a liquid state, it is necessary to allow for the operation of chance. In most of his novels, Zeno in fact seeks to produce a different brand of Naturalism, one that will avoid determinism and will afford him a better understanding of his society, which, unlike Zola's industrialized France, was an agrarian colonial system ruled by the backward, superannuated Spanish Empire. Zeno has the additional distinction of being the first Puerto Rican narrator to create a school. Inspired by his example, a group of younger novelists began writing in the Naturalist vein: Matías González García (1866-1938), José Elías Levis (1871-1942), and Ramón Juliá Marín (1878-1917).

In poetry, Francisco Gonzalo ("Pachín") Marín's verse, although not as well-wrought as that of his near-contemporary, the Parnassian poet-patriot José de Diego (1866-1918), is interesting for the influence it shows of the *Versos sencillos* (Simple Verses; 1891) of the Cuban revolutionary and precursor of *modernismo*, José Martí (see the section on

Cuba). Like many of Martí's most successful poems, Marín's verses, particularly those in his posthumously published book, *En la arena* (In the Sand; 1898), are antirhetorical in tone and tend to be concise and direct in their lyricism. Indeed, although Marín could write love lyrics as tender as Gautier's, his most characteristic poetry shows a defiant, heroic attitude that was altogether new in the Puerto Rican tradition; as Marín himself wrote, "My rough verses on the page I stamp/ like an iron brand upon a carpet."

III

With the Spanish-Cuban-American War of 1898, and the United States invasion of Puerto Rico that same year, there began a new period of cultural readjustment and revalorization. The Spanish masters were gone, replaced by the "Yankee" colonial authorities. In purely administrative, governmental matters, the change was not drastic; during the first decades of the century, American generals and civilians appointed by Washington ruled the island in much the same way as the Spanish had. But the ideological system that the Puerto Rican elite had created as it fought its political battles and wrote its texts began to suffer profound commotions. The American invasion had put an end to a brief experiment in political autonomy with which Spain had belatedly tried to contain its rebellious Caribbean colonies. It was an experiment that, for the first time, had given landowners and professionals a semblance of political power and the possibility of governing the country in a manner that suited their class interests. The invasion had also put a halt to the desperate efforts of the most radical sector of the Puerto Rican dominant class to achieve the island's independence. Drastic ideological shifts were the order of the day. While many independence leaders like Hostos and Betances remained true to their convictions and denounced Puerto Rico as either a colony of Spain or the United States, others who held key positions in the Puerto Rican conspiratorial scene at the time, like J. J. Henna and Roberto H. Todd, had always covertly wished Puerto Rico to be annexed to the United States, and they now openly proclaimed their annexationism. Those who had been autonomists under Spain were now torn between their loyalty to the "Mother Country" and the new freedoms offered by the Americans, while the pro-Spanish *incondicionales*, while lamenting the change in sovreignty, felt that, as long as their economic interests were untouched, they could live with the Americans, and many also joined the annexationist fold. It is important to note, however, that most members of the Creole intelligentsia still leaned towards autonomy or independence from the new colonial power. The Puerto Rican masses, on the other hand, comprised of a vast rural proletariat, a smaller population of urban laborers, and highly class-conscious craftsmen like the *tabaqueros* (tobacco workers), held their collective breath, not knowing whether their own centuries-old struggle for economic and social justice would be fulfilled or ignored by the Americans.

Contrary to what some Puerto Rican literary historians have claimed, literature was not lacking during this period. It is true, nevertheless, that the political crisis of the American takeover kept many members of Puerto Rico's Creole intelligentsia busy making speeches, writing newspaper articles, and generally trying to make sense of the new situation. Zeno Gandía, for example, was among those who suspended novelistic activity in order to work at convincing the Americans to grant Puerto Rico its independence; but many others continued to write and to publish. It was during the first decades of the twentieth century that Zeno's Naturalist disciples published their major novels: Levis's *Mancha de lodo* (Mud Stain; 1903), González García's *Gestación* (Gestation; 1904), and Juliá Marín's *Tierra adentro* (Inland; 1911) and *La gleba* (Clod of Earth; 1912). In these novels, which have yet to receive the critical attention they deserve, Puerto Rican narrators chronicled the social and cultural impact of the American invasion with almost journalistic immediacy.

Once again we find during this period a foreign literary movement receiving a skeptical welcome as it arrives on Puerto Rican shores. This time it was Spanish American *modernismo* (Modernism). Literary critics have always said that Modernism, like Romanticism, "arrived late" in Puerto Rico. Aside from the fact that in literature belatedness is not necessarily a handicap, the truth is that most of the major turn-of-the-century Puerto Rican writers became aware of the new literary movement almost as soon as it appeared. Zeno Gandía, for instance, though himself not a Modernist was a lifelong friend of one of the founding figures of the movement, the Cuban José Martí, whom he first met in Spain, where Zeno was studying medicine and Martí, banished from Cuba, studied law. Another example is that of the Asturias-born Puerto Rican critic Manuel Fernández Juncos (1846-1928), who corresponded during the 1890s with Modernism's most important figure, Rubén Darío (see the chapter on Nicaragua).

Like Romanticism before it, Modernism suffered a critical refraction as it entered the Puerto Rican literary scene. But this time the degree of acceptance of Modernism by Puerto Rican authors was determined less by their political conservatism or liberalism than by their vision of what Puerto Rican culture was or should be. Indeed, the American takeover's most dramatic and immediate effect on Puerto Rican intellectual life was the immense importance the island's intelligentsia suddenly gave to the very concept of culture. As we have seen, a certain notion of Puerto Rican culture had previously existed as part of the rhetorical arsenal of the Creoles under Spanish rule. But the existence of a native, autonomous Puerto Rican culture, with its attendant sense of nationhood, had rarely been invoked by the nineteenth-century intellectuals as a justification for Puerto Rico's autonomy or independence.

Instead, autonomy or independence were considered desirable, mainly because they would enable the island to escape the backwardness in which, in every sense, Spain had kept it during its long colonial rule. By and large, despite their expressions of love for their homeland, most nineteenth-century Puerto Rican intellectuals were imbued with the idea of progress, and all agreed on the essentially Hispanic character of Puerto Rican culture. They would have been mystified and shocked by the interest shown by their twentieth-century descendants in the folklore of the *jíbaro* (the Puerto Rican peasant) or, later, of the blacks. The United States' takeover changed that, however. Displaced by allpowerful masters who spoke a different tongue and had different customs and who, moreover, intended to impose their alien culture on the Puerto Ricans, the elite realized that culture would be an important factor in their dealings with the "Gentlemen from the North," as José de Diego ironically referred to the Americans. The Puerto Rican patricians also realized that culture was in fact one of the few areas of island life over which they still had some power. The cosmopolitanism and exoticism of Modernism's early stages was thus not well received by the main Puerto Rican turn-of-the-century writers, most of whom were desperately trying to produce a new, coherent model of Puerto Rican culture that would sustain their claim that Puerto Rico was a nation and not just "a bunch of people" who could be bought and sold between two empires.

By and large, the most outstanding Puerto Rican Modernists—José de Diego (1866-1918) and Luis Lloréns Torres (1878-1944) in poetry, and, in prose, Nemesio Canales (1878-1923)—had such an idiosyncratic and critical view of the movement that some critics, without questioning their importance, have denied them their status as representative Puerto Rican Modernists. Nevertheless, Diego, Lloréns, and Canales are the three major literary figures of this period, and they cannot be ignored.

Although they did their share of formal innovation in verse and prose and made frequent use of the topics and symbols of Modernist writing (swans, femmes fatales, orientalism, and the like), what these writers found most useful in Modernism was the new ideas it contained about the nature of literature and culture. A profound knowledge of the aims and methods of philology, the nineteenth-century science of language and textuality, had allowed the Spanish American Modernists to develop a notion of literature and culture as artifice, as the product of a conscious intellectual endeavor, rather than of spontaneous, natural generation. (Although, for contingent political reasons, this artificiality of culture was often still hidden beneath the Romantic myth of culture's telluric roots).

José Martí quoted in one of his chronicles these revealing words from the influential French philologist Ernest Renan: "Human history is not a chapter in Zoology. Man is a rational and moral being. Free will stands above the base influence of the *Volksgeist*. A nation is a soul, a spiritual principle created out of the past, with its life in the present, and any great assemblage of men of sound minds and generous hearts can create the moral consciousness that constitutes a nation." This idea of national culture as an artificial construct, laboriously put together by an intellectual elite, was probably Modernism's most profound legacy to Puerto Rican letters. This explains in part why, in many of their poems and prose works, the major Puerto Rican Modernists turned to the modality of *criollismo* (Creolism) in a conscious attempt to define the particularity of Puerto Rican culture and to find its adequate symbolic representation.

Lloréns Torres was a key figure in this endeavor. In the Creolist poems collected in his two main books, *Voces de la campana mayor* (Voices of the Great Bell; 1935) and *Alturas de América* (Heights of America; 1940), Lloréns outlines the principal symbol of the new concept of Puerto Rican culture: the figure of the jíbaro and his folklore. Lloréns, along with his disciple Virgilio Dávila (1869-1943), saw in the jíbaro the perfect symbolic figure for the new concept of Puerto Rican culture espoused by the Creole elite. This concept retained some qualities of the old liberal Romantic notion of Puerto Rican culture: for one thing, it was still essentially Hispanophilic. However, unlike that of the Romantics, the Hispanophilia of the Creolists, and of their intellectual heirs in the Generation of 1930, was a nostalgic gesture that needed to be reconciled with their somewhat contradictory claim that Puerto Rican culture was unique and not a mere prolongation of Spanish culture. For the Creolists and the Generation of 1930, Puerto Rican culture needed to be linked to the Hispanic past but also to be rooted in the insular landscape. The figure of the jíbaro fulfilled this harmonizing symbolic role perfectly. As codified by Lloréns, Dávila, and others, the archetypal Puerto Rican was the peasant from the mountainous coffee-growing region of the interior, the free-living, impoverished white descendant of the Spanish conquistadors, with deep roots in the land, yet also linked by his language and folklore to his Peninsular past. That this picture was hardly that of the real Puerto Rican peasant, who was often of mixed blood and subjected to the exploitative labor of the coffee and sugar plantations, did not seem to matter. It also did not seem to matter that a large sector of the Puerto Rican population is black or mulatto. What mattered was that now these writers had an apparently coherent notion of Puerto Rican culture with which to oppose the Americanization policy imposed by the United States colonial regime.

Although Lloréns was the precursor of this new concept of culture, it fell to the intellectuals of the so-called Generation of 1930 to give it solidity and intellectual legitimacy. This brilliant group of men and women, most of whom had not even been born at the time of the American invasion, produced a true Renaissance in Puerto Rican scholarship and literature and helped give new direction to Puerto Rico's stagnant political scene. Furthermore, they succeeded in forcing the abolition of obligatory English-language instruction in Puerto Rican public schools, thus assuring that Puerto Rico would remain firmly within the Spanish-speaking world. In the essays on cultural criticism of Antonio S. Pedreira (1899-1939), particularly in his polemical *Insularismo* (Insularism; 1934) and *La actualidad del jíbaro* (The Present-Day Pertinence of the Jíbaro; 1935), in the literary criticism of Margot Arce (1904) and Concha Meléndez (1895-1984), in the poetry of Francisco Manrique Cabrera (1908-78), in the novel *La llamarada* (The Fire Storm; 1935) by Enrique Laguerre (1906), in *Cuentos para fomentar el turismo* (Stories to Promote Tourism; 1946) by Emilio S. Belaval (1903-72), and *Terrazo* (Ground; 1947) by Abelardo Díaz Alfaro (1919), the notion of Puerto Rican culture as a specifically Hispanic, white, and Catholic regional offshoot of Western culture was reaffirmed.

The literary ideology within which many of these intellectuals worked was based on the irrationalist philosophy popularized by Ortega y Gasset in his *Revista de Occidente* (Journal of the West), particularly on the ideas of Oswald Spengler in his influential *The Decline of the West* (1917). Their work thus had much in common with that of many other Spanish American intellectuals of the same period who, in response to

United States dominance in hemispheric affairs as well as to the social and political changes brought to Spanish America by an increased modernization, used the conceptual apparatus of German *Lebensphilosophie* (Vitalistic Philosophy) to redefine their respective national identities: Samuel Ramos and José Vasconcelos in Mexico, Fernando Ortiz and Jorge Mañach in Cuba, and Ezequiel Martínez Estrada in Argentina (see the pertinent national sections).

Not surprisingly, however, the most Spenglerian of the Generation of 1930 was also their foremost dissident, the poet Luis Palés Matos (1898-1959). Of all the Puerto Rican intellectuals of his generation, Palés was the one most closely attuned to the neoprimitivistic vogue in Western avant-garde art during the twenties and thirties. His reading of Spengler, whom the poet Juan Antonio Corretjer (1908-85), in a 1936 article, called "the intellectual apostle of the black man's emergence into the European artistic hemisphere," led him to espouse a broader, anthropologically oriented notion of culture not limited to the products of the elite (as many other members of the 1930s movement still believed), and consequently to point out the importance of the black contribution to the Puerto Rican ethos. In his book of Afro-Antillean poems, *Tuntún de pasa y grifería* (1937), Palés implicitly debated the view of Puerto Rican culture held by most of the island's intellectuals at that time. For Palés, as for important Cuban and other Caribbean cultural figures, Antillean culture as a whole was a mulatto culture, the product of the synthesis of European and African racial and cultural elements on the soil of the Antilles.

Palés's poems, although immensely popular, gave rise to an acrimonious debate within Puerto Rican intellectual community. In various essays, the poets J. I. de Diego Padró (1896-1974), Luis Antonio Miranda (1896-1975), and Graciany Miranda Archilla (1910) furiously attacked Palés's Afro-Antilleanism. Palés defended his views with vigor and clarity in various essays and interviews. In a 1932 article, he stated: "We in the Antilles . . . should take Lloréns Torres and the Cuban poets [Nicolás] Guillén and [Emilio] Ballagas as our point of departure. These poets, each in their own way, have raised the ideal framework for a typically Antillean poetry and are directing our verse towards its logical and natural channel. Lloréns, however, confines himself to portraying the jíbaro, the peasant of pure Spanish blood who has adapted himself to the tropics, and avoids the other racial nucleus that has so nobly intermingled with us and that because of its fecundity, its strength and its lively nature has impressed unmistakable characteristics into our psychology, giving it, precisely, its true Antillean character. I am referring to the blacks. An Antillean poetry that excludes this powerful element seems to me to be almost impossible." Despite some deficiencies (he has been accused, like other advocates of Negrism, of caricaturing blacks and of simplifying a very complex social and ethnic situation), Palés's position on the question of Puerto Rican culture was the most advanced and radical of any of the island's intellectuals at the time—so radical, in fact, that it was not accepted by the vast majority of Puerto Rican intellectuals, many of whom saw Palés's criticism of Puerto Rican racism as politically divisive.

One of the few 1930s writers who sided with Palés, Tomás Blanco (1897-1975), also helped to weaken the impact of his ideas with his soothing tract, *El prejuicio racial en Puerto Rico* (Racial Prejudice in Puerto Rico; 1942). Blanco, against all historical evidence, claims that racial prejudice is nonexistent in Puerto Rican society and that whatever racial prejudice exists is mostly due to United States influence. A brilliant essayist in his own right, as is shown by his *Prontuario histórico de Puerto Rico* (Historical Summary of Puerto Rico; 1935), written in reply to Pedreira's *Insularismo*, Blanco nevertheless helped to perpetuate the Creolist myth of the jíbaro as the cornerstone of Puerto Rican society and culture. This myth would not begin to fall apart until the late sixties and early seventies, when the socioeconomic order produced by the Popular Democratic Party in the forties and fifties assumed crisis proportions.

IV

As might be expected, the Puerto Rican avant-garde movements of the twenties and thirties were, like Puerto Rican Modernism, subdued in terms of formal innovation, although ideologically up-to-date. Moreover, the avant-garde ideas about art and society that had begun to reach Puerto Rico at that time produced more than just Palés's Afro-Antilleanism. The poet Evaristo Ribera Chevremont (1896-1976), whom one might call the Puerto Rican "impresario of the avant-garde" (as Roger Shattuck called Apollinaire), had brought from his stay in Spain during the early 1920s the free verse forms and socially concerned poetry. Although Chevremont soon moved away from avant-gardism and social poetry, these concerns were taken up by another major poet, Corretjer. Politically radical from his youth, Corretjer blended Creolism with avant-garde poetic forms and deeply felt social and political concerns to create what has been called a Neocreolist poetry. Corretjer saw himself as an heir to the combative tradition of Pachín Marín; in his main poetic works—*Agüeybana* (1932), *Amor de Puerto Rico* (Love of Puerto Rico; 1937), *El leñero* (The Wood Seller; 1944), and *Alabanza en la Torre de Ciales* (Praise in the Tower of Ciales; 1953)—the jíbaros are portrayed in a less idealized fashion than in other works of the period. They are seen not so much as symbols of Puerto Rican nationhood as concrete, historical men and women, members of an exploited rural proletariat. After his political initiation in the socially conservative Nationalist Party of Pedro Albizu Campos (1893-1965), Corretjer moved closer to Marxist ideas and began to rethink the question of Puerto Rican culture in those terms. Nevertheless, his ideas, developed during his frequent stays in prison and disseminated in newspaper articles and in verses, did not begin to have an impact until the mid-1970s.

The avant-garde also stimulated the rise of numerous women poets, the most outstanding of whom are Julia de Burgos (1914-53) and Clara Lair (1895-1974). The works of these poets, particularly Burgos's *Poemas en veinte surcos* (Poems in Twenty Furrows; 1938) and *El mar y tú y otros poemas* (The Sea and You and Other Poems; 1958), and Lair's *Arras de cristal* (Promises Made of Glass; 1937), helped to undermine the male-oriented aspects of the 1930s vision of culture and broadened the range of Puerto Rican literary expression to include the feminine experience. Burgos in particular is recognized not only as a great poet, but also as a forerunner of contemporary Puerto Rican feminism.

In prose narrative, the authors of the 1930s movement generally avoided avant-gardist experimentation, writing novels and short stories that usually dealt with rural themes and followed the conventions of literary "realism." In the works of Laguerre, Belaval, and Díaz Alfaro, for example, the jíbaro, seen as the archetypal Puerto Rican, is portrayed as an embattled, tragic figure who transcends his misery by means of his perennial stoicism and occasional quick-wittedness (jibería). However, in the years following the Second World War, and partly as a consequence of the dramatic socioeconomic changes that occurred in the island in the postwar years, a younger generation of writers arose that brought avant-garde forms and an urban thematics to Puerto Rican narrative prose. Some literary histories, following Ortega y Gasset's generational scheme, refer to it as the Generation of 1945, but Corretjer characterized it better when, in one of his articles, he named it the Desperate Generation. Its most prominent figures in the area of prose narrative are José Luis González, René Marqués (1919-79), Pedro Juan Soto (1928), José Luis Vivas Maldonado (1926), and Emilio Díaz Valcárcel (1929).

The reasons for Corretjer's designation become clear if one looks at Puerto Rican history during this period. The thirties, forties, and early fifties saw the rise of a widespread and influential nationalist movement in Puerto Rico that found its political expression in the Nationalist Party headed by Pedro Albizu Campos and its subsequent repression by the American colonial authorities. The social reformism of the Roosevelt administration in Washington during the Depression, along with the Americans' renewed realization of Puerto Rico's strategic importance during the Second World War, caused American influence to be exerted on Puerto Rican society during those years as never before, and in different ways.

To begin with, the Nationalists were persecuted and their leaders incarcerated. New military and naval installations on the island were established, and existing ones were enlarged. A group of reformist politicians from the Creole elite, headed by a minor poet and astute politician, Luis Muñoz Marín (1898-1980), was encouraged by the Washington government to form a new political party (the Popular Democratic Party: PPD) and to launch a populist movement that, significantly, took the silhouette of a jíbaro as its symbol and promised the peasants "Pan, Tierra, Libertad" (Bread, Land, Freedom). Eventually, the PPD was to become the main force in Puerto Rican politics, and Muñoz the first Puerto Rican governor elected by his own people. As a further concession, the American government, feeling the pressure of the burgeoning postwar anticolonialist movements around the world, ratified the political formula of the Estado Libre Asociado (Free Associated State, misleadingly called Commonwealth in English-language documents) proposed by the PPD for Puerto Rico. Under this formula, Puerto Rico was granted a degree of autonomous government, although it still does not possess international political sovreignty and numerous agencies of the U.S. government—including the Postal Service, Army, Navy, and FBI—continue to operate in the island.

In addition, shortly before the establishment of the Estado Libre Asociado, the PPD-controlled government had begun a crash industrialization program, code named Project Bootstrap, aimed at changing Puerto Rico from a predominantly agrarian, sugar-producing country into an industrial one, a sort of Caribbean Hong Kong. Soon after, the large-scale emigration of Puerto Ricans to New York was encouraged by the government as a safety valve for the problems of rural unemployment and urban overcrowding caused by Project Bootstrap. The intellectuals of the 1940s, all of whom were nationalists of one sort or another, saw the fortunes of nationalism wax and wane, and saw the Creolist rhetoric regarding the jíbaro and the Hispanic essence of Puerto Rican nationality appropriated and diluted by the PPD-dominated government. If one adds to this the impact of McCarthyism in Puerto Rican politics of the fifties, it is not surprising that these writers grew "desperate."

José Luis González was the precursor, with his book of short stories, *El hombre en la calle* (The Man in the Street; 1948). In it, he spearheaded the return of Puerto Rican narrative to the urban thematics previously cultivated by the nineteenth-century Naturalist novel, but making use of the avant-garde narrative techniques (flashbacks, stream-of-consciousness, multiple narrators) gleaned from readings of English-language authors such as Joyce, Faulkner, and Dos Passos. Needless to say, because of his commitment to social realism, González's narrative avant-gardism is very moderate; he is by no means a Puerto Rican James Joyce. In any case, González's characters were no longer jíbaros but, rather, working-class men and women caught between their impoverished rural origins and the demands of urban, industrialized life in San Juan or New York. González had been active both in literature and in politics at an early age: at seventeen, he had already published a book of short stories, *En la sombra* (In the Shadow; 1943), and he was among the founders of the Puerto Rican Communist Party. Although González's initial impact on Puerto Rican narrative was great, his influence in the Puerto Rican literary scene was diminished by his expatriation from the island during the 1950s due to McCarthyist persecution (he now resides in Mexico and is a Mexican citizen), and his contributions were soon overshadowed by those of René Marqués.

Descended from a wealthy landowning family, Marqués studied agronomy, but he soon became more interested in literature. During the 1950s, the flamboyant and charismatic playwright, essayist, and narrator was a perennial first-prize winner at the annual Ateneo Puertorriqueño short story competition and the most visible of the angry young men of the Desperate Generation. With plays like *La carreta* (*The Oxcart*; 1952), which dealt with the rural exodus produced by Project Bootstrap, short story collections like *Otro día nuestro* (Another of Our Days; 1955) and *En una ciudad llamada San Juan* (In a City Called San Juan; 1960), and novels like *La víspera del hombre* (Eve of Man; 1959), Marqués raised the technical standards of each of those genres and set the tone for much of the prose writing of his generation. The tone of that writing was generally one of existential anguish and profound anxiety, permeated by a nostalgia for the vanishing (and idealized) rural way of life. Invoking the works of existentialist thinkers from Unamuno to Heidegger and Sartre, Marqués produced a violent and tragic vision of Puerto Rican culture that owed much to that produced by the 1930s writers. Although the jíbaro was no longer a central symbol in this notion of culture, he remained in the background as a nostalgic emblem of the basic Puerto Rican values being eroded by the industrialization and militarization of the island, values that were still considered to be purely Hispanic. The main departure in the new concept of culture developed by Marqués and the other writers of his generation was, above all, its anguished groping for new values, for a stable foundation on which to (re)build Puerto Rican culture at a time when the island's economy and society were undergoing drastic changes.

Not surprisingly, their obsession with existential questions led some writers of the Desperate Generation to cultivate the theater with an abundance and intensity never before seen in Puerto Rican literary history. The groundwork for the theatrical renaissance of the forties and fifties had been laid, as with the other literary genres, by the Generation of 1930. As actor, director, and playwright, Emilio S. Belaval was a key figure in the theater of the thirties, although many of his major plays were published much later during the fifties: *La muerte* (Death; 1953), *La Hacienda de los Cuatro Vientos* (Four Winds Farm; 1959), and *La vida* (Life; 1959). Other important thirties playwrights were Manuel Méndez Ballester (1909), who wrote realist plays about the exploitation of the peasantry like *El clamor de los surcos* (Plaint of the Furrows; 1938) and *Tiempo muerto* (Idle Time; 1940); Fernando Sierra Berdecía (1903-62), whose play *Esta noche juega el joker* (The Joker Plays Tonight; 1938) is among the first literary works dealing with Puerto Ricans in New York; and Luis Rechani Agrait (1902), who specialized in political satires like *Mi señoría* (My Lordship; 1940).

But it is in the late forties and fifties that Puerto Rican theater attains maturity with technically innovative and ideologically profound plays like *María Soledad* (1947), *Vejigantes* (Mummers; 1958), and *Sirena* (Mermaid; 1959) by Francisco Arriví (1915); and *La carreta, La muerte no entrará en Palacio* (Death Shall not Enter the Palace; 1959), and *Los soles truncos* (*The House on Cristo Street*; 1958) by René Marqués. During the late fifties, the Institute of Puerto Rican Culture began sponsoring a yearly theater festival in which these plays were showcased, along with newer productions by authors like Gerard Paul Marín (1922), Luis Rafael Sánchez (1936), Myrna Casas (1934), and Jaime Carrero (1931). Gradually, during the sixties and seventies, Puerto Rican theater moved away from the existential thematics of the Desparate Generation towards a broader sort of social and cultural criticism. This was embodied in plays that were often highly experimental like Sánchez's *Los ángeles se han fatigado* (The Angeles Are Weary; 1960), *La pasión según Antígona Pérez* (The Passion According to Antígona Pérez; 1968), and his recent *Quíntuples* (Quintuplets; 1985); and Carrero's *Pipo Subway no sabe reír* (Pipo Subway Doesn't Know How to Laugh; 1971), *La caja de caudales FM* (The FM Safe; 1979), and *El Lucky Seven* (Lucky Seven; 1979). Thematically, many of Carrero's plays deal with the lives and problems of Neoricans, Americans of Puerto Rican descent, and particularly with the question of the existence of a separate Neorican cultural identity. Some of Carrero's plays were originally written in English, thus straddling the linguistic barrier that traditionally separates Neorican literature from that of the "Island."

Indeed, the inclusion of Neorican literature as part of Puerto Rican literature as a whole is a topic that began to be debated in the early sixties and is still to be fully resolved. Most Puerto Rican critics from the "Island" would argue that the language used by a writer determines literary tradition, and since most Neorican writers write in Enlgish, their work belongs to the United States literary tradition.

V

By the late 1960s, it became clear that the 1930s notion of Puerto Rican culture, which still lived on in school curricula and in some political rhetoric, and the remodeled version of it proposed by Marqués and the writers of his generation, were both completely useless as instruments for the critical analysis and truthful representation of Puerto Rican reality. They had always been useless for that purpose, of course, since their original function had been basically defensive: they had been ideological bastions erected by intellectuals from the Creole elite to guard against American cultural penetration on the one hand, and against the burgeoning, unruly forces of Puerto Rican popular culture on the other. During the 1960s, however, a series of circumstances occurred that allowed the rise of a more open and critical view of Puerto Rican culture. To mention just a few: outside Puerto Rico there were political events like the

Cuban Revolution, with its turn towards socialism in the early sixties, and the widespread protests against the Vietnam War and the draft; in the cultural sphere, there was the worldwide malaise expressed in the sixties youth rebellion on the one hand, and on the other the growing prominence of Spanish American narrative in the so-called boom of Spanish American fiction. Locally, political events like the succession crisis of 1967-68, when Luis Muñoz Marín stepped down as governor of Puerto Rico only to see his party, the PPD, lose its first elections in a quarter-century, were also significant. One can also point to the increased social mobility produced in Puerto Rico by the transition to an industrialized society, along with the failure of Project Bootstrap to provide a solid economic foundation for the island's future development. These and similar factors helped to foment a profound critical consciousness in Puerto Rican intellectuals and artists. The only precedent for this in Puerto Rican intellectual history would be the radical abolitionism and anticolonialism of the late Romantics. Nevertheless, the implications of the contemporary Puerto Rican critical consciousness are more far-reaching, since they not only concern politics but also representation, in the broadest sense of the term.

Not surprisingly, the rebirth of the critical spirit in Puerto Rican intellectual endeavors has favored the development of essayistic and narrative prose. The most influential Puerto Rican writers to arise during the late sixties and early seventies are short story writers and novelists like Luis Rafael Sánchez, Edgardo Rodríguez Juliá, Ana Lydia Vega (1946), Rosario Ferré (1938), and Manuel Ramos Otero (1948), among others. Also influential have been some older authors who have turned to the essay in recent years, like González and Corretjer, the importance of whose journalistic and essayistic work was only recently recognized. Poetry has not had as great an impact on current Puerto Rican literature, despite the collective merit of the poets clustered around the journals *Guajana* (1962-77)—Andrés Castro Ríos (1942), Vicente Rodríguez Nietzsche (1942), José Manuel Torres Santiago (1940), Edwin Reyes (1944), and Antonio Cabán Vale (1942)—and *Mester* (1967-70)—Salvador López González (1937), Jorge María Ruscalleda Bercedóniz (1944), Iván Silén (1944), and Carmelo Rodríguez Torres (1941).

The leader, or *adelantado* (scout), as the critic Josemilio González (1918) called him, of the new Puerto Rican literature is without a doubt Luis Rafael Sánchez. In his only book of short stories so far, *En cuerpo de camisa* (In Casual Dress; 1966) and in his best-selling novel, *La guaracha del Macho Camacho* (*Macho Camacho's Beat*; 1976), Sánchez brought into Puerto Rican writing the semiotic sophistication of the best contemporary Spanish American narrative, along with an irreverent sense of humor that intensifies the critical nature of his texts. From a thematic point of view, it would seem that Sánchez has merely sought to renew the old Palesian notion of Puerto Rican culture as a mulatto culture, since many of his characters are black or mulatto, and they openly exhibit common Puerto Rican attitudes about race and social class. Certainly there is in Sánchez's work a willingness to confront issues of race discrimination and class conflict that were rarely addressed directly in previous Puerto Rican narratives and essays. Nevertheless, in his texts Sánchez goes beyond Palés towards a critique of the very notion of culture and its use as the basis for a discourse about Puerto Rico and its people. Sánchez has been the first Puerto Rican writer (since Zeno Gandía, perhaps) to bring the question of Puerto Rican culture within a representational problematics; in other words, to deal not so much with what Puerto Rican culture *is* but with the metaphors and symbolic systems that are used to represent it and, in a sense, to create it.

La guaracha del Macho Camacho offers a new approach to the problematics of Puerto Rican culture, one which takes information theory as its point of departure and performs a critical, even parodic, reading of Palés's theory of culture. *Tuntún de pasa y grifería*, along with Zeno's *La charca*, is one of the many classics of Puerto Rican literature that are reinscribed in a parodic key within Sánchez's text. However, if in *Tuntún* Palés presented a triumphant and utopian view of Caribbean culture as the harmonious fusion of diverse races and cultures, *La guaracha*'s more critical view presents Puerto Rican culture as an utterly fragmented entity, torn apart not by natural forces but by class struggles and by the systematic interference of the American-controlled mass media and their attendant consumer society. *La guaracha* abounds in metaphors taken from the world of radio and television, and a key metaphor in it is the concept of "interference" or "static" itself. Puerto Rican culture is metaphorizred in Sánchez's novel as a cacophony of mutually interfering radio and TV emissions, which, like the "snow" on a TV screen, "freeze" Puerto Rican culture into a fragmented muddle. Palés's allegorical figure for the underlying harmony of Caribbean culture, the "Mulata-Antilla," reappears in Sánchez's text as the TV singer and dancer Iris Chacón, whose frantic rhythms seem to tear her apart like a sugar mill out of control. Instead of Palés's Spenglerian vitalism, in which the reproductive fecundity of the Mulata-Antilla guarantees the continued existence of Caribbean culture, Sánchez's novel takes place in an atmosphere of crisis, where reproduction is overwhelmed by dissemination, vitalism is submerged by the death principle, synthesis is an illusion, and criticism becomes Puerto Rican culture's last line of defense. Despite *La guaracha*'s pessimistic view, the dazzling clarity with which Sánchez was able to define the problematics of culture in Puerto Rico today and his vigorous and effective defense of the value of modern literature as the most critical and radically honest form of representation, because it does not attempt to present itself as the truth, allowed other contemporary Puerto Rican writers to engage more freely and forcefully in the critical analysis of Puerto Rican culture.

The two most brilliant contemporary writers to have appeared in Sánchez's wake are Ana Lydia Vega and Edgardo Rodríguez Juliá. In her recent book of short stories, *Encancaranublado* (Overcast Sky; 1983), Vega explores the Caribbean dimension of the problematics of culture defined by Sánchez, a dimension only implied in *La guaracha*. The stories in *Encancaranublado* deal with events and characters from all over the Caribbean region; Haitians, Cubans, Dominicans, Puerto Ricans, as well as people from the Lesser Antilles, appear in these stories in ways reminiscent of Palés's Afro-Antillean poetry. As in *Tuntún*, many of Vega's characters are black or mulatto, and they are sometimes very close to becoming stereotypes. Indeed, another Palesian trait in *Encancaranublado* is Vega's overt recourse to allegory and parable in order to represent, in a condensed manner, topics and problems that would require volumes of detailed discussion. This is particularly true of the title story, "Encancaranublado," a tale of three castaways, one Haitian, one Dominican, one Cuban, who wind up in the same boat on the high seas and who are picked up by an American Navy ship where all the menial labor is done by Puerto Ricans, as well as in "Puerto Rican Syndrome" and "Historia de arroz con habichuelas" (History of Rice with Beans). Allegory in Vega's short stories is not only a sort of narrative shorthand, however, but, as in Palés's "Mulata-Antilla" poem, it becomes the basis for a utopian vision of the reconciliation of opposites, a plea for consensus.

In contrast, Rodríguez Juliá's remarkable testimonial narrative, *El entierro de Cortijo* (Cortijo's Burial; 1983) seeks to go beyond *La guaracha*'s "textual" approach to Puerto Rican culture and Vega's allegorical and utopian visions in order to seek out the empirical reality that underlies the fictions of Sánchez and Vega. Thus, instead of dealing with a fictional musician like Macho Camacho, Rodríguez Juliá will speak about the historic Rafael Cortijo; instead of alluding to abstract and occasionally nameless characters as Vega does, he will speak of recognizable present-day people like the *salsa* (literally, "sauce") musicians Cheo Feliciano and Maelo Rivera. Taking journalistic discourse as his model, Rodríguez Juliá chronicles a brief but hopefully revealing moment in the life of a certain sector of Puerto Rican society: the burial of Cortijo by the black and mulatto population of the northeastern outskirts of San Juan, of Villa Palmeras and the Lloréns Torres housing project. In an earlier book, *Las tribulaciones de Jonás* (Jonas's Tribulations; 1981), Rodríguez Juliá had taken as his point of departure a similar event, but one that affected a larger sector of Puerto Rican society: the burial of Luis Muñoz Marín.

True to *El entierro de Cortijo*'s testimonial and journalistic impulse, the narrator becomes a roving eye and ear, taking in all the disparated incidents that occurred on that sweltering afternoon when the precursor of salsa music was buried. The narrative flows and meanders asystematically, in a sort of Brownian motion, trying to attune itself to the rhythm of the events described. But *Cortijo* is more than an exercise in jounalistic reporting. Throughout the book, the narrator, who is identified as Rodríguez Juliá himself, inserts his own reflections, opinions, theories, and even fictions, into his discourse. Belying its claims to orality, Rodríguez Juliá's book is full of textual reminiscences, not only of the poetry of Palés Matos but also of the old eighteenth- and nineteenth-century essays on manners, by means of which authors as diverse as Joseph Addison, Honoré de Balzac, Mariano José de Larra, and, in Puerto Rico, Manuel Alonso, aimed to produce a physiognomy of national culture, a coherent, organic model of nationhood. Frequently, Rodríguez Juliá describes in his book the persons he sees as folk prototypes, with precise details of speech, dress, and behavior that serve to place that person within a broader social structure. But these are simply gestures, traces of an earlier way of conceiving culture. The idea of culture that underlies *Cortijo* is a far more sophisticated one. Rodríguez Juliá's vision of Puerto Rican culture is very close to Sánchez's; here, once again, Puerto Rican culture is viewed as a jumble of conflicting and contradictory gestures that interfere with each other and rarely allow order to emerge from the chaos of opposing viewpoints. Significantly, in both *La guaracha* and *Cortijo* we find the metaphor of Puerto Rican culture as a slow, almost chaotic procession: the monumental traffic jam in *La guaracha* and the disorganized funeral cortege in *Cortijo*. In *La guaracha*, social and cultural chaos arises not only from the perturbing noises of the mass media, but also from the absence of a figure of paternal (or even maternal) authority able to produce a new order out of chaos. The graffiti Senator Reynosa reads in *La guaracha* proclaiming that "Muñoz is coming, repent!" only underscore the absence of the father figure: *La guaracha* was written while Muñoz Marín was still alive, but living in Italy in a sort of self-imposed exile. What Rodríguez Juliá presents in *Cortijo* (as he did in *Jonás*) is the moment of transition itself, the moment of loss, when the patriarch dies with no one to take his place. In the ensuing disorder, History assumes the form of a funeral cortege, a slow and painful procession towards an open grave. Ultimately, Rodríguez Juliá's attempt to ground his thoughts about Puerto Rican culture on an empirical, although asystematic, basis leads him to dissolve the very notion of culture as an organic, intelligible system: Cortijo's death is also the death of authority and of the author. As the young people who attend the funeral dance a *guaguancó* in front of Cortijo's grave, an orgiastic, dyonysian disorder seems to be taking over in literature as in the real world.

Another dimension of the problematics of culture in Puerto Rico is explored in the fiction of Rosario Ferré. Although less spectacular than the work of Sánchez, Vega, and Rodríguez Juliá, Ferré's short stories and novelettes, collected in *Papeles de Pandora* (Pandora's Papers; 1976) and in her recent *Maldito amor* (Accursed Love; 1986), have consistently and tellingly explored the role of women in the Puerto Rican ethos. In short stories like "La muñeca menor" (The Youngest Doll), "La bella durmiente" (Sleeping Beauty), and "Cuando las mujeres quieren a los hombres" (When Women Love Men) from *Papeles de Pandora*, Ferré criticizes the feminine stereotypes common in Puerto Rican culture and points out their roots in the class system. *Papeles de Pandora* is the first successful attempt at writing fiction in Puerto Rico from a feminine, if not feminist, viewpoint, and it has served as a model for futher experiments in feminist fiction, like *Vírgenes y mártires* (Virgins and Martyrs; 1981), a book of short stories by Ana Lydia Vega and Carmen Lugo Filippi (1940).

If criticism indeed thrives on crisis, then, in view of the island's current economic slump and explosive social situation, Puerto Rican literature will probably continue being profoundly critical and self-critical, and will continue to increase in quantity and quality. This was recently confirmed with the publication of Luis Rafael Sánchez's long-awaited second novel, *La importancia de llamarse Daniel Santos* (The Importance of Being Named Daniel Santos; 1989). In a bid to reach a broader Latin American readership, this novel deals with the life and times of the Puerto Rican pop singer Daniel Santos, whose fifty-year-long artistic career spanned virtually all the Americas, from New York and Havana to Mexico City and Lima. It also contains a strong essayistic element, in which Sánchez reflects on the relation between mass culture, society, and literature in Latin America. In a similar cosmopolitan vein, Ana Lydia Vega's most recent book of short stories, *Pasión de historia* (A Passion for History; 1987), whose title story won the prestigious Juan Rulfo International Short Story Award in Paris in 1984, uses the format of the detective story and the film noir to explore some of Vega's favorite topics: Caribbean and Puerto Rican identity, feminism, and pop culture. And Edgard Rodríguez Juliá has cemented his reputation as one of the most productive, ambitious, and talented of the new Puerto Rican narrators with the publication of his massive novel set in an imaginary eighteenth-century Puerto Rico, *La noche oscura del Niño Avilés* (The Dark Night of the Child Avilés; 1984), as well as with two further collections of his documentary narratives: *Una noche con Iris Chacón* (A Night With Iris Chacón; 1986) and *El cruce de la habia de Guánica* (Crossing Guánica Bay; 1989). English and French translations of Sánchez's *Daniel Santos* are currently being prepared, an event that should give these works a further international resonance.

Not since the 1930s has Puerto Rican literature seen such a vigorous and youthful literary endeavor. Unlike their precursors in the 1930s, however, with their self-absorbed preoccupation about Puerto Rico's national identity, contemporary Puerto Rican writers have sought greater contacts with their counterparts in the rest of the Spanish-speaking world. In this, they have benefitted from the increased internationalization of today's Spanish American literature as a whole, and, for the first time in decades, they are being received and recognized as equals by their colleagues in the world literary scene. Furthermore, although the principal strength of Puerto Rican literature at the present time is concentrated in the short story and the novel, poetry and literary criticism are not far behind, and it is to be expected that the next decades will see a flowering of these two genres as well.

VI

To conclude this summary of Puerto Rican literature, mention should be made of the key role played by literary magazines in Puerto Rican literary history. From the "ladies' journals" of the nineteenth century, like Tapia y Rivera's *La azucena* (White Lily; 1870-71, 1874-77) to Luis

Lloréns Torres's *Revista de las Antillas* (Antillean Review; 1913-15), Antonio S. Pedreira's *Indice* (Index; 1929-31), and Ferré's *Zona de carga y descarga* (Loading and Unloading Zone; 1972-75), to mention some of the most outstanding, Puerto Rican literary magazines have fulfilled the vital function of keeping channels of communication alive, not only among Puerto Rican intellectuals, but also between Puerto Rico and the rest of the world. Special mention must go to the two journals sponsored and edited by Nilita Vientós (1908). First *Asomante* (Dawning; 1945-70) and then *Sin nombre* (Nameless; 1970-85) constitute the longest-lived journals in Puerto Rican literary history. They have been the principal instruments in the fight of Puerto Rican writers against the island's cultural isolation, particularly from the rest of Spanish America, abetted by the United States and the Puerto Rican annexationists. In spite of Puerto Rico's lack of political sovreignty and a juridically recognized international status, Puerto Rican artists and intellectuals have valiantly, and, in general, successfully, struggled to keep their country within the Hispanic orb and to represent it, in the semiotic as well as the political sense of the term, before the other nations of the world, as they will probably continue to do long after Puerto Rico's vexing "status question" is finally resolved.

BIBLIOGRAPHY

Babín, María Teresa. *The Puerto Ricans' Spirit: Their History, Life and Culture*. New York: Macmillan, 1979. A translation of Babín's 1959 *Panorama de la cultura puertorriqueña*. Although its focus goes beyond literature, it is the closest thing in English to a history of Puerto Rican literature.

Babín, María Teresa, and Stan Steiner, eds. *Borinquen. An Anthology of Puerto Rican Literature*. New York: Vintage Books, 1974. The most widely available English reference on Puerto Rican literature. Contains a broad selection of translations from Puerto Rican writers up to the 1960s, with introductions and an informative general prologue.

Cabrera, Francisco Manrique. *Historia de la literatura puertorriqueña*. Río Piedras: Editorial Cultural, 1979. First published in 1956, Manrique's history has already been superseded by newer literary histories such as González's and Rivera de Alvarez's (see below). Nevertheless, it is an important work in the history of Puerto Rican literary criticism, since many of the later literary histories have been written in reply to its now-dated 1930s interpretation of Puerto Rican culture.

Foster, David William. *Puerto Rican Literature: a Bibliography of Secondary Sources*. Westport, Conn.: Greenwood Press, 1982. A comprehensive registry of general references, references on special topics, and critical books and essays on specific authors.

González, José Luis. *Literatura y sociedad en Puerto Rico*. México, D.F.: Fondo de Cultura Económica, 1976. González's compelling revisionary interpretation of Puerto Rican literature up to the late nineteenth century from a Marxist-influenced perspective.

González, José Luis. *El país de cuatro pisos y otros ensayos*. Río Piedras: Ediciones Huracán, 1980. Contains influential essays on the relationship between literature and Puerto Rican national identity.

González, Josemilio. *La poesía contemporánea de Puerto Rico (1930-1960)*. San Juan: Instituto de Cultura Puertorriqueña, 1972. A history of contemporary Puerto Rican poetry, up to the 1960s.

Morfi, Angelina. *Historia crítica de un siglo de teatro puertorriqueño*. San Juan: Instituto de Cultura Puertorriqueña, 1980. A comprehensive history of Puerto Rican theater.

Phillips, Jordan B. *Contemporary Puerto Rican Drama*. New York: Plaza Mayor, 1972. A good general introduction in English.

Quiles de la Luz, Lilian. *El cuento en la literatura puertorriqueña*. Río Piedras: Editorial de la Universidad de Puerto Rico, 1968. A history of the Puerto Rican short story.

Rivera de Alvarez, Josefina. *Literatura puertorriqueña: su proceso en el tiempo*. Madrid: Ediciones Partenón, 1983. By far the most complete and up-to-date Puerto Rican literary history available, it includes the very young contemporary authors of the so-called Generation of 1975. While it suffers from a good deal of critical impressionism, its erudition is impeccable and detailed, and Rivera de Alvarez provides readers with abundant information even about minor writers. Rivera de Alvarez is also the author of the indispensable two-volume *Diccionario de la literatura puertorriqueña* (1967).

EL SALVADOR
Paul W. Borgeson, Jr.
University of Illinois

I

If a country's literary and cultural evolution can be determined by its socioeconomic and political circumstances, that country is El Salvador; and if a nation may be periodically so plunged into the morass of repression, rigidly heirarchical social structures (read "strictures"), and political violence as to all but paralyze literary creativity, again El Salvador would be the case to examine. El Salvador's cultural situation is exceptionally acute: whereas countries like Mexico, Peru, and others have suffered similar problems and still produced strong literatures, in El Salvador circumstances have conspired to limit the ability to produce literature of aesthetic merit and penetrating content.

El Salvador possesses a people largely homogeneous in racial and cultural heritage, highly unified geographically and in their nationalistic feelings, and recognized as hard-working and selfless. In this small country, densely populated, seriously overfarmed, and with overriding social problems, literature has been, all too often, an escape from national life: a false and dangerous refuge in the picturesquely romanticized countryside and the unrecognizably idealized *campesino* (rural farmer). And in more recent decades, political activism has been the preferred route to social change: for many, literature has proven too slow, too easily manipulated, and too indirect to deal with the ongoing emergency.

Constants in the literary ambience of El Salvador include the absence of strong and open publishing houses; exceptionally limited (and even less circulated) press runs; frequent censorship, voluntary and imposed, pre- and postpublication alike; literature of and from exile, often not available at all at home; an educational system whose lack of basic texts, insistence on rote learning, and traces of social classism restrict the number of people able to partake of literature; lack of an internal (much less external) market for writers and their consequent dependence on a full-time profession (an obvious vulnerability); the very real danger to the committed artist; control of the media by the classical triumvirate of oligarchy, military, and (less, it would seem, today) church. In short, the very existence today of a Salvadoran literature of merit, and especially of one that serves society by challenging it, is a moving testimony to the spirit of resistance and the individual tenacity of the Salvadoran people.

II

That of El Salvador is among the latest literatures to emerge in Latin America. Like the rest of Central America (save Guatemala), El Salvador possesses only the faintest vestiges of pre-Columbian literature. Secondly, what today is El Salvador was, during the colonial period, a province of the Captaincy General of Guatemala, itself dependent (with some variations) on the Viceroyalty of New Spain (today's Mexico). Hence, the early period finds Salvadoran cultural activity inextricably bound up with that of Guatemala. The earliest intellectuals in El Salvador were often Spaniards, books arrived slowly and piecemeal, and there was no university until independence. Hence, we must accept the verdict of Salvadoran critics and historians that the country's own literature begins with the remaking of culture that liberation from Spain first made possible. Anthologies of Salvadoran poetry, for example, typically begin with Francisco Gavidia (1863-1955) or Miguel Alvarez Castro (1795-1856).

III

The fusion of literary with social issues in Salvadoran writing will alternate, as in most countries, with evasionist, "pure" art. In the literature of El Salvador, however, the tendency (the necessity, perhaps) of escape into idealization has been dominant.

The earliest Salvadoran literature, then, is identified as that of independence. It is principally patriotic and exhortative, consisting of oratory, essays, and journalistic writings: the essays and speeches of José Simeón Cañas (1767-1835), Manuel José Arce (1787-1847), and José Matías Delgado (1765-1833), heroes of El Salvador's emancipation. The first Salvadoran poetry is often considered to be that of Alvarez Castro, neoclassical in form, patriotic in themes ("Al ciudadano José del Valle" [To Citizen José del Valle; 1884]), but also with some early Romantic subjectivity. Alvarez Castro also set a precedent for Salvadoran writers by being active in many other fields (politics, journalism, music, government).

In the nineteenth century, the theater barely existed in El Salvador. The first play of record was produced in 1814, and the first by a Salvadoran only in 1842, *Morazánida* (Epic of Morazán) by Francisco Díaz (1812-45); Diáz also wrote poetry of quite varied themes, from the epigrammatic to the patriotic.

Full-blown Romanticism, which dominated the Latin American nineteenth century, has marked the literature of El Salvador ever since. The Modernist movement that followed (1880s to 1920s) owed as much to the Romantics as to the French Symbolists and Parnassians; and since in El Salvador Modernism never had the same impact as in other countries, there has been a greater continuity of certain tendencies—emotionalism, subjectivity, lyricism dominant over narrative, national typologies, and presence of the physical environment, often humanized—than in perhaps any other country. Indeed, popular taste still tends to gravitate to the major poets of the nineteenth century and to those of the twentieth who owe them an artistic debt. The principal precursor of Romanticism in El Salvador is José Batres Montúfar (1809-44), who is claimed by both El Salvador and Guatemala. Other notable Romantics, more fully within the movement, include Enrique Hoyos (1810-59), whose *Apóstrofes* (Apostrophes; 1845) is a short work that generally avoids Romanticism's tendency to sticky sweetness; Juan José Bernal (18411905), whose later verse presented Biblical themes with epic style: *Recuerdos de Tierra Santa* (Memories of the Holy Land; 1894) and *Los evangelistas: bocetos bíblicos* (The Evangelists: Biblical Sketches; 1895); and Isaac Ruiz Araujo (1850-81), Ignacio Gómez (1813-76), Juan José Cañas (1826-1918), and Francisco Esteban Galindo (1850-96), whose drama *Las dos flores, o Rosa y María* (The Two Flowers, or Rosa and María) was presented in 1872—a full thirty years after the first Salvadoran play.

During the Romantic period, El Salvador also produced the first women poets, now largely forgotten, but continued to lack a true novel. Later Salvadoran Romanticism sees the formation of the country's first literary groups (a trend whose importance will grow with time), the opening of the National University (by decree in 1870), the founding of the Salvadoran chapter of the Royal Academy of the [Spanish] Language (1873), and the establishment of the Academy of Sciences and Belles

Lettres (whose journal was published 1888-94). To sum up this time, El Salvador's literature was more creative and abundant in poetry than in prose, the latter being largely dedicated to humanistic theorizations. Writers regularly crossed generic lines with a resultant dispersion of effort and a general reluctance to take any of the genres beyond their established limits.

As in other Central American countries, the 1880s were a time of ferment in Salvadoran letters. The work of Francisco Gavidia is considered by many to be the first truly Salvadoran literature. This energetic and imaginative spirit was of great importance to Rubén Darío (see the essay on Nicaragua), particularly in the adaptation of French verse forms and their musicality to Spanish (that of the Alexandrine in particular). Gavidia's own abundant work covers all genres and with nearly equal felicity. In his lifetime he became the dominant writer and thinker of his country, received many public honors, and left abundant translations that helped open El Salvador to world literary currents more than ever before. Like Darío, he stands today, for many, as not only the founder of Modernism in his country, but of a national literature of universal perspectives.

During the Modernist period, the theater was renovated with the help of Gavidia, and journalism by Román Mayorga Rivas, a Nicaraguan. Mayorga also made a major contribution to Salvadoran poetry by assembling the *Guirnalda salvadoreña* (Salvadoran Anthology; 1884-86). For the first time, many of the anthologized poets could become known not only within their country but elsewhere as well. The *Guirnalda* remains an important resource today.

Arturo Ambrogi (1875-1936), another multigeneric author, is today best known for his short stories, and for being among the first in El Salvador to invest this young genre with the discipline and perspicacity it demands. His stories, such as those of *Cuentos y fantasías* (Stories and Fantasies; 1895), mark the emergence of his own unique voice and of the short story of aesthetic, and not merely documentational, merit. Ambrogi includes a dose of regional language and customs, but covers varied themes, and was a polished stylist influenced by the Modernists.

As the nineteenth century closed, Salvadoran literature was beginning to emerge from what has justly been called "colonial retrospection." El Salvador, as yet, was a country with a respectable amount of writing but with little real literature and even less that could properly be called its own. The writer typically was economically privileged, at least in comparison to the rural and urban masses, and, even more perhaps than in other countries, tended to write from that position: El Salvador also lacked any significant popular literature, a situation that has changed only recently.

IV

The turn of the century finds El Salvador largely in a neofeudal condition, with an oligarchy no less self-interested than today and with a literature all too often drowning in a lyricism disinvolved with lived reality: a compensation that tolerated complacency toward the country's social paralysis. Songs to the laboriousness of the campesino or the beauty of the Salvadoran countryside, while legitimate themes, nevertheless ignored other truths equally important and more pressing. No equivalent emerges in El Salvador to the Realistic-Naturalistic literature of, for example, Chile, where denunciations of the situation of mine workers helped open eyes to an urgent human tragedy. Not all Salvadoran writers disregarded social reality, however. The Juan Montalvo Society attempted for a short time to turn readers to social issues: the result, foreseeably, was exile and excommunication. The country's official concern was not to have its shortcomings revealed but to develop economically on largely North American models. This was, then, hardly a time (rarely in El Salvador has there been one) when denunciation of injustice would be tolerated.

Alberto Masferrer (1868-1932) was the outstanding social philosopher of El Salvador during his lifetime. His vast production covers the decrepitude of the Romantic impulse, partakes of Modernism, and extends into the Vanguard innovations of the late 1920s and 1930s. His progressive ideas (and ideals) covered a range of thought from social structures to metaphysics, economics, and Latin Americanism. His clear prose is principally expository, although he also left a small body of verse, some of which is collected in *El rosal deshojado* (The Leafless Rosebush; 1935).

In other prose developments, what many consider a novel was finally written by a Salvadoran: *Roca Celis*, by Manuel Delgado (1908). Its value is less artistic than to stimulate more advanced work. Other prose writers, such as Luis Lagos y Lagos (1870-1913), continued the recording of local customs.

As Modernism declined, still without distinguished poets in El Salvador, one name stands out: Carlos Bustamante (1891-1955), who maintained a singularly high level of achievement and a voice both varied and rich, capable of ranging from the near-epic to intimate confession. "Mi caso" (My Case; undated), for example, has a quiet lyricism that suggests rather than overstating. Bustamante represents the change toward the coming literature of the Vanguard. Other transitional figures are Julio Enrique Avila (1892-1968), who broke from regular metrical verse but kept a rhyme scheme; Alberto Rivas Bonilla (1891), best known for his short fictions; Vicente Rosales y Rosales (1894-1980), in whose verse music stands out more than the anecdotal; Gilberto González y Contreras (1900-54), known for his use of the haiku (of which the Vanguard would be fond); and José Llerena, hijo (1895-1943). Alfredo Espino (1900-28) has long been the consecrated poet of modern El Salvador, by far the most read and surely the least controversial in his themes. His verses of sentimental quietism (*Jícaras tristes* [Sad Water-Gourds; 1936]) represent to many newer poets and critics the escapism of earlier Salvadoran literature: for Manlio Argueta, for example, Espino's work has actually restricted El Salvador's artistic development and delayed literature's recognition of exploitation and poverty.

Claudia Lars (pseud. of Carmen Brannon, 1899-1974) is the first Salvadoran woman writer to achieve both a substantive body of work and wide recognition. Her prose and poetry are, for the time, appropriately sentimental, yet they rarely fall into the neo-Romantic pitfall, staying always on a level of considerable stylistic and formal control and maintaining a certain distance (both aesthetic and emotional) from the subject matter. Both anguish and hope are judiciously counterbalanced in her verse. A few of her many works are *Canción redonda* (Round Song; 1937), *Sonetos* (Sonnets; 1946), *Sobre el angel y el hombre* (On Angel and Man; 1962), *Tierra de infancia* (Land of Childhood; 1958).

Lars and Salarrué (pseud. of Salvador Salazar Arrué, 1899-1975) coincide chronologically with the Vanguard, but neither belongs to it. In the case of Lars, it is for reasons of form and style. Salarrué is simply a special case in Salvadoran letters, first because he is one of the few to be widely read elsewhere, and secondly by the very nature of his work. Salarrué has specialized (of itself exceptional) in the short story and the novel. He is one of the few writers anywhere to reproduce the speech of children in highly local language without sounding paternalistic. One must read Salarrué aloud: near-phonetic spelling is used, and a great deal of the delight of his tales lies precisely in hearing (not just seeing) his youthful protagonists in action. The narrator subordinates himself to his characters and their situations, often humorous and touchingly insightful suggestions of the resourcefulness and resilience of Salvadorans and others. His best-known works include *Cuentos de barro* (Clay Stories; 1933) and *Cuentos de cipotes* (Stories of Children; 1945). Salarrué's love for language itself is confirmed in the experimentation and the vivid imagery of his best poetry, collected in *Algunos poemas de Salarrué* (A Few Poems by Salarrué; 1971), which do show some Vanguard influence.

As in the poems of Salarrué and Claudia Lars, the Salvadoran Vanguard is moderate in tone and its approach to literature. Whereas in other countries this movement was highly iconoclastic and experimental, in El Salvador poets generally preferred to adapt the new techniques and ideas to their own tradition and aesthetics. Socialistic ideas occasionally appear and, more often than before, we find literature depicting daily life recognizably. The poet considered El Salvador's first Vanguardist is Pedro Geoffroy Rivas (1907-1980), whose verse is relatively daring in its use of metaphor and in its social content. Serafín Quiteño (1907) exemplifies the moderate view of poetry in his use of classical forms along with free verse.

The refusal of Salvadoran writers fully to adopt current literary isms facilitated the transition from the Vanguard to modern Salvadoran verse, which begins in the 1940s. Geoffroy Rivas in particular announces what had only been sporadic before: a literature that faces reality without blinking. In 1941 six young poets formed Gruposéis (Groupsix), which would set a course for change together with the Círculo Literario Universitario (University Literary Circle). Antonio Gamero (1915) and Osvaldo Escobar Velado (1917-61) stand out, especially Escobar: *Volcán en el tiempo* (Volcano in Time; 1955), *Cristoamérica* (Christamerica; 1959).

In contrast to poetry, the novel of El Salvador has continued to be a hinterland. One critic listed Salvadoran novels previous to 1945 and came up with only eleven, including *Roca Celis*. The most widely read novels since are likely *Jaraguá* (1950) by Napoleón Rodríguez Ruiz (1908); *Las tinajas* (The Waterjugs; 1940) by Ramón González Montalvo (1908); and *Vidal Cruz* (1949), by José Edgardo Salgado (1914). All are rural novels, more typical of what would have been a neo-Realistic narrative than of the modern novel: tales of the land with traces of *Doña Bárbara* (the famous novel by Rómulo Gallegos; see the section on Venezuela) and even some Romantic qualities. The novel continues to be a difficult genre for El Salvador today.

The short story has gone farther: being easier to publish and otherwise circulate, it has, along with poetry, been El Salvador's leading contribution to Latin American writing. Hugo Lindo (1917) has published a great number of books, widely admired and, as usual, covering the major genres. His poetry is noted for its formal control and religious themes; in the short story some pieces contain an element of the fantastic. Lindo contrasts directly with the writers of Gruposéis: his is a cultured and intellectual literature, concerned with wide-ranging human problems more than with social change. He is surely the Salvadoran writer most frequently recognized with literary prizes and diplomatic appointments. Representative works include the short stories of *Guaro y champaña* (Moonshine and Champagne; 1947); *Varia poesía* (Diverse Poems; 1961); the novel *El anzuelo de Dios* (God's Hook; 1963); and the short stories of *Espejos paralelos* (Parallel Mirrors; 1974).

V

Again stressing that Salvadoran writers tend not to specialize in a single literary genre, the interest of space suggests a grouping of the most recent generations by their apparent preference and best achievements. In the theater, for example, two names stand out: Walter Béneke (1923) and Waldo Chávez Velasco (1932). The latter has published several volumes of short stories, such as *Cuentos de hoy y de mañana* (Stories of Today and of Tomorrow; 1963). His theatrical production, not extensive, is marked by lyrical language, as in *Fábrica de sueños* (Dream Factory; 1957). Better known for his theater is Béneke, whose *Funeral Home* (titled in English) has been widely translated and is an effective presentation of moral and cultural conflict.

The short story has at least one outstanding proponent who should be much better known outside of his country: Alvaro Menén Desleal (the ironic pseudonym for Alvaro Menéndez Leal, 1931; *[des]leal* means [dis]loyal). His play *Luz negra* (Black Light; 1967) is perhaps even better known than Béneke's *Funeral Home*, but we consider his short stories more representative of his work. And they are excellent: tightly structured, surprising, and dramatic, written in a prose perfectly suited to being a source of pleasure without distracting from a unified reading experience. Menén has been awarded many prizes for his narratives, among the best collections of which are *Cuentos breves y maravillosos* (Short and Marvelous Stories; 1963), *Una cuerda de nylon y oro* (A Tether of Nylon and Gold; 1969), and *Revolución en el país que edificó un castillo de hadas* (Revolution in the Country that Built a Fairy Castle; 1971). A number of his tales contain an element of fantasy akin to

Magical Realism and suggest a certain affinity to the Argentines Jorge Luis Borges and Julio Cortázar (see the section on Argentina).

El Salvador continues to be a country of poets—or at least one that produces them, whether or not they can remain at home. In the period since 1950 or so, a number with great promise have emerged; socially awake and literarily skilled, they often suggest that alleged conflicts between the revolutionary and the artist are a product of a distorted view of art and life. Among these provocative writers are Claribel Alegría (born in Nicaragua, 1924), with *Anillo de silencio* (Ring of Silence; 1948), *Cenizas de Izalco* (Ashes of Izalco Volcano; 1966), and *Album familiar* (Family Album; 1982); Tirso Canales (pseud. of José Antonio Canales, 1930), socially committed poet and playwright who wrote *Los ataúdes* (The Coffins; 1963) in collaboration with Rodríguez Ruiz and the essay *El artista y la contradicción fundamental de la época* (The Artist and the Fundamental Contradiction of the Times; 1966); and Alfonso Quijada Urías (1940), whose poetry and short stories have been influential on younger and more activist Salvadorans (*Estados sobrenaturales y otros poemas* [Supernatural States and Other Poems; 1971]) and *Otras historias famosas* [Other Famous Stories; 1974]). With Dalton (see below), Quijada Urías is probably the most significant of his group. Also deserving of mention are Roberto Armijo (1937), *Homenajes y otros poemas* (Homages and Other Poems; 1979); Manlio Argueta (1935), initially a poet but far better known for his novels *El valle de las hamacas* (The Valley of Hammocks; 1970—the title refers to San Salvador), *Caperucita en la Zona Roja* (Little Riding Hood in the Red Zone; 1977), and *Un día en la vida* (*One Day of Life*; 1981); José Roberto Cea (1939); and Italo López Vallecillos (1932).

The majority of the writers of this last group are not only multi-faceted, but far more than any generation before them have studied and promoted Salvadoran literature. It is also to be noted that nearly all these men and women have spent much of their time in exile as a result of their literary and political activity.

We close this segment with the Salvadoran writer most read and admired of his generation: Roque Dalton García (1935-1975). Like his contemporaries, Dalton was a political activist and dedicated his literature in large measure to revealing to his countrymen and women (and to others) a living reality, divested of romanticized evasions but with a highly intimate vision that avoids abstraction. He moves from the specific to the general, in contrast to the homilistic paternalism found in others. Dalton's travels and exiles led him to become well known throughout Latin America, and his writings are translated into numerous languages; Dalton is unquestionably the most influential Salvadoran writer of his time. Principal works include *La ventana en el rostro* (The Window in the Face; 1961), *Taberna y otros lugares* (Tavern and Other Places; 1969), *Las historias prohibidas del Pulgarcito* (The Prohibited Tales of Little Flea; 1974—El Salvador is often referred to as the "little flea" of Central America because of its size), *Pobrecito poeta que era yo* (Poor Little Poet that I Was; 1976), and *Poemas clandestinos* (Clandestine Poems; 1981).

VI

Salvadoran literature is a faithful reflection of national experience, both directly, through revelatory and didactic writings, and indirectly, through reluctance or the absolute impossibility of writing about such matters. The true literature of El Salvador largely remains yet to be written; in the last decades the task has been taken on. It is to be hoped that the valor and capacity to continue their struggle, which the Salvadoran people have reaffirmed time and time again, will produce a culture and a literature giving adequate expression to their qualities and to the liberation of their spirit.

BIBLIOGRAPHY

Argueta, Manlio. *Poesía de El Salvador*. San José, Costa Rica: Editorial Universitaria Centroamericana, 1983. The most recent anthology of Salvadoran poetry, with a short but provocative introduction; much more representative of social verse than previous collections.

Barbero, Edmundo. *Panorama del teatro en El Salvador*. San Salvador: Editorial Universitaria, 1979. Extensive prologue summarizing the development of Salvadoran theater and outlining an extensive project for publication of its major productions, of which this is the first (and apparently only) volume; plays by Francisco Gavidia and Joaquín Emilio Aragón.

Barraza Meléndez, Martín. *Trayectoria del cuento salvadoreño*. Bogotá: Pontificia Universidad Católica Javeriana, 1961. Short and not

very daring study of the Salvadoran short story; examines principally Ambrogi, Salarrué, and Francisco Herrera Velado, plus
several others.

Membreño, María B. de. *Literatura de El Salvador*. San Salvador:
Tipografía Central, 1960? Idiosyncratic compilation of documents and commentary; part anthology and part literary history,
it covers other areas of cultural life as well; for browsing.

Toruño, Juan Felipe. *Desarrollo literario de El Salvador*. San Salvador:
Ministerio de Cultura, 1958. The principal source of Salvadoran
literary history, thoroughly researched and reasonably balanced
in perspectives, although at times impressionistic.

URUGUAY
William H. Katra
University of Wisconsin-Eau Claire

I

Defiance and defensive pride are the two themes that characterize the national literary expression in Uruguay's first century as an independent country. Its small size and buffer location between Argentina and Brazil, the two South American giants, accounted for the country's marginal importance in the developments of the region and the largely responsive, rather than protagonist, role assumed by its writers and intellectuals. During the first decades of national life, two themes permeate Uruguay's cultural discourse. First, there was the humiliation of the population in the face of continual infringements on national sovereignty by foreign interests and its sensed inferiority in comparison to the politically expansive and economically preponderant Argentines, especially those of the Province of Buenos Aires. And second, there was the growing conflict between the rural folk, with their traditional, Spanish culture, and the expansive urban experience, fueled by an immigrant population, that embraced the ideas and objectives of European progress.

By the end of the nineteenth century, when the urban experience had succeeded in extending hegemony over the rural areas, the Uruguayan writers' deep-seated defensiveness became directed toward a new issue, that of modernization. The rapid changes to society were unsettling: the new predominance of a large immigrant population, the spread of light industries, and the mushrooming growth of the capital city. Political instability continued, but it was now aggravated by the boom-bust swings of the economic cycle. Historians point to the growing prosperity and rising expectations of the population. But the country's foremost writers accentuated a growing sense of vulnerability by treating the timeless themes of the countryside and the inner security of the spirit. But literature inevitably yielded to life. Unavoidable world market forces and the irresistible lure of a Janus-faced progress would usher the country, and its reluctant writers, into the simmering caldron of twentieth-century life.

Montevideo, located on the left bank of the Uruguay and Plata (Plate) Rivers, was already destined to play second city to Buenos Aires—in spite of its far superior harbor—when the Spanish crown created the Viceroyalty of the Rio de la Plata in 1776. Buenos Aires grew rapidly on account of its new role as capital of the region and its convenient location for servicing the growing transatlantic trade with Europe. Meanwhile, daily life in Montevideo—initially settled as an impediment to the expansionist ambitions of Brazil—altered between concerns of the fortress and the countryside. By the outbreak of the independence movement in 1810, Buenos Aires already boasted of a significant population, commercial influence, and a relatively developed urban and European-oriented culture; however, Montevideo—some one-hundred-and-fifty miles across the estuary—languished as a dusty outpost for contraband trade of hides and dried meat for principally English manufactured imports.

The major impetus for the independence movement was provided by the enlightened leaders in Buenos Aires, who abounded in idealism and ambition but lacked in prudent, realistic policies. While they waged war upon the enemy Spanish forces, they simultaneously maneuvered to bring the outlying areas of the now defunct colonial administration under its centralized authority. The population of Montevideo supported the first objective, but they stalwartly resisted the second. It was José Gervasio Artigas who led the Banda Oriental (Left Bank) in the development of far-sighted social and economic reforms—called by detractors aspects of a "gaucho democracy"—and united the rest of the fluvial provinces in the Federalist struggle for preserving local autonomy in the face of the hegemonic pretensions of Buenos Aires's cultured minorities.

The wide-spread sentiment of Montevideans regarding these struggles and their exceptional leader, Artigas, were fittingly recorded in the verses of Bartolomé Hidalgo (1788-1822). Although others—José Prego de Olivera (1750-1814) and Eusebio Valdenegro (1786-1818), for example—had preceded him as poets of this land, Hidalgo was the first to capture the colorful oral tradition of the predominantly rural population in written gauchesque verses. In his childhood he was employed by Artigas's father and developed a friendship with the future national leader, under whom he served as a soldier against the English in 1811. Although he cultivated different genres of poetry, the *cielitos* (Creole tunes) written in the gaucho idiom during the siege of Montevideo between

1812 and 1814 won him wide acclaim for their faithful expression of the unlettered soldiers' love for liberty and justice, hatred of the English and the Spaniards, and wry humor. While these early verses often appear dry and overly didactic to the modern reader, the three "Diálogos" (Dialogues), written between 1821 and 1822 when Hidalgo lived in Buenos Aires exile, are considered among the best of the gauchesque genre. Their genuinely popular flavor and the playful portrait of customs, sentiments, and social types account for the immense popularity that they enjoyed in Hidalgo's day. He expressed the mistrust of the Creole population toward the "cultured" minorities of the metropolis—and perhaps implicitly the ingrained fear of Uruguayans of an arrogant and powerful Buenos Aires. Present-day gauchesque singers such as Alfredo Zitarrosa have found in these verses an unequaled poetic protest against social and economic injustice.

For two decades following independence, the valiant resistance to alternating attempts by Portuguese and Porteño (or Buenos Aires) forces to bring the Banda Oriental under their respective jurisdictions, hardly provided conducive circumstances for flourishing cultural activity. Representative of the period is Francisco Acuña de Figueroa (1791-1862), whose long life of unselfish service to the young country did not exclude long periods of Brazilian exile and suffering due to material want. His abundant production of neo-classical poems, that treat patriotic, religious, satiric, and civic themes, appeared continually in the pages of the local press. A late convert to the cause of independence, his participation in defense of Montevideo from 1812 to 1814 provided the material for his most ambitious work, the *Diario histórico del sitio* (Historical Diary of the Siege; 1857), a rhymed chronicle of undisputed historical value in its treatment of the most important events of the conflict with Spain, and its eulogies of the country's notable leaders at the time, with the noticeable omission of Artigas. He also authored the "Himno nacional" (National Hymn), written in 1833 under the inspiration of Spanish poet Quintana, whose revised version of 1845 is that still sung today on official and patriotic occasions.

The anti-Artigas sentiments of Acuña accompanied an attraction to the European ideals of the early liberals in the Rioplatense region, who did not eschew alliance with the Brazilian empire in their goal of curtailing the power of the rural landowners, the caudillos. Between 1820–the year of Artigas's final defeat and path to exile in Paraguay—and 1825 the region was dominated by Brazil under the name of the Cisplatine Province. But anti-Brazilian sentiment grew, as did Buenos Aires's fear of

Brazil's growing presence in the region. The 1825 excursion from Buenos Aires to Uruguayan territory of the "Immortal Thirty-Three," under the leadership of Juan Antonio Lavalleja, brought an end to the decade-long Brazilian occupation. In 1828, Brazil and Argentina, under pressure from the British, renounced any geographic ambitions and formally recognized the definitive independence of the new buffer state, the República Oriental del Uruguay.

II

Independence, however, hardly brought social and political stability. In the faction ridden political environment, there were two predominant groupings: the Blancos (or Whites), headed by General Manuel Oribe, that represented the interests of the large landowners and were allied to the government of Juan Manuel de Rosas in neighboring Buenos Aires; and the Colorados (or Reds), led first by Lavalleja and then by General Fructuoso Rivera, who found their principal base of support in the incipient bourgeois population of Montevideo, and supported the cause of Argentina's exiled liberal or unitarian party against the Argentine dictator.

The social and political divisions of the country—between city and countryside, between the owners of slaughter houses and ranches and the poor gaucho workers—receive expression in the gauchesque poems of Manuel de Araucho (1803-42), that were written between 1828 and 1835. The greater part of his poetic and theatrical writing followed the then popular neoclassical norms—a good example is his ode "A la batalla de Ituzaingó" (To the Battle of Ituzaingó), that was presented in 1832 in the Casa de Comedias. His two gauchesque poems, the first of their type ever published in Montevideo, appeared in *Un paso en el Pindo* (A Pass in the Pindo; 1835), that was dedicated to General Oribe. In one of these poems, Araucho's imitation gaucho voice, expressing itself in the popular epistolary form, called attention to the harm that would come to the country if the "dotores" (the book-learned minority) of the city were to succeed in realizing their project of constituting a national bank. The second poem treated more specifically the injustices suffered by the gaucho at the hands not only of the large landowners, but also the owners of medium and small commercial enterprises.

In 1838, General Rivera's ouster of Oribe from power in Montevideo initiated the Guerra Grande (The Great War), which was highlighted by the nine-year siege of Montevideo by Blanco forces with the support of Buenos Aires. The seige accompanied a period of intense intellectual and cultural activity among the relatively small urban population of 35,000, the majority of whom were recent European immigrants.

Within Montevideo, the educated youth of the region's patrician familes viewed in epic terms their struggle against Oribe and Rosas. Their liberal social and political ideals were flavored by a distinctively romantic temperament, that was well in keeping with their passionate readings of Rousseau, Byron, Musset, and later, Chateaubriand. The leading figures of first generation of romantics—Andrés Lamas (1817-91), Adolfo Berro (1819-41), Alejandro Magariños Cervantes (1825-93), and Juan Carlos Gómez (1820-82)—hailed from the patrician families of the city, were educated in the elite institutions there and abroad, and promoted the European countries' growing influence in their city. They viewed their city and their small cultured public as surrounded by the vestiges of barbarism and intellectual darkness. The public that they projected for their writings was for the most part foreign or European readers, whom they depicted as their brothers in the spirit and their allies in colonizing and transforming their primitive land.

Ironically, the rigors and deprivations caused by the siege inspired a poetic reaction. After service in defense of the city during the day, many of these activist-intellectuals passed the long hours of the afternoon and evening in cultural pursuits. The heatedly contested poetic competitions of 1841 and 1843, in honor of the region's independence from Spain three decades earlier, pitted neo-classical versifiers against the more impetuous romantics. Foremost among the former was Acuña de Figueroa, while the latter were led by Lamas and the youthful Argentine exiles. At the same time, Melchor Pacheco y Obes (1809-55), suffering sickness and material deprivation in Brazilian exile, composed some of the period's most memorable romantic verse, that mournfully celebrated his distant homeland and the idyllic love of the wife he had left behind. Later, when he would be fulfilling the indispensable services of directing Montevideo's defense, and then representing Uruguay in the French court, he would find time to compose other important verses of philosophical theme.

In the sieged city, journalistic activity also flourished. There were as many as sixteen different newspapers—but perhaps an average of ten at any one time—actively publishing for the small literate population. Many of these newspapers were headed by the energetic exile population and existed for the sole purpose of denouncing the crimes of the Rosas government. Others disseminated among a willing reading public the liberal and pre-Positivist (i.e., the thought of Claude Henri de Rouvroy, comte de Saint-Simon, and others) ideas that would constitute the philosophical foundation for the moral, cultural, and political transformation that was ambitioned by these urban intellectuals of liberal persuasion.

Undoubtedly, it was the Argentine exiles, through their journalistic writing, who provided the major impetus for spiritual and theoretical rennovation. The failed uprising of Juan Lavalle against the Argentine dictator, Rosas, in 1829 brought to East Bank shores Juan Cruz and Florencio Varela, Miguel Cané, and Valentín Alsina, among others. After 1835 the participants of the Rebellion of the South sought similar exile. Between 1838 and 1840 perhaps the most renown group of refugees from Rosas's persecution found its way to Montevideo, the activists of Joven Argentina (Young Argentina), or later known as the Asociación de Mayo (May Association): Juan Bautista Alberdi, Juan María Gutiérrez, Vicente Fidel López, José Mármol, José Rivera Indarte, Bartolomé Mitre, and Esteban Echeverría (see section on Argentina). Added to this remarkable gathering were several learned Europeans, for example future Italian patriot Giuseppe Garibaldi, who had also sought refuge in the besieged city from political reaction in their respective societies.

Most noteworthy of this contribution from the Argentine exiles were Alberdi's articles on romantic literature, philolsophy, and political liberty; the journalistic writings of Rivera Indarte attacking Rosas; the essays of Cané and others expounding upon the fundamental ideas of Saint-Simon; and Florencio Varela's proposals for political reform and an alliance with France and England against the Rosas tyranny. Of significance also was the publication of Mármol's romantic, patriotic poetry, in addition to Echeverria's expanded *Dogma socialista* (Socialist Dogma; 1846) and other essays in which this important thinker defined with greater precision his advanced ideas on government, education, and society. Even the impetuous Domingo F. Sarmiento (1811-88), perhaps the maximum proponent for the romantic generation's social program of imposing the ideas and institutions of "civilization" over the region's recalcitrant rural "barbarism," participated—albeit briefly—in the Montevidean dialogue. In *Viajes por Europa, Africa y América* (Travels Through Europe, Africa and America; 1849-51), he described Montevideo in 1846, strife-torn after ten years of siege and blockade by the Rosas government, as hardly in a situation to take advantage of this potpourri of progressive ideas: the city and region were rapidly becoming transformed, with "one people arriving and another dying." This was Sarmiento's manner of depicting the shifting racial and ethnic balance of the region and predicting the path of Europeanized development that River Plate society and culture would subsequently follow.

Among the Uruguayans participating in this romantic movement, Lamas was undoubtedly the leader. From the pages of *El Iniciador* (The Initiator), founded in conjunction with Alberdi and others in 1838, he articulated the liberal program that denounced the region's feudal social and economic structures inherited from the Spanish colonial past, and promoted in vague terms the democratic, nationalistic objectives of a youth committed to progress. His energetic actions as Montevideo's *jefe político* (city manager) throughout most of the seige, merited the respect of friend and foe alike. In 1845 he published a series of newspaper articles, later collected in book form under the title *Apuntes sobre las agresiones del Dictador arjentino D. Juan Manuel de Rosas, contra la independencia de la República Oriental del Uruguay* (Notes on the Agressions of the Argentine Dictator Juan Manuel de Rosas, against the Independence of Uruguay; 1849), which provided detailed documentation of the Argentine dictator's abuses, and anticipated by only months Sarmiento's definitive rendering of the "civilization versus barbarism" thesis that justified the hegemonic pretentions of—in Angel Rama's words—the *ciudad letrada* (the cultured city) over the retrograde power of the rural caudillo and the backward customs of the rural interior. In "Manifiesto de 1855" (1855 Manifest), he proposed a politics of conciliation as a solution to the chronic in-fighting between the country's dominant political groupings. Although his efforts in 1848 and 1852 to win the support of Brazil in the struggle against Rosas brought upon him the condemnation of nationalistic detractors, those same actions earned him wide esteem at the time in his circle of leaders that were committed to the agenda of progress.

The Argentine liberals brought about the defeat of Rosas in 1852, but they had to wait another whole decade before achieving their definitive victory over the caudillos of the interior. As in the past, the politics of Buenos Aires played a preponderant role in influencing public life in Montevideo. The Mitre administration's wrath against the caudillos of the interior did not stop with the extermination of the followers of Peñalosa and Felipe Varela, but also sought similar victories in Uruguay and Paraguay. In 1863 it supported the assault led by Colorado General Flores, and assisted by Brazil, against the ruling Blanco party in Montevideo. With Flores in power shortly thereafter, the governments of the three coastal countries then led their Triple Alliance against the only

goverment of the region still resisting liberal implantations of free economic trade and financial dependence in front of Great Britain: the
landlocked country of Paraguay. In Uruguay, it was a period of intense
factional rivalry between the city and the countryside, Colorados and
Blancos. The spirit of tolerance and moderation had dissolved with the
terrible seige bombing of the Uruguayan city of Paysandú by Flores and
the Brazilian fleet, and would repeat itself a thousand times over in the
slaughter of Paraguayan troops by the joint Argentine-Brazilian command. The liberals' monopoly of the new instruments of war—the
steam-powered destroyer, the Remington automatic—could not snuff out
entirely the traditional orientation of the country's minority rural population. But through these instruments the *patriciado de doctores* (the pa-
triciate of the educated minority) succeeded in reducing the power of the
rural caudillos, centralizing the power of the state, opening its borders
up to international trade and investments, and inaugurating a new era of
immigration, agriculture, and material progress.

The culture of the country from the 1850s to the 1880s was dominated by the liberals, who had helped to consolidate the patrician state.
Juan Carlos Gómez (1820-84), alternating between Montevideo and
Buenos Aires, was the most influential voice in the intrepid liberal press,
that urged unrelenting war against the caudillos and the creation of a
Rioplatense nation that would unite all the former Spanish colonies of
the region. Domingo Ordoñana (dates unknown), producer and land
owner in addition to writer and militant, was the foremost proponent of
militarism and the application of technology to create a modernized
agricultural sector. And lastly, José Pedro Varela (1845-89), who had
assimilated the most fertile ideas of the epoch with regard to public
education, became the region's most persuasive advocate for the moral
and intellectual elevation of the common people. With a vision unsurpassed for his period, he predicated the work ethic, agricultural colonization and small-scale agriculture as means for fortifying the institution of
the family and the stability and prosperity of the small stable nation-state.

The spirit of optimism that reigned in liberal society did not leave its
testimony in a strong and memorable production of expressive literature.
In the 1840s Lamas, in addition to the Argentines Echeverría, Alberdi,
Cané, and Sarmiento, had postulated the necessity of creating a truly
"national" literature as a means of enhancing the spirit of the nation-state
they were intent upon constituting. With this inspiration, Magariños
Cervantes wrote the novel *Caramurú* (1850), with less than brilliant re-

sults. The romantic poetry of the period was slightly more memorable. Gómez's amorous verses stand out on account of his success in going beyond the obvious models of Hugo and Lamartine and capturing an authentic interior dimension. That, in addition to some few verses of Berro constituted the highlights of the *Album de poesías* (Album of Poetry) that Magariños Cervantes would prepare in 1885. Add to these voices the small and almost forgotten book by José Pedro Varela entitled *Ecos perdidos* (Lost Echoes; 1865) and the confident poetic affirmation in *Notas de un himno* (Notes about a Hymn; 1877) by José Zorrilla de San Martín (1855-1931), and one will have surveyed the best of the country's lyrical tradition up to the end of the century.

An estimable romantic narrative, featuring the character types and customs of the period, can be found in the English language writings of Guillermo Enrique (William Henry) Hudson (1841-1922). Born near Buenos Aires in 1833 of North American parents, he visited much of Uruguay on horseback between 1868 and 1869 and observed first hand one chapter of the civil strife—what he called "wars of crows and pies"—that consumed the country's energies almost without interruption for fifty years until 1910. His *The Purple Land* (1885) described in memorable fashion the countryside, character types, rural customs, and urban intrigues. The color referred to in the title pertained to the spilled blood of a people whose "vicious natures are disguised in human shape," whose "crimes surpassed all others, ancient or modern." This hardly flattering appraisal carried over to his English-speaking countrymen, who were described as languishing in idleness and progressively succumbing to the primitive culture of the nearly deserted countryside. But perhaps of greater transcendence was the transformation of the protagonist: his gradual conversion to a gaucho way of life in spite of all the vicissitudes experienced. Indeed, this glorification of gaucho life had an immense impact upon the largely English-reading public of the time.

III

Meanwhile, the country was undergoing profound transformations, especially in and around the capital city, where the settlement of immigrants, primarily from Spain and Italy, increased the region's population nearly sevenfold in the last half of the century alone. New light-industrial and service jobs meant the rise of a numerous middle class, which found its spokesmen among a university-educated elite. The

604 Handbook of Latin American Literature

latter, favoring a liberal, Europeanized, direction for the country's development, slowly gained ascendancy over the Creoles, whose power base was in the interior.

Although Uruguay did not witness the bloody massacres, as did Argentina during the 1860s, of desperate and rebellious rural workers (the *montonera*) at the hands of crack troops from the capital city, the changes affecting the rural population were nevertheless significant. The fencing of range land for raising improved stock began in earnest in the 1870s; the expansion of the railroads to rural centers of production typified the 1880s; importation of improved breeding stock marked the 1890s—all of this meant increased profits for the relatively small number of large cattle-producing landowners, whose hide, salted meat, and, more recently, wool exports continued to dominate the country's export economy. Yet those landowners who refused to jump on the modernizing bandwagon faced increasing economic pressure. Vying for predominance were new groups of middle-class immigrant landowners, whose commercial success in grain cultivation, wool and milk production, increased the economic pressure on the old breed of relatively inefficient cattle producers. All of this contributed to the increased marginalization of the poor rural population of gaucho peons, and was interpreted as a threat to the traditional way of life enjoyed until then by the rural society headed by the caudillo. The last sparks of rural resistance to inevitable change were the failed uprisings of 1897 and 1904 led by Blanco chieftan, Aparicio Saravia, whose heroic figure straddled the line between legend and anachronism.

The surviving fragments of ballads and songs from the region's oral tradition, that were assiduously collected by folklorists and anthropologists a half-century later—foremost among whom was Lauro Ayestarán (1913-66), in *La primitiva poesía gauchesca en el Uruguay, Vol. I* (The Primitive Gauchesque Poetry in Uruguay, Vol. I; 1950)—provided sketchy documentation of the sense of marginalization and impending destruction that were widely felt in rural areas. The educated gauchesque poets, who imitated the language of the illiterate gaucho and internalized their sentiments, provided a written expression of this important chapter of national cultural history. The most accomplished of these gauchesque bards was Antonio D. Lussich (Luciano Sánchez, pseud.; 1848-1929), whose *Los tres gauchos orientales* (The Three Uruguayan Gauchos; 1872), anticipated by months José Hernández's *Martín Fierro* (see chapter on Argentina). The two poets were united not only by friendship, but also by similar historical situations: the poetic motivation of each was in part a response to the failed rural uprisings of 1870 (led respectively by Timoteo Aparicio in Uruguay and Ricardo López Jordán in Argentina) in which each poet played a significant role. Lussich's poem specified to a greater degree the political circumstances at the root of the unjustices suffered by the rural population. This poem, as well as in its equally popular sequel, *El matrero Luciano* (The Outlaw Luciano; 1873), treated instances of corruption and electoral fraud occasioned by the Colorado Party. But the major topic of Lussich's poems was the agitated and imperiled existence of the seminomadic gaucho. Like Hernández, Lussich's major accomplishment was the artistic liberation of a rude but noble rural protagonist from the pejorative stigma of a "barbaric," vice-ridden people.

Lussich's poems, like that of Hernández, must be considered as "elegies," in that they sang praise of a race and a class then politically and economically defeated and on the verge of social extinction. This was because the rapidly changing social, technological, and productive conditions in the countryside had brought about an equally significant transformation in the life of the gaucho: from semiautonomous free-dom-loving range rider to obedient ranch hand or rural proletariat. The few gaucho survivors were now offered an ironic consolation: immortali-zation in the pages of the national literary production. In truth, the end of the century saw the imperative in urban cultural and political circles to construct a "national identity" by presenting the mythified gaucho as prototype of the country's population, and by projecting Artigas, the maximum caudillo in its young history, as founder of the Uruguayan State.

The cultural transformation of Artigas—who in life had been the origin of instability in the countryside—into foundational ideomyth justi-fying the modernized state, is especially intriguing. Especially important in this project of cultural revisionism was the theatrical production, *Arti-gas* (1898), by Washington P. Bermúdez (1847-1913), and the essays: *La epopeya de Artigas* (The Epic Poem of Artigas; 1910), by Zorrilla de San Martín, which had been vaguely anticipated two decades earlier in *La leyenda patria* (The Patriotic Legend; 1879); and "La grandeza de Arti-gas" (The Greatness of Artigas; 1915), by José Enrique Rodó (1872-1917). This literary expression found support in the revisionist historical studies by several writers, including Eduardo Acevedo Díaz (1851-1924), Carlos María Ramírez (1847-1898), and Angel Floro Costa (1838-1906).

Cultural phenomena related to this literary immortalization of the gaucho involved large segments of the urban population. Montevideo during the 1890s was the scene of frequent visits from Argentina by the Podestá brothers, whose popular theater treating the gaucho outlaw, Juan Moreira, captured the imagination of the new urban public, many of whom were themselves of gaucho extraction or sons and daughters of recent immigrants eager to embrace the symbols of a new nationality. The period also witnessed the widespread popularity of three other institutions: the Creole circus, that featured folklore music and rodeo events; Creole clubs, that provided the opportunity for urban youths to celebrate the dress, customs, and culture of the rural past; and a new pulp literature, taking the form of cheap novels and magazines, that sensationalized the exploits of mythified gaucho outlaws. It was a curious sociopsychological phenomenon: the imagination of the middle and working-class urban public romanticized the period of the country's historical past when gaucho society still predominated and when a substantial European immigrant population was only the starry-eyed projection of liberal dreamers.

The gaucho phenomenon was also felt in the cultural experience of the educated middle class and the cultural elite, that evolved from popular elegy to poetic anachronism. The stage witnessed several plays featuring protagonists who were humanized gaucho outlaws: *Juan Soldao* (Soldier Juan; Argentina, 1891), by Orosmán Moratorio (1852-98), and *Julián Giménez* (1894), by Abdón Arózteguy (1853-1926). At the time this last play was considered by some groups as the "true national drama of the Uruguayans." Toward the end of the century, the gauchesque genre experienced a further revival through the widely-read Creolist magazine, *El fogón* (*The Campfire*; 1895-1913). Still enthusiastically recited in countryside gatherings from this generally conventional outpouring of romantic, nativist sentiment, are the poems of Spanish-born José Alonso y Trelles (El Viejo Pancho, pseud.; 1857-1924).

The high point of this literary vindication of the gaucho—and, indirectly, of the chronic clashes waged by Blanco Party loyalists against the Colorados, was the series of historical novels by Acevedo Díaz: *Ismael* (Ishmael; 1888), *Nativa* (Native; 1890), and *Grito de gloria* (The Battle-Cry of Glory; 1893), followed by two other works treating gaucho themes, *Soledad* (Solitude; 1894), and *Lanza y sable* (Spear and Sabre, 1914). At the age of nineteen, while studying law at the University of Montevideo, Acevedo lent his support to the revolutionary cause of Blanco Party leader Timoteo Aparicio; this experience initiated a lifelong involvement in politics, which resulted in his appointment to several positions of importance in public administration, as well as periods of exile in Argentina. The two themes continually reiterated in literary as well as political writing were his high regard for traditional rural values and his esteem for the gaucho's bravery and civic virtue in the country's historical development.

In Acevedo's extensive writing on Uruguayan history and society, there was also an element of nationalist reaction against the strong urban and "culturalist" biases of the country's early romantic tradition, in addition to Argentine liberal historians (primarily Sarmiento, Mitre, and V. F. López), whose writings demonstrated an inability to comprehend Uruguayans' long-standing desire for local autonomy and short-lived experience with grass-roots democracy; similarly offensive was the liberal writers' calumnious portrait of José Artigas as a primitive gaucho demagogue. Acevedo internalized the defensiveness of his countrymen toward their powerful and arrogant neighbor; ironically, he celebrated his society's relative marginalization, which meant in a positive vein its greater immunity to the domination of powerful economic interests and foreign commercial agents, in addition to its greater resistance to imported cultural and artistic norms. These reasons explain in part Acevedo's focus on the past and his epic and romantic treatment, but with traces of realism, of the gaucho's positive role in the country's independence and struggle against foreign invaders. In later works, the more overt political thesis in support of the gaucho and the rural-oriented Blanco Party lessened artistic impact. But Acevedo's exaltation of his country's passions, tragedy, and struggles counterbalanced the "barbaric" depiction of the region's rural heritage, as propagated by those contemporaries who placed their literary talents at the service of an ethnocentric, Europeanized program for national modernization.

Given the frustrated promises of independence and tortuous civil wars, it is understandable that Uruguayan writers of the second half of the nineteenth century sought the realization of poetic and nationalist ideals in literary creation: essayists and dramatists in the mythification of Artigas, Acevedo in the nostalgic recreation of an idealized past, and Zorrilla de San Martin in the lyrical unreality of Rousseauistic Indian life. Although Zorrilla's long narrative poem, *Tabaré* (1888), enjoyed enormous popularity in its day, and although many critics have judged its formal attributes to be almost unrivaled in Hispanic-American letters, its melancholic, plastic beauty hardly appeals to contemporary artistic tastes. This poem of ghosts and theological investigation spoke to the inventive capacity of a literary mind and not to lived historical reality. With notable exceptions (the Jesuits in Paraguay, Artigas, some Argentine leaders), the expansive white population in the region scornfully abused the Indians and then massacred or drove them away. In truth, the European colonists and their descendants hardly considered the primitive, nomadic Indians of the River Plate region to be the stuff for poetic treatment. Zorrilla's aesthetic cultivation of the exotic Tabaré, son of Charrúa father and Spanish mother, could only have been written in a land where the natives had already disappeared.

IV

Approaching the new century, the changes announced prophetically by liberal modernizers a half-century earlier were already social fact. Some nationalist writers continued to emphasize the negative aspects of this modernization: the foreign powers' continued meddling in the affairs of the country (and perhaps their fueling of the almost ceaseless internal political struggles), and the dramatic alteration of the country's demography, ethnic composition, and political power base. However, these complaints gradually waned as a consequence of the country's exceptional economic prosperity. Especially after 1875, there reigned an optimistic climate indicative of the country's full employment (in urban areas), high salaries, widespread possibilities for upward mobility, incipient urban industrialization, growth of the middle classes, expansion of communication, energy, housing, education, and health facilities, and a lessening of social and political tensions that accompanied the institutionalization of democratic practices. This general optimism was nowhere more evident than in the countryside: benign international market conditions all but excluded the country's cattle producers from the business cycles and crises that periodically devastated other regions. Until the Great Depression of the 1930s, the view from the countryside saw Uruguay enjoying an almost uninterrupted prosperity—an exceptional position in comparison to the rest of the countries of Latin America.

The tumultuous changes occurring in the country became the focus of a revitalized theater, behind the lead of Florencio Sánchez (1875-1910), who was perhaps the most talented playwright in the country's history. Sánchez, of a poor family in Montevideo, overcame the desillusionment experienced as supporter of the Savaria revolution before the turn of the century, and went on to become a spokesman for anarchist and socialist causes. His ideological militancy, however, never contaminated the sincere human vision that his plays always communicated. Most widely acclaimed were his dramas treating the conflicts between the city and the countryside, between the virtuous Creole population of the rural areas and the hardworking and often money-grabbing immigrant farmers. A parallel theme was inter-generational conflict within the creole family, where progressive youths with universalist orientation challenged the traditional beliefs and retrograde practices of their elders. *M'hijo el dotor* (My Son, the Doctor; 1904), *La gringa* (The Italian Girl; 1904)—whose title refers to the daughter of Italians—and especially *Barranca abajo* (Downhill; 1905) highlighted the pride and self-respect of the Creoles who, nevertheless, were despised by the new immigrant farmers on account of their servile, pacific orientation, and perceived slothfulness, laziness, and resistance to progress. Sánchez depicted the Creoles as fatally losing out to the ambitious newcomers. Although the immigrants brought to the countryside a badly needed work ethic and the necessary capital for the technological transformation of rural labors, these positive contributions were undermined by their unconstrained ambition, obedience to hollow materialist values, and disrespect for the Creole population's solid family orientation.

In the next decade, similar themes would continue to assert themselves in the theater. The most highly regarded was *El león ciego* (The Blind Lion; 1912), by Ernesto Herrera (1886-1917)—praised as "that barbaric work . . . that cyclical tragedy"—that lamented the disappearance of the rural caudillo who had faithfully interpreted the will of the rural masses. The play's protagonist, the aged caudillo Gumersindo, was a survivor of the civil wars who was now manipulated by the professional politicians of the city for their own ambitions. *Sangre de hermanos* (Fraternal Blood; 1917), by Francisco Imhof (1880-1937), treated related themes: the condemnation of the fratricidal barbarism of the traditional caudillo, and the ambiguous desire for material progress that nevertheless ignored social justice.

New urban themes also began to invade the repertoire. As in neighboring Buenos Aires, a flurry of dramatic productions borrowed from the techniques of the popular *sainete* (one-act farse) in their stylization of a new national character type: the fear-inspiring, resentful *guapo*, or clever lower-class urban hustler. On stage, the sad musical strains of the tango were also immortalized, along with the familiar tango themes of desillusionment, nostalgia for bygone days, and sense of impending disaster. Herrera's *El pan nuestro* (Our Daily Bread, 1914) projected these themes onto middle-class protagonists residing in Madrid. Their realistic tragedy drew upon many similar cases occuring in Montevideo itself: the loss of a job due to links with financial fraud was but the starting point for a descent into degrading misery.

Whereas Sánchez and Herrera symbolically redeemed the Creole population of minifundia rural producers and ranch hands, now in decline, Javier de Viana (1868-1926) and Carlos Reyles (1868-1938) summarily condemned it to wither away in ignominy. Both hailed from traditional landowner families, which accounts in part for the disdain for what they perceived as the lazy, indolent, often violent gaucho farmhands. Viana, remembered primarily as a short story writer, flavored his own observations of rural life with the naturalist tint learned from Zola, Maupassant, and Turgenev. Although his stark, vibrant descriptions of rural life are memorable, his characters often fail to arouse the sympathy of the contemporary reader. His claustrophobic determinism shrouded them in brutal instincts and offensive vices. As such, he merely reinforced the racist inclinations of writers like Carlos Octavio Bunge (1875-1918) and José Ingenieros (1877-1925), who believed that the mixed-race gaucho possessed an inferior genetic composition that doomed him to marginality or extinction.

Reyles's novels—*La raza de Caín* (The Race of Cain; 1900), *El terruño* (The Native Soil; 1916), and *El gaucho Florido* (The Gaucho Florido; 1932)—also portrayed base, degenerate gaucho protagonists, as they came to be viewed through the naturalism-tinted lens of the doctrinaire writer. But there were two themes that distinguished his writing from Viana's. The first was the depiction of the new class of urban intellectuals as weak, indecisive, and impractical beings prone to ineffective or illusory contemplation. The second, very much related, was his depiction of rural property owners as that social group best able to offer the social and moral leadership for a sound state. This brand of Creolist narrative in both Viana and Reyles therefore served a mediating function in portraying rural life and land ownership as secure from the instability that plagued other sectors of society; it was also one indication of the rural oligarchy's defensive stance toward social and political, but definitely not economic, challenges from the country's expanding urban sectors.

Montevideo, meanwhile, had become dramatically altered. Visitors called it a maritime city neither blessed nor plagued with the dramatic cosmopolitanism of neighboring Buenos Aires or Rio de Janeiro. With 200,000 people, and half again as many in the immediately surrounding areas, greater Montevideo contained fully a third of the country's

1,000,000 population. Progress was immediately evident in the tele-
phones, gas-lit streets, and electric trolleys. But after the market crash
of 1890 import-substitution industrialization stagnated and European
immigration slumped considerably. Now, "pueblos de ratas" (rat-infested
slums), which girdled the metropolitan area, offered miserable residence
to unemployed and predominately illiterate country folk whose rural
livelihood had disappeared with the advent of fenced-in ranches.

Not surprisingly, there arose an urban expression that corresponded
to the Creolist defensiveness in the face of society's encroaching modernization. This movement, called by literary critics Modernismo (Modernism), prevailed in elitist cultural circles throughout Latin America during
the initial decades of the present century. While expressing the desire
for artistic, philosophical, and spiritual renovation, its adherents also
sought to avoid consideration of social and political problems and rejected the positivist orientation then prevailing in intellectual and political
circles. Foremost among Uruguay's Modernists was José Enrique Rodó,
whose *Ariel* (1900) and *Motivos de Proteo* (Motives of Proteus; 1909)
became objects of cult-like reverence in intellectual and student circles
across Latin America. Indeed, this first work set the tone and anticipated many of the themes of the continent-wide Arielist Generation of 1900:
a celebration of the cultural and linguistic bonds uniting the Hispanic-American countries, a sensed superiority of the Latin American spirit
in contrast to the materialism that reigned in the United States, an affirmation of the intellectual elite's mission of cultivating aesthetic and spiritual values in the lesser-educated masses, and the flight from social and
political turmoil through the cultivation of an interior artistic and moral
reign.

Paradoxical about Rodó and many Modernist writers was that they,
although writing for the cultured minorities, hailed generally from ruined
middle-class families and had directly experienced the excruciating trials
of economic necessity. A proteismo—or intense optimism of the spirit—was in many cases merely the other side of the coin for deep pessimism toward sordid reality. But instead of embracing the cause of the
new urban proletariat and the anarchist or socialist movements that
sought worker organization as a protection against exploitation, Rodó
argued for the need of "aristocratic values" and the emergence of a select
cultural elite that would lead the youth of society toward the restoration
of a past classical harmony. This discourse of cultural privilege differed
in form, but not in substance, from the reactionary social and political
program of the now rivaled, but hardly beleaguered, rural oligarchy.

In this light, Rodó's curious inversion of identities from Shakespeare's *The Tempest* becomes comprehensible: Ariel was his choice to represent the "natural" or "spiritual" Latin American citizen, and Caliban—formerly Shakespeare's brutish Caribbean native—was now used in reference to the mediocre, utilitarian population of the United States. Critics have traditionally explained this new association in the light of the near universal affront experienced by Latin Americans with the "big-stick" seizure of Panama and the yellow journalism-inspired belligerency that resulted in the United States's seizure of Cuba and Puerto Rico at the conclusion of the Spanish-American War. My own interpretation for Rodó's switch of identities, one that enriches but does not supplant the first, points to his internalization of the sentiments felt by the white European immigrants who had "arrived" and had definitively displaced the indigenous and Creole population. The disdain of Europeanized intellectuals in previous generations for gaucho "americanismo" received new expression in Rodó's contempt for the "degenerate" democratic "americanismo" of the United States and, implicitly, for the urban workers whose new militancy challenged the status quo in his own land. Having experienced a fall from economic fortune during his childhood, Rodó developed an ingrained fear and hatred of the "coarse multitudes." In short, Rodó's *arielista* elitism and corresponding contempt for the popular classes typified the general reaction of Latin America's middle-class intellectuals toward the turbulence that announced the possibility for rapid social change.

V

And yet, Rodó's airy optimism stood as a prophesy of the dramatic transformations that would occur before his untimely death in 1917: the democratic revolution, which occurred under the leadership of two-time national president José Batlle y Ordóñez (1903-07; 1911-15). Batlle set the foundation for Latin America's most stable constitutional government, whose progressive labor programs and "moral" legislation (laws for divorce, protection of illegitimate children, the end of the death penalty) were to earn for Uruguay the nickname of Switzerland of the West. This remarkable leader channeled the energetic immigrant population and harnessed the militant urban workers in successfully disputing the power of the landed oligarchy. Such a political program complemented a strengthening of the state in order to exert greater control over the economic activities of foreign enterprises and to redistribute more equitably the increasing national wealth.

The intense ideological furor previously typifying the country's intellectual, cultural, and political environments, found a point around which there was no significant dispute: the legitimacy of the new welfare state. Luis Alberto de Herrera, the kingpin of the Blanco Party, verbally sparred with Colorado leaders over programmatic trifles, but embraced what was most fundamental: the reformist order guaranteeing progress as well as social and political stability. Carlos Vaz Ferreira (1872-1958), with wide prestige in philosophical circles, provided a theoretical justification for the protection that economic interests now enjoyed in front of political power, in *Sobre la propiedad de la tierra* (On the Ownership of Land; 1918). With the same result, anarchists and socialists joined the bandwagon of progress by abjuring the legacy of the country's caudillos, denouncing the squalor of the growing metropolis, and idealizing the rural masses as paragons of virtue and civilization. Socialist Party leader Emilio Frugoni (1880-1969), at different moments excelling as poet, journalist, and essayist, led the radical movement toward an endorsement of the new status quo. His essay, *La epopeya de la ciudad* (The Epic Story of the City; 1927), glorified the city, while his widely disseminated writings on Marxist theory singled out the countryside, latifundium, cattle ranching, feudalism, and caudillos, as the multiple fonts of evil. In this return to the worn Manichean formula of civilization versus barbarism used by liberal activists three-quarters of a century before, the socialists and anarchists joined the tacit political alliance that sacralized order, stigmatized any form of violence, and in no moment threatened the vital interests of the conservative classes. Yet the benefits were manifest: a bullish economy, observable material progress, and in the city a fairly homogenous sharing of the social wealth.

Interestingly, Uruguay's writers largely ignored these remarkable transformations, that elevated the country above the drugery of social problems and economic scarcity that characterize almost every other Latin American country. Very possibly, those writers have believed that their capital city, distanced from the cultural and political epicenters of Latin America and the West, hardly provided credible support for the literary adventure. According to Mario Benedetti, writers, deep down in their consciousness, found disagreeable Montevideo's pseudo-European color, which seemed false and somewhat hypocritical. But this reaction revealed their own shameful insincerity: like Montevideo, they rejected America with their backs toward the country; they gazed toward Europe and the sea, but all that fell within their field of vision was a river with shifting international currents.

Vanguardism was one such movement: European inspiration caused a brief local glitter, but, unlike what occurred across the estuary, failed to ignite or inspire a subsequent national expression of consequence. Heading the list of Vanguard poets was Julio Herrera y Reissig (1875-1910), whose physical sickness and eccentric bohemian lifestyle were representative of the period. His was a poetry for a refined, sophisticated reading public, with its abundance of erudite metaphors and allusions to Latin and Arcadian names. And yet his perverse themes, grotesque images, and exuberant parody aimed at jarring the sensitivities of the cultural establishment. His most respected collection, *Los éxtasis de la montaña* (The Ecstasies of the Mountain; 1904), continued with this implicit challenge to society by evading modern and urban themes and recreating instead a timeless, unchanging pastoral world. Like Rodó, his guiltless, literary world served as a bulwark against irrepressible melancholy and subconscious fears triggered by the transformations occurring in his midst.

Evasion through literature was the sign of the times. Delmira Agustini (1886-1914) and María Eugenia Vaz Ferreira (1875-1924), although not as thoroughly identified with Modernist or Vanguard currents as Herrera, nevertheless suffered from a similar despondency and sought a comparable transcendence in lyrical creation. The poetry of Agustini, which expressed intense eroticism and rebelliousness of woman facing traditional submission to the male, has been revived recently by readers of feminist orientation. Of interest here is the poet's expression of her uncontrollable fascination with love, which accompanied disenchantment, a failed marriage, and a violent death. Less dramatic was the empty world expressed in the poetry of Vaz Ferreira. Against the nothingness experienced by a "shipwrecked" humanity, art, even though it was a "dead-end alley," constituted the most accessible and socially acceptable refuge from anguish.

Severe health problems and highly idiosyncratic temperament that led to intense psychological anguish were two characteristics that all of the Modernist writers mentioned above held in common. Does this chance convergence of personal circumstances invalidate the ideological interpretation, which views Uruguayan Modernism as one manifestation of the middle class intellectual's revolt, albeit aesthetic, against the predominant positivist values of the newly modernized environment? The addition of one more name, Horacio Quiroga (1878-1937), to the list of disturbed Modernist writers merely heightens our perplexity.

Quiroga's lifelong experiences with sickness, family tragedy, personal despair, geographical exile, and intense commitment to the literary task, were well in keeping with the Modernist pattern. He was born and raised in Uruguay, but after 1900 he resided primarily in Argentina. He began publishing his short stories after the turn of the century under the strong influence of Modernist poets and Edgar Allan Poe. His best stories, which still inspire immense respect among Latin American readers, combined a mysterious, metapsychological element to material based on his own experiences in the tropical Province of Misiones in northeast Argentina: *Cuentos de amor, de locura y de muerte* (*Tales of Love, Madness and Death*; 1917), *Cuentos de la selva* (*Tales of the Jungle*; 1918), *Anaconda* (1921), *La gallina degollada y otros cuentos* (*The De-headed Chicken and Other Stories*; 1925), and *Los desterrados* (*The Exiles*; 1926). In life and literature, Quiroga demonstrated that the quality of man's life was in personal struggle, sometimes against the primitive elements of a hostile nature, sometimes against the quirks of his own fate. But that lonely struggle was far preferred to life in society. Several of his stories reveal a scornful attitude toward the machinery of society and civilized man's senseless rational drive. Social organization increased rather than lessened difficulties; carefully conceived plans generally ended in futility or destruction. Man consequently wrecked havoc on the animal or natural world because of his inability to understand them. Quiroga's writing, like that of the other talented writers of his generation, offered testimony to the bitter confrontation of the writer with his society at the beginning of the present century, which in so many other respects promised the fulfillment of the continent's long deferred dreams.

The writing of the 1920s contrasted decidedly with the nihilism and passionate evasion of the Modernist generation. It was a period of fresh encounter with personal and national reality; literature and art affirmed the triumphant bourgeois spirit. This Golden Decade witnessed a flowering of creative talent in several fields: Eduardo Fabini and Luis Cluzeau Mortet composed a music overflowing with national essences; Pedro Figari systematically painted the nation's heritage of black candombes, gaucho life, and rural landscape. The poetry of Frugoni, Fernán Silva Valdés (1887-1975), Romildo Risso (1882-1946), and Pedro Leandro Ipuche (1889-1976) treated themes of everyday life and Montevidean street scenes, the new industrial society with its autos, airplanes, and growing mechanization of life. Also evident was a playful and at times daring irreverence, which sometimes crossed over into caustic irony. The culmination of this celebratory expression was the poetry of Juana de Ibarbourou (1895-1979). Her peaceful provincial life as mother and faithful wife were reflected in a poetry that won enthusiastic readers across the continent for its expression of youthful zest for life and warm monogamous passion. Her cult of "light, beauty, flowers, full, and healthy life" reflected the heyday of Uruguay's national experience. The dreams of Artigas, Batlle, and Varela all seemed well on the path toward realization.

VI

The blind forces of history had other plans, however. The Great Depression of the 1930s brought to a screeching halt the "benevolent" development of Uruguay's economy, exposing the flimsy façade of prosperity and social harmony that had deflected critical attention away from vast, unresolved problems. Foremost among these were the highly skewed distribution of land ownership in the interior, scarce investment of capital in the country's principal areas of production, especially the cattle industry, astronomic public debt owed primarily to British banks, highly dependent nature of the national market (Julio Herrera y Obes remarked in 1890 that while President of the country his responsibilities were akin to those of "the manager of a large cattle ranch, whose board of directors met in London"), and high consumption of imported goods whose purchase was possible only as long as Uruguayan exports remained in demand. The depression brought about a drastic reduction of international trade and, consequently, a virtual standstill of Uruguayan economic life. Soon to follow was the 1933 coup d'état by Colorado leader Gabriel Terra and supported by the country's dominant classes, that dissolved the inefficient executive council and restored the presidency. For broad sectors of a desillusioned population, however, the change confirmed their fear of the fragility and impotence of the democratic state. In retrospect, this period constituted not merely a periodic low point of an inescapable business cycle, as it later came to be viewed for northern hemisphere countries in which economic activity slowly recovered and then surpassed previous standards. Instead, it became the benchmark in Uruguayan national history that indicated a chronic decline that has continued, and even increased, up through the present.

The crisis sparked a surge of essayistic writing that questioned the status of the country's institutions and the recent failure of its democratic experience. Throughout the previous decade Justino Zavala Muniz (1898-1968) had revealed in several essays the treasons, discrimination, and plundering of the rural sector that was taking place under the country's democratic mask. These explosive themes now populated his theater: *La cruz de los caminos* (The Crossing of the Roads; 1933), *En un rincón del Tacuarí* (In a Remote Corner of Tacuarí; 1938), and *Alto Alegre* (Happy Stop; 1940). Frugoni, in *La revolución del machete. Panorama político del Uruguay* (The Revolution of the Machete. Political Panorama of Uruguay; 1935), denounced the failure of the state to alter the country's economic and productive structures. Alberto Zum Felde (1887-1976), in *El ocaso de la democracia* (The Decline of Democracy; 1939), honed in on the fatal weakness of the Batlle order, that it was "mere formalism without true substantial content." This work was merely the midpoint of Zum Felde's remarkable intellectual contribution: for over forty years he would offer the most authoritative and penetrating insights to the country's and continent's intellectual history: *Proceso Histórico del Uruguay* (Historical Process of Uruguay; 1919), *Indice crítico de la literatura hispanoamericana*. Vol. I: *La ensayística*; Vol. II: *La narrativa* (Critical Index of Hispanoamerican Literature. Vol. I: The Essay; Vol. II: The Narrative; 1954, 1959).

In spite of the impending gloom descending over Uruguayan society during the 1930s and 1940s, or perhaps because of it, the poetic "epidemic" continued unabated. The link between subjective lyrical expression and sociopolitical context is difficult to draw in all cases. Nevertheless some trends of the new poetry written by those born in the first decade of the century seem significant: an apparent inner turmoil was suppressed through an emphasis on formal beauty. Two of the most outstanding writers were Sara de Ibáñez (1910-71) and Clara Silva (1903-76). With the poetry of the former, an overly ornate expression and the excessive attention to technique accompanied an insensitivity to human issues. Egocentric verses communicated an anguished rift between physical and spiritual love. Silva's narrative expression displayed a similar solipsistic tendency in the expression of an intimate female conscience consumed by sexual fears and resentments, and suffering from tremendous difficulties in relating to the surrounding world. Only these two writers rose above the mundane artistic standards of the now-threatened welfare epoch: the predominant trend was for "bureaucratized" creativity to seek canonization in the comforts provided through the state's generous retirement benefits.

Other poets of the same generation expressed more directly the spiritual anguish that was beginning to be recognized as a sign of the times. Liber Falco (1906-55), in *Tiempo y tiempo* (Time and Time; 1940 to 1956), melancholically attempted to transcend the fear he felt in the face of an upended universe through the search for solidarity with the humble order of things. The poetic trajectory of Juan Cunha (1910-85) revealed a somewhat different temperament: youthful lyrical enthusiasm fell to the silence masking crisis, only to surge forth again after 1951 in a mature expression of the poet's resentful solitude amidst silent streets and secured front doors.

Was the flowering of magical and fantastic literature during this same period a psychological mediation for writer and public alike against the discomfort caused by social and political turmoil? On the other side of the estuary, Jorge Luis Borges and Adolfo Bioy Casares (see section on Argentina) were the obvious precursors of the fantastic, that since the 1930s has remained prominent in Rioplatense literature. In Uruguay, two names stand out: Quiroga and Felisberto Hernández (1902-64). Undisputable was the new stage in Hernández's narrative trajectory at the beginning of the 1940s, with its evocations tinged with fantasy. Works like *Nadie encendía las lámparas* (Nobody Lit the Lamps; 1947) and *La casa inundada* (The Flooded House; 1960) revealed a mischievous curiosity for the gloomy and the prohibited. With satirical tone, and recurring frequently to freudian symbols, Hernández constructed ambiguously comic narrations over absurd or hallucinatory topics, that nevertheless maintained contact with the plausible. Although this exuberant exercise of the imagination was not well received by critics at the time, in recent decades it has come to interest a wide circle of readers.

The resurgence of Creolist expression midway through the 1920s, and lasting beyond the 1940s, possibly responded to the same sensed discomfort on the part of several writers with the problems experienced in the urban sector. The majority of their stoical, self-reliant rural protagonists were the product not of information gained through direct experience or contact, but rather of impersonal investigation and authentic but reflected sentiments. On the lighter side were the seventeen celebratory works of Serafín J. García (1908-85), that united gauchesque stories, poems, and countryside legends. Similar in tone was Juan José Morosoli (1899-1957), who explicitly characterized his narrative as a nostalgic turn toward the mythical past, which had the objective of eulogizing the "natural childhood" of the countryside resident. A less optimistic view predominated in other noteworthy works, however. The ugly narrative world of Francisco Espínola (1901-73), which offered the Creolist equivalent to the urban squalor depicted by Argentine Roberto Arlt, emphasized the barren psychological landscape of a rural population consumed by anguish and remorse. The sole work of Victor Dotti (190755), *Los alambradores* (The Fencemakers; 1929), was a classic of the period for its depiction of the overbearing solitude of the primitive rural setting that contributed to the hardened, emotionless character of the gaucho. The most outstanding novels of Enrique Amorim (1900-60)—*La carreta* (The Cart; 1932) and *El caballo y su sombra* (The Horse and its Shadow; 1941)—portrayed the physical and moral misery of the rural population, who sometimes was "devoured" by the primitive natural forces of the plains. His narrative, which was not limited to rural themes, continually demonstrated the author's angry disillusionment with the inert bureaucratic structures of modern society. Lastly, Julio C. da Rosa (1920), publishing in the 1950s and early 1960s, depicted compassionate yet naive countryside natives who stoically resisted society's corrupting presence and its sometimes harsh intrusions into their world.

It might be true that Uruguay, a land of small happenings, hardly offered inspiration for great novelists. Perhaps the only exception to this was Juan Carlos Onetti (1909), even though his difficult, morose works have never enjoyed the exuberant mass reading public of the more recent "boom" writers: *El pozo* (*The Pit*; 1939), *Tierra de nadie* (*No Man's Land;* 1941), *La vida breve* (*The Short Life*; 1950), *El astillero* (*The Shipyard*; 1961), and *Juntacadáveres* (*The Bodysnatcher*; 1964). Possibly the alienated, solitary writer, who resembled his protagonists in this regard, never intended that his fiction address the lived problems of society. Nevertheless, the work of no other writer rivaled his forceful depiction of River Plate society before midcentury, resigned to passivity and impotence and exiled to a history deprived of events.

El astillero represented the culmination of Onetti's previous novels and for that reason offered the best diagnosis of the total defeat suffered by his countrymen. The novel's setting was significant: the region's shipbuilding industry, which once had led the world in productivity and quality workmanship, now faced financial ruin without clients or workers. Larsen, the protagonist, might well be compared to Uruguayan society at the time of the market crash, with his thirty years of high living on dirty money and dirty women. Although immobilized by his wretched surroundings, Larsen was nevertheless treated with pity by the writer: the protagonist was just another victim who had to suffer the punishment inflicted upon him by adverse circumstances, with the timid hope of realizing his own liberation. He stood apart from the vulgar daily life that surrounded him, unable to sustain a dialogue with others or influence his own destiny. His situation was symbolic of the country's failed promise to develop an effective relationship with the world. It was testimony to a fickle global order that first ascended, then marginalized, a small portion of humanity, by relegating them to stagnate before the toppled idols of their own dreams.

The country's depressed situation, as depicted by Onetti, became aggravated in the late 1930s and 1940s with the wave of political reaction and intolerance that jarred the West: the rise of fascism and militarism, followed by the outbreak of hostilities in Spain and then the rest of Europe. In general, it was a period of deferred or deflected literary and artistic creativity.

The ensuing national crisis continued to be recorded in the pulse beat of the lyrical poets. Those born in the 1920s who began publishing in the 1940s—Mario Benedetti (1920), Humberto Megget (1926-51), Ida Vitale (1924), Amanda Berenguer (1921), Carlos Brandy (1923), and Idea Vilariño (1920)—largely continued in the path of their predecessors: superficial hermeticism often masked disillusionment with a mediocre, corrupt world. The titles of Vilariño's collections were representative in communicating perplexity before an irredeemable, hostile world: *Paraíso perdido* (Paradise Lost; 1949), *Abandono y fantasmas* (Abandonment and Ghosts; 1950), *Por aire sucio* (Through Dirty Air; 1950). In this last work, a sense of spiritual desolation predominated: "I no longer now no longer want to reach out / move the hand nor the glance / nor the heart. I no longer now no longer desire / the dirty, dirty, dirty light of day."

While the national decline led many writers to a literature emphasizing an imaginative or subjective dimension, others favored political relevance in narrative, the essay, and criticism. Amorim was the first important literary figure to embrace the Communist cause, while Dotti represented the writer whose creative talents were sacrificed for political objectives. Dionisio Trillo Pays (1909-71) and Alfredo Dante Gravina (1913) popularized a largely realist narrative treatment of urgent social problems and the effect of these on individuals. The narratives of Carlos Martínez Moreno (1917-86) used as novelistic backdrops the Spanish Civil War, the Bolivian Revolution, and later the Castro experience in Cuba. *El paredón* (The Wall; 1962), perhaps one of the finest novels of the period, integrated political testimony with human drama: the Uruguayan visitor in Cuba agonized over the relevance of that country's tumultuous revolutionary experience for his own land, where "everyone suffered from a paradisiacal quietism, where everything breathed order, good sense, austerity, equilibrium, and prudence."

Of far greater transcendence in the intellectual life of the country was the founding of the weekly journal *Marcha* in 1939 by Carlos Quijano (1900-82). For over four decades *Marcha* would provide a germinating thrust to the country's intellectual life. On the social and political levels, *Marcha* symbolized the radicalization of the middle class intellectual who sought solidarity with the organized working class in order to achieve a profound restructuring of social institutions. Of particular importance was the journal's advocation of governmental initiative in the subdivision of the country's latifundia, an objective which even the far-sighted Batlle y Ordóñez had never seriously entertained. Unfortunately, this publishing effort would never budge significantly the country's prudent, cautious population, even in front of a widening crisis. However, its section dedicated to literature and art, at different moments under the enlightened direction of Onetti, Emir Rodríguez Monegal (1921-85), Angel Rama (1926-85), and Jorge Ruffinelli (1943), provided a forum for the continent's most outstanding writers and thinkers, and established Uruguay as a cultural mecca in the Third World.

VII

After the glimmer of a possible recovery in the early 1950s, the country's economy again experienced a sharp deterioration. The surprise, disbelief, and panic that gripped the country inevitably contributed to the Blanco Party's victory in the national elections of 1958, which ended the Colorado's dominance for nearly a century. This "mental earthquake" triggered a rapid growth in labor union membership and leftist political activity on the part of workers and public employees.

The polar night therefore continued for Uruguayan society, but this did not extend into the area of literary production. Instead, by the beginning of the sixties a new spirit of commitment, which accompanied a significant blossoming of creative energy, began to prevail. The profuse production of Onetti, Amorim, Martínez Moreno, Da Rosa, Gravina, Morosoli, and other experienced writers monopolized bookstore windows. But slowly, the works of a new generation of participants began to have impact. Jorge Onetti (1930), Hiber Conteris (1933), Fernando Aínsa (1937), and Eduardo Galeano (1940) had been nurtured on the ideas of literary engagement that prevailed in artistic circles of postwar Europe and had been weaned on the rising expectations triggered by the region's brief relapse into prosperity during the Korean War, the not altogether negative experience with populist government, and the optimism accompanying Castro's incipient revolution in Cuba. But there were others hailing from older generations—Antonio Larreta (1922), Carlos Maggi (1922), Andersson Banchero (1925), and Benedetti—who also attempted to breathe an ethical spirit into a literature of responsibility which spoke to the climate of instability and change. All these writers rejected the former generation's mocking, alienated attitude and its refuge in aesthetic games. In theater, narrative, and verse, they sought to distance themselves from false folklorisms, where literature served a social role of preserving archaic linguistic and institutional forms. In their majority, they embraced the ideals of the conflictive and divided political Left, yet refused to convert their work into propagandistic or ideological weapons. Instead, their narrative craft demonstrated differing personal responses to the national crisis. The disconformity of these writers was expressed through bored or passionless adolescent protagonists adrift in the bourgeois world; or in their appropriation of a common, functional language to describe the pop-cultural and social world of the proletariat. Yet others traced through crude realistic techniques the heated social struggles, rude erotic encounters, and inner turbulence of an outwardly conformist people.

A revived theater contributed enormously to the artistic awakening of the period, in spite of the inevitable challenge to middle class attention by the cinema and, after 1960, television. To this end, the contribution of Larreta as actor, director, producer, and playwright was fundamental. His plays, *La sonrisa* (The Smile; 1950) and *Oficio de tinieblas* (Profession of Darkness; 1954), stood out for their exploration of moral and psychological aspects of bourgeois society that was constructed upon hypocrisy and lies. Treating similar themes were the neorealist pieces of Jacobo Langsner (1927, Rumania), *Los ridículos* (The Ridiculous Ones; 1951), and *Los artistas* (The Artists; 1954), in which exaggerated everyday language was the dramatic vehicle for depicting internalized tensions that frequently erupted into violence. Even more important were the dramas of Maggi—*La biblioteca* (The Library; 1957), *La trastienda* (The Backroom; 1958), and *La gran viuda* (The Famous Widow; 1959), which continued this inquisition of national reality. Targets for Maggi's expressionistic stage, in addition to his moralizing criticism of customs in the popular essay, *El Uruguay y su gente* (Uruguay and its People; 1963), were the fragile myths of welfare security due to the state's unwieldy bureaucracy, and the false, inauthentic cultural life of the middle class. Unfortunately, a distorted identification with a mythified Creole past detracted from the force of Maggi's otherwise virulent criticisms and highbrow satires.

The writer of the period who offered the most forceful form of literary commitment was Mario Benedetti. His novels, *La tregua (The Truce* 1960) and *Gracias por el fuego* (Thanks for the Light; 1965), in addition to his bestselling collection of short stories, *Montevideanos* (The Montevideans; 1959), all undisparagingly portrayed the mundane, hedonistic personality types that predominated in River Plate society. Their trivial concerns, when not vociferously rendered, resembled infantile laments. Love was their misnomer for unfulfilled desires and obscene gestures. An apparent cordiality in social interaction masked acute exasperation that often exploded into violence. Within these unimaginative and passionless beings there lurked a fury of repressed passions and resentments. With self-effacing affection, Benedetti drew the archetypical figures and institutions of a comic, hallucinatory world.

The intellectually charged environment from the 1960s on gave rise to the most significant flowering of essayistic writing to be produced in the country since the days of Rodó and Vaz Ferreira in the first decades of the century. Uruguay's liberal educational system and its active cultural life accounted, at least in part, for the fortunate constellation of several thinkers whose writings on national and hemispheric concerns were to win continent-wide attention. Heading the list was Carlos Real de Azúa (1915-77), whose encyclopedic knowledge, that was often communicated through a disordered, complex—but never superficial—style, bridged traditional disciplines. Of note were his penetrating analyses of the country's oligarchical structures and their links with foreign interests: *El impulso y su freno* (The Impulse and its Brake; 1958), *El patriciado uruguayo* (The Dignity of Uruguayan Patricians; 1961), and *Historia visible e historia esotérica* (Visible History and Esoteric History, 1975). Carrying the analysis of national dependency and foreign imperialism into the cultural realm was Benedetti's *El escritor latinoamericano y la revolución posible* (The Latin American Writer and the Possible Revolution; 1974). Also of wide dissemination was *Historia del imperialismo norteamericano* (History of North American Imperialism; 1977), in which Vivián Trías (1922-80) recreated Marxist categories in relation to the peculiar characteristics of Latin America. A study with immediate symbolic importance on account of its mythification of revolutionary leader, Raúl Sendic, and its justification of armed conflict as the authentic road to revolutionary change, was *La rebelión de los cañeros* (The Rebellion of the Sugarcane Workers; 1969), by Mauricio Rosencof (1933)—a work whose themes had been anticipated in a most important theatrical production, *Los caballos* (The Horses; 1967). Culminating this radical inquiry into the region's underdevelopment was Galeano's *Las venas abiertas de América Latina: cinco siglos del pillaje de un continente* (*Open Veins of Latin America: Five Centuries of the Pillage of a Continent*; 1971). This work, that went through thirty-five editions and several translations in its first ten years of publication, has become required reading for serious students of Latin America everywhere.

While several accomplished writers anguished over the nation's problems, a substantial group of aspiring creators communicated a more complacent, idyllic image of national life. In 1963 Rama called attention to preponderance of certain themes in the writings of Silvia Lago (1932), Claudio Trobo (1936), and Alberto Paganini (1932): the imitated tedium of Italian cinematographer Antonioni, an erotic gymnastics that followed the trendy *nouvelle vague*, and a skepticism and even cynicism that accompanied hedonistic life styles. In an essay published the following year, Benedetti identified a similar tendency, which he summarized as *literatura de balneario* (Vacation-Beach Literature). Repeatedly depicted in this new expression was a generic protagonist whose personality and activities were intimately identified with the setting of his "exploits": the nation's sunny beaches ("fishing, sports, bikinis, vitamins, sensation of health, umbrellas pointing toward the sun, toasted leisure, bare backs, *mate* gourds and thermoses, transistor radios, gambling houses, erotic invitation . . ."). He was skilled at flirting, arguing, and misunderstanding, the country's "three specialties." But rarely, if ever, did he engage in *action* or enter into the country's troublesome streets or conflict-ridden countryside. This complacent expression captured well the widespread tendency (outside of intellectual circles, at least) to make a fetish of the country's democracy and project its two World Cup championships to the proportion of an illusory world vision.

VIII

Whereas the postmodern literary adventure in the Northern Hemisphere has been inspired by the dubious successes of progress, in Uruguay writers have responded to precisely the opposite. By the late 1960s the country's wool and meat exports, whether measured in quantity or monetary value, were less than thirty years earlier. Investment in light industry had come to a virtual standstill, and in many sectors was even declining. Ninety percent of the country's rural establishments continued to be either too large or too small for efficient production. The national debt was burgeoning, and unemployment remained high. The general standard of living, which was previously the highest in Latin America, began to fall precipitously.

Uruguay's younger writers, following the lead of Latin American writers in general, rejected the Neorealism of the previous generation in their quest for a more appropriate means to participate in the pan-Occidental cultural dialogue. Their total rejection of contemporary society, not only as experienced in perennially troubled Uruguay, but also in the logocentric, patriarchal, postcapitalist West, went hand-in-hand with the search for new, redeeming structures. This legitimization crisis took many narrative forms. First, there was blossoming of fantastic and experimental literature that began to appear in full force after 1967. Indeed, the writings of Silva Vila, José Pedro Díaz (1921), and Armonía Etchepare (Armonía Somers, pseud.; 1914), followed the patterns established earlier by Borges and Felisberto Hernández, in emphasizing complex mental configurations, metaphysical questions, and the zone of the unreal, while paying scant attention to lived social issues. Similar was the writing of Mercedes Rein (1931), who depicted in *Zoologísmos* (Zoologisms; 1967) a phantasmagoric, confused world in the throes of disintegration. Through her expressionistic lens, the old bourgeoisie, now anachronistic in function and values, still exercised its influence, but through Baroque, overly sumptuous, even absurd gestures. Teresa Porzekanski (1945), in *El acertijo y otros cuentos* (The Guessing Game and Other Stories; 1967), later followed by *Historias para mi abuela* (Stories for My Grandmother; 1970), narratively traced the frozen forms and gestures of a gerontocratic society that was tensely balanced between the living and the dead. With Robbe-Grillet-like behaviorism, Gley Eyherabide (1934) emphasized the rich suggestiveness of disconnections between beings and objects. In *El otro equilibrista y veintisiete más* (The Other Tight-Rope Walker and Twenty-Seven More; 1967) his belabored descriptions of trivial everyday objects and situations revealed a fragmented, disarticulated reality. And lastly, the highly praised stories of Cristina Peri Rossi (1941), fruit of the country's most unrestrained libertarian imagination, presented a tense, unsettling vision of unreality. The titles to her story collections, *Los museos abandonados* (Abandoned Museums; 1968) and *Indicios pánicos* (Indications of Panic; 1970), suggested the macabre subjective landscape of a frustrated population for whom a sense of satisfaction or self-realization was gained only through the desperate flight of the imagination.

Paralleling the writers' literary terrorism against a moribund culture was the urban guerrilla war of the Tupamaros. This name was synonymous with liberation struggle, having originated in Peru's sixteenth century (the Indian leader Túpac Amaru), and then appropriated in 1810 by the Banda Oriental's gaucho horsemen in their skirmishes against Spanish and Portuguese oppressors. 1969 saw the seizure, by this group of the city of Pando, an event that fanned the imagination of the militant sectors of the population, but also called into action the previously dormant national security forces. For three years the rebels, organized in an extensive underground network, challenged the country's power elite through audacious kidnappings, bank seizures and prison escapes, events graphically recorded in Constantin Costa Gavra's widely commented movie, *State of Siege* (1973). By the mid-1970s, this play at revolution had been brutally suppressed, and at an enormous price: several hundred thousand exiles, hundreds of extrajudicial killings by military and security forces, the highest proportion of political prisoners for any country in the West, and the dismemberment of democratic institutions by a ruthless military regime.

The severity of the repression took most observers by surprise and made a sorry mockery of an earlier assessment that the country offered a "fortunate and sensible exception to the 'barbaric' tragedies" of other countries in South America's southern cone. Writers were singled out for "exemplary" punishment: Conteris, Rosencof, Nelson Marra (1942), and—briefly—Juan Carlos Onetti were jailed, some of them tortured. *Marcha*, after more than 30 years of publishing its independent progressive views on society and culture, was forcibly shut down in 1974. Journal archives were burned, historical research was prohibited, the quoting of Artigas became sufficient grounds for official reprisals. Much of the country's literary heritage, in addition to the works of many contemporary U.S. and European writers, was proscribed from public bookshelves; on the prohibited list appeared titles by Acevedo Díaz, Rodó, Morosoli, Espínola, and Benedetti. Popular protest singers Alfredo Zitarrosa and Daniel Viglietti were decreed dangerous nonpersons. This spirit of intolerance bordered on the ludicrous with the ban from radio broadcast of several tangos written and sung by Carlos Gardel, who had died a half-century before. Benedetti depicted this environment of Draconian control in a poem of 1979: "prohibited the silences, the unanimous shouts / miniskirts and labor unions / artigas and gardel." The shock experienced as a result of the military's severe extrajudicial measures seemed to produced its intended result: thousands of intellectuals fled the country, while most of those remaining chose "inner exile" in the form of self-censorship and silence.

Many of the country's most outstanding writers, from their distinct vantage points in exile, slowly internalized and then expressed in their writing the horror story experienced by those who remained behind. Sometimes, it was an "emergency literature" that was conceived with the objective of raising a shout of protest against the reigning inhumanity. Representative was Benedetti's *Pedro y el capitán* (Pedro and the Captain; 1979), a theater piece that portrayed the existential situation of an incarcerated political activist and the self-justifications of his military torturer. Sometimes this expression took the form of the intimate reckoning with one's own shambled existence. This was the stuff of Peri Rossi's 1970 collection of short stories, *Indicios pánicos* and her 1975 poetic collection, *Descripción de un naúfrago* (Description of a Shipwreck Victim). Of similar origin was Galeano's narrative, *La canción de nosotros* (The Song We Sing; 1975), as well as his "aesthetic-realist" testimony, *Días y noches de amor y de guerra* (Days and Nights of Love and War; 1979).

IX

With the new decade, the names of younger writers began to challenge the editorial predominance of the more established literary personalities, although it is too early to tell whether or not this signaled the rise of a new artistic or social sensitivity. Much of this writing continued to emphasize an intense preoccupation with the convulsed political reality of the country and the resultant suffering of its population. Social novels cast fictionalized action against the backdrop of true-to-life circumstances, while poetically recreating documentary material. Also prominent was an autobiographical expression by members of this dislocated generation who had grown to maturity in the streets of Caracas, Paris, Madrid, or Munich, but whose identity behind the doors of their rented dwellings still remained nostalgically *oriental*. Similar topics would also occupy the imagination of older writers: in 1981 Martínez Moreno published his fictionalized study of militarism, *El color que el infierno me escondiera* (The Color Hell Holds for Me; 1981), and Galeano completed the three volumes of his lyrical documentary of Latin American history, *Memoria del fuego* (*Memory of Fire*, 1982-87).

This terrible drama for Uruguayan society and literature was somewhat appeased in 1985, when the military bosses allowed the partial reestablishment of constitutional government and the first election of a civilian president in twelve years. Many writers and artists who had belatedly relocated elsewhere were reluctant to leave new jobs and livelihoods. Through their efforts a strain of Uruguayan literature would continue to thrive in foreign lands. A different type of literary commitment awaited those writers who had remained or who had chosen to return. It was they who assumed the task of rebuilding a culture and a literature in the face of economic depression and weakened cultural institutions. Inevitably, these problems would affect the tone and topic of Uruguayan literature into the forseeable future.

BIBLIOGRAPHY

Benedetti, Mario. *Literatura uruguaya, siglo XX: ensayo*. 2nd expanded ed. Montevideo: Alfa, 1969. The various essays treating the outstanding writers of this century offer judicious and penetrating insights with regard to both ideological and formal qualities.

Bollo, Sarah. *Literatura uruguaya, 1807-1975*. Montevideo: Universidad de la República, 1976. Biobibliographical data is given for over 400 writers and poets, with brief critical descriptions. The appendix offers useful generational groupings and lists of important periodicals.

Englekirk, John E., and Margaret M. Ramos. *La narrativa uruguaya: estudio crítico-bibliográfico*. Berkeley: University of California Press, 1967. The eighty-page historical overview of Uruguayan narrative is followed by an impressive 220-page "register" of over 400 authors, that provides exhaustive details about editions, contents, and critical commentary on published works.

Franco, Jean. *The Modern Culture of Latin America: Society and the Artist*. Rev. ed. Baltimore: Penguin Books, 1970. Although treating Latin America in general, its brief social and ideological commentary about the important twentieth-century Uruguayan writers is noteworthy.

Rama, Angel. *La generación crítica 1939-1969.* I: *Panoramas.* Montevideo: Arca, 1972. Insightful and detailed treatment, often repetitive, of artistic and intellectual currents, with elucidating studies on the principal writers and poets.

Real de Azúa, Carlos. *Antología del ensayo uruguayo contemporáneo.* Montevideo: Universidad de la República, 1964. Biobibliographical information and penetrating criticisms given in the introductory sections for forty of the country's most outstanding essayists and literary critics.

Real de Azúa, Carlos. *Un siglo y medio de cultura uruguaya.* Montevideo: 1958. In-depth, often penetrating, treatment of the genesis and outgrowths of writers' ideas, but not outstanding with regard to literary qualities.

Rela, Walter. *Historia del teatro uruguayo: 1808-1968.* Montevideo: Banda Oriental, 1969. The fact-filled narrative tracing the development of Uruguayan theater is supplemented by a chronological table of plays by Uruguayan writers, a long bibliography, and helpful indexes.

Rela, Walter. *Literatura uruguaya: bibliografía selectiva.* Tempe: Arizona State University, Center for Latin American Studies, 1986. An essential registry of works and critical studies.

Rela, Walter. *Literatura uruguaya: tablas cronológicas, 1835-1985. Indice de publicaciones periódicas, 1838-1986.* Montevideo: Universidad Católica del Uruguay, 1986. Detailed chronologies on the essay, theater, poetry, and narrative.

Rodríguez Monegal, Emir. *Literatura uruguaya del medio siglo.* Montevideo: Alfa, 1966. Detailed treatment of the literary, cultural and artistic currents from 1958, with brief reference to significant writers and tendencies of the early century. The work singles out five principal creators in each of narrative, poetry, theater, and essay for extended, penetrating study.

Trigo, Abril. *Caudillo, estado, nación: literatura, historia e ideología en el Uruguay.* Gaithersburg, MD: Hispamérica, 1990. An authoritative ideological reading of those events and literary works (particularly dramatic) most impregnated with sociopolitical significance.

Visca, Arturo Sergio. *Aspectos de la narrativa criollista.* Montevideo: Biblioteca Nacional, 1972. This largely stylistic study, at times without social or ideological insights, focuses on more than twenty Creolist writers, going back to 1880.

Zum Felde, Alberto. *Proceso intelectual del Uruguay y crítica de su literatura*. Montevideo: Imprenta Nacional Colorada, 1930. The country's most respected literary and intellectual historian expands his 1921 *Crítica de la literatura uruguaya* into a three-volume inclusive treatment of political and artistic currents. While ignoring many social and ideological issues, it offers detailed analyses of narrative plots and characters.

VENEZUELA
John Beverley
University of Pittsburgh

I

When Rómulo Gallegos published *Doña Bárbara* in 1929, some seventy-five percent of the population of Venezuela lived in the countryside, twenty-five percent in the cities and major towns. The dominant economic form was still the traditional latifundio, the dominant economic activity production of agricultural commodities (sugar, coffee, cacao, beef, hides) for export. In the last half century, because of a very rapid and uneven process of capitalist industrialization, a demographic mutation has taken place. At present, eighty percent of the population of Venezuela (which has roughly quadrupled since 1927) is located in the urban sector, and of this eighty percent, sixty percent is concentrated in eight large cities. The capital city of Caracas has grown from a somewhat bucolic colonial city of two or three-hundred thousand residents to a metropolitan labyrinth with a population of over three million today. Concurrently, the dominant economic sectors have shifted from agriculture to the advanced technologies of the oil and iron ore extractive industries and to import-substitution manufacturing and merchandising enterprises, some under private, others under state ownership. The urban population is articulated into a new spectrum of class relationships by the economic shift: industrial, state, and financial elite; urban petty bourgeoisie; white-collar middle strata of bureaucrats, technicians, and professionals; a partly unionized blue-collar proletariat; and, most strikingly, the extensive subproletariat of the *ranchos* (shanty towns), the so-called marginal population driven off the countryside but not yet integrated into the capitalist labor market.

In 1966, the novelist Adriano González León complained in an interview that modern Venezuelan narrative had failed to confront the structural and syntactic innovations of a Joyce, what he termed Kafka's "metaphysics of disorientation and the void," and the "explosive energy" of Faulkner and the U.S. novel in general. It remained, he argued, a provincial narrative, anachronistic in both its themes and techniques.

What is the relation between these two phenomena, the one concerning an "elite" level of cultural production (the novel), the other a fundamental transformation of the economic, political, and demographic structure of modern Venezuela? Around an answer to this question, we will trace a trajectory of the development of Venezuelan literature in its coincidence with the major social and political forces that have shaped that country's history from the moment of independence in the early nineteenth century to the near present. There are three key literary-ideological points in this trajectory: the heyday of Liberal Romanticism in the mid and late nineteenth century; the crisis of Liberalism and the rise of a populist social realism in the 1920s and 1930s; finally, the "modernization crisis" of the 1960s and the emergence of a Venezuelan boom in narrative and poetry.

II

The breakup of the Spanish American empire and the consequent formation of nation-states like Venezuela out of its diverse parts in the early nineteenth century represented the effect of an emerging class aspiring to become dominant: the creole bourgeoisie located in the urban centers of the colonial system and deriving its cohesion and identity as a class from its involvement in import/export trade with first Spain, then the world market. The ideological expression of this class was an adaptation of European and North American Liberalism that revolved around three basic principles: 1) free trade, based on the principle of "mutual advantage" derived via the unhindered operation of the international market from the specialization of Latin American countries as producers and exporters of foodstuffs and raw materials in exchange for importation of commodities elaborated by European industrial capitalism (principally English to begin with); 2) diffusionism, the principle of encouraging the penetration of Latin America by foreign capital and technology, channeled through the urban centers into the "interior"; 3) republicanism, or the organization of the nation-state as a representative democracy, centralized around the urban network and controlled politically by the bourgeoisie. As André Gunder Frank has shown, the essence of the social project of the Liberal bourgeoisie in Latin America may be expressed in the formula: metropolis-center (Europe) > metropolis-periphery (Latin American cities) > interior (traditional latifundio), where the direction of transfer of economic value flows towards the center, while the direction of political and cultural control flows from the center. Quite consciously, Liberal ideology made the motor of sociocultural change exogenous by opening up Latin America to what was seen as the progressive operation of the world market and of capital investment by Europe and North America.

Latin American Romanticism both stems from and acts as a sustaining expression—an ideological practice—for the Latin American nineteenth century Liberal project. Romanticism involves an implicit conception of history, society, and the role of the individual both as leader and follower, a conception expressing the need to create through a psychic catharsis and prolonged pedagogical "uplifting" a new American character structure free from the inheritances of the colonial period.

Among these inheritances was not, however, a well-developed tradition of colonial literary production such as existed in the urban centers (Lima, Mexico City, Bogotá, later Buenos Aires) of the major vice-royalties. This is not to say that Venezuela lacked entirely a colonial literature. There are the inevitable chronicles and "histories" of the province, such as *Historia de la conquista y población de Venezuela* (History of the Conquest and Settlement of Venezuela; 1723) by José Oviedo y Baños (1671-1738), generally considered the first expression of Venezuelan literary nationalism; a Baroque *costumbrismo* (sketches of daily life) in, for example, *Teatro de Caracas* (Theater of Caracas; 1770?) by Blas José Terrero (1735-1802), or the four-volumes of *Relación de visitas* (Travel Digest; 1791) by Bishop Mariano Martí (1721-1794); and a variety of forms of poetry, including the popular, mestizo ballads called *aguinaldos* and lyrics in Indian languages. But there is no Venezuelan figure comparable to, say, Sor Juana Inés de la Cruz (see the section on Mexico). Venezuelan national literature is, in a sense, a Liberal invention.

Liberalism saw the development of a national literature as a way to create a mentality appropriate for the consolidation of the newly independent nations under the hegemony of an enlightened bourgeois despotism. In this process, the writer conceives of himself as a sort of Moses, "informing" the mass of the population, which is seen as still submerged in semibarbarism, lacking rational self-consciousness and an emancipatory will to power. Romantic literature is nationalistic in the sense that it attempts to construct a vision of a new American cosmos. But within this cosmos, the human and natural elements of the new republics find their proper place and use in terms of their integration into the evolving social project of the Liberal bourgeoisie (which, in the fashion of French Republicanism, invests itself with the character of being a movement of universal human emancipation).

The characteristic narrative genres of Romanticism are forms like the epic of the conquest of the interior or the rural idyll that elevate the class project of the urban bourgeoisie to the level of a national enterprise deserving and demanding the allegiance of all social groups: "civilization versus barbarism". The Romantic "Adam" who actualizes in his person the qualities of the future Liberal utopia is typically the Byronic intellectual/young officer/businessman (sometimes a blend of all three) who directs the process of social integration of the interior, inviting (pedagogically) or obliging (militarily) other social classes and peoples to cancel their own interests and identity and subjugate themselves to his "civilizing" will, which is deemed the condition for their own human emancipation. This hero is the product of the city, which irradiates itself through his action into the national body politic. By contrast, the characteristic villain of Romantic narrative is the particularist egotism of the latifundista elite (provincial caudillos and cruel landowners) that fragments the unity of the body politic and leaves it in a state of cultural and economic childhood.

Liberal Romanticism finds its most characteristic expression in nineteenth-century Venezuelan writing in the literary work of Simón Bolívar (1783-1830) himself; in the nostalgic Bolivarism of such "Romantic histories" as *Venezuela heroica* (Heroic Venezuela; 1881) by Eduardo Blanco (1840-1912), or the *Biografía de José Félix Ribas* (Biography of José Félix Ribas; 1859) by Juan Vicente González (1810-66), which consecrate for Venezuelan creole nationalism something like the North American myth of the founding fathers; in the poems, essays, and social *costumbrismo* of Liberal pedagogues like Andrés Bello (1781-1865), the greatest of Venezuela's nineteenth-century intellectuals: "Silva a la agricultura de la zona tórrida" (Song to Tropical Agriculture; 1826); Simón Rodríguez (1771-1854): *Sociedades americanas* (American Societies; 1840); Francisco Lazo Martí (1868-1909): "Silva criolla" (Creole Song; 1901); or Juan Antonio Pérez Bonalde (1846-92): "Vuelta a la patria" (Coming Home; 1890). The text that perhaps best represents Liberal Romanticism in Venezuela is from the end of the nineteenth century: the novel *Peonía* (1890) by Manuel Romero García (1861-1917), a variant of the oligarchic rural idyll whose founding model was *María* by the Colombian novelist Jorge Isaacs (see the section on Colombia).

Peonía is written in a pseudoautobiographical first-person singular. It concerns a young engineer, Carlos, recently graduated from college in Caracas, who is invited to visit his uncle Pedro at his hacienda, Peonía. Don Pedro, a brutal and ignorant man, symbolizes the backwardness of the conservative rural oligarchy. He is engaged in a dispute with his brother Nicolás over the boundaries of his estate (Nicolás is the "good" landowner, friendly to his workers and progressive in outlook). During his visit, Carlos falls in love with his cousin Luisa, Pedro's daughter. He is forced to return to Caracas for a time, where he is arrested and exiled as a political discontent. Eventually, he is able to return to Peonía to reclaim Luisa and presumably become the new heir to the hacienda. However, the servants and peasants of the estate have rebelled against Don Pedro's brutality and, just as Carlos arrives, they set fire to the house. Pedro and his family perish in the fire. Luisa dies in Carlos's arms.

III

As a late nineteenth-century novel, *Peonía* reflects not only the traditional Liberal allegorical coordinates of civilization versus barbarism, city versus "interior," reason and science versus instinct, elite versus mass. It also suggests, particularly in the sections concerning Carlos's imprisonment and exile, a crisis at the center of the Liberal project itself, which has revealed instead of the expected utopia of Progress and Democracy something much more sinister.

By holding that Adam Smith's "unseen hand" of the marketplace destined the Latin American republics to specialize in agricultural exports, Liberalism imposed on them a built-in limitation. Since the creole bourgeoisie was intermediary between the direct production of commodities in the interior and their eventual destination on the international market, it possessed no great impulse to transform the character of agricultural production per se. It placed the latifundio and the indigenous sectors under the political control of the city; it linked the city with the interior and the world market through the building of railway and transportation networks; it developed port facilities, rationalized fiscal and tariff policies, and so on. But it did not fundamentally transform the structure of production relations and techniques in the countryside nor the conditions of life of the peasantry. Investment in and development of new areas of production was largely handed over to foreign capital and was centered mainly in raw material extraction (oil, rubber, minerals).

Because of this limitation, in none of the Latin American republics did the desired objective of Liberalism resolve itself purely; it was always conditioned by various forms of international dependence (commodity prices, imperialist foreign policy rivalry) and the national alliances, compromises, practical forms of power necessary to safeguard its basic economic interests. Hence the tragicomedy of the Liberal century that Gabriel García Márquez traces so elegantly in his *Cien años de soledad* (*One Hundred Years of Solitude*; see the section on Colombia): "uplifting" democratic presidents in the fashion of Argentina's Domingo Faustino Sarmiento (see the section on Argentina) in alternation with reactionary military despotisms; the "positivist" dictatorships of the late nineteenth century; the unending civil wars between Conservatives and Liberals in which issues are either forgotten or futile, since neither side can decisively defeat the other.

In Venezuela it is the dictatorship of Juan Vicente Gómez, straddling most of the first third of the twentieth century, that comes to represent a sort of dystopian apotheosis of the nineteenth-century Liberal project. The rural latifundio is linked to the port city via the river network, the provincial market centers, the railways. It produces—primitively but lucratively—cacao, coffee, sugar, beef, and leather for an export trade controlled by a newly cosmopolitan urban bourgeoisie with its homes, servants, stock exchange, banks, clubs, warehouses, shipping firms, university, and the like. State power is exercised via the iron-handed patriarch, who can hold in balance the economic and political rivalries of the landowners and the bourgeoisie and at the same time welcome the entry of foreign capital to exploit the nation's resources in the name of a self-evident "progress" (self-evident since the national bourgeoisie is incapable financially, politically, and technically of undertaking such a project itself).

In this situation, Liberalism must redefine and reenergize itself as a formative national ideology. As long as the rural masses remain in a state of economic apathy and immiseration barely on the margin of the money economy, there is no room for profitable capitalist expansion beyond production for export, since the sector of national consumption is stagnant, limited to the privileged latifundistas and Creole bourgeoisie and a small middle class whose consumption needs can be serviced by imports. The indirect revenues accruing to Venezuela from the oil industry, as well as the social and technological spin-offs of the presence of highly-articulated monopoly capitalist enclaves in the country, provide over time, however, a basis for the formation of a *desarrollista* (developmentalist) faction of the bourgeoisie. This group will gradually differentiate itself from the import-export intermediary model of the traditional bourgeoisie, in particular, by supporting economic measures that depend in turn on the development of Venezuelan industry and markets (e.g., import substitution). In this process, it is seen as essential that sections of the peasantry be freed from their bondage to the latifundio and capacitated both as consumers and industrial workers. This will put at the center of political and social struggle the issue of agrarian reform. At the same time, "from below," so to speak, there is throughout the 1920s increased labor and peasant militancy: in 1925, for example, there is a general strike in the vast oil fields around Lake Maracaibo.

In Venezuela, the first inklings of this new bourgeois project appear in the Generation of 1928, so named because of the widespread student demonstrations in that year against the Gómez dictatorship. The decisive political product of the Generation of 1928 and the major shaping force in modern Venezuelan history is Rómulo Betancourt (1908-81) and his Acción Democrática (Democratic Action) party. Acción Democrática will structure itself as a mass populist party, seeking to ally the sectors of the bourgeoisie and petty bourgeoisie cramped by the dictatorship and the oligarchic structure of social and economic power inherited from the nineteenth century with the awakening peasant and working class movement. It will advocate a nationalist program based on the necessity of land reform, nationalization of natural resource production (particularly oil), mass public education, development subsidized by the state of national manufacture and industry, improvement in the living standards of the working population, free trade unions and peasant leagues, and full political democracy.

Acción Democrática and parties like it represent a decisive new stage of bourgeois ideology in Latin America, a transition from traditional Liberalism to a variety of forms of populist nationalism (but not to socialism, as Betancourt signals by disaffiliating his organization from the Venezuelan communist movement in the 1930s). The dominant literary tendencies of the 1930s and 1940s will correspond to this shift.

IV

Rómulo Gallegos (1884-1969) and the writers immediately following him, like the early Guillermo Meneses (1911-77)—*Campeones* (Champions; 1939), *El mestizo José Vargas* (The Mestizo José Vargas; 1946); Ramón Díaz Sánchez (1903-68)—*Mene* (1936), *Cumboto* (1948); Julián Padrón (1910-54)—*Madrugada* (Dawn; 1939), *Clamor campesino* (Peasant Outcry; 1945); Miguel Otero Silva (1908)—*Fiebre* (Fever; 1939), *Oficina No. 1* (Office Number One; 1961), *Casas muertas* (Dead Houses; 1955); or Antonio Arráiz (1903-62)—*Puros hombres* (All Men; 1938); and in theater César Rengifo (1905) represent the culminating phase of what Venezuelan criticism calls "the cycle of *Peonía*": the development in the 1930s and 1940s of a Venezuelan novel of the land based on agrarian themes and reflecting a new sense of national pride (*criollismo* [Creolism]). The antecedents of this generation are in Venezuelan positivism and Modernism—Rufino Blanco Fombona (1874-1944), Manuel Díaz Rodríguez (1871-1927), Gonzalo Picón Febres (1860-1918), José Gil Fortoul (1862-1943)—and in the mordant satire of two key early twentieth-century novelists: José Rafael Pocaterra (18901955)—*Política feminista* (Feminist Politics; 1913), *Cuentos grotescos* (Grotesque Stories; 1922), and Teresa de la Parra (1898-1936)—*Ifigenia* (1924), *Las memorias de Mamá Blanca* (The Memoirs of Mother Blanca; 1929). But the 1930s novelists abandon the psychological introspection of Pocaterra and Parra. Their novels, and the parallel movement in poetry represented by Andrés Eloy Blanco (1897-1955), are works of social description and protest seeking to break Venezuela out of the violent rural apathy, to criticize American imperialism, and to integrate the mestizo peasantry into national life, to represent the new labor movement, to provoke if not a social revolution at least fundamental reforms of the sort espoused by Acción Democrática (most of these writers oscillate politically between nationalism and communism).

Gallegos's mature work, beginning with *Doña Bárbara* (1929)—in a sense, the founding text of Acción Democrática—coincides exactly with the political ferment of the Generation of 1928 in which Gallegos himself, like many of these writers, is a direct participant. *Doña Bárbara* follows the narrative-allegorical scheme of *Peonía* and Liberal romance. A young lawyer, Santos Luzardo, returns from Caracas to inherit the family estate in the *llanos*—the cattle-raising section of Venezuela—where he had spent his youth. His task is to restore the estate, which has been allowed to decay. His efforts put him in conflict with his neighbor, Doña Bárbara, who symbolizes, like don Pedro in *Peonía*, rural backwardness and bossism (*caudillismo*), and her ally, a sinister North American entrepreneur named Mr. Danger. Complications ensue when Santos falls in love with Bárbara's bastard daughter Marisela. Eventually, he defeats Bárbara, who disappears mysteriously, leaving Santos and Marisela to marry and merge the two haciendas.

The character of Doña Bárbara is clearly meant by Gallegos to resonate the Liberal image of the undeveloped interior as the "child" or "body" of the nation that must be made subject to a civilizing will. Her human development is strategically fixated at the age of fifteen when she witnesses the murder of a young wanderer she has fallen in love with—Asdrúbal—and is raped by his killers, a traumatic scene she returns to throughout the action and in her apparent suicide at the novel's end. She is identified directly with the state of nature, the violent llano and rivers, something moved only by superstition, instinct, animal cunning, and fear that cannot plan, that is finally powerless before Santos. (It goes without saying the association Bárbara-*barbarie* [barbarism] is sexist.) Santos Luzardo is the typical Liberal civilizer, holding in his head the image—"complex, ideal and perfect as a brain"—of the city. Evidently Bárbara symbolizes an anarchic human force and a rich but difficult nature (the Venezuelan mestizo personality, the llano) that if it can be "broken," trained, "put to work," is capable of tremendous accomplishments. The redemption of the daughter, Marisela, and her conversion into Santos's wife acts as a narrative signifier for this process of social incorporation.

But there are also senses in which the novel moves beyond the paradigm of nineteenth-century Liberalism. For one thing, Liberalism establishes, as we have noted, the dependency of the latifundio on the city but leaves its essential structure intact. Santos wants to transform the latifundio, to replace it, in effect, with capitalist farming. He wants to enclose the property he has clear title to with barbed wire, ending the traditional transhumance system of the llano and the intricate property disputes (counterfeit cattle brands, water rights, etc.) it gives rise to.

The relation that Santos establishes with his workers and with Marisela makes of his ranch, Altamira (High Point; by contrast, Bárbara's ranch is called El Miedo—Fear), the allegorical microcosm of the political alliance between the progressive national bourgeoisie and the peasantry. Gallegos's interest in racial mixing or *mestizaje* as the basis of the Venezuelan national character—it is a theme he will explore at length in his later novels of the 1930s, like *Cantaclaro* (1934), *Canaima* (1935), or

Pobre negro (Poor Black; 1937)—works to much the same effect. Marisela is, like her mother, a mestizo; her marriage with Santos provides an image of a new national elite that dissolves the traditional white monopoly on power and privilege. By contrast, Liberal writing, despite its folklore and costumbrismo and its nominal commitment to democracy, was represented basically by a white, Europeanizing vision of social progress that often took the form (the underside, so to speak, of the Romantic epic) of the genocide of native populations and racial *blanqueamiento* (whitening) via massive immigration from Europe.

Some of the writers associated with the concerns of the Generation of 1928 go further than Gallegos in their depiction of rural poverty and violence, moving towards a Marxist sense of class struggle in the countryside and in the new oil fields and mines (Julián Padrón and Miguel Otero Silva, for example). They coincide with Gallegos, however, in producing what we may characterize as a kind of populist realism bound up with the new political and cultural forces that emerge in Venezuela as elsewhere in Latin America in the decade of the 1930s, forces that will reach their culminating point at the end of the 1950s in close relation with the dynamic of the Cuban revolution.

V

We may now return to the issue raised at the beginning of this account by Adriano González León's remarks on the formal conservatism of Venezuelan literature. It should be clear that they are directed in particular against the whole tradition of Gallegos and the cycle of *Peonía*. González León belonged to the literary young Turks of groups like Sardio and Techo de la Ballena (Roof of the Whale) who began to champion in the late 1950s an attitude of iconoclasm towards the great Realist novels of the land of the preceding generation and who sought inspiration in an unstable amalgam of existentialism, Marxism, and literary Modernism (in the English-language sense of the term). The new writers resurrected, as an alternative to social realism, the experimental, introspective, and antiregionalist narrative and poetry associated with a group of writers of the 1930s and 1940s who constitute in diverse ways (they are far from forming a coherent generation or literary tendency) what has come to be known as *vanguardista* (avant-garde) writing. They include Julio Garmendia (1898)—*La tienda de muñecos* (The Marionette Store; 1927); the later Guillermo Meneses—e.g., *El falso cuaderno de*

Narciso Espejo (Narciso Mirror's False Notebook; 1952); Arturo Uslar Pietri (1906)—*Las lanzas coloradas* (Colored Spears; 1930), *El camino de El Dorado* (The Path to El Dorado; 1947); and Enrique Bernardo Núñez (1895-1964), whose *Cubaagua* (1931) and *La galera de Tiberio* (Tiberias's Galley; 1938) are regarded as precursors of "magic realism" in the Latin American novel of the 1950s.

The linearity of the plots of novels like *Doña Bárbara*, the recognizableness in social reality of their characters, their symbolic transparency as allegories of progressive and reactionary forces in Venezuelan history: these formal elements are not separate from what we might call the content of these novels as ideological discourse. They are meant to be popular, to give the Venezuelan of whatever social class understandable images—positive and negative heroes like the social realist novels of the Stalin period in Russia—which can be emulated, learned from. They aim to produce a sort of collective national myth that will draw into action even the lowest strata of society. Gallegos's sense of the possibility of a progressive national history and cultural development is built into the providential logic of his plots where all the contradictory, interlocked elements function to produce the desired "awakening" or reform. The sort of technical innovations González León finds missing are precisely those which if introduced into a Gallegos novel would problematize its communicative efficiency. To put this another way, González León in suggesting Joyce, Kafka, and Faulkner as the models for contemporary Venezuelan narrative was implicitly questioning the relation between Gallegos's style of social realism and the ideological presuppositions it is founded on. Why?

The defeat of the dictatorship of Marcos Pérez Jiménez in the insurrections of 1958 marks the triumph of the democratic national revolution proposed by the Generation of 1928 and frustrated in the first Acción Democrática government of 1947 in which Gallegos himself was elected president. From 1958 to the present, Acción Democrática will be the major shaping force in Venezuelan politics, consolidating the power of the national bourgeoisie and simultaneously managing to maintain control over the peasant and labor movements. A piecemeal agrarian reform completes the transformation of the countryside into a sector dominated by capitalist production models. The stranglehold of the latifundio is ended; "desarrollo para adentro" (development inwards) becomes the slogan of the new state and private entrepreneurs. In fallow hacienda lands mushroom housing projects, industrial parks, shanty towns to house the rural population flocking to the cities. Royalties on oil exports (which in the 1960s are still controlled by U.S. and European petroleum companies) feed the process of industrialization and modernization. Caracas metamorphoses into a sort of Latin American Los Angeles, girded with freeways, smog, housing shortages, skyscrapers, monumental traffic jams. A society of nouveaux riches appears side by side with idealistic middle class students devoted to political terrorism, urban gangs of rancho delinquents, technocrats, government bureaucrats, political police (the dreaded DIGEPOL), unionized workers in the new industrial parks, immigrants from Spain and Italy. Spanish colonial gives way to neo-Bauhaus in architecture; the traditional *coplas llaneras* (ranch songs), so admired by Gallegos, to North American "acid rock."

Gallegos's Santos Luzardo embodied two basic civilizing impulses: *cercar* (fence in) and *poblar* (populate). Venezuela's contemporary development has shown in practice that these impulses are contradictory. The agrarian reform, instead of populating the interior, forces masses of peasants who can no longer maintain themselves in the countryside into the cities where they form the unproductive subproletariat of the ranchos. While broad sectors of the population and the national space are in fact drawn into a highly articulated capitalist consumer economy, the polarization between city and countryside increases and sudden wealth on the one side is accompanied by staggering pauperization on the other. If anything, the new capitalism involves an increasing dependence on and domination by multinational capital that expresses itself in distortions on the level of language and culture. (González León cites a Chrysler press release to symbolize Venezuela in the 1960s: "Venezuela is rolling. And it's rolling in cars and trucks made in Venezuela. Chrysler is rolling along in step with the progress of a great democratic nation.") Finally, the transition from peonage to blue- or white-collar employment in modern enterprises is still fundamentally a transition from one form of class servitude to another, and the new antagonisms implicit in a capitalist economy begin to surface once the honeymoon of the populist alliance is over.

Symptomatic of the contradictions of the new phase of bourgeois hegemony is the armed struggle that convulses every level of Venezuelan life between 1960 and 1968. The Venezuelan Communist Party (PCV), also a product of the popular and intellectual ferment of the Generation of 1928, had traditionally allied itself with Acción Democrática around the program of a national democratic revolution, and it had played a major role in preparing the defeat of the Pérez Jiménez dictatorship. In 1960, together with a large section of AD itself that breaks away to form the MIR (Movement of the Revolutionary Left), the PCV launches its cadre into an urban and rural guerrilla war, charging Betancourt has betrayed the democratic program and is handing the country over to continued U.S. domination. The aim is to duplicate the achievement of the Cuban revolution, to create a political force that in extending the limits of the populist program to their utmost will create the preconditions for Venezuela's transition to socialism. The main guerrilla organization is the FALN—Frente Armada de Liberación Nacional (Armed Front for National Liberation).

The literary fellow travelers of the armed struggle—what one writer has called Venezuela's "izquierda cultural" (cultural left)—are writers like Adriano González León (1931) himself—in his *País portátil* (Portable Homeland; 1968), the representative novel of the 1960s in Venezuela; Salvador Garmendia (1928)—*Los pequeños seres* (Small People; 1959), *Los habitantes* (The Dwellers; 1961), *La mala vida* (The Bad Life; 1968); Argenis Rodríguez (1935)—*Entre las breñas* (In the Thicket; 1964); José Santos Urriola (1927)—*La hora más oscura* (The Darkest Hour; 1969); José Balza (1939)—*Largo* (Slow; 1968); Luis Britto García (1941)—*Vela de armas* (Deposition of Arms; 1970), *Rajatabla* (At Any Price; 1970); Domingo Miliani (1934)—*Recuentos* (Retold; 1969); Carlos Noguera (1943)—*Historias de la calle Lincoln* (Stories of Lincoln Street; 1971); Orlando Araujo (1928)—*Venezuela violenta* (Violent Venezuela; 1968); José Vincente Abreu (1927)—*Se llamaba SN* (Its Name Was S.N.; 1964), *Las cuatro letras* (The Four Letters; 1969); and, in the theater, Isaac Chocrón (1932)—*Asia y el lejano oriente* (Asia and the Far East; 1966); and José Cabrujas (1937)—*Profundo* (Deep; 1971).

Latin American boom writing in general shows a tendency to fuse literary Modernism with the apocalyptic thematics of what one critic (Hernán Vidal) has called "a crepuscular and dreamlike spectacle." This is a particularly apt description of Venezuelan new narrative centered on the experience of the armed struggle. *País portátil* concerns a young militant in the urban guerrilla underground who is traveling across Caracas to deliver weapons and plans for an action. The narrative is pure Joycean interior monologue. He goes over in his mind the intricate Kabbalah of the guerrilla: safe houses, pass words, synchronizations of actions. A kaleidoscope of fragmentary impressions of the city passes before him: faces, shops, traffic jams, police, sirens, student demonstrations. These are mixed with memories, anecdotes, family histories from his childhood in the countryside. His passage is from one violence to another, one fear to another. His odyssey culminates, like the history of his rural ancestors, in a sterile act of rebellion. His guerrilla group has been betrayed; the DIGEPOL is closing in: "¿Qué hacer? Imposible salvar nada. No hay tiempo, no hay calle, no hay camino, no hay un carajo" (What to do? Impossible to save anything. There's no time, there's no street, there's no road, there's fuck all").

The city is a violent and chaotic labyrinth in a novel like Balza's *Largo*. Torture is both a metaphor for consciousness and a material reality. The hero has lost the cohesion and sense of connection to history that characterizes Santos Luzardo. He is the faceless servant of the bourgeois apparatus who expects "a promotion at forty" (Garmendia; *Los pequeños seres*); the young guerrilla torn between idealism and fear; the rootless juvenile delinquent of the ranchos: that is, people who live either at the margin of society or who have lost themselves within it. Narrative technique mirrors this decomposition of personality; it becomes subjective, schizophrenic. Past and present, memory, desire, and reality meet and separate in intricate series of overlapping planes. Plot takes on something of the random simultaneity of the city itself. The new narrative is seconded by an iconoclastic new-wave poetry, centered around the work of figures like Guillermo Sucre (1933), Rafael Cadenas (1930), Ramón Palomares (1935), Juan Calzadilla (1931), Edmundo Aray (1936), Gustavo Pereira (1940), and Rafael José Muñoz (1928).

It is clear that this is a writing that is post-Liberal in its structuring assumptions, one that no longer reproduces the pattern of becoming in a stable space and time characteristic of narrative realism, a writing that is a reaction on the aesthetic level to the whole project of capitalist modernization and consumerism. But is it a revolutionary writing? There was a good deal of posturing by the Venezuelan boom writers as to how their experimentalism was the equivalent in literature of the vanguard action of the guerrilla group celebrated in Régis Debray's popular manual, *Revolución en la revolución* (Revolution in the Revolution; 1961). But this was in a sense to beg the question: to the extent that the Venezuelan armed struggle was unable to develop a broad popular base, something increasingly evident after 1965 when the Communist Party pulls out and leaves its direction in the hands of young leftists, it was itself a peculiar but not uncharacteristic form of Liberal heroism that appealed to the idealism of new middle- and upper-class youth. Venezuelan writing in the 1960s intended to transgress the limits of Liberal ideology in both its traditional and populist forms; it pointed tacitly or explicitly to the need for solving the problems of Venezuela's *anti-desarrollo* (antidevelopment) by following the model of the Cuban revolution, still very much in its heroic phase. At the same time, however, there is a sense in which this writing, with its emphasis on the novel, the mobile, the gratuitous, the chaotic, the carnavalesque, reproduces the very conditions of anomie and alienation it pretends to question, making of the text a sort of private utopia or psychedelic trip capable of producing a catharsis in a reading public disoriented by what the Mexican writer Carlos Fuentes was to call "the sudden presence of modernity": the shock of the new.

Despite its declared identification with the Left, Venezuelan boom writing was less successful in many ways than the earlier novel of the land it displaced in evoking those social forces—particularly the new working class—that have begun to emerge in the last fifty years. The literary form that perhaps best represents these forces is the so-called *testimonio* (testimony), a semidocumentary, first-person narrative in which the "author" (or speaker) of the story is also its real protagonist.

Testimonio is a hybrid literary form in which a professional writer edits into book or story form the tape-recorded oral narrative of an informant. Venezuela has been one of the countries in Latin America where testimonio has been most developed and popularized, particularly in the years 1970-75 by the left-wing publishing house Editorial Fuentes in Caracas. Two main types emerged. First, there are neopicaresque narratives derived from the life of the subproletariat of the ranchos or urban slums or from 1960s drug culture. They include, for example, the prison testimonio *Retén de Catia* (Catia Lockup; 1972) by Juan Sebastián Aldana (dates unknown), *Pito de oro* (The Golden Whistle; 1973), about drug addiction, by Clara Posani (dates unknown), and the classic *Soy un delincuente* (I'm a Juvenile Delinquent; 1974) by Ramón Antonio Brizuela (1952-73; he was killed in a shoot-out with the police). The second group includes memoirs by men and women who were involved in the armed struggle. The best of many are perhaps *Aquí no ha pasado nada* (Nothing Happened Here; 1972) by the journalist Angela Zago (1943?) and *FALN Brigada Uno* (FALN: First Brigade; 1973) by Luis Correa (dates unknown). It is interesting to note that testimonios have been the basis for a number of scripts in Venezuela's rapidly developing movie and television industry.

Part of the convention of the testimonio is precisely its apparently "extraliterary" character, its appeal to the immediacy of a popular voice representing its own experience of life and history without formal or stylistic manipulation or a strong authorial presence. Testimonios are narrations "from below," so to speak, usually by people who otherwise would have no access to producing literature. It would be wrong to think of them as primarily "documentary" in character, however. Consciously or unconsciously, testimonio in Venezuela, as elsewhere in Latin America, appeared as a *literary* alternative to the experimentalism and cosmopolitanism of the boom writers. It offers what is in effect a new form of literary narrative—no longer something that could be called precisely a novel—produced not by the traditional Latin American "author" as a class-bound figure in both the colonial and national periods, but by those social classes and groups that are struggling for their full human development and expression. Testimonio is the voice of something that is coming into being, and as a literary form is itself still unstable and hard to classify. It represents, in this sense, the moment of—again in the English-language sense—a Postmodernism in Venezuelan literature.

BIBLIOGRAPHY

Araujo, Orlando. *Narrativa venezolana contemporánea.* Caracas: Editorial Tiempo Nuevo, 1972. On the boom writers.

Belrose, Maurice. *La sociedad venezolana en su novela (1890-1935).* Maracaibo: Universidad de Zulia, 1979. On the "cycle of *Peonía.*"

Chacón, Alfredo. *La izquierda cultural venezolana (1958-1968).* Caracas: Editorial Fuentes, 1971. Overview and anthology of the literary fellow travelers of the Venezuelan armed struggle in the 1960s.

Díaz Seijas, Pedro. *La antigua y la moderna literatura venezolana.* Caracas: Ediciones Armitano, 1966. A useful general history and anthology.

Diccionario general de la literatura venezolana. Mérida: Centro de Investigaciones Literarias, 1974. Useful reference work.

Liscano, Juan. *Panorama de la literatura venezolana actual.* Caracas: Publicaciones Españolas, 1973. The best general survey of modern Venezuelan literature.

Medina, José Ramón. *50 años de literatura venezolana (1918-1968).* Caracas: Monte Avila, 1969. Examines twentieth-century literature.

Miliani, Domingo. *Tríptico venezolano.* Caracas: Fundación de Promoción Cultural, 1985. Essays on Venezuelan narrative, intellectual history, and literary criticism by the country's most important contemporary critic.

Monasteri, Rubén. *Un enfoque crítico del teatro venezolano*. Caracas: Monte Avila, 1975. On theater.

Osorio, Nelson. *La formación de la vanguardia literaria en Venezuela*. Caracas: Biblioteca de la Academia Nacional de la Historia, 1985. Important revision of Venezuelan avant-garde writing in the 1920s and 1930s.

Páes Puma, Mauro. *Orígenes de la poesía colonial venezolana*. Caracas: Consejo Municipal, 1979. Excellent study and anthology of colonial poetry, including indigenous writers.

Picón Salas, Mariano. *Literatura venezolana*. Caracas, 1940. This classic literary history, which has had various subsequent editions, reflects the vision of the Generation of 1928.

Subero, Efraín. *El primer poema de tema venezolano*. Caracas: Centro de Investigaciones Literarias de UCAB, 1973. See the essay "En torno a la literatura colonial y folklórica" on colonial and folkloric literature.

Uslar Pietri, Arturo. *Letras y hombres de Venezuela*. México, D.F.: Fondo de Cultura Económica, 1948. A personal overview by one of Venezuela's important modern writer-critics.

Vilda, Carmelo. *Proceso de la cultura venezolana: I (1498-1830); II (1830-1930); III (1935-1985)*. Caracas: Centro Gumilla, 1984. Very helpful overview of Venezuelan culture and literature published in pamphlet form.

LATINO WRITING IN THE UNITED STATES

Santa Arias
and
Erlinda Gonzales-Berry
University of New Mexico

I

Latinos in the United States have been writing fiction, writing their selves, and writing about their experiences ever since the first explorers came to America five hundred years ago. The existence of numerous historical and legal documents, poems, and fictional narratives treating travel, exploration, war, love, the unknown, and the struggle for survival testifies to the rich literary and oral tradition created by the conquistadors and missionaries. These beginnings were testimonies of the fears and conflicts of those who were sent to the unexplored north with the promise of finding the fabled riches and thereby changing their already disillusioning foray into the New World. The written chronicles of these expeditions have, in common with the contemporary cultural manifestations of Latinos in this country, a manifestation of individual experience of rupture and displacement produced by their new historical reality. In these early cultural manifestations of the Spanish explorers, one can find the foundations of Latin American literary discourse and, moreover, the foundations of the Latino cultural expression in the United States. The testimonial and legal documents of the northern frontier were crucial in the self-defense and criticism of the conditions in which the explorers lived at the time, after serving and risking their lives for the Spanish Crown. The legacy of the chronicles—called *crónicas* in Spanish, a major genre of the written culture of the Conquest—and the critical interpretation of those early years of exploration and conquest, is still so alive in the texts written by Latinos that it can not be ignored. We can state that Latino literary discourse, as the expression of the colonial/colonized subject, provides vivid testimony of cultural conflict, disruption of identity, and change and adaptation. Significantly, this testimony can serve as an instrument of empowerment.

With the progressive transformation of literary studies into cultural studies, and with sociohistorical and feminist criticism demonstrating that literary texts are products with sociohistorical referents, ethnic writing has become the center of much attention of literary critics, professional organizations, and publishers, not only in the United States but also in Latin America and Europe. Still, forms that are specifically Latino, Afro-American, or Asian-American in nature, whether poetry or other forms of cultural expression, are continually threatened by the dominance of Euro-American aesthetic concepts. However, the 1980s have represented an attempt to demarginalize Latino discourses with increased exposure in academic scholarship, university programs like American Studies, Ethnic Studies, English and Spanish departments, and mainstream media. Another important change of the 1980s was the addition of popular culture and mass media to the cultural studies agenda. All these factors have contributed to a reconceptualization of the United States not as a "melting pot," but as a multicultural and multicentric space, along with recognition of the crucial role played by ethnic minorities.

The civil rights movement of the 1960s gave rise to the creation of many Latino journals, newspapers, and small presses that, while often unrecognized by the academy, nevertheless provided a forum for the articulation of Latino culture. Currently, several journals dealing with Latino culture in the United States, like *Melus, Third Woman, Bilingual Review/La revista bilingüe, Boletín del Centro de Estudios Puertorriqueños* (Bulletin of the Center for Puerto Rican Studies), *The Americas Review* (formerly *Revista chicano-riqueña* [Chicano-Puerto Rican Review]) are beginning to receive broader recognition. These journals of Latino culture publish creative and critical culture texts, language and sociohistorical research essays, reviews and visual art. They have become a new vehicle of promotion and diffusion of Latino cultural expression and interpretation, and they appeal not only to the academic community, but also to a larger audience interested in the evolving "self" of Latino culture.

Many Latino writers like Oscar Hijuelos (1951), Elena Castedo (1940), Sandra Cisneros (1954), and Jimmy Santiago Baca (1952) have broken into the commercial world by signing contracts with major publishing companies. Oscar Hijuelos's the *Mambo Kings Play Songs of Love* (1989), published in translation by Ediciones Firuela in Madrid in

1990, won the Pulitzer Prise in the same year. Elena Castedo's first novel, *Paradise* (1990), translated by the author, was a finalist for the 1991 National Book Award. Also, the bilingual edition, with English translation by David William Foster, of Aristeo Brito's *El diablo en Texas* (*The Devil in Texas*; 1976) received the 1990 Western States Book Award in fiction. Other writers who began writing in Spanish, such as Elías Miguel Muñoz (1954) and Roberto Fernández (1951), have switched to English, mainly to expand their readership and publication opportunities. This move of Latino cultural expression from the margins to the center and the increasing attention on the borderland worlds of ethnic communities open up a new set of questions and needs for redefinition. Notwithstanding the success and recognition of some of the Latino writers and their texts by mainstream critics and institutions, their referent remains centered on the experience of exile and Latin America.

Many worlds overlap in Latino literary discourse articulating new positions. It is the cultural expression of a borderland space where language, class, gender, and racial ethnicity are the interrelated themes in the Latino ethos. As expressed not only in the content of the text, but in the rhetorical and formal construction of expression, language and identity have been major concerns of Chicanos, Boricuas (Puerto Ricans), and Cuban American writers. We cannot claim that the dominant language of expression has been English; in the last decade Latinos have been writing in English, Spanish, or both. Interlinguality has been one of the most dominant signifying elements in the writing of identity and creation of a Latino text. In the sixties it was the strongest form of counterdiscourse, an expression of self-affirmation and the articulation of identity. This stylistic preference, while expanding metaphorical possibilities, also placed the ideological perspective in the foreground.

Latinas, that is to say Latino women, have been writing for a long time. This is evident when one takes a close look at the works produced by women in the nineteenth century, many of them still waiting in archives for publication and study. It has been in the last two decades, with the rise of the civil rights movement and the impact of the Anglo-feminist movement in the United States, that we have seen the emergence and widespread use of feminist perspectives by women of color on culture, politics, and the literary expression of their experience. A prominent theme in the writing of Latinas has been the call for a trans-Latina solidarity in order to fight patriarchy and double marginalization. In this period the voices of this doubly oppressed group began to be heard in the call for action in the public as well as in the private sphere. In narrative, female characters begin to appear who act not as images of male-edifying alterity, but rather as women struggling with the contradictions that permeate daily life in a sexist society.

The publication of critical and creative anthologies by Latinas or women of color has made an impact in the reception and perception of Latino discursive production. Among the most important collections are: *Hispanic Women Write* (1983), edited by Evangelina Vigil (1949); *Cuentos: Stories by Latinas* (1983), edited by Alma Gómez (1953), Cherríe Moraga (1952), and Mariana Romo-Carmona (1952); *Breaking Boundaries: Latina Writings and Critical Readings* (1989), edited by Asunción Horno-Delgado (1956), Eliana Ortega (1942), Nina M. Scott (1937), and Nancy Saporta Sternbach (1949); and *Making Face, Making Soul* (1990), edited by Gloria Anzaldúa (1942). Another important source dedicated only to Chicana (Chicano women writers) literary discourse is the edited collection of critical essays entitled *Chicana Creativity and Criticism: Charting New Frontiers in American Literature* (1988) by María Herrera-Sobek (1942) and Helena Viramontes (1954). To the literary expression of Chicana, Puerto Rican, and Cuban American we have to add the literary production of the Chilean Marjorie Agosín (1955) and the Dominican Julia Alvarez (1950).

When we address the issue of Latino literary discourse, we must acknowledge that it is a dynamic and pluricultural form of expression that goes beyond the Chicano, Cuban, and Puerto Rican production. It is impossible to ignore the written expression of the diaspora from Central America, South American, and many non-Spanish-speaking countries that has become part of the Latino community, for the voices of these exiles are also beginning to be heard as a contribution to the formation of a new transnational culture. Many writers who form part of what has been called exile literature view their work as existing within the literary canon of their country of origin. However, some of these writers are beginning to write about their exile experience and to be included in anthologies of ethnic American writers. One important publication is a 1990 number of the *Americas Review* dedicated to exile literary discourse, *Paradise Lost or Gained?: the Literature of Hispanic Exile*, edited by Fernando Alegría and Jorge Rufinelli.

Without denying the relevance of other more recently arrived Latin American immigrants, the decision has been to dedicate most of this survey to the evolving discursive practices of the three most visible groups: Chicanos, Puerto Ricans, and Cuban Americans. Not only are they the largest groups, but their presence and their literary production on North American soil extends back four hundred years in the case of Chicanos, and in that of Puerto Ricans and Cubans, over a century. It is not our intention to suggest that the latter share a homogeneous experience. Chicanos, people of Mexican descent, can claim their presence in the United States Southwest since the earliest Spanish colonies of the sixteenth century, though Mexican inmigrants in the twentieth century have ventured beyond that region. The steady flow of immigration of Mexicans to this country is owed to the proximity of Mexico and to the demand of the American industries for cheap labor. Puerto Ricans have been American citizens since 1917 when the Jones Act was approved by the Congress of the United States. The political status of the island with regard to the United States was first that of a territory; subsecuently it became a Commonwealth (Estado Libre Asociado) in 1952. As a consequence of this status the Puerto Rican working class has been emigrating to the United States since the end of the nineteenth century in search of a better life. Even though Cuban presence in the United States dates from the nineteenth century, the major influx occured as a consequence of the 1959 Cuban Revolution. These Cubans are, consequently, political exiles rather than working class immigrants.

II. Chicano Literature

One of the most patently visible facets of Chicanos' efforts in the sixties and seventies to assert themselves through a form of cultural nationalism was a burgeoning corpus of creative literature that, above all, served as a vehicle of self-knowledge. In their task of accumulating evidence for a collective self-portrait, Chicano writers, in the literary production of the last two-and-a-half decades, have explored their past, revitalized and mystified their cultural values, and examined what it means to exist in the interstices and on the borders of two monolithic cultures.

Initially called a renaissance phenomenon, this corpus of literature did not develop in a vacuum. It is based on a solid literary tradition that has its origins in the exploration and settlement of the Southwest by inhabitants of Mexico and Spain more than four centuries ago. Luis Leal elucidates the background of Chicano literature of the prerenaissance period by pointing out four distinct stages of development (18-30). During the Hispanic phase, 1542-1821, he includes dozens of chronicles and travel journals, among them the *Naufragios y comentarios* (The Journey of Alvar Nuñez Cabeza de Vaca; 1542) by Alvar Núñez Cabeza de Vaca (1490-1557), *Relación del descubrimiento de las siete ciudades de Cíbola* (*Account of the Discovery of the Seven Cities of Cibola*; 1539) by Fray Marcos de Niza (ca. 1510-ca. 1570), and Pedro de Castañeda (dates unknown) *Relación de la jornada de Coronado* (The Journey of Coronado; 1542). One of the most important works of this period, an epic poem of 34 vergillian cantos by Gaspar Pérez de Villagrá (1555-1620), *Historia de la Nueva México* (History of New Mexico; 1610), was unfortunately cast into the category of good history and bad poetry by an early reader. Only in recent years has it begun to receive the attention it merits as a literary text and to be recognized as the first epic of North American Literature. A broad variety of oral genres, introduced from Spain and Mexico to the northern borderlands and those created in the region, shored up the corpus of expressive culture of the Spanish period. In this category we can point to the *romances* (ballads), *coplas* (couplets), *cuentos* (legends), *décimas* (ten line verses), *autos sacramentales* (religious dramas), *pastorelas* (shepards plays), many of which exist today in the memories of the older generation.

There was no hiatus of production during the Mexican Period (1821-48) and, in addition to the continued vitality and evolution of the oral genres, we can point to specific works such as Lorenzo de Zavala's *Viaje a los Estados-Unidos de Norte America* (Journey to the United States of North America; 1834), an ethnographic narrative by Gerónimo Boscana (1776-1831) called *Chinigchinich* (1846), *Pastorela en dos actos* (Pastorale in Two Acts; 1828), the anonymous historical drama, *Los Tejanos* (The Texans) performed in New Mexico in 1846. This plays treats the invasion of New Mexico by a military unit from the Republic of Texas in 1841. The dramatic account of this historical event introduces a recurring theme in Chicano folklore and literature: Mexicans pitted against Anglos survive against technological or other advantages by resorting to cunning strategies.

The second half of the nineteenth century, Leal's Transition Period (1848-1910), was indeed a period of prolific literary production. This was the result of new opportunities for 1) production with the availability of presses, and 2) the education of a greater numbers of mexicanos. Scholars have recovered hundreds of samples of poems and short stories from newspapers and other sources from this period. Although most of this work displays the then popular romantic tendencies in Mexican literature, a motivating force was to affirm cultural identity by positing the written word as an amulet against imminent displacement. Published narrative works from this period include *The Squatter and the Don: Descriptive of Contemporary Occurrances in California* (1885) by María Amparo Ruiz de Burton (dates unknown), and published under the pseudonym C. Loyal, *Hijo de la tempesdad* (Son of the Tempest; 1892) and *Tras la tormenta la calma* (Calm After the Storm; 1892) by Eusebio Chacón (1869-1948). Ruiz de Burton's is perhaps the earliest published Chicano novel and is unique because it is one of the few pieces by women extant from that period. The novel focuses on the appropriation of land in California by the invading Americans and the demise of the landowning class of Californios. Mariano Vallejo's five volume manuscript, which formed a substantial chunk of Bancroft's history of California, deals with the same phenomenon. But without doubt the most important subgenre of this period for contemporary Chicano literary scholars was the corrido. A vital oral genre until the 1930s, it was an explicit instrument of symbolic resistance to hegemonic forces on the border. Its function as a paradigm for a discourse of resistance, which forms the backbone of much of contemporary Chicano narrative, is acknowledged by many scholars today (Saldívar 26-42).

During the twentieth century we see a tapering off of literary production by Chicanos. Perhaps this can be attritubed to the effects of English language spread, as fewer and fewer mexicanos wrote in Spanish. We might also attribute the reduced literary activity of what Leal calls the Period of Interaction (1910-43) to the fact that the voices of mexicanos were appropriated by mainstream writers who purported to speak on their behalf. Some notable exceptions are found in writers who continued to use Spanish, such New Mexican poets Felipe Maximiliano Chacón (1873-1948) and Vicente Bernal (1888-1926) and journalists Daniel Venegas (dates unknown) and Jorge Ulica (1870-1926). The latter had a distinguished career as a journalist and used this medium for satirizing both American customs and Mexicans who remained greenhorns and failed to learn English. A wonderful parodic and carnivalesque novel by Daniel Venegas, *Don Chipote o cuando los pericos mamen* (Don Chipote or When the Parrots Suckle; 1928) also belongs to this period. In this novel, the exiled Mexican author delivers a biting critique of the United States for condoning the exploitation of Mexican workers. The text exorts Mexicans to accept the fact that it is better to remain in Mexico, poor indeed, but free from the humiliation and suffering that awaits them in the United States. In addition, Nicolás Kanellos has called attention to the vitality of Spanish language theater throughout the Southwest in the twenties, "with Los Angeles and San Antonio supporting more than twenty houses that were showing everything from melodrama to *zarzuela* [operettas] to vaudeville, and with tent theaters travelling to smaller towns and cities throughout the five southwestern states" (Kanellos, *Hispanic Theatre* 9).

In English we have a number of women writing, among them Nina Otero Warren (1885-?) and María Cristina Mena (dates unknown). Mena's short stories tend to be of the picturesque and romanticizing variety that did little more than conform to Anglo stereotypes of Mexican Americans. Otero Warren's *Old Spain in Our Southwest* (1936) enunciates a plaintive lament against displacement of New Mexicans from the land, but the power of her lament is lost in a nostalgic cloud of mystification. Yet we must keep in mind that these writers wrote despite great obstacles considering the role of women during their time, and, lest critics feel tempted to trivialize their work, we must recognize that their voices speak from a position of silence and marginality more marked than that of their male counterparts.

The Los Angeles Zoot Suit riots of 1943 mark for Leal the beginning of the contemporary or Chicano Period. While scores of young Chicanos demonstrated their patriotism by defending their country in World War II, their younger siblings were being beaten and left naked on the streets by American soldiers waiting to be shipped off to war. The Axis powers did not waste time in pointing out the contradictory position held by the United States as it defended the world in the name of democracy and justice, yet resorted to violent tactics to cope with its "Mexican problem" at home. It was in the wake of these events that Mexican Americans realized that patriotism was no guarantee against discrimination, and it was this awareness that planted the seeds for a Chicano consciousness that was to bear fruit two decades later. Though there are few writers from the earlier years of this period—Josefina Niggli (1910), Mario Suárez (1925), Fray Angélico Chávez (1910)—it is not until the late 1960s and early 1970s that a significant number of Chicanos began to produce works that self-consciously proclaimed their affiliation to a sociopolitical movement that called attention to the marginalized social position of *la raza* (the race) in the United States and sought avenues through which Chicanos could establish themselves as agents of their own social and political destiny. Niggli's *Mexican Village* (1945) tells the story of a son of a Mexican woman and an Anglo father who travels to Mexico in search of ancestral roots. There seems to be a strong message implicit in this story for Mexican Americans who were beginning to tread the waters of assimilation. Suárez, in his short stories that appeared in the

Arizona Quarterly in 1947, augured the dawning of contemporary Chicano literature in his sensitive portrayal of Mexican Americans, whom he called Chicanos, who struggled to create for themselves a space somewhere between Mexican and American cultures in which to accommodate their difference.

Some literary historians argue that José Antonio Villarreal's (1924) *Pocho* (1959) is the work that marks the beginning of the contemporary Chicano literary period. The word *pocho* of the title is a term used by Mexicans to refer to their culturally demexicanized kin living in the United States. Though published in 1959 by Doubleday Press, this text was not "discovered" by Chicanos until the late 1960s when it was proclaimed by some to be the "first Chicano novel." Its protagonist is a young Mexican American male caught between an outdated system of patriarchal heroic values nurtured during the Mexican Revolution and the values offered by a dominant culture that tempts with the lure of assimilation even as it oppresses and marginalizes the Chicano working class. While it appears, at the end, that the protagonist forsakes his father's values in favor of assimilation, the ending is sufficiently ambiguous so as to allow some critics to see it as a paradigmatic work for the novel of the renaissance and for others to dismiss it as the antithesis of those works that will clearly assume a stance of contestation in relation to the mainstream canon.

All literary historians do agree, however, that by the time of the appearance of El Teatro Campesino Chicano literature had implanted itself as an inexorable cultural phenomenon in the United States. Writing in a bilingual mode, as did many in the movement period, Luis Valdez (1940) drew international attention for his agitprop *actos* (acts) that brought to formal and informal stages (flatbed trucks on which skits were performed for members of picket lines) the plight of the striking farm workers united by César Chávez in 1965. Valdez's theater combined Brechtian techniques with contemporary social concerns and pre-Columbian themes to create an exciting and powerful politically committed theater. Over the years Valdez's work has evolved into more complex and sophisticated theater. *Zoot Suit* (1977), for example, still retained some of the characteristics of his early political and mythical theater, but stock figures gave way to more psychologically developed characters. Other dramatists of the Chicano period to have received wide critical attention are Estella Portillo Trambley (1936) (*Sor Juana and Other Plays*; 1983), Cherríe Moraga (*Giving Up the Ghost*; 1989), and Carlos Morton (1947) (*The Many Deaths of Danny Rosales*; 1986). Morton, in a satirical style introduced in a play called *Adán y Eva* (Adam and Eve), first published in *El grito* (The Shout; 1974), relies on parody for his acerbic attacks on racist and distorted accounts of Chicano history. *The Many Deaths of Danny Rosales* is an exception in that its theme of police brutality calls for a treatment more attuned to the precepts of social realism, though the work certainly contains some lyrical and symbolic embellishments. New Mexican dramatist, Denise Chávez (1948), has received more attention for her novel *Last of the Menu Girls* (1986) than for her theater. Yet she has written close to thirty plays. Of these, *Plaza* (The Square) was staged by La Compañía de Teatro de Albuquerque at the Edinburgh Film Festival in 1984.

An important event in the development of Chicano literature of the movement years was the establishment of Quinto Sol Publications. The initial efforts of this Berkeley-based group produced a journal, *El grito*, which focused on issues in the social sciences but gradually gave more attention to creative literature. Quinto Sol's announcement in 1970 of a literary prize for the best Chicano work gave impetus to the production of longer narrative works. Bruce-Novoa calls attention to the importance of this prize in the formation of Chicano literary canon; he in fact claims that the first three recipients, Tomás Rivera (1935-84), Rudolfo Anaya (1937), and Rolando Hinojosa (1929) became the Chicano Big Three-- that is, the most widely read and studied Chicano writers (*Retrospace* 135). Rivera's *...Y no se lo tragó la tierra* (*"And the Earth Did Not Part"*; 1971) certainly establishes what was to be the trend, if not in the Chicano novel *per se*, then certainly regarding the criteria whereby novels would be admitted in the emerging canon: the individual's search for identity, the significance of which is grasped only in relation to his community's collective identity. Its simple language, its short "skin and bones" narrative sketches, and its depiction of Chicano "everyman" make this a very accessible work. But it is its almost perfect balance between the individual and the collective search for meaning in a world distorted by greed and its understated unveiling of oppressive ideologies in his depiction of the experiences of Texas migrant workers that make this one of the best Chicano texts.

The second winner of the Quinto Sol Prize, Anaya's *Bless Me, Ultima* (1972), is a consciously wrought romance that posits the *nuevo mexicano* (New Mexican) cultural ethos as the backdrop against which the young protagonist embarks upon a heroic quest for goodness and beauty. Subsequent titles by this widely read author are *Heart of Aztlan* (1976), *Tor-*

tuga (1979), *The Legend of La Llorona: A Short Novel* (1984), *The Silence of the Llano: Short Stories* (1982), and *A Chicano in China* (1986).

The third author to receive the Quinto Sol Prize was Rolando Hinojosa. In *Estampas del Valle y otras obras* (Sketches of the Valley and Other Works; 1972) Hinojosa sets down the primary characteristics that will appear and reappear in two decades of novelistic production: formal experimentation, a brilliant stylization of oral language, and an understated ironic humor. Each of his subsequent novels, *Generaciones y semblanzas* (Biographies and Lineages; 1977), winner of Casa de las Américas prize in 1976 under the title *Klail City y sus alrededores* (Klail City and Environs; 1976); *Mi Querido Rafa* (*Dear Rafe*; 1981); *Partners in Crime* (1985); *Rites and Witnesses: A Comedy* (1982); *Claros varones de Belken* (*Fair Gentlemen of Belken County*; 1986); and *Becky and Her Friends* (1990), forms a microtext in a broader macrotext called the Klail City Death Trip Series. In the series, Hinojosa explores the development of the Chicano community in the Rio Grande Valley of Texas in the context of deeply ingrained structures of domination and equally ingrained patterns of resistance and contestation.

Other important novels of the first decade of production were *The Plum Plum Pickers* (1969) by Raymond Barrio (1921), *The Autobiography of a Brown Buffalo* (1972) and *The Revolt of the Cockroach People* (1973) by Oscar Zeta Acosta (1935-?), *Chicano* (1970) by Richard Vásquez (1928), *The Road to Tamazunchale* (1975) by Ron Arias (1941). One of the most acclaimed works of fiction written by a Chicano, the latter includes mythic motifs that bear a strong mark of Latin American literary magic realism.

In the literature of the "movement years" two tendencies were apparent, tendencies that are universally recognized as important stages in the development of emerging national or ethnic literatures. The first of these reveals a marked preoccupation with the question of cultural identity, manifesting itself through an elaborate examination of cultural themes and mystification. Most obvious was the nostalgic treatment of pre-Columbian culture, particularly Aztec motifs, among them the myth of Aztlán. Chicano authors took this ancient Aztec legend and converted it into a contemporary myth that allowed them to reclaim their ancient indigenous roots that had been hidden by colonial and postcolonial discourses of domination. But more important, the myth allowed Chicanos to reclaim the Southwest as the homeland and with one swift stroke of the pen, to lay claim to their status as foreigners in their ancestral dwelling. It is no accident that so many titles of the early movement years bear the word Aztlán. In addition to the elaboration of pre-Columbian motifs and imagery, we see a marked tendency toward Hispanic *costumbrismo*. The ways of the *barrio* (Chicano neighborhood), a description of the folk that inhabit the barrio, customs, traditions, values all found their way onto the written page. The oral genres were likewise transformed into literary motifs.

Through the assertion of the values and virtues of their own culture, writers were now in a position to react against the forces of exclusion and marginalization. The newly discovered sense of self-determination becomes so bold as to engender a feeling of superiority reminiscent of attitudes of Latin American *arielistas* (followers of Ariel) in confrontation with *el gran coloso del norte*. The latter literally means "the great collosus of the north" and was a term used in reference to the United States. We clearly see this attitude in Sergio Elizondo's agonistic poem, "Perros" ("Dogs") from his collection *Perros y antiperros* (Dogs and Antidogs; 1972): "Chavalo, más fuerte es el amor/que me mueve dentro/que un siglo de motores" (Dude, stronger is the love/that moves me inside/than a century of motors).

In this battle of literary images Chicano culture emerges spiritually victorious as did Latin American culture in the famous poem of the Nicaraguan Rubén Darío (1867-1916) in which he reminds North America that "Y, pues contáis con todo, falta una cosa ¡Dios!" (Now then, you've everything on your side, save God!). The essence of this moral victory is best summed up in an influential text of the movement years (1971): "Our ideals, our way of looking at life, our traditions, our sense of brotherhood and human dignity, and the deep love which have prevailed in spite of the gringo, who would rather have us remade in his image and likeness; materialistic cultureless, colorless, monolingual, and racist" (*Chicano Manifesto* 46).

This phase in the development of Chicano literature is most visible in poetry, much of which was written in a bilingual form. The signifying dimension of this interlingual mode was intractably political. Both in form and content this poetry indicted the dominant culture for economic exploitation, for racial discrimination, for relegating Chicanos to the margins of history through silence, or worse, through misrepresentation. That it did so in a mixture of Spanish and English, and in a broad variety of linguistic registers, including the most informal registers, leaves no doubt that the implied audience was a grassroots Chicano audience, and that its primary motive was to call for change and for action. Poets who engaged in the writing of bilingual "movement poetry" were Ricardo

Sánchez (1941), Alurista (1947), José Antonio Burciaga (1940), Sergio Elizondo (1930), José Montoya (1932), Margarita Cota-Cárdenas (1941), Raúl Salinas (1934), Carmen Tafoya (1951), Abelardo Delgado (1931). By the 1980s, however, the radical practice of writing in mixed codes had practically disappeared. Perhaps desiring to reach a broader audience, Chicano poets wrote almost exclusively in English. One could, of course, also suggest that the cooptation of the sociopolitical ethnic movements of the 1970s led to an abandonment of explicitly political concerns among Chicano writers. This does not mean that their work ceased to assume a contestatory stance against the literature of the mainstream canon that had never considered Chicano cultural expression worthy of inclusion. *Where Sparrows Work Hard* (1981) by Gary Soto (1952), *Shaking off the Dark* (1984) by Tino Villanueva (1941), *Whispering to Fool the Wind* (1982) by Alberto Ríos, *Chants* (1984) by Pat Mora (1942), *Women Are Not Roses* (1984) by Ana Castillo (1953), *My Wicked, Wicked Ways* (1988) by Sandra Cisneros, stand out in this decade.

An interesting phenomenon within the corpus of Chicano literature has been the production of works of fiction written exclusively in Spanish. Among the important ones are Margarita Cota-Cárdenas, *Puppet* (1985), Sergio Elizondo, *Muerte en una estrella* (Death on a Star; 1984), Miguel Méndez-M. (1930), *Peregrinos de Aztlán* (*Pilgrims in Aztlán*; 1974), and *El sueño de Santa María de las Piedras* (*The Dream of Santa María de las Piedras*; 1986), Alejandro Morales (1944), *Caras y vino nuevo* (*Old Faces and New Wine*; (1975), *La verdad sin voz* (*Death of an Anglo*; 1979), Aristeo Brito (1942), *El Diablo en Texas* (*The Devil in Texas*; 1974), Sabine Ulibarrí (1919), *Tierra Amarilla* (Tierra Amarilla: Stories of New Mexico; 1971), *Mi abuela fumaba puros* (*My Grandma Smoked Cigars and Other Stories of Tierra Amarilla*; 1979), Rivera's *Y no se lo tragó la tierra* (*And the Earth Did Not Part*; 1971) and the bulk of the production of Rolando Hinojosa. The training of all these writers in graduate programs in Hispanic language and literature has allowed them not only to write sustained works in Spanish, but also to draw upon aesthetic tendencies of Peninsular and Latin American literature. Ulibarrí's work, for example, is steeped in the *costumbrista* (local color) tradition of nineteenth-century Spanish letters, and Hinojosa's intertextual ties to Galdós are striking. The works of Méndez, Cota-Cárdenas, and Morales call attention to their filiation with the experimental and postmodern techniques of the Latin American novel of the sixties and seventies: temporal and spatial disjunctions, multiple points of view, pushing language to the limits, bearing testimony to social oppression. Should it surprise us to find these very characteristics in novels written by Chicano professors of Latin American literature? Likewise, it should not surprise us that their works have had special attraction for some scholars of Latin American Literature in American universities. Unfortunately, since the majority of Chicanos have been educated in English rather than Spanish, there is a limited reading audience among Chicanos for these works and their authors have indeed been brave to write in Spanish. Each year we see fewer titles published in Spanish. Thus the polemic of the early years regarding the appropriate national categorization of Chicano literature—did it belong in the canon of United States literature or did it belong to Mexican lettres?—has become a moot point. Of course the place of this literature will be determined by the future status of the Spanish language in the United States. The steadily increasing demographic figures, including both native born and immigrant Latinos, auger a bright future.

By the 1980s it was apparent that Chicano literature, shored up with a burgeoning corpus of literary criticism, had begun to mature. The tight and polished fiction of Gary Soto, Rolando Hinojosa, and Arturo Islas (1938-91), the award-winning poetry of Jimmy Santiago Baca, but more important the blossoming of work by Chicanas, all bear witness to the process of maturation.

A perusal of the bibliographies of Chicano literature of the 1960s and 1970s will show that very few women were being published. Those whose work began to enter the Chicano canon early on were Estela Portillo, Bernice Zamora (1938), Angela de Hoyos (1945), Lorna Dee Cervantes (1954), Alma Villanueva (1944), Evangelina Vigil. But in the 1980s we see a proliferation of works written by Chicanas, particularly in the genres of poetry and fiction. If the literature of the movement years offered a discourse of resistance against hegemonic practices, it continued to manifest its own patriarchal discourse of domination. While women writers were initially reticent to confront this contradiction for fear of jeopardizing the broader collective agenda, it was not long before they began to deal openly with the issues of sexism. Sandra Cisneros's *House on Mango Street* (1983) lays before the reader the image of women trapped in tenements looking out the windows at public life. Her protagonist rejects the path to entrapment and opts for a house, and by extension, a life inscribed by her own hand. Ana Castillo's *The Mixquiahuala Letters* (1986) examines the price women must pay in exchange for independence, as her protagonist casts a sardonic glance at a past in which she and her friend sought male affection on their own terms.

Gloria Anzaldúa's *Borderlands/La Frontera: the New Mestiza* (1987), in a style that eludes genre specificity, speaks of crossing cultural, linguistic, sexual, and psychological borders in her search for a *mestiza* consciousness. With each new Chicana writer the literary space expands to include daring but honest treatment of heretofore taboo topics such as physical abuse, rape, incest, heterosexual and lesbian sexuality. If in the 1960s and 1970s Chicano writers politicized the text, in the 1980s Chicanas expanded the meaning of politics to include gender. Chicano males are beginning to respond both in their own creative writing and in their literary criticism to the challenge laid forth by Chicanas to cultural values and aesthetic forms that privilege patriarchal paradigms.

Building on Hispanic and American literary traditions and on a strong folk base and oral tradition, Chicano and Chicana writers, during the past two and a half decades, have inscribed in the realm of the fictionalized world, with its infinite dimensions of possibilities, the very broad and heterogeneous nature of "the Chicano experience." They have revised the history written about them and have offered in its stead new models of signification within which Chicanos stand not as objects, but rather as agents of their imagined worlds.

II. Puerto Ricans

José Luis González (1926), one of the most recognized Puerto Rican writers in Latin America, broke new ground when he addressed the importance to the Island's debates regarding the significance of Puerto Rican migration to the United States and the polemical nature of their literary production. Like René Marqués (1919-79), Pedro Juan Soto (1928), Emilio Díaz Valcárcel (1929), and Enrique Laguerre (1906), among many others, González has dealt in his writing with the emigrant experience in the United States. Notwithstanding the fact that he addresses this issue in his own work, in short story collections such as *En Nueva York y otras desgracias* (In New York and Other Disgraces, 1973) and *Paisa* (Compatriate, 1950), he still claims that the most authentic literary expression of the Puerto Ricans in the United States is going to be the one produced by the offspring of the emigres, "ya en la década del cuarenta pensaba y decía yo que la expresión literaria más auténtica de los emigrados puertorriqueños en Norteamérica tendría que ser la que sus descendientes produjeran algún día, necesariamente en lengua inglesa" (already in the 1940s I was thinking and saying that the most authentic literary expression of the Puerto Rican emigrants in North America would have to be the literature that their decendents would necesarily produce in the English language) (*El país de los cuatro pisos* 102).

Nevertheless, we have to acknowledge that the first Puerto Ricans to write in the United States were the expatriate political elite seeking the independence of Puerto Rico from Spain during the last decades of the nineteenth century. Figures such as Ramón Emeterio Betances (1827-99), Lola Rodríguez de Tió (1843-1924), and Eugenio María de Hostos (1839-1903) disseminated important political essays and literary texts from New York (see the essay in this volume on Puerto Rican literature). The nationalist discourse and the political experience of Puerto Ricans cannot be studied as an isolated case. We are compelled by the circumstances in which these texts were produced to study them in conjunction with the parallel Cuban experience. Lola Rodríguez de Tió, poet and revolutionary, author of "La Borinqueña" (this is the femenine adjective derived from the indigenous name, Borinquen, for the Island), the national anthem of Puerto Rico, wrote during her exile in New York in 1893: "Cuba y Puerto Rico son/de un pájaro las dos alas/ reciben flores y balas/en el mismo corazón." (Babín 82) (Cuba and Puerto Rico are/the two wings of a bird,/they receive flowers and bullets/on the very same heart.) These popular verses gave clear evidence of Puerto Rican and Cuban solidarity and the collective efforts that took place in the United States during their liberation struggle.

In the nineteenth century there was a thriving Spanish-language press in New York, Florida, the Southwest, and California. In the last decades of the nineteenth century the Latino literary and cultural institutions were expanding mainly because of "the political and cultural ferment caused by the Cuban war for independence and the Spanish American War" (Horno 238). Journals and newspapers like *La gaceta ilustrada* (The Illustrated Gazette), *Las novedades* (Novelties), and *El porvenir* (The Future); the *Revista popular* (The Popular Journal) and the Cuban *La patria* (The Homeland), and, into the twentieth century, *La opinión* (The Opinion), *La prensa* (The Press), *Sangre latina* (Latin Blood), *Revista pan-americana* (Pan-American Journal), and *La paz y el trabajo* (Peace and Labor), were publishing some of the most important political activists. These publications played a key role in the political, social, and cultural movements of Puerto Ricans and Cubans, as well as Spanish immigrants who arrived in the United States as a result of the mass exile provoked by the Spanish civil war in the 1930s. After the Great Depression and the repatriation of Mexican immigrants in the Southwest, many of these newspapers and small presses were forced to close.

It is significant to our discussion of Puerto Rican literature in the United States that the first written expression of Puerto Ricans and Cubans here was the anticolonialist discourse crucial to the formation of a nation. The critical stance against colonialism together with writing as an expression of solidarity and as an instrument for political action have permeated the cultural production of Puerto Ricans, Cubans, and all Latino populations. Francisco Gonzalo "Pachín" Marín (1863-97) and Arturo Alfonso Shomburg (1874-1938) are important political activists who published in Hispanic newspapers at the turn of the century. Shomburg was very important within the African American community and one of the founders of the Harlem Renaissance. Literary and cultural critics sense the obligation to rescue from obscurity these publications that express most freely the nationalist hopes for liberation for their home country.

During the first half of the twentieth century, texts whose inspiration was the Puerto Rican experience in New York began to appear. Salient among them are *Esta noche juega el jóker* (The Joker Plays Tonight; 1938) by Fernando Sierra Berdecía (1903-62) and the novels of José I. Diego Padró (1899-1974). Julia de Burgos (1914-53), Clemente Soto Vélez (1905), Juan Antonio Corretjer (1908), important poets from the Island, lived in the United States and their work, to a certain extent, reflects this experience of exile. Julia de Burgos and Clemente Soto Vélez stayed in the United States to become a source of inspiration for the younger generation of Nuyorican poets, that is Puerto Rican poets from New York, as is shown by the Sandra María Esteves (1948), "A Julia y a mí" (To Me and Julia), and Martín Espada (1957), "Clemente's Bullets."

Besides the works of José Luis González, the generation of the 1950s, working very much within the Latin American tradition, produced some classical texts dealing with the Puerto Rican experience in New York. Texts such as Pedro Juan Soto's *Spiks* (1954), René Márques's *La carreta* (The Oxcart; 1953), and Emilio Díaz Valcálcel's *Harlem todos los días* (Harlem Everyday; 1972) represent the misfortune, cultural shock, and experience of oppression suffered by the working class immigrants.

As Juan Flores (1943) points out, one can find in the 1950s a "view from within" in the texts of Puerto Ricans who came here to stay and considered the barrio home. Authors like Jesús Colón (1901-74), *A Puerto Rican in New York and Other Sketches* (1961), Bernardo Vega

(1885-1965), *Memorias de Bernardo Vega* (Memoirs of Bernardo Vega; 1977), and Jaime Carrero (1931), *Pipo Subway no sabe reír* (Pipo Subway Doesn't Know How to Laugh; 1973) were key figures in writing and chronicling of the lives and struggles of the Puerto Rican community.

The *Memorias de Bernardo Vega* represents one of the most insightful and invaluable narratives of the Puerto Rican migrant experience. It is a first-hand account of Puerto Rican working-class existence in New York from the last decades of the nineteenth century to the 1940s. The *Memorias* can be classified as an autobiography, a chronicle, or a testimonial novel, but most importantly as a political document that testifies to the political consciousness in the Puerto Rican community during those pioneer years. Bernardo Vega was a cigar worker, activist in the independence movement, and a trade union activist. Narrative strategies of the nineteenth-century literary culture acquired in the workplace were deployed in Vega's text. The *tabaquerías* (cigar factories) in Puerto Rico and Cuba were more than work centers, they were cultural centers where historical, philosophical, and literary texts were read to the workers. This tradition, that promoted political and literary sophistication among the workers, and brought by Cubans to Tampa, soon was to be spread to workplaces in New York.

The last three decades marked an important moment in the cultural history of Puerto Ricans in New York. Prose writing, directly linked to the earlier *memorias* and testimonies of the Puerto Rican community, becomes the preferred mode of expression. Written in English, *Down These Mean Streets* (1967) by Piri Thomas (1928), and *Nilda* (1974) by Nicholasa Mohr (1935) represent the best autobiographical fiction produced by Boricuas. Mohr's *El Bronx Remembered* (1975), *In Nueva York* (1977), and *Rituals of Survival: a Woman's Portfolio* (1984) depict a different vision of life in New York for the Puerto Rican. These Nuyorican narratives of survival gave new direction and strength to a Puerto Rican literary tradition that was evolving as a testimonial expression of a national minority. Beyond the individual self, these texts represent the collective self's contradictions and confusion between mainstream American and Puerto Rican popular culture and their everyday struggle.

One of the dominant themes in the Nuyorican literary expression has been the commitment to self-understanding and how that self is related to the world. This positioning has led most of the Nuyorican poets and prose writers to take a stance, to confront the ambivalence that is a consequence of the colonial condition of the Island and of Puerto Ricans in the mainland. Sandra María Esteves has stated: "The Nuyorican poetry of today is an affirmation of political struggle. It is an acute aware-ness of the North American condition which manifests itself at the core of every individual. Ultimately, it is a statement of determination, to dream, perhaps to hope, to determine, to give birth, to mold, to survive that confrontation victoriously" (Horno 168).

With the foundation in the late 1960s and early 1970s of the Young Lords and other political organizations, such as Resistancia Puertorrique-ña (Puerto Rican Resistance), the 1972 foundation of the MINP Com-mittee (Movimiento de la Izquierda Nacional Puertorriqueña [National Puerto Rican Leftist Movement]), the Puerto Rican Socialist Party U. S. Section, many Puerto Rican poets and cultural advocates, like Pedro Pietri (1944), Felipe Luciano (1947), and Miguel Algarín (1941) took to the streets to demonstrate with political activists demanding better hous-ing, education, and health programs for Puerto Ricans. The establish-ment of La Tertulia (the literary circle) and Miguel Algarín's Nuyorican Poet's Cafe as performance venues and cultural organizations with a clear political agenda, like Taller Boricua (the Boricua workshop), were some of the notable events that confirmed the ways in which Puerto Ricans were engaging the dominant instutions by creating their own space to perform and promote their creative work.

The oral character of Nuyorican poetry makes it a unique discursive manifestation, the impact of which is very much dependent on perfor-mance. A masterful example of this process is a scene in a Young Lords' documentary film in which we see Pedro Pietri declaming his title poem *Puerto Rican Obituary* (1973) from a church. Many poets such as Tato Laviera (1950) and Miguel Algarín consciously exploit orality and performance in order to reach and involve their audiences. Dependent on the musical structure of Caribbean rhythms of African origin, poets perform in order to give life to their work and to add an emotional and dramatic dimension that makes the reception of their texts a more com-plete and powerful experience.

Mainly because of their performative dimension, poetry and theater became not only some of the most common mediums of expression, but key vehicles of consciousness-raising in the late sixties and seventies. John C. Miller points out that we have to call the period in New York between 1965 and 1977 the New Rican or Nuyorican theater phase (Ka-nellos, *Hispanic Theater* 27). In this period, cultural organizations that promoted theater and traveling companies were founded, and Puerto Rican theater and poetry were performed in the streets of the barrios, jails, and work centers. Nuyoricans poets who have become recognized as playwrights are Miguel Piñero (1946-1988) (*Short Eyes*; 1975), Tato Laviera (195070) and Miguel Algarín (*Olú Clemente*; 1979), and Pedro Pietri (*Play for the Page, Not for the Stage*; 1980 and *The Masses are Asses*; 1984). This very vital and politically effective mode of expression has all but disappeared. Currently, it has been upstaged by more traditional Spanish and Latin American theater.

The poetry written in Spanish, with some exceptions, does not reflect the urban experience of the working class Puerto Rican in New York. It is very difficult to characterize the poetic texts of Etnairis Rivera (1949) (*WY dondequiera* [WY Wherever; 1974] and *María del mar morivi-ví* [María of the Moriviví Sea; 1976]), Luz María Umpierre (1947) (*Una puertorriqueña en Penna* [A Puerto Rican in Pennsylvania; 1974]), Ivan Silén (1944) (*Después del suicidio* [After the suicide; 1970]) *Los poemas de Fili Melé* [Fili Mele's Poems; 1976], *El miedo del Pantócrata* [The Pantocrator's Fear; 1981], and *La biografía* [The Biography; 1984]), and Alfredo Villanueva Collado (*Grimorio* [Angst; 1986] and *La voz de la mujer que llevo dentro* [The Voice of the Woman Within Me; 1990]). These poetic texts engage to a certain extent the U. S. experience, but they also include the political situation of the Island, the feelings of nostalgia for Puerto Rico, and other themes like romantic love and hetero- and homoeroticism.

For many Puerto Ricans on the Island, it has been very difficult to deal with the returning migration. The disdain and prejudice against the language and culture of the Puerto Ricans in New York is indeed apparent. Jaime Carrero, with *Raquelo tiene un mensaje* (Raquelo Has a Message; 1970), and Pedro Juan Soto, with *Ardiente suelo, fría estación* (Burning Soil, Cold Season; 1961) have shown their strong concern for this issue by producing novels on it. The "Nuyorican" writer, as well as other Latinos, has to address two "Others": Puerto Rican insularist and the United States dominant culture. Writers like Nicholasa Mohr and Tato Laviera have raised the issue of the marginalization and exclusion on the Island of the children of those who were forced to emigrate as workers. Mohr has stated:

> Because I am a daughter of the Puerto Rican Diaspora, English is the language that gives life to my work, the characters I create, and that stimulates me as a writer. It has also been a vital component in the struggle for my very survival....
> Later, when some of us returned to the Island, it was clear to see that according to the position one's family held, and the

color of one's skin, one could hold a better job and have a higher place in society. It was also evident that those children of the poor and dark migrants who have been forced out more than two generations before, and who returned either with intentions to relocate or merely to visit, were not always welcomed. They were quickly labeled and categorized as outsiders, as "gringos" and "Nuyoricans." Indeed, proof of the false legacy that so many of us inherited from our elders was painfully clear. (Horno 113-114)

While the tension between the two groups continues to be a concern, a more ardent issue is that of redefining and valorizing Nuyorican selfhood, its cultural expression, and its relation to the broader Latino/Latin American communities. In 1980 the renewed *Revista chicano-riqueña* (now *Americas Review*) published an insightful statement titled "New York Puerto Rican Literature" by Tato Laviera:

New York Puerto Rican Literature in two languages/three forms, Spanish, Spanglish and English, abounds inside the *callejones* of New York. Literature deep in embroidered richness, vernaculars of Indian Jíbaros inside Black English talk, centered in classical Spanish verses, three political ideologies: statehood, commonwealth and independence, all actively pursuing the Boricua land in diversified poetic expression. Literature of urban brick-cold minority realities; literature of music, growing and strong; literature of motherhood as determined as ever; literature called development; forward fast-tongued, struggling to keep afloat. All in all, New York Latino literature, ready to gain control, meaning literary movement is vibrant, eighty-achieving, oral, *de boca [by mouth]*, emerging from the soul-gut experiences *de nuestra gente [our people], pa'arriba, pa'lante, qué vale!* [Upwards and forward, its worth the effort]. (iv)

Tato Laviera redefines "New York Puerto Rican literature" through his work and reflection. For him, more than the written word, it is Latino music that inspires him and offers him a way of surviving and of voicing the self. But more importantly, he posits the idea of his work as a dialogic act defined by the political ideologies, by the multiculturality of New York, and by the cold urban enviroment so alien to Puerto Ricans. Laviera, with his collections of poems *La Carreta Made a U-Turn* (The

Oxcart Made a U-Turn; 1984), *AmeRican* (1985), *Enclave* (1985), and *Mainstream Ethics* (1988), and Louis Reyes Rivera, with *Who Pays the Cost* (1977) and *This One for You* (1983), not only have celebrated the Puerto Rican spirit in New York and confronted prejudice on two fronts, but have offered critical insights into the problems of colonialism and the colonial mentality of Puerto Ricans on the Island. Moreover, they have shown a strong concern in their poetry with racism, constructing a poetic text where the daily racial strife and confrontation with multiple social others is at the core of their work. Besides Tato Laviera, other important new poets that began to publish and acquire attention in the 1980s have been Aurora Levins-Morales (1954) and Rosario Morales (1930) with their book *Getting Home Alive* (1986) and Martín Espada with *The Immigrant Iceboy Bolero* (1982), *Trumpets from the Island of Their Eviction* (1987) and, recently published by Curbstone Press, *Rebellion is the Circle of a Lover's Hand* (1990).

The dual poetic composition produced by Aurora and Rosario is a book of collective and personal memories that is succesful in articulating the experiences of diversity, political oppression, and solidarity between women of all races in the United States. Aurora Levins-Morales presents in her refletions and poetry a cultural heritage that defines her and will define her children no matter where they are born:

> My children will hear stories about the *coquis* and coffee
>   flowers, about hurricanes and roosters crowing in the
>   night,
>   and will dig among old photographs to understand the
>   home-
>   sick sadness that sometimes swallows me.... Perhaps
>   they
>   will lie in bed among the sounds of the rainforest, and
>   it will
>   be the smell of eucalyptus that calls to them in their
>   dreams. (27; the coqui is a kind of small tree frog
>   indigenous to the island of Puerto Rico, known for its
>   distinct and melodious night call)

And in a very powerful, singular poem that Aurora and Rosario co-create that vibrates in dialogue, they write:

I am what I am.

A child of the Americas.
A light-skinned mestiza of the Caribbean
A child of many diaspora, born into this continent at a cross
roads.
I am Puerto Rican. I am U. S. American.
I am New York Manhattan and the Bronx.
A mountain-born, country-bred, homegrown jíbara child,
up from the shtetl, a California Puerto Rican Jew.
A product of New York ghettos I have never known.
I am an inmigrant
and the daughter and granddaughter of immigrants.
We didn't know our forbears' names with a certainty.
They aren't written anywhere.
First names only, or mija, negra, ne, honey, sugar, dear. (212)

As Lourdes Rojas points out, Rosario and Aurora "are equally proud
of their historical past and cultural present. They are aware of being a
product of many diasporas, drawing strength equally from all of their
roots and they also are cognizant of, and committed to, their historical
present" (Horno 175). As we see in the work of Aurora and Rosario,
writing for Latinos serves as a mechanism to tell the story of lives of
marginality, reaffirm our cultural identity, and create solidarity not only
between Latinos, but between all immigrants, "children of the Americas."

Inspired in the civil rights movement of the 1960s, Martín Espada
voices the oppression and injustices committed against Puerto Ricans
and Latinos in the United States. One important aspect of his work,
besides the solidarity that he manifests with other Latino communities
in the United States, is the connection and commitment with Latin
American social and political processes. Martín Espada, who writes in
English, has made an attempt in his latest book, *Rebellion is the Circle
of a Lover's Hands* (1991), to reach the Spanish speaking people by
publishing an exceptional bilingual edition in which the Spanish translation captures the "sound" of the original version.

Recently, Juan Flores made this important statement: "Puerto Rican
writing in the United States, even in this initial testimonial stage, needs
to be read as a colonial literature. Its deeper problematic makes it more
akin to the minority literatures of oppressed groups than to the literary
practice and purposes of ethnic immigrants" ("Puerto Rican Literature"
213). When one tries to redefine Puerto Rican literature in relation to
the expression of other minorities, a Pandora's box is opened. For Puer-

to Ricans on the Island, it is very hard to accept the texts written in English about an experience outside of Puerto Rico as part of their national literary tradition. But, as José Luis González articulated so long ago: "las raíces nacionales de un escritor no están necesaria ni esencialmente en los personajes o en los ambientes de sus obras, sino en su persona misma, en su particular visión de la realidad, cualquier realidad" (*El país de los cuatro pisos* 105). (The national roots of a writer are not necessary to the work nor do they form part of the essence of his fictional worlds. They pertain rather to his own persona and to his particular vision of reality, what ever that may be.)

III. Cuban Americans

Cuban writing in the United States addresses a variety of issues, ranging from the exile experience, social and political oppression, and race relations to pre-Castro Cuba, language and cultural conflicts, and assimilation. It comprises a complex and diverse cultural manifestation whose major contributors during the past thirty years have been the generation that migrated to the United States after the Cuban revolution and their children. However, one cannot ignore the long, preexisting cultural history of Cubans in the United States nor their contributions to mainland culture in music, dance, and literature.

It is a common perception that the Cuban presence in the United States is a result of the exodus after the rise to power of Fidel Castro in 1959. But, as we have stated of the Puerto Rican experience, the history of Cuban immigration, and consequently of Cuban cultural manifestation in this country, needs to be studied from the final decades of the nineteenth century. During this period literary figures and leaders of the independence movement in Cuba, such as José Martí (1853-95) who, while living in the United States, wrote and published some of their most important works.

As a result of the War of Independence, many Spanish and Cuban owners of cigars factories in Cuba relocated to the United States. Tampa became one of the favorite cities for this group. Nicolás Kanellos has pointed out that the reasons for this relocation were of a political and economic nature: the immigrants sought to avoid the hostilities of the Cuban War of Independence, to be nearer to their primary markets, and to avoid import duties (*History of Hispanic Theater* 146). As a consequence of this relocation, mutual aid societies were founded, such as the

Círculo Cubano (Cuban Circle), the Centro Obrero (Workers' Center), and the Unión Martí-Maceo (Martí-Maceo Union), which served as cultural community centers for the tobacco workers. During the 1890s and through the 1920s these societies played an important role in the organization and consciousness-raising process of the tobacco workers. With cultural events like poetry readings, theater performances, and musical events, they created a space that allowed them to cultivate their cultural heritage and at the same time address the social and political issues that concerned them.

During this period, a national Cuban theater was created, which had immediate repercussions in the cultural activities of the Cubans in Tampa. Inspired by the Italian *Commedia dell'Arte* and the Spanish *sainetes* (one-act farce) the Cuban *teatro bufo* (bufo theater) was born. The *teatro bufo* was a musical farce that combined parody and satire to represent the oppressive social and political situation of Cubans, their feelings of nationalism, and the reaffirmation of cultural identity. To depict the essence of Cuban culture and conflict, Afro-Cuban music and dance and set-piece characters like *el negrito* (the little black boy), *la mulata* (mulatto woman) and *el gallego* (the Galician) were employed. *Teatro bufo* was destined to achieve popularity on the theatrical stages of Havana, New York, and Tampa during the 1920s.

The relocated Spanish and Cuban cigar factory owners in Tampa aided the creation of the Hispanic theater there. The tobacco workers were quite vocal about the quality of the performances; Kanellos states that "their families knew the difference between good and mediocre shows and were quite demanding, if newspaper critiques are indicative" (*History of Hispanic Theater* 147). Tampa became one of the stopping points of many of the best Spanish and Cuban touring companies. The factory owners brought from Cuba professional playwrights, directors, and actors and soon some of the tobacco workers were involved in the production of plays, as well.

Cuban playwrights carried to Tampa their literary heritage, but soon they began to stage plays that dealt with their particular binational social and political situation. In the Circulo Cubano were popular plays such as *Un tabaquero huelguista* (A Tabacco Striker; 1924), *Huelga general* (General Strike; 1934), *Las máquinas torcedoras o la máquina de la industria* (The Twister or the Industrial Machine; 1929), and farces such as *El espiritista* (The Spiritualist; 1925), *Boda de papa Montero* (Papa Montero's Wedding; 1925), *Molde de suegra* (Mother-in-Law's Pattern; 1926), and *Los amores de Clara* (Clara's Loves; 1926).

During the 1940s and 1950s Cuban influence played a major role in the mainland cultural scene with its Afro-Cuban musical and dance heritage. It is significant that this forgotten cultural history has been recalled by Oscar Hijuelos in his most recent novel, *The Mambo Kings Play Songs of Love* (1990), winner of the 1989 Pulitzer Prize. This novel recreates one of the most influential times in Latin music, the era of the mambo craze, the cha-cha-cha, and the rumba. It is the story of two Cuban brothers, known as the Mambo Kings, who come to New York in the 1940s, César and his brother, Néstor. Their relationships with urban life, women, fame, and music is narrated by Eugenio Castillo, the son of Néstor.

Eugenio, in search of his father, offers us the memories of his uncle in order to tell the story of the Mambo Kings, beginning with their start as musicians in the Oriente province of Cuba. He tells us of their immigration to the Cuban enclave in Manhattan, the beginnings of their ensemble performances at clubs throughout New York, through their achievement of stardom when Desi Arnaz invites them to play "Beautiful María of My Soul" on his show, *I Love Lucy*. Their appearance on this show represents the climax of their careers. Cuban melancholy drives Néstor to his death and César begins to drift in and out of the music scene, finally ending up totally unrecognized and alcoholic.

The Mambo Kings, their music, and their experiences portray vividly the dynamics of the exile experience: marginality, struggle for survival, nostalgia, and displacement. One of the most important aspects of the novel is the manner in which music becomes the center of the narrative. Music is the reason the musicians move to New York in search of better opportunities, the mechanism of expression of the brothers' feelings of love and sorrow, and the inspiration that guides Hijuelos to textualize the male experience of exile, love, success, and failure.

The literary history of the Cubans in the United States during the 1940s and 1950s lacks exposure and research. The attention of critics has been on the 1960s and the major exodus of middle- and upper-class intellectuals to Latin America, Spain, and the United States. Most of the writers from this first postexodus generation are very political, conservative, and antirevolutionary. Novels by some writers of this group, such as *De buena cepa* (From Good Stock; 1967) and *Entre todo y el nada* (Between All and Nothing; 1976) by René de Landa (1922); *Territorio libre* (Free Territory; 1967), *Los dioses ajenos* (Another's Gods; 1971), and *El palacio de la furia* (The Palace of Fury; 1976) by Luis Ricardo Alonso (1929); *El sitio de nadie* (No One's Place; 1972) by Hilda Perera

(1926), among others, have been called anti-Castro novels by critics, because of their depiction of the repressive nature of the revolution.

Matías Montes Huidobro (1931), critic, playwright, and novelist, with *Los desterrados al fuego* (Exiled to the Fire; 1975) presents a prime example of a novel very much within the Latin American tradition of the exile experience that grapples with the feelings of alienation and displacement of the emigrés. This winner of the Fondo de Cultura Económica prize for first novel, awarded by the Mexican publishing house of the same name, is a first-person narrative about the psychological difficulties produced by the sudden break from the motherland. It depicts the interior journey of the narrator-protagonist in his search for cultural identity, and the acceptance of his loss and final healing.

With the Cuban revolution, many well-known playwrights, in addition to those above mentioned, Montes Huidobro, José Sánchez-Boudy (1928), José Cid Pérez (1906), Julio Matas (1931), and Celedonio González (1923) moved to the United States. Their plays have been published, but not many have been successfully staged. This generation of playwrights was influenced by the experimental theater movement in Cuba during the 1950s. Besides continuing the cultural themes of the Cuban tradition they began to incorporate themes that were related to their new historical reality, the political experience of the exile.

Coming to terms with the Cuban revolution, the adjustment to a new space, and the dynamics of cultural struggle and adaptation have become common themes in the literary expression of Cubans in general. This transition began in the 1970s when we witnessed the creation of *Areito* (1975), an important magazine treating cultural and sociopolitical issues that came to accept and support the Cuban revolution, and the publication of literary works by the children of those who left Cuba after Castro's rise to power. The writers of this generation, many of them writing in Spanish, others in English, some in both, include Lourdes Casal (1938-81), Enrique Sacerío Garí (1945), Eliana Rivero (1941), Rafael Catalá (1942), and Dolores Prida (1943). Eliana Rivero has pointed out:

> Some of these writers do not share with their parents' generation an ideological rejection of Third World views; they have become politicized during their confrontation with injustices in the American system, mostly during their college years in the middle and the late sixties (the civil rights movement and the Viet Nam anti-war movement). Many of them have come to accept the historical existence of the Cuban revolution as an

> irrevocable fact, and although they affiliate with the various positions of the political spectrum, most feel identified with the social struggles of minority groups in the United States, and with those of other Latin American peoples. ("Hispanic Literature" 184)

Areito, the post-emigration generation, and the creation of the Center for Cuban Studies marked a very important moment of transition in the cultural history of Cubans in this country. This moment represented an acceptance of the revolution and a movement towards an understanding of the political, social, and cultural issues that affect minorities.

Bruce-Novoa stated in the essay "Hispanic Literature in the United States" that he excluded the literary production of Cubans in his essay because they consider themselves exiles more than U. S. citizens or permanent residents and their literature is still essentially Latin American (*Retrospace* 27). But he predicts:

> The younger generations will probably change this tendency, having grown up for the most part in the U. S. A. and experiencing Cuba only through the nostalgic memories of their elders. But that literature lies in the future and, thus, outside the concerns of this essay. (*Retrospace* 27-28)

The 1980s have witnessed the rise of the voices of this younger generation of Cuban American or "Cubish" writers who were raised in the United States. The exile experience is no longer the major preoccupation. Nevertheless, images of Cuba are present in their work and the exile experience of their parents is still manifest, but they have come to identify with the social struggles of other minorities in the United States.

Defining the cultural and political position of Cubans as a national minority and the depiction of the Cuban community and its culture in the United States are the major aims of Cuban American writers today. It is in poetry and theater that Cuban American literature has emerged. However, in such novels of Hilda Perera's *¡Felices Pascuas!* (Merry Christmas!; 1977) and Roberto Fernández's *La vida es un special* (Life Is on Special; 1981) and *La montaña rusa* (The Roller Coaster; 1985) we find a change in focus to emphasize Cuban life and culture in the United States. Fernández's novel is the first to deal with the experience of Cubans living in Miami's Little Havana. Humorous and absurd situations are employed to represent the experience of exile. These novels and the works of other writers represent a transition between the old and new realities, which requires the forging of a new cultural and linguistic identity.

Compared with Chicano and Puerto Rican theatrical literary production, few Cuban American plays are written and staged and fewer still are published. In spite of that situation, Cuban playwrights continue to write. During the 1980s playwrights such as Iván Acosta (1943), Omar Torres (1945), and Dolores Prida have used humorous and satirical situations to represent the cultural shock, contradictions, and struggle of the Cuban and Latino community. Plays such as Acostas's *El Super* (The Manager; 1982), Prida's *Coser y cantar* (Sewing and Singing; 1981), and Torres's *Dreamland Melody* (1982) have been successful in their portrayal of the adjustment of the Cuban family in the United States.

Dolores Prida, through her poetry as well as her plays, has been one of the few Cuban American women writers who has joined the group of Latinas addressing problems of *machismo* and discrimination faced by women. One of her most successful plays to address this issue has been *Beautiful Señoritas* (1977), which exposes the ways in which male chauvinism and Catholicism have repressed Latinas. In *Coser y cantar*, "a one-act bilingual fantasy for two women," Prida presents two characters, Ella (she) and She, having a bilingual conversation about their lives and debating about their Hispanic heritage and the American influence on them. The play's originality comes from the protagonists jointly representing the two aspects of the split personality of a Cuban immigrant.

In the last twenty years, many Cuban American writers began to use both languages in their literary production. Carolina Hospital (1957), a poet and literary critic, published an anthology which she titled *Los atrevidos* (1988; Those Who Dare). She calls the young bilingual and bicultural generation born after 1940 *los atrevidos* because they are taking a risk writing in English and acknowledging a new historical reality. Describing their work, she points out:

> Even though we can point to specific cultural legacies, in reality all of these writers are affected by a mosaic of cultural traditions, as well as an underlying exile consciousness. The sense of severance and rupture, provoked by this exile consciousness, manifests itself at structural, rather than thematic, levels. The personas in the poems or the novels are trapped by physical limitations in the environment or by their own inabilities to reconcile with their sense of alienation. Conflicts arise at all

dimensions: linguistic, cultural and ideological. Oppositions predominate in the texts and it is from these tensions that emerges a daring creativity. (Hospital 18)

Some of the poets of this generation are Iraida Iturralde (1954), Ricardo Pau-Llosa (1954), Gustavo Pérez Firmat (1949), Esperanza Rubido (1949), Roberto Fernández, and Elías Miguel Muñoz. In their work we find themes inspired in the civil rights movement of the 1960s, also present in the production of Chicanos and Puerto Ricans. Cuba and Miami are strong motifs in this generation. Ricardo Pau-Llosa writes:

> Beneath us the city toys
> with itself, and we descend
> into its tinkertoy order,
> its honeyed crime lights
> that cast a phoney day
> on brittle ghettos
> and sidewalks clean
> of human shadows. A few inches
> to the south another country
> has thrown up its own parody
> of salsa mispelled signs.
> The bayside condos
> rise like glassy Venus
> from the concrete shore,
> and catch our shooting
> star lights for a fragment of windows and seconds.
> They mirror themselves,
> opaque vanities the size
> of my thumb. I pale
> my cheek against the pane
> as the runaway jolt
> blurs us into our city. (Hospital 49-50)

The contrast between *aquí y allá* (here and there) is unavoidable, the link with Cuba is unbreakable.

One of the most prominent poets of this generation, Gustavo Pérez Firmat, also a well known literary critic, describes his poems as "schizo-paranoics" because they are between the uniqueness and multiplicity of reality. Bilingualism and biculturalism are present through all his work. In the prologue to his section in *Triple Crown* he states:

> Para ser cubano en North Carolina hay que estar loco. Es una locura que me hace pensar en la locura o manía poética de los griegos (Rosa tiene razón: soy un maniático), y es esa manía la que da lugar a estos poemas schizo, multiplicados por tres y divididos entre el español y el inglés. (Durán 125)

> To be a Cuban in North Carolina you have to be crazy. It is the kind of craziness that makes me think about the insanity or poetic mania of the Greeks (Rosa is right: I am a maniac), and it is that mania that gives rise to these schizo poems, multiplied by three and divided between Spanish and English.

In the poem "Son/Song" the line between poetry and music is elusive; every line he writes is charged with meaning and song.

> Sometimes I get
> the fee
> ling that eve
> ry word I writ
> e deserves a li
> ne to itself.
> So cha, so cha, so cha
> cha
> cha
> rged with me
> aning, with son
> g, do they see
> m. (Durán 140)

Caribbean music, with its African rhythms, set the tone for Cuban and Nuyorican poetry, as we can see in Gustavo Pérez Firmat and Nuyoricans like Víctor Hernández Cruz (1949) in his collection of poetry, *Rhythm, Content & Flavor* (1989), and Tato Laviera's poems. It inspires them and gives form and rhythm to their literary expression in all genres. Reproducing the rhythm of Latin music in poetry or finding in it a source of inspiration have served as another means for affirmation of cultural identity. Moreover, in the 1960s and 1970s salsa music was massively popular and influential in New York, Miami, and Puerto Rico as a manifestation of solidarity, and even as an instrument of empowerment.

Cuban Americans are no longer a foreign group living here for a short period of time. The younger generations recognize this and manifest it in their writing. They are finding their voice and telling their story. Images of Cuba are interwoven throughout their texts, but their immigrant history is what is unique to them. Through writing they reveal and explain themselves and they record and preserve their own and their parents' experiences. Cuban writing in all genres, from its earliest expressions to the most recent manifestations, shows a strong concern for its immigrant history. But this experience is approached from diverse ideological perspectives. In the literary production of the 1980s, Chicanos, Puerto Ricans, and other Latinos share their preoccupation with language, marginality, and ethnic identity. But on the other hand, Cuban literary expression is unique because they cannot forget the political events that caused the Cuban diaspora.

IV

The proliferation of Latino literary expression in the United States and the importance recently placed on it by American critics represent a challenge for Latin Americans. The challenge is to recognize the discourse of those who left or who stayed on their lands after the "take over" by the United States, discourses that have not been heard and that constitute an Other that has been previously denied. The written expression of Latinos, with its articulation of life in the margins, its search for self-definition, and its struggle to define its own voice, is a product of the pluricultural experience and heritage and represents one of the most rich and significant elements of the American and Latin American cultural tradition.

The articulation of the margins has taken many forms. Criticism itself is a unique cultural expression that serves as a bridge for understanding and making visible the way the Latin American and the U. S. Latino literary traditions differ from and at the same time dialogue with one another. The construction of a critical discourse is another form of textualizing and defining the self. Recently, Gloria Anzaldúa in her introduction to *Making Face, Making Soul* (1990) claimed that it is vital that women of color and ethnic minorities occupy the theorizing space:

we need *teorías* [theories] that will enable us to interpret what happens in the world, that will explain how and why we relate to certain people in specific ways, that will reflect what goes on between inner, outer and peripheral "I"s within a person and between the personal "I"s and the collective "we" of our ethnic communities. *Necesitamos teorías* [We need theories] that will rewrite history using race, class, gender and ethnicity as categories of analysis, theories that cross borders, that blur boundaries.... (xxv)

The same way that Latino writing lives in the "in-between," the critical theory that is used to interpret it needs, for Anzaldúa, to overlap many "worlds" and to be "partially inside and partially outside of the Western frame of reference" (xxvi). With the discussions and debates of postmodernism and cultural politics in American academia, there has been an opening towards theories of discourse that take into account the voices of those constituted as an "Other." As part of cultural studies and feminist cultural theory, the emphasis has been placed on articulating the margins and the voices that have been repressed or silenced. But this revision and change comes from two directions: from the institutional perspective and from the authors who speak from the margins themselves. The creation of "mestizaje theories," as Anzaldúa puts it, can be viewed as another expression of Latino self-definition, a desire for full speech and correction of the misrepresentation of Latinos. This critical practice will cross over and complete Latin American literary history.

We must recognize that the political events of this century, including the exile diaspora from Argentina, Chile, Uruguay, El Salvador, Cuba, throughout many other countries, have produced a body of texts in all genres, fiction and nonfiction, that has brought a part of Latin America to the United States. These voices of exile, intermingling with those of Chicanos and Puerto Ricans, form a much stronger and different voice of solidarity that, as Juan Flores and George Yúdice have explained, "do not aspire to enter an already given America but to participate in the construction of a new hegemony dependent upon their cultural practices and discourses" (73). The creation and criticism of a theoretical framework for the study of Latin American literary discourse should continue from within Latin America, Europe and the United States, but only alongside the study of Latino literature in the United States.

BIBLIOGRAPHY

Algarín, Miguel, and Miguel Piñero. *Nuyorican Poetry: an Anthology of Puerto Rican Words and Feelings*. New York: Morrow, 1975. Collection of New York City poets that attempts to define and characterize the "new" Nuyorican poetry.

Anzaldúa, Gloria, ed. *Making Face, Making Soul: Creative and Critical Perspectives by Women of Color*. San Francisco: An Aunt Lute Foundation Book, 1990. Creative, critical, and theoretical essays on the literary discourse of women of color.

Babín, Maria Teresa, and Stan Steiner, eds. *Borinquen: an Anthology of Puerto Rican Literature*. New York: Alfred A. Knopf, 1974. Collection of essays, poetry, and songs from the colonial period to the present that reflects social, political, and cultural concerns of Puerto Ricans in the Island and the United States.

Barradas, Efraín, and Rafael Rodríguez, eds. *Herejes y mitificadores: muestra de poesía puertorriqueña en los Estados Unidos*. Río Piedras, P.R.: Ediciones Huracán, 1980. With an excellent introduction, this bilingual anthology seeks to introduce to Puerto Ricans on the Island representative poets who write about the collective experience of their U.S. community.

Brown Ruoff, A. LaVonne, and Jerry W. Ward, eds. *Redefining American Literary History*. New York: Modern Language Association of America, 1990. Includes both a summary of the debates on the revision of the American literary canon and the important essays by Nicolás Kanellos, "Orality and Hispanic Literature in the United States"; Juan Flores, "Puerto Rican Literature in the United States: Stages and Perspectives"; and Juan Bruce-Novoa, "Canonical and Noncanonical Texts: a Chicano Case Study."

Bruce-Novoa, Juan. *Retrospace. Collected Essays on Chicano Literature*. Houston: Arte Público Press, 1990. Important articles on the history and theory of Chicano literature in perspective with other Latino groups in the United States.

Bruce-Novoa, Juan. *Chicano Poetry: a Response to Chaos*. Austin: University of Texas Press, 1982. A collection of essays employing close textual analysis of the work of one Chicana and eleven Chicano poets. Seeks to unveil the poet's response to the threat of loss in the deep structure of the poem.

Calderón, Héctor, and José David Saldívar. *Criticism in the Borderlands: Studies in Chicano Literature, Culture and Ideology*. Durham:

Duke University Press, 1991. An outstanding collection of essays addressing a variety of cultural issues from a poststructuralist perspective. Essays by José Limón, Rosaura Sánchez, Renato Rosales, and Norma Alarcón, among others.

Durán, Roberto, Judith Ortíz Cofer, and Gustavo Pérez Firmat. *Triple Crown*. Tempe: Bilingual Press, 1987. Collections of poems by the three authors.

Flores, Juan, and George Yúdice. "Living Borders/Buscando America: Languages of Latino Self-Formation." *Social Text* 24 (1990) 57-84. Critical interpretation of Latino culture from a sociohistorical perspective.

Gonzales-Berry, Erlinda. *Pasó por aquí: Critical Essays on the New Mexican Literary Tradition, 1542-1988*. Albuquerque: University of New Mexico Press, 1989. Includes essays of a historical and analytical nature on early chroniclers, Juan Gaspar de Villagrá, folk and secular drama, Fray Angélico Chavez, Cleofas Jaramillo, Eusebio Chacón, Fabiola C. de Baca, Rudolfo Anaya, and others. Contributors include Luis Leal, Juan Bruce-Novoa, Tey Diana Rebolledo, Genaro Padilla, and Francisco Lomelí.

González, José Luis. *El país de los cuatro pisos y otros ensayos*. Río Piedras, P.R.: Ediciones Huracán, 1989. The title essay is one of the most controversial texts to address Puerto Rican political culture. Also, another important essay included in this collection is "El escritor en el exilio."

Herrera-Sobek, María, and Helena María Viramontes, eds. *Chicana Creativity and Criticism: Charting New Frontiers in American Literature*. Special issue of *The Americas Review* 15: 3-4 (1987). The entire number is devoted to Chicana literature and art, and criticism of works. Contains five excellent essays on Chicana literature, three on general topics, one on Cisneros's *House on Mango Street*, and one on the works of Helena María Viramontes and Cherríe Moraga.

Herrera-Sobek, María, and Helena María Viramontes, eds. *Beyond Stereotypes: The Critical Analysis of Chicana Literature*. Binghamton, N.Y.: The Bilingual Press, 1985. A collection of six essays by leading critics of Chicano literature on general topics (e.g., "Humor in Chicana Literature") and specific writers (e.g., Gina Valdés, Sylvia Lizárraga, Estela Portillo Trambley, and Alma Villanueva).

Horno-Delgado, Asunción, Eliana Ortega, Nina M. Scott, and Nancy Saporta Sternbach, eds. *Breaking Boundaries: Latina Writings and Critical Readings*. Amherst: University of Massachusetts Press, 1989. Excellent critical essays that include Chicanas, Puertorriqueñas, Cubanas, and other Latinas. Essays on individual writers serve as an example of the most important critical issues that dominate Latina writing.

Hospital, Carolina. *Cuban American Writers: Los Atrevidos*. Princeton, N.Y.: Ediciones Ellas, 1988. Included in this poetry collection are Gustavo Pérez Firmat, Elias Miguel Muñoz, Lourdes Gil, Roberto Fernández, Ricardo Pau-Llosa, Jorge Guitart, and Carolina Hospital, among others.

Kanellos, Nicolás. *A History of Hispanic Theater in the United States: Origins to 1940*. Austin: University of Texas Press, 1990. Excellent history of Hispanic theater organized around the cities where it developed and had its major impact.

Kanellos, Nicolás, ed. *Biographical Dictionary of Hispanic Literature in the United States*. Westport, Conn.: Greenwood Press, 1990. Includes Puerto Ricans, Cubans, and other Hispanic writers. Each entry has a brief biography of the author, a discussion of the major themes of his or her work, a survey of criticism and a bibliography.

Kanellos, Nicolás, ed. *Hispanic Theater in the United States*. Houston: Arte Público Press, 1984. Collection of essays dealing with various aspects of Hispanic theater. Essays by John C. Miller, Tomás Ybarra Fausto, and Jorge A. Huerta, among others.

Lattin, Vernon, ed. *Contemporary Chicano Fiction: a Critical Survey*. Binghamton, N.Y.: Bilingual Press, 1986. A collection of essays on the Chicano novel with several articles on Oscar Acosta, Rolando Hinojosa, and Rudolfo Anaya.

Leal, Luis. "Mexican American Literature: A Historical Perspective." 18-30 *Modern Chicano Writers*. Joseph Sommers and Tomás Ybarra-Frausto, eds. Englewood Cliffs, N.J.: Prentice Hall, 1979. A study of Chicano literary history.

Rendón, Armando. *Chicano Manifesto*. New York: Macmillan, 1971. A text re-visioning Chicano history and identity.

Rivero, Eliana. "Hispanic Literature in the United States: Self Image and Conflict." *Revista chicano-riqueña* 13 (1985), 173-192. Excellent introduction to Latino literature sociohistorical issues.

Rodríguez de Laguna, Asela, ed. *Images and Identities: the Puerto Rican in Literature*. New Brunswick, N.J.: Transaction, 1987. Divided into six parts, this book presents essays by some of the most recognized Puerto Rican and Nuyorican creative writers and their perspective on Puerto Rican culture and literature.

Rodríguez del Pino, Salvador. *La novela chicana escrita en español: cinco autores comprometidos*. Ypsilanti: Bilingual, 1982. Examines the Spanish language novels of Tomás Rivera, Rolando Hinojosa, Alejandro Morales, Aristeo Brito, and Miguel Méndez-M. The interpretive essays are developed around the theme of alienation.

Saldívar, José David, ed. *The Rolando Hinojosa Reader: Essays Historical and Critical*. *Revista chicano-riqueña* 12.3-4 (1984). A collection of essays on Rolando Hinojosa's "Klail City Death Trip Series." Excellent contributions by Rosaura Sánchez, Hector Calderón, Ramón Saldívar, Margarita Cota-Cárdenas, and Rolando Hinojosa, among others.

Saldívar, Ramón. *Chicano Narrative: the Dialectics of Difference*. Madison: University of Wisconsin Press, 1990. This is a monograph that addresses critical issues such as writing the self, race, class, gender, rewriting of history and popular culture in chicano literature.

Sánchez, Marta. *Chicana Poetry: a Critical Approach to an Emerging Literature*. Berkeley: University of California Press, 1985. A feminist analysis of four Chicana poets: Alma Villanueva, Lorna Dee Cervantes, Lucha Corpi, and Bernice Zamora.

Shirley, Carl, and Francisco Lomelí, eds. *The Dictionary of Literary Biography: Chicano Series*. Detroit: Gale Press, 1989. A collection of bibliobiographic essays on Chicano writers by leading critics of Chicano literature.

Silén, Iván, ed. *Los paraguas amarillos: los poetas latinos en Nueva York*. Binghamton, N.Y.: Bilingual Press, 1984. Collection of poetic texts by Latin American writers who live in New York and write in Spanish, with the exception of Pedro Pietri.

Sommers, Joseph, Tomás Ybarra-Frausto, eds. *Modern Chicano Writers*. Englewood Cliffs, N.J.: Prentice-Hall, 1979. A collection of essays on various critical approaches to Chicano literature.

Tatum, Charles. *Chicano Literature*. Boston: Twayne, 1982. A literary history that attempts to give a panoramic view of the development of Chicano literature from its origins to 1980s.

PARALITERATURE
Chuck Tatum
University of Arizona

The continuing debate among theorists over the definition and inter-relationship of "elite," "popular," and "mass" culture again was brought into sharp focus with the Museum of Modern Art's exhibition entitled, "High and Low: Modern Art and Popular Culture." The museum directors' intent was to illustrate that it is never easy to separate the high and low culture into rigidly defined categories and that they often share a common inspiration in "scraps of newsprint, theatrical posters and commercial labels, in the sullen scrawls of prisoners and delinquents, or in the lurid imagery of the funnies" (Danto 656). Arthur Danto, an eminent art historian, recounts in his review of the exhibition that he has often been attacked by elitists for, among other sins, defending Andy Warhol as a philosophical genius and giving "Pop Art" a position of dignity in contemporary art history. In an eloquent defense of his "maverick" status among established arbiters of good and bad taste, Danto points out that it was the genius of Wittgenstein to find philosophical inspiration in Street and Smith's *Detective Story Magazine* and the genius of Sartre to discover phenomenological truth in a conversaton with Raymond Aron.

While Danto applauds the exhibition's directors for their boldness and wisdom, he recognizes that other critics have responded harshly and critically to the conflation of aesthetic categories that should never have been brought together under one roof.

The varied responses to the Museum of Modern Art's exhibition are paralleled in countless debates over the relative merits of popular culture and its place within society itself as well as within traditionally defined forms of artistic expression like painting, cinema, architecture, or literature. Yet despite the resistance to accept popular culture's role in what is defined as "elite culture," it is undeniable that the former suffuses the latter. Danto and others have convincingly demonstrated this. In terms of Latin American literature, it is difficult to identify a monographic study of writers like Jorge Luis Borges, Carlos Fuentes, Jorge Amado, Gabriel García Márquez, Manuel Puig, or Elena Poniatowska without coming across some reference to the presence of popular culture in their works. At the same time, there are many forms of popular culture in Latin America that exist autonomously outside of any direct relation to elite culture.

It is thus appropriate to review the phenomenon of paraliterature in Latin America, which is manifested independently in multiple forms and is reflected in the works of well-known writers. In order to better understand the dynamics of paraliterature in terms of the multiple and complicated relationships among its creators and audiences, a brief review of major theoretical approaches to popular culture itself would be instructive.

Theoretical Approaches to Popular Culture

In general terms, there are two dominant views of the production and consumption of popular culture: 1) it is imposed from without and above subordinated peoples by the forces of domination; 2) it is made from within and below structures of domination by subordinated peoples themselves. The first view, by far the most widely accepted, is that of mass cultural theorists and has evolved out of concepts developed by individuals associated with the Frankfurt Institute for Social Research (founded at the University of Frankfurt in 1923) who later emigrated to the United States. For our purposes the writings of Theodor Adorno are particularly important, specifically his 1967 reconsideration of his earlier thinking, "Culture Industry Reconsidered" (Adorno). In this essay, Adorno associates mass culture with "culture industry" in order to distinguish the former from popular culture, which he considers to be a spontaneous expression arising directly from the masses. His analysis of a culture industry is somewhat mechanistic and betrays his utter disdain for its manifestations, especially when contrasted to forms of high culture. Those who control the culture industry deliberately conflate spheres of high and low art (spheres that Adorno thinks have justifiably been separate for thousands of years) into a consumable product for the masses. Technical capabilities as well as administrative and economic concentration make such a product readily available to be passed on to consumers from above. Contrary to what the culture industry would have us believe, the consumer is considered as the object rather than the subject of a process that cynically lulls us into accepting "the master's voice." The culture industry has no interest in the specific content or formation of individual artistic expression, but rather in transforming works into various cultural commodities; works have value only in relation to their potential as commodities to be foisted on the masses, particularly the masses in the most economically developed countries, where a higher generation of capital is possible.

Stuart Hall and Paddy Whannel have given us a useful composite overview of mass culture adherents' stance that include the following characteristics: 1) Power and techniques to manipulate the culture industry is concentrated in a few hands and many are employed to carry out its most nefarious ends. The ethics of salesmanship and persuasion pervades all aspects of public life. 2) Artistic creativity has been snuffed out in favor of cultural products mass-produced for a large and unthinking consumer audience. 3) Individuals' worth in society is judged solely on the basis of their potential as consumers, and they are mere passive receivers of cultural products, unable to make judgments or meaningful discriminations. 4) Electronic and print mass media play an increasingly important role in creating a pseudoworld in which our experiences are reorganized into stereotypes and distortions of ourselves and our reality. 5) The world created by mass media is unambiguously defined so that subtle distinctions become increasingly blurred. 6) Folk art, popular art that arises from below, and high art are all subsumed into mass culture, which has no respect for tradition, values, or aesthetics that do not serve its purposes. 7) Conformity rather than true expression of individuality is emphasized. The cult of personality—actors, politicians, sports heroes—dominates. 8) Consumers live passively in a dreamlike world stripped of their own aspirations and sense of themselves.

This is, indeed, a most depressing picture of mass culture society in which various cultural products play an important role as commodities designed to maintain a false sense of reality and to satisfy passive consumer tastes. However, the critical/theoretical view of these products does evolve to become more sophisticated and more useful in interpreting them. In terms of cultural texts—the term is used broadly to include traditionally defined written texts as well as texts in a wider sense—the last thirty years have seen a number of approaches come into fashion and then fade. Structuralism, for example, while it provided a useful means to break down a text into its component formal parts, tended to conceptualize the reader as "an overly passive recipient of narrative meanings" (Ashley 136). In addition, given its emphasis on the formal qualities of the text, it deemphasized the fact that the reading of the text takes place in a cultural context. Ultimately, structuralism's dominant emphasis on scientifically precise analysis made it relatively useless in considering the role of the reader in constructing the text.

Some of the varieties of poststructuralism that emerged in France in the 1960s react against structuralism's scientific emphasis and are more useful in considering the popular culture text within a broader context of the reader as well as the reading process itself. While the many theories that became prominent during this period varied greatly, they do seem to share a common sense of a "total culture" in which both readers and texts are shaped (Ashley 136). Within this wider social, political, and material context, the concept of ideology formulated by Louis Althusser and others is central. Althusser's "lived ideology" greatly expands its narrow definition from an orthodox Marxist notion of false consciousness to a sense that it is "embedded in all levels of social existence, penetrating even the most commonplace institutions, occurrences, and social interactions" (Ashley 137). He broadly views institutions as "ideological apparatuses" that promote a dominant account "of the way that things are." Popular fiction and other forms of paraliterature would constitute such apparatuses because they are ideologically charged texts that complicitly invite us to share their producers' dominant account of the world. While Althusser does not view the reader as an automaton who mechanistically responds to the "hailing" of the ideological message embedded in the text, he is at least skeptical that the reader of certain texts (e.g., popular fiction) can resist. Thus both Althusserian and post-Althusserian ideological criticism must be used with great caution so as not to distort the reader as well as the text itself.

Deconstructionist criticism of the 1970s and 1980s also rejects structuralism's rigidly scientific concept of the author and the popular fiction text. As for most poststructuralist theory, literary meaning is highly elusive and no longer unitary as it was for Adorno and the structuralists. Readers of deconstructionist criticism are well acquainted with the notion of the text's incoherencies, dislocations, contradictions, silences, and absences. Regarding popular fiction, Pierre Macherey in *A Theory of Literary Production* shows that literary language itself is highly contradictory; while it attempts to explain, to clarify, the fact that it is based in ideology makes this intent suspect. As a good deconstructionist, he insists that what popular texts do not say is as important as what they attempt to say (Ashley 141).

A version of mass culturalist theory dominant in Latin America in the late 1960s and 1970s (and found even today) is the cultural imperialism thesis, a corollary of the dependency theory of economic development in vogue among social scientists and economists fifteen to twenty years ago. Briefly stated, the dependency model originated in the extensive Latin American debate on the problems of underdevelopment. It emerged from the convergence of two intellectual trends: one that can be roughly identified as neo-Marxist and the other rooted in an earlier Latin American discussion of economic development that coalesced into the United Nations' Economic Commission for Latin America (ECLA) in the 1950s.

Several important aspects of the dependency phenomenon need to be emphasized: the penetration of multinational corporations in the underdeveloped economies of Third World countries; the political objectives and foreign aid policies of developed countries; and the subordinate position of underdeveloped countries in the international market system. Parallel to the importance of the relationships between developed and underdeveloped countries are the structures of internal relationships within each underdeveloped country. The center/periphery dichotomy that characterizes the macrocosm is duplicated microcosmically within each of these countries. Urban concentrations of economic and political power (whose interests are often allied and coincide with those of the developed countries and multinationals) form centers in their relationship to less powerful urban and rural peripheries which would be forced to adopt capitalist, consumption-oriented production priorities that disadvantage a country's lower economic sectors.

The cultural imperialist thesis that grows out of the dependency model of development focuses on the role that various cultural industries and mass media—radio, television, photonovels, comic books, music, newspapers, advertising, etc.—play within the underdeveloped economies and societies of Third World nations. While advocates of this view of dominant/subordinate countries' relationships in the socioeconomic, political, and cultural sphere clearly adhere to the Frankfurt School's concept of mass culture as imposed from without and above, they do not betray the same attitude of disregard toward "low" culture as, for example, Adorno. They are suspicious only of those forms of "low" culture that are manipulated by powerful economic interests to promote capitalist consumerism.

Armand Mattelart, one of the principle formulators of the cultural imperialism thesis, views as essential the process of ideological transference—attitudes, behavior, and life models—that accompany developed countries' economic penetration and imperial foreign policies. He considers cultural imperialism as a model of organization of power that seeks a homogenization, a demobilization, disorganization, and subsequently a consensus. "A people deprived of its culture, its customs, its own style of life, is just as defenseless as if it had been robbed of its raw materials" (Torrecilla 69). Mattelart believes that an integral aspect of cultural imperialism is a "correlation of forces, a combination of national and international forces," whereby creole bourgeoisies direct programs of cultural nationalism that facilitate the penetration of foreign interests of monopoly capital. These programs may vary from underdeveloped country to country, but their relationship to external forces is always the same: large national cultural industries such as electronic and print media depend both financially and for their sources of news on foreign counterparts. Mattelart warns against considering cultural imperialism as a kind of *deus ex machina*, a conspiratorial external force that manipulates domestic cultural industries. Rather, he believes that each underdeveloped society has its own state apparatus that is very well adapted to its particular culture and class structure and generates cultural messages not perceived as foreign. Transnational or multinational corporations and interests are much more important in the generation of cultural messages than the foreign governments of developed countries.

An early and somewhat crude application of the cultural imperialism thesis was Ariel Dorfman and Armand Mattelart's 1972 book, *Para leer el Pato Donald: comunicación de masa y colonialismo* (Reading Donald Duck: Mass Communication and Colonialism). It is a study of the capitalist values and behaviors embedded in Disney comic books highly popular in Chile before and during the presidency of Salvador Allende (1970-73). From an analysis of the comic book's content the authors extrapolate to the dangers that these seemingly inoffensive stories pose to Chilean children during their formative years. They view these values as reflective of the "American Dream of Life" that a United States-based cultural industry imposes upon Third World countries in order to guarantee its own economic and political dominance.

As discussed above, Mattelart later refined his model to eliminate the *deus ex machina* element. Greater sophistication also characterized other studies that the Dorfman/Mattelart work gave rise to. Several of these will be discussed in the following sections on various paraliterary forms.

Herbert I. Schiller, one of the most articulate and prolific proponents of the cultural imperialism thesis, has discussed at length the objectives and operations of multinational corporations in the specific area of communications. He contends that "the basic economic ogranizational unit in the modern world capitalist economy is the multinational corporation. A few hundred of these giant agglomerations of capital, largely American-owned dominate the global market in the production and distribution of goods and services" (164). A primary concern of Schiller and other theorists revolves around the destructive cultural consequences that multinational corporations have on Third World societies, especially on the behavior and world view of their audiences.

All of the above critical/theoretical approaches tend to view popular culture in general and paraliterature in particular as a cultural phenomenon that is imposed from above. A radically different view would position popular culture as made from within and below. John Fiske, a proponent of this approach, believes that popular culture "is made by subordinate peoples in their own interests out of resources that also, contradictorily, serve the economic interests of the dominant" (2). Part of it is always outside the control of hegemonic forces for it is a culture of conflict that always "involves the struggle to make social meanings that are in the interests of the subordinate and that are not those preferred by the dominant ideology." Creators and consumers of popular culture have the choice of either resisting or evading structures of dominance. He offers as examples of this choice girl fans of Madonna who resist patriarchal meanings of female sexuality by constructing their oppositional ones. Surfers on the other hand avoid structures of dominance by "evading social discipline, evading ideological control and positioning" (2). He would agree with the deconstructionists when he asserts that meanings can never be identified in a popular culture text but must be constructed within wider social life and in relation to other texts. Moreover, popular texts are inadequate in themselves and are completed only when taken up by people within their everyday culture. Readers give meaning to these texts only when their textual messages are relevant to their everyday lives. Fiske views "relevance" as central to popular culture for it minimizes the differences between text and life, aesthetics and everyday experience. Relevance is produced for readers from the intersection of the textual and the social (6). The subordinate, which for Fiske constitute the majority of producers and consumers of popular culture, hold semiotic power—that is the power to construct oppositional meanings (10). This potential to semiotically resist differentiates his readers from those envisioned by Frankfurt School Marxists, structuralists, and poststructuralists such as Adorno, Barthes, Althusser, and Macherey.

Fiske's optimistic view of the production and consumption of popular culture as having the power to construct oppositional meanings is at least partially shared by Néstor García Canclini, John Beverley, and Marc Zimmerman whose analyses are also rooted in the writings of Gramsci and Althusser, as well as in those of more contemporary Marxist theorists of popular culture such as Ernesto Laclau, Chantal Mouffe, Jean Baudrillard, and Pierre Bourdieu. In his 1982 study, *Las culturas populares en el capitalismo* (Popular Cultures in Capitalism), García Canclini examines the transformations that indigenous Mexican arts, crafts, and popular festivals have undergone within the context of late capitalism in a developing industrialized economy. Like Fiske, he believes that not only does culture represent a society, it also serves the function of "reelaborating" social structures and inventing new ones (43). He demonstrates how, in the past few decades, Tarascan and other Indian groups' production of arts and crafts and celebration of their festivals have lost their symbolic meaning through, among other things, their reification in museums and their reproduction for economic purposes by dominant capitalist interests. His program for initiating a contrahegemonic basis for popular cultural forms includes the organization of the producers of these forms—in fact, the organization of the entire popular sector—into cooperatives and unions, thus allowing indigenous groups to reassert control over the means of production and distribution they once had. Related to this is the reappropriation of the symbolic meaning of their products, a process that involves strategies for the progressive control over the spaces and mechanisms of distribution—i.e., removing their products and festivals from museums, governments stores, tourist markets, etc. (161).

Beverley and Zimmerman share García Canclini's optimism—all of their works are characterized by a strong Gramscian and Althusserian faith in the subaltern classes—in the potential of producers of popular culture to develop contrahegemonic forms of cultural resistance. Beverley and Zimmerman's 1990 monograph, *Literature and Politics in the Central American Revolutions*, is built on the assumption that society "is not some essence that is prior to representation but rather the product of struggles over meaning and representation." This perspective, itself an offshoot of Laclau and Mouffe's thesis, allows them "to consider the ways in which literature [including paraliterary forms such as popular poetry], rather than being simply a reflection or epiphenomenon of the social as in the traditional base-superstructure model, is constitutive—in historically and socially specific ways—in some measure of it" (ix). The authors endeavor to show how poetry, including literary expressions within the dominant Spanish-speaking Creole-mestizo cultural tradition as well as recent voices of the indigenous, non-Spanish-speaking peoples, has been a materially decisive force in the revolutions of Guatemala, El Salvador, and Nicaragua. However, in focusing on poetry, they do not exclude other forms of indigenous and mestizo oral culture such as the traditional *corrido* (ballad) and new styles of popular music and hybrid folk music (*la nueva trova* [the new trove]), street theater, storytelling, *refranes* (sayings), myth and superstition, and forms of rumor and gossip (xiv).

Paraliterary Forms

Given the broad consideration that many contemporary theorists give to what constitutes a text, it is both acceptable and desirable to discuss a wide variety of paraliterary forms common to Latin America: comic books and comic strips, single-panel cartoons, photonovels, posters, pop occult texts, *literatura de cordel* (literature on a string), detective fiction, and testimonial and documentary literature. While several of these forms might not meet, in a strict sense, a traditional definition of paraliterature, they certainly can be "read" in the same manner as a literary text is read.

Comic Books and Comic Strips

As is the case of many other forms of paraliterature (as well as popular culture in general) in Latin America, very little research has been done on comic books and comic strips with the exception Argentina, Brazil, and Mexico. Scant information is available on the evolution of comic books and comic strips; nonetheless, it is generally recognized that the former developed from the latter that became popular in Latin America during the first third of this century (Hinds 82). Comic strips published in newspapers were initially translations of North American ones and even later native varieties closely resembled those produced by their northern neighbor. Humor and fantasy were the most popular categories published in Mexican newspapers such as *El heraldo* and *El universal*, in Argentine magazines such as *Tit-bits*, and in Brazilian publications such as *O Tico-Tico*, a newspaper devoted to comics.

The comic book proper did not begin to be produced until the 1930s with the creation in Mexico of *Los supersabios* (The Super Wisemen; 1936) and *La familia Burrón* (The Burrón Family; 1937). The latter, a humorous saga of an urban lower-middle-class family, is still published today by Gabriel Vargas, its original creator. In Argentina the humor comic book *Patoruzú* appeared in 1931. Its creator, Dante Quintero, uses his main character, a Pampas Indian, to poke fun at the pretentions of urban society. Publications such as *El Tony* (1928) and *Pif-Paf* (1937) were devoted entirely to comics (both comic strips and comic books). Brazil's first genuine comic books, *Gibi mensal* (Monthly Gibi), began to be published during the late 1930s.

The 1950s began to see the decline of the comic book in the United States but its climb to new popular heights in some Latin American countries, particularly in Mexico. Manuel de Landa began to publish a pocket-size comic book and individual artists and entrepeneurs founded their own companies. Guillermo Parra and Yolanda Vargas Dulché joined to establish Editorial Argumentos, which eventually published one of Latin America's best-selling comic books, *Lágrimas, risas y amor* (Tears, Laughter, and Love), a title dominated by highly formulaic romance themes. Rius (Eduardo del Río) began creating a subversive political comic book, *Los supermachos* (The Super Studs), in the mid-1960s. When his editors cancelled his contract after several years, he went on to create and publish an equally controversial comic book, *Los agachados* (The Downtrodden). Other notable titles that began appearing in Mexico in the 1960s are: *Kalimán*, a superhero comic book that would soon become—and still is—Mexico's most popular comic book; the Western comic book *El Payo*; and the slapstick humor-adventure comic book *Chanoc*; the adventure comic book *Torbellino*; and the detective thriller *La novela policiaca* (Police Tales).

Argentina's best known comic strip during the past thirty years is *Mafalda* (1965-mid-1970s) by Joaquín Salvador Lavado (Quino). The strip's main character, Mafalda, is a precocious young girl, world-wise way beyond her age. She and her cohorts, a cast of children, constantly question the logic and sanity of the adult world, which they see as corrupted by materialist values, violence, deceit, etc. (Mesón). In addition to this comic strip, perhaps Latin America's most popular, other satirical strips have caught the popular imagination. For example, Roberto Fontanarrosa's *Las aventuras de Inodoro Pereira* (The Adventures of

Inodoro Pereira) pokes fun at Argentina's sacred Gaucho tradition. The main character has been described as a "paradigmatic gaucho" (Foster, "Gauchomanía") whose image Fontanarrosa manipulates to critique an essential aspect of the national mythos as well as its corrosive nature in the present.

Brazil has also emerged as a center of comic book and comic strip activity during the contemporary period. Alves Pinto (Ziraldo), through his comic strip *Perere*, takes a swipe at Brazilian values, society, and culture while taking care not to become overly caustic. Maurício de Sousa, a successful publisher and entrepeneur, has created several important comic books including *Mónica* and *Cebolinha*. Other creators of note are Daniel Azulay, Floriano Hermeto, Gedeone Malagola, and Henfil. Henfil's comic strips are aimed at undercutting the superficiality and falseness of Brazilian values much like Lavado's *Mafalda* vis-à-vis Argentina.

Mexico, Argentina, and Brazil have been the centers of comic strip and comic book production in Latin America for almost five decades, but there are important titles in other countries as well. For example, in Peru Juan Acevedo has created a socially conscious comic book called *Cuy* whose main character, a rodent, is contrasted to Disney's counterpart Mickey Mouse. In Cuba during the Castro era the comic strip *Gugulandia* has maintained an incessant critique of nonsocialist countries. While they had a short history, the Chilean comic books *Cabro chico* (Little Kid) and *La firme* (The Upstanding One) stand, along with *Gugulandia*, as excellent examples of politically alternative comics. Both were published for two years during the height of the Salvador Allende era (1971-73) (Kunzle, "Chile's *La firme*; Woll).

The study of Latin American comic strips and comic books during the past twenty years has been heavily influenced by Dorfman and Mattelart's 1972 book, *Para leer el Pato Donald: comunicación de masa y colonialismo* (*Reading Donald Duck: Mass Communications and Colonialism*), already discussed. While in retrospect the authors' analysis of the Disney comic book *Donald Duck* seems simplistic in both its methodology and application, their work spawned many others. Some are more refined, while others do not transcend the original work's mechanistic predisposition toward oversimplifying complex sociopolitical and cultural phenomena. Dorfman himself (with Manuel Jofré) went on to publish *Supermán y sus amigos del alma* (Superman and His Bosom Buddies) and *Reader's nuestro que estás en la tierra* (Our Reader's Digest Who Art on Earth). In the first, the authors analyze the American popular culture hero, the Lone Ranger, as well as the Chilean comic strip *Mampato*. While Armand Mattelart has published several monographic studies since 1971, they will not be discussed here because they deal more with mass culture in general rather than with paraliterature per se.

Other studies of comic books and comic strips that come under the Dorfman/Mattelart sphere of influence are: 1) Irene Hérner's *Mitos y monitos: historietas y fotonovelas en México* (Myths and Figures: Comic Books and Photonovels in Mexico) which clearly falls under the shadow of Dorfman and Mattelart's influence. Yet it is not limited, as is their 1972 book, by sweeping generalizations and extrapolations based solely on content analysis. In addition to a discussion of content, Herner provides valuable information on the structure of the Mexican comic book (and photonovel) industry, as well as some rare statistics on readership. 2) The Mexican critic Higilio Alvarez Constantino clearly views comic books imported from the United States as threats to the country's cultural integrity. In his book, *La magia de los cómics coloniza nuestra cultura* (The Magic of Comics Colonizes Our Culture), Higilio Alvarez Constantino sees comic books and other cultural industries such as television as ideological threats to a people who are just emerging from economic, political, and cultural underdevelopment. He challenges Mexican readers to protect their national heritage and cultural sovereignty through the creation of massive educational and legislative resistance to the continued incursion of foreign values, largely American. 3) Miguel Angel Gallo in his *Los cómics: un enfoque sociológico* (The Comics: a Sociological Focus) also sees the comic book as a foreign invention designed to aid and abet economic imperialism by perpetrating the worst capitalist attitudes and mores upon an unsuspecting reading public. He claims that Mexican and other Latin American readers become contaminated by exported United States ideological stances on matters such as racism, collective political action, the subjugation of women and minorities, violence, and historical immobility.

The other major theoretical approach used to examine Latin American comic books and comic strips can be generally classified as semiological. While not always adhered to rigorously, Umberto Eco is cited in a number of studies that examine a restricted range of works. Several of these semiotically oriented approaches have appeared in the Mexican publication *El cómic es algo serio* (The Comic Book Is a Serious Matter), the most interesting being short article, by David Alfie and Leobardo Cornejo, the first a general discussion of the possibilities of semiotics as applied to comics, the second an interesting but somewhat truncated analysis of Rius's *Los supermachos* and *Los agachados*.

Perhaps the most thorough monographic treatment of comic books is Harold E. Hinds, Jr., and Charles Tatum's forthcoming *Not for Children Only: The Mexican Comic Book in the 1970s*. The book includes a long introductory survey of Mexican comic book history, the industry, readership, and critical works, and individual chapters on representative titles: *Kalimán*-superhero comic book; *Lágrimas, risas y amor*-romance comic book; Rius's *Los supermachos* and *Los agachados*-political comic books; the post-Rius *Los supermachos*; *Chanoc*-adventure comic book; *El Payo*-Western comic book; *La familia Burrón*-family comic book; *La novela policiaca*-detective comic book. Each chapter is divided into sections dealing with an overview of the specific comic book's content and artistic features, a comparison with its North American counterparts, and a discussion of how it reflects contemporary Mexico. In the final chapter, the authors weigh the titles discussed in previous chapters against the cultural imperialism thesis concluding that Mexican comic books of the 1970s generally do not fit the model.

While many other studies could be cited, they do not in general follow any discernible theoretical/critical approach nor are they particularly thorough or interesting.

Single-Panel Cartoons

Unlike comic books and comic strips that are of more recent vintage, the single-panel cartoon in Latin America has its roots deeply planted in the nineteenth century. Its early history is closely related to the development of mass circulation newspapers during the post-colonial period in the Spanish and Portuguese-speaking young republics and the emergence of readership interest in political figures and events (Lindstrom, "The Single-Panel Cartoon" 208). While there is no causal relationship, its rise in popularity parallels an active period of newspaper and magazine caricature art in the United States.

Regarding the latter phenomenon, John J. Johnson has traced the history of the portrayal of Latin America in United States caricatures. Much like these political single-panel cartoons, caricatures in Latin American publications initially were characterized by explicit references to important events and specific labeling of public figures. While creators of single-panel cartoons could not count on their readers' familiarity with national history or contemporary events, they did assume that they had been liberally educated, especially in the humanities and fine arts. For example, cartoons often contained allusions to classical mythology or European history.

The twentieth century marked a significant change in emphasis as the themes and material for the single-panel cartoon broadened to appeal to a wider, not so highly educated, readership as before. Magazines like Buenos Aires's *Caras y caretas* (Faces and Masks) dealt with human foibles and poked fun at conventions and attitudes more widely shared by the general populace (Fraser). In Mexico Guadalupe José Posada's skeleton etchings, which mercilessly satirized prominent public officials, social institutions, class values and mores, etc., were designed to appeal to proletarian tastes. His cartoons were initially distributed on the streets in the form of inexpensive mass produced sheets, thus representing for many who have studied his art a democratization of the form itself (Lindstrom, "The Single-Panel Cartoon" 209). Another Mexican artist, José Clemente Orozco, is often associated with Posada, one of his mentors, especially his biting and sharply critical attacks on conservative politicians and social fat cats.

Among single-panel cartoonists prominent today are the Mexican Eduardo del Río (Rius) who is best known for his comic books and illustrated books; the Uruguayan Hermenegildo Sábat, an established artist who has turned to cartooning in order to appeal to a wider audience; the Brazilian Luis Fernando Veríssimo, a founder of the generally scandalous publication *Pato Macho* (Stud Duck); the Colombian Gonzalo Angarita who takes aim in his cartoons at would-be social climbers and nouveaux riches; and the Venezuelan Pedro León Zapata, an excellent graphic artist whose cartoons sometimes suffer from their being limited to very specific situations.

Eduardo del Río is probably one of the best-known political illustrators in Latin America, although his artistry is not particularly remarkable. He originally drew cartoons for the popular Mexico City magazine *Siempre* and later contributed to a host of publications including a health food periodical and an occasional political satire publication, *El garrapato* (The Scrawl). His 1968 publication, *Caricaturas rechazadas* (Rejected Caricatures), deals with a wide variety of subjects including political corruption, the virtues of socialism, holistic health, the plight of the Mexican Indian, United States imperialism, and the exploitation of the Chicano.

Compared to critical studies of some other paraliterary forms, there is a paucity of thoughtful or theoretically oriented criticism of single-panel cartoons. Although some excellent descriptive overviews of cartooning in specific Latin American countries do provide a reasonably good perspective, there is little approaching the richness of criticism on comic books or even photonovels. An exception is Naomi Lindstrom's 1980 study of cartooning in Argentina from the 1940s through the 1970s in which she examines single-panel cartoons appearing in mass-audience magazines within the context of Peronism and post-Peronism. Focusing on Willy (Guillermo) Divito's magazine *Rico Tipo* (Big Shot), Landrú's (Juan Carlos Columbres) *Tía Vicenta* (Aunt Vicenta), Quino (pseudonym of Joaquín S. Lavado), and Roberto Fontanarrosa, she shows how Argentine cartooning has consistently during the past thirty years become more radical and more deliberate in its questioning of fundamental social structures. Lindstrom's 1985 overview of single-panel cartoons is an extremely valuable source of information on this critically neglected paraliterary genre. In her assessment of future research in this area, Lindstrom wryly comments that "everything" needs to be done. She cites Johnson's work on Latin America in United States caricature as a model of criticism that is badly needed on home-grown single-panel cartoons. Elizabeth K. Baur and Eco's semiological studies of media and other paraliterary forms as well as sex-role approaches are cited as worthy models to follow.

Photonovels

After the comic book, the photonovel is perhaps the paraliterary form that has been most disparaged as, at best, worthless, and, at worst, an assault upon Latin America's moral fiber. Photonovels are, next to the comic book, the most widely distributed printed material in Latin America. These romantic stories presented in book form as balloon-captioned photographs seem to suffer the same neglect as comic books, at least among Latin America's reading public; few admit to reading them, nobody seems eager to produce them, and no respectable educational institution or archive would deign to collect and preserve them. They are, then, as ephemeral as comic books, for once they are bought from newsstands or have served their purpose at neighborhood rental markets, they seem to disappear. Only the most persistent collector—usually someone with a scholarly interest in these short books of photos—will possess sufficient back numbers to draw any meaningful conclusions about their content, ideological underpinnings, artistic features, etc.

As the United States was the initial source for Latin American comic strips and comic books, Europe was the source for photonovels. They have been traced as far back as 1834 and are linked to the introduction of commerical photography (Saint-Michel). France was the biggest producer of *roman-photo*, largely because of the prominence there of photography and later the movie industry; by mid-twentieth century photonovels had become a byproduct of the still photographs used in films. However, the continuous, moving and speaking image of the film could only become a discontinuous, static, and mute image on the printed page (Flora, "Photonovels" 150). It was the del Duca brothers in Italy who first produced a commercially successful photonovel—*fumetti* for the "cloud of smoke" dialogue bubbles above the characters' heads—in 1945 based on the highly successful 1932 Hollywood movie, *Grand Hotel*. The collection of captioned photographs were very soon translated into other languages like French and Spanish and began to be distributed internationally.

Spain soon began producing its own photonovels based on its growing film industry and drawing on a tradition of romantic tales for women. Spanish *fotonovelas* were exported to northern Latin America, while Italian *fumetti* were exported to the Southern Cone, especially Argentina. The Spanish romantic photonovel, *Corín Tellado*, became enormously popular among literate, middle-class women readers and was eventually produced in Latin America itself.

As Flora has indicated, the Latin American production of photonovels initially took advantage of several factors including: close ties with Italian production companies, the rise in popularity of magazines in the 1950s, the development of a strong printing industry particularly in the southern cone, the strengthening of film industries in the southern cone, the establishment of viable television industries, the strong linkages between Italy and its immigrant populations in countries such as Argentina and Brazil. Photonovel production was first limited to these two countries but later moved to Chile, Mexico, and Miami (after 1959 by the Cuban exile community).

Photonovel production in Argentina reached its apogee during the economic boom of the 1950s and 1960s. Photonovels became very popular among the working class. Later, when television began expanding, concurrent photonovel and *telenovela* (soap opera) production became common as actors moved easily back and forth between the two media.

With the beginning of a series of largely military regimes in Brazil after 1964, photonovels struck a conservative course. Those produced domestically by Editora Abril (an extension of the Argentinian Editorial Abril) were mainly very similar to imports and translations of Italian and Argentinian photonovels. Only *Sétimo céu* (Seventh Heaven) used Brazilian materials and emphasized Brazilian themes.

The dominant type of photonovel in Latin America through the 1970s was the so-called *rosa*, which in formulaic fashion posits innocent but poor women against wealthy but corrupt women to win over rich men who must choose between their base instincts and noble and virtuous feelings. The poor women usually win out after much suffering and sacrifice; even when they or the men they love die, they are at least reunited in heaven. In order to satisfy strict political and religious censorship as well as to enhance sales, these *fotonovelas rosas* (rose-colored photonovels) generally avoid national themes and settings. They are often sanitized beyond any recognition that they have been produced in Latin America, and the characters are generally European in behavior and appearance.

Coinciding with mass rejection of dictatorship and a generally greater political consciousness among its readership, some photonovels in the mid-1970s began to turn toward indigenous themes, characters, and settings. The Peruvian photonovel *Simplemente María* (Just Mary) is representative of such a shift away from the evasion and escapism of the *rosa* toward a more realistic portrayal of Latin American reality. María is a young, illiterate girl of Indian descent who is betrayed by an upper middle-class student. He leaves her pregnant to fend for herself and her child. Notably, although she accepts her destiny, she does continue to struggle to better herself.

The *fotonovela suave* (soft photonovel) also came into prominence in the mid-1970s. Flora speculates that the new orientation it reflected toward more middle-class concerns was in response to the working-class readership's growing tired of the *rosa*'s repetitiousness (Flora, "*Fotonovelas*" 525). The *suave* far exceeded sales expectations as its production was distributed among a large number of publishers. Advertising was included by Southern Cone companies but restricted in Mexico and the Andean countries. The distribution of *suaves* was monopolized by very few companies often with multinational linkages.

The third type of photonovel popular in Latin America is the *roja* (red), which deals much more explicit than *rosas* or *suaves* with sex and sexuality and male physical violence against women. The explicitness of *rojas* is immediately evident in their covers; scantily clad women are portrayed in sexually explicit positions, and in many cases scenes of violence or implied violence are depicted. On the other hand, *rosas* and *suaves* covers tend to strike a tenderly romantic note. Expressed female sexuality, which is seen as threatening to societal and familial harmony, inevitably ends in tragedy. Flora has observed that the covers (as well as the content) of *rojas*—not unlike the two other photonovel genres—promote an individualistic mode of problem solving rather than collective action or political change; they promote unsolidarity (Flora, "Photonovels" 161). Despite their explicitness, the underlying morality of *rojas* is essentially the same as that of *rosas* and *suaves*: any significant deviation from traditional values and accepted norms of behavior is deemed unacceptable and is punished.

An extreme version of the *fotonovela roja* is the *picaresca* (picaresque) which thrived in Mexico in the late 1970s during a period of relaxed censorship. *Rojas*'s covers and content often border on soft pornography, but the *picaresca* crosses over the line into hard pornography with its prurient photos and portrayal of sex as an end in itself. Apparently meant to appeal to the imagination of young males, sex-starved voluptuous women are frequently depicted pursuing men who can satisfy their insatiable physical longing.

As in the case of alternative comic books such as *Los agachados*, *Los supermachos*, *La firme*, *Gugulandia*, and *Cabro chico*, there are also alternative photonovels that markedly contrast with the four types just described. One example is a collectively produced photonovel out of Ecuador that encouraged organization among indigenous groups (Parlato, Parlato, and Cain). Another example is Southern California project that produced a variety of photonovels for the local Spanish-speaking population (Torres).

Studies of the Latin American photonovel are, if anything, more influenced than comic book studies by the mass culturalist criticism associated with Adorno and, in Latin America, with Dorfman and Mattelart's *Para leer el Pato Donald*. Cornelia Butler Flora is a preeminent critic who has devoted much of her scholarship since the early-1970s to photonovels. Her earliest work focuses on the *fotonovela rosa*'s propensity toward individual actions rather than collective solutions. She compares the photonovel's depiction of the female as a passive, subordinate creation simililar to that of women's magazine fiction, and concludes that the message is basically the same in both forms of paraliterature (Flora, "The Passive Female"). A 1978 study was more global in nature as she and Jan Flora attempted to link a structural analysis of the genre with economic and political factors (Flora and Flora). Her 1989 study examines the political economy of photonovel production across Latin America. As in preceding studies, she sees the photonovel as "another medium where decodification of resistance [to the ideological hegemony of the dominant class] can occur" (Flora, "The Political Economy" 215). However, what is notable about this study and what differentiates it from earlier ones is her focus on the reader rather than content. Basing her line of reasoning on Eco's notion of "common frames" she examines how readers apply their own life experiences to give meaning to a particular photonovel as well as to the genre or subgenre as a whole. She then traces how variations in these "negotiated readings" increased as the material itself diversified between 1950 and 1982. Her latest study is particularly noteworthy because it shows the importance of social interaction for meaning even in mass culture.

Michèle Mattelart's studies focus on the photonovel as "a purveyor of the culture of feminine oppression" (Flora, "The Photonovels" 164). Not unlike Ariel Dorfman and Armand Mattelart's conclusion about the Disney comic book in *Para leer el Pato Donald*, Michèle Mattelart sees the photonovel genre as a "commercial adaptation to the new exigencies of a consumption society." She relates social status to the property of consumption and not to ownership of means presented as an individual characteristic. An individual's inability to survive and advance up the socioeconomic ladder is due neither to an intrinsic personality defect nor to the structural predisposition that makes them possible. In all of her studies, Michèle Mattelart reveals the dual norms of conduct for men and women; women are urged to maintain their virginity in order to make more possible the courting and marrying of middle- and upper-middle-class men, their means to achieving societal acceptance and economic security. Her 1977 book, *La cultura de la opresión feminina* (The Culture of Female Oppression), is the clearest and most systematic treatment of the message of feminine oppression in any Latin American paraliterary form. In it as well as in later essays, she follows a Marxist analysis with semiotic echoes; in this sense, she does not closely synchronize with the growing body of feminist criticism during the late 1970s and the early 1980s.

Jane Hill and Carole Browner have also done important gender-inflected work on the photonovel, but their conclusion is quite different from Mattelart's. Their analysis of Mexican photonovels reveals that gender does not form the major hierarchy between characters; it is instead social class reinforced by rural and urban differences. They found that "goodness" was consistently associated with lower-class characters, while "evil" was almost inevitably attributed to upper-class characters, both regardless of gender.

Flora, Michèle Mattelart, and Hill and Browner view the Latin American photonovel as a potentially influential instrument in forming and reinforcing traditional, nonprogressive values and behaviors. Other critics view them quite differently. For example, Fernando Curiel, an avid reader of photonovels, believes they developed out of Mexican cultural roots and therefore should be considered as a legitimate mass medium, not an inferior popular culture form with corrosive effects.

Posters

Posters straddle a line between art and paraliterature and could reasonably be included as an example of either. They are a text in a traditional sense with written words and a text in a way that poststructuralist theory broadly considers the term: that is, they can be "read" just as a literary work is read. Moreover, posters in the Latin American context are public texts often found on building walls and meant to be read by passersby; they are generally not hidden away in museums as artistic artifacts preserved for their aesthetic particularity. They are usually designed with a specific audience in mind and contain a political or social message expressed explicitly and overtly. In this sense, they fall within a Latin American tradition of popular artistic expression that has its roots in the "painted walls" of the Aztecs and other indigenous cultures.

Contemporary Argentina provides a rich source of poster art arising from the political turmoil and change that has besieged its populace for the past twenty years. According to Lyman Chaffee, this medium has developed in Buenos Aires with a definable "infrastructure of illustrators and technicians, concepts and themes, interest group sponsors, sophisticated stylistic forms, printing shops, visual placement for maximum impact, and cadre system for quick placement throughout the city" (Chaffee, "Poster and Political Propaganda" 80). He views poster art as a means of communicating with the city's politicized masses by democratizing the mass media and bringing political messages directly to the general public. Its messages, which are accessible and comprehensible, tell not only of injustice and suffering but call the people to rally around a new set of ideals and leadership.

An excellent comparison of the manner in which poster art differs within a more repressive political climate is provided by Chaffee in his study of public art in contemporary Paraguay, one of the least politicized countries in the Southern Cone, due mainly to the dominance of the authoritarian regime of General Alfredo Stroessner until very recently (Chaffee, "Popular Culture"). Because of the extreme risk of affixing posters to public walls without detection by a state police apparatus faithful to the regime, one tends to find displayed only officially sanctioned posters sponsored by approved groups and political parties. As would be expected, opposition groups use graffiti writing that can be applied easily and quickly on walls with relatively less risk of detection.

Posters were also common in Cuba, Chile, and Nicaragua at various times during the past twenty years. In Cuba, posters have been officially sponsored by the Castro government as one of many means of communicating revolutionary messages to the populace. The most widely circulated posters were those published in the early 1970s by OSPAAAL, the Organization of Solidarity with the Peoples of Africa, Asia, and Latin America (Kunzle, "Nationalist"). The dominant message is one of Latin American unity in resistance against imperialism. Unlike the political posters in Argentina and Paraguay, the Cuban posters were meant for exportation as well as for domestic display on public *vallas* or billboards. The Chilean Popular Unity government of Salvador Allende published posters from 1970 to 1973, but unlike Cuban posters, which communicated with "a vanguard, semiotic urgency" (Kunzle, "Nationalist" 147), those in Chile incorporated more individual, personal viewpoints. In addition, they were circulated privately and generally not made available to a wide public as in Cuba. The Nicaraguan revolutionary government also used posters, but seemed to prefer larger-format wall murals in the Mexican muralist tradition displayed on *rótulos de carretera* (highway billboards) where they would be seen by passing motorists and pedestrians. Many of these murals were produced collectively by internationalist brigades from other countries who came to Nicaragua in the early 1980s in support of the post-Somoza government. Some murals were commissioned to advance official causes such as the literacy campaign.

Literatura de Cordel

The pamphlet stories in verse known commonly by readers and critics as *folhetos* (pamphlets) or *literatura de cordel* are largely found in

Brazil. These "stories on a string" (so-called because of the manner in which they are hung from a string for display in markets and other public places) were once limited to northeastern Brazil, but due to demographic and technological changes they have spread to other regions and especially to major southern cities such as Rio de Janeiro, São Paulo, and Brasilia (Slater).

The *folheto* is typically a small four by six-and-a-half inch booklet printed on newspaper weight paper consisting of eight, sixteen, thirty-two, or sixty-four uncut pages—that is, multipliers of its fourfold pages. Its stanzas typically are of six or seven lines. Of note are its covers, which not only are artistically interesting but also functionally serve to indicate to the illiterate would-be reader its contents. Major popular artists create blockprints or *xilogravuras* designed to make the booklet more attractive. The author and/or publisher's name usually appear above the title on the cover page, and a likeness of the author as well as advertising appear on the back page.

It is generally agreed that the *folheto* first appeared in the late nineteenth century in northeastern Brazil, but its development prior to then is sketchy at best. Critics have speculated that it developed out of several folk or popular literature traditions, including the oral balladry or *romanceiro* tradition, the Portuguese chapbook tradition, the Brazilian improvised verse dialogues or contests, biblical stories or exemplum, the folktale known in Brazil as the *trancoso*, and a variety of African and Brazilian-Indian elements (Slater 3). Some critics have noted the similarity between the *folheto* and the *corrido* compositions popular in Mexico and elsewhere, but whereas the *corrido* composer sings accompanying himself with a guitar, the popular poet chants his ballad without music in order to turn the pages and sell his product to an eager public.

As Slater has observed, while many *folhetos* are humorous and a few are obscene or pornographic, almost all of them carry a solemn and unambiguous message arising out of its hero or heroine's test of character, which either he or she passes or fails. These series of trials link the *folheto* with a popular religious tradition of worldly saints or sinners that give it its distinct moral character (12).

Most *folheto* buyers are white Brazilians who seem to respond favorably to the predominant portrayal of Indians and blacks as villains. The incorporation of African-Brazilian elements has increased as the paraliterary form has become more urbanized. One finds a good deal of folk religious cultism included and usually viewed critically as a mysterious activity and power associated with nefarious and evil forces.

The development of *literatura de cordel* as an economically viable body of literature was delayed until the late nineteenth century, largely because of the low number of potential literate buyers and the lack of an effective distribution system. Once both of these conditions were met, economic viability quickly transformed the *cordel* into a definable popular phenomenon. At the same time, the increasing economic prosperity of Brazil's northeastern interior brought printing presses to its commercial centers. The mass migration from rural areas to urban centers in the past twenty-five years also has included *cordel* poets who have left northeastern Brazil to relocate in coastal cities such as Fortaleza and Recife as well as major cities in the south.

Cordel authors range from young teenagers to old people. Although the large majority have been men, women have played a prominent role in the editing and synthesizing of their author-husbands and fathers' original creations. The predominance of men is directly related to a historically strong gender bias among northeastern Brazil's lower classes—while some writers come from privileged households, the majority belong to the subsistence farmer class—towards educating males before, or at the expense of, females. In addition, the full-time commitment required to market the product has conflicted with woman's traditional role as the homemaker, housekeeper, and primary parent. Many writers trace their interest in and introduction to *cordel* writing to an older relative who practiced this popular art form (Slater 23).

The production of a *folheto* from start to finish is usually a one-person or family operation including its writing, printing, and distribution. Most creators start their careers as vendors who have to perform parts of the *folheto* in order to attract buyers in a highly competitive open market. The aspiring poet-vendor must then attract enough capital to have his verse printed and distributed. Many more prominent poets published and sold their own work until the past decade.

Rustic hand presses located in small shops and houses have steadily given way to large, technologically advanced presses associated with powerful commercial interests devoted to profit making. This has also altered *cordel* literature in major ways as large-scale distributors have supplanted local distribution networks and poet-performers are decreasingly involved in marketing their own product. Although it is still possible to witness poets chanting the traditional *toada* (chant), it is a rapidly disappearing form of popular expression. At present, only three publishers account for approximately forty percent of all *folhetos* printed each year and just one is a traditional regional press.

Most scholarship on *literatura de cordel* is descriptive, focusing on its origins, development, types, poets, and themes. A number of recent studies can be loosely classified as structural analyses. While these represent an improvement over previous studies, they tend not to take into consideration economic, social, and cultural factors that have affected the *folheto*'s transformation from a largely popular art form to one that recently has become mass produced and mass distributed. Structural studies also frequently ignore the genre's performance aspect and the response and involvement of the audience. Slater's study has the virtue of giving some attention to these two aspects as well as to the reasons for its transformation.

Pop Occult Literature

Popular occult literature by Latin American authors is readily available in many countries, yet it has generally been neglected as a subject of serious study. Perhaps this is due to the fact that few of these books with ghostly cover art that deal with a variety of occult themes are authored by writers generally considered "serious." Unlike detective fiction, popular occult literature seems to have nobody of the stature of a Borges, Viñas, or Fuentes that would surely attract wider critical attention.

Some of the common themes found in these texts are: "psi" research, mystics, out-of-body travel, prophecy, spells, apocalyptic thought, and heresy. Naomi Lindstrom, in the only serious study of this paraliterary genre, has proposed a typology for considering the mass of texts available on the Latin American market: those in which extraordinary individuals whose privileged access to the arcane world come through exceptional sensitivity, purity, or other virtue; works sponsored by formally constituted theosophical societies and represented as authoritative theophilosophical doctrine; those works that rely on the authors' assumption of a non-Western identity and entitled to voice the "wisdom of the East" (Lindstrom, "Latin American Pop Occult Texts").

A representative example of the first type is Lauro Neiva's 1975 *Os mortos ensinam aos vivos* (The Dead Teach the Living) which is characterized by a heterogeneous collection of journalistic and other materials such as: the mutagenic properties of Strontium 90; counterculture cures through spiritism and shock therapy; Brazilian spirit cults' spiritual-holistic healing; and a disquisition on the concept of Karma. In examining the ideological implications of the Brazilian text, Lindstrom finds a decided conservative nationalist orientation, especially in the author's championing of Brazilian spirit cults and his invocation, "Brazil; you are the future of the world" (161). Chilean Elcira Pinticart de W.'s 1977 *El cultivo de las rosas* (The Flowering of the Roses) is another example of the first type, as the author self-servingly characterizes herself as being endowed with a special sensitivity to natural phenomena. Like Neiva, Pinticart attempts to legitimate her parapsychological discoveries by overlaying them with a pseudoscientific methodology. Lindstrom finds her ideological bent to be conservative, growing out of the traditional feminine role she defines for herself.

Luis Eduardo Pérez Pereyra is an example of a writer who promotes a theosophist position, in his case, as an alternative to doctrinaire Christian mystical writings. His nonpopulist ideas are reflected in his belief that only a few enlightened individuals are endowed with truth and that only they can spiritually lead the misinformed masses towards it. He uses the Uruguayan writer José Enrique Rodó's positivism to legitimate his own "reasoned" theosophism.

Strictly speaking, the third category of popular occult writings that express a reliance on non-Western identity and mastery of a non-Western way of knowing do not fall within Latin American paraliterary works. Nonetheless, as Lindstrom has pointed out, the extensive popularity in Latin America of foreign writers such as Lobsand Rampa should at least be of interest to scholars. Rampa is an Englishman with an acquired Tibetan identity; his works have been translated and widely distributed throughout Latin America. Like other writers in the first two categories, he also promotes dependence on spiritual gurus endowed with special powers and insight.

Because popular occult texts are marketed as mass-produced consumer items, they deserve our attention. Future research might consider readers' responses to them as well their sometimes overt references to social and political structures and reliance on respected Latin American writers such as the Chilean Gabriela Mistral and Rodó.

Detective Fiction

Not unlike the comics and the photonovel, a key to understanding the development of detective fiction (*literatura policial*) in Latin America is its relationship to the genre in the United States and Europe; it first left its mark in Latin America as an imported paraliterary form (Simpson). While detective fiction has undergone much change since its origins in the midnineteenth century, there are basically two types that have dominated not only in the United States and Europe but in Latin America as well: the classic whodunit or the puzzle-novel (*novela de enigma* or *relato problema* in Spanish and *romance policial* in Portuguese) and the hard-boiled (*serie negra* or *novela dura* in Spanish and *romance policial norteamericano* in Portuguese). Although the classic can be traced to Edgar Allan Poe's detective Dupin, stories its early history is associated more with British authors. Similar to much paraliterature, its formula is simple and readily identifiable: a detective (usually endowed with unusual powers of deductive reasoning) solves a crime that is presented as a puzzle with no obvious answer. The detective uses not only his—most of the detectives of the classic were male—native intelligence, but also a finely honed knowledge of human behavior to relentlessly pursue a solution to the crime, which is presented at the end of the story. The second type, the hard-boiled, represents a later development in detective fiction. Unlike the classic, it is associated almost exclusively with United States writers. Raymond Chandler, one of its originators, spoke for many young writers who had tired of the "papier-maché villains and detectives of exquisite and impossible gentility" of the classic tradition. As the name describes, the hard-boiled writers meant to give detective fiction a flavor of authenticity of life as viewed from its sometimes seamy underside. It is thus characterized by more action, sex, and violence and less genteel reasoning than the classic. Hard-boiled writers tend to emphasize crime as symptomatic of an overall corrupt society in contrast to classic writers who insist on seeing the criminal act as an aberration in an otherwise sane and ideal society.

While both classic and hard-boiled detective fiction writers have been popular in translation in Latin America since the 1930s, relatively few native writers have devoted themselves to the genre. Some critics place the blame on Latin American publishers claiming that they are far more interested in investing in a time-tested product that guarantees lucrative returns—works in translation—than risking financially to promote their own authors. Publishers, in turn, blame the readership for resisting home-grown writers in preference for works in translation. A more esoteric reason focuses on what some authors perceive as "the fundamental incompatibility of Latin American realities with the ideology codified in the structures and conventions of the predominant whodunit" (Simpson 19). For example, the Mexican social gadfly Carlos Monsiváis believes that Latin American reality is simply not structured to accomodate detective fiction. The judicial and the police systems in most countries simply do not resemble those in Europe or the United States (Simpson 24).

Despite the plausibility of these and other reasons, Simpson points out that there is a considerable body of detective fiction by Latin American writers. Moreover, it is generally less formulaic and standardized than its European or United States counterparts. She points out that Latin American writers intentionally model their works on both classic and hard-boiled patterns, yet this allows them to emphasize the differences of their own works. She has identitied the juxtapostion of the two texts in one narrative structure as a palimpsest, a strategy that allows native writers to work with formulas and standard patterns in new and innovative ways to, for example, express views about moral issues and social problems and to question the ideological assumptions of the model (Simpson 23). Not unlike the comic book and the photonovel, detective fiction has a very strong presence in some Latin American countries and is practically nonexistent in others. Argentina, Uruguay, Brazil, Mexico, and Cuba are the countries in which this paraliterary genre has been most popular.

1932 marks the publication of the first full-length Argentinian detective novel (Sauli Lostal's *El enigma de la calle Arcos* [The Mystery of Arcos Street]), but it wasn't until the 1940s that detective fiction in Argentina ceased to come under heavy foreign influence. It was only in the 1940s that Argentine writers began to publish works on a regular basis. Jorge Luis Borges and other elite writers' predilection for detective stories is well-known, but their works are by no means the only ones to appear during this period. Initially, it was the classic or *relato problema* model that dominated; it wasn't until the 1950s that hard-boiled or the *novela dura* became acceptable as well.

Leonardo Castellani (better known by his pseudonym Jerónimo del Rey) began to publish in the 1930s and hit full stride in later decades with the publication of a series of stories featuring Padre Ducadelia, which are somewhat reminiscent of G.K. Chesterton's Father Brown novels. Castellani's fictional priest-detective Ducadelia represents an unusual native-grown protagonist different from those dominant in foreign imports. Representative of a rebellious Catholic Church that heavily identifies with the poor, Padre Ducadelia associates with social outcasts and is openly critical of repressive institutions including the political system and the conservative official Church. In Simpson's opinion, Castellani stands out as "an iconoclastic figure in Argentine literary history" (Simpson 33). He stands out as an exception to most other contemporary Argentinian writers who cultivate a more refined version of detective fiction. Jorge Luis Borges is of course a singular representative of this type of Argentine detective fiction. During the 1930s, he regularly included works by fellow writers in a literary supplement of the Buenos Aires newspaper *Crítica*. He also wrote fondly of G. K. Chesterton's works and then published his much anthologized intellectual short story "La muerte y la brújula" ("Death and the Compass") in 1942.

Unlike Castellani, who used detective fiction to criticize conservative and reactionary political elites, Borges and other elitist writers, like Manuel Peyrou, Adolfo Bioy Casares, and Enrique Anderson Imbert, used it in the 1940s to satirize Juan Domingo Perón and his populist sociopolitical idelology. Frequently their tales are cryptic, but beneath a veneer of apparent cerebral detachment lies an attack on the "undesirable elements" that had been swept into power with Perón's presidential triumph. Their class-related disdain for the new political order was expressed through finely wrought parody and satire. Examples are *Seis problemas para don Isidro Parodi* (Six Problems for Don Isidoro Parodi; 1942) by H. Bustos Domecq (the pseudonym used by Borges and Bioy Casares) and *Un modelo para la muerte* (Death Model; 1946) by Suárez Lynch (another pseudoynm used by the two authors). Andrés Avellaneda has shown how in the first work the authors associate various human traits and weaknesses with the lower classes who were among Perón's most rabid supporters (Simpson 37). He has also demonstrated how the second work, written in an almost impenetrable *lunfardo* (an Italian-based underworld argot), also satirizes the lower classes and reveals the authors' elitist ideology. Bioy Casares authored his own works (e.g., "El perjurio de la nieve" [The Perjury of Snow; 1944]) as well as one in collaboration with his wife Silvina Ocampo: *Los que aman odian* (Those Who Love Hate; 1946). Manuel Peyrou's *El estruendo de las rosas* (*The Thunder of the Roses*; 1948) is one of the most imporant detective novels of the 1940s to be critical of the Peronist regime. It is a thinly veiled whodunit that takes place in a European country; nonetheless, the author's critique of Peronist nationalism is at least implicit.

By the 1970s the *novela dura* had completely replaced the *relato problema* in Argentina. Ricardo Piglia, as editor of Editorial Tiempo Contemporáneo's "Serie Negra" (Black Series), played a major role in popularizing *duras*. Unlike their United States counterpart, the hard-boiled, at least those published by Piglia, are decidedly political in taking a critical, adversarial stance towards dominant institutions and public officials. *Chicho Grande* (1953) by Pedro Pago (a pseudonym of David Viñas) provides an early model for this type of detective fiction by presenting a depraved aspect of lower-class existence and the criminal underground in Buenos Aires. Juan Carlos Martini's novel *El agua en los pulmones* (Water in the Lungs; 1973) portrays a corrupt society brought on by the breakdown of capitalism. Manuel Puig's *The Buenos Aires Affair* (1973) is only minimally a detective novel despite its subtitle, "novela policial"; nonetheless, it is included here because it represents yet another example of how an elite writer uses paraliterary forms and strategies. Puig actually parodies the hard-boiled detective novel as he sets out to demonstrate how "alien and alienating ideological images and models of discourse" (Hollywood films, United States detective fiction) serve to create violence due to repressed eroticism (Simpson 59). In his "Homenaje a Roberto Arlt" (Homage to Arlt; 1975), Ricardo Piglia parallels his search for Arlt's personality to that of the detective who sets out to solve a mystery; the crime, in the literary sense, is the text itself for it contains all the hidden secrets necessary to track down the perpetrator, i.e., the writer.

As in Argentina, foreign detective fiction in translation has been far more popular in Brazil than works by native authors. In addition, although there were Brazilian writers actively writing detective fiction during the early part of the twentieth century—Henrique Maximiniano Coelho Neto, Afrânio Peixoto, José Joaquim de Campos Medeiros de Albuquerque, and Viriato Correa—a solid core of such writing has never been in evidence in Brazil as in Argentina. Luiz Lopes Coelho is generally considered to have produced the first authentically Brazilian detective figure with a series of works not begun until the 1960s. Maria Alice Barroso's *Quem matou Pacífico?* (Who Killed Pacífico?), the first serious "literary" detective work, was not published until 1969. The 1970s and the 1980s have seen some very interesting forms of experimentation with the detective genre including: hybrid *crime-reportagem* (crime report) texts that are sensationalist and social protest literature at the same time, extended chronicles that discuss contemporary events, and some detective works that comment on contemporary social issues (Simpson 62). In addition, parodies and spoofs of detective fiction seems to have become quite popular during the past twenty years. As in Argentina, well-known writers—Coelho Neto, Peixoto, Jorge Amado, and João Guimarães Rosa—have on occasion ventured into detective fiction. Yet despite detective fiction's health during the latter part of the twentieth century, it never caught the Brazilian public's imagination as it did in Argentina. While this is due to a variety of factors, one important consideration is the strong influence British culture in general and British detective fiction in particular had on Argentina.

Mexico had a solid detective short story tradition by the 1930s and 1940s associated with writers such as Antonio Helú, Pepe Martínez de la Vega, and María Elvira Bermúdez, but the detective novel never did become an important genre. As in both Argentina and Brazil, elite writers experimented with detective fiction but did not devote themselves to it; the best-known works in this genre are: Rodolfo Usigli's *Ensayo de un crimen* (Rehearsal of a Crime; 1976), Paco Ignacio Taibo II's *Días de combate* (Battle Days; 1976) and *Cosa fácil* (Something Easy; 1977), Vicente Leñero's *Los albañiles* (The Masons; 1964) and *El doble crimen de los Flores Muñoz* (The Double Crime of the Flores Muñozes; 1985), José Emilio Pacheco's *Morirás lejos* (You Will Die Faraway; 1967), Rafael Bernal's *El complot mongol* (The Mongol Plot; 1969), and Carlos Fuentes's *La cabeza de la Hidra* (*Hydra Head*; 1978). Perhaps the most interesting of these works is Leñero's recent work, *El doble crimen de los Flores Muñoz*, which is based on a real crime extensively covered in the Mexican press. It is a hybrid form of documentary and fiction somewhat reminiscent of Truman Capote's chiller *In Cold Blood*, which also was rooted in brutal reality. A 1982 anthology of Mexican detective stories, *El cuento policial mexicano* (The Mexican Detective Story), points to a promising group of younger writers who could serve to revitalize the genre; Luis Arturo Ramos is representative of this group.

Detective fiction in Cuba is heavily associated with the 1959 Cuban Revolution; it was virtually nonexistent before. As could be expected, much of the fiction published in Cuba in the past twenty-five years bears a strong mark of Cuban socialist views, values, and aspirations. Ignacio Cárdenas Acuña's 1971 detective novel *Enigmas para un domingo* (Mysteries for a Sunday) is the beginning of a very active period of detective fiction. As has been the case with other forms of artistic expression in Cuba, the government created virtually overnight a detective fiction contest; it began in 1972 as Concurso Aniversario del Triunfo de la Revolución (Contest Celebrating the Triumph of the Revolution) and immediately served as catalyst for detective fiction production. With the possible exception of Argentina, detective fiction is nowhere more popular than in Cuba (Simpson 97). Quite logically, this government-sponsored contest has produced works with a socialist ideological bent. In this sense, the annnual detective fiction contest is similar to the Premio Casa de las Américas (Casa de las Américas Prize) which recognizes progressive international and national works of several genres. Conventional detective formulas and conventions are revised along socialist lines. For example, the protagonist, rather than being an independent detective, is a state police officer who typically investigates "crimes against the state." He is assisted by the common people committed to socialist ideals in tracking down a perpetrator of counterrevolutionary actions. Necessarily, the police officer does not come from the upper classes, nor is he more educated than others; rather, he is a classless representative of the State who functions in its behalf (Simpson 101). Juan Angel Cardi's *El American Way of Death* (The American Way of Death; 1980) is one of the best and most technically sophisticated works of Cuban detective fiction. Unlike many other novels, this one is able to establish a healthy distance from strictly ideological concerns to comment as metafiction on the detective genre itself. In the same vein, Arnaldo Correa's 1982 collection of detective stories, *El terror* (The Terror), gives more weight to narrative demands than to didactic ends. In addition, as Simpson astutely asserts, "the admission of the existence of an acceptable, or at least expected, level of criminal activity in Cuban society . . . represents a major reversal of the pattern in Cuban detective fiction that conveys an image of a society in which no counterrevolutionary, subversive criminal activity is tolerated, and in which no other kind of crime exists because the socioeconomic system that is its source has been eliminated" (Simpson 115).

Testimonial/Documentary Literature

An adequate definition of testimonial/documentary literature is more elusive than for most other paraliterary forms. Some would claim that most Latin American literature (particularly its narrative) constitutes a sociohistorical document owing to its historically strong ties to reality. For example, Foster ("Latin American Documentary Novel") has pointed out that together the novels of social realism (narratives written between 1848 and 1916) and contemporary novels treating the conflicts of Latin American society (such as the so-called dictator novel) have emerged "as an especially productive form of documentary" (Foster 41). However, quite apart from this strong documentary vein running through Latin American fiction for almost 150 years there is an impressive array of

documentary and nonficton narrative referred to as "testimonial literature."

Trying to arrive at a meaningful definition of documentary/testimonial
literature is extremely difficult given the fact that a wide range of works
is generally included under such a label, ranging from the relatively raw
testimony of a Domitila Barrios Chungara or a Rigoberta Menchú to a
highly literary manipulation of a horrific experience such as Manuel
Puig's *El beso de la mujer araña* (*Kiss of the Spider Woman*; 1976). A
more useful approach to documentary/testimonial literature would be to
place it along a continuum of authorial mediation and participation in
the recreation of a specific event, series of events, or a generalized situation directly grounded in social reality. It is important to recognize at
the outset that no published work is entirely unmediated, for even the
case of *"Si me permiten hablar...": testimonio de Domitila, una mujer de
las minas de Bolivia* ("If I May Speak": Testimony of Domitila, a Woman
of the Bolivian Mines; 1977) a transcriber/editor mediated her original
testimony. Nonetheless, this work bears far less mediation that those of
Puig. The outline below progresses along a line from works with less to
more authorial mediation and participation.

Some of the characteristics of direct testimony would be: the pre-
existence of an indisputable sociohistorical occurrence or situation—the
exploitative conditions in Bolivian mines, subsistence farming in a Guatemalan feudal *hacienda* system, guerrilla warfare during the Cuban Revolution—that lends itself to a discursive version or interpretation of such
a reality; a high degree of referentiality with its creator having a specific
view of the world; intertextual in that it assumes, either explicitly or
implicitly, another version (another text) vis-à-vis its referent (Prada
Oropeza 8). Moreover, direct testimonial discourse possesses a decided
intentionality in bringing to a situation or occurrence a test, justification,
or confirmation of its truth or certainty, at least as defined by its author
who witnesses and testifies to its veracity. Testimonial discourse is
generally seen as distinct from strictly fictional discourse in its avoidance
of literary devices, but at the same time it has measurable aesthetic value
that differentiates it from, say, journalistic reporting. The Cuban writer
Miguel Barnet considers the rise of testimonial/documentary discourse
as a challenge and possible alternative to traditional Latin American
literature itself (285-286). The essential quality he assigns the former is
the very minor role that the authorial ego plays in the conscious creation
of a work.

TESTIMONIAL LITERATURE WITH MINIMAL MEDIATION

Huillca: habla un campesino peruano (Huillca; a Peruvian Peasant Speaks; 1974) consists of simple but powerful words spoken by a Peruvian highland *campesino*. Quetchua Huillca relates a simple autobiographical account of growing up with his mother and siblings on a small plot of land and eking out a subsistence in the shadow of a wealthy hacienda. Like Domitila's testimony, his words probably have lost little in the process of being transcribed and edited. *"Si me permiten hablar"* is a Bolivian woman's testimony given before a meeting of the International Women's Year held in Mexico City in 1975. We are struck by the directness of her words, which relate a very personal tale of suffering, violence, and repression of a woman who had dedicated her life to gaining justice for the Bolivian miner. While her words were transcribed and edited by the Brazilian educator Moema Viezzer, the reader is struck by their forcefulness and Domitila Barrios de Chungara's strength of will. *Me llamo Rigoberta Menchú* (My Name is Rigoberta Menchú; 1983) like Domitila and Huillca, consists of testimony given directly to a sympathetic audience. The words of this Guatemalan Indian woman have been transcribed and edited, that is, shaped by an educated interviewer/editor. Nonetheless, like the two preceding examples of testimonial literature, this work puts us in as direct contact with a social reality as any written text.

Guerrilla warfare during the past forty years in countries such as Cuba, Guatemala, and Nicaragua have yielded what Juan Duchesne has identified as "narraciones guerrilleras" (guerrilla narratives). Examples of these testimonial narratives are: the Argentine Ernesto Che Guevara's *Pasajes de la guerra revolucionaria* (Passages on the Revolutionary War; 1969) and his *Diario en Bolivia* (Bolivian Diary; 1972), the first a direct account of the pre-1959 campaign against Bautista's regime in Cuba, the second a running diary of waging guerrilla warfare in Bolivia; Omar Cabezas Lacayo's *La montaña es algo más que una inmensa estepa verde* (The Mountain is Something More than an Immense Green Steppe; 1982) about a guerrilla's political awakening and participation in the resistance movement against the Nicaraguan Somocista dictatorship; Mario Payeras's *Los días de la selva* (Jungle Days; 1980) relating the activities of a guerrilla group in the Quiché area of Guatemala between 1972 and 1976.

A related type of paraliterature resulted from testimony given by Chileans who witnessed or directly participated in the events surrounding the 1973-Pinochet coup against Salvador Allende and the subsequent rounding up, torture, and death of thousands of Unidad Popular and other leftists. Ariel Dorfman has found that most of these testimonials share in common a strong desire to accuse the perpetrator of these crimes, to remember the suffering and travails of those pursued, to give moral support to those still involved in the struggle, and to analyze the root causes for the 1973 conflagration and its aftermath. Some examples of these works are: Alejandro Witker's *Prisión en Chile* (Prison in Chile; 1975), Rodrigo Rojas's *Jamás de rodillas* (Never on My Knees; 1974), Rolando Carrasco's *Prigué* (1977), Aníbal Quijada Cerda's *Cerco de púas* (Barbed Wire; 1977), and Manuel Cabieses's *Chile: 11808 horas en campos de concentración* (Chile: 11808 Hours in Concentration Camps; 1975).

WORKS WITH A GREATER DEGREE OF MEDIATION AND AUTHORIAL PARTICIPATION IN THEIR CREATION

The extraordinarily long title of Gabriel García Márquez's specifically documentary narrative, *Relato de un náufrago que estuvo diez días a la deriva en una balsa sin comer ni beber, que fue proclamado héroe de la patria, besado por las reinas de la belleza y hecho rico por la publicidad, y luego aborrecido por el gobierno y olvidado para siempre* (*The Story of a Shipwrecked Sailor, Who Drifted on a Life Raft for Ten Days without Food or Water, Was Proclaimed a National Hero, Kissed by Beauty Queens, Made Rich through Publicity, and Then Spurned by the Government and Forgotten for All Time*; 1970), gives an overview of the work. The Colombian author's subsequent introduction, which resulted in a "recontextualization in his presentation of the narrative in book form" (Foster, "Latin American Documentary Narrative" 50), led to a major political scandal and contributed to García Márquez's ten-year exile from his country. Elena Poniatowska's *La noche de Tlatelolco* (*Massacre in Mexico*; 1971) documents the events surrounding the demonstration and subsequent massacre that occurred on October 2, 1968 in La Plaza de las Tres Culturas in Mexico City. The author skillfully weaves together fragments of newspaper reports, radio and television interviews, personal interviews, and dramatic photographs in order to recreate the horror that marked this watershed in contemporary Mexican history.

Some other works that should be included under the category of documentary literature are the following. Rodolfo Walsh's *Operación masacre* (Operation Massacre; 1957), which Foster has identified as "easily the most authentic example of documentary narrative in Latin American fiction," is a blending of materials gathered in the author's investigations and narrative strategies "to make a rhetorically effective presentation of an actual event" (Foster, "Latin American Documentary Narrative" 142). Miguel Barnet's *Biografía de un cimarrón* (Biography of a Runaway Slave; 1966), is a documentary narrative divided between the author's recreation of a former slave's—*cimarrón* is used in the Caribbean to designate a runaway slave—personal suffering before the abolition of slavery in Cuba and several other cultural and social aspects of Cuban society prior to the island's independence from Spain in 1898. Hernán Valdés's *Tejas Verdes: diario de un campo de concentración* (Tejas Verdes: Diary of a Concentration Camp; 1974) is a recreation of the author's month of internment in a concentration camp immediately after the 1973 Chilean coup against Salvador Allende. It is rich in detail about the techniques and horror of political torture in official and unofficial camps and jails, secret police, and death squads in a suddenly repressive political situation. To the above works could be added: Enrique Medina's *Las muecas del miedo* (Grimaces of Fear; 1981) and his *Con el trapo en la boca* (With a Rag in Her Mouth; 1983); Marta Lynch's *La penúltima versión de Colorada Villanueva* (The Penultimate Version of Colorada Villanueva; 1979) and her *Informe bajo llave* (Report under Wraps; 1983); Oscar Hermes Villordo's *La brasa en la mano* (A Hot Coal in His Hand; 1983); and Fernando Alonso's *Goliat o la noche de los milagros* (Goliath or the Night of Miracles; 1983); Jacobo Timerman's *Prisoner without a Name, Cell without a Number* (1981; first published in English and only subsequently in Spanish as *Prisionero sin nombre, celda sin número*).

The Incorporation of Paraliterature in Explicitly Literary Texts

The use of paraliterature is not a recent phenomenon in Latin America; as already discussed, Borges and Bioy Casares created highly exquisite detective fiction almost forty years ago. However, Latin American novelists during the past twenty years have drawn increasingly on paraliterature and other forms of popular culture to create works that, if nothing else, are more accessible to a wider reading public than many of the cerebral Borgian-like texts. While one could speculate endlessly to try to explain this literary trend, a possible analogy can be drawn with the use of myths and archetypal patterns to stimulate and activate the reader's psychologically sensitive triggers—complexes, tendencies, primeval images—in order to maximize contact with the text and to bring about a fuller emotive and cognative response (Solotorevsky 17).

The use of and response to popular culture modes is complex and varied from text to text. The Argentinian novelist Manuel Puig, perhaps more successfully than most other contemporary Latin American writers, has used popular culture with interesting results. His first commercially successful novel, *La traición de Rita Hayworth* (*Betrayed by Rita Hayworth*; 1968), signaled Puig's innovative use of different forms of popular and mass cultural media. American films of the 1930s and the 1940s form the backdrop for what is otherwise a banal personal history of a provincial youth's passage from childhood into adolescence. The dazzling world of the Ginger Rogers-Fred Astaire, Rita Hayworth-Tyrone Powers and other movies becomes Toto's escape from a confusing and conflictive time in his young life as the former gradually supplants the latter. Puig's 1973 novel, *Boquitas pintadas* (*Heartbreak Tango*), draws on popular tango and bolero verses, quotations from popular magazines such as *Nuestra vecindad* (Our Neighborhood), *Mundo femenino* (Woman's World), and *País elegante* (Elegant Country), a radio sopa opera, mortuary commemorative plates, and popular advertising clichés. This technique serves to seduce the reader into a fictional everyday world that contrasts with her/his own, characterized by rampant dehumanization and alienation. *Boquitas pintadas* serves as a parody of such popular culture forms as the highly escapist *fotonovela rosa* and the *folletín* (serial novel). Puig's novel *The Buenos Aires Affair* (1973) is, in turn, a parody of the detective novel just as Borges's 1956 short story "La muerte y la brújula" was almost two decades before. While Puig's tone and attitude are playful, Borges's are mocking and acerbically ironic. In his 1976 novel, *El beso de la mujer araña*, Puig relies heavily on incorported fragments from sentimentally romantic films and popular songs.

Julio Cortázar was no stranger to paraliterature. In 1975, he created a comic book, *Fantomas contra los vampiros multinacionales* (Fantomas against the Multinational Vampires), in which he attempts to bridge the gap between mass culture and politics. His 1973 novel, *Libro de Manuel* (*A Manual for Manuel*), is a virtual compendium of microtexts incorporated in the overall structure of the novel. The majority of these texts are taken from periodical literature, especially newspaper articles, that refer directly and indirectly to events unfolding in Argentina at the very time of the novel's writing. Cortázar's urgency to express his opposition to a repressive political regime and his solidarity with its victims is heightened by the use of journalistic accounts that shortly before had reported violence against a civilian population, the persecution of political dissidents, and the general carnage and upheaval in Argentine society (McCracken).

Mario Vargas Llosa's novel *La tía Julia y el escribidor* (*Aunt Julia and the Scriptwriter*; 1981) represents a quantitative leap over Cortázar's novel in terms of the amount of incorporated popular culture material. Pedro Camacho's radio soap operas (*radionovelas* and *radioteatros*) are as extensive as Marito and Julia's amorous relationship in the novel. The chapters devoted to the former material are not contextualized by the writer's comments, thus leading the reader to believe that they are as important as the relationship itself.

Other examples of literary works that utilize popular culture are: Roberto Arlt's play, *Los trescientos millones* (Three-Hundred Million Pesos; 1931); several of José Agustín's novels including *La tumba* (*The Tomb*; 1967) and *De perfil* (In Profile; 1966); Gustavo Sainz's novel *Gazapo* (1965); and Luis Rafael Sánchez's novel *La guaracha del Macho Camacho* (*Macho Camacho's Beat*; 1976).

BIBLIOGRAPHY

Adorno, Theodor W. "Culture Industry Reconsidered." *New German Critique* 6 (1975): 495-514.

Alfie, David. "Semiología del cómic." *El cómic es algo serio*. México, D.F.: Ediciones Eufesa, 1982.

Althusser, Louis. "Ideology and Ideological State Apparatuses." *Lenin and Philosophy and Other Essays*. New York: Monthly Review Press, 1971. 127-186.

Ashley, Bob. *The Study of Popular Fiction: A Source Book*. London: Pinter Publishers, 1989.

Barnet, Miguel. "La novela testimonio. Socio-literatura." 280-302. *Testimonio y literatura*. Eds. René Jara and Hernán Vidal.

Barthes, Roland. *The Pleasure of the Text*. New York: Hill and Wang, 1975.

Baur, Elisabeth K. *La historieta como experiencia didáctica*. Trans., Pablo Klein. México, D.F.: Editorial Nueva Imagen, 1976.

Bennett, Tony. "Marxism and Popular Fiction." *Literature and History* 7.2 (1981): 98-125.

Beverley, John, and Marc Zimmerman. *Literature and Politics in the Central American Revolutions*. Austin: University of Texas Press, 1990.

Bourdieu, Pierre. *Distinction: A Social Critique of the Judgment of Taste*. Trans., R. Nice. Cambridge: Harvard University Press, 1984.

Cawelti, John G. "The Concept of Formula in the Study of Popular Literature." *Journal of Popular Culture* 3 (1969): 381-390.

Cawelti, John G. *Adventure, Mystery and Romance*. Chicago: University of Chicago Press, 1976.

Chaffee, Lyman. "Poster and Political Propaganda in Argentina." *Studies in Latin American Popular Culture* 5 (1986): 78-89.

Chaffee, Lyman. "The Popular Culture Political Persuasion in Paraguay." *Studies in Latin American Popular Culture* 9 (1990): 127-148.

Constantino, Higilio Alvarez. *La magia de los cómics coloniza nuestra cultura*. México, D.F., 1978.

Cornejo, Leobardo. "Semiótica de *Los supermachos* y *Los agachados* de Rius." *El cómic es algo serio*. México, D.F.: Ediciones Eufesa, 1982.

Curiel, Fernando. *Fotonovela rosa, fontonovela roja*. México, D.F.: Universidad Nacional Autónoma de México, 1980. Cuadernos de Humanidades, 9.

Danto, Arthur. "High and Low at MoMA." *The Nation* (November 26, 1990): 658.

Dorfman, Ariel. "Código político y código literario: el género testimonio en Chile hoy." 170-234. *Testimonio y literatura*. Eds. René Jara and Hernán Vidal.

Dorfman, Ariel. *Reader's Nuestro que estás en la tierra*. México, D.F.: Editorial Nueva Imagen, 1980.

Dorfman, Ariel, and Manuel Jofré. *Supermán y sus amigos del alma*. Buenos Aires: Editorial Galerna, 1974.

Dorfman, Ariel, and Armand Mattelart. *Para leer el Pato Donald: comunicación de masa y colonialismo*. Valparaíso: Ediciones Universitarias de Valparaíso, 1971.

Duchesne, Juan. "Las narraciones guerrilleras: configuración de un sujeto épico de nuevo tipo." 85-137. *Testimonio y literatura*. Eds. René Jara y Hernán Vidal.

Eagleton, Terry. *Literary Theory. An Introduction.* Oxford: Basil Black-well, 1983.

Eco, Umberto. *Apocalípticos e integrados ante la cultura de masas.* Trans., Andrés Boglar. México, D.F.: Editorial Lumen, 1968.

Fiske, John. *Reading the Popular.* Boston: Unwin and Hyman, 1989.

Flora, Cornelia Butler. "*Fotonovelas*: Message Creation and Reception." *Journal of Popular Culture* 14.3 (1980): 524-534.

Flora, Cornelia Butler. "Photonovels." 151-172. In *Handbook of Latin American Popular Culture.* Eds. Harold E. Hinds, Jr., and Charles Tatum.

Flora, Cornelia Butler. "The Passive Female: Her Comparative Image by Class and Culture in Women's Magazine Fiction." *Journal of Marriage and the Family* 33 (August 1971): 435-444.

Flora, Cornelia Butler. "The Political Economy of *Fotonovela* Production in Latin America." *Studies in Latin American Popular Culture* 8 (1989): 215-230.

Flora, Cornelia Butler. "Roasting Donald Duck: Alternative Comics and Photonovels in Latin America." *Journal of Popular Culture* 18 (1984): 163-183.

Flora, Cornelia Butler, and Jan L. Flora. "The *Fotonovela* as a Tool for Class and Cultural Domination." *Latin American Perspectives* 5.1 (1978): 134-150.

Foster, David William. "Gauchomanía y gauchofobia en *Las aventuras de Inodoro Pereyra* de Roberto Fontanarrosa." 109-131. *Literature and Popular Culture in the Hispanic World.* Ed. Rose S. Minc. Also as Chapter 4 of his *From Mafalda to Los Supermachos: Latin American Graphic Humor as Popular Culture.* Boulder: Lynne Reinner Publishers, 1989.

Foster, David William. "Latin American Documentary Narrative." *PMLA; Publications of the Modern Language Association* 99.1 (1984): 41-55. Also as Chapter 1 of his *Alternate Voices in the Contemporary Latin American Narrative.* Columbia: University of Missouri Press, 1985.

Foster, David William. "Mafalda: An Argentine Comic Strip." *Journal of Popular Culture* 14 (1980): 497-508. Also as Chapter 5 of his *From Mafalda to Los Supermachos: Latin American Graphic Humor as Popular Culture.* Boulder: Lynne Reinner Publishers, 1989.

Franco, Jean. "What's in a Name? Popular Culture Theories and Their Limitations." *Studies in Latin American Popular Culture* 1 (1982): 5-14.

Fraser, Howard. *Magazines and Masks: Caras y caretas as a Reflection of Buenos Aires, 1898-1908*. Tempe: Center for Latin American Studies, Arizona State University, 1987.

Gallo, Miguel Angel. *Los cómics: un enfoque sociológico*. México, D.F.: Ediciones Quinto Sol, n.d.

García Canclini, Néstor. *Las culturas populares en el capitalismo*. México, D.F: Editorial Nueva Imagen, 1982.

Hall, Stuart, and Paddy Whannel. *The Popular Arts*. London: Hutchinson, 1964.

Helguera, J. León. 1987. "Notes on a Century of Colombian Cartooning: 1830-1930." *Studies in Latin American Popular Culture* 6 (1987): 259-280.

Hérner, Irene. *Mitos y monitos: historietas y fotonovelas en México*. México, D. F.: Universidad Nacional Autónoma de México/Editorial Nueva Imagen, 1979.

Hill, Jane, and Carole Browner. "Gender Ambiguity and Class Stereotyping in the Mexican *Fotonovela*." *Studies in Latin American Popular Culture* 1 (1982): 43-64.

Hinds, Harold E., Jr. "Comics." *Handbook of Latin American Popular Culture*. Eds. Harold E. Hinds, Jr., and Charles Tatum. 81-110.

Hinds, Harold E., Jr., and Charles Tatum, eds. *Handbook of Latin American Popular Culture*. Westport, Conn.: Greenwood Press, 1985.

Hunt, Nancy L., and David G. LaFrance. "Palomo's '*El cuarto reich*': Economic Disaster, Torture and Other Laughs." *Studies in Latin American Popular Culture* 2 (1983): 36-43.

Jameson, Fredric. "Ideology, Narrative Analysis and Popular Culture." *Theory and Society* 4 (1977): 543-559.

Jara, René, and Hernán Vidal, eds. *Testimonio y literatura*. Minneapolis: Institute for the Study of Ideology and Literature, 1986.

Johnson, John J. *Latin America in Caricature*. Austin: University of Texas Press, 1980.

Kunzle, David. "Chile's *La firme* vs. ITT." *Latin American Perspectives* 5.1 (Winter 1978): 119-133.

Kunzle, David. "Nationalist, Internationalist and Anti-Imperialist Themes in the Public Revolutionary Art of Cuba, Chile and Nicaragua." *Studies in Latin American Popular Culture* 2 (1983): 141-157.

Laclau, Ernesto, and Chantal Mouffe. *Hegemony and Socialist Strategy: Towards a Radical Democratic Politics*. Trans. Winston Moore and Paul Cammack. London: Verso, 1985.

Lindstrom, Naomi. "Latin American Pop Occult Texts: Implicit Ideolo gy." *Studies in Latin American Popular Culture* 2 (1983): 158-170.

Lindstrom, Naomi. "The Single-Panel Cartoon." 207-228. In *Handbook of Latin American Popular Culture*. Eds. Harold E. Hinds, Jr., and Charles Tatum.

Lindstrom, Naomi. "Social Commentary in Argentine Cartooning: from Description to Questioning." *Journal of Popular Culture* 14 (Winter 1980): 509-523.

Mattelart, Michèle. *La cultura de la opresión femenina*. México, D.F.: Ediciones Era, 1977.

McCracken, Ellen. "*Libro de Manuel* and *Fantomas contra los vampiros multinacionales*: Mass Culture, Art, and Politics." 69-78. *Literature and Popular Culture in the Hispanic World*. Ed. Rose S. Minc.

Mesón, Danusia L. "*Mafalda* y la crítica pura (?) de la razón y el orden." 101-108. *Literature and Popular Culture in the Hispanic World*. Ed. Rose S. Minc. 101-108.

Minc, Rose S., ed. *Literature and Popular Culture in the Hispanic World*. Gaithersburg, Md.: Ediciones Hispamérica, 1981.

Palacios, Julia Emilia. "*Torbellino*: Towards an Alternative Comic Book." *Studies in Latin American Popular Culture* 5(1986): 186-195.

Parlato, Ronald, Margaret Burres Parlato, and Bonnie J. Cain. *Fotonovela and Comic Books: The Use of Popular Graphic Media in Development*. Washington, D.C.: Agency for International Development, 1980.

Prada Oropeza, Renato. "De lo testimonial al testimonio. Notas para un deslinde del discurso-testimonio." 7-21. *Testimonio y literatura*. Eds. René Jara and Hernán Vidal.

Saint-Michel, Serge. *Le Roman-Photo*. Paris: Libraire Larousse, 1979.

Schiller, Herbert I. *Communication and Cultural Domination*. White Plains, N.Y.: International Arts and Sciences Press, 1976.

Simpson, Amelia S. *Detective Fiction from Latin America*. Rutherford, N.J.: Fairleigh Dickinson University Press, 1990.

Slater, Candace. *Stories on a String. The Brazilian Literatura de cordel*. Berkeley: University of California Press, 1982.

Solotorevsky, Myrna. *Literatura*. *Paraliteratura*. Gaithersburg, Md.:
     Ediciones Hispamérica, 1988.
Torrecilla, Arturo. "Cultural Imperialism, Mass Media and Class Strug-
     gle: An Interview with Armand Mattelart." Trans. Mary C.
     Axtmann. *Insurgent Sociologist* 9.4 (Spring 1980): 69-79.
Torres, Kay. "Colectivo El Ojo y la fotonovela." *Obscur: Magazines of
     the Los Angeles Center Photographic Studies* 2.5 (1983): 18-23.
Woll, Allen J. "The Comic Book in a Socialist Society: Allende's Chile,
     1970-1973." *Journal of Popular Culture* 9 (Spring 1976): 1039-
     1045.

FILM
John King
University of Warwick

I

The decade of the 1990s will witness a number of significant anniver-saries: 1992, the quincentenary of the "Discovery" of Latin America; one hundred years of cinema, which could be said to correspond to one hundred years of modernity and/or solitude in the subcontinent; 2000, a date that evokes millenarian and apocalyptic desires and fears. It is an appropriate conjuncture to review the developing histories of cinemas in Latin America. Instead of attempting a comprehensive overview of the many different processes and tendencies at work over the past century, this chapter selects a number of key films that serve as signposts to the larger design.

Cinema emerged as a modern and popular cultural medium. The words "modern" and "popular" will require close attention. If the moder-nity of cinema referred to the new scientific and technological advances, the possibility of new and mobile ways of seeing, then "peripheral" mo-dernity in Latin America would always be moving in the shadow cast by uneven development: "The notion of 'correct' technique assumes the legitimacy of 'universal' values embedded in the equipment and the raw material, themselves products of advanced technology.... The technology embedded in the means of production facilitates the equivocal transfer of the economic notion of underdevelopment to the level of culture" (Ismail Xavier, quoted in Johnson, *The Film Industry* 22). The very technology of cinema, cameras, film stock, and expertise all came from outside, although these could be exploited by local adventurers or entre-preneurs. Latin America competed, on unequal terms, with the high-cost technological advances of cinema: many national industries took years, for example, to convert to sound; a great number of these industries today work with annual funds equivalent to the budget of one small-scale

Hollywood feature. The dominant Hollywood model also universalized a "correct" way of filming and a "correct" way of seeing. Filmmakers would consistently be working within or against this set of values, in a marketplace geared to the production, distribution, and exhibition of the Hollywood product. Hollywood also acted as a rather perverse ethnographer of Latin America, "creating" an image of a landscape and a people south of the border. All these tensions are alluded to in the Brazilian Nelson Pereira dos Santos's film, *Como era gostoso o meu francês* (How Tasty Was My Little Frenchman; 1971), which reworks one of the foundational stories of Latin American culture, the "encounter" between European whites and indigenous peoples.

II

> Sou um tupi tangendo um alaúde...
> Galicismo a berrar nos desertos da América
> (I am a Tupi Indian strumming a lute....
> Gallicism bellowing in the deserts of America)
> (Mário de Andrade, *Hallucinated City*)

"Latest news from Terra Firme": The first words of Pereira dos Santos's film set up a reading that refers both to the early colonial history of Brazil (named Terra Firme), but also to the present. Jean, the potentially tasty Frenchman of the film title, is part of a French Huguenot expedition to Brazil in the mid-sixteenth century, a time when France was threatening the Portuguese Crown's authority and settlement in the New World. Both colonial powers were initially interested in a species of dyewood known as "brazil," and the brazil-wood trade became a lucrative business. Jean is captured by the Tupinamba Indians and sentenced to death in several months time. While awaiting this death, he lives as one of the tribe; is provided with a wife, Sebiopepe; and goes in to battle with the tribe using the advanced "technologies" of canon and gunpowder, before he meets his ritual death and is ingested by the community. A final shot sees Sebiopepe gnawing contentedly at his neck bone.

The film constantly undermines the European (and by extension North American and white Brazilian middle-class) vision of "otherness." It provides captions of a number of written accounts from sixteenth-century chroniclers, voyagers, and clerics that give an official version of the process and justification of colonization. These are ironically undermined by the screen images that reveal the cultural shocks and clashes of this first "encounter." From the outset, the "civilized" spectators' ironic, superior detachment is questioned. Most of the dialogue is in Tupi and is translated into Portuguese subtitles. The spectator is used to reading subtitles for "foreign" films, not for his or her own language. Colonization, if Todorov and other linguistic critics are right, was achieved through knowledge of language and an ability to translate and thus understand and manipulate the other's motives and mentalities. It also imposed the language of the colonizer on indigenous peoples. Jean is initially captured by Portuguese adventurers and their allies, the Tupiniquim Indians. Very quickly the Tubinamba (supposedly allies of French settlers) overrun the Tupiniquim and capture both the Portuguese and the solitary Frenchman. In order to determine who their "allies" are, the Tupinamba leader sets the Europeans a linguistic "test." The Portuguese recite a cooking recipe (eating, greed, gluttony, digestion is an ironic lietmotif that pervades the film), while the Frenchman says enigmatically in French: "The savages walk naked and we walk unrecognized." The Indian leader cannot understand these strange tongues. Europeans cannot be differentiated through linguistic difference or superiority: they are all barbarians (the term barbarian, we remember, comes from the Greek and referred to those who could not speak the language of Athens and instead bleated like sheep). All Europeans, in the end, are exploiters, not "allies," and Jean is only kept alive since he persuades his captors that he understands how to fire two captured canons. It is his technical skill, rather than his culture, that makes him useful.

Throughout the film, the contrast and contradictions between the European individual and the indigenous communities are teased out. Even though Jean soon walks naked and shaves off his body hair, becomes a hunter and gatherer, and is granted an Indian wife, he cannot become assimilated. When his wife Sebiopepe tells him of an indigenous creation myth of the God Maira who taught the community how to make fire and move from caves into houses and village communities, Jean immediately identifies with the God. He does not hear the rest of the myth, that the tribe eventually kill their God. Similarly he is particularly attracted to the Indian woman when he finds a gold coin in her navel. His discovery of the gold and his attempted escape with this bullion are linked to a number of incidents in the film when Europeans attempt to exploit the "hidden wealth" of Brazil. He wants to escape with both the gold and his other "plunder," Sebiopepe, but she foils this plan by shooting him in the leg with an arrow. Jean later goes to war successfully alongside the Tupinamba, firing his canons to great effect, and returns thinking that his bravery will be rewarded by his release. He does not realize that it is now, as a true warrior, that he really merits death and ingestion by the tribe. Sebiopepe rehearses with him the ritual of his killing and tells him that he must behave like a warrior and a true man. When the final ritual is enacted, however, he breaks down and utters a curse in French that can only be read as a prophecy by the viewer. "Soon my people will arrive in ever increasing numbers to avenge my death and destroy you all."

Cannibalism is the main point of resistance in this otherwise melancholic idyll. Here Pereira dos Santos takes up the line of argument expounded by the Brazilian modernists of the 1920s, in particular by Oswald de Andrade in his "Anthropophagous Manifesto" of 1928, which argued that Brazilian culture and society need not always be a poor, underdeveloped relation of European and North American technology and development, but could assimilate, eat, digest, and rework the best of foreign influences, while evacuating the rest. The dichotomy foreign/national could be overcome in a new synthesis, an act of creative revenge against the colonial powers. Oswald's contemporary Mário de Andrade was not so sanguine about this process, as the epigraph at the beginning of this section reveals. To be a Tupi with a lute, a gallicism bellowing in the deserts of America suggests not synthesis, but rather painful and perhaps irreconcilable contradictions. His great novel of 1928, *Macunaíma*, points to these absurdist contradictions. When the Brazilian cineaste Joaquim Pedro de Andrade made a successful film of *Macunaíma* in 1969, he pointed also to the destructive elements of cannibalism: "Cannibalism has merely institutionalized itself, cleverly disguised itself. The new heroes, still looking for a collective consciousness, try to devour those who devour us. But, still weak, they are themselves transformed into products by the media and consumed. The Left, while being devoured by the Right, tries to discipline and purify itself by eating itself—a practice that is simply the cannibalism of the weak. Meanwhile, voraciously, nations devour their people" (quoted in Johnson and Stam 83). *How Tasty Was My Little Frenchman* moves between these different readings. At times it seems to express a utopian hope for a return to a primitive "Golden Age" society, but it is also extremely conscious of the need to live in history, a history marked by brutal encounters, hierarchies, and wars. In the tropics, as Ismail Xavier puts it, "civilization is the result of an illegitimate invasion that, imagined as a search for paradise, actually destroyed the well-balanced world of those living far from European culture." In these terms, "Civilization *is* the Other".

This film therefore, introduces a number of issues that need to be kept clearly in focus in the developing history of Latin American cinema. It highlights binary oppositions like Europe/America, Hollywood/Latin American Cinema, technology/underdevelopment, elite/popular, international/national and shows that within each country there is a constant process of digestion or transculturation, an awareness of the hybrid nature of cultural formations. This foundational story of a first "encounter between two worlds" points to the necessary mediations that take place between and within these "worlds" throughout history.

The Brazilian modernists of the 1920s, Oswald and Mário de Andrade, constantly negotiated the space between the fear and desire of the "Hallucinated City" (Mário's term) and the backwardness of the surrounding countryside. The eponymous transformative hero Macunaíma embarks on a journey from the Amazon to São Paulo in order to recover a magical talisman now in the possession of a São Paulo based Italo-Brazilian industrialist, Venceslau Pietro Pietra, who tries to eat our hero on numerous occasions. Both the novel and the later film make great comic play of the shock of the new experienced by Macunaíma in the metropolis, a world of speed, of crisscrossing electric cables and tram lines, of cars and new inventions, of European immigrants speaking a variety of tongues, a mixture of races, Germans, Italians, Jews, Russians, Brazilian blacks, Indian and whites, cities that are "maelstroms of perpetual tension, disintegration, assimilation, and renewal." They offer, in Bakhtin's terms, a "polyphony" of voices and experiences that do not become assimilated in any "melting pot," but rather generate dynamic tensions. The birth of cinema in Latin America coincides with this confused modernity. It takes firm root in the growing cities, and the city itself becomes a central motif of early cinema.

III

La ciudad del ensueño (The City of Dreams) was the title of a popular Argentine film of 1922 by Argentina's most tenacious and prolific early film maker, José Agustín Ferreyra. He referred, of course, to Buenos Aires. A year later Jorge Luis Borges wrote in a poem on the "Mythical Foundation of Buenos Aires": "Hard to imagine that Buenos Aires had any beginning/ I think of it as eternal as air and water." The city acquired a privileged space in the imaginary of its artists and writers. Small wonder: Buenos Aires held twenty percent of Argentina's population by 1930, a percentage that would increase every year due to internal migration. At the turn of the century, Argentina was one of the richest countries in the world, supplying beef and cereals to the world market. The wide boulevards and elegant town houses in Buenos Aires proclaimed that here was a city that aspired to be the Paris of the southern hemisphere, a metropolis positioned ambiguously on the periphery of the world. To this bustling commercial bureaucratic city flocked immigrants mainly from Spain and Italy. The nation's population grew from around 1,200,000 in 1852 to roughly eight million by 1914 as a result of immigration. In 1920, three out of every four adults in the central district of the city of Buenos Aires were born in Europe.

Buenos Aires, like other cities in Latin America that emerged in the early twentieth century, developed a highly sophisticated elite culture. There was also a strong popular culture expressed in popular melodrama, farces, music hall, tango, cinema, serialized novels, women's magazines, and political newsletters. Buenos Aires becomes important as a physical space and as a cultural myth, as Beatriz Sarlo has argued so convincingly: "The modern is also a form of feeling and a mode of experiencing the social, technological, and spatial changes brought about by capitalism. The artists represent and challenge, virtually at the same time, a body of new and traumatic experiences..., optimism in the face of a world in the process of transformation, and melancholy in the face of an irretrievable past." The street offers change, but it can also be transformed into myth: in early Argentine cinema, we find the recuperation of a neighborhood (*barrio*) street, where the city can resist the stigma of modernity. These streets become the privileged space for the tango lyrics of the twenties and thirties. The neighborhood streets also offer a black-cloth to the sentimental melodramas of José Ferreyra in the 1930s that starred the actress and singer Libertad Lamarque. The lyrics of the tango, like these early melodramas, contrast modernity and tradition: a protagonist is often stranded in the world of modernity ("Anclado en Paris"—anchored in Paris), dreaming and singing nostalgically of his mother, friends, the lover's nest (*bulín*), the barrio. Early sentimental literature and serialized novels offer similar plots for the new cinema, fueling both fears and desires.

Argentine talkies became extremely popular by exploiting these codes, the ingénue in the world of modernity, the prostitute with the heart of gold, the barrio as the site of homespun wisdom, simple melodramatic plots punctuated by song, the tango in particular. Similar patterns can be observed in Mexico and in Brazil, the two other main national industries of the first half of the century. Hollywood was well aware of the success of this formula and made several "Argentine" films starring the legendary Carlos Gardel specifically for a Latin American audience. His films often had to be stopped and rewound so that audiences could enjoy again El Mudo (the Mute) singing "Mi Buenos Aires querido" (My Beloved Buenos Aires) or "El día que me quieras" (The Day When You Love Me). Only Libertad Lamarque could compete with Gardel's popularity in the 1930s. Her life story, like that later of Evita Perón, seemed to come out of the plot of a tango melodrama. Born of humble origins in the provinces, she moved to the city and worked her way up through cabaret and vaudeville, ekeing out a meagre existence in a world of duplicitous men and false glamour. She wrote the script of, and starred in, the 1936 film *Ayúdame a vivir* (Help Me Live), directed by Ferreyra, which propelled her into stardom. This film set a style for the musical in Argentina in which the song lyrics, as in operetta or its Spanish cousin, the *zarzuela*, are built into the script as moments of dramatic punctuation. Gardel films stop by contrast when the star sings a song. There is one unforgettable scene in *Ayúdame a vivir* when a rich young man drags his latest drunken catch up a stairway towards a bedroom. The door opens, the couple intertwine, but over her shoulder the women catches sight of the demure Libertad Lamarque waiting patiently for her unfaithful man. A series of horrified close-up glances are exchanged between the three protagonists until Lamarque bursts into a song of righteous indignation, condemning the treachery and duplicity of men. The new immigrants to the city flocked to such movies and could empathize with the heroine, who was pure and moral, struggling against the odds.

As urbanization became more complex and Argentine cinema more secure, more complex urban dramas were possible. Perhaps the most interesting of the pre-1950 period was Luis César Amadori's *Dios se lo pague* (God Bless You; 1948). The location is the central streets of Buenos Aires, where an extremely intelligent beggar plies his trade outside a church and outside an aristocratic club. The narrative begins in a comic picaresque mode as a rather unsuccessful tramp is taught by his wise mentor how to extract money from passersby, who can understand psychology at a glance. One of the alms givers, a beautiful, but distracted young woman, soon becomes, however, the focus of the narrative, and comedy gives way to a more nuanced, sophisticated discussion of the

female protagonist's viewpoint as one source of identification for the
spectator. She is a woman of limited means (she is soon thrown out of
her boarding hotel for nonpayment of bills) who haunts the salons and
gaming houses of the rich in search of a satisfying relationship and financial security. This aristocratic gaming house is raided by the police and
she takes shelter with the tramp on the street outside. He advises her
to give up such haunts and seek love and fortune in other areas. Immediately his advice seems to become a reality as, next morning, she receives a bouquet of orchids and a ticket to the opera, Wagner's *Lohengrin*. In the opera house, the melodrama literally takes on its dictionary
definition as a dramatic narrative in which music marks the emotional
effects. A mysterious man appears in her box and explains the relevant
parts of the opera. Lohengrin, knight of the Grail, comes to champion
Elsa against her detractors. His one stipulation is that he must first
obtain her promise never to question him about his name and origins.
Bewitched by the opera, she goes to live with him on these terms, exchanging a life of random desire for a suffocating life of plenty.

As the narrative develops, the spectator gradually discovers that the
tramp and the mysterious millionaire she has married are one and the
same person. He lives on the street in order to obtain a clear perspective on the hypocrisy of life. He is a man who many years earlier had
been a worker cheated by his employer out of a patent he was developing. His first wife subsequently hanged herself in abject misery, and
he was apprehended trying to take revenge on the employer. This revenge clouds his vision and prevents any true engagement with life or
with the woman he now keeps in a gilded cage. After many narrative
twists both characters find a true humility and love ("Give what you have
and ask for what you desire"), and their new life begins in the church
where the millionaire/tramp had begged for many years. The film re-
verses the ending of *Lohengrin*. In the opera, Elsa finds out who her
champion is, and thus revealed, he must return to his father, Parsifal,
while Elsa swoons lifeless. Here recognition brings reconciliation: the
grail is not always somewhere else but, it is argued, in our reach. The
melodrama uses its urban locations to great effect: the central streets in
which dandies and tramps rub shoulders, the *arrabal* or working-class
outskirts where the protagonist carved out a precarious living and was
duped; the factory; the aristocratic salons, the site of conspicuous consumption and of the delights and snares of the modern; the town house
where Elsa is kept a prisoner and finally the church that resolves the
tensions and blesses the new union. The interiors allow the family melo-

drama to develop with a claustrophobic intensity, and the streets offer an examination of history and social tensions. The sophistication and assurance of the film was recognized in an Oscar nomination in 1948.

IV

Melodrama is the dominant mode of film narration up to the 1950s in Latin America, often combined with music and comedy. In Mexico, as critic Ana López points out, two basic melodramatic tendencies "developed between 1930 and 1960: family melodramas that focused on the problems of love, sexuality and parenting and epic melodramas that reworked national history, especially the events of the Mexican Revolution...although the two categories are somewhat fluid, with some family melodramas taking place in the context of the Revolution." Melodrama has until recently been dismissed in Latin America as escapist false consciousness and as failed political realism or failed tragedy. Recent criticism has begun to rethink the function of melodrama as a site of popular resistance. Jesús Martín Barbero argues that by "melodramatizing everything, through family relationships, the popular classes take revenge, in their own way, upon the commodification of life and dreams" (quoted in Rowe and Schelling 108). Melodrama also offers an opposition to the dominance of Hollywood as Carlos Monsiváis points out: "If competition with North America is impossible, artistically or technically, the only defense is excess, the absence of limits of the melodrama" (quoted in López, "Tears and Desire"). Melodrama in Mexico also played an important part in reconstructing the nation and the national imaginary after the upheavals of the Revolution, affirming the dynamism of Mexican history, the beauty and expressiveness of the landscape and the harmonious and civic responsibility of its inhabitants. The group that established the "image" for the decade of the 1940s in Mexico was the director Emilio Fernández, the cinematographer Gabriel Figueroa, the producer Agustín Fink, scriptwriter Mauricio Magdaleno, and the actors Dolores del Río and Pedro Armendáriz.

Fernández's visionary mystical exposition of Mexican history and landscape is best expressed in films like *Flor silvestre* (Wild Flower; 1943) and *María Candelaria* (1943). Carlos Monsiváis has the exact phrase for these works, "*autos sacramentales* [religious plays] of Mexicanness," offering not realism, but rather lofty visions of courage, the grandeur of the land, machismo and the feminine spirit ("Gabriel Figueroa"). He was

Mexico's John Ford. Figueroa's eloquent photography captures, in allegorical fashion, the moment of Adam and Eve in the garden of Mexico, the expressive physiognomies of the main characters, which harmonize with the expressive nature of the landscape: its lowering clouds, the emblematic plants, the play of light and dark, the shadows cast by the heat of the sun. Mexico, for Fernández, is elemental, atavistic, the site of primal passion and violence, from which a new progressive nation can be forged.

The face of the woman in the work of Fernández—a face that depicted moral and physical perfection—was that of Dolores del Río who, in 1943, succumbed to the blandishments of the Mexican film industry in an attempt to revive her waning acting career. In Hollywood from 1925 to 1942, she had appeared in twenty-eight films as the instinctual savage who could be tamed by love and Western culture, or as the more distant, exotic beauty. She had star appeal, but this was beginning to fade by the early forties. Fernández persuaded her to play a humble Mexican girl in *Flor silvestre*. The muralist Diego Rivera hinted that this would do her international reputation no harm; according to Fernández's daughter Adela, Rivera said, "You have an excellent opportunity to play in a film that is so Mexican, for the Europeans are rediscovering Mexico and are attracted by all the mysteries contained here" (Fernández 191). For whatever reason, the Hollywood legend became a humble peasant girl who falls in love with the landowner's son and marries him in secret against the wishes of his despotic father. The story is told in flashback from a moment in the "present," when an elderly Dolores del Río stands with her son and looks over the lands that were once a hacienda and are now owned collectively. The didactic purpose of the family unit is made immediately, as the camera pans slowly across the landscape and the voice of Dolores del Río recounts how "back then" (before the Revolution), very few people owned the land. "No one can live without a little piece of land." Yet the fight for land engenders violence and sacrifice. "Here," she says to her son, an upright young man in military uniform, "your father was born and died." The scene dissolves, and the next frame takes us into a church adorned with flowers where Esperanza (Del Río) and José Luis (Armendáriz) are married. The camera concentrates on the severe and expressive beauty of their faces, a morally and physically perfect couple thrown into the maelstrom of social change. It seems as if their love is doomed, for José Luis is the landowner's son and Esperanza is of lowly status. All the peasant characters express a similar fatalism: inequality is God's law. Only José Luis expresses his dissent:

"the land belongs to those who work it, suffer on it and dream of it....
God made us equal."

Interspersed by songs, mariachi bands, and comic interludes the
tragedy unfolds. Esperanza's pure love melts the heart of José Luis's
mother, but the Revolution intervenes. José Luis has been thrown out
of his father's hacienda (only the intervention of the women of the family
prevent the father from killing the son), and lives in a simple home with
the pregnant Esperanza and two loyal peons. The Revolution breaks out
and the house is visited by sympathetic revolutionaries. José Luis is
warned that the Revolution has unleashed both positive and negative
forces: bands of desperados are hijacking the legitimate aspirations of the
people and commiting acts of banditry. Two such bandit leaders (one
played with malicious relish by Fernández himself), kill José Luis's father, sack the hacienda, kidnap Esperanza, now with child, and in a
mounting tragic spiral of violence, execute José Luis, who sacrifices himself for his wife and child and, by extension, for his country. The film
ends with Dolores del Río's moralistic gloss: "The blood spilled in so
many years of struggle by thousands of men who, like your father, believed in goodness and in justice, was not sterile. On this bloodstained
ground, the Mexico of today has been raised, in which new life now
beats."

A new land forged in blood and in conflict. Yet the strong images
in the film illustrate violence rather than reconciliation: José Luis walking
through the devastated family house, his spurs clinking in the eery silence, while the Trío Calaveras sing the *corrido* (ballad) "El hijo desobe-
diente" (The Disobedient Son); José Luis stringing up the dead body of
the bandit leader who killed his father, leaving it swinging above his
father's grave; Esperanza fleeing her cabin with her baby, stumbling
across a dark landscape, pursued in a cloud of dust by Fernández on
horseback; Esperanza clinging to José Luis before he is to be shot. In
such scenes, Fernández achieves a tragic intensity that gives the lie to the
mature Esperanza's moralistic ending and the easy acceptance of the
nation's social contract.

Similarly lofty sentiments and aching purity are to be found in Argentina's national melodrama *La guerra gaucha* (The Gaucho War, directed by Lucas Demare in 1942) which focused on the Independence
period of 1814-18 when Güemes and his gaucho militia battled in Alto
Perú against the forces of Spain. All soical sectors in Salta—the local
aristocrats, the town sacristan, the gaucho forces—join in a successful
guerrilla war. Even a captured, wounded Peruvian officer is taught to

realize that his loyalties lie with the future of Latin America rather than with imperial Spain. Some spectacular, if rudimentary, battles, and the evocative landscape of the North, help to make a successful epitaph to "those who lived and died, the nameless ones, those who waged the gaucho war."

V

Comedy was the final successful element of Latin American movies in the early period, in the rearguard action against the Hollywood invasion of the 1920s and 1930s. Though the image could be understood everywhere, surely, cineastes argued, vernacular language and music were specific to particular cultures. They were right up to a point. Although by the 1930s Hollywood movies occupied some 95 percent of screen time throughout Latin America, there was still a small space for the singers and comedians who were an integral part of popular urban culture, in vaudeville, in short theatrical comic sketches, in tents and circuses and in the naissant industry of the radio. Mario Moreno—Cantinflas—began his life as a circus entertainer, as a dancer, a tumbler, and a comedian. He achieved great popular success before being taken up by the film industry. With his greasy shirt, crumpled sagging trousers, and large scuffed shoes, he epitomized the *pelado*, the scruffy street-wise neighborhood pícaro (the *arrabal* occupied a similar real and symbolic space in Mexico to the one we have already mapped out in Argentina), who deflates the pomposity of political and legal rhetoric. *Cantinflismo*, acting like Cantinflas, becomes a mode of speech where, delivered at breakneck speed, words go in desperate search of meaning. In his third film (*Ahí está el detalle* [That's the Crux of the Matter]; 1940), in the final court scene, he so disrupts the proceedings that the judge and the officials end up using the same nonsense language. In such movies, he ridiculed the pomposity of the middle classes and the empty rhetoric of politicians. Part of his popularity lay in his comic critique of social injustice. Roger Bartra, the Mexican critic, recounts a typical boutade: when Cantinflas was asked if work was a good thing, he replied, "if it were good, the rich would have got in on the act." But as Bartra points out, his is a conformist critique that "proposes flight rather than struggle, elusiveness rather than opposition (Bartra 176).

In these films, the marginal pelado, a figure of potential threat, becomes the inoffensive *peladito* (i.e., a diminutive pelado). *El gendarme desconocido* (The Unknown Policeman; 1941) offers one of his most successful guises: the policeman who is really a peladito. The film is prefaced by an unnecessary "health warning": "Our policemen are respectable and brave." Cantinflas is offering here an imaginary police force, one that is unnecessary, since the foundations of the system are kept firmly in place. Cantinflas's nonsense words and his extraordinary physical dexterity (limbs contort into impossible positions, just as words float free) are applauded by all classes. The cinema discovers the marketplace for a simple form of mass humor, which is delivered with a sardonic smile and an impossible arching of the eyebrows (Monsiváis, *Escenas* 88). In *Patrullero 777* (Patrol Man 777; 1985), one of the countless remakes of *El gendarme desconocido*, Cantinflas uses one of his favorite verbal gags. Cantinflas is talking on the telephone. All the cinema audience can hear is his replies, which offer modulations of surprise, anxiety, and complicity: "You don't say. You DON'T say. You don't SAY." This conversation lasts for several minutes. When he eventually comes off the phone, his colleague asks him what message his interlocutor gave. Cantinflas answers, eyebrows arching, hand swinging, "Beats me. He didn't say." Audiences greeted this with hoots and screams of laughter.

It is difficult to disagree with Roger Bartra's severe critique of these films: "The confused verbalism of Cantinflas is not a critique of the demagoguery of politicians: it rather legitimates them. With gestures and mimicry—parallel to the nonsense of the flow of words—Cantinflas insinuates that there is another interpretation, something hidden. That other reality invoked by the nodding of the head and the movement of his eyebrows and hips is a world of illegal advantages, of sexuality without eroticism, of power without representation, of wealth without work. There is an invitation to bribery and con tricks: the rules of the game are based on a lumpen venality that allows the Mexican to evade the police, swindle idiots, escape homosexuality, manage facile sex with other women while avoiding being cuckolded themselves. The pelado lives in a world that, in order to function, needs to be oiled permanently" (Bartra 180-181). The Mexicans in these films lack sense, but they do display emotion. And yet for many, the temporary victories of the peladito had a huge attraction. It was not merely empty political rhetoric that caused Diego Rivera to include Cantinflas in his magnificent mural in the Insurgentes Theater as a defender of the poor. Not a defender to lead them out of misery, but a man who could alleviate this misery with a few good or terrible gags (Monsiváis, *Escenas* 93).

Comedy and music were foregrounded also in Brazil's popular genre, the *chanchada* (a blend of music and comedy), which had its origins in Brazilian comic theater and in music and dance forms revolving around carnival. Two of Brazil's greatest comics, Oscarito and Grande Otelo, became stars of this genre, which was produced and reproduced in countless films of the 1930s and 1940s. Recent critics have pointed to the radical, subversive potential of some of these films that deliberately parody and laugh away the pretensions of Hollywood big-budget movies, genres, and the star system. In this analysis, laughter becomes the tool of the oppressed. It is equally clear, however, that most chanchadas worked within the paradigms analyzed above in relation to Cantinflas, offering "an idealized and inconsequential image of Brazilians, crystallized in a perpetually playful Río de Janeiro?" (João Luís Viera, quoted in Johnson and Stam 27). These films were very popular and attracted large Brazilian audiences. However, it was the mission of the young film directors of the 1950s, the *Cinema Novo* (new cinema) movement, to reveal this "popular" form as cheap, exploitative commercialism. It was the duty of the filmmaker, they felt, to reveal to the people the "real" conditions of their oppression.

VI

There was little avant-garde exploration of the medium of cinema itself in the movies up to the 1950s. If theorists of modernism like Walter Benjamin talked of the inherent radical and experimental nature of cinema, their arguments found few echoes among the practitioners. Some of these early films, however, did have a raw energy that became dissipated as the laws of the marketplace demanded rapid reproduction, a steady supply of closed-flow forms. The Mexican industry of the 1940s became a mini-Hollywood within Latin America by successfully exploiting two or three fixed genres.

A reaction to this increased commodification of the popular occurred in the 1950s and 1960s, part of a process that could draw on, but also quickly transcended, the European models of neorealism and the "new wave." It opposed the dominant idealisms by arguing that the experiences and actions of men and women are formed by concrete environments, that histories are made up of the aspirations, victories, often crushing defeats of real people who do not necessarily follow the plangent rhythms of singing *charros* (gentlemen horsemen). It was the duty of the filmmaker to tap into this experience, which could be done in a variety of roles: teacher, prophet, ethnographer, dispassionate observer. Most prominent cineastes of this period were fired by marxist, socialist principles, and they put their cameras at the service of developmentalism or the maximum utopia of revolutionary social change. It was a fruitful period in terms of producing a corpus of remarkable film and generating a series of complex theoretical debates, the notion of a Third Cinema still current today. One of the most complex and interesting directors of this period was Glauber Rocha and his film *Deus e o diabo na terra do sol* (God and the Devil in the Land of the Sun, released outside Brazil as *Black God, White Devil*; 1963) can offer a way into his formal and thematic concerns.

Black God is set in the Northeast of Brazil, in the desolate, drought-ridden sertão (badlands). Glauber has talked of the hunger and violence that marks the Latin American condition: "We know—since we made those ugly, sad, films, those screaming, desperate films in which reason has not always prevailed—that this hunger will not be assuaged by moderate government reforms and that the cloak of technicolour cannot hide, but rather only aggravates its tumors. Therefore, only a culture of hunger can qualitatively surpass its own structures by undermining and destroying them. The most noble cultural manifestation of hunger is violence." Glauber's characters share this exasperation and reach "moments of truth" though violence. Glauber radically rejects the dominant forms and language of industrial cinema, denies the universality of Hollywood, and seeks consistently to invent a language to express this necessary, liberating violence.

The site of the sertão was used by several Brazilian Cinema Novo directors, Glauber, Nelson Pereira dos Santos, and Ruy Guerra, to expose the problems of unequal development and the oppression of rural landowners. The city, the urban middle classes, and the proletariat are largely absent from these early films, since up until the coup of 1964 intellectuals like Glauber broadly supported the developmental nationalism of presidents like Kubitschek and Goulart that gave prominence to modernization led by progressive elements of a national bourgeoisie. The countryside, therefore, was the site of underdevelopment, of false consciousness that had to be overcome before progress was possible. Yet the problems were more complex than this simple analysis. The Northeast was also a place of messianic religious revolt and social banditry, the black god (Sebastião) and white devil (Corisco) of the English title of Glauber's film. One strong memory in the film is that of the

Canudos rebellion of 1893-97, in which a fanatic rebel priest led a band of peasants and social outcasts in opposing the new Republic. The dispossessed peasants of the run-down sugar plantations resented the incursion of modern capitalism and stoutly defended God and the old Empire. In 1893, Antônio the Counselor led this movement of some thirty thousand people against the modern secular state. They survived for several years, rebuffing the weight of the Republican army. The revolt became the stuff of written record, from Euclides da Cunha's *Rebellion in the Backlands* (see the section on Brazil) to Mario Vargas Llosa's *The War of the End of the World* (see the section on Peru), but also importantly of popular memory, a legend sung by the troubadours of the Northeast and recorded in the popular broadsheets known as *cordel* (literally, string, an allusion to how the broadsheets are displayed for sale in the public markets; see section on Paraliterature).

Another important form of rebellion in the backlands was banditry, something that has been called "social banditry." It is unclear whether these groups of outlaws, the *cangaços* who raided farms and settlements in the Northeast, were indeed "social" rebels, but they have been so anointed in popular memory. The ballads and poems sing of the legendary *cangaçeiro* (outlaw) Lampião as a Robin Hood figure. He was active from the 1920s until he was killed in 1938. Corisco in the film is a survivor of Lampião's massacre, a killing of the poor as a form of euthanasia. The cangaçeiro had already been taken up as a popular myth in cinema, when the Vera Cruz company, an ill-fated attempt to modernize cinema in the late 1940s and early 1950s, produced the lyrical *O cangaçeiro* (The Outlaw; directed by Lima Barreto in 1953), which tells of a young cangaçeiro who falls in love with a rural schoolteacher and has to confront his gang with the implications of his new way of thinking. Glauber was therefore not dealing merely with simple religious bigotry, but with a set of beliefs inscribed in popular consciousness and popular memory and in the broadsheets of popular poetry that set out social contradictions in terms of a mythical struggle between God and the Devil (Rowe and Schelling 91). The film, therefore, takes the form of a journey through different alienated forms of protest.

Two peasants, Manuel and Rosa, look for salvation from drought and oppression. Manuel sees the messianic leader Sebastião just before he kills the local *coronel* (literally, colonel—i.e., political boss), who has swindled him out of cattle. He flees with Rosa to the protection of Sebastião's movement. From the initial shots it is clear that Glauber is not interested in "realism" as a narrative mode, preferring Brechtian devices of theatricality and ritual. Randal Johnson accurately observes that the "narrative plays on contrast, juxtaposing sometimes agonizing temporal dilations with frenetic camera movements and rapid montage. The tension that builds up in the drawn-out dilated sequences is violently released in the synthetic ones, thereby reflecting the very lives of the protagonists" (Johnson, *Cinema Novo* 130). The narrative viewpoint is also ambiguous. The blind singer Julio comments on the action, but his "viewpoint" is often contradicted by the filmic diegesis or by a "superior" narrator who can see further and more clearly than Julio and the two characters. The musical score also underlines this complexity, giving a baroque texture by its play of silence and saturation, in which Brazil's great regional composer Heitor Villa-Lobos vies with popular ballads or with the screams and chants of Sebastião's followers.

As the movement of the film indicates, Manuel and Rosa (although she has a much clearer vision than he) must transcend popular religiosity and anarchic social violence. Sebastião repeats a phrase by Antônio the Counselor that "the sertão will become the sea, the sea the sertão": this is the apocalyptic promise born out of death and resurrection, out of the enduring battle between St. George and the Dragon. Sebastião and Corisco represent important stages in this utopian journey "to the sea." Antonio das Mortes, the existential bounty hunter, the "killer of cangaçeiros" helps to free Manual and Rosa so that they can "tell their story." Towards the end of the film the chorus on the soundtrack announces clearly that "The land belongs to man, not to God nor to the Devil." As critic Ismail Xavier points out, "the future becomes concrete at the end of the film. After the death of the *cangaçeiro* and after running round in circles for most of the film, Manuel and Rosa run through the sertão in a straight line and the screen is taken over by the image of the sea, reaffirming the certainty of the Revolution. By contrasting heaven and hell and the present (suffering) and the future (plenty), via the juxtaposition of the sertão and the sea, Rocha represents the revolution as a process of migration, a search for heaven on earth."

VII

Jorge Sanjinés began making documentaries in Bolivia in the early 1960s. He soon realized that the gap between the (middle-class, white, male) filmmaker and the "people" was enormous and should become part of his theoretical analysis of the filmmaking process itself: "We began to realize that the people were not interested in seeing films that did not contribute to anything, films that merely satisfied their curiosity to see themselves reflected on the screen. We realized that the people knew much more about misery than any filmmaker who might aspire to show it to them. Those workers, miners, and peasants are the protagonists of misery in Bolivia. Except for bringing tears to the eyes of a few pious liberals, the kind of films we were making were good for nothing" (quoted in Burton 38). In a volume of theoretical writing about cinema, carefully and aptly named *Teoría y práctica de un cine junto al pueblo* (Theory and Practice of a Moviemaking alongside the People; 1979), Sanjinés makes a telling point about the gap between the filmmaker and the indigenous communities in the Andes, a gap that had to be bridged before he and his group could make *Yawar Mallku* (Blood of the Condor; 1968). They found a theme, the forced sterilization of women in the countryside by United States agencies like the Peace Corps, which gave substance to the nature of imperialism, otherwise just a distant abstraction to local communities. One lesson it seemed had been learned: not to use "abstractions" like the nation, the state, imperialism in indigenous communities whose relationship to time, space, and social relations was very different. The "story" would have to be relevant to their lived experiences. Another lesson, the need to speak Quechua or Aymara, the Indian languages, was also learned, but without any understanding of what language implied in cultural terms. Sanjinés tells that when the film crew went up to the chosen Indian village, a long and difficult journey, they found that the people ignored them, treated them with mistrust, and refused to cooperate. After two weeks, when the project was about to fall through, they realized that they were approaching the community in the wrong way. They had contacted the mayor, thinking that he was the appropriate power, but then "we realized that the mayor did not have power. The power was really democratic, it resided in an assembly. The individual was only important as part of a collectivity" (personal interview, 1986). They then asked for the village assembly to discuss their project and have the local shaman read the coca leaves to verify their honesty. In this way, they were accepted. The scene of the shaman verifying the truth came to be used in the film.

Yawar Mallku moves between the country and the city, the isolated Indian settlements and the capital, which increasingly attracts migrant workers seeking a better life as an escape from rural poverty, only to find the marginal squalor of the shantytowns. The narrative present charts the increasingly desperate attempts of a city based Indian, Sixto, to obtain blood for his dying brother Ignacio, who has been wounded and brought to the city by his wife. Flashbacks establish why the brother was wounded. He was a local Indian leader in the mountains who gradually discovered that the infertility of his own wife and of the other women in the region was due to sterilization operations carried out by three young North American Peace Corps workers. The community takes revenge by castrating the two North American men, and the police capture, shoot, and leave for dead several villagers, including Ignacio.

Sanjinés does not work with simple Manichaean oppositions. Life in the Indian village is grindingly poor and harsh. Yet the community still remains a community, which articulates a different cultural universe with non-Western notions of time and history. On several occasions we see how ritual is used as a formalization of everyday life that reasserts cosmology and history, and how oral cultures (as opposed to the written rules and regulations of the city) organize and encode their existence through "a variety of action and locations that include ritual, theater, music, pilgrimages, artifacts, narratives, and the ways in which the earth itself is perceived as patterned with lines and significant points" (Rowe and Schelling 53). Such cultural strength keeps alive the possibility of a utopian future, here signaled in the raised guns of Indian resistance that is the final image of the film. This moment is prefigured in a ritual when Ignacio fills himself with light at dawn, an action that seems to signify, with the emergence of the sun, the coming of a new age in a cyclical view of history, the age of the Incas and of Indian civilization (Rowe and Schelling 52). The millenarian promise, brought to the Andes by the Franciscan missionaries in the sixteenth century, argues that existing power structures set up by Spanish colonialism (and later North American neocolonialism) can be reversed. This utopian desire is linked to the Andean concept of *pacha kuti*, "the turning upside down and inside out of time and space." Even though the Indian leader dies in the hospital, his spirit is resurrected in his previously alienated, city dwelling brother, who returns to the community and to the struggle: "The notion of historical change is also articulated with the idea that the lower or inside world...will exchange places with our present world. The lower world, region of chaos and fertility, becomes the source of the future, an extension of the belief that the dead return to present time and space through the growing season" (Rowe and Schelling 55). Similarly, even though this community is now part of the global order of capitalist relations (roads significantly link it to the city, the Indians meet the Peace

Corps workers on the road), it is not seen as totally subordinated to capitalist "modernity."

Yet the film also argues that it is utopian to suggest that precapitalist culture can resist successfully the lure and the shock of the new. Up to seventy percent of the population of Latin America now live in cities; cultures are mediated by the city. The second half of the film concentrates on the world of La Paz, on the world of the textile worker Sixto, who initially denies his Indian origins and tries to become integrated into a society that, as the film shows in its odyssey through the city, is rigidly stratified topographically and in racial and class terms. In his desperate search for blood and plasma, Sixto is faced with the indifference of the middle-class order, and the indifference and "difference" of this society's white, North Americanized, wealthy ruling order. This awareness allows the spirit of his brother to be reborn in him, in a necessary rebellion in the Andes.

Perhaps no political film has ever had such an immediate and lasting impact. The government tried to stop the screening of the film in La Paz on 17 July 1969, but a huge public demonstration changed this ruling. It started up a public debate and a campaign against the activities of the Peace Corps, which was expelled from Bolivia by General Torres in May 1971. But the film did not satisfy the Ukamau group at the level of form, since it still seemed to impose the cultural expectations of the dominant classes on the indigenous people. The language of the film was seen to be alien to this sector with its constant use of flashbacks and suspense and its examination of individual psychologies. It should be remembered that the nation-state of Bolivia is the result of creole domination over the Indian Aymara, Quechua, and Guarani nations, a domination that was only partially successful. Even by 1976, with the increasing growth of urbanization, over a fifth of the population still spoke no Spanish. It was not enough, therefore, for Ukamau to film with dialogue in the native languages, for there was "a formal conflict at the level of the medium itself, which did not correspond to the internal rhythms of our people or their profound conception of reality. The substantial difference lay in the way in which the Quechua-Aymara people conceive of themselves collectively, in the nonindividualistic form of their culture" (Sanjinés, "We Invent" 31). This attitude would mean rethinking forms that privilege the individual over the social: the close-up, the psychological examination of individual motivation, the standard conventions of the fiction film. Filmmaking for the group would in the future deal with the history of the collective, seeking to reactivate the popular memory denied by the hegemonic powers.

VIII

The question of popular memory and popular resistance was a feature of these landmark 1960s films. Fictional films like *Yawar Mallku* had a strong documentary focus. It was the documentary that was seen to have a flexibility, immediacy, and a didactic purpose appropriate to these times. Julianne Burton has recently edited a wide-ranging analysis of the social documentary in Latin America that maps the field in great detail. This short survey takes one key moment from Argentina as its example.

In Argentina, Fernando Birri is seen to be the precursor of the social documentary. He opened a film school in Santa Fe and produced several significant documentaries based on the surrounding community. The documentary *Tire dié* (Throw Us a Dime; 1958) was a group project by some eighty students who observed and recorded the local children of a shanty town who daily risked their lives running along a main railway line begging for coins. The film developed as a dialogue with the local community: a first version was shown to different audiences and the final cut was made after incorporating their suggestions. It was, in many ways, their film. Birri's work was important for sixties filmmakers in his emphasis on national popular cinema, his attempt to adopt and transform neorealism in the context of Latin America, and his effort to break with the distribution and exhibition circuits of commercial cinema, incorporating new working-class and peasant audiences into more democratic cultural practices. Fernando Birri's *Tire dié* is quoted in the film under discussion in this section, Fernando Solanas and Octavio Getino's *La hora de los hornos* (The Hour of the Furnaces; 1966-68).

La hora demands in its obsessively authoritative voice-over that it be read as a political act, a concrete intervention in history. It cannot be understood outside the context of late sixties militancy in Argentina, although the theoretical essay that followed the film, "Towards a Third Cinema," has become a seminal text for discussing Latin American, African, and Asian cinema. *La hora* was filmed and initially shown clandestinely under the Onganía dictatorship (1966-70). It was made by a group of militant, radical Peronists. Space precludes any detailed analysis of how the populist president Juan Domingo Perón (1946-55), who was abhorred by most middle-class intellectuals, became, during his exile in Spain in the 1960s, transformed into a Third World, nationalist figure. Even though Perón was ousted by the military in 1955 and Peronism was banned from the political arena, the movement still mobilized powerful resources in the urban lower-middle and working classes, in the trade union confederation, in the myth of Evita ("Volveré y seré millones" [I will return as millions]), and in Perón's own messianic promise of a second coming. Subsequent military and civilian governments found it difficult to correct the imbalances of the Peronist economic legacy, and as society reeled between military and civilian governments, so Perón grew in stature as the alternative to the spiral of decline. Faced with this decline and spurred by the imaginative proximity of social change and revolution (in particular the example of Cuba), a number of artists and intellectuals, among other sectors, became politicized and fought the government in all areas of political and cultural activity. Onganía seemed to epitomize everything that was corrupt about the Argentine state: he abandoned politics, imposed a severe economic stabilization plan, intervened brutally in the universities, seized magazines, shut down theaters on moral grounds, and closed radio news services and television shows.

The response of young intellectuals varied in sophistication, but the dominant strands of thought were nationalist, populist anti-imperialist, and in many cases Peronist. The European "universalist" model was called into question for having distorted national development. A number of research institutes in Argentina and in Latin America explored the links between dependency and underdevelopment and provided theoretical justification for rejecting the old tradition of uncritically assimilating the latest European trends. Concepts such as "the people," "the national," "the Third World" were given a new positive value, and significantly the rhetoric was "Latin Americanist." *La hora* is a complex example of these aspirations and desires (for recent analyses of the radicalization of Argentine intellectuals in the 1960s, see Terán; Sigal).

The colossal work lasting four and a half hours is divided into three parts. Part I, "Neocolonialism and Violence," deals with Argentina's economic and cultural dependency on Europe. Part II, "An Act for Liberation," talks of Peronism as a force for change in government, both when in power, from 1946 to 1955, and in exile. Part III, "Violence and Liberation," contains a series of interviews with militants discussing the best way of achieving revolutionary transformation. The first five minutes of Part I bombard the viewer with images demanding active engagement. The film begins with a dark screen and a relentless, rhythmical drumming. After thirty seconds there is a flare of light (prefiguring the beacon of independence alluded to in the title of the film, a quotation from the Cuban José Martí) and there follows an accelerating montage of documentary clips, showing violence and resistance on the streets, photographs, captions advancing out of the screen, epigraphs from a cluster of "revolutionary" leaders or theoreticians, Aimé Césaire, Fidel Castro, Che Guevara, and Solanas's particular Argentine pantheon: Perón, Raúl Scalabrini Ortiz, and Juan José Hernández Arregui. Latin America, a caption proclaims, "is a continent at war." This introduction sets the tone of the historical/political analysis and also points to the inventiveness and experimental nature of its formal composition. Especially in Part I—the two subsequent parts are more "traditional" in a documentary sense—Solanas and the Cinema Liberation Group interweave in a vivid tapestry a number of different materials: commercials, interviews, newsreels, and still photos. The film quotes filmmakers like Birri, the Brazilian Leon Hirszman, and the Cuban Santiago Alvarez, crosscuts fiction and documentary, *cinema verité* and operatic stylization, always restless, always demanding (cf. Stam). The first part is divided into thirteen sections covering history, the country, daily violence, the port city, the oligarchy, the system, political violence, neoracism, dependency, cultural violence, cultural models, the ideological war, all ending with "the option," a five minute shot of Che Guevara's face in death, the choice of death that is the choice also of a life of liberation, of self-awareness.

While the film is formally complex, the historical analysis and the omniscient narration are ideologically Manichaean, at the service of revolutionary Peronism and popular nationalism. It follows the analysis of Argentine nationalist critics such as Juan José Hernández Arregui, Arturo Jauretche, and Jorge Abelardo Ramos in terms of its stark contrasts: on the one hand, the national consciousness—Latin American identity defined in terms of suffering, exploitation, and resistance—and on the other hand, imperialism, the dependent oligarchy, and the colonized middle sectors. One important set of images contrasts the brutality and poverty of regional areas like Tucumán with superficially "swinging" Buenos Aires, full of psychedelic lights, flower children, and miniskirts. The mask of modernization is stripped off to reveal the "true" nature of Argentine society, one, which, it is argued, must be changed immediately.

The film is structured as a political act, an exceptional moment of communication. At the end of Part II, a voice declares: "Now the film

is pausing, it opens up for you to continue it. Now you have the floor."
At the beginning of the second part, the film quotes Frantz Fanon, a
passage that neatly summarizes its intentions: "The political meeting is
a liturgical act, it is a privileged moment for men and women to hear
and speak. To politicize is to open up the spirit, awaken the spirit, give
birth to the spirit, it is, as Césaire says, a means of 'inventing souls.' If
it is necessary to involve the whole world in the fight for common salvation, then there are no clean hands, no spectators, no innocents.... Every
spectator is a coward or a traitor." After making the film, Solanas and
Getino theorized their concerns in a seminal, bombastic essay titled
"Towards a Third Cinema." They argue that in Argentina and in the
Third World generally, filmmakers must pose an alternative to both the
"first" cinema, Hollywood, and the "second" cinema, the *auteur* cinema,
which does not commit itself to popular struggle. The only alternative
is a third cinema, the cinema of liberation.

La hora had a huge impact under the Onganía dictatorship, and it
was shown by clandestine organizations in private houses, on the shop
floor, or in villages. Viewing it with the benefit of hindsight, its faith in
Peronism seems pathetically misplaced and the tone of its argument
stridently naive. Such a caveat cannot, however, deny the radical impact
of the film and its directors in the late sixties and early seventies. It was
part of a massive wave of social unrest and militancy that was brutally
suppressed by internecine political rivalry in the mid-seventies and the
military dictatorship of 1976.

IX

The first part of *La hora de los hornos* ends with a photograph of the
seemingly smiling, wise, and serene face of the dead Che Guevara.
Memorias del subdesarrollo (Memories of Underdevelopment) was directed in 1968 in Cuba, in a year entitled "The year of the heroic guerrilla."
It is perhaps the most accomplished Cuban feature film of the decade,
and it puts on the agenda the whole question of commitment to a revolution under seige and in particular the intellectual's commitment to a
wider society. The director, Tomás Gutiérrez Alea, puts himself into the
fictional narrative, together with a number of important revolutionary
intellectuals who include the writer Edmundo Desnoes, whose novel
serves as a basis for the screenplay. The protagonist, Sergio, is a failed
writer, caught in an existentialist trap, unable to communicate through

the written word, unable to communicate with a wider society. The film charts his trajectory and his decline through his relationship with other intellectuals and with a series of emblematic female characters.

The function of the intellectual in the Revolution had been on the agenda throughout the 1960s of generating heated debates, expulsions, repressions, and exiles. Fidel's "Words to the Intellectuals" of 1961 had stated that "Inside the Revolution, everything; outside the Revolution, nothing," and Che had written convincingly about the difficult transition of those artists marked by "original sin" as a consequence of their traditional role as an outside "critical conscience" of society toward becoming more actively, "organically" (to use Gramsci's terms), engaged in social processes.

Gutiérrez Alea himself gives an excellent introduction to his main protagonist:

> In one sense Sergio represents the ideal of what every man with that particular kind of [bourgeois] mentality would like to have been: rich, good looking, intelligent, with access to the upper social strata and to beautiful women who are very willing to go to bed with him. That is to say, people identify to a certain degree with him as a character. The film plays with this identification.... But then what happens? As the film progresses, one begins to perceive not only the vision that Sergio has of himself, but also the vision that reality gives to *us*, the people who made the film. They correspond to our vision of reality and also to our critical view of the protagonist. Little by little the character begins to destroy himself precisely because reality begins to overwhelm him, for he is unable to act. At the end of the film, the protagonist ends up like a cockroach squashed by his fear, by his impotence, by everything. (quoted in Burton 119)

From the opening sequences, this play of identification and rejection is built up subtly. Sergio's appearance, his sense of humor, his sense of irony, his caustic comments on other members of his class, all engage the viewer. Yet it is clear, from the moment when he bids his wife goodbye (she is leaving for Miami) or when he surveys the city from his balcony, that he is always keeping reality at a distance, seeing through glass, through telescopes or, in an interesting scene of erotic voyeurism, through the mask of his wife's stockings, pulled over his head. This inability to form social relationships is seen in his treatment of four women characters. He patronizes and molds his wife as a perverse sculptor, only to abandon her as wearisome; he toys with, seduces, and is soon bored by a young working-class girl; he has erotic fantasies about his maid, but is inhibited by class background to understand a provincial girl from the countryside; he dreams of an ideal "European" girlfriend whom he abandoned as a young man in order to pursue business interests. Women are for casual colonization or for masturbatory dreams. While he can understand the colonial mentality of a writer such as Hemingway—there is a significant scene shot in Hemingway's house—who used Cuba as a site for his own fantasies of exoticism and machismo, he cannot apply this analysis to himself.

The spectators must therefore reexamine those values that have made them identify with Sergio. Importantly also, Sergio is a writer, suffering from acute writer's block (his typewriter in an early scene jams on the word *joder*: the revolutionary process is literally "screwing him up," but he cannot understand why). He is an intellectual with access to Alea himself at the offices of the Cuban film institute, ICAIC. Sergio takes his young pickup to ICAIC to get her an audition. With Alea they see a series of pornographic film clips the director had found lying around the ICAIC studios, a remnant of Batista's censors. The director says that he will use them in a film he is making. Forever the pessimist, Sergio asks if it will be released, and the director answers affirmatively. The film will be a collage, he says, that will include a bit of everything. Alea here makes an important point about working with and through underdevelopment. Cuban filmmakers can only aspire to an "imperfect cinema," to use the Cuban Julio García Espinosa's term: they do not have access to big budgets, new technologies, the sophistication of an industrial system. In this film Alea takes several sequences from one position on the street. He does this, he once remarked, since the old camera that he was using was so heavy that it could not be moved too often or too far from the ICAIC offices. Yet there are ways in which scarcity can be turned into a "signifier" by shaping old material or found objects such as the censored film clips into new dynamic collages. In the early years of the Revolution, Cuban cinema concentrated on newsreels and documentaries: these were the immediate concerns of a new society with pressing ideological concerns and limited budgets. Feature films only begin to be made systematically in the late 1960s. Yet Alea can creatively use this footage: the film is a blend of documentary and fictional elements. One documentary scene, the televised trials of the Bay of Pigs mercenaries, where the prisoners deny their individual responsibility in the invasion, makes a telling point about the relationship between the individual and the group. Sergio buys a book about these trials, *Moral burguesa y revolución* (Bourgeois Morality and Revolution) by the Argentine León Rozitchner, condemns his friend's bourgeois codes, but once again cannot read his own life in these pages. The documentary film footage makes clear that there must be a more considered reflection on the responsibility of the individual in society. Overall the film reveals the gap between the filmmaker and his fictional character and the necessary commitment of the artist, albeit in conditions of scarcity.

The time scale of the film is important. It was made in 1968, but refers to an earlier period in the decade, from the Bay of Pigs invasion in April 1961 to the Missile Crisis of October 1962. It deals with the consolidation of the Revolution in the face of U.S. imperialist aggression, portraying a Revolution in process, a people constantly alert, and the need for commitment in all sectors of society. These were all-important sentiments for the late sixties in a country trying to survive the tight economic blockade and overcome external political and military interference and a stagnating economy that relied increasingly on the monoculture of sugar. *Memorias* supports this process of mobilization, but not in any black-and-white way. It shows that the Revolution is made up not of stereotyped exemplary new men and women, but of individuals still crossed by contradictory desires and aspirations.

Towards the end of *Memorias*, Sergio is cooped up in his increasingly claustrophobic flat, while outside these ordinary people mobilize in defense of the Revolution during the Missile Crisis. On television, Castro gives his memorable speech where he proclaimed that: "No one is going to inspect our country because we grant no one the right. We will never renounce the sovereign prerogative that within our frontiers, we will make all the decisions and we are the only ones who will inspect anything. Anyone intending to inspect our country should be ready to come in battledress." Sergio scans a newspaper: a cartoon shows a man with a question mark over his head. At the end of the cartoon strip, the question mark flattens him into the ground. There is no space for individual questioning when it denies active engagement with social reality.

X

"The female figure has been a recurrent cipher of national identity in Cuban cinema for nearly three decades. Expressing the individual sacrifices and collective struggles that have shaped the modern Cuban nation, established filmmakers as well as aspiring directors have seen in the figure of the Cuban women the embodiment of the ideals of the nation" (D'Lugo). There has indeed been a conscious attempt in Cuba to invest meaning in the "imaginary community" that is the nation through the role of gender issues. The overcoming of machismo is seen as one of the firm bases of revolutionary society. This symbolic struggle does not merely work on the level of the imaginary: it is also rooted in progressive legislation such as the Family Code of 1974, which established conditions of equality and responsibility within marriage. ICAIC has made a number of important films on the subject, nearly all directed, in a significant irony, by men. Sara Gómez, a notable exception to this pattern, directed *De Cierta Manera* (One Way or Another; 1974). She died, tragically, of asthma before the final cut of the film could be made. It was completed by Alea and García Espinosa.

The narrative deals with Yolanda, a young and enthusiastic school-mistress sent out to Las Yaguas, a community that was rebuilt on the site of one of Havanna's worse slums. She develops a relationship with a factory worker, Mario, who must adapt to her more progressive ideas and also rethink his old friendship with Humberto, who, with the excuse of visiting an ailing mother, takes several days off work with his girl-friend. Men, the old codes demand, should stick together, but Mario refuses to cover up for his friend. The film begins and ends with Humberto's hearing at a worker's council and Mario's denunciation of his friend: the narrative is thus framed by a discussion on revolutionary responsibility and, in particular, *male* responsibility.

Yolanda is the main focus of this narrative that blends documentary and fiction. Yolanda operates within the fiction, but she also steps out of this narrative to address the spectator directly on several occasions. Documentary sequences interrupt the flow and the pleasure of the romance narrative. The scene of the worker's council is followed by a documentary showing the slum conditions before the model housing development was erected. This blending of fiction and documentary draws the spectators into an awareness of their real social conditions and the debates surrounding the many processes taking place. The film argues from this early segment that model housing estates have no function if the mentality remains underdeveloped. The historical roots of machismo, identified as the main enemy of progress, are traced in a conversation between Yolanda and Mario, back to the imposition and survival of African religious cults, in this case the Abacúa society. Both African and Hispanic culture, it is argued, are bastions of male chauvinism. Here once again the fiction is interrupted by a documentary section on the Abacúa sects. The lumpen and working-class elements of Havana and Matanzas—mainly black (the film also deals with issues of race with sensitivity)—have not been incorporated successfully into the Revolution. Mario's partial conversion is seen as a victory for Yolanda, but her revolutionary ideals are put firmly to the test in a world of single mothers, rebellious children, and machista workers. Two main characters, the single mother "La Mexicana" and her disruptive child Lázaro, are drawn from real life. The gap between the "imagined" community and reality remains great. Mario's conversion is only partial. He feels that in denouncing his friend he acted "like a woman." "After all it's men who made the Revolution," he states. Yolanda finds Miraflores confusing and complex, as she confesses to the camera: "I graduated from different schools. Then I came here, and all this was a different world, one I thought no longer existed." Throughout the film Gómez presents problems rather than offering easy solutions (for a detailed reading of this film, see Chanan 285-292).

XI

This survey of "new" cinemas of the 1960s and early 1970s ends with a consideration of Miguel Littín's *El chacal de Nahueltoro* (The Jackal of Nahueltoro; 1969). By the late 1960s, new cinema had become a generalized Latin American movement. In 1967 a Chilean doctor and cineaste, Aldo Francia, organized a "Meeting of Latin American Filmmakers" at the Viña del Mar film festival. The festival saw the arrival of delegates from seven countries and films from nine. The meeting put forward an ambitious set of resolutions concerning future collaborative work and the sharing and dissemination of material, many of which remain elusive goals twenty-five years later. Chilean filmmakers at the festival found that they shared the ideals and aspirations of the movement and a sense of optimism for the future. Raúl Ruiz makes the point: "Suddenly we found ourselves with a cinema that in a very obvious and natural way, without any cultural inferiority complex, was being made with very few resources, with the resources that we could acquire, and with a freedom that earlier Latin American and European cinema did not have. Suddenly we found ourselves with all the advantages. Glauber Rocha's *Black God, White Devil* is Sartre's 'Devil' and 'God,'\ but it is also many more things. It is a cinema that has no problem in quoting, accepting, and swallowing Sartre, without any complex, while remaining very Brazilian." Littín shares in this optimism that cinema in South America had found a number of expressive languages and could be in the vanguard struggle for social change.

El chacal focuses on a true story of a man who murdered a homeless woman and her five children in a hopeless act of violence and drunkenness. He is arrested, put in prison, and executed. In 1960 the sensationalist press painted the man as a "jackal," but Littín is at pains to show how social conditions act as breeding grounds for drunkenness, violence, and despair. The film was released a year before the Popular Unity government under Allende came to power, towards the end of the Christian Democrat period of office. The Christian Democrats had proclaimed that they would develop a social policy for marginal groups and promised to create a hundred-thousand landholders among landless peasants to help alleviate cases such as the one so tragically highlighted in 1960. By examining this incident, Littín implies that the Christian Democrat rhetoric had not become a reality. Conditions had improved very little throughout the 1960s: the Marxist parties, it is argued, should be allowed to set the country on the Chilean road to socialism.

As in several films discussed earlier, the narrative is framed by a series of "documentary" devices. Littín spent several years researching the case, and he provides an analysis that provides layers of competing information. On the sound track, language relates to different forms of power. The instrumental language of the legal depositions gives a cold reading: José murdered a woman and five children and according to section X of the penal code, he is condemned to death. José, who learns to read and write in prison, signs his own death warrant. The sensationalist press and radio reports, often accompanied by noises of police sirens and a braying crowd, extract the crime from its social context: José, is a jackal, a monstrous aberration who must be sacrificed to the multitude's need for blood and revenge. The sympathetic reporter, who in the second half of the film tries to help José and extract the reasons for his action, becomes, in a significant shift, a mouthpiece for José, carrying on and making known the words of the downtrodden, who by definition have no access to language. Finally there are José's own words, fumbling, halting, barely articulate, which recount the story of the murder and his own brutal, poverty-stricken background.

The image track articulates what José does not have the words to express. In a series of flashbacks from the moment of his arrest—which is captured in a cinéma-verité, documentary style, privileging a hand-held camera that swirls in and out of the crowd scenes (López, "At the Limits")—certain key moments of José's childhood and adolescence are explored. The tone is one of great compassion, capturing the bewildered alienation of a tiny child of eight, homeless and rejected; the back-breaking servility of his adolescence; the hopelessness of a young adult drifting penniless through a stricken rural landscape, where the majority have no access to land. José moves the way he speaks: he shuffles, eyes downcast, or stares bewildered and uncomprehending. Drink offers temporary anesthesia or causes wild rages, as when he kills the homeless widow who showed him a brief moment of kindness by offering him water. Having killed her, he is propelled to kill her five children, "so that they should not suffer any more." These scenes offer a merciless critique of a society that allows the conditions of rural misery to go unresolved, preventing even minimum forms of sociability. Significantly, José is arrested at a dance in a rural bar when he is dancing a *cueca* (a type of Chilean folk dance), a tiny glimpse of community that is soon annihilated.

The second half of the film charts José's socialization in prison and his execution. After the vigorous pace of the first sections, which constantly shift narrative perspective and point of view, these scenes build slowly and relentlessly to their inevitable outcome. Ironically, it is in prison that José finds the community denied him in his earlier years. Initially he shuffles around the prison compound, just as he shuffled around the rural landscape, but a football rolls towards him. A voice asks him to kick the ball back. Hesitantly, he picks up the ball, then launches a vigorous kick. The scene ends with a freeze-frame of his face, for the first time smiling. In prison he plays on a football team, he learns literacy skills, makes baskets and guitars, is taught significant moments of Chilean history. The classroom scene ironically explores the nationalist rhetoric of the history teacher, who harangues his bewildered class about the virtues of patriotism, the state and the nation, abstractions that mean nothing to the prisoners. The state, the nation, the church, it is argued, need scapegoats. José, the scapegoat, is literally driven out of the town (civilized society) and "stoned" to death to expiate the sins of society. Is redemption possible for him? The bold words on his prison walls read "redemption not deprivation," and José in many way redeems himself by taking responsibility for his actions and by finding a "family," useful work, and a community. On several occasions, the film alludes to images of Christ's suffering: when José is captured, he is brought back between two policeman on horseback, his arms extended like a cross; the seat on which he is executed has a similar form to the cross; his guards play dice outside his cell, an allusion, perhaps to Christ's jailers who gambled for his garments. As in Littín's later film *La tierra prometida* (The Promised Land; 1974), there is a contrast between state religion and the religion of the poor—José achieves redemption on his own terms. The mass murderer is a man of great dignity. It is society that denies its inhabitants that possibility of self-respect. That is the ultimate crime.

XII

By the mid-1970s the political project of new cinema as a vanguard movement for revolutionary social change lay in ruins. A wave of military dictatorships swept through the Southern Cone. The 1964 coup in Brazil led to a more extreme dictatorship between 1968 and 1971. In Bolivia, General Hugo Banzer ruled with repressive severity between 1971 and 1978. In Uruguay, the military overthrew one of Latin America's most stable democracies in 1973. Later the same year, the armed forces under General Pinochet ended Chile's three-year experiment of democratic revolutionary change. In Argentina, after the death of Perón in 1974, the country was torn by near civil war, a violence that was extended and systematized when the military took power in 1976. The intellectual community suffered the same fate as those in the wider community: imprisonment, murder, torture, exile, or extreme censorship. In Cuba, the decade saw ideological austerity and a marked slowing down in the pace of artistic experimentation. Only a few state-led initiatives in Andean countries and in Mexico gave cinema any signs of vigor.

Fernando Solanas was one of many intellectuals forced into exile. His analysis of the state of exile took many years to find funding and was eventually released in 1985: *Tangos, el exilio de Gardel* (Tangos, the Exile of Gardel). *Tangos* concentrates on a group of exiled artists and intellectuals in Paris and explores the ways in which they are distanced from, yet still preserve, their national identity. The artistic troupe seeks to create a *tanguedia* (a tango tragedy/comedy) based on their own exile experi-

ence and also on tango, which in itself contains both comedy and tragedy. The film is very deliberately also a *tanguedia*, analyzing the anguish
of separation through the expressive forms of tango. Tango is made to
represent many aspects of the Argentine experience. It is the quintessen-
tial popular song and dance form in Argentina. As a dance, it maintains
certain steps and rhythms unchanged since the turn of the century. But
these are combined into new sequences by the dance troupe in the film
(the new musical combinations are set out by Argentina's most famous
jazz-tango musician Astor Piazzolla). The film is divided into chapters
introduced by a group of young musical performers, the children of the
exiles, caught ambiguously between France and Argentina. The lyrics of
their tangos are composed by Solanas himself. Argentine culture has a
tradition, Solanas argues, that constantly renews itself despite displacement and extraterritoriality. The lyrics of tango, as indicated earlier in
this chapter, deal with exile and return: a narrator, often far from his or
her native land ("Anclado en Paris"—anchored in Paris) speaks of the
longing for the city of Buenos Aires and its sense of place. The most
famous tango singer of all, Carlos Gardel, represents the image and
voice of the tango, and he is a folk myth in Agentina. He evokes nostalgia, but also personifies for Solanas a truly Argentine popular culture.

The film deals with memories of the various exiles suffered by the
troupe themselves, far from friends and Argentina, "the daily confrontations between the tragic and the absurd: mannequins in the dance hall
representing the disappeared and the tortured; stylized exploding or
deflating bodies literalizing the emotions of the troupe" (Newman).
Solanas himself plays a small cameo role in which he becomes dismem-
bered as a mannequin and literally explodes in frustration at the difficulties of financing and mounting the project. There is an attempt by the
group to maintain contact with artistic creation in Argentina itself. The
scriptwriter of the *tanguedia*, Juan Uno, supposedly lives in Argentina
and the composer Juan Dos, in exile, tries to make sense of his words,
written on scraps of paper or received by telephone. (There is a clear
homage to the Julio Cortázar of *Rayuela* [*Hopscotch*; 1963; see the section on Argentina], who danced a similar hopscotch between Europe and
Argentina.) The film explores the pain of the central characters, in
particular that of the lead female dancer who remembers a disappeared
husband, tries to make sense of everyday existence, and fuel a desire to
create, despite the fact that the funding of the project is shaky and the
potential audience unclear.

Yet the film cannot remain in the vast rehearsal room of the *tanguedia*, the theatrical location of suffering and creation, for it needs to reconstruct a political message, the renovation of Peronism. In the beginning of the final sequence "Volver" (Going Home), as Kathleen Newman accurately points out, the narrative focuses in on a small tableau. Gerardo, an intellectual who now works as a security man, has a dream in which he is visited by San Martín, the Argentine Independence hero, and by Carlos Gardel, who was of French origin. Both these men died far from Argentina, Gardel in a plane crash in Colombia and San Martín in France after decades of exile. All three men listen to Gardel's tango "Volver." They represent a familiar Peronist triumvirate of a "progressive" military man (Perón was a soldier, and one of the props of Peronism was at least the tacit support of the armed forces); the "people" as represented by Gardel, the soul and "voice" of Argentina; and the intellectual, the political theorist. A similar group would sit round "a table of dreams" in Solanas's next film *Sur* (Southside; 1988), which deals with the painful return of Argentina to democracy. It does not appear that Gerardo questions his radical analysis of the early 1970s: only the brutality of the military, it seems, interrupted a viable political process. The "return" is linked to the return of Peronism. The lessons of radicalism, its authoritarian backlash, and the fracturing of a nation, so painfully explored in the Chilean Raúl Ruiz's *Diálogos de exilados* (Dialogue of Exiles) made in 1974, also in Paris, are seen here to be elided. History has shown that the survival of Peronism has been ensured, at least in the short term, by Menem, a president who has dismantled most of its basic tenets. When Solanas criticized this president in 1991, a hit squad wounded him in the leg. Like *La hora de los hornos*, *Tangos* reveals a director of great formal invention whose political analysis still resists nuance. Yet just as *La hora* is probably still the best known political documentary of the sixties, so *Tangos* has brought to a wide audience in Latin America, Europe, and the United States the huge emotional impact of the pain of the exile experience. In *Diálogo de exilados*, Ruiz quoted Brecht ironically: "The best school of dialectic is emigration, the most skillful dialecticians are exiles. It is change that forces them into exile, and they are only interested in change.... If their adversaries prevail over them, they calculate the price they must have paid for their victory and they have a sharp eye for contradiction." Solanas is not the most nuanced dialectician. The exile experience did, however, generate a number of important fictional films and, in particular, documentaries. Chilean cineastes were most active in this area.

XIII

In 1982 the Argentine filmmaker María Luisa Bemberg and her producer, Lita Stantic (who runs the most successful women's independent production company in Latin America, GEA Cinematográfica), began work on the script of *Camila*, based on the true story of Camila O'Gorman, a woman from the Argentine aristocracy who eloped with a priest during the Rosas dictatorship of the mid-nineteenth century and was executed, with her lover, for sexual immorality and blasphemy. Throughout the year's elaboration of the script, they did not know if they would be allowed to film in Argentina. The military dictatorship was crumbling in the aftermath of the Falklands/Malvinas war, but democratic succession was not yet assured. Bemberg had already encountered hostile censorship when in her earlier *Señora de nadie* (No One's Woman; 1982) she had attempted to include a homosexual in her exploration of the marginal status of a separated woman. "They told me that it was a very bad example of Argentine mothers and that we couldn't put, in their phrase, a *maricón* (fag), in the film. The colonel (who ran the National Film Institute) said that he would rather have a son who had cancer than one who was a homosexual, so I couldn't do it" (quoted in King, "Assailing" 161). To get around censorship, they signed a coproduction contract with Spain to guarantee release in the Spanish market at least. Shooting began, however, the day after Alfonsín's election victory in December 1983, and the project could proceed without fear of overt censorship. The project was, nonetheless, kept under close scrutiny by the Catholic hierarchy, which ranks among the most reactionary in Latin America. The film managed to disarm some ecclesiastical criticism by having Camila seduce the priest, but it also makes it very clear that patriarchal values are inscribed in an alliance of large landowners and the Catholic Church. In December 1986, the Church tried to force the state television channel not to show the film over the Christmas period since it was perceived as undermining traditional worship.

The film is also transparently clear in its use of history as a commentary on the recent events of the so-called dirty war against subversion in Argentina (1976-82). The dictatorship of Juan Manuel de Rosas has always been viewed by liberal intellectuals as a site of a clash between liberal civilization and autarchic barbarism. The writers of the Rosas dictatorship, in exile in Chile or in Montevideo—Domingo Faustino Sarmiento, Esteban Echeverría, José Mármol—produced a great deal of protest literature in Manichaean terms, including Sarmiento's vertebral *Facundo* (1848). Camila O'Gorman was, of course, their contemporary, but her story would not fit neatly into the River Plate romantic mode, which inscribed women characters like the heroine of Mármol's *Amalia* (1851-55) as ethereal clichés of perfect womanhood. In her life, and in this film, Camila subverts such neat stereotypes. Anti-Peronist writers in the 1940s, such as Adolfo Bioy Casares and Jorge Luis Borges, wrote savage attacks on the government through allegorical references to the Rosas period. It took Borges, however, a number of years to realize that the "gentlemen" (his term) who overthrew the Peronists in 1976 were in fact engaged in a campaign of systematic murder. Just before his death in 1986, Borges attended the trials of the military and came out in tears saying that the armed forces had behaved in a way that he found un-imaginable. It was Bemberg, not Borges, who had the imagination to show the horrors of the recent past: the two young lovers sacrificed by Rosas clearly prefigure the deaths of so many young people in the "dirty" war.

Interestingly, Bemberg chooses melodrama as her narrative mode, which, as we have seen, has a strong tradition in Latin America. Like many filmmakers of the Alfonsín period, including Luis Puenzo with his Oscar-winning *La historia oficial* (The Official Story; 1986), Bemberg works within "mainstream" narratives. The oppositional practices of the 1960s, "political" as opposed to "commercial" cinema, were in general not appropriate to the conditions of the 1980s, which were ruled by the mar-ketplace and the increasing globalization of the media industries. Also, new movies were not calls to arms, but rather a reflection on the recent past.

Bemberg deploys melodramatic elements very skilfully "as constitu-ents of a system of punctuation, giving expressive color and chromatic contrast to the story-line by orchestrating the emotional ups and downs of the intrigue" (Gledhill 30). The spectacle and moral polarizations of *Camila* do not manipulate the audience (as a mere "tear-jerker"), but instead serve as points of clarification and identification. For, as critic Christine Gledhill has noted, the characters of successful melodrama become objects of pathos because they are constructed as victims of forces that lie beyond their control and/or understanding. But pathos, unlike pity, appeals to the understanding as well as to the emotions. The spectator is involved with the characters, but can exercise pity only by evaluating signs that the protagonists cannot have access to.

The opening credit sequence sees the arrival of a carriage to what seems to be an idyllic country house. Camila as a child is waiting with the household to greet La Perichona, her grandmother, who was the lover of an executed politician of the Independence period, Liniers. She became a *cause célèbre*, branded as a spy and as a transgressor. She is now being delivered to her family under house arrest, condemned as prisoner to live out her days as a literal "mad woman in the attic." The small child is seen to have an immediate bond with her grandmother, despite the disapproving looks of her father. The grandmother asks her, "Do you like love stories?" In the early scenes of the film, Camila visits her grandmother's "forbidden" room where desire is stigmatized as madness. From the outset, therefore, the spectator is given a reading of the melodrama that explores the terrible consequences of desire colliding with reality. The idyllic country house is seen as the bastion of the patriarchal order. Camila's permitted movement is between the house and the church, where the sermon and the confessional once more reaffirm the traditional order. When she moves in the street or in bookshops (she is an avid reader: literature also releases desires), male members of the family attempt to control her space. Ironically, radically, the male bastions of the sermon and the confessional become the privileged site of the transgression. A young priest arrives and speaks out in his sermons against injustice. In the confessional, where sin is usually admitted and absolved, Camila confesses her desires: the seduction takes place as a play of looks through the confessional grille and through a frank exchange of views and sentiments that cannot be condemned as sinful.

The spectator can thus clearly perceive the contrast between the traditional patriarchal family and the utopian family established by the lovers, between state power and love and between traditional and progressive Catholicism. When Rosas's gangs of state terror kill and maim, placing the liberal bookseller's head in public view on a spike, the parallels between them and the anonymous killers of the "dirty war" become inescapable. The film also undermines the stereotypes enshrined in such codes as the nineteenth-century "cult of the womenhood," a blend of piety, purity, domesticity, and submissiveness, or the idea of the "fallen woman," a character who populates literature and film and who must be punished for the transgression of sexual mores. The lovers are condemned to death by patriarchal powers: the dictator Rosas; Camila's father; opportunistic opposition goups (e.g., Sarmiento from exile) who try to score political points under the banner of morality; and the Catholic hierarchy.

Camila also allowed Argentine audiences a form of collective catharsis, enabling them to experience in public emotions that had to remain private during the years of the dictatorship. Two million people wept at the story of Camila O'Gorman, which was their own story, an astonishing figure for Argentine cinema. For many months, the film outgrossed the main Hollywood features, *ET* and *Porky's*.

XIV

Camila benefited from credits given by the State under the Alfonsín regime. Brazilian cinema in the 1970s and the 1980s was largely funded by credits from the state body, Embrafilme. The Cinema Novo "outsiders" of the early 1960s became the chief beneficiaries of the state and many critical films were made mainly from "within" the system. In Mexico under President Echeverría in 1970-76 and in the last year, 1991, under Salinas de Gortari, filmmaking has flourished. Filmmakers have constantly debated the problem of state funding, of becoming swallowed up by the "philanthropic ogre," Octavio Paz's celebrated image for the state. At the moment of writing, with a deepening economic crisis throughout Latin America, state subsidies are declining everywhere, and the chill winds of the market threaten to blow away many of the achievements of the last thirty years. While filmmakers question the limitations imposed by working with the state, they realize only too well the further limitations imposed by working without state support. The search for funds leads to increasingly complex coproduction arrangements with, for example, European producers, and such coproductions, which often include foreign "stars" as a necessary marketing strategy, question the whole basis of the "national" in a media world of increasing globalization.

The North American industry has always controlled a large proportion of screen time all over Latin America. National cinema has only, therefore, a small percentage of its own "natural" market. Thus, "unable to depend even on home markets for a return on investments and lacking access to significant ancillary markets (television, cable, video), unprotected Latin American film industries have lacked the capital necessary to sustain continuous production on a large scale. Inevitably, the result has been the underdevelopment of most national film industries" (Johnson, "In the Belly"). As we have seen, Mexico, Argentina, and Brazil have the strongest "industries" in Latin America and their brief moments of visibility have normally been made possible by state support. Such was the case in Mexico from 1970 to 1976 when, after the massacre at Tlatelolco in 1968, the state sought to woo the intellectual field. Many different resources were poured into cinema, and few could resist these blandishments. The government supported national and also "exile" cinema. The Chilean, Miguel Littín, made his high-budget, internationalist, Third World epic *Actas de Marusia* (Letters from Marusia; 1975) in Mexico. The state had an ability to pay for, and absorb, films that were critical of the government, such as *Cascabel* (Rattlesnake; 1976). Talented directors like Arturo Ripstein and Jaime Hermosillo made some of their best work in this period. But perhaps the most significant film to reveal the extent of the freedom of filmmaking under Echeverría is *Canoa* (1975), directed by Felipe Cazals. The film is firmly based on events that took place on 14 September 1968 in the village of San Miguel Canoa, a few miles from the city of Puebla. Five young employees of the University of Puebla on a climbing expedition were forced by torrential rain to seek shelter in the village and were later set upon by a mob of villagers led by the Catholic priest, who accused them of being communist student subversives out to desecrate the church. Two of the group were hacked to death, together with a villager who gave them shelter; the other three were dragged to the main square, where their lives were saved only by the opportune arrival of the police. The incident is a vivid comment on the force of antistudent hysteria generated by the government and the press in the months preceding this massacre (and the massacre in Tlatelolco one month later). It also stresses the uneven development of Mexican society where, only minutes away from a sophisticated urban capital, local communities are still prey to reactionary messianic forces.

The script was written by Tomás Pérez Turrent, who also published a book on the making of the film. This work stresses the meticulous documentation and reconstruction of the events. As in *El chacal de Nahueltoro*, the force of the "real" becomes an important narrative device. The exact timing of each incident is indicated on the screen as the boys move unknowingly to their fate. Both scriptwriter and director had access to the survivors of the massacre who, initially reluctantly, were drawn into the research for the film and later into the film itself. As part of its "realist effect," the film intercuts reconstructed "documentary" footage in the main narrative. The "documentary" serves two functions. First it shows, in a long early sequence, the nature of poverty, isolation, feudalism and Catholic bigotry in Canoa. It also serves as a Brechtian device, an attempt at distancing the spectator from the hypnotic terror of the events. For example, when an ax smashes through the door that shelters the boys from the braying crowd, the narrative cuts to a later "documentary" statement by the priest. However, if Cazals is using Brechtian devices, they do not succeed. His strength lies in the visceral: the meticulous plotting of the events and the orchestration of a mounting tension and the horrible force of real events.

After two presidencies of neglect, Mexican cinema, with the support of President Carlos Salinas de Gortari, is once again showing signs of health. In 1991, as cinema stagnated all over Latin America, Mexican cinema was showered with prizes and favorable critical attention. Even Octavio Paz, long-term scourge of the philanthropic ogre, now openly supported what he perceived to be the modernization of the PRI under Salinas. His periodical, *Vuelta* (Return), no longer contains articles critical of state power. Once again, the state allowed cinema to film "difficult" subjects. Jorge Fons, for example, made *Rojo amanecer* (Red Dawn; 1990) on the student massacre at Tlatelolco. Several features were also made by women. It is too recent to have these films firmly in focus, but this recovery illustrates one significant point. If cinema is to survive, it must be through a considered mixture of private and public funding.

XV

Carlos Sorin's *La pelicula del rey* (A King and His Movie; 1985) neatly encapsulates the enthusiasms, but also the difficulties of current film production. The film recounts a young filmmaker's desperate attempt to tell the story of Orelie Antoine de Tounens, a Frenchman who in 1861 founded the kingdom of Araucania and Patagonia. The Frenchman's deranged utopic quest is mirrored by that of the filmmaker. Independent filmmaking in a world of global media struggles is an almost unnegotiable anachronism. The director in this film is very reminiscent of the "peripheral" German Werner Herzog, whose world is that of scapegoats, of self-tormented egomaniacs, of supermen fighting losing battles in a world dominated by advanced technology (Elsaesser). If Herzog has the demented drive to force hundreds of Amazon Indians to pull a boat over a mountain range in *Fitzcarraldo*, the Argentine filmmaker has no money to keep his cast or his extras together, as his backers withdraw financial support. He needs an epic battle scene, but the huge troupe of marauding Indians is in the end played by two or three reluctant horses and actors. The director is comically positioned as an underdog, but also as an overreacher. Yet there is no real critique offered of his utopian desire. When the director is forced to abandon the shooting, and retreats to the city on a battered bus, a gleam comes into his eye: another mad project is being formulated. Making films on the periphery of an increasingly deregulated transnational world of signs and electronic impulses is obviously a quixotic venture, but one that seems always necessary. In the present unstable political and cultural environment, there is still a generation of filmmakers with an idea in their heads and a camera in their hands, to use Glauber Rocha's famous phrase. García Márquez, a willing general in this particular industrial labyrinth, summed up this mood of optimism in a speech made at the inauguration of the Latin American Film Foundation in 1985: "Between 1952 and 1955, four of us who are now on board this boat studied at the Centro Sperimentale in Rome: Julio García Espinosa, [Cuban] Vice Minister of Culture for Cinema, Fernando Birri, the great pope of the New Latin American cinema, Tomás Gutiérrez Alea, one of its most notable craftsmen and I, who wanted nothing more in life than to become the filmmaker I never became.... The fact that this evening we are still talking like madmen about the same thing, after thirty years, and that there are so many Latin Americans from all parts and from different generations also talking about the same thing, I take as one further proof of an indestructible idea" (quoted in *Anuario 88* 1).

BIBLIOGRAPHY

Anuario 88. La Habana: Escuela Internacional de cine y TV, 1988.

Bartra, Roger. *La jaula de la melancolía: identidad y metamorfosis del mexicano*. México, D.F.: Grijalbo, 1987.

Burton, J. *Cinema and Social Change in Latin America: Conversations with Film-makers*. Austin: University of Texas Press, 1986.

Chanan, Michael. *The Cuban Image*. London: British Film Institute, 1985.

D'Lugo, Marvin. "Transparent Women: Gender and Nation in Cuban Cinema." In A. López, M. Alvarado, J. King, eds. *Mediating Two Worlds: the Americas and Europe*. London: British Film Institute, forthcoming.

Elsaesser, Tomas. "Hyper-Retro-or Counter Cinema: European Cinema and Third Cinema between Hollywood and Art Cinema." In A. López, M. Alvarado, J. King, eds. *Mediating Two Worlds: the Americas and Europe*. London: British Film Institute, forthcoming.

Fernández, Adela. *El Indio Fernández: vida y mito*. México, D.F.: Panorama, 1986.

Gledhill, C., ed. *Home Is Where the Heart Is*. London: British Film Institute, 1987.

Johnson, Randal. *Cinema Novo x 5: Masters of Contemporary Brazilian Film*. Austin: University of Texas Press, 1984.

Johnson, Randal. *The Film Industry in Brazil: Culture and the State*. Pittsburgh: University of Pittsburgh, 1987.

Johnson, Randal. "In the Belly of the Ogre: Cinema and State in Latin America." In A. López, M. Alvarado, J. King, eds. *Mediating Two Worlds: the Americas and Europe*. London: British Film Institute, forthcoming.

Johnson, Randal, and Robert Stam, eds. *Brazilian Cinema*. Cranbury, N.J.: Associated University Press, 1982.

King, John. "Assailing the Heights of Macho Pictures." 158-170. In S. Bassnett, ed., *Knives and Angels: Women Writers in Latin America*. London: Zed, 1990.

King, John. *Magical Reels: A History of Cinema in Latin America*. London: Verso, 1990. For a detailed bibliography of critical works on Latin American cinema in English, see the bibliography of this work. Some sections of this essay are drawn from this book. The author thanks the editors of Verso for their permissions.

López, Ana. "At the Limits of Documentary." 412-417. In J. Burton, ed., *The Social Documentary in Latin America*. Pittsburgh: University of Pittsburgh Press, 1990.

López, Ana. "Tears and Desire: Women and Melodrama in the 'Old' Mexican Cinema." In A. López, M. Alvarado, J. King, eds. *Mediating Two Worlds: the Americas and Europe*. London: British Film Institute, forthcoming.

Monsiváis, Carlos. *Escenas de pudor y liviandad*. México, D.F.: Grijalbo, 1988.

Monsiváis, Carlos. "Gabriel Figueroa: la institución del punto de vista." *Artes de México*, nueva época 2 (Winter 1988): 65.

Newman, Kathleen. "National Cinema after Globalisation: Fernando E. Solanas' *Sur* and the Exiled Nation." In A. López, M. Alvarado, J. King, eds. *Mediating Two Worlds: the Americas and Europe*. London: British Film Institute, forthcoming.

Pérez Turrent, Tomás. *Canoa: historia de un hecho vergonzoso*. Puebla: Universidad Autónoma de Puebla, 1984.

Rocha, Glauber. "The Aesthetics of Hunger." 13-14. In Michael Chanan, ed., *Twenty-Five Years of the New Latin American Cinema*. London: British Film Institute, 1983.

Rowe, William, and Vivian Schelling. *Memory and Modernity: Popular Culture in Latin America*. London: Verso, 1991.

Ruiz, Raúl. "No hacer más una película como si fuera la última." *Araucaria de Chile* 11 (1980): 102.

Sanjinés, Jorge. "We Invent a New Language through Popular Culture." *Framework* 10 (1979): 31.

Sanjinés, Jorge, and Grupo Ukamau. *Teoría y práctica de un cine junto al pueblo*. México, D.F.: Siglo XXI, 1979.

Sarlo, Beatriz. "Cultural Mixture." In A. López, M. Alvarado, J. King, eds. *Mediating Two Worlds: the Americas and Europe*. London: British Film Institute, forthcoming.

Sigal, Silvia. *Intelectuales y poder en la década del sesenta*. Buenos Aires: Puntosur, 1991.

Stam, Robert. "*The Hour of the Furnaces* and the Two Avant-gardes." 251-266. In J. Burton, ed. *Social Documentary in Latin America*. Pittsburgh: University of Pittsburgh Press, 1990.

Terán, Oscar. *Nuestros años sesentas*. Buenos Aires: Puntosur, 1991.

Todorov, Tzvetan. *La Conquête de l'Amérique: la question de l'autre*. Paris: Seuil, 1982.

Xavier, Ismail. "El Dorado as Hell." In A. López, M. Alvarado, J. King, eds. *Mediating Two Worlds: the Americas and Europe*. London: British Film Institute, forthcoming.

INDEX OF NAMES

(Alphabetization follows the norms of the Library of Congress)

Abbad y Lasierra, Iñigo, 556
Abente y Lago, Victoriano, 477
Abramo, Livio, 489
Abreu, José Vicente, 643
Abreu Gómez, Ermilio, 362
Abril, Pablo, 514
Abril, Xavier, 515
Aceval, Benjamín, 475
Acevedo Díaz, Eduardo, 605-607, 626
Acevedo Hernández, Antonio, 131-134, 154, 158
Acosta, Agustín, 242
Acosta, Iván, 677
Acosta, Oscar, 352, 354
Acosta de Samper, Soledad, 197, 198
Acuña, Manuel, 386
Acuña de Figueroa, Francisco, 597, 599
Adán, Martín, 515, 517, 545
Addison, Joseph, 577
Adolph, José B., 538, 539
Adonias Filho. See Aguiar, Adonias
Adorno, Theodor, 688, 690, 691, 694, 704
Adoum, Jorge Enrique, 301, 306, 308, 311
Agosín, Marjorie, 652
Aguiar, Adonias (Adonias Filho), 177
Aguiar, Adriano M., 477
Aguilar Mora, Jorge, 430, 437-438
Aguilera, Julio Fausto, 329
Aguilera, Rodolfo (Fito), 465
Aguilera Garramuño, Marco Tulio, 212, 213
Aguilera Malta, Demetrio, 301, 302, 305, 312

Aguirre, Isidora, 164, 165
Aguirre, Juan Bautista, 293, 294
Aguirre, Lope de, 181
Aguirre, Nataniel, 70-72
Agurcia, Mercedes, 352
Agustín, José, 436-438, 723
Agustini, Delmira, 614
Aínsa, Fernando, 622
Alas, Leopoldo, 240
Alba, Patricia, 547
Albán, Laureano, 224, 225
Albán Gómez, Ernesto, 312
Alberdi, Juan Bautista, 6, 7, 33, 600-602
Alberti, Rafael, 199, 486
Albizúrez Palma, Francisco, 331
Alcalde, Alfonso, 151
Alcázar, Ligia, 462
Aldana, Juan Sebastián, 645
Alegría, Ciro, 518, 520-522, 528, 532, 548, 550
Alegría, Claribel, 591
Alegría, Fernando, 151, 163, 652
Aleijadinho, 97, 98
Aleixandre, Eduardo, 199, 200
Alemán, José María, 457
Alemán, Mateo, 370
Alemán, Vicente. See Barrera, Claudio
Alencar, José de, 101-105
Alexis, Jacques Stéphen, 337, 338, 343
Alfaro, Eloy, 298
Alfaro, Ricardo J., 455
Alfie, David, 698
Alfonseca, Miguel, 278
Algarín, Miguel, 667, 668
Allende, Isabel, 161, 165, 171, 175

Almeida, Manuel Antônio de, 103
Alonso, Carmen de. See Carrasco Barrios, Margarita
Alonso, Fernando, 721
Alonso, Luis Ricardo, 266, 674
Alonso, Manuel, 558-560, 577
Alonso y Telles, José, 606
Alsina, Valentín, 600
Altamirano, Ignacio, 380, 385, 386, 406
Althusser, Louis, 690, 694
Alurista, 661
Alva Ixtlilxóchitl, Fernando de, 363, 364
Alvarado, Elvia, 353
Alvarado, Huberto, 328
Alvarado, Pedro de, 320
Alvarado de Ricord, Elsie, 461
Alvarez, José Sixto, 15
Alvarez, Julia, 652
Alvarez, Santiago, 751
Alvarez, Soledad, 280
Alvarez Baragaño, José, 253
Alvarez Castro, Miguel, 584, 585
Alvarez Constantino, Higilio, 698
Alvarez Gardeazábal, Alvaro, 210, 211
Alvarez Lleras, Antonio, 211
Alvarez Sáenz, Félix, 543
Alves, Castro, 100
Amado, Jorge, 111, 417, 688, 715
Amadori, Luis César, 735
Amaya Amador, Ramón, 351
Ambrogi, Arturo, 586
Amorim, Enrique, 619-621
Ananía, José, 29
Anaya, Rudolfo, 658
Anchieta, José de, 97
Anderson Imbert, Enrique, 3, 31, 714
Andrade, Carlos Drummond de, 111, 116, 200
Andrade, Joaquim Pedro de, 732
Andrade, Jorge, 118
Andrade, Mário de, 108, 109, 119, 120, 730, 732, 733
Andrade, Oswald de, 105, 108, 109, 117, 119, 732, 733
Andreiev, Leonid, 24
Andreve, Guillermo, 458
Angarita, Gonzalo, 700
Angel, Albucía, 212, 213

Angulo y Guridi, Javier, 273
Anjos, Augusto dos, 107
Antequera, José de, 469
Anzaldúa, Gloria, 652, 663, 680, 681
Apollinaire, Guillaume, 276, 568
Appleyard, José Luis, 486
Aquinas, Thomas, 473
Arango, Luis Alfredo, 329
Arango y Parreño, Francisco de, 241
Araucho, Manuel de, 598
Araujo, Orlando, 643
Aray, Edmundo, 644
Arce, Manuel José, 584
Arce, Margot, 566
Arcocha, Juan, 265
Ardila, Julio, 464
Ardissone, José Luis, 489
Arellano, Jorge Eduardo, 446
Arenal, Humberto, 262
Arenas, Braulio, 151
Arenas, Reinaldo, 266
Arévalo Martínez, Rafael, 323, 324
Argandoña, Frontaura, 84, 85
Arguedas, Alcides, 75-77, 79, 80
Arguedas, José María, 416, 509, 519, 521-523, 525, 532, 548, 550
Argüello, Lino, 447
Argüello, Santiago, 447
Argueta, Manlio, 588, 591
Arias, Arturo, 331
Arias, Augusto, 310
Arias, Ron, 659
Arias de Saavedra, Hernando, 469
Arias Suárez, Eduardo, 195
Arias Trujillo, Bernardo, 195
Aridjis, Homero, 434
Arlt, Roberto, 22, 48, 54, 619, 715, 723
Armendáriz, Carlos, 737, 738
Armijo, Roberto, 591
Aron, Raymond, 687
Arosemena, Justo, 454
Arosemena, Mariano, 454
Arosemena, Pablo, 455
Arózteguy, Abdón, 606
Arráiz, Antonio, 638
Arreola, Juan José, 413
Arrieta, Rafael Alberto, 21
Arriví, Francisco, 572

Arrufat, Antón, 256
Artel, Jorge, 188
Artiles, Freddy, 258
Arzáns Orsúa y Vela, Bartolomé, 67, 68, 70
Ascasubi, Hilario, 9
Asís, Jorge, 40, 41, 52
Asturias, Miguel Angel, 320, 323, 325-327, 352
Asunción Silva, José, 187, 197-199
Auden, W. H., 514
Avelino, Andrés, 275
Avellaneda, Andrés, 714
Avila, Julio Enrique, 588
Avila Jiménez, Antonio, 77
Avilés Blonda, Máximo, 277
Avilés Fabila, René, 430
Ayala, Eligio, 482
Ayala, Eusebio, 482
Ayestarán, Lauro, 604
Ayusto, Juan José, 278
Azaña y Llano, Josefa de, 503, 504
Azara, Félix de, 472
Azevedo, Aluísio, 101
Azevedo, Alvares de, 100
Azevedo, Arthur, 117
Azofeifa, Isaac Felipe, 224
Azuela, Mariano, 396-398, 400, 404, 405, 413, 417
Azulay, Daniel, 697

Babot, Jarl Ricardo, 464
Baca, Jimmy Santiago, 650, 662
Bacardí Moreau, Emilio, 247
Báez, Cecilio, 478, 481
Baeza, Flores, 276
Bahr, Eduardo, 352
Bakhtin, Mikhail, 283
Bakunin, Mikhail A., 143
Balboa, Silvestre de, 227, 228, 259
Balbuena, Bernardo de, 371
Ballagas, Emilio, 567
Ballivián, Vicente, 69
Ballón Aguirre, Enrique, 550
Balza, José, 643, 644
Balzac, Honoré de, 577
Banchero, Andersson, 622
Banchs, Alberto, 31

Bancroft, Hubert Howe, 655
Bandeira, Manuel, 117
Baquero, Gastón, 243, 254
Baquíjano y Carrillo, José, 505
Barahona, José Porfirio, 353
Barba, Eugenio, 529
Barba Jacob, Porfirio. See Osorio, Miguel Angel
Barbero, Jesús Martín, 737
Barbieri, Vicente, 27
Barbosa, João Alfredo, 117
Barco Centenera, Martín del, 471
Bareiro, Francisco Luis, 478
Bareiro Saguier, Rubén, 486, 487
Barletta, Leónidas, 22
Barnet, Miguel, 265, 718, 721
Barnoya, José, 330
Barrera, Claudio, 351, 353, 354
Barrera, Isaac J., 289
Barrera Valverde, Alfonso, 308
Barreto, Afonso Henriques de Lima, 107, 119, 744
Barrett, Rafael, 479
Barrio, Raymond, 659
Barrios, Agustín, 482
Barrios, Eduardo, 154, 155, 157, 158
Barrios Chungara, Domitila, 718, 719
Barros, Daniel, 154
Barros Arana, Diego, 140
Barroso, Maria Alice, 715
Barthes, Roland, 694
Bartra, Roger, 740, 741
Bastidas, Antonio, 291
Bataille, Georges, 422
Batres Montúfar, José, 322, 585
Battilana de Gásperi, Raúl, 481
Baudelaire, Charles, 198, 275, 422, 459
Baudrillard, Jean, 694
Baur, Elizabeth K., 701
Bazán, Juan F., 485
Beaumarchais, Pierre-Augustin Caron de, 136
Bécquer, Gustavo Adolfo, 127, 143, 152, 230, 459, 477, 558, 559
Bedregal, Yolanda, 82
Belaúnde, Víctor Andrés, 510
Belaval, Emilio S., 566, 569, 572
Beleño, Guillermo E., 465

Beleño, Joaquín, 464
Belli, Carlos Germán, 544, 545
Belli, Gioconda, 450
Bello, Andrés, 135-141, 558, 634
Bello, Inés. See, Echeverría Bello de Laraín Alcalde, Inés
Bellolio, Walter, 307
Bemberg, María Luisa, 763
Benarós, León, 27
Bendaña, Armando, 330
Benedetti, Mario, 613, 620, 622-624, 627
Benedetto, Antonio di, 34
Béneke, Walter, 590
Benítez, Alejandrina, 559
Benítez, Fernando, 433
Benítez, María Bibiana, 557, 559
Benítez Rojo, Antonio, 266
Benjamin, Walter, 742
Berceo, Gonzalo de, 136, 138
Berenguer, Amanda, 620
Bergeaud, Eméric, 337
Beristaín y Souza, José Mariano, 376
Bermúdez, Alenka, 329
Bermúdez, Hernán Antonio, 354
Bermúdez, María Elvira, 716
Bermúdez, Ricardo J., 460
Bermúdez, Washington P., 605
Bermúdez de la Torre, Pedro José, 503
Bernal, Juan José, 585
Bernal, Rafael, 716
Bernal, Vicente, 655
Bernárdez, Francisco Luis, 21
Berro, Adolfo, 599, 603
Betances, Ramón Emeterio, 558, 560, 562, 664
Beverley, John, 694
Bianchi, Soledad, 176
Bilac, Olavo, 107
Bilbao, Francisco, 134, 135
Billanueva, Marta, 144
Bioy Casares, Adolfo, 30, 618, 714, 721, 764
Birri, Fernando, 749, 751, 769
Blanco, Andrés Eloy, 638
Blanco, Eduardo, 634
Blanco, Guillermo, 164, 165
Blanco, Tomás, 568
Blanco Fombona, Rufino, 138, 638

Blest Gana, Alberto, 127, 135, 137, 140, 142, 143, 157
Bloch, Ernst, 283
Bocanegra, Matías de, 371
Bogado Gondra, Basilio, 489
Bogado Gondra, Juan Félix, 489
Boh, Luis Alberto, 489
Bolívar, Simón, 634
Bombal, María Luisa, 134, 144, 160, 161
Bonasso, Miguel, 44
Bonifáz Nuño, Rubén, 416
Bonilla, Abelardo, 218
Bonilla, Ronald, 224
Bonomini, Angel, 31
Borda Leaño, Héctor, 82
Borges, Fermín, 256
Borges, Jorge Luis, 21, 29-31, 48, 56-58, 116, 185, 200, 282, 352, 484, 515, 591, 618, 625, 688, 710, 713, 714, 721, 722, 733, 764
Borja, Arturo, 305, 306, 310
Borjas, Edilberto, 353
Borrero, Dulce María, 242
Borrero, Juana, 231
Boscana, Gerónimo, 654
Bosch, Juan, 276, 278
Bosco, Eduardo, 27
Bosi, Alfredo, 117
Botero, Juan José, 195
Botero Restrepo, Jesús, 195
Boti, Regino, 242
Boullosa, Carmen, 435-436
Bourdieu, Pierre, 694
Braga, Rubem, 117
Brañas, César, 325, 326, 329
Brandy, Carlos, 620
Brannon, Carmen. See Lars, Claudia
Brasseur de Bourbourg, Charles Etienne de, 318, 319
Brau, Salvador, 560
Bravo, José Antonio, 542, 543
Bravo de Lagunas y Villela, Josefa, 503
Bray, Arturo, 483
Brecht, Bertolt, 762
Brene, José, 259, 260
Breton, André, 151, 276
Brierre, Jean F., 336
Brinton, Daniel, 319

Brito, Alonso A., 350
Brito, Aristeo, 651, 661
Britto García, Luis, 643
Britton, Rosa María, 466
Brizuela, Ramón Antonio, 645
Brocha Gorda. See Jaimes, Julio Lucas
Brouchard, Carl, 36
Browner, Carole, 705, 706
Bruce-Novoa, Juan, 658, 676
Brull, Mariano, 242
Brunet, Marta, 144, 160, 161
Bryce Echenique, Alfredo Marcelo, 531, 532, 535-537, 540, 542, 543
Buenaventura, Enrique, 211
Buero Vallejo, Antonio, 81
Buitrago, Fanny, 212, 213
Bullrich, Silvina, 51
Bunge, Carlos Octavio, 610
Burciaga, José Antonio, 661
Burgos, Julia de, 569, 665
Burton, Julianne, 749
Bustamante, Carlos, 587
Bustamante, Ricardo José, 71
Bustamante y Ballivián, Enrique, 512
Bustos Domecq, Honorio, 30, 714
Byrne, Bonifacio, 242
Byron, George Gordon, 136, 459, 599

Caballero, Bernardino, 475, 477
Caballero Calderón, Eduardo, 197, 202
Cabán Vale, Antonio, 574
Cabañas, Esteban. See Colombino, Carlos
Cabello de Carbonera, Mercedes, 509
Cabeza Lacayo, Omar, 719
Cabieses, Manuel, 720
Cabotín. See Carrillo, Enrique A.
Cabral, Manuel de, 276, 278
Cabrales, Luis Alberto, 448
Cabrera, Francisco Manrique, 566
Cabrera, Lydia, 248, 249
Cabrera Infante, Guillermo, 252, 264, 265
Cabrujas, José, 643
Cadalso, José, 136
Cadenas, Rafael, 644
Caicedo, Andrés, 212, 213
Calabi Abaroa, Guido, 81

Calancha, Antonio de la, 66
Caldera, Daniel, 154
Calderini, Gustavo, 489
Calderón de la Barca, Pedro, 136, 138, 363, 373
Calderón y Badillo, Juana, 503
Calero Orozco, Adolfo, 449
Callado, Antonio, 117
Calvetti, Jorge, 27
Calvo, Carlos, 475, 480
Calvo, César, 543
Calzadilla, Juan, 644
Camacho Ramírez, Arturo, 199
Camarano de Sucre, Yolanda, 465
Cambaceres, Eugenio, 14
Camões, Luis de, 97
Campero Echazú, Octavio, 77
Campo, Angel de, 391
Campo, Estanislao del, 9, 10
Campoamor, Ramón de, 558
Campobello, Nellie, 414, 435
Campos, Julieta, 423
Campos, Marco Antonio, 431
Campos Cervera, Herib, 486
Campos Medeiros de Albuquerque, José Joaquim de, 715
Camps, David, 259, 261
Canales, José Antonio, 591
Canales, Nemesio, 564, 565
Canales, Tirso. See Canales, José Antonio
Cañas, Alberto, 224
Cañas, José Marín, 222
Cañas, Juan José, 585
Cancela, Arturo, 21
Candanedo, César A., 463, 464
Cândido, Antonio, 117
Cané, Miguel, 12, 600, 602
Cane'K, Caby Domatilia, 330
Canese, Jorge, 489, 490
Canese, Ricardo, 489
Cantinflas, 740, 741
Capoche, Luis, 65
Capote, Truman, 190, 716
Carballido, Emilio, 416, 426
Cárcamo, Jacobo, 353
Cardenal, Ernesto, 225, 448-450
Cárdenas, Bernardino de, 469

Cárdenas, Eliécer, 305, 307, 308
Cárdenas, Raúl de, 256, 260
Cárdenas Acuña, Ignacio, 716
Cardi, Juan Angel, 717
Cardona, Alcira, 82
Cardona, Jenaro, 220, 221
Cardona Peña, Alfredo, 224
Cardoso, Lúcio, 111
Cardoza y Aragón, Luis, 328
Cardozo, Efraim, 485
Carías Reyes, Marcos, 350, 352
Carlyle, Thomas, 473
Caro, Miguel Antonio, 197, 198, 200, 207
Carpentier, Alejo, 248-251, 265, 283, 338, 344
Carpio, Manuel, 381
Carranza, Eduardo, 199
Carrasco Barrios, Margarita, 144, 145
Carrasquilla, Tomás, 185, 193, 194, 197, 211
Carrera Andrade, Jorge, 305, 306, 310, 311
Carrera, Margarita, 329
Carrero, Jaime, 573, 666, 668
Carrillo, Enrique A., 510
Carrillo, Francisco, 544
Carrió de la Vandera, Alonso, 501, 502
Carrión, Alejandro, 289
Carrión, Miguel de, 247
Cartagena Portolatín, Aída, 276, 284
Carvajal, Iván, 312
Carvajal, María Isabel, 221
Carvajal, Mario, 207, 208
Casaccia, Gabriel, 483, 484
Casal, Julián del, 230, 232, 233, 243
Casal, Lourdes, 675
Casas, Bartolomé de las, 123, 271, 320, 321, 327, 363, 364, 446, 470, 500
Casas, Myrna, 573
Caso, Antonio, 76
Castañeda, Pedro de, 654
Castañeda, Salvador, 429
Castañeda Aragón, Gregorio, 188
Castedo, Elena, 650, 651
Castellani, Leonardo, 713, 714
Castellanos, Dora, 200
Castellanos, Jesús, 247
Castellanos, Juan de, 180, 181, 196

Castellanos, Rosario, 415, 416, 431, 435
Castellanos Moya, Horacio, 353, 355
Castellón, Pedro Angel, 230
Castelnuovo, Elías, 22, 28, 50
Castera, Georges, 335
Castillo, Abelardo, 37
Castillo, Ana, 661, 662
Castillo, Eduardo, 197
Castillo, Efraím, 285
Castillo, Florencio del, 218
Castillo, Otto René, 329
Castillo, Roberto, 353
Castillo y Guevara, Francisca Josefa de, 180, 182, 183
Castrillo, Primo, 82
Castro, Fidel, 751
Castro, Gil de, 127
Castro Ríos, Andrés, 574
Castro Saavedra, Carlos, 200
Castro Titu Cusi Yupanqui, Diego de, 499
Catalá, Rafael, 675
Cazals, Felipe, 767
Cea, José Roberto, 591
Centeno de Osma, Gabriel, 497
Centurión, Juan Crisóstomo, 477
Cepeda Samudio, Alvaro, 185, 187, 189, 190, 211
Cerna, Ismael, 323
Cerruto, Oscar, 78, 82, 85-89
Cervantes, Lorna Dee, 662
Cervantes Saavedra, Miguel de, 136, 180, 403, 484, 502
Césaire, Aimé, 151, 751, 752
Ceselli, Juan José, 28, 48
Cesped, Man, 77
Céspedes, Augusto, 78, 80
Cestero, Tulio, 274
Cetina, Gutierre de, 370
Chacón, Eusebio, 655
Chacón, Felipe Maximiliano, 655
Chacón Nardi, Rafaela, 254
Chaffee, Lyman, 706, 707
Chamorro, Delfín, 477
Champs, Olga, 188
Chandler, Raymond, 46, 712
Changmarín, Carlos Francisco, 463, 465
Chaplin, Charles, 152

Charry Lara, Fernando, 199
Chase, Alfonso, 223
Chateaubriand, François René de, 136, 296, 599
Chauvel, Marie, 338
Chaves, Julio César, 485
Chaves de Ferreiro, Ana Iris, 485
Chávez, Angélico, 656
Chávez, Denise, 658
Chávez, Fernando, 300
Chávez Velasco, Waldo, 590
Chesterton, Gilbert Keith, 713
Chiáppori, Atilio, 31
Chiarella Kruger, Jorge, 529
Chirinos Arrieta, Eduardo, 548
Chirveches, Armando, 77
Chocano, José Santos, 324, 506, 511, 513, 514, 549
Chocrón, Isaac, 643
Chong Ruiz, Eustorgio, 463, 465
Chuez, Enrique, 465
Chumacero, Alí, 416
Churata, Gamaliel, 519
Cid Pérez, José, 675
Cienfuegos, Edwin, 331
Cienfuegos, Julia Guillermina, 329
Cieza de León, Pedro, 65, 66, 499
Cisneros, Antonio, 545, 546
Cisneros, Sandra, 650, 661, 662
Cocteau, Jean, 515
Cohen, Marcelo, 44, 59
Cojulún Bedoya, Carlos, 331
Colchado Lucio, Oscar, 543
Coll, Mauricio, 261
Collazos, Oscar, 437
Colombino, Carlos, 486
Colón, Jesús, 665
Columbres, Juan Carlos, 701
Columbus, Christopher, 176, 177, 181, 271
Colunje, Gil, 457
Concolorcorvo. See Carrió de la Vandera, Alonso
Congrains, Enrique, 525, 526
Conteris, Hiber, 622, 626
Conti, Haroldo, 43
Contreras, Francisco, 138
Córdoba, Matías de, 322

Córdoba y Salinas, Diego de, 66
Corneille, Pierre, 504
Cornejo, Leobardo, 698
Cornejo Polar, Antonio, 550
Coronel Urtecho, José, 448, 449
Correa, Arnaldo, 717
Correa, Julio, 483
Correa, Luis, 645
Correa, Viriato, 715
Corretjer, Juan Antonio, 567, 569, 570, 574, 665
Cortázar, Julio, 31, 34, 35, 39, 57, 116, 213, 532, 537, 591, 722, 723, 761
Cortés, Alfonso, 447
Cortés, Hernán, 361, 367, 368
Cossa, Roberto M., 37
Costa, Cláudio Manuel da, 98
Costa Gavra, Constantin, 626
Costa du Rels, Adolfo, 81
Costantini, Humberto, 37, 44
Cota-Cárdenas, Margarita, 661
Cote Lemus, Eduardo, 200
Coutinho, Afrânio, 117
Covarrubias, Francisco, 237
Cox, Mariana, 143, 144
Crespo Paniagua, Renato, 81
Cruchaga Santa María, Angel, 145, 146
Cruz, Juan, 600
Cruz Ayala [Alón], José de la, 477
Cruz e Sousa, João da, 107
Cuadra, Angel, 255
Cuadra, Fernando, 164
Cuadra, José de la, 301, 302
Cuadra, Monolo, 448
Cuadra, Pablo Antonio, 448-450
Cuervo, Rufino José, 197, 198, 200
Cuesta, Jorge, 400, 402, 403
Cuesta y Cuesta, Alfonso, 305
Cueto, Alonso, 543
Cueva, Agustín, 289, 313
Cueva, Juan de la, 370
Cuevas, José Luis, 422
Cunha, Euclides da, 107, 119, 744
Cunha, Juan, 618
Curiel, Fernando, 706
Cuzzani, Agustín, 36

d'León, Omar, 450

Dal Masetto, Antonio, 37, 44
Dalton García, Roque, 329, 591, 592
Dante Alighieri, 329
Danto, Arthur, 687
Darío, Rubén, 16, 18, 69, 72-75, 187, 199, 140, 142, 310, 324, 349, 443, 446-449, 458, 480, 510, 563, 586, 660
Dávalos, Jaime, 52
Dávalos, Juan Santiago, 486
Dávalos, René, 489, 490
Dávila, Juan, 446
Dávila, Virgilio, 565, 566
Dávila Andrade, César, 311
Dávila Vázquez, Jorge, 305
Debesa, Fernando, 164
Debravo, Jorge, 225
Debray, Régis, 644
Decoud, Diógenes, 477, 480
Decoud, Héctor Francisco, 477
Decoud, José Segundo, 476, 477
del Duca brothers, 702
Deleuze, Gilles, 115
Delgado, Abelardo, 661
Delgado, José Matías, 584
Delgado, Manuel, 587
Delgado, Rafael, 388, 389
Delgado, Washington, 544, 546
Deligne, Gastón Fernando, 273
Delmar, Meira. See Champs, Olga
Demare, Lucas, 739
Denevi, Marcos, 31
Denis, Villard, 336
Denis de Icaza, Amelia, 457
Depestre, René, 336
Derrida, Jacques, 115
Descartes, René, 473
Desnoes, Edmundo, 262, 752
Día Arrieta, Hernán, 143
Dias, Gonçalves, 100
Díaz, Eugenio, 197, 198
Díaz, Francisco, 585
Díaz, Jorge, 164-167
Díaz, José Pedro, 625
Díaz, Juan O., 463
Díaz, Otilio Vigil, 275
Díaz, Zoraida, 458
Díaz Alfaro, Abelardo, 566, 569
Díaz Blaitry, Tobías, 463

Díaz Covarrubias, Juan, 382, 383
Díaz del Castillo, Bernal, 320, 367, 368
Díaz Diocaretz, Myriam, 165, 173, 174
Díaz Loyola, Carlos, 140, 146, 150, 152, 163
Díaz Lozano, Argentina, 351
Díaz Machicao, Porfirio, 78
Díaz Mirón, Salvador, 71, 391-393
Díaz Pérez, Rodrigo, 486
Díaz Rodríguez, Manuel, 638
Díaz Sánchez, Ramón, 638
Díaz Valcárcel, Emilio, 570, 663, 665
Díaz Villamil, Antonio, 80
Díaz Xebutá Quej, Francisco, 318, 319
Dickens, Charles, 136
Dickmann, Max, 22
Diego, Eliseo, 242
Diego, Gerardo, 199
Diego, José de, 561, 564, 565
Diego Padró, José. I. de, 567, 665
Diez-Canseco, José, 517
Dios Peza, Juan de, 386
Dios Restrepo, Juan de, 193, 197
Discépolo, Armando, 49, 53
Discépolo, Enrique Santos, 53
Divito, Willy (Guillermo), 701
Dobles, Fabián, 222
Dobles, Julieta, 224
Dobles Segreda, Luis, 220
Domínguez, José Antonio, 348
Domínguez, Manuel, 480
Domínguez, Ramiro, 486
Domínguez Camargo, Hernando, 180, 182, 183
Donoso, José, 134, 164-166, 168, 169, 172, 175, 532
Donoso Pareja, Miguel, 305, 307
Dorfman, Ariel, 165, 692, 697, 698, 704, 705, 720
Dorr, Nicolás, 256, 257, 259
Dos Passos, John, 420, 571
Dostoyevsky, Fyodor Mikhailovich, 422
Dotti, Victor, 619, 620
Dourado, Autran, 117
Draghi Lucero, Juan, 52
Drago Bracco, Adolfo, 323
Dragún, Osvaldo, 36
Droguett, Carlos, 150, 162

Duarte, Juan Pablo, 273
Duchesne, Juan, 719
Dumas, Alexandre, 136
Duncan, Quince, 223
Duque López, Alberto, 212, 213
Durand, Luis, 158
Durand, Oswald, 334, 335
Durón, Juan Fidel, 351

Echavarría, Rogelio, 194
Echavarría Vilaseca, Encarnación, 273
Echeverría, Aquileo J., 224
Echeverría, Esteban, 3-5, 600, 602, 764
Echeverría Bello de Laraín Alcalde,
  Inés, 144
Echeverría Mejía, Arturo, 195
Eco, Umberto, 698, 701, 705
Edwards, Jorge, 164-166, 168-171
Edwards Bello, Joaquín, 155-157
Egaña, Juan, 128-132
Egüez, Ivan, 305, 306
Eguiara y Eguren, Juan José de, 376
Eguren, José María, 511, 512, 514, 545,
  548, 549
Egusquiza, Juan Bautista, 477
Elizondo, Salvador, 423-425
Elizondo, Sergio, 660, 661
Eltit, Diamela, 174, 175
Eluard, Paul, 276
Emerson, Ralph Waldo, 136, 146, 230
Ercilla y Zúñiga, Alonso de, 123-127,
  130, 174-177, 470, 471
Escardó, Rolando, 253
Escoba, Ticio, 489
Escobar, Alberto, 549, 550
Escobar, Benjamín, 475
Escobar Velado, Osvaldo, 589
Escoto, Julio, 352, 354
Escribá, Ligia, 330
Eslava, Jorge, 547
Espada, Martín, 665, 670
Espaillat, Margarita L. de, 281
Espejo, Eugenio, 293, 294, 296
Espino, Alfredo, 58
Espínola, Francisco, 619, 627
Espinoza, Mario, 164
Espinoza Medrano, Juan de, 497
Espronceda, José de, 136, 139, 457, 558

Esquivel, Julia, 329
Esteves, Sandra María, 665, 666
Estévez, Abilio, 259
Estigarribia, Antonio, 476, 484
Estigarribia, José Félix, 482
Estorino, Abelardo, 234, 256, 258, 259
Estrada, Angel de, 12
Estrella, Ulises, 305, 312
Estupiñán Bass, Nelson, 304, 305
Etchepare, Armonía, 625
Etienne, Franck, 334, 335
Evia, Xacinto de, 291
Eyherabide, Gley, 625
Ezeiza, Gabino, 9

Fábrega, Demetrio J., 458
Fajardo, Julio José, 200
Falco, Liber, 618
Fallas, Carlos Luis, 222
Fanon, Frantz, 752
Fariña Núñez, Eloy, 478, 479
Faulkner, William, 189, 190, 213, 571,
  632, 641
Favia Souza, Manuel de, 497
Feijóo, Samuel, 253
Felipe, Carlos, 234, 246
Fernández, Emilio, 737-739
Fernández, Francisco, 237
Fernández, Gerardo, 258, 261
Fernández, Heriberto, 481
Fernández, León, 446
Fernández, Macedonio, 23, 48
Fernández, Mauro, 219
Fernández, Pablo Armando, 253, 263
Fernández, Roberto, 651, 676, 678
Fernández de Lizardi, José Joaquín, 372,
  378-380, 382, 383, 387, 388, 390
Fernández de Oviedo, Gonzalo, 271, 446
Fernández de Valenzuela, Fernando, 183
Fernández Juncos, Manuel, 563
Fernández Mejía, Abel, 277
Fernández Moreno, Baldomero, 27
Fernández Moreno, César, 27, 28
Fernández Retamar, Roberto, 243, 253
Ferré, Rosario, 574, 578, 580
Ferreira, José Ribamar, 117
Ferreira Filho, João Antônio, 117
Ferreiro, Adolfo, 489

Ferreiro, Oscar, 485
Ferrer, Rolando, 255, 257
Ferrer Valdés, Manuel, 462
Ferreyra, José Agustín, 733-735
Feuillet, Tomás Martín, 457
Fielding, Henry, 136
Fierro, Humberto, 305, 306, 310
Figueroa, Francisco, 328
Figueroa, Gabriel, 737, 738
Figueroa Navarro, Alfredo, 462
Fijman, Jacobo, 21
Filloy, Juan, 48
Fink, Agustín, 737
Firmin, Anténor, 338
Fiske, John, 693, 694
Flacón, César, 517
Flaubert, Gustave, 550
Flora, Cornelia Butler, 702-705
Flores, José Asunción, 483
Flores, Juan, 665, 671, 681
Flores, Manuel M., 386
Flores, Marco Antonio, 331
Flores, Mario, 81
Flores, Oscar, 352, 353
Flores Saavedra, Mery, 82
Florit, Eugenio, 254
Floro Costa, Angel, 605
Fons, Jorge, 768
Fonseca, Rubem, 117, 423
Fontanarrosa, Roberto, 696, 697, 701
Foppa, Aleida, 329
Ford, Aníbal, 54
Ford, John, 738
Fornaris, José, 229
Fortoul, José Gil, 638
Foster, David William, 651, 717, 721
Foucault, Michel, 115, 142
Francia, Aldo, 757
Francisco, Ramón, 278
Francovich, Guillermo, 82
Frank, Waldo, 26, 517
Fray Mocho. See Alvarez, José Sixto
Freire Esteves, Gomes, 478
Freud, Sigmund, 200
Freyre, Carolina, 69
Frías, Heriberto, 390, 391, 397
Frisancho, Jorge, 547, 548
Frugoni, Emilio, 613, 615, 617

Fuenmayor, Alfonso, 187
Fuenmayor, José Félix, 187-189
Fuentes, Carlos, 212, 357, 358, 360, 361,
    412, 414, 418-421, 432, 485, 532, 537,
    538, 645, 688, 710, 716
Fuentes, José Lorenzo, 262
Fuentes, Manuel Atanasio, 506
Fuentes y Guzmán, Francisco Antonio
    de, 321
Fulleda León, Gerardo, 259

Gagnini, Carlos, 220
Gaitán Durán, Jorge, 200
Galarza Zavala, Jaime, 306
Galeano, Eduardo, 53, 622, 624, 627, 628
Galeano, José Antonio, 489
Galeano, Maneco, 489
Galich, Franz, 330
Galich, Manuel, 323
Galindo, Francisco Esteban, 585
Galindo, Néstor, 71
Galindo, Sergio, 417
Gallardo, Sara, 51
Gallegos, Daniel, 224
Gallegos, Rómulo, 325, 326, 589, 631,
    638-642
Gallegos Lara, Joaquim, 301, 302, 304
Gallo, Miguel Angel, 698
Galván, Manuel de Jesús, 274
Gálvez, Manuel, 19, 20, 23, 39
Gamarra, Abelardo, 510
Gambaro, Griselda, 37, 52
Gamboa, Federico, 390, 391, 397
Gamboa, Octavio, 200, 207, 208
Gamero, Antonio, 589
Gamero de Medina, Lucila, 348, 349
Gana, Federico, 137, 143, 158
Gandi, Carla, 173, 174
Gandolfi Herrero, Arístides, 22
Gangotena, Alfredo, 310, 311
Gantier, Joaquín, 81
Garay, Blas, 478
Garbett, Jorge, 489
Garbuglio, José Carlos, 117
García, Charlie, 43
García, Germán Leopoldo, 41
García, José Joaquín, 233
García, Santiago, 211

García, Serafín J., 618
García Calderón, Francisco, 510
García Calderón, Ventura, 510, 511, 514, 519
García Canclini, Néstor, 694
García Espinosa, Julio, 754, 756, 769
García Godoy, Federico, 274
García Goyena, Rafael, 295, 322
García Herreros, Manuel, 188, 189
García Lorca, Federico, 152, 199
García Márquez, Gabriel, 179, 182, 185, 187-191, 210-213, 353, 415, 532, 537, 550, 551, 636, 688, 720, 769
García Marruz, Fina, 254
García Mérou, Martín, 12
García Monge, Joaquín, 220
García Moreno, Gabriel, 297, 298
García Ponce, Juan, 421, 423-425, 430
García Vega, Lorenzo, 242
Garcilaso de la Vega, 136, 138, 371
Garcilaso de la Vega, El Inca, 66, 470, 471, 500, 501, 518, 548, 549, 551
Gardel, Carlos, 627, 735, 760-762
Garibay K., Angel María, 363, 365
Garmendia, Julio, 640, 643, 644
Garro, Elena, 414, 415, 426, 435
Gaspar de Francia, José, 473, 474, 479
Gassendi, Pierre, 473
Gastelu, Angel, 242
Gatón Arce, Freddy, 276
Gatti, Gustavo, 486
Gautier, Théophile, 559
Gautier Benítez, José, 559, 560, 562
Gavidia, Francisco, 584, 586
Geel, María Carola, 144
Geenzier, Enrique, 459
Gelly, Juan Andrés, 475
Genet, Jean, 200
Gerchunoff, Alberto, 18, 49, 50
Gertner, María Elena, 164
Getino, Octavio, 749, 752
Giaconi, Claudio, 164
Giardinelli, Mempo, 58
Gíaz de Guzmán, Ruy, 471, 472
Gibson Moller, Percy, 514, 526
Gide, André, 276
Gilbert, Enrique Gil, 301
Gill, Juan Bautista, 475

Girón Cerna, Carlos, 323
Girondo, Oliverio, 21, 27
Girri, Alberto, 27
Giusti, Roberto F., 23
Gledhill, Christine, 764
Godoi, Juansilvano, 477
Godoy, Juan, 151, 162
Godoy Alcayaga, Lucila, 144, 146
Goethe, Johann Wolfgang von, 136, 422
Gogol, Nicolai, 403
Goldemberg, Isaac, 542
Goligorsky, Eduardo, 37
Gomes, Alfredo Dias, 118
Gómez, Alma, 652
Gómez, Ignacio, 585
Gómez, Juan Carlos, 599, 602, 603
Gómez, Miguel Angel, 27
Gómez, Sara, 756, 757
Gómez Bas, Joaquín, 31
Gómez Bueno de Acuña, Dora, 483
Gómez de Avellaneda, Gertrudis, 230, 234-236, 238
Gómez Escobar, Francisco, 195
Gómez Hermosilla, José, 138
Gómez-Martínez, José Luis, 87
Gómez Perasso, José Antonio, 489
Gómez Restrepo, Antonio, 207
Gómez Rojas, José Domingo, 159, 160, 163
Gómez Rosa, Alexis, 281
Gómez Sanjurjo, José María, 486
Gómez y Carrillo, Enrique, 324
Gondra, Manuel, 480
Góngora, Luis de, 97, 371, 497, 503
Gonzaga, Tomás Antônio, 98
González, Celedonio, 266, 675
González, José Luis, 556, 570, 571, 574, 663, 665, 672
González, Josemilio, 574
González, Juan Vivente, 634
González, Natalicio, 481, 483
González, Otto-Raúl, 328
González, Pedro Antonio, 140
González, Rafael, 261
González Camargo, Joaquín, 198
González Dávila, Gil, 446
González Davison, Fernando, 331
González de Cascorro, Raúl, 258

González de Eslava, Hernán, 370
González del Valle, Alcíbiades, 490
González García, Matías, 561, 563
González Lanuza, Eduardo, 21
González León, Adriano, 631, 640-643
González Martínez, Enrique, 396, 398, 413
González Montalvo, Ramón, 589
González Peña, Carlos, 362
González Prada, Manuel, 71, 507, 508, 514, 548
González Suárez, Federico, 298
González Tuñón, Enrique, 21, 29
González Tuñón, Raúl, 21, 29
González Vigil, Ricardo, 551
González y Contreras, Gilberto, 588
González Zeledón, Manuel, 220, 221
Gorki, Maxim, 24
Gorostiza, Carlos, 36
Gorostiza, Celestino, 403
Gorostiza, José, 401
Gorriti, Juana Manuela, 50
Gosálvez, Raúl Botehlo, 79, 81
Gramsci, Antonio, 694, 753
Granados, Blanca, 329
Granata, María, 27
Gravina, Alfredo Dante, 620, 621
Gregorio, Jesús, 260
Greiff, León de, 194, 195, 199
Groot, José Manuel, 197, 198, 200
Grotowski, Jerzy, 529
Groussac, Paul, 39
Guanes, Alejandro, 478
Guardia, Gloria, 465
Guardia y Ayala, Víctor de la, 456
Guarnieri, Gianfrancesco, 118
Gudiño Kieffer, Eduardo, 35, 39
Gudiño Kramer, Luis, 35
Guerra, Lucía, 161, 165
Guerra, Ruy, 743
Guevara, Ernesto Che, 719, 751-753
Guggiari, José Patricio, 482
Guido, Beatriz, 34
Guido y Spano, Carlos, 16
Guillén, Alberto, 515
Guillén, Jorge, 199
Guillén, Nicolás, 244, 245, 253, 275, 567
Guillén Pinto, Alfredo, 79

Guillén Zelaya, Alfonso, 350
Guimarães, Bernardo, 101
Güiraldes, Ricardo, 23, 24, 48
Gullar, Ferreira. See Ferreira, José Ribamar
Gunder Frank, André, 632
Gusmán, Luis, 44
Gutiérrez, Carlos Federico, 348
Gutiérrez, Eduardo, 13
Gutiérrez, Ignacio, 259, 261
Gutiérrez, Joaquín, 222
Gutiérrez, Juan María, 600
Gutiérrez, Miguel, 542
Gutiérrez Alea, Tomás, 752-754, 756, 769
Gutiérrez González, Gregorio, 185, 192
Gutiérrez Nájera, Manuel, 391-393, 510
Guzmán, Augusto, 78
Guzmán, Martín Luis, 395, 404, 405
Guzmán, Nicomedes, 158, 162, 163
Guzmán Cruchaga, Juan, 146

Hahn, Oscar, 165, 173
Halac, Ricardo, 37
Hall, Stuart, 698
Halmar, Augusto d' 145, 159, 162, 163
Hamel, Teresa, 145
Harris, Tomás, 176
Harte, Bret, 158
Hayes, Rutherford B., 475
Hebreo, León, 501
Heidegger, Martin, 572
Heiremans, Luis Alberto, 164, 165
Heker, Liliana, 51
Helgott, Sarina, 529
Helú, Antonio, 716
Hemingway, Ernest, 521, 537, 754
Henríquez Ureña, Max, 273
Henríquez y Carvajal, Federico, 273
Heraud, Javier, 545
Herder, Johann Gottfried, 137
Heredia, José María, 227-229, 234, 459
Herken Krauer, Juan Carlos, 489
Hermeto, Floriano, 697
Hermosillo, Jaime, 767
Hernández, Eugenio, 260
Hernández, Felisberto, 618, 625
Hernández, Gaspar Octavio, 459

Hernández, José, 10, 604, 605
Hernández, Leopoldo, 259
Hernández, Luisa Josefina, 426
Hernández, Miguel, 486
Hernández, Pero, 470, 471
Hernández Arana Xahilá, Francisco, 318
Hernández Arregui, Juan José, 751
Hernández Cobos, José Humberto, 328
Hernández Cruz, Víctor, 679
Hernández Franco, Tomás, 276
Hernández Rueda, Lupo, 277, 281
Hérner, Irene, 698
Herrera, Darío, 458
Herrera, Ernesto, 609, 610
Herrera, Flavio, 325
Herrera Sevillano, Demetrio, 460
Herrera-Sobek, María, 652
Herrera y Mendoza, Juana de, 503
Herrera y Reissig, Julio, 614
Herzog, Werner, 768
Hevia, Aniceto, 160
Hibbert, Fernand, 337
Hidalgo, Alberto, 514, 515
Hidalgo, Bartolomé, 596, 597
Hijuelos, Oscar, 650, 674
Hill, Jane, 705, 706
Hinds, Jr., Harold E., 699
Hinojosa, Rolando, 658, 659, 661, 662
Hinostroza, Rodolfo, 545, 546
Hirszman, Leon, 751
Hojeda, Diego de, 502
Holmberg, Eduardo Estanislao, 31
Horno-Delgado, Asunción, 652
Hospital, Carolina, 677
Hostos, Eugenio María de, 273, 560-562, 664
Hoyos, Angela de, 662
Hoyos, Enrique, 585
Huanay, Julián, 525, 526
Hudson, William Henry, 603
Huerta, David, 431, 432, 438
Huerta, Efraín, 412, 413, 417
Hugo, Victor, 481, 558, 603
Huidobro, Vicente, 145-148, 150-152, 163, 513
Huillca, Quetchua, 719
Humboldt, Alexander von, 137
Hunneus, Ester, 144

Hurtado, Osvaldo, 306

Ibáñez, Sara de, 617
Ibarbourou, Juana de, 516, 616
Ibargüengoitia, Jorge, 417, 418, 434
Icaza, Jorge, 300, 301
Imhof, Francisco, 609
Incháustegui Cabral, Héctor, 276, 278
Inclán, Luis G., 383, 385
Ingenieros, José, 610
Insfrán, Pablo Max, 478
Ipuche, Pedro Leandro, 615
Irala Burgos, Adriano, 486
Irisarri, Antonio José de, 322
Irving, Washington, 136
Isaacs, Jorge, 179, 185, 207-209, 634
Islas, Arturo, 662
Iturralde, Iraida, 678
Izaguirre, Carlos, 351

Jácome, Gustavo Alfredo, 305
Jaimes, Julio Lucas, 69, 70
Jaimes Freyre, Ricardo, 69, 72-74
Jameson, Fredric, 429
Jamis, Fayad, 253
Jara, Cromwell, 543
Jara, Marta, 145
Jara Idrovo, Efraín, 311
Jaramillo, Carlos Eduardo, 312
Jaramillo Agudelo, Darío, 196, 212, 213
Jaramillo Arango, Rafael, 195
Jaramillo Levi, Enrique, 466
Jauretche, Arturo, 31, 751
Jerez, Francisco de, 499
Jiménez, Juan Ramón, 199
Jiménez, Líliam, 328
Jiménez, Manuel de Jesús, 219
Jiménez, Max, 220
Jiménez Borja, Arturo, 528
Jiménez de Quesada, Gonzalo, 180, 181
Jitrik, Noé, 2, 33, 54, 55
Joffré, Sara, 528
Jofré, Manuel, 697
Johnson, John J., 699, 701
Johnson, Randal, 745
Jotabetche. See Vallejo, José Joaquín
Jover Peralta, Anselmo, 483

Jovii, Paulo, 181
Joyce, James, 276, 571, 631, 641
Juana Inés de la Cruz, 183, 296, 366,
  371-375, 380, 392, 402, 414, 415, 435,
  470, 503, 504, 633
Juárez Toledo, Enrique, 328
Juliá Marín, Ramón, 561, 563, 569

Kafka, Franz, 189, 152, 631, 641
Kanellos, Nicolás, 655, 672, 673
Kastos, Emiro. See Dios Restrepo,
  Juan de
Keyserling, Count Herman von, 26
Klein, Herbert S., 83
Koch-Grünberg, Theodor, 109
Kon, Daniel, 43
Kordon, Bernardo, 29
Korsi, Demetrio, 459
Krauch, Jorge, 489
Kropotkin, Petr A., 143

La Fontaine, Jean de, 334
Labarca, Amanda, 145
Labarca Hubertson, Angela, 144
Labrador Ruiz, Enrique, 248, 249
Laclau, Ernesto, 694
Lafforgue, Jorge, 54
Lafourcade, Enrique, 164
Lago, Silvia, 624
Lagos y Lagos, Luis, 587
Laguerre, Enrique, 566, 569, 663
Laínez, Daniel, 351, 354
Laíno, Domingo, 481
Lair, Clara, 569
Lamarque, Libertad, 734, 735
Lamartine, Alphonse Marie Louis de
  Prat de, 136, 459, 603
Lamas, Andrés, 599, 601, 602
Lamas de Rodríguez Alcalá, Teresa, 482
Lamborghini, Osvaldo, 35, 42
Landa, Manuel de, 696
Landa, René de, 674
Landívar, Rafael, 321, 322
Landrú. See Columbres, Juan Carlos
Lange, Norah, 21, 27
Langsner, Jacobo, 622
Laparra de La Cerda, Vicenta, 323
Lara, Jesús, 78, 79

Laraque, Paul, 336
Larra, Mariano José de, 135, 136, 138,
  139, 382, 577
Larreta, Antonio, 622
Larreta, Enrique, 16
Lars, Claudia, 588, 589
Las Heras, César Alonso de, 485
Laso, Jaime, 164
Lastarria, José Victorino, 135
Latorre, Mariano, 158, 162
Lauer, Mirko, 545, 551
Laurenza, Roque Javier, 462
Lavado, Joaquín Salvador (Quino), 696,
  697, 701
Lavalle, José Antonio de, 506
Laviera, Tato, 667-670, 679
Lavín Cerda, Hernán, 173
Lazo Martí, Francisco, 634
Leal, Luis, 653
Leante, César, 262, 266
Leão, José Joaquim de Campos, 117
Ledesma, Luis Manuel, 281
Ledru, André Pierre, 557
Leis, Raúl, 464
Leitón, Roberto, 78
Leiva, Jorge Ernesto, 206
Leiva, Raúl, 328
Lemus, William, 331
Leñero, Vicente, 417, 425, 426, 434, 716
León, Luis de, 136, 138
León Mera, Juan, 288, 289, 295-297
León-Portilla, Miguel, 66, 363
León Zapata, Pedro, 700
Léry, Jean de, 97
Lévi-Strauss, Claude, 97
Levins-Morales, Aurora, 670, 671
Levis, José Elías, 561, 563
Lewis, Samuel, 455
Leyes de Chaves, María Concepción,
  482
Lezama Lima, José, 232, 242-245, 249,
  253, 263
Lhérisson, Justin, 337
Libertella, Héctor, 35
Libio Pitty, Dimas, 465
Liendo y Goicoechea, José Antonio de,
  218, 219
Lihn, Enrique, 152, 153. 172

Lillo, Baldomero, 137, 143, 158
Lima, Luiz Costa, 117
Lima Barreto. See Barreto, Afonso
    Henriques de Lima
Lindo, Hugo, 589
Lindstrom, Naomi, 701, 710, 711
Lins, Osman, 117
Lión, Luis de, 330
Lisboa, Antônio Francisco. See Aleija-
    dinho
Lispector, Clarice, 112-114
Littín, Miguel, 757, 758, 760, 767
Llanos, Antonio, 207, 208
Llerena, José, 588
Llona, Teresa María, 515
Lloréns Torres, Luis, 564-567, 580
Loayza, Luis, 535, 536, 543
Lockward, Antonio, 278
Lomboy, Reinaldo, 162
Londoño, Víctor M., 197
Longfellow, Henry Wadsworth, 230
Lopes Coelho, Luiz, 715
López, Ana, 737
López, Carlos Antonio, 474-477, 480-482
López, José Hilario, 184
López, Lucio Vicente, 12
López, Luis Carlos, 186-188
López, René, 242
López, Venancio, 477
López, Vicente Fidel, 600, 607
López Albújar, Enrique, 516, 517, 519
López de Blomberg, Ercilia, 477
López de Gómara, Francisco, 368
López de Mesa, Luis, 207
López Degregori, Carlos, 547
López Gómez, Adel, 195
López González, Salvador, 574
López Grenno, Gregorio, 489
López Pineda, Julián, 350
López Portillo y Rojas, José, 388, 389,
    397
López Vallecillos, Italo, 591
López Velarde, Ramón, 398, 399, 402,
    514
López y Fuentes, Gregorio, 405, 406
Lora y Lora, José Eufemio, 511
Lostal, Sauli, 713
Loveira, Carlos, 247

Loyal, C. See Ruiz de Burton, María
    Amparo
Luaces, Joaquín Lorenzo, 236, 237
Luciano, Felipe, 667
Luco Cruchaga, Germán, 154
Lugo Filippi, Carmen, 578
Lugones, Leopoldo, 16-20, 24
Lukács, Georg, 283
Lussich, Antonio D., 604, 605
Luz y Caballero, José de la, 241
Lynch, Eliza Alicia, 476
Lynch, Marta, 34, 50, 721
Lyra, Carmen, 221

Machado de Assis, Joaquim Maria, 103-
    106, 109, 119, 120
Macherey, Pierre, 690, 694
Mafud, Julio, 33
Magalhães Gandavo, Pero de, 96
Magariños Cervantes, Alejandro, 599,
    602, 603
Magdaleno, Mauricio, 406, 737
Maggi, Carlos, 622, 623
Magón. See González Zeledón, Manuel
Mahautiere, Duvivier de la, 334
Mailer, Norman, 55
Maíz, Fidel, 475
Majol, Manuel, 15
Malagola, Gedeone, 697
Maldonado, Pedro Vicente, 293, 294
Maldonado, Ricardo, 355
Mallarmé, Stéphane, 422
Mallea, Eduardo, 26
Mañach, Jorge, 567
Manjarrez, Héctor, 431, 437
Mann, Thomas, 422
Mansilla, Lucio Victorio, 12, 13
Mansur, Osvaldo, 44
Manzano, Juan Francisco, 238, 240
Manzi, Homero. See Manzione, Ho-
    mero
Manzione, Homero, 53
Marcos, Plínio, 118
Marechal, Leopoldo, 32, 47
Mariani, Roberto, 22
Mariátegui, José Carlos, 508, 516, 518,
    519, 521, 548

Marín, Francisco Gonzalo, 560-562, 665
Marín, Gerard Paul, 573
Marín del Solar, Mercedes, 144
Marinello, Juan, 242
Marlowe, Philip, 46
Mármol, José, 5, 600, 764
Marof, Tristán. See Navarro, Gustavo
Marqués, Lina, 329
Marqués, René, 570-573, 663, 665
Marra, Nelson, 626
Marré, Luis, 253, 254
Marrero Aristy, Ramón, 276
Marrero Marengo, Ricardo, 478
Marroquín, José Manuel, 185, 197, 198, 200
Marsicovétere y Durán, Miguel, 323
Martel, Julián. See Miró, José
Martelli, Juan Carlos, 44
Martí, José, 71-73, 231-234, 239, 240-242, 245, 246, 260, 324, 474, 561-563, 565, 672, 751
Martí, Mariano, 633
Martínez, Carlos Dámaso, 44
Martínez, Gregorio, 542
Martínez, José de Jesús, 461
Martínez, José Luis, 363, 365,
Martínez, Luis A., 299, 300
Martínez, Nela, 302
Martínez, Reinaldo, 485
Martínez, Tomás Eloy, 44, 47
Martínez de Irala, Domingo, 469
Martínez de la Rosa, Francisco, 68, 69
Martínez de la Vega, Pepe, 716
Martínez de Navarrete, José Manuel, 376
Martínez Estrada, Ezequiel, 25, 26, 31, 32-34, 567
Martínez Luján, Domingo, 511
Martínez Moreno, Carlos, 620, 621, 628
Martínez Rivas, Carlos, 448, 449
Martínez Torres, Olga, 328
Martínez Villena, Rubén, 242
Martini, Juan Carlos, 35, 44, 715
Mártir de Anghiería, Pedro, 446
Martos, Marcos, 545
Marx, Karl, 24, 200, 143, 151
Masferrer, Alberto, 587
Masó, Fausto, 266

Massís, Mahfud, 151
Mastretta, Angeles, 435-436
Mastronardi, Carlos, 21, 27
Matas, Julio, 256, 675
Mateo, Andrés L., 285
Mateo, Catarino, 330
Matos, Gregório de, 97, 98, 120
Matta, Guillermo, 140
Mattelart, Armand, 691, 692, 698, 704, 705
Mattelart, Michèle, 705, 706
Matto de Turner, Clorinda, 508, 509, 514, 517, 519
Maupassant, Guy de, 17, 510, 610
Mavila, José Enrique, 529
Maya, Rafael, 207
Mayorga Rivas, Román, 447, 586
Mazó, Ricardo, 486
Médez, Luz, 329
Medina, Enrique, 40, 41, 721
Megget, Humberto, 620
Meireles, Cecília, 117
Mejía, Epifanio, 193
Mejía, José, 295
Mejía, Merardo, 351
Mejía Nieto, Arturo, 351
Mejía Sánchez, Ernesto, 448
Mejía Vallejo, Manuel, 195, 196
Meléndez, Concha, 566
Meléndez, Juan, 66
Melgar, Mariano, 505, 506
Melo, Juan Vicente, 422, 423
Melo Neto, João Cabral de, 116
Mena, María Cristina, 656
Menchú, Rigoberta, 330, 718, 719
Mendés, Catulle, 478
Mendes, Murilo, 116, 117
Méndez, Francisco, 328
Méndez Ballester, Manuel, 572
Méndez-M., Miguel, 661
Méndez Mina, Gloria, 329
Méndez Pereira, Octavio, 455
Mendinaceli, Carlos, 80
Mendive, José María, 230
Mendizábal, Raúl, 547
Mendoza, Diego de, 66
Mendoza, Jaime, 77, 79
Mendoza, María Luisa, 430

Mendoza, Pedro, 470
Mendoza Varela, Eduardo, 199
Menén Desleal, Alvaro. See Menéndez Leal, Alvaro
Menéndez Leal, Alvaro, 590
Menéndez y Pelayo, Marcelino, 135, 136, 140, 548
Meneses, Guillermo, 638, 640
Menkos-Deka, Carlos, 330
Meschonnic, Henry, 282
Mesonero Romanos, Ramón de, 139
Mexía de Fernangil, Diego, 503
Meza Nicholls, Alejandro, 211
Michelet, Jules, 481
Mieses Burgos, Franklin, 276
Miguel, María Esther de, 37
Milanés, José Jacinto, 230, 231, 234, 236
Miliani, Domingo, 643
Milla, José, 322
Millán, Gonzalo, 173
Miller, Henry, 200
Miller, Jeannette, 280
Miller, John C., 667
Mir, Pedro, 271, 276, 284
Miranda, Luis Antonio, 567
Miranda Archilla, Graciany, 567
Miró, José, 14
Miró, Ricardo, 458
Mirón Alvarez, Oscar, 328
Mistral, Gabriela, 144-147, 150, 152, 163, 173, 515, 516, 711
Mitre, Bartolomé, 283, 476, 600, 601, 607
Mohr, Nicholasa, 666, 668
Molina, Enrique, 27, 28
Molina, Horacio Jorge, 21
Molina, Juan Ramón, 349
Molina Vijil, Manuel, 348
Molinari, Ricardo, 21
Molinas Rolón, Guillermo, 478
Mompox, Fernando de, 469
Mon y Velarde, Juan Antonio, 192
Monge, Carlos Francisco, 224
Monsiváis, Carlos, 378, 430, 432, 712, 737
Montaigne, René de, 123
Montalbetti Solari, Mario, 547
Montalvo, Juan, 288, 289, 295-298, 300, 587

Montaner, Carlos Alberto, 266
Monte, Domingo del, 241
Monte, Félix María del, 273
Monteforte Toledo, Mario, 325, 326
Montenegro, Carlos, 248, 249
Montes-Huidobro, Matías, 255, 259, 266, 675
Montoya, José, 661
Monvel, María, 144
Moock, Armando, 154
Mora, Pat, 661
Moraga, Cherríe, 652, 657
Morales, Alejandro, 661
Morales, Beltrán, 450
Morales, Mario Roberto, 331
Morales, Rosario, 670, 671
Morales Santos, Francisco, 329
Morán, Diana, 461
Moratorio, Orosmán, 606
More, Federico, 514
Moreano, Alejandro, 305, 308
Moreno, Fulgencio R., 481
Moreno, Mario. See Cantinflas
Moreno-Durán, R. H., 212, 213
Moreno Jiménez, Domingo, 275
Morinigo, José Nicolás, 489
Morisseau-Leroy, Félix, 334, 335
Moro, César, 515
Morosoli, Juan José, 618, 621, 626
Morris, Andrés, 352
Morton, Carlos, 657, 658
Moscote, José Dolores, 455
Mouffe, Chantal, 694
Moyano, Daniel, 37, 44
Mujía, María Josefa, 71
Mujica Láinez, Manuel, 31
Müller, Herbert, 164
Muñoz, Diego, 158
Muñoz, Elías Miguel, 651, 678
Muñoz, Rafael, 417
Muñoz, Rafael José, 644
Muñoz Marín, Luis, 570
Murena, Héctor A., 32, 34, 51
Murillo, Rosario, 450
Musil, Robert, 422
Musset, Alfred de, 459, 599
Mutis, Alvaro, 199
Mutis, José Celestino, 183, 196

Nájera, Francisco, 330
Najlis, Michèle, 450
Nalé Roxlo, Conrado, 21
Nandino, Elías, 419
Naranjo, Carmen, 223
Navarro, Gustavo, 78
Navarro, Noel, 262
Navarro Luna, Manuel, 242
Neiva, Lauro, 710, 711
Nejar, Carlos, 117
Neruda, Pablo, 199, 133, 145, 148-150, 152, 153, 163, 275, 311, 353, 484, 486, 513
Nervo, Amado, 391
Neto, Henrique Maximiniano Coelho, 715
Netzahualcóyotl, 365
Newman, Kathleen, 762
Newton, Isaac, 473
Nieto, Juan José, 187
Nietzsche, Friedrich, 115, 411
Niggli, Josefina, 656
Niño Guzmán, Guillermo de, 543
Niza, Marcos de, 654
Noboa Caamuño, Ernesto, 305, 306, 310
Noguera, Carlos, 489
Noriego Hope, Carlos, 406
Novás Calvo, Lino, 248, 249
Novo, Salvador, 402, 416
Nunes, Benedito, 117
Núñez, Apolinar, 281
Núñez, Enrique Bernardo, 641
Núñez, Estuardo, 549
Núñez, Rafael, 187
Núñez, Sergio, 300
Núñez Cabeza de Vaca, Alvar, 469-471, 654

O'Gorman, Edmundo, 360, 361
O'Hara, Edgar, 547
O'Leary, Juan E., 481, 482
O'Reilly, Alejandro, 556
Obaldía, María Olimpia de, 459
Obeso, Candelario, 186-188
Obligado, Carlos, 16
Obligado, Rafael, 12
Obregón, Carlos, 200
Ocampo, Silvina, 30, 31, 714

Ocampo, Victoria, 26, 31
Ocaña, Diego de, 67
Ocantos, Carlos María, 15
Ochoa López, Moravia, 462, 465
Ochoa Velásquez, Angela, 350
Odio, Eunice, 224, 225
Olave, Pablo de, 549
Olavide, Pablo de, 504
Olivari, Nicolás, 21
Oliver Labra, Clarilda, 254
Olmedo, José Joaquín de, 295
Oña, Pedro de, 175, 176
Onetti, Juan Carlos, 619-622, 626
Onís, Federico de, 144
Oquendo de Amat, Carlos, 512
Ordoñana, Domingo, 602
Oreamuno, Yolanda, 222, 223
Orestes Nieto, Manuel, 462
Orgambide, Pedro, 37, 44
Orihuela, Roberto, 261
Orozco, Olga, 27, 28, 47, 48
Orozco, José Clemente, 399, 700
Orphée, Elvira, 37
Orrego Luco, Luis, 137, 143, 155, 156
Orrego de Uribe, Rosario, 144
Orsuna, Pedro de, 181
Ortea, Juan Isidro, 273
Ortega, Eliana, 652
Ortega, Julio, 528, 529, 545, 550, 551
Ortega, Ramón, 350
Ortega y Gasset, José, 566, 569
Ortiz, Adalberto, 303, 304
Ortiz, Fernando, 567
Ortiz, José Concepción, 483
Ortiz, Juan L., 48
Ortiz de Montellano, Bernardo, 402
Ortiz Guerrero, Manuel, 481, 483
Osorio, Luis Enrique, 211
Osorio, Miguel Angel (Porfirio Barba Jacob), 194, 324
Osorio Lizarazo, José A., 197, 201, 202
Osses, Esther María, 461
Otelo, Grande, 742
Otelo, Oscarito, 742
Otero, Leandro, 263
Otero Reich, Raúl, 77, 78
Otero Silva, Miguel, 638, 639
Otero Warren, Nina, 656

Ovalle, Alonso de, 177
Oviedo, Jorge Luis, 353
Oviedo, José Miguel, 550, 551
Oviedo y Baños, José, 633
Owen, Gilberto, 402, 403
Oyarzún, Mila, 144
Ozores, Renato, 463, 464

Pachacuti Yampi Sal Camayagua, Santa
   Cruz, 66
Pacheco, Cristina, 434
Pacheco, José Emilio, 366, 418, 423, 429,
   431-434, 716
Pacheco y Obes, Melchor, 599
Padilla, Herberto, 254
Padrón, Julián, 640
Paganini, Alberto, 624
Pago, Pedro. See Viñas, David
Palacio, Pablo, 301, 303, 304
Palacios, Arnold, 206
Palés Matos, Luis, 567, 568, 575-577
Pallais, Azarías H., 447
Palma, Clemente, 510
Palma, Ricardo, 69, 507, 508, 510, 528,
   548, 549, 551
Palma y Román, Angélica, 510
Palmério, Mário, 111
Palomares, Ramón, 644
Pane, Ignacio A., 480
Pané, Román, 271
Pardo, Jorge Eliécer, 205
Pardo García, Germán, 199
Pardo y Aliaga, Felipe, 506
Paredes, Rigoberto, 355
Paredes Candia, Rigoberto, 76, 77
Pareja Diezcanseco, Alfredo, 301, 303,
   305
Parodi, Enrique, 477
Parra, Guillermo, 696
Parra, Hernando de la, 233
Parra, Nicanor, 151-153, 172
Parra, Teresa de la, 638
Parra del Riego, Juan, 514
Parra Sandoval, Rodrigo, 212, 213
Pasamanik, Luisa, 51
Paso, Fernando del, 423, 429-434
Pasos, Joaquín, 448, 449
Pastor Benítez, Justo, 483

Pau-Llosa, Ricardo, 678
Paula Rendón, Francisco de, 194
Pavese, Cesare, 486
Payeras, Mario, 330, 719
Payno, Manuel, 382, 386, 387
Payró, Roberto J., 19
Paz, Marcela, 144
Paz, Octavio, 16, 76, 160, 200, 358, 359,
   363, 366, 373, 410-413, 418-419, 421,
   427-429, 431, 433, 434, 766, 768
Pazos Kanki, Vicente, 68, 69
Pecci, Antonio, 489
Pedreira, Antonio S., 566, 568, 580
Pedroni, José B., 29
Peix, Pedro, 283, 284
Peixoto, Afrânio, 715
Pellegrini, Aldo, 28
Pellicer, Carlos, 402
Pellicer, Eustaquio, 15
Peña, Horacio, 450
Pena, Luís Carlos Martins, 117
Peralta, Alejandro, 519, 544
Peralta, Bertalicia, 462
Peralta y Barnuevo, Pedro, 470, 503, 504
Perdomo, José Luis, 331
Pereira, Gustavo, 644
Pereira dos Santos, Nelson, 730, 732,
   743
Pereira Rodríguez, José, 605
Perera, Hilda, 262, 265, 674, 676
Péret, Benjamín, 151
Pereyra, Diómedes de, 79
Pérez, José Joaquín, 273
Pérez, Raúl, 305
Pérez Alfonseca, Ricardo, 274
Pérez Chaves, Emilio, 489
Pérez de Villagrá, 654
Pérez de Zambrana, Luisa, 230
Pérez Firmat, Gustavo, 678, 679
Pérez Galdós, Benito, 240, 661
Pérez Maricevich, Francisco, 485
Pérez Pereyra, Luis Eduardo, 711
Pérez Rosales, Vicente, 137, 157
Pérez Torres, Raúl, 309
Pérez Turrent, Tomás, 767
Peri Rossi, Cristina, 626, 627
Perón, Evita (Eva Duarte), 735, 750
Perón, Juan Domingo, 31, 714, 749-751

Pesado, José Joaquín, 381
Peyrou, Manuel, 31, 714
Phelps, Anthony, 336
Piazzolla, Astor, 761
Picchetti, Leonor, 37
Picón Febres, Gonzalo, 638
Pietri, Pedro, 667, 668
Piglia, Ricardo, 44, 45, 54, 57, 58, 714
Piñera, Virgilio, 234, 243, 246, 255-257, 262, 263
Piñero, Miguel, 667
Pinticart de W., Elcira, 711
Pinto, Alves, 697
Pinto, Manuel María, 72, 73
Pita, Santiago de 233
Pitol, Sergio, 422, 423, 434
Pizarnik, Alejandra, 51
Pla, Josefina, 485, 490
Pla, Roger, 34
Plácido. See Valdés, Concepción
Pocaterra, José Rafael, 638
Podestá, los hermanos, 606
Podestá, Manuel T., 15
Poe, Edgar Allan, 198, 478, 510, 558, 559, 615, 712
Polo, Sancho. See Rabasa, Emilio
Poma de Ayala, Felipe Guamán, 66, 499, 500, 548
Pombo, Rafael, 198
Ponce, Javier, 308, 312
Ponce, Marco Antonio, 351
Poniatowska, Elena, 428-431, 433-435, 688, 720
Porchia, Antonio, 48
Porras, Belisario, 455
Porras Barrenechea, Raúl, 549
Portillo, Estela, 662
Portillo Trambley, Estella, 657
Portocarrero, Elena, 528
Portogallo, José. See Ananía, José
Porzekanski, Teresa, 625
Posada, Guadalupe José, 700
Posani, Clara, 645
Prada Oropeza, Renato, 90
Prado, Pedro, 145-147
Preciado, Antonio, 312
Prego de Olivera, José, 596
Price, Hannibal, 338

Price-Mars, Jean, 338, 340, 342
Prida, Dolores, 675, 677
Prieto, Adolfo, 1, 33
Prieto, Guillermo, 381, 382
Prieto, Jenaro, 155
Prieto, Justo, 483
Proaño, Federico, 298
Prosdocimi, María del Carmen, 281
Proust, Marcel, 537
Prud'homme, Emilio, 273
Puenzo, Luis, 764
Puga, María Luisa, 435-436
Puig, Manuel, 38, 39, 44, 57, 58, 213, 437, 438, 688, 715, 718, 721

Qorpo-Santo. See Leão, José Joaquim de Campos
Queiroz, Raquel de, 414
Quesada, José Luis, 355
Quevedo, Francisco de, 97, 152, 503
Quezada, Jaime, 173
Quijada Cerda, Aníbal, 720
Quijada Urias, Alfonso, 591
Quijano, Carlos, 621
Quino. See Lavado, Joaquín Salvador
Quiñones, Delia, 329
Quintana, Manuel José, 348, 597
Quintero, Dante, 696
Quintero, Héctor, 260
Quintero, José Agustín, 230
Quiroga, Horacio, 511, 615, 618
Quiroga Santa Cruz, Marcelo, 86, 90
Quiteño, Serafín, 589

Rabasa, Emilio, 387, 388, 397
Rabelais, François, 109
Rabinovich, José, 50
Radrigán, Juan, 168
Ral, Adelaida, 240
Rama, Angel, 601, 621, 624
Ramírez, Alexis, 355
Ramírez, Armando, 438
Ramírez, Carlos María, 605
Ramírez, Ignacio, 381, 385
Ramírez, Sergio, 448, 449
Ramos, Agustín, 429
Ramos, Graciliano, 110, 111, 120
Ramos, Jorge Abelardo, 751

Ramos, José Antonio, 245-248, 258
Ramos, Lilia, 221
Ramos, Luis Arturo, 434, 716
Ramos, Samuel, 76, 407, 597
Ramos Otero, Manuel, 574
Rampa, Lobsand, 711
Rawet, Samuel, 117
Real de Azúa, Carlos, 623
Recalde, Facundo, 481
Recavarren de Zizold, Catalina, 515
Rechani Agrait, Luis, 572
Rêgo, José Lins do, 110
Reguera Saumell, Manuel, 256
Rein, Mercedes, 625
Renan, Ernest, 565
Rengifo, César, 638
Requena, María Asunción, 164
Restrepo Jaramillo, José, 195
Revueltas, José, 409, 410, 412, 413, 428, 432
Rey, Jerónimo del. See Castellani, Leonardo
Rey Sosa, Rodrigo, 331
Reyes, Alfonso, 200, 362, 363, 395, 398
Reyes, Chela, 144
Reyes, Edwin, 574
Reyes Basoalto, Neftali, 148
Reyes Ortiz, Félix, 72
Reyes Rivera, Louis, 670
Reyles, Carlos, 610
Reyna, Bessy, 466
Reynolds, Gregorio, 72
Reynoso, Oswaldo, 525, 526, 535, 536
Ribadeneira, Edmundo, 305
Ribera Chevremont, Evaristo, 568
Ribeyro, Julio Ramón, 525, 528, 531, 532, 535, 536, 538-540, 543
Ricardo, Antonio, 498
Riedemann, Clemente, 176
Riera, Mario, 464
Riesco, Laura, 542
Rimbaud, Arthur, 198, 151, 422
Río, Dolores del, 737-739
Río, Eduardo del, 696, 699, 700
Ríos, Alberto, 661
Ríos, Edda de los, 489
Ríos, Edmundo de los, 535
Ríos, Juan, 526, 528

Ripstein, Arturo, 767
Risco, René del, 278
Risso, Romildo, 615
Ritter, Jorge R., 485
Rius. See Río, Eduardo del
Riva Agüero, José de la, 510, 511, 548
Rivarola Matto, María, 485
Rivas, Alvaro de, 136
Rivas, Lucinda, 329, 330
Rivas, Pedro Geoffroy, 589
Rivas Bonilla, Alberto, 588
Rivera, Andrés, 44, 46
Rivera, Diego, 399, 420, 738, 741
Rivera, Etnaris, 668
Rivera, Jorge B., 54, 57
Rivera, José Eustasio, 179, 203-205, 325, 326
Rivera, Pedro, 462, 465
Rivera, Tomás, 658, 661
Rivera Indarte, José, 600
Rivera Martínez, Edgardo, 543
Rivera Saavedra, Juan, 528, 529
Rivero, Eliana, 675
Riveros, Juan Pablo, 176
Roa Bastos, Augusto, 473, 486, 487, 490
Robbe-Grillet, Alain, 200, 625
Rocha, Glauber Pedro de Andrade, 743, 744, 758, 769
Rocha, Luis, 450
Rodas, Ana María, 329
Rodó, José Enrique, 479, 605, 611, 612, 614, 623, 626, 711
Rodrigues, Nélson, 117
Rodríguez, Argenis, 643
Rodríguez, Augusto, 463
Rodríguez, José Carlos, 489
Rodríguez, Luis Felipe, 247
Rodríguez, Simón, 634
Rodríguez Alcalá, Guido, 489
Rodríguez Cerna, Carlos, 323
Rodríguez de la Cámara [del Padrón], Juan, 218
Rodríguez de Tió, Lola, 560,, 561, 664
Rodríguez Freyle, Juan, 179-182
Rodríguez Galván, Ignacio, 381
Rodríguez Herrera, Mariano, 262
Rodríguez Juliá, Edgardo, 574, 576-579
Rodríguez Monegal, Emir, 621

Rodríguez Nietzsche, Vicente, 574
Rodríguez Ruiz, Napoleón, 589, 591
Rodríguez Santos, Justo, 242
Rodríguez Torres, Carmelo, 574
Roepka, Gabriela, 164
Roffé, Reina, 51
Roggiano, Alfredo A., 27
Rojas, Angel F., 304
Rojas, Gonzalo, 151, 172
Rojas, Jorge, 185, 199
Rojas, Lourdes, 671
Rojas, Manuel, 159, 161-163
Rojas, Raquel, 489
Rojas, Ricardo, 20, 26
Rojas, Rodrigo, 720
Rojas Garcés, Delia, 144
Rojas Herazo, Héctor, 185, 189-191, 211-213
Rojas y Cañas, Ramón, 506
Rokha, Pablo de. See Díaz Loyola, Carlos
Rokha, Winet de, 144
Román, Sabrina, 281
Romano, Eduardo, 48
Romanos, Mesonero, 382
Romero, Elvio, 486
Romero, José Rubén, 417
Romero, Marcela, 543
Romero, Soledad, 329
Romero del Valle, Emilia, 549
Romero García, Manuel, 634
Romo-Carmona, Mariana, 652
Romualdo, Alejandro, 544
Ros-Zanet, José Guillermo, 461
Rosa, João Guimarães, 112, 114-116, 120, 487, 715
Rosa, Juan de la, 131-133
Rosa, Julio C. da, 619, 621
Rosa, Ramón, 348
Rosales, César, 27
Rosales y Rosales, Vicente, 588
Rosas de Oquendo, Mateo, 503
Rose, Juan Gonzalo, 544
Rosencof, Mauricio, 624, 626
Rouge, Delie, 144
Roumain, Jacques, 337
Roumer, Emile, 336
Roura, Nelson, 489

Rousseau, Jean-Jacques, 136, 473, 599
Rovinski, Samuel, 223, 224
Rozitchner, León, 755
Rozsa, Jorge, 81
Ruales, Huilo, 309
Rubén, Humbert, 489
Rubião, Murilo, 117
Rubido, Esperanza, 678
Rueda, Manuel, 281
Ruffinelli, Jorge, 621, 652
Ruffinelli, Luis, 483
Ruiz, Jorge Eliécer, 200
Ruiz, Raúl, 757, 762
Ruiz Araujo, Isaac, 585
Ruiz de Alarcón, Juan, 369, 504
Ruiz de Burton, María Amparo, 655
Ruiz Gómez, Darío, 196
Ruiz Nestosa, Jesús, 489
Ruiz Rosas, Alonso, 547
Rulfo, Juan, 413-415
Ruscalleda Bercedóniz, Jorge María, 574

Sábat, Hermenegildo, 700
Sabato, Ernesto, 31, 32, 34, 55-57
Sabella, Andrés, 158
Sabines, Jaime, 417
Sabino, Fernando, 117
Sacerío Garí, Enrique, 675
Saco, José Antonio, 241
Sáenz, Carlos Luis, 221
Sáenz, Dalmiro, 34
Saenz, Jaime, 82, 86, 88, 89
Sáenz Morales, Ramón, 448
Saer, Juan José, 44
Sáez de Ovecure, Diego, 322
Sahagún, Fray Bernandino de, 363, 364
Sainz, Gustavo, 436-438, 723
Salarrué. See Salazar Arrué, Salvador
Salazar Arrué, Salvador, 448, 588, 589
Salazar Bondy, Sebastián, 507, 525-527
Salazar Herrera, Carlos, 222
Salazar y Torres, Agustín, 371
Sales, Miguel, 255
Salgado, José Edgardo, 589
Salinas, Pedro, 199, 544
Salinas, Raúl, 661
Salmón, Raúl, 81
Salvador, Francisco, 352

Sam Cop, Enrique Luis, 330
Samayoa Chinchilla, Carlos, 325, 326
Samper, Darío, 199
Samper, José María, 197, 203
Sánchez, Florencio, 485, 608, 610
Sánchez, Héctor, 205
Sánchez, José María, 463
Sánchez, Luciano. See Lussich, Antonio D.
Sánchez, Luis Alberto, 548
Sánchez, Luis Rafael, 573-579, 723
Sánchez, Néstor, 35
Sánchez, Ricardo, 660, 661
Sánchez Aizcorbe, Alejandro, 543
Sánchez Borbón, Guillermo, 463
Sánchez-Boudy, José, 266, 675
Sánchez de Tagle, Francisco Manuel, 376
Sánchez Hernani, Enrique, 547
Sánchez León, Abelardo, 545-547
Sánchez Quell, Hipólito, 485
Sancho de la Hoz, Pedro, 499
Sandoval y Zapata, Luis de, 371
Sanguily, Manuel, 242
Sanín Cano, Baldomero, 193
Sanjinés, Jorge, 745-748
Santa Cruz, Nicomedes, 516
Santacilia, Pedro, 230
Santacruz Pachacuti, Joan de, 499
Santiago, Silviano, 117
Santiván, Fernando, 144
Santiváñez, Róger, 547
Santo Tomás, Domingo de, 289
Santos Urriola, José, 643
Saporta Sternbach, Nancy, 652
Sarduy, Severo, 263, 264
Sarlo, Beatriz, 55, 734
Sarmiento, Domingo Faustino, 6-8, 12, 33, 34, 474, 476, 600, 602, 607, 636, 764, 765
Sarmiento de Gamboa, Pedro, 65, 499
Saroyan, William, 190
Sartre, Jean-Paul, 200, 572, 687, 758
Sarusky, Jaime, 262
Scalabrini Ortiz, Raúl, 21, 25, 26, 29, 751
Schiller, Herbert I., 692, 693
Schlegel, August Wilhelm von 137
Schlegel, Friedrich, 137

Schleiermacher, Friedrich Ernst Daniel, 137
Schmidl, Utz (Ulrico), 470
Schulz Solari, Alejandro, 23, 31
Schwarz, Roberto, 117
Scorza, Manuel, 524
Scott, Nina M., 652
Scott, Walter, 136, 137
Sebreli, Juan José, 33
Seguera, Mito, 489
Segundo de Silvestre, Luis, 197, 198
Segura y Cordero, Manuel Ascensio, 506
Selva, Salomón de la, 448
Serrano, Gil. See Candanedo, César A.
Shakespeare, William, 136, 403, 612
Shattuck, Roger, 568
Shaw, George Bernard, 403
Shimose, Pedro, 91, 92
Shomberg, Arturo Alfonso, 665
Sicardi, Francisco, 15
Sierra, Stella, 461
Sierra Berdecía, Fernando, 572, 665
Sieveking, Alejandro, 164
Sigüenza y Góngora, Carlos de, 371-373
Silén, Iván, 574, 668
Silva, Clara, 617
Silva, Medardo Angel, 305, 310
Silva Jiménez, Georgina, 144
Silva Valdés, Fernán, 615
Simeón Cañas, José, 584
Simó, Manuel, 281
Simpson, Amelia S., 713
Sinán, Rogelio, 459, 460, 462, 464
Siqueiros, Alfaro, 399
Skármeta, Antonio, 150, 165, 437
Slater, Candace, 708, 710
Smith, Adam, 635
Smith, Octavio, 242
Socorro Rodríguez, Manuel del, 184
Soffia, Joãe Antonio, 140
Solanas, Fernando, 749, 751, 752, 760-762
Solano, Vicente, 295
Solano López, Francisco, 474-476
Solar, Xul. See Schulz Solari, Alejandro
Solares, Ignacio, 434
Solari Swayne, Enrique, 527
Solarte, Tristán. See Sánchez Borbón,

Guillermo
Soler, Ricaurte, 455
Soler Puig, José, 262
Sologuren, Xavier, 544
Solórzano, Carlos, 323, 324
Somers, Armonía. See Etchepare, Armonía
Sophocles, 334, 403
Soriano, Osvaldo, 44, 46
Sorin, Carlos, 768
Sorrentino, Fernando, 31
Sosa, Julio B., 463
Sosa, Roberto, 354
Sosnowski, Saúl, 49
Soto, Gary, 661, 662
Soto, León A., 458
Soto, Marco Aurelio, 348
Soto, Pedro Juan, 570, 663, 665, 668
Soto Borda, Clímaco, 197, 201
Soto Hall, Máximo, 323, 325
Soto Rovelo, Roberto, 352
Soto Vélez, Clemente, 665
Sousa, Maurício de, 697
Souza, Márcio, 117
Spengler, Oswald, 566
Spota, Luis, 417, 430, 435
St. Aude, Magloire, 336
Staël, Madame de, 136
Stantic, Lita, 763, 764
Stefanich, Juan 481
Steinbeck, John, 520
Sterne, Laurence, 104, 136, 437
Storni, Alfonsina, 23, 50
Stroesner, Alfredo, 484, 488
Suárez, Clementina, 350
Suárez, Francisco, 473
Suárez, Gastón, 81
Suárez, Marco Fidel, 197, 198, 202, 207
Suárez, Mario, 656
Suárez Figueroa, Sergio, 81
Suárez Romero, Anselo, 238
Suassuna, Ariano, 118
Suáznavar, Constantino, 354
Sucre, Guillermo, 644
Süssekind, Flora, 117
Svanascini, Osvaldo, 31
Sylvain, Georges, 334
Szichman, Mario, 41

Tablada, Juan José, 398, 399
Taboada Terán, Néstor, 79
Tafoya, Carmen, 661
Tagle, María, 144
Taguada, 131-134
Taibo II, Paco Ignacio, 716
Talavera, Natalicio, 475
Tamayo, Franz, 72, 74, 75, 77
Tamayo Vargas, Augusto, 549
Tanco, Félix, 237
Tapia y Rivera, Alejandro, 559, 560, 580
Tatum, Charles, 699
Teillier, Jorge, 146, 153
Tejeda, Luis de, 53
Tejera, Gil Blas, 464
Telles, Lygia Fagundes, 117
Terralla Landa, Esteban de, 504
Terrazas, Francisco de, 370
Terrero, Blas José, 633
Teurbe Telón, Miguel, 230
Thomas, Piri, 666
Thomson, Augusto Geomine, 159
Thorndike, Guillermo, 538, 539
Tiempo, César, 27
Tinajero, Fernando, 305, 312
Tizón, Héctor, 44
Tobías Rosa, José María, 350
Tolentino, Marianne de, 281
Tolstoy, Leo, 143, 510
Tomás Cuellar, José de, 382
Toranzos Bardel, Fortunato, 478
Torga, Rudi, 489
Torre, Gerardo de la, 429
Torre Reyes, Carlos de la, 308
Torres, Omar, 677
Torres Bodet, Jaime, 402, 403
Torres Santiago, José Manuel, 574
Torri, Julio, 395
Traba, Marta, 37
Trejo Fuentes, Ignacio, 434
Trevisan, Dalton, 117
Triana, José, 256, 258, 259
Trías, Vivián, 623
Trillo Pays, Dionisio, 620
Trinidad Reyes, José, 347-349
Tristán, Flora, 549
Trobo, Claudio, 624
Trouillot, Michel-Rolph, 335

Turcios, Froylán, 349
Turgeniev, Ivan, 158, 610
Turla, Leopoldo, 230

Ubidia, Abdón, 305, 308
Ugarte, Manuel, 20, 25, 26
Ugarte, María, 281
Ugarte Cahmorro, Guillermo, 527
Ulibarrí, Sabine, 661
Ulica, Jorge, 655
Umpierre, Luz María, 668
Unamuno, Miguel de, 572
Ureña de Mendoza, Nicolás, 273
Ureña Henríquez, Salomé, 273
Ureta, Alberto, 512
Uribe, Pedro Antonio, 210
Uribe Piedrahita, César, 195
Urondo, Francisco, 42
Urteaga, José Carlos, 529
Urteaga Cabrera, Luis, 542
Usigli, Rodolfo, 76, 407, 716
Uslar Pietri, Arturo, 641

Valcárcel, Luís E., 517
Valdano Morejón, Juan, 289
Valdelomar, Abraham, 506, 514, 515
Valdenegro, Eusebio, 596
Valdés, Concepción, 229, 234
Valdés, Diógenes, 281
Valdés, Hernán, 721
Valdez, Luis, 657
Valdivia, Pedro, 176, 177
Valdivieso, Jaime, 164
Valdivieso, Mercedes. See Valenzuela
  Alvarez, Mercedes
Valdovinos, Arnaldo, 482
Valencia, Gerardo, 207
Valencia, Guillermo, 207
Valencia Goelkel, Hernando, 200
Valenzuela, Luisa, 51
Valenzuela Alvarez, Mercedes, 161, 164
Valera Benítez, Rafael, 277
Valera y Morales, Félix, 241
Valéry, Paul, 326
Valladares, Alejandro, 354
Valladares, Armando, 255
Vallbona, Rima de, 223
Valle, José Cecilio del, 348

Valle, Luz, 329
Valle, Rafael Heliodoro, 350
Valle, Rosamel del, 145
Valle y Caviedes, Juan del, 503
Vallegos, Rogue, 485
Vallejo, César, 275, 353, 506, 509, 513,
  514, 516, 517, 531, 543-545, 548, 551
Vallejo, José Joaquín, 135, 157
Vallejo, Mariano, 655
Valls, Jorge, 255
Vanasco, Alberto, 31
Vanegas, Juan de Dios 448
Varela, Alfredo, 28
Varela, Blanca, 544
Varela, Florencio, 600
Varela, José Pedro, 602, 603
Vargas, Gabriel, 696
Vargas, Germán, 187
Vargas Dulché, Yolanda, 696
Vargas Llosa, Mario, 212, 213, 485, 494,
  530-538, 540-543, 550, 551, 723, 744
Vargas Osorio, Tomás, 197, 199
Vargas Vicuña, Eleodoro, 525
Vargas Vila, José María, 197, 200, 201
Varona, Enrique José, 242
Vasconcelos, José, 144, 395, 402, 518,
  567
Vásconez, Javier, 309
Vásquez, Richard, 659
Vásquez Méndez, Gustavo, 82, 86, 89
Vaz de Caminha, Pero, 96
Vaz Ferreira, Carlos, 613, 623
Vaz Ferreira, María Eugenia, 614
Vázquez, Juan, 272
Vázquez, Miguel Angel, 328, 331
Vázquez Méndez, Gonzalo, 89, 90
Vedrines, Jules, 275
Vega, Ana Lydia, 574, 576-579
Vega, Bernardo, 665, 666
Vega, Julio de la, 82
Vega, Lope de, 138, 304, 363, 503
Vegas Seminario, Francisco, 517
Veiga, José J., 117
Veintimilla de Galindo, Dolores, 296
Vela, Arqueles, 406
Velasco, Juan de, 293-295
Velasco Mackenzie, Jorge, 307
Velásquez, Samuel, 193, 194

Velázquez, Roberto A., 478
Vélez Ladrón de Guevara, Francisco
  Antonio, 183
Veloz Maggiolo, Marcio, 279, 281, 284
Venegas, Daniel, 655
Vera, Pedro Jorge, 301, 305, 306
Verbitsky, Bernardo, 28
Vergara, José Manuel, 164, 165
Vergara y Vergara, José María, 184, 185,
  196, 197
Verge, Pedro, 284
Veríssimo, Erico, 117
Veríssimo, Fernando, 700
Verlaine, Paul, 198
Vial, Román, 154
Viana, Javier de, 610
Viana, Luz de, 144
Vianna Filho, Oduvaldo, 118
Viaud Renaud, Jacques, 278
Vicens, Josefina, 435
Vicioso, Abelardo, 271, 277
Vicioso, Chiqui, 281
Vico, Giambattista, 362
Vicuña, Cecilia, 173
Vicuña Mackenna, Benjamín, 135, 137,
  140
Vidal, Hernán, 643
Vidales, Luis, 194, 199
Vientós, Nilita, 580
Viera, João Luís, 742
Viezzer, Moema, 719
Vigil, Evangelina, 652, 662
Viglietti, Daniel, 627
Vila, Silva, 625
Vilalta, Maruxa, 426-427
Vilariño, Idea, 620
Vilela, Luiz, 117
Villa-Lobos, Heitor, 745
Villagra Marsal, Carlos, 486, 487
Villalobos, Arias de, 371
Villalobos, Rosendo, 71
Villanueva, Alma, 662
Villanueva, Tino, 661
Villanueva Collado, Alfredo, 668
Villareal, José Antonio, 657
Villarejo, José S., 482
Villaroel, Gaspar de, 291, 292
Villatoro, José Luis, 329

Villaurrutia, Xavier, 402, 403, 416
Villaverde, Cirilo, 238-240
Villegas, Abelardo, 426
Villegas, Juan, 151
Villegas, Víctor, 277
Villordo, Oscar Hermes, 37, 39, 721
Viñas, David, 1, 33, 44, 54, 55, 710, 715
Viñas, Ismael, 33
Vinueza, Humberto, 312
Vinyes, Ramón, 186
Víquez, Pío, 219
Viramontes, Helena, 652
Viscarra Fabre, Guillermo, 77
Vitale, Ida, 620
Vitier, Cintio, 242
Vitoria, Francisco de, 218
Vivas Maldonado, José Luis, 570
Vizcardo y Guzmán, Juan Pablo, 505
Vodanovic, Sergio, 164
Voltaire (François-Marie-Arouet), 473

Walker Martínez, Carlos, 140
Walsh, María Elena, 51
Walsh, Rodolfo, 42, 720
Warhol, Andy, 687
Wernicke, Enrique, 29
Westphalen, Emilio Adolfo, 515, 516
Whannel, Paddy, 689
Whitman, Walt, 152, 511
Wiesse, María, 512
Wiezell, Elsa, 485
Wilcock, Juan Rodolfo, 27
Wilde, Eduardo, 12
Wilms Montt, Teresa, 144
Wilson, Carlos Guillermo, 466
Witker, Alejandro, 720
Wittgenstein, Ludwig, 687
Wolff, Egon, 164-168
Wyld Ospina, Carlos, 325

Xavier, Ismail, 732, 745
Ximénez, Francisco, 318, 320, 321

Yan, Mari. See Yáñez, María Flora
Yáñez, Agustín, 76, 408-410, 413
Yáñez, María Flora, 160
Yánez Cossío, Alicia, 306, 307
Yerovi, Leonidas, 511

Yllescas, Edwin, 450
Ynsfrán, Edgar, 484
Young Núñez, César, 461
Yúdice, George, 681
Yunque, Alvaro, 22

Zachrisson, Boris A., 465
Zago, Angela, 645
Zalamea Borda, Eduardo, 197, 201
Zaldumbide, Julio, 298
Zamora, Bernice, 662
Zamudio, Adela, 71, 72
Zapata, Luis, 438
Zapata Olivella, Manuel, 212, 213
Zarco, Francisco, 382
Zavala, Lorenzo de, 654
Zavala Cataño, Víctor, 528
Zavala Guzmán, Simón, 311
Zavala Muniz, Justino, 617

Zavaleta, Carlos E., 525
Zeitlin, Israel. See Tiempo, César
Zenea, Juan Clemente, 232, 255
Zeno Gandía, Manuel, 560, 561, 563, 575
Zeta Acosta, Oscar, 659
Zimmerman, Marc, 694
Ziraldo. See Pinto, Alves
Zitarrosa, Alfredo, 596, 627
Zola, Emile, 155, 158, 159, 479, 561, 610
Zorilla, José, 136
Zorilla, Rafael Augusto, 275
Zorilla de San Martín, José, 477, 603,
    605, 607
Zubizarreta, Carlos, 485
Zubizarreta, Gonzalo, 486
Zucolillo, Aldo, 489
Zum Felde, Alberto, 617
Zurita, Raúl, 165, 174

1526